SEE WEB LINKS

For recommended web links for this title, visit www.
oxfordreference.com/page/lawlinks when you see this sign.

The most authoritative and up-to-date reference books for both students and the general reader.

Accounting
Animal Behaviour
Archaeology
Architecture and Landscape Architecture
Art and Artists
Art Terms
Arthurian Literature and Legend
Astronomy
Battles
Bible
Biology
Biomedicine
British History
British Place-Names
Business and Management
Card Games
Chemical Engineering
Chemistry
Christian Art and Architecture
Christian Church
Classical Literature
Computing
Construction, Surveying, and Civil Engineering
Cosmology
Countries of the World
Critical Theory
Dance
Dentistry
Ecology
Economics
Education
English Etymology
English Grammar
English Idioms
English Literature
English Surnames
Environment and Conservation
Everyday Grammar
Film Studies
Finance and Banking
Foreign Words and Phrases
Forensic Science
Geography
Geology and Earth Sciences
Hinduism
Human Geography
Humorous Quotations

Irish History
Islam
Journalism
Kings and Queens of Britain
Law
Law Enforcement
Linguistics
Literary Terms
London Place-Names
Mathematics
Marketing
Mechanical Engineering
Media and Communication
Medical
Modern Poetry
Modern Slang
Music
Musical Terms
Nursing
Opera Characters
Philosophy
Physics
Plant Sciences
Plays
Pocket Fowler's Modern English Usage
Political Quotations
Politics
Popes
Proverbs
Psychology
Quotations
Quotations by Subject
Reference and Allusion
Rhyming
Rhyming Slang
Saints
Science
Scottish History
Shakespeare
Slang
Social Work and Social Care
Sociology
Statistics
Synonyms and Antonyms
Weather
Weights, Measures, and Units
Word Origins
Zoology

Many of these titles are also available online at www.oxfordreference.com

A Dictionary of

Law

EIGHTH EDITION

Edited by JONATHAN LAW

OXFORD
UNIVERSITY PRESS

Great Clarendon Street, Oxford, OX2 6DP,
United Kingdom

Oxford University Press is a department of the University of Oxford.
It furthers the University's objective of excellence in research, scholarship,
and education by publishing worldwide. Oxford is a registered trade mark of
Oxford University Press in the UK and in certain other countries

© Market House Books 1983, 1990, 1994, 1997, 2002, 2006, 2009, 2013, 2015

The moral rights of the author have been asserted

First edition 1983 as *A Concise Dictionary of Law*
Second edition 1990
Third edition 1994
Fourth edition 1997
Fifth edition 2002
Sixth edition 2006
Seventh edition 2009
Seventh edition reissued with new covers and updates 2013
Eighth edition 2015

Impression: 1

Published in the United States of America by Oxford University Press
198 Madison Avenue, New York, NY 10016, United States of America

British Library Cataloguing in Publication Data

Data available

Library of Congress Control Number: 2014946124

ISBN 978-0-19-966492-4

Printed in Great Britain by
Clays Ltd, St Ives plc

Contents

Preface

This dictionary, now in its eighth edition, has been written by a distinguished team of academic and practising lawyers. With its easy-to-use format and emphasis on accessible language, it is designed to meet the needs of four main categories of reader:

- legal professionals, who sometimes need a quick, portable, and reliable reference source;
- students following law courses at all levels, who require clear explanations of legal concepts and terminology;
- professionals in other fields (e.g. business people, local government officers, accountants, and social workers), who require some knowledge of the law in their work;
- laypeople who are affected by the law as homebuyers, consumers, motorists, and employees and in various aspects of family life (e.g. divorce, inheritance).

Each article begins with a clear definition of the entry word (or words) which, in most cases, is followed by a more detailed explanation or description of the concepts involved. Legal jargon is avoided wherever possible.

This new edition reflects many recent changes in the law and legal system. If any provisions of new legislation were not in force at the time of publication, the entries to which they apply will indicate the direction of the proposed changes. The growing importance of European law, international law, and human rights law has been recognized in the updating of the text.

References to important new cases, with full citations, have likewise been added wherever this seems particularly relevant. These will be particularly valuable to law students but, owing to the ready availability of case-law materials online, can be followed up quite easily by those who have no access to a law library. An introduction to the legal resources now available on the Internet is another important feature of this edition (see Appendix II). There is also a centre section aimed specifically at students: the Writing and Citation Guide provides detailed advice on how to write and present essays on legal subjects.

An asterisk (*) placed before a word in a definition indicates that additional relevant information will be found under this article. Some entries simply refer the reader to another entry, indicating either that they are synonyms or abbreviations or that they are most conveniently explained in one of the dictionary's longer articles. Finally, the use of the pronoun "he" (rather than "he or she") in entries has been adopted purely to simplify the construction of sentences; it does not imply that the subject matter relates exclusively or primarily to males.

J.L.

2014

Credits

Editor of the sixth, seventh, and eighth editions

Jonathan Law BA

Editor of the earlier editions

Elizabeth A. Martin MA

Contributors for the eighth edition

Nicholas Acomb LLB, TEP   *Solicitor*
Owain Blackwell BA, LLM   *Head of Law (LLB), University of Bolton*
Simon R. Brown LLB   *Solicitor, Head of Department of Law, Buckinghamshire New University*
Sandra Clarke MA   *Barrister; Acting Head, School of Law, University of Greenwich*
David Collison CTA (Fellow), FCA, TEP   *Tax consultant*
Mike Cuthbert LLM, BA, BSC, FRSA   *Senior Tutor in Law, University of Northampton*
Kim Everett LLB   *Principal Lecturer and Teaching Fellow in Law, University of Greenwich*
Margaret Ford BA, MBA
Barbara Harvey LLB, LLM   *Principal Lecturer in Law, Leicester De Montfort Law School*
P. D. Martin Jackson BSC, PGDip law, BVC   *Barrister; Senior Lecturer in Law, University of Greenwich*
Brian Jones LLB, Mphil   *Senior Lecturer in Law, University of Bolton*
Rowena Meager LLB, BCL   *Barrister, Lecturer in Law, University of Buckingham*
Anne E. Morris LLB   *Honorary Senior Research Fellow, School of Law and Social Justice, University of Liverpool*
Michael Ottley LLB, LLM   *Senior Lecturer in Law, University of Greenwich*
David Rigg LLB, LLM   *Barrister, Senior Lecturer in Law, University of Bolton*
Nicholas J. Simpson MA   *Solicitor*
E. Susan Singleton LLB   *Solicitor*
John Wadham BSC, MSC   *Solicitor; Executive Director, Interights*

Contributors for the first edition

Martin R. Banham-Hall LLB   *Solicitor*
Bernard Berkovits LLB   *Lecturer in Law, University of Buckingham*
P. J. Clarke BCL, MA   *Barrister; Fellow and Tutor in Law, Jesus College, Oxford*
Letitia Crabb LLB, LLM   *Solicitor; Lecturer in Law, University College of Wales, Aberystwyth*
J. W. Davies LLB, MA, BCL   *Fellow of Brasenose College, Oxford*
B. Russell Davis MA, LLB   *Barrister*
J. D. Feltham BA, MA   *Fellow of Magdalen College, Oxford*
Judith Lewis LLB   *Solicitor*
Keith Uff MA, BCL   *Lecturer in Law, University of Birmingham*

abandonment *n.* **1.** The act of giving up a legal right, particularly a right of ownership of property. Property that has been abandoned is *res nullius* (a thing belonging to no one), and a person taking possession of it therefore acquires a lawful title. An item is regarded as abandoned when it can be established that the original owner has discarded it and is indifferent as to what becomes of it: such an item cannot be the subject of a theft charge. However, property placed by its owner in a dustbin is not abandoned, having been placed there for the purpose of being collected as refuse. In marine insurance, abandonment is the surrender of all rights to a ship or cargo in a case of *constructive total loss. The insured person must do this by giving the insurer within a reasonable time a **notice of abandonment**, by which he relinquishes all his rights to the ship or cargo to the insurer and can treat the loss as if it were an actual total loss. **2.** In civil litigation, the relinquishing of the whole or part of the claim made in an action or of an appeal. Any claim is now considered to be abandoned once a *notice of discontinuance is served, under Part 38 of the *Civil Procedure Rules. **3.** The offence of a parent or guardian leaving a child under the age of 16 to its fate. A child is not regarded as abandoned if the parent knows and approves steps someone else is taking to look after it. The court may allow a child to be adopted without the consent of its parents if they are guilty of abandonment.

abatement *n.* **1.** (of debts) The proportionate reduction in the payment of debts that takes place if a person's assets are insufficient to settle with his creditors in full. **2.** (of legacies) The reduction or cancellation of legacies when a solvent estate is insufficient to cover all the legacies provided for in the will or on intestacy after payment of the deceased's debts. The Administration of Estates Act 1925 (sch 1 pt II) provides that general legacies, unless given to satisfy a debt, abate in proportion to the amounts of those legacies; specific and demonstrative legacies then abate if the estate is still insufficient to pay all debts, and a demonstrative legacy also abates if the specified fund is insufficient to cover it. For example, A's estate may comprise a painting, £3,000 in his savings account, and £7,000 in other money; there are debts of £1,000 but his will leaves the painting to B, £5,000 from the savings account to C, £8,000 to D, and £2,000 to E. B will receive the painting, C's demonstrative legacy abates to £3,000, and after the debts are paid from the remaining £7,000, D's and E's general legacies abate proportionately, to £4,800 and £1,200 respectively. When annuities are given by the will, the general rule is that they are valued at the date of the testator's death, then abate proportionately in accordance with that valuation, and each annuitant receives the abated sum. All these rules are subject to any contrary intention being expressed in the will. **3.** (in land law) Any reduction or cancellation of money payable. For example a lease may provide for an abatement of rent in certain circumstances, e.g. if the building is destroyed by fire, and a purchaser of land may claim an abatement of the price if the seller can prove his ownership of only part of the land he contracted to sell. **4.** (of nuisances) The termination, removal, or destruction of a *nuisance. A person injured by a nuisance has a right to abate it. In doing so, he must not do more damage than is necessary and, if removal of the nuisance requires entry on to the property from which it emanates, he will generally have to give notice to the wrongdoer. A local authority can issue an abatement notice to control statutory nuisances. **5.** (of proceedings) The termination of civil proceedings by operation of law, caused by a change of interest or status (e.g. bankruptcy or death) of one of the parties after the start but before the completion of the proceedings. An abatement did not prevent either of the parties from bringing fresh proceedings in respect of the same cause of action. Pleas in abatement have been abolished; in modern practice any change of interest or status of the parties does not affect the validity of the proceedings, provided that the cause of action survives.

abduction *n.* Wrongfully taking away or detaining another person, usually by force or fraud. *See* CHILD ABDUCTION; FALSE IMPRISONMENT; KIDNAPPING.

abet *vb. See* AID AND ABET.

ABH *See* ACTUAL BODILY HARM.

ab initio [Latin] From the beginning. If a contract is void (say for *mistake) *ab initio*, this has the consequence that no innocent third parties can acquire rights under any subsequent contract (*Bell v Lever Bros* [1932] AC 161 (HL) (Lord Atkin)).

ab intestato [Latin: from an intestate] Describing an inheritance from someone who dies without leaving a valid will.

abortion *n.* The removal of an embryo or foetus from the uterus at a stage in the pregnancy when it is deemed incapable of independent survival (*see* VIABLE). Under the Offences Against the Person Act 1861 (s 58) abortion is a criminal offence unless carried out in accordance with the provisions of the Abortion Act 1967, which sets out the grounds upon which a termination is legal (s 1). Generally, a termination is lawful if the pregnancy has not exceeded 24 weeks and if the continuance of the pregnancy would involve a greater risk to the physical or mental health of the pregnant woman than having an abortion. In some circumstances a termination is permitted after 24 weeks, for example if there is a substantial risk that the child if born would be seriously handicapped or if the continuance of the pregnancy would involve grave permanent injury to the physical or mental health of the pregnant woman. The abortion must be carried out in an approved hospital or clinic and two medical practitioners must certify that the termination is necessary for one of the reasons set out in the Act. The distinction between abortion and contraception is a crucial one. A recent case, *R (Smeaton on behalf of SPUC) v Secretary of State for Health* [2002] EWHC 610 (Admin), [2002] 2 FLR 146, ruled that use of the "morning after pill", which prevents the implantation of the fertilized egg in the womb, did not constitute an abortion. Doctors are not obliged to perform abortions if they can prove that they have a conscientious objection to so doing. A husband cannot prevent his wife having a legal abortion if she so wishes. *Compare* CHILD DESTRUCTION.

absconding *n.* The failure of a person to surrender to the custody of a court in order to avoid legal proceedings. *See also* SURRENDER TO CUSTODY.

absence *n.* (in court procedure) The nonappearance of a party to litigation or a person summoned to attend as a witness. Part 39 of the *Civil Procedure Rules sets out the consequences of a party's failure to attend the trial in civil proceedings. In criminal proceedings a summary trial may take place in the absence of the accused or in the absence of the prosecutor under the Magistrate Courts Act 1980.

absente reo [Latin] The defendant being absent.

absent-mindedness *n. See* NON-INSANE AUTOMATISM.

absent parent *See* NON-RESIDENT PARENT; CHILD SUPPORT MAINTENANCE.

absolute *adj.* Complete; unconditional; not relative or qualified. A **rule absolute** is an order that can be enforced at once, in contradistinction to a **rule nisi**, which commands the opposite party to appear on a day therein named and show cause why he should not perform the act or submit to the terms therein set forth. In default of his appearance or showing good cause, the rule is made absolute. *See* DECREE ABSOLUTE; DECREE NISI.

absolute assignment *See* ASSIGNMENT.

absolute discharge *See* DISCHARGE.

absolute interest In ascertaining the income tax treatment of a beneficiary's entitlement to the estate of a deceased person it is first necessary to determine whether the beneficiary has an absolute interest or a **limited interest**. The beneficiary has an absolute interest in the *residuary estate if that residue is payable to him, of right, as soon as the residue has been ascertained (Income Tax (Trading and Other Income) Act 2005 s 650(1)). He has a limited interest if his right to the estate, once ascertained, is only to the income arising from the residue (s 650 (2)).

absolute privilege The defence that a statement cannot be made the subject of an action for *defamation because it was made in Parliament, in papers ordered to be published by either House of Parliament, in judicial proceedings or a fair and accurate contemporaneous report of judicial proceedings, or in an official communication between certain officers of State. Under the Defamation Act 1996, the defence was extended to reports of proceedings of the European Court of Justice. The Defamation Act 2013 now applies it to all courts of other countries and territories outside the UK and to certain international courts and tribunals. Under certain circumstances defined by the 1996 Act the absolute privilege accorded to statements or proceedings in Parliament may be waived (**waiver of privilege**) to permit evidence to be adduced in an action for defamation. *Compare* QUALIFIED PRIVILEGE.

absolute right A right set out in the *European Convention on Human Rights that cannot lawfully be interfered with, no matter how important the public interest in doing so might be. Absolute rights include *freedom of thought, conscience, and religion and the prohibitions on *torture, *inhuman treatment or punishment, and *degrading treatment or punishment. *Compare* QUALIFIED RIGHT.

absolute theory of sovereign immunity A theory that long prevailed, particularly in the UK, that a foreign state could not be impleaded (i.e. sued) before a municipal tribunal in any circumstances. The doctrine of *sovereign immunity was originally devised to uphold mutual respect between monarchs by according immunity to the exercise of their state functions within foreign jurisdictions. However, the 20th century saw the rise of industrial enterprises funded and controlled by the state: to accord immunity to such enterprises gave them an unfair commercial advantage and the absolute view of state immunity was gradually abandoned by the international community. The UK was one of the last states to respect the traditional view. The common-law position was altered so as to conform to the new world norm by the Court of Appeal in *Trendtex Trading Corpn v Central Bank of Nigeria* [1977] QB 529 (CA). The statutory position was altered by the State Immunity Act 1978. An additional restriction on state immunity arose out of the case of *R v Bow Street Metropolitan Stipendiary Magistrate, ex p Pinochet Ugarte (No. 3)* [1999] 2 WLR 827 (HL). Here it was held by the House of Lords that the Criminal Justice Act 1988 removed immunity from a former head

a

of state with regard to acts carried out in the exercise of his official functions if such acts were a breach of **jus cogens* (e.g. acts of torture and genocide).

absolute title Ownership of a *legal estate in registered land with a guarantee by the state that no one has a better right to that estate. An absolute title to freehold land is equivalent to an estate in fee simple in possession in unregistered land. **Absolute leasehold title**, unlike *good leasehold title, guarantees that the lessor has title to grant the lease. (*Compare* POSSESSORY TITLE; QUALIFIED TITLE.) The title may be subject to:

- *encumbrances and other entries noted on the register by means of substantive registration (e.g. a registered legal charge or land charge);
- noted interests, such as that of a beneficiary under a trust, which may be protected by means of a *notice or *restriction on the register rather than by substantive registration;
- *overriding interests (which by their nature do not appear on the register and must be ascertained by search and enquiry).

See also LAND REGISTRATION.

abstracting electricity The offence, punishable with up to five years' imprisonment and/or a fine, of dishonestly using, wasting, or diverting electricity. This offence may be committed by someone who bypasses his electricity meter or reconnects a disconnected meter or who unlawfully obtains a free telephone call (though there is a more specific and potentially less serious offence to deal with this). Bypassing a gas or water meter could constitute *theft of the gas or water. In *Low v Blease* [1975] Crim LR 513 it was held that electricity could not be stolen as it is not property within the meaning of section 4 of the Theft Act 1968. Computer hackers were formerly charged with offences of abstracting electricity until the Computer Misuse Act 1990 made *hacking a specific criminal offence.

abstraction of water The taking or impounding of water from a river or other source of supply. It normally requires a licence from the *Environment Agency but there are exceptions; primarily, when less than 20 cubic metres of water per day are taken, when the water is for domestic or agricultural use (excluding spray irrigation), or when it is removed in the course of fire-fighting or land drainage. Further restrictions come into force when river or groundwater levels are low. The legislative framework for water abstraction is contained primarily in the Water Resources Act 1991 as amended by the Water Act 2003.

abstract of title Written details of the *title deeds and documents that prove an owner's right to dispose of his land or an interest in this. An abstract generally deals only with the *legal estate and any equitable interests that are not *overreached. An owner usually supplies an abstract of title before *completion to an intending purchaser or mortgagee, who compares it with the original title deeds when these are produced or handed over on completion of the transaction. An abstract of title to registered land consists of *official copies of the entries in the register and details of any other documents necessary to prove the owner's title, such as a marriage certificate proving a woman's change of surname. For unregistered land, the abstract of title must usually trace the history of the land's ownership from a document at least 15 years old (the *root of title) and give details of any document creating encumbrances to which the land is subject. An abstract of title formerly comprised extracts, often in abbreviated note form, but now generally comprises duplicate copies of the relevant documents (an **epitome of title**). An abstract or epitome, with each copy document marked as examined against the original, may be sufficient in itself to deduce title; for instance, when a title is split into lots, the purchaser of each lot may be required to accept an examined abstract or epitome in lieu of the original title deeds, accompanied by an *acknowledgment and undertaking.

abuse of a dominant position Unlawful activities by large businesses, i.e. usually those having a market share of at least 40% in at least one EU state. Examples of such activities, which are contrary to *Article 102 of the Treaty on the Functioning of the European Union (previously Article 82 Treaty of Rome) and the UK Competition Act 1998, include refusing to supply an existing customer and engaging in *predatory pricing. The European Commission and the *Office of Fair Trading can fine businesses up to 10% of annual worldwide group turnover for breach of Article 102. High fines include €497M against Microsoft in 2004, €280.5M for continued breach in 2006/07, and a final record additional €899M in 2008 for continued lack of compliance. In the UK Napp Pharmaceuticals was fined £3.21M for abuse of a dominant position contrary to the Competition Act 1998 but this was reduced to £2M on appeal.

abuse of a position of trust It is an abuse of a position of trust for a person over the age of 18 years (A) to engage in sexual activity with a person under the age of 18 (B), where A looks after B in a care institution wherein B is accommodated and cared for, including a hospital, independent clinic, care home, residential care home, private hospital, community home, voluntary home, children's home, a home provided under section 82(5) of the Children Act 1989, or a residential family care centre. Four criminal offences under the Sexual Offences Act 2003 involve an abuse of a position of trust: sexual touching (s 16), engaging in sexual activity in a child's presence (s 17), causing or inciting a child to engage in sexual activity (s 18), and causing a child to watch a sexual act (s 19). The maximum sentence for committing a sexual offence involving an abuse of trust is five years' imprisonment.

abuse of process A tort where damage is caused by using a legal process for an ulterior collateral purpose. (*See also* MALICIOUS PROSECUTION.) Actions that are obviously frivolous, vexatious, or in bad faith can be stayed or dismissed by the court as an abuse of process.

abusive behaviour *See* THREATENING BEHAVIOUR.

abutter *n.* The owner of premises adjoining the property of another.

ABWOR Assistance by way of representation. *See* LEGAL AID.

ACAS Advisory Conciliation and Arbitration Service: a statutory body established under the Employment Protection Act 1975; the composition and functions of ACAS are now governed by Parts IV and VI of the Trade Union and Labour Relations (Consolidation) Act 1992. ACAS was set up to promote the improvement of industrial relations and the development of *collective bargaining. In its conciliation function it may intervene, with or without the parties' consent, in a *trade dispute to offer facilities and assistance in negotiating a settlement.

ACAS does not itself arbitrate in such disputes, but with the consent of both parties it may refer a dispute to the *Central Arbitration Committee or to an independent arbitrator.

ACAS may give free advice to employers, employees, and their respective representatives on matters of employment or industrial relations. It issues codes of practice giving guidance on such matters as disciplinary procedures and *dismissal procedures and *disclosure of information to trade unions. It may also conduct inquiries into industrial relations problems, either generally or in relation to particular businesses, and publish the results after considering the views of parties directly affected. ACAS can charge for its services when it considers that this is appropriate.

ACAS employs **conciliation officers** who may assist parties to an application to an *employment tribunal to reach a settlement before the hearing. The law on conciliation generally is contained in the Employment Tribunals Act 1996. Pre-claim conciliation was originally optional but the Enterprise and Regulatory Reform Act 2013 amends the Employment Tribunals Act 1996 so that anyone intending to make a claim to a tribunal must first contact ACAS about their claim. *See also* SETTLEMENT AGREEMENT.

The **ACAS Arbitration Scheme** is a scheme set up under the Employment Rights (Dispute Resolution) Act 1998 to encourage the resolution of employment disputes between employer and employee without involving an employment tribunal. An ACAS appointed arbitrator gives a decision binding on the parties as to whether the dismissal was fair or unfair. The scheme is voluntary and take-up has been low.

((())) SEE WEB LINKS
• Website of ACAS

acceleration *n.* The coming into possession of a *future interest in any property at an earlier stage than that directed by the transaction or settlement that created the interest. For example, a landlord's interest in *reversion is accelerated if the tenant surrenders the lease before it has expired. When a will bequeaths an interest for life that lapses (e.g. because the legatee dies before the testator), the interest of the person entitled in *remainder is accelerated and takes effect immediately the testator dies.

acceptance *n.* Agreement to the terms of an *offer that, provided certain other requirements are fulfilled, converts the offer into a legally binding contract. If the method by which acceptance is to be signified is indicated by the offeror, that method alone will be effective (*Holwell Securities Ltd v Hughes* [1974] 1 WLR 155 (CA)). If it is not, acceptance may be either express (by word of mouth or in writing) or inferred from the offeree's conduct; for example, if he receives goods on approval and starts to make use of them (*Beta Computers (Europe) Ltd v Adobe Systems (Europe) Ltd* [1996] FSR 367). The acceptance must always, however, involve some action on the part of the person to whom the offer was made: the offeror cannot assert that his offer will be treated as accepted unless the offeree rejects it (*Felthouse v Bindley* (1862) 11 CBNS 869). The validity of an acceptance is governed by four principal rules:

(1) It must take place while the offer is still in force, i.e. before it has lapsed (*see* LAPSE OF OFFER) or been revoked (*see* REVOCATION OF OFFER).

(2) It must be on the same terms as the offer. An acceptance made subject to any variation is treated as a *counteroffer.

(3) It must be unconditional, thus an acceptance **subject to contract** is not a valid acceptance.

(4) It must be communicated to the offeror. Acceptance by letter is treated as communicated when the letter is posted (*Adams v Lindsell* (1818) 1 B & Ald 681, 106 ER 250), provided that both parties are aware that communication is to be by post (*Henthorn v Fraser* [1892] 2 Ch 27 (CA)). Telex, and therefore probably e-mail, is equated with the telephone, so that communication takes place only on receipt (*Entores Ltd v Miles Far East Corp* [1955] 2 QB 327).

However, when the offer consists of a promise to confer a benefit on whoever may perform a specified act, the offeror waives the requirement of communication as a separate act. If, for example, he offers a reward for information, a person able to supply the information is not expected to accept the offer formally. The act of giving the information itself constitutes the acceptance, the communication of the acceptance, and the performance of the contract (*New Zealand Shipping Co Ltd v Satterthwaite (AM) & Co Ltd* [1975] AC 154 (PC)).

acceptance of a bill The written agreement by the person on whom a *bill of exchange is drawn (the **drawee**) that he will accept the order of the person who draws it upon him (the **drawer**). The acceptance must be written on the bill and signed. The signature of the drawee without additional words is sufficient, although generally the word "accepted" is used as well. Upon acceptance the drawee becomes the acceptor and the party primarily liable upon the bill. *See also* QUALIFIED ACCEPTANCE.

acceptance *supra protest* (acceptance for honour) A form of *acceptance of a bill of exchange to save the good name of the drawer or an endorser. If a bill of exchange has been either the subject of a *protest for dishonour by nonacceptance or protested for better security, and it is not overdue, any person who is not already liable on the bill may, with the consent of the holder, accept the bill *supra protest*. Such an acceptance must be written on the bill, indicate that it is an acceptance for honour, and be signed. The acceptor for honour engages that he will pay the bill on due presentment if it is not paid by the drawee, provided that it has been duly presented for payment and protested for nonpayment and that he receives notice of these facts. He is liable to the holder and to all parties to the bill subsequent to the party for whose honour he accepted.

access *n.* Formerly, the opportunity to visit a child that was granted (at the discretion of the court) to its parent when the other parent had the care and control of the child after divorce or when a custodianship order was in force. Since the Children Act 1989 came into force the concept of access has been replaced by that of *contact. *See also* SECTION 8 ORDERS.

accession *n.* **1.** The formal agreement of a country to an international *treaty. The term is applied to the agreement of a country to become a member state of the European Union. Member states accede to the Treaty of Rome or any other EU treaty by signing **accession agreements**. **2.** The process of a member of the royal family succeeding to the throne, which occurs immediately on the death or abdication of the previous sovereign. **3.** The right to all that one's own property produces, e.g. the fruit of trees or the young of animals, and to all that becomes added to or incorporated with it either naturally or artificially, e.g. land formed by gradual deposits of soil (*see* ALLUVION) or buildings erected on, or trees, vines, etc., planted in one's ground.

access land Land to which the public has or will have access for the purposes of open-air recreation under the Countryside and Rights of Way Act 2000. It includes land shown as open country (mountain, moor, heath, or down) on a map in conclusive form issued by an appropriate countryside body (the Countryside Agency or the Countryside Council for Wales) or as common land, or land situated more than 600 metres above sea level, or land that has been dedicated as access land. *See* RIGHT TO ROAM.

accessory *n.* **1.** One who *aids and abets or *counsels or *procures someone else to commit a crime. A secondary party to an offence – i.e. one who participates in it but does not bring about the *actus reus* directly – may still be regarded by the law as liable. Section 8 of the Accessories And Abettors Act 1861 (as amended by the Criminal Law Act 1977) states: "Whosoever shall aid, abet, counsel or procure the commission of any indictable offence. . . . shall be liable to be tried, indicted and punished as the *principal offender." Similar provision is made in respect of summary offences under section 44 of the Magistrates' Courts Act 1980. **2.** One who knowingly assists a person who has committed an indictable offence with the intention of *impeding apprehension or prosecution.

accessory liability in breach of trust If a stranger knowingly and dishonestly assists a trustee in a *breach of trust he will be liable as an accessory (*Royal Brunei*

a

Airlines Sdn Bhd v Tan [1995] 2 AC 378 (PC)). He will not usually have received any trust assets; however, in consequence of his **dishonest assistance** in the breach he will be personally liable to account to the trust for any losses arising from his actions. Such a person is sometimes referred to as a *constructive trustee, but this terminology is problematic and best avoided. The test for "dishonesty" is an objective one (*Barlow Clowes International v Eurotrust International* [2005] UKPC 37, [2006] 1 WLR 1476). *See also* LIABILITY FOR RECEIPT.

access to neighbouring land Under the Access to Neighbouring Land Act 1992 one landowner has a right to go onto the land of another for the purpose of carrying out necessary repairs or maintenance to his own property. An **access order** can be granted by the County Court; this will specify the extent of the access and any compensation to be paid. The access order must be registered to be binding on future purchasers of the land to which access has been granted (*see* LAND REGISTRATION).

accident *n. See* FATAL ACCIDENTS; MISTAKE; ROAD TRAFFIC ACCIDENTS.

accident record book A record kept by the police of details of the accidents they have investigated. Access to this is usually requested by solicitors acting in subsequent litigation relating to *road traffic accidents. The Association of Chief Police Officers Traffic Committee has issued guidelines on charges for such reports.

accomenda *n.* A contract made by an individual with the master of a vessel, to whom he entrusts personal property to be sold for their joint account.

accommodation bill A bill of exchange accepted by an **accommodation party**, i.e. a person who signs without receiving value and for the purpose of lending his name (i.e. his credit) to someone else. An accommodation party is liable on the bill to a *holder for value.

accomplice *n.* One who is a party to a crime, either as a *principal or as an *accessory. *See also* CORROBORATION.

accord and satisfaction The purchase by one party to a contract of a release from his obligations under it when the other party has already performed his side of the bargain. A release of this one-sided nature constitutes a **unilateral discharge** of the contract; unless granted by deed, it can at common law be effected only by purchase, i.e. by a fresh agreement (accord) for which new consideration (satisfaction) is given. If, for example, A is due to pay £1000 on a particular date to B for contractual services rendered, B might agree to accept £900 paid on an earlier date, the earlier payment constituting satisfaction. *Compare* BILATERAL DISCHARGE. *See also* ESTOPPEL.

account *n.* A remedy at common law and (more importantly) in equity requiring one party to a relationship (e.g. a partner or trustee) to account to the other(s) for moneys received or due. It may be pursued in addition to a claim for another remedy, such as damages, or as a substantive remedy in its own right. An **order to account** can fulfil two functions: firstly, it can quantify the amount of the profit or loss being pursued; secondly, it can impose liability to make payment. An order to account may be made where a fiduciary makes unauthorized profits or receives a bribe, for example. Cases: *Boardman v Phipps* [1967] 2 AC 46 (HL); *AG for Hong Kong v Reid* [1994] 1 AC 324 (PC).

accounting period The period for which a company makes up its accounts. *Corporation tax is imposed on the profits measured for an accounting period (Corporation Taxes Act 2009 s 8). For this purpose, an accounting period cannot exceed 12 months. Certain events, notably a company ceasing to trade, are specified by statute as causing the end of an accounting period, even though the company may not make up its accounts to that date. *See also* FINANCIAL YEAR.

accounting practice The financial reporting of any enterprise necessitates a measure of the profit (or loss) generated during the period covered by the report and, usually, also a balance sheet showing assets minus liabilities at the reporting date. The manner in which profits, assets, and liabilities are measured is the accounting practice of the enterprise. The Accounting Standards Board and the International Accounting Standards Board issue *Financial Reporting Standards, which specify the accounting practices to be adopted by a company. These statements are commonly referred to as **generally accepted accounting practice** (**GAAP**). It is of the essence of the income tax charge (and the corporation tax charge for companies) that tax is levied on the profit of a business. Increasingly, tax law has taken accounting practice as the rule to determine the amount of profit on which tax is imposed. This is far from the approach of judges in the 19th century, who considered the court as arbiter of the measure of profit for tax purposes. A modern judgment that would appear to assert the supremacy of accounting practice is that of Lord Millet, who in 2000 ruled that: "There was no basis on which a taxpayer could challenge an assessment based on its own financial statements as long as these were prepared in accordance with ordinary accounting principles, showed a true and fair view of its affairs, and were not inconsistent with the statute" (*IRC v Secan Ltd* (2000) 74 TC 1). This is a substantial move away from the view expressed by Lord Denning in 1972: "A judge may reject the accountant's evidence, or he may accept it" (*Heather v C-E Consulting Group Ltd* (1972) 48 TC 293, 323E–H).

In the Finance Act 2000, statute, for the first time, used the concept of normal accounting practice to enact anti-avoidance legislation. A company is prohibited from obtaining a tax advantage by triggering a capital gain on the sale of its future rents. The prohibition is effected by requiring companies to draw up accounts for tax purposes in accordance with "normal accounting practice", which is considered to outlaw such accounting treatment (s 110). Intriguingly, the way in which the statute is worded has the effect that future pronouncements by the Accounting Standards Board (or the International Accounting Standards Board) in this area are automatically given statutory effect. Thus, a manner of measuring profit for tax purposes that is permitted in one year may be outlawed the following year, without there being any statutory change.

More recently, a number of specific provisions in the Taxes Acts have defined the scope of the provision by reference to "generally accepted accounting practice", rather than by providing a statutory definition. A notable example is the relief (now 225% of the amount expended) for the cost of research and development. The adoption of this approach within tax statute is not without difficulty. First, the accounting standards followed in the UK and Europe differ from those followed in the USA and other jurisdictions. Second, accountants regard all accounting standards as subject to the overriding requirement that the treatment in the accounts should give a "true and fair view" of the state of affairs of the business. This can mean that different accountants apply accounting standards differently.

( ) SEE WEB LINKS

• Website of the Financial Reporting Council: includes a list of standards currently in issue

accounting records *See* BOOKS OF ACCOUNT.

account monitoring order An order of the court requiring a financial institution to provide certain information held by them relating to a customer for the purposes of an investigation (Glossary to the Criminal Procedure Rules). Section 370 of the Proceeds of

Crime Act 2002 sets out the requirements to be met in applying for the order. *Compare* CUSTOMER INFORMATION ORDER.

account of profits A remedy that a claimant can claim as an alternative to damages in certain circumstances, e.g. in an action for breach of *copyright. A successful claimant is entitled to a sum equal to the monetary gain the defendant has made through wronging the claimant.

accounts *pl. n.* Statements of a company's financial position prepared annually. A company is under a duty to "keep adequate accounting records" in order to show the day-to-day entries of money received and expended by the company and the extent of its assets and liabilities (Companies Act 2006 s 386). The annual accounts consist of a *balance sheet, a *profit and loss account, a statement of total recognized gains and losses and, if required, a cash-flow statement. The accounts must present a "true and fair view" of the company's financial position (Companies Act 2006 s 393) and, where appropriate, are to be kept in a form prescribed by the Act. Depending on the type of company, the accounts are accompanied by a directors' report, a directors' remuneration report, and an auditor's report. A private company has nine months after the end of the company's accounting reference period to file its accounts: a public company has six months after the end of that period (Companies Act 2006 s 442). Section 437 of the Companies Act 2006 requires the directors of a public company to lay the accounts before a *general meeting of the company. As a private company is not obliged under the Companies Act 2006 to hold an annual general meeting, there is no general requirement to lay the accounts before a general meeting of a private company. Listed companies are additionally required to ensure the accounts (and reports) are available on a website (Companies Act 2006 s 430). Small and medium-sized companies can avoid the filing requirements relating to the accounts if they are exempt from audit and deliver abbreviated accounts (Companies Act 2006 s 444–45). Members are entitled to be sent copies of the accounts. *See also* BOOKS OF ACCOUNT; SUMMARY FINANCIAL STATEMENT.

accreditation *n.* The process by which diplomats are exchanged between nation states. Diplomats present their own credentials (hence the word) to the host government's appropriate representative.

accretion *n.* The process by which new land formations are legally assimilated to old by a change in the flow of a water channel. In contrast to *avulsion, this process involves a very slow, near imperceptible, natural action of water and other elements. It would include, for example, the natural diversion of a boundary river leaving an island, sandbank, or dry land where it previously flowed, the formation of islands at a river mouth, and additions to a delta by the deposit of sand and soil upon the shoreline. Accretion will allow the beneficiary state to legitimately claim title to the new land so created. *See also* THALWEG, RULE OF THE.

For cases in which acquisition of territory by accretion has arisen, *see The Anna* (1805) 5 C Rob 373 (Lord Stowell) and *Secretary of State for India v Chellikani Rama Roa* (1916) 32 TLR 652 (PC). There is a large volume of US decisions concerning accretion; the classic illustration of a finding of both accretion and *avulsion can be found in the *Chamizal Arbitration* 5 AJIL 785 (1911) concerning the path of the Rio Grande.

accrue *vb.* To become a legally enforceable claim or right. For example, a *cause of action usually accrues on the date that the claimant suffers injury.

accruer *n.* A provision in a will under which the subject matter of a failed gift accrues or is added to some other gift that has an independent effect under the terms of the will. An example would be a legacy in a will of "£10,000 to such of my brothers as shall survive me and if more than one in equal shares". If one brother predeceases the testator, his share will be added or accrue to the surviving brothers' shares. *Compare* SUBSTITUTIONAL LEGACY.

accumulation *n.* The continual addition of the income of a fund to the capital, so that the fund grows indefinitely. Before the Accumulation Act 1800 accumulation was permitted for the length of the perpetuity period (i.e. lives in being plus 21 years: *see* RULE AGAINST PERPETUITIES). The periods for which accumulation is now permitted are shorter; they are listed in the Law of Property Act 1925 and the Perpetuities and Accumulations Act 1964 and include a period of 21 years from the date of the disposition, the period of the life of the settlor, and the duration of the minority of any person mentioned in the disposition. Income is often directed to be accumulated if (for example) the beneficiary is a minor, or the interest in his favour is protected or contingent, or if the terms of a trust are discretionary.

accumulation and maintenance settlement (A and M settlement) A *discretionary trust that fulfils three conditions: (1) the terms of the settlement require that beneficiaries obtain an *interest in possession at a specified age, not exceeding 25; (2) whilst under the specified age, any income not advanced to the beneficiary must be accumulated; (3) either (a) the period from the creation of the trust to the creation of the interest in possession is less than 25 years or (b) all beneficiaries are children of a common grandparent. Formerly, a transfer of property into such a settlement was a *potentially exempt transfer and there was no immediate charge to *inheritance tax. However, following the changes made by the Finance Act 2006 (sch 20) it is no longer important to determine whether or not a settlement satisfies these conditions. Inheritance tax is, in general, charged on the transfer of property into any type of settlement, unless the trust is for the benefit of a disabled person or a bereaved minor. From April 2008 all existing A and M settlements were reclassified for tax purposes as either *18-25 trusts or *relevant property trusts.

accusare nemo se debet [Latin] No one is bound to accuse himself or herself.

accusatorial procedure (adversary procedure) A system of criminal justice in which conclusions as to liability are reached by the process of prosecution and defence. It is the primary duty of the prosecutor and defence to press their respective viewpoints within the constraints of the rules of evidence while the judge acts as an impartial umpire, who allows the facts to emerge from this procedure. Common-law systems usually adopt an accusatorial procedure. *See also* BURDEN OF PROOF. *Compare* INQUISITORIAL PROCEDURE.

acknowledgment *n.* **1.** The admission by a debtor that a debt is due or a claim exists. **2.** Confirmation by the signatory to a document that the signature on the document is his own.

acknowledgment and undertaking Confirmation in a *title deed that a person may see and have copies of relevant deeds not in his possession (acknowledgment), with a promise from the holder of them to keep them safely (undertaking). Thus when part of an owner's land is sold, he keeps his deeds to the whole but in the conveyance gives this acknowledgment and undertaking to the purchaser, who can then prove his title to the part from copies of the earlier deeds and by calling for production of the originals. In the majority of cases the vendor gives the purchaser all title documents relating solely to the land conveyed, and an acknowledgment and undertaking is only necessary when this does not happen. Note that personal representatives and fiduciary owners will normally give only an acknowledgment, no undertaking. Breach of an undertaking gives rise to an action in damages.

acknowledgment of service A defendant who intends to contest proceedings brought against him by a claimant must respond to the claim by filing an acknowledgment of service under Part 10 of the * Civil Procedure Rules (CPR) and/or by filing a *defence under Part 15 of the CPR. Acknowledgments of service are used if the defendant is unable to file a defence within the required time or if the defendant intends to dispute the jurisdiction of the court under Part 11 of the CPR. By acknowledging service a defendant is given an extra 14 days for filing the defence. In effect this means that the defendant has a 28-day period after *service of the claim before the defence must be served. Once the defendant has returned the relevant section of the acknowledgment of service form, the court must notify the claimant in writing. The claimant may obtain judgment in *default if the defendant fails to file an acknowledgment of service or a defence within the specified time periods.

a coelo usque ad centrum [Latin: from the heavens to the centre of the earth] *See* CUIUS EST SOLUM EIUS EST USQUE AD COELUM ET AD INFEROS.

ACP states The African, Caribbean, and Pacific states that are associated together by the Georgetown Agreement of 1975 and that (with the exception of Cuba) signed the Cotonou Agreement with the EU in 2000. The Agreement, which covers such issues as foreign aid, trade, investment, human rights, and governance, succeeded the Lomé Convention, which had not addressed human rights and governance issues. There are 79 signatories (2013). The Agreement replaced unilateral trade preferences that the EU had with the ACP countries under the Lomé Convention with economic partnership agreements involving reciprocal obligations. The aim is free access to markets between the EU and ACP countries. The Agreement also provides for the ACP least-developed countries (LDCs) to be treated differently from ACP non-LDCs.

acquiescence *n.* Express or implied *consent. In law, care must be taken to distinguish between mere knowledge of a situation and positive consent to it. For example, in the defence of *volenti non fit injuria* an injured party will not be regarded as having consented to a risk simply because he knew that the risk existed (*Smith v Baker & Sons* [1891] AC 325 (HL)).

acquired rights *See* RELEVANT TRANSFER.

acquis communautaire [French] The body of *Community legislation and judgments of the *European Court of Justice by which all EU member states are bound.

acquisition fraud *See* MISSING TRADER INTRA-COMMUNITY FRAUD.

acquittal *n.* A decision by a court that a defendant accused of a crime is not guilty. A court must acquit a defendant following a verdict of *not guilty or a successful plea of *autrefois acquit* or *autrefois convict*. Once acquitted, a defendant cannot be retried for the same crime unless there is important new evidence (*see* DOUBLE JEOPARDY); however, an acquittal in a criminal court does not bind civil courts.

acte clair [Law French: clear point] A matter so obvious as not to need legal argument. In recent decades the concept of *acte clair* has become important in European law. Where a matter of European Community law arises before a domestic tribunal and there is doubt as to the interpretation of the law, the tribunal is bound by the Treaty on the Functioning of the European Union (formerly Treaty of Rome) to refer the matter under Article 234 to the European Court of Justice. However, where the domestic tribunal feels that the point in law is sufficiently well defined (for example, by previous case law before the European Court of Justice) they claim there is an *acte clair* and decline to submit the matter under Article 234 (*R v Secretary of State, ex p Schering* [1987] 1 CMLR 277).

act in pais [Law French] A thing done out of court and not a matter of record.

action *n.* A proceeding in which a party pursues a legal right in a civil court. *See also* IN PERSONAM; IN REM.

actio personalis moritur cum persona [Latin: a personal action dies with the person concerned] A maxim stating that actions of tort or contract are destroyed by the death of either the injured or the injuring party. Modern statutes mean that this is rarely the case. However, before the passing of the Fatal Accidents Act 1846 acceptance of this notion meant that in actions in negligence it was better for a doctor to kill his patient outright than to injure him. This situation arose because it was originally believed that the primary function of tort was to punish and not to compensate for damage caused. The maxim still survives in the law of *defamation ("you cannot defame the dead").

actio popularis (actio communis) [Latin: action of the people] In public international law, an action brought to vindicate an interest that is of general importance to the international community, as distinct from an interest vested more particularly in the state that wishes to institute proceedings. The *International Court of Justice has held that a right of *actio popularis* "is not known to international law as it stands at present" (*South West Africa Cases: Ethiopia and Liberia v South Africa (Second Phase)* ICJ Reports (1966)): proceedings in defence of legal rights or interests require those rights or interests to be clearly vested in those who claim them, even though it is not necessary to show that the claimant state would suffer direct material injury by any abrogation. Although the notion of *actio popularis* is in some respects associated with that of *erga omnes* obligations, the two are distinct and (to the extent that they are accepted) each may exist independently of the other.

actio quanti minoris [Latin: action of how much less] An action in which the purchaser of a good claims a reduction of the price proportionate to the reduction in value caused by a defect. Under the Sales of Goods Act 1979 s 48C(1)(a), where there is a minor defect in the product (and hence a breach of the implied term of satisfactory quality (s 14)), then "the buyer can require the seller to reduce the purchase price of the goods in question to the buyer by an appropriate amount."

active trust (special trust) A trust that imposes duties on the trustee other than that of merely handing over the trust property to the person entitled to it (*compare* BARE TRUST). These duties may impose a specific obligation on the trustee or confer a discretion on him.

activity requirement A requirement that may be imposed by a sentencing court as part of a *community order or a *suspended sentence order under the Criminal Justice Act 2003. Section 201 of the Act requires that the offender carries out a specified activity, typically one designed to make reparation to the victim or to make the offender less likely to reoffend (e.g. by acquiring basic literacy skills). Under the Criminal Justice and Immigration Act 2008 an activity requirement may also be imposed as part of a *youth rehabilitation order.

act of a stranger A defence to an action in *nuisance or under the *rule in *Rylands v Fletcher*, where the damage is caused by the independent and unforeseeable act of a

a

stranger over whom the defendant has no control (*Perry v Kendrick's Transport Ltd* [1956] 1 WLR 85).

act of God An event due to natural causes (storms, earthquakes, floods, etc.) so exceptionally severe that no-one could reasonably be expected to anticipate or guard against it. It may be used as a defence but is unlikely to succeed (*Greenock Corporation v Caledonian Railway* [1917] AC 556 (HL)). *See* FORCE MAJEURE.

Act of Parliament (statute) A document that sets out legal rules and has (normally) been passed by both Houses of *Parliament in the form of a *Bill and agreed to by the Crown (*see* ROYAL ASSENT). Under the Parliament Acts 1911 and 1949, however, passing of public Bills by the House of Lords can be dispensed with, except in the case of Bills to extend the duration of Parliament or to confirm provisional orders. Subject to these exceptions, the Lords can delay Bills passed by the House of Commons; it cannot block them completely. If the Commons pass a money Bill (for example, one giving effect to the Budget) and the Lords do not pass it unaltered within one month, it may be submitted direct for the royal assent. Any other Bill may receive the royal assent without being passed by the Lords if the Commons pass it in two consecutive sessions and at least one year elapses between its second reading in the first session and its third reading in the second (*Jackson & others v AG* [2005] UKHL 56).

Every modern Act of Parliament begins with a **long title**, which summarizes its aims, and ends with a **short title**, by which it may be cited in any other document. The short title includes the calendar year in which the Act receives the royal assent (e.g. The Competition Act 1998). An alternative method of citation is by the calendar year together with the Chapter number allotted to the Act on receiving the assent or, in the case of an Act earlier than 1963, by its regnal year or years and Chapter number. Regnal years are numbered from the date of a sovereign's accession to the throne, and an Act is attributed to the year or years covering the session in which it receives the royal assent. (*See also* ENACTING WORDS.) An Act comes into force on the date of royal assent unless it specifies a different date or provides for the date to be fixed by ministerial order.

Acts of Parliament are classified by the Queen's Printer as public general Acts, local Acts, and personal Acts. **Public general Acts** include all Acts (except those confirming provisional orders) introduced into Parliament as public Bills. **Local Acts** comprise all Acts introduced as private Bills and confined in operation to a particular area, together with Acts confirming provisional orders. **Personal Acts** are Acts introduced as private Bills and applying to private individuals or estates. Acts are alternatively classified as **public Acts** or **private Acts** according to their status in courts of law. A public Act is judicially noticed (i.e. accepted by the courts as a matter of general knowledge). A private Act is not, and must be expressly pleaded by the person relying on it. All Acts since 1850 are public unless they specifically provide otherwise.

act of state An act, often involving force, of the executive of a state, or committed by an agent of a sovereign power with its prior approval or subsequent ratification, that affects adversely a person who does not owe allegiance to that power. The courts have power to decide whether or not particular conduct constitutes such an act, but if it does, they have no jurisdiction to award any remedy. The so-called **act of state doctrine** holds that, in the absence of a treaty, the courts of no state can question the validity or legality of the acts of state of another sovereign state or of its agents. If such questioning is thought necessary, it is to be confined to diplomatic channels. The classic statement of this doctrine is that made by Chief Justice Fuller in the decision of the US Supreme Court in *Underhill v Hernandez* 168 US 250, 252 (1897). A good English example of the application of the doctrine can be found in *Buttes Gas and Oil Co v Hammer* [1982] AC 888, in which the House of Lords held that issues relating to the sovereignty of a foreign state over territory, the extent of its territorial sea, and its continental shelf jurisdiction were inherently non-justiciable in the municipal courts of the United Kingdom. The modern law on this doctrine has severely curtailed the number of acts that can be included within its compass. *See* SOVEREIGN IMMUNITY.

actual bodily harm (ABH) Any hurt or injury calculated to interfere with the health or comfort of the victim. *Assault causing actual bodily harm is a summary or indictable offence carrying a maximum punishment of five years' imprisonment. The hurt need not be serious or permanent in nature, but it must be more than trifling (*R v Miller* [1954] 2 QB 282). It is enough to show that pain or discomfort has been suffered, even though no bruising is evident. Psychiatric injury (more than mere anxiety or fear) may constitute actual bodily harm (*R v Chan-Fook* [1994] 2 All ER 552).

actual military service *See* PRIVILEGED WILL.

actual notice Knowledge that a person has of rights adverse to his own. If a purchaser of unregistered land has actual notice of an interest that is not required to be registered as a land charge, and which will not be overreached on the sale to him, he will be bound by it. The doctrine of notice plays no part in registered land, where it has been replaced by the rules of registration. *See also* CONSTRUCTIVE NOTICE; IMPUTED NOTICE.

actual total loss (in marine insurance) A loss of a ship or cargo in which the subject matter is destroyed or damaged to such an extent that it can no longer be used for its purpose, or when the insured is irretrievably deprived of it. If the ship or cargo is the subject of a *valued policy, the measure of indemnity is the sum fixed by the policy; if the policy is unvalued, the measure of indemnity is the insurable value of the subject insured. *Compare* CONSTRUCTIVE TOTAL LOSS.

actus reus [Latin: a guilty act] The prohibited conduct or behaviour that the law seeks to prevent. Although commonly referred to as the "guilty act" this is rather simplistic, as the *actus reus* includes all the aspects of the crime except the accused's mental state (*see* MENS REA). In most cases the *actus reus* will simply be an act (e.g. appropriation of property is the act of theft) accompanied by specified circumstances (e.g. that the property belongs to another). Sometimes, however, the *actus reus* may be an *omission to act (e.g. failure to prevent death may be the *actus reus* of manslaughter: *R v Stone and Dobinson* [1977] QB 354) or it may include a specified consequence (death resulting being the consequence required for the *actus reus* of murder or manslaughter). In certain cases the *actus reus* may simply be a state of affairs rather than an act (*Winzar v Chief Constable of Kent* (1983) *The Times* 28 March 1983).

actus reus non facit reum nisi mens sit rea [Latin: an act is not necessarily a guilty act unless the accused has the necessary state of mind required for that offence] The maxim that, generally, a person cannot be guilty of a crime unless two elements are present: the *actus reus* ("guilty act") and the *mens rea* ("guilty mind"). Most criminal offences require (1) an *actus reus* (conduct "external" to the defendant's thoughts and intentions) and (2) a *mens rea* (a specific state of mind on the part of the accused).

ad colligenda bona [Latin] To collect the goods. The court may grant *letters of administration *ad colligenda bona* to any person to deal with specified property in an estate when that property might be endangered by delay. The purpose of the grant is to collect in and preserve assets. For example, if part of the estate consists of perishable goods the court may grant administration *ad colligenda bona* to any suitable person to allow him to sell or otherwise deal with those goods for the benefit of the estate. This is a limited grant only and ceases on the issue of a full grant of representation to the persons entitled to deal with the whole estate. In one case, such a grant was issued to the Official Solicitor on an application by HM Revenue and Customs when the executors of the deceased's will delayed applying for probate.

additional voluntary contribution (AVC) An additional payment that may be made by an employee to a *pension scheme in order to increase the benefits available from his pension fund on retirement. AVCs can be paid into an employer's scheme or into a scheme of the employee's choice (a free-standing AVC); they can be made free of tax within HM Revenue limits.

address for service The address, which a party to court proceedings gives to the court and/or the other party, to which all the formal documents relating to the proceedings should be delivered. Notices delivered at that address (which may be, for example, the address of his solicitors) are binding on the party concerned. Relevant rules are contained in Part 6 of the *Civil Procedure Rules. *See* SERVICE.

adduce *vb*. To put forward in evidence.

ademption *n*. The cancellation or reduction of a specific *legacy because the subject matter of the gift is no longer part of the testator's estate at his death, or the testator no longer has power to dispose of it, or there is nothing conforming to the description of it in the will. For example, if the will bequeaths a particular house that the testator sold during his lifetime, or if after making a will giving a legacy to his child the testator gives the child property constituting a *portion, the legacy is in each case adeemed. The gift of the house is cancelled and the child's legacy is reduced by the amount of the portion (*see also* SATISFACTION). Ademption need not occur by the testator's own deed; for example, an Act of Parliament that nationalized a company in which the testator had shares would cause a legacy of those shares to adeem. Neither a general legacy nor a demonstrative legacy can be affected by ademption. An express clause in a will may provide the legatee with a *substitutional legacy if ademption should occur.

ad hoc [Latin: for this] For a particular purpose, case, or occasion only.

ad idem [Latin: towards the same] Indicates that the parties to a transaction are in agreement. *See* CONSENSUS AD IDEM.

ADIZ *See* AIR DEFENCE IDENTIFICATION ZONE.

adjective law The part of the law that deals with practice and procedure in the courts. *Compare* SUBSTANTIVE LAW.

adjournment *n*. (in court procedure) The postponement or suspension of the hearing of a case until a future date. Civil courts have the power to adjourn hearings under Part 3 of the *Civil Procedure Rules and criminal courts have the power to adjourn proceedings under the *Criminal Procedure Rules.

adjudication *n*. The formal judgment or decision of a court or tribunal.

adjudication order Formerly, a court order that made a debtor bankrupt. It was replaced by a *bankruptcy order.

adjustment *n*. **1.** The determination of the amount due under a policy of insurance. **2.** The working out by an average adjuster of the rights and liabilities arising in a case of general *average.

ad litem [Latin: as regards the action] A **grant *ad litem*** is the appointment by a court
of a person to act on behalf of an estate in court proceedings, when the estate's proper
representatives are unable or unwilling to act. For example, the Official Solicitor may
be appointed administrator *ad litem* when a person wishes to claim against the estate
under the Inheritance (Provision for Family and Dependants) Act 1975 (*see* FAMILY
PROVISION) but the personal representatives are not willing to act, or nobody is entitled to
a grant, or the only person entitled to a grant is the litigant himself. Once the proceedings
in question are over, application may be made by the estate's proper representatives
for a general grant, whereupon the grant *ad litem* will terminate. A **guardian *ad litem***
is the former name for a *litigation friend responsible for the conduct of legal
proceedings on behalf of someone else (typically, a minor). *See* CHILDREN'S GUARDIAN.

administration *n.* **1.** The period in which the affairs, business, and property of a
company is managed by a qualified *insolvency practitioner known as an **administrator**.
The provision is contained in schedule B1 of the Insolvency Act 1986. The administrator
can be appointed either by the court under an *administration order or by the company,
its directors, or a *qualifying floating charge holder. The administrator must perform his
functions in the interests of the company's creditors as a whole, in accordance with the
following three objectives, which are in descending order of importance:

(a) To rescue the company as a going concern (the primary purpose);
(b) To achieve a better result for the company's creditors than would be achieved if the
      company were wound up; and
(c) To realize property to make a distribution to one or more secured or preferential
      creditors.

2. The collection of assets, payment of debts, and distribution to the beneficiaries
of property in the estate of a deceased person. *See also* GRANT OF REPRESENTATION.
3. The granting of *letters of administration in the estate of a deceased person to an
*administrator, when there is no executor under the will. **4.** The process of carrying
out duties imposed by a trust in connection with the property of a person of unsound
mind or a bankrupt.

administration action Application made by the *personal representatives of the
estate of a deceased person, or by a beneficiary or creditor of the estate, for an order that
the court take over the administration of the estate. Once such an order has been made,
the powers of the personal representatives to deal with the estate cannot be exercised
without sanction of the court.

administration bond A guarantee by a third party, often an insurance company, to
make good any loss arising if a person to whom letters of administration have been
granted fails to deal properly with the estate. The court usually requires an
administration bond as a condition of granting letters of administration only when the
beneficiaries are considered to need special protection, e.g. when the administrator lives
abroad or where there has been a dispute as to who should administer the estate.

administration of poison *See* POISON.

administration order **1.** An order made in a county court for the administration
of the affairs of a *judgment debtor. The order normally requires the debtor to pay his
debts by instalments: so long as he does so, the creditors referred to in the order cannot
enforce their individual claims by other methods without the leave of the court.
Administration orders are issued when the debtor has multiple debts but it is thought
that his bankruptcy can be avoided. Relevant rules are set out in Order 39 of the County
Court Rules, at schedule 2 to the *Civil Procedure Rules. **2.** An order made by the

court under the Insolvency Act 1986, directing that, during the period for which it is in force, the affairs, business, and property of a company shall be managed by an administrator appointed by the court. In order for the court to grant such an order it must be satisfied that the company cannot or is unlikely to be able to pay its debts when due *and* that the order is likely to allow for the three stated objectives of an *administration.

The Insolvency Act does not specify a period for the duration of the order: it remains in force until the administrator is discharged, by the court, having achieved the purpose(s) for which the order was granted or having decided that the purpose cannot be achieved.

While the order is in force the company may not be wound up; no steps may be taken to enforce any security over the company's property or to repossess goods in the company's possession, except with the leave of the court, and no other proceedings or other legal processes may be initiated or continued, against the company or its property, except with the court's leave.

administration pending suit *See* PENDENTE LITE.

administration period The period during which the estate of a deceased person is administered. The administration period begins at the date of death and is completed when *personal representatives have ascertained the value of the deceased's *residuary estate.

Administrative Court A section of the *Queen's Bench Division of the High Court that hears *judicial review cases.

Administrative Justice and Tribunals Council A body created by the Tribunals, Courts and Enforcement Act 2007 to oversee *administrative tribunals and inquiries. Under the Public Bodies Act 2011 it was abolished as of 19 August 2013.

administrative law The branch of *public law governing the exercise of powers and duties by public authorities. It is particularly concerned with the control of public power by *judicial review and by non-judicial mechanisms such as individual and collective *ministerial responsibility, and the work of the *Parliamentary Ombudsman, the *Commissions for Local Administration, and other Commissioners or Ombudsmen. There is no universally accepted demarcation of the area of administrative law, but it conventionally includes tribunals and inquiries as well as central and local government.

administrative letter *See* COMFORT LETTER.

administrative powers Discretionary powers of an executive nature that are conferred by legislation on government ministers, public and local authorities, and other bodies and persons for the purpose of giving detailed effect to broadly defined policy. Examples include powers to acquire land compulsorily, to grant or refuse licences or consents, and to determine the precise nature and extent of services to be provided. Administrative powers are found in every sphere of public administration, including town and country planning, the regulation of public health and other environmental matters, the functioning of the welfare services, and the control of many trades, professions, and other activities. Their exercise is subject to judicial control by means of the doctrine of *ultra vires.

administrative receiver A *receiver who, under the terms of a debenture secured by floating *charge, takes control of all (or substantially all) of a company's assets. Subject to certain exceptions, an administrative receiver cannot be appointed by the holder of a floating charge in respect of any floating charge created after 15 September 2003 (in accordance with the Insolvency Act 1986, as amended by the Enterprise Act 2002). *See also* INSOLVENCY PRACTITIONER.

administrative tribunal A body established by or under Act of Parliament to decide claims and disputes arising in connection with the administration of legislative schemes, normally of a welfare or regulatory nature. The tribunals exist outside the ordinary courts of law, but their decisions are subject to judicial control by means of the doctrine of **ultra vires* and in cases of *error of law on the face of the record. Under the Tribunals, Courts and Enforcement Act 2007 the jurisdictions of many existing tribunals were transferred to two new bodies, the *First-tier Tribunal and the *Upper Tribunal. *Compare* DOMESTIC TRIBUNAL. *See also* COURTS AND TRIBUNALS SERVICE, HM.

administrator *n.* **1.** A person appointed by the court to collect and distribute a deceased person's estate when the deceased died intestate, his will did not appoint an executor, or the executor refuses to act. An administrator's authority to deal with the estate does not begin until the court has granted *letters of administration. The Non-Contentious Probate Rules 1987 (r 20 and r 22) lay down the order in which people are entitled to a *grant of representation. *Compare* EXECUTOR. **2.** *See* ADMINISTRATION.

Admiralty Court A court forming part of the *Queen's Bench Division of the High Court whose jurisdiction embraces civil actions relating to ships and the sea. *Puisne judges hear cases with the assistance of nautical assessors. The court's work includes cases about collisions, damage to cargo, prizes (*see* PRIZE COURT), and salvage, and in some cases *assessors may be called in to sit with the judge. The distinctive feature of the court's procedure is the action **in rem,* under which the property that has given rise to the cause of action (usually a ship) may be "arrested" and held by the court to satisfy the claimant's claim. In practice, it is usual for the owners of the property to give security for its release while the action is proceeding. If the claim is successful, the property held or the sum given by way of security is available to satisfy the judgment. Until 1971 the Admiralty Court was part of the *Probate, Divorce and Admiralty Division of the High Court. Since the Access to Justice Act 1999, all Admiralty proceedings are allocated to the *multi-track.

admissibility of evidence The principles determining whether or not particular items of evidence may be received by the court. The central principle of admissibility is *relevance. All evidence that is sufficiently relevant is admissible and all that is not sufficiently relevant is inadmissible. However, evidence that is relevant may be inadmissible if it falls within the scope of one of the *exclusionary rules of evidence. *See also* CONDITIONAL ADMISSIBILITY; MULTIPLE ADMISSIBILITY.

admissibility of records In civil proceedings, documents containing information (records) are admissible under the Civil Evidence Act 1995 as evidence of the facts stated in them. Before the introduction of the 1995 Act such documents and records were admissible only if they came within an exception to the rules prohibiting the use of *hearsay evidence. In criminal cases, the hearsay rules in relation to business documents are now to be found in section 117 of the Criminal Justice Act 2003. Under this provision, such records are generally admissible if oral evidence would be admissible as evidence of the matter, the document was created or received by a person acting in the course of a trade, business, profession, or other occupation, or as the holder of a paid or unpaid office, and the person who supplied the information contained in the records had (or may reasonably be supposed to have had) personal knowledge of the matters dealt with.

admission *n*. **1.** In civil proceedings, a statement by a party to litigation or by his duly authorized agent that is adverse to the party's case. Admissions may be **informal** (i.e. in a document or by word of mouth) or **formal** (i.e. made in a statement of case or in reply to a request for further information). **2.** In criminal proceedings, a statement by the defendant admitting an offence or a fact. Admissions may be informal or formal. An informal admission is called a *confession. A formal admission must comply with section 10 of the Criminal Justice Act 1967 and may be made either before or at the hearing, but if not made in court, it must be in writing and signed by the defendant or his legal adviser. A formal admission may be made in respect of any fact about which *oral evidence could be given and is *conclusive evidence of the fact admitted at all criminal proceedings relating to the matter, although it may be withdrawn at any stage with the permission of the court. A plea of guilty to a charge read out in court is a formal admission. *See also* CAUTION.

admonition *n*. A reprimand from a judge to a defendant who has been discharged from the further prosecution of an offence.

adoption **1.** The process by which a parent's legal rights and duties in respect of an unmarried minor are transferred to another person or persons. Adoption can only take place by means of an **adoption order** made by the family proceedings court, the county court, or the High Court. After the adoption order the child's natural parents are no longer considered in law to be the parents of the child, and the child is henceforth regarded as the legal child of the adoptive parents. Adoption is different from any other court order affecting children, such as a *residence order, because it extinguishes the *parental responsibility held by anyone before the making of the order.

The law on adoption is now contained in the Adoption and Children Act 2002. Detailed procedural rules and accompanying practice directions for all proceedings involving adoption were issued by the Family Procedure Rule Committee in 2005.

Unlike previous legislation, the 2002 Act is based on an explicit statement that the paramount consideration in deciding whether or not a child should be adopted must be the welfare of that child throughout his or her life. The court must, when reaching its decision, take into account all relevant circumstances, including (if possible) the child's wishes. The court should direct its mind not only to what the child might gain from adoption, but also to what the child might lose, for example, his or her links with existing wider family members. The court will be aided in reaching its decision by consulting experts, such as social workers or psychiatrists. It may also appoint a *children's guardian to act in the child's best interests.

There are many provisions in the Children and Adoption Act 2002 designed to make sure that any adoption will be in the child's best interest. For example, an adoption agency is expressly required, when placing a child, to give due consideration to the child's religious persuasion, ethnic origin, and cultural background. There are also rules as to who may adopt and who may be adopted. The 2002 Act breaks new ground in allowing, for the first time, unmarried couples, whether heterosexual or same sex, to adopt a child together (effective from December 2005). Under the Act, every local authority must set up and maintain an *adoption service, and these are carefully controlled. Since 2003 adoption support services, including financial support as well as advice and counselling, are available to adoptive parents.

Normally a child cannot be adopted without the consent of each of its parents or guardians, but a court may make an adoption order against the parents' wishes if it considers it to be in the child's best interest to do so. In the case of a child who is in local authority care under a *care order, the court may make a *placement order without the parents' consent. Since the Children Act 1989 the court has an option of making a *residence order instead of an adoption order, so that parental responsibility may be shared with the birth parents. It can also make a *contact order in addition to an adoption order, so that the child can continue to maintain links with his birth family (*see* POST-ADOPTION CONTACT).

The Registrar General must keep a register containing details of all adoption orders, which any member of the public may consult. An adopted child over the age of 18 has a right to a copy of his original birth certificate, thereby enabling him to find out who his natural parents are. Although natural parents can register their interest in contacting their children who have been adopted, they have no corresponding right to trace these adopted children. The **Adoption Contact Register** contains the names and addresses of all adopted persons who are over the age of 18, have a copy of their birth certificate, and wish to contact a relative, together with the details of relatives who wish to make contact with an adopted person. **2.** Reliance by a court on a rule of international law that has not been expressly made part of the law of the land but is not inconsistent with it. **3.** The decision of a local authority or similar body to bring into force in their area an Act of Parliament conferring powers on them at their option.

(⊕) SEE WEB LINKS

- Introduction to the Adoption Contact Register from the GOV.UK website
- Website of the British Agencies for Adoption and Fostering

adoption agency A local authority or an approved *adoption society. The role of the agency is to decide whether prospective adopters are suitable and whether a placement of a particular child with prospective adopters should be approved.

adoption leave Time off work available to adoptive parents when a child is newly placed for adoption. It is available to an individual or to one member of a couple (although the other may qualify for *paternity leave). To qualify for leave, an employee must have worked continuously for the employer for 26 weeks ending with the week in which they are notified of being matched with a child for adoption.

Adopters are entitled to up to 26 weeks' **ordinary adoption leave** followed by up to 26 weeks' **additional adoption leave**. Leave may start from the date of the child's placement or from a fixed date that can be up to 14 days before the expected date of placement. During leave, most adopters are entitled to **Statutory Adoption Pay** (**SAP**) from their employers. This is payable for up to 39 weeks. The rate of Statutory Adoption Pay is the same as the standard rate of Statutory Maternity Pay (*see* MATERNITY RIGHTS). Adopters must inform their employers of their intention to take adoption leave within seven days of being notified by their adoption agency that they have been matched with a child for adoption, unless this is not reasonably practicable. Employees are protected from suffering detriment or unfair dismissal for reasons related to taking, or seeking to take, adoption leave. Employees who believe they have been treated unfairly can complain to an *employment tribunal. *See also* DEPENDANTS' LEAVE; PARENTAL LEAVE; PATERNITY LEAVE.

adoption service Under the Children and Adoption Act 2002 the different services, collectively, that local authorities must provide within their area in order to meet the needs of *adoption. These services include provision of accommodation for pregnant women and mothers, making arrangements for placing children with prospective adopters, and advising people with adoption problems. In addition, each local authority must provide **adoption support services**, such as advice and counselling, and health, education, and cultural services.

adoption society A group of people organized to make arrangements for the adoption of children. Adoption societies must be approved by the Secretary of State before acting as such.

adoptive relationship A legal relationship created as a result of an *adoption order. The persons adopting a child are known as **adoptive parents** and other relatives as **adoptive relatives**. The laws of *affinity are, however, not altered by the new adoptive relationship.

ADR *See* ALTERNATIVE DISPUTE RESOLUTION.

ad referendum [Latin: subject to reference] Denoting a contract or other matter that is subject to agreement by other parties and finalization of the details.

adulteration *n.* The mixing of other substances with food. It is an offence of *strict liability under the Food Act 1984 to sell any food containing a substance that would endanger health. It is also an offence to mix dangerous substances into food with the intention of selling the mixture.

adultery *n.* An act of sexual intercourse between a male and female not married to each other, when at least one of them is married to someone else. Intercourse for this purpose means penetration of the vagina by the penis; any degree of penetration will suffice (full penetration is not necessary). Receiving donor insemination does not constitute adultery, nor does anal intercourse or non-penetrative sex. Adultery is one of the five facts that a petitioner may rely on under the Matrimonial Causes Act 1973 as evidence to show that the marriage has irretrievably broken down. However, in addition to the adultery, the petitioner must show that she or he finds it intolerable to live with the respondent; this need not be as a consequence at the adultery (*Cleary v Cleary* [1974] 1 WLR 73 (CA)). *See* DIVORCE.

ad valorem [Latin: to value] According to or in proportion to the value of something. Thus an *ad valorum* duty is levied in accordance with the value of the goods concerned, as opposed to their quantity.

advance decision A legally recognized decision (often described as a **living will**) regulated by the Mental Capacity Act 2005, in which a mentally capable adult identifies specified treatment (e.g. a blood transfusion) that should not be carried out in the event that he loses capacity. Generally, there is no requirement that the decision be in writing unless it relates to life-saving treatment (in which case it must be in writing and witnessed by a third party). In order to be effective the directive must be valid (e.g. the patient must not have withdrawn it or done anything inconsistent with the decision: *HE v A Hospital NHS Trust* [2003] EWHC 1017 (Fam), [2003] FLR 408). It must also be applicable to the treatment in question. For this reason advance directives need careful drafting. A medical professional who provides treatment in contravention of an advance directive that he knows to be valid and applicable is potentially committing a tortious or criminal act.

advance information In criminal proceedings, information about the case against an accused provided by the prosecution to the defence as part of the pretrial *disclosure of information. More specifically, the term refers to information disclosed as part of the *mode of trial procedure now governed by part 21 of the Criminal Procedure Rules.

advancement *n.* **1.** The power, in a trust, to provide capital sums for the benefit of a person who is an infant or who may (but is not certain to) receive the property under a settlement. The term is a shortened form of **advancement in the world** and has the connotation of providing a single or lump sum from the trust fund for a specific purpose of a permanent nature; examples include sums payable on marriage, to buy a house for the beneficiary, or to establish the beneficiary in a trade or profession. Until 1925 a power of advancement had to be specifically included in any settlement: a statutory power now exists, under section 32 of the Trustee Act 1925, subject to contrary intention. No person may receive by way of advancement more than half that to which he could ever become entitled. **2.** A presumption, arising in certain circumstances, that if one person makes a voluntary transfer to another or purchases property in the name of another, the property is intended for the advancement of that other person and will be held beneficially by that person and not on *resulting trust for the person who provides or purchases it. The presumption of advancement arises when a father or other person in the position of a parent (*in loco parentis*) purchases property for, or makes a voluntary transfer of property to, a child. The presumption does not automatically arise in the case of a mother. Until 1882 a married woman could not, during marriage, own property. However, her automatic exclusion from the presumption now seems nonsensical (especially as a mother now has a statutory duty to maintain her children), although she will in many cases be found to be "in the position of a parent". The presumption of advancement has been held to exist when a husband makes a voluntary transfer to, or purchases property for, his wife (though not *vice versa*), and occasionally a man for his mistress, but the strength (and perhaps even the existence) of this presumption has been doubted (*Pettitt v Pettitt* [1970] AC 777 (HL)). The presumption of advancement, in so far as it subsists, may be rebutted by evidence that advancement was not intended. This evidence may be *parol evidence.

Section 199 of the Equality Act 2010 seeks to abolish the presumption of advancement on grounds of sex equality; however, this provision has not so far (2014) been brought into force.

adversary procedure *See* ACCUSATORIAL PROCEDURE.

adverse inference An inference that may be drawn contrary to a defendant's interest in a criminal case under sections 34–37 of the Criminal Justice and Public Order Act 1994. The Act provides that the court may draw such inferences as appear proper from the defendant's failure to mention facts when questioned or charged, his silence at trial, his failure to account for objects, substances, or marks when arrested, and his failure or refusal to account for his presence at a particular place when arrested. The European Court of Human Rights has held that adverse inferences are not *per se* a breach of Article 6 of the European Convention on Human Rights, which protects the right to a *fair trial (*John Murray v United Kingdom* (1996) 22 EHRR 29).

adverse occupation Occupation of premises by a trespasser to the exclusion of the owner or lawful occupier. *Trespass in itself is not usually a criminal offence, but if the premises are residential and were being occupied, the trespasser (whether or not he used force in order to enter) is guilty of an offence under the Criminal Law Act 1977 if he refuses to leave when asked to do so by the displaced *residential occupier or a protected intending occupier (or by someone acting on behalf of them). A protected intending occupier includes a purchaser, someone let in by the local authority, Housing Corporation, or a housing association with written evidence of his claim to the premises, or someone holding a lease, tenancy, or licence with two years to run. Under the Criminal Justice and Public Order Act 1994, such a person may obtain an interim possession order. This differs from an ordinary possession order in that it is much quicker, may be heard in the absence of those on the property, and involves the police in enforcement. Once the proper procedure has been followed and the applicant has shown a good case for possession, an order will require those on the land to leave within 24 hours. Remaining on the premises or re-entry within 12 months is a *summary offence, punishable by a *fine on level 5 and/or six months' imprisonment. A uniformed constable has a power of *arrest. It is also an offence to make false or misleading statements in making or resisting such an order. Similar penalties apply on summary conviction, but on *indictment a maximum of two years' imprisonment and/or a fine may be imposed.

Usually it is a summary offence for a stranger or the landlord to use violence to gain entry to premises when it is known that there is someone on those premises opposed to such an entry. However, a displaced residential occupier or a protected intending occupier who has asked the person to leave may call on the police for assistance. A police constable may arrest anyone who refuses to leave for the *summary offence of adverse occupation of residential premises. Furthermore, it is not an offence if a constable, a displaced residential occupier, or a protected intending occupier (or their agents) uses force to secure entry. *See* FORCIBLE ENTRY.

adverse possession The occupation of land to which another person (the **paper owner**) has title, with the intention of possessing it as one's own. The leading case on adverse possession is *Pye v Graham* [2002] UKHL 30, [2003] 1 AC 419. That case confirmed that, in order to adversely possess land, the adverse possessor ("squatter") must dispossess the paper owner by exercising exclusive physical possession of the land with the intention of possessing it to the exclusion of all others, without the consent of the paper owner.

The effect of adverse possession depends upon whether the land is registered or unregistered, and on the date of the adverse possession. If the land is unregistered, the effect of the Limitation Act 1980 is that in most cases adverse possession for 12 years or more extinguishes the title of the paper owner. The squatter becomes legally entitled to the land. In the case of registered land, where the limitation period of 12 years has been completed before 13 October 2003, 12 years' adverse possession will oblige the paper owner to hold the land on trust for the squatter under section 75 of the Land Registration Act 1925. The squatter is entitled to apply to the Land Registry to have the title transferred into his name. Where the limitation period of 12 years has not been completed before 13 October 2003, the Land Registration Act 2002 applies. After 10 years' adverse possession, the squatter may apply to be registered as the proprietor of the land. The Land Registrar will write to the registered proprietor and others interested in the land (such as mortgagees) to inform them of the application. Those notified have 65 working days to reply objecting to the application. If no objection is received, the squatter will be registered as proprietor in place of the original paper owner. If an objection is received, the paper owner has a further two years to eject the squatter; otherwise he can make a further application to be registered as proprietor. In a few exceptional cases, the squatter may be registered as proprietor despite the paper owner's objections, for example in cases where the real boundary between two properties has been in its present position for more than 10 years but the filed plan shows a different boundary.

A person who enters a residential building as a trespasser, knowing that he is a trespasser, and who lives or intends to live in the building is committing a criminal offence under the Legal Aid, Sentencing and Punishment of Offenders Act 2012 s 144. The offence is committed even if the squatter entered as a trespasser before the Act came into force. Adverse possession cannot be based upon a criminal act, and the Land Registry has made it clear that applications for registration will not be accepted from squatters who are in breach of this provision.

adverse witness A witness who gives evidence unfavourable to the party who called him. Unless the witness is deemed a *hostile witness, his credibility may not be attacked by the party calling him (although contradictory evidence may be called). If, however, the witness is deemed hostile the party calling him may be allowed to introduce evidence of a previous inconsistent statement made by that witness. *See also* UNFAVOURABLE WITNESS.

advice on evidence The written opinion of counsel identifying the issues raised in a civil or criminal case and advising counsel's instructing solicitor in relation to the evidence to be called at trial.

advisory jurisdiction The jurisdiction of the *International Court of Justice under which it can render legal opinions, similar in kind to declaration (*see* DECLARATORY JUDGMENT) under English municipal law. In contrast to the contentious jurisdiction of the Court, states are not parties to the proceedings and there is no claimant or defendant to the action. The Court proceeds by inviting states or international organizations to provide information to assist the Court in its determination of point of law at issue.

The authority of the International Court of Justice to give advisory opinions is found under Article 96 of the UN Charter. Under this Article the Court is empowered to give such opinions on legal questions at the request of the UN Security Council or the General Assembly. Moreover, the power to request advisory opinions on legal questions arising within the scope of their activities also resides in other organs of the United Nations and its specialized agencies if they have been authorized by the General Assembly to do so.

When an advisory opinion is sought upon a question actually pending between two states each of them is entitled to have an *ad hoc* judge on the bench. The request for an advisory opinion must be made by the United Nations to assist it in the discharge of its function; provided the opinion relates to a legal question it is immaterial that it affects political issues (*Admission of New Members Case* [1948] ICJ Rep 57). Consent is not required for an advisory opinion. Among the International Court of Justice's most prominent advisory opinions are *UN Admissions (Competence of General Assembly) Case* [1950] ICJ Rep 15; *Genocide Reservations Case* [1951] ICJ Rep 15; and *PLO UN Mission Case* [1988] ICJ Rep 12.

ad vitam aut culpam [Latin: for life or until blame] The principle that once appointed, certain office holders can only be removed for wrongdoing. In England judges were traditionally appointed on this basis to prevent their being dismissed for political reasons (Act of Settlement 1700 art 3 (7)). For judges, retirement is now governed by section 76 of the Judicial Pensions and Retirement Act 1993.

advocacy qualification A qualification authorizing a person to act as an *advocate under the provisions of the Courts and Legal Services Act 1990. There are separate qualifications for different levels of the court system, but the rights of those already entitled to appear as advocates at any level of the system at the time when the Act came into force are preserved.

advocate *n.* **1.** One who exercises a *right of audience and argues a case for a client in legal proceedings. In magistrates' courts, the county courts, tribunals, coroners' courts, and the European courts both *barristers and *solicitors have the right to appear as advocates. In most Crown Court centres, the High Court, the Court of Appeal, and the House of Lords barristers have traditionally had exclusive rights of audience. However, the provisions of the Courts and Legal Services Act 1990 allow solicitors with appropriate experience to qualify for rights of audience similar to those of barristers and acquire *advocacy qualifications for the Crown Court, High Court, Court of Appeal, and House of Lords. In many tribunals there are no rules concerning representation, and laymen may appear as advocates. Advocates no longer enjoy immunity from law suits for negligence in relation to civil or criminal litigation. **2.** In Scotland, a member of the Faculty of Advocates, the professional organization of the Scots Bar.

Advocates-General Senior law officers who assist the *European Court of Justice in its task of reaching a judgment in the cases brought before it. They are characterized by their independence and impartiality. Following the hearing of the case they deliver in open court an "opinion" that is not binding on the judges, but which reflects the views of someone with the same standing as a judge.

advowson *n.* A right of presenting a clergyman to an ecclesiastical living. The advowson is an incorporeal *hereditament that gives the owner (or patron) the right to nominate the next holder of a living that has fallen vacant. It may exist **in gross** (i.e. independently of any ownership of land by the person entitled) or may be **appendent** (i.e. annexed to land so that it may be enjoyed by each owner for the time being). The right is usually associated with the lordship of a manor.

aequitas est quasi aequalitas *See* EQUALITY IS EQUITY.

affidavit *n.* A sworn written statement of evidence used mainly to support certain applications and, in some circumstances, as evidence in court proceedings. The person who makes the affidavit must swear or affirm that the contents are true before a person authorized to take oaths in respect of the particular kind of affidavit. Under Part 32 of the *Civil Procedure Rules applications for *search orders, *freezing injunctions, or any order requiring an occupier to permit another to enter his land must be supported by affidavit evidence. Affidavits must comply with the criteria listed in Practice Direction 32. *See also* ARGUMENTATIVE AFFIDAVIT.

affiliation order Formerly, an order of a magistrates' court against a man alleged to be the father of an illegitimate child, obliging him to make payments towards the upkeep of the child. Affiliation proceedings have been abolished by the Family Law Reform Act 1987 and financial provision for illegitimate and legitimate children is now the same (*see* CHILD SUPPORT MAINTENANCE).

affinity *n.* The relationship created by marriage between a husband and his wife's blood relatives or between a wife and her husband's blood relatives. Some categories of people related by affinity are forbidden to marry each other (*see* PROHIBITED DEGREES OF RELATIONSHIPS). The relationship of blood relatives is known as *consanguinity. *See also* INCEST.

affirm *vb.* **1.** To confirm a legal decision, particularly (of an appeal court) to confirm a judgment made in a lower court. **2.** To promise in solemn form to tell the truth while giving evidence or when making an *affidavit. Under the Oaths Act 1978, any person who objects to being sworn on *oath, or in respect of whom it is not reasonably practicable to administer an oath, may instead affirm. Affirmation has the same legal effects as the taking of an oath. **3.** To treat a contract as continuing in existence, instead of exercising a right to rescind it for *misrepresentation or other cause (*see* VOIDABLE CONTRACT) or to treat it as discharged by reason of repudiation or breach (*see* BREACH OF CONTRACT). Affirmation is effective only if it takes place with full knowledge of the facts. It may take the form of an express declaration of intention to proceed with the contract; alternatively, that intention may be inferred from conduct (if, for example, the party attempts to sell goods that have been delivered under a contract voidable for misrepresentation). Lapse of time without seeking a remedy may be treated as evidence of affirmation (*Clough v London and North Western Railway Co* (1871) LR 7 Exch 26).

affirmative resolution *See* DELEGATED LEGISLATION.

affray *n*. The offence of using or threatening, other than by words alone, unlawful violence. The conduct must be such as would have caused a reasonable person to fear for his safety, though no such person need be present. The defendant must intend to use or threaten violence or, alternatively, must be aware that his conduct may be violent or threaten violence (*R v Smith* [1997] 1 Cr App R 14). The offence is found in the Public Order Act 1986, though it can be committed in private as well as in public places. It replaces the common-law offence of affray and is punishable on indictment with up to three years' imprisonment and/or a fine or, on summary conviction, by imprisonment for a term not exceeding six months or by a fine. A constable may arrest without warrant anyone he reasonable suspects is committing affray. *See also* ASSAULT; RIOT; VIOLENT DISORDER.

affreightment *n*. A contract for the carriage of goods by sea (the consideration being called **freight** and the carrier the **freighter**). It can be either a *charterparty or a contract whose terms are set out in the *bill of lading.

African, Caribbean, Pacific Group (ACP Group) The 79 countries in the developing world that are signatories to the **Cotonou Agreement** of June 2000, which establishes a partnership with the European Union. The main objectives of the Agreement are the reduction of poverty in ACP countries and the integration of these states with the rest of the global economy. Most ACP countries were former colonies of EU member states.

AGA *See* AUTHORIZED GUARANTEE AGREEMENT.

age discrimination The law governing age discrimination was introduced in 2006 and is now found in the *Equality Act 2010. Age discrimination is unlawful in employment and (from April 2012) in the provision of goods, facilities, and services. It covers direct and *indirect discrimination, *victimization, and *harassment. However, it differs from the other "protected characteristics" in that direct discrimination may be defended if it is objectively justified. There is also a range of exceptions where the general rules will not apply, including age-based concessions and state benefits.

There are no longer upper age limits on unfair dismissal and redundancy claims and employers cannot set compulsory retirement ages or force an employee to retire unless this can be justified as a proportionate means of achieving a legitimate aim (*Seldon v Clarkson Wright and Jakes* [2012] UKSC 16, [2012] ICR 716).

agency *n*. **1.** The relationship between an *agent and his principal. **2.** The business carried on by an agent.

agency workers Workers who are supplied to an employer by an agency, usually on a temporary or contingent basis. Agency workers have always lacked employment protection rights. Some protection was provided by the Conduct of Employment Agencies and Employment Businesses Regulations 2003 but employment rights remain a problem as it can be difficult to establish who, if anyone, is the employer. Such workers are sometimes said to have a "triangular" working relationship, in that they do their work for the client but may be paid by the agency. They may have a contract with the agency, with the client or, sometimes, with neither (*Montgomery v Johnson Underwood Ltd* [2001] EWCA Civ 318, [2001] ICR 819). In order to decide whether such a worker is an employee the courts have looked for a regular pattern of mutual obligations between the parties (*Consistent Group Lts v Kalwak and others* [2008] EWCA Civ 430, [2008] IRLR 505). The courts have been willing to consider the possibility of an implied contract of employment between a worker and the client who is using his services, but this would rarely be the case (*James v London Borough of Greenwich* [2008] EWCA Civ 35, [2008] IRLR 302).

Agency workers have, however, benefited from the Agency Workers Regulations 2010 which implemented the EU **Agency Workers Directive** 2008/104. The Regulations provide a right to "equal treatment" when an agency worker has undertaken the same role, whether on one or more assignments, with the same hirer for 12 continuous weeks. Agency workers have the right to bring a claim in an employment tribunal if assignments are structured so as to avoid the scope of the Regulations. "Equal treatment" means the agency worker should enjoy the same basic working and employment conditions as he would have been entitled to if recruited by the hirer under a *contract of employment to do the same job. Basic working and employment conditions cover pay and working time protections (e.g. rest breaks; annual leave entitlement).

The Regulations do not give a right to complain about *unfair dismissal or claim certain other employment rights because they do not make agency workers "employees". To that extent earlier case law remains relevant.

agent *n*. A person appointed by another (the **principal**) to act on his behalf, often to negotiate a contract between the principal and a third party. If an agent discloses his principal's name (or at least the existence of a principal) to the third party with whom he is dealing, the agent himself is not normally entitled to the benefit of, or be liable on, the contract. An **undisclosed principal** is one whose existence is not revealed by the agent to a third party; he may still be entitled to the benefit of, and be liable on, the contract, but in such cases the agent is also entitled and liable. However, an undisclosed principal may not be entitled to the benefit of a contract if the agency is inconsistent with the terms of the contract or if the third party shows that he wished to contract with the agent personally.

A **general agent** is one who has authority to act for his principal in all his business of a particular kind, or who acts for the principal in the course of his (the agent's) usual business or profession. A **special agent** is authorized to act only for a special purpose that is not in the ordinary course of the agent's business or profession. The principal of a general agent is bound by acts of the agent that are incidental to the ordinary conduct of the agent's business or the effective performance of his duties, even if the principal has imposed limitations on the agent's authority. But in the case of a special agent, the principal is not bound by acts that are not within the authority conferred. In either case, the principal may ratify an unauthorized contract. An agent for the sale of goods sometimes agrees to protect his principal against the risk of the buyer's insolvency. He does this by undertaking liability for the unjustifiable failure of the third-party buyer to pay the price of the goods. Such an agent is called a *del credere* **agent**. *See also* COMMERCIAL AGENT; MERCANTILE AGENT.

agent provocateur A person who actively entices, encourages, or persuades another person to commit a crime that would not otherwise have been committed and then reports the person to the authorities (*see* ENTRAPMENT). The agent provocateur may be regarded as an accomplice in any offence committed as a result of this intervention; however, the fact that the principal was enticed, encouraged, or persuaded by the agent provocateur provides no defence for the principal.

age of consent The age at which a person can legally consent to sexual intercourse, or to an act that would otherwise constitute sexual assault. This age is 16.

aggravated assault *See* ASSAULT.

aggravated burglary *See* BURGLARY.

aggravated damages Compensatory *damages that are awarded when the conduct
of the defendant or the surrounding circumstances increase the injury to the claimant by
subjecting him to humiliation, distress, or embarrassment, particularly in such torts as
assault, false imprisonment, and defamation. *Compare* EXEMPLARY DAMAGES.

aggravated trespass *See* TRESPASS.

aggravated vehicle-taking An offence concerning so-called **joyriding**, created by
the Aggravated Vehicle Taking Act 1992 and inserted in The Theft Act 1968 (s 12A). The
offence arises when a motor vehicle that has been unlawfully taken is driven in a
dangerous manner on a public road, causing an accident resulting in injury to another
person or damage to property or to the vehicle itself. Any person who either (i) took the
vehicle or (ii) drove it or rode in it knowing that it was taken without the owner's consent
may be guilty of the offence.

aggregates levy A tax imposed on the commercial exploitation of rock, gravel, or
sand by the Finance Act 2001 (s 16–49 cc 4–10). The tax is charged on all supplies made
on or after 1 April 2002.

aggression *n.* (in international law) According to the General Assembly Resolution
(3314) on the Definition of Aggression 1975, the use of armed force by one state against
the sovereignty, territorial integrity, or political independence of another state or in any
way inconsistent with the Charter of the United Nations. The Resolution lists examples of
aggression, which include the following:

(1) invasion, attack, military occupation, or annexation of the territory of any state by the
    armed forces of another state;
(2) bombardment or the use of any weapons by a state against another state's territory;
(3) armed blockade by a state of another state's ports or coasts;
(4) the use of a state's armed forces in another state in breach of the terms of the
    agreement on which they were allowed into that state;
(5) allowing one's territory to be placed at the disposal of another state, to be used by
    that state for committing an act of aggression against a third state;
(6) sending armed bands or guerrillas to carry out armed raids on another state that are
    grave enough to amount to any of the above acts.

The first use of armed force by a state in contravention of the UN Charter is prima facie
evidence of aggression, although the final decision in such cases is left to the Security
Council, who may also classify other acts as aggression. The Resolution declares that no
consideration whatsoever can justify aggression, that territory cannot be acquired by acts
of aggression, and that wars of aggression constitute a crime against international peace.
See also HUMANITARIAN INTERVENTION; MARTENS CLAUSE; OCCUPATION; OFFENCES
AGAINST INTERNATIONAL LAW AND ORDER; USE OF FORCE; WAR; WAR CRIMES.

agreement *n.* (in international law) *See* TREATY.

agreement for a lease A contract to enter into a *lease. Special rules govern the
creation of such a contract. Before 27 September 1989, a contract to grant a lease was
unenforceable unless it was evidenced in writing (Law Property Act 1925 s 40) or
evidenced by a sufficient act of *part performance (such as taking possession and paying
rent). Since 27 September 1989, a contract to grant a lease for not more than three years
may be made orally or by any kind of written agreement so long as it does not give rise to
a *future lease. A contract to grant a longer lease must be in writing, incorporating all the
terms of the agreement, and signed by the parties (Law of Property (Miscellaneous
Provisions) Act 1989 s 2). A contract that does not comply with these requirements is void

a

irrespective of performance unless it gives rise to a constructive or resulting trust (Law of Property (Miscellaneous Provisions) Act 1989; *Yaxley v Gotts* [1999] EWCA Civ 3006, [2000] Ch 162).

agrément *n*. The formal diplomatic notification by a state that the diplomatic agent selected to be sent to it by another state has been accepted, i.e. is *persona grata* and can consequently become accredited to it. The *agrément* is the reply to a query by the sending state, which precedes the sent diplomat's formal nomination and accreditation. This type of mutual exchange by two states over their diplomatic representation is called **agréation** and is an informal method of determining that the representative is acceptable to the host state before the final appointment is made. The mere expression of a wish may reasonably be enough to prevent an appointment from being made. However, once *agrément* has been made, good cause alone justifies a demand that it be cancelled. *See also* PERSONA NON GRATA.

agricultural holding A tenancy of agricultural land under the Agricultural Holdings Act 1986. Tenants have special statutory protection and there is a procedure to fix rent by arbitration if the parties cannot agree. The landlord normally has to give at least one year's notice to quit. The tenant can usually appeal to *Agricultural Land and Drainage to decide whether the notice to quit should operate. The landlord is entitled to compensation at the end of the tenancy if the holding has deteriorated and the tenant is at fault; the tenant can claim compensation at the end of the tenancy for disturbance and for improvements he has made. The 1986 Act gives the security of tenure. No new Agricultural Holdings Act tenancies may be created after 1 September 1995 (*see* FARM BUSINESS TENANCY). Tenancies and licences to those working the land may give security of tenure under the Housing Act 1988 if the tenants are qualifying workers (working on the land as defined in the Act) and otherwise qualify. *See* ASSURED AGRICULTURAL OCCUPANCY.

Agricultural Land and Drainage (AL&D) An independent statutory body that now forms part of the *First-tier Tribunal (Property Chamber). Its main role is in settling disputes between agricultural tenants and landlords arising from tenancy agreements held under the Agricultural Holdings Act 1986. AL&D also considers applications under the Land and Drainage Act 1991 in respect of drainage issues between neighbours.

agricultural property relief An *inheritance tax relief available on the transfer of agricultural land and buildings when certain qualifying conditions are met. A farmhouse can qualify for agricultural property relief.

aid and abet To assist in the performance of a crime either before or during (but not after) its commission. Aiding usually refers to material assistance (e.g. providing the tools for the crime), and abetting to lesser assistance (e.g. acting as a look-out or driving a car to the scene of the crime). Aiders and abettors are liable to be tried as *accessories. Mere presence at the scene of a crime is not aiding and abetting (*R v Allan* [1965] 1 QB 130: here the defendant passively watched a fight but there was no evidence to show that his mere presence offered encouragement). The prosecution must prove that the defendant had knowledge that he was assisting the *principal in the commission of the crime. *See also* IMPEDING APPREHENSION OR PROSECUTION.

Air Defence Identification Zone (ADIZ) A zone, which can extend in some cases up to 300 miles beyond the territorial sea, established for security reasons by some states off their coasts. When entering the ADIZ all aircraft are required to identify themselves, report flight plans, and inform ground control of their exact position. *See also* AIRSPACE.

airforce law *See* SERVICE LAW.

air pollution *See* POLLUTION.

airspace *n.* In English law and international law, the ownership of land includes ownership of the airspace above it, by application of the maxim **cuius est solum, eius est usque ad coelum et ad inferos* (whoever owns land, it is theirs up to the heavens and down to hell); outer space, however, is not considered to be subject to ownership.

In English law an owner has rights in as much of the airspace above his land as is necessary for the ordinary use of his land and the structures on it. This constraint reflects an overriding public interest in aerospace technology, which would be threatened were consent to be required for aircraft or satellites passing over land (*Bernstein v Skyviews* [1978] QB 479). Within these limits a projection over one's land (such as a signboard or even a very tall crane) can be a trespass (*Kelsen v Imperial Tobacco Co* [1957] 2 QB 334) and pollution of air by one's neighbour can be a nuisance (*St Helens Smelting Co v Tipping* (1865) 11 HL Cas 642). Pollution of air is also controlled by various statutes. There is no natural right to the free flow of air from neighbouring land, but **easements for the flow of air through a defined opening (such as a window or a ventilator) can be acquired. Civil aircraft flying at a reasonable height over land do not commit trespass (Civil Aviation Act 1982 s 76(1)), but damages can be obtained if material loss or damage is caused to people or property.

In international law, national airspace, including airspace above the internal waters and the territorial sea, is under complete and exclusive sovereignty of the subjacent state. As a result, apart from aircraft in distress, any use of national airspace by non-national aircraft requires the official consent of the state concerned. This can be granted unilaterally or more commonly (in respect of commercial flights) through a bilateral treaty, usually on conditions of reciprocity. *See* TERRITORIAL WATERS.

alcohol treatment requirement A requirement that may be imposed by a sentencing court as part of a **community order or a **suspended sentence order under the Criminal Justice Act 2003. It requires that the offender undergoes treatment to reduce or eliminate his dependency on alcohol. The requirement cannot be imposed without the offender first expressing his willingness to comply.

alderman *n.* A senior member of a local authority, elected by its directly elected members. Active aldermanic rank now exists only in the **City of London, having been phased out elsewhere by the Local Government Act 1972. County, district, and London borough councils can, however, appoint past members to honorary rank in recognition of eminent service. The term was originally synonymous with "elder" and is of Anglo-Saxon derivation.

aleatory contract An agreement of which the effects, with respect both to the gains and losses, whether to all parties or to some of them, depend on an uncertain event. Classically, this would be a **gaming contract. At common law a wager was a legal contract, which the courts were bound to enforce, so long as it was not against morality, decency, or sound policy (*Johnson v Lumley* (1852) 12 CB 468).

alibi *n.* [from Latin: elsewhere] A defence to a criminal charge alleging that the defendant was not at the place at which the offence was committed at the time of its alleged commission and so could not have been responsible for it. If the defendant proposes to introduce alibi evidence, details of his alibi should be provided to the prosecution.

alien *n.* A person who, under the law of a particular state, is not a citizen of that state. Aliens are usually classified as **resident aliens** (domiciled in the host country) or **transient aliens** (temporarily in the host country on business, study, etc.). They are normally subject to certain civil disabilities, such as being ineligible to vote. For the purposes of UK statute law an alien is defined by the British Nationality Act 1981 (in force from 1 January 1983) as a person who is neither a Commonwealth citizen, nor a British protected person, nor a citizen of the Republic of Ireland. At common law, a distinction is drawn between friendly and **enemy aliens**. The latter comprise not only citizens of hostile states but also all others voluntarily living in enemy territory or carrying on business there; they are subject to additional disabilities. *See also* ALLEGIANCE; DUE DILIGENCE; JUS SANGUINIS.

alienable *adj.* Capable of being transferred: used particularly in relation to real property. *See also* RULE AGAINST INALIENABILITY.

alienation *n.* The transfer of property (particularly real property) from one person to another. *See also* RESTRAINT ON ALIENATION.

alieni juris [Latin: of another's right] Describing the status of a person who is not of full age and capacity. *Compare* SUI JURIS.

alimentary trust *See* PROTECTIVE TRUST.

alimony *n.* Formerly, financial provision made by a husband to his wife when they are living apart. Alimony is now known as *maintenance or *financial provision.

aliunde *adj.* [Latin: from elsewhere] From a source outside the document currently under consideration. Evidence *aliunde* may be considered where the meaning of a document (e.g. a will) is otherwise unclear.

allegation *n.* Any statement of fact in a *statement of case, *affidavit, or *indictment.

allegiance *n.* The duty of obedience owed to a head of state in return for his protection. It is due from all citizens of that state and its dependencies and also from any *alien present in the state (including enemy aliens under licence; for example, internees). A person who is declared by the British Nationality Act 1981 not to be an alien but who has a primary citizenship conferred by a state other than the UK is probably governed by the same principles as aliens so far as allegiance is concerned.

allocation *n.* The stage in civil litigation when a decision is made as to how the case is to be dealt with. Under Part 26 of the *Civil Procedure Rules after each of the parties has completed and filed a *directions questionnaire, allocation is made to one of three **tracks**:

- the *small claims track, which is the normal track for cases worth less than £10,000 and where the value of any claim for personal injuries is not more than £1,000;
- the *fast track, which is the normal track for cases worth between £10,000 and £25,000 and for which the small claims track is not the normal track and where the trial is likely to last for no longer than one day; and
- the *multi-track, which is the normal track for cases worth more than £25,000 and for which the small claims track or the fast track is not the normal track.

When deciding the track for a claim the court has regard to various factors, including the financial value of the claim, the nature of the remedy sought, and the likely complexity of the facts, law, or evidence. *See also* CASE MANAGEMENT.

allocation questionnaire Under earlier versions of the *Civil Procedure Rules, a questionnaire that was served on both parties in civil litigation. The completion of this document enabled the court to allocate the case to the most appropriate track (*see* ALLOCATION). The completed form included such information as the monetary value of the claim, the complexity of the case, the number of litigants involved, and whether there were any counterclaims. From April 2013 allocation questionnaires were replaced by *directions questionnaires.

allocution (allocutus) *n.* The formal procedure in which the court asks a person who has just been convicted whether he has "legal cause to show why judgment should not be pronounced against him", or anything else to say before being sentenced. In practice, it is an opportunity for the convicted person to state any mitigating factors that might make a less severe punishment appropriate.

allograph *n.* A document not written by any of the parties to which it applies: the opposite of an autograph.

allotment *n.* A method of acquiring previously unissued shares in a *limited company in exchange for a contribution of capital. An application for such shares will often be made on the *flotation of a *public company or on the privatization of a state-owned industry. The company accepts the application by dispatching a **letter of allotment** to the applicant stating how many shares he has been allotted; he then has an unconditional right to be entered in the *register of members in respect of those shares. If he has been allotted fewer shares than he has applied for, he receives a cheque for the unallotted balance (an application must be accompanied by a cheque for the full value of the shares applied for). *See also* AUTHORIZED CAPITAL; RETURN.

all-ports warning system A system, operated by the police through the police national computer broadcast system, whereby details of a child at risk of abduction are circulated to immigration officers at ports and airports, who will then assist the police in trying to prevent that child from leaving the country. Before instituting a **port alert** the police must be convinced that the complaint is genuine and that the danger of removal is real and imminent. In the case of children aged 16 or 17 a court order is required. *See* CHILD ABDUCTION.

alluvion *n.* Land imperceptibly gained from the sea or a river by the washing up of sand and soil so as to form firm ground. The title to such land is discussed in Blackstone's *Commentaries* Vol. 2 p. 261.

alteration *n.* A change that, when made in a legal document, may affect its validity. An alteration in a will is presumed to have been made after execution and the alteration will therefore be invalid. However, it will be valid if it is proved to have been made before execution or if it was executed in the same way as the will itself. If the alteration is duly attested by the testator and the witnesses placing their initials or signatures by it, it is presumed to be valid (Wills Act 1837 s 21). If an invalid alteration completely obliterates the original words, it is treated as a blank space. If the original words can still be read, they remain effective. Alterations in deeds are presumed to have been made before execution. Alterations made after execution do not affect the validity of the deed if their purpose is to correct an obvious error. If, however, a material alteration is made to a deed after execution without the consent of the parties, the deed may become void in part. *See also* AMENDMENT; OBLITERATION.

alteration of share capital An increase, reduction (*see* REDUCTION OF CAPITAL), or any other change in the *authorized capital of a company. If acting in accordance with the

Companies Act 2006 s 617, a limited company can increase its authorized capital as appropriate. It can also rearrange its existing authorized capital (e.g. by consolidating 100 shares of £1 into 25 shares of £4 or by subdividing 100 shares of £1 into 200 of 50p) and cancel unissued shares. Unless the articles of association provide otherwise, these powers may be exercised by an *ordinary resolution.

alternative dispute resolution (ADR) Various methods of resolving civil disputes otherwise than through the normal trial process. Under Part 1 of the *Civil Procedure Rules the court will encourage the parties to use an alternative dispute resolution procedure if the court considers this appropriate, and should facilitate the use of such procedures. *See also* ARBITRATION; MEDIATION; CONCILIATION.

(⊕) SEE WEB LINKS
- Website of the ADR Group
- Website of the Centre for Effective Dispute Resolution

alternative finance arrangements A term applied in the Finance Acts to certain lending arrangements that comply with Islamic law. Muslims may refuse to enter into an arrangement that requires the payment of interest, this being contrary to the Koranic prohibition on *riba*. In order to provide financing for housing and business purchases, several alternative financing structures have been developed, notably *murabaha* (sale with deferred enhanced payment), *mudaraba* (advancing capital in exchange for a share of profits), *wakala* (an agent investing money on behalf of a principal), and diminishing *musharaka* (a joint ownership arrangement used to finance the purchase of property or some other asset). The Finance Act 2005 (s 46–47) and Finance Act 2006 (s 95) introduce a tax code under which UK tax is levied on the lender and relief is granted to the borrower as if (broadly) a proportion of each payment were interest. *See also* ISTISNA'A.

Alternative Investment Market (AIM) *See* STOCK EXCHANGE.

alternative verdict A verdict of not guilty of the offence actually charged but guilty of some lesser offence not specifically charged. Such a verdict is only permitted when there is insufficient evidence to establish the more serious offence but the evidence given is sufficient to prove the lesser offence. If, for example, in a murder case there is evidence that the defendant lacked *malice aforethought, an alternative verdict of manslaughter may be returned.

ambiguity *n.* Uncertainty in meaning. In legal documents ambiguity may be patent or latent. A **patent ambiguity** is obvious to anyone looking at the document; for example, when a blank space is left for a name. A **latent ambiguity** at first appears to be an unambiguous statement, but the ambiguity becomes apparent in the light of knowledge gained other than from the document. An example is "I give my gold watch to X", when the testator has two gold watches. In general, *extrinsic evidence can be used to clarify latent ambiguities, but not patent ambiguities. Extrinsic evidence cannot be used to give a different meaning to words capable of ordinary interpretation.

ambulatory *adj.* (of a will) Taking effect not from when it was made but from the death of the testator. Thus descriptions of property bequeathed or of beneficiaries are taken to refer to property or persons existing at that time. The will remains revocable until death.

ameliorating waste Alterations made by a tenant that improve the land he leases. *See* WASTE.

amendment *n*. **1.** Changes made to legislation, for the purpose of adding to, correcting, or modifying the operation of the legislation. **2.** Changes made to the *statement of case used in civil litigation. The relevant rules are at Part 17 of the *Civil Procedure Rules. When a statement of case has been served, a party may only amend it with the written consent of all the other parties or with the permission of the court. *See also* DEPARTURE. **3.** An alteration of a *treaty adopted by the consent of the *high contracting parties and intended to be binding upon all such parties. An amendment may involve either individual provisions or a complete review of the treaty.

a mensa et thoro [Latin] From board and bed. A decree of divorce *a mensa et thoro* was the forerunner of the modern judicial separation order. *See also* A VINCULO MATRIMONII.

amerce *vb*. An archaic term meaning to punish with a fine.

AMHP *See* APPROVED MENTAL HEALTH PROFESSIONAL.

amicus curiae [Latin: friend of the court or tribunal] A non-party who gives evidence before the court so as to assist it with research, argument, or submissions. For example, in the House of Lords decision on whether to allow the extradition of General Pinochet their lordships sought an independent expert opinion on the matter of diplomatic immunity. For that purpose they called upon an expert in this field, David Lloyd Jones QC, to assist the court.

amnesty *n*. An act erasing from legal memory some aspect of criminal conduct by an offender. It is most frequently granted to groups of people in respect of political offences and is wider than a *pardon, which merely relieves an offender of punishment.

Amsterdam Treaty The EU treaty signed in Amsterdam in 1997 (in force from 1 May 1999), which amended provisions of the *Treaty of Rome (European Community Treaty) and the *Maastricht Treaty (Treaty on European Union). Among other effects, the Amsterdam Treaty increased the powers of the European Parliament by extending the *codecision procedure to all areas covered by qualified majority voting and enabled the *Social Chapter to be incorporated into the Treaty of Rome.

analytical jurisprudence A branch of *legal positivism that attempts to provide analytical tools by which the law and legal concepts are most accurately and rigorously described. It involves the examination of legal reasoning, legal interpretation, and the efficacy of laws and legal systems.

ancient lights An *easement acquired by lapse of time (*see* PRESCRIPTION) resulting from 20 years' continuous enjoyment of the access of light to the claimant's land without any written consent from the owner of the land over which the easement is claimed.

ancillary credit business A business involved in credit brokerage, debt adjusting, debt counselling, debt collecting, or the operation of a credit-reference agency. **Credit brokerage** includes the effecting of introductions of individuals wishing to obtain credit to persons carrying on a *consumer-credit business. **Debt adjusting** is the process by which a third party negotiates terms for the discharge of a debt due under *consumer-credit agreements or *consumer-hire agreements with the creditor or owner on behalf of the debtor or hirer. The latter may also pay a third party to take over his obligation to discharge a debt or to undertake any similar activity concerned with its liquidation. **Debt counselling** is the giving of advice (other than by the original creditor and certain others) to debtors or hirers about the liquidation of debts due under consumer-credit agreements or consumer-hire agreements. In **debt collecting**, someone other than the creditor takes steps to procure the payment of debts owing to him. A creditor may engage a debt collector for this purpose. A **credit-reference agency** collects information concerning the financial standing of individuals and supplies this information to those seeking it. The Consumer Credit Act 1974 provides for the licensing of ancillary credit businesses and regulates their activities. The Consumer Credit Act 2006 extended the definition of such businesses to include debt administration.

ancillary probate A grant of probate to an executor appointed under a foreign jurisdiction to enable him to deal with assets of the deceased in the UK.

ancillary relief A court order incidental to another order or application. It usually refers to a *financial provision order or a *property adjustment order made in the course of proceedings for divorce, separation, or nullity under the Matrimonial Causes Act 1973. Such orders are made on or after granting the decree.

ancillary restraint A restriction that is imposed as part of a larger transaction. In relation to the EU *merger rules, there is a notice setting out for how long and on what terms ancillary restraints are permitted in the context of such arrangements.

angary *n.* The right of belligerent states to make use of (or destroy if necessary) neutral property on their own or on enemy territory or on the open sea, for the purpose of offence and defence. Traditionally, the right (*jus angariae*) was restricted to the belligerent laying an *embargo on and seizing neutral merchant ships in its harbours and compelling them and their crews to transport troops, ammunition, and provisions to certain places on payment of freight in advance. However, all sorts of neutral property, including vessels or other means of transport, arms, ammunition, provisions, or other personal property, may be the object of the modern right of angary, provided the articles concerned are serviceable to military ends and wants. It has been contended that one ground for distinction between angary and other forms of *expropriation (i.e. requisition) is the quantum of compensation. In cases of angary full compensation is payable, whereas in other cases of expropriation less than full compensation may suffice.

animals *pl. n.* For purposes of civil liability in England, animals are classified as belonging to a dangerous or a nondangerous species (Animals Act 1971). A dangerous species is one not commonly domesticated in the British Isles, whose fully grown members are likely to cause severe damage, or any damage they do cause will be severe. The keeper of an animal of a dangerous species is strictly liable for any damage it causes. Liability for damage done by other animals arises either under the Animals Act, if the animal was known by its keeper to have characteristics not normally found in that species, or only normally found in particular circumstances, which made it likely to cause that kind of damage; or under ordinary rules of tort liability. Thus carelessly allowing a dog to stray on the highway can make the keeper liable in negligence if it causes an accident, and excessive smell from a pig farm can be an actionable nuisance (*Wheeler v Saunders* [1996] Ch 19).

The Animals Act also imposes *strict liability for damage done by trespassing livestock, which includes cattle, horses, sheep, pigs, goats, and poultry. The keeper of a dog that kills or injures livestock is liable for the damage, except when the livestock was injured while straying on the keeper's land. If livestock is worried by a dog, the owner of the livestock (or the owner of the land on which the livestock lives) may kill or injure the dog to protect the livestock.

In Scotland, there is strict liability for damage caused by animals belonging to a species likely to kill or severely injure persons or animals or cause material damage to property under the Animals (Scotland) Act 1987. The Act also excuses the killing or injuring of an animal that attacks or harries people or livestock.

Dangerous wild animals may require a licence under the Dangerous Wild Animals Act 1976 (*see* DANGEROUS ANIMALS). Keeping dogs of a species bred for fighting is an offence under the Dangerous Dogs Act 1991. The use of *guard dogs is controlled by the Guard Dogs Act 1975. Other statutes protect various species, control importation of animals, and deal with animal diseases.

animus *n.* [Latin] Intention. The term is often used in combination; for example, **animus furandi** – the intention to steal; **animus manendi** – the intention to remain in one place (for the purposes of the law relating to *domicile); **animus donandi**: – the intention to transfer property.

animus testandi [Latin: a mind to make a will] *See* TESTAMENTARY INTENTION.

annexation *n.* (in international law) The acquisition of legal sovereignty by one state over the territory of another, usually by *occupation or conquest. Annexation is now generally considered illegal in international law, even when it results from a legitimate use of force (for example, in self-defence). An example can be found in UN Security Council Resolution 242 (1967) dealing with Israel's annexation of the Golan Heights from Syria, the Gaza Strip from Egypt, and the West Bank from Jordan as a consequence of their action in self-defence in the June (Six Day) War of 1967. The resolution emphasized "the inadmissibility of the acquisition of territory by war . . . ". UN General Assembly Resolution 2949 (1972) also reaffirms "that the territory of a State shall not be the object of occupation or acquisition by another State resulting from the threat or use of force . . . ". The annexing state is not bound by pre-existing obligations of the state annexed.

annual general meeting (AGM) A meeting of the members of a *public company required to be held each calendar year. Not more than 18 months should elapse between meetings, and 21 days' written notice (specifying the meeting as the annual general meeting) must usually be given. AGMs are concerned with the accounts, directors' and auditor's reports, dividends, the election of directors, and the appointment and remuneration of the auditor. Other matters are treated as *special business. Under the Companies Act 2006 a private company is no longer required to hold an AGM; however, section 303 of the Act enables 10% of members of a private company to requisition a general meeting (5% where more than 12 months has elapsed since the last *general meeting).

Annual Investment Allowance A *capital allowance available from 2008. It enables a business to offset 100% of its capital expenditure in any one year against corporation tax, to a current limit of £25,000 (Finance Act 2011 s 11(2); there was a temporary limit of £250,000 in 2012–14). The allowance, which is available to businesses of any size or legal form, replaces the various first-year allowances on specified plant and machinery previously available to small and medium-sized companies.

annual return A document that registered companies are required by law to send to *Companies House, usually each year. It includes information concerning the type of company and its business activities, the registered office, directors, company members, and certain company debts. It is open to public inspection. Failure to file the return is a criminal offence and may lead to the company being removed from the register and fined.

annual value of land The annual rent that might reasonably be expected from letting land or buildings, if the tenant pays all usual rates and taxes while other expenses (including repairs) are borne by the landlord. It is used in assessing business *rates. HM Revenue and Customs carries out the valuation.

annuity *n.* A sum of money payable annually for as long as the beneficiary (**annuitant**) lives, or for some other specified period (e.g. the life of another person (*pur autre vie*) or the minority of the annuitant). An annuity left by will is treated as a pecuniary legacy. An annuity may be charged on, or directed to be paid out of, a particular fund or it may be unsecured. A **joint annuity**, in which money is payable to more than one annuitant, terminates on the death of the last survivor. *See also* RENTCHARGE.

annulment *n.* **1.** A declaration by the court that a marriage was never legally valid. In all cases of nullity except nonconsummation, a decree of annulment will only be granted within three years after the celebration of the marriage. *See also* NULLITY OF MARRIAGE. **2.** The cancellation by a court of a *bankruptcy order, which occurs when it considers that the debtor was wrongly made bankrupt, when all the debts have been paid in full, or when the court approves a *voluntary arrangement. The power of annulment is discretionary. Annulment does not affect the validity of any sale of property or other action that has already taken place as a result of the bankruptcy order. **3.** The cancellation of *delegated legislation by resolution of either House of Parliament. **4.** The setting aside of legislation or other action by the *European Court of Justice.

annus et dies [Latin] A year and a day. At common law, the Crown was entitled to take possession of the lands of a person convicted of felony and to exploit them without reserve for a year and a day. This was known as the **right of year, day, and waste**.

answer *n.* A *statement of case served by the respondent to a petition. It is equivalent to the *defence served by the defendant in response to a claim form.

antecedents *pl. n.* An accused or convicted person's *previous convictions or history of bad *character. Traditionally, such evidence has been admissible only for the purpose of determining sentence after conviction but, under the Criminal Justice Act 2003, evidence of the defendant's bad character may be admitted in determining guilt under certain conditions. Where the defendant's antecedents are admitted for the purpose of determining sentence, the allegations must be capable of being proven and, if challenged by the defence, the prosecution must prove the allegations under the general rules of evidence. If the allegations are not proven through admissible evidence, the court may not consider them in passing sentence.

ante litem motam [Latin: before controversy moved] Denoting things written or said before litigation commenced.

antenuptial agreement *See* PRENUPTIAL AGREEMENT.

antenuptial settlement *See* MARRIAGE SETTLEMENT.

anti-avoidance provisions A cluster of statutory provisions designed to stop certain arrangements that would otherwise reduce the taxpayer's tax liability. The main anti-avoidance provisions concern:

- so-called dividend stripping and bond washing (Taxes Act 1988 s 729–30, those sections introduced in 1937 and 1938);
- manufactured dividends (Corporation Taxes Act 2010 s 780–804);
- transactions in securities (Corporation Taxes Act 2010 s 731–751);
- an arrangement entered into by the Beatles whereby they sold their future income to a company in exchange for a (pre-1965 non-taxable) capital sum received (Corporation Taxes Act 2010, s 752–757).

From 2013 statute provides a *General Anti-Abuse Rule aimed at negating any tax advantage arising from "abusive action". *See also* ACCOUNTING PRACTICE; TAX AVOIDANCE.

anticipatory breach *See* BREACH OF CONTRACT.

anticipatory self-defence In effect, a pre-emptive strike by one state against another. Such action is of doubtful legality under the United Nations Charter. Some jurists have argued that such action was considered justifiable under customary international law and that the right to act upon this basis has been expressly preserved under Article 51 of the Charter. This, however, is merely an argument: it has never been granted legitimacy by the international community. An example can be found in the Security Council's treatment of the British plea of self-defence in the Harib Fort incident in 1964. In that case, the UK had bombed a fort in the Yemen that it claimed had been used as a base for mounting a series of raids into the South Arabian Federation (then a British protectorate). The UK argued that there was every reason to believe that such raids would continue and that the bombing was therefore a legitimate measure of anticipatory self-defence. The Security Council, however, rejected the idea of anticipatory self-defence against attacks that were not imminent and condemned the British action as an illegal *reprisal. The Council has taken a similar stance in relation to Israeli claims based upon a similar justification. *See* SELF-DEFENCE.

anticompetitive practice An unfair practice by a business that is in breach of either the Chapter I prohibition of the Competition Act 1998 or *Article 101 of the Treaty on the Functioning of the European Union (formerly Treaty of Rome). Examples of such practices include refusing to supply goods, operating discriminatory terms, and forcing purchasers to buy goods or services they do not want (tying clauses). Anticompetitive practices may be investigated by the *Office of Fair Trading under the Competition Act 1998. Such practices, when carried out by companies in a dominant position, can lead to fines of 10% of the business's annual turnover under UK and EU competition law.

antidumping *n. See* DUMPING.

antisocial behaviour order *See* ASBO.

antitrust law *n. See* COMPETITION LAW.

Anton Piller order *See* SEARCH ORDER.

apology *n.* A defence to an action for *defamation (1) in cases of unintentional defamation, where the defendant innocently and without negligence defamed the claimant but has offered a suitable correction and apology and has paid compensation, or (2) in cases where a libel is published in a newspaper or periodical without malice or gross negligence and an apology is published before the start of the action. In addition to providing a defence in these cases, the fact that the defendant has made or offered to make an apology may always be taken into account in mitigation of damages. *See also* OFFER OF AMENDS.

a posteriori [Latin: from the later (i.e. from effect to cause)] Describing or relating to reasoning based on deductions from observation or known facts, i.e. inductive reasoning. *Compare* A PRIORI.

appeal *n.* An application for the judicial examination by a higher tribunal of the decision of any lower tribunal. In modern English practice most appeals are limited to a review of the decision of the lower tribunal using a transcript or note of the evidence heard by that tribunal. In some circumstances there may be a full *rehearing in which witnesses are recalled and fresh evidence may be introduced. The appellate tribunal may in general make any order that the lower tribunal could have made, but there are some statutory restrictions upon this power; for example, in criminal cases the Court of Appeal may not impose a more severe sentence than the trial court. Appellate tribunals are usually reluctant to overrule the decisions of lower tribunals on questions of fact even when they have the power to do so; consequently argument on appeals can be directed towards legal errors allegedly committed at the trial. In some cases (e.g. appeals by *case stated from magistrates' courts) the appeal may by law be confined to questions of law. Appeal may be contrasted with **review**, in which the higher tribunal is confined to an examination of the *record of the lower tribunal's proceedings (i.e. excluding evidence tendered). *See also* APPELLATE JURISDICTION.

appeal in Revenue matters An appeal may be made against a Revenue notice or assessment by giving notice to the inspector within 30 days of its issue. An appeal can be against (a) an assessment on the individual; (b) a notice; (c) a Revenue amendment of a self-assessment; (d) a penalty assessment; (e) a notice requiring the production of documents; and (f) delay in completing enquiries into a self-assessment. The appeal will be made either to the General Commissioners, a body of lay persons assisted by a qualified clerk, or the Special Commissioners, who are highly qualified persons. Sometimes the legislation reserves a particular appeal to one or other body; otherwise the choice lies with the taxpayer. Other methods of appeal include seeking the opinion of the court (*A-G v National Provincial Bank Ltd* (1924) AC 262). It is also sometimes possible to enter an originating summons, as in *Buxton v Public Trustee* (1962) 41 TC 235.

appeals system *See* APPELLATE JURISDICTION.

Appeal Tribunal Until 2008, a tribunal that heard appeals from decisions on claims for social security benefits. Such appeals are now heard by a section of the Social Entitlement Chamber of the *First-tier Tribunal.

appellant *n.* A person who makes an *appeal to a court that has the jurisdiction to hear appeals, such as the Court of Appeal.

Appellate Committee *See* HOUSE OF LORDS.

appellate jurisdiction The power of a judge to hear *appeals from a previous court decision. Appellate jurisdiction in the **criminal courts** is determined by the nature of the offence. In the case of a *summary offence, appeals by the defendant against conviction and/or sentence in the magistrates' court are to the Crown Court. Appeals from magistrates' courts are to the High Court or Divisional Court of the Queen's Bench Division if an appeal by the prosecution or defence is by way of *case stated on a point of law. Appeals from the Crown Court can also be by way of case stated but only if the Crown Court had previously heard the appeal from the magistrates' court. Higher appeals are restricted to those from the High Court or Divisional Court on a point of law of general public importance. In the case of an *indictable offence, appeals by the defendant against conviction and/or sentence in the Crown Court are to the Court of Appeal (Criminal Division). Reference to the Court of Appeal may also be made (1) by the Attorney General due to an unduly light sentence, (2) by the Attorney General on a point of law following acquittal (although the earlier acquittal will not be affected), or (3) by the Home Secretary for consideration following conviction. A further appeal to the Supreme Court by the defence or prosecution is only available on a point of law of general public importance and with permission.

Appellate jurisdiction in the **civil courts** was substantially revised as a result of the Access to Justice Act 1999. Part IV of that Act seeks to ensure that appeals are heard by the next most appropriate level of judge, rather than the next highest court, as was the position before the introduction of the *Civil Procedure Rules. The Lord Chancellor is able "by order" to vary routes of appeal if he considers it appropriate; such an order is now in place in the form of the Access to Justice Act 1999 (Destination of Appeals) Order 2000.

A circuit judge in the county court is now able to hear appeals from the *small claims track, provided that the judge sitting at first instance was a district judge. A single High Court judge is able to consider civil and criminal appeals in contempt of court cases; criminal appeals by way of case stated from magistrates' courts and the Crown Courts; and civil appeals from High Court masters, district judges, and county court circuit judges. As an exception, civil appeals from High Court masters, district judges, and county court circuit judges will be to the Court of Appeal if the previous court matter was either (1) a final decision made in a *multi-track claim or in specialist proceedings or (2) an appeal itself from a county court judge. Two or more High Court judges sitting as a Divisional Court may also hear appeals. In the Chancery Divisional Court, appeals may be heard from certain tribunals and from the county courts for such matters as bankruptcy appeals. In the Family Divisional Court, appeals may be heard from the magistrates' courts and the county courts, typically in respect of financial provision in cases of divorce and separation. In the Queen's Bench Divisional Court, appeals may be heard from the magistrates' courts, the Crown Court, and various tribunals by way of case stated and in matters of *judicial review and *habeas corpus. The Court of Appeal (Civil Division) is able to hear appeals from the county courts by way of the *leapfrog procedure (Court of Appeal) and appeals from the High Court and various tribunals. The Supreme Court will hear appeals primarily from the Court of Appeal but can hear appeals from the High Court under the leapfrog procedure (Supreme Court).

In matters of European Community law, the *European Court of Justice has the authority to overrule any national court, criminal or civil. Individuals, groups, or organizations who consider themselves to be victims of a breach of the *European Convention on Human Rights, and who have failed to find a remedy in the national courts, may appeal to the Court of Human Rights in Strasbourg.

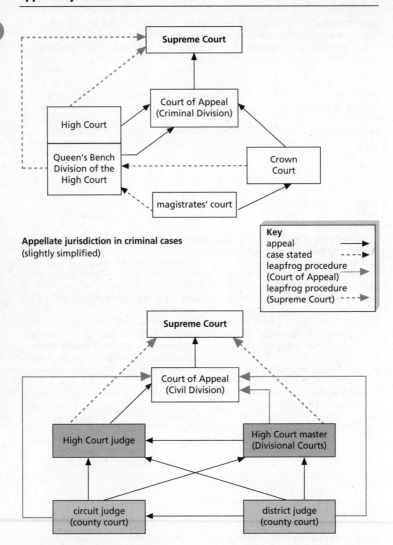

Appellate jurisdiction in criminal cases
(slightly simplified)

Key
appeal
case stated
leapfrog procedure
(Court of Appeal)
leapfrog procedure
(Supreme Court)

Appellate jurisdiction in civil cases
(slightly simplified)
Since the introduction of the Civil Procedure Rules in 1999, appeals are
heard by the next most appropriate level of judge, rather than the next
level of court.

applicable law The laws of a jurisdiction that apply to a particular transaction or agreement. Many countries are signatories of the international Rome Convention (1980; in force from 1 April 1991), which provides that the parties' choice of law will be respected and, in the absence of a term in the relevant agreement, the country's laws with the closest connection with the contract will apply.

applicant *n.* A person who applies for something, especially court relief.

applying the proviso *See* PROVISO.

appointed day The date specified in an Act of Parliament (or in a commencement order) for its coming into force.

appointee *n.* **1.** A person in whose favour a *power of appointment is exercised. **2.** A person selected for a particular purpose.

appointment *n.* *See* POWER OF APPOINTMENT.

appointor *n.* A person given a *power of appointment to exercise.

approbate and reprobate To accept and reject. A person is not allowed to accept the benefit of a document (e.g. a deed of gift) but reject any liabilities attached to it.

appropriation *n.* **1.** (in administrative law) The allocation of a sum of money to a particular purpose. The annual Appropriation Act authorizes the issue from the Consolidated Fund of money required to meet government expenditure and allocates it between departments and by reference to itemized heads of expenditure. **2.** (in criminal law) *See* THEFT. **3.** (in probate law) The transfer by *personal representatives of a particular asset in satisfaction of a legacy or share of the estate. For example, a testator leaves a legacy of £1,000 to A; part of the estate comprises shares in ICI and, rather than paying A in cash, the personal representatives appropriate shares in ICI to A to the value of £1,000 in satisfaction of the legacy. Personal representatives' authority to appropriate is conferred by section 41 of the Administration of Estate Act 1925 and requires the consent of the beneficiary (which is normally dispensed with by an express term of the will).

appropriation of payments The allocation of one or more payments to one particular debt out of several owed by a debtor to the same creditor. The power of allocation belongs in the first instance to the debtor, but if he does not make an appropriation at the time of payment, then the creditor may do so. In the case of current accounts, in the absence of an express appropriation, payments are normally appropriated to the oldest outstanding debt.

appropriations in aid Day-to-day revenue received by government departments and retained to meet expenditure instead of being paid into the Consolidated Fund.

approved clinician A person approved by the appropriate national authority to act as a clinician in charge of a particular episode or type of treatment in respect of a patient with a *mental disorder. *Compare* RESPONSIBLE CLINICIAN.

approved mental health professional (AMHP) Under the Mental Health Act 2007, a person approved by a local social-services authority to fulfil certain roles relating to the detention of mentally disordered patients (*see* MENTAL DISORDER). The term replaces and widens that of **approved social worker**, used in the Mental Health Act 1983.

approximation of laws The process by which member states of the EU change their national laws to enable the free market to function properly. It is required by the Treaty of Rome. *Compare* HARMONIZATION OF LAWS.

appurtenant *adj.* Attached or annexed to land and enhancing the land or its use. An *easement must be appurtenant to a *dominant tenement but a *profit *à prendre* need not. Thus a right of way over land in Yorkshire granted to a Sussex landowner does not benefit his Sussex property and is not an easement, but a right to shoot game over the Yorkshire land could give a man in Sussex (whether landowner or not) a valid profit *à prendre*.

a priori [Latin: from the previous (i.e. from cause to effect)] Describing or relating to reasoning that is based on abstract ideas, anticipates the effects of particular causes, or (more loosely) makes a presumption that is true as far as is known, i.e. deductive reasoning. *Compare* A POSTERIORI.

arbitrary punishment *See* PUNISHMENT.

arbitration *n.* The determination of a dispute by one or more independent third parties (the **arbitrators**) rather than by a court. Arbitrators are appointed by the parties in accordance with the terms of the *arbitration agreement or in default by a court. An arbitrator is bound to apply the law accurately but may in general adopt whatever procedure he chooses and is not bound by the *exclusionary rules of the law of evidence; he must, however, conform to the rules of *natural justice. In English law, arbitrators are subject to extensive control by the courts, with respect to both the manner in which the arbitration is conducted and the correctness of the law that the arbitrators have applied, although this control was loosened to some extent by the Arbitration Act 1996. The judgment of an arbitrator is called his **award**, which can be the subject of an *appeal to the High Court on a question of law under the provisions of the Arbitration Act 1996. In some types of arbitration it is the practice for both parties to appoint an arbitrator. If the arbitrators fail to agree about the matter in dispute, they will appoint an **umpire**, who has the casting vote in making the award. English courts attach great importance to arbitration and will normally stay an action brought in the courts in breach of a binding arbitration agreement. *See also* ALTERNATIVE DISPUTE RESOLUTION.

The modern origins of international arbitration can be traced to the Jay Treaty (1784) between the USA and the UK, which provided for the determination of legal disputes between states by mixed commissions. The *Hague Conventions of 1899 and 1907 contained rules of arbitration that have now become part of customary international law. The 1899 Conventions created the Permanent Court of Arbitration, which was not strictly speaking a court but a means of providing a body of arbitrators on which the parties to a dispute could draw. Consent to arbitration by a state can be given in three ways: (1) by inclusion of a special arbitration clause in a treaty; (2) by a general treaty of arbitration, which arranges arbitration procedures for future disputes; and (3) by a special arbitration treaty designed for a current dispute.

Examples of arbitration include the *Clipperton Island Arbitration (France v Mexico)* (1932) 26 AJIL 390; the *Tinoco Arbitration* (1923) 1 RIAA 369; and the *Canada/France Maritime Delimitation Arbitration* (1992) 31 ILM 1145. Sadly, some arbitration decisions have been ignored, e.g. the *Beagle Channel Arbitration (Chile v Argentina)* (1977) 52 ILR 93, in which the pope acted as mediator.

Arbitration between a state and a foreign national can be facilitated through the medium of the International Centre for Settlement of Investment Disputes (ICSID) based in Washington DC. Article 25 of the 1965 Convention on the Settlement of Investment Disputes Between States and Nationals of Other States extends to ICSID jurisdiction over investment disputes between "a Contracting State . . . and *a national of another contracting State.*"

arbitration agreement A contract to refer a present or future legal dispute to *arbitration. Such agreements are of two kinds: those referring an existing dispute to arbitration and those relating to disputes that may arise in the future. The second type is much more common. No particular form is necessary, but the agreement should name the place of arbitration and either appoint the arbitrator or arbitrators or (more usually) define the manner in which they are to be appointed in the absence of agreement between the parties. The agreement should also set out the procedure for appointing an umpire if two arbitrators are involved and they fail to agree.

arbitration clause An express term of a contract in writing (usually of a commercial nature) constituting an agreement to refer disputes arising out of the contract to *arbitration.

archipelago *n.* A collection of islands (including parts of islands, interconnecting waters, and other natural features) so closely interrelated that they form an intrinsic geographical, economic, and political entity, or which historically have been regarded as such. An example is the Galápagos Islands. In contrast, an **archipelagic state** has been defined by the Convention on the Law of the Sea (1982) as a state comprising one or more archipelagos; it may also include other islands. An example of an archipelagic state is the Bahamas. *See also* TERRITORIAL WATERS.

arguendo *adv.* [Latin: for the sake of argument] A term sometimes used by lawyers and judges when they wish to explore the implications that follow from a particular point (often a fact asserted by a hostile party) without accepting that the point at issue is indeed true.

argumentative affidavit An *affidavit containing not only allegations of fact but also arguments as to the bearing of those facts on the matter in dispute.

armchair principle A rule applied in the *interpretation of wills, enabling circumstances existing when the will was made to be used as evidence to elucidate the meaning of words appearing in the will. For example, such evidence may establish the identity of a beneficiary referred to in the will only by a nickname. The phrase originates from a well-known judicial observation that one may, when construing a will, "place [oneself] in the testator's armchair and consider the circumstances by which he was surrounded when he made his will".

arraign *vb.* To start a criminal *trial on indictment by calling the defendant by name, putting the charges to him by reading the *indictment, and asking him whether he pleads guilty or not guilty. The defendant then pleads to the indictment. Arraignment will now normally occur at the *plea and case management hearing.

arrangement *n.* **1.** (in commercial and company law) *See* DEED OF ARRANGEMENT; SCHEME OF ARRANGEMENT; VOLUNTARY ARRANGEMENT. **2.** (in international law) *See* TREATY.

array *n. See* CHALLENGE TO JURY.

arrest *n.* The apprehension of a person suspected of criminal activities. Most arrests are made by police officers, although anybody may, under prescribed conditions, effect an arrest. In some cases the officer will have a *warrant of arrest signed by a magistrate, which must be shown to the accused (though not necessarily at the time of arrest).

However, a warrant is not required for an *indictable offence and the Serious Organized Crime and Police Act 2005 effectively gives the police the power to arrest any person where they consider this to be necessary for any of a wide range of reasons (*see* ARRESTABLE OFFENCE). When an arrest is made, the accused must be told that he is being arrested and given the ground for his arrest. The arresting police officer has power to search the person he is arresting for any property that may be used in evidence against him. Anyone making or assisting in an arrest may use as much force as reasonable in the circumstances. Resisting lawful arrest may constitute the crime of *assault or *obstructing a police officer. A person who believes he has been wrongfully arrested may petition for *habeas corpus and may sue the person who arrested him for *false imprisonment. *See also* BAIL; CAUTION; DETENTION; REMAND.

arrestable offence A former category of offence defined by the Police and Criminal Evidence Act 1984. Any offence carrying a fixed mandatory penalty or a sentence of at least five years' imprisonment was automatically an arrestable offence. However, a large number of other crimes were also specified to be arrestable offences even though they did not fulfil these conditions. Where a police officer had reason to suspect that an arrestable offence either had been, or was about to be, committed he enjoyed specific powers of arrest, entry of premises, and search that did not apply in the case of a non-arrestable offence. The distinction between arrestable and other offences was abolished by the Serious Organized Crime and Police Act 2005, which effectively gives the police the power to arrest anyone where they have reason to consider this "necessary". The other specific powers that applied in the case of arrestable offences have been transferred to the category of *indictable offences.

arrested development Formerly, under the Mental Health Act 1983, a category of *mental disorder comprising lack of intelligence and social functioning. The Mental Health Act 2007 amended the 1983 Act to create a single category of mental disorder or disability.

arrived ship *See* LAY DAYS.

arson *n.* The intentional or reckless destruction or damaging of property by fire without a lawful excuse. There are two forms of arson corresponding to the two forms of *criminal damage in the Criminal Damage Act 1971. Aggravated arson (triable on indictment) carries a maximum sentence of life imprisonment. Simple arson (triable summarily) carries a sentence of up to six months' imprisonment or a fixed fine.

article *n.* A clause in a document. The plural, **articles**, is often used to mean the entire document, e.g. *articles of association.

Article 101 A provision of the Treaty on the Functioning of the European Union (previously Treaty of Rome) that prohibits anticompetitive agreements the aim or effect of which is to restrict, prevent, or distort competition in the EU (*see also* COMPETITION LAW). Article 101 (formerly 81 and before that 85) applies directly in all member states (*see* COMMUNITY LEGISLATION) and is often used against *cartels; it only applies when the agreement affects trade between member states. Agreements that infringe the Article are void and unenforceable; third parties have the right to bring actions for damages if they have suffered loss through the operation of such agreements. Infringement of the Article may result in EU fines of up to 10% of annual worldwide turnover. In the UK there are very similar provisions in the Competition Act 1998, which prohibit anticompetitive agreements under Chapter I of that Act. *See also* BLOCK EXEMPTION.

Article 102 A provision of the Treaty on the Functioning of the European Union (previously Treaty of Rome), with direct effect throughout the EU (*see* COMMUNITY LEGISLATION), that prohibits *abuses of a dominant position by businesses in the EU. Examples of breaches of Article 102 (formerly 82 and before that 86) include refusing to supply an existing customer (for example, when it has begun to operate in competition with the dominant company), selectively reducing prices to stop competition from competitors (*see* PREDATORY PRICING), unfair or excessive prices, tying clauses, and refusing to license *intellectual property rights. Article 102 only prohibits such conduct if the business is dominant, i.e. if it enjoys a market share of 40% or more in the EU (or a substantial part of it). The rules only apply when the conduct affects trade between member states. There is a very similar prohibition in the Chapter II prohibition of the Competition Act 1998, which holds that abuse of a dominant position will breach UK law if it has effects in the UK.

Article 267 Reference A provision of the *Treaty on the Functioning of the European Union (formerly the Treaty of Rome) entitling national courts to refer matters of EU law to the European Court of Justice for a determination. The case ultimately returns to the national court for a final judgment. Such a procedure is known as a "267 reference". Article 267 (formerly Article 234, originally Article 177) is a provision of the Treaty that empowers the Court of Justice to decide such issues as how the Treaty should be interpreted and whether or not the European Commission or other bodies have acted properly. *See* ACTE CLAIR.

articles of association Regulations for the management of a registered company. They form, together with any relevant resolutions or agreements, the company's constitution. Model statutory articles for different types of company are provided by the Companies (Model Articles) Regulations 2008.

artificial insemination *See* HUMAN ASSISTED REPRODUCTION.

artificial nutrition and hydration The use of invasive feeding tubes or injections to keep a patient alive. In medical ethics there is much debate over when such treatment may be withheld or withdrawn from patients who have no prospect of recovery, especially in the case of patients who are unable to communicate their wishes. When other intensive treatments are judged *futile, artificial nutrition and hydration become what are known as *extraordinary means of prolonging life. Legally, it is permissible to withdraw such treatment when it is no longer in the patient's interests and when the intention is not to kill the patient, even though this must be the inevitable result (*see* DOCTRINE OF DOUBLE EFFECT). In cases of patients in a *persistent vegetative state, the matter must be referred to the courts.

artificial person *See* JURISTIC PERSON.

ASBO Anti-Social Behaviour Order: a court order that prohibits the defendant from doing anything described in the order. Under the Crime and Disorder Act 1998, an ASBO may be imposed on an individual providing that the person has acted in an anti-social manner, that is to say, in a manner likely to cause harassment, alarm, or distress to one or more persons not of the same household as himself, and that such an order is necessary to protect relevant persons from further anti-social acts by him. ASBOs may be imposed either as an alternative to criminal prosecution or following a conviction in criminal proceedings.

ascertained goods *See* UNASCERTAINED GOODS.

asportation *n. See* LARCENY.

assault *n.* An intentional or reckless act that causes someone to be put in fear of immediate physical harm. Actual physical contact is not necessary to constitute an assault (for example, pointing a gun at someone may constitute an assault (*R v Lamb* [1967] 2 QB 981): the word is often loosely used to include both threatening acts and physical violence (*see* BATTERY). Assault is a form of *trespass to the person and a crime as well as a tort: an **ordinary** (or **common**) **assault**, as described above, is a *summary offence punishable by a fine and/or up to six months' imprisonment. Certain kinds of more serious assault are known as **aggravated assaults** and carry stricter penalties. Examples of these are assault with intent to resist lawful arrest (two years), assault occasioning *actual bodily harm (five years), maliciously wounding or inflicting grievous bodily harm (five years), and maliciously wounding or causing grievous bodily harm with intent (life imprisonment). *See also* AFFRAY; SEXUAL ASSAULT.

assault by penetration A criminal offence under the Sexual Offences Act 2003, in which a person (A) intentionally penetrates the vagina or anus of another person (B) with part of his body or anything else, where the penetration is sexual, where B does not *consent to the penetration, and where A does not have a reasonable belief that B consents. Whether A's belief in B's consent is reasonable is to be determined having regard to all the circumstances, including any steps A has taken to ascertain whether B consents. The *mens rea* element for assault by penetration in the 2003 Act sets a standard of negligence whereby the defendant's honest but unreasonable belief in his victim's consent will not negate liability. Formerly, the defendant's honest belief in the victim's consent would negate liability, irrespective of whether that belief was reasonable (*DPP v Morgan* [1976] AC 182 (HL)). The maximum penalty for assault by penetration is life imprisonment. Unlike *rape, which can only be committed as a principal by a man, assault by penetration can be committed as a principal by both men and women. *See also* SEXUAL ASSAULT.

assault of a child under 13 by penetration It is a specific criminal offence under the Sexual Offences Act 2003 to engage in sexual penetration with a child under the age of 13. Consent is irrelevant to determining whether the offence has been committed. A person commits the offence if he intentionally penetrates the vagina or anus of another person with a part of his body or anything else, where the penetration is sexual, and where the other person is under 13. The maximum penalty is life imprisonment. The victim cannot be convicted as an accessory to this offence, even if the offence takes place with the victim's voluntary assistance, since the offence is designed to protect the victim (*R v Tyrrell* (1894) 1 QB 710 (CCR)). *Compare* RAPE OF A CHILD UNDER 13; SEXUAL ACTIVITY WITH A CHILD.

assault on a police constable in the execution of his duty A person is guilty of a specific offence if he assaults a constable in the execution of his duty, or assaults a person assisting a constable in the execution of his duty (Police Act 1996 s 89). The offender does not need to know that the person he is assaulting is a constable.

Assembly of the European Communities *See* EUROPEAN PARLIAMENT.

assent *n.* The process under which *personal representatives are able to transfer property (real or personal) to a beneficiary of the estate. It is simply an indication by the personal representatives that the property is not needed for the administration of the estate and that the property may pass to the beneficiary. No formality is required for personal property but an assent in writing is required for real property (Administration of Estates Act 1925 s 36).

assent procedure A procedure introduced by the Single European Act 1986 that gave greater powers to the *European Parliament over the unelected European Commission. It applied when there was a single reading of a new legislative measure in the Parliament: Parliament either assented by an absolute majority to the measure as presented to it or rejected it; it did not have a power to amend the measure. Under the Lisbon Treaty of 2007 the assent procedure has been replaced by the *ordinary legislative procedure in nearly all areas; where it is retained, it is known as the **consent procedure**. *Compare* CODECISION PROCEDURE; COOPERATION PROCEDURE.

assessment of costs The method by which the amount of costs payable by one party to another, or payable by a client to his solicitor, is determined by an officer of the court. Before the introduction of the *Civil Procedure Rules in 1999, this was called **taxation of costs**. Assessments may be summary or detailed. In a **summary assessment**, the court determines the amount payable immediately at the end of the hearing. In this instance, the court can call for whatever evidence is available at the time (e.g. brief fee) to determine the amount. This is the preferred method of assessment in *fast track trials. Summary assessment can only be carried out by the judge who heard the case at the time. In contrast, a **detailed assessment** involves the quantification of costs to a *costs officer, who considers the amount at some stage after the hearing. Detailed assessments are mostly carried out by district judges in the county courts but there is a dedicated office, the Senior Courts Costs Office, for the High Court and the Court of Appeal.

assessor *n.* A person called in to assist a court in trying a case requiring specialized technical knowledge. The High Court and the Court of Appeal have wide powers to appoint assessors to assist them in any action, but this power is rarely exercised except in Admiralty cases. Assessors will not give oral evidence and will not be open to cross-examination or questioning. In cases involving questions of navigation and seamanship, it is the invariable practice to appoint assessors who are Elder Brethren of Trinity House. In proceedings to review an *assessment of costs a practising solicitor and a *costs officer are usually appointed to assist the judge.

assets *pl. n.* Physical property and/or rights that have a monetary value and are capable of being those of a *juristic person or a natural person (i.e. a human being). They can comprise real assets (real property) and personal assets (personal property). In respect of a juristic person, such as a corporation, assets include fixed or capital assets (those identified as being held and used on a continuing basis in the business activity, e.g. machinery) and current or circulating assets (those not intended to be used on a continuing basis in the business activity but realized in the course of trading).

In respect of a natural person who is deceased, assets comprise all real and personal property that forms part of the deceased's estate and is available for the payment of the deceased's debts and liabilities. *See also* FAMILY ASSETS; WASTING ASSETS.

For purposes of *capital gains tax, which is charged on the *disposal of an asset, assets are defined in accordance with the declaration that: "All forms of property shall be assets" (Taxation of Chargeable Gains Act 1992 s 21(1)). In *O'Brien v Benson's Hosiery (Holdings) Ltd* [1979] STC 735 (HL), the House of Lords held that the rights an employer has by virtue of a contract of employment with an employee constitute an asset for capital gains tax purposes. The fact that the rights cannot be assigned is irrelevant. In calculating *entrepreneurs' relief a distinction is made between *business assets and any other assets. Certain classes of assets are specifically exempted from capital gains tax, notably a person's principal private residence.

assignment *n.* **1.** The transfer of a *chose in action by one person (the **assignor**) to another (the **assignee**). By the rules of the common law, this was not permissible. If, for example, A was owed a contract debt by B, he could not transfer his right to C so as to enable C to sue B for the money owed. The assignment of certain choses in action is now authorized and governed by particular statutes. For example, the Companies Act 1985 allows shares in a company to be transferred in the manner prescribed by the company's articles of association. These, however, are special cases; in general, choses in action, whether legal (e.g. the benefit of a contract) or equitable (e.g. a right under a trust), can be transferred either by equitable assignment or, under the Law of Property Act 1925, by statutory assignment. For an **equitable assignment**, no formality is required. It is sufficient that the assignor shows a clear intention to transfer ownership of his right to the assignee. If, however, it is a legal chose that is assigned, the assignor must be made a party to any proceedings by the assignee to enforce the right. In the above example, C can sue B for the debt, but he must join A as co-claimant or (if A refuses to lend his name to the action in this way) as co-defendant. A **statutory assignment** under the Law of Property Act 1925 is sometimes referred to as a **legal assignment**, but since it may relate to an equitable chose in action as well as a legal one this is not wholly accurate. It enables the assignee to enforce the right assigned in his own name and without joining the assignor to the proceedings even if it is a legal chose. There are three requirements for its validity: it must be absolute; it must be in writing; and written notice of it must be given to the person against whom the right is enforceable. For these purposes, an **absolute assignment** is one that transfers the assignor's entire interest to the assignee unconditionally. If less than his entire interest (e.g. part of a debt) is transferred, or if any condition is attached to the transfer (e.g. that the consent of a third party be obtained), the assignment is not absolute. An assignment need not, however, be permanent to be absolute, and this is exemplified by the mortgage of a chose in action. If A, who owes money to C, assigns to C as security for that debt a debt due to him from B, with the proviso that C will reassign the debt if A settles what is due to him, the assignment is absolute despite the proviso for reassignment.

   The assignment of contractual rights (which must be distinguished from *novation) is subject to certain restrictions. For reasons of public policy, the holder of a public office must not assign his salary nor a wife her right to maintenance payments awarded in matrimonial proceedings. Rights to the performance of personal services, as under contracts of employment, are also incapable of being assigned. *Intellectual property rights must be assigned or transferred by document in writing signed by the assignor. *Stamp duty land tax is payable on assignments of property if the value transferred is over the prescribed limit. **2.** The transfer of the whole of the remainder of the term of a lease. A tenant may assign his lease unless there is a covenant against it: there is often a covenant against assignment without the landlord's consent. The landlord cannot charge a fee for giving his consent unless there is express provision for this in the lease and he may not withhold his consent unreasonably. Less commonly, a lease may contain a covenant that prohibits any assignment at all. Where a lease contains a covenant against assigning without the landlord's consent, such consent not to be unreasonably withheld, the landlord has certain statutory duties. He must give the tenant notice of his decision within a reasonable time of the tenant requesting consent; the notice must give reasons for any refusal of consent, or conditions attached to acceptance; and the conditions themselves must not be unreasonable (Landlord and Tenant (Covenants) Act 1995). *See also* BUSINESS TENANCY.

assisted suicide The act of helping someone to commit *suicide Under the Suicide Act s 2 a person commits a crime if he intentionally performs an act that is capable of encouraging or assisting another to commit, or to attempt to commit, suicide. This covers a variety of acts, ranging from giving someone a lethal dose of pills to arranging for them to go abroad to a country where assisted suicide is legal. The Director of Public Prosecutions has a discretion whether to prosecute (s 2(4)) and in many cases has chosen not to do so. Following the widely publicized case of *Purdy v Director of Public Prosecutions* [2009] UKHL 45, the DPP published a document setting out the circumstances in which a prosecution is likely. The offence of assisting suicide may also be committed where an individual sets up a website or publishes materials that promote suicide. It is important to note that respecting a competent patient's right to refuse life-saving treatment is not legally regarded as helping them die (*see* ADVANCE DECISION). Case: *R (Pretty) v DPP* [2001] UKHL 61, [2002] 1 AC 800. *See also* EUTHANASIA; PHYSICIAN-ASSISTED SUICIDE.

(⊕) SEE WEB LINKS
• The DPP's guidance for prosecutors in cases of assisted suicide

assize *n.* **1.** An assize court or council. In modern times assizes were sittings of High Court judges travelling on circuits around the country with commissions from the Crown to hear cases. These commissions were either of oyer, terminer, and general gaol delivery, empowering the judges to try the most serious criminal cases, or of *nisi prius*, empowering them to try civil actions. These assizes were abolished by the Courts Act 1971, and the criminal jurisdiction of assizes was transferred to the Crown Court. At the same time, the High Court was empowered to hear civil cases anywhere in England and Wales without the need for a special commission. **2.** A statute or ordinance, e.g. the Assize of Clarendon, Novel Disseisin.

associated operations Two or more operations that are considered in terms of their combined effect when calculating the *transfer of value chargeable to *inheritance tax. In such cases the transfer of value is measured as the reduction in the estate caused by the various operations considered in aggregate (Inheritance Tax Act 1984 s 268). Case law demonstrates that operations are not associated merely by virtue of taking place at the same time, nor by different persons choosing to perform similar acts. For two operations to be associated, it would appear that, either, the two operations concern the same property (Inheritance Tax Act 1984 s 268(1)(a) or one operation is dependent on the other (*Rysaffe Trustee Co (CI) v IRC* [2003] EWCA Civ 356, [2003] STC 536).

association agreement An agreement between a member state of the European Union and a non-EU country or organization, as provided for in Article 217 of the Treaty on the Functioning of the European Union (formerly Treaty of Rome). The agreement, which may be with a country, a union of states, or an international organization, establishes an association involving reciprocal rights and obligations, common action, and special procedures.

assumpsit *n.* [Latin: he has undertaken] Historically, an action at common law for the recovery of damages arising from a person's failure to do something he had promised to do (whether expressly or implicitly). It was thus an early form of suit for *breach of contract.

assurance *n. See* INSURANCE.

assured agricultural occupancy A form of *assured tenancy in which the tenant is an agricultural worker living in a *tied cottage. This kind of tenancy replaced *protected occupancies from 15 January 1989.

assured shorthold tenancy A kind of *assured tenancy at the end of which the landlord is entitled to recover possession without having to show one of the usual grounds for possession of an assured tenancy. This kind of tenancy was introduced by the Housing Act 1988, replacing **protected shorthold tenancies**. Under the 1988 Act the landlord was obliged to give the tenant notice before the grant of the tenancy that it was an assured shorthold tenancy. However, under the Housing Act 1996, from 28 February 1997 the requirement for the landlord to serve a notice is removed, and all new tenancies are automatically assured shortholds unless otherwise agreed. If a landlord wants to give the tenant security under an assured tenancy, this must be specifically created; if this is not done, the tenancy is an assured shorthold without *security of tenure. A tenant can apply to a rent assessment committee if he thinks the rent of the tenancy is excessive. The committee can fix a new rent if they think that the rent is significantly higher than that of other assured tenancies in the area. However, government regulations may restrict this right in certain areas or in certain circumstances.

The landlord may obtain possession at any time when he would have been entitled to do so contractually, by giving two months' notice and specifying that the tenancy is an assured shorthold tenancy. No order for possession may be made in the first six months of the tenancy.

assured tenancy A form of tenancy under the Housing Act 1988 that is at a market rent but gives *security of tenure. The premises may be furnished or unfurnished. This kind of tenancy replaces *protected tenancies except those in existence before the Housing Act 1988 came into force. Former assured tenancies under the Housing Act 1980 (where different provisions applied) are converted into the new kind of assured tenancy.

To qualify as an assured tenancy, the premises must be let as a separate dwelling, within certain rateable value limits. There are certain exceptions, such as when the landlord lives in another part of the same premises. Under the Housing Act 1996, from 28 February 1997 all new residential tenancies are *assured shorthold tenancies without security of tenure, unless a notice is specifically served stating that the parties are creating an assured tenancy.

The rent is an open market rent agreed between the landlord and tenant, and it is not registered. However, the landlord must give the tenant notice if he intends to increase the rent, and the tenant can then apply to a *rent assessment committee if he thinks the increase is excessive. The rent assessment committee determines the rent at the current market value. There are limits on the frequency of rent increases.

The landlord can only regain possession on certain statutory grounds. These include: nonpayment of rent; that the landlord formerly lived in the dwelling and requires it again for his own use; that the tenant is a *nuisance neighbour or may become a nuisance; and that alternative accommodation is available (the court has discretion in this last case).

When the tenant of an assured tenancy dies, his spouse, civil partner, or cohabitee has a right, in certain circumstances, to take over the tenancy as successor to the deceased tenant. An assured tenant cannot usually assign the tenancy without the landlord's consent. *See also* STATUTORY PERIODIC TENANCY.

asylum *n.* Refuge granted to an individual whose *extradition is sought by a foreign government or who is fleeing persecution in his native state. This can include refuge in the territory of a foreign country (**territorial asylum**) or in a foreign embassy (**diplomatic asylum**). The latter is particularly contentious as it is a derogation from the sovereignty of the territorial state; moreover, diplomatic asylum may only be granted in cases of an alleged political offence and not in cases involving common-law crimes. Diplomatic asylum is well recognized in Latin American states. Conventions relating to it include the Havana Convention of 1928, the Montevideo Convention of 1933, and the

Caracas Convention of 1954. The nature of diplomatic asylum was defined in the *Asylum Case (Columbia v Peru)* [1950] ICJ Rep 266.

On the issue of granting **political asylum** to refugees the applicable law is contained in the Convention Relating to the Status of Refugees 1951 (UKTS 39 (1954) Cmd 9171), which came into force in 1954 and to which the UK is a party. The original 1951 Convention only extended refugee status to those displaced by events occurring in Europe and elsewhere before 1 January 1951. This wording was subsequently removed by the Protocol Relating to the Status of Refugees (1967) (UKTS 15 (1969) Cmnd 3906). The 1951 Convention defined a refugee as a person with a "well founded fear of being persecuted for reasons of race, religion, nationality, membership of a particular social group or political opinion, [who] is outside the country of which that person is a national and is unable or, owing to such a fear, is unwilling to return to it" (art 1(A) (2)).

One of the safeguards for the refugee is the right of *non-refoulement set out in Article 33 of the Convention. However, the effectiveness of this Article is undermined by the fact that it is up to each state to determine whether an individual comes under the classification of refugee contained in Article 1 of the Treaty.

In the UK, the procedures for applying for political asylum and for appealing against a negative decision have been significantly tightened up by the Immigration and Asylum Act 2002, the Nationality, Immigration and Nationality Act 1999, the Asylum and Immigration (Treatment of Claimants etc.) Act 2004, and the Immigration, Asylum and Nationality Act 2006. *See also* DEPORTATION; IMMIGRATION.

at sea *See* PRIVILEGED WILL.

attachment *n.* A court order for the detention of a person and/or his property. Attachment can be used by the courts for the punishment of *contempt of court.

attachment of earnings An order made under the Attachment of Earnings Act 1971 by which a court orders the payment of judgment debts and other sums due under court orders (e.g. maintenance) by direct deduction from the debtor's earnings. Payment is usually in instalments, and the debtor's employer is responsible for paying these to the court.

attempt *n.* (in criminal law) Any act that is more than merely preparatory to the intended commission of a crime; such an act is itself a crime. Section 1 (i) of the Criminal Attempts Act 1981 provides:- "If, with intent to commit an offence to which this section applies, a person does an act which is more than merely preparatory to the commission of the offence, he is guilty of attempting to commit the offence." For example, shooting at someone but missing could be attempted murder, but merely buying a revolver would not. One may be guilty of attempting to commit a crime that proves impossible to commit (e.g. attempted theft from an empty handbag: *see* IMPOSSIBILITY).

attendance centre A nonresidential institution that offenders under the age 25 may be ordered to attend if they have not previously been sentenced to prison or detention in a young offender institution. Attendance, which is outside normal school or working hours, is for periods of up to 3 hours on a single day, to a minimum of 12 hours and a maximum of 36 hours. An **attendance centre requirement** may be imposed in the form of a *community order, a *suspended sentence order, or a *youth rehabilitation order.

attestation *n.* The signature of witnesses to the making of a *will or *deed. Under the Wills Act 1837 as amended the testator must sign or acknowledge his signature (*see* ACKNOWLEDGMENT) in the presence of two witnesses who must both be present at the same time and who must each sign (attest) in the testator's presence. The signature of each party to a deed must be attested by one witness. *See also* EXECUTION OF WILL.

attorney *n*. A person who is appointed by another and has authority to act on behalf of another. *See also* POWER OF ATTORNEY.

Attorney General The principal law officer of the Crown. The Attorney General is usually a Member of Parliament of the ruling party and holds ministerial office, although he is not normally a member of the Cabinet. He is the chief legal adviser of the government, answers questions relating to legal matters in the House of Commons, and is politically responsible for the *Crown Prosecution Service, *Director of Public Prosecutions, *Treasury Solicitor, and *Serious Fraud Office. He is the leader of the English Bar and presides at its general meetings. The consent of the Attorney General is required for bringing certain criminal actions, principally ones relating to offences against the state and public order and corruption. The Attorney General sometimes appears in court as an *advocate in cases of exceptional public interest, but he is not now allowed to engage in private practice. He has the right to terminate any criminal proceedings by entering a *nolle prosequi*. See also* SOLICITOR GENERAL.

attornment *n*. An act by a bailee (*see* BAILMENT) in possession of goods on behalf of one person acknowledging that he will hold the goods on behalf of someone else. The attornment notionally transfers possession to the other person (constructive possession) and can thus be a delivery of goods sold.

auction *n*. A method of sale in which parties are invited to make competing offers (**bids**) to purchase an item. The auctioneer, who acts as the agent of the seller until fall of the hammer, announces completion of the sale in favour of the highest bidder by striking his desk with a hammer (or in any other customary manner). Until then any bidder may retract his bid and the auctioneer may withdraw the goods. The seller may not bid unless the sale is stated to be subject to the seller's right to bid. Merely to advertise an auction does not bind the auctioneer to hold one. However, if he advertises an auction without reserve and accepts bids, he will be liable if he fails to knock the item down to the highest outside bidder. An auctioneer who discloses his agency promises to a buyer that he has authority to sell and that he knows of no defect to the seller's title; he does not promise that the buyer of a specific chattel will get a good title.

Auctions can either result in a sale between a business seller and consumer buyer or between consumers (non-traders) who are both selling and buying. The law applicable differs depending on if a business sale is involved. Sales on eBay and similar sites on the internet are often by way of auction and can either be from a business to a consumer or consumer to consumer. Significant amounts of UK government contracting are now undertaken by way of online electronic auction.

auction ring A group of buyers who agree not to compete against each other at an auction with a view to purchasing articles for less than the open-market value. The profit earned thereby is shared among the members of the ring, or a second "knock-out" auction is held in private by the members of the ring with the article being sold to the highest bidder and the profit shared among the members. Under the Auctions (Bidding Agreements) Acts 1927 (as amended by the Criminal Justice Act 1967) and 1969 it is a criminal offence for a dealer to participate in an auction ring and a seller is given the right to set aside the contract of sale if one of the purchasers is a dealer in a ring.

audi alteram partem *See* NATURAL JUSTICE.

Audit Commission Currently, a statutory public body that takes responsibility for audit arrangements in respect of local government and the National Health Service in England and Wales. It is expected to be abolished under the Local Audit and Accountability Bill that is currently going through Parliament. Under the Bill, local authorities will choose their own auditors and a new decentralized audit system covering local government, police, and health bodies will be established. The Financial Reporting Council will become the primary regulator and the National Audit Office will prepare and maintain the Code of Audit Practice and Guidance for auditors.

audit exemption All companies are required to appoint auditors, unless exempt (Companies Act 2006 s 475). Small and dormant companies are exempt (s 477, s 480) where the directors of such companies provide a statement to that effect on the company's balance sheet. However, an exempt company must hold an audit if member (s) holding at least 10% of any class of shares demand one (s 476). A small company is an exempt company if two of the following requirements are met: (1) the company has an annual turnover of £6.5 million or less; (2) the total assets of the company are £3.26 million or less; (3) the company has 50 or fewer employees. A company is not required to appoint an auditor where the directors reasonably resolve that audited accounts are unlikely to be required (s 485, s 489).

auditor *n.* A person or firm appointed to examine the *books of account and the *accounts of a registered company and to report upon them to company members. An **auditor's report** must state whether or not, in the auditor's opinion, the accounts have been properly prepared and give a true and fair view of the company's financial position. The Companies Act sets out the qualifications an auditor must possess and also certain rights to enable him to fulfil his duty effectively.

authentication *n.* A distinct procedural step at the conclusion of a *treaty at which the definitive text of the treaty is established as correct and authentic and not subject to further modification.

authority *n.* **1.** Power delegated to a person or body to act in a particular way. The person in whom authority is vested is usually called an *agent and the person conferring the authority is the principal. **2.** A governing body, such as a *local authority, charged with power and duty to perform certain functions. **3.** A judicial decision or other source of law used as a ground for a legal proposition. *See also* PERSUASIVE AUTHORITY.

authorized capital (nominal capital) The total value of the shares that a registered company is authorized to issue in order to raise capital. The authorized capital of a company limited by shares (*see* LIMITED COMPANY) must be stated in the statement of capital and initial holdings (a requirement for registration of a company), as must the number and nominal value of the shares (Companies Act 2006 s 10). For example, an authorized capital of £120,000 may be divided into 120 000 shares of £1 (the **nominal value**) each. If the company has issued 100 000 of these shares, it is said to have an **issued capital** of £100,000 and retains the ability, without an increase in capital (*see* ALTERATION OF SHARE CAPITAL), to issue further shares in future. If the company has received the full nominal value of the shares issued, its *paid-up capital equals its issued capital. Where a company has not yet called for payment (*see* CALL) of the full nominal value, it has **uncalled capital**. **Reserve capital** is that part of the uncalled capital that the company has determined (by *special resolution) shall not be called up except upon a winding-up. A public company must have authorized share capital of at least £50,000 or the prescribed euro equivalent (Companies Act 2006 s 763).

authorized guarantee agreement (AGA) An agreement made between landlord and tenant on an *assignment of the lease to a third party, whereby the tenant guarantees the performance of the terms of the lease by the assignee (Landlord and Tenant (Covenants) Act 1995). The tenant cannot be required to give such a guarantee unless the lease expressly provides for an AGA.

authorized investments Formerly, those investments in which a trustee was permitted to invest trust property as set out in the Trustee Investments Act 1961. A much wider *general power of investment has now been given to trustees by the Trustee Act 2000.

authorized securities *See* AUTHORIZED INVESTMENTS.

automatic reservation A *reservation to the acceptance by a state of the compulsory jurisdiction of the *International Court of Justice. This is made under the *optional clause of the Statute of the Court, which permits an accepting state to unilaterally claim the right to determine the scope of its reservation.

automatism *n. See* INSANITY; NON-INSANE AUTOMATISM.

autopsy (post-mortem) *n.* The examination of a body after death in order to establish the cause of death. Autopsies are frequently requested by coroners (*see* INQUEST).

aut punire aut dedere [Latin: either punish or surrender] In extradition law, the doctrine that offenders must be either punished by the state of refuge or surrendered to the state that can and will punish them.

autrefois acquit [French: previously acquitted] A *special plea in bar of arraignment claiming that the defendant has previously been acquitted by a court of competent jurisdiction of the same (or substantially the same) offence as that with which he is now charged or that he could have been convicted on an earlier indictment of the same (or substantially the same) offence. When this plea is entered the judge determines the issue. If the plea is successful it bars further proceedings on the indictment. The plea may be combined with one of *not guilty. The Criminal Justice Act 2003 allows for retrial in a limited range of offences where there is new and compelling evidence that the acquitted person is guilty of the offence and a retrial is in the interests of justice. *See also* DOUBLE JEOPARDY; NEMO DEBET BIS VEXARI.

autrefois convict [French: previously convicted] A *special plea in bar of arraignment claiming that the defendant has previously been convicted by a court of competent jurisdiction of the same (or substantially the same) offence as that with which he is now charged or that he could have been convicted on an earlier indictment of the same (or substantially the same) offence. When this plea is entered the judge determines the issue. If the plea is successful it bars further proceedings on the indictment. The plea may be combined with one of *not guilty. The Criminal Justice Act 2003 allows for retrial in a limited range of offences where there is new and compelling evidence that the acquitted person is guilty of the offence and a retrial is in the interests of justice. *See also* DOUBLE JEOPARDY; NEMO DEBET BIS VEXARI.

autre vie *See* ESTATE PUR (OR PER) AUTRE VIE.

auxiliary jurisdiction The jurisdiction exercised by the *Court of Chancery to aid a claimant at common law; for example, by forcing a defendant to reveal documents and thus provide necessary evidence for his case. Auxiliary jurisdiction was rendered obsolete by the Judicature Acts 1873–75.

AVC *See* ADDITIONAL VOLUNTARY CONTRIBUTION.

aver *vb.* To allege as true (in pleadings). A statement making such an allegation is an **averment**.

average *n.* **1.** (in marine insurance) A loss or damage arising from an event at sea. **2.** A reduction in the amount payable under an insurance policy in respect of a partial loss of property. All marine insurance policies are subject to average under the Marine Insurance Act 1906 as amended by the Consumer Insurance (Disclosure and Representations) Act 2012; other policies may be subject to average if they contain express provision to that effect (an **average clause**).

In maritime law, the expression **general** (or **gross**) average is used in relation to certain acts, to the losses they cause, and to the rights of contribution to which they give rise. A **general-average act** consists of any sacrifice or expenditure made intentionally and reasonably to preserve property involved in a sea voyage. For example, the jettisoning of some of a ship's cargo to keep it afloat during a storm is a general-average act. The loss directly resulting from a general-average act is called **general-average loss** and is borne proportionately by all whose property has been saved. The owner of jettisoned cargo, for example, is entitled to a contribution from other cargo owners as well as the shipowners; such a contribution is called a **general-average contribution**. The principle of general average is common to the laws of all maritime nations, but the detailed rules are not uniform. To overcome conflict of law, a standard set of rules was agreed in the 19th century at international conferences of shipowners and others held at York and Antwerp. These, known as the **York–Antwerp rules**, do not have the force of law, but it is common practice to incorporate them (as subsequently amended) in contracts of *affreightment, thereby displacing national laws. The basic principle is that an insured who has suffered a general-average loss may recover the whole of it from his underwriters without enforcing his rights to contribution; these become enforceable by the underwriters instead.

By contrast, **particular average** (also called **simple** or **petty average**) relates purely to marine insurance. It consists of any partial loss that is not a general-average loss (for example, the damage of cargo by seawater). It is therefore borne purely by the person suffering it and is frequently covered by a policy only in limited circumstances.

A ship sold **free from average** is free from any claims whatsoever.

((⊕)) SEE WEB LINKS

• The latest version of the York–Antwerp Rules, as prepared by the Comité Maritime International

a vinculo matrimonii [Latin] From the bond of marriage. A decree of divorce *a vinculo matrimonii* allowed a spouse to remarry and was the forerunner of the modern divorce decree. *See also* A MENSA ET THORO.

avoid *vb.* To set aside a *voidable contract.

avulsion *n.* A sudden and violent shift in the course of a river that leaves the old riverbed dry. This could be caused by such natural forces as floods, tidal waves, or hurricanes. The alteration of territory by this means does not affect the title to territory; thus new claims by a state that would appear to benefit from the rapid geological change would be disbarred. The classic illustration of this was in the *Chamizal Arbitration* (1911) 5 AJIL 782 concerning land boundary changes made by the changing course of the Rio Grande between the USA and Mexico. The USA claimed that the new tract had been formed by the process of slow erosion and *accretion. Mexico contended that it had been formed by avulsion. By a convention of 1910 the controversy was submitted to arbitration and the Commission held that part of the tract was due to "slow and gradual erosion" (accretion) but that another part resulted from "the great flood of 1864" (avulsion) and should therefore be assigned to Mexico.

avoidance of disposition order An order by the High Court preventing or setting aside a transaction by a husband or wife that was made to defeat his (or her) spouse's claim to financial provision. A transaction, such as a gift, made within three years before the application is presumed to have been made in order to defeat the spouse's claim if its effect would be to defeat her claim. But a sale of property to a purchaser in good faith will not be set aside.

award *n. See* ARBITRATION.

backed for bail Describing a warrant for arrest issued by a magistrate or by the Crown Court to a police officer, directing him to release the accused, upon arrest, on bail under specified conditions. The police officer is bound to release the arrested person if his sureties are approved.

bail *n.* The release by the police, magistrates' court, or Crown Court of a person held in legal custody while awaiting trial or appealing against a criminal conviction. Conditions may be imposed on a person released on bail by the police. A person granted bail undertakes to pay a specified sum to the court if he fails to appear on the date set by the court (*see also* JUSTIFYING BAIL). This is known as **bail in one's own recognizance**. Often the court also requires guarantors (known as **sureties**) to undertake to produce the accused or to forfeit the sum fixed by the court if they fail to do so. In these circumstances the bailed person is, in theory, released into the custody of the sureties. Judges have wide discretionary powers as to whether or not bail should be granted, and for what sum. Normally an accused is granted bail unless it is likely that he will abscond, or interfere with witnesses, or unless he is accused of murder, attempted murder, manslaughter, rape, or attempted rape and has a previous conviction for such an offence. The accused, and the prosecution in limited circumstances, may appeal.

bailee *n. See* BAILMENT.

bail hostel Accommodation for persons of no fixed address who have been released on bail.

bailiff *n.* **1.** An officer of a court (usually a county court) concerned with the service of the court's processes and the enforcement of its orders, especially warrants of *execution authorizing the seizure of the goods of a debtor. The term is often loosely applied to a *High Court Enforcement Officer. **2.** A judicial official in Guernsey (Royal Court Bailiff).

bailiwick *n.* The area within which a *bailiff or *sheriff exercises jurisdiction.

bailment *n.* The transfer of the possession of goods by the owner (the **bailor**) to another (the **bailee**) for a particular purpose. Examples of bailments are the hiring of goods, the loan of goods, the pledge of goods, and the delivery of goods for carriage, safe custody, or repair. Ownership of the goods remains in the bailor, who has the right to demand their return or direct their disposal at the end of the period (if any) fixed for the bailment or (if no period is fixed) at will. This right will, however, be qualified by any *lien the bailee may have over the goods. Bailment exists independently of contract. But if the bailor receives payment for the bailment (a **bailment for reward**) there is often an express contract setting out the rights and obligations of the parties. A bailment for which the bailor receives no reward (e.g. the loan of a book to a friend) is called a **gratuitous bailment**.

bailor *n. See* BAILMENT.

balance sheet A document presenting in summary form a true and fair view of a company's financial position at a particular time (e.g. at the end of its financial year). It must show the items listed in either of the two formats set out in the Companies Act 2006. In theory, this represents the amount that would be available for the benefit of members if the company were immediately wound up and liabilities were discharged out of the proceeds of selling its assets. *See* ACCOUNTS.

bank holidays Days that are declared holidays for the clearing banks and are kept as public holidays under the Banking and Financial Dealing Act 1971 or by royal proclamation under this Act. In England and Wales there are currently eight bank holidays a year: New Year's Day (or, if that is a Saturday or Sunday, the following Monday), Good Friday, Easter Monday, May Holiday (the first Monday in May), Spring Bank Holiday (the last Monday in May), Summer Bank Holiday (the last Monday in August), and Christmas Day and the following day (or, if Christmas Day is a Saturday or Sunday, the following Monday and Tuesday).

bankruptcy *n.* The state of a person who has been adjudged by a court to be insolvent. The court orders the compulsory administration of a bankrupt's affairs so that his assets can be fairly distributed among his creditors. Bankruptcy proceedings are started by a **bankruptcy petition**, which may be presented to the court by:

(1) a creditor or creditors;
(2) a person affected by a *voluntary arrangement to pay debts set up by the debtor under the Insolvency Act 1986;
(3) the Director of Public Prosecutions;
(4) the debtor himself.

The grounds for a creditors' petition are that the debtor appears to be unable to pay a debt for which a statutory demand has been made or that a court has ordered him or her to pay. The debt must amount to at least £750. The grounds for a petition by a person bound by a voluntary arrangement are that the debtor has not complied with the terms of the arrangement or has withheld material information. The Director of Public Prosecutions may present a petition in the public interest under the Powers of Criminal Courts Act 1973. The debtor may also present a petition on the grounds of being unable to pay his debts.

Once a petition has been presented, the debtor may not dispose of any property. The court may halt any other legal proceedings against the debtor. An interim receiver may be appointed. This will usually be the *official receiver, who will take any necessary action to protect the debtor's estate. A special manager may be appointed if the nature of the debtor's business requires it.

The court may make a **bankruptcy order** at its discretion. Once this has happened, the debtor is an *undischarged bankrupt, who is deprived of the ownership of all property and must assist the official receiver in listing it, recovering it, protecting it, etc. The official receiver becomes manager and receiver of the estate until the appointment of a **trustee in bankruptcy**. The bankrupt must prepare a statement of affairs for the official receiver within 21 days of the bankruptcy order. A *public examination of the bankrupt may be ordered on the application of the official receiver or the creditors, in which the bankrupt will be required to answer questions about his or her affairs in court.

Within 12 weeks the official receiver must decide whether to call a **meeting of creditors** to appoint a trustee in bankruptcy. The trustee's duties are to collect, realize, and distribute the bankrupt's estate. The trustee may be appointed by the creditors, the court, or the Secretary of State and must be a qualified *insolvency practitioner or the official receiver. All the property of the bankrupt is available to pay the creditors, except for the following:

- equipment necessary for him to continue in employment or business;
- necessary domestic equipment;
- income required for the reasonable domestic needs of the bankrupt and his family.

The court has discretion whether to order the sale of a house in which a spouse or children are living.

    All creditors must prove their claims to the trustee. Only unsecured claims can be proved in bankruptcy. When all expenses have been paid, the trustee will divide the estate. The Insolvency Act 1986 sets out the order in which creditors will be paid (*see* PREFERENTIAL DEBTS).

    The bankruptcy may end automatically after one year, but in some cases a court order is required. The bankrupt is discharged and receives a certificate of discharge from the court.

(⊕) SEE WEB LINKS
- Information on bankruptcy (and alternative procedures) from the Insolvency Service website

banning order *See* FOOTBALL HOOLIGANISM.

banns *pl. n.* The public announcement in church of an intended marriage. Banns must be published for three successive Sundays if a marriage is to take place in the Church of England other than by religious licence or a superintendent registrar's certificate. *See also* MARRIAGE BY CERTIFICATE; MARRIAGE BY RELIGIOUS LICENCE.

bar *n.* **1.** A legal impediment. **2.** An imaginary barrier in a court of law. Only Queen's Counsel, officers of the court, and litigants in person are allowed between the bar and the *bench when the court is in session. **3.** A rail near the entrance to each House of Parliament beyond which nonmembers may not pass but to which they may be summoned (e.g. for reprimand).

Bar *n.* *Barristers, collectively. To be **called to the Bar** is to be admitted to the profession by one of the Inns of Court.

Bar Council (General Council of the Bar of England and Wales) The governing body for barristers both practising and non-practising. Through the **Bar Standards Board** it issues a code of conduct to which all barristers are obliged to adhere, maintains standards within the Bar, and considers complaints against barristers. *See also* COUNCIL OF THE INNS OF COURT.

(⊕) SEE WEB LINKS
- Website of the Bar Council: includes careers information, ethical and practice guidance for barristers, and guidance on finding and instructing a barrister
- Website of the Bar Standards Board: includes the current code of conduct

bareboat charter A form of boat or ship hire in which the hirer assumes full control and possession of the vessel, pays all charges and expenses, and provides master and crew. A bareboat charter may end with the hirer acquiring title in the vessel; in this case it is known as a **charter for demise** or **demise charter**. *See also* CHARTERPARTY.

bare licensee A person who uses or occupies land by permission of the owner but has no legal or equitable interest in it. Such permission is personal to him; thus he cannot transfer it. He cannot enforce it against a third party who acquires the land from the owner. His permission can be brought to an end at any time and he must leave the property with "all reasonable speed". If he does not do so he becomes a trespasser (*see* TRESPASS). *See also* LICENCE.

bare trust (naked trust, simple trust) A trust under which the trustee is under no obligation except to hold the trust property in trust for an adult beneficiary who is *sui juris* and to deal with the trust property only as instructed by the beneficiary (*compare* ACTIVE TRUST). A bare trustee is therefore a *nominee.

Where assets are held on a bare trust, the *capital gains tax charge arises on the beneficiary and not on the trustee. For capital gains tax purposes, a trust is treated by statute as a bare trust if the beneficiary has the exclusive right to require the property to be passed to him, subject only to satisfying any outstanding charge, lien, or other right. (However, *see Stephenson v Barclays Bank Trust Co Ltd* [1975] 1 WLR 882 (Ch); *Crowe v Appleby* [1975] 1 WLR 885; *Booth v Ellard* [1980] STC 555).

For tax purposes, there may also be a bare trust where property is held for an infant or an adult without mental capacity. However, for such property to be treated as being held on a bare trust the incapacity (whether by virtue of age or mental condition) of the beneficiary must be the only reason for his not being absolutely entitled (*Tomlinson v Glyn's Executor and Trustee Co* [1980] 45 TC 607).

barratry *n.* **1.** Any act committed wilfully by the master or crew of a ship to the detriment of its owner or charterer. Examples include scuttling the ship and embezzling the cargo. Illegal activities (e.g. carrying prohibited persons) leading to the forfeiture of the ship also constitute barratry. Barratry is one of the risks covered by policies of marine insurance. **2.** The former common-law offence (abolished by the Criminal Law Act 1967) of habitually raising or inciting disputes in the courts.

barring of entailed interest *See* ENTAILED INTEREST.

barrister *n.* A legal practitioner admitted to plead at the Bar. A barrister must be a member of one of the four *Inns of Court, by whom he is **called to the Bar** when admitted to the profession. To qualify as a barrister it is necessary to have either a qualifying law degree or to have completed a graduate diploma in law. It is then necessary to complete the Bar Vocational Course, colloquially known as "bar school." Thereafter barristers take a pupillage, which is usually with a set of chambers, before seeking a permanent place as a "tenant". The primary function of barristers is to act as *advocates for parties in courts or tribunals, but they also undertake the writing of opinions and some of the work preparatory to a trial. Their general immunity from law suits in negligence for criminal and civil litigation has been abolished. With certain exceptions a barrister may only act upon the instructions of a *solicitor, who is also responsible for the payment of the barrister's fee. Barristers have the right of audience in all courts: they are either *Queen's Counsel (often referred to as **leaders** or **leading counsel**) or *junior barristers. *See also* ADVOCACY QUALIFICATION.

baseline *n.* The line forming the boundary between the *internal waters of a state on its landward side and the territorial sea on its seaward side (*see* TERRITORIAL WATERS). Other coastal state zones (the contiguous zone, *exclusive economic zone, and exclusive fishing zone) are measured from the baseline.

basic award *See* COMPENSATION.

basic intent Any criminal offence for which *recklessness or *negligence will suffice to establish the *mens rea element may be considered an offence of basic intent. *Compare* SPECIFIC INTENT. *See also* INTOXICATION.

battered child A child subjected to physical violence or abuse by a parent, step-parent, or any other person with whom he is living. A battered child may be protected if the other parent (or person who is looking after him) applies for an injunction under the Family Law Act 1996, but only if the child is living, or might reasonably be expected to live, with the applicant. The Act applies to children under 18. When a child is suffering, or likely to suffer, significant harm, a local authority may apply for a *supervision order or *care order under the Children Act 1989. *See also* EMERGENCY PROTECTION ORDER.

battered spouse or cohabitant *See* DOMESTIC VIOLENCE.

Battered Woman Syndrome A psychological syndrome suffered by a person (typically a woman) as a result of prolonged and extreme physical and emotional abuse by her partner. Battered Woman Syndrome has informed the basis for partial defence to murder in cases where the battered woman kills her abusive partner, although there is no formal legal defence properly referred to as Battered Woman Syndrome; rather, the evidence of abuse and its psychological effects upon the battered woman may provide the basis for a defence of *loss of control or *diminished responsibility (*R v Ahluwhalia* [1992] 4 All ER 889 (CA)). While Battered Woman Syndrome has been criticized for its failure to account for the wide range of responses that battered women may experience in response to severe abuse, it has provided one set of reasons explaining why battered women may be unable to escape from an abusive partner.

battery *n.* The intentional or reckless application of physical force to another person. Common battery is a criminal offence (punishable with a fine and/or six months' imprisonment) as well as a tort, even if no actual harm results. The *consent of the victim is a defence to common battery. If actual harm does result, however, the consent of the victim will provide a defence only when the injury is inflicted for good reason (e.g. in the course of a sport or medical treatment). Consent has been rejected as a defence where actual harm was inflicted in the course of consensual sado-masochistic activities (*AG's Reference (No 6 of 1980)*[1981] 2 All ER 1057). *Compare* ASSAULT; GRIEVOUS BODILY HARM.

bay *n.* A well-marked roughly semicircular indentation on a coastline. What does or does not constitute a bay can be of relevance in determining a state's control of its coastal waters. The test is a geographical one, taking into account relative dimensions and configuration. The following three considerations have been taken into account when making this determination: (1) the depth of the indentation relative to the width of its mouth; (2) the economic and strategic importance of the indentation to the coastal state; and (3) the seclusion of the indentation from the highway of nations on the open sea. The above factors, however, do not apply to a small number of so-called "historic bays". These have been claimed as internal waters on the basis of historic title. For example, the estuary of the River Plate in Argentina is claimed as internal waters, as is the vast Hudson Bay of Canada, which embraces about 580000 square miles. *See also* TERRITORIAL WATERS.

bearer *n.* The person in possession of a bill of exchange or promissory note that is payable to the bearer.

beauty contest A method used by an employer contemplating entering a *single-union agreement, in which a number of unions are invited to present proposals for collective bargaining arrangements within an establishment. After reviewing the proposals the company decides to recognize the union that best meets its criteria.

bed and breakfasting The sale of shares on one day and their repurchase the next day. This has traditionally been undertaken in order to trigger a loss that can then be put against gains that would otherwise be subject to *capital gains tax. The taxation of Chargeable Gains Act 1992 s 106A makes the arrangement ineffective for shares sold and repurchased within a 30 day period. There are, however, no provisions that stop the bed and breakfasting of other assets and the arrangement is sometimes made for e.g. works of art. An imaginative use of the bed and breakfast anti-avoidance provisions was demonstrated in *Davies v Hicks* [2005] STC 850, in which the taxpayer contrived to avoid a tax charge on a sale for £1,676,000 when a trust was moved from UK trustees to trustees in Mauritius.

Beddoe order An order made by the court granting trustees permission to incur expense on behalf of the trust by bringing or defending an action. An application for such an order must be made prior to the trustees' engaging in litigation if protection is to be acquired. The order protects the trustees against claims by the beneficiaries that the action should not have been brought and enables the trustees to recover the costs from the trust property. If an order has not been obtained, these consequences may not follow, and the trustees may be personally liable to the beneficiaries for any loss incurred on behalf of the trust and also may themselves have to pay any costs to the trust arising from the action. The name derives from the case *Re Beddoe* (*Downes v Cottam*) [1893] 1 Ch 547.

belligerent communities, recognition of The formal acknowledgment by a state of the existence of a civil war between another state's central government and the peoples of an area within its territorial boundaries. Such recognition brings about the conventional operation of the rules of war, in particular those humanitarian restraints upon the combatants introduced by the international law of armed force. Another result of recognition of belligerency is that both the rebels and the parent central government are entitled to exercise belligerent rights and are subject to the obligations imposed on belligerents. Following recognition, third states have the rights and obligations of *neutrality. *Compare* INSURGENCY.

bench *n.* **1.** Literally, the seat of a judge in court. The bench is usually in an elevated position at one side of the court room facing the seats of counsel and solicitors. **2.** A group of judges or magistrates sitting together in a court, or all judges, collectively. Thus a lawyer who has been appointed a judge is said to have been **elevated to the bench**.

Benchers (Masters of the Bench) *pl. n.* Judges and senior practitioners who form a governing body for each of the Inns of Court. They are recruited by co-option and elect one of their number annually to be the Treasurer. Benchers are responsible for admission of students and calls to the Bar and exercise disciplinary powers over the members of the Inn. Appeal from their decisions is to the Lord Chancellor and "visitors" (i.e. High Court Judges sitting for the appeal).

bench warrant A warrant for the arrest of a person who has failed to attend court when summoned or subpoenaed to do so or against whom an order of committal for contempt of court has been made and who cannot be found. The warrant is issued during a sitting of the court.

beneficial interest The rights of a beneficiary in respect of the property held in trust for him. Taxation is (generally) concerned with beneficial ownership and not with legal title. Thus, if the name of A appears on the Land Registry certificate, but A is holding the land on behalf of C, D and E, income arising from the land is assessed on C, D, and E; capital gains tax is charged on C, D, and E when the land is sold. *See also* BARE TRUST; EQUITABLE INTERESTS.

beneficial owner An owner who is entitled to the possession and use of land or its income for his own benefit. Under the Law of Property Act 1925 a person who for valuable *consideration conveys land as beneficial owner gives implied covenants

(1) that he has the right to convey it;
(2) for quiet enjoyment (i.e. that the transferee takes possession free from adverse claims to the land);
(3) that the land is free from encumbrances other than any specified in the conveyance;
(4) for further assurance (i.e. that the transferor will do anything necessary to cure any defect in the conveyance);
(5) when the land is leasehold (a) that the lease is valid and subsisting and (b) that the convenants in the lease have been performed and the rent paid.

When the owner of a legal estate is not the beneficial owner (e.g. a mortgagee, trustee, or personal representative) his only implied covenant in a conveyance of the land is that he has not himself created any encumbrance.

beneficiary *n.* **1.** A person entitled to benefit from a *trust. The beneficiary holds a *beneficial interest in the property of which a *trustee holds the legal *interest. A beneficiary was formerly known as the **cestui que trust**. **2.** One who benefits from a will.

beneficiary principle The principle that, for a trust to be valid, there must be a human *beneficiary capable of enforcing the trust. Exceptions to the beneficiary principle are *charitable trusts and a limited number of *purpose trusts that are commonly referred to as "trusts of imperfect obligation". It has been held that indirect human beneficiaries satisfy the beneficiary principle (*Re Denley's Trust Deed* [1969] 1 Ch 373).

benefits in kind Goods or services supplied by an employer to an employee. A director or employee receiving benefits in kind from his employer (and, sometimes, from third parties) is (generally) subject to income tax on the cost suffered by the employer in providing the benefit (Income Tax (Earnings and Pensions) Act 2003 s 63–220).

benevolent purposes Purposes that are for the public good but not necessarily charitable. They are wider than *philanthropic purposes. If a trust is constructed as being for "charitable *or* benevolent" purposes it will not be charitable (*Chichester Diocesan Fund and Board of Finance v Simpson* [1944] AC 341 (HL)). *See* CHARITABLE TRUST.

Benjamin order An order made by the court for the distribution of assets on death when it is uncertain whether or not a beneficiary is alive. The order authorizes the personal representatives of the deceased (who will be administering the estate) to distribute the property on the basis that the beneficiary is dead (or on some other basis); the personal representatives are therefore protected from being sued if the beneficiary is in fact alive and entitled. The beneficiary may, however, trace the trust property (*see* TRACING TRUST PROPERTY). The name derives from the case *Re Benjamin* [1902] 1 Ch 723.

bequeath *vb.* To dispose by will of property other than land. *Compare* DEVISE. *See* LEGACY.

bequest *n.* A gift by will of property other than land. *Compare* DEVISE. *See* LEGACY.

bereaved minor's trust As defined by the Inheritance Tax Act 1984 s 71(A), a *trust established under a will for the minor child of the testator. Under such a trust the child must become entitled to the assets of the trust on or before attaining 18. No additional *inheritance tax charges are incurred when the capital is distributed out of the trust to the child. A *statutory trust for the minor child of an *intestate also qualifies as a bereaved minor's trust.

bereavement, damages for *See* FATAL ACCIDENTS.

bereavement benefit A benefit payable to widows, widowers, and (since December 2005) civil partners (*see* CIVIL PARTNERSHIP), subject to conditions set out in the Welfare Reform and Pensions Act 1999. It consists of a bereavement payment (made as a lump sum), a widowed parent allowance (where applicable), and a bereavement allowance.

Berne Convention The Berne Convention for the Protection of Literary and Artistic Works: an international convention of September 1886 that sets out ground rules for protection of *copyright at national level; it has since been amended several times. Many nations are signatories to the Convention, including the UK and, more recently, the United States. *See also* TRIPS.

best-evidence rule A rule, formerly of central importance, requiring that a party must call the best evidence that the nature of the case will allow. At common law an aspect of the best evidence rule required a party relying on the contents of a document at trial to produce the original document. This aspect of the rule is now of diminished importance, although under the *Civil Procedure Rules original documents should be made available for inspection by the other parties before the hearing and by the judge at the hearing.

best interests 1. (in medical law) Where an adult lacks capacity, the Mental Capacity Act 2005 provides that any decision relating to medical care or treatment should be taken in accordance with that patient's best interests. The decision will be taken by the relevant health care professional or, in the event of a dispute, by the courts or a court-appointed *deputy (not, it is to be noted by the patient's relatives). In reaching the decision, the decision-maker is directed by section 4 to consider various factors, including (*inter alia*) the person's past and present wishes and feelings and the beliefs and values that would be likely to influence his decision if he had capacity. The decision-maker should also, if practical and appropriate, consult those caring for the patient or interested in his welfare. It is to be noted that an alternative to the "best interests" test, that of *substituted judgment, is preferred in some jurisdictions (e.g. the USA). 2. (in family law) *See* WELFARE PRINCIPLE.

best value A requirement under the Local Government Act 1999 that *local authorities must have regard to economy, efficiency, and effectiveness when exercising their functions and must make arrangements to secure continuous improvement.

Beth Din The Jewish religious court, the London branch of which is historically the supreme Jewish legal authority for several Commonwealth countries and is also consulted by Batei Din throughout Europe. The court handles all areas of Jewish law, including questions of marriage, divorce, and conversion. With the consent of the parties it can also hear civil disputes, such as commercial disputes between businesses.

bias *n. See* NATURAL JUSTICE.

bid *n. See* AUCTION.

bigamy *n.* The act of going through a marriage ceremony with someone when one is already lawfully married to someone else (Offences Against the Person Act 1861 s 57). Bigamy is a crime, punishable by up to seven years' imprisonment; however, there is a defence if the accused honestly and reasonably believed that his or her first spouse was dead or that their previous marriage had been dissolved or annulled or was void. There is also a special defence if the accused's spouse has been absent for at least seven years, and is therefore presumed by the accused to be dead, even if he does not have positive proof of the death. Even though a person is found not guilty of the crime of bigamy, the bigamous marriage will still be void if that person had a spouse living at the time that the second marriage was celebrated.

bilateral contract (synallagmatic contract) A contract that creates mutual obligations, i.e. both parties undertake to do, or refrain from doing, something in exchange for the other party's undertaking. The majority of contracts are bilateral in nature. *Compare* UNILATERAL CONTRACT.

bilateral discharge The ending of a contract by agreement, when neither party has yet performed his obligations under it (an **executory contract**). Each party supplies consideration for the agreement to discharge by releasing the other from his existing obligations. *Compare* unilateral discharge (*see* ACCORD AND SATISFACTION).

bill *n.* **1.** Any of various written instruments; for example, a *bill of exchange, a *bill of indictment, or a *bill of lading. **2.** A written account of money owed; for example, a *bill of costs.

Bill *n.* A draft of a proposed *Act of Parliament, which must (normally) be passed by both Houses before becoming an Act. Bills are either public or private, and the procedure governing their passing by Parliament depends basically on this distinction. In general, a **public Bill** is one relating to matters of general concern; it is introduced by the government or by a private member (**private member's Bill**). In the House of Commons the government sets aside certain Fridays for debate on private member's Bills, and a ballot at the beginning of each session of Parliament determines the members whose Bills are to have priority on those days. A private member's Bill that is not supported by the government stands little chance of successfully completing all stages and becoming an Act. The government sometimes prefers a private member to sponsor a particularly controversial Bill that they themselves support; for example, the Abortion Act 1967 was introduced by a private member (David Steel) and was successful because it had the support of the government of the day. A public Bill, unless predominantly financial, can be introduced in either House (less controversial Bills are introduced in the Lords first). The Bill is presented by the minister or other member in charge, passed by being read three times, and then sent to the other House. Its first reading is a formality, but it is debated on second and third readings, between which it goes through a Committee stage and a Report stage during which amendments may be made. A Bill that has not become an Act by the end of the session lapses; if reintroduced in a subsequent session, it must go through all stages again.

A **private Bill** is one designed to benefit a particular person, local authority, or other body, by whom it is presented. It is introduced on a petition by the promoter, which is preceded by public advertisement and by notice to those directly affected. Its Committee stage in the first House is conducted before a small group of members, and evidence for and against it is heard. Thereafter, it follows the procedure for public Bills.

A **hybrid Bill** is a government bill that is purely local or personal in character and affects only one of a number of interests in the same class. For example, a government Bill to nationalize one only of several private-sector airlines would be hybrid. A hybrid Bill proceeds as a public Bill until after second reading in the first House, after which it is treated similarly to a private Bill.

bill of costs An account of *costs prepared by a solicitor in respect of legal services he has rendered his client. In general a solicitor may be required to furnish his client with a bill unless they have made an agreement in writing to the contrary. If no such agreement has been made the solicitor may not, without the permission of the High Court, sue for **recovery of costs** until one month after the bill of costs has been delivered. Until August 2009 any client dissatisfied with a bill could require his solicitor to obtain a **remuneration certificate** from the Law Society; the certificate would either confirm that the fee was fair and reasonable or substitute a lower fee. Under the Solicitors (Non-Contentious Business) Remuneration Order 2009 a dissatisfied client no longer has this option but may make a complaint about the bill to the Legal Complaints Service. In contentious (i.e. litigious) matters the bill is subject to *assessment of costs. *See also* COSTS DRAFTSMAN.

bill of exchange An unconditional order in writing, addressed by one person (the **drawer**) to another (the **drawee**) and signed by the person giving it, requiring the drawee to pay on demand or at a fixed or determinable future time a specified sum of money to or to the order of a specified person (the **payee**) or to the bearer. If the bill is payable at a future time the drawee signifies his *acceptance, which makes him the party primarily liable upon the bill; the drawer and endorsers may also be liable upon a bill. The use of bills of exchange enables one person to transfer to another an enforceable right to a sum of money. A bill of exchange is not only transferable but also negotiable, since if a person without an enforceable right to the money transfers a bill to a *holder in due course, the latter obtains a good title to it. Much of the law on bills of exchange is codified by the Bills of Exchange Act 1882 and the Cheques Act 1992.

bill of indictment A formal written document containing the charges to which the accused will plead at trial in the Crown Court. Under Part 14 of the *Criminal Procedure Rules the prosecution is required to draw up the indictment within prescribed time limits. The bill is normally preferred by delivering it to the Crown Court Officer. After it has been signed by the officer, the bill becomes the *indictment on which the defendant is tried.

bill of lading A document acknowledging the shipment of a consignor's goods for carriage by sea (*compare* SEA WAYBILL). It is used primarily when the ship is carrying goods belonging to a number of consignors (a general ship). In this case, each consignor receives a bill issued (normally by the master of the ship) on behalf of either the shipowner or a charterer under a *charterparty. The bill serves three functions: it is a receipt for the goods; it summarizes the terms of the contract of carriage; and it acts as a document of title to the goods. A bill of lading is also issued by a shipowner to a charterer who is using the ship for the carriage of his own goods. In this case, the terms of the contract of carriage are in the charterparty and the bill serves only as a receipt and a document of title. During transit, ownership of the goods may be transferred by delivering the bill to another if it is drawn to bearer or by endorsing it if it is drawn to order. It is not, however, a *negotiable instrument.

The responsibilities, liabilities, rights, and immunities attaching to carriers under bills of lading are stated in the **Hague Rules**. These were drawn up by the International Law Association meeting at The Hague in 1921 and adopted by an International Conference on Maritime Law held at Brussels in 1922. They were given effect in the UK by the Carriage of Goods by Sea Act 1924 and so became known in the UK as the Hague Rules of 1924. They were amended by the Brussels Protocol 1968, effect being given to the amendments by the Carriage of Goods by Sea Act 1971. The Rules, which are set out in a schedule to the Act, apply to carriage under a bill of lading from any port in Great Britain or Northern Ireland to any other port and also to carriage between any of the states by which they have been adopted. Every bill issued in Great Britain or Northern Ireland to which the Rules apply must state that fact expressly (the clause giving effect to this requirement is customarily referred to as the **paramount clause**). The Hague Rules were completely rewritten in 1978 in a new treaty known as the **Hamburg Rules** (ratified by 34 countries so far), which drastically alter the privileged position of a sea carrier as compared to other carriers. However, they have not yet been generally adopted – indeed, it is estimated that they govern less than 5% of world maritime trade.

(((●))) SEE WEB LINKS
- Full text of the Hague Rules
- Full text of the Hamburg Rules

bill of rights A formal document that sets out the fundamental or most important rights of the citizens or residents of a country. The English Bill of Rights of 1689, for example, set out a number of such rights, including freedom of speech for Parliament and the prohibition of cruel and unusual punishments. A bill of rights is often part of the constitution of the state and gives courts (sometimes only the supreme court) the power to enforce compliance with such rights. In the USA the Supreme Court can even strike down legislation if it does not comply with the US Bill of Rights. In other countries the relationship between the legislature and the court's duty to promote compliance with a bill of rights is more complex.

Most bills of rights include the core civil and political rights such as liberty, freedom of expression, and fair trial and due process (see, for example, the *European Convention of Human Rights). Some, such as the South African Bill of Rights, also contain socioeconomic rights, such as a right to food, water, health care, proper housing, and a healthy environment.

The *Human Rights Act currently functions as the United Kingdom's Bill of Rights. In 2011 the government set up a Bill of Rights Commission to consider replacing the Act with a British Bill of Rights; however, this body failed to reach agreement before it disbanded in 2012.

bill of sale A document by which a person transfers the ownership of goods to another. Commonly the goods are transferred conditionally, as security for a debt, and a **conditional bill of sale** is thus a mortgage of goods. The mortgagor has a right to redeem the goods on repayment of the debt and usually remains in possession of them; he may thus obtain false credit by appearing to own them. An **absolute bill of sale** transfers ownership of the goods absolutely. The Bills of Sale Acts 1878 and 1882 regulate the registration and form of bills of sale. The *Civil Procedure Rules set out certain formalities in relation to litigation concerning bills of sale under these statutes.

bind over An order issued by a magistrates' court or by the Crown Court directing the person subject to the order to *keep the peace or be of *good behaviour or by the Crown Court directing the person to come up for judgment. A bind over to keep the peace or be of good behaviour is often used as a means of case disposal in minor cases, whereby the prosecution agrees not to proceed in exchange for the defendant's agreement to be bound over for a stated period. If the defendant breaks any of the conditions of the order during this period, he will forfeit a specified sum of money. A bind over to come up for judgment may be used as a substitute for sentencing in the Crown Court, whereby the defendant agrees to be bound by certain conditions following conviction. If the defendant breaks any of the conditions, he will be brought back before the court and sentenced. *See* RECOGNIZANCE.

birth certificate A certified copy of an entry of birth in the register of births, deaths, and marriages, which comprises evidence of the detail there stated. *See* REGISTRATION OF BIRTH.

black cap Formerly, a cap worn by an English judge on the most solemn occasions, most notably when passing sentence of death. Contrary to popular belief, the cap was not itself an emblem of the death sentence; rather, it was a normal part of judicial full dress, as worn by judges on all especially formal occasions.

blacklist *n.* A list that contains details of members of trade unions, and in particular details of trade-union activists, compiled with a view to being used by outside bodies, usually employers and their associations, for the purpose of discrimination in relation to the recruitment and treatment of workers. The utilization of such lists is prohibited by the Employment Relations Act 1999 (Blacklists) Regulations 2010. This includes selling, supplying, compiling, or using lists for the purposes of recruitment and discriminatory treatment.

blackmail *n.* The crime of making an unwarranted demand with menaces for the purpose of financial gain for oneself or someone else or financial loss to the person threatened. The menaces may include a threat of violence or of detrimental action, e.g. exposure of past immorality or misconduct (Theft Act 1968 s 21). Blackmail is punishable by up to 14 years' imprisonment. As long as the demand is made with menaces, it will be presumed to be unwarranted, unless the accused can show both that he thought he was reasonable in making the demand and that he thought it was reasonable to use the menaces as a means of pressure. *See also* THREAT.

Black Rod, Gentleman Usher of the An official of the House of Lords whose title derives from his staff of office – an ebony rod surmounted with a gold lion. The office originated as usher of the Order of the Garter in the 14th century; the parliamentary appointment dates from 1522. Black Rod is responsible for maintaining order in the House and summons members of the Commons to the Lords to hear a speech from the throne.

blasphemy *n.* Statements or writings that deny – in an offensive or insulting manner – the truth of the Christian religion, the Bible, the Book of Common Prayer, or the existence of God. Blasphemy is a crime at common law, and if it is published there is no need to show an intention to shock or insult or an awareness that the publication is blasphemous. Prosecutions for blasphemy are now rare and it has been suggested that the crime be abolished.

blight notice A statutory notice by which an owner-occupier can require a public authority to purchase land that is potentially liable to compulsory acquisition by them and therefore cannot be sold at full value on the open market. The land may, for example, be shown in a development plan to be prospectively required for the authority's purposes or it may be designated in published proposals as the site of a future highway.

blind trust A trust in which the settlor transfers property to trustees to be held on trust for his own benefit on the basis that he will not know the nature of the investments being made by the trustees. This type of arrangement would prevent the settlor from being vulnerable to accusations of conflicts of interest between his private and professional life and is typically used by politicians and other public figures.

blockade *n.* The act of a belligerent power of preventing access to or egress from the ports of its enemy by stationing a ship or squadron in such a position that it can intercept vessels attempting to approach or leave such ports. A neutral merchant vessel trying to break through a blockade is liable to capture and condemnation by the captor's *prize court. A blockade is practically always carried out by a warship or warships of a belligerent, although in certain circumstances it may be effected by land batteries commanding the approach to a blockaded port. In the latter case it must be supported by a naval force sufficient to warn off innocent and capture offending vessels attempting to enter (*The Circassian* (1864) 2 Wall 135, 149).

block exemption Exemption from *Article 101 of the Treaty on the Functioning of the European Union (previously Treaty of Rome) for certain types of anticompetitive agreements that fall within the scope of special EU regulations that have direct effect in the EU (*see* COMMUNITY LEGISLATION). Block exemptions exist in a number of different areas, including *vertical agreements, research and development, specialization, and *technology transfer. The regulations are published in the EU's *Official Journal*; any agreement that complies with the regulations will be exempt from Article 101. Many contracts in the EU are drafted to comply with the block exemption regulations by using the wording of those regulations in the agreements themselves. EU block exemptions provide an automatic exemption from the provisions of UK competition law in the Competition Act 1998.

(⊕) SEE WEB LINKS

• The Europa website provides details of all EU antitrust rules and block exemptions

blood relationship *See* CONSANGUINITY.

blood specimen *See* SPECIMEN OF BLOOD.

blood test **1.** An analysis of blood designed to show that a particular man could not be the father of a specified child (it cannot establish that the person *is* the father). The court may order blood tests in disputes about paternity, but a man cannot be compelled to undergo the test against his will. His refusal may, however, lead the court to draw adverse conclusions. Any attempt to take blood without consent would be trespass. *See also* DNA FINGERPRINTING. **2.** *See* SPECIMEN OF BLOOD.

blue bag Traditionally, a bag to carry a barrister's robes. When a person is called to the bar, by tradition he is provided, as part of his outfit, with a blue bag to carry his robe and wig box. If later on he is in a case with a Queen's Counsel as his leader, it is the privilege of the QC, if he thinks the junior has played his part well, to present him with a **red bag**.

blue book A form of government publication, such as a report of a committee, inquiry, or royal commission, published in blue covers. *See also* PARLIAMENTARY PAPERS.

bodily harm *See* ACTUAL BODILY HARM; ASSAULT; GRIEVOUS BODILY HARM.

body corporate *See* CORPORATION.

boilerplate *n.* **1.** A standard form of words used in drafting contracts or other legal documents. **2.** A standard form or document that can be modified to cover various cases.

Bolam test In cases of alleged clinical *negligence, a test used to determine the standard of care owed to a patient by doctors. The case *Bolam v Friern Hospital Management Committee* (1957) 1 WLR 583 established that there can be no breach in the duty of care so long as the doctor acted in accordance with a responsible body of medical opinion. Subsequent cases have challenged this test, requiring the doctor to behave "reasonably" or "logically" regardless of the body of medical opinion (*Bolitho v City and*

Hackney Health Authority [1998] AC 232 (HL)). The Bolam test applies only to cases of medical treatment and not to information given at *consent.

bomb hoax A deception in which one or more people are led to believe that an explosion is likely to occur that will cause physical injury or damage to property. A bomb hoax may constitute *blackmail (if accompanied by a demand), public nuisance, threats to damage property (an offence under the Criminal Damage Act 1971), or wasting the time of the police (under the Criminal Law Act 1967). Under the Criminal Law Act 1977 it is a special statutory offence, punishable by imprisonment for up to five years and/or a fine, to place or send an object anywhere with the intention of leading someone to believe that it is likely to explode and cause harm. It is also an offence falsely to tell anyone that a bomb has been placed in a certain place or that some other object is liable to explode.

bona vacantia [Latin: empty goods] Property not disposed of by a deceased's will and to which there is no relation entitled on intestacy. Under the Administration of Estates Act 1925 s 46, such property passes to the Crown, the Duchy of Lancaster, or the Duke of Cornwall. In practice it is usually used to make *ex gratia* payments, at the discretion of the Crown, Duchy, or Duke, to any dependants of the deceased and anyone else for whom he might reasonably have been expected to provide.

bond *n.* **1.** A deed by which one person (the **obligor**) commits himself to another (the **obligee**) to do something or refrain from doing something. If it secures the payment of money, it is called a **common money bond**; a bond giving security for the carrying out of a contract is called a **performance bond**. **2.** A document issued by a government, local authority, company, or other public body undertaking to repay long-term debt with interest. **Bond issues** are issues of debt securities by a borrower to investors in return for the payment of a subscription price.

bonus issue (capitalization issue, scrip issue) A method of increasing a company's issued capital (*see* AUTHORIZED CAPITAL) by issuing further shares to existing company members. These shares are paid for out of undistributed profits of the company, the *share premium account, or the *capital redemption reserve. The bonus issue is made to shareholders in proportion to their existing shareholding (e.g. a 1 for 2 bonus issue means that shareholders receive an extra free share for every two shares they hold).

books of account (accounting records) Records that disclose and explain a company's financial position at any time and enable its directors to prepare its *accounts. The books (which registered companies are required to keep by the Companies Act 2006) should reveal, on a day-to-day basis, sums received and expended together with details of the transaction, assets and liabilities, and (where appropriate) goods sold and purchased. Public companies must preserve their books for six years, private companies for three years. Company officers and *auditors (but not members) have a statutory right to inspect the books.

borough *n.* An area of local government, abolished as such (except in *Greater London) by the Local Government Act 1972. A *district may, however, be styled a borough by royal charter. Originally, a borough was a fortified town; later, a town entitled to send a representative to Parliament.

borough court An inferior *court of record for the trial of civil actions by charter, custom, or otherwise in a borough. All remaining borough courts were abolished in 1974 by the Local Government Act 1972.

borstal *n.* An institution to which young offenders (aged 15 to 20 inclusive) could be sent before June 1983 instead of prison. Young offenders who commit a sufficiently serious offence are now subjected to a *detention and training order. *See also* JUVENILE OFFENDER.

bottomry *n. See* HYPOTHECATION.

boundary *n.* (in international law) An imaginary line that determines the territorial limits of a state. Such boundaries define the limitation of each state's effective *jurisdiction. They are three-dimensional in nature in that they include the *airspace and subsoil of the state, the *terra firma* within the boundary, and the maritime domain of the state's internal waters and territorial sea. *See also* ACCRETION; AVULSION; THALWEG, RULE OF THE.

boundary commissions Independent bodies established under the Parliamentary Constituencies Act 1986 to carry out periodic reviews of parliamentary constituencies for the purpose of recommending boundary changes to take account of shifts in population. In 2000 the functions of the commission for England were transferred to the newly created *Electoral Commission), which was also mandated to set up **Boundary Committees** for Wales, Scotland, and Northern Ireland.

Bournewood gap A legal loophole that has enabled adults without mental capacity but who are compliant to be hospitalized and treated for psychiatric problems without the procedural safeguards offered by the Mental Health Act 1983. The European Court of Human Rights has ruled that such practice violated a patient's right to liberty (*HL v UK* App no 45508/99 (2004) 40 EHRR 761). As a result the Mental Capacity Act 2005 has been amended (2007) to provide a new framework, referred to as the *Deprivation of Liberty Safeguards.

brain death *n.* Permanent functional death of the centres in the brainstem that control breathing, heart rate, and other vital reflexes. Brain death may be judged to have occurred even where the heart beat can be maintained with a mechanical ventilator. In medical law, particular problems arise when a potential organ donor is being kept artificially alive. Legally, two independent medical opinions are required before brain death is agreed and organs can be removed.

breach of close Entry on another's land without permission: a form of *trespass to land. A close is a piece of land separated off from land owned by others or from common land.

breach of confidence 1. The unauthorized disclosure of confidential information. Originally, this referred quite narrowly to information arising from a confidential situation, transaction, or relationship (*Duchess of Argyll v Duke of Argyll* [1967] Ch 302). However, with the enactment of the Human Rights Act 1998, which gives effect to the provision of the *European Convention on Human Rights (art 8) that "Everyone has the right to respect for his private and family life, his home and his correspondence", the courts have extended the tort of breach of confidence to protect certain aspects of personal *privacy (*Campbell v Mirror Group Newspapers Ltd* [2004] UKHL 22, [2004] AC 457). A pre-existing confidential relationship is no longer required: a duty of confidence is imposed whenever a person receives information he knows or ought to know is fairly and reasonably to be regarded as confidential. The claimant's article 8 right to privacy must be balanced against the article 10 right to freedom of expression (*McKennitt v Ash* [2006] EWCA Civ 1714). The obligation of confidence has been extended to protect an exclusivity agreement between a celebrity and a magazine (*Douglas v Hello! Ltd* [2007]

UKHL 21, [2008] 1 AC 1). **2.** Failure to observe an injunction granted by the court to prevent this. The injunction is most commonly granted to protect commercial information or *trade secrets but may also be granted, for example, to protect the secrecy of communications made between husband and wife during marriage or, possibly, between cohabitants during their period of cohabitation. The laws protecting confidential information exist at common law and will only restrain the dissemination of truly confidential information. Information that has been disclosed anywhere in the world, unless it was disclosed under conditions (usually a contract) of confidence, cannot subsequently be prevented from disclosure by the courts, as such a prohibition would be pointless.

breach of contract An actual failure by a party to a contract to perform his obligations under that contract or an indication of his intention not to do so. An indication that a contract will be breached in the future is called **repudiation** or an **anticipatory breach**, and may be either expressed in words or implied from conduct. Such an implication arises when the only reasonable inference from a person's acts is that he does not intend to fulfil his part of the bargain. For example, an anticipatory breach occurs if a person contracts to sell his car to A, but sells and delivers it to B before the delivery date agreed with A. The repudiation of a contract entitles the injured party to treat the contract as discharged and to sue immediately for *damages for the loss sustained. The same procedure applies to an actual breach if it amounts to breach of a *condition (sometimes referred to as **fundamental breach**) or breach of an *innominate term when the consequences of breach are sufficiently serious. In either an anticipatory or actual breach, the injured party may, however, decide to *affirm the contract instead. When an actual breach amounts to breach of a *warranty, or breach of an innominate term and the consequences of breach are not sufficiently serious to allow for discharge, the injured party is entitled to sue for damages only. However, most commercial agreements provide a right to terminate the agreement even when the breach is minor, thus overriding the common law principle described here. The process of treating a contract as discharged by reason of repudiation or actual breach is sometimes referred to as *rescission or repudiation, but this latter term is clearly confusing. Other remedies available under certain circumstances for breach of contract are an *injunction and *specific performance. *See also* INDUCING BREACH OF CONTRACT.

breach of privilege *See* PARLIAMENTARY PRIVILEGE.

breach of statutory duty Breach of a duty imposed on some person or body by a statute. The person or body in breach of the statutory duty is liable to any criminal penalty imposed by the statute, but may also be liable to pay damages to the person injured by the breach if he belongs to the class for whose protection the statute was passed. Not all statutory duties give rise to civil actions for breach. If the statute does not deal with the matter expressly, the courts must decide whether or not Parliament intended to confer civil remedies. Many actions for breach of statutory duty arise out of statutes dealing with *safety at work (*Ziemniak v ETPM Deep Sea Ltd* [2003] EWCA Civ 636), [2003] 2 All ER (Comm) 283).

breach of the peace The state that occurs when harm is done or likely to be done to a person or (in his presence) to his property, or when a person is in fear of being harmed through an *assault, *affray, or other disturbance. At common law, anyone may lawfully arrest a person for a breach of the peace committed in his presence, or when he reasonably believes that a person is about to commit or renew such a breach. To breach the peace is a crime in Scotland; elsewhere, magistrates may *bind over a person to keep the peace. *See also* ARREST; OFFENCES AGAINST PUBLIC ORDER.

breach of trust Any improper act or omission by a trustee or other person in a fiduciary position contrary to the duties imposed upon him by the terms of the trust, by statute, or at common law. A breach need not be deliberate or dishonest. In all cases the trustee is personally responsible to the beneficiaries and is liable for any loss caused to the trust.

break clause A clause often contained in a *fixed-term lease that provides for an option to terminate the tenancy before the end of the term at a particular time or when a particular event occurs.

breakdown of marriage See MARITAL BREAKDOWN.

breathalyser *n.* A device, approved by the Secretary of State, that is used in the preliminary *breath test to measure the amount of alcohol in a driver's breath. A breathalyser should not be used within 20 minutes after consuming alcohol or on a suspect who has just been smoking.

breath specimen See SPECIMEN OF BREATH.

breath test A preliminary test applied by a uniformed police officer by means of a *breathalyser to a driver whom he suspects has alcohol in his body in excess of the legal limit, has committed a traffic offence while the car was moving, or has driven a motor vehicle involved in an accident. The test may be administered on the spot to someone either actually driving, attempting to drive, or in charge of a motor vehicle on a road or public place or suspected by the police officer of having done so in the above circumstances. If the test proves positive (*see* DRUNKEN DRIVING), the police officer may arrest the suspect without a warrant and take him to a police station, where further investigations may take place (*see* SPECIMEN OF BREATH). It is an offence to refuse to submit to a breath test unless there is some reasonable excuse (usually a medical reason), and a police officer may arrest without warrant anyone who refuses the test. The offence is punishable by a fine, endorsement (carrying 4 points under the *totting-up system), and discretionary disqualification. A police officer has the power to enter any place in order to apply the breath test to someone he suspects of having been involved in an accident in which someone else was injured or to arrest someone who refused the test or whose test was positive.

brewster sessions The annual meetings of licensing justices to deal with the grant, renewal, and transfer of licences to sell intoxicating liquor. See LICENSING OF PREMISES.

bribery *n.* Under the Bribery Act 2010, an individual who gives, offers, or promises "financial or other advantage" to induce another individual to act "improperly" in the performance of a "relevant function or activity" commits the offence of bribery (s 1). A "relevant function or activity" is defined as "any function of a public nature; any activity connected with a business, trade or profession; any activity performed in the course of a person's employment; or any activity performed by or on behalf of a body of persons whether corporate or unincorporated" (s 3). Such a function is performed "improperly" when the performance breaches: (i) a reasonable expectation of good faith or impartiality; or (ii) a reasonable expectation of how a person in a position of trust should behave (s 4–5). The Act likewise makes it an offence to accept or solicit bribes (s 2) and creates the specific offence of bribing foreign public officials (s 6). The maximum penalty for these offences is 10 years' imprisonment together with an unlimited fine.

Under the Act a commercial organization commits an offence where it fails to prevent bribery on its behalf by any "associated person" (s 7–9). The offence is one of *vicarious liability; even where there is no deliberate wrongdoing or direct knowledge on the part of the organization, it will be guilty of this offence where such bribery occurs and it can not show that it has "adequate procedures" to prevent its occurrence.

Before the passage of the 2010 Act, the term "bribery" referred specifically to the common-law offence of making improper payments to judges, magistrates, or other judicial officers. Offences relating more generally to the improper influencing of public servants and other persons in a position of trust were referred to as **corruption** and given statutory definition by the Public Bodies Corrupt Practices Act 1889, the Prevention of Corruption Act 1906, and the Prevention of Corruption Act 1906. These Acts were all repealed by the 2010 Act.

bridleway Under the Highways Act 1980, a *highway over which the public has a right of way on foot and a right of way on horseback or leading a horse, with or without a right to drive animals along the highway. *Compare* CARRIAGEWAY; DRIFTWAY; FOOTPATH.

brief *n.* **1.** A document or bundle of documents by which a solicitor instructs a barrister to appear as an advocate in court. A brief usually comprises a **backsheet**, typed on large brief-size paper giving the title of the case and including the solicitor's instructions, which is wrapped around the other papers relevant to the case. The whole bundle is tied up with red tape in the case of a private client, white tape if the brief is from the Crown, and green tape if from one of the land authorities. **2.** A colloquial name for a barrister, as in "my brief is Mr Jones".

brief fee The fee payable to a barrister for taking on a *brief; the payment covers all preparatory work, such as reading of documents and research into the law, as well as the first day in court. For any additional days in court, a *refresher is usually payable.

bright line A clearly defined rule of law that means that a legal issue can be easily and objectively determined. Where there is no bright line, the law might be ambiguous and each case might turn on its own individual facts.

British citizenship One of three forms of citizenship introduced by the British Nationality Act 1981, which replaced citizenship of the UK and Colonies. The others were British Dependent Territories citizenship (now *British Overseas Territories citizenship) and *British Overseas citizenship.

On the date on which it came into force (1 January 1983), the Act conferred British citizenship automatically on every existing citizen of the UK and Colonies who was entitled to the *right of abode in the UK under the Immigration Act 1971. As from that date, there have been four principal ways of acquiring the citizenship – by birth, by descent, by registration, and by naturalization. A person acquires it by birth if he is born in the UK and his father or mother is either a British citizen or settled in the UK (i.e. resident there, and not restricted by the immigration laws as to length of stay). If born outside the UK, he acquires it by descent if one of his parents has British citizenship (but not, normally, if that citizenship was itself acquired by descent). The British Nationality (Falkland Islands) Act 1983 made special provision to confer British citizenship on those people with connections with the Falkland Islands. The British Nationality (Hong Kong) Act 1997 gave additional rights to certain people from Hong Kong to acquire British citizenship. Finally, the British Overseas Territories Act 2002 extended full British citizenship to nearly all British Overseas Territories citizens, most of whom now hold both forms of citizenship. Registration may be applied for by a minor, but adults are eligible only if they have particular links with the UK. In some cases (e.g. British Overseas Territories citizens, British Overseas citizens, British protected persons, and British subjects with certain residential qualifications), it is a right; in others, it is at the discretion of the Secretary of State. Any adult may apply for naturalization but there are residential and other requirements (e.g. proof of good character), and its grant is always discretionary. The Nationality, Immigration and Asylum Act 2002 imposes a condition that applicants should demonstrate a knowledge of British life and culture. Under the Borders, Citizenship and Immigration Act 2009 the naturalization process can be shortened if the applicant undertakes voluntary community work.

A registered or naturalized citizen may be deprived of his citizenship if he obtained it improperly, behaves disloyally, or is sentenced during the first five years to imprisonment exceeding one year. The Immigration, Asylum and Nationality Act 2006 also contains several provisions empowering the Home Secretary to deprive a person of British citizenship (or right of abode) if it is considered that such deprivation is "conducive to the public good" (s 56). For example, the Australian *Guantanamo Bay inmate David Matthew Hicks applied for British citizenship based on his maternal heritage (as allowed by the 2002 Act). Hicks was granted citizenship on 5 July 2006, but stripped of it several hours later under section 56 of the 2006 Act.

British Commonwealth *See* COMMONWEALTH.

British National (Overseas) A form of British nationality that those who were British Dependent Territories citizens by virtue of a connection with Hong Kong may acquire by registration. They ceased to be British Dependent Territories citizens on 1 July 1997.

British Overseas citizenship One of three forms of citizenship introduced by the British Nationality Act 1981 to replace citizenship of the UK and Colonies. On the date on which it came into force (1 January 1983), the Act conferred the citizenship automatically on every existing citizen of the UK and Colonies who did not qualify for either of the other new forms (*British citizenship and British Dependent Territories citizenship, now *British Overseas Territories citizenship). Acquisition as from that date has been by registration only, and this is confined almost completely to minors. The right to register as a British Overseas citizen was further limited by the Nationality, Immigration and Asylum Act 2002. A British Overseas citizen may become entitled to registration as a British citizen by virtue of UK residence.

British Overseas Territories citizenship One of three forms of citizenship introduced (as **British Dependent Territories Citizenship**) by the British Nationality Act 1981 to replace citizenship of the UK and Colonies. The others are *British citizenship and *British Overseas citizenship. The relevant territories for the purposes of this form of citizenship are listed in a schedule to the Act; they include Bermuda and Gibraltar, among others.

On the date on which it came into force (1 January 1983), the Act conferred the citizenship automatically on a large number of existing citizens of the UK and Colonies on the grounds of birth, registration, or naturalization in a dependent territory or descent from a parent or grandparent who had that citizenship on one of those grounds. As from that date, acquisition (and deprivation in the case of registered or naturalized citizens) have been governed by principles similar to those applying to British citizenship, except that acquisition by registration relates almost exclusively to minors. The right to register as a British Overseas Territories Citizen was further limited by the Nationality, Immigration and Asylum Act 2002. A British Overseas Territories citizen can become entitled to registration as a British citizen by virtue of UK residence. On 1 July 1997, those who were British Dependent Territories citizens by virtue of a connection with Hong Kong ceased to be British Dependent Territories citizens. However, they were entitled to acquire a new form of British nationality, known as *British National (Overseas), by registration. The British Overseas Territories Act 2002 extended full British citizenship (including the *right of abode) to nearly all British Overseas Citizens, most of whom now hold both types of citizenship.

British protected person One of a class of people defined as such by an order under the British Nationality Act 1981 or the Solomon Islands Act 1978 because of their connection with former protectorates, protected states, and trust territories. A British protected person may become entitled to registration as a British citizen by reason of UK residence.

British subject Under the British Nationality Act 1948, a secondary status that was common to all who were primarily citizens either of the UK and Colonies or of one of the independent Commonwealth countries. This status was also shared by a limited number of people who did not have any such primary citizenship, including former British subjects who were also citizens of Eire (as it then was) or who could have acquired one of the primary citizenships but did not in fact do so.

Under the British Nationality Act 1981 (which replaced the 1948 Act as from 1 January 1983), the status of British subject was confined to those who had enjoyed it under the former Act without having one of the primary citizenships; the expression *Commonwealth citizen was redefined as a secondary status of more universal application. The Act provided for minors to be able to apply for registration as British subjects and for British subjects to become entitled to registration as British citizens by virtue of UK residence.

Broadmoor A hospital providing high-security psychiatric services at Crowthorne, near Camberley, in Berkshire. It treats dangerous and violent patients (previously known as criminal lunatics) who are sent to it. *See* SPECIAL HOSPITAL.

brothel *n.* A place used for the purpose of female or male *prostitution. A contract for the hiring or letting of a brothel is void (as being contrary to public policy) and under the Sexual Offences Act 1956 (s 33–36) it is an offence for a landlord to let premises knowing that they are to be used as a brothel (*Kelly v Purvis* [1983] AC 663 (QB)). It is also an offence for someone to help or manage a brothel or for a tenant or occupier of any premises to permit the premises to be used as a brothel.

Brussels Convention An international convention of 1968 that determines which courts will have jurisdiction in relation to international disputes (*see* FOREIGN JUDGMENTS). Generally, if a contract provides that a certain country's courts will hear any disputes that arise, this will be respected. The Convention also provides rules when the parties have not chosen a forum for their disputes. Many EU states are individually a party to the Convention; the UK signed up to it in 1978 and enacted it into national law in 1982.

brutum fulmen [Latin: senseless thunderbolt] An empty threat; any judgment or decree that is unenforceable or void.

Bryan Treaties (Bryan Arbitration Treaties) The series of treaties, signed at Washington in 1914, that established permanent commissions of inquiry. They are named after William Jennings Bryan, the US Secretary of State at the time. Such inquiries were designed to resolve differences between the United States of America and a large number of foreign states. The treaties were not all identical, but had the following key feature in common: the *high contracting parties agreed (1) to refer all disputes that diplomatic methods had failed to resolve to a Permanent International Commission for investigation and report, and (2) not to begin hostilities before the report was submitted. *See also* INQUIRY.

Budget *n. See* Chancellor of the Exchequer.

buggery (sodomy) *n.* Anal intercourse by a man with another man or a woman, or bestiality by a man or a woman. The offence of buggery no longer exists. However, anal intercourse without consent may constitute *rape under section 1 of the Sexual Offences Act 2003 and sexual intercourse with animals may be prosecuted under section 69.

bugging *n. See* electronic surveillance.

building lease A lease under which the tenant covenants to erect specified buildings on the land. Sometimes the lease only begins when the buildings have been erected. At the end of the lease the buildings generally become the property of the landlord. It used to be common for residential property to be built under a building lease, usually for 99 years, under which the landlord would let to a builder at a rent that ignored the value of the buildings (*ground rent), and the builder would sell the lease to a tenant. Under a lease of this kind, the tenant may acquire a statutory right to purchase the freehold under the Leasehold Reform Act 1967.

building preservation notice A notice by a local planning authority (*see* town and country planning) that places a building regarded as suitable for listing and in danger of demolition or alteration under temporary control as a *listed building, pending a decision on its listing by the Secretary of State.

building scheme A defined area of land sold by a single vendor in plots for (or following) development, each plot being sold subject to similar *restrictive covenants that are clearly intended to benefit the whole. For example, restrictive covenants prohibiting trade or excessive noise are frequently imposed on the sale of plots on a housing estate, to maintain the character of the estate as a whole. The law allows the owner of any plot in a building scheme to enforce such covenants against any other plot owner, even though neither was a party to the document that imposed the covenants.

building society A corporation established under the Building Societies Act 1986 for the purpose of making loans to its members on the security of mortgages on their homes, out of funds invested by its members. Generally a building society's security must be a first legal mortgage on the borrower's home. However, the Building Societies Act 1986 now empowers societies to lend on the security of second mortgages and to provide a wide range of banking and other financial services.

Bullock order A form of order for the payment of costs in civil cases sometimes made when the claimant has, in the court's opinion, reasonably sued two defendants but has succeeded against only one of them. The order requires the claimant to pay the successful defendant's costs but allows him to include these costs in those payable to him by the unsuccessful defendant. The order takes its name from the case *Bullock v London General Omnibus Co* [1907] 1 KB 264. It should be distinguished from a **Sanderson order** (from the case *Sanderson v Blyth Theatre Co* [1903] 2 KB 533), in which the unsuccessful defendant is ordered to pay the costs of the successful defendant directly.

burden of proof The duty of a party to litigation to prove a fact or facts in issue. Generally the burden of proof falls upon the party who substantially asserts the truth of a particular fact (the prosecution or the claimant). A distinction is drawn between the **persuasive** (or **legal**) **burden**, which is carried by the party who as a matter of law will lose the case if he fails to prove the fact in issue; and the **evidential burden** (**burden of adducing evidence** or **burden of going forward**), which is the duty of showing that there is sufficient evidence to raise an issue fit for the consideration of the *trier of fact as to the existence or nonexistence of a fact in issue.

The normal rule is that a defendant in a criminal case is presumed to be innocent until he is proved guilty; it is therefore the duty of the prosecution to prove its case by establishing both the *actus reus* of the crime and the *mens rea*. It must first satisfy the evidential burden to show that its allegations have something to support them. If it cannot satisfy this burden, the defence may submit or the judge may direct that there is *no case to answer, and the judge must direct the jury to acquit. The prosecution may sometimes rely on presumptions of fact to satisfy the evidential burden of proof (e.g. the fact that a woman was subjected to violence during sexual intercourse will normally raise a presumption to support a charge of rape and prove that she did not consent). If, however, the prosecution has established a basis for its case, it must then continue to satisfy the persuasive burden by proving its case beyond reasonable doubt (*see also* PROOF BEYOND REASONABLE DOUBT). It is the duty of the judge to tell the jury clearly that the prosecution must prove its case and that it must prove it beyond reasonable doubt; if he does not give this clear direction, the defendant is entitled to be acquitted.

There are some exceptions to the normal rule that the burden of proof is upon the prosecution. The main exceptions are as follows:

(1) When the defendant admits the elements of the crime (the *actus reus* and *mens rea*) but pleads a special defence, the evidential burden is upon him to create at least a reasonable doubt in his favour. This may occur, for example, in a prosecution for murder in which the defendant raises a defence of self-defence.

(2) When the defendant pleads *coercion, *diminished responsibility, or *insanity, both the evidential and persuasive burden rest upon him. In this case, however, it is sufficient if he proves his case on a balance of probabilities (i.e. he must persuade the jury that it is more likely than not that he was insane than not).

(3) In some cases statute expressly places a persuasive burden on the defendant; for example, a person who carries an *offensive weapon in public is guilty of an offence unless he proves that he had lawful authority or a reasonable excuse.

burglary *n.* The offence, under the Theft Act 1968, of either: (A) entering a building, part of a building, ship, or inhabited vehicle (e.g. a caravan) as a trespasser (*R v Collins* [1973] QB 100) with the intention of committing one of three specified crimes in it (**burglary with intent** – Theft Act 1968 s 9 (1) (a); or (B) entering it as a trespasser only but subsequently committing one of two specified crimes in it (**burglary without intent** – Theft Act 1968 s 9 (1) (b). The three specified crimes for burglary with intent are (1) *theft; (2) inflicting *grievous bodily harm; and (3) causing *criminal damage. In 2003 the offence of burglary with intent to rape was replaced by that of trespass with intent to commit a sexual offence (Sexual Offences Act s 63). The two specified offences for burglary without intent are (1) stealing or attempting to steal; and (2) inflicting or attempting to inflict grievous bodily harm. Burglary is punishable by up to 14 years' imprisonment. **Aggravated burglary** (Theft Act 1968 s 10), in which the trespasser is carrying a weapon of offence, explosive, or firearm (*R v Kelly* (1992) 97 Cr App R 245), may be punished by a maximum sentence of life imprisonment. The Crime (Sentences) Act 1997 provides for an automatic three-year minimum sentence for third-time burglars, although judges may give a lesser sentence if the court considers the minimum would be unjust in all the circumstances. *See also* REPEAT OFFENDER.

business *n.* For *value-added tax purposes, an activity is a business (and, hence, potentially liable to VAT) if it amounts to an "economic activity" within the meaning of the EU Sixth Directive, as interpreted by the European Court of Justice (*Welcome Trust Ltd v Customs and Excise Commissioners* [1994] VAT Decision 12206). Elsewhere in the

Taxes Acts, the meaning of the term "business" seems to derive from the context. A "property business" is the aggregate of all lettings carried on by one taxpayer, income tax on property income being levied on the profits of the taxpayer's single "property business". The courts have generally considered that every *company carries on a business, that being the essential nature of a company. Sometimes, the business is merely holding shares in other companies (*see* INVESTMENT COMPANY). When computing profits on which an income tax charge is imposed, deductions are made for expenditure with a business purpose. No deductions are made for expenditure with a domestic purpose, nor (generally) where there is *duality of purpose.

business asset   When calculating that part of a capital gain that is chargeable to *capital gains tax, *entrepreneurs' relief is available where the gain arises on the disposal of business assets. (Prior to its abolition in 2008, taper relief was similarly available on the disposal of business assets.) For entrepreneurs' relief, the following are treated as business assets:

- shares and securities in a trading company (listed or unlisted), where 5% or more of the shares have been held;
- an asset used for the purposes of trade carried on by an unlisted trading company;
- an asset held for the purposes of trade carried on by the taxpayer, either alone or in partnership.

Assets held by trustees are treated as business assets if they fulfil the requirements outlined above for individuals.

business liability   Liability (contractual or tortious) for a breach of obligations or duties arising in the course of a business (which can include the activities of a government department or local or public authority) or from the occupation of business premises. The Unfair Contract Terms Act 1977 and, for consumer contracts, the Unfair Terms in Consumer Contracts Regulations 1999 limit the extent to which a person may rely on terms in his contracts that attempt to exclude or restrict his business liability (*see* EXCLUSION AND RESTRICTION OF NEGLIGENCE LIABILITY).

business name   The name under which a sole trader, partnership, limited liability partnership, or company carries on business. The choice of a business name is restricted by sections 1192–99 of the Companies Act 2006, so that (for example) a misleading name may not be used. In the case of an individual or ordinary partnership, the names and addresses of the individuals concerned must be disclosed in documents issuing from the business (for example, receipts) and upon business premises, in accordance with the Companies Act 2006 sections 1200–06. The disclosure requirements for a company and a limited liability partnership are provided for by sections 82–85 of the Companies Act and the Companies (Trading Disclosures) Regulations 2008. Contravention of the Act may lead to a fine and an inability to enforce contracts. The use of a business name is also restricted by the tort of *passing off. *See also* COMPANY NAME.

business property relief   A relief (often at 100%) is given against the value of qualifying property for the purpose of computing any *inheritance tax charge. The relief is applied to six categories of property:

- an interest in a business;
- unquoted shares in a (broadly) trading company;
- a controlling interest of quoted shares in a (broadly) trading company;
- unquoted securities of a company controlled by the person making the *transfer of value;

- land, building, machinery or plant used for the trade of a company controlled by the transferor or by a partnership in which he was a partner;
- settled property consisting of land or buildings used for the purposes of a trade carried on by the transferor.

business tenancy A *tenancy of premises that are occupied for the purposes of a trade, profession, or employment. Business tenants have special statutory protection (Landlord and Tenant Act 1954 Part II). If the landlord serves a notice to quit, the tenant can usually apply to the courts for a new tenancy. If the landlord wishes to oppose the grant of a new tenancy he must show that he has statutory grounds, which may include breaches of the tenant's obligations under the tenancy agreement or the provision of suitable alternative accommodation by the landlord. Otherwise the court will grant a new tenancy on whatever terms the parties agree or, if they cannot agree, on whatever terms the court considers reasonable.

Under the Landlord and Tenant (Covenants) Act 1995 when business tenancies are assigned the new tenant generally takes over the covenants (or promises and warranties) of the first tenant in the lease except when otherwise agreed. Previously the old tenant was always liable, even after *assignment, if a subsequent tenant defaulted on the lease. If the lease expressly provides for it, the former tenant may, however, be required to guarantee his assignee's obligation by way of *authorized guarantee agreement.

"but for" test See CAUSATION.

buyer *n.* The party to a contract for the sale of goods who agrees to acquire ownership of the goods and to pay the price. See also PURCHASER.

byelaw *n.* A form of *delegated legislation, made principally by local authorities. District and London borough councils have general powers to make byelaws for the good rule and government of their areas, and all local authorities have powers to make them on a wide range of specific matters (e.g. public health). Certain public corporations also make byelaws for the regulation of their undertakings. A statutory power to make byelaws includes a power to rescind, revoke, amend, or vary them. By contrast with most other forms of delegated legislation, byelaws are not subject to any form of parliamentary control but take effect if confirmed by a government minister. It is common for central government to prepare draft byelaws that may be made by such authorities as choose to do so. Byelaws are, however, subject to judicial control by means of the doctrine of *ultra vires.*

Cabinet *n.* A body of *ministers (normally about 20) consisting mostly of heads of chief government departments but also including some ministers with few or no departmental responsibilities; it is headed by the *Prime Minister, in whose gift membership lies. As the principal executive body under the UK constitution, its function is to formulate government policy and to carry it into effect (particularly by the initiation of legislation). The Cabinet has no statutory foundation and exists entirely by convention, although it has been mentioned in statute from time to time, e.g. in the Ministers of the Crown Act 1937, which provided additional salaries to "Cabinet Ministers". The Cabinet is bound by the convention of **collective responsibility**, i.e. all members should fully support Cabinet decisions; a member who disagrees with a decision must resign. If the government loses a vote of confidence, or suffers any other major defeat in the House of Commons, the whole Cabinet must resign.

cabotage *n.* Transport services provided in one member state of the EU by a carrier of another state. Article 91 (formerly 71 and before that 75) of the Treaty on the Functioning of the European Union (previously Treaty of Rome) provides that the Council of the European Union may lay down proposals in relation to the conditions under which nonresident carriers may operate transport services within a member state.

CAC *See* CENTRAL ARBITRATION COMMITTEE.

Cafcass *See* CHILDREN AND FAMILY COURT ADVISORY AND SUPPORT SERVICE.

Calderbank letter (Calderbank offer) Formerly, a letter sent by one party to a civil action, in which a remedy other than debt or damages is claimed, to another offering to compromise the action on terms specified in the letter. The first such letter was sent in the case *Calderbank v Calderbank* [1976] Fam 93 (CA). Calderbank offers are now (since the introduction of the *Civil Procedure Rules in 1999) generally known as *Part 36 offers. However, the term remains in use in family proceedings. Calderbank letters may be referred to only when the question of costs rises.

call *n.* **1.** A ceremony at which students of the Inns of Court become barristers. The name of the student is read out and he is "called to the Bar" by the Treasurer of his Inn. Call ceremonies take place four times a year, once in each dining term. **2.** A demand by a company under the terms of the articles of association or an ordinary resolution requiring company members to pay up fully or in part the nominal value of their shares. Unless the articles provide otherwise, calls must be made equally upon all shareholders of the same class. Calls should be distinguished from **instalments**, which become due upon a date predetermined at the time the shares were issued. *See also* PAID-UP CAPITAL.

calling the jury Announcing the names of those selected to serve on a jury as a result of a ballot of the jury panel.

Calvo clause A clause in a contract stating that the parties to the contract agree to rely exclusively on domestic remedies in the event of a dispute. The insertion of such a clause in a contract was an attempt, originally by Latin American countries, to eliminate diplomatic intervention should a dispute arise with a foreign national: by making such a contract the foreign national was said to have renounced the protection of his government. The clause, which is named after the Argentine jurist Carlos Calvo (1824–1906), is in effect in most cases superfluous – firstly, because diplomatic intervention belongs to the state only, and thus cannot be renounced by an individual; and secondly, because the exhaustion of local remedies is always taken to be a *condition precedent to appealing for diplomatic intervention. Since the 1930s such clauses have not been used in international disputes.

cancellation *n.* **1.** (in equity) An order by the court that specified documents should no longer have effect. This may occur when a document has fulfilled its purpose but its continued existence could lead to improper claims against its maker. **2.** (in commercial law) The right to cancel a commercial contract after it has been entered into. The right to cancel exists generally for contracts concluded at a distance (*see* DISTANCE SELLING), such as mail order and Internet sales when the contract is with a *consumer, and in particular in such sectors as time-share sales and consumer credit.

cannabis *n.* A drug obtained from the crushed leaves and flowers of the hemp plant (*Cannabis sativa*). Cannabis is defined as a *controlled drug of Class B.

cannon-shot rule The rule by which a state has territorial sovereignty of that coastal sea within three miles of land. Its name derives from the fact that in the 17th century this limit roughly corresponded to the outer range of coastal artillery weapons and therefore reflected the principle *terrae dominum finitur, ubi finitur armorium vis* (the dominion of the land ends where the range of weapons ends). The rule is now not widely recognized: many nations have established a 6- or 12-mile coastal limit. *See also* TERRITORIAL WATERS.

canonical disability *See* IMPOTENCE.

canon law (ecclesiastical law) Church law, such as the Roman Catholic Code of Canon Law and, in England, the law of the Church of England. Unless subsequently becoming *legislation or *custom, it is not part of the laws of England but is binding on the clergy and lay people holding ecclesiastical office, e.g. churchwardens. *See* ECCLESIASTICAL COURTS.

CAP *See* COMMON AGRICULTURAL POLICY.

capacity of a child in criminal law *See* DOLI CAPAX.

capacity to consent to medical treatment *See* COMPETENT PATIENT; INCOMPETENT PATIENT.

capacity to contract Competence to enter into a legally binding agreement. The main categories of persons lacking this capacity in full are minors, the mentally disordered, the drunk, and corporations other than those created by royal charter.

A minor is capable of making valid contracts for *necessaries and is also bound by any beneficial contract of service into which he enters (i.e. any contract of employment or training that is advantageous to him taken as a whole). Certain contracts of a proprietary nature (e.g. tenancy agreements, agreements to buy company shares, and partnership agreements) are voidable in that a minor may repudiate them either before he comes of age or within a reasonable time thereafter. If he fails to repudiate, he becomes fully bound. All other contracts made by a minor are unenforceable unless ratified by the minor when he comes of age (*see* RATIFICATION) unless the Minors Contracts Act 1987 applies. This Act gives the court the right to require the transfer of property acquired by a minor under a contract when it is just and equitable to do so and improves the rights of adults contracting with minors.

A contract made by a person who is mentally disordered or drunk is voidable if the other party knows that his disorder or drunkenness will prevent him from understanding what he is doing. This means that, subject to certain limitations, he can set the contract aside by *rescission.

A corporation incorporated by royal charter has full contractual capacity, but a statutory corporation has power to contract only for purposes connected with the objects for which it was incorporated. Other contracts are *ultra vires* and void.

capias *n.* [Latin: that you take] One of a group of writs of assistance conferring certain supplemental powers upon the sheriff in respect of the enforcement of judgment. Such writs are now obsolete.

capital 1. (share capital) A fund representing the contributions given to the company by shareholders in return for their *shares. These assets are intended to protect the interests of any creditors in the event of a *limited company encountering financial difficulties, and there are rules under the Companies Act 2006 to ensure that this fund is not reduced unless it is absolutely necessary. Each share is assigned a **nominal** or **par value** to enable each holder to measure his interest in and liability to the company. In a company limited by shares the liability of a shareholder is limited to the unpaid purchase price of the share. If a company is able to command a market price for a share that is above the nominal value assigned to it, the difference is said to represent a **premium**. The total number of shares and their nominal values must be stated in the capital clause of the *memorandum of association. *See* AUTHORIZED CAPITAL. **2.** *See* LOAN CAPITAL.

capital allowance A tax allowance for businesses on capital expenditure on particular items. These include *machinery and plant, industrial buildings, agricultural buildings, mines and oil wells, energy-saving equipment, and scientific equipment. For other types of capital expenditure neither the capital cost nor the depreciation is allowable against tax. From 1 April 2012, the first £25,000 of expenditure attracts 100% *Annual Investment Allowance. Expenditure in excess of this sum attracts a capital allowance (usually at 20% per year).

In order to claim a capital allowance, the asset for which the allowance is claimed must belong to the person in consequence of a payment (Capital Allowances Act 2002 s 167–70). The courts have interpreted the word "belong" by reference to concepts of property law. In *Stokes v Costain Property Investment Ltd* [1984] STC 204 (CA) the Court of Appeal held that the tenant was not able to claim capital allowances for a lift installed by the tenant as, under general landlord principles, the act of installing the lift made the lift the property of the landlord. A similar decision on fixtures was given in *Melluish v BMI(3) Ltd* [1994] STC 802 (CA).

capital gains tax (CGT) A tax on *chargeable gains arising from chargeable *disposals of chargeable *assets. Events treated as disposals include not only the sale or exchange of an asset but also the complete loss or destruction of an asset (Taxation of Chargeable Gains Act 1992 s 24(1), the vesting of trust property (s 71), or the receipt of a capital sum in relation to an asset (s 22). A *gift may be a chargeable disposal.

CGT was introduced in 1965 and applies only to gains accruing since 5 April 1965. For disposals on or after 6 April 1988, CGT effectively imposes only on gains accruing since

31 March 1982. To remove from the charge to tax increases in value that arise purely as a result of inflation, a measure of relief (*indexation allowance) is applied to gains made by a company. Since 1998 individuals have not been given relief for the effect of inflation; however, the rate of tax applied to a capital gain made by an individual is lower than the rate of tax on income. Gains made by an individual may attract *entrepreneurs' relief. *See also* HOLDOVER RELIEF; ROLLOVER RELIEF.

(⊕) SEE WEB LINKS
• CGT area of the HM Revenue and Customs website

capitalization issue *See* BONUS ISSUE.

capital money Money arising from the sale, mortgage, etc. of land held on a {trust of land} or from *settled land. It is important that capital money is paid to two or more trustees of land: if it is paid to a sole trustee, equitable interests in the land may not be overreached, and the purchaser may be bound by them (*Williams & Glyn's Bank Ltd v Boland* [1981] AC 487). Capital money arising from settled land must be paid to the trustees of the settlement, not the *tenant for life.

capital punishment Death imposed as a punishment for crime. Capital punishment for murder was abolished in the UK under the Murder (Abolition of Death Penalty) Act 1965. The death penalty continued to exist for a small number of offences, such as *piracy and *treason. The ratification by the UK of the Sixth and Thirteenth Protocols of the *European Convention on Human Rights and the introduction of the *Human Rights Act 1998 has meant that the death penalty is now completely abolished, even in respect of acts in times of war. Its reintroduction would be a violation of the Human Rights Act and, at an international level, a breach of a treaty obligation.

capital redemption reserve A fund established to protect creditors by ensuring that the assets representing a company's *capital are not reduced. In limited circumstances a company is permitted to buy back its own shares. If this is provided for by a term in the original share contract the company **redeems** its own shares. If no such term exists the company makes a **purchase of its own shares**. In either case the value of the capital sum will be reduced by the amount of the purchase or redemption unless an equal amount is transferred to a reserve that is subject to the same restrictions as the capital.

capitulation *n.* **1.** An agreement under which a body of troops or a naval force surrenders upon conditions. The arrangement is a bargain made in the common interest of the contracting parties, one of which avoids the useless loss that is incurred in a hopeless struggle, while the other, besides also avoiding loss, is spared all further sacrifice of time and trouble. A capitulation must be distinguished from an **unconditional surrender**, which need not be effected on the basis of an instrument signed by both parties and is not an agreement. **2.** A system of extraterritorial jurisdiction, based partly upon custom and partly upon treaties of unilateral obligation, in which cases relating to foreign citizens were tried before diplomatic or consular courts operating in accordance with the laws of the states concerned. The practice is now obsolete, being a clear breach of the right of sovereign equality between states.

caravan *n.* Any structure adapted for human habitation and capable of being moved from one place to another, either by being towed or being transported on a motor vehicle or trailer. *See also* UNAUTHORIZED CAMPING.

care and control Formerly, the right to the physical possession and control of the day-to-day activities of a minor. *See* PARENTAL RESPONSIBILITY; SECTION 8 ORDERS.

care contact order An order of the court allowing a local authority to restrict *contact with a child in care (*see* CARE ORDER). Under the Children Act 1989 s 34(1) there is a presumption that children in care will have reasonable contact with their parents (including unmarried parents) or those who have had care of them. In an emergency a local authority may refuse to allow contact for not more than seven days where it is satisfied that it is necessary to do so in order to safeguard or promote the child's welfare.

careless and inconsiderate driving Driving a mechanically propelled vehicle on a road or other public place without due care and attention, or without reasonable consideration for other persons using the road or place (Road Traffic Act 1988 s 3). This is a *summary offence for which the maximum penalty is a *fine at level 4 on the standard scale and it carries 3–9 penalty points under the *totting-up system; *disqualification is discretionary. *See also* CAUSING DEATH BY CARELESS OR INCONSIDERATE DRIVING.

careless statement *See* NEGLIGENT MISSTATEMENT.

care order A court order placing a child under the care of a local authority under the Children Act s 31. An application for a care order is generally made by a local authority, although it can be made by the NSPCC or a person authorized by the Secretary of State. The court has the power to make a care order only when it is satisfied that a child is suffering or likely to suffer significant harm either caused by the care (or lack of care) given to it by its parents, or because the child is beyond parental control (the so-called **threshold criteria**). The phrase "significant harm", as defined in the Children Act, means ill treatment (including sexual abuse and forms of treatment that are not physical) or the impairment of health (either physical or mental) or development (whether physical, intellectual, emotional, social, or behavioural). Once the court is satisfied that the threshold criteria have been satisfied, it must decide whether a care order would be in the best interests of the child. In so doing, it should scrutinize the *care plan drawn up in respect of the child. The court may, instead of making a care order, make a *supervision order or a *section 8 order. Since the coming into force of the Human Rights Act 1998, the court must ensure that the granting of a care order will not be in breach of Article 8 (which guarantees a right to *family life); the court must be satisfied that any intervention by the state between parents and children is proportionate to the legitimate aim of protecting family life. A care order gives the local authority *parental responsibility for the child who is the subject of the order. Although parents retain their parental responsibility, in practice all major decisions relating to the child are made by the local authority. While the child is in care, the local authority cannot change the child's religion or surname or consent to an adoption order or appoint a guardian. There is a presumption that parents will have reasonable contact with their children while in care; if the local authority wishes to prevent this, it must apply for a court order to limit such contact. A parent with parental responsibility, the child itself, or the local authority may apply to discharge a care order. No care order can be made with respect to a child who is over the age of 16. Before the Crime and Disorder Act 1998 came into force a care order could only be made if the threshold criteria were met. Now, however, the family proceedings court has the power to make a care order if a child is in breach of a *child safety order. It is important to distinguish between a child who is the subject of a care order and one who is being provided with *voluntary accommodation by a local authority.

care plan Each local authority is required by the Children Act 1989 s 31A to prepare a care plan in respect of a child it is looking after. The purpose of a care plan is to safeguard and promote the welfare of the child in accordance with the local authority's duties under the Children Act 1989. The plan will address such matters as where the child is to be placed and the likely duration of such a placement, arrangements for contact between the child and its family, and what the needs of the child are and how these might be met. When a court is deciding whether or not to make a *care order or a *supervision order in respect of a child, the care plan is of crucial importance and must be scrutinized carefully. The plan should be kept under review and revised if necessary.

care proceedings *See* CARE ORDER.

Care Quality Commission for England An independent body set up by the Health and Social Care Act 2008. The Commission took over the functions of three previously existing bodies: the *Healthcare Commission; the *Mental Health Act Commission; and the Commission for Social Care Inspection, all of which were abolished by the Act.

((⊕)) SEE WEB LINKS
• Website of the Care Quality Commission for England

carer's allowance A taxable benefit under the Social Security Acts, payable in certain circumstances to a person of working age who is not gainfully employed because he is regularly and substantially engaged in caring for a severely disabled relative. Until 2003 it was known as **invalid care allowance**.

Care Standard Appeals Tribunal A body established by the Protection of Children Act 1999 that hears appeals on a variety of matters in relation to persons and organizations working with children. For example, a person may appeal against the inclusion of his name on the list of those considered to be unsuitable to work with children (the *PoCA list) or against a refusal to register him as a childminder.

cargo *n.* Goods, other than the personal luggage of passengers, carried by a ship or aircraft. Normally (but not necessarily in relation to insurance) "cargo" denotes the whole of a ship's loading. Under a ship's charterparty, the freight payable to the shipowner is normally calculated at a rate per tonne of cargo. Unless otherwise agreed, the duty of the charterer is to provide a full and complete cargo: if he fails to do this, he is liable for damages known as **dead freight**.

carousel fraud *See* MISSING TRADER INTRA-COMMUNITY FRAUD.

carriage of goods by air The act of carrying goods by air, which is normally under a contract between the consignor and a *carrier. International carriage has been the subject of several international conventions: Warsaw (1929), The Hague (1955), Guadalajara (1961), Guatemala (1971), and Montreal (1975). The UK is party to a number of these Conventions, which have been given effect by the Carriage by Air Acts 1932, 1961, and 1962 and the Carriage by Air and Road Act 1979 (in part not yet in force). They deal with such matters as the nature and limit of the carrier's liability, who can sue and be sued, the right to stop in transit, the documentation of air carriage, and time limits for complaint.

Special rules apply if the goods are dangerous. The International Civil Aviation Organization (ICAO)'s Technical Instructions for the Safe Transport of Dangerous Goods by Air and the International Maritime Dangerous Goods (IMDG) Code are the two international agreements regulating the carriage of dangerous goods by air and sea.

carriageway A *highway over which the public have a right of way with vehicles, on foot, or on horse and a right to drive livestock. *Compare* BRIDLEWAY; DRIFTWAY; FOOTPATH.

carrier *n.* One who transports persons or goods from one place to another. Carriage is normally under a contract that may affect or limit the duties otherwise imposed by law, but such contracts may be subject to statutory control. Carriers of goods are bailees of the goods consigned. A **common carrier** is one who publicly undertakes to carry any goods or persons for payment on the routes he covers. A common carrier is subject to three common-law duties: (1) he must, if he has space, accept any goods of the type he carries or any person; (2) he must charge only a reasonable rate; and (3) he is strictly liable for all loss or damage to goods in the course of transit (*but see* INHERENT VICE). All other carriers are **private carriers**, and they owe only a duty of reasonable care.

carrier's lien The right of a common *carrier to retain possession of goods he has carried until he has been paid his freight or charge.

cartel *n.* **1.** A national or international association of independent enterprises formed to create a *monopoly in a given industry. Usually cartels involve an agreement between businesses not to compete with one another that is secret, verbal, and often informal. Typically, cartel members may agree on:

- prices;
- output levels;
- discounts;
- credit terms;
- which customers they will supply;
- which areas they will supply;
- who should win a contract (bid rigging).

Each of the above types of agreement is prohibited by the Competition Act 1998 in the UK and *Article 101 of the *Treaty on the Functioning of the European Union. In addition, the Enterprise Act 2002 makes it a criminal offence for individuals dishonestly to take part in certain specified cartels, essentially those that involve price fixing, market sharing, limitation of production or supply, or bid rigging. Cartels can occur in almost any industry and can involve goods or services at the manufacturing, distribution, or retail level. Some sectors are more susceptible to cartels than others because of the structure or the way in which they operate. The UK competition authorities believe these are mostly where:

- there are few competitors;
- the products have similar characteristics, leaving little scope for competition on quality or service;
- communication channels between competitors are already established;
- the industry is suffering from excess capacity or there is general recession.

2. An agreement between belligerent states for certain types of nonhostile transactions, especially the treatment and exchange of prisoners.

case *n.* **1.** A court *action. **2.** A legal dispute. **3.** The arguments, collectively, put forward by either side in a court action. **4.** (action on the case) A form of action abolished by the Judicature Acts 1873–75.

case law The body of law set out in judicial decisions, as distinct from *statute law. *See also* PRECEDENT.

case management Under the * Civil Procedure Rules (CPR), the procedure for managing civil cases introduced from 1999. Under this regime, the judge becomes the case manager. A case is allocated to one of three **tracks**, depending on the value of the dispute and the complexity of the case: the *small claims track, *fast track, or *multi-track.

Each case is actively managed by the judge on a court-controlled timetable with the aims of encouraging and facilitating cooperation between the parties, identifying the areas in dispute, and encouraging settlement. The court can control progress and even "strike out" an action. In considering the benefits of a particular way of hearing it can use a range of procedural devices to enforce discipline against lawyers and parties not complying with CPR *pre-action protocols and/or *Practice Directions, including costs sanctions and refusing an extension of time.

With effect from 1 April 2013 the case management regime includes an explicit element of **costs management** by the court. Each party is required to submit a costs budget at an early stage of the proceedings and parties are encouraged to agree these budgets between themselves wherever possible. The court may at any stage make a **costs management order** and if it does so will thereafter control the parties' budgets in respect of recoverable costs. A **costs capping order** may also be made against all or any of the parties.

case management conference (CMC) Under the *Civil Procedure Rules, a central feature of *case management at which the judge reviews the progress of the case preparation, including the degree of compliance with *Practice Directions and *pre-action protocols. Legal representatives who are to attend the trial should normally attend this hearing and the judge is able to make further directions as are considered necessary. A CMC may be either an oral hearing, or if specifically directed, via telephone conference. A case management conference may also be used in some family cases. *See* PRETRIAL REVIEW. *See also* PLEA AND CASE MANAGEMENT HEARING.

case stated A written statement of the facts found by a magistrates' court or tribunal submitted for the opinion of the Divisional Court on any question of law or jurisdiction involved. Any person who was a party to the proceedings or is aggrieved by the decision can request the court or tribunal to state a case. *See* APPELLATE JURISDICTION.

casus belli [Latin: occasion for war] An event giving rise to war or used to justify war. The only legitimate *casus belli* now is an unprovoked attack necessitating self-defence on the part of the victim.

casus foederis [Latin: case for the alliance] The event upon the occurrence of which it becomes the duty of one ally to render assistance to the other. Thus, in the case of a defensive alliance, the *casus foederis* occurs when war is declared or commenced against one of the allies. Treaties of alliance very often define precisely the event that is to be regarded as the *casus foederis*. However, many alliances have been concluded without such precise definition and, consequently, disputes have arisen between the parties as to whether the *casus foederis* has, in fact, occurred.

casus omissus [Latin] A circumstance not provided for by common law or statute; a gap in the law. Where such a gap exists in a statute, particularly one of a penal nature, it is not for the judge to bridge such a gap. Case: *Fisher v Bell* [1961] QB 394, 400 (Lord Parker CJ).

catching bargain (unconscionable bargain) A contract on very unfair terms. An example is the sale of a future interest in property at a gross undervalue, made by someone with expectations to succeed to the property who is in immediate need of money. Such a contract may be set aside or modified by a court of equitable jurisdiction.

causa causans [Latin: cause causing] The real, proximate, or main cause of something; the final link in the chain of *causation. It is not to be confused with the *causa* *sine qua non* – the cause without which something could not have occurred. Determining the *causa causans* can be a vital factor in establishing negligence actions in tort.

causa sine qua non *See* CAUSATION.

causation *n.* The relationship between an act and the consequences it produces. It is one of the elements that must be proved before an accused can be convicted of a crime in which the effect of the act is part of the definition of the crime (e.g. murder). Whatever other causes may have effected the bringing about of the *actus reus*, it needs to be shown that the defendant's behaviour did, in a significant way, contribute to the *actus reus*. In *R v White* [1910] 2 KB 124, White gave poison to his mother who died. However, medical evidence proved that the mother had died from a heart attack and that the poison was in no way connected to the death. Therefore the defendant's behaviour did not contribute in any way to the resulting death.

Causation is a question of both 1) fact and 2) law and in both cases this is a question for the jury to decide:

1) Factual causation: it must be shown that, "but for" the defendant's act, the event would not have occurred. The act must be a *causa sine qua non* ("cause without which") of the event. a test sometimes known as the **"but for" test**.

2) Legal causation: the defendant's act must be an operative and substantial cause of the consequence. His act need not be the sole cause, but must make a significant and not trivial (*de minimis non curat lex*) contribution to the result. For example, if a doctor takes a blood sample from a patient who has been stabbed and is dying the taking of the blood will weaken the patient, but the doctor's role in the patient's death is minimal and causally insignificant.

Sometimes a new act or event (*novus actus* (or *nova causa*) *interveniens*) may break the legal chain of causation and relieve the defendant of responsibility. The chain of causation between the defendant's act and the resulting consequences will be broken if another unforeseeable act occurs and if "the second cause is so overwhelming as to make the original [act] merely part of the history" (Lord Parker CJ in *R v Smith* [1959] 2 QB 35 at 42-43).

In tort it must be established that the defendant's tortious conduct caused or materially contributed to the damage to the claimant before the defendant can be found liable for that damage. In order to determine factual causation, courts adopt the same "but for" test used in criminal cases: "but for" the defendant's tortious conduct, would the claimant's loss have occurred (*Barnett v Chelsea and Kensington Hospital Management Committee* [1969] 1 QB 428)? However, this test is inadequate for cases of concurrent or cumulative causes, where the actions of two or more tortfeasors are each sufficient to produce the damage. Where there is more than one possible cause there are several tests that may be applied. For example, did the defendant's negligence materially increase the risk of injury (*Mc Ghee v National Coal Board* [1973] 1 WLR 1)? Similarly, was the defendant's breach of duty a material cause of the injury? One of five causes will not suffice to establish liability (*Wilsher v Essex Area Health Authority* [1988] AC 1074). In order for causation to be established on the balance of probabilities, it requires at least a 51% chance that the defendant's actions caused the damage (*Hotson v East Berkshire Health Authority* [1987] AC 750).

Where the defendant's negligence has caused the loss of a business deal, claimants may be awarded damages for **loss of a chance** (*Stovold v Barlows* [1995] NPC 154). However, claimants are unlikely to succeed for loss of a chance of recovery after medical *negligence (*Gregg v Scott* [2005] UKHL 2, [2005] 2 AC 176).

cause *n.* **1.** A court *action. **2.** *See* CAUSATION.

Cause Book The book recording the issue of claim forms in the *Central Office of the Senior Courts and certain later stages of the court proceedings.

Cause List A list of cases to be heard, displayed in the precincts of a court. The *Daily Cause List* lists all cases for trial in the Royal Courts of Justice and its outlying buildings. It also contains the **warned list** of cases about to be listed for hearing.

cause of action The facts that entitle a person to sue. The cause of action may be a wrongful act, such as *trespass; or the harm resulting from a wrongful act, as in the tort of *negligence.

causing a child to watch a sexual act It is a criminal offence under the Sexual Offences Act 2003 for a person, for the purpose of obtaining sexual gratification, to intentionally cause a person under the age of 16 (child) to watch any third person engaging in sexual activity, or to look at an image of any person engaging in sexual activity (as, for example, causing a child to look at a pornographic image). If the child is between the ages of 13 and 16, the defendant's mistaken belief that the child is over the age of 16 will negate his liability, providing that belief is both honestly held and reasonable. If the child is under the age of 13, the defendant's mistaken belief that the child is over 16 will not negate his liability, irrespective of whether that belief is honestly held and reasonable. The maximum sentence is 10 years' imprisonment.

causing death by careless driving when under the influence of drink or **drugs** The offence committed by someone whose driving while unfit through drink or drugs or driving over the prescribed limit (*see* DRUNKEN DRIVING) results in the death of another person. For this offence, which was created by the Road Traffic Act 1991, the driving must be judged careless (*see* CARELESS AND INCONSIDERATE DRIVING; CAUSING DEATH BY CARELESS OR INCONSIDERATE DRIVING) rather than dangerous (*compare* CAUSING DEATH BY DANGEROUS DRIVING); the maximum punishment is five years' imprisonment and compulsory *disqualification.

causing death by careless or inconsiderate driving An offence inserted into the Road Traffic Act 1988 (s 2B) by the Road Safety Act 2006 (s 20): it is committed by a person who causes the death of another person while driving without due care and attention, or without reasonable consideration for other road users. The offence covers those cases where a person's driving leads to fatal consequences but the standard of driving does not amount to being dangerous nor is the driver under the influence of drink or drugs.

causing death by dangerous driving The offence committed by someone guilty of *dangerous driving that results in the death of another person. It is defined by the Road Traffic Act 1988 s 1 (as amended by the Road Traffic Act 1991) and replaces the former offence of causing death by reckless driving (defined in the Road Traffic Act 1988). If the danger is such that there is an obvious and serious risk of injury to another person or significant damage to property – and the driver either recognizes the risk or fails to give any thought to the possibility that such a risk exists – this will constitute reckless *manslaughter in addition to causing death by dangerous driving. The maximum penalty for causing death by dangerous driving is fourteen years' imprisonment and compulsory *disqualification for not less than two years.

causing loss by unlawful means An unlawful interference with the actions of a third party in which the claimant has an economic interest, with an intention to cause loss to the claimant. Acts are only unlawful if they are actionable by the third party in civil law. The torts of "interfering with contractual relations" and *intimidation are now encompassed within this tort (*OBG Ltd v Allan* [2007] UKHL 21, [2008] 1 SC 1). *See also* INDUCING BREACH OF CONTRACT; INTERFERING WITH TRADE OR BUSINESS.

caution *n.* **1.** (in criminal law) a. A warning that should normally be given by a police officer, in accordance with a code of practice issued under the Police and Criminal Evidence Act 1984, when he has grounds for believing that a person has committed an offence and when arresting him. The caution is in the following terms: "You do not have to say anything. But it may harm your defence if you do not mention when questioned something which you later rely on in court. Anything you do say may be given in evidence." The caution must be given before any questions are put. If a person is not under arrest when a caution is given, the officer must say so; if he is at a police station the officer must also tell him that he is free to leave and remind him that he may obtain legal advice. The officer must record the caution in his pocket book or the interview record, as appropriate. *See* RIGHT OF SILENCE. b. A warning by a police officer, on releasing a suspect when it has been decided not to bring a prosecution against him, that if he is subsequently reported for any other offence, the circumstances relating to his first alleged offence may be taken into account. It is common practice for the police to give this type of caution, although the procedure has no statutory basis and there are no legal consequences if it is not followed. **2.** (in land law) Formerly, a document lodged at the Land Registry by a person having an interest in registered land, requiring that no dealing with that land be registered until the cautioner has been notified, so that he may lodge an objection. For example, a caution might have been lodged by someone who was induced by fraud to convey his land, in order to prevent the fraudulent transferee from registering his title. Since 13 October 2003 cautions against dealings have been replaced by unilateral *notices.

caution against first registration A caution that may be lodged at the Land Registry by any person claiming to have ownership of, or an interest in, unregistered land. The effect of the caution is to oblige the registrar to notify the cautioner of any application for first registration of that land, and of the cautioner's right to object to that registration. The cautioner then has 15 days to object. The owner of the legal estate to which the caution relates has a right to apply for cancellation of the caution, as do some others interested in the land. If the unregistered land could itself be registered in the name of the cautioner (for example, he has a freehold estate) then he should apply for first registration of the land himself, rather than lodging a caution.

caveat *n.* [from Latin: let him beware] A notice, usually in the form of an entry in a register, to the effect that no action of a certain kind may be taken without first informing the person who gave the notice (the **caveator**). For example, if there are doubts as to the validity of a will, or who is entitled to administer an estate, or reservations about the executors, the lodging of a caveat by any person at any Probate Registry assures that a *grant of representation is not issued without the caveator being notified of the application for a grant and being given chance to object.

caveat actor [Latin] Let the doer be on his guard.

caveat emptor [Latin: let the buyer beware] A common-law maxim warning a purchaser that he could not claim that his purchases were defective unless he protected himself by obtaining express guarantees from the vendor. The maxim has been modified by statute: under the Sale of Goods Act 1979 (a consolidating statute), contracts for the sale of goods have implied terms requiring the goods to correspond with their description and any sample and, if they are sold in the course of a business, to be of satisfactory quality and fit for any purpose made known to the seller. Each of these implied terms is a *condition of the contract. However, in many commercial contracts the vendors attempt to exempt themselves from liability for breach of these terms. This will usually be valid unless the exclusion is unreasonable or unfair under the law relating to unfair contract terms. These statutory conditions do not apply to sales of land, to which the maxim *caveat emptor* still applies as far as the condition of the property is concerned. However, a term is normally implied that the vendor must convey a good *title to the land, free from encumbrances that were not disclosed to the purchaser before the contract was made.

caveat subscriptor [Latin] Let the person signing (e.g. a contract) be on his guard.

caveat venditor [Latin] Let the seller be on his guard.

CCGs *See* CLINICAL COMMISSIONING GROUPS.

CCRC *See* CRIMINAL CASES REVIEW COMMISSION.

CE [French *Communauté européenne*: European Community] A marking applied to certain products, such as toys and machinery, to indicate that they have complied with certain EU directives that apply to them, including *electromagnetic compatibility. A CE marking is not a quality mark, but it indicates that health and safety and other legislation has been complied with. The manufacturer or first importer into the EU must apply the CE marking; fines can be levied for breach of the rules.

Central Arbitration Committee (CAC) A statutory body, established under the Employment Protection Act 1975 (consolidated into the Trade Union and Labour Relations (Consolidation) Act 1992), that consists of a chairman and members appointed by the Secretary of State for Business, Innovation and Skills from persons nominated by *ACAS. The Committee determines disputes relating to: (1) arbitration in *trade disputes referred by ACAS with the consent of both parties; (2) *disclosure of information to trade unions; (3) recognition and derecognition of trade unions for the purpose of *collective bargaining (*see* RECOGNITION PROCEDURE); and (4) specified issues in relation to the introduction and operation of *European Works Councils.

When the Committee makes an award of pay and/or conditions of employment in a case where an employer has failed to disclose information, these generally become incorporated in the contracts of employment of individual employees and are enforceable in the courts.

Central Criminal Court The principal *Crown Court for Central London, usually known from its address as the **Old Bailey**. The senior circuit judge at the court has the ancient title **Recorder of London** and his deputy is known as the *Common Serjeant. By tradition, the Lord Mayor of London and any City aldermen may sit on the judges' bench but they do not play any part in hearings.

Central Office The administrative organization of the *Senior Courts in London, from which claim forms are issued. Its business is superintended by the Queen's Bench Masters (*see* MASTERS OF THE HIGH COURT), one of whom sits each day as **practice master** to give any directions that may be required on questions of practice and procedure.

certificate of incorporation A document issued by the Registrar of Companies after the *registration of a company, certifying that the company is incorporated (*see* INCORPORATION). For a *limited company, the certificate also certifies that the company members have limited liability, and for a *public company the fact that it is a public company. The validity of the incorporation cannot thereafter be challenged.

Certification Officer (CO) An official first appointed in 1975 when his principal function was to certify trade unions as independent in order that they could benefit from various legislative rights. The office is now governed by the Trade Union and Labour Relations (Consolidation) Act 1992 and its powers were extended by the Employment Act 1999. The CO remains responsible for certifying the independence of trade unions but also has administrative and judicial functions, which include the maintenance of a list of trade unions and employers' associations, supervision of trade-union accounts and mergers between unions, and determination of complaints concerning trade-union elections and political funds. The CO can hear certain complaints from union members against the union, including those relating to disciplinary action against a member where the member is complaining about a breach of the union's rules. The CO is appointed by the Secretary of State for Business, Innovation and Skills but operates independently of government. The Annual Report shows the business of the CO and provides statistics on trade union membership.

certiorari *n.* [Latin: to be informed] *See* QUASHING ORDER.

certum est quod certum reddi potest [Latin] If something is capable of being made certain, it should be treated as certain. For example, a landlord can only distrain for rent (*see* DISTRESS) if the amount of rent is certain. However, if the amount of the rent is capable of being ascertained, it is treated as certain.

cessante ratione legis, cessat lex ipsa [Latin: when the reason for a law ceases, the law itself ceases] The principle that when the grounds that gave rise to a law cease to exist, the law itself ceases to exist. A good example of this can be found with regard to the immunity of advocates as discussed by Lord Hoffmann in *Arthur J S Hall & Co v Simons* [2002] 1 AC 615 (HL).

cessate grant 1. A grant (e.g. of a lease) renewing a previous grant that has lapsed. **2.** A second *grant of representation issued when the first grant was conditional or limited in some way and the condition or limitation has either been fulfilled or the original grantee has died leaving it unfulfilled. It is usually required when the estate of the deceased has not been fully administered but unlike a grant *de bonis non administratis* it operates as a re-grant of the whole estate rather than the unadministered part. For example, where *letters of administration are issued to a guardian for the use and benefit of a minor named as executor, a cessate grant is required when the minor reaches 18. *See* GRANT FOR THE USE AND BENEFIT.

cesser *n.* The premature termination of some right or interest. For example, if land is held in trust for A for life so long as he does not marry and then for B, there is a cesser of A's life interest if he marries. A mortgage under which the mortgagor attorns tenant of the mortgagee (*see* ATTORNMENT) provides for cesser on redemption: thus the tenancy ends whenever the debt is repaid.

cesser clause A clause inserted in a charterparty when the charterer intends to transfer to a shipper his right to have goods carried. It provides that the shipowner is to have a lien over the shipper's goods for the freight payable under the charterparty, and that the charterer's liability for that freight will cease accordingly on shipment of a full cargo.

cession *n.* The transfer of sovereignty over a territory by means of a treaty. This may either be a peace treaty (e.g. the peace treaty between France and Germany in 1871 that made Alsace-Lorraine part of the German empire), a treaty to exchange territory (e.g. the treaty of 1890 whereby the UK ceded Heligoland to Germany in exchange for Zanzibar), or more rarely a treaty bestowing a gift. *See also* DERIVATIVE TITLE.

cestui que trust [Norman French, from *cestui à que trust*, he for whom is the trust] Formerly, a beneficiary under a trust.

cestui que use [Norman French, from *cestui à que use*, he to whose use] A person to whose use (i.e. for whose benefit) property was held by another. The modern equivalent is the *beneficiary. *See* USE.

cestui que vie [Norman French, from *cestui à que vie*, he for whose life] A person for whose life an interest in property is held by another person. *See* ESTATE PUR (OR PER) AUTRE VIE.

CET *See* COMMON EXTERNAL TARIFF.

CFP *See* COMMON FISHERIES POLICY.

CFSP (common foreign and security policy) *See* EUROPEAN UNION; MAASTRICHT TREATY.

CGT *See* CAPITAL GAINS TAX.

chain of executorship (chain of representation) A rule under the Administration of Estates Act 1925 s 7 by which the executor of someone who was himself a sole or surviving executor stands, on the latter's death, in his place as executor of the testator who appointed him. Thus, if A appoints B as his only executor and B in turn appoints C as his own executor, then if A dies and subsequently B dies having already taken out a grant of probate of A's will, then C, on taking out of a grant of probate of B's will, becomes the executor of both A and B. The rule does not apply on intestacy or to an administrator, and the chain is broken by the failure of a testator to appoint an executor or a failure to obtain probate. *See also* DE BONIS NON ADMINISTRATIS.

chain of title The successive instruments conveying *real property, commencing with the original grant or other source and including the conveyance to the person claiming title.

challenge to jury A procedure by which the parties may object to the composition of a jury before it is sworn. Formerly, a challenge could be **peremptory** (with no reason for the challenge being given) or **for cause**. Peremptory challenges were abolished by the Criminal Justice Act 1988, but in some circumstances the prosecution may be entitled to ask that a juror "stand by" as he is about to take the oath. This is usually where either (a) the defence agrees with the prosecution that a juror is totally unsuitable or (b) the Attorney General has ordered a security check on the jury in a case involving terrorism or national security. Either party may challenge for cause. This may be **to the array**, in which the whole panel is challenged by alleging some irregularity in the summoning of the jury (such as bias or partiality on the part of the jury summoning officer); or **to the polls**, in which individual jurors may be challenged. A challenge for cause is made immediately before the juror is sworn, and may be made on the grounds that the juror is not qualified to serve or is biased. Any challenge to jurors for cause is tried by the trial judge.

chambers *pl. n.* **1.** The offices occupied by a barrister or group of barristers. (The term is also used for the group of barristers practising from a set of chambers.) **2.** The private office of a judge, master, or district judge. Most *interim proceedings are held in chambers (in private) and the public is not admitted, although judgment may be given in open court if the matter is one of public interest. **3.** A three-judge panel of the *International Court of Justice that may be resorted to as an alternative to the complete 15-member court. Use of the chambers can, for example, be found in the *Gulf of Maine Case* [1984] ICJ Rep 246.

champerty *n. See* MAINTENANCE AND CHAMPERTY.

Chancellor of the Exchequer The minister who, as political head of the Treasury, is responsible for government monetary policy, raising national revenue (particularly through taxation), and controlling public expenditure in the UK. Each year he presents to Parliament a **Budget** (usually in March) proposing changes in revenue and taxation and a statement (in November) proposing government expenditure.

Chancery Division The division of the *High Court of Justice created by the Judicature Acts 1873–75 to replace the *Court of Chancery. The work of the Division is principally concerned with matters relating to real property, trusts, and the administration of estates but also includes cases concerned with company law, patents and other *intellectual property, and confidentiality cases. It may hear some *appeals. The head of the Division was formerly known as the *Vice Chancellor; under the Constitutional Reform Act 2005 this office was retitled **Chancellor of the High Court**. *See also* APPELLATE JURISDICTION; COMPANIES COURT.

Chancery Masters *See* MASTERS OF THE HIGH COURT.

change of name A natural person (i.e. a human being) may change his or her *surname simply by using a different name with sufficient consistency to become generally known by that name. A change is normally given formal publicity (e.g. by means of a statutory declaration, deed poll, or newspaper advertisement), but this is not legally necessary. A woman can also change her surname through operation of law on getting married. A young child, however, has no power to change its surname, nor does one parent have such a power without the consent of the other. (An injunction may be sought to prevent a parent from attempting to change a child's name unilaterally.) When a mother has remarried after divorce or is living with another person, and wishes to change the name of the child to that of her new partner, a court order must be obtained and the welfare of the child will be the first and paramount consideration. A person's Christian name (i.e. a name given at baptism) can, under ecclesiastical law, be changed only by the bishop on that person's subsequent confirmation.

   A *juristic person may change its name but may be subject to formal procedure before the change of name takes effect; for example, for a company limited by shares, a change of name is possible only on the passing of a special resolution of the company at an extraordinary or annual general meeting.

change of position A defence to a claim for restitution for unjust enrichment first formally recognized by Lord Goff in *Lipkin Gorman v Karpnale Ltd* [1991] 2 AC 548 (HL). The defence allows the defendant to set against his enrichment the amount of disenrichment that he has sustained but would not otherwise have sustained had it not been for the enrichment. In *Lipkin Gorman* the enriched casino was liable to make restitution for amounts received from a compulsive gambler who had obtained the stake money dishonestly. However, the extent of the casino's liability was reduced by the amount it had paid out in winnings to the gambler.

Chapter VII The chapter of the United Nations Charter that is headed: "Action with respect to threats to the peace, breaches of the peace and acts of aggression" and includes Articles 39–51 of the Charter. Those who devised the UN Charter were acutely aware of the failure of the former Covenant of the League of Nations in respect of *collective security, namely (1) that it left it open to member states to respond, or not respond, to the call for military aid and (2) it provided no machinery or system for organizing League forces in advance or for coordinating such responses as members might make. Chapter VII addressed such problems by empowering the Security Council to orchestrate such collective actions under Articles 42 and 43. Under Articles 43–47 advance preparation of collective action was to be made through a *Military Staff Committee. Article 51 creates a right to *self-defence for member states; controversially, it is held to have preserved the wider scope of self-defence in customary international law. A use of force not brought under Chapter VII of the UN Charter is illegal. The consequences of this can be great when one is assessing the matter of *war crimes. *See also* ENFORCEMENT ACTION.

character *n.* (in the law of evidence) **1.** The reputation of a party or witness. Evidence of the reputation for truthfulness of a witness may be given in both civil and criminal cases. However, in civil cases the reputation of a party is not admissible unless it is directly in issue, as it may be in an action for *defamation. In criminal cases the accused may call evidence of his good character and in certain circumstances may be entitled to a good character direction. The Criminal Justice Act 2003 abolished most of the existing rules on evidence of bad character, introducing new restrictions on raising the bad character of witnesses and permitting wider reference to a defendant's bad character. The Act provides that evidence of the defendant's bad character (defined by section 99 as "evidence of or a disposition towards misconduct") is only admissible if:

- all parties to the proceedings agree to the evidence being admissible;
- the evidence is adduced by the defendant himself or is given in answer to a question asked by him in cross-examination and intended to elicit it;
- it is important explanatory evidence;
- it is relevant to an important matter in issue between the defendant and the prosecution;
- it has substantial probative value in relation to an important matter in issue between the defendant and a co-defendant;
- it is evidence to correct a false impression given by the defendant;
- the defendant has made an attack on another person's character.

See also ANTECEDENTS. **2.** Loosely, the disposition of a party.

charge *n.* **1.** A formal accusation of a crime, usually made at the police station after *interrogation. A decision to charge a suspect will normally be taken by the *Crown Prosecution Service. *See also* INDICTMENT. **2.** Instructions given by a judge to a jury. A defendant is also said to be put in the charge of the jury when a trial is commenced. **3.** A legal or equitable interest in land, securing the payment of money. It gives the creditor in whose favour the charge is created (the **chargee**) the right to payment from the income or proceeds of sale of the land charged, in priority to claims against the debtor by unsecured creditors. Under the Law of Property Act 1925 the only valid legal charges are: (1) a *rentcharge payable immediately and for a fixed period or in perpetuity; (2) a charge by way of legal *mortgage; and (3) certain charges arising under statute (e.g. under the Charging Orders Act 1979). All others take effect as equitable interests. All mortgages and charges over registered land must be registered to be enforceable against purchases of the land; both legal mortgages and *equitable charges over unregistered land must be registered as land charges unless the mortgagee or chargee holds the title deeds as security (*see* REGISTRATION OF ENCUMBRANCES). **4.** An interest in company property created in favour of a creditor (e.g. as a *debenture holder) to secure the amount owing.

Charges must be registered at Companies House in accordance with chapter A1 of part 25 of the Companies Act 2006. Chapter A1 introduces an exemption-based system and permits electronic filing of charges, with effect from 13 April 2013. A **fixed charge** is attached to specific assets (e.g. premises, plant and machinery) and while in force prevents the company from dealing freely with those assets without the consent of the lender. A **floating charge** does not immediately attach to any specific assets but "floats" over all the company's assets until *crystallization. Until this point the company is free to deal freely with such assets; this type of charge is suitable for current assets (e.g. cash, stock in trade), whose values must necessarily fluctuate (*Re Yorkshire Woolcombers Association Ltd* [1903] 2 Ch 284). In the event of the company not paying the debt the creditor can secure the amount owing in accordance with the terms of the charge. If the company goes into liquidation (*see* WINDING-UP) the order for repayment of debts laid down under the Insolvency Act 1986 is that fixed-charge holders are paid before floating-charge holders. A charge can also be created upon shares. For example, the articles of association usually give the company a *lien in respect of unpaid *calls, and company members may, in order to secure a debt owed to a third party, charge their shares, either by a full *transfer of shares coupled with an agreement to retransfer upon repayment of the debt or by a deposit of the *share certificate.

chargeable gain That part of the gain arising on *disposal of a chargeable asset that is subject to *capital gains tax (or, in the case of a company, to corporation tax). The chargeable gain is calculated after adjusting the difference between selling price and purchase cost in accordance with the provisions of the Taxation of Chargeable Gains Act 1992. This involves making certain specified deductions in the amount of the gain, such as those arising from *indexation allowance (an allowance for inflation), *entrepreneurs' relief, and the personal allowance for capital gains tax.

charge by way of legal mortgage *See* MORTGAGE.

chargé d'affaires In most instances, the second-ranking official amongst an embassy's delegation. His or her duty is to take charge (hence the name) of the diplomatic mission and premises in the absence of the principal diplomat.

charge sheet A document in which an officer at a police station records an accusation against a suspect. It normally also gives details of his name and those of his accusers, who should sign the sheet.

charges register *See* LAND REGISTRATION.

charging clause A clause in a trust entitling a trustee to charge for his services. When a solicitor or some other professional person is appointed trustee, he is usually authorized to charge for his services. In the absence of such a clause, and subject to there being no contrary intention expressed, the Trustee Act 2000 (s 29) enables the reasonable remuneration of professional trustees (except sole trustees or charitable trustees).

charging order A court order obtained by a judgment creditor by which the judgment debtor's property (including money, land, and shares) becomes security for the payment of the debt and interest. The relevant procedure is set out in Part 73 of the *Civil Procedure Rules.

charitable trust A trust whose purposes are regarded by the law as being charitable. Charitable trusts enjoy many advantages including exemption from many forms of taxation, the ability to claim tax paid by its donors by way of *gift aid, lack of necessity for there to be human beneficiaries (*see* BENEFICIARY PRINCIPLE), and the nonapplication of the *rule against perpetual trusts. For a purpose to be charitable it must comply with the provisions of the Charities Act 2006, which sets out the meaning of "charitable purpose" in section 2. The 2011 Act consolidated the earlier Charities Act 2006 with other charity legislation. Prior to the enactment of the 2006 Act, which modernized charity law, there was no statutory definition of charity: in determining whether trusts were charitable it was necessary to refer to judicial precedent, the starting point being the four "heads" of charity identified by Lord Macnaghten in the decision in *Commissioners for Special Purposes of Income Tax v Pemsel* [1891] AC 531 (HL) (Pemsel's case). Despite the introduction of a new statutory definition of "charity" and "charitable purpose", section 4 of the 2011 Act (as s 4 of the earlier 2006 Act) expressly preserves and incorporates the law prior to its enactment.

charity *n.* A body (corporate or not) established for one of the charitable purposes specified by statute (*see* CHARITABLE TRUST). A charity is subject to the control of the High Court in the exercise of its jurisdiction with respect to charities. With certain exceptions, all charities are required to be registered with the *Charity Commission.

Charity Commission A statutory body, now governed by the Charities Act 2011, generally responsible for the administration of charities. The Commissioners are responsible for promoting the effective use of charitable resources, for encouraging the development of better methods of administration, for giving charity trustees information and advice on matters affecting charity, and for investigating and checking abuses. The Commissioners maintain a computerized register of charities and decide whether or not a body should be registered; an appeal from their decision may be made to the High Court or the *Charity Tribunal (for decisions made after 18 March 2008). Their Annual Reports (published by the Stationery Office) indicate how the Commissioners operate and how they are allowing the law of charity to develop.

(⊕) SEE WEB LINKS
• Website of the Charity Commission

Charity Tribunal An independent body established under the Charities Act 2006 to hear appeals against decisions of the *Charity Commission, to hear applications for review of decisions of the Charity Commission, and to consider references from the Attorney General or the Charity Commission on points of law. The Charity Tribunal only has jurisdiction in respect of Charity Commission decisions made on or after 18 March 2008 and is now governed by the Charities Act 2011.

charter *n.* **1.** A document evidencing something done between one party and another. The term is normally used in relation to a grant of rights or privileges by the Crown; for example, the grant of a royal charter to a university. **2.** A constitution, e.g. the Charter of the United Nations.

charter for demise *See* BAREBOAT CHARTER.

Charter of Fundamental Rights The Charter of Fundamental Rights of the European Union brings together the principles of the *European Convention on Human Rights, the European Social Charter, and Community law as they relate to the rights of EU citizens. The Charter has been recognized by the EU since the meeting in Nice in December 2000 but did not become legally binding upon the member states until 2009 when the *Treaty of Lisbon was ratified and came into force. (The *Constitutional Treaty of 2004 had previously incorporated the Charter but did not itself become law.)

charterparty *n.* A written contract by which a person (the **charterer**) hires from a shipowner, in return for the payment of freight, the use of his ship or part of it for the carriage of goods by sea. The hiring may be either for a specified period (a **time charter**) or for a specified voyage or voyages (a **voyage charter**), and the charterer may hire the ship for carrying either his own goods alone or the goods of a number of shippers, who may or may not include himself. A special type of charterparty is the *bareboat charter: it is analogous to a lease of land and gives the charterer full possession and control of the ship. The normal charterparty is a **simple charter**, under which the shipowner retains possession and control and the primary rights of the charterer are confined to placing goods on board and choosing the ports of call. A number of standard forms (known by codenames such as Austwheat and Shelltime) have been developed for use in particular trades. *See also* BILL OF LADING; CESSER CLAUSE.

chastisement *n.* Physical punishment as a form of discipline. A parent or guardian has traditionally held the common-law right to inflict reasonable and moderate punishment on his children; however, an amendment to the Children Act 2004 has removed this as a defence in cases in which the child is caused actual bodily harm. A parent or guardian was also formerly entitled to authorize someone else *in loco parentis* to inflict chastisement, such as a school. Corporal punishment is now illegal in both state and private schools, whether or not the parent consents. A husband does not have the right to chastise his wife, nor a wife her husband. Illegal chastisement may amount to one of the *offences against the person.

chattel *n.* Any property other than freehold land (*compare* REAL PROPERTY). Leasehold interests in land are called **chattels real**, because they bear characteristics of both real and personal property. Tangible goods are called **chattels personal**.

cheat *n.* A common-law offence, now restricted to defrauding the public revenue (e.g. the tax authorities). No act of deceit is required. It is enough if one dishonestly fails to make VAT or other tax returns and to pay the tax due.

check-off *n.* A system whereby an employer deducts union membership fees from a member's wages during the calculation of those wages and pays them over to the union. Such deductions are regulated by the Deregulation (Deduction from Pay of Union Subscriptions) Order 1998. These require that an employer must obtain the workers' written authorization before making deductions; the authorization remains valid unless and until withdrawn.

cheque *n.* A *bill of exchange drawn on a banker payable on demand. Since a cheque is payable on demand it need not be presented to the drawee bank for acceptance. A cheque operates as a mandate or order to the drawee bank to pay and debit the account of its customer, the drawer. The Cheques Act 1992 gave legal force to the words "account payee" on cheques, making them nontransferable.

cheque card A card issued by a bank to one of its customers containing an undertaking that any cheque signed by the customer and not exceeding a stated sum will be honoured by the bank. This is normally subject to certain conditions; for example, the cheque must be signed in the presence of the payee, the signature must correspond with a specimen on the card, and the payee must write the card number on the reverse of the cheque. The bank thus undertakes to the payee of the cheque that the cheque will be honoured regardless of the state of the customer's account with the bank.

Chicago School **1.** *See* ECONOMIC ANALYSIS OF LAW. **2.** *See* POSITIVIST SCHOOL OF CRIMINOLOGY.

chief constable The rank held by the chief officer of every police force in the United Kingdom except the City of London Police and the Metropolitan Police. The title is also held *ex officio* by the president of the Association of Chief Police Officers under the Police Reform Act 2002.

chief rent *See* RENTCHARGE.

child *n.* **1.** A young person. There is no definitive definition of a child: the term has been used for persons under the age of 14, under the age of 16, and sometimes under the age of 18 (an *infant). Each case depends on its context and the wording of the statute governing it. For the purposes of the Children Act 1989 and the Family Law Act 1996 a child is a person under the age of 18. **2.** An offspring of parents. In wills, statutes, and other legal documents, the effect of the Family Law Reform Act 1987 is that there is a presumption that (unless the contrary intention is apparent) the word "child" includes any illegitimate child (*see* ILLEGITIMACY). Adopted children are treated as the legitimate children of their adoptive parents. *See also* CHILD OF THE FAMILY; QUALIFYING CHILD.

child abduction A criminal offence under the Child Abduction Act 1984; it consists of taking or detaining a child under the age of 16, without lawful authority or reasonable excuse, so as to remove the child from or keep him out of the lawful control of any person having lawful control of the child.

The further offence of **child abduction by a person connected with the child** is committed by taking or being responsible for the sending away of a child out of the UK without the consent of everyone with *parental responsibility for that child, unless the court has granted permission to do so. This means that a parent will be committing an offence if he or she removes their child without the permission of the other parent, so long as that other parent has parental responsibility. The exception to this rule is that a parent with a *residence order can remove his or her child from the jurisdiction for a period of up to one month (Children Act 1989 s 13(2)). An offence will not be committed if the parent who removed the child did so in the belief that the other parent had consented, or would have consented had he or she known of the circumstances. A parent who fears that his or her child may be abducted can apply to the court for a *specific issue order and may ask the police to initiate a port alert (*see* ALL-PORTS WARNING SYSTEM). The courts have the power to order the return of a child's passport or that a passport be not issued for the child. *See also* HAGUE CONVENTION ON THE CIVIL ASPECTS OF INTERNATIONAL CHILD ABDUCTION.

child abuse *See* ABUSE OF A POSITION OF TRUST; ASSAULT OF A CHILD UNDER 13 BY PENETRATION; CAUSING A CHILD TO WATCH A SEXUAL ACT; ENGAGING IN SEXUAL ACTIVITY IN THE PRESENCE OF A CHILD; FAMILIAL CHILD SEXUAL OFFENCES; RAPE OF A CHILD UNDER 13; SEXUAL ACTIVITY WITH A CHILD; SEXUAL ASSAULT OF A CHILD UNDER 13.

child arrangements order A proposed new order that will set out the arrangements for the bringing up of a child in cases of dispute between separating parents, replacing the currently existing *contact orders and *residence orders. The intention is to move away from potentially loaded terms such as "residence" and "contact", which have often become a source of contention between parents, and to focus attention on practical issues concerning the day-to-day care of the child. The government published draft legislation to this effect in 2012.

child assessment order An order of the court made under the Children Act 1989 s 43 when a local authority or the NSPCC has concerns for a child's welfare in circumstances when the child's parents are refusing to allow the child to be medically or otherwise examined. The order authorizes such an examination but, importantly, does not confer *parental responsibility on the applicant. If a local authority fears that a child is in immediate danger, or when it is denied access to a child, an *emergency protection order should be applied for rather than a child assessment order.

child being looked after by a local authority See LOOKED-AFTER CHILD.

child cruelty Under the Children and Young Persons Act 1933 (s 1) any person aged 16 or over who has responsibility for any person under that age commits the offence of child cruelty if he wilfully assaults, ill-treats, neglects, abandons, or exposes that young person, or causes or procures him to be assaulted, ill-treated, neglected, abandoned, or exposed in a manner likely to cause him unnecessary suffering or injury to health.

child destruction An act causing a *viable unborn child to die during the course of pregnancy or birth before it has an existence independent of its mother. If carried out with the intention of causing death, and if it is proved that the act was not carried out in good faith in order to preserve the mother's life, the offence is subject to a maximum punishment of life imprisonment. Governed by the Infant Life (Preservation) Act 1929 (s 1), this offence fills the gap between murder (the unlawful killing of a living being) and *abortion, which is the procuring of a miscarriage.

child employee A child of compulsory school age (i.e. between 5 and 16 years) who undertakes paid work. Subject to certain exceptions, such employment is prohibited in Britain, and any employment under the age of 13 years is completely prohibited. Children are prohibited from working in industrial undertakings, factories, or mines. There are narrow exceptions for work in theatres and films, sports, work experience and/or training, and light work, with strict conditions attached in each case. In many cases these exceptions require that prior authorization is obtained from a local authority with respect to the proposed work (see the Children and Young Persons Act 1933, as amended by the Children (Protection at Work) Regulations 1998 and 2000).

In particular, children falling within some of the above exceptions must not work for more than two hours on any school day (outside school hours) or for more than 12 hours a week during term times. Work must not start before 7 a.m. or after 7 p.m. These restrictions can be relaxed for working time during school holidays and for children between 13 and 15 years of age. Night work by children is prohibited between 8 p.m. and 6 a.m., and children working more than four hours daily are entitled to a one-hour break from work. Local authorities are also empowered to regulate further the employment of children under byelaws. Byelaws may differ from authority to authority.

Workers aged 16 and 17 are referred to as **young** or **adolescent workers**. Their employment is restricted (see the Working Time Regulations 1998, as amended). They may work no more than 8 hours a day and no more than 40 hours a week. No young worker may work at night (10 p.m. to 6 a.m. or 11 p.m. to 7 a.m.). They are entitled to 12 consecutive hours' rest between each working day, two days' weekly rest, and a 30-minute rest break when working longer than 4½ hours. They are also entitled to four weeks' paid annual leave.

child in care A child who is the subject of a *care order under the Children Act 1989 s 31. It is important to note that not all children who are being looked after by a local authority are the subjects of care orders; some of these children may be being accommodated by the local authority on a voluntary basis (see VOLUNTARY ACCOMMODATION). See also LOOKED-AFTER CHILD.

Child Maintenance Service See CHILD SUPPORT MAINTENANCE.

child of the family A person considered under the Matrimonial Causes Act 1973, the Domestic Procedures and Magistrates' Courts Act 1978, and the Children Act 1989 to be the child of a married couple, although not necessarily born to or adopted by them, on the grounds that he or she has been treated by them as their own child. Courts have powers to make orders in favour of children of the family in all *family proceedings.

child of unmarried parents *See* ILLEGITIMACY.

Child Protection Conference A conference that decides what action should be taken by the local authority in respect of a child believed to be at risk of suffering harm. The conference comprises representatives of those bodies concerned with the child's welfare, including the NSPCC, social services, the police, the health and education authorities, and the probation service. Parents have no absolute right to attend the Child Protection Conference but are usually excluded only in exceptional circumstances.

child protection in divorce The legal rules designed to safeguard the position of children of divorcees. In the past courts would routinely make orders for custody and access in respect of children on divorce. The Children Act 1989, however, introduced a presumption of non-interference; i.e. the court will assume that parents are able to make their own arrangements for their children and will only make an order if it is necessary to do so, for example when the parents are in disagreement. Divorce courts have wide powers to make financial provision and property adjustment orders in favour of *children of the family, as well as any *section 8 orders necessary to safeguard the child's welfare. If the court is concerned about the welfare of a child before it, it may direct a local authority to investigate the child's circumstances with a view to determining whether intervention is necessary.

Children and Family Court Advisory and Support Service (Cafcass) An amalgamation of three former services: the Guardian ad Litem Service, the Family Court Welfare Service, and the Official Solicitor's children's department. Cafcass looks after the interests of children involved in court proceedings. It works with children and their families and advises the court on what it considers to be in the best interests of individual children.

children and young people's plan A document that all local authorities are under a duty to provide under the Children Act 2004. It sets out all the services available to children in the locality, including health services, youth justice, and voluntary and community services.

children in care *See* CHILD IN CARE; CARE ORDER.

children in need Those children designated by the Children Act 1989 as being in need of special support and provision by the *local authority. Local authorities have a duty to provide certain services for such children. Children in need include disabled children and children who are unlikely to maintain a reasonable standard of health or development without the provision of these special *support services.

Children's Commissioner A post created in Wales under the Care Standards Act 2000 and in England by the Children Act 2004. Independent of government, the role of the Commissioner is to promote awareness of the views and interests of children. He is not generally permitted to conduct investigations into the cases of individual children, but is allowed to do so where the case has wider policy relevance for other children not directly involved.

children's guardian A person appointed by the court to protect a minor's interests in proceedings affecting his interests (such as adoption, wardship, or care proceedings), formerly known as a **guardian *ad litem***. Since the Children Act 1989 came into force the role of guardians has increased and they must ensure that the options open to the court are fully investigated. However, if a child is deemed capable of instructing a solicitor on his own behalf, he may do so even if this conflicts with the interests of the guardian.

child safety order An order made by a magistrates' court that enables local authorities to intervene when a child under the age of 10 (who cannot be prosecuted in criminal proceedings by virtue of his age) behaves antisocially or disruptively. The order was introduced by the Crime and Disorder Act 1998. An application for an order is made by a local authority on the grounds that the child has committed, or is in danger of committing, acts that could constitute an offence were he over 10 years old or that have caused, or are likely to cause, harassment, alarm, or distress. The requirements imposed under the order are a matter for the court and might include, for example, attendance at school, avoiding contact with disruptive and older children, and not visiting such areas as shopping centres unsupervised. The purpose of the requirements imposed is either to ensure that the child receives appropriate care, protection, and support and is subject to proper control, or to prevent the repetition of the kind of behaviour that led to the child safety order being made. Breach of the order may lead to the court making a *care order in respect of the child. *See also* PARENTING ORDER.

child support maintenance The amount that a **non-resident parent** (i.e. one who does not live with the child concerned) must pay as a contribution to the upkeep of his or her *qualifying child. Where the non-resident parent's weekly income is £200 or more the amount payable is currently based on the following percentages of his or her gross weekly income: 12% for one qualifying child; 16% for two qualifying children; and 19% for three or more qualifying children. This is subject to a ceiling of £800 per week. Where the non-resident parent has gross weekly income of more than £800 the amount payable reduces to 9%, 12%, or 15% respectively for weekly income above £800 but less than £3,000. These amounts are reduced where a non-resident parent has other "relevant children" (children for whom he or his partner receives child benefit). A reduced rate is payable where the non-resident parent's income is less than £200 but more than £100. Where the non-resident's income is £100 or less or he or she, or his or her partner, is receiving prescribed benefits or a pension a flat rate of £5 is payable).

Under the Child Support Act 1991 the **Child Support Agency** (**CSA**) became responsible for the assessment, collection, and enforcement of maintenance for children, rather than the courts. These responsibilities were transferred to a new body, the **Child Maintenance and Enforcement Commission** (**CMEC**), in 2008 and subsequently (2012) to the **Child Maintenance Service**. As a general rule it is to the statutory maintenance service that a parent must turn for maintenance for his or her child; the courts however do have the power to make payments in certain cases, for example in respect of a disabled child or where a child requires money to meet the cost of his education. Parents are now encouraged to enter into "family-based arrangements" before having recourse to the statutory service. The statutory body has wide powers of enforcement: it can for example make an order for payment to be deducted directly from wages.

( ) SEE WEB LINKS

• Introduction to child maintenance from the GOV.UK website: includes a child-maintenance calculator

child tax credit *See* TAX CREDIT.

child witness *See* COMPETENCE; VIDEO EVIDENCE; WITNESS.

Chiltern Hundreds, stewardship of the An appointment that, as a nominal office of profit under the Crown, disqualifies its holder from membership of the House of Commons. Although the appointment has been a sinecure since the 18th century, it has been retained as a disqualifying office to enable members to give up their seats during the lifetime of a parliament (a member cannot by law resign his seat). After obtaining the stewardship (an application for which is never refused), the member resigns the office so as to make it available for re-use.

A second office used for the same purpose is the stewardship of the **Manor of Northstead**. The law relating to both these offices is now contained in the House of Commons Disqualification Act 1975.

chose *n.* A thing. Choses are divided into two classes. A **chose in possession** is a tangible item capable of being actually possessed and enjoyed, e.g. a book or a piece of furniture. A **chose in action** is a right (e.g. a right to recover a debt) that can be enforced by legal action.

Church of England The established Church in England, of which the sovereign is the supreme head. Structurally, the Church consists of the two provinces of Canterbury and York, which are divided into dioceses, and these into parishes. For each province there is an archbishop (that of Canterbury being Primate of All England, and that of York Primate of England), and for each diocese a bishop. A suffragan bishop has no diocese of his own but assists an archbishop or a diocesan bishop. The archbishops and other senior bishops are members of the House of Lords.

The governing body of the Church is the General Synod (formerly the Church Assembly, but renamed and reconstituted by the Synodical Government Measure 1969). It consists of a House of Bishops, a House of Clergy, and a House of Laity and has legislative functions. A **Measure** passed by each House and granted the royal assent following a resolution of each House of Parliament has the force of an Act of Parliament. There are also diocesan synods, and certain matters require the approval of a majority of these before they can be finally approved by the General Synod. The Dioceses Measure 1978 authorizes the reorganization of diocesan structure and the creation of area synods, to which diocesan synods may delegate functions. *See also* ECCLESIASTICAL COURTS.

CIF contract (cost, insurance, freight contract) A type of contract for the international sale of goods by which the seller agrees not only to supply the goods but also to make a contract of carriage with a sea carrier, under which the goods will be delivered at the contract port of destination, and a contract of insurance with an insurer, to cover them while they are in transit. The seller performs his contract by delivering the relevant documents to the buyer: an invoice specifying the goods and their price, a *bill of lading evidencing the contract of carriage, a policy of insurance, and any other documents specified in the contract. The contract will normally provide for payment against documents. The risk of accidental loss or damage normally passes to the buyer on or as from shipment. CIF is a defined *Incoterm under *Incoterms 2010*.

circuit administrator A civil servant having responsibility for the administration of the courts within a circuit (*see* CIRCUIT SYSTEM). He liaises closely with the *presiding judge of the circuit in the allocation of resources and particularly the sittings of judges and recorders.

circuit judge Any of the judges appointed under the provisions of the Courts Act 1971 from among those who have had a seven-year Crown Court or county court *advocacy qualification, or who are *recorders, or who have held a full-time appointment of at least three years duration in one of the offices listed in the Courts Act 1971. They sit in the *county courts and the *Crown Court and may, by invitation of the Lord Chief Justice, sit as High Court judges. All judges of county courts and other judges of comparable status were made circuit judges in 1971.

circuit system The system of dividing England and Wales into regional **circuits** for the purpose of court administration. It is based upon the traditional regional groupings adopted by the Bar and consists of the South-Eastern, Western, Midland and Oxford, Wales and Chester, Northern, and North-Eastern circuits. Each circuit is administered by a *circuit administrator and supervised by two *presiding judges. *See also* CIRCUIT JUDGE.

The term circuits also refers to representative and professional bodies of barristers who (usually) practice in the respective geographical locales. Their role is to advance the interests of their members.

circumstantial evidence (indirect evidence) Evidence from which the judge or jury may infer the existence of a fact in issue but which does not prove the existence of the fact directly. *Compare* DIRECT EVIDENCE.

citation *n.* **1.** A document issued by the court on application of a person interested in a deceased person's estate calling upon the party cited to show cause why a particular step should not be taken. This could be a citation to take out probate, to accept or refuse a grant, or to propound a will (i.e. prove that a will is valid). **2.** A detailed reference to a legal case, piece of legislation, or legal authority. For advice on citation see the WRITING AND CITATION GUIDE at the centre of this volume.

citator *n.* A publication, such as the Law Reports Index or the All England Law Reports Consolidated Tables and Index, Table volume, that enables lawyers and law students to find the status of a case in the light of subsequent cases: that is, whether it has been followed, distinguished, applied, etc. and if so, by which cases. This process can now be undertaken using electronic media such as LexisNexis and Westlaw.

citizen of the European Union A form of citizenship established by the *Maastricht Treaty of 1992. Every person holding the citizenship of a member state is automatically a citizen of the EU; this status does not have to be applied for and does not replace their national citizenship.

citizen's arrest An *arrest by anyone other than a police officer. Such an arrest is lawful.

citizenship of the UK and Colonies A form of citizenship created by the British Nationality Act 1948. By the British Nationality Act 1981, it was replaced as from 1 January 1983 by *British citizenship, British Dependent Territories citizenship (now *British Overseas Territories citizenship), and *British Overseas citizenship.

City Code on Takeovers and Mergers A body of rules regulating those engaged in the conduct of *takeovers and *mergers of public companies. It is administered by the **Panel on Takeovers and Mergers**, including representatives from major financial and business institutions. The principal aim of the Code is to ensure that company members (rather than the directors) decide upon the merits of accepting a bid, that they are fully informed about what is going on, and that shareholders of the same class are treated equally in the event of a takeover or merger. Under the Companies Act 2006 the rules are required to give effect to the EU Takeovers Directive (s 943) and a ruling by the Panel is, to the extent specified in the rules, and subject to any appeal or review, of binding effect (s 945).

City of London That part of *Greater London which, for local government purposes, is administered by the Corporation of London. In addition to special powers under ancient royal charters, the Corporation has all the functions of a London borough council, which it exercises principally through a Court of Common Council consisting of the Lord Mayor, aldermen elected for life, and common council men elected annually. Limited governmental functions are exercised through a separate Court of Aldermen, and formal functions through a Court of Common Hall.

civil court A court exercising jurisdiction over civil rather than criminal cases. In England the principal civil *courts of first instance are the *county courts and the *High Court. *Magistrates' courts have limited civil jurisdiction, mainly confined to family and matrimonial proceedings.

civil law 1. The law of any particular state, now usually called *municipal law. **2.** Roman law. **3.** A legal system based on Roman law, as distinct from the English system of *common law. **4.** *Private law, as opposed to *public law, military law, and ecclesiastical law.

civil liability contribution The right of a person who is liable for damage to recover from any other person who is liable for the same damage a contribution to represent that person's share of responsibility for the damage. When two or more people are liable for causing the same damage, the injured person is entitled to recover full compensation for his losses from any one of them. The wrongdoer who is sued may then ask for contribution from the other wrongdoers. Since the Civil Liability (Contribution) Act 1978, the right to contribution is available in all forms of civil liability, whether tort, breach of contract, breach of trust, or otherwise. The court assesses the amount of contribution on the basis of what would be just and equitable, taking into account the parties' responsibility for the damage.

Civil List The sum authorized by statute to be paid annually out of the *Consolidated Fund for meeting the expenses of the royal household and for making allowances to certain members of the royal family. It may be increased in amount by Treasury order, but this is liable to annulment by the House of Commons. Certain members of the royal family have volunteered to be taxed on their Civil List allowances.

civil partnership A new legal status, created by the Civil Partnership Act 2004, that confers analogous rights to those conferred by marriage on same-sex couples who register their relationship. To be eligible to form a civil partnership, the parties must be over 16 years of age, of the same sex, and not related to each other within the *prohibited degrees. The partnership can be dissolved by the granting by a court of a **dissolution order**, on proof by the applicant that the partnership has irretrievably broken down. This must be evidenced by one of four facts: (1) that the respondent has behaved in such a way that the petitioner can no longer be reasonably expected to live with him; (2) that the applicant and the respondent have lived apart for at least two years and the respondent consents to a dissolution order being made; (3) that the applicant and the respondent have lived apart for at least five years; (4) that the respondent has deserted the petitioner for at least two years. On the dissolution of a partnership, the courts have powers to make provision for *financial relief that mirror those contained in the Matrimonial Causes Act 1973 for married couples. A civil partner can now obtain, in the same way as a spouse, matrimonial home rights (now known simply as *home rights) and has the same rights as a spouse in relation to inheritance under the intestacy rules and under the Inheritance

(Provision for Family and Dependants) Act 1975. The Children Act 1989 as amended now gives a civil partner the same rights as a *step-parent to apply for *parental responsibility in respect of a child.

Statutory instruments issued under the authority of the Finance Act 2005 (s 103) have the effect that civil partners are treated for tax purposes as if they were married persons. Thus, a transfer of assets (whether at death or during lifetime) from one civil partner to the other is exempt from *inheritance tax. No capital gain is triggered by the gift of an asset from one civil partner to the other. When a settlement is established under which it is possible for a settlor's civil partner to receive benefit, income and gains arising are taxed on the settlor, in the same way as would apply if it were possible for the settlor's spouse to receive benefit.

Civil Procedure Rules (CPR) A procedural code that was enacted in 1998 and revoked the *Rules of the Supreme Court with effect from 26 April 1999. The Rules, a result of the reforms proposed by Lord Woolf's *Access to Justice* (Final Report) 1996, govern proceedings in the civil cases of the Court of Appeal (Civil Division), the High Court, and the county courts. The CPR is supplemented by *Practice Directions and *pre-action protocols. The Rules have no application in certain areas, including the Mental Health Act 1983 Part IV, and have limited application to family proceedings.

((⊕)) SEE WEB LINKS
• Full text of the Civil Procedure Rules, with Practice Directions, from the Ministry of Justice website

civil protection Establishments and units organized or authorized by the competent authorities to carry out operations intended to protect the civilian population against the dangers of hostilities or disasters and to help it to recover from the immediate effects of these. Arrangements for civil protection are now contained in the Civil Contingencies Act 2004. The Act introduces a broadly defined concept of emergency, which includes hostile attack by a foreign power, terrorist attacks, and events that threaten serious harm to human welfare or the environment. It requires local government, the emergency services, and various central government bodies to make plans and arrangements for coping with emergencies and provides for the Crown to exercise *emergency powers.

civil remedy *See* REMEDY.

Civil Service The body of *Crown servants that are employed to put government policies into action and are paid wholly out of money voted annually by Parliament. Civil servants include the administrative and executive staff of central government departments (e.g. the Home Office and Treasury), including *executive agencies (e.g. the Land Registry and the Prison Service). The Civil Service is politically impartial and permanent, thereby providing stable administration notwithstanding changes of government. The police (not being Crown servants), the armed forces (not being civil), government ministers, and those (e.g. judges) whose salaries are charged on the Consolidated Fund are not civil servants.

Civil Service Commission The body that regulates recruitment to the Civil Service, ensuring that appointments are on merit after fair and open competition. It helps promote the Civil Service values of honesty, integrity, objectivity, and impartiality, and hears complaints under the Civil Service Code. The Commission is independent of both the Civil Service and the government.

civil wrong An infringement of a person's rights, for which the person wronged may sue for damages or some other civil remedy. Examples are *torts and *breaches of contract.

claim *n.* A demand for a remedy or assertion of a right, especially the right to take a particular case to court (right of action). The term is used in civil litigation. *See also* CLAIM FORM; PART 20 CLAIM.

claimant *n.* A person applying for relief against another person in an action, suit, petition, or any other form of court proceeding. Before the introduction of the *Civil Procedure Rules in 1999, a claimant was called a **plaintiff**. *Compare* DEFENDANT.

claim form (in civil proceedings) A formal written statement setting out details of the claimant, defendant, and the remedy being sought. The claim form may also contain details of the claim (the **particulars of claim**); alternatively, these can be served separately. Since the introduction of the *Civil Procedure Rules in 1999, the usual method of initiating civil proceedings is by issuing a claim form under Part 7 of the Rules; all previous methods (e.g. writ of summons, originating summons) have now been rendered obsolete. *See also* PART 8 CLAIM FORM; STATEMENT OF CASE.

claim of privilege *See* PRIVILEGE.

Claim Production Centre (CPC) An organization within the administrative structure of the *county courts system for the production of summonses issued by large-scale users of the county court, particularly utilities companies. It is located in Northampton. Around 90% of all claims are now dealt with in electronic form through the **County Court Bulk Centre (CCBC)**, which was established on the same site in 1990. Where the defendant contests the claim (or some part of it), the matter is transferred to the local county court.

class gift A gift to people of a certain specified category (e.g. "to my daughters"), rather than to people named individually, (e.g. "to my daughters A and B").

classical school of criminology One of the two major schools of *criminology. Originating in the 18th century and rooted in philosophical *utilitarianism, it sees man as a rational self-seeking being whose acts are freely chosen. Faced with alternative courses of action, he will weigh up the risks and benefits of each and act so as to maximize his pleasure and minimize his pain. This explains both the existence of crime and the need for a rational penal policy in which the threat of PUNISHMENT is used to deter criminal behaviour. To be an effective deterrent, punishment must be swift, certain, and proportionate to the offence.

From the late 19th century the classical school was challenged by the *positivist school of criminology, which downplays the role of free will and emphasizes the various social and psychological forces that may drive an individual to crime. More recently, aspects of the classical approach have been revived in so-called **rational choice theory**, which highlights the opportunistic element in many crimes and stresses the role of surveillance and environmental design (e.g. better street lighting) in crime prevention.

classification of animals *See* ANIMALS; DANGEROUS ANIMALS.

class rights Rights that attach to a clearly defined class of share (e.g. preference *shares) or are conferred upon a person for so long as he is a holder of any shares. In the latter case shareholders become a class in their own right. Typical class rights would relate to *dividends, return of capital on a *winding-up, or the right to appoint a director to the board. Class rights may only be altered either in accordance with a clause in the constitutional documents of the company (*see* ARTICLES OF ASSOCIATION) or with the consent of the class affected (Companies Act 2006 s 630). Shareholders from the class affected who did not agree to the alteration and who hold not less that 15% of the issued shares of the class may apply to court to have the change cancelled within 21 days (Companies Act 2006 s 633).

clause *n.* **1.** A subdivision of a document. A clause of a written contract contains a term or provision of the contract. Clauses are usually numbered consecutively (1, 2, etc.); subclauses may follow a clause, numbered 1.1, 1.1.1, etc. **2.** A section of a *Bill.

clean break The principle, enshrined in the Matrimonial Causes Act 1973 s 25A, that upon divorce, the court should exercise its powers so that that each spouse is financially independent of the other after the divorce if it is just and reasonable to do so. Generally this will involve the court requiring one spouse to pay to the other a lump sum instead of continuous periodical payments. In practice a clean break is generally only imposed where the parties are very wealthy or in a short childless marriage or where both spouses have well-established careers. Where it considers that a party could adjust without undue hardship to the termination of financial support in the foreseeable future, the court can also make a deferred clean break order under which periodical payments will terminate after a specified period. The Child Support Act 1991 makes it possible for a parent with care of a child to apply directly to the Child Support Agency for a maintenance assessment even when the divorce court has achieved a clean break (*see* CHILD SUPPORT MAINTENANCE).

clean hands A phrase from a *maxim of equity: he who comes to equity must come with clean hands, i.e. a person who makes a claim in equity must be free from any taint of fraud with respect to that claim. For example, a person seeking to enforce an agreement must not himself be in breach of it.

clearance *n.* **1.** A certificate acknowledging a ship's compliance with customs requirements. **2.** An indication from a taxing authority that a certain provision does not apply to a particular transaction. The procedure is only available when specified by statute, as, for example, on the reorganization of a company's share capital, on the demerger of a company's trade, and on a company's purchase of its own shares. Exceptionally, the Revenue grants a clearance under the extra-statutory concessional treatment whereby a dividend paid on the winding-up of a company is subject to capital gains tax and not to income tax.

Clerk of the House The principal permanent officer of the House of Commons.

Clerk of the Parliaments The principal permanent officer of the House of Lords.

clerk to the justices (justices' clerk, magistrates' clerk) A person who has a five-year magistrates' court qualification, or a barrister or solicitor of not less than five years' standing as an assistant to a magistrates' clerk, who is appointed to assist magistrates in court, particularly by giving advice about questions of law and matters of practice or procedure. The clerk or one of his staff will sit in court with the justices in order to advise them, but should not retire with them when they consider their verdict. On their request, he may advise them in private during their retirement, but should return to the court when his advice has been given. *See also* MAGISTRATES' COURT.

client *n.* A person who employs a solicitor to carry out legal business on behalf of himself or someone else. The relationship between a solicitor and his client is a *fiduciary one and any other transactions between them may be affected by *undue influence. Except in very limited circumstances under the direct access scheme, a solicitor's client cannot consult a barrister directly but only through his solicitor: the solicitor is therefore the barrister's client.

climate change levy A tax charged on the supply of electricity, gas, coal, and coke, as they are supplies that are regarded as leading to global warming. The levy is imposed by the Finance Act 2000 (sch 6) on any supply made on or after 1 April 2001.

Clinical Commissioning Groups (CCGs) Self-governing bodies within the *National Health Service that now commission most NHS services; they replaced the system of *Primary Care Trusts (PCTs) from 1 April 2013. CCGs have taken on many functions of the PCTs and in addition some functions previously undertaken by the Department of Health. All GP practices belong now to a CCG and the groups also include other health professionals, such as nurses. CCGs commission most services, including planned hospital care, rehabilitative care, urgent and emergency care (including out-of-hours), most community health services, and mental health and learning disability services. CCGs can commission any service provider that meets NHS standards and costs: these can be NHS hospitals, social enterprises, charities, or private sector providers.

clog or fetter on the equitable right to redeem Any provision in a *mortgage deed to prevent redemption on payment of the debt or performance of the obligation for which the security was given. Such provisions are void. An example is an option contained in the mortgage deed for the mortgagee to purchase the mortgaged property before or after the mortgage has been redeemed (*Jones v Morgan* [2001] EWCA Civ 995). **Unconscionable** provisions in a mortgage (for example, one to prevent redemption for 100 years) are also void. However, a company may issue irredeemable *debentures. A provision that would otherwise be unconscionable may be valid if the transaction containing it is a commercial arrangement rather than a mortgage. Thus, such provisions in mortgages of public houses or garages by their tenants or owners to breweries or oil companies will be upheld, provided that they do not infringe the contractual rules against *restraint of trade. Under the Unfair Terms in Consumer Contracts Regulations 1994 unfair redemption penalties may also be subject to challenge.

cloning *n.* The asexual production of a human organism that is genetically identical to a currently existing or previously existing human being. This is accomplished by replacing the nucleus of an egg with the nuclear material of a donor cell. If the resulting embryo is implanted into a womb with the aim of producing a child, this is referred to as **reproductive cloning**, a process which is currently unlawful under the Human Reproductive Cloning Act 2001. Where the cloned embryo is created in order to produce cells that will be transplanted into a person suffering from some disability or illness, the process is referred to as **therapeutic cloning**. Such a process may be lawful if licensed by the *Human Fertilization and Embryology Authority.

close *n.* Land that is enclosed.

close company A company under the control of its directors or five or fewer **participators**. The participators have or are entitled to acquire a share or interest in the capital or income of the company and can include *loan creditors. Special tax provisions apply to such companies.

closed-shop agreement A collective agreement requiring members of a particular group of employees to be or become members of a specified trade union.

A **pre-entry agreement** is one that prohibits an employer from engaging a relevant employee unless he is already a member of the union concerned. A **post-entry agreement** requires employees to join the specified union within a certain time after the employment commences.

Under the Trade Union and Labour Relations (Consolidation) Act 1992, all employees are free to join a trade union or not, as they wish. If an employer takes action, short of dismissal, against an employee to enforce membership of a union, the employee can complain to an *employment tribunal, which can order the employer to pay him compensation. Dismissal for failure to belong to a trade union is automatically unfair (*see* INADMISSIBLE REASON). In this case there are special minimum rates of *compensation payable. If, as a result of trade union pressure, an employer dismisses an employee for failing to belong to a union, the employer can join the union as a party to the dismissal proceedings and pass the liability to pay compensation on to the union.

A union that attempts to enforce a closed shop by industrial action loses the immunity from legal action that it would otherwise have if the action was in furtherance of a *trade dispute.

The effect of these provisions is that, while closed-shop agreements are not in themselves illegal, they are unenforceable by either employers or unions.

close investment holding company Any *close company that does not exist wholly or mainly to carry on a trade on a commercial basis or to hold land that is let to unconnected persons. A close investment holding company is subject to corporation tax at the full rate on its profits; it cannot benefit from the lower rates and reliefs that are available to other companies.

close of pleadings Formerly, a stage in the course of pleading in an action in the High Court that occurred 14 days after service of the reply, defence to counterclaim, or defence. This stage has been taken over by the functions of *case management and track *allocation.

closing order An order made by a local housing authority under the Housing Act 1985 prohibiting the use of a house, which it considers unfit for human habitation, for any purpose not approved by the authority.

closure *n.* The curtailing of debate on a question, particularly in the House of Commons, by carrying a motion (which cannot itself be debated) "that the question be now put". The result is that a vote on the question under debate must be taken immediately. *Compare* GUILLOTINE.

CLS *See* CRITICAL LEGAL STUDIES.

club *n.* An association regulated by rules that bind its members according to the law of contract. Club property is either vested in trustees for the members (**members' club**) or owned by a proprietor (often a company limited by guarantee; *see* LIMITED COMPANY) who operates the club as a business for profit (**proprietary club**). The committee is usually liable for club debts in the case of a members' club; the proprietor in the case of a proprietary club.

CMA *See* COMPETITION AND MARKETS AUTHORITY.

CMC *See* CASE MANAGEMENT CONFERENCE.

Coase theorem A concept often invoked in the *economic analysis of law. Named after the Nobel laureate Ronald Coase (1911–2013), it defines an "efficient" outcome as one in which the net sum of social wealth is maximized. The theorem is especially applicable to the law of *tort, where it can be used to test the extent to which the rules produce such an "efficient" outcome. The simple version of the Coase theorem may be stated as follows: where there are minimal transaction costs and clearly defined property rights, the "efficient" result will occur regardless of the choice of legal rule. However, avoiding accidents through safety measures inevitably incurs costs; the approach adopted by Coase therefore is that an "efficient" rule is one that minimizes the sum of accident costs and prevention costs, because such a rule will normally reduce social wealth the least. *Compare* PARETO EFFICIENCY; KALDOR-HICKS EFFICIENCY.

coastal waters *See* EXCLUSIVE ECONOMIC ZONE; FISHERY LIMITS; TERRITORIAL WATERS.

code *n.* A complete written formulation of a body of law, (e.g. the *Code Napoléon* in France). A code of English law does not exist, but a few specialized topics have been dealt with in this way by means of a *codifying statute (e.g. the Sale of Goods Act 1893, re-enacted with modifications by the Sale of Goods Act 1979).

codecision procedure A procedure introduced by the *Maastricht Treaty under which the *European Parliament gained a power to veto certain legislative proposals. If the *Council of the European Union and the European Parliament fail to agree after a second reading of the proposal by the Parliament, a **conciliation committee** of the Council and Parliament will attempt to reach a compromise. If no compromise is reached, the Parliament can reject the measure by absolute majority voting. Under the *Lisbon Treaty the codecision procedure was extended to most legislative areas and renamed the *ordinary legislative procedure. *Compare* ASSENT PROCEDURE; COOPERATION PROCEDURE.

Code for Crown Prosecutors Guidance issued by the Director of Public Prosecutions to the *Crown Prosecution Service under the Prosecution of Offenders Act 1985 on the general principles to be applied when making decisions about prosecutions. Crown Prosecutors must be satisfied that there is sufficient evidence to provide a realistic prospect of conviction and that a prosecution is needed in the public interest.

(((())) SEE WEB LINKS

• The Code for Crown Prosecutors

code of practice **1.** A body of rules for practical guidance only, or that sets out professional standards of behaviour, but does not have the force of law, e.g. the Highway Code. Under the provisions of the Fair Trading Act 1973 and the Enterprise Act 2002 the *Office of Fair Trading has the duty of encouraging trade associations to prepare and distribute to their members codes of practice for guidance in safeguarding and promoting the interests of UK consumers. Several such codes have been approved. Codes of practice have also been published by *ACAS, the Health and Safety, Equal Opportunities, and Racial Equality Commissions, and the Secretary of State for Work and Pensions, providing guidance to employers, employees, and their representatives on the fulfilment of their statutory obligations in relevant fields.

Generally, failure to comply with a code of practice does not automatically expose the party in breach to prosecution or any civil remedy. It may, however, be relied on as evidence tending to show that he has not fulfilled some relevant statutory requirement. **2.** Any of the codes issued by the Home Secretary under the Police and Criminal Evidence Act 1984 and approved by Parliament (the **PACE codes**); the codes were revised in 2004 and again in 2010. **Code A** deals with the exercise by police officers of statutory powers to search a person or a vehicle without first making an arrest. It also deals with the need for a police officer to make a record of a stop or encounter. **Code B** deals with police powers to search premises and to seize and retain property found on premises and persons. **Code C** sets out the requirements for the detention, treatment, and questioning of people in police custody by police officers. **Code D** concerns the main methods used by the police to identify people in connection with the investigation of offences and the keeping of accurate and reliable criminal records. **Code E** deals with the tape recording of interviews with suspects in the police station. **Code F** deals with the visual recording with sound of interviews with suspects. **Code G** deals with powers of arrest under section 24 of the Police and Criminal Evidence Act 1984 as amended by section 110 of the Serious Organised Crime and Police Act 2005. **Code H** deals with the detention and questioning of terrorism suspects in police custody.

codicil *n.* A document supplementary to a will, which is executed with the same formalities under the Wills Act 1837 (*see* EXECUTION OF WILL) and adds to, varies, or revokes provisions in the will. It must be proved with the will *see* PROVING A WILL. A codicil confirming a will normally republishes the will (*see* REPUBLICATION OF WILL) and may revive a will that has been revoked if that is the testator's clear intention. If many changes are made to the will it is better to execute a new will.

codifying statute A statute that sets out the whole of the existing law (i.e. both statute law and common law) on a particular subject. Such statutes are extremely rare; an example is the Law of Property Act 1925. *Compare* CONSOLIDATING STATUTE. *See also* INTERPRETATION.

coercion *n.* A defence available only to married women who have committed a crime (other than murder or treason) in the presence of, and under pressure from, their husbands. Its scope is unclear but may be wider than that of *duress in that it may cover economic and moral as well as physical pressure, though unlike duress it has to be proved (*see* BURDEN OF PROOF). If a wife is acquitted on grounds of coercion, her husband may be liable for the offence in question through his wife's innocent agency and/or for a crime involving a *threat.

cognates *pl. n.* Persons descended from a common ancestor.

cohabitants *pl. n.* Unmarried sexual partners who are living in a long-term stable relationship. English law, unlike that of some other jurisdictions, provides no coherent approach towards cohabitation and, unless a specific statutory provision provides otherwise, cohabitants are treated in law no differently than two strangers. The most crucial legal difference between a married and an unmarried couple is that, in the event of the relationship breaking down, the courts have no power to require one partner to transfer property to the other or to pay maintenance. The other important distinction is that if one party dies intestate (i.e. without making a will), then the remaining unmarried partner, unlike a spouse, has no automatic right to inherit all or part of the estate. An application can be made, however, under the Inheritance (Provision for Family and Dependants) Act 1975. In relation to any children, the distinction between "illegitimate" and "legitimate" children has now almost disappeared (*see* ILLEGITIMACY). An *unmarried father will automatically have parental responsibility for any child born after December 1993 if he is registered as the child's father on the child's birth certificate. Unmarried partners are protected under *domestic violence legislation, although the degree of protection offered is slightly less than that offered to their married counterparts. Normally statutes conferring rights on cohabitants apply only to heterosexual partners; however, a recent case decided that the phrase "as husband and wife" includes same-sex couples (*Ghaidan v Mendoza* [2002] 3 FCR 591 (CA)). This decision gave a homosexual partner the right to succeed to a tenancy on the death of his partner but could have wider implications. Same-sex partners now have the right to register a *civil partnership.

co-imperium *n.* Joint rule by two or more states of an entity that has a distinct international status (*compare* CONDOMINIUM). An example is the occupation and rule of Germany after 1945 by the four victorious powers.

collateral **1.** *adj.* Describing the relationship between people who share a common ancestor but are descended from him through different lines of descent. *See also* CONSANGUINITY. **2.** *adj.* Ancillary; subordinate but connected to the main subject, etc. **3.** *n.* Security that is additional to the main security for a debt (or an advantage to the mortgagee that is additional to the payment of interest). For example, a lender may require as collateral the assignment of an insurance policy in addition to the principal security of a mortgage on the borrower's home.

collateral advantage The situation in which a contracting party uses his stronger bargaining position to obtain terms that are advantageous to him, often disproportionately so, over and above the benefits conferred upon him by the core contract itself. Such an advantage may be conferred upon one of the parties to a contract by the inclusion of an *option to purchase or a **solus* tie, for example. Clauses that confer a collateral advantage in the context of a mortgage contract, thereby clogging or fettering the mortgagor's *equitable right to redeem, are susceptible to being struck down by the court.

collateral benefits Benefits received from a third party by the victim of a tortious injury in consequence of the injury, such as insurance money, sick pay, disability pensions, loans, social security benefits, or gifts from a disaster appeal fund. Some collateral benefits are taken into account when assessing the damages to be paid by the person liable for the injury; others, such as insurance money and gifts, are not.

Under the Social Security (Recovery of Benefits) Act 1997, the amount of social security benefits received by the victim for the first five years after injury, or until the making of the compensation payment (whichever is earlier), must be deducted from the total damages awarded by the court, or agreed by way of settlements, and be repaid to the state. Compensation under the Act is treated as having three elements; loss of earnings, cost of care, and loss of mobility. State benefits can only be deducted from the relevant head of damages awarded. No benefits can be deducted from damages awarded for pain and suffering.

collateral contract A subsidiary contract that induces a person to enter into a main contract. For example, if X agrees to buy from Y goods made by Z, and does so on the strength of Z's assurance as to the high quality of the goods, X and Z may be held to have made a collateral contract consisting of Z's promise as to quality given in consideration of X's promise to enter into the main contract with Y.

collective bargaining Negotiations between trade unions (acting for their members) and employers or employers' associations about terms and conditions of employment. Under the Trade Union and Labour Relations (Consolidation) Act 1992, a **collective agreement** (an agreement between trade union and employer resulting from collective bargaining) is not legally binding unless it is in writing and specifically states the parties' intention to be bound. Unenforceable collective agreements frequently include terms (relating to pay, discipline, etc.) that will become incorporated in individual employees' binding contracts of employment (*Edinburgh Council v Brown* [1999] IRLR 208). The written *statement of terms of employment, which the employer must give under the Employment Rights Act 1996, must refer the employee to the collective agreement, which must be reasonably accessible to him. Terms of a collective agreement that discriminate on grounds of any of the protected characteristics covered by the *Equality Act 2010 may be challenged by individuals in a court or employment tribunal and may be declared void. When a collective agreement provides that individual employees' contracts will circumscribe their right to strike, the employees will only be bound if their contracts contain that provision and the collective agreement was negotiated by an *independent trade union, is in writing, and is readily accessible to employees during working hours. The parties to a collective agreement containing procedures for determining complaints of unfair dismissal may apply to the Secretary of State for an order that those procedures be substituted for the statutory jurisdiction of employment tribunals. An order will only be made if the agreement was negotiated by an independent trade union, identifies the employees affected, and gives them remedies as beneficial as the statutory scheme and a right to independent arbitration or adjudication. *See also* DISCLOSURE OF INFORMATION; RECOGNITION PROCEDURE.

collective redundancy The proposed dismissal as redundant by an employer of 20 or more employees. In such a situation the employer is required, under the Trade Union and Labour Relations (Consolidation) Act 1992, to disclose information (*see* DISCLOSURE OF INFORMATION) and to consult with elected workers' representatives or representatives of a recognized trade union with a view to reaching agreement about ways of avoiding the dismissals, reducing the numbers of employees to be dismissed, and mitigating the consequences of the dismissals. If the employer fails to comply with these requirements the union may complain to an employment tribunal who may, if the complaint is upheld, issue a *protective award. Employment tribunals have held that notification of impending redundancies must take place at the earliest opportunity in order that representations by the union may be taken into account (Case C-188/03 *Junk v Kuhnel* [2005] IRLR 310 (ECJ)).

collective responsibility *See* CABINET.

collective security The centralized system of international rules, now embodied in the Charter of the United Nations, that governs the collective resort to force under the authority of the United Nations for the purpose of maintaining or restoring international peace and security. An example is the action by the international community during the Gulf War of 1991. It should be noted that the precise legal justification of this conflict is uncertain, the UN Security Council Resolution 678 stating only that its legal basis was under *Chapter VII of the UN Charter. Justification for the military action against Iraq undertaken by the USA and its allies in 2003 was claimed under the UN Security Council resolutions made at the time of the previous Gulf conflict, notably Resolutions 660 and 678. The legality of such a use remains highly doubtful. *See also* ENFORCEMENT ACTION.

collective trespass *See* TRESPASS.

collision clause (running-down clause) A clause in a marine insurance policy binding the underwriters to indemnify the insured in respect of any damages in tort he may be liable for as a result of his ship colliding with another. At common law, such a policy covers only the insured's physical losses. The clause is customarily restricted to three quarters of the damages in question. When two vessels collide, the damage done to each is added together and treated as a common loss. It is divided between insurers according to the proportion of blame attributable to each ship or, if this cannot be determined, equally.

collusion *n.* **1.** An improper agreement or bargain between parties that one of them should bring proceedings against the other. Collusion is no longer a bar to divorce or nullity proceedings, but it may affect the validity of a declaration of legitimacy. **2.** Any comparing of evidence between witnesses that intentionally or accidentally results in the evidence being tainted.

colony *n*. A territory that forms part of the Crown's dominions outside the UK. Although it may enjoy internal self-government, its external affairs are controlled by the UK government.

colourable *adj*. Describing that which is one thing in appearance but another in substance; for example, a symbolic residence in a parish for the purpose of qualifying for marriage there.

combat immunity A common law doctrine that operates to exclude civil liability for negligence and deliberate damage to property or person committed by the armed forces during certain combat operations.

comfort letter (administrative letter) Formerly, a letter sent by the Competition Directorate of the European Commission following a notification for exemption or *negative clearance of a commercial agreement that might infringe EU *competition law. Individual notifications for clearance under Article 101 of the Treaty on the Functioning of the European Union are no longer possible.

comitology A process in which the *European Commission, when implementing EU law, has to consult special advisory committees made up of experts from the various EU countries. The procedure is designed to ensure that, wherever possible, any measure put forward reflects the situation in each member state.

comity *n*. **1.** (*comitas gentium*) Neighbourly gestures or courtesies extended from one state to another, or others, without accepting a legal obligation to behave in that manner. Comity is founded upon the concept of sovereign equality among states and is expected to be reciprocal. It is possible for such practices, over a period of time and with common usage, to develop into rules of *customary international law, although this requires such behaviour to acquire a binding or compelling quality. *See* CUSTOM; OPINIO JURIS. **2.** *See* JUDICIAL COMITY.

Command Papers Documents that the government, by royal command, presents to Parliament for consideration. They include **white papers** and **green papers**. The former contain statements of policy or explanations of proposed legislation; the latter are essentially discussion documents.

command responsibility A criminal offence under the *International Criminal Court Act 2001. It provides that a military commander is responsible for offences committed by forces under his effective command and control where he knew, or should have known, that his forces were committing such offences and failed to take all necessary and reasonable measures to prevent their commission.

commercial agent An *agent who solicits business from potential customers on behalf of a principal. In the EU the contracts of many commercial agents are governed by directive 86/653, which gives them substantial rights to claim compensation or an indemnity on termination of their agency agreement and implies other terms into their contracts; for example, in relation to payment of commission and notice periods for termination of the agreement. In Great Britain this directive is implemented by the Commercial Agents (Council Directive) Regulations 1993 as amended with similar regulations for Northern Ireland.

Commercial Court A court forming part of the *Queen's Bench Division of the High Court and specializing in the trial of commercial cases, notably those relating to shipping, commodity trading, and large commercial transactions. Many of the court's cases arise from the awards of arbitrators (*see* ARBITRATION). The judges of the court are nominated by the Lord Chief Justice from among the Queen's Bench *puisne judges who have special experience of commercial matters.

commission *n.* **1.** Authority to exercise a power or a direction to perform a duty; for example, a commission of a *justice of the peace. **2.** A body directed to perform a particular duty. Examples are the *Charity Commission and the *Law Commission. **3.** A sum payable to an *agent in return for his performing a particular service. This may, for example, be a percentage of the sum for which he has secured a contract of sale of his principal's property. The circumstances in which a commission is payable depend on the terms of the contract between principal and agent. The terms on which commission is paid to a *commercial agent are set down in the EU directive 86/653. **4.** Authorization by a court or a judge for a witness to be examined on oath by a court, judge, or other authorized person, to provide evidence for use in court proceedings. The procedure is used when the witness is unlikely to be able to attend the hearing (e.g. because of illness). If the witness is still unable to attend when the court hearing takes place the written evidence is read by the court.

Commissioner *n.* (in the EU) *See* EUROPEAN COMMISSION.

commissioner for oaths A person appointed by the Lord Chief Justice to administer oaths or take affidavits. By statute, every solicitor who holds a *practising certificate has the powers of a commissioner for oaths, but he may not exercise these powers in proceedings in which he is acting for any of the parties or in which he is interested. Thus when an affidavit must be sworn, the client cannot use his own solicitor but must go to another solicitor to witness the swearing.

Commission for Local Administration in England A commission established by the Local Government Act 1974 to investigate complaints by the public of injustice suffered through maladministration by local authorities and certain other bodies. It consists of the *Parliamentary Ombudsman and two **Local Government Ombudsmen** for the various regions. Certain matters (e.g. decisions affecting the public generally and the conduct of criminal investigations) are outside their competence. Complaints to an Ombudsman must normally be made in writing, either directly or through a member of the local authority concerned. Ombudsmen's reports are sent to the complainant and the authority concerned and are also made public. Separate arrangements exist for Scotland, Wales, and Northern Ireland.

(⊕) SEE WEB LINKS
• Website of the Local Government Ombudsman for England

Commission for Racial Equality (**CRE**) A body appointed by the Home Secretary under the Race Relations Act 1976 with the general aim of promoting equality of opportunity and good relations between different racial groups. Since 1 October 2007 the functions of the CRE have been integrated into the *Equality and Human Rights Commission.

Commission of the European Communities *See* EUROPEAN COMMISSION.

committal for sentence The procedure whereby a person convicted in a magistrates' court is sent to the Crown Court for sentencing when the sentencing powers of the magistrates' court are not considered sufficient.

committal in civil proceedings An order that a person be committed to prison that may be used as a punishment for *contempt of court (e.g. where there has been disobedience of an order of the court or disruption of court proceedings).

committal proceedings Formerly, a preliminary hearing in a magistrates' court held before a case was sent to be tried before a jury in the Crown Court. s. There were two forms of committal proceedings under section 6 of the Magistrates' Courts Act 1980: committal without consideration of the evidence or committal with consideration of the evidence. No oral evidence was heard. The prosecution had to establish a prima facie case before the case could be committed to the Crown Court and the defence could make a submission of no case to answer. The test for the magistrates was whether the prosecution evidence taken at its highest was such that a jury properly directed could not properly convict on it (*R v Galbraith* [1981] 1 WLR 1039). Committal hearings for indictable-only offences were abolished in 2001 and committal hearings where the accused was charged with an *offence triable either way and had elected to be tried in the Crown Court were abolished in 2013.

Committee of the Regions (CoR) An EU advisory body set up in 1994 and composed of representatives of regional and local authorities. It has to be consulted before EU decisions are taken on those matters specified by the treaties: these include regional policy, the environment, and transport.

Committee of the whole House A committee of which all members of the House of Commons or the House of Lords are members. In the Lords it sits for the committee stage of all public Bills. In the Commons the committee stage is normally taken by a *standing committee, but major Bills (particularly if controversial) are sometimes referred instead to a whole House committee. Certain matters concerning expenditure and taxation were formerly considered by the whole House sitting as the **Committee of Supply** or the **Committee of Ways and Means**, but since 1967 they have been dealt with by the House sitting as such.

common *n.* A *profit *à prendre* enjoyed by a number of landowners over *common land. A right of common may be *appurtenant, in gross (i.e. independent of any *dominant tenement), or *pur cause de vicinage* ("by reason of neighbourhood": the right to allow animals grazing common land to stray onto adjoining common land). They generally comprise rights of pasture (grazing), piscary (fishing), turbary (rare; a right to take turf), *ferae naturae* (a right to take animals), *estovers, etc., and unless they exist in gross are usually limited to the reasonable needs of the dominant tenements.

Common Agricultural Policy (CAP) The agricultural policy of the EU as set out in Articles 32–38 of the Treaty of Rome. The overall aims of the CAP are to increase agricultural productivity, ensure a fair standard of living for the agricultural community, stabilize markets, assure the availability of supplies, and ensure that supplies reach consumers at a reasonable price. The Treaty is supplemented by a wide range of EU directives in this field. *See also* INTERVENTION.

common assault *See* ASSAULT.

Common Budget *See* COMMON EXTERNAL TARIFF.

common carrier *See* CARRIER.

common design The intention assumed to be shared by those engaged in a joint illegal enterprise: each party is liable for anything done during the pursuance of that enterprise, including any unexpected consequences that arise (*R v Bainbridge* [1960] 1 QB 129). If, however, one of the parties does something that was not agreed beforehand, the others may not be held responsible for the consequences of this act (*Davies v DPP* [1954] AC 378 (HL)). *See also* ACCESSORY.

common duty of care The duty of an occupier of land or premises to take reasonable care to see that visitors will be reasonably safe in using the premises for the purposes for which they are invited or permitted to be there (Occupiers' Liability Act 1957 s 2(2)). *See* OCCUPIER'S LIABILITY.

Common External Tariff (CET) The tariff of import duties payable on certain goods entering any member state of the European Union from non-EU countries. The CET prevents the distortion of trade that would occur if member states set their own import duties on products coming into their state from outside the EU. The Tariff contributes to the **Common Budget** of the EU, from which subsidies due under the *Common Agricultural Policy are paid.

Common Fisheries Policy (CFP) A fishing policy agreed between members of the European Community in 1983. It lays down annual catch limits (*quotas) for each state for major species of fish, a 12-mile exclusive fishing zone for each state, and an equal-access zone of 200 nautical miles from its coast, within which any member state is allowed to fish. There are some exceptions to these regulations. The CFP is handled by the European Commission's Fisheries Directorate General. It was reviewed in 1992 and subjected to major reforms (including severe cuts in quotas) in 2002. *See also* FISHERY LIMITS.

common form probate *See* NON-CONTENTIOUS PROBATE BUSINESS.

common heritage of mankind principle The principle that areas of Antarctica, the sea bed, and outer space should not be monopolized for the benefit of one state or group of states alone, but should be treated as if they are to be used to the benefit of all mankind. For example, Article 4 of the Moon Treaty 1979 states that exploration "shall be the province of all mankind and shall be carried out for the benefit and in the interests of all countries, irrespective of their degree of economic or scientific development". *See* RES COMMUNIS.

commonhold *n*. A third way of owning land, in addition to *freehold and *leasehold, that was introduced into England and Wales by the Commonhold and Leasehold Reform Act 2002. It is intended for developments in which individual properties, such as flats, houses, or shops, are owned and occupied by separate persons, but there are common parts, such as stairways and walkways, that need to remain in central ownership and to be maintained. The Act was passed to remedy defects in the most common way of holding such land, namely long leases.

Each separate property in a commonhold development is a **unit**; the owner is a **unit-holder**. The body owning the common parts is the **commonhold association**, a private company limited by guarantee. Each unit-holder is a member of that company. The company membership is limited to the unit-holders, and the memorandum and articles of the company must specify the land in relation to which the association exercises function, and whose business it is to own and manage the common parts. The commonhold association will also need to create a **Commonhold Community**

Statement (CCS) setting out the rules and regulations of the particular community. The commonhold association with its common parts and all the associated units will be registered at the Land Registry. It will be possible for leasehold developments to convert to commonhold, but only by the consent of all parties.

The Act has not been used as widely as anticipated, so there is currently little commonhold land.

common land Land subject to rights of *common. The Commons Registration Act 1965 provides for the registration with local authorities of all common land in England and Wales, its owners, and claims to rights of common over it. Subject to the investigation by Commons Commissioners of disputed cases, and to exceptions for land becoming or ceasing to be common land, registration provides conclusive evidence that land is common land and also of the rights of common over it. Rights could be lost by failure to register.

common law **1.** The part of English law based on rules developed by the royal courts during the first three centuries after the Norman Conquest (1066) as a system applicable to the whole country, as opposed to local customs. The Normans did not attempt to make new law for the country or to impose French law on it; they were mainly concerned with establishing a strong central administration and safeguarding the royal revenues, and it was through machinery devised for these purposes that the common law developed. Royal representatives were sent on tours of the shires to check on the conduct of local affairs generally, and this involved their participating in the work of local courts. At the same time there split off from the body of advisers surrounding the king (the *curia regis*) the first permanent royal court – the *Court of Exchequer, sitting at Westminster to hear disputes concerning the revenues. Under Henry II (reigned 1154–89), to whom the development of the common law is principally due, the royal representatives were sent out on a regular basis (their tours being known as circuits) and their functions began to be exclusively judicial. Known as *justiciae errantes* (wandering justices), they took over the work of the local courts. In the same period there appeared at Westminster a second permanent royal court, the *Court of Common Pleas. These two steps mark the real origins of the common law. The judges of the Court of Common Pleas so successfully superimposed a single system on the multiplicity of local customs that, as early as the end of the 12th century, reference is found in court records to the custom of the kingdom. In this process they were joined by the judges of the Court of Exchequer, which began to exercise jurisdiction in many cases involving disputes between subjects rather than the royal revenues, and by those of a third royal court that gradually emerged – the Court of King's Bench (*see* COURT OF QUEEN'S BENCH). The common law was subsequently supplemented by *equity, but it remained separately administered by the three courts of common law until they and the Court of Chancery (all of them sitting in Westminster Hall until rehoused in the Strand in 1872) were replaced by the *High Court of Justice under the Judicature Acts 1873–75. **2.** Rules of law developed by the courts as opposed to those created by statute. **3.** A general system of law deriving exclusively from court decisions.

common-law marriage **1.** A marriage recognized as valid at common law although not complying with the usual requirements for marriage. Such marriages are only recognized today if (1) they are celebrated outside England and there is no local form of marriage reasonably available to the parties or (2) they are celebrated by military chaplains in a foreign territory (or on a ship in foreign waters), and one of the parties to the marriage is serving in the Forces in that territory. The form of marriage is a declaration that the parties take each other as husband and wife. **2.** Loosely, the situation of two unmarried people living together as husband and wife (*see* COHABITANTS). It is often believed that legal rights attach to such a relationship. This is not the case.

common mistake *See* MISTAKE.

common money bond *See* BOND.

Common Serjeant The title held by the second most senior *circuit judge at the *Central Criminal Court. It was formerly an ancient office of the City of London, first mentioned in its records in 1291. Serjeants-at-law were the highest order at the English Bar from the 13th or 14th centuries until the King's Counsel took priority in the 17th century. Until 1873 the judges of the common law courts were appointed from the serjeants; the order of serjeants was dissolved in 1877.

Commonwealth (British Commonwealth) *n.* A voluntary association consisting of the UK and many of its former colonies or dependencies (e.g. protectorates) that have attained full independence and are recognized by international law as separate countries. The earliest to obtain independence (e.g. Canada and Australia) did so by virtue of the Statute of Westminster 1931, but the majority have been granted it individually by subsequent Independence Acts. Some (such as Canada and Australia) are still technically part of the Crown's dominions; others (e.g. India) have become republics. All accept the Crown as the symbol of their free association and the head of the Commonwealth.

Commonwealth citizen Under the British Nationality Act 1948, a status synonymous with that of *British subject. By the British Nationality Act 1981 (which replaced the 1948 Act as from 1 January 1983 and gave the expression British subject a very limited meaning), it was redefined as a wide secondary status. It now includes every person who is either a British citizen, a British Overseas Territories citizen, a British National (Overseas), a British Overseas citizen, a British subject (in its current sense), or a citizen of one of the independent Commonwealth countries.

commorientes *pl. n.* [Latin] Persons who die at the same time or when the order of death is uncertain. Under the Law of Property Act 1925 s 184, commorientes are presumed (so far as the devolution of their property is concerned) to have died in order of seniority. Thus a bequest by the younger to the elder is treated as having lapsed. However, this rule may be displaced by a contrary intention expressed in a will by use of a *survivorship clause. Note also that under the Administration of Estates Act 1925 s 45(2A) (as amended by the Law Reform (Succession) Act 1995), where an intestate dies after 1 January 1996 a surviving spouse will only take on the intestacy if she or he survives the intestate by 28 days. The commorientes rule does not apply for inheritance tax purposes – the Inheritance Tax Act 1984 s 4(2) provides that where the order of deaths is uncertain it is assumed neither person survived the other.

community *n.* A *local government area in Wales, as set out in the Local Government (Wales) Act 1994, consisting of a division of a *county or a county borough and equivalent to an English civil parish. All communities have meetings and many have an elected community council, which is a *local authority with a number of minor functions (e.g. the provision of allotments, bus shelters, and recreation grounds). A community council may by resolution call its area a town, itself a town council, and its chairman the town mayor, either in Welsh or in English.

Community dimension (in EU mergers law) *See* MERGER.

community home An institution for the accommodation and maintenance of children and young persons in care. Community homes are provided by local authorities and voluntary organizations under the Children Act 1989. A local authority may be liable for the acts of children in community homes.

community interest company A *limited company registered under sections 26-63 of the Companies (Audit, Investigations and Community Enterprise) Act 2004. Registration requires the approval of the Regulator of Community Interest Companies who must be satisfied that the company satisfies the "community interest test", namely, that a reasonable person would consider that the company's activities are being carried on for the benefit of the community. A company formed for a political purpose cannot be registered as a community interest company. There are limitations as to the amount of dividends such a company can pay to its members.

Community law (EU law) The law of the European Union (as opposed to the national laws of the member states). It consists of the treaties establishing the EU (together with subsequent amending treaties), *Community legislation, and decisions of the *European Court of Justice. Any provision of the treaties or of Community legislation that is directly applicable or directly effective in a member state forms part of the law of that state and prevails over its national law in the event of any inconsistency between the two.

Community Legal Service *See* LEGAL AID.

Community legislation Laws made by the *European Parliament acting jointly with the *Council of the European Union and the *European Commission. Each body has legislative powers but most legislation is now made by the Parliament and Council, based on proposals by the Commission. The role of the Parliament in the legislative process was strengthened under the Single European Act 1986 and the Maastricht Treaty 1992 but most decisively under the 2007 Treaty of Lisbon (*see* ORDINARY LEGISLATIVE PROCEDURE). Community legislation is in the form of regulations, directives, and decisions. **Regulations** are of general application, binding in their entirety, and directly applicable in all member states without the need for individual member states to enact these domestically (*see* COMMUNITY LAW). **Directives** are addressed to one or more member states and require them to achieve (by amending national law if necessary) specified results. They are not directly applicable – they do not create enforceable Community rights in member states until the state has legislated in accordance with the directive: the domestic statute then creates the rights for the citizens of that country. A directive cannot therefore impose legal obligations on individuals or private bodies, but by its **direct effect** it confers rights on individuals against the state and state bodies, even before it has been implemented by changes to national law, by decisions of the European court. **Decisions** may be addressed either to states or to persons and are binding on them in their entirety. Both the Council and the Commission may also make **recommendations**, give **opinions**, and issue *notices, but these are not legally binding.

community of assets (community of property) The sharing of ownership of matrimonial property, such as the home and furniture, as an automatic consequence of marriage. This is not a feature of English law. *See* FAMILY ASSETS.

community order A sentence that may be ordered under the Criminal Justice Act 2003 imposing one or more of 12 specified requirements: an *unpaid work requirement, an *activity requirement, a *programme requirement, a *prohibited activity requirement, a *curfew requirement, an *exclusion requirement, a *residence requirement, a *mental health treatment requirement, a *drug treatment requirement, an *alcohol treatment requirement, a *supervision requirement, and (in the case of an offender aged under 25) an *attendance centre requirement. In certain cases the court may additionally impose an electronic monitoring requirement. Under the Criminal Justice and Immigration Act 2008 the system of community orders was extended to offenders aged 18 or under in the form of *youth rehabilitation orders. The same Act provides that adult community orders can only be imposed where: (i) the offence is imprisonable; or (ii) the offender has been convicted and fined on three previous occasions. *See also* SUSPENDED SENTENCE.

Community Patent A proposed European Union *patent that is likely to become available in 2014; it will consist of a single, unitary, centrally enforceable patent to cover all the member states of the EU except Spain and Italy. The EU Community Patent is distinct from the current European Patent, which is granted under the European Patent Convention and does not have unitary effect.

community patient A patient subject to a *Community Treatment Order.

community punishment order *See* UNPAID WORK REQUIREMENT.

community rehabilitation order *See* SUPERVISION REQUIREMENT.

community sentence A sentence that consists of or includes a *community order or a *youth rehabilitation order.

Community Trade Mark (CTM) A *trade mark that is registered for the whole of the European Union. It can be obtained by application to national trade mark offices or the Community Trade Mark Office at Alicante, Spain. The European Commission adopted the Regulation for the Community Trade Mark, Regulation 40/94, on 20 December 1993; UK legislation was included in the Trade Marks Act 1994. Marks are registered for a period of ten years and may be renewed on payment of fees.

(⊕) SEE WEB LINKS

• Information on the Community Trade Mark from the website of the Office of Harmonization for the Internal Market: includes case law

Community Treatment Order (CTO) An order made under the Mental Health Act 1983 (as amended by the Mental Health Act 2007) in respect of a patient who has been detained for treatment, which discharges the patient subject to certain conditions. The conditions will be those deemed necessary (i) to ensure that the patient receives medical treatment; (ii) to prevent the risk of harm to the patient's health or safety; and (iii) to protect other persons (s 17A). The order is made by the patient's *responsible clinician with the support of an *approved mental health professional. All CTO patients—so-called **community patients**—are required to make themselves available for medical examination and can be recalled to hospital by notice in writing (exercisable immediately).

commutation *n.* **1.** The modification of a prison sentence so as to make the punishment to which a person has been condemned less severe. **2.** An ad hoc exercise of executive clemency by which the Home Secretary (in the monarch's name) shortens the duration of a sentence at any time for any reason without reference to any standards.

commutative contract *See* CONTRACT OF EXCHANGE.

Companies Court A court forming part of the *Chancery Division of the High Court. It deals with matters arising out of the Companies Act and other related statutes.

Companies House The office of the Registrar of Companies (*see* REGISTRATION OF A COMPANY). Companies with a registered office in England or Wales are served by the registry at Cardiff; those in Scotland by the registry in Edinburgh. Certain documents lodged there are open to inspection. These documents include the *accounts of limited companies, the *annual return, any *prospectus, the *memorandum and *articles of association, and particulars of the directors, the secretary, the *registered office, some types of company *charge, and notices of liquidation.

(⊕) SEE WEB LINKS

• Companies House website: includes guidance on incorporating and winding up a company

company *n.* An association formed to conduct business or other activities in the name of the association. Most companies are incorporated (*see* INCORPORATION) and therefore have a legal personality distinct from those of their members. Incorporation is usually by registration under the Companies Act 2006 (*see* REGISTRATION OF A COMPANY) but may be by private Act of Parliament (*see* STATUTORY COMPANY), by a public general Act (public corporation), or by royal charter (**chartered company**). Shareholders and directors are generally protected when the company goes out of business. *See* COMMUNITY INTEREST COMPANY; FOREIGN COMPANY; LIMITED COMPANY; PRIVATE COMPANY; PUBLIC COMPANY; UNLIMITED COMPANY; WELSH COMPANY.

In the *corporation tax legislation, a "company" means any body corporate or unincorporated association (Taxes Act 1988, s 832(1),(2)) but does not include a partnership, a local authority, or a local authority association (*Frampton (Trustees of the Worthing Rugby Football Club) v IRC* [1987] STC 273; *Blackpool Marton Rotary Club v Marin* [1988] STC 823). Authorized unit trusts are treated as if they were companies (Taxes Act 1988 s 468).

company meeting *See* GENERAL MEETING.

company member A person who holds *shares in a company or, in the case of a company that does not issue shares (such as a company limited by guarantee), any of those who have signed the founding documents or have been admitted to membership by the directors. *See* LIMITED COMPANY.

company name (registered name) The title of a registered company, as stated in the application for registration, on the company's certificate of incorporation, and in the *Register of Companies. The names with which companies can be registered are restricted (*see* BUSINESS NAME). The name must appear clearly in full outside the *registered office and other business premises, upon the company seal, and upon certain documents issuing from the company, including notepaper and invoices (Companies Act 2006 s 82–85; Companies (Trading Disclosure Regulations) 2008). Noncompliance is an offence and fines can be levied. Under the Insolvency Act 1986, it may be an offence for a director of a company that has gone into insolvent liquidation to re-use the company name (Insolvency Act 1986 s 216). *See also* CHANGE OF NAME; LIMITED COMPANY.

company secretary An officer of a company whose role will vary according to the nature of the company but will generally be concerned with the administrative duties imposed upon the company by the Companies Act (e.g. delivering documents to *Companies House). Under the Companies Act 2006 (s 271) every public company is required to have a company secretary who must be qualified to act as such. A private company is no longer required to have a company secretary (Companies Act 2006 s 270).

compellable witness A witness who may lawfully be required to give evidence and who may be punished for *contempt of court for refusal. In principle every person who is competent to be a witness is compellable. In criminal proceedings, the spouse or civil partner of the accused is generally competent and compellable as a witness for the defence. However, the spouse or civil partner of the accused is not normally compellable as a witness for the prosecution. *See* COMPETENCE.

compensation *n.* Monetary payment to compensate for loss or damage. When someone has committed a criminal offence that caused personal injury, loss, or damage, and he has been convicted for this offence or it was taken into account when sentencing for another offence, the court may make a **compensation order** requiring the offender to pay compensation to the person suffering the loss (with interest, if need be). The power of the court to make compensation orders is governed by the Powers of Criminal Courts (Sentencing) Act 2000 sections 130–34. Magistrates' courts may make orders in respect of compensation. The court must take into account the offender's means and should avoid making excessively high orders or orders to be paid in long-term instalments. If the offender cannot afford to pay both a fine and compensation, priority should be given to payment of compensation. A compensation order may be made for funeral expenses or bereavement in respect of death resulting from an offence other than a death due to a motor-vehicle accident. Potential claimants and maximum compensation for bereavement are the same as those under the Fatal Accidents Act 1976 (*see* FATAL ACCIDENTS). An order may only be made in respect of injury, loss, or damage (other than loss suffered by a person's dependants in consequence of his death) due to a motor-vehicle accident if (1) it is for damage to property occurring while it was outside the owner's possession in the case of offences under the Theft Act 1968, or (2) the offender was uninsured to use the vehicle and compensation is not payable under the *Motor Insurers' Bureau agreement. A court that does not award compensation must give reasons. Victims of *criminal injury may apply for compensation under the *Criminal Injuries Compensation Scheme. Under the Theft Act 1968, a *restitution order in monetary terms may be made when the stolen goods are no longer in existence; this kind of order is equivalent to a compensation order. Compensation orders may be made in addition to, or instead of, other sentences. A court must order a parent or guardian of an offender under the age of 17 to pay a compensation order on behalf of the offender unless the parent or guardian cannot be found or it would be unreasonable to order him to pay it.

A person who has been wrongfully convicted of a criminal offence may apply to the Home Secretary for compensation, which is awarded upon the assessment of an independent assessor.

An *employment tribunal may order an employer to pay compensation to an employee who has been unfairly dismissed (*see* UNFAIR DISMISSAL). The compensation comprises a **basic award** of a sum equivalent to the statutory *redundancy payment to which a redundant employee would be entitled (with a minimum of £5,500 (2013) when dismissal is for certain automatically unfair reasons including trade union activity), and a **compensatory award** representing the loss that the employee suffers because of the dismissal. Under the Enterprise and Regulatory Reform Act 2013, the compensatory award will be capped at one year's pay or £74,200, whichever is the lower, and the calculation will be based on the statutory definition of a week's pay in the Employment Rights Act 1996, thus excluding pension contributions and fringe benefits.

Additional compensation may be awarded if the employer does not comply with an order by the tribunal to re-employ the employee; the additional award will be between 26 and 52 weeks' pay. Limits on the amount of weekly pay that can be used in these calculations are set by regulations made by the Secretary of State for Business, Innovation and Skills and reviewed annually. In 2013, the limit on a week's pay was £450. The tribunal may reduce any compensation by an appropriate proportion when the employee's conduct has contributed to his dismissal. Compensation may also be adjusted where either party fails to comply with a relevant code of practice. The employee is under the same duty to mitigate his loss as someone claiming damages in the courts. Thus if he unreasonably refuses an offer of a new job he will not be compensated for his continued unemployment thereafter. If the employee was dismissed for his failure to enter into a *closed-shop agreement, following pressure by a trade union for his dismissal, the employer can pass on to the trade union the liability to pay compensation. Compensation may also be awarded by an employment tribunal when there is a finding of unlawful discrimination. In such cases there is no upper limit on the amount of damages. This award can also include an amount for hurt feelings.

compensation culture A culture in which many citizens have come to believe that for all ills that befall them another must be to blame, and that *compensation by way of *damages should therefore be sought. It is often alleged that such a culture has become prevalent in the UK during recent decades. This attitude has major implications for, amongst others, the insurance industry.

competence *n.* (of witnesses) The legal capacity of a person to be a *witness. Every person of sound mind and sufficient understanding is generally competent as a witness. A child is competent to give evidence unless it appears to the court that the child is incapable of giving intelligible testimony. However, a child below the age of 14 years may only give *unsworn evidence. The spouse or civil partner of an accused is generally competent and compellable as a witness for the defence, and is also competent (but not normally a *compellable witness) as a witness for the prosecution.

competent patient (patient with capacity) A patient who has the mental capacity to *consent to medical treatment. The Mental Capacity Act 2005 defines a competent patient as one who is able to take a decision for himself, i.e. who can understand and retain the information relevant to the decision, weigh that information as part of the process of making the decision, and communicate that decision (s 3(1)). The distinction between a competent patient and an *incompetent patient is crucial: whereas consent is required before treating the former, it is not required from the latter. The wishes of a competent patient must be respected and he is entitled to refuse any medical intervention, even life-saving treatment. The Mental Capacity Act specifies that a medical professional should presume that a patient is competent unless there is evidence to the contrary: a person is not to be treated as incompetent merely because he makes an unwise decision (*Re C* (*Adult: Refusal of Treatment*) [1994] 1 FLR 31; *Re B* (*Adult: Refusal of Medical Treatment*) [2002] EWHC 429 (Fam)).

Competition and Markets Authority (CMA) A new body that combines the functions of the former Competition Commission, which handled competition law and its enforcement in the UK, and the *Office of Fair Trading. It was established under the Enterprise and Regulatory Reform Act 2013 and began operating in April 2014.

competition law The branch of law concerned with the regulation of *anticompetitive practices, *restrictive trade practices, and *abuses of a dominant position or market power. Such laws prohibit *cartels and other commercial restrictive agreements. In the UK the Competition Act 1998 and Enterprise Act 2002 contain the legislative provisions. Throughout the EU, *Articles 101 and 102 of the Treaty on the Functioning of the European Union and regulations made under those provisions contain the legal rules in this area, which constitute EU competition law. In the USA competition law is known as **antitrust law**.

competitive tendering The introduction of competition into the provision of public services with the aim of improving the cost-effectiveness and quality of these services. It affected a wide range of public bodies, from local authorities to the prison service:

public services were supplied by the body (usually a private-sector company) that submitted the most competitive tender for the service in question. Examples of services most commonly provided by this means were refuse collection, the provision of school meals, and residential care for the elderly. These rules were principally contained in the Local Government Acts 1988 and 1992. The Local Government Act 1999 abolished compulsory competitive tendering and replaced it with a duty to provide *best value, whereby authorities must have regard to economy, efficiency, and effectiveness when exercising their functions.

complainant *n.* In criminal proceedings, a person who makes a formal *complaint that an offence has been committed. In relation to rape or other sexual offences the complainant is the person against whom the offence is alleged to have been committed. In such cases the complainant is allowed by statute to remain anonymous; evidence relating to her previous sexual experience cannot be given (unless the court especially rules otherwise).

complaint *n.* **1.** The document used to start certain types of criminal proceedings in a magistrates' court, or the process of using such a document to start proceedings. **2.** A formal allegation of a crime. *See* COMPLAINANT.

completely constituted trust In general, a valid *declaration of trust becomes "completely constituted" when legal title to the trust property is transferred to the trustee(s); the only exceptions are where the *rule in *Re Rose* applies or where it would be unconscionable for an intended voluntary transfer of property to be resiled from (*Penington v Waine* [2002] 4 All ER 215). In some cases, such as where there is a self-declaration of trust, the trust is completely constituted by the declaration itself but in others it is necessary to deliver the trust property to the trustee. When dealing with certain types of property, specific formalities must be complied with for a trust to be completely constituted. For example, a declaration of a trust of shares will require transfer of the shares and this will involve the completion and registration of a certificate transferring the same. An **incompletely constituted trust** will be void.

completion *n.* (in land law) The point at which ownership of land that is the subject of a contract for its sale changes hands. The purchaser hands over any unpaid balance of the price in exchange for the title deeds and a valid conveyance of the land to him if the land is unregistered. If the land is registered, the purchaser receives a simple form of transfer that must be lodged at the appropriate District *Land Registry.

composition *n.* An agreement between a debtor and his creditors discharging the debts in exchange for payment of a proportion of what is due. The debtor may have to register the agreement as a *deed of arrangement. *See also* SCHEME OF ARRANGEMENT; VOLUNTARY ARRANGEMENT.

compos mentis [Latin: possessed of mind] Of sound mind: sane. A valid contract must be made by someone who is *compos mentis. See* CAPACITY TO CONTRACT.

compound *vb.* **1.** To make a *composition with creditors. **2.** *See* COMPOUNDING AN OFFENCE.

compounding an offence The offence of accepting or agreeing to accept *consideration for not disclosing information that might assist in convicting or prosecuting someone who has committed an *indictable offence (consideration here does not include reasonable compensation for loss or injury caused by the offence: Criminal Law Act 1967 s 5). There is also a special statutory offence of advertising a reward for stolen goods on the basis that "no questions will be asked" or that the person producing the goods "will be safe from inquiry" (Theft Act 1968 s 23).

compound settlement A settlement of land arising from a series of trust instruments, e.g. a resettlement following the barring of an *entailed interest. Under the Settled Land Act 1925 the trustees of the original settlement (or if there are none, those of the resettlement) are treated as the trustees of the compound settlement. Thus the tenant for life is always able to overreach the interests of all other beneficiaries (*see* OVERREACHING).

compromis d'arbitrage [French] Agreements between states to submit disputes between them to an arbitration tribunal. *See also* ARBITRATION.

compromise *n.* The settlement of a disputed claim by agreement between the parties. Any court proceedings already started are terminated. The terms of the settlement can be incorporated in a judgment by the court (called a **consent order**) or the terms can form a contract between the parties.

compromise agreement *See* SETTLEMENT AGREEMENT.

compulsory jurisdiction The capacity of an international tribunal to order and thus compel states to litigate a dispute before it. The compulsory jurisdiction of the *International Court of Justice, under Article 36(2) of its Statute, depends on voluntary declarations in advance by the states concerned. This is known as the *optional clause.

compulsory purchase The enforced acquisition of land for public purposes, by statutory authority and on payment of compensation. Authority may be given for a specific acquisition, but public and local authorities have wide powers to acquire any land required for particular functions, such as education. These powers are normally exercised under the Acquisition of Land Act 1981, and compensation is assessed under the Land Compensation Acts 1961 and 1973. A compulsory purchase order is submitted for confirmation to the appropriate government minister, whose decision is preceded by an inquiry into public objections. In most cases the procedure includes the service of a *notice to treat on the landowner, who then negotiates compensation. Any dispute about compensation is decided by the Lands Chamber of the *Upper Tribunal. *See also* SPECIAL PROCEDURE ORDERS.

compulsory winding-up (compulsory liquidation) A procedure for winding up a company by the court based on a petition made under circumstances listed in the Insolvency Act 1986. The main grounds for this type of petition are that the company is unable to pay its debts or that the court is of the opinion that it is in the interests of the company that a *just and equitable winding-up should be made (Insolvency Act 1986 s 122). Any director, *contributory, or creditor of the company, the supervisor of a *voluntary arrangement, or the Secretary of State may make such a petition (Insolvency Act 1986 s 124). The *winding-up is conducted by a *liquidator, who is supervised by the court, a *liquidation committee, and the Department of Business, Innovation and Skills.

computer documents (in the law of evidence) A document produced by a computer may be admissible as real evidence or as hearsay evidence: in criminal proceedings the admissibility of such evidence is now governed by the Criminal Justice Act 2003.

computer misuse *See* HACKING.

concealment *n. See* NONDISCLOSURE.

concealment of securities The offence (punishable by up to seven years' imprisonment) of dishonestly concealing, destroying, or defacing any **valuable security**, will, or any document issuing from a court or government department for the purpose of gain for oneself or causing loss to another. Valuable securities include any documents concerning rights over property, authorizing payment of money or the delivery of property, or evidencing such rights or the satisfying of any obligation.

concentration *n.* (in EU law) The technical term for a *merger.

concert party (consortium) An agreement (which may or may not be legally binding) between a number of people to acquire shares in a company in order to accumulate a significant holding of its voting shares. Under the Companies Act 2006 and rules administered by the Panel on Takeovers and Mergers anyone becoming interested in 3% or more of the voting shares of a public company must disclose this to the company; a member of a concert party is deemed to be interested not only in his own shares but also in those of other consortium members. Such disclosure may enable a company to counter a *takeover; it may also trigger rules relating to partial offers, which may make it necessary for the consortium to offer to buy the remaining shares. *See also* SARs. *Compare* DAWN RAID.

conciliation *n.* **1.** (in civil disputes) *See* ACAS; ALTERNATIVE DISPUTE RESOLUTION. **2.** A procedure of peaceful settlement of international disputes. The matter of dispute is referred to a standing or *ad hoc* commission of conciliation, appointed with the parties' agreement, whose function is to elucidate the facts objectively and impartially and then to issue a report. The eventual report is expected to contain concrete proposals for a settlement, which, however, the parties are under no legal obligation to accept. Added impetus to this method of dispute resolution was given by the UN Draft Resolution on Conciliation of Disputes Between States and the Convention on Conciliation and Arbitration 1992. Sadly, conciliation failed completely to resolve the disputes arising from the break-up of the former state of Yugoslavia in the 1990s. *See also* GOOD OFFICES; MEDIATION.

conclusive evidence Evidence that must, as a matter of law, be taken to establish some fact in issue and that cannot be disputed. For example, the certificate of incorporation of a company is conclusive evidence of its incorporation.

concurrent interests Ownership of land by two or more persons at the same time; for example, *joint tenancy and *tenancy in common.

concurrent jurisdiction That part of the jurisdiction of the *Court of Chancery before the Judicature Acts 1873–75 that was enforced equally in the common law courts; equity usually took jurisdiction because the common law remedies were inadequate. Since the Judicature Acts the jurisdiction of all divisions of the High Court has been concurrent in name, but certain remedies (for example, specific performance and injunction) are more commonly sought in the Chancery Division. *Compare* EXCLUSIVE JURISDICTION.

concurrent lease A lease granted by a landlord to run at the same time as another lease of the same premises. The effect is that the lessee of the concurrent lease acquires the rights and duties of the landlord in relation to the other lease.

concurrent planning (twin-track planning) The planning involved in placing certain children who are in local-authority care with carers who are approved to both foster and adopt. Initially, the plan requires that the carers should work constructively to return the child to its parents. If it becomes apparent that this will not happen within a reasonable time, the carers will continue to look after the child and apply to adopt him. The aim of concurrent planning is to reduce the number of moves experienced by a child in care.

concurrent sentence A *sentence to be served at the same time as one or more other sentences, when the accused has been convicted of more than one offence. Concurrent sentences are usually terms of imprisonment, and in effect the accused serves the term of the longest sentence. Alternatively the court may impose **consecutive sentences**, which follow on from each other.

concurrent tortfeasors *See* JOINT TORTFEASORS.

condition *n.* **1.** A major term of a contract. It is frequently described as a term that goes to the root of a contract or is of the **essence of a contract** (*see also* TIME PROVISIONS IN CONTRACTS); it is contrasted with a **warranty**, which is a term of minor importance. Breach of a condition constitutes a fundamental breach of the contract and entitles the injured party to treat it as discharged, whereas breach of warranty is remediable only by an action for damages, subject to any contrary provision in a contract (*see* BREACH OF CONTRACT). A condition or a warranty may be either an *express term or an *implied term. In the case of an express term, the fact that the contract labels it a condition or a warranty is not regarded by the courts as conclusive of its status (*L Schuler AG v Wickman Machine Tools Sales Ltd* [1974] AC 235 (HL)). *See also* INNOMINATE TERMS. **2.** A provision that does not form part of a contractual obligation but operates either to suspend the contract until a specified event has happened (a **condition precedent**) or to bring it to an end in certain specified circumstances (a **condition subsequent**). When X agrees to buy Y's car if it passes its MOT test, this is a condition precedent; a condition in a contract for the sale of goods that entitles the purchaser to return the goods if dissatisfied with them is a condition subsequent.

conditional admissibility The *admissibility of evidence whose *relevance is conditional upon the existence of some fact that has not yet been proved. The courts permit such evidence to be given conditionally, upon proof of that fact at a later stage of the trial. Such evidence is sometimes said to have been received *de bene esse.

conditional agreement An agreement that will take effect, if at all, upon the happening of some uncertain event.

conditional discharge *See* DISCHARGE.

conditional fee agreement (CFA) An agreement, which must be in writing, between lawyer and client for legal services in litigation that the lawyer will not be entitled to all or some of his normal fees if the case is lost. This is popularly known as a **no win, no fee** agreement. In return for accepting the risk of such an agreement, the lawyer is entitled to charge a higher fee (by claiming a higher *uplift) if successful. If the claimant loses the case, he may have to pay the other party's costs. The litigation is therefore not entirely risk-free, although insurance, for which premiums are charged, can be taken out to accommodate this risk. The conditions on which a conditional fee agreement may be made (including the type of proceedings in which they are available and the maximum percentage increase in fees allowed) are prescribed under the Courts and Legal Services Act 1990, the Access to Justice Act 1999, and the Legal Aid, Sentencing and Punishment of Offenders Act 2012. For most areas of law conditional fee agreements are unlawful, but they are allowed for certain limited categories of cases, including personal injury cases. *See also* DAMAGES-BASED AGREEMENT; MAINTENANCE AND CHAMPERTY; SUCCESS FEE.

conditional interest An interest that is liable to be forfeited, on the occurrence of a specified event, at the instance of the person who created it; for example, when A conveys land to B in fee simple subject to a rentcharge and reserves a right of forfeiture for nonpayment. Under the Law of Property (Amendment) Act 1926 a conditional interest in land qualifies as a *fee simple absolute in possession and can therefore exist as a legal estate. *Compare* CONTINGENT INTEREST; DETERMINABLE INTEREST.

conditional sale agreement A contract of sale under which the price is payable by instalments and ownership is not to pass to the buyer (although he is in possession of the goods) until specified conditions relating to the payment of the price or other matters are fulfilled. The seller retains ownership of the goods as security until he is paid. A conditional sale agreement is a *consumer-credit agreement; it is regulated by the Consumer Credit Act 1974 as amended by the Consumer Credit Act 2006, if the buyer is an individual and the agreement is not otherwise exempt.

condition precedent *See* CONDITION.

condition subsequent *See* CONDITION.

condominium *n.* **1.** Joint sovereignty over a territory by two or more states (the word is also used for the territory subject to joint sovereignty). For example, the New Hebrides Islands in the South Pacific were a Franco-British condominium until 1980. Sovereignty is joint, but each jointly governing power has separate jurisdiction over its own subjects. *Compare* CO-IMPERIUM. **2.** Individual ownership of part of a building (e.g. a flat in a block of flats) combined with common ownership of the parts of the building used in common.

condonation *n.* Forgiving a matrimonial offence or turning a blind eye to it. Formerly a bar to divorce, it is no longer relevant in divorce proceedings.

confederation *n.* A formal association of states loosely bound by a treaty, in many cases one establishing a central governing mechanism with specified powers over member states but not directly over citizens of those states. In a confederation, the constituent states retain their national sovereignty and consequently their right to *secession. *Compare* FEDERAL STATE.

conference *n.* **1.** A meeting of members of the House of Lords and the House of Commons appointed to attempt to reach agreement when one House objects to amendments made to one of its Bills by the other. **2.** A meeting between counsel and a solicitor and client to discuss a case in which they are engaged. Conferences usually take place at counsel's chambers. If the barrister involved is a QC, the meeting is called a **consultation.**

confession *n.* An *admission, in whole or in part, by an accused person of his guilt. A confession is defined in section 82 of the Police and Criminal Evidence Act 1984 (PACE) as any statement wholly or partly adverse to the person who made it, whether made to a person in authority or not and whether made in words or otherwise. At common law, confessions were admissible if made voluntarily, i.e. not obtained as a result of some threat or inducement held out by a person in authority (such as a police officer). They are now governed by section 76 of PACE, which requires the prosecution, if called upon to do so, to prove beyond a reasonable doubt that the confession was not obtained by oppression of the person who made it or as a result of anything that was likely to render the confession unreliable. A confession may also be ruled to be inadmissible under section 78 of PACE if it appears to the court that, having regard to all of the circumstances, including the circumstances in which the evidence was obtained, the admission of the evidence would have such an adverse effect upon the fairness of the proceedings that the court ought not to admit it (as, for example, where a suspect has wrongfully been denied access to legal advice).

confession and avoidance A pleading in the *defence that, while admitting or assuming the truth of the material facts alleged in the particulars of claim (the **confession**), seeks to avoid or destroy the legal consequences of those facts by alleging further facts constituting some defence to the claim (the **avoidance**). An example is a plea of self-defence to an action for assault.

confidential communication The mere fact that a communication is confidential does not in itself make it inadmissible; it will only be so if it is within the scope of an evidentiary *privilege, such as legal professional privilege.

confidential information *See* BREACH OF CONFIDENCE.

confidentiality *n.* (in medical law) A strong and longstanding obligation, arising out of common law, that requires doctors to keep any personal information about their patients private. A doctor automatically assumes such an obligation during a patient consultation. Sometimes it is permissible or even obligatory to breach a patient's confidence, e.g. when a patient suffers from a notifiable disease. Interestingly, HIV has not been made a notifiable disease in the UK, in order to encourage patients to come forward for testing and treatment. This means that it is the legal responsibility of the patient to inform any potential sexual partners that he or she has the virus; the doctor is legally required to provide suitable advice on safe sex but must not breach confidentiality. *See also* PRIVACY.

confiscation order An order that requires an offender convicted by the Crown Court of an *indictable offence, who has benefited by at least £5,000 from that offence (or an offence taken into consideration), to pay a sum that the court thinks fit (Proceeds of Crime Act 2002). Magistrates may make such orders only in relation to a limited class of offences (e.g. offences relating to the supply of video recordings of unclassified work). The order is enforced like a *fine and is in addition to any other sentence. The High Court may make a restraint order prohibiting the transfer or disposal of realizable property held by a person when proceedings have been instituted against him for a relevant offence. *See also* CONTROLLED DRUGS.

conflict of laws *See* PRIVATE INTERNATIONAL LAW.

confusion of goods The mixing of goods of two or more owners in such a way that their original shares can no longer be distinguished. The owners hold the goods in common, in proportion to their shares. One owner may be awarded possession of the mixture, if he has best right to it, subject to him compensating the other owner for his proportion.

conjugal rights The rights of either spouse of a marriage, which include the right to the other's consortium (company), cohabitation (sexual intercourse), and maintenance during the marriage. There is, however, no longer any legal procedure for enforcing these rights. The old action for restitution of conjugal rights was abolished in 1971 and a husband insisting on sexual intercourse against the wishes of his wife may be guilty of *rape. *See also* CONSUMMATION OF A MARRIAGE.

connivance *n*. Behaviour of a person designed to cause his or her spouse to commit a matrimonial offence, such as adultery. Connivance is no longer an absolute bar to divorce, but may still be evidence that the marriage has not irretrievably broken down.

conquest *n*. The acquisition by military force of enemy territory followed by its formal annexation after the cessation of hostilities. It does not include the acquisition of land as a term of a peace treaty (*see* CESSION). The acquisition of territory after a war in the absence of any peace treaty, because the defeated state has ceased to exist, is known as *debellatio* or **subjugation**. Conquest is not now regarded as a legitimate means of acquiring territory, and hence conferring valid title, as Article 2(4) of the UN Charter expressly prohibits aggressive war and Article 5(3) of General Assembly Resolution 3314 (XXIX) of 1975 effectively nullifies any legal title acquired in this way.

consanguinity (blood relationship) *n*. Relationship by blood, i.e. by descent from a common ancestor. People descended from two common ancestors are said to be of the **whole blood**. If they share only one ancestor, they are of the **half blood**. *Compare* AFFINITY.

conscience clause A clause in a law or contract that allows a person to be exempted from certain actions of which he morally disapproves. For example, in the contract of employment for doctors there is usually a conscience clause concerning exemption from carrying out abortions.

consecutive sentences *See* CONCURRENT SENTENCE.

consensus ad idem [Latin: agreement on the same thing] The agreement by contracting parties to identical terms that is necessary for the formation of a legally binding contract. *See* ACCEPTANCE; MISTAKE; OFFER.

consent *n*. **1.** Agreement by choice, by one who has the freedom and capacity to make that choice. Consent is essential in a number of circumstances. For example, contracts and marriages are invalid unless both parties give their consent. Consent must be given freely, without duress or deception, and with sufficient legal competence to give it. The law also recognizes the implied consent that arises in everyday situations, such as accepting that you may be jostled on a crowded train or in a busy shop.

In criminal law, issues of consent arise mainly in connection with offences involving violence and sexual acts. In looking at consent as a defence the courts will consider the degree of harm (you could not, for example, consent to being killed) and the purpose of the activity (*R v Donovan* [1934] 2 KB 498; *R v Brown* [1994] 1 AC 212; *R v Laskey, Jaggard and Brown* App. No 109/95 (1997) 24 EHRR 39). For public-policy reasons, a victim's consent to conduct that foreseeably causes him *actual bodily harm is no defence to a charge involving ABH, *wounding (although *see R v Wilson* [1997] QB 47), or *homicide; in other cases the defendant should be acquitted if the magistrates or jury have a reasonable doubt not only as to whether the victim had consented but also as to whether he thought the victim had consented. The Sexual Offences Act 2003 (s 74-75) creates both a conclusive and an evidential presumption regarding consent. Where the defendant intentionally deceived the complainant as to the nature or purpose of the relevant act (*R v Williams* [1923] 1 KB 340) or the defendant intentionally induced the complainant to consent to the relevant act by impersonating a person known personally to the complainant (*R v Elbekkay* [1995] Crim LR 163), it is conclusively presumed that the victim did not consent to the relevant act. Where anyone used violence against the victim, caused her to fear that immediate violence would be used against her or another person (*R v Olugboja* [1981] 3 All ER 433), or where the victim was unlawfully detained, unconscious, unable to communicate, or involuntarily intoxicated, it is presumed as an evidential matter that the victim did not consent to the relevant act. *See also* AGE OF CONSENT; BATTERY; CONVEYANCE; RAPE. **2.** (in medical law) Agreement to undergo medical treatment or to participate in medical research. Four conditions must apply for consent to be valid: (1) the patient must be given sufficient information (*see* INFORMED CONSENT); (2) the patient must be competent, i.e. he must have the capacity to understand, retain, and weigh up the information and to make a rational decision; (3) the patient must be in a position to decide voluntarily, i.e. without external pressure; and (4) the patient must communicate his decision. Real or valid consent provides a legal defence against the charge of *battery (trespass against the person). To avoid such a charge, a doctor must ensure that the patient has understood, at least in broad terms, what the treatment entails. An action for *negligence may be brought if the doctor discloses insufficient information or fails to answer the patient's questions. *See also* COMPETENT PATIENT; INCOMPETENT PATIENT.

The law requires consent to be evidenced in writing only in special cases, such as recruiting a subject to a clinical trial. The need to obtain informed consent before proceeding with treatment is precluded in three circumstances: emergency, incompetence, and *therapeutic privilege.

conservation area An area designated as such by a local planning authority (*see* TOWN AND COUNTRY PLANNING) because it is of special architectural or historic interest the character of which ought to be preserved or enhanced. Each building in the area becomes protected as if it were a *listed building, and trees not protected by a *tree preservation order may only be lopped, felled, etc., after notice to the authority.

consideration *n.* **1.** An act, forbearance, or promise by one party to a contract that constitutes the price for which he buys the promise of the other (*Dunlop v Selfridge* [1915] AC 847 (HL)). Consideration is essential to the validity of any contract other than one made by deed. Without consideration an agreement not made by deed is not binding; it is a *nudum pactum* (naked agreement), governed by the maxim *ex nudo pacto non oritur actio* (a right of action does not arise out of a naked agreement).

The doctrine of consideration is governed by four major principles:

(1) A **valuable consideration** is required, i.e. the act, forbearance, or promise must have some economic value. **Good consideration** (natural love and affection or a moral duty) is not enough to render a promise enforceable (*Thomas v Thomas* (1842) 2 QB 851, 114 ER 330).

(2) Consideration need not be adequate but it must be sufficient. Not to be adequate in this context means that it need not constitute a realistic price for the promise it buys, as long as it has some economic value. If X promises to sell his £250,000 house to Y for £25,000, Y is giving valuable consideration despite its inadequacy. £1 is often the consideration in commercial contracts. That it must be sufficient means sufficient in law. A person's performance of, or promise to perform, an existing duty usually cannot in law constitute consideration (*Stilk v Myrick* (1809) 2 Camp 317, 170 ER 1168; *Williams v Roffey Bros & Nicholls (Contractors) Ltd* [1990] 1 QB 1 (CA)).

(3) Consideration must move from the promisee. Thus if X promises to give Y £1,000 in return for Y's promise to give employment to Z, Z cannot enforce Y's promise, for he has not supplied the consideration for it.

(4) Consideration may be executory or executed but must not be past. A promise in return for a promise (as in a contract of sale) is **executory consideration**; an act or forbearance in return for a promise (as in giving information to obtain a reward) is **executed consideration**. However, a completed act or forbearance is **past**

consideration in relation to any subsequent promise. For example, if X gives information to Y gratuitously and Y then promises to reward him this is past consideration, which does not constitute consideration (*Eastwood v Kenyon* (1840) 113 ER 482 (QB)).

2. For *capital gains tax purposes, the actual amount received on the *disposal of an asset, in money or money's worth. Any receipt is potentially liable to be treated as consideration. Consideration can include the right to a further sum if, for example, profit targets are received (*Marren v Ingles* [1980] STC 500 (HL)). Such consideration is an asset, the disposal of which creates a second capital gain. For VAT, a consideration in something other than money must be capable of being expressed in money (Case 154/80 *Staatssecretaris van Financiën v Coöperatieve Aardappelenbewaarplaats GA* [1981] ECR 445).

consistory court *See* ECCLESIASTICAL COURTS.

Consolidated Criminal Practice Direction *n.* A consolidation of existing *Practice Directions, Practice Statements, and Practice Notes as they affect proceedings in the Court of Appeal (Criminal Division), the Crown Court, and the magistrates' courts; it does not include the Practice Directions relating to costs.

Consolidated Fund The central account with the Bank of England maintained by the government for receiving public revenue and meeting public expenditure. Most payments from it are authorized annually by Consolidated Fund Acts, but some (e.g. judicial salaries) are permanent statutory charges on it.

consolidating statute A statute that repeals and re-enacts existing statutes relating to a particular subject. Its purpose is to state their combined effect and so simplify the presentation of the law. It does not aim to alter the law unless it is stated in its long title to be a consolidation with amendments. An example of a consolidating statute is the Trade Union and Labour Relations (Consolidation) Act 1992. *Compare* CODIFYING STATUTE. *See also feature* RULES AND PRINCIPLES OF STATUTORY INTERPRETATION.

consolidation of actions In civil proceedings, a procedure by which two or more cases may be amalgamated. It is generally necessary to show that some common question of law or fact will arise in all the cases. The purpose of consolidation is to save costs and time. The power to consolidate proceedings is an aspect of the court's general powers of management as set out in Part 3 of the *Civil Procedure Rules.

consolidation of mortgages The right of a mortgagee who has taken mortgages on two or more properties from the same mortagor to require the mortgagor to redeem all of the mortgages or none, provided that the contractual date of redemption (*see* POWER OF SALE) for all of them has passed. The right arose because it was considered unfair to a mortgagee to have one security redeemed when another, given by the same mortgagor, might be inadequate to secure that loan. Since 1881 at least one of the mortgage deeds must show an intent to allow consolidation for the mortgagee to exercise the right. *Compare* TACKING.

consortium *See* CONCERT PARTY.

conspiracy *n.* **1.** An agreement between two or more people to behave in a manner that will automatically constitute an offence by at least one of them (e.g. two people agree that one of them shall steal while the other waits in a getaway car). The agreement is itself a statutory crime, usually punishable in the same way as the offence agreed on, even if it is not carried out (*see* INCHOATE). *Mens rea*, in the sense of knowledge of the facts that make the action criminal, is required by at least two of the conspirators, even if the crime agreed upon is one of *strict liability. One may be guilty of conspiracy even if it is impossible to commit the offence agreed on (for example, when two or more people conspire to take money from a safe but, unknown to them, there is no money in it: *see also R v Shivpuri* [1986] 2 All ER 334). A person is, however, not guilty of conspiracy if the only other party to the agreement is his (or her) spouse. Nor is there liability when the acts are to be carried out in furtherance of a trade dispute and involve only a summary and nonimprisonable offence. Incitement to conspire and attempt to conspire are no longer crimes.

Some forms of criminal conspiracy still exist at common law. These are now limited to: (1) conspiracy to *defraud (e.g. to commit fraud, theft, obtain property by deception, or infringe a copyright) or to cause an official to act contrary to his public duty; (2) conspiracy to corrupt public morals (*see* CORRUPTION OF PUBLIC MORALS); and (3) conspiracy to outrage public decency (this might include an agreement to mount an indecent exhibition). **2.** A conspiracy to injure a third party is a tort if two or more people act together to cause loss to that party. For **lawful means conspiracy** intention to injure must be the predominant purpose, rather than protection of one's own financial or trade interests. **Unlawful means conspiracy** requires a shared intention of using "unlawful means" to injure the third party. In this context "unlawful" includes committing a crime, as well as a wrong actionable in civil law (*Total Network SL v Revenue and Customs Commissioners* [2008] UKHL 19, [2008] 2 WLR 711).

constable *n. See* POLICE OFFICER.

constituency *n.* An area of the UK for which a representative is elected to membership of the *House of Commons or the *European Parliament. *See also* BOUNDARY COMMISSIONS.

Constituency Members Members of the *London Assembly each of whom represents one of the 14 London constituencies. Constituency Members are elected every four years by voters in London, at the same time as *London Members and the *Mayor of London are elected. Each of the 14 London constituencies returns one member.

constitution *n.* The rules and practices that determine the composition and functions of the organs of central and local government in a state and regulate the relationship between the individual and the state. Most states have a written constitution, one of the fundamental provisions of which is that it can itself be amended only in accordance with a special procedure. The constitution of the UK is largely unwritten. It consists partly of statutes, for the amendment of which by subsequent statutes no special procedure is required (*see* ACT OF PARLIAMENT), but also, to a very significant extent, of *common law rules and *constitutional conventions.

constitutional conventions Practices relating to the exercise of their functions by the Crown, the government, Parliament, and the judiciary that are not legally enforceable but are commonly followed as if they were. One of the most important is that the Crown must exercise its constitutional powers only in accordance with the advice of ministers who collectively command the support of a majority of the House of Commons. There is no single reason why conventions are observed. For example, it is a very old convention that Parliament must be summoned at least once a year. If that were not to happen, there would be no annual Finance Act and the government would be able to function only by raising illegal taxation. By contrast, if the Crown broke the convention that the royal assent must not be refused to a Bill duly passed by Parliament, illegal conduct would not necessarily follow (although the future of the monarchy could well be at risk). The basic reason for obeying conventions is to ensure that the machinery of government should function smoothly; conventions have not been codified into law and therefore can be modified informally to meet changing circumstances. Case: *AG v Jonathan Cape Ltd* [1976] QB 752 (*Spycatcher* case).

Constitutional Treaty of the European Union Following the signing of the *Treaty of Nice in 2001, a convention was established to provide a simplified single document that would represent a "constitution for the EU". The Constitutional Treaty, which provided for the creation of an EU President and foreign minister and further limited the right of national veto, was signed by member states in October 2004 and was due to come into force in 2006. However, following unfavourable referendums in France and Belgium in 2005 it was not ratified and did not become law. The 2007 *Lisbon Treaty has many similarities with the Constitutional Treaty: it was ratified in 2009.

constitutive theory The proposition that the existence of a state can only begin with its formal or implied *recognition by other states. The constitutive theory of recognition insists that only the positive act of recognition creates the new *international legal personality. *Compare* DECLARATORY THEORY.

construction *n. See* INTERPRETATION.

Construction Industry Scheme (CIS) A set of statutory provisions that require a person making a payment to a subcontractor in (usually) the building industry to deduct tax at basic rate from all payments made, unless the recipient produces a certificate provided by the Revenue permitting payment to be made without deduction of tax. The current CIS commenced on 6 April 2007.

constructive *adj.* Describing anything that is deemed by law to exist or to have happened, even though that is not in fact the case.

constructive desertion Behaviour by one spouse causing the other to leave the matrimonial home. If the behaviour is so bad that the party who leaves is forced to do so, it is the spouse who stays behind who is considered, in law, to have deserted, and not the spouse who actually left. A petition for divorce may therefore be brought, after two years, on the ground of *desertion by the spouse who remained behind.

constructive dismissal Termination of a contract of employment by an employee because his employer has shown that he does not intend to be bound by some essential term of the contract, including the implied term of mutual trust and confidence. Although the employee has resigned, he has the same right to apply to an employment tribunal as one who has been unfairly dismissed by his employer (*Western Excavating (ECC) v Sharp* [1978] QB 761). *See also* UNFAIR DISMISSAL.

constructive fraud (legal fraud) Any of certain forms of unintentional deception or misrepresentation (*compare* FRAUD). The concept is applied by equity to those cases in which the courts will not enforce or will set aside certain transactions (e.g. contracts) because it is considered unfair or unconscionable for a person to insist on the transaction being completed. This unfairness may be inferred from the terms of the transaction (when these are such that no person with proper advice would have entered the transaction) or from the relationship of the parties (for example, that of solicitor and client or of trustee and beneficiary).

constructive notice Knowledge that the law presumes a person to have even if he is actually ignorant of the facts. A purchaser of unregistered land has constructive notice of all matters that a prudent purchaser would discover on inspection of the property or proper investigation of the title (Law of Property Act 1925 s 199). It has also been held that a purchaser has constructive notice of the rights of any person (such as a spouse) who may reside on the property but is not an owner of the legal estate and therefore does not appear on the title deeds (*Kingsnorth v Tizard* [1986] 1 WLR 783). A purchaser of unregistered land is bound by all matters of which he has constructive, as well as actual, notice unless those matters are void against him for want of registration under the Land Charges Act 1972. Those dealing with registered companies have constructive notice of the contents of documents open to public inspection at *Companies House. *See also* ACTUAL NOTICE; IMPUTED NOTICE.

constructive total loss A loss of a ship or cargo that is only partial but is treated for the purposes of a marine insurance policy as if it were an *actual total loss. This may occur when an actual total loss either appears unavoidable (e.g. when a perishable cargo becomes stranded indefinitely) or can only be prevented by incurring expenditure greater than the value of the ship or cargo. In estimating the cost of repairs for this purpose, general average contributions by other insurers are left out of account, but the expense of salvage operations is a relevant factor. The insured must serve a notice of *abandonment of the ship or cargo on the underwriters. This must be unconditional and served within a reasonable time of his learning of the loss; once accepted by the underwriters, it is irrevocable. The underwriters become liable to indemnify him as for a total loss and in return are entitled to all his rights in the ship or cargo.

constructive trust A trust that arises by operation of the law. It is a form of *implied trust and is exempt from compliance with formalities by section 53(2) of the Law of Property Act 1925. There are two recognized types of constructive trust: the **institutional constructive trust** and the **remedial constructive trust**. English law recognizes only the former. An institutional constructive trust automatically comes into being when certain circumstances arise; for example, when a person in a fiduciary position makes an unauthorized profit or when a stranger meddles in a trust. In a domestic setting, a constructive trust may be found to exist when the legal owner of property attempts to deny the rights of another person (usually a cohabitee) who has contributed either directly or indirectly to the purchase of the property, or where the legal owner tries to deny an express agreement to share ownership of the property (*Lloyds Bank v Rosset* [1991] 1 AC 107 (HL); *Oxley v Hiscock* [2004] 3 All ER 703 (CA); *Stack v Dowden* [2007] UKHL 17). By contrast, a remedial constructive trust is a tool of the court that is used at the discretion of the judge to provide a remedy. In those jurisdictions that recognize them, remedial constructive trusts are often used to reverse the unjust enrichment of the defendant, thereby giving effect to *restitution. English law has not been prepared to accept the remedial constructive trust (*Westdeutsche Landesbank Girozentrale v Islington London Borough Council* [1996] AC 669 (HL)).

constructive trustee A person who holds title to property that it is established he holds on constructive trust for another. He is not necessarily subject to the same duties and liabilities as the trustee of an *express trust. Until the court concludes that a constructive trust has arisen, the constructive trustee will probably be unaware that he is holding the property on trust for another. Once an individual's status as a constructive trustee has been established, he will be under a duty to the trust, although the extent of his liability may vary from case to case, depending upon the circumstances.

Where personal liability to *account has been imposed upon a fiduciary for receiving an unauthorized profit, or upon a stranger for dishonest assistance or for receiving property in *breach of trust, the courts have often referred to this personal liability as "liability to account as a constructive trustee". This use of terminology is misleading and has been criticized (*Paragon Finance v D B Thakerar & Co* [1999] 1 All ER 400 (CA)).

construe *vb.* To interpret a (legal) document in writing.

consul *n.* A *diplomatic agent commissioned by a sovereign state to reside in a foreign city, to represent the political and trading interests of the sending state, and to assist in all matters pertaining to the commercial relations between the two countries. *See also* DIPLOMATIC MISSION.

consumer *n.* A private individual acting otherwise than in a course of a business. Consumers are often given greater legal protection when entering into contracts, for example by having a right to avoid certain unfair terms or to cancel the contract (*see* CONSUMER PROTECTION; DISTANCE SELLING). Many regulations define "consumer" in a particular manner.

consumer-credit agreement A *personal-credit agreement in which an individual (the debtor) is provided with credit. Unless exempted, consumer-credit agreements are regulated by the Consumer Credit Act 1974 as amended by the Consumer Credit Act 2006, which contains provisions regarding the seeking of business, entry into agreements, matters arising during the currency of agreements, default and termination, security, and judicial control. A loan to an individual businessman for business purposes can be a consumer-credit agreement. There used to be a maximum financial level above which the protection did not apply that has been abolished.

consumer-credit business Any business that comprises or relates to the provision of credit under *consumer-credit agreements regulated by the Consumer Credit Act 1974. With certain exceptions, e.g. local authorities, a licence is required to carry on a consumer-credit business.

consumer-credit register The register kept by the *Office of Fair Trading, as required by the Consumer Credit Act 1974, relating to the licensing or carrying on of *consumer-credit businesses or *consumer-hire businesses. The register contains particulars of undetermined applications, licences that are in force or have at any time been suspended or revoked, and decisions given under the Act and any appeal from them. The public is entitled to inspect the register on payment of a fee.

consumer goods Goods normally supplied for private use or consumption. The Unfair Contract Terms Act 1977 provides that if consumer goods prove defective when used otherwise than exclusively for business purposes as a result of negligence of a manufacturer or distributor, that person's *business liability cannot be excluded or restricted by any guarantee under which the goods are sold. Under the Consumer Protection Act 1987, suppliers of all consumer goods must ensure that the goods comply with the *general safety requirement. Otherwise they commit a criminal offence.

consumer-hire agreement An agreement made by a person with an individual, a partnership, or with some other unincorporated body (the **hirer**) for the *bailment of goods to the hirer; the agreement must not be a *hire-purchase agreement and must be capable of subsisting for more than three months. The concept thus does not include a hiring to a company. Consumer-hire agreements, unless exempted, are regulated by the Consumer Credit Act 1974. *Compare* CONSUMER-CREDIT AGREEMENT.

consumer-hire business Any business that comprises or relates to the bailment of goods under *consumer-hire agreements regulated by the Consumer Credit Act 1974. With certain exceptions, e.g. local authorities, a licence is required to carry on a consumer-hire business.

consumer protection The protection, especially by legal means, of consumers (those who contract otherwise than in the course of a business to obtain goods or services from those who supply them in the course of a business). It is the policy of current legislation to protect consumers against unfair contract terms. In particular they are protected against terms that attempt to exclude or restrict the seller's implied undertakings that he has a right to sell the goods, that the goods conform with either description or sample, and that they are of satisfactory quality and fit for their particular purpose (Unfair Contract Terms Act 1977). EU directive 93/13 renders unfair terms in consumer contracts void; it is implemented in the UK by the Unfair Terms in Consumer Contracts Regulations 1999. The *Office of Fair Trading runs a special unfair terms unit, which investigates cases in this field. It also issues special guidance to businesses on unfair terms in particular sectors. There is also provision for the banning of unfair *consumer trade practices under the Consumer Protection from Unfair Trading Regulations 2008. Consumers (including individual businesspeople) are protected when obtaining credit (Consumer Credit Act 1974) and there is provision for the imposition of standards relating to the safety of goods under the Consumer Protection Act 1987 and the General Product Safety Regulations 2005. There are, in addition, many legislative measures that are product-specific, such as toy safety regulations. *See also* PRODUCT LIABILITY.

(⊕) SEE WEB LINKS
- Advice on consumer issues from the Citizens Advice Service
- Website of the Office of Fair Trading: includes details of consumer regulations and approved codes of practice
- Website of Consumer Focus, the statutory consumer organization established in 2008

consumer trade practice Any practice carried on in connection with the supply of goods (by sale or otherwise) or services to consumers. These practices include the terms or conditions of supply and the manner in which they are communicated to the consumers, the promotion of the supply of goods or services, the methods of salesmanship employed in dealing with consumers, the way in which goods are packed, or the methods of demanding or securing payment for goods or services. Under UK legislation consumer trade practices are controlled by the Minister and the *Office of Fair Trading.

consummation of a marriage The "completion" of a marriage by an act of sexual intercourse. It is defined for these purposes as complete penetration of the vagina by the penis (although ejaculation is not necessary). A marriage may be consummated despite the use of a contraceptive sheath. If a spouse is incapable of consummation or refuses without good reason to consummate the marriage, these may be grounds for *annulment of the marriage. If one of the partners refuses to arrange an additional marriage ceremony (e.g. in a church) without which he knows his spouse will not agree to have intercourse, this may be a good reason for the spouse's refusal to have intercourse. In this case it is the partner who refused to arrange the ceremony who is regarded as not having consummated the marriage, even though that partner is willing to have intercourse.

contact *n.* (in family law) The opportunity for a child to communicate with a person with whom that child is not resident. The degree of contact may range from a telephone call to a long stay or even a visit abroad, and the court may formalize such arrangements by making a contact order (*see* SECTION 8 ORDERS). The question of contact after a child has been adopted is becoming a contentious issue. *See also* CARE CONTACT ORDER.

contact order A court order requiring the person with whom a child is living to allow the child to visit or stay with the person named in the order (typically the other parent). Such an order usually requires face to face meetings, but can also involve indirect contact such as e-mails or letters. The whole question of contact has become one of major importance recently; case law indicates that under the European Convention of Human Rights, contact is a right of both the child and the parent that can only be interfered with if there is sound justification for so doing. The leading case on the principles applicable to contact is the Court of Appeal's decision in *Re M (Contact: Welfare test)* [1995] 1 FLR 274 (CA). There is a strong presumption in favour of contact, but each case must be decided on its merits and in some cases the fundamental and emotional need of a child to have contact with both of his parents might be outweighed by the depth of harm the child might suffer. Where a parent is violent, the court must carefully weigh up the risk against the positive benefits of contact, and of particular importance will be the willingness of that parent to change his conduct (*Re L (Contact: Domestic Violence)* [2000] 2 FLR 334).

contemporanea expositio [Latin: contemporaneous interpretation] The interpretation of a document in the sense in which it would have been interpreted at the time of its making. This principle is applied particularly to the interpretation of ancient documents.

contempt of court **1.** (civil contempt) Disobedience to a court order or process, such as breach of an injunction. If an injunction is served on a defendant with a **penal notice** attached, breach of the injunction can result in the defendant being imprisoned. **2.** (criminal contempt) Conduct that obstructs or tends to obstruct the proper administration of justice. At common law criminal contempt includes the following:

- deliberately interfering with the outcome of legal proceedings, e.g. by bribing or intimidating witnesses, the jury, or a judge;
- **contempt in the face of the court**, e.g. using threatening language or creating a disturbance in court;
- scandalizing the court by "scurrilous abuse" of a judge going beyond reasonable criticism or attacking the integrity of the administration of justice;
- interfering with the general process of administration of justice, e.g. by disclosing the deliberations of a jury, even though no particular proceedings are pending.

Under the Contempt of Court Act 1981 it is a statutory contempt to publish to the public, by any means, any communication that creates a substantial risk that the course of justice in particular legal proceedings will be seriously impeded or prejudiced, if the proceedings are active. It is also contempt under the Act to obtain or disclose any particulars of jury discussions and to bring into court or use a tape recorder without permission. Contempt of court is a criminal offence punishable by a prison sentence and/or a fine.

contempt of Parliament *See* PARLIAMENTARY PRIVILEGE.

contemptuous damages A very small sum of *damages awarded when, although the claimant is technically entitled to succeed, the court thinks that the action should not have been brought. Contemptuous damages are sometimes awarded in actions for defamation where harm to reputation is deemed minimal (*Grobbelaar v News Group Newspapers Ltd* [2002] UK UL 40, [2002] 1 WLR 3024).

contentious business Business of a solicitor when there is a contest between the parties involved, especially litigation. It is important in relation to *costs, since different rules govern contentious and noncontentious costs.

contentious probate business Disputed applications to the court relating to the validity of wills and the administration of estates. *See also* PROBATE; PROBATE ACTION.

contiguous zone *See* TERRITORIAL WATERS.

continental shelf The sea bed and the soil beneath it that is adjacent to the coast of a maritime state and outside the limits of the state's territorial waters. The 1958 Geneva Convention on the Continental Shelf limits the extent of the shelf to waters less than 200 metres deep or, beyond that limit, to waters that are of such a depth that exploitation of the natural resources of the sea bed is possible. The coastal state is granted exclusive sovereign rights of exploitation over mineral resources and nonmoving species in its continental shelf, provided that this causes no unreasonable interference to navigation, fishing, or scientific research. The 1982 Conference on the Law of the Sea extends the continental shelf, in some cases, to a distance of 200 nautical miles from the baselines around the coast from which the breadth of the territorial sea is measured. It also makes special provisions for delimiting the continental shelf between states with adjacent or opposite coastlines, but does not lay down rules of law for such delimitation. Rocks that cannot sustain human habitation do not have a continental shelf. *See also* LAW OF THE SEA.

contingency fee *See* SUCCESS FEE.

contingent interest An interest that can only come into being upon the occurrence of a specified event (for example when A conveys land to B provided he marries). As a contingent interest can only come into being in the future, if at all, it cannot exist as a legal estate in land. Before 1997, such a transaction created a settlement to which the Settled Land Act 1925 applied. From 1997, such a transaction gives rise to a *trust of land under the Trusts of Land and Appointment of Trustees Act 1996. Contingent interests are consequently *equitable interests only. *Compare* CONDITIONAL INTEREST; DETERMINABLE INTEREST.

contingent legacy A bequest that only takes effect if a particular condition is fulfilled, e.g. a bequest "to A if he shall marry within five years".

continuous bail Bail granted by a magistrates' court directing the accused to appear at every time and place to which the proceedings may from time to time be adjourned, as opposed to a direction to appear at the end of a fixed period of remand (Bail Act 1976; Magistrates' Courts Act 1980 s 128).

continuous employment The period for which a person's employment in the same business has subsisted. Under the Employment Rights Act 1996, employees have the right to claim certain statutory remedies only if they have been continuously employed for certain minimum periods. The required period of continuous employment necessary to bring an *unfair dismissal action if employment began after April 2012 is two years, unless it is for an automatically unfair *inadmissible reason in which case there is no minimum period required. There is no minimum period required where dismissal is because of the employee's political beliefs, but such a dismissal is not automatically unfair and the employer may seek to justify it as being reasonable. The right of employees to statutory redundancy payments and to *guarantee payments arises after two years' and one month's continuous employment, respectively. The statutory minimum period of *notice to terminate an employee's contract also depends on his period of continuous employment in the business. When a business changes ownership as a going concern, the employee's period of continuous employment under both the old and the new employer counts in calculating the total (*see also* RELEVANT TRANSFER). When an employee is unjustifiably dismissed without notice, the minimum notice to which he was entitled under the statute is added to the actual period of employment in calculating whether or not he has served the minimum continuous period. Part-time employees are subject to the same rules as full-time employees (*see* PART-TIME WORKER).

Periods during which an employee was on strike do not break the continuity, but are excluded from his total period of continuous employment. Continuity is not broken when a woman is absent due to pregnancy or childbirth, provided she takes up her right to return to work (*see* MATERNITY RIGHTS).

contraband *n.* **1.** Goods whose import or export is forbidden. **2.** (contraband of war) Goods (such as munitions) carried by a neutral or belligerent's vessel (ship or aircraft) during wartime and destined for the use of one belligerent power against the other (or capable of being so used). Arms and other goods of a military nature were traditionally referred to as **absolute contraband**, while goods having peaceful uses, but nevertheless of assistance to a belligerent, were **conditional contraband**. The distinction, though formally retained, has effectively been abolished. Belligerent states are expected to issue contraband lists in order to exercise the right of capture. Goods being carried to enemy territory in an enemy ship are contraband even if they belong to a neutral power. The other belligerent is entitled to seize and confiscate such goods. *See also* PRIZE COURT; SEARCH OF SHIP.

contra bonos mores [Latin] Against good morals. It is a matter of controversy to what extent the criminal law should, or does, prohibit immoral conduct merely on the ground of its immorality. The tendency in recent years has been to limit legal intervention in matters of morals to acts that cause harm to others. However, there are still certain offences regarded as essentially immoral (e.g. *incest). There are also offences of conspiring to corrupt public morals (although *corruption of public morals is not in itself criminal) and of outraging (or conspiring to outrage) public decency, although the scope of these offences is uncertain. *See also* CONSPIRACY.

contract *n.* A legally binding agreement. Agreement arises as a result of *offer and *acceptance, but a number of other requirements must be satisfied for an agreement to be legally binding.

(1) There must be *consideration (unless the contract is by deed).
(2) The parties must have an *intention to create legal relations. This requirement usually operates to prevent a purely domestic or social agreement from constituting a contract (*see also* HONOUR CLAUSE).
(3) The parties must have *capacity to contract.
(4) The agreement must comply with any formal legal requirements. In general, no particular formality is required for the creation of a valid contract. It may be oral, written, partly oral and partly written, or even implied from conduct. Certain transactions are, however, valid only if effected by deed (e.g. transfers of shares in British ships) or in writing (e.g. promissory notes, contracts for the sale of interests in land, and guarantees that can at law only be enforced if evidenced in writing).
(5) The agreement must be legal (*see* ILLEGAL CONTRACT).
(6) The agreement must not be rendered void either by some common-law or statutory rule or by some inherent defect, such as operative mistake (*see* VOID CONTRACT).

Certain contracts, though valid, may be liable to be set aside by one of the parties on such grounds as misrepresentation or the exercise of undue influence (*see* VOIDABLE CONTRACT).

contract of employment (contract of service) A contract by which a person agrees to undertake certain duties under the direction and control of the employer in return for a specified wage or salary. The contract need not be in writing, but under the Employment Rights Act 1996 the employee must be given a written *statement of terms of employment. Implied in every contract of employment are a duty of mutual confidence and trust, the employer's duty to protect the employee from danger and risks to his health, and the employee's duty to do the work to the best of his ability. Employees who have been continuously employed in the same business for certain minimum periods (*see* CONTINUOUS EMPLOYMENT) have statutory rights, relating for example to *unfair dismissal and *redundancy, that do not apply to the self-employed. A self-employed person is engaged under a contract for services and owes his employer or customer no other duty than to complete the specified work in accordance with the terms of the individual contract; he is not otherwise under the direction or control of the employer as to how or when he works.

Termination of a contract of employment in breach of the terms of the contract is *wrongful dismissal and may be remedied in the county court or the High Court or by an employment tribunal. In such an action the court is not concerned with "fairness" but purely with compensating for a breach of the terms of the contract (*Horkulak v Cantor Fitzgerald International* [2004] EWCA Civ 1287, [2005] ICR 402).

contract of exchange (commutative contract) A barter contract in which property is transferred from one party to the other in return for other property. No money passes from one party to the other. A contract of exchange of goods is not governed by the Sale of Goods Act 1979. *Compare* SALE OF GOODS.

contract of record A judgment or recognizance enrolled in the record of the proceedings of a *court of record, implying a debt that arises from the entry on the record and not from any agreement between the parties.

contract of sale *See* SALE; SALE OF GOODS.

contract of service *See* CONTRACT OF EMPLOYMENT.

contractual tenancy A *lease or tenancy that gives the tenant exclusive possession for a term at a rent against the landlord, but that does not create the legal estate of *term of years absolute, because the landlord does not have the capacity to create such an estate (*Bruton v London and Quadrant Housing Trust* [2000] 1 AC 406 (HL)).

contra proferentum [Latin: against the one putting it forth] The principle that ambiguities in documents should be construed against the drafter. This canon of construction is predicated on the assumption that a person who produces a document has the capacity to avoid ambiguities when drafting it. It is often applied by the courts when construing claimed exclusion or limitation of liability clauses in contracts. Thus, the court will view such a clause very strictly. If it fails to apply to the exact circumstance that took place, the defendant will have been deemed to have failed to have satisfactorily excluded his liability in law. Case: *White v John Warwick & Co Ltd* [1953] 1 WLR 1285 (Ch).

contribution *n*. The payment made by each of two or more people in respect of damage or a loss for which they are jointly liable. In tort, when two or more people are jointly liable for the same damage and the person injured has recovered his losses from one of them, that person may seek contributions from the other tortfeasors (*see* CIVIL LIABILITY CONTRIBUTION; JOINT TORTFEASORS). In the case of a general-average loss (*see* AVERAGE), any person who has sustained the loss is entitled to contributions from others with an interest in the property. *See also* PART 20 CLAIM.

contributory   *n.* Any of the past or present members of a company, who are potentially liable to contribute to the company's assets in the event of a *winding-up. The maximum liability is limited, in a company limited by shares (*see* LIMITED COMPANY), to the amount unpaid on shares (*see* CALL). A past member remains liable for this amount if *winding-up follows within one year.

contributory negligence   A person's carelessness for his own safety or interests, which contributes materially to damage suffered by him as a result partly of his own fault and partly of the fault of another person or persons. Thus careless driving, knowingly travelling with a drunken driver, and failure to wear a seat belt are common forms of contributory negligence in highway accidents. The Law Reform (Contributory Negligence) Act 1945 granted a general power to apportion damages. The effect of contributory negligence is to reduce the claimant's damages by an amount that the court thinks just and equitable. The defence is most common in actions for negligence, but can be pleaded in some other torts, e.g. *nuisance, *rule in *Rylands v Fletcher*, *breach of statutory duty, or under the Animals Act 1971 (*see* ANIMALS). Contributory negligence may also be a defence to some actions for breach of contract. It is not a defence to *conversion or intentional trespass to goods (Torts (Interference with Goods) Act 1977).

controlled drugs   Dangerous drugs that are subject to criminal regulation. In the Misuse of Drugs Act 1971 these are grouped in three classes: A, B, and C. Class A is the most dangerous and includes opium and its natural and synthetic derivatives (e.g. morphine and heroin), cocaine, and Ecstasy. Class B includes amphetamines and C – the least dangerous class – includes anabolic steroids and benzodiazepine antidepressants. It is an offence to possess a controlled drug or to supply or offer it to another.

    Under the Drug Trafficking Offences Act 1986, the Crown Court must impose a *confiscation order when a person who has benefited from drug trafficking is sentenced for a related offence. The amount of the order is the proceeds of the offender's trafficking or, if less, the amount realizable from his property. Imprisonment follows any default. The Act also penalizes those assisting in the retention of drug trafficking proceeds or disclosing information likely to prejudice a drug trafficking investigation. Under the Crime (Sentences) Act 1997 there is an automatic seven-year minimum sentence on third-time dealers in Class A drugs. However, judges may give a lesser sentence if the court considers the minimum would be unjust in all the circumstances. *See also* REPEAT OFFENDER.

controlled foreign company   In order to limit the ability of a multinational group of companies to enjoy profit without any charge to UK tax, statute imposes a corporation tax charge on a UK company for profits generated by a "controlled foreign company" (CFC). The definition of a CFC and the mechanism for achieving this aim were both substantially revised by the Finance Act 2012 sch 20. A CFC is a company that is not resident in the UK but is controlled by persons (companies or individuals) resident within the UK. Profits of a CFC are charged on its UK resident corporate owners (but not on individuals owning the company) if they fall within what the Act describes as the "business profits gateway" or the "financial profits gateway". Broadly, these are defined with the intention of bringing into charge profits that commercially may be expected to have arisen in the UK, if tax planning arrangements had not been effected to move the profits out of UK tax charge. Thus a subsidiary in a tax haven trading by using the assets of its UK parent is likely to have the subsidiary's profits charged on the parent, by virtue of it being identified as a controlled foreign company.

controlled tenancy   A type of *protected tenancy that sometimes occurred with tenancies created before 6 July 1957. From 28 November 1980 all controlled tenancies were converted into *regulated tenancies.

controlled trust A trust of which one or more solicitors or their employees are sole trustees. Such trusts are subject to special accounts rules made under the Solicitors Act 1974; breaches of these rules may be reported to the Solicitors' Disciplinary Tribunal.

controller *n.* (in company law) Strictly, one who holds shares conferring a majority of the *voting power that can be exercised at a general meeting. In practice, effective control can often be exercised by a director with no voting power or a minority of it if he is able to manipulate *proxy voting. *See also* SUBSIDIARY COMPANY.

control orders *See feature* TERRORISM.

contumacy *n.* A refusal to appear in court when legally summoned or disobedience to the rules and order of a court.

convention *n.* **1.** A *treaty, usually of a multilateral nature. The International Law Commission prepares draft conventions on various issues for the progressive development of international law. Article 38(1)(a) of the Statute of the *International Court of Justice, when citing the sources of law it recognizes, refers to "international conventions, whether general or particular establishing rules expressly recognised by the contesting states." **2.** A written document adopted by international organizations for their own regulation. **3.** *See* CONSTITUTIONAL CONVENTIONS.

conventionality thesis *See* LEGAL POSITIVISM.

Convention right Any right protected under the *European Convention on Human Rights that is included in the *Human Rights Act 1998. When an issue arises in a case in relation to a convention right it is said to be "engaged".

conversion *n.* **1.** (in tort) The tort of wrongfully dealing with a person's goods in a way that constitutes a denial of the owner's rights or an assertion of rights inconsistent with the owner's. Wrongfully taking possession of goods, disposing of them, destroying them, or refusing to return them are acts of conversion. Mere negligence in allowing goods to be lost or destroyed was not conversion at common law, but is a ground of liability under the Torts (Interference with Goods) Act 1977. The tort does not extend to intangible property such as contractual rights (*OBG Ltd v Allan* [2007] UKHL 21, [2008] 1 AC 1). The claimant in conversion must prove that he had ownership, possession, or the right to immediate possession of the goods at the time of the defendant's wrongful act (*see also* JUS TERTII). Subject to some exceptions, it is no defence that the defendant acted innocently. **2.** (in equity) The changing (either actually or fictionally) of one kind of property into another. For example, if land is sold the interest of those entitled to the property changes from an interest in the land to an interest in the money that represents it. Before 1926 (and to a lesser extent thereafter) it was important to know whether a person entitled to property had interests in land or in the proceeds of its sale: to leave the determination of these rights to be decided by the precise moment of a sale could have led to uncertainty and injustice. The doctrine of conversion stated that if there was a **duty to convert** the property, equity would assume the property to have been converted forthwith: "equity looks on that as done which ought to have been done" (*see* MAXIMS OF EQUITY). This doctrine was abolished with effect from 1 January 1997 by the Trusts of Land and Appointment of Trustees Act 1996.

converted tenancy A tenancy that was converted from a *controlled tenancy into a *regulated tenancy. From 28 November 1980 all controlled tenancies were converted into regulated tenancies.

conveyance *n.* **1. a.** A document (other than a will) that transfers an interest in land. To convey a legal estate in land, the conveyance must be by deed. **b.** Transfer of an interest in land by means of this document. *See* CONVEYANCING. **2.** Any vehicle, vessel, or aircraft manufactured or subsequently adapted to carry a driver. It is a statutory offence punishable by up to six months' imprisonment and a fine, for anyone to take a conveyance for his own or someone else's use (albeit temporary) without the owner's consent or to drive or be transported in a conveyance knowing that it has been taken without consent (Theft Act 1968 s 12). The meaning of "conveyance" does not include pedal cycles or rowing boats. *See also* AGGRAVATED VEHICLE-TAKING; INTERFERING WITH VEHICLES.

conveyancing *n.* The procedures involved in validly creating, extinguishing, and transferring ownership of interests in land. Only a practising solicitor or *licensed conveyancer may charge a fee for undertaking the most essential parts of such transactions. Under the Law of Property (Miscellaneous Provisions) Act 1989 contracts for the sale or disposition of land must be made in writing. Apart from preparing the deeds or other documents by which the transaction is effected, certain investigative steps are usually required. The sale and purchase of a residential house in England or Wales will generally involve the following:

(1) Preparation of a contract by the vendor's solicitor defining the terms of the transaction, describing the property concerned, and disclosing *land charges and other interests in it that will affect the purchaser.

(2) The vendor usually supplies a **Seller's Property Information Form** giving details of such potential problems as disputes over boundaries, the construction or treatment of buildings, compliance with planning authorities' requirements, and liability for maintenance of shared facilities. Otherwise, these matters are dealt with in written inquiries from the purchaser's solicitor seeking assurances from the vendor.

(3) *Official search by the purchaser's solicitor in the local land charges register to ensure there are no undisclosed charges that could bind the purchaser. The local authority is also asked to disclose other information, such as proposals for building new roads near the property.

(4) If the purchaser is raising a *mortgage towards the price, his solicitor will ensure that the funds will be available at the appropriate time.

(5) The purchaser's solicitor may then negotiate alterations to the draft contract with the vendor's solicitor, in order to ensure its compliance with the purchaser's requirements and to cover points arising from the earlier inquiries and search.

(6) When there is a chain of sales and purchases dependent on one another, the solicitors for the parties involved liaise with one another through all steps of the transactions, particularly in arranging a date for completion.

(7) The parties become legally committed to buy and sell respectively upon *exchange of contracts. It is then usual for the purchaser to pay a percentage of the price to the vendor's solicitor as a deposit.

(8) The vendor's solicitor prepares and delivers an epitome or *abstract of title to the purchaser's solicitor, who studies it to ensure that the vendor's title is proved in accordance with the contract. As final checks on the vendor's title, he conducts an official search in the *Land Registry or the *Land Charges Department as appropriate, and raises *requisitions on title requiring the vendor to clear any defects or adverse interests revealed by the abstract or search.

(9) The purchaser's solicitor prepares the deed (usually a conveyance, transfer, or assignment) by which the property is to be transferred to his client, and has its terms approved by the vendor's solicitor. He also ensures that the purchaser's mortgage deed (if any) is in order.

(10) In preparation for completion, the purchaser's solicitor arranges with the necessary parties for the funds to be available on the completion date and ensures that the necessary deeds will be executed by that date.

(11) On completion, the purchaser's solicitor checks the vendor's original *title deeds against the epitome (or abstract) of title, and takes possession of them together with the deed of transfer. He hands over the price, and the transaction is then legally completed.

(12) After completion, the transfer deed is produced to HM Revenue and Customs, and any *stamp duty land tax paid by the purchaser's solicitor on his client's behalf. He also gives formal notice of the transaction when appropriate; for example, when a leasehold interest is purchased, the lessor must usually be notified. As the land will need to be registered on completion, the purchaser's solicitor lodges the relevant deeds with the Land Registry. *See also* ELECTRONIC CONVEYANCING.

conviction *n.* **1.** (for the purposes of the Bail Act 1976) In criminal proceedings, a finding of *guilty, or an acquittal on the ground of insanity. In a magistrates' court, a finding that the accused carried out the act for which he was charged (*see* SUMMARY CONVICTION). **2.** (for the purposes of the Rehabilitation of Offenders Act 1974) Any finding (except one of insanity), either in criminal proceedings or in care proceedings, that a person has committed an offence or carried out the act for which he was charged. *See also* SPENT CONVICTION.

cooperation procedure A procedure introduced by the *Single European Act 1986 that allowed the *European Parliament to impede the adoption of proposed legislation by the *Council of the European Union. If, after a second reading, Parliament voted by an absolute majority to reject the measure, this could only be overturned by a unanimous decision of the Council. The cooperation procedure was extended to new areas of policy by the *Maastricht Treaty but was subsequently repealed by the *Lisbon Treaty, which introduced the *ordinary legislative procedure. *Compare* ASSENT PROCEDURE; CODECISION PROCEDURE. *See also* ORDINARY LEGISLATIVE PROCEDURE.

copyhold *n.* Formerly, ownership of land enforceable only in the court of the lord of the manor and not protected by the sovereign's courts (*see* FEUDAL SYSTEM). The owner's title comprised a copy of an entry in the rolls of the lord's court. By the Law of Property Act 1922 copyhold tenure was abolished and existing copyholds were converted into freeholds.

copyright *n.* The exclusive right to reproduce or authorize others to reproduce artistic, dramatic, literary, or musical works. It is conferred by the Copyright, Designs and Patents Act 1988, which also extends to sound broadcasting, cinematograph films, and television broadcasts (including cable television). Copyright lasts for the author's lifetime plus 70 years from the end of the year in which he died; it can be assigned or transmitted on death. EU directive 93/98 requires all EU states to ensure that the duration of copyright is the life of the author plus 70 years. Copyright protection for sound recordings lasts for 50 years from the date of their publication (although in 2009 there were proposals to extend this period; for broadcasts it is 50 years from the end of the year in which the broadcast took place. Directive 91/250 requires all EU member states to protect computer *software by copyright law. The principal remedies for breach of copyright (known as **piracy**) are an action for *damages and *account of profits or an *injunction. It is a criminal offence knowingly to make or deal in articles that infringe a copyright. *See also* BERNE CONVENTION; HACKING.

co-respondent *n.* In a petition of divorce under the Matrimonial Causes Act 1973, the party with whom a married person is alleged to have committed adultery and who, if named, is normally made a party to divorce proceedings.

coroner *n.* An officer of the Crown whose principal function is to investigate deaths suspected of being violent or unnatural. He will do this either by ordering an *autopsy or conducting an *inquest. The coroner also holds inquests on *treasure trove. Coroners are appointed by the Crown from among barristers, solicitors, and qualified medical practitioners of not less than five years' standing. There are limited rules governing the procedure of the coroner's court. The function of the coroner is purely to investigate the circumstances of a particular event: he does not make decisions as to who may be to blame.

corporate manslaughter An offence introduced by the Corporate Manslaughter and Corporate Homicide Act 2007. It occurs where the death of a person (such as an employee or a customer) has been caused by a gross breach of a relevant *duty of care owed to that person by the company and the breach involved a serious failing by senior management in the way the company's activities were organized or managed (*R v Cotswold Geotechnical Holdings Ltd* [2011] EWCA Crim 1337, [2011] All ER 100). The offence can be committed only by companies and certain other organizations (including partnerships, trade unions, and some government departments). In Scotland the offence is known as *corporate homicide*.

The same Act abolished the common-law offence of manslaughter by gross negligence in regard to corporations. Individuals, such as directors of a company, can be prosecuted under the common law for the offence of *manslaughter (*R v Kite* [1996] 2 Cr App R (S) 295 (CA); *R v P&O European Ferries (Dover) Ltd* (1990) 93 Cr App R 72 (CA); *Re AG Ref No 2 of 1999* [2000] QB 796).

corporate personality *See* INCORPORATION.

corporate trustee *See* TRUST CORPORATION.

corporate venturing scheme (CVS) A scheme designed to encourage established companies to invest in ordinary shares of (generally) trading companies of the same kind as those qualifying under the *Enterprise Investment Scheme; the scheme encourages the investing and qualifying companies to form mutually beneficial corporate venturing relationships. Companies investing through the CVS may obtain *corporation tax relief (at 20%) on the amount invested provided that the shares are held for at least three years after issue or, if later, three years after the trade for which the money was raised begins. Investing companies also obtain relief for most allowable losses on the shares and deferral of corporation tax when a chargeable gain from the disposal of CVS shares is reinvested in a new CVS investment.

corporation (body corporate) *n.* An entity that has legal personality, i.e. it is capable of enjoying and being subject to legal rights and duties (*see* JURISTIC PERSON) and possesses the capacity of succession. A **corporation aggregate** (e.g. a *company registered under the Companies Acts) consists of a number of members who fluctuate from time to time. A **corporation sole** (e.g. the *Crown) consists of one member only and his or her successors. *See also* INCORPORATION.

corporation tax A tax on the worldwide profits of limited companies and certain other bodies resident in the UK. Corporation tax started on 6 April 1966 (before this date companies paid income tax and profits tax). It applies to all bodies corporate and unincorporated associations, including limited companies, building societies, cooperative societies, unit trusts, and investment trusts, but excluding local authorities.

The tax is based on the profits shown in the company's audited accounts after adding back certain nonallowable deductions, which include depreciation of *machinery and plant. *Annual Investment Allowance and other *capital allowances are deductible for corporation tax purposes, as are losses carried forward from earlier years. Larger companies now pay corporation tax in instalments. Other companies pay corporation tax nine months after the end of the company's chargeable accounting period. *Chargeable gains are included in total profits for corporation tax purposes and are, thus, subject to the same rate of tax as applies to trading and other profits.

The rate of corporation tax depends on the size of the profits in the accounting period. If profits are less than £300,000, tax is levied at 20%; if profits exceed £1,500,000, tax is levied at 23%. Profits between these limits attract a marginal rate of 23¾%. A foreign company is subject to corporation tax on profits of any trade it has in the UK.

(⊕) SEE WEB LINKS

• Corporation Tax area of the HM Revenue and Customs website

corporeal hereditament *See* HEREDITAMENT.

corpus delicti [Latin: the body of the offence] The proof that the crime has been committed. Originally this referred literally to the corpse of a murdered person. It now refers to the factual evidence of the crime.

corroboration *n.* Evidence that confirms the accuracy of other evidence "in a material particular". In general, English law does not normally require corroboration and any fact may be proved by a single item of credible evidence. A judge has a discretion to indicate to the jury the dangers of relying on particular evidence. Guidelines were laid down by the Court of Appeal in *R v Makanjuola, R v Easton* [1995] 3 All ER 730 (CA). Corroboration remains mandatory in cases of *treason and *perjury and for opinion evidence as to some matters, such as *speeding, though other historical requirements have been abolished.

corrupt and illegal practices Offences defined by the Representation of the People Act 1983 in connection with conduct at parliamentary or local elections. Corrupt practices, which include bribery and intimidation, are the more serious of the two. The most frequent illegal practice is spending by a candidate in excess of the amount authorized for the management of his campaign.

corruption *n. See* BRIBERY.

corruption of public morals Conduct "destructive of the [moral] fabric of society". It is uncertain if such acts are crimes, although those who published "directories" of prostitutes or magazine advertisements encouraging readers to meet the advertisers for homosexual purposes have been found guilty of conspiring to corrupt public morals. Cases: *Shaw v DPP* [1962] AC 220 (HL); *Knuller Ltd v DPP* [1973] AC 435 (HL). *See also* CONSPIRACY; CONTRA BONOS MORES.

cost, insurance, freight *See* CIF CONTRACT.

costs *pl. n.* Sums payable for legal services. A distinction is drawn between **contentious** and **noncontentious costs** (broadly, the distinction between costs relating to litigious and nonlitigious matters). Solicitors' costs are normally divided into **profit**

costs (representing the solicitor's profit and overheads) and **disbursements** (any out-of-pocket expenses he may have incurred in the conduct of the case).

In civil litigation the court has a wide discretion to make an award in respect of the costs of the case, but the general principle applied is that the loser of the case must pay the costs of the winner (this was previously known as **costs follow the event**). The court will order on what basis the costs will be assessed. In normal adversary litigation this is the **standard basis**, in which the loser pays a reasonable sum in respect of all costs reasonably incurred by the winning party (*see also* INDEMNITY BASIS). If the court does not make an order for payment of fixed costs (i.e. the amount allowed in respect of solicitors' charges), or fixed costs are not provided for, the amount of costs payable will be determined by the court or by a *costs officer (*see* ASSESSMENT OF COSTS). *See also* COSTS IN ANY EVENT; COSTS IN THE CASE; COSTS RESERVED.

costs draftsman A person (usually a legal executive rather than a qualified solicitor) who specializes in drawing up *bills of costs. Some work in solicitors' firms and some in independent firms of costs specialists.

costs in any event An order for costs made in *interim proceedings by which the winner of the hearing in question shall be paid the costs of that stage in the proceedings whatever the outcome of the trial. *Compare* COSTS IN THE CASE.

costs in the case An order for costs made in *interim proceedings by which the costs of the hearing in question are payable in accordance with the order for costs to be made at the final trial. This will usually have the effect that they are paid by the overall loser of the litigation. *Compare* COSTS IN ANY EVENT.

costs management *See* CASE MANAGEMENT.

costs officer The judge or officer of the court who determines the amount of costs payable in a detailed *assessment of costs. The costs officer may be a **costs judge** (an official of the Senior Courts, formerly known as a **taxing master**), a district judge, or an authorized officer of a county court, a district registry, the Principal Registry of the Family Division, or the Senior Courts Costs Office.

costs reserved An order for costs made in *interim proceedings by which the costs of the hearing in question are reserved for the decision of the trial judge rather than decided by the master or district judge at the hearing itself.

costs thrown away Costs either unnecessarily incurred by a party as a result of some procedural error committed by the other party or properly incurred but wasted as a result of a subsequent act of the other party (e.g. by amending the claim form or statement of case).

Cotonou Agreement *See* AFRICAN, CARIBBEAN, PACIFIC GROUP.

council housing Residential accommodation provided for renting by local authorities (primarily by district and London borough councils, who, as housing authorities, have a general statutory duty to meet housing needs in their areas). Authorities may build new properties and acquire existing ones for the purpose. The allocation and management of housing stock is in general within their sole discretion, but statute does impose certain priorities (e.g. towards homeless persons) and the Housing Act 1980 (now repealed) gave their tenants a measure of security of tenure. There are also financial restraints, such as restrictions on the proportion of capital receipts available for house building, imposed by central government. Certain tenants of council housing have the right to purchase the freehold of a council house or a long lease of a council flat at a discount. The Housing Act 1988 introduced measures under which council housing can be transferred to the private rented sector if tenants so desire. A new regulatory framework for social housing was introduced by the Housing and Regeneration Act 2008, which established the *Tenant Services Authority. *See also* HOMES AND COMMUNITIES AGENCY.

councillor *n.* (in local government) *See* LOCAL AUTHORITY.

Council of Europe A European organization for cooperation in various areas between most European (not just EU) states. The assembly of the Council of Europe elects the judges of the European Court of Human Rights. The Council's fundamental role is the maintenance of pluralist liberal democracy and economic stability in Europe. To this end member states have endorsed the preservation of individual rights as being a, if not the, vital method of achieving these aims. The Constitution of the Council of Europe provides that each member must ensure "the enjoyment by all persons within its jurisdiction of human rights and fundamental freedoms." This provision was implemented by the creation of two human rights treaties, the *European Convention on Human Rights1950 and the *European Social Charter 1961.

Council of the European Union (Council of Ministers) The organ of the EU that is primarily concerned with the formulation of policy and (in conjunction with the *European Commission and *European Parliament) the adoption of *Community legislation. The Council consists of one member of government of each of the member states of the Community (normally its foreign minister, but other ministers may attend instead for the consideration of specialized topics), and its presidency is held by each state in turn for periods of six months. The Council is serviced by a Committee of Permanent Representatives (COREPER). This consists of senior civil servants of each state and its primary function is to clarify national attitudes for the assistance of the Council in reaching its decisions. It also disposes on behalf of the Council of matters that are not controversial. Decisions of the Council are taken by a unanimous vote (*see also* VETO) or, in most cases, by **qualified majority voting (qmv)**. Each member state has a number of votes approximately proportional to the size of its population, with a total of 352 votes; in qmv 260 votes are necessary to pass a measure. In addition, any country can require that the countries in favour must account for 65% or more of the total EU population. *Compare* EUROPEAN COUNCIL.

Council of the Inns of Court A body, comprising representatives of the four *Inns of Court, that meets with the *Bar Council and the Bar Standards Board to formulate and coordinate policy for the profession. When the Council of the Inns of Court and Bar Council disagree, the latter's policy is implemented if it has the support of two-thirds of the members of the bar. The Council also convenes panels to deal with disciplinary matters involving barristers.

council tax A form of local tax levied on all private households (with some exceptions) to contribute to the cost of local government. In general, all the residents of a dwelling are jointly liable to pay the tax. Council tax was introduced by the Local Government Finance Act 1992 and took effect from April 1993, replacing the community charge. The tax is based on the capital value of the dwelling owned or rented by the occupiers. Each dwelling is assessed to see which of eight price bands (A to H) it falls within. The amount of the charge is set by the local council.

The amount payable can be reduced by discounts (e.g. there is a 25% discount where only one adult occupies the property), benefits for those on low incomes, and reductions for disabilities where homes are adapted for disabled persons. Council tax is a personal charge. When ownership of a property is transferred, the liability to unpaid council tax remains with the person on whom it was assessed.

counsel **1.** *n.* A barrister, or barristers collectively. **2.** *v.* In criminal law, to encourage or advise a principal in the commission of an offence. Counselling is one form of accessory liability in criminal law (*see also* AID AND ABET; PROCURE). An accessory may be held liable for having counselled the principal's offence, irrespective of whether the accessory's counselling was causally related to the principal's offence (*R v Calhaen* [1985] QB 808).

Counsellors of State Persons appointed under the Regency Acts 1937 to 1953 to exercise royal functions while the sovereign is ill (but not totally incapacitated, in which case the functions pass to a *regent) or temporarily absent from the UK. They are appointed by the sovereign by letters patent, which must specify the functions delegated to them. These must not include the function of dissolving Parliament, except on the sovereign's express instructions, or that of creating new peers. The persons to be appointed are the sovereign's spouse and the four next in line to the throne (omitting anyone not qualified to be Regent or intending to be abroad during the period of delegation).

count *n. See* INDICTMENT.

counterclaim *n.* In civil proceedings, a claim brought by a defendant in response to the claimant's claim, which is included in the same proceedings as the claimant's claim. A counterclaim asserts an independent cause of action but is not also a defence to the claim made in the action by the claimant. It is an example of a *Part 20 claim. *See also* SET-OFF.

counterfeiting *n.* It is an offence for a person to make a copy of a currency note or of a protected coin intending that he or another shall pass or tender it as genuine (Forgery and Counterfeiting Act 1981 s 14).

countermeasures *pl. n.* Actions, military or economic, taken in response to the conduct of another state that are not necessary or justifiable as *self-defence. As with other forms of force, the unilateral use of such countermeasures may be illegal under the UN Charter unless it be approved by a UN Security Council resolution. *See* ANGARY; ANTICIPATORY SELF-DEFENCE; REPRISALS.

counteroffer A response to an *offer, made to the offeror by the offeree, that seeks either to introduce a new term or to vary an existing term of the offer. Such a response must itself satisfy the definition of an offer, i.e. it must contain a firm commitment to be bound by the specified terms. The effect of a counteroffer is to extinguish the original offer and the counteroffer then becomes the communication that is capable of *acceptance (*Hyde v Wrench* (1840) 3 Beav 334).

countertrade *n.* A form of trading in which an exporter of goods or services undertakes to accept goods or services (rather than money) from the importer in exchange.

county *n.* A first-tier *local government area in England (outside Greater London) or Wales. The Local Government Act 1972 created 45 counties for England and 8 for Wales, dividing the former into 6 metropolitan and 39 nonmetropolitan counties. The metropolitan counties – Greater Manchester, Merseyside, South Yorkshire, Tyne and Wear, West Midlands, and West Yorkshire – were abolished and their functions transferred generally to district councils by the Local Government Act 1985. The Local

Government (Wales) Act 1994 reorganized local government areas in Wales; on 1 April 1996 all the existing counties and *districts were replaced by 11 counties and 11 **county boroughs**, each administered by a single-tier (unitary) council. In some parts of England *unitary authorities have replaced *county councils; this has resulted in the reorganization of certain county areas. *See also* PRESERVED COUNTY.

county council A *local authority whose area is a *county. A county council has certain exclusive responsibilities (e.g. education, fire services, highways, and refuse disposal) and shares others (e.g. recreation, town and country planning) with the councils of the districts in its area. The *Local Government Commission for England began work in 1992 on restructuring local government areas with a view to establishing single-tier local authorities (*see* UNITARY AUTHORITY), which has led to the abolition of certain county councils.

county court Any of the civil courts forming a system covering all of England and Wales, originally set up in 1846. The area covered by each court does not invariably correspond to the local government county boundary. Under Part 7 of the *Civil Procedure Rules, which sets out the rules for starting cases, the county court retains an unlimited jurisdiction for claims in contract and tort. It will hear some appeals (*see* APPELLATE JURISDICTION). Each court has a *circuit judge and a *district judge.

County Court Bulk Centre (CCBC) *See* CLAIM PRODUCTION CENTRE.

course of employment The scope of the work a person is employed to do. An employer may be held responsible under the principle of *vicarious liability for his employee's wrongful acts if they are necessarily incidental to his work, or authorized (expressly or by implication) by the employer, or, though not in any way authorized, are a wrongful way of doing something he was employed to do. Case: *Lister v Hesley Hall Ltd* [2001] UKHL 22, [2002] 1 AC 215.

court *n.* **1.** A body established by law for the administration of justice by *judges or *magistrates. **2.** A hall or building in which a court is held. **3. a.** The residence of a sovereign. **b.** The sovereign and her (or his) family and attendants or officials of state.

Court for Consideration of Crown Cases Reserved A court created by the Crown Cases Act 1848 for considering questions of law arising out of the conviction of a person for treason, felony, or misdemeanour and reserved by the trial judge or justices for the consideration of the court. Its jurisdiction was exercised by the judges of the *High Court, at least five of whom had to sit together. The Court was abolished in 1907 and its jurisdiction transferred to the *Court of Criminal Appeal, which had wider powers.

Court Martial Under the Armed Forces Act 2006, a court convened to try offences against *service law. It consists of a legally qualified *judge advocate and between three and seven serving officers (depending on the seriousness of the offence to be tried). The court may include warrant officers, provided that the accused is of a rank below that of the court members concerned, and civilian members, if a civilian who is subject to service discipline is being tried. The finding and any sentence awarded are determined by a majority of the votes of the members of the court (the judge advocate has no vote on the finding).

Since 1951 there has been a Court Martial Appeal Court, which consists of the Lord Chief Justice and other members of the Senior Courts. A convicted person may appeal to the Court against the conviction and (from 1 April 1997) against sentence. Either he or the *Director of Service Prosecutions may then appeal to the House of Lords.

When a member of the armed forces is charged with conduct committed in the UK that is an offence under both service law and the ordinary criminal law, the trial may in certain serious cases (e.g. treason, murder, manslaughter, and rape) be held by the ordinary criminal courts (and is in practice frequently held by them in other cases). Provision exists to ensure that a person cannot be tried twice for the same offence. *See also* SERVICE CIVILIAN COURT.

Court of Appeal A court created by the Judicature Acts 1873–75. The Court exercises *appellate jurisdiction over all judgments and orders of the High Court and most determinations of judges of the county courts. In some cases the Court of Appeal is the *court of last resort, but in other cases its decisions can be appealed to the *Supreme Court, with permission of the Court of Appeal or the Supreme Court. The Court is divided into a **Civil Division** (presided over by the *Master of the Rolls) and a **Criminal Division** (presided over by the *Lord Chief Justice). The ordinary judges of the Court are the *Lords Justices of Appeal, but other specific office holders and High Court judges may, by invitation, also sit in the Court.

Court of Arches The ecclesiastical court of appeal from the consistory court (*see* ECCLESIASTICAL COURTS), which has the jurisdiction of the former provincial Court of Archbishop of Canterbury. The judge of the court, the **Dean of Arches**, hears appeals from bishops or their chancellors, deans and chapters, and archdeacons. The court's name is derived from its original location, the church of St Mary-le-Bow, whose steeple was erected upon arches.

Court of Chancery The original court of *equity, presided over by the *Lord Chancellor. By the Judicature Acts 1873–75 its jurisdiction was merged into that of the High Court, of which it became the *Chancery Division.

Court of Chivalry An ancient feudal court having jurisdiction over questions relating to armorial bearings and questions of precedence. It is not a *court of record.

Court of Common Pleas One of the three courts of *common law into which the *curia regis* was divided (the others being the *Court of Queen's Bench and the *Court of Exchequer) whose jurisdiction was merged into that of the High Court by the Judicature Acts 1873–75. It became the **Common Pleas Division**, which in 1880 was merged into the *Queen's Bench Division.

Court of Criminal Appeal A court created by the Criminal Appeal Act 1907 to take over the jurisdiction formerly exercised by the *Court for Consideration of Crown Cases Reserved. Its powers were greatly extended, particularly in considering questions of fact as well as law, but it was abolished by the Criminal Appeal Act 1966 and its jurisdiction transferred to that of the *Court of Appeal (Criminal Division).

Court of Ecclesiastical Causes Reserved A court created by the Ecclesiastical Jurisdiction Measure 1963 and having both original and appellate jurisdiction covering the provinces of Canterbury and York. Its original jurisdiction is to hear and determine proceedings in which a person in Holy Orders is charged with an offence against ecclesiastical law involving matters of doctrine, ritual, or ceremonial and all suits of *duplex querela*. Its appellate jurisdiction is in respect of appeals from decisions of consistory courts involving matters of doctrine, ritual, or ceremonial. The court comprises five judges and three diocesan or ex-diocesan bishops. *See also* ECCLESIASTICAL COURTS.

Court of Exchequer One of the three courts of *common law into which the *curia regis* was divided (the others being the *Court of Queen's Bench and the *Court of Common Pleas) whose jurisdiction was merged into that of the High Court by the Judicature Acts 1873–75. It became the **Exchequer Division**, which in 1880 merged into the *Queen's Bench Division. The judges of the Exchequer were known as **Barons**.

court of first instance 1. A court in which any proceedings are initiated. 2. Loosely, a court in which a case is tried, as opposed to any court in which it may be heard on appeal.

Court of First Instance *See* GENERAL COURT.

Court of Justice of the European Communities *See* EUROPEAN COURT OF JUSTICE.

court of last resort A court from which no appeal (or no further appeal) lies. In English law the *House of Lords is usually the court of last resort (although some cases may be referred to the *European Court of Justice). However, in some cases the *Court of Appeal is by statute the court of last resort.

Court of Probate A court created in 1857 to take over the jurisdiction formerly exercised by the ecclesiastical courts in relation to the granting of probate and letters of administration. By the Judicature Acts 1873–75 the jurisdiction of the court was transferred to the *Probate, Divorce and Admiralty Division of the High Court.

Court of Protection A court that administers the property and affairs of persons lacking mental capacity to make the relevant decisions for themselves. The court, which was established under the Mental Capacity Act 2005, is responsible for appointing *deputies to make decisions on behalf of such a person; it can also intervene in disputes about *lasting power of attorney.

Court of Queen's Bench Until 1875, one of the three courts of *common law into which the *curia regis* was divided (the others being the *Court of Common Pleas and the *Court of Exchequer). Its principal functions were the trial of civil actions in contract and tort and the exercise of supervisory powers over inferior courts. By the Judicature Acts 1873–75 its jurisdiction was transferred to the *Queen's Bench Division of the High Court. When the sovereign was a king, it was known as the **Court of King's Bench**.

court of record A court whose acts and judicial proceedings are permanently maintained and recorded. In modern practice the principal significance of such courts is that they have the power to punish for *contempt of court. *See also* CONTRACT OF RECORD.

Court of Session A Scottish court corresponding to the Senior Courts in England and Wales. It consists of an Outer House (corresponding to the *High Court) and an Inner House (corresponding to the *Court of Appeal).

court of summary jurisdiction *See* MAGISTRATES' COURT.

court order *See* ORDER.

Courts and Tribunals Service, HM A government agency created on 1 April 2011 that merges the former Tribunals Service and HM Courts Service into one integrated body. The Service is responsible for the administration of central government tribunals and the criminal, civil, and family courts in England and Wales and of non-devolved tribunals in Scotland and Northern Ireland.

(((●))) SEE WEB LINKS

• Website of HM Courts and Tribunals Service

covenant *n. See* DEED; LEASE; RESTRICTIVE COVENANT.

covenant running with the land 1. A *restrictive covenant affecting freehold land and binding or benefiting third parties who acquire the land. A restrictive covenant runs with the land of the covenantee if it is intended to benefit, and is capable of benefiting, land owned by the covenantor (the *dominant tenement) (*Tulk v Moxhay* (1842) 2 Ph 774). A covenant created before 1926 will bind a purchaser **for value** of the legal estate in the *servient tenement if he has notice of it; a covenant created after 1925 will not bind a purchaser of the legal estate **for money or money's worth** unless it is registered (*see* REGISTRATION OF ENCUMBRANCES). A positive covenant (i.e. an obligation to perform an act) does not run with the land (*Rhone v Stephens* [1994] 2 AC 310). **2.** In a lease, a covenant, either restrictive or positive, that "touches and concerns" the land, i.e. one that affects the nature, value, or enjoyment of the land, and will bind successors in title of the landlord and the tenant provided there is *privity of estate between them.

covenant to repair A clause contained in most *leases that sets out each party's obligations to carry out repairs. The standard of repair depends on the terms of the covenant, the kind of property, and the nature of the surrounding area. The general rule is that the property must be maintained in the condition that a reasonable tenant of that property would expect. The person carrying out the repairs must restore the property to the condition it was in before the damage or want of repair arose: this is the case even if the property was damaged or in disrepair at the commencement of the lease. In the case of a block of flats or offices, the landlord is often responsible for external, and the tenant for internal, repairs. When one party alone is responsible for repairs, this is more likely to be the landlord in the case of a short lease and the tenant in the case of a longer lease. A landlord is liable by statute to repair the structure and exterior and the appliances for heating and sanitation in a dwelling house let for less than seven years (Landlord and Tenant Act 1985 s 11).

If the tenant does not fulfil his repairing obligations the landlord's remedies are *forfeiture or suing the tenant for damages. The measure of damages is the difference in value of the premises as they stand and the value of the premises fully repaired (Landlord and Tenant Act 1928 s 18). If the landlord is in breach of covenant, the tenant's remedies are as follows: he can sue for damages (including costs of alternative accommodation if required); he can sue for *specific performance, a court order to compel the landlord to carry out his obligations; or, if he is sure that the landlord is in breach of covenant and he has told the landlord about the breach, he can carry out the repairs himself and recover the cost from the landlord.

coverture *n.* Formerly, the status of a woman during, and arising out of, marriage. At common law a wife "lost" her own personality, which became incorporated into that of her husband, and could only act under his protection and "cover". Married women no longer suffer disabilities as a result of coverture. *See also* UNITY OF PERSONALITY.

covin *n.* A secret agreement between two or more persons to act in a way that injures the legitimate rights of another; collusion.

CPC *See* CLAIM PRODUCTION CENTRE.

CPR *See* CIVIL PROCEDURE RULES.

CPS *See* CROWN PROSECUTION SERVICE.

credit *n.* **1.** The agreed deferment of payment of a debt. Under the Consumer Credit Act 1974, credit also includes any other form of financial accommodation, including a cash loan. It does not include the charge for credit but does include the total price of goods hired to an individual under a *hire-purchase agreement less the aggregate of the deposit and the total charge for credit. **2.** (in the law of evidence) The credibility of a witness. It may be inferred by the *trier of fact from the witness's demeanour and the evidence in the case. A witness may be cross-examined as to credit by reference to his bias, *previous convictions (where allowed by the Criminal Justice Act 2003), previous inconsistent statements, reputation for untruthfulness, or any physical or mental disability affecting the credibility of his evidence.

credit card A plastic card, issued by a bank or finance organization, that enables its holder to obtain credit when making purchases. The use of credit cards usually involves three contracts:

(1) A contract between the company issuing the credit card and the cardholder whereby the holder can use the card to purchase goods and, in return, promises to pay the credit company the price charged by the supplier. The holder normally receives monthly statements from the credit company, which he may pay in full within a certain number of days with no interest charged; alternatively, he may make a specified minimum payment and pay a high rate of interest on the outstanding balance.
(2) A contract between the credit company and the supplier whereby the supplier agrees to accept payment by use of the card and the credit company agrees to pay the supplier the price of the goods supplied less a discount.
(3) A contract between the cardholder and the supplier, who agrees to supply the goods on the basis that payment will be obtained from the credit company.

credit for guilty plea The reduction in sentence that an offender is entitled to on account of having pleaded guilty to the offence. In determining the appropriate sentence, the sentencing court must take into account (i) the stage in proceedings at which the offender indicated his intention to plead guilty, and (ii) the circumstances in which the indication was given (Criminal Justice Act 2003 s 144). The credit given can range from a one-third reduction of the appropriate sentence where an offender pleads guilty at the very first reasonable opportunity, to a one-tenth reduction where an offender changes his plea during the course of the trial. Different considerations apply when sentencing offenders for murder.

credit limit **1.** The maximum credit allowed to a debtor. **2.** (under the Consumer Credit Act 1974) The maximum debit balance allowed on a running-account credit agreement during any period.

creditor *n.* **1.** One to whom a debt is owed. *See also* JUDGMENT CREDITOR; LOAN CREDITOR; SECURED CREDITOR; UNSECURED CREDITOR. **2.** (under the Consumer Credit Act 1974) The person providing credit under a *consumer-credit agreement or the person to whom his rights and duties under the agreement have passed by assignment or operation of law.

creditors' committee A committee that may be appointed by creditors to supervise the trustee appointed to handle the affairs of a bankrupt. A committee consists of between three and five creditors and their duty is to see that the distribution of the bankrupt's assets is carried out as quickly and economically as possible. *See* BANKRUPTCY.

credit sale agreement A contract for the sale of goods under which the price is payable by instalments but the contract is not a *conditional sale agreement, i.e. ownership passes to the buyer. A credit sale agreement is a *consumer-credit agreement; it is regulated by the Consumer Credit Act 1974 if the buyer is an individual and the agreement is not otherwise exempt.

crime *n.* An act (or sometimes a failure to act) that is deemed by statute or by the common law to be a public wrong and is therefore punishable by the state in criminal proceedings. Every crime consists of an *actus reus* accompanied by a specified *mens rea* (unless it is a crime of *strict liability), and the prosecution must prove these elements of the crime beyond reasonable doubt (*see* BURDEN OF PROOF). Some crimes are serious wrongs of a moral nature (e.g. murder or rape); others interfere with the smooth running of society (e.g. parking offences). Most *prosecutions for crime are brought by the Crown Prosecution Service (although they can also be initiated by private people); some require the consent of the *Attorney General. Crimes are customarily divided into *indictable offences (for trial by judge and jury) and *summary offences (for trial by magistrates); some are hybrid (*see* OFFENCE TRIABLE EITHER WAY). The *punishments for a crime include life imprisonment (e.g. for murder), imprisonment for a specified period, suspended sentences of imprisonment, conditional discharges, community orders, binding over, and fines; in most cases judges have discretion in deciding on the punishment (*see* SENTENCE). Some crimes may also be civil wrongs (*see* TORT); for example, theft and criminal damage are crimes punishable by imprisonment as well as torts for which the victim may claim damages.

crimes against humanity *See* WAR CRIMES.

crimes against peace *See* WAR CRIMES.

Criminal Cases Review Commission (CCRC) An independent public body set up in 1997 to investigate possible miscarriages of justice. It can refer cases to the appeal courts.

(⊕) SEE WEB LINKS
• Guide to the CCRC from the Ministry of Justice

criminal conviction certificate A certificate given to those who request details of information held about their criminal records. The certificate is obtained from the *Criminal Records Bureau, which was set up under the Police Act 1997.

criminal court A court exercising jurisdiction over criminal rather than civil cases. *Summary offences and some *indictable offences are tried by *magistrates' courts; the more serious indictable offences are committed or sent to the *Crown Court for trial.

criminal damage The offence of intentionally or recklessly destroying or damaging any property belonging to another without a lawful excuse (Criminal Damage Act 1971 s 1). It is punishable by up to ten years' imprisonment. There is also an aggravated offence, punishable by a maximum sentence of life imprisonment, of damaging property (even one's own) in such a way as to endanger someone's life, either intentionally or recklessly. Related offences are those of threatening to destroy or damage property and of possessing anything with the intention of destroying or damaging property with it. *See also* ARSON.

Criminal Injuries Compensation Scheme A state scheme for awarding payments from public funds to victims who have sustained *criminal injury, on the same basis as civil damages would be awarded (*see also* COMPENSATION). Damage to property is not included in the scheme. The scheme is administered by a board that may refuse or reduce an award (1) if the claimant fails to cooperate in providing details of the circumstances of the injury or in assisting the police to bring the wrongdoer to justice, or (2) because of the claimant's activities, unlawful conduct, or conduct in connection with the injury. Dependants of persons dying after sustaining criminal injury may also claim awards. The board may apply for a county court order directing a convicted offender wholly or partly to reimburse the board for an award made. The Criminal Injuries Compensation Act 1995 (in force from 1 April 1996) set out new rules for payment. *See also* RIOT.

criminal injury For purposes of the *Criminal Injuries Compensation Scheme, any crime involving the use of violence against another person. Such crimes include rape, assault, arson, poisoning, and criminal damage to property involving a risk of danger to life. Traffic offences other than a deliberate attempt to run the victim down are not included. Such injuries include pregnancy, disease, and mental distress attributable either to fear of immediate physical injury (even to another person) or to being present when another person sustained physical injury.

criminal investigation in Revenue matters The duties of officers of HM Revenue and Customs can include an investigation to decide whether a criminal act has been performed. Where there are reasonable grounds for believing that a criminal offence has been committed, the Revenue officer undertaking the investigation has powers and responsibilities under the Police and Criminal Evidence Act 1984 (PACE). Originally, these powers and responsibilities were restricted to officers of HM Customs and Excise. However, following the merger of HM Customs and Excise with the Inland Revenue in 2005, the Finance Act 2007 s 82 extends the powers to all officers of HM Revenue and Customs who undertake investigations. These include powers of search, of seizure, and of arrest. Responsibilities of the investigating officer imposed by PACE include the requirement to give a criminal caution and to record interviews that take place after the point of time at which there is reasonable suspicion that a criminal offence has been committed.

criminal libel *See* LIBEL.

Criminal Procedure Rules The procedural code governing the practices to be followed in the criminal courts, made under the Courts Act 2003 with effect from April 2005. Criminal Procedure Rules apply in all criminal cases in magistrates' courts and in the Crown Court, and in all cases in the Criminal Division of the Court of Appeal. *See also* CONSOLIDATED CRIMINAL PRACTICE DIRECTION.

(⊕) SEE WEB LINKS
• Full text of the Criminal Procedure Rules from the Ministry of Justice website

Criminal Records Bureau An agency of the Home Office that provides for full and enhanced checks to be undertaken on individuals with regard to any criminal records they may have, and for this information to be passed (with their consent) to bodies registered for that purpose. The Bureau, which was set up under the Police Act 1997, also supply a *criminal conviction certificate to individuals on request.

criminology *n.* The study of crime. Criminology is an interdisciplinary field that combines aspects of legal theory and the substantive legal disciplines with approaches based on psychology, sociology, and moral philosophy. Its subjects include the nature and definition of crime, its forms and incidence, its causes, and crime prevention. Historically, two main approaches have dominated, the classical school and the positivist school. The *classical school of criminology emphasizes the role of free will and rational choice in criminal behaviour and the use of punishment to deter it. By contrast, the *positivist school of criminology seeks the causes of crime in biological, psychological, and sociological factors largely outside the control of the individual offender. Most modern approaches to criminology can be seen to have their roots in one or other of these schools, although recent decades have seen the development of so-called "integrative" and "realist" theories that seek to combine elements of both. *See also* PENOLOGY.

critical criminology *See* POSITIVIST SCHOOL OF CRIMINOLOGY.

critical legal studies (CLS) A radical approach to jurisprudence that developed in the USA in the 1970s. It expresses a broadly Marxist critique of the substantive doctrines of the law (*see* MARXIST LEGAL THEORY), but draws on philosophy, literary criticism, psychoanalysis, linguistics, and semiotics as well as politics and economics. In its early stages, CLS was distinctive in two respects: first, it was located within legal scholarship rather than sociology or political science; secondly, it sought to address the inequities of legal doctrine. Although often described as a successor of *legal realism, its view of the notion of the indeterminacy of law is in fact much more radical. Whereas the US realists regarded indeterminacy as being confined to a certain class of cases, CLS theorists contend that law is radically indeterminate in the sense that the class of available legal materials rarely, if ever, logically or causally entails a unique outcome. It rejects conventional liberal conceptions of law that draw a fundamental distinction between law-making by the legislature, on the one hand, and interpretation of the law by the judiciary, on the other. Since CLS regards the law as indeterminate, judges are perceived as typically deciding cases by making new law, a view inconsistent with liberal ideology.

critical race theory (CRT) A radical movement within *jurisprudence that traces its origin to a conference held in Madison, Wisconsin, in 1989. Sometimes called **outsider jurisprudence**, it sets out to challenge the conventional liberal approach to civil rights issues, in particular the notion that there can be a colour-blind view of social justice. CRT regards the privileged position occupied by mostly White, middle-class academics as a major obstacle to a comprehensive exposure of the racism that is seen to permeate the law, its rules, concepts, and institutions. Adherents generally argue that only those who have themselves suffered the indignity and injustice of discrimination can be the authentic voices of marginalized racial minorities. The law's formal constructs reproduce, it is claimed, the reality of a privileged male White elite, whose culture, way of life, attitudes, and norms constitute the prevailing "neutrality" of the law.

cross-appeals *pl. n.* Appeals by both parties to court proceedings when neither party is satisfied with the judgment of the lower court. For example, a defendant may appeal against a judgment finding him liable for damages, while the claimant may appeal in the same case on the ground that the amount of damages awarded is too low.

cross-examination *n.* The questioning of a *witness by a party other than the one who called the witness. It may be **to the issue**, i.e. designed to elicit information favourable to the party on whose behalf it is conducted and to cast doubt on the accuracy of evidence given against that party; or **to credit**, i.e. designed to cast doubt upon the credibility of the witness. *Leading questions may be asked during cross-examination. *See also* CREDIT.

Crown *n.* The office (a *corporation sole) in which supreme power in the UK is legally vested. The person filling it at any given time is referred to as the **sovereign** (a **king** or **queen**: *see also* QUEEN). The title to the Crown is hereditary and its descent is governed by the Act of Settlement 1701 as amended by His Majesty's Declaration of Abdication Act 1936 (which excluded Edward VIII and his descendants from the line of succession). The majority of governmental powers in the UK are now conferred by statute directly on ministers, the judiciary, and other persons and bodies, but the sovereign retains a limited number of common law functions (known as *royal prerogatives) that, except in exceptional circumstances, can be exercised only in accordance with ministerial advice. In practice it is the minister, and not the sovereign, who today carries out these common law powers and is said to be the Crown when so doing.

At common law the Crown could not be sued in tort, but the Crown Proceedings Act 1947 enabled civil actions to be taken against the Crown (*see* CROWN PROCEEDINGS). It is still not possible to sue the sovereign personally.

Crown Agents for Overseas Governments and Administrations A body operating under the Crown Agents Act 1979 to provide commercial, financial, and professional services to overseas governments, international bodies, and public authorities. After the discovery of heavy financial losses between 1968 and 1974, the body was restructured by the 1979 Act and a tribunal of inquiry was set up to investigate its activities during those years.

Crown Court A court created by the Courts Act 1971 to take over the jurisdiction formerly exercised by *assizes and *quarter sessions, which were abolished by the same Act. It is one of the Senior Courts of England and Wales. The Crown Court has an unlimited jurisdiction over all criminal cases tried on *indictment and also acts as a court for the hearing of appeals from *magistrates' courts. Unlike the courts it replaced, the Crown Court is one court that can sit at any centre in England and Wales designated by the Lord Chancellor. *See also* THREE-TIER SYSTEM.

Crown Court rules Rules regulating the practice and procedure of the *Crown Court. The rules are made by the Crown Court Rule Committee under a power conferred by the Courts Act 1971.

Crown privilege The right of the Crown to withhold documentary evidence in any legal proceedings on the grounds that its disclosure would injure the public interest. It was expressly preserved by the Crown Proceedings Act 1947 (*see* CROWN PROCEEDINGS) but has now been replaced by the doctrine of *public interest immunity.

Crown proceedings Actions against the Crown brought under the Crown Proceedings Act 1947. The prerogative of perfection (the King can do no wrong; *see* ROYAL PREROGATIVE) originally resulted in immunity from legal proceedings, not only of the sovereign personally but also of the Crown itself (including government departments and all other public bodies that were agencies of the Crown). It gradually became possible, however, to take proceedings against the Crown for damages for breach of contract or for the recovery of property. The form of the proceedings was a **petition of right** (not an ordinary action), and the procedure governing them was eventually regulated by the Petition of Right Act 1860. The Crown Proceedings Act 1947 replaced petitions of right by ordinary actions. It also made the Crown liable to action for the tort of any servant or agent committed in the course of his employment, for breach of its duties as an employer and as an occupier of property, and for breach of any statutory duty that is binding on the Crown. It did not affect the presumption of *interpretation that statutes do not bind the Crown; nor did it affect *Crown privilege.

Formerly, members of the armed forces were unable to sue the Crown in tort for death or personal injury caused by a fellow member of the armed forces while on duty. This right was extended to them by the Crown Proceedings (Armed Forces) Act 1987, but controversially the right was not made retrospective. Recent case: *Smith & Others v Ministry of Defence* [2013] UKSC 41, [2013] WLR (D) 239.

Crown Prosecution Service (CPS) An organization created by the Prosecution of Offences Act 1985 to conduct the majority of criminal prosecutions. Its head is the *Director of Public Prosecutions, who is answerable to Parliament through the *Attorney General. The CPS is independent of the police and is organized on a regional basis, each region having a **Chief Crown Prosecutor**. It also advises police forces on matters related to criminal offences.

Crown servant Any person in the employment of the Crown (this does not include police officers or local government employees). The Crown employs its servants at will and can therefore dismiss them at any time. However, since 1971 statute has given civil servants the right to bring proceedings for *unfair dismissal before employment tribunals. A civil servant can bring proceedings against the Crown for arrears of pay but a member of the armed forces cannot. Crown servants are subject to the Official Secrets Act 1989. Since the 1980s the number of Crown servants has been reduced substantially, as the government has pursued a policy of *privatization of former public-sector functions. Some bodies have become *executive agencies.

CRT *See* CRITICAL RACE THEORY.

cruelty *n.* Formerly, behaviour serious enough to injure a spouse's physical or mental health. Cruelty is no longer a basis in itself for granting a divorce or orders in magistrates' courts but it would constitute *unreasonable behaviour under the Matrimonial Causes Act 1973 s 1(2)(b).

crystallization *n.* An event or a condition that is complied with, causing a floating *charge to stop "floating" over a company's fluctuating assets (e.g. cash, stock-in-trade) and to fasten upon the existing assets (and value) at that time. This will occur when a *receiver has been appointed under the terms of the charge to arrange payment of the debt from assets subject to the charge. Alternatively, other events or conditions may be stated under the terms of the charge when created (e.g. that the company goes into liquidation (*see* WINDING-UP) or by notice to the company by the holder of the charge (*Re Brightlife Ltd* [1987] Ch 200). Until crystallization the company is free to deal with assets subject to the charge as it wishes.

CSA Child Support Agency. *See* CHILD SUPPORT MAINTENANCE.

CTM *See* COMMUNITY TRADE MARK.

CTO *See* COMMUNITY TREATMENT ORDER.

cuius est solum, eius est usque ad coelum et ad inferos [Latin: whoever owns land it is theirs up to the heavens and down to hell] A maxim, attributed to the 13th-century jurist Accursius, that describes the vertical extent of an owner's right in land; this is taken to include the substrata, the surface, and *airspace. The maxim was approved by the Supreme Court in *Bocardo SA v Star Energy UK Onshore Ltd* [2010] UKSC 35, [2011] 1 AC 380 in relation to oil wells far below the surface of the ground. In principle, any incursion onto land below the surface will be a trespass. However, some minerals are vested in the Crown by common law (gold and silver) and others by statute (e.g. oil and gas). Rights to airspace are limited to the height required for ordinary use of the land (*Bernstein v Skyviews* [1978] QB 479).

culpa tenet suos auctores [Latin: a fault binds its own authors] A maxim meaning that the only person liable for a fault is he who is the direct author of it. Thus it would exclude *vicarious liability.

cum testamento annexo [Latin: with the will annexed] A grant of *letters of administration with the will annexed is made where the deceased's will does not appoint executors or where the executors named do not prove the will (Supreme Court Act 1981 s 119; Non-Contentious Probate Rules 1987 r 20).

cur. adv. vult (c.a.v.) [Latin: *curia advisari vult*, the court wishes to consider the matter] An abbreviation in law reports indicating that the judgment of the court was delivered not extempore at the end of the hearing but at a later date.

curfew requirement A requirement that an offender remains at a specified place at particular times. A curfew requirement may be imposed as part of a *community order, a *suspended sentence order, or a *youth rehabilitation order. Under the Legal Aid, Sentencing and Punishment of Offenders Act 2012 s 81, the maximum specified curfew period is increased from 12 hours to 16 hours, and the maximum period for which the curfew may be in place is increased from 6 to 12 months.

curtain principle One of the three principles of *land registration: that details of interests under trusts should be kept off the register. The interests will be overreached when the land is sold, so purchasers do not need to know the details (*see* OVERREACHING). *See also* INDEMNITY PRINCIPLE; MIRROR PRINCIPLE.

curtilage *n.* A piece of ground lying immediately next to and belonging to a dwelling, typically a courtyard or garden with any outbuildings etc. In the USA, curtilage is an important concept in those parts of the common law relating to privacy, trespass, and search and seizure; in the UK it is now cited chiefly in local planning rules and the listed buildings legislation.

custodian trustee A trustee who has care and custody of trust property; other trustees (the **managing trustees**) are responsible for its management.

custody *n.* **1.** Imprisonment or confinement. The current policy behind the use of custody was established in the Criminal Justice Act 1991 and has been consolidated by the Powers of Criminal Courts (Sentencing) Act 2000 and the Criminal Justice Act 2003. There is a twin-track approach, under which long custodial sentences will be levied on very serious crimes, particularly those of violence, but custody may be replaced with *community sentences for the less serious ones. The Powers of Criminal Courts (Sentencing) Act 2000 establishes a framework for custodial sentencing that reflects this proportionality principle and includes a policy of reducing prison for non-serious offences. To this end, section 79 of the Act introduces a "custody threshold" that has to be surmounted before any court can impose a custodial sentence, and section 80 imposes limits on the length of any custodial sentence given. **2.** (in family law) Formerly, the bundle of rights and responsibilities that parents (and sometimes others) had in relation to a child. "Custody", which featured in various statutes, has now been replaced by the concept of *parental responsibility introduced by the Children Act 1989.

custody time limit The maximum period for which a person may be kept in custody before being brought to trial. These maximum periods are governed by section 22 of the Prosecution of Offences Act 1985 and the Prosecution of Offences

(Custody Time Limits) Regulations 1987; they may only be extended by an order of the judge.

custom *n*. A practice that has been followed in a particular locality in such circumstances that it is to be accepted as part of the law of that locality. In order to be recognized as customary law it must be reasonable in nature and it must have been followed continuously, and as if it were a right, since the beginning of legal memory. Legal memory began in 1189, but proof that a practice has been followed within living memory raises a presumption that it began before that date. Custom is one of the four sources of international law (*see* CUSTOMARY INTERNATIONAL LAW). Its elaboration is a complex process involving (1) the accumulation of state practice, (2) the practices of international organizations, (3) the decisions of international and national courts on disputed questions, and (4) the mediation of jurists. One essential ingredient in transforming mere practice into obligatory customary law is *opinio juris*.

customary international law What might be called the "common law" of the law of nations. It consists of a vast body of detailed rules that, until the dawn of the 20th century, constituted the chief body of *international law. Many of these rules, such as those relating to maritime law, had their origin in the practice of a single state, the UK, which was able to impose its will until the rules came to be accepted by other states. Other rules, notably those relating to commercial transaction, had their origin in the voluntary practice of a small number of states and, being found useful and convenient, were gradually adopted by other states until the established practice became a binding rule. Customary law was thus almost of its nature an uncertain law. For this reason, during the 20th century increasing use was made of black-letter treaties to supersede customary law. *See* CUSTOM.

customer information order An order requiring a financial institution to provide certain information held by them relating to a customer for the purposes of an investigation into the proceeds of crime (Glossary to the Criminal Procedure Rules). *Compare* ACCOUNT MONITORING ORDER.

customs duty A charge or toll payable on certain goods exported from or imported into the UK. Customs duties are charged either in the form of an *ad valorem* duty, i.e. a percentage of the value of the goods, or as a specific duty charged according to the volume of the goods. All goods are classified in the Customs Tariff but not all goods are subject to duty. HM Revenue and Customs administers and collects customs duties. Membership of the EU has required the abolition of import duties between member states and the establishment of a *Common External Tariff. *Compare* EXCISE DUTY.

CVS *See* CORPORATE VENTURING SCHEME.

cybercrime *n*. Crime committed over the Internet. No specific laws exist to cover cybercrime, but such crimes might include *hacking, distributing or possessing (i.e. downloading) obscene images of children (*see* OBSCENE PUBLICATIONS), *defamation over the Internet, *copyright infringement, and *fraud.

cycle track A route over which riders of pedal cycles have a right of way. It is an offence under the Cycle Tracks Acts 1984 to place a motor vehicle on a cycle track.

cyngor *n*. The Welsh title for the council of a county or a county borough.

cy-près doctrine [French: *cy*, here; *près*, near] A doctrine that in some circumstances enables a gift to charity that would otherwise fail to be diverted to another related charitable purpose. If, for example, the purpose for which a charitable gift is made cannot be achieved in exactly the way intended, or if the funds available are more than sufficient to achieve the purpose, the court or the Charity Commissioners may make a scheme for the funds to be applied to a charitable purpose as close as possible to the original one. If the gift fails after it has come into effect, cy-près will operate automatically. If a gift fails at its inception, the application of the doctrine will depend on a court's perception of the settlor's intention; to apply the funds of cy-près, a general charitable intention must be found. Applications for a cy-près scheme are governed by part 6 of the Charities Act 2011.

Daily Cause List *See* Cause List.

damage *n.* Loss or harm. Not all forms of damage give rise to a right of action; for example, an occupier of land must put up with a reasonable amount of noise from his neighbours (*see* NUISANCE), and the law generally gives no compensation to relatives of an accident victim for grief or sorrow, except in the limited statutory form of damages for bereavement (*see* FATAL ACCIDENTS). Damage for which there is no remedy in law is known as *damnum sine injuria*. Conversely, a legal wrong may not cause actual damage (*injuria sine damno*). If the wrong is actionable without proof of damage (such as trespass to land) and no damage has occurred, the claimant is entitled to nominal damages. Most torts, however, are only actionable if damage has been caused (*see* NEGLIGENCE). In *libel and some forms of *slander, damage to reputation was traditionally presumed; the Defamation Act 2013 now requires serious harm to the claimant's reputation to have occurred or to be likely to occur. In the case of a body trading for profit, such harm is equated with serious financial loss.

damages *pl. n.* A sum of money awarded by a court as compensation for a tort or a breach of contract. Damages are usually a *lump-sum award (*see also* PROVISIONAL DAMAGES). The general principle is that the claimant is entitled to full compensation (*restitutio in integrum*) for his losses. **Substantial damages** are given when actual damage has been caused, but **nominal damages** may be given for breach of contract and for some torts (such as trespass) in which no damage has been caused, in order to vindicate the claimant's rights. Damages may be *aggravated by the circumstances of the wrong. In exceptional cases in tort (but never in contract) *exemplary damages may be given to punish the defendant's wrongdoing. Damages may be classified as unliquidated or liquidated. **Liquidated damages** are a sum fixed in advance by the parties to a contract as the amount to be paid in the event of a breach. They are recoverable provided that the sum fixed was a fair pre-estimate of the likely consequences of a breach, but not if they were imposed as a *penalty. **Unliquidated damages** are damages the amount of which is fixed by the court. Damages may also be classified as *general and special damages.

The purpose of damages in tort is to put the claimant in the position he would have been in if the tort had not been committed. Recovery is limited by the rules of *remoteness of damage (*Overseas Tankship (UK) v Morts Dock & Engineering Co. (The Wagon Mound)* [1961] AC 388 (PC)). The claimant must take reasonable steps to mitigate his losses and so may be expected to undergo medical treatment for his injuries or to seek alternative employment if his injuries prevent him from doing his former job. Damages may also be reduced for the claimant's *contributory negligence. The purpose of damages in contract is to put the claimant in the position he would have been in if the contract had been performed, but, as in the case of damages in tort, recovery is limited by rules relating to remoteness of damage (*Hadley v Baxendale* (1854) LR 9 Exch 341, 156 ER 145). Again as in the case of torts, the claimant is also under a duty to take all reasonable steps to mitigate his losses and cannot claim compensation for any loss caused by his failure to do this. If, for example, a hotel reservation is cancelled, the hotelier must make all reasonable attempts to relet the room for the period in question or as much of it as possible.

Damages for breach of the *Human Rights Act1998 follow principles of *just satisfaction developed by the European Court of Human Rights (*R (Greenfield) v Secretary of State for the Home Department* [2005] UKHL 14, [2005] 1 WLR 673).

damages-based agreement (DBA) A form of no win, no fee agreement in which a claimants lawyers are paid a percentage of any damages that are recovered. Until April 2013 DBAs were permitted only in employment tribunal cases; however, the Damages-Based Agreements Regulations 2013 extend this type of agreement to civil litigation. The lawyer can claim up to 25% of damages (excluding damages for future care and loss) in personal injury cases; 35% of damages in employment tribunal cases; and 50% of damages in all other cases. *See also* CONDITIONAL FEE AGREEMENT.

damnum sine injuria esse potest [Latin: there may be damage or injury inflicted without any wrong being done] The principle that a claimant who has suffered damage in consequence of the act of another may not be entitled to recover compensation because the defendant's act was not in law wrongful. For example, in *Mayor of Bradford v Pickles* [1895] AC 587 (HL) the House of Lords refused to intervene against a landowner who, annoyed by the refusal of a municipal authority to purchase his plot in connection with a water-supply scheme, intercepted underground water percolating in undefined channels through his land to an area owned by the corporation. The landowner committed no breach of the law in acting as he did so; although the municipal authority suffered damage (to their water supply) they did not suffer a wrong in law.

dangerous animals Animals the keeping or use of which is regulated by statute because of their propensity to cause damage. Under the Dangerous Wild Animals Act 1976, the keeping of apes, bears, crocodiles, porcupines, tigers, venomous snakes, and other potentially dangerous animals requires a local-authority licence. A list of the animals classified as dangerous wild animals is contained in a schedule to the 1976 Act. The Dangerous Dogs Act 1991 made the breeding, sale, or possession of dogs belonging to a type bred for fighting (e.g. pit bull terriers) an offence, enabled similar restrictions to be imposed in relation to other dogs presenting a danger to the public, and made it an offence to let a dog get dangerously out of control in a public place. Under the Anti-Social Behaviour, Crime and Policing Bill (2013), the offence of being in charge of an out-of-control dog will be extended to cover private property, including people's houses. The use of *guard dogs is strictly controlled by the Guard Dogs Act 1975.

dangerous driving The offence of driving a motor vehicle in such a way as to fall far below the standard that would be expected of a competent and careful driver, or in a manner that would be considered obviously dangerous by a competent and careful driver (Road Traffic Act 1988 s 2). The maximum penalty on indictment is two years' imprisonment and/or a fine; on summary trial, it is six months' imprisonment and/or a fine. *Disqualification is compulsory with endorsement of between 3 and 11 penalty points. Forfeiture of the vehicle used may also be ordered (Powers of the Criminal Courts (Sentencing) Act 2000 s 143). *See also* CAUSING DEATH BY DANGEROUS DRIVING.

dangerous machinery An employer is under a duty to safeguard employees from dangerous machinery. By the Factories Act 1961, all dangerous parts of machinery must be securely fenced, unless they are in such a position or of such construction that they are as safe as if they were securely fenced. The Mines and Quarries Act 1954 deals with the safety of machinery in mines and quarries, and the EU Machinery Directive and attendant regulations also lay down rules in this field. The Health and Safety at Work Act 1974 contains general provisions on *safety at work. *See also* DEFECTIVE EQUIPMENT.

dangerous offender One who commits, as a principal or accessory, certain violent or sexual offences specified in the Criminal Justice Act 2003 (sch 15) where the court is of the opinion that there is a significant risk to members of the public of serious harm occasioned by the commission by him of further specified offences. Under a sentencing scheme introduced by the 2003 Act, dangerous offenders will be given an extended sentence of imprisonment, which is a determinate sentence of which the defendant must serve at least half. The defendant may be released during the second half of the sentence, providing he receives a positive recommendation from the Parole Board. In addition to the extended sentence provisions under the Act, dangerous offenders must also receive extended supervision periods of up to five years for nonviolent offenders and up to eight years for violent offenders. The dangerous-offender sentencing scheme under the 2003 Act replaces the custodial sentencing schemes in the Powers of Criminal Courts (Sentencing) Act 2000, under which offenders convicted of a violent or sexual offence were subjected to "longer than commensurate" sentencing when this was deemed necessary to protect the public from serious harm, and where offenders convicted of a second serious offence received automatic life sentences.

dangerous things *See* RULE IN RYLANDS V FLETCHER.

DA notice A notice issued by the Defence, Press and Broadcasting Advisory Committee requesting editors and broadcasters not to publish certain information regarded as prejudicial to national security. The notice, which is not legally enforceable, may well cover material that is not restricted from publication under the *Official Secrets Acts. In June 2013, for example, a DA notice was issued asking the media to desist from publishing any articles about UK involvement in the US PRISM programme, an electronic surveillance and data-gathering operation. Until 1993 DA notices were known as **D notices**.

database *n.* An organized collection of information held on a computer. Databases are usually protected by *copyright in the UK under the Copyright, Designs and Patents Act 1988 and the EU directive 96/9 (implemented by the Copyright and Rights in Databases Regulations 1997). Copyright protects the structure, order, arrangement on the page or screen, and other features of the database in addition to the information in the database itself.

data protection Safeguards relating to personal data, i.e. personal information about individuals that is stored on a computer and on "relevant manual filing systems". In the UK the principles of data protection, the responsibilities of data controllers, and the rights of data subjects are governed by the Data Protection Act 1998, which came into force in 2000. The 1998 Act extends the operation of protection beyond computer storage, replaces the system of registration with one of notification, and demands that the level of description by data controllers under the new Act is more general than the detailed coding system previously required. Under the 1998 Act, the eight principles of data protection are:

(1) The information to be contained in personal data shall be obtained, and personal data shall be processed, fairly and lawfully.

(2) Personal data shall be held only for specified and lawful purposes and shall not be used or disclosed in any manner incompatible with those purposes.

(3) Personal data held for any purpose shall be relevant to that purpose and not excessive in relation to the purpose(s) for which it is used.

(4) Personal data shall be accurate and, where necessary, kept up to date.

(5) Personal data held for any purpose shall not be kept longer than necessary for that purpose.

(6) Personal data shall be processed in accordance with the rights of data subjects.

(7) Appropriate technical and organizational measure shall be taken against unauthorized and unlawful processing of personal data and against accidental loss or destruction of, or damage to, personal data.

(8) Personal data shall not be transferred to a country or territory outside the European Union unless that country or territory ensures an adequate level of protection for the rights and freedoms of data subjects in relation to the processing of personal data.

Data controllers must now notify their processing of data (unless they are exempt) with the **Information Commissioner** via the telephone, by requesting, completing, and returning a notification form, or over the Internet. Notification is renewable annually; a data controller who fails to notify his or her processing of data, or any changes that have been made since notification, commits a criminal offence.

The Information Commissioner can seek information from and ultimately take enforcement action against data controllers for noncompliance with their full obligations under the 1998 Act. Appeals against decisions of the Commissioner may be made to the **Data Protection Tribunal**. Apart from non-notification, strict liability criminal offences under the 1998 Act include:

- obtaining, disclosing (or bringing about the disclosure), or selling (or advertising for sale) personal data, without consent of the data controller;
- obtaining unauthorized access to data;
- asking another person to obtain access to data;
- failing to respond to an information and/or enforcement notice.

Data subjects have considerable rights conferred on them under the 1998 Act. They include:

- the right to find out what information is held about them;
- the right to seek a court order to rectify, block, erase, and destroy personal details if these are inaccurate, contain expressions of opinion, or are based on inaccurate data;
- the right to prevent processing where such processing would cause substantial unwarranted damage or substantial distress to themselves or anyone else;
- the right to prevent the processing of data for direct marketing;
- the right to compensation from a data controller for damage or damage and distress caused by any breach of the 1998 Act.

(⊕) SEE WEB LINKS
- Information and guidance from the Information Commissioner's Office

dawn raid **1.** An offer by a person or persons (*see* CONCERT PARTY) to buy a substantial quantity of shares in a public company at above the market value, the offer remaining open for a very short period (usually hours). Because of the speed required smaller shareholders may have little opportunity to avail themselves of the offer. Rules restrict the speed at which such acquisitions can be made. *See* SARs. **2.** An unannounced visit by officials of the European Commission or the UK Office of Fair Trading investigating cartels or other breaches of the competition rules under *Articles 81 and 82 of the Treaty of Rome or under the Competition Act 1998.

days of grace The three days that were added to the time of payment fixed by a *bill of exchange not payable on demand before the Banking and Financial Dealings Act 1971 came into force. A bill drawn on or after 16 January 1972 is payable in all cases on the last day of the time of payment fixed by the bill or, if that is a nonbusiness day, on the succeeding business day.

DBA *See* DAMAGES-BASED AGREEMENT.

dead letter An Act of Parliament that is still theoretically enforceable but has long since ceased to be applied as law. Such a statute awaits repeal, most likely by the Statute Law Revision Acts.

death *n. See* BRAIN DEATH; REGISTRATION OF DEATH.

death penalty *See* CAPITAL PUNISHMENT.

de bene esse [Latin: of well-being] Denoting a course of action that is the best that can be done in the present circumstances or in anticipation of a future event. An example is obtaining a *deposition from a witness when there is a likelihood that he will be unable to attend the court hearing.

debenture *n.* A document that acknowledges and contains the terms of a loan (usually to a company). The loan may be unsecured (a **naked debenture**). More usually, however, the debenture will be subject to a *charge and will contain the terms of the charge (e.g. the right to appoint a *receiver or a *crystallization event). Debentures may be issued to a single creditor or in a series to several creditors in order to raise finance for a company. In the case of the latter, a trust may be created and contained within the debenture in favour of such creditors. This enables the company to appoint a trustee for debenture holders to ensure that the financial activities of the company are managed in the interests of the group of creditors. Finance raised by the issue of debentures is known as *loan capital. This is contrasted with share *capital, the holders of which are *company members.

de bonis asportatis [Latin: of goods carried away] One form of trespass to goods (*see* TRESPASS), not distinguished in modern law from other direct interferences with the possession of goods.

de bonis non administratis [Latin: of unadministered goods] A second grant of *letters of administration of the estate of a deceased person when administration has previously been granted to someone who has himself died before completing the administration of the estate leaving no executor, so that the *chain of executorship is broken. This second grant enables the administration of the estate of the deceased person to be completed.

debt *n.* **1.** A sum of money owed by one person or group to another. **2.** The obligation to pay a sum of money owed.

debt adjusting *See* ANCILLARY CREDIT BUSINESS.

debt collecting *See* ANCILLARY CREDIT BUSINESS.

debtor *n.* **1.** One who owes a debt. *See also* JUDGMENT DEBTOR. **2.** (under the Consumer Credit Act 1974) The individual receiving credit under a *consumer-credit agreement or the person to whom his rights and duties under the agreement have passed by assignment or operation of law.

debtor-creditor agreement A *consumer-credit agreement regulated by the Consumer Credit Act 1974. It may be:

(1) a *restricted-use credit agreement to finance a transaction between the debtor and a supplier in which there are no arrangements between the creditor and the supplier (e.g. when a loan is paid by the creditor direct to a dealer who is to supply the debtor);

(2) a restricted-use credit agreement to refinance any existing indebtedness of the debtor's to the creditor or any other person;

(3) an unrestricted-use credit agreement (e.g. a straight loan of money) that is not made by the creditor under arrangements with a supplier in the knowledge that the credit is to be used to finance a transaction between the debtor and the supplier.

debtor-creditor-supplier agreement A *consumer-credit agreement regulated by the Consumer Credit Act 1974. It may be:

(1) a *restricted-use credit agreement to finance a transaction between the debtor and the creditor, which may or may not form part of that agreement (e.g. a purchase of goods on credit);

(2) a restricted-use credit agreement to finance a transaction between the debtor and a supplier, made by the creditor and involving arrangements between himself and the supplier;

(3) an unrestricted-use credit agreement that is made by the creditor under pre-existing arrangements between himself and a supplier in the knowledge that the credit is to be used to finance a transaction between the debtor and the supplier.

deceit *n.* A tort that is committed when someone knowingly (i.e. without belief in its truth) or recklessly (i.e. careless whether it be true or false) makes a false statement of fact intending that it should be acted on by someone else and that person does act on the false statement and thereby suffers damage (*Derry v Peek* (1889) 14 AC 337 (HL)). *See* FRAUD.

deception *n.* A false representation, by words or conduct, of a matter of fact (including the existence of an intention) or law that is made deliberately or recklessly to another person. Deception itself is not a crime, but until January 2007 there were six imprisonable crimes involving deception:

(1) Obtaining property.

(2) Obtaining an overdraft, an insurance policy, an annuity contract, or the opportunity to earn money (or more money) in a job or to win money by betting. These two offences are punishable by up to ten years' imprisonment.

(3) Obtaining any services (e.g. of a driver or typist or the hiring of a car).

(4) Securing the remission of all or part of an existing liability to make payment (whether one's own or another's) with intent to make permanent default in whole or in part.

(5) Causing someone to wait for or forego a debt owing to him.

(6) Obtaining an exemption from or abatement of liability to pay for something (e.g. obtaining free or cheap travel by falsely pretending to be a senior citizen).

These offences were repealed by the Fraud Act 2006 as from 15 January 2007; however, as the Act has no retrospective effect, the old law applies to offences committed before this date. It is not an offence to deceive someone in any other circumstances, provided there is no element of *forgery or *false accounting. *See also* FRAUD.

decisions of the EU *See* COMMUNITY LEGISLATION.

declaration *n*. **1.** (in the law of evidence) An oral or written statement not made on oath. The term is mainly applied to certain types of out-of-court statement that have traditionally been considered admissible as an exception to the rule against *hearsay evidence; for example, a *declaration concerning pedigree or a *declaration concerning public or general rights. *See also* STATUTORY DECLARATION. **2.** A discretionary remedy involving a finding by the High Court as to a person's legal status, rights, or obligations. A declaration cannot be directly enforced, but is frequently sought both in private law (e.g. to answer a question as to nationality or rights under a will) and in public law (e.g. to test a claim that delegated legislation or the decision of some inferior court, tribunal, or administrative authority is *ultra vires*). In both public and private law the applicant must show standing, i.e. that the issue affects him directly. *Compare* QUASHING ORDER. *See also* JUDICIAL REVIEW.

declaration against interest A *declaration by a person who has subsequently died which he knew, when he made it, would be against his pecuniary or proprietary interest.

declaration concerning pedigree A *declaration made by a person who has subsequently died, or to be inferred from family conduct, concerning a disputed pedigree of a blood relation or the spouse of a blood relation. The declaration must have been made before the dispute in which it is tendered as evidence had arisen. A declaration concerning pedigree has traditionally been admissible at common law as an exception to the hearsay rule.

declaration concerning public or general rights A *declaration made by a person concerning the reputed existence of a public or general right. **Public rights** affect everyone (e.g. a public *right of way) while **general rights** affect a class of people (e.g. a right of *common). An oral or written declaration concerning public or general rights has traditionally been admissible at common law as an exception to the hearsay rule, for example when the maker of the declaration has since died.

declaration in course of duty A *declaration by a person who has subsequently died made while pursuing a duty to record or report his acts.

declaration of incompatibility A declaration by a court (High Court or above) that a statute (or part of a statute) is incompatible with the *European Convention on Human Rights. Before making such a declaration, the court must try to interpret or give effect to the legislation "so far as it is possible to do so . . . in a way which is compatible with the Convention rights". A declaration of incompatibility does not in itself invalidate the legislation but a fast-track procedure can be used by the government to ensure that Parliament amends it.

declaration of intention *See* OFFER.

declaration of parentage A declaration by a court under the Family Law Act 1986 as to whether a named person is or was the parent of another person. Normally the court will only hear an application where the applicant has a sufficient personal interest in the outcome of the case. The most effective way of determining paternity is through the use of scientific tests (e.g. blood tests or now, more commonly, DNA tests). The court has a general power to order such tests, but may not order an adult to undergo them without that party's consent. However a refusal may lead the court to draw adverse inferences (e.g. that a particular man is the father of the child). A "bodily sample" may be taken from a child under the age of 16 where (a) the person with care and control of the child consents or (b) the court considers that a test would be in the best interests of the child. The courts generally do order tests, taking the view that in most cases the interest of the child will be best served by knowing the truth *(Re F (A Minor: Paternity test)* [1993] 1 FLR 598 (CA); *Re H (Paternity: Blood test)* [1996] 2 FLR 65 (CA); *Re K (Specific issue order)* [1999] 2 FLR 280; *Re T (Paternity: ordering blood tests)* [2001] 2 FLR 1190). A similar declaration of parentage can be made under the Child Support Act 1991 (*see* CHILD SUPPORT MAINTENANCE).

declaration of trust A statement by the legal owner of property indicating that this property is to be held on trust. No specific words are necessary, as long as the intention to declare a trust is made clear. *Precatory words will not be sufficient (*Lambe v Eames* (1871) 6 Ch 597; *Re Adams and the Kensington Vestry* (1884) 27 Ch D 394). In most cases, the person intended to be trustee holds the property once a valid declaration of trust has been made. However, a declaration of a trust where the trust property is land is subject to certain formalities, detailed in the Law of Property Act 1925 s 53(1)(b). Non-compliance renders such a trust unenforceable. *See* EXPRESS TRUST.

declaratory judgment A judgment that merely states the court's opinion on a question of law or declares the rights of the parties, without normally including any provision for enforcement. A claim for declaration may, however, be combined with one for some substantive relief, such as damages.

declaratory theory The proposition that a state has capacity (and personality) in international law as soon as it exists in fact (that is, when it becomes competent in municipal law). This capacity is generated spontaneously from the assertion by the community that it is a judicial entity. When socially organized, the new state is internally legally organized, and hence competent to act in such a way as to engage itself in international responsibility. Thus, according to this theory, *recognition does not create any state that did not already exist. *See* INTERNATIONAL LEGAL PERSONALITY. *Compare* CONSTITUTIVE THEORY.

decompilation (reverse engineering) *n.* The process of taking computer *software apart, usually by way of converting executable program code (the object code version of a program) into a higher level programming language so that it can be read by people. Under EU directive 2009/24 (which replaced directive 91/250), computer software is protected by *copyright throughout the EU. However, a very limited right to decompilation is given in that directive for the defined purpose of writing an interoperable program, under certain very strict conditions. Any provision in a contract to exclude this limited right will be void. In the UK the original 1991 directive is implemented by the Copyright (Computer Programs) Regulations 1992 by way of amendments to the Copyright, Designs and Patents Act 1988.

decree *n.* **1.** A law. **2.** A court order. *See also* DECREE ABSOLUTE; DECREE NISI.

decree absolute A decree of divorce, nullity, or presumption of death that brings a marriage to a legal end, enabling the parties to remarry. It is usually issued six weeks after the *decree nisi (unless there are exceptional reasons why it should be given sooner). A list of decrees absolute is kept at the Divorce Registry and access to it is open to the public.

decree nisi A conditional decree of divorce, nullity, or presumption of death. For most purposes the parties to the marriage are still married until the decree is made absolute. During the period between decree nisi and decree absolute the Queen's Proctor or any member of the public may intervene to prevent the decree being made absolute and the decree may be rescinded if obtained by fraud.

decree of presumption of death and dissolution of marriage An order made under the Matrimonial Causes Act 1973 s 19 that presumes the death of a spouse and thereby dissolves the marriage. The court can grant such a decree if the petitioner is able to show that there are reasonable grounds for believing that the other party to the marriage is dead. In practice, this means that the other party will have been continually absent from the petitioner for a period of seven years or more and that the petitioner has no reason to believe that he or she has been alive during that period. The effect of granting the decree is that the petitioner is free to remarry.

deductions *pl. n.* (in employment law) Sums deducted from an employee's wages. The Employment Rights Act 1996 provides strict rules on what can be deducted from wages. Permitted deductions include those for income tax, National Insurance, and pension contributions (for employees who have agreed to be part of an employer's pension scheme). Deductions are also allowed when there has been an overpayment of wages or expenses in the past, when there has been a strike and wages are withheld, or when there is a court order, such as an order from the Child Support Agency or a court attachment of earnings order. There are special rules for those in retail employment.

deed *n.* A written document that must make it clear on its face that it is intended to be a deed and validly executed as a deed. Before 31 July 1990, all deeds required a seal in order to be validly executed, but this requirement was abolished by the Law of Property (Miscellaneous Provisions) Act 1989. A deed executed since that date by an individual requires only that it must be signed by its maker in the presence of a witness, or at the maker's direction and in the presence of two witnesses, and delivered. Deeds executed by companies require before delivery the signature of a director and secretary, or two directors, of the company; alternatively, if the company has a seal, the deed may be executed by affixing the company seal. If the deed is a contractual document, it is referred to as a **specialty**. A promise contained in a deed is called a **covenant** and is binding even if not supported by *consideration. Covenants may be either express or implied. A deed normally takes effect on delivery; actual delivery constitutes handing it to the other party; constructive delivery involved (in strict theory) touching the seal with the finger, and saying words such as "I deliver this as my act and deed". If a deed is delivered but is not to become operative until a future date or until some condition has been fulfilled, it is called an **escrow**. The **recitals** of a deed are those parts that merely declare facts and do not effect any of the substance of the transaction. They are usually inserted to explain the reason for the transaction. The **operative part** of a deed is the part that actually effects the objects of the deed, as by transferring land. The **testatum** (or **witnessing part**) constitutes the opening words of the operative part, i.e. "Now this deed witnesseth as follows". The **premises** are the words in the operative part that describe the parties and the transaction involved. The **parcels** are the words in the premises that describe the property involved. The **testimonium** is the concluding part, beginning "In witness whereof", and containing the signatures of the parties and witnesses. The *locus sigilli* is the position indicated for placing the seal. When a deed refers to itself as "these presents", "presents" means present statements. The advantage of a deed over an ordinary contract is that the limitation period is 12 rather than 6 years (*see* LIMITATION) and no *consideration is required for the deed to be enforceable. *See also* DEED POLL.

deed of arrangement A written agreement between a debtor and his creditors, when no *bankruptcy order has been made, arranging the debtor's affairs either for the benefit of the creditors generally or, when the debtor is insolvent, for the benefit of at least three of the creditors. A deed of arrangement is regulated by statute and must be registered with the Insolvency Service within seven days. It may take a number of different forms: it may be a *composition, an *assignment of the debtor's property to a trustee for the benefit of his creditors, or an agreement to wind up the debtor's business in such a way as to pay his debts. The debtor usually agrees to such an arrangement in order to avoid bankruptcy. A similar arrangement can be agreed after a bankruptcy order is made, but this is regulated in a different way (*see* VOLUNTARY ARRANGEMENT).

deed of covenant A *deed containing an undertaking to pay an agreed amount over an agreed period. Certain tax advantages could be obtained through the use of covenants, particularly in the case of four-year covenants in favour of charities. This was superseded by *gift aid in April 2000.

deed of family arrangement *See* DEED OF VARIATION.

deed of gift A *deed conveying property from one person (the donor) to another (the donee) when the donee gives no *consideration in return. The donee can enforce a deed of gift against the donor. Gifts made other than by deed are not generally enforceable (*but see* PART PERFORMANCE).

deed of variation (deed of family arrangement) A deed by which the beneficiary under a will or an intestacy redirects the gift to some other person (who may or may not be a beneficiary of the estate). Provided this is done within two years of the deceased's death and statutory requirements are complied with, the redirection is not treated as a gift for inheritance tax or capital gains tax purposes by the beneficiary giving up his interest (Inheritance Tax Act 1984 s 144; Taxation of Chargeable Gains Act 1992 s 62). In *Soutter's Executry v IRC* [2002] STC (SCD) 385 executors attempted to vary a trust that arose at the death but ceased before the date of the deed of variation: it was held that this was not a valid deed of variation.

deed poll A *deed to which there is only one party; for example, one declaring a *change of name.

deemed *adj.* Supposed. In the construction of some documents (particularly statutes) an artificial construction is given to a word or phrase that ordinarily would not be so construed, in order to clarify any doubt or as a convenient form of drafting shorthand.

deemed domicile For the purpose of *inheritance tax, an individual who is not domiciled in the UK is nevertheless subject to inheritance tax on property situated throughout the world if he has been resident in the UK for more than 16 out of the 20 years prior to the occasion of charge. The rule also applies inheritance tax on a global basis for three years after an individual has lost a *domicile within a constituent part of the UK (Inheritance Tax Act 1984 s 267). The concept of deemed domicile applies to inheritance tax only: it has no relevance for income tax or capital gains tax.

deep seabed area Under the 1982 United Nations Law of the Sea Treaty, this is defined as being the ocean floor and its subsoil beyond the limits of national jurisdiction. Thus, it constitutes that area beneath the oceans that does not come within any of the coastal zones. The resources within such an area are the *common heritage of mankind. Under the Treaty an organization nominated the **International Seabed Authority** will control deep seabed mining in the area.

de facto [Latin: in fact] Existing as a matter of fact rather than of right. The government may, for example, recognize a foreign government *de facto* if it is actually in control of a country even though it has no legal right to rule (*see* RECOGNITION). *Compare* DE JURE.

***de facto* carers** *See* SOCIAL PARENTS.

de facto director A person who is not legally or formally appointed as a director of a company but may be regarded as such as a matter of fact, because (for example) he is allowed to occupy the position of director or assumes the responsibilities of a director (*Ultraframe v Fielding* [2005] EWHC 1638 (Ch), [2005] All ER (D) 397; *Statek Corporation v Alford* [2008] EWHC 32 (Ch), [2008] BCC 266).

defamation *n.* The *publication of an untrue statement about a person that tends to lower his reputation in the opinion of right-thinking members of the community (*Sim v Stretch* [1936] 2 ALL ER 1237 (HL)) or to make them shun or avoid him. The Defamation Act 2013 introduced a further threshold test, providing that a statement is not defamatory unless serious harm to the claimant's reputation has been caused or is likely to occur. Defamation is usually in words, but pictures, gestures, and other acts can be defamatory. In English law, a distinction is made between defamation in permanent form (*see* LIBEL) and defamation not in permanent form (*see* SLANDER). This distinction is not made in Scotland. The remedies in tort for defamation are damages and injunction.

In English law, the basis of the tort is injury to reputation, so it must be proved that the statement was communicated to someone other than the person defamed. In Scottish law, defamation includes injury to the feelings of the person defamed as well as injury to reputation, so an action can be brought when a statement is communicated only to the person defamed. If the statement is not obviously defamatory, the claimant must show that it would be understood in a defamatory sense (*see* INNUENDO). It is not necessary to prove that the defendant intended to refer to the claimant. The test is whether reasonable people would think the statement referred to him, but the defendant may escape liability for **unintentional defamation** by making an *offer of amends (*see also* APOLOGY). Other defences are *truth (formerly known as justification), *honest opinion (formerly known as, fair comment), *absolute privilege, and *qualified privilege. The 2013 Act also extends privilege to *peer-reviewed statements in scientific or academic journals. A new statutory defence is created for operators of websites in respect of statements posted by third parties; the defence is lost if the operator fails to remove the defamatory posting after having been notified by a claimant who is unable to identify the poster sufficiently to take action against him in person.

All those involved in the publication of a defamatory statement, such as printers, publishers, and broadcasting companies, are liable and every repetition of a defamatory statement is a fresh publication, giving rise to a new cause of action. A mere distributor of a book, newspaper, etc., may have a defence of **innocent dissemination** if he was not the author, editor, or commercial publisher; took reasonable care in relation to the publication, and did not know and had no reason to know of its defamatory contents (Defamation Act 1996 s 1). The Defamation Act 1996 introduced a summary procedure for claims of less than £10,000 to be heard by a judge alone but did not otherwise change the rule that the jury and not the judge decides on the damages in defamation cases. The *limitation period was reduced to one year. The Defamation Act 2013 now provides for trial without jury unless the court orders otherwise.

default *n.* Failure to do something required by law, usually failure to comply with mandatory rules of procedure. If a defendant in civil proceedings is in default by failing to file an acknowledgement of service or a defence, the claimant may obtain **judgment in default** under Part 12 of the *Civil Procedure Rules.

default notice A notice that must be served on a contract breaker before taking action in consequence of his breach. Under the Consumer Credit Act 1974 a default notice must be served on a debtor or hirer in breach of a regulated agreement before the creditor or owner is entitled to terminate the agreement; to demand earlier payment of any sum; to recover possession of any goods or land; to treat any right conferred on the debtor or hirer by the agreement as terminated, restricted, or deferred; or to enforce any security. The notice must specify the nature of the breach, what action (if any) is required to remedy it, and the date before which that action is to be taken. If the breach is not capable of remedy, the notice must specify the sum (if any) required in compensation and the date before which it is to be paid.

default summons Formerly, a summons used to initiate proceedings in the county courts when the only relief claimed was the payment of money. Under the *Civil Procedure Rules, such claims are now made by *claim forms under Part 7 of the Rules.

defeasance *n.* A condition providing that, upon the performance of a certain act or the occurrence of a certain event, an estate or interest created shall be void. A *mortgage is a deed that contains a clause of defeasance.

defect *n.* **1.** A fault or failing in a thing. The defect may be obvious (a **patent defect**) or it may not be apparent at first (a **latent defect**). In a sale of goods, the buyer usually has a legal remedy against a professional seller if the goods have a latent defect. If there is a patent defect he usually has no such remedy if he had an opportunity to inspect the goods before purchase. *See also* SATISFACTORY QUALITY. **2.** (defect in a product) A fault in a product as defined in the Consumer Protection Act 1987. A defect exists in products under the Act when the safety of the products is not what people generally are entitled to expect. In determining what people are entitled to expect, reference should be made to the way in which the goods are marked, any warnings issued with them, and the time of supply. The Act implements EU directive 85/374 on *product liability. Under the Latent Damage Act 1986 the time limit to bring legal actions (*see* LIMITATION) is extended to a period of three years from when the latent defect becomes apparent.

defective equipment An employer's duty to provide his employees with a safe system of work, so far as is reasonably practicable, includes the provision and maintenance of safe tools and equipment (including materials) for the job. The employer is liable to an employee injured by a defect in the equipment he provides, even if the defect was due to the fault of some third party, such as the manufacturer of the equipment. This area is heavily regulated by European directives, resulting in, for example, the Personal Protective Equipment Regulations 2002, the Provision and Use of Work Equipment Regulations 1998, and the Work at Height Regulations 2005. *See also* SAFETY AT WORK.

defective premises Liability for defects in the construction of buildings can arise both at common law, in contract and tort, and by statute. In addition to any liability they may incur for breach of contract, builders, architects, surveyors, etc., are liable in tort on ordinary principles for *negligence and may also be in breach of statutory duties; for example, the duty imposed by the Defective Premises Act 1972, in respect of work connected with the provision of a dwelling, to see that the dwelling will be fit for habitation. A landlord who is responsible for repairs, or who has reserved the right to enter and carry out repairs, may be liable for damage caused by failure to repair not only to his tenants, but also to third parties who could be expected to be affected by the defects. For the liability of occupiers of premises, *see* OCCUPIER'S LIABILITY.

defective products *See* PRODUCT LIABILITY.

defectum sanguinis [Latin: failure of blood] Lack of an heir.

defence *n.* **1.** In civil proceedings, the response by a defendant to service of a claim. Once a claim form or particulars of claim have been served on the defendant, he is under an obligation to respond. If he does not file a defence, judgment in default may be entered against him under Part 12 of the *Civil Procedure Rules. Generally, a defence must be filed within 14 days of service of the claim. The defendant may obtain an extension of a further 14 days by filing an *acknowledgment of service under Part 10 of the Civil Procedure Rules. **2.** In civil and criminal proceedings, an issue of law or fact that, if determined in favour of the defendant, will relieve him of liability wholly or in part. *See also* GENERAL DEFENCES.

defence statement In criminal proceedings, a written statement setting out in general terms the nature of the accused's defence. A defence statement must comply with the requirements set out in the Criminal Procedure and Investigations Act 1996. It should include any particular defences on which the accused intends to rely, indicate the matters of fact on which he takes issue with the prosecution, set out why he takes issue with the prosecution, and indicate any point of law (including any point as to the admissibility of the evidence) that he wishes to take. A defence statement must also give particulars of any *alibi, including details of any alibi witness. If at trial the accused puts forward a defence different from that set out in the defence statement, the court or jury may draw such inferences as appear proper in deciding whether the accused is guilty of the offence concerned. In proceedings before the Crown Court the accused must serve a defence statement where the prosecutor has provided initial disclosure. In proceedings before the magistrates court the accused may choose to serve a defence statement.

defendant *n.* A person against whom court proceedings are brought. *Compare* CLAIMANT.

deferred debt In bankruptcy proceedings, a debt that by statute is not paid until all other debts have been paid in full.

deferred sentence A sentence that is determined after a period of delay to allow the court to assess any change in the person's conduct or circumstances after his conviction.

deforcement *n.* The withholding of lands or tenements from the rightful owner.

defrauding *n.* Any act that deprives someone of something that is his or to which he might be entitled or that injures someone in relation to any proprietary right. It is a crime (a form of *conspiracy at common law) to conspire to defraud someone. *See also* CHEAT; DISHONESTY.

degrading treatment or punishment Treatment that arouses in the victim a feeling or fear, anguish, and inferiority capable of humiliating and debasing the victim and possibly breaking his physical or moral resistance (*Ireland v UK* (1978) Series A no 25 2 EHRR 25). The prohibition on degrading treatment or punishment is set out in Article 3 of the European Convention on Human Rights and the *Human Rights Act 1998. This right is an *absolute right; such treatment can never be justified as being in the public interest, no matter how great that public interest might be. Public authorities have a limited but positive duty to protect this right from interference by third parties.

de jure [Latin] As a matter of legal right. *See* RECOGNITION. *Compare* DE FACTO.

del credere agent [Italian: of trust] *See* AGENT.

delegated legislation (subordinate legislation) Legislation made under powers conferred by an Act of Parliament (an enabling statute, often called the parent Act). The bulk of delegated legislation is governmental: it consists mainly of *Orders in Council and instruments of various names (e.g. orders, regulations, rules, directions, and schemes) made by ministers (*see also* GOVERNMENT CIRCULARS). Its primary use is to supplement Acts of Parliament by prescribing the detailed and technical rules required for their operation; unlike an Act, it has the advantage that it can be made (and later amended if necessary) without taking up parliamentary time. Delegated legislation is also made by a variety of bodies outside central government, examples being *byelaws, the *Civil Procedure Rules, and the codes of conduct of certain professional bodies (*see also* ORDERS OF COUNCIL).

Most delegated legislation (byelaws are the main exception) is subject to some degree of parliamentary control, which may take any of three principal forms:

(1) a simple requirement that it be laid before Parliament after being made (thus ensuring that members become aware of its existence but affording them no special method or opportunity of questioning its substance);

(2) a provision that it be laid and, for a specified period, liable to annulment by a resolution of either House (**negative resolution** procedure);

(3) a provision that it be laid and either shall not take effect until approved by resolutions of both Houses or shall cease to have effect unless approved within a specified period (**affirmative resolution** procedure).

In the case of purely financial instruments, any provision for a negative or affirmative resolution refers to the House of Commons alone. (*See also* STATUTORY INSTRUMENT; SPECIAL PROCEDURE ORDERS.)

All delegated legislation is subject to judicial control under the doctrine of *ultra vires*. Delegated legislation is interpreted in the light of the parent Act, so particular words are presumed to be used in the same sense as in that Act. This rule apart, it is governed by the same principles as those governing the *interpretation of statutes. *See also* SUBDELEGATED LEGISLATION.

delegation *n.* **1.** The grant of authority to a person to act on behalf of one or more others, for agreed purposes. **2.** *See* VICARIOUS LIABILITY.

delegatus non potest delegare [Latin] A person to whom something has been delegated cannot delegate further, i.e. one to whom powers and duties have been entrusted cannot entrust them to another. The rule applies particularly when the delegate possesses some special skill in the performance of the duties delegated, or when personal trust is involved. The rule does not apply if there is express or implied authority to delegate. Trustees, for example, have always been entitled to employ agents when this was necessary (for example, they can employ solicitors to do legal work). Since 1925, a trustee may delegate any business of the trust to an agent provided that he does so in good faith. Further, since 1971, any trustee may delegate, for a period not exceeding one year, any trusts, powers, or discretions he has; this delegation may be repeated.

de lege ferenda [Latin: of (or concerning) the law that is to come into force] A phrase used to indicate that a proposition relates to what the law ought to be or may in the future be.

de lege lata [Latin: of (or concerning) the law that is in force] A phrase used to indicate that a proposition relates to the law as it is.

delivery *n.* The transfer of possession of property from one person to another. Under the Sale of Goods Act 1979, a seller delivers goods to a buyer if he delivers them physically, if he makes **symbolic delivery** by delivering the document of title to them (e.g. a *bill of lading) or other means of control over them (e.g. the keys of a warehouse in which they are stored), or if a third party who is holding them acknowledges that he now holds them for the buyer. In **constructive delivery**, the seller agrees that he holds the goods on behalf of the buyer or the buyer has possession of the goods under a hire-purchase agreement and becomes owner on making the final payment.

demanding with menaces *See* BLACKMAIL.

demerger *n.* The split of a company or a group of companies carrying on two or more trades, so that different persons after the demerger own the different trades. The Corporation Taxes Act 2010 ss 1073–1117 provides reliefs so a demerger is not treated as a payment of a dividend for tax purposes.

de minimis non curat lex [Latin] The law does not take account of trifles. It will not, for example, award damages for a trifling nuisance. The *de minimis* rule applies in a number of other areas, including EU *competition law.

demise (in land law) **1.** *vb.* To grant a lease. **2.** *n.* The lease itself.

demise charter *See* BAREBOAT CHARTER.

demise of the Crown The death of the sovereign. The Crown, in fact, never dies: the accession of the new sovereign takes place at the moment of the demise, and there is no interregnum.

demonstrative legacy *See* LEGACY.

demoted tenancy A tenancy granted by a social landlord that has lost the security of tenure it would normally enjoy owing to the antisocial behaviour of the tenant or a member of his household. Demoted tenancies were introduced by the Anti-Social Behaviour Act 2003.

demur *vb.* To object formally to a pleading. Such an objection is a **demurrer**.

demurrage *n.* Liquidated *damages payable under a charterparty at a specified daily rate for any days (**demurrage days**) required for completing the loading or discharging of cargo after the *lay days have expired. The word is also commonly used to denote the unliquidated damages to which the shipowner is entitled if, when no lay days are specified, the ship is detained for loading or unloading beyond a reasonable time.

demutualization *n.* The reincorporation as a *public company of a *building society or an insurance company that has previously been a *mutual society.

Department for Constitutional Affairs (DCA) A UK government department created in 2003 from the former *Lord Chancellor's Department. Its principal responsibilities were running the courts and justice system, upholding legal and human rights, and modernizing the constitution in terms of the Constitutional Reform Act 2005. Associated bodies included the Office for Judicial Complaints and the Judicial Appointments Commission. The Secretary of State for Constitutional Affairs was the Lord Chancellor. The responsibilities of the DCA transferred to the new *Ministry of Justice in May 2007.

departure *n.* (in civil proceedings) The introduction of a new allegation of fact or the raising of a new ground or claim inconsistent with the party's earlier claim. Under Part 17 of the *Civil Procedure Rules *amendments to *statements of case may be made with the written consent of all the other parties or with the permission of the court. The court will generally allow amendments so that the real dispute between the parties can be adjudicated upon, provided that any prejudice to the other party caused by the amendment can be compensated for in costs.

dependant *n.* A person who relies on someone else for maintenance or financial support. On the death of the latter, the courts now have wide discretionary powers to award financial provision to dependants out of the estate of the deceased. The list of dependants includes not only spouses, former spouses, children, and children of the family, but anyone (e.g. a lover, housekeeper, or servant) who was being maintained to some extent by the deceased immediately before his death. *See also* REASONABLE FINANCIAL PROVISION.

dependants' leave Under the Employment Rights Act 1996, employees are entitled to a reasonable amount of unpaid time off work in the following situations:

- to provide assistance when a dependant falls ill, is pregnant (not including time off after the birth, which is *paternity leave or *parental leave), or is injured or assaulted;
- to make arrangements for the provision of care for a dependant who is ill or injured, or in consequence of the death of a dependant;
- because of the unexpected disruption or termination of arrangements for the care of a dependant;
- to deal with an incident that involves a child of the employee and occurs unexpectedly in a period during which an educational establishment the child attends is responsible for him (in school time).

A dependant is a husband, wife, civil partner, child or parent, or other relative or person who reasonably relies on the employee for assistance. Case: *Royal Bank of Scotland Plc v Harrison* [2009] ICR 116. *See also* ADOPTION LEAVE; MATERNITY RIGHTS.

dependent relative revocation The doctrine that if a testator revokes his will in the mistaken belief that a particular result will ensue, or that a particular set of facts exists when it does not, then the revoked will may still hold good. For example, if a testator destroys his will, in the mistaken belief that thereby an earlier will would be revived, the destroyed will will be held not to have been revoked. Similarly, a testator may revoke his will, intending to make another; the revoked will holds good if the testator subsequently makes no new will or an invalid one.

dependent state A member of the community of states with qualified or limited status. Such states possess no separate statehood or sovereignty: it is the parent state alone that possesses *international legal personality and has the capacity to exercise international rights and duties.

dependent territory A territory (e.g. a colony) the government of which is to some extent the legal responsibility of the government of another territory.

de plano [Latin: summarily] In civil litigation, a procedural device used to settle a case without trial where there is no disagreement on material issues of fact. *See* SUMMARY JUDGMENT.

deponent *n.* A person who gives testimony under oath, which is reduced to writing for use on the trial of a cause.

deportation *n.* The removal from a state of a foreign national. In the UK this is authorized in the case of any person who does not have *right of abode by the Immigration Act 1971 (as amended by the Immigration and Asylum Act 1999 and the

Nationality, Immigration and Asylum Act 2002) and by the UK Borders Act (2007). A foreign national may be ordered to leave the country in five circumstances: if he has overstayed or broken a condition attached to his permission to stay; if (he being 17 or over) a court recommends deportation on his conviction of an offence punishable with imprisonment; if he is convicted of a crime and sentenced to 12 months or longer in prison (*see* FOREIGN NATIONAL OFFENDERS); if the Secretary of State thinks his deportation to be for the public good; or if another person to whose family he belongs is deported. Appeals against deportation orders are made to the *Immigration and Asylum Tribunal, except where the individual served with the order is held to be a threat to national security; in this case the appeal must be made to the Special Immigration Appeals Commission (SIAC) established under the Special Immigration Appeals Commission Act 1997. The Immigration Act 1988 restricts the right of appeal in the case of those who have failed to observe a condition or limitation on their leave to enter the UK. The Immigration and Asylum Act 2000, the Nationality, Immigration and Asylum Act 2002, and the Immigration, Asylum and Nationality Act 2006 all give additional powers to order those present in the UK without permission to leave, either when they have overstayed or obtained leave to remain by deception or when they were never granted leave to remain. The legislation also provides for the removal of asylum claimants under standing arrangements with other EU member states (*R v Secretary of State for the Home Department, ex p Khan* [1995] 2 All ER 540 (CA)). Under the *European Convention on Human Rights there is an absolute prohibition against deporting a person to a country where he risks being tortured. In international law the term *expulsion is usually preferred to deportation in those cases where an individuals legal right to remain is terminated by the state. *See also* DUBLIN CONVENTION.

depose *vb*. To make a *deposition or other written statement on oath.

deposit *n*. **1.** A sum paid by one party to a contract to the other party as a guarantee that the first party will carry out the terms of the contract. The first party will forfeit the sum in question if he does not carry out the terms, even if the sum is in excess of the other party's loss. If the contract is completed without dispute the deposit becomes part payment. In land law a deposit is usually made by a purchaser when exchanging contracts (*see* EXCHANGE OF CONTRACTS) for the purchase of land. The contract stipulates whether the recipient (usually the vendor's solicitor or estate agent) holds the deposit as agent for the vendor, in which case the vendor can use the money pending *completion of the transaction, or as stakeholder, in which case the funds must remain in the stakeholder's account until completion or (in the case of a dispute) a court has decided who should have it. If the contract is rescinded the purchaser is entitled to the return of his deposit. **2.** The placing of title deeds with a mortgagee of unregistered land as security for the debt. A mortgagee not protected by deposit of title deeds (such as a second mortgagee of unregistered land) registers his mortgage (*see* REGISTRATION OF ENCUMBRANCES) and is then entitled to receive the title deeds from prior mortgagees after the redemption of their security. All mortgages of registered land must be registered to be binding on purchases of the land.

deposition *n*. In civil proceedings, a statement made on oath before a judge or an examiner of the court under Part 34 of the *Civil Procedure Rules. The court may order an examiner of the court to take depositions from any witnesses who are (for example) ill or likely to be abroad at the time of the hearing. At the taking of the deposition the witness is examined and cross-examined as if he was giving evidence at trial; the evidence of the witness is recorded in full. A deposition may be given in evidence at a hearing or at trial. *See also* LETTER OF REQUEST.

deprave *vb.* To make morally bad. The term is used particularly in relation to the effect of *obscene publications. A person is considered to have been depraved if his mind is influenced in an immoral way, even though this does not necessarily result in any act of depravity.

Deprivation of Liberty Safeguards (DOLS) A framework introduced in 2009 under the Mental Capacity Act 2005 (as amended by the Mental Health Act 2007) to protect the rights of adult patients who require treatment in a hospital or care home in conditions that might amount to a deprivation of liberty, but are incapable of giving consent to these restrictions (*see* INCOMPETENT PATIENT). Individuals who fall within the remit of the safeguards would include those with severe learning difficulties, people suffering from dementia, and those with brain injuries. In such cases authorization to deprive a patient of liberty must be sought from the relevant local authority or the NHS *Clinical Commissioning Group, which will then carry out various assessments to determine whether such a deprivation is in the patient's best interests.

The safeguards were introduced to close the legal loophole known as the *Bournewood gap, following a ruling by the European Court of Human Rights that the rights of patients in these circumstances had been violated (*HL v UK* App (2004) 40 EHRR 761). The DOLS do not apply to persons detained under the Mental Health Act 1983 (*see* MENTAL DISORDER), which offers a separate framework of safeguards.

deputy *n.* A person appointed by the court under section 16 of the Mental Capacity Act 2005 to take decisions relating to the personal welfare of someone lacking capacity. A deputy has the power to give or refuse *consent to medical treatment.

derecognition *n.* A process whereby notice is given to terminate union recognition in an establishment or company. Employees continue to have the right to belong to a trade union, but the employer no longer negotiates collectively: terms and conditions previously the subject of *collective bargaining are negotiated individually or with groups of employees unconnected with trade unions, resulting in a **personal contract**. *See also* RECOGNITION PROCEDURE.

deregulation *n.* **1.** The controls imposed by governments on the operation of markets, such as is allowed for under the Deregulation and Contracting Out Act 1990. **2.** A movement in the EU to reduce rules at Community level that could be better set at national level (*see* SUBSIDIARITY).

derivative claim A claim brought under section 260 of the Companies Act 2006 by a member of a company on behalf of the company for a wrong done to it. Such a claim, formerly available at common law, is an exception to the rule in *Foss v Harbottle* (1843) 2 Hare 461, namely, that the proper claimant to bring a claim for a wrong done to a company is the company itself. To bring a derivative claim, the member must show a prima facie case in accordance with section 261 of the Companies Act and obtain the permission of the court to continue with the claim. Section 260 of the Companies Act provides that the member must establish that there has been an actual or proposed act or omission involving negligence, default, breach of trust, or breach of duty by a director, former director, or shadow director of the company and that the company has a cause of action arising from such a breach. Where the court is satisfied that there is a prima facie case, it has the power, inter alia, to give directions as to the evidence to be provided by the company and, on hearing the application, to give or refuse permission to continue the claim. Under section 263 of the Companies Act, the court must refuse to give permission where it is satisfied that a person acting in accordance with section 172 of the Act (duty to promote the success of the company) would not seek to continue with the claim, or where the act has been authorized or ratified by the company. Where this is not the case, factors the court can take into account in deciding whether to allow the claim to proceed include: whether the member is acting in good faith (*Barrett v Duckett* [1995] 1 BCLC 243 (CA)); the importance that a person acting in accordance with section 172 of the Act would attach to continuing the claim (*Franbar Holdings Ltd v Patel* [2008] EWHC 1534 (Ch), [2008] WLR (D) 220; *Kiani v Cooper* [2010] EWHC 577 (Ch), BCC 463); whether the act in the circumstances would be likely to be authorized or ratified by the company; whether the company has decided not to pursue the claim; whether the member could pursue an action in his own right (*Franbar Holdings Ltd v Patel*); and the views of other members who have no personal interest (*Smith v Croft* (No 2) [1988] Ch 114). Any decision by the company to ratify the conduct of a director amounting to a breach of duty must be taken by the members, the votes of the director as member not counting, unless consent is unanimous (Companies Act s 239). The common law and equitable rules on acts that are incapable of ratification are preserved by the Act. Examples of cases in which the court has allowed a claim to proceed (albeit in some cases limited to disclosure of documents) are *Kiani v Cooper* [2010] BCC 463; *Stainer v Lee* [2010] EWHC 1539 (Ch); and *Phillips v Fryer* [2012] EWHC 1611 (Ch).

derivative deed A deed that is supplemental to another, whose scope it alters, confirms, or extends. An example is a deed admitting a new partner to a firm on terms set out in a principal deed executed by the original partners.

derivative title A claim of sovereignty over a territory, that territory having previously belonged to another sovereign state. Derivation of title to territory involves the transfer (*cession) of title from one sovereign state to another.

derivative trust *See* SUB-TRUST.

derogation *n.* Lessening or restriction of the authority, strength, or power of a law, right, or obligation. Specifically: **1.** (in the European Convention on Human Rights) A provision that enables a signatory state to avoid the obligations of some but not all of the substantive provisions of the rest of the Convention in time of war or other public emergency threatening the life of the nation (Article 15).

Following the terrorist attacks on the USA of 11 September 2001 and the passing of the Antiterrorism, Crime and Security Act 2001, the UK government derogated from Article 5 of the Convention. This derogation was necessary because that Act allowed the detention by the Secretary of State of certain foreign nationals merely on the basis that they were suspected of involvement in terrorism. That provision was declared to be in breach of the Convention by the House of Lords in December 2004 (*A v Secretary of State for the Home Department* [2004] UKHL 56, [2005] 2 AC 68) and abandoned in March 2005. Subsequently the Grand Chamber of the European Court of Human Rights followed the reasoning of the House of Lords and also found a violation of the Convention (*A v UK* (App no 3455/05) (2009) 49 EHRR 29). **2.** (in EU law) An exemption clause that permits a member state of the EU to avoid a certain directive or regulation. Sometimes member states are allowed a longer than normal time to implement an EU directive.

desertion *n.* **1.** The failure by a husband or wife to cohabit with his or her spouse. Desertion usually takes the form of physically leaving the home, but this is not essential: there may be desertion although both parties live under the same roof, if all elements of a shared life (e.g. sexual intercourse, eating meals together) have ceased. Desertion must be a unilateral act carried out against the wishes of the other spouse, with the intention of bringing married life to an end (*animus deserendi*). If it is continuous for more than two years, it may be evidence that the marriage has irretrievably broken down and entitle the deserted spouse to a decree of *divorce. *See also* CONSTRUCTIVE DESERTION. **2.** An offence under the Armed Forces Act 2006 committed by a member of the armed forces who leaves or fails to attend at his unit, ship, or place of duty without lawful authority. He must intend to remain permanently absent from duty or intend to avoid a period of active service.

design right Legal protection for the external appearance of an article, including its shape, configuration, pattern, or ornament. A design right is distinct from a *patent, which protects the internal workings of the article. The right entitles the owner to prevent others making articles to the same design. Design rights in the UK are either registered (*see* REGISTERED DESIGN) or unregistered. Registered designs must have aesthetic appeal; they are protected under the Registered Designs Act 1949 as amended and last for a maximum of 25 years provided renewal fees are paid. Unregistered designs, which came into existence in 1989, are protected under the Copyright, Designs and Patents Act 1988. In the EU an unregistered design right lasts for three years from the point at which the design is first disclosed or made available to the public in some manner. In the UK unregistered rights last for ten years from the end of the calendar year in which the design was first made into a marketable product. The date at which the design was first fixed in a tangible form is also taken into account, and the duration should not exceed 15 years from the end of the calendar year in which the design was first recorded. The UK's ten-year duration is split into two five-year periods: exclusive rights are retained for the first five years, but during the remaining five years other parties are allowed to apply for licenses to the design (for which royalties can be charged). For UK designers, both the UK and EU rights can exist at the same time. It is also possible to register an EU-wide Community Design Right that provides protection in all EU member states. In 2012 some changes to UK design law were proposed by the Intellectual Property Office (IPO).

de son tort *See* EXECUTOR DE SON TORT; TRUSTEE DE SON TORT.

desuetude *n.* [Latin: disuse] The condition of a legal term or measure that has fallen into disuse over time. For example, the Treason Act of 1351 is still in force today. Under this Act, the crime of high treason is made out if anyone "violate" the King's companion, the King's eldest daughter if she was unmarried (even presumably if she were to give her consent), or the wife of the King's eldest son and heir. It is arguable that these offences, though still within an enforceable statute, have fallen into desuetude and in consequence would not be enforced by a court of law today. Until the entry into force of section 36 of the Crime and Disorder Act 1998, the death penalty could be enforced for acts of treason by English courts.

detention *n.* Depriving a person of his liberty against his will following *arrest. The Police and Criminal Evidence Act 1984 closely regulates police powers of detention and detained persons' rights. In general, detention of adults without charge is allowed only when it is necessary to secure or preserve evidence or to obtain it by questioning; it should only continue beyond 24 hours (to 36 hours) in respect of serious indictable offences (e.g. rape, kidnapping, causing death by dangerous driving) when a superintendent or more senior officer reasonably believes it to be necessary. Magistrates' courts may then authorize a further extension without charge for up to 36 hours, which can be extended for another 36 hours, but the overall detention period cannot exceed 96 hours.

If the ground for detention ceases, or if further detention is not authorized, the detainee must either be released or be charged and either released on *bail to appear before a court or taken before the next available court. An arrested person held in custody may have one person told of this as soon as practicable, though if a serious arrestable offence is involved and a senior police officer reasonably believes that this would interfere with the investigation, this can be delayed for up to 36 hours. The detainee has a broadly similar right of access to a solicitor. Under the *Terrorism Act 2006 the period for which terrorist suspects may be detained without charge was extended from 14 days to 28 days.

detention and training order (DTO) A custodial sentence that may be passed on a person aged 12 or over but under 17 (*see* JUVENILE OFFENDER). The offence must be such that it would be punishable by imprisonment if committed by an adult. The minimum detention period for the order is 4 months and the maximum period is 2 years. Normally, half the sentence is served in detention and half in the community under the supervision of a probation officer or other responsible person. DTOs replaced secure training orders (for 12–14 year olds) and detention in a young offender institution (for 15–17 year olds) in 2000.

detention for assessment *See* MENTAL DISORDER.

detention for treatment *See* MENTAL DISORDER.

determinable interest An interest that will automatically come to an end on the occurrence of some specified event (which, however, may never happen). For example, if A conveys land to B until he marries, B has a determinable interest that would pass back to A upon his marriage. But if B dies a bachelor the *possibility of a reverter to A is destroyed and B's heirs acquire an absolute interest. An interest that must end at some future point (e.g. a *life interest) is not classified as a determinable interest, but one that could end during a person's life (for example a *protective trust) is so classified. A determinable legal estate in land prior to 1925 was known as a **determinable fee**, but under the Law of Property Act 1925 it can now exist only as an equitable interest. It is exceptionally difficult to distinguish between a determinable interest and a *conditional interest. *Compare* CONTINGENT INTEREST.

deterrence *n. See* PUNISHMENT.

devastavit *n.* [Latin: he has wasted] The failure of a personal representative to administer a deceased person's estate promptly and in a proper manner. For example, if he pays in full a legacy subject to the possibility of *abatement he is personally liable for the loss suffered by other beneficiaries and caused by his *devastavit*. He may also be liable if, for example, he disposes of an asset in the estate at an undervalue, even if acting in good faith.

development *n.* (in *town and country planning) Generally, the carrying out of any building or other operation affecting land and the making of any material change in the use of any buildings or land. Development does not include alterations to buildings not materially affecting their external appearance or changes of use that fall within certain **use classes** prescribed by statutory instrument. For example, office use is a use class and a mere change in the type of office business is not development. All development requires planning permission, other than "permitted development" under a general development order. The demolition of houses to provide car parking and a landscaped area is not development.

development plan *See* TOWN AND COUNTRY PLANNING.

deviation *n.* (in marine insurance) The departure of a ship from an agreed course. A ship must follow the course specified in a voyage or mixed insurance policy (*see* TIME

POLICY); if no course is specified, the ship must follow the usual course for the voyage. Deviation discharges the underwriters from all liability for subsequent loss (even though it may not increase the risk) unless it is caused by circumstances beyond control or is justified on certain very limited grounds (e.g. to ensure the safety of the ship or to save human life, but not merely to save property). Unreasonable delay may also amount to deviation. Insurance cover does not revive when the ship rejoins the original course. Between the parties to a voyage charter, the possibility of deviation is normally the subject of an express deviation clause in the *charterparty. For goods carried under a *bill of lading, permitted deviation is dealt with by the Hague Rules.

devil 1. *n.* A junior member of the Bar who does work (usually settling statements of case or writing opinions) for a more senior barrister under an informal arrangement between them and without reference to the senior's instructing solicitor. The Junior Counsel to the Treasury is sometimes referred to as the **Attorney General's devil**. 2. *vb.* To act as a devil.

devise 1. *n.* A gift by will of *real property (*compare* BEQUEST; LEGACY); the beneficiary is called the **devisee**. A devise may be **specific** (e.g. "my house, Blackacre, to A"), **general** (e.g. "all my real property to B"), or **residuary** (e.g. after a specific devise "...and the rest of my real property to C"). 2. *vb.* To dispose of real property by will.

devolution *n.* 1. The delegation by the central government to a regional authority of legislative or executive functions (or both) relating to domestic issues within the region. The word is most commonly used in the context of such functions in Scotland, Wales, and Northern Ireland. For example, the Scotland Act 1998 devolved power to the *Scottish Parliament, enabling it to make certain Acts in some areas of policy and to alter income tax. However, the UK parliament reserved power to make laws for Scotland. The Government of Wales Act 1998 gave limited administrative powers to the *Welsh Assembly and further legislation has given the Assembly a legislative function. The Northern Ireland Act 1998 established an elected *Northern Ireland Assembly with a power sharing executive and power was devolved in December 1999. However, the Northern Ireland Act 2000 enables power to revert to the UK parliament, suspending the Northern Ireland Assembly until the Secretary of State makes a restoration order. The Assembly was in a state of suspension from October 2002 until May 2007, when devolved power was restored. 2. The passing of property from one owner to another, which may occur on death or sale, as a gift, by operation of law, or in any other way.

dictum *n.* [Latin: a saying] An observation by a judge with respect to a point of law arising in a case before him. *See also* OBITER DICTUM.

dies non juridicus [Latin] A day upon which the courts do not sit, such as a Sunday.

digital signature Data appended to a unit of data held on a computer, or a cryptographic transformation of a data unit, that allows the recipient of the data unit to prove its source and integrity and protects against forgery. The International Standards Organization defined this means of identification and protection. An *electronic signature, as defined by the Electronic Communications Act 2000, has a similar effect in relation to a commercial agreement.

dilapidation *n.* A state of disrepair. The term is usually used in relation to repairs required at the end of a lease or tenancy.

diminished responsibility An abnormality of mental functioning that does not constitute *insanity (*R v Seers* [1984] 79 Cr App 261 CA) but is a partial defence to a charge of murder. Under the Coroners and Justice Act 2009, the phrase abnormality of mental functioning replaces abnormality of mind in the earlier legislation; the abnormality must also have arisen from a recognized medical condition (*R v Dowds* [2012] EWCA Crim 281 (CA), [2012] 1 Cr App R 455). To serve as a defence, the abnormality of mental functioning must substantially impair the defendants ability: (i) to understand the nature of his conduct; (ii) to form a rational judgment; and (iii) to exercise self-control. It has been liberally interpreted to cover such conditions as depression or *irresistible impulse (*R v Vinagre* (1979) 69 Cr App R 104). If the defendant proves the defence, he is convicted of *manslaughter. *See also* BATTERED WOMAN SYNDROME; DOMESTIC VIOLENCE; INTOXICATION; LOSS OF CONTROL.

diplomatic agent One of a class of state officials who are entrusted with the responsibility for representing their state and its interests and welfare and that of its citizens or subjects in the jurisdiction of another state or in international organizations. Diplomatic agents can be generally classified into two groups: (1) heads of mission and (2) members of the staff of the mission having diplomatic rank. *See also* DIPLOMATIC IMMUNITY; DIPLOMATIC MISSION.

diplomatic immunity The freedom from legal proceedings in the UK that is granted to members of diplomatic missions of foreign states by the Diplomatic Privileges Act 1964. This Act incorporates some of the provisions of the Vienna Convention on Diplomatic Relations (1961), which governs diplomatic immunity in international law. The extent of the immunity depends upon the status of the member in question, as certified by the Secretary of State. If he is a member of the mission's diplomatic staff, he is entitled to complete criminal immunity and to civil immunity except for actions relating to certain private activities. A member of the administrative or technical staff has full criminal immunity, but his civil immunity relates only to acts performed in the course of his official duties. For domestic staff, both criminal and civil immunity are restricted to official duties. The so-called **diplomatic bag** is immune from search and seizure, as are the premises of the mission.

Similar immunities are granted to members of Commonwealth missions by the Diplomatic and other Privileges Act 1971, and to members of certain international bodies under the International Organisations Acts 1968 and 1981. Under the Diplomatic and Consular Premises Act 1987, the Secretary of State may remove diplomatic status from diplomatic or consular premises that are being misused.

diplomatic mission A body composed of government officers representing the interests and welfare of their state who have been posted abroad (by the sending state) and operate within the jurisdisdiction of another state (the receiving state). This mission will be accorded protection by the receiving state in accordance with the rules of *diplomatic immunity. *See also* DIPLOMATIC AGENT.

direct evidence (original evidence) **1.** A statement made by a witness in court offered as proof of the truth of any fact stated by him. *Compare* HEARSAY EVIDENCE. **2.** A statement of a witness that he perceived a fact in issue with one of his five senses (percipient evidence) or that he was in a particular physical or mental state. *Compare* CIRCUMSTANTIAL EVIDENCE.

direct examination *See* EXAMINATION-IN-CHIEF.

directions questionnaire Under the latest *Civil Procedure Rules, a questionnaire that is served on both parties after the defendant has filed a defence; its purpose is to assist the court in allocating the case to the most appropriate track (*see* ALLOCATION). As such, it replaces the *allocation questionnaire for all cases in which a defence is received on or after 1 April 2013. There are now two separate questionnaires: one for cases that the court has provisionally allocated to the *small claims track; and one for cases that may be allocated to either the *fast track or the *multi-track. Failure to return a completed questionnaire and any accompanying documents by the date specified may result in the claim (or the defence) being struck out.

direction to jury Instructions by a judge to a jury on a point of law (e.g. the definition of the crime charged or the nature and scope of possible defences). Failure to direct correctly may be grounds for an appeal if any resulting conviction is deemed unsafe.

directives of the EU *See* COMMUNITY LEGISLATION.

Direct Labour Organization A local government division, staffed by local government employees, that submits bids for services in competition with private-sector companies when these services are put out to compulsory *competitive tendering.

directly applicable law Any provision of the law of the European Union that automatically forms part of the national law of the member states. EU regulations are directly applicable. *See* COMMUNITY LAW; COMMUNITY LEGISLATION.

directly effective law Any provision of the law of the European Union that is not *directly applicable but that grants individual rights against the state with immediate effect (i.e. before it has been implemented by domestic legislation). EU directives have direct effect (*Van Duyn v Home Office* [1974] 1 WLR 1107 (Ch), case 41/74 [1974] ECR 1337). *See* COMMUNITY LAW; COMMUNITY LEGISLATION.

director *n.* An officer of a company appointed by or under the provisions of the *articles of association. Directors may have a contract of employment with the company (**service directors** and *managing directors) or merely attend board meetings (**nonexecutive directors**). (*See also* SHADOW DIRECTOR.) Contracts of employment can be inspected by company members (Companies Act 2006 s 239); contracts of two years or more duration require approval by ordinary resolution (Companies Act 2006 s 188). Usually, general management powers are vested in the directors acting collectively, although they may delegate some or all of these powers to the managing director. Directors act as agents of their company, to which they owe *fiduciary duties (in the performance of which they must consider the interests of both company members and employees) and a *duty of care (Companies Act 2006 s 170–77). Transactions involving a conflict between their duty and their personal interests are regulated by the Companies Act 2006 (in particular s 175, s 177, and s 182–214). Directors can be dismissed by *ordinary resolution despite the terms of the articles or any contract of employment, but dismissal in these circumstances is subject to the payment of damages for breach of contract (Companies Act 2006 s 168). Under the Company Directors Disqualification Act 1986, directors may be disqualified for *fraudulent trading or *wrongful trading and conduct that makes them unfit to be concerned in the management of companies.

Remuneration of directors for their services may be due under a contract of employment or determined by the general meeting. Particulars appear in the *accounts and, if a listed company, in the directors' remuneration report.

Director of Public Prosecutions (DPP) The head of the * Crown Prosecution Service (CPS), who must be a lawyer of at least ten years' general qualification. The DPP is appointed by the *Attorney General and discharges his functions under the superintendence of the Attorney General. The DPP, through the CPS, is responsible for the conduct of all criminal prosecutions instituted by the police and he may intervene in any criminal proceedings when it appears to him to be appropriate. Some statutes require the consent of the DPP to prosecution.

Director of Service Prosecutions (DSP) The head of the **Service Prosecuting Authority (SPA)**, who must be a lawyer of at least ten years' general qualification. The DSP, through the SPA, is responsible for the conduct of all service prosecutions before the *Court Martial and the *Service Civilian Court under the Armed Forces Act 2006. The DSP is appointed by the Queen and discharges his functions under the superintendence of the *Attorney General.

directors' authority to act A director's authority to act on behalf of a company may be based on actual or apparent authority. **Actual authority** is either express or implied. **Express authority** is an explicit conferring of authority on a director from, for example, the *articles of association or a contract of employment (*SMC Electronics Ltd v Akhter Computers Ltd* [2001] 1 BCLC 433 (CA)). **Implied authority** comprises usual authority (i.e. those powers that fall within the usual scope of the office to which the individual has been appointed) or authority based on the conduct of the partiesas, for example, where a director on previous occasions has been allowed by his principal to act in excess of his authority (*Hely-Hutchinson v Brayhead Ltd* [1968] 1 QB 549). **Apparent** (or **ostensible**) **authority** is the authority of an agent as it appears to others: i.e., the particular agent has been held out by their principal as possessing the requisite authority (*Freeman & Lockyer v Buckhurst Park Properties (Mangal) Ltd* [1964] 2 QB 480).

directors' duties Obligations owed by a director of a company. The purpose of such duties, which are based on the common law and equitable principles, is to safeguard the interests of the company. The duties are owed to the company (Companies Act 2006 s 170) and apply also to *shadow directors to the extent provided for by common law or equitable principles (s 170(5)). The Companies Act sets out seven "general" duties:

- the duty to act within the powers of the company's constitution and to exercise the powers for the purposes for which they are conferred (s 171) (*Howard Smith Ltd v Ampol Petroleum Ltd* [1974] AC 821(PC));
- the duty to act in good faith to promote the success of the company for the benefit of its members as a whole (s 172) (*Re Smith & Fawcett Ltd* [1942] Ch 304);
- the duty to exercise independent judgment (s 173) (*Fulham Football Club Ltd v Cabra Estates plc* [1994] 1 BCLC 363(CA));
- the duty to exercise reasonable care, skill, and diligence (s 174) (*Re City Equitable Fire Insurance Co Ltd* [1925] Ch 407);
- the duty to avoid conflicts of interest (s 175) (*Regal (Hastings) Ltd v Gulliver* [1942] 2 AC 134(HL));
- the duty not to accept benefits from third parties (s 176) (*Boston Deep Sea Fishing Co v Ansell* [1888] 39 Ch D);
- the duty to declare an interest in any proposed transaction or arrangement with the company (s 177).

disability discrimination *See* DISABLED PERSON; DISCRIMINATION.

disability living allowance A tax-free benefit payable to those under 65 who have had a disability requiring help for at least three months and are likely to need such help for at least a further six months. It has two components: a care component, payable at three rates to those needing help with personal care; and a mobility component, payable at two rates to those aged three or over who need help with walking. The rates depend on the level of help required. For most claimants disability living allowance was replaced by a **Personal Independence Payment** from April 2013. Claimants over 65 continue to receive the allowance and there are no plans to replace it for those under the age of 16.

Disability Rights Commission (DRC) A body established in 2000 by the Disability Rights Commission Act 1999 to monitor the working of the Disability Discrimination Acts 1995–2005 and to promote equality of opportunity for disabled people. Since 1 October 2007 the functions of the DRC have been integrated into the *Equality and Human Rights Commission.

disabled person Under the Equality Act 2010 (as previously under the Disability Discrimination Act 1995), a person who has a physical or mental impairment that has a substantial and long term effect on his abilities to carry out day-to-day activities (although some conditions, including HIV and multiple sclerosis, qualify from the point of diagnosis). The Act makes it unlawful to discriminate against a person solely because he has a disability (e.g. refusing to employ someone who is qualified to do the job simply because he has cerebral palsy or because she is partially sighted). Where the *discrimination results from a reason arising from the disability, the employer is allowed a defence of justification (e.g. where a wheelchair user is refused employment because the office is up a steep flight of stairs and there is no lift). The employer is, however, under a duty to make *reasonable adjustments in relation to the disabled person. These might include alterations to premises (e.g. a stairlift) or to working conditions. Disabled persons are also protected from *indirect discrimination, *harassment, and *victimization. The law applies to all employers, regardless of size. The legislation is overseen by the *Equality and Human Rights Commission as successor to the Disability Rights Commission. *See also* MENTAL DISABILITY; PRE-EMPLOYMENT HEALTH QUESTIONNAIRES.

disablement benefit *See* INDUSTRIAL INJURIES DISABLEMENT BENEFIT.

disabling statute A statute that disqualifies a person or persons of a specified class from exercising a legal right or freedom that he or they would otherwise enjoy.

disbar *vb.* To expel a barrister from his *Inn of Court. The sentence of disbarment is pronounced by the *Benchers of the barrister's Inn, subject to a right of appeal to the judges who act as visitors of all the Inns of Court.

disbursement *n.* A cost incurred by a solicitor or barrister while acting on behalf of a client.

discharge *n.* Release from an obligation, debt, or liability, particularly the following. **1.** *Discharge of contract. **2.** The release of a debtor from all *provable debts (with minor exceptions) at the end of *bankruptcy proceedings. In certain circumstances discharge is automatic. In other cases, the debtor or the official receiver may apply to the court for an **order of discharge**. This may be subject to conditions, such as further payments by the debtor to his creditors out of his future income, or it may be suspended until the creditors receive a higher proportion of the amount due to them. After discharge the debtor is freed from most of the disabilities to which he was subject as an *undischarged bankrupt. **3.** The release of a convicted defendant without imposing a punishment on him. A discharge may be absolute or conditional. In an **absolute discharge** the defendant is not punished for the offence. His conviction may, however, be accompanied by a *compensation order or by *endorsement of his driving licence or *disqualification from driving. A **conditional discharge** also releases the defendant without punishment, provided that he is not convicted of any other offence within a specified period (usually three years). If he is convicted within that time, the court may sentence him for the original offence as well. Three conditions are required for the court to order a discharge: (1) that a community sentence is not appropriate; (2) that the punishment for the offence must not be fixed by law; and (3) that the court thinks it inadvisable to punish the defendant in the circumstances.

discharge of contract The termination of a contractual obligation. Discharge may take place by: (1) *performance of contract; (2) express agreement, which may involve either *bilateral discharge or unilateral discharge (*see* ACCORD AND SATISFACTION); (3) *breach of contract; or (4) *frustration of contract.

disclaimer *n.* The refusal or renunciation of a right, claim, or property. A beneficiary under a will may disclaim (i.e. reject) his gift at any time after the death of the testator as long as he has not accepted any benefit from the gift. The disclaimed property then passes to other beneficiaries entitled under the will or under the intestacy rules. A trustee may disclaim a trust if he has not yet accepted it; once he has accepted his trusteeship he may no longer disclaim it but he may resign (*see* RETIREMENT OF TRUSTEES). Trusts and powers are normally disclaimed by deed.

disclosure *n.* **1.** (in contract law) *See* NONDISCLOSURE; UBERRIMAE FIDEI. **2.** (in company law) **a.** A method of protecting investors that relies on the company disclosing and publishing information, which is then evaluated by the investors, their advisers, and the press. *See also* STOCK EXCHANGE. **b.** A method of regulating the conduct of directors and promoters by requiring them, on *fiduciary principles or by statutory provisions, to disclose to the company any relevant information, e.g. an interest in a contract with the company.

disclosure and inspection of documents Disclosure by a party to civil litigation under Part 31 of the *Civil Procedure Rules of the *documents in his possession, custody, or power relating to matters in question in the action and their subsequent inspection by the opposing party. Before the introduction of the Civil Procedure Rules in 1999, this procedure was called **discovery and inspection of documents**. Directions for disclosure generally take place at the *allocation stage or the *case management conference and, unless the court directs or the parties agree otherwise, there will normally be a direction for **standard disclosure**. This involves a reasonable search by each party to disclose documents on which that party intends to rely, documents that may be adverse to their own case or another party's case, documents that support another party's case, and documents that are required to be disclosed by any relevant *Practice Direction. Once a party has served a list of documents, the other party, together with any co-defendants, must be allowed to inspect the documents referred to in the list. However, some documents, although they must be disclosed in the list, may be privileged and thus exempted from the requirement to produce them for inspection (*see* PRIVILEGE). The court also has power under Part 31 of the Civil Procedure Rules to direct that **specific disclosure** and/or inspection be made. *See also* FAILURE TO MAKE DISCLOSURE; NONDISCLOSURE.

disclosure of information 1. (in employment law) The communication by an employer to employees and their trade-union representatives of information relevant to *collective bargaining, proposed *redundancies, and the preservation of employees' health and *safety at work. Under the Trade Union and Labour Relations (Consolidation) Act 1992, employers must disclose the following information to the representatives of a recognized *independent trade union or to other employee representatives where there is no recognized trade union.

(1) Information that is essential for the maintenance of good industrial relations or for the formulation of wage and related demands. The duty to disclose this information only arises if the union requests the information. When disclosure would damage national security or harm the business (apart from its effect on collective bargaining), or the information is *sub judice* or relevant only to particular individuals, disclosure need not be given. Guidelines on disclosure are published by *ACAS (*see also* CODE OF PRACTICE). When an employer refuses to disclose essential information, the *Central Arbitration Committee is empowered on the application of the trade union to make awards of wages and conditions that are ultimately enforceable in the courts.

(2) Details of any collective redundancies proposed by the employer. It must give the union 45 days' notice when 100 or more employees are to be made redundant over a period of 90 days or less, and 30 days' notice when between 20 and 99 redundancy dismissals are proposed within a 90-day period. The employer's notice must specify the reason for the proposals, the numbers and job descriptions of employees involved, the way in which employees have been selected for redundancy, and the procedures for their dismissal. It must consider any representations made by the union, but need not comply with its demands. If the employer fails to give the required notice, the union can apply to an employment tribunal, which may make a *protective award to the redundant employees. Additionally, employers are required to notify the Secretary of State *before* giving notice to terminate an employee's contract (Case C-188/03 *Junk v Kühnel* [2005] IRLR 310 (ECJ)).

Under the Health and Safety at Work Act 1974, an employer must give his employees at large such information, instruction, and supervision as will ensure their health and safety so far as is reasonably practicable. He must also give copies of any relevant documents to safety representatives appointed by a recognized trade union. **2.** (in criminal proceedings) The duty of disclosure of evidence by the prosecution, and of certain specified matters by the defence, under the Criminal Procedure and Investigations Act 1996 as amended by the Criminal Justice Act 2003. In criminal proceedings, the prosecution has a duty to disclose material relevant to an investigation but which does not form part of the prosecution case. In particular, the prosecution must provide the defence with copies of, or access to, any material that might reasonably be considered capable of undermining the prosecution case or of assisting the case for the accused. The defence duty of disclosure in criminal proceedings includes the requirement to serve a *defence statement; the requirement to give notice of the intention to call (and details of) defence witnesses; and the requirement to give notice of the decision to instruct (and details of) an expert witness. **3.** *See* BREACH OF CONFIDENCE.

disclosure of interest The duty of local authority members to disclose (at the time or by prior notice to the authority) any pecuniary interest, direct or indirect, that they or their spouses have in any matter discussed at a local authority meeting. They must also abstain from speaking and voting on it. Breach of the duty is a criminal offence.

discontinuance of action *See* NOTICE OF DISCONTINUANCE.

discontinuous lease A *lease in which the tenant's right to possession is not for a single continuous period but rather for, say, two weeks per year for five years. Such an arrangement is most common with holiday properties and is sometimes called a **timeshare lease**.

discovery *n.* (in international law) A method of acquiring territory in which good title can be gained by claiming previously unclaimed land (*terra nullius*). In the early days of European exploration it was held that the discovery of a previously unknown land conferred absolute title to it upon the state by whose agents the discovery was made. However, it has now long been established that the bare fact of discovery is an insufficient ground of proprietary right.

The distinction between acquisition by *cession and acquisition by discovery was based upon the difference between organized and unorganized societies. The North Island of New Zealand, for example, was treated as a case of acquisition by cession; whereas the South Island, which was largely uninhabited and not generally under the rule of any chiefs, was treated as a case of discovery. Equally, since the discoverers believed that the Australian aborigines were incapable of intelligent transactions with respect to land, Australia was treated as a *terra nullius*.

discovery and inspection of documents *See* DISCLOSURE AND INSPECTION OF DOCUMENTS.

discretion *n. See* JUDICIAL DISCRETION.

discretionary trust A trust under which the trustees are given discretion as to who, within a class chosen by the settlor, should receive trust property and how much each should receive. A settlor must give some indication as to the limits of the class of people he intends to benefit, but the trustees do not need to have an exhaustive list (*McPhail v Doulton* [1971] AC 424 (HL)). A beneficiary under a discretionary trust has no enforceable right to any part of the property or its income, and thus no *interest in possession in the trust property until such time as an appointment is made in favour of one or more of the class of beneficiaries (*Gartside v IRC* [1968] AC 553 (HL); *Sainsbury v IRC* [1970] Ch 712; *Re Smith* [1928] Ch 915). Such trusts are often very difficult to distinguish from *trust powers and *powers of appointment held by trustees.

Discretionary trusts have been invaluable in planning to mitigate liability to tax, but recent fiscal legislation has greatly reduced their advantages. Most discretionary trusts are now *relevant property trusts for tax purposes. *See* ACCUMULATION AND MAINTENANCE SETTLEMENT.

discrimination *n.* Treating a person less favourably than others on grounds unrelated to merit, usually because he or she belongs to a particular group or category. The *Equality Act 2010 governs unlawful discrimination. As well as direct discrimination, this may involve *indirect discrimination, *victimization, or *harassment. It is unlawful to discriminate on grounds of any of the "protected characteristics" in the Act: these include on grounds of sex (including gender reassignment), sexual orientation, religion or belief, disability, and age. *See* AGE DISCRIMINATION; POSITIVE DISCRIMINATION; RACE DISCRIMINATION; SEX DISCRIMINATION.

disentailing deed A deed used to bar (convert into a *fee simple) an *entailed interest.

disentailment *n.* The barring of an *entailed interest.

dishonest assistance *See* ACCESSORY LIABILITY IN BREACH OF TRUST.

dishonesty *n.* An element of liability in *theft, *abstracting electricity, *deception, *handling stolen goods, and some related offences. To convict of such offences the magistrates or jury must be satisfied that what was done was dishonest by the ordinary standards of honest and reasonable people and that the defendant realized this at the time (*R v Ghosh* [1982] QB 1053 (CA)).

dishonour *n.* (in commercial law) Failure to honour a bill of exchange. This may be by nonacceptance, when a bill of exchange is presented for *acceptance and this is refused or cannot be obtained (or when *presentment for acceptance is excused and the bill is not accepted); or by nonpayment, when the bill is presented for payment and payment is refused or cannot be obtained (or when presentment is excused and the bill is overdue and unpaid). In both cases the holder has an immediate right of recourse against the drawer and endorsers, but *foreign bills that have been dishonoured must first be protested (*see* PROTEST). *See also* NOTICE OF DISHONOUR.

dismissal *n.* (in employment law) The termination of an employee's contract of employment by the employer. An employer usually dismisses the employee by giving him the required period of *notice, but dismissal without notice may be justified in certain circumstances (e.g. for gross misconduct). An employer's failure to renew a fixed-term employment contract also counts as dismissal. An employee having the required length of service in the business (*see* CONTINUOUS EMPLOYMENT) can apply to an employment tribunal if he is unfairly dismissed (*see* UNFAIR DISMISSAL); the tribunal can order his *reinstatement or *re-engagement or can award him *compensation. An employee dismissed for *redundancy after two years' continuous employment in the business is entitled to a *redundancy payment under the Employment Rights Act 1996. An employee dismissed without due notice or before his fixed-term contract expires can also claim damages in the courts for *wrongful dismissal. *See also* DISMISSAL PROCEDURES; STATEMENT OF REASONS FOR DISMISSAL.

dismissal of action In civil proceedings, the termination of a claim in favour of the defendant. An order for dismissal of a claim may be made by the court on an application for *summary judgment under Part 24 of the *Civil Procedure Rules. *See* STRIKE OUT.

dismissal procedures In a claim for *unfair dismissal the *employment tribunal must consider whether, in addition to the employer being able to show a reason for the dismissal that is listed in the Employment Rights Act 1996, the employer acted reasonably (fairly) in treating the reason as justifying dismissal. An important part of deciding the fairness of a dismissal is the question of whether the employer followed a fair procedure. This would include, in appropriate cases, a warning, a hearing, and the possibility of an appeal. Guidance as to the kind of procedures an employer should follow in order to behave fairly are laid down in the *ACAS Code of Practice on Discipline and Grievance. If either party does not follow the Code, it is open to the tribunal to make adjustments in any compensation that is awarded.

disorderly house A *brothel or a place staging performances or exhibitions that tend to corrupt or deprave and outrage common decency. It is a misdemeanour at common law to keep a disorderly house (*R v Tan* [1983] QB 1053).

disparagement of goods *See* SLANDER OF GOODS.

disposal *n.* Although *capital gains tax (CGT) is charged when there is a disposal of an *asset, statute does not define disposal. It is declared that the receipt of a capital sum in relation to an asset may be treated as a disposal for the purpose of CGT (Taxation of Chargeable Gains Act 1992 s 22). When an asset is transferred to trustees, there is a disposal even if the settlor is the only person entitled to receive capital from the trust (*Re Paradise Motor Company Ltd* [1968] 1 WLR 1125 (CA)). In contrast, there is not a CGT disposal when an asset is transferred to a nominee (Taxation of Chargeable Gains Act 1992 s 60). Similarly, the passing of an asset from *personal representatives to the beneficiary under a will or intestacy is not a disposal for CGT purposes.

Certain events are treated as deemed disposals for CGT purposes, giving rise to a capital gain. These include the death of a life tenant of a trust and the vesting of a beneficial interest in property by a beneficiary reaching the age specified in the trust deed. A disposal under an unconditional contract takes place when the contract is made, and not on completion; a disposal under a conditional contract is made when the condition is satisfied.

There can be a difference between the person who makes the disposal and the person liable for the tax liability. In *Jerome v Kelly* [2004] UKHL 25, [2004] STC 887 the disposal was made by an individual, who then assigned his interest to trustees; the House of Lords held that the tax liability arose on the trustees, and not on the individual who made the disposal.

disposal of uncollected goods The sale by a bailee of goods in his possession or under his control when the bailor is in breach of an obligation to collect them (*see* BAILMENT). When the original contract does not require the bailor to collect the goods, the bailee may, by giving notice, impose such an obligation. The relevant statutory provisions in the Torts (Interference with Goods) Act 1977 lay down conditions relating to the giving of notice of the bailee's intention to sell, allowing the bailor a reasonable opportunity to collect. The bailee should adopt the best method of sale available and must account to the bailor for the proceeds of sale less any sum due before he gave notice of intention to sell. There is provision for a bailee to have a sale authorized by a court.

disposition *n.* **1.** (in land law) The transfer of property by some act of its owner, e.g. by sale, gift, will, or exchange. **2.** (in the law of evidence) The tendency of a person (especially the accused) to act in a particular way. *See also* ANTECEDENTS; CHARACTER.

disqualification *n.* Depriving someone of a right because he has committed a criminal offence or failed to comply with specified conditions. Disqualification is usually imposed in relation to activities requiring a licence, and in particular for traffic offences. In the case of many traffic offences, the court has discretion to disqualify drivers for a stated period. There are also a number of traffic offences for which disqualification for at least 12 months is compulsory (unless the offender can show special reasons relating to the circumstances of the offence, not to his personal circumstances). These offences are:

(1) manslaughter;
(2) *causing death by dangerous driving (the minimum disqualification period here is two years);
(3) *causing death by careless or inconsiderate driving;
(4) *dangerous driving;
(5) driving or attempting to drive while unfit;
(6) driving or attempting to drive with excess alcohol in the breath, blood, or urine (*see* DRUNKEN DRIVING);
(7) failure (in certain cases) to provide a *specimen of breath, blood, or urine;
(8) racing or speed trials on the highway.

If a person is convicted for a second time within ten years of a driving offence involving drink or drugs, he must be disqualified for at least three years. The courts may also disqualify anyone who commits an indictable offence of any kind involving the use of a car. There is also a *totting-up system of endorsements, which can result in disqualification. When someone is disqualified from driving, his licence will usually also be endorsed with details of the offence (but not with any penalty points for the purpose of totting up). The court may also make a *driving-test order. A person who has been disqualified from driving may apply to have the disqualification removed after two years or half the period of disqualification (whichever is longer) or, when he has been disqualified for ten years or more, after five years. *See also* DRIVING WHILE DISQUALIFIED.

dissentiente *adj.* [Latin] Dissenting from one's brother judges and making a speech to this effect. It is often abbreviated to **diss** in citations of cases.

dissolution *n.* **1.** The legal termination of a marriage by a decree of divorce, nullity, or *presumption of death or of a *civil partnership by the granting of a dissolution order. **2.** The dissolving of a *registered company. This can be achieved on the completion of a *winding-up (as provided for by sections 201–03 and 205 of the Insolvency Act 1986) or by the Registrar of Companies striking it off the companies register as "defunct", because he has reasonable cause to believe that the company is no longer carrying on business or has failed to file accounts (Companies Act 2006 s 1000). Directors of a company can likewise apply to the Registrar of Companies to have the company struck off (Companies Act 2006 s 1003). The company can be restored to register subsequently on application by petition and payment of the relevant fee (Companies Act 2006 s 1024–34). **3.** *See* PARLIAMENT.

distance selling The sale of goods or services to a consumer in which the parties do not meet, such as sale by mail order, telephone, digital TV, email, or the Internet. The EU distance selling directive 97/7, implemented from October 2000 in the UK by the Consumer Protection (Distance Selling) Regulations 2000 as amended, contains the relevant law. In particular, consumers have rights to certain information about the contract to be entered into and, in many cases, the right to cancel the contract within a certain period, often seven working days from the day after receipt of the goods. The right applies whether the goods are defective or not, but it does not apply in certain important categories (such as auctions, betting, goods specifically made for a consumer, and food that will deteriorate). The Consumer Rights Directive 2011/83 will make minor changes to the legislation when implemented in the UK and elsewhere by June 2014.

distinguishing a case The process of providing reasons for deciding a case under consideration differently from a similar case referred to as a *precedent.

distortion of competition *See* ARTICLE 101.

distrain *vb.* To seize goods by way of *distress.

distress *n.* The seizure of goods as security for the performance of an obligation. The two principal situations covered by the remedy of distress are (1) between landlord and tenant when the rent is in arrears (*see* DISTRESS FOR RENT); and (2) when goods are unlawfully on an occupier's land and have done or are doing damage. In the latter case the occupier may detain the chattel until compensation is paid for the damage.

distress for rent Formerly, the common law right for a landlord to seize a tenant's goods to secure payment of rent arrears. If the tenant failed to pay the rent arrears after distress had been levied, the landlord could sell the goods and keep the amount due. The common law right will be abolished when the Tribunals, Courts and Enforcement Act 2007 s 71 comes into force. In the case of a lease of commercial premises, the landlord may use the procedure for taking control of goods governed by the Tribunals, Courts and Enforcement Act 2007 sch 12 to secure payment of arrears of rent.

distressing letters *See* SENDING DISTRESSING LETTERS.

distribution *n.* **1.** The process of handing over to the beneficiaries their entitlements under a deceased person's will or on his intestacy. **2.** Any payment made by a company to a shareholder. There are two separate types of distribution, either of which can be in cash or in kind. An **income distribution** is a distribution during the life of a company and is made out of profits that the company has generated up to the time of the distribution. A **capital distribution** is a payment made on the winding up of a company and may include repayment of the company's share capital. An income distribution to an individual is subjected to income tax; a capital distribution received by an individual is subjected to capital gains tax (with rare exceptions).

district *n.* A *local government area in England (outside Greater London) consisting of a division of a *county. The Local Government Act 1972 divided the 6 metropolitan and 39 nonmetropolitan counties in England into 36 metropolitan and 296 nonmetropolitan districts, respectively, and the 8 counties in Wales into 37 districts. The 6 metropolitan counties were abolished by the Local Government Act 1985 and their functions transferred generally to the metropolitan district councils, which became single-tier authorities. A district may be styled a borough by royal charter granted on the petition of the *district council. The Welsh counties and districts were abolished by the Local Government (Wales) Act 1994, being replaced on 1 April 1996 by 22 *unitary authorities (11 counties and 11 county boroughs). Unitary authorities were introduced in certain nonmetropolitan areas of England in 1996–98.

district council A *local authority whose area is a *district. A district council has certain exclusive responsibilities (e.g. housing and local planning) and shares others (e.g. recreation, town and country planning) with the council of the county to which the district belongs. Some responsibilities (e.g. education and the personal social services) belong to the district council if the district is metropolitan, but to the county council if it is not. If a district has the style of borough, its council is called a borough council and its chairman the mayor. In the 1990s the Local Government Commission for England carried out a review of local authorities with a view to establishing *unitary (single-tier) authorities. This led to wider powers for district councils and to some amalgamations and boundary revision.

district judge In the county courts, a judicial officer appointed by the Lord Chancellor from solicitors or barristers of not less than five years' standing. The district judge supervises interim (interlocutory) and post-judgment stages of the case, but can also try civil cases within a financial limit defined by statute. They may also try family cases. District judges were formerly known as **district registrars**. Part-time district judges are known as deputy district judges.

district judge (magistrates' court) A barrister or solicitor of not less than seven years' standing, appointed by the Lord Chancellor to sit in a magistrates' court on a full-time salaried basis: formerly (before August 2000) called a **stipendiary magistrate**. Metropolitan district judges (magistrates' court) sit in magistrates' courts for Inner London; other magistrates sit in large provincial centres. They have power to perform any act and to exercise alone any jurisdiction that can be performed or exercised by two justices of the peace, except the grant or transfer of any licence. In other respects their powers are the same as other justices.

district probate registry *See* PROBATE REGISTRY.

district registry An office of the High Court outside London, corresponding in function to the *Central Office. There are district registries in all major towns and cities in England and Wales. However, only a limited number of district registries exercise full powers in relation to proceedings in the *Chancery Division.

distringas *n.* [Latin: that you distrain] A writ, now obsolete, commanding the sheriff to distrain on a person for a certain purpose. In modern practice it has been replaced by a *stop notice, sometimes called a **notice in lieu of *distringas***, which prevents dealings in securities that are subject to a *charging order.

disturbance *n.* **1.** The infringement of a right, e.g. the obstruction of a right of way. **2.** The removal of a person's rights under a statutory power. For example, compensation for disturbance may be payable to a landowner if his land is compulsorily acquired by a local authority.

dividend *n.* A payment declared either by the directors of a company **(interim dividend)** or at the *annual general meeting (**final dividend**) as being payable to shareholders from profits available for distribution. The payment is determined by reference to the terms of the *share contract; it is an agreed fixed rate for preference shares but will vary with the fortunes of the company for the holders of ordinary shares.

divisible contract *See* PERFORMANCE OF CONTRACT.

division *n.* The taking of a vote on any matter in either House of Parliament.

Divisional Court A court consisting of not less than two judges of one of the Divisions (Queen's Bench, Chancery, and Family) of the High Court. Their function is to hear appeals in various matters prescribed by statute; they also exercise the supervisory jurisdiction of the High Court over inferior courts. Most of this jurisdiction is exercised by the Queen's Bench Division, which also hears applications for *judicial review in the *Administrative Court and appeals by way of *case stated from magistrates' courts.

Divisions of the High Court *See* CHANCERY DIVISION; FAMILY DIVISION; QUEEN'S BENCH DIVISION.

divorce *n.* The legal termination of a marriage and the obligations created by marriage, other than by a decree of nullity or presumption of death. The present law on divorce dates from 1969. Before this, the law required proof of a *matrimonial offence (adultery, cruelty, or desertion of three years). The current law is contained in the Matrimonial Causes Act 1973, which provides that there is only one ground for divorce, namely that the marriage has irretrievably broken down. Proceedings are initiated by either spouse filing a **petition for divorce**, stating the facts that have led to the marital breakdown and accompanied by a *statement of arrangement for children. (Divorce proceedings may not be started within the first year of a marriage.) Irretrievable breakdown of a marriage may only be evidenced by one of the following five facts:

(1) that the respondent has committed *adultery and the petitioner finds it intolerable to live with the respondent;

(2) that the respondent has behaved in such a way that the petitioner cannot reasonably be expected to live with the respondent (*see* UNREASONABLE BEHAVIOUR);

(3) that the respondent has deserted the petitioner for at least two years (*see* DESERTION);

(4) that the parties have lived apart for at least two years and the respondent consents to a divorce;

(5) that the parties have lived apart for at least five years.

A respondent in a two-year separation case can apply for a postponement of the divorce until the court is satisfied that the petitioner has made fair and reasonable financial provision for the respondent. In a five-year separation case the court has the power to bar divorce if it believes that grave financial or other hardship would result from the dissolution and that it would be wrong to dissolve the marriage; however, this power is rarely exercised.

Divorce is a two-stage process. The first stage is the granting of a *decree nisi; six weeks later the petitioner may apply for a *decree absolute. The marriage is not terminated until the decree absolute has been granted. Uncontested divorce cases are heard under the *special procedure; the majority of cases are now dealt with in this way. Divorce courts have wide powers under the Matrimonial Causes Act 1973 to make orders in respect of children and to adjust financial and property rights. *See also* CHILD PROTECTION IN DIVORCE; FINANCIAL PROVISION ORDER; MAINTENANCE AGREEMENT; PROPERTY ADJUSTMENT ORDER.

Divorce Registry The section of the Family Division of the High Court with jurisdiction over divorce proceedings.

DNA fingerprinting (genetic fingerprinting) A scientific technique in which an individual's genetic material (DNA) is extracted from cells in a sample of tissue and analysed to produce a graphic chart that is unique to that person. The technique may be used as *evidence of identity in a criminal or civil case and has been notably successful in both paternity and rape cases. **DNA samples** (e.g. of hair) may be taken from suspects in accordance with the Police and Criminal Evidence Act 1984 and after conviction for any offence punishable by imprisonment.

DNAR order *See* DO NOT ATTEMPT RESUSCITATION ORDER.

dock *n.* [from Flemish: hutch, pen] In some courts, the enclosed place in which a prisoner is held during his trial.

dock brief The obsolete procedure by which a defendant to a criminal charge could, on indictment, select any barrister in the court who was not otherwise engaged to represent him, on payment of a nominal fee.

docket *n.* **1.** An abstract or brief written entry in a court record or a book in which brief entries of acts done in court are made. **2.** An agenda for the cases about to appear before the court. Hence, to say that a court has a full docket usually means that it is booked to hear many cases.

doctrine of double effect The doctrine that where a single action will forseeably have both a good and a bad outcome, a person may perform this action provided that (a) he intends only the good outcome, (b) the bad outcome is not disproportionate to the good, and (c) the good outcome is not a direct consequence of the bad. The doctrine has often been applied to dilemmas in medical law. The classic example occurs where a terminally ill patient requires high doses of pain relief that will also hasten his death. In such a case the law holds that the doctor may supply the necessary dosage without this being considered tantamount to *euthanasia, even though the outcome will be the same.

doctrine of incorporation The doctrine that rules of international law automatically form part of municipal law. It is opposed to the **doctrine of transformation**, which states that international law only forms a part of municipal law if accepted as such by statute or judicial decisions. It is not altogether clear which view English law takes with respect to rules of customary *international law. As far as international treaties are concerned, the sovereign has the power to make or ratify treaties so as to bind England under international law, but these treaties have no effect in municipal law (with the exception of treaties governing the conduct of war) until enacted by Parliament. However, judges will sometimes consider provisions of international treaties (e.g. those relating to *human rights) in applying municipal law. It has been said that directives of the European Community have the force of law in member states, but practice varies widely (*see* COMMUNITY LEGISLATION).

document *n.* Something that records or transmits information, typically in writing on paper. For the purposes of providing evidence to a court, documents include books, maps, plans, drawings, photographs, graphs, discs, tapes, soundtracks, and films (*see also* COMPUTER DOCUMENTS). Some legal documents are only valid if they meet certain requirements (*see* DEED; WILL). Under Part 31 of the *Civil Procedure Rules documents that are to be used in civil proceedings must be disclosed to the other party in a procedure known as *disclosure and inspection of documents. In court, the original of a document should be produced in most cases (*see* BEST-EVIDENCE RULE). Statements in public documents and records are generally admissible as an exception to the hearsay rule.

documentary evidence Evidence in written rather than oral form. The admissibility of a document depends upon (1) proof of the authenticity of the document and (2) the purpose for which it is being offered in evidence. If it is being offered to prove the truth of some matter stated in the document itself it may be necessary to consider the application of the rule against hearsay (*see* HEARSAY EVIDENCE) and its many exceptions.

document of title to goods A document, such as a *bill of lading, that embodies the undertaking of the person holding the goods (the bailee) to hold the goods for whoever is the current holder of the document and to deliver the goods to that person in exchange for the document.

"dog-leg" claim A claim for *breach of trust by a beneficiary against the directors of a *trust corporation. The directors would not, under normal company law principles, be potential targets for a trust beneficiary; the directors ordinarily owe duties solely to the company, the trust corporation. However, in circumstances where the trust corporation is not prepared or able to pursue its own directors for breach of *fiduciary duty and has no assets out of which a claim by beneficiaries for breach of trust may be satisfied, the beneficiaries may wish to pursue the directors of the trust corporation directly. The "dog-leg" claim has been used in an attempt to circumvent the general principle that a director cannot be pursued personally for a breach of duty to the company; it argues that a claim for breach of trust arising because of the breach of duty by individual directors of a trust corporation is held on trust for the beneficiaries. Such a claim has, however, received a very lukewarm reception. A "dog-leg" claim was considered arguable in *HA v JAPT* [1997] OPLR 123; however, other attempts to assert such a claim have failed (*Gregson v HAE Trustees* [2008] EWHC 1006 (Ch), [2008] WLR (D)146; *Alhamrani v Alhamrani* [2007] JRC 026 (a decision of the Royal Court of Jersey)).

dogs *pl. n.* See ANIMALS; DANGEROUS ANIMALS; GUARD DOG.

doli capax [Latin] Capable of wrong. A child under the age of 10 is deemed incapable of committing any crime. Above the age of 10 children are *doli capax* and are treated as adults, although they will usually be tried in special youth courts (with the exception of homicide and certain other grave offences) and subject to special punishments. Formerly, there was a rebuttable presumption that a child between the ages of 10 and 14 was also *doli incapax* (incapable of wrong). This presumption has now been abolished (Crime and Disorder Act 1998 s 34). *See* JUVENILE OFFENDER.

DOLS See DEPRIVATION OF LIBERTY SAFEGUARDS.

domain name An Internet address, which may be protected under *trade mark law.

domestic premises A private residence, used wholly for living accommodation, together with its garden, yard, and attached buildings (such as garages and outhouses).

domestic tribunal A body that exercises jurisdiction over the internal affairs of a particular profession or association under powers conferred either by statute (e.g. the disciplinary committee of the Law Society) or by contract between the members (e.g. the disciplinary committee of a trade union). The decisions of these tribunals are subject to judicial control under the doctrine of **ultra vires* and, if they are statutory, when there is an *error of law on the face of the record. *Compare* ADMINISTRATIVE TRIBUNAL.

domestic violence Any incident of violence, threatening behaviour, or abuse (psychological, physical, sexual, financial, or emotional) between adults who are or have been intimate partners or family members, regardless of gender or sexuality. Persons who are subject to domestic violence (or those afraid of future violence) may seek protection in a number of ways. Under the Family Law Act 1996 an application can be made to the court for a *non-molestation order or an *occupation order. A non-molestation order directs the other partner not to molest, annoy, or use violence against the applicant. Breach of such an order is a crime under section 42A. An *occupation order entitles the applicant to remain in occupation of the matrimonial home and may prohibit, suspend, or restrict the abusive partner's right to occupy the house. The court must attach a power of arrest to an occupation order if the abuser has used or threatened violence against his or her partner. This gives a constable the power to arrest without warrant the abuser if he or she is in breach of the order. In cases of emergency an order without notice may be granted. In theory, a criminal prosecution for *assault or for harassment under the Protection from Harassment Act 1997 could be brought but in practice this is seldom used by victims of domestic violence. Under the Housing Act 1985, local authorities have a duty to supply emergency accommodation to those made homeless when they have left their homes because of domestic violence.

Those who have been subjected to continued beatings by their partners over a period of time may plead *provocation or *diminished responsibility if charged with the murder of their partner. *See* BATTERED WOMAN SYNDROME.

domicile *n.* The country that a person treats as his permanent home and to which he has the closest legal attachment. A person cannot be without a domicile and cannot have two domiciles at once. He acquires at birth a **domicile of origin**. Normally, if his father is then alive, he takes his father's domicile; if not, his mother's. He retains his domicile of origin until (if ever) he acquires a **domicile of choice** in its place. A domicile of choice is acquired by making a home in a country with the intention that it should be a permanent base. It may be acquired at any time after a person becomes 16 and can be replaced at will by a new domicile of choice. *See* LEX DOMICILII.

dominant tenement Land having the benefit of an *easement (e.g. a right of way) or profit *à prendre* (e.g. the right to fish) over other land, known as the **servient tenement**.

dominium *n.* [Latin: power] **1.** Absolute ownership of property, involving the right to use, enjoy, profit from, and dispose of the property at will. **2.** The power of a state to exercise supreme authority (absolute *sovereignty) over all persons and things within its territory.

donatio mortis causa [Latin: a gift on account of death] An immediate gift of real or personal property made by a donor who expects to die in the near future. The gift must be made to take complete effect only on the death of the donor and there must be delivery of the property or something amounting to delivery. The latter requirement has been held to be satisfied by a transfer of the means or part of the means of obtaining the property or a transfer of the indications of title to the property (e.g. title deeds). The donor must make the transfer with the intention of relinquishing ownership of the property but may withdraw from that intention at any time prior to death and thereby defeat the gift. If the donor does not die the gift will be revoked. In practice such gifts are extremely rare.

Do Not Attempt Resuscitation order (DNAR order) An instruction, usually made by a patient while mentally competent and recorded in his notes, requesting the doctor to desist from performing resuscitation in the event of heart failure. In the past, elderly patients have often been subject to DNAR orders without their knowledge.

double criminality The rule in *extradition procedures that, in order for the request to be complied with, the crime for which extradition is sought must be a crime in both the requesting state and the state to which the fugitive has fled. The offence need not have the same name and it need not have the same element to make it criminal (*Collins v Loisel* 259 US 309 (1922)). *See also* EXTRADITION TREATY; SPECIALITY.

double jeopardy A defence to a prosecution for a crime, raising the claim that the accused is being placed on trial for a second time for the same offence. The so-called double jeopardy rule stated that no person may be twice put in jeopardy of life or limb for the same offence. Following the entry into force of the Criminal Justice Act 2003 the double jeopardy rule was altered (s 75). The new measures only apply to serious offences (i.e. those carrying a maximum sentence of life imprisonment and for which the consequences for victims or society as a whole are particularly serious) such as murder, manslaughter, and rape. A retrial may now be allowed if compelling new evidence comes to light against the person originally acquitted at the trial. Examples of such evidence include DNA or fingerprint tests or a new witness coming forward. The measures permit the police to reinvestigate a person acquitted of serious offences in these circumstances, and enable the prosecuting authorities to apply to the Court of Appeal for an acquittal to be quashed and for a retrial to take place where the court is satisfied that the new evidence is highly probative of the case against the acquitted person. Consent must also be obtained from the *Director of Public Prosecutions before the reinvestigation and the retrial can take place. *See also* AUTREFOIS ACQUIT; AUTREFOIS CONVICT.

double portions *pl. n. See* RULE AGAINST DOUBLE PORTIONS.

double probate A second grant of *probate in respect of the same estate in favour of an executor who was not a party to the first grant. This occurs when the executor has not renounced his executorship and has a power to apply for a grant of probate at a later time than the original grant because, for example, of *power reserved by that executor.

double taxation relief A number of different mechanisms designed to either reduce or avoid multiple tax charges where the same item of income is liable to taxation by more than one jurisdiction. The USA taxes income of US citizens wherever it arises and wherever the citizen is resident. The UK taxes income wherever it arises to a person resident in the UK, and taxes income arising in the UK to persons resident anywhere in the world. Other jurisdictions have similarly ambitious practices in raising tax revenue. It is, thus, commonplace for one source of income to be potentially subject to more than one tax charge.

Under the UK tax system, several different methods of double taxation relief are available:

(1) relief is given under a treaty between the UK and another jurisdiction by the treaty declaring that income of a specified nature is exempt from tax in one of the two jurisdiction;

(2) credit against UK tax is given by such a treaty for foreign tax paid;

(3) where there is no treaty, or no provision in a treaty, a system of "unilateral relief" may allow the crediting of a foreign tax payment against the UK tax liability;

(4) any foreign tax paid that is not otherwise relieved is treated as an expense in calculating the income subject to UK tax.

Equivalent provisions apply for tax on capital gains and, to a restricted extent, to taxation imposed on an estate at death. The UK has double taxation treaties for income tax/ corporation tax with 124 countries and for inheritance tax with only 10 countries. Interpretation of double taxation relief treaties has given difficulty to the courts. The Vienna Convention on the Law of Treaties 1969 (Article 31) requires that a treaty be interpreted in good faith and that terms in the treaty be interpreted in the light of their object and purpose. These are concepts that are inherently foreign to English law and have led to decisions such as *Sportsman v IRC* [1998] STC 289, in which it was held that a treaty should not be interpreted so as to allow a taxpayer to pay no tax in either country.

DPP *See* DIRECTOR OF PUBLIC PROSECUTIONS.

draft *n*. **1.** An initial unsigned agreement, treaty, or piece of legislation, which is not yet in force. **2.** An order for the payment of money, e.g. a banker's draft.

Drago doctrine The doctrine that states cannot employ force in order to recover debts incurred by other states. In 1902 the combined fleets of Great Britain, Germany, and Italy mounted a blockade of Venezuela with the object of enforcing contractual and other claims against that country. This led Dr Drago, foreign minister of the Argentine Republic, to formulate the doctrine now known by his name, which states that "a public debt cannot give rise to the right of intervention, and much less to the occupation of the soil of any American nation by a European power".

driftway *n*. A *highway over which there exists a right to drive cattle, accompanied by persons either on foot or mounted.

driver *n*. For purposes of the Road Traffic Acts, anyone who uses the ordinary controls of a vehicle (i.e. steering and brakes) to direct its movement. This includes anyone steering a car when the engine is off or when being towed by another vehicle.

driving licence An official authority to drive a motor vehicle, granted upon passing a driving test. A renewable provisional driving licence, valid for 12 months, may be granted to learner drivers, but the holder of a provisional licence may not drive a motor car on a public road unless accompanied by a qualified driver and unless he displays "L" plates on the front and rear of the vehicle.

A full licence may be obtained by anyone who has passed the Department of Transport driving test, which is carried out by the Driving Standards Agency (an executive agency) and is now preceded by a written test, or held a full licence issued in Great Britain, Northern Ireland, the Isle of Man, or the Channel Islands within ten years before the date on which the licence is to come into force. It is normally granted until the applicant's 70th birthday. After the age of 70, licences are granted for three-year periods. The applicant must disclose any disability and may be asked to produce his medical records or have a medical examination.

An applicant will not normally be granted a licence if he is suffering from certain types of disability, including epilepsy, sudden attacks of disabling giddiness or fainting, or a severe mental illness or defect. In the case of epilepsy, however, he may still be granted a licence if he can show that he has been free of all attacks for at least two years or that he has only had attacks during sleep for more than three years. If an applicant for a licence has diabetes or a heart condition, is fitted with a heart pacemaker, has been treated within the previous three years for drug addiction, or is suffering from any other disability (e.g. loss or weakness of a limb) that would affect his driving, the grant of a licence is usually discretionary.

It is an offence to knowingly make a false statement in order to obtain a driving licence, not to disclose any current *endorsements, or not to sign one's name in ink on the licence. A police officer may require a driver to show his driving licence or produce it personally at a specified police station within five days. He may also ask to see the licence of someone whom he believes was either driving a vehicle involved in an accident or had committed a motoring offence. Failure to produce one's licence in these circumstances carries a fine. *See also* DRIVING WITHOUT A LICENCE.

Under the Road Traffic (New Drivers) Act 1995, with effect from 1 June 1997, a driver who is convicted of an endorsable offence and who has accumulated 6 or more penalty points (*see* TOTTING UP) within two years of passing a driving test will have his licence revoked and must retake the test. When the Road Safety Act 2006 (s 34) is brought into force, it will offer an element of retraining for repeat offenders and enable those who successfully complete one of the new range of courses to have penalty points removed from their licence. This is intended to act as an incentive for repeat offenders, who will benefit from a reduced risk of *disqualification on reaching 12 or more penalty points.

driving-test order An order by the court that a person who has been convicted of an offence that is subject to *disqualification should be disqualified from driving until he passes a test showing that he is fit to drive. The order should only be made where there is reason to suspect that the person is not fit to drive; for example, because he is very old or unwell, and has shown evidence of incompetence in his driving. It is not meant as a punishment but to protect the public.

driving while disqualified An offence committed by the *driver of a motor vehicle on a public road when he is disqualified from driving (*see* DISQUALIFICATION). This is an endorsable offence (carrying 7 penalty points under the *totting-up system) and the courts have discretion to impose a further period of disqualification.

driving while unfit *See* DRUNKEN DRIVING.

driving without a licence An offence committed by the *driver of a motor vehicle on a public road without a *driving licence or provisional driving licence valid for the vehicle he is driving. If the circumstances are such that he would in fact have been refused a licence had he applied for one, or if he fails to comply with the conditions applicable to a provisional licence, his licence (if he subsequently obtains one) will usually be endorsed (the endorsement carries 2 penalty points under the *totting-up system) and the court has discretion to order disqualification from driving (if he applies for a licence during the disqualification period). Otherwise this is not an endorsable offence.

driving without insurance An offence committed by a *driver who uses or allows someone else to use a motor vehicle on a public road without valid *third-party insurance. The offence is one of *strict liability (except when an employee is using his employer's vehicle) and applies even if, for example, the insurance company who issued the insurance suddenly goes into liquidation. The offence is punishable by a fine, endorsement (it carries 6–8 penalty points under the *totting-up system), and disqualification at the discretion of the court.

drugs *pl. n. See* CONTROLLED DRUGS.

drug treatment requirement A requirement that may be imposed by a sentencing court as part of a *community order or a *suspended sentence order under the Criminal Justice Act 2003 or as part of a *youth rehabilitation order under the Criminal Justice and Immigration Act 2008. The offender is required to undergo treatment to reduce his dependency on drugs or his tendency to misuse drugs. A drug treatment requirement can only be imposed with the consent of the offender.

drunken driving Driving (*see* DRIVER) while affected by alcohol. Drunken driving covers two separate legal offences.

(1) **Driving while unfit**. It is an offence to drive or attempt to drive a motor vehicle on a road or public place when one's ability to drive properly is impaired by alcohol or drugs. Drugs include medicines (such as insulin for diabetics), and the offence appears to be one of *strict liability. It is also an offence to be in charge of a motor vehicle on a road or in a public place while unfit to drive because of drink or drugs, but the defendant will be acquitted if he can show that there was no likelihood of his driving the vehicle in this condition (for example, if he arranged for someone else to drive him if he became drunk). A police officer can arrest without a warrant anyone whom he reasonably suspects is committing or has been committing either of these offences; he may also (except in Scotland) enter any place where he believes the suspect to be, using force if necessary.

(2) **Driving over the prescribed limit**. It is an offence to drive or attempt to drive a motor vehicle on a road or in a public place if the level of alcohol in one's breath, blood, or urine is above the specified prescribed limit (35 micrograms of alcohol in 100 millilitres (ml) of breath; 80 milligrams (mg) of alcohol in 100 ml of blood; 107 mg of alcohol in 100 ml of urine: Road Traffic Act 1988 s 11). It is also an offence to be in charge of a motor vehicle on a road or in a public place when the proportion of alcohol is more than the prescribed limit, subject to the same defence as in being in charge while unfit. Both these offences are offences of strict liability: it is therefore not a defence to show that one did not know that the drink was alcoholic or that it exceeded the prescribed limit. The normal way in which offences involving excess alcohol levels are proved is by taking a *specimen of breath for laboratory analysis, but this is not necessary if the offence can be proved in some other way (for example, by evidence of how much a person drank before driving). There is no power to arrest a person on suspicion of committing or having committed an offence of this sort before administering a preliminary *breath test.

Most charges involving drinking and driving are brought under the offence of driving over the prescribed limit rather than driving while unfit, but the powers to administer a breath test or to take a specimen of breath for analysis apply to both offences. The penalties for either of these offences are a fine and/or imprisonment, *endorsement, and obligatory *disqualification (in cases of driving or attempting to drive) or discretionary disqualification (in cases of being in charge). Under the *totting-up system, the discretionary disqualification offences carry 10 penalty points and the compulsory disqualification offences carry 3–11 penalty points (which are only imposed if there are special reasons preventing disqualification). *See also* CAUSING DEATH BY CARELESS DRIVING WHEN UNDER THE INFLUENCE OF DRINK OR DRUGS; OFFENCES RELATING TO ROAD TRAFFIC.

drunkenness *n.* *Intoxication resulting from imbibing an excess of alcohol. It is an offence to be drunk in a public place.

DSP *See* Director of Service Prosecutions.

dualism *n.* *See* monism.

duality *n.* A principle of UK income tax and corporation tax under which expenditure is not deductible in computing the profits subject to tax if the expenditure has a dual purpose. A deduction in computing trading profits is therefore denied for any expense not incurred wholly and exclusively for the purposes of the trade. In *Mallalieu v Drummond* [1983] STC 665 (HL), Mallalieu was a barrister who sought to deduct the cost of clothes bought to wear in court, such clothes being required by rules of court etiquette. The House of Lords held that the clothes performed the function of providing warmth and decency to Miss Mallalieu, as well as satisfying the court rules. This duality of purpose denied a deduction for the expense of purchasing the court clothes. The duality principle refuses relief by apportionment of a payment but permits relief where a wholly business expenditure can be identified by dissection of a payment (*Gazelle v Servini* [1995] STC 324).

dubitante *adj.* [Latin] Doubting. The term is used in law reports in relation to a judge who is doubtful about a legal proposition but does not wish to declare it wrong.

Dublin Convention A convention signed by EU member states in 1990; its purpose was to identify the member state responsible for examining an *asylum claim by a non-EU national and more generally to prevent abuse of the asylum system. In general, any claim should be dealt with by the state through which the asylum seeker first entered the EU. The convention came into force for the original signatories in 1997 and is now consolidated into the Dublin II Regulation 343/2003.

duces tecum [Latin: you shall bring with you] *See* witness summons.

due diligence The legal obligation of states to exercise all reasonable efforts to protect *aliens and their property in the host state. Such aliens must have been permitted entry into the host state. If there is a failure or lack of due diligence, the state in default is held responsible and liable to make compensation for injury to the alien or to the alien's estate. *See* state responsibility.

dum casta vixerit [Latin] As long as she lives chastely. A clause sometimes inserted in a separation agreement, freeing the husband from the terms of the agreement (e.g. maintenance obligations) if his wife commits adultery.

dumping *n.* The sale of goods abroad at prices below their normal value. Within the EU dumping regulations prohibit the sale of goods at below normal value. **Countervailing** (or **antidumping**) **duties** may be ordered on certain imported goods to prevent dumping.

dum sola [Latin] While single: the status of a single woman or widow.

duplex querela [Latin: double complaint] The procedure in ecclesiastical law for challenging a bishop's refusal to admit a presentee to a benefice.

duplicity *n.* The error of alleging two or more separate offences in one count of an *indictment. The count is then said to be void for duplicity and must be corrected.

A duplicitous indictment does not permit a jury to return a verdict on each distinct offence.

durante absentia [Latin: during the absence of] Describing a grant of *letters of administration of a deceased's estate to some person interested in the estate while the personal representative is abroad. *See also* LIMITED ADMINISTRATION.

duress *n.* Pressure, especially actual or threatened physical force, put on a person to act in a particular way. Acts carried out under duress usually have no legal effect; for example, a contract obtained by duress is voidable (*see also* ECONOMIC DURESS; UNDUE INFLUENCE). In criminal law, when the defendant's power to resist is destroyed by a threat of death or serious personal injury or by circumstances, he will have a defence to a criminal charge, although he has the *mens rea* for the crime and knows that what he is doing is wrong (*R v Graham* [1982] 1 WLR 294). Duress is not a defence to a charge of murder as a principal (i.e. to someone who actually carries out the murder himself), nor is it a defence to aiding and abetting murder (*R v Howe* [1987] AC 417 (HL)). The threat need not be immediate; it is sufficient that it is effective; for example a threat in court to kill a witness may constitute duress and thus be a defence to a charge of perjury, even though it cannot be carried out in the courtroom (*Hudson and Taylor* [1971] 2 QB 202). However, the defence is unavailable to someone who failed to take available alternative action to avoid the threat. *See also* COERCION; EXCUSE; NECESSITY; SELF-DEFENCE.

During Her (or His) Majesty's pleasure A phrase colloquially used to describe the period of detention imposed upon a defendant found not guilty by reason of *insanity. Such a person was consequently known as a **pleasure patient**. The defendant must still be admitted to a hospital specified by the Home Secretary (either a local psychiatric hospital or a *special hospital) and remain there until otherwise directed, but the phrase "during Her Majesty's pleasure" is no longer used in the statute.

"Dutch courage" *See* INTOXICATION.

duty *n.* **1.** A legal requirement to carry out or refrain from carrying out any act. *Compare* POWER. **2.** A payment levied by the state, particularly on certain goods and transactions. Examples are *customs duty, *excise duty, and *stamp duty.

duty of care The legal obligation to take reasonable care to avoid causing damage. There is no liability in tort for *negligence unless the act or omission that causes damage is a breach of a duty of care owed to the claimant. There is a duty to take care in most situations in which one can reasonably foresee that one's actions may cause physical damage to the person or property of others (*see* NEIGHBOUR PRINCIPLE). The duty is owed to those people likely to be affected by the conduct in question. Thus doctors owe a duty of care to their patients (*Bolam v Friern Hospital Management Committee* [1957] 1 WLR 583 (QB)) and users of the highway have a duty of care to all other road users (*Nettleship v Weston* [1971] 2 QB 691). However, there is no general duty to prevent other persons causing damage or to rescue persons or property in danger. Liability for careless words is more limited than liability for careless acts (*see* NEGLIGENT MISSTATEMENT) and there is no general duty not to cause *economic loss or *psychiatric injury. The existence and scope of the duty of care will depend upon all the circumstances of the case and the relationship between the parties. The courts have developed a three tier test to determine whether a duty of care exists (*Caparo Industries plc v Dickman* [1990] 2 AC 605 (HL)), and in novel cases courts are mindful of a range of policy issues. Most duties of care are the result of judicial decisions;

however, some are contained in statutes, such as the Occupier's Liability Act 1957 (*see* OCCUPIER'S LIABILITY).

duty solicitors *Solicitors who attend by rota at magistrates' courts in order to assist and advise defendants who are otherwise unrepresented.

duty to convert (in equity) *See* CONVERSION.

dying declaration An oral or written statement by a person on the point of death concerning the cause of his death. At common law, a dying declaration was admissible at a trial for the murder or the manslaughter of the declarant as an exception to the rule against *hearsay evidence, provided that he would have been a competent witness had he survived (*see* COMPETENCE). Case law required that the person making the dying declaration must have had a "settled, hopeless expectation of death". The current law is found in the Criminal Justice Act 2003.

easement *n.* A right enjoyed by the owner of land (the **dominant tenement**) to a benefit from other land (the **servient tenement**). An easement benefits and binds the land itself and therefore continues despite any change of ownership of either dominant or servient tenement, although it will be extinguished if the two tenements come into common ownership (*compare* QUASI-EASEMENT). It may be acquired by statute (for example, local Acts of Parliament), be expressly granted (e.g. by *deed giving a right of way), arise as an *implied easement (e.g. an easement of support from an adjoining building), or be acquired by *prescription. (*See also* PROFIT À PRENDRE.) An easement can exist as either a legal or an equitable interest in land. Only easements created by statute, deed, or prescription and held on terms equivalent to a *fee simple absolute in possession or *term of years absolute qualify as **legal easements** and are binding on all who acquire the unregistered servient tenement or any interest in it. Expressly created legal easements must be registered against the title of the servient tenement, or they will not bind future purchases of that tenement. All others are **equitable easements** and must generally be registered to be enforceable against a purchaser. Under section 62 of the Law of Property Act 1925, when land is conveyed, all easements appertaining to it automatically pass with it without the necessity for express words in the conveyance. *See also* REGISTRATION OF ENCUMBRANCES.

easement of necessity An *easement that is implied into a transfer of land because the land would be completely unusable without it. The most common example is the case of a "landlocked close" – a piece of land that has no access from the highway. An easement of necessity may be implied in favour of the person disposing of the land (**implied reservation**) or in favour of the person receiving the land (**implied grant**).

EBRD *See* EUROPEAN BANK FOR RECONSTRUCTION AND DEVELOPMENT.

EC *See* EUROPEAN COMMUNITY.

ecclesiastical courts Courts responsible for the administration of the ecclesiastical law of the Church of England. They comprise **consistory courts**, which are the courts of each diocese, for enforcing discipline among the clergy; the *Court of Arches and the **Chancery Court of York**, which hear appeals from consistory courts in their respective provinces; the *Judicial Committee of the Privy Council, which hears appeals from the provincial courts in matters not involving doctrine, ritual, or ceremonial; and the *Court of Ecclesiastical Causes Reserved.

ecclesiastical law *See* CANON LAW.

ecolabel *n.* A label with the EU logo that is used on products that comply with environmental requirements in particular directives.

⊕ SEE WEB LINKS

• Information on ecolabels from the Europa website

economic analysis of law A theory of law, usually seen as a modern form of *utilitarianism, based largely on the proposition that a rational human being will always act to maximize his satisfactions: if he wants something badly enough, he will therefore be prepared to pay for it. Richard Posner (1939–), one of the leading exponents of this approach, attempts to demonstrate that the development of a great many common law rules can be explained by this simple fact. Judges frequently decide hard cases by choosing an outcome that will maximize the wealth of society. Thus, in the development of the law of *negligence, Posner argues, the imposition of liability normally depends on what is most efficient economically. By "wealth maximization" Posner means a situation in which goods and other resources are in the hands of those people who value them most (i.e. those who are willing and able to pay more to have them); society maximizes its wealth when all its resources are distributed in such a way that the sum of everyone's transactions is as high as possible. For Posner and other adherents of the so-called **Chicago School** this is as it should be; their analysis is thus both descriptive and normative. *See also* COASE THEOREM; KALDOR-HICKS EFFICIENCY; PARETO EFFICIENCY.

economic duress Historically within contract law, a claim that a contract was voidable for *duress could only be successful if a threat to the person (i.e. physical duress) had induced the contract (*Skeate v Beale* (1840) 11 Ad & El 983, 113 ER 688). Now, however, a contract may be voidable for economic duress. The essential elements are that an illegitimate threat is made (e.g. to breach an existing contract or to commit a tort) and that the injured party has no practical alternative to agreeing to the terms set out by the person making the threat. Additional case: *Universe Tankships Inc of Monrovia v International Transport Workers Federation* [1983] 1 AC 366 (HL). *See also* VOIDABLE CONTRACT.

economic loss The courts distinguish between financial or economic loss resulting from physical damage, which is generally recoverable, and **pure economic loss**, which does not result from personal injury or damage to property belonging to the claimant (*Spartan Steel & Alloys v Martin & Co (Contractors) Ltd* [1972] QB 27 (CA)). For pure economic loss the courts impose a much more limited *duty of care.

Economic Social Council of the United Nations (ECOSOC) A UN body designed to promote the observance of human rights and the general welfare of the rights of the individual. ECOSOC conducts studies and produces reports on economic, cultural, social, educational, and health matters.

e-conveyancing *n. See* ELECTRONIC CONVEYANCING.

ECSC *See* EUROPEAN COAL AND STEEL COMMUNITY.

ECU (European Currency Unit) *n.* A currency medium and unit of account of the *European Monetary System, which was replaced by the euro in 1999 (*see* EUROPEAN MONETARY UNION). The ECU was used in the *Exchange Rate Mechanism, and some bonds were issued by member states in ECUs.

education authorities The authorities responsible for the statutory system of education introduced by the Education Act 1944, i.e. the Secretary of State for Education and Skills and local education authorities (LEAs). In England and Wales the latter are county councils or unitary councils and, within *Greater London, the London borough councils. The Education Reform Act 1988 introduced measures under which schools could, with the approval of the Secretary of State, opt out of local education authority control to become grant-maintained schools. A new framework for schools was established under the School Standards and Framework Act 1998 and the Education

Acts of 2002 and 2005. This consisted of a three-part structure of community schools (controlled by the LEAs), voluntary schools (often with a distinctive religious ethos), and foundation schools (the former grant-maintained schools, now funded by the LEAs rather than centrally). The Education and Inspections Act 2006 included the provision for a foundation school to set up a charitable foundation (or trust) to support the school. The aim of such trust schools, which remain LEA-maintained schools, is to use experience, energy, and expertise from other schools and professions as a lever to raise standards. Academy schools were introduced in 2000 and free schools (academies by law) in 2011; these are state funded but free from LEA control. Relevant legislation includes the Education Act 2011 and the Academies Act 2010.

education supervision order A court order, applied for by a local education authority under the Children Act 1989 s 36, in respect of a child of compulsory school age whom it is felt is not being properly educated. The effect of the order is to place the child under the supervision of a social worker who will in general seek to ensure regular school attendance. It is a criminal offence to persistently fail to comply with the supervisor. If a child fails to comply the local authority might as a last resort apply for a *care order. *See also* SCHOOL ATTENDANCE PROCEDURES.

EEA *See* EUROPEAN ECONOMIC AREA.

EEC (European Economic Community) *See* EUROPEAN COMMUNITY.

EEZ *See* EXCLUSIVE ECONOMIC ZONE.

effective date of termination The date on which a contract of employment comes to an end, i.e. the date of expiry of any *notice given or of a fixed-term contract or the date of the employee's dismissal or resignation if no notice is given. However, an employee dismissed without the statutory minimum notice to which he was entitled is treated as having worked for that period after his dismissal for the purpose of calculating whether or not his length of service (*see* CONTINUOUS EMPLOYMENT) qualifies him to apply to an employment tribunal in respect of unfair dismissal and in relation to calculating his weeks' pay and basic award (*see* COMPENSATION). The effective date of termination marks the start of the three month period in which the dismissed employee may present a claim to the *employment tribunal.Case: *Fox Maintenance Ltd v Jackson* [1978] ICR 110.

effective remedy A right contained in Article 13 of the *European Convention on Human Rights but not incorporated directly by the *Human Rights Act 1998. The Article stipulates that the state must provide systems that give effective remedies for violations and arguable claims of violations of the other rights contained in the Convention. This article requires that such systems and procedures can both determine such claims and provide for redress for those violations that are substantiated.

effects doctrine The jurisdiction of a state is normally confined to its territorial extent. However, in the area of economic regulation, especially in anti-monopoly (trust) legislation, US courts in particular have shown a willingness to extend US domestic legislation beyond territorial boundaries. Tribunals in the US (for example, in *US v Watchmakers of Switzerland Information Center Inc* 133 F Supp 40 (1955) have adopted the view that whenever activity abroad has consequences or effects within the USA that are contrary to municipal legislation, then the US courts are empowered to make orders requiring the disposition of patent rights and other property of foreign corporations etc. The Court of Justice of the European Communities has applied a similar principle in respect of company subsidiaries (*A Ahlstrom Oy v Commission* [1988] ECR 5193 (Woodpulp Case)).

EFTA *See* European Free Trade Association.

eggshell skull rule The rule that a *tortfeasor cannot complain if the injuries he has caused turn out to be more serious than expected because his victim suffered from a pre-existing weakness, such as an unusually thin skull. A tortfeasor must take his victim as he finds him (*Smith v Leech Brain & Co Ltd* [1962] 2 QB 405).

18–25 trust A *trust established for the benefit of a young person, who becomes absolutely entitled to the trust property on or before his 25th birthday. An 18–25 trust can now only be created by the will of the young person's parent or step-parent (until April 2008 it could also be created by converting an existing *discretionary trust). The trust is charged to *inheritance tax (i) on settlement; (ii) when any distribution is made to the beneficiary, he or she being over 18 years old; and (iii) when the beneficiary becomes absolutely entitled, he or she being over 18 years old.

ei qui affirmat, non ei qui negat, incumbit probatio [Latin] The proof lies upon him who affirms, not upon him who denies. The rule is adopted because the negative does not admit of the direct and simple proof of which the affirmative is capable.

EIS *See* Enterprise Investment Scheme.

ejusdem generis [Latin: of the same kind] *See* interpretation.

Elder Brethren *See* assessor.

election *n.* **1.** The process of choosing by vote a member of a representative body, such as the House of Commons or a local authority. For the House of Commons, a **general election** involving all UK constituencies is held when the sovereign dissolves Parliament and summons a new one; a **by-election** is held if a particular constituency becomes vacant (e.g. on the death of the sitting member) during the life of a Parliament. Local government elections (apart from those to fill casual vacancies) are held at statutory intervals (*see* local authority). The conduct of elections is regulated by the Representation of the People Acts 1983 and 1985. The Representation of the People Act 2000 made some changes to electoral registration and absent voting and allowed for experiments involving innovative electoral procedures. Other changes make it easier for the disabled to vote and created an offence of supplying false particulars on a nomination form. Voting is secret and normally in person, but any elector can obtain a postal vote without having to specify a reason. The only requirement is that the applicant is included in the Register of Electors. Applications for a particular election must be received by the Electoral Registration Officer six working days before an election. Different rules apply in Northern Ireland. Any dispute as to the validity of the election of a Member of Parliament or a local government councillor is raised on an **election petition**, which is decided by an **election court** consisting of two High Court judges. *See also* franchise; free elections. **2.** A doctrine of equity, commonly applied to wills, based on the principle that a person must accept both benefits and burdens under one document, or reject both. It arises when there are two gifts in one document, one of A's (the creator's) property to B and one of B's property to C. B must choose whether to accept the gift of A's property to him and transfer his own property to C, or to reject both gifts.

election court *See* election.

election petition *See* election.

elective resolution   Formerly, a decision by all the members of a *private company to dispense with complying with specified provisions of the Companies Act 1985, for example holding an *annual general meeting. The requirement for such a resolution was removed by the Companies Act 2006.

elector *n.* **1.** A person entitled to vote at an *election. For parliamentary and local government elections, a **register of electors** is maintained. A new register comes into force on 16 February each year and governs elections held during the following 12 months. It records electors by reference to their residence on the preceding 10 October (the qualifying date) and includes people who will become 18 (and so entitled to vote) in the year following its publication. Inclusion on the register is a requirement for voting. A person on it cannot be prevented from voting but incurs penalties if he votes without in fact being entitled to do so. *See* FRANCHISE. **2.** (in equity) One who makes an election.

Electoral Commission   An independent public body created in terms of the Political Parties, Elections and Referendums Act 2000. Its duties include reporting on the conduct of *elections (including general parliamentary elections, elections to the European Parliament, and elections to the devolved parliaments for Scotland, Wales, and Northern Ireland) and referendums. It is also empowered to review and report on a range of associated matters, such as the redistribution of seats, the formation and funding of political parties, and political advertising, and to provide advice and assistance to political parties, returning officers, and others. The functions of the Boundary Commission and the Local Government Commission for England have been transferred to the Electoral Commission, which is also mandated to establish Boundary Committees for Wales, Scotland, and Northern Ireland. The Commission is required to maintain registers of political parties and to exercise certain regulatory functions in relation to their financing.

(⊕) SEE WEB LINKS

• Website of the Electoral Commission

electricity *n. See* ABSTRACTING ELECTRICITY.

electromagnetic compatibility   The capability of electromagnetic products, such as computer equipment, machines, etc., to be used together without special modification. The EU electromagnetic compatibility directive, which is now part of English law, sets out the minimum requirements to ensure that the use of computers, etc., does not cause interference with other electromagnetic products. *See also* CE.

electronic conveyancing **(e-conveyancing)**   The transfer of land by electronic means instead of by paper documents. The framework for such *conveyancing has been set in place by the Electronic Communications Act 2000 and the Land Registration Act 2002. No date has yet been announced for the bringing into force of the relevant provisions of the 2002 Act, but the land registers are kept in electronic form and it is already possible to discharge mortgages electronically. The Land Registry announced in 2013 that further development of electronic conveyancing had been suspended for the foreseeable future. *See* LAND REGISTRATION.

electronic data interchange **(EDI)**   The use of electronic data-transmission networks to exchange information. Significant commercial contracts set out the terms on which such information is supplied, and much commerce is now done on this basis (known as **paperless trading**), either through a closed network called an **intranet**, to which only members of a limited group have access, or through an open network, i.e. the Internet. Some international legal rules have been agreed in this field, including the

Uniform Rules of Conduct for Interchange of Trade Data by Teletransmission (*See* UNCID).

electronic signature An item of data incorporated into or associated with an electronically transmitted document that fulfils the function of a written signature. Under the Electronic Communications Act 2000 electronic signatures are recognized in legal proceedings and as having legal effect. An electronic signature can be purchased from such bodies as the Post Office and the London Chamber of Commerce on production of relevant identification documents. *See also* DIGITAL SIGNATURE.

electronic surveillance The use of *telephone tapping, hidden microphones (bugging) or cameras, or similar means to obtain evidence. Telecommunications interception evidence is normally inadmissible at trial in England but evidence obtained by other means of electronic surveillance may be admissible. The Police Act 1997 provides for a system in which independent commissioners of police oversee the arrangements and investigate complaints in relation to intrusive *surveillance operations.

eleemosynary corporation [from Latin: *eleemosyna*, alms] Originally, a lay (rather than an ecclesiastical) charity. An eleemosynary corporation is now a charity directed to the relief of individual distress.

embargo *n.* The detention of ships in port: a type of *reprisal. Ships of a delinquent state may be prevented from leaving the ports of an injured state in order to compel the delinquent state to make reparation for the wrong done. A good illustration of this was the action of Great Britain in 1839, when she captured and laid embargo upon Sicilian vessels, because the two Sicilies had granted a sulphur monopoly in violation of a commercial treaty. Such a *reprisal would now be, arguably, a breach of Article 2(1) of the United Nations Charter. *See also* ANGARY.

embassy *n.* Under the Vienna Convention on Diplomatic Relations 1961, the function or the position of an ambassador. The term is also used to refer to the building in which the diplomatic functions are undertaken (the correct formal term for this being the "premises").

embezzlement *n.* The dishonest appropriation by an employee of any money or property given to him on behalf of his employer. Before 1969 there was a special offence of embezzlement; it is now, however, classified as a form of *theft.

emblements *pl. n.* Cultivated crops that are normally harvested annually. A tenant for life of settled land may continue to harvest crops he has sown if his interest in the land ceases for any reason other than by his own act. For example, he may continue to harvest his crops if his interest ends on the death of another person but not if his interest was for life until remarriage and he remarries. When he dies, his personal representatives are entitled to reap for the benefit of his estate any crops sown by him before his death.

embracery *n.* The former common-law crime of attempting to influence a jury corruptly in favour of one party in a trial by promises, persuasions, entreaties, money, entertainments, or the like. By the mid 1970s the offence was considered obsolete, the conduct in question being dealt with by either *perverting the course of justice or *contempt of court (Criminal Justice and Public Order Act 1994 s 51). Embracery was abolished as a separate offence by the Bribery Act 2010 (*see* BRIBERY).

embryo selection The process by which embryos created by IVF are selected for implantation. The practice of **preimplantation genetic diagnosis** (**PGD**) means that it is now possible to select an embryo that does not have, or is not likely to have, a particular disability, or to select an embryo with certain characteristics. PGD requires a licence from the *Human Fertilization and Embryology Authority (HFEA), which will only allow the procedure where there is a significant risk of a serious genetic condition being present in the embryo. Licences have been granted to allow the selection of an embryo that is a genetic match to an existing child suffering from a genetic illness. Tissue from a child conceived in this way – popularly known as a **saviour sibling** – can be used to treat the older brother or sister. **Sex selection**, i.e. the selection of an embryo for implantation on the basis of gender, is only allowed by the HFEA to avoid a risk of a genetic illness, not for social reasons.

emergency powers Powers conferred by government regulations during a **state of emergency**. The existence of such a state is declared by royal proclamation under the Emergency Powers Acts 1920 and 1964 and the Civil Contingencies Act 2004. A proclamation, which lasts for one month but is renewable, may be issued whenever there is a threat (e.g. a major strike or natural disaster) to the country's essentials of life. The regulations made may confer on government departments, the armed forces, and others all powers necessary to secure the supply and distribution of necessities and the maintenance of public peace and safety. *See also* CIVIL PROTECTION.

emergency protection order A court order under the Children Act 1989 that gives a local authority or the NSPCC the right to remove a child to suitable accommodation for a maximum of eight days (with a right to apply for a seven-day extension) if there is reasonable cause to believe a child is suffering or is likely to suffer significant harm unless the order is made. The order gives the applicant *parental responsibility in so far as it promotes the welfare of the child (*see* WELFARE PRINCIPLE). In some cases it may be preferable to remove the abuser from the home rather than the child. The Children Act 1989 provides for the inclusion of an *exclusion requirement in an emergency protection order. The effect of this is to exclude the abuser from the family home. The order may only be made when another person in the same household as the child consents to the exclusion order and is able and willing to care properly for the child. *See also* SECTION 47 ENQUIRY.

eminent domain *See* EXPROPRIATION.

emoluments *pl. n.* A person's earnings, including salaries, fees, wages, profits, and benefits in kind (e.g. company cars). The distinction between emoluments (subject to income tax) and earnings (subject to national insurance) is explored in *HMRC v Forde & McHugh Ltd* [2012] EWCA Civ 692.

empanel *vb.* To select a jury to try an issue before a court.

employee *n.* A person who works under the direction and control of another (the *employer) in return for a wage or salary. An employee works for the employer under a "contract of service", whereas an independent contractor who is contracted to perform a specific task works under a "contract for services". The distinction is crucial since employees enjoy more protection under the employment legislation. The question as to whether someone is or is not an employee is governed by tests laid down by the courts over many years and can be far from clear (*Lane v Shire Roofing Co (Oxford) Ltd* [1995] IRLR 493 (CA); *James v London Borough of Greenwich* [2008] EWCA Civ 35, [2008] IRLR 302). *See* CONTRACT OF EMPLOYMENT; EMPLOYER AND EMPLOYEE; WORKER.

employees' inventions Products, equipment, or techniques invented by an employee in the course of his employment. Under the Patents Act 1977 section 39, these belong to the employer if the invention was made in the course of the employee's normal duties and these were likely to lead to an invention or in the course of any duties involving a special obligation to further the employer's business. These provisions cannot be changed in a contract of employment. The employee may, however, be awarded compensation by the Comptroller General of Patents, Designs and Trademarks if the invention is of outstanding benefit to the employer (this virtually never applies). Copyright works also belong to the employer if the employee produces them in the course of his employment (*LIFFE Administration and Management v Pinkava* [2007] EWCA Civ 217, [2007] ICR 1489).

employees' share scheme A method of sharing company profits with employees either by distributing shares already paid up by the company, either to the employees themselves or to trustees for them, or by conferring upon them options to acquire shares on favourable terms. Certain schemes carry tax concessions.

employer *n.* A person who engages another to work under his direction and control in return for a wage or salary (*see also* CONTRACT OF EMPLOYMENT). Companies are **associated employers** if one of them controls the other or others or if they are themselves controlled by the same company.

employer and employee The relationship between the parties to a *contract of employment. (It was formerly known as **master and servant**.) The relationship is governed by the express and implied terms of the contract and by statutory rules that the contract cannot exclude. These relate, for example, to *unfair dismissal, *redundancy, *maternity rights, *trade union membership and activity, and health and *safety at work. On the principle of *vicarious liability, third parties may hold an employer responsible for certain wrongs committed by his employee in the course of his employment.

SEE WEB LINKS
• Guide to employment rights from the TUC's WorkSMART website

employers' association An organization whose members are wholly or mainly employers and whose principal purposes include the regulation of relations between employers and workers or trade unions. Under the Trade Union and Labour Relations (Consolidation) Act 1992, employers' associations have similar legal status to *trade unions, being immune from certain civil legal proceedings in tort relating to interference with contracts and restraint of trade.

employer's liability The liability of an employer for breach of his duty to provide for his employees competent fellow-workers, safe equipment, a safe place of work, and a safe system of work, including adequate supervision (*Wilson and Clyde Coal Co Ltd v English* [1938] AC 57 (HL) 141). This includes a duty not to cause *psychiatric injury (*Barber v Somerset CC* [2004] UKHL 13, [2004] 1 WLR 1089; *Hartman v South Essex Mental Health and Community Care NHS Trust* [2005] EWCA Civ 6, [2005] ICR 782). Liability can be in tort for damages for *negligence and for *breach of statutory duty under statutes providing for *safety at work; there are also criminal penalties. *See* DANGEROUS MACHINERY; DEFECTIVE EQUIPMENT.

Employment Appeal Tribunal (EAT) A statutory body established to hear appeals from *employment tribunals. The original composition of the EAT was a High Court judge as chairman and two or four lay members with special knowledge or experience as employers' or employees' representatives. From June 2013 a judge will normally sit alone. The EAT can only hear appeals on questions of law, not fact. The EAT may allow or dismiss an appeal or, in certain circumstances, remit the case to the employment tribunal for further hearing. From 2013 fees are incurred by anyone wishing to bring an appeal:

the issue fee (£400) is paid when the claim is submitted and the hearing fee (£1,200) is paid prior to the full hearing. Those on low incomes may qualify for a remission of the fees. The parties may be represented at the hearing by anyone they choose, who need not have legal qualifications. The EAT cannot enforce its own decisions; thus, for example, when an employer fails to comply with an order for compensation that the EAT upholds, separate application must be made to the court to enforce the order. A party may appeal to the Court of Appeal from a decision of the EAT, but only with the leave of the EAT or the Court of Appeal. The Employment Tribunals Act 1996 sets out the jurisdiction of the EAT. The EAT does not generally order either party to pay the other's costs, except when the appeal is frivolous, vexatious, misconceived, or improperly conducted.

Employment (Framework) Directive An EU directive (Council Directive 2000/78) that prohibits *discrimination on grounds of religion or belief, disability, age, or sexual orientation. It covers employment, training, and membership of workers', employers', or professional organizations.

employment income As may be expected from a taxing statute, the Income Tax (Earnings and Pensions) Act 2003 gives a very wide definition of the "employment income" that is subject to tax under that statute. Employment income means any salary, wages or fee, gratuity, other profit, or incidental benefit of any kind obtained by an employee if it is for money or money's worth or "anything else that constitutes an emolument of the employment". In case this definition is not wide enough, Parliament has added to the definition of employment income "any amount treated as earnings" and "any amount which counts as employment income". Thus a payment for breach of an employment contract is taxed as employment income, as is the cost to the employer of providing a *benefit in kind for an employee. A payment for termination of an employment is brought within the statutory definition of employment income by the Income Tax (Earnings and Pensions) Act 2003 s 402. A special tax code is applied, which may exempt from income tax the first £30,000 received (s 403).

employment tribunal (ET) Any of the bodies established under the employment protection legislation to hear and rule on certain disputes between employers and employees or trade unions relating to statutory terms and conditions of employment. Originally called **industrial tribunals**, they were renamed in 1998. They are governed by the Employment Tribunals Act 1996. The tribunals hear, amongst other cases, complaints concerning *unfair dismissal, *redundancy, *discrimination, *equal pay, *maternity rights, and complaints of unlawful deductions from wages under the Employment Rights Act 1996 (Part II). Tribunals sit in local centres in public and may consist of a legally qualified chairman (the employment judge) and two independent laymen but employment judges may also sit alone. There is a power in the Enterprise and Regulatory Reform Act 2013 also to allow "legal officers" to decide certain claims, if the parties agree. This is aimed at speeding up the process. An ET cannot enforce its own awards (this must be done by separate application to a court) and it can conduct its proceedings informally. Strict rules of evidence need not apply and the parties can present their own case or be represented by anyone they wish at their own expense. The tribunal has powers to declare a dismissal unfair and to award *compensation, which is the usual remedy, but they also have power to order the *reinstatement or *re-engagement of a dismissed employee.

Before conducting a full hearing of the case, the tribunal may conduct a pre-hearing review to assess the strength of the case. If the review suggests that the claim of defence is unlikely to succeed, the tribunal may require the claimant or the employer to pay a deposit. The maximum that can be required is £1,000. Costs are not normally awarded against an unsuccessful party but may be payable if a deposit has been required and the case is unsuccessful (in which case the deposit will go towards the costs) or where the tribunal finds that a party has acted vexatiously or unreasonably.

From 2013 fees must be paid by anyone bringing a claim. The level of fee varies according to the type of case. For unfair dismissal, the issue fee will be £250 and the hearing fee is £950. Those on low incomes may be eligible for remission of the fees.

The Enterprise and Regulatory Reform Act 2013 gives tribunals the discretion to impose a financial penalty on an employer where there has been a breach of a worker's employment rights and the tribunal considers that the employer's behaviour in committing the breach had one or more aggravating features, such as malice, or where the employer has repeatedly breached those rights. The maximum penalty is £5,000. If the employer complies within 21 days the penalty is reduced by 50%. The penalty is payable to the Government, not the claimant.

An appeal on a point of law arising from any decision of an ET may be heard by the *Employment Appeal Tribunal.

• Website of the employment tribunals

EMS *See* European Monetary System.

EMU *See* European Monetary Union.

EN *See* Euro Norm.

enabling statute A statute that confers rights or powers upon any body or person.

enacting words The introductory words in an *Act of Parliament that give it the force of law. They follow immediately after the long title and date of royal assent, unless preceded by a preamble, and normally run: "Be It Enacted by the Queen's most Excellent Majesty, by and with the advice and consent of the Lords Spiritual and Temporal, and Commons, in this present Parliament assembled, and by the authority of the same, as follows . . .". A special formula is used in cases when the Parliament Acts 1911 and 1949 apply (*see* Act of Parliament).

enactment *n.* An Act of Parliament, a Measure of the General Synod (*see* Church of England), an order, or any other piece of subordinate legislation, or any particular provision contained in any of these (e.g. a particular section or article). Delegated legislation is not an enactment for the purposes of the Local Government Act 1992.

en banc [French: on the bench] Describing a hearing, often of an appeal, that is heard by all the judges of a court rather than a panel.

encroachment *n.* The act of extending one's own rights at the expense of others, particularly by taking in adjoining land to make it appear part of one's own. If the encroachment is acquiesced in for 12 years, the land taken is considered to be annexed to the land of the person who made the encroachment.

encumbrance (incumbrance) *n.* A right or interest in land owned by someone other than the owner of the land itself; examples include easements, leases, mortgages, and restrictive covenants. When title to the land is registered (*see* land registration), encumbrances other than overriding interests are recorded in the Charges Register. Certain encumbrances affecting unregistered land will only be enforceable against third parties if registered at the Land Charges Registry. *See also* registration of encumbrances.

endorsement *n.* **1.** The procedure in which the particulars of a driving offence are noted on a person's driving licence. When the court orders endorsement for an offence carrying obligatory or discretionary *disqualification but the driver is not disqualified, the endorsement also contains particulars of the number of penalty points imposed for the purposes of *totting up. When the court orders disqualification, only the particulars of the offence are noted. The courts can order endorsement upon a conviction for most traffic offences (the main exceptions being parking offences) and in many cases they must order an endorsement, unless there are special reasons (e.g. a sudden emergency) why they should not. A person whose licence is to be endorsed must produce it for the court; if he does not do so, his licence may be suspended. A driver whose licence has been endorsed may apply to have a new "clean" licence after a certain number of years has elapsed (usually 4 years, but 11 in the case of offences involving *drunken driving). Under the Road Traffic (New Drivers) Act 1995, with effect from 1 June 1997, a driver who is convicted of an endorsable offence and who has accumulated 6 or more penalty points within two years of passing a driving test has his licence revoked and must retake a driving test. **2.** The signature of the holder on a bill of exchange, which is an essential step in negotiating or transferring a bill payable to order. The endorsement must be completed by delivering the bill to the transferee. An **endorsement in blank** is the bare signature of the holder and makes the bill payable to bearer. A **special endorsement** specifies the person to whom (or to whose order) the bill is payable (e.g. "Pay X or order"). An endorser, by endorsing a bill, takes on certain obligations to the holder or a subsequent endorser. **3.** The noting on a document of details of a later transaction affecting the subject matter of that document. For example, a beneficiary in whose favour a personal representative executes an *assent of property may require details of the assent to be written (**endorsed**) on the document containing the *probate or *letters of administration. Equally, a purchaser of a plot forming part of a larger plot of land may require a note or memorandum of the conveyance to him to be endorsed on the title deeds relating to the whole plot.

endowment *n.* **1.** The provision of a fixed income for the support of a charity. **2.** Any property belonging permanently to a charity.

enforcement action Any action, authorized by the United Nations Security Council, to enforce *collective security under *Chapter VII (i.e. Articles 39–51) of the UN Charter. As such it stands as one of the very few legal justifications for *use of force in international law. Strictly, any enforcement action can only be justified under Article 42 of the Charter, which requires agreement by member states to place their armed forces at the disposal of the UN (*see* MILITARY STAFF COMMITTEE). However, although the theory of enforcement action would seem to be that of concerted action by members under Article 42, such a limitation is not expressly stated in the Charter. Article 39 was worded so widely as to allow the Security Council, using the implied powers allowed for by that Article, to bypass this problem and authorize that member states voluntarily furnish armed forces to be under the unified command of one member state. Upon the basis of such implied power, an enforcement action was justified under Security Council recommendations under Article 39 in order to defend Korea (1950) and to liberate Kuwait in the first Gulf conflict (1991).

enforcement notice A notice by a local planning authority (*see* TOWN AND COUNTRY PLANNING) that requires certain steps to be taken within a specified time to remedy an alleged breach of planning control. An example of such a breach would occur if development was carried out without planning permission or contrary to conditions attached to planning permission. A local planning authority that has notice of a breach of planning control has, however, a discretion as to whether to enforce against that breach. Appeal against the notice may be made to the Secretary of State on various grounds, including the ground that the development is one for which planning permission ought to be granted. *see also* STOP NOTICE.

enforcement of judgment In civil proceedings, the processes by which the judgments and orders of a court may be enforced. Under the * Civil Procedure Rules (CPR) judgments and orders for the payment of money (including the payment of costs) may be enforced by a variety of methods, including a writ of *fieri facias* or warrant of execution; a *Third Party Debt Order; a *charging order; an attachment of earnings order; and the appointment of a *receiver. Under Part 70 of the CPR a *judgment creditor may use any method of enforcement that is available, and may use more than one method (either at the same time or one after another).

Judgments for possession of land may be enforced by a *writ of possession or a warrant of possession. Judgments for delivery of goods may be enforced by a *writ of delivery or a warrant of delivery. *See also* COMMITTAL IN CIVIL PROCEEDINGS; INJUNCTION; SEQUESTRATION.

enforcer *n.* A third party to a trust who is neither a trustee nor a beneficiary but who can be appointed under the trust instrument for the purposes of ensuring that the trust is carried out in accordance with its terms. Although such a role is recognized in some jurisdictions, English law remains attached to the *beneficiary principle, under which a trust is only valid where there is a human beneficiary who is able to enforce the trust. (The only exceptions are charitable trusts, where the terms are enforced by the Crown, and a very limited class of *purpose trusts.) Support has grown in some academic quarters for the replacement of the beneficiary principle with a broader **enforcer principle**, under which the terms of a trust can be enforced by designated persons who are not beneficiaries.

enfranchise *vb.* **1.** To give to a person or class of people the right to vote at elections. **2.** To give to an area or a class of people the right to be represented on an elected body.

enfranchisement of tenancy A method for acquiring the freehold or an extended lease of a leasehold house. A tenant has a statutory right of enfranchisement when he has a long lease (exceeding 21 years). The tenant's rights to enfranchise are governed by the Commonhold and Leasehold Reform Act 2002.

engagement to marry An agreement, verbal or in writing, to marry at a future date. Such agreements are no longer treated as enforceable legal contracts, and no action can be brought for breach of such an agreement or to recover expenses incurred as a result of the agreement. Engagement rings are deemed to be absolute gifts and cannot be recovered when an engagement is broken. There is a special statutory provision that property rights between engaged parties (for example, in respect of a house purchased with a view to marriage) are to be decided in accordance with the rules governing property rights of married couples.

engaging in sexual activity in the presence of a child It is a criminal offence under section 11 of the Sexual Offences Act 2003 for a person over the age of 18 to engage in sexual activity when a person under the age of 16 (child) is present or is in a place from which the sexual activity can be observed, and the defendant knows or believes that the child is aware, or the defendant is intending that the child should be aware, that the defendant is engaging in the sexual activity. If the child is between the ages of 13 and 16, the defendant's mistaken belief that the child is over the age of 16 will negate his liability, providing that belief is both honestly held and reasonable.

If the child is under the age of 13, his mistaken belief that the child is over 16 will not negate his liability, irrespective of whether that belief is honestly held and reasonable. The maximum sentence is 10 years' imprisonment.

engross *vb.* To prepare a fair copy of a deed or other legal document ready for execution by the parties.

enlarge *vb.* (in land law) To acquire further rights in land, thereby increasing one's interest to some greater estate or interest. For example, a *tenant in tail may enlarge his interest into a fee simple by executing a disentailing deed (*see* ENTAILED INTEREST).

enrolment *n.* The registration of an act or document on an official record. It used to be obligatory to enrol many documents in the Enrolment Office, a department of the Chancery Division. Nearly all such obligations were abolished by the Judicature Acts 1873–75.

entailed interest An *equitable interest in land under which ownership is limited to a person and the heirs of his body (either generally or those of a specified class). Such heirs are still those who would inherit under the law of intestacy as it applied before the Administration of Estates Act 1925. Since 1997, no new entailed interests can be created. An attempt to do so creates an absolute interest instead (Trusts of Land and Appointment of Trustees Act 1996 sch 1 para 5).

enter *vb.* **1.** (in the law of *burglary) To make "an effective and substantial" entry as a trespasser (*R v Collins* [1973] QB 100). This does not necessarily require entry of the whole of the defendant's body. **2.** (in land law) *See* ENTRY INTO POSSESSION.

entering judgment A procedure in civil courts in which a judgment is formally recorded by the court after it has been given. Under Part 40 of the *Civil Procedure Rules a judgment or order will normally be drawn up by the court unless the court orders a party to draw it up, or a party, with the permission of the court, agrees to draw it up. Every judgment or order must bear the date on which it was given or made and must be *sealed by the court.

Enterprise Investment Scheme (EIS) A scheme to encourage investment in unlisted companies. The EIS gives income tax relief of 20% on investments to individuals who invest from £500 to £100,000 in any one year in shares issued by UK trading companies not quoted on the Stock Exchange. Gains on the sale of shares issued under this scheme are also exempt from capital gains tax. Investors can hold paid directorships of the companies; there is also income and capital gains tax relief on losses. Companies providing private housing on assured tenancies are excluded from the scheme. Tax relief of 50% of an investment up to £100,000 made between 6 April 2012 and 5 April 2017 is also available under the **Seed Enterprise Investment Scheme** (Finance Act 2012 sch 6).

entire contract *See* PERFORMANCE OF CONTRACT.

entrapment *n.* Deliberately enticing a person into committing a crime in order to secure his conviction, as by offering to buy drugs from him. The English courts do not recognize entrapment as a defence. However, a court may stay proceedings as an abuse of the court's process or rule that certain evidence is inadmissible on the ground that the admission of the evidence would have such an adverse effect on the fairness of the proceedings that it ought not to be admitted (Police and Criminal Evidence Act 1984 s78). Entrapment may also be used as a reason for mitigating a sentence. *See also* AGENT PROVOCATEUR.

entrepreneurs' relief A *capital gains tax relief available from April 2008 (when it replaced taper relief). Where an individual makes a disposal that attracts entrepreneurs' relief, tax is charged at a special low rate of 10%. In order to qualify for the relief, the disposal must be by an individual and of a *business asset. Entrepreneurs' relief is denied if the asset has been held for less than a year. The special 10% tax rate given by the relief is applied only to the first £5 million of gains made by any one individual.

entry into possession The act of going upon land to assert some right over it. For example, a lease usually gives the landlord the right to enter and take possession if the tenant fails to pay the rent or commits a breach of covenant. A mortgagee has the right to recover possession from a defaulting mortgagor who is in possession. In general, such rights of entry cannot be enforced unless the court orders the defaulter to give up possession.

entry without warrant Entry by a police officer onto private premises without the authority of a warrant. This is in general unlawful except with the occupier's consent (which is revocable), but it is permitted by statute for the purpose of arresting for *indictable offences and in certain circumstances to search premises (*see* POWER OF SEARCH); it is also allowed at common law to stop an actual or apprehended breach of the peace.

Environment Agency A non-departmental public body established under the Environment Act 1995. It is responsible for protecting the environment in England, notably by controlling *pollution, regulating *waste disposal, and managing water resources (including fisheries and flood defences). The Agency issues licences, permits, and authorizations, such as those required for the industrial *abstraction of water or commercial carriage of waste.

(⊕) SEE WEB LINKS

• Website of the Environment Agency: includes information on waste management and environmental permitting

environmental degradation In international law, a depletion of the earth's resources through *pollution that transcends territorial boundaries. Global warming creating desertification and the slow destruction of ice at the poles would be obvious examples.

epitome of title *See* ABSTRACT OF TITLE.

Equality Act 2010 An Act that consolidates, harmonizes, and extends the whole body of legislation passed to outlaw various types of *discrimination over the previous 40 years. The Equality Act specifies nine **protected characteristics** that may be the basis of unlawful discrimination: age, disability, gender reassignment, marriage and civil partnership, pregnancy and maternity, race, religion or belief, sex, and sexual orientation. In doing so, the Act repeals and replaces the earlier legislation that related to these characteristics, including the Equal Pay Act 1970, the Sex Discrimination Act 1975, the Race Relations Act 1976, the Disability Discrimination Act 1995, the Employment Equality (Religion or Belief) Regulations 2003, the Employment Equality (Sexual Orientation) Regulations 2003, the Employment Equality (Age) Regulations 2006, the Equality Act 2006 (pt 2), the Equality Act (Sexual Orientation) Regulations 2007.

The Act applies in a number of areas other than employment, including education, transport, and the provision of goods and services. Discrimination may be direct or indirect (*see* INDIRECT DISCRIMINATION). It may arise from a mistaken belief that someone has a protected characteristic (for example, treating someone less favourably because they are believed to be gay), or because of a person's association with someone who has a protected characteristic (for example, where someone is treated less favourably because their child is disabled). The Act also covers *victimization and *harassment.

Employers must not discriminate against or victimize applicants or employees on the basis of any of the protected characteristics. It is also unlawful to harass or sexually harass applicants or employees. There are special rules for discrimination on grounds of pregnancy and maternity, and for the discrimination that arises where an employer fails to make *reasonable adjustments for a disabled employee. Discrimination in employment may relate to decisions about who to employ and on what terms, access to promotion, training, and other benefits, and dismissal or any other detriment. Sex discrimination in pay is dealt with in the provisions relating to *equal pay (referred to in the Act as "equality of terms"). The Act also makes unenforceable any terms of employment that prevent someone from disclosing their pay to others, or terms that try to prevent people from asking colleagues about their pay, where the purpose is to find out whether a difference in pay is connected with a protected characteristic (for example, sex). Under the Act employers may, but are not required to, take positive action where one of several equally qualified candidates belongs to a group identified by one or more of the protected characteristics and perceived to be socially or economically disadvantaged or subject to discrimination. Such positive action is distinct from *positive discrimination, which remains unlawful. There are a number of exceptions that apply to the employment sphere, including where having one of the protected characteristics is an occupational requirement and that can be justified as being a proportionate means of achieving a legitimate aim. There are also special exceptions that apply in the case of religion or belief and in the case of age.

The Act extends the public sector *equality duty to all nine protected characteristics.

Individuals who suffer discrimination under the terms of the Act may bring a complaint in the *employment tribunal for employment-related matters or in the courts for matters relating to the provision of goods and services. The new *Equality and Human Rights Commission also has enforcement powers. The field is heavily influenced by European law (*see* EMPLOYMENT (FRAMEWORK) DIRECTIVE; EQUAL TREATMENT DIRECTIVE; RACE DIRECTIVE).

Equality and Human Rights Commission (EHRC) A non-departmental public body established under the Equality Act 2006. It is accountable for its public funds but independent of government. The Commission brings together the work of three previous bodies – the Equal Opportunities Commission, the Commission for Racial Equality, and the Disability Rights Commission – and assumes responsibility for equality in the areas of age, sexual orientation, and religion or belief. The remit of the commission is to promote and monitor human rights; and to protect, enforce, and promote equality across the nine "protected characteristics" – age, disability, gender, race, religion and belief, pregnancy and maternity, marriage and civil partnership, sexual orientation, and gender reassignment. Its enforcement powers include inquiries into general equality issues (for example, sex discrimination in the finance industry) and assessments of whether public bodies are complying with the public sector {equality duty}.

((⊕)) SEE WEB LINKS

• Website of the EHRC: provides information on human rights, public-sector equality duties, and best practice for employers

equality clause A clause in a contract of employment stipulating that if a woman is employed on similar work to that of a man in the same employment, or on work rated as equivalent or of equal value to his, then the terms of her contract (including, but not restricted to, pay) must place her in no less favourable a position than the man.

A contract not containing such a clause (either directly or as a result of some collective agreement) is deemed to include one by virtue of the Equality Act 2010. Case: (*Hayward v Cammell Laird Shipbuilders Ltd* [1988] IAC 894 (HL)). *See also* EQUAL PAY; SEX DISCRIMINATION.

equality duty The *Equality Act 2010 imposes a duty, on public bodies (e.g. local authorities) to have due regard to certain matters when exercising their functions. These are: (1) eliminating conduct that is prohibited by the Act; (2) advancing equality of opportunity between people who share a "protected characteristic" and people who do not share it; and (3) fostering good relations between people who share a protected characteristic and people who do not share it. Previously the equality duty applied only in relation to race, disability, and sex. It now covers all the protected characteristics in the Equality Act, except that the second and third matters do not apply to the protected characteristics of marriage and civil partnership.In addition to the general duty, regulations may impose specific duties on public bodies. The specific duties applicable in England are far less detailed than those that apply in Scotland and Wales.

Failure to comply with the duty does not create a right for individuals to sue the public body. Enforcement is by the *Equality and Human Rights Commission. The duty is, however, enforceable by way of *judicial review by an individual or group (*R (Williams) v Surrey County Council* [2012] EWHC 867 (QB)), [2012] RqLR GS6.

equality is equity [from Latin: *aequitas est quasi aequalitas*] A *maxim of equity stating that if there are no reasons for any other basis of division of property, those entitled to it shall share it equally.

equality of arms A concept that has been created by the European Court of Human Rights in the context of the right to a *fair trial (Article 6). Equality of arms requires that there be a fair balance between the opportunities afforded the parties involved in litigation (for example, each party should be able to call witnesses and cross-examine the witnesses called by the other party). In some circumstances this may require the provision of financial support to allow a person of limited means to pay for legal representation (*Airey v Ireland* (App no 6289/73) [1981] (ECHR 1)).

Equal Opportunities Commission (EOC) A body established by the Sex Discrimination Acts 1975 and 1986 to work towards eliminating discrimination on grounds of sex or marital status, to promote equality of opportunity between the sexes, and to keep the working of the Acts, and of the Equal Pay Act 1970, under review. Since 1 October 2007 the functions of the EOC have been integrated into the *Equality and Human Rights Commission. *See* SEX DISCRIMINATION.

equal pay The requirement of the *Equality Act 2010 that men and women in the same employment must be paid at the same rate for like work or work rated as equivalent or of equal value. They are in the same employment if they work at the same establishment (or if one works at an establishment that includes the other's) and they work for the same or an associated *employer. The establishments must also be those at which the terms and conditions of employment are observed generally or for employees of the relevant description. "Like work" is work that is broadly similar, where any differences between the man's work and the woman's are not of practical importance (*Capper Pass Ltd v Lawton* [1976] IRLR 366 (EAT)). Work is rated as equivalent when the employer has undertaken a study to evaluate his employees' jobs in terms of the skill, effort, and responsibility demanded of them and the woman's job is given the same grade as the man's (*Eaton Ltd v Nuttall* [1977] IRLR 71 (EAT)). If the employer has no job-evaluation scheme, an independent expert is appointed by an employment tribunal to evaluate the two jobs to see if they are of equal value. Thus when the employer's job-grading system or the expert's report recognizes that the woman's job is as demanding as the man's, they are entitled to equal pay even though the nature of the work they do is very different. An employer's job-evaluation system can be challenged on the basis that it is discriminatory (Case C-237/85 *Rummler v Dato-Druck Gmbh* [1986] ECR 2101). *See also* EQUALITY CLAUSE.

The Enterprise and Regulatory Reform Act 2013 allows for regulations to be made that will require an employment tribunal to order employers to carry out equal pay audits where they have been found to have breached equal pay law. Regulations may provide that an employment tribunal may order an employer to pay a penalty not exceeding £5,000 for failure to comply with an equal pay audit order. It is not intended that firms will be required to publish the results of any audit.

There is a Code of Practice on Equal Pay, as issued by the Equality and Human Rights Commission in 2010. The Code is admissible in evidence in any tribunal proceedings.

equal treatment The requirement, enshrined in the Treaty of Rome, that nationals of one EU state moving to work in another EU state must be treated in the same way as those workers of the state to which they have moved. There must be *free movement of workers throughout the EU and no discrimination in relation to pay, social security, and tax benefits. *See* EQUAL PAY.

Equal Treatment Directive An EU directive (Council Directive 76/207) that prohibited *discrimination on grounds of sex in employment, training, membership of workers', employers', or professional organizations, and some aspects of social security. It operated along with other sex equality directives, including the Equal Pay Directive (75/117). EU Directive 2006/54, on the implementation of the principle of equal opportunities and equal treatment of men and women in matters of employment and occupation, consolidated and amended (in accordance with case law from the *European Court of Justice) seven separate Directives relating to sex equality. The Directive covers equal treatment of men and women in relation to: equal pay; access to employment, vocational training, and promotion; working conditions; occupational social security schemes; it also deals with the burden of proof in sex discrimination cases.

The Equal Treatment Directive (Council Directive 2004/113) covers equal access for women and men to the supply of goods and services, including insurance.

equitable *adj.* **1.** Recognized by or in accordance with the rules of equity: applied to distinguish certain concepts used in both common or statute law and in equity. For example, assignments and mortgages can be either legal or equitable. **2.** Describing a right or concept recognized by the Court of Chancery. **3.** Just, fair, and reasonable. For example, a document may have two meanings, one strict and the other (the equitable construction) more benevolent.

equitable assignment *See* ASSIGNMENT.

equitable charge **1.** *See* EQUITABLE MORTGAGE. **2.** A *charge created by designating specific property for the discharge of some debt or other obligation. No special form of words is necessary to create an equitable charge, manifested intention being sufficient. *See* GENERAL EQUITABLE CHARGE.

equitable easement *See* EASEMENT.

equitable estate A right in property recognized by the Court of Chancery, as distinct from a *legal estate recognized in common law courts (*see* ESTATE). Equitable estates reflected legal interests but could be more flexible (*compare* SHIFTING USE; SPRINGING

USE). Before 1926, most types of estate could exist either at law or in equity; since 1925 only a limited number of legal estates can exist; all other interests in land are called *equitable interests. The term equitable estate is now technically incorrect.

equitable estoppel *See* ESTOPPEL.

equitable execution Means of enforcing the judgment of a court when the judgment creditor cannot obtain satisfaction from the normal methods of *execution. For example, the creditor may appoint a receiver to manage the defendant's property or he may obtain an injunction to prevent the defendant from dealing with the property. These remedies are often regarded as relief granted by the court, rather than as execution.

equitable interests Interests in property originally recognized by the Court of Chancery, as distinct from legal interests recognized in the common-law courts. They arose in cases when it was against the principles of *equity for a person to enforce a legal right. Originally equitable rights (e.g. a trust, or the *equity of redemption under a mortgage) were enforceable against the person with a legal right over the property in question. Later, however, those who were given the property by the holder of the legal interests took it subject to equitable interests; later still, anyone who bought property knowing of the equitable interests was bound by them. In the developed law, everyone took property subject to equitable interests except those who bought it and neither knew nor ought to have known of the equitable interests (i.e. a bona fide *purchaser for value without notice). Since 1925, equitable interests may be protected by the doctrine of *overreaching, under the system of *land charges, or by notice.

equitable lease An agreement for the grant of an interest in land on terms that correspond to a *legal lease but do not comply with the necessary formal requirements of a legal lease. For example, if L purports to grant T a lease for seven years but the transaction is effected by simple written contract to grant a lease rather than by deed, the court may enforce the contract to grant the lease between the parties. This follows the principle that "equity looks upon that as done which ought to be done" (*see* MAXIMS OF EQUITY) (*Walsh v Lonsdale* (1820) 21 Ch D 9). Further, T's rights under the contract could be registered as an *estate contract and thus bind any third party acquiring L's interest in the land.

equitable lien *See* LIEN.

equitable mortgage (equitable charge) A *mortgage under which the mortgagee does not obtain a legal interest in the land. An equitable mortgage may arise as follows:
(1) If the mortgagor has only an *equitable interest in the land, he can only grant an equitable mortgage. For example, a mortgage granted by a beneficiary under a *trust of land could only be equitable.
(2) An equitable mortgage will arise if the mortgage is not made by deed (a requirement for legal mortgages). The contract for the mortgage must nevertheless be made in writing.
(3) If a charge by way of legal mortgage of registered land is not entered onto the register, it takes effect in equity only (Land Registration Act 2002 s 27(1)).

equitable presumptions An inference by equity that where a given set of facts exists, this gives rise to the assumption that other facts follow. For example, the presumption of *advancement means that a father who makes a voluntary transfer to his child is deemed to have intended to make a *gift. Other examples of an equitable presumption include the presumption of a *resulting trust and the presumption of equality (*see* EQUALITY IS EQUITY).

equitable remedies Means granted by *equity to redress a wrong. Since the range of legal remedies was originally very limited, equity showed great flexibility in granting remedies, which were discretionary: the conduct of the parties, particularly that of the claimant, was taken into account (*see* CLEAN HANDS). The main equitable remedies are now *specific performance, *rescission, *cancellation, *rectification, *account, *injunction, and the appointment of a *receiver. These remedies may be sought in any division of the High Court or, in some instances, in the county courts; they are still discretionary in nature, although the discretion is often exercised on established lines.

equitable rights Rights recognized by *equity. *See* EQUITABLE INTERESTS; EQUITABLE REMEDIES.

equitable right to redeem The mortgagor's right to pay off the loan secured on his property, even after the date to redemption as stated in the mortgage deed has passed, and have the mortgage discharged. The court may strike down any term that provides a *collateral advantage to the mortgagee, or any *clogs or fetters on the equitable right to redeem if it determines that the clog or fetter unfairly interferes with the mortgagor's inviolable right to redeem. Such collateral advantages or clogs or fetters are generally contained within the terms of the mortgage (although not exclusively so: see *Lewis v Frank Love Ltd* [1961] 1 WLR 261 (Ch)) and include such provisions as an option to purchase (*Samuel v Jarrah Timber & Wood Paving Corporation Ltd* [1904] AC 323 (HL)) or a *solus* tie (*Noakes & Co Ltd v Rice* [1902] AC 24 (HL)).

equitable waste Alterations made by a tenant that cause damage to the leased property. *See* WASTE.

equity *n.* **1.** That part of English law originally administered by the *Lord Chancellor and later by the *Court of Chancery, as distinct from that administered by the courts of *common law. The common law did not recognize certain concepts (e.g. uses and trusts) and its remedies were limited in scope and flexibility, since it relied primarily on the remedy of damages. In the Middle Ages litigants were entitled to petition the king, who relied on the advice of his Chancellor, commonly an ecclesiastic ("the keeper of the king's conscience"), to do justice in each case. By the 15th century, petitions were referred directly to the Chancellor, who dealt with cases on a flexible basis: he was more concerned with the fair result than with rigid principles of law (hence the jurist John Selden's jibe that "equity varied with the length of the Chancellor's foot"). Moreover, if a defendant refused to comply with the Chancellor's order, he would be imprisoned for contempt of the order until he chose to comply (*see* IN PERSONAM). In the 17th century conflict arose between the common-law judges and the Chancellor as to who should prevail; James I resolved the dispute in favour of the Chancellor. General principles began to emerge, and by the early 19th century the Court of Chancery was more organized and its jurisdiction, once flexible, had ossified into a body of precedent with fixed principles. The Court of Chancery had varying types of jurisdiction (*see* AUXILIARY JURISDICTION; CONCURRENT JURISDICTION; EXCLUSIVE JURISDICTION) and many of its general principles were stated in the form of *maxims of equity; equity had (and still has) certain doctrines (*see* ELECTION; CONVERSION; RECONVERSION; PERFORMANCE OF CONTRACT; SATISFACTION). Under the Judicature Acts 1873–75, with the establishment of the High Court of Justice to administer both common law and equity, the Court of Chancery was abolished (though much of its work is still carried out by the *Chancery Division). The Judicature Acts also provided that in cases in which there was a conflict between the rules of law and equity, the rules of equity should prevail. The main areas of equitable jurisdiction now include *trusts, *equitable interests over property, relief against *forfeiture and penalties, and *equitable remedies. Equity is thus a regulated scheme of legal principles, but new developments are still possible ("equity is not past the age of child-bearing"): recent examples of its creativity include the *freezing injunction and the *search order. **2.** An equitable right or claim, especially an *equitable interest, or *equity of redemption, or *mere equity. **3.** A share in a limited company.

equity of redemption The full bundle of a mortgagor's rights in the mortgaged property, subject to the rights of the mortgagee. The equity of redemption is more commonly referred to simply as the "equity" and is generally equivalent to the value of the property less the outstanding debt secured against it. For example, a property worth £500,000 subject to an outstanding mortgage of £250,000 will have equity to the value of £250,000. This equity can support further borrowing (subject to issues of priority) and can be gifted by will.

equity's darling *See* PURCHASER FOR VALUE WITHOUT NOTICE.

***erga omnes* obligations** [Latin: towards all] (in international law) Obligations in whose fulfilment all states have a legal interest because their subject matter is of importance to the international community as a whole. It follows from this that the breach of such an obligation is of concern not only to the victimized state but also to all the other members of the international community. Thus, in the event of a breach of these obligations, every state must be considered justified in invoking (probably through judicial channels) the responsibility of the guilty state committing the internationally wrongful act. It has been suggested that an example of an *erga omnes* obligation is that of a people's right to *self-determination.

ERM *See* EXCHANGE RATE MECHANISM.

error *n.* A mistake of law in a judgment or order of a court or in some procedural step in legal proceedings. A **writ of error** was formerly used to instruct an inferior court to send records of its proceedings for review by a superior court. It was abolished in civil cases by the Judicature Acts 1873–75 and in criminal cases by the Criminal Appeal Act 1907 and replaced by the modern system of *appeal.

error juris nocet [Latin: Error of law injures] A legal maxim sometimes used to distinguish *mistakes of law from mistakes of fact.

error of law on the face of the record A mistake of law that is made by an inferior court or tribunal in reaching a decision and is apparent from the record of its proceedings. The decision can be quashed by the High Court in *judicial review proceedings by the remedy of *quashing order except in the case of a *domestic tribunal with purely contractual powers. *See also* ULTRA VIRES.

escape *n.* The common-law offence of escaping from lawful custody. The custody may be in prison or a police station, or even in the open air. The escaper need not have been charged with any offence, provided his detention is lawful (e.g. he may be detained to provide a *specimen of breath). Nor is it necessary for him to commit any act of breaking out. It is also an offence to help the escape of a prisoner and to permit a prisoner who is detained in relation to a criminal matter to escape. If someone actually breaks out of a building in which he is lawfully confined he commits a separate offence of **prison breaking**. Case: *R v Dhillon* [2006] 1 WLR 1535.

escrow *n. See* DEED.

espionage *n. See* SPYING.

espousal of claim The action by which a state undertakes to gain redress of a grievance on behalf of one of its subjects or citizens. *see also* EXHAUSTION OF LOCAL REMEDIES.

essence of a contract *See* CONDITION.

estate *n.* **1.** (in land law) Technically, the duration of *tenure in land (*Walsingham's Case* (1573) 2 Plowd 547). In strict legal theory, the Crown has ownership of all land in England and Wales. All others hold an estate (a period of time for which the tenure will last) of the Crown. In practice, the **freehold estate** *fee simple absolute in possession is indistinguishable from absolute ownership. Other freehold estates exist, such as the *life interest and the *fee tail, but these are far less common and will exist as part of a trust or settlement and be equitable rather than legal. The **leasehold estate** or *term of years absolute is the estate held by a tenant from a landlord. It, like the fee simple absolute in possession, is capable of being a legal estate. **2.** (in revenue law) The aggregate of all the property to which a person is beneficially entitled. It covers not only tangible property, but also equitable rights, debts, and any other rights capable of being reduced to a money value (*O'Neill v IRC* [1988] STC (SCD) 110; *Melville v IRC* [2001] EWCA Civ 1247, [2001] STC 271). There is no rule that prevents an asset from being in two different individuals' estates at the same time. **Excluded property**, which includes most reversionary interests and certain foreign matters, is not taken into account for the death charge (*see* INHERITANCE TAX).

estate agent A person who introduces prospective buyers and sellers of property to each other. Such a person may be a member of a professional body but is in any event regulated by the Office of Fair Trading (OFT), under the Estate Agents Act 1979. The Property Misdescription Act 1991 prohibits estate agents from making false or misleading statements about property in the course of their business; making such statements is punishable by a fine. From October 2008 all estate agents are required to register with the Ombudsman for Estate Agents or another redress scheme that has been approved by the OFT. *See also* MISDESCRIPTION.

estate contract A contract in which the owner of land agrees to create or convey a legal estate in the land; for example, he may contract to grant a lease or to sell or he may grant a valid option to purchase. The contract confers on the purchaser an equitable interest that is enforceable against third parties if registered. *See* REGISTRATION OF ENCUMBRANCES.

estate for years Ownership of land subsisting by reference to a period of time. *See* TERM OF YEARS.

estate owner The owner of a *legal estate in land.

estate pur (or per) autre vie [from Norman French: *autre vie*, other life] An interest in property for the lifetime of someone else. If A is given property for B's life, A is the tenant *pur autre vie* and will hold the property during the lifetime of B (the *cestui que vie*). If A dies before B, the persons entitled under A's will or on his intestacy will take the interest for the remainder of B's life; if B dies before A, A's interest thereupon terminates. The interest is a kind of *life interest and an estate of freehold, i.e. it could be inherited; since 1925 it has been an *equitable interest only.

estate rentcharge *See* RENTCHARGE.

estate subsisting at law *See* LEGAL ESTATE.

estoppel *n.* [from Norman French *estouper*, to stop up] A rule of evidence or a rule of law that prevents a person from denying the truth of a statement he has made or from denying the existence of facts that he has alleged to exist. The denial must have been acted upon (probably to his disadvantage) by the person who wishes to take advantage of the estoppel or his position must have been altered as a result. There are several varieties of estoppel.

- **Estoppel by conduct** (or *in pais*) arises when the party estopped has made a statement or has led the other party to believe in a certain fact.
- **Estoppel by deed** prevents a person who has executed a deed from saying that the facts stated in the deed are not true.
- **Estoppel by record** (or *per rem judicatam*) prevents a person from reopening questions that are *res judicata* (i.e. that have been adjudicated upon by a court of competent jurisdiction). *See also* ISSUE ESTOPPEL.

There are two forms of **equitable estoppel** – promissory and proprietary. The doctrine of **promissory estoppel** applies when one party to a contract promises the other (by words or conduct) that he will not enforce his rights under the contract in whole or in part. Provided that the other party has acted in reliance on that promise, it will, though unsupported by consideration, bind the person making it: he will not be allowed subsequently to sue on the contract. When applicable, the doctrine thus modifies the common-law rules relating to *accord and satisfaction. Under the doctrine of **proprietary estoppel**, the courts can grant a discretionary remedy in circumstances where an owner of land has implicitly or explicitly led another to act detrimentally in the belief that rights in or over land would be acquired. The remedy may take the form of the grant of a *fee simple in the property (*Pascoe v Turner* [1979] 1 WLR 431), the grant of a short-term occupational *licence, or even a monetary sum equivalent to the value of the detriment suffered by the claimant in reliance upon the expectation (*Jennings v Rice* [2003] P & CR 8 (CA)). The court will always seek to do the minimum necessary to satisfy the equity. The scope of proprietary estoppel was subject to extensive review by the House of Lords in *Yeoman's Row Management Ltd v Cobbe* [2008] UKHL 55, [2008] 1 WLR 1752 and *Thorner v Major* [2009] UKHL 18, [2009] 1 WLR 76.

estovers *pl. n.* The right to cut timber for certain purposes from land not in one's own absolute ownership. The right arises in favour of a lessee or *tenant for life under a settlement of the land and it can exist as a *profit *à prendre*. Estovers comprise the right to take timber as: (1) **house bote**, for repairing a dwelling or for use as firewood in it; (2) **plough bote**, for repairing farm implements; and (3) **hay bote**, for repairing fences. In each case the lessee or tenant may take only sufficient timber for present needs and not for future requirements. Estovers as profits *à prendre* are usually *appurtenant.

Estrada doctrine The doctrine that *recognition of a government should be based on its *de facto* existence, rather than on its legitimacy. It is named after Don Genero Estrada, the Mexican Secretary of Foreign Affairs who in 1930 ordered that Mexican diplomats should issue no declarations that amounted to a grant of recognition: he felt that this was an insulting practice and offended against the sovereignty of other nations. In 1980 the UK, USA, and many other states adopted the Estrada doctrine. *Compare* TOBAR DOCTRINE.

estreat [from Old French *estrait*] **1.** *n.* an extract from a record relating to *recognizances and fines. **2.** *vb.* To forfeit a recognizance, especially one given by the surety of someone admitted to bail, or to enforce a fine.

ethnic minority A group numerically inferior to the rest of the population of a state whose members are nationals of that state and possess cultural, religious, or linguistic characteristics distinct from those of the total population and show, if only implicitly, a sense of solidarity, directed towards preserving their own social customs, religion, or language. The attempted extirpation of an ethnic minority by the forces of the majority within a state (known as **ethnic cleansing**) can be regarded as a crime against humanity (*see* WAR CRIMES) justifying humanitarian intervention.

ETSI *See* EUROPEAN TELECOMMUNICATIONS STANDARDS INSTITUTE.

EU *See* EUROPEAN UNION.

EU law *See* COMMUNITY LAW.

Euratom *See* EUROPEAN ATOMIC ENERGY COMMUNITY.

euro *See* EUROPEAN MONETARY UNION.

Eurogroup A body comprising the finance ministers of the 17 member states of the European Union that have adopted the euro as their national currency. Only these states are permitted to vote on questions relating to the euro and its associated monetary policy. The Eurogroup was set on a formal legal basis by Protocol 14 of the *Lisbon Treaty.

Euro Norm (EN) A European standard adopted by European standards bodies, such as CEN (the European Standardization Committee) and CENELEC (the European Electrotechnical Standardization Committee), in place of a national standard, such as those produced in the UK by the British Standards Institution (BSI).

European arrest warrant An arrest warrant designed to strengthen cooperation between the national jurisdictions of the member states of the EU by eliminating the use of *extradition. Based on a Framework Decision adopted in June 2002, these warrants have been issued since January 2004.

European Atomic Energy Community (Euratom) The organization set up under the Treaty of Rome (1957) by the six members of the *European Coal and Steel Community and effective from 1 January 1958. Euratom was formed to create the technical and industrial conditions necessary to establish the nuclear industries and direct them to peaceful use to obtain a single energy market. *See* EUROPEAN COMMUNITY.

European Bank for Reconstruction and Development (EBRD) An intergovernmental bank set up in 1990 to provide loans for industrial and commercial projects in the countries of central and eastern Europe. Membership includes all the countries of the European Union and the Organization for Economic Cooperation and Development, as well as the central and eastern European countries. The EU provided 51% of the initial capital. The bank's headquarters are in London.

European Central Bank (ECB) A central bank of the *European Union to which member states who have adopted * European Monetary Union (EMU) are committed by the *Maastricht Treaty. The ECB was set up in 1998 and became active in 1999, as the governor of economic and monetary policy throughout the Union. It works closely with the central banks of the states participating in EMU.

European Coal and Steel Community (ECSC) The first of the European Communities, established by the *Paris Treaty (1951) and effective from 1952. The ECSC created a common market in coal, steel, iron ore, and scrap between the member states, and it coordinated policies of the member states in these fields. The Treaty expired in July 2002 after 50 years in force. The original members were Belgium, France, West Germany, Italy, Luxembourg, and the Netherlands. These six countries, in 1957,

signed the *Treaty of Rome setting up the European Economic Community.
See EUROPEAN COMMUNITY.

European Commission (Commission of the European Communities) An organ
of the European Union formed in 1967, having both executive and legislative functions. It
is composed of 28 Commissioners (one from each member state) who must be nationals
of member states and are appointed by member states by mutual agreement; their
appointment must be approved by the *European Parliament. Each Commissioner
assumes responsibility for a particular field of activity and oversees the department
(**Directorate General**) devoted to that field. Once appointed, the Commissioners must
act in the interests of the EU; they are not to be regarded as representatives of their
countries and must not seek or take instructions from any government or other body.
Each Commissioner is appointed for a (renewable) four-year period. The Commission's
executive functions include administration of Community funds and ensuring that
Community law is enforced (*see* EUROPEAN COURT OF JUSTICE). Its legislative functions
consist primarily of submitting proposals for legislation to the *Council of the European
Union and the *European Parliament, in some cases on the orders of the Council and in
others on its own initiative. It also has legislative powers of its own, partly under the
*Lisbon Treaty and partly by virtue of delegation by the Council, but only on a limited
range of subjects (*see* COMMUNITY LEGISLATION).

European Community (EC) An economic and political association of European
states that originated as the **European Economic Community** (**EEC**). It was created by
the *Treaty of Rome in 1957 with the broad object of furthering economic development
within the Community by the establishment of a **Common Market** and the
approximation of the economic policies of member states. Its more detailed aims
included eliminating customs duties internally and adopting a common customs tariff
externally, the following by member states of common policies on agriculture and
transport, promoting the free movement of labour and capital between member states,
and outlawing within the Community all practices leading to the distortion of
competition (*see* ARTICLE 101). Two of its institutions, the *European Parliament and the
*European Court of Justice, were shared with the *European Coal and Steel Community
(established in 1951) and the *European Atomic Energy Community (Euratom;
established in 1957); the separate executive and legislative bodies of these three
European Communities were merged in 1967 (*see* EUROPEAN COMMISSION; COUNCIL
OF THE EUROPEAN UNION).

The *Single European Act 1986, given effect in the UK by the European Communities
(Amendment) Act 1986, contains provisions designed to make "concrete progress"
towards European unity, including measures to establish a *Single Market for the free
movement of goods, services, capital, and persons within the Community: the Single
Market came into operation on 1 January 1993. In February 1992 the member states
signed the Treaty on European Union (*see* MAASTRICHT TREATY). This amended the
founding treaties of the Communities by establishing a *European Union based upon the
three Communities; renamed the EEC the European Community; and introduced new
policy areas with the aim of creating closer economic, political, and monetary union
between member states. The Treaty came into force on 1 November 1993; it was
amended by the *Amsterdam Treaty. The European Community was finally dissolved
(as an entity distinct from the European Union) with the ratification of the *Lisbon
Treaty in 2009.

The changes in UK law necessary as a result of her joining the EEC were made by the
European Communities Act 1972.

European Community Treaty *See* TREATY OF ROME.

European company *See* Societas Europaea.

European Convention on Human Rights A convention, originally formulated in 1950, aimed at protecting the *human rights of all people in the member states of the *Council of Europe. Part 1 of the Convention, together with a number of subsequent protocols, define the rights and freedoms that each signatory state must guarantee to all within its jurisdiction, although states may derogate from the Convention in respect of particular activities (*see* derogation). The Convention established a Commission on Human Rights (now abolished) and a **Court of Human Rights** in Strasbourg. The Court may hear complaints (known as applications) either by one state against another or from an individual, group, or nongovernmental organization claiming to be a victim of a breach of the Convention. The Court cannot deal with any complaint, however, unless the applicant has first tried remedies in the national courts ("exhausted domestic remedies"). All complaints must be made not later than four months from the date on which the decision against the applicant was made in the national courts (or the date of the alleged violation if there is no effective national remedy). The Court will only investigate a complaint if it is judged to fulfil the specific conditions that make it admissible. The Court has power to make a final ruling, which is binding on the state parties, and in some cases to award compensation.

Despite the fact that the UK took perhaps the most significant part in writing and inspiring the Convention, and was the first to sign and to ratify it, the Convention articles only came into force in the UK also as a matter of domestic law on 2 October 2000. This followed the entry into force of the *Human Rights Act 1998.

European Convention on State Immunity An international convention of 1972 setting out when and how member states of the European Community (now the European Union) may sue or be sued (by other states or by individuals). It is in force only in those EU states that have signed up to the convention. *See also* immunity.

European Council A body consisting of the heads of government of the member states of the European Union. It is not a formal organ of the EU (*compare* Council of the European Union), but meets three times a year to consider major developments of policy. It inspired, for example, the *European Monetary System.

European Court of Human Rights *See* European Convention on Human Rights.

European Court of Justice **(ECJ, Court of Justice of the European Communities)** An institution of the European Union that has three primary judicial responsibilities. It interprets the treaties establishing the European Community; it decides upon the validity and the meaning of *Community legislation; and it determines whether any act or omission by the European Commission, the Council of the European Union, or any member state constitutes a breach of *Community law.

The Court sits at Luxembourg. It consists of 28 judges appointed by the member states by mutual agreement and assisted by 8 *Advocates-General. Proceedings before the Court involve written and oral submissions by the parties concerned. Proceedings against the Commission or the Council may be brought by the other of these two bodies, by any member state, or by individual persons; proceedings to challenge the validity of legislative or other action by either Commission or Council are known as proceedings for **annulment**. Proceedings against a member state may be brought by the Commission, the Council, or any other member state. Appeals from the *General Court go to the ECJ. The decisions of the Court are binding and there is no appeal against them.

The Court also has power, at the request of a court of any member state, to give a preliminary ruling on any point of Community law on which that court requires clarification.

European Currency Unit *See* ECU.

European Economic and Social Committee (EESC) An EU advisory body founded in 1957 to represent employers, trade unions, farmers, consumers, and other interest groups. Its views are taken into account by the European Parliament, Council of Ministers, and Commission.

European Economic Area (EEA) A free-trade area encompassing the 28 member states of the *European Union and the member states (excluding Switzerland) of the *European Free Trade Association (EFTA), i.e. Norway, Iceland, and Liechtenstein. The EEA Agreement, which contains many provisions similar to the *Treaty of Rome, was signed in 1992 and came into force on 1 January 1994. The EEA has its own institutions, such as the EFTA Court of Justice and the EFTA Surveillance Authority (ESA), and many of the EU *Single Market directives and other legislative measures apply within it, although it does not have a budget.

European Economic Community *See* EUROPEAN COMMUNITY.

European Free Trade Association (EFTA) A trade association formed in 1960 between Austria, Denmark, Norway, Portugal, Sweden, Switzerland, and the UK, with Finland, Iceland, and Liechtenstein joining later. The current members are Iceland, Liechtenstein, Norway and Switzerland as the other members left on joining the *European Union (or its earlier communities). EFTA is a looser association than the EU, dealing only with trade barriers rather than generally coordinating economic policy. EFTA is governed by a council in which each member has one vote; decisions must normally be unanimous and are binding on all member countries. EFTA has bilateral agreements with the EU. All tariffs between EFTA and EU countries were abolished finally in 1984 and a free-trade area now exists between EU and EFTA member states (*see* EUROPEAN ECONOMIC AREA).

European Monetary System (EMS) A financial system formed in March 1979 to develop closer cooperation in monetary policy among members of the European Community in advance of the liberalization of capital. It included the * Exchange Rate Mechanism (ERM) to stabilize exchange rates between member states as a precursor to *European Monetary Union. Directive 88/361 removed restrictions on the movement of capital between people resident in the member states. Article 102A of the Single European Act 1986 inserted a new Article (now called Article 98) into the Treaty of Rome to refer to the EMS.

European Monetary Union (EMU) The establishment of a common currency for member states of the European Union. The *Maastricht Treaty specified three stages for achieving EMU, starting with participation in the *Exchange Rate Mechanism. The second stage created the European Monetary Institute, which coordinated the economic and monetary policy of member states. The third stage, achieved by January 1999, locked member states into a fixed exchange rate, activated the *European Central Bank, and introduced the single currency, the **euro** (divided into 100 cents), for all noncash transactions (national currencies continued in use for cash transactions). In 2002 euro notes and coins came into circulation in those states within the system.

European Parliament An institution of the EU, formerly called the **Assembly of the European Communities**. Members of the European Parliament (**MEPs**) are drawn from member states of the EU but group themselves politically rather than nationally. There are 751 seats as from 2014, of which the UK has 73. In the case of the UK, MEPs are elected under the European Assembly Elections Act 1978 for constituencies comprising two or more UK parliamentary constituencies.

The European Parliament's power and influence derive chiefly from its power to amend, and subsequently to adopt or reject, proposed EU legislation (including the EU's budget). Its powers in the legislative process were extended under the Single European Act 1986, under the Maastricht Treaty by the introduction of the *cooperation, *codecision, and *assent procedures, and most decisively under the *Lisbon Treaty, which introduced the *ordinary legislative procedure. The Parliament may also put questions to the Council and the Commission and, by a motion of censure requiring a special majority, can force the resignation of the whole Commission (but not of individual Commissioners). Under the Maastricht Treaty it can now veto the appointment of a new Commission.

The European Parliament holds its sessions in Strasbourg, but its Secretariat-General is in Luxembourg and its committees meet in Brussels. The elected Parliament serves a term of five years, after which elections are held.

European Patent Court (Unified Patent Court) A proposed court that will exercise specialized jurisdiction in patent disputes throughout the EU, thus avoiding the need for multiple litigation in up to 28 member states. An agreement to establish such a court was signed by 25 EU states (all the current members except Poland, Spain, and Croatia) in 2013. The court is expected to be based in London.

European Public Prosecutor As proposed by the European Commission in 2000, an independent body with authority to investigate and prosecute fraud and other crimes affecting the financial interests of the EU. The *Lisbon Treaty includes an article allowing for the establishment of such a prosecutor.

European Social Charter A Charter signed by the member states of the *Council of Europe in 1961 that aims to protect social and economic rights, such as safe working conditions, medical assistance, vocational training, the right to work, to just conditions of work, to safe and healthy working conditions, to social welfare services, etc. The 46 European states that have ratified the Social Charter are obliged to submit reports on a two-yearly basis, examining the effectiveness with which the Charter has been implemented within their jurisdiction. Membership is restricted to democratic countries.

European Telecommunications Standards Institute (ETSI) The organization that sets standards for the telecommunications industry throughout Europe. Established in 1988, it is made up of representatives of the telecommunications industry.

European Union (EU) The 28 nations that have joined together to form an economic community with common monetary, political, and social aspirations. The EU came into being on 1 November 1993 according to the terms of the *Maastricht Treaty. It comprises the three European Communities (*see* EUROPEAN COMMUNITY), extended by the adoption of a common foreign and security policy (CFSP), which requires cooperation between member states in foreign policy and security, and cooperation in justice and home affairs.

The original members of the European (Economic) Community were Belgium, France, Germany, Italy, Luxembourg, and the Netherlands, which signed the *Treaty of Rome in 1957. The UK, the Republic of Ireland, and Denmark joined in 1972, Greece in 1981, and Spain and Portugal in 1986. After the creation of the EU, Austria, Sweden, and Finland joined in 1995; Cyprus, the Czech Republic, Estonia, Hungary, Latvia, Lithuania, Malta, Poland, Slovakia, and Slovenia in 2004; Bulgaria and Romania in 2007; and Croatia in 2013.

European Works Council (EWC) A council, set up by a special negotiating body, consisting of both employee and management representatives established at European level for the purpose of informing and consulting with employees on transnational issues. The requirement to set up such councils originated from the European Works Council Directive 1994. This was revised by Directive 2009/38. The 1994 Directive was implemented by the UK through the Transnational Information and Consultation of Employees Regulations 1999, and the amended Directive by the Transnational Information and Consultation of Employees (Amendment) Regulations 2010 which came into force in 2011. The Regulations apply to undertakings or groups with at least 1000 employees across member states of the European Economic Area and at least 150 employees in each of two or more of those member states. The Regulations set out the procedures for negotiating an EWC agreement, the enforcement mechanisms, provisions on confidentiality, and statutory protections for employees who are members of such a group when asserting their rights or performing duties under the Regulations. Disputes over procedural matters in setting up an EWC are heard by the *Central Arbitration Committee. Complaints of a failure to establish an EWC, or a failure to operate the system properly once set up, are heard by the *Employment Appeal Tribunal. Employment protection disputes with respect to individual employees go to an *employment tribunal.

eurotort *n.* A directly effective rule of EU law (*see* COMMUNITY LEGISLATION), breach of which gives the person injured a remedy in British courts in the form of an action in tort for breach of statutory duty. *See also* COMMUNITY LAW.

euthanasia *n.* The act of taking life to relieve pain. The term is a wide one and covers **voluntary euthanasia**, where the sufferer's life is ended at his or her specific request, **non-voluntary euthanasia**, where a person is unable to express his or her wishes (e.g. a baby or a person in a *persistent vegetative state, and **involuntary euthanasia**, where a person is killed without his own or any proxy authority. Involuntary euthanasia is always illegal, whereas the legality of voluntary and non-voluntary euthanasia depends in general as to whether it is passive or active. Generally, euthanasia is illegal and will amount to murder or *assisted suicide where active steps are taken (e.g. the administration of a drug) to terminate life, even where the motive is a compassionate one. Passive euthanasia, for example the withdrawal of life-saving treatment, is legal if done in the patient's best interest (*Airedale NHS Trust v Bland* [1993] AC 78 (HL)). *See also* ARTIFICIAL NUTRITION AND HYDRATION; EXTRAORDINARY MEANS.

eviction *n.* The removal of a tenant or any other occupier from occupation. Under the Protection from Eviction Act 1977 the eviction of a *residential occupier, other than by proceedings in the court, is a criminal offence. It is also an offence to harass a residential occupier to try to persuade him to leave (*see* HARASSMENT OF OCCUPIER). If a mortgagee can take possession peaceably, no court order is required (*Ropaigealach v Barclay's Bank plc* [2000] QB 263). Many tenants have statutory protection and the landlord must prove to a court that he has appropriate grounds for possession. Under the Housing Act 1988 a tenant may claim damages for unlawful eviction. *See also* AGRICULTURAL HOLDING; ASSURED SHORTHOLD TENANCY; ASSURED TENANCY; BUSINESS TENANCY; LONG TENANCY; PROTECTED TENANCY; SECURE TENANCY; RESTRICTED CONTRACT; TRESPASS.

The Protection from Harassment Act 1997 allows the court to impose a restraining order against a tenant who is harassing a neighbour, which might require the harasser to be evicted (*see* NUISANCE NEIGHBOURS).

evidence *n.* That which tends to prove the existence or nonexistence of some fact. It may consist of *testimony, *documentary evidence, *real evidence, and, when admissible, *hearsay evidence. The law of evidence comprises all the rules governing the presentation of facts and proof in proceedings before a court, including in particular the rules governing the *admissibility of evidence and the *exclusionary rules. *See also* CHARACTER; CIRCUMSTANTIAL EVIDENCE; CONCLUSIVE EVIDENCE; DIRECT EVIDENCE; EXTRINSIC EVIDENCE; PRIMARY EVIDENCE; SECONDARY EVIDENCE; VIDEO EVIDENCE.

evidenced in writing *See* UNENFORCEABLE CONTRACT.

evidence-in-chief In court proceedings, the evidence given by a witness for the party who called him. Part 32 of the *Civil Procedure Rules provides that where a witness is called to give evidence at trial, his witness statement shall stand as his evidence-in-chief unless the court orders otherwise. He may be cross-examined on his witness statement whether or not the statement or any part of it was referred to during his *examination-in-chief. In criminal proceedings evidence-in-chief will nearly always take the form of live evidence in court.

evidence in rebuttal Evidence offered to counteract (**rebut**) other evidence in a case. Under the Civil Evidence Act 1995 evidence of a *previous statement by a witness may be adduced in civil proceedings to rebut a suggestion that his evidence has been fabricated. Under the Criminal Justice Act 2003 a previous statement by a witness, admitted in criminal proceedings as evidence to rebut a suggestion that his oral evidence has been fabricated, is admissible as evidence of any matter stated of which oral evidence by that witness would be admissible.

evidence obtained illegally Evidence obtained by some means contrary to law. At common law, if evidence was obtained illegally (e.g. where there had been a search of premises without a search warrant), that evidence was not inadmissible as a matter of law, but the court might exclude it as a matter of discretion where its prejudicial effect outweighed its probative value. The Police and Criminal Evidence Act 1984 preserves this common law discretion and also provides that the court may refuse to allow evidence on which the prosecution proposes to rely if, having regard to all the circumstances including the circumstances in which the evidence was obtained, the admission of the evidence would have such an adverse effect on the fairness of the proceedings that the court ought not to admit it. In cases involving illegally obtained evidence the court will also have regard to the provisions of the *European Convention on Human Rights and the *Human Rights Act 1998. *See also* CONFESSION.

evidence of character *See* CHARACTER.

evidence of disposition *See* DISPOSITION.

evidence of identity Evidence that tends to prove the identity of a person. A person's identity may be proved by *direct evidence (even though this may involve a witness giving *opinion evidence) or by *circumstantial evidence. *Secondary evidence of an out-of-court identification by a witness (as where the witness has picked the accused out in the course of a video identification or an identification parade) may also be given to confirm the witness's testimony. In criminal cases, the case of *R v Turnbull* [1977] QB 224 (CA) provides that whenever the case against an accused depends wholly or substantially on the correctness of an identification of the accused that the defence alleges to be mistaken, the judge should warn the jury of the special need for caution before convicting the accused in reliance on the correctness of the identification. The judge should also direct the jury to examine closely the circumstances in which the identification was made. When the quality of the identification evidence is good, the jury can be left to assess the value of the identifying evidence even though there is no other evidence to support it. However, when the quality of the identifying evidence is poor, as for example when it depends solely on a fleeting glance or on a longer observation made in difficult conditions, the judge should withdraw the case from the jury and direct an acquittal unless there is other evidence that goes to support the correctness of the identification.

Code D of the *codes of practice established under the Police and Criminal Evidence Act 1984 concerns the main methods used by the police to identify people in connection with the investigation of offences. These include video identification (where the witness is shown moving images of a known suspect, together with similar images of others who resemble the suspect); identification parades (where the witness sees the suspect in a line of others who resemble the suspect); and group identification (where the witness sees the suspect in an informal group of people). Code D also deals with identification by fingerprints; identification using footwear impressions; and identification by using body samples to generate a DNA profile for comparison with material obtained from the scene of a crime or a victim. *See* DNA FINGERPRINTING.

evidence of opinion *See* OPINION EVIDENCE.

evidence of user Evidence of the manner in which the parties to a contract have acted. In a limited number of circumstances, evidence of user is admissible to assist the court in resolving a dispute between the parties as to their precise obligations. It may, for example, help to clarify an ambiguity in the wording of the contract or an allegation that written terms have been varied by oral agreement.

evidential burden *See* BURDEN OF PROOF.

EWC *See* EUROPEAN WORKS COUNCIL.

ex abundanti cautela [Latin: out of abundant caution] A saying applied to any legal step (e.g. insertion of a clause in a contract) taken as a precaution against an event that is judged to be very unlikely but not impossible.

ex aequo et bono [Latin] As a result of fair dealing and good conscience, i.e. on the basis of *equity. The phrase refers to the way in which an international tribunal can base its decision not upon conventional law but on what is just and fair to the parties before it. Article 38 of the Statute of the *International Court of Justice provides that "if the parties agree the Court may decide a case *ex aequo et bono*". In point of fact this provision has never been implemented for the practical reason that in no case before the Court have the parties agreed to allow its use.

examination *n.* The questioning of a witness on oath or affirmation. In civil and criminal proceedings, a witness called to give evidence at trial may be subject to *examination-in-chief, *cross-examination, and *re-examination. *See also* COMMISSION.

examination-in-chief (direct examination) The questioning of a witness by the party who called him to give evidence. *Leading questions may not normally be asked, except on matters that are introductory to the witness's evidence or are not in dispute. The purpose of examination-in-chief is to elicit facts favourable to the case of the party conducting the examination. It is followed by a *cross-examination by the opposing party. In civil proceedings, Part 32 of the *Civil Procedure Rules provides that where a witness is called to give evidence at trial, his witness statement shall stand as his *evidence-in-chief unless the court orders otherwise, and he may be cross-examined on his witness statement whether or not the statement or any part of it was referred to during his examination-in-chief. *See also* HOSTILE WITNESS.

examined copy *See* ABSTRACT OF TITLE.

examining justice A magistrate, carrying out his function of checking that a case appears (on the face of the prosecution case papers) to exist against an accused before the case is put forward for trial in the Crown Court. *See also* COMMITTAL PROCEEDINGS; SENDING FOR TRIAL.

excepted estate A deceased person's estate where the requirement for the delivery of a full *inheritance tax account is dispensed with under regulations made under the Inheritance Tax Act 1984 s 256. This is the case, for example, where the total value of the estate is less than the inheritance tax threshold or is less than £1 million and exempt from inheritance tax because the estate passes to a surviving spouse or civil partner.

excepted perils Risks expressly excluded from the cover given by an insurance policy.

exchange of contracts The point at which a purchaser of land exchanges a copy of the sale contract signed by him for an identical copy signed by the vendor. At that point the contract becomes legally binding on both parties and the purchaser acquires an *equitable interest in the land. He will not acquire the legal estate until *completion and registration.

exchange of medical reports The exchange of medical reports in personal injury actions in the hope that they can be agreed before the hearing of the case, thus saving time and expense. The exchange of reports that are intended to be relied on at the hearing is compulsory, unless the court's permission not to disclose is obtained. The court also has power to order disclosure of medical reports by persons not party to the proceedings, such as a hospital authority.

Exchange Rate Mechanism (ERM) A component of the *European Monetary System under which the central banks of participating countries could not allow their currencies to fluctuate more than a certain percentage above (the ceiling rate) or below (minimum rate) a central rate, which was set in *ECUs. The system served as a precursor to full * European Monetary Union (EMU), which was achieved in 1999–2002. From 1999, states may join **ERM II**, which is based on the euro and supervised by the *European Central Bank. All countries joining the EU are now required to join ERM II as soon as this is judged economically practicable.

Exchequer *n.* The department within Government that receives and controls the national revenue. *See* CHANCELLOR OF THE EXCHEQUER; COURT OF EXCHEQUER.

excise duty A charge or toll payable on certain goods produced and consumed within the UK (*compare* CUSTOMS DUTY). Formerly, the term was applied solely to duty imposed on beer, ale, cider or other commodities. Current law, however, imposes excise duty on licences, such as those required for the possession of a gun, or for dealing in game, or for the sale of beer, wine, and spirits.

excluded material Material held in confidence, including personal records and journalistic documents or records. A warrant enabling access to excluded material for the purposes of a criminal investigation can only be obtained from a circuit judge. *See* SPECIAL PROCEDURE MATERIAL.

exclusion and restriction of contractual liability *See* EXEMPTION CLAUSE.

exclusion and restriction of negligence liability The Unfair Contract Terms Act 1977 provides that a person cannot exclude or restrict his *business liability for death or injury resulting from negligence. Nor can he exclude or restrict his liability for other loss or damage arising from negligence, unless any contract term or notice by which he seeks to do so satisfies the requirement of reasonableness (as defined in detail in the Act). For the purposes of this provision, negligence means the breach of any contractual or common-law duty to take reasonable care or exercise reasonable skill or of the *common duty of care imposed by the Occupiers' Liability Acts 1957 and 1984. There are similar provisions in relation to consumer contracts in the Unfair Terms in Consumer Contracts Regulations 1999.

exclusionary rules In the law of *evidence, rules prohibiting the proof of certain facts or the proof of facts in particular ways.

exclusion requirement **1.** A requirement that may be imposed by a sentencing court as part of a *community order or a *suspended sentence order under the Criminal Justice Act 2003 or as part of a *youth rehabilitation order under the Criminal Justice and Immigration Act 2008. An offender is prohibited from entering a specific place or area for a period of up to two years. Compliance is usually monitored by electronic tagging. **2.** A requirement in an *emergency protection order or an interim care order that a person who is suspected of having abused a child is excluded from the child's home. A *power of arrest may be attached to the order.

exclusive economic zone (EEZ) A zone defined by Articles 55–75 of the UN Convention on the Law of the Sea as comprising that area of sea adjacent to a coastal state not exceeding 200 miles from the *baseline of the territorial sea. The state shall have sovereign rights over the zone for the purpose of exploring and exploiting, conserving, and managing the living and nonliving resources of the sea, seabed, and subsoil within it. *See also* HIGH SEAS; LAW OF THE SEA; TERRITORIAL WATERS.

exclusive jurisdiction **1.** That part of the jurisdiction of the *Court of Chancery that belonged to the Chancery alone. The jurisdiction ceased after the Judicature Acts 1873–75, but the matters under exclusive jurisdiction (e.g. trusts, administration of estates) are now dealt with in the Chancery Division. *Compare* CONCURRENT JURISDICTION. **2.** A clause in a commercial agreement providing that only the English, Scottish, or other courts will be entitled to determine disputes between the parties. Normally agreements provide that the parties agree to submit to either the exclusive or the nonexclusive jurisdiction of particular courts. If no such clause is included, international conventions, such as the Brussels and Lugano conventions, determine which courts have jurisdiction. EU regulation 44/2001 contains provisions in this area applicable from January 2001, under which customers are given a right to bring proceedings in their home state in some cases.

excusable homicide The killing of a human being that results in no criminal liability, because it took place by misadventure (an accident not involving gross negligence). *See* HOMICIDE.

excuse *n.* A category of defences in criminal law reflecting a determination that the defendant is not criminally blameworthy for having engaged in what was, none the less, criminally wrongful conduct. *Insanity and involuntary *intoxication are often commonly assumed to be central examples of excuse. It is often said that excuse defences focus on the actor, whereas *justification defences focus on the act: actors are excused, actions are justified. *See also* DURESS.

ex debito justitiae [Latin: from what is owed] Stated of a remedy that the court has no discretion to refuse. Thus, the applicant has the remedy as of right.

executed *adj.* Completed. A contract that has been carried out by both parties is said to have been executed, and *consideration that has been actually given for a contract is described as **executed consideration**. *See also* EXECUTED TRUST. *Compare* EXECUTORY.

executed trust (perfect trust) A trust in which the interests of all the beneficiaries have been set out and clearly defined by the settlor. *Compare* EXECUTORY TRUST.

execution *n.* **1.** The process of carrying out a sentence of death imposed by a court. *See also* CAPITAL PUNISHMENT. **2.** The enforcement of the rights of a *judgment creditor. The term is often used to mean the recovery of a debt only, especially by seizure of goods belonging to the debtor under a writ of *fieri facias* or a warrant of execution. *See also* ENFORCEMENT OF JUDGMENT; EQUITABLE EXECUTION. **3.** The completion of the formalities necessary for a written document to become legally valid. In the case of a *deed, for example, this comprises the signing and delivery of the document. *See also* EXECUTION OF WILL.

execution against goods *See* FIERI FACIAS.

execution of will The process by which a testator's will is made legally valid. Under the Wills Act 1837 s 9, the will must be signed at the end by the testator or by someone authorized by him, and the signature must be made or acknowledged (*see* ACKNOWLEDGMENT) by the testator in the presence of at least two witnesses, present at the same time, who must themselves sign the will or acknowledge their signatures in the testator's presence. A will witnessed by a beneficiary or the beneficiary's spouse is not void, but the gift to that beneficiary or spouse is void (Wills Act 1837 s 15). A clause in a will permitting an executor to charge for his services is not treated as a gift for the purposes of section 15, so that an executor may act as a witness without forfeiting his charges (Trustee Act 2000 s 28).

executive agency A semi-autonomous agency that is responsible for delivering a service according to the policy and resources framework of a central government department. Executive agencies do not have a separate legal existence from their "parent" government department and operate under powers delegated by ministers. They therefore remain part of the *Civil Service. Each agency is headed by a chief executive who reports to the minister of the department concerned. They are designed to deliver public services more effectively and efficiently and play no role in the development of policy. The intention is that central government should become purely policy-making, leaving service delivery entirely to specialized executive agencies. Examples include the Prison Service, the Passport Agency, Companies House, and the Royal Mint.

executor *n.* A person appointed by a will to administer the testator's estate. A deceased person's property is vested in his executors, who are empowered to deal with it as directed by the will from the time of the testator's death. They must, however, usually obtain a grant of *probate from the court in order to prove the will and their right to deal with the estate. Appointment as an executor confers only the power to deal with the deceased's property in accordance with his will, and not beneficial ownership, although an executor may also be a beneficiary under the will. *Compare* ADMINISTRATOR.

executor *de son tort* [French: by his own wrongdoing] A person who deals (intermeddles) with a deceased person's assets without the authority of the rightful personal representatives or of the court. He is answerable to the rightful personal representatives and to the creditors of the estate for any acts done without such authority and for any assets of the estate that come into his hands.

executor's oath A written statement sworn by executors or administrators of an estate; it accompanies an application for a *grant of representation (Non Contentious Probate Rules 1987, r 8). *See also* OATH.

executor's year The period of a year, starting from the death of the deceased, within which nobody can compel his *personal representatives to distribute the estate, even if the testator has directed payment of a legacy before the expiry of that period (Administration of Estates Act 1925 s 44). The complexity of an estate and the nature of the assets may justify personal representatives taking longer than this.

executory *adj*. Remaining to be done. A contract that has yet to be carried out is said to be an **executory contract**, and *consideration that has still to be given for a contract is described as **executory consideration**. *See also* EXECUTORY INTEREST; EXECUTORY TRUST. *Compare* EXECUTED.

executory interest (mainly historical) An interest in property that arises or passes to a particular person on the occurrence of a specified event. For example, when property is settled in trust "for A, but for B if he marries Mary", then B has an executory interest. Under the Law of Property Act 1925 executory interests in land can only exist as equitable interests. *Compare* REMAINDER; REVERSION.

executory trust (imperfect trust) A trust in which the general intention of the settlor has been declared but the specific terms and limitations are not completely set out. Such trusts often arise in family settlements where the intention is to provide for any future children. A *discretionary trust is an executory trust. A beneficiary under an executory trust has no enforceable right to any part of the trust property. *Compare* EXECUTED TRUST.

exemplary damages (punitive damages, vindictive damages) Damages given to punish the defendant rather than (or as well as) to compensate the claimant for harm done. Such damages are exceptional in tort, since the general rule is that damages are given only to compensate for loss caused. They can be awarded in some tort actions: (1) when expressly authorized by statute; (2) to punish oppressive, arbitrary, or unconstitutional acts by government servants; (3) when the defendant has deliberately calculated that the profits to be made out of committing a tort (e.g. by publishing a defamatory book) may exceed the damages at risk. In such cases, exemplary damages are given to prove that "tort does not pay" (*Rookes v Barnard* [1964] AC 1129). Exemplary damages cannot be given for breach of contract.

exemption clause A term in a contract purporting to exclude or restrict the liability for breach of obligation of one of the parties in specified circumstances. The courts do not regard exemption clauses with favour. If such a clause is ambiguous, they will interpret it narrowly rather than widely. If an exclusion or restriction is not recited in a formal contract but is specified or referred to in an informal document, such as a ticket or a notice displayed in a hotel, it will not even be treated as a term of the contract unless reasonable steps were taken to bring it to the notice of the person affected at the time of contracting (*Parker v South Eastern Railway* (1877) 2 CPD 416, All ER 166). The Unfair Contract Terms Act 1977 and Unfair Terms in Consumer Contracts Regulations 1999 contain complex provisions limiting the extent to which a person can exclude or restrict his *business liability towards consumers. In addition, the 1977 Act subjects certain types of exemption clause to a test of reasonableness, even in a business-to-business transaction. The Office of Fair Trading runs an unfair terms unit to monitor such clauses and enforce the 1999 Regulations. Other statutes forbidding the exclusion or restriction of particular forms of liability are the Defective Premises Act 1972, the Consumer Protection Act 1987, and the Road Traffic Act 1988. *See also* EXCLUSION AND RESTRICTION OF NEGLIGENCE LIABILITY; INTERNATIONAL SUPPLY CONTRACT.

exempt supply A supply that is specified by the Value Added Taxes Act 1994 as being exempt from a charge to *value-added tax. As VAT is a European tax, subject to EU legislation, an exemption under UK law is either a reflection of the general exemption in the Sixth Council Directive of 17 May 1997 Articles 13–16 or is given as a *derogation to the UK under Article 27 of that Directive. Schedule 9 of the Value Added Taxes Act 1994 specifies exempt supplies in 15 categories:

(1) land;
(2) insurance;
(3) postal services;
(4) betting, gaming, and lotteries;
(5) finance;
(6) education;
(7) health and welfare;
(8) burial and cremation;
(9) trade unions, professional, and other public interest bodies;
(10) sport and physical education;
(11) works of art, etc.;
(12) fund-raising events;
(13) cultural services;
(14) certain supplies the *input tax on which is irrecoverable;
(15) investment gold.

See also ZERO-RATED SUPPLY.

exequatur *n.* A certificate issued by a host state that admits and accords recognition to the official status of a *consul, authorizing him to carry out consular functions in that country. The sending state grants the consular official a commission or patent, which authorizes the consul to represent his state's interests within the host state. The term originally referred to a temporal sovereign's authorization of a bishop, or a papal decree, within his jurisdiction.

ex gratia [Latin] Done as a matter of favour. An *ex gratia* payment is one not required to be made by a legal duty.

exhaustion of local remedies The rule of *customary international law that when an *alien has been wronged, all municipal remedies available to the injured party in the host country must have been pursued before the alien appeals to his own government to intervene on his behalf. This is a customary precondition to any *espousal of claim by a state on behalf of a national based upon foreign soil. Case: *Interhandel Case (Switzerland v US)* [1959] ICJ Rep 6.

exhaustion of rights A free-trade principle which holds that, once goods are put on the market, owners of *intellectual property rights in those goods, who made the goods or allowed others to do so under their rights, may not use national intellectual property rights to prevent an import or export of the goods. Within the EU these rules derive from Articles 34–36 (previously 28–30 and before that 30–36) of the Treaty on the Functioning of the European Union. *See also* FREE MOVEMENT.

exhibit **1.** *n.* A physical object or document produced in a court, shown to a witness who is giving evidence, or used in conjunction with an *affidavit or a witness statement. Physical objects produced for the inspection of the court (such as a murder weapon in a criminal trial) are referred to as *real evidence. The Practice Direction to Part 32 of the *Civil Procedure Rules sets out provisions dealing with exhibits in civil proceedings. **2.** *vb.* To refer to an object or document in an *affidavit or a witness statement.

ex nudo pacto non oritur actio [Latin: a right of action does not arise out of a naked agreement] *See* CONSIDERATION.

ex officio [Latin] By virtue of holding an office. Thus, the Lord Chief Justice is *ex officio* a member of the Court of Appeal.

***ex officio* magistrate** A magistrate by virtue of holding some other office, usually that of mayor of a city or borough. Most *ex officio* magistrateships were abolished by the Justices of the Peace Act 1968 and the Administration of Justice Act 1973, but High Court judges are justices of the peace *ex officio* for the whole of England and Wales and the Lord Mayor and aldermen are justices *ex officio* for the City of London.

exordium *n.* The introductory part of a writing or speech. Classically, the exordium of a will identifies the testator, establishes his place of residence, declares the instrument to be the testator's last will, and revokes all prior testamentary dispositions.

ex parte (ex p) [Latin] **1.** On the part of one side only. An *ex parte* hearing is defined in the Glossary to the *Criminal Procedure Rules as a hearing where only one party is allowed to attend and make submissions. However, the term *ex parte* is no longer generally used in civil proceedings, having been replaced by the phrase *without notice. **2.** On behalf of. This term is used in the headings of law reports together with the name of the person making the application to the court in the case in question, for example in applications for *judicial review.

expatriation *n.* A person's voluntary action of living outside his native country, either permanently or during his employment abroad, whereby he renounces or loses allegiance to his former state of nationality. *Compare* DEPORTATION.

expectant heir A person who has an interest in remainder or in reversion in property or a chance of succeeding to it (interest in expectancy). An unconscionable contract with an expectant heir (e.g. in which he sells his inheritance at an undervalue in order to raise cash) may be set aside by the court.

expert opinion *See* OPINION EVIDENCE.

Expiring Laws Continuance Acts Statutes formerly passed annually to continue in force for a further year a number of miscellaneous Acts that were originally stated to remain in force for one year only. The renewal of temporary statutes is now effected individually.

explanatory notes Notes produced by the government department responsible for a particular public Act to explain the legislation to readers who are not legally qualified. Although the notes are published with the Act they are not part of the legislation and do not have legal force. The practice was introduced in 1999.

explosive *n.* Any substance made in order to achieve an explosion that causes damage or destruction or intended to be used in that way by a person who possesses it. If someone committing *burglary has an explosive with him, he is guilty of aggravated burglary, punishable with a maximum of life imprisonment. The Explosive Substances Act 1883 creates special offences of (1) causing an explosion that is likely to endanger life or cause serious damage to property (even if no harm or damage is actually done); (2) attempting to cause such an explosion; and (3) making or possessing an explosive with the intention of using it to endanger life or to seriously damage property. Under the Offences Against the Person Act 1861 (s 28-30), it is an offence to injure anyone by means of an explosion, to send or deliver an explosive to anyone, or to place an explosive near a building, ship, or boat with the intention of causing physical injury.

export bans *Anticompetitive practices that have the effect of banning the resale of products from one EU territory in another state of the EU. Export bans have long been held to infringe the competition rules in *Article 101 of the Treaty on the Functioning of the European Union; they can lead the European Commission to levy fines of up to 10% of annual worldwide group turnover. Examples of practices that infringe the rules include clauses in contracts banning exports; an export ban in a written contract will be void when Article 101 applies. However, when the *vertical agreements regulation 330/2010 applies it is permitted to restrict an exclusive distributor from actively soliciting sales outside its territory. It is not permissible to prevent a distributor from advertising on a website as this is regarded as "passive" rather than "active" selling. In addition, practices that have the effect of bolstering or imposing an export ban are forbidden, including buying up all *parallel imports, marking products solely for the purposes of tracing them to stop parallel importation, and sending faxes to, or otherwise putting pressure on, dealers not to engage in parallel importation.

ex post facto [Latin: by a subsequent act] Describing any legal act, such as a statute, that has retrospective effect.

exposure *n.* Under the Sexual Offences Act 2003 (s 66) a person is guilty of exposure if he or she intentionally exposes his or her genitals and intends that someone else will see them and be caused alarm or distress. This will not normally include such activities as nude swimming or sun-bathing, "streaking", or naked protests and the like. However, where the exposure (by a man or a woman) goes far beyond generally accepted standards of decency and at least two people could have seen it, it may amount to the common-law offence of **indecent exposure**, even if it cannot be shown that anyone actually saw the exposure or was upset by it. Public nudity may also amount to an offence under the terms of the Public Order Act 1986 (s 5).

expressio unius est exclusio alterius [Latin: the inclusion of the one is the exclusion of the other] *See* INTERPRETATION.

express term A provision of a contract, agreed to by the parties, that is either written or spoken. Such a provision may be classified as a *condition, a *warranty, or an *innominate term. *Compare* IMPLIED TERM.

express trust A trust created expressly by the settlor, i.e. by stating directly his intention to create a trust. There is no need for formal words provided that the intention to create a trust is clear from the documents or from the oral statements of the settlor, but most express trusts are contained in documents that have been professionally drafted. (If the trust property is land evidence in writing is required, as section 53 (1)(b) of the Law of Property Act applies, if the trust is to be enforceable.) For there to be an express trust it is also necessary for the "three certainties" to be satisfied (*Knight v Knight* (1849) 3 Beav 148): certainty of intention, certainty of subject matter, and certainty of objects (beneficiaries). *Compare* IMPLIED TRUST.

expropriation *n.* The taking by the state of private property for public purposes, normally without compensation (*compare* COMPULSORY PURCHASE, which carries with it a right to compensation). The right to expropriate is known in some legal systems as the right of **eminent domain**. In the UK, expropriation requires statutory authority except in time of war or apprehended war (*see* ROYAL PREROGATIVE).

ex proprio motu (**ex mero motu**) [Latin: of his own motion] Describing acts that a court may perform on its own initiative and without any application by the parties.

expulsion *n.* In international law, the termination by a state of an alien's legal entry and right to remain. This is often based upon the ground that the alien is considered undesirable or a threat to the state. Grounds for expulsion have included the following: conviction of a crime compromising public security; vagabondage; vice; disease; spying and political intrigue; resistance to the law; and abuse of the national flag. Case: the *Buffalo Case* (1903) UN Rep IX 445. *See also* DEPORTATION.

extended sentence A sentence longer than the maximum prescribed for a particular offence, which was formerly imposed on persistent offenders under certain circumstances. The power to impose extended sentences was abolished by the Criminal Justice Act 1991.

extinguishment *n.* The cessation or cancellation of some right or interest. For example, an *easement is extinguished if the dominant and servient tenements come into the same ownership. Mere *non-user of an easement, however, will not cause it to be extinguished unless an intention to abandon it can be shown (*Benn v Hardinge* (1992) 66 P & CR 246).

extortion *n.* A common-law offence committed by a public officer who uses his position to take money or any other benefit that is not due to him. If he obtains the benefit by means of menaces, this may also amount to blackmail.

extradition *n.* The surrender by one state to another of a person accused or convicted of committing an offence in the territorial jurisdiction of the latter, which being competent to try and punish him demands his surrender. Extradition from the UK relates to surrender to foreign states (*compare* FUGITIVE OFFENDER) and is governed by the Extradition Act 2003. There must be an *extradition treaty between the UK and the state requiring the surrender. The offence alleged must be a crime in the UK as well as in the requesting state, it must be both covered by the treaty and within the list of extraditable offences contained in the Act itself, and it must not be of a political character. *See also* DOUBLE CRIMINALITY.

extradition treaty A treaty under the terms of which a state agrees to deport a fugitive criminal (or suspect) to the state where the offence was committed or to the fugitive's state of nationality (*see* EXTRADITION). In the latter case the crime in question must be one that is a breach of the municipal law of the national committed outside the territorial boundaries of the state of which he is a citizen. Extradition treaties are bilateral in character and there is a lack of uniformity in their provisions and in their interpretation. However, they invariably contain the following three features:

(1) the state that has custody will not surrender the fugitive unless *prima facie* evidence of his guilt is submitted to them;

(2) no political offenders will be surrendered;

(3) no surrender will be made unless adequate assurances are given that the accused will not on that occasion be tried for any offence other than the crime for which he is surrendered.

extrajudicial divorce A divorce granted outside a court of law by a nonjudicial process (such as a *ghet or a *talaq). An extrajudicial divorce will not be recognized in the UK if it takes place in the UK, Channel Islands, or Isle of Man. *See also* OVERSEAS DIVORCE.

extraordinary general meeting *See* GENERAL MEETING.

extraordinary means In medical law, treatments used to prolong a person's life that are not regarded as beneficial (i.e. they do nothing to promote recovery or relieve suffering) and that may even be burdensome to the patient. Recent cases have established the principle that there is no legal obligation to prolong life by extraordinary means. "Extraordinary" does not mean unusual: treatments that are considered routine may be classed as extraordinary when they are no longer clinically effective. *See* ARTIFICIAL NUTRITION AND HYDRATION.

extraordinary rendition A euphemism for the extrajudicial transfer of individuals from one state to another. The term arose in relation to the recent US practice of transferring suspected terrorists to countries known to torture prisoners or to employ harsh interrogation techniques that may rise to the level of torture – methods that would be illegal under US federal law. As well as violating the commonly accepted *jus cogens* rule against torture in public international law, the practice also violates international treaty obligations, in particular the *European Convention on Human Rights 1950 (as brought into UK law by the Human Rights Act 1998 and the Criminal Justice Act 1988). The most explicit provision on extraordinary rendition can be found in Article 3 of the UN Convention Against Torture and Other Cruel, Inhuman or Degrading Treatment or Punishment, which states that no state party "shall expel, return ('refouler') or extradite a person to another State where are substantial grounds for believing that he would be in danger of being subjected to torture". In December 2005 the British police launched an investigation into persistent claims that the CIA used British airports to transport around 200 terrorist suspects for torture in secret camps abroad. The British government denied any knowledge of the use of British airports for such a purpose.

extraterritoriality *n.* A theory in international law explaining *diplomatic immunity on the basis that the premises of a foreign mission form a part of the territory of the sending state. This theory is not accepted in English law (thus a divorce granted in a foreign embassy in England is not obtained outside the British Isles for purposes of the Recognition of Divorces Act 1971). Diplomatic immunity is based either on the theory that the diplomatic mission personifies – and is entitled to the immunities of – the sending state or on the practical necessity of such immunity for diplomacy.

extrinsic evidence (parol evidence) Evidence relating to matters referred to in a document that is not itself included in that document. Extrinsic evidence cannot generally be given to contradict or alter the terms of a written document such as a judicial record or a contract, but such evidence may be admissible where there are allegations of mistake, illegality, or fraud. Extrinsic evidence may also be admissible in aid of interpretation of a document. *See also* PAROL EVIDENCE RULE.

ex turpi causa non oritur actio [Latin: no action can be based on a disreputable cause] The principle that the courts may refuse to enforce a claim arising out of the claimant's own illegal or immoral conduct or transactions. Hence parties who have knowingly entered into an *illegal contract may not be able to enforce it and a person injured by a fellow-criminal while they are jointly committing a serious crime may not be able to sue for damages for the injury.

fact *n.* An event or state of affairs known to have happened or existed. It may be distinguished from law (as in *trier of fact) or, in the law of evidence, from opinion (*see* OPINION EVIDENCE). The **facts in issue** are the main facts that a party carrying the persuasive *burden of proof must establish in order to succeed, for example the elements of the offence or parts of the *cause of action; in a wider sense they may include subordinate or collateral facts, such as those affecting the *credit of a witness or the *admissibility of evidence. *See also* FACTUM.

factor *n.* An agent entrusted with the possession of goods (or documents of title representing goods) for the purposes of sale. A factor is likely to fall within the definition of a *mercantile agent in the Factors Act 1889 and to have the powers of a mercantile agent. A factor has a *lien over the goods entrusted to him that covers any claims against the principal arising out of the agency.

factum *n.* [Latin] **1.** A *fact or statement of facts. For example, a ***factum probans*** (*pl.***facta probantia***) is a fact offered in evidence as proof of another fact, and a ***factum probandum*** (*pl. ***facta probanda***) is a fact that needs to be proved. **2.** An act or deed. *See also* NON EST FACTUM.

failure to maintain The failure of either spouse to provide reasonable maintenance for the other or to make a proper contribution towards the maintenance of any children of the family during the subsistence of the marriage. Upon proof of such failure, family proceedings courts have jurisdiction to make orders for unsecured periodical payments and for lump-sum orders not exceeding £1,000. The divorce county courts and High Court have power to make orders for periodical payment (which may also be secured by a charge on the property of the respondent spouse) and for lump-sum orders (of any sum). It is no longer necessary to prove **wilful neglect to maintain** (i.e. deliberate withholding of maintenance). Under the Child Support Act 1991, application for periodical payments for children can now usually be made directly to the Child Support Agency (*see* CHILD SUPPORT MAINTENANCE) rather than the court.

failure to make disclosure Failure of a party to disclose documents as required by a direction for disclosure (*see* DISCLOSURE AND INSPECTION OF DOCUMENTS). This will lead to an application to the court for an order compelling disclosure. Unless the court gives permission under Part 31 of the Civil Procedure Rules, a party may not rely on any document where he has failed to disclose this document or failed to permit inspection by the other party.

fair comment Formerly a defence to an action for *defamation that the statement made was fair comment on a matter of public interest. Under the Defamation Act 2013 it was replaced by a defence of *honest opinion.

fair dismissal *Dismissal of an employee when a tribunal decides that an employer has acted reasonably in dismissing the employee and that the dismissal was for a lawful reason, i.e. on the grounds of the employee's capability, qualifications, or conduct; redundancy; the fact that it would be illegal to continue employing the employee; or some other substantial reason. *Compare* UNFAIR DISMISSAL.

fair rent Rent fixed by a rent officer or rent assessment committee for the holder of a *protected or *statutory tenancy. The rent is registered in relation to the property. When fixing the rent, no account is taken of the scarcity of rented property and therefore the rent is often lower than a market rent. The rent of *assured tenancies is fixed by agreement between the landlord and tenant. The tenant can apply to a *rent assessment committee to determine the rent if the landlord wishes to increase it. The committee must fix the rent at the amount the landlord could obtain on the open market. There is no registration of rent for assured tenancies, but the rents determined by rent assessment committees are recorded and this information is available to the public.

fair trial A right set out in Article 6 of the *European Convention on Human Rights and the *Human Rights Act1998. The right to a fair trial applies in civil and criminal proceedings and includes the right to a public hearing (subject to some exceptions) by an independent and impartial tribunal established by law. It has been interpreted as requiring that the state may sometimes need to provide legal aid for a litigant: *Airey v Ireland* App No 6289/73 [1981] ECHR 1. In criminal cases there are also the following specified rights: the *presumption of innocence; the right to be told the details of the case against you; to have time and facilities to prepare a defence and to instruct lawyers (with financial support where necessary); to call witnesses and examine the witnesses for the prosecution; and to have the free assistance of an interpreter. *See also* EQUALITY OF ARMS.

fairway *n.* The mid-channel of a navigable river, extending as near to the shore as there is sufficient depth of water for ordinary navigation.

fair wear and tear A phrase often found in repairing covenants in leases. When a tenant is not obliged to repair fair (reasonable) wear and tear occurring during his tenancy, he must nevertheless do any repairs to prevent consequential damage resulting from the original wear and tear. For example, if a slate blows off a roof the tenant is not liable to repair it, but he ought to prevent the rain entering through the hole and doing more damage.

falsa demonstratio non nocet [Latin: a false description does not vitiate] A rule applied where a description of something in a legal document (e.g. a will) is made up of more than one part, and one part is true, but the other false: if the part that is true describes the subject with sufficient legal certainty, then the untrue part will not vitiate the document.

false accounting An offence, punishable by up to seven years' imprisonment, committed by someone who dishonestly falsifies, destroys, or hides any account or document used in accounting or who uses such a document knowing or suspecting it to be false or misleading (Theft Act 1968 s 17). The offence must be committed for the purpose of gain or causing loss to another. There is also a special offence (also punishable by up to seven years' imprisonment) committed by a company director who publishes or allows to be published a written statement he knows or suspects is misleading or false in order to deceive members or creditors of the company. *See also* FORGERY.

false imprisonment Unlawful restriction of a person's freedom of movement, not necessarily in a prison. Any complete deprivation of freedom of movement is sufficient, so false imprisonment includes unlawful arrest and unlawfully preventing a person leaving a room or a shop. The restriction must be total: it is not imprisonment to prevent a person proceeding in one direction if he is free to leave in others (*Bird v Jones* (1845) 7QB 742). False imprisonment is a form of *trespass to the person, so it is not necessary to prove that it has caused actual damage. It is both a crime and a tort of strict liability. Damages, which may be *aggravated or *exemplary, can be obtained in tort and the writ of *habeas corpus is available to restore the imprisoned person to liberty.

false plea (sham plea) A statement of case that is obviously frivolous or absurd and is made only for the purpose of vexation or delay. A court may order a statement of case that would adversely affect the fair trial of a case to be struck out or amended.

false pretence The act of misleading someone by a false representation, either by words or conduct. The former offence of obtaining property by false pretences now comes under the general offence of *fraud. *See also* DECEPTION.

false statement *See* PERJURY.

false trade description A description of goods made in the course of a business that is false in respect of certain facts (*see* TRADE DESCRIPTION). Offences committed prior to 26 May 2006 were governed by the Trade Descriptions Acts 1968 and 1972, whereby it was an offence to apply a false trade description to goods either directly, by implication, or indirectly (e.g. by tampering with a car's mileometer or painting over rust on the bodywork). It was also an offence to supply or offer to supply goods to which a false trade description is attached. These offences were triable either summarily or on indictment (in which case they carried a maximum two years' prison sentence). This legislation was repealed by the Consumer Protection from Unfair Trading Regulations 2008, which are supplemented by the Business Protection from Misleading Marketing Regulations 2008.

falsification of accounts *See* FALSE ACCOUNTING.

familial child sexual offences The Sexual Offences Act 2003 creates a number of offences, all formerly categorized as incest, relating to sexual activities amongst family members: these include sexual activity with a child family member (s 25), inciting a child family member to engage in sexual activity (s 26). Sexual activity includes any form of intentional touching that is sexual in nature. The maximum sentence is 14 years' imprisonment.

family *n.* A group of people connected by a close relationship. For legal purposes a family is usually limited to relationships by blood, marriage, civil partnership, or adoption, although sometimes (e.g. for social security purposes) statute expressly includes other people, such as common-law wives (*see* COMMON-LAW MARRIAGE). The courts have interpreted the word "family" to include unmarried couples living as husband and wife in permanent and stable relationships. In *Ghaidan v Mendoza* [2002] 3 FCR 591 (CA) the court interpreted the word "family" in the Rent Act 1977 to include the gay partner of a deceased tenant.

family assets Property acquired by one or both parties to a marriage to be used for the benefit of the family as a whole. Typical examples are the *matrimonial home, furniture, and car. There is no special body of law dealing with family assets as such, but the courts have wide discretion to make orders in relation to such assets upon dissolution of the marriage and have developed flexible guidelines to apply in the case of family assets. Thus, one spouse will often acquire a share in the home owned by the other, by reason of his or her contributions to the welfare of the family and its finances.

family assistance order A court order under the Children Act 1989 that a probation officer, or an officer of a local authority, should advise, assist, and befriend a particular child or a person closely connected with the child (such as a parent) in order to provide short-term support for the family. The order can only be made with the consent of the person it concerns (other than the child) and has effect for up to six months.

Family Court A proposed new court that is intended to hear family law matters in place of the three tiers of court that currently do so (the county court, the *family proceedings court, and the Family Division of the High Court). It is intended that all levels of the family judiciary should sit in the new court, with cases being allocated according to their complexity. The Family Division of the High Court will continue to exercise exclusive jurisdiction over cases involving its *inherent jurisdiction or requiring international work. The government published draft legislation to this effect in 2012.

Family Division The division of the *High Court concerned with *family proceedings and noncontentious probate matters. Until 1971, it was known as the *Probate, Divorce and Admiralty Division. It may hear some appeals (*see* APPELLATE JURISDICTION). The chief judge of the Division is called the President.

Family Intervention Tenancy Where a possession order for council or housing association-owned residential property has, or could have, been made against a tenant in consequence of anti-social behaviour, the landlord may (since 1 January 2009) offer a Family Intervention Tenancy. Such tenancies, usually granted for 6 to 24 months, lack *security of tenure, have limited protection from eviction, and must be accompanied by a behaviour support agreement. If the tenancy is not determined, the tenant may be offered an introductory, starter, secure, or assured tenancy on expiry of the Family Intervention Tenancy.

Family Justice Council A body created in 2002 to monitor the effectiveness of the family justice system and to advise on reforms where necessary. It is administered by the Ministry of Justice.

(⊕) SEE WEB LINKS
• Webpage of the Family Justice Council

family life Article 8 of the *European Convention on Human Rights and the *Human Rights Act1998 guarantee respect for family life. The right to family life extends beyond formal relationships and legitimate arrangements (*Marckx v Belgium* (App no 6833/74) [1979] ECHR 2). This right is a *qualified right: the public interest can be used to justify an interference with it providing that this is prescribed by law. The *right to marry and found a family is contained in Article 12 of the Convention.

family name *See* SURNAME.

family proceedings All court proceedings under the inherent jurisdiction of the High Court that deal with matters relating to the welfare of children (*see* WELFARE PRINCIPLE). Before 1989 the court's powers to make orders concerning children varied, depending on the level of the court and the proceedings involved. The Children Act 1989, together with the Family Proceedings Rules 1991, rationalized the court's powers and created a unified structure of the High Court, county courts, and magistrates' courts. A Family Procedure Rule Committee was established in 2003 to lay down a single set of procedural rules for all levels of court. The ambit of family proceedings is very wide, including proceedings for *divorce, *domestic violence, children in care (*see* CARE

ORDER), adoption, and *wardship and applications for a *parental order under
section 54 of the Human Fertilization and Embryology Act 2008.

family provision Provision made by the courts out of the estate of a deceased person
in favour of his family or *dependants. The court may award a family provision if it is
satisfied that the provision made for the applicant either by the deceased person or by
the law of intestacy is, in the circumstances, unreasonable.

farm business tenancy A tenancy created under the Agricultural Tenacies Act 1995.
A farm business tenancy will be established where there is a grant of a tenancy on or
after 1 September 1995 of land to be used for the purposes of agriculture. The regime
does not provide automatic security of tenure; the tenancy may be determined by
notice of intention to terminate by either party as long as at least one year's notice is
given. The tenancy may allow diversification into businesses other than agriculture.
There is provision for compensation for tenants' improvements at the end of the
tenancy, provided they were carried out with the consent of the landlord. *Compare*
AGRICULTURAL HOLDING.

farming *n*. Special tax provisions apply for farming. For income tax, profits can be
averaged. Inheritance tax relief at 100% is usually available against the value of farm land
and machinery used for farming. The Income Tax (Trading and Other Income) Act 2005
s 876 states that farming means the occupation of land wholly or mainly for the purpose
of husbandry. Husbandry is declared not to include market gardening. In 1925 the
Court of Session equated "husbandry" with a trade that depends on the use of "fruits
of the land occupied" (*Lean and Dickson v Ball* (1925) 10 TC 341, 345). In that case,
intensive poultry rearing was held to be husbandry.

fast track The track to which a civil case is allocated when the amount claimed
exceeds £10,000 but is less than £12,000 (*see* ALLOCATION). The fast track provides a
streamlined procedure in order to ensure that any legal and other costs remain
proportionate to the amount claimed. It achieves this through the use of standard
directions by the court, a fixed timetable of about 30 weeks between directions and trial,
a trial of one day only, no oral expert evidence to be used in trial, and costs being fixed
dependent on the level of advocacy used.

fatal accidents By the Law Reform (Miscellaneous Provisions) Act 1934, a right of
action by (or against) a deceased person survives his death and can be brought for the
benefit of (or against) his estate. Thus if a person is killed in a motor accident due to
the negligence of the driver, an action can be brought against the driver in the name
of the deceased; any damages obtained become part of the deceased's estate. Actions
for defamation of a deceased person and claims for certain types of loss are excluded
from the Act and do not survive death.

The Fatal Accidents Act 1976, amended by the Administration of Justice Act 1982 and
the Civil Partnership Act 2004, confers the right to recover damages for loss of support
on the dependants of a person who has been killed in an accident, if the deceased
would have been able to recover damages for injury but for his death. The class of
dependants who may sue is defined by statute and includes such persons as spouses,
former spouses, civil partners, former civil partners, common law spouses, parents,
children, brothers, and sisters. The main purpose of the action is to compensate
dependants for loss of the financial support they could have expected to receive from
the deceased. However, **damages for bereavement** may be claimed on the death of
a spouse or civil partner by the surviving spouse or civil partner, or on the death of an

unmarried minor child by the parents. The amount awarded is currently fixed at £12,980. Funeral expenses can be recovered if incurred.

federal state A state formed by the amalgamation or union of previously autonomous or independent states. A newly created federal state is constitutionally granted direct power over the subjects or citizens of the formerly independent states. As such, the new federal state becomes a single composite international legal person. Those former entities that comprise it have consented to subsume their former sovereignty into that of the federal state, although they retain their identity in municipal law. Examples of federal states include the USA and Switzerland. *Compare* CONFEDERATION.

fee *n.* A legal estate (other than leasehold) in land that is capable of being inherited. Since the Law of Property Act 1925 the term's only modern significance is in the phrase *fee simple absolute in possession. All other such estates that formerly existed in fee are now equitable interests only.

fee farm rent *See* RENTCHARGE.

fee simple absolute in possession The freehold estate: one of only two forms of ownership of land that, under the Law of Property Act 1925, can exist as a legal estate (*see also* TERM OF YEARS ABSOLUTE). All others take effect as equitable interests. **Fee simple** indicates ownership that is not liable to end upon any person's death, with the expiration of time, or on the failure of a particular line of heirs. **Absolute** means that the owner's rights are not conditional or liable to terminate on the occurrence of any event (except the exercise of a right of *re-entry – Law of Property (Amendment) Act 1926). **In possession** means that the owner's rights are immediate, thus future interests do not qualify, but possession need not imply actual physical occupation (for instance, a person in receipt of rents and profits can be said to be in possession).

fee tail A legal estate in land that was abolished by the Law of Property Act 1925. It can now exist only as an equitable *entailed interest, and no new entailed interests can be created since 1997.

felony *n.* Formerly, an offence more serious than a *misdemeanour. Since 1967 the term has been abandoned (although it is retained in pre-1967 statutes that are still in force) and the law formerly relating to misdemeanours now applies to felonies. *See also* ARRESTABLE OFFENCE; INDICTABLE OFFENCE; SUMMARY OFFENCE.

female genital mutilation (FGM) Circumcision of the female genitalia that is not medically necessary. The Female Genital Mutilation Act 2003 makes it a criminal offence for anyone to perform as a principal, or to aid and abet, counsel, or procure, FGM within the UK, and for UK nationals or permanent residents of the UK to do so inside or outside the UK.

feme covert [Anglo-French] A married woman, under the *coverture of her husband.

feme sole [Anglo-French] An unmarried woman. The term includes a widow or divorcée or a woman whose marriage has been annulled.

feminist legal theory A broad movement that seeks to show how conventional legal theory, far from being gender-blind, ignores the position and perspective of women. Feminist writers examine the inequalities to be found in the criminal law (especially in rape and domestic violence), family law, contract, tort, property, and other branches of the substantive law, including aspects of public law. Four principal strands of feminist thought may be identified. **Liberal feminism** regards persons as autonomous, rights-bearing agents and accentuates the values of equality, rationality, and autonomy. Its central claim is that since women and men are equally rational they ought to have the same opportunities to exercise rational choices. **Radical feminism** regards this view as misguided since, by asserting women's similarity to men, it merely assimilates women into the male domain. Because men dominate women, the issue is ultimately one of power. Reforming the law is, by itself, unlikely to satisfy the demands of women at work, in the home, or simply as human beings. **Difference feminism** likewise rejects an idea of formal equality which, it contends, obscures the real differences between men and women. Instead, it seeks to expose the unstated premises of the law's substance, practice, and procedure by demonstrating the various forms of discrimination implicit in the criminal law, the law of evidence, tort law, and the process of legal reasoning itself. **Postmodern feminism**, in rejecting the existence of any objective truths, treats such concepts as "equality", "gender", and even "woman" with deep scepticism (*see* POSTMODERNIST LEGAL THOUGHT).

ferry *n*. A public highway by boat across water connecting places where the public have rights (usually of way) granted by royal charter or acquired by *prescription.

feudal system A political, economic, and social system in which the main social bond was the relationship between the Lord and others and in which this personal relationship was inseparable from a proprietary relationship that existed between them. It was introduced into England as a result of the Norman Conquest (1066). At its centre was the doctrine of **tenures**. All the land in the country was regarded as being owned by William I as the result of his conquest, and thereafter only the Crown could own land. The subject could merely hold it on a tenure, either directly from the Crown or indirectly through an intermediate superior. Such lands as William did not retain in his own possession he parcelled out to his barons. Holding directly from him, they were known as **tenants-in-chief**, and the tenures on which they held were **knight service** (which involved a duty to render military service for a specified number of days in each year), **sergeanty** (the performance of personal services), or **frankalmoign** (services of a religious character). Tenants-in-chief subgranted portions of their lands to lesser men to hold by tenure from them, the lesser men did likewise, and so on. The process of subgranting was called **subinfeudation**, and a man's immediate superior was known as his **mesne lord**. The principal tenures by which land was held through subinfeudation were knight service, frankalmoign, and **socage** (the rendering of agricultural or other services of a fixed nature, including the payment of money). All these tenures were free tenures. Much land was, however, held by unfree tenure, known as *copyhold: its tenant (a villein) was required to give any type of labour demanded of him.

   The system of tenures did not continue as an active force for more than a few centuries. The services to be performed were gradually commuted to money payments (**quit rents**), tenures were virtually reduced to socage and copyhold by the Statute of Military Tenures (or Tenures Abolition Act) 1660, and copyhold was converted into socage by the Law of Property Act 1922. However, the theory that the subject cannot own the land itself remains at the roots of land law; what he can own is an *estate in land, which entitles him to enjoy the land as much as if he did own it.

FGM *See* FEMALE GENITAL MUTILATION.

fiat justicia ruat coelum [Latin: Let there be justice, though the heavens fall] A maxim stating that justice must be done, whatever the consequences.

fiction *n.* An assumption that something is true irrespective of whether it is really true or not. In English legal history fictions were used by the courts during the development of forms of court action. They enabled the courts to avoid cumbersome procedures, to make remedies available when they would not be otherwise, and to extend their jurisdiction. For example, the action of *trover was originally based on the defendant's finding the claimant's goods and taking them for himself. In time, it became unnecessary to prove the "finding": a remedy was granted on the basis only of proving that the goods were the claimant's and that the defendant had taken them.

fiduciary [from Latin: *fiducia*, trust] **1.** *n.* A person, such as a trustee, who holds a position of trust or confidence with respect to someone else and who is therefore obliged to act solely for that person's benefit. **2.** *adj.* In a position of trust or confidence. Fiduciary relationships include those between trustees and their beneficiaries, company promoters and directors and their shareholders, solicitors and their clients, and guardians and their wards.

fieri facias (*fi. fa.*) [Latin: you should cause to be done] A High Court writ of execution to enforce the payment of a debt when judgment has been entered against the debtor. The writ can also be used to enforce a judgment for payment of damages. The writ is addressed to the *High Court Enforcement Officer requiring him to seize the property of the debtor in order to pay the debt, interest, and costs. In the county courts execution is levied by bailiffs under a warrant of execution.

fieri feci [Latin: I have caused to be done] The report of the *High Court Enforcement Officer or other appropriate officer saying how much he has recovered by levying execution under a writ of *fieri facias*.

fi. fa. *See* FIERI FACIAS.

filing *n.* The act of delivering a deed, mortgage, or other legal document to the officer who is authorized by law to receive it and preserve it for a particular purpose, e.g. a court clerk.

final act A document containing a formal summary of the proceedings of an international conference. The signature appended to the final act is not regarded as binding on the signatory state with regard to the treaties it refers to. For the document to be binding, a separate signature is required followed by *ratification. In rare circumstances, the final act can constitute a *treaty.

final judgment The *judgment in civil proceedings that ends the action, usually the judgment of the court at trial. Appeal against a final judgment may be made without leave of the court. *Compare* INTERIM JUDGMENT.

Finance Bill A parliamentary Bill dealing with taxation matters, introduced each year to enact the Budget proposals. In recent years, the normal parliamentary programme has started with the Budget in March or April, with the year's Finance Bill being published a few weeks later. The Finance Bill then passes through the committee stages of the House of Commons, after which it goes for a formal Lords reading as, constitutionally, the House of Lords is unable to amend a money bill. The Finance Bill then receives royal assent, typically in the first week of July. *See also* MONEY BILL.

financial assistance The provision of funds etc. by a company to enable a person to acquire shares in that company. Such assistance is unlawful where it is in contravention of sections 678(1) and 679(1) of the Companies Act 2006. Section 678(1) provides that where a person is acquiring shares in a *public company, it is not lawful for that company to give financial assistance directly or indirectly for the purposes of the acquisition before, during, or after the acquisition. Section 679(1) provides a similar prohibition in relation to a public company that is a subsidiary of a private holding company. There are, however, exceptions. These include where the company lends money in the ordinary course of business, e.g. where a bank customer borrows money to buy shares in the bank, or where the financial assistance is authorized by some other provision of company law, e.g. for the purpose of an *employees' share scheme. The most significant exception, however, is contained in section 678(2) of the Companies Act, which states that a public company can give such assistance where this is an incidental part of some larger purpose of the company and it is given in good faith in the interests of the company.

financial provision order An order for periodical payments or a lump sum made for the purpose of adjusting the financial position of the parties to a marriage and any children of the family. Such orders may be made on or after the granting of a decree of divorce, nullity, or judicial separation or when one party to the marriage has failed to provide, or to make a proper contribution towards, reasonable maintenance for the other or a child of the family. On divorce, judicial separation, or nullity, the court also has the power to make *property adjustment orders. In determining whether to make financial provision orders, the court has a very wide discretion under section 25 of the Matrimonial Causes Act 1973. It has an overriding duty to give first consideration to the welfare of any child under the age of 18 years and to try to achieve a *clean break wherever possible. The Act lists seven matters that the court must take into account as part of the circumstances it is to consider. These include: the financial resources and needs each of the parties has or is likely to have in the foreseeable future; the age of the parties and the length of the marriage; the standard of living enjoyed by the family before the breakdown of the marriage; the contributions that each of the parties has made to the welfare of the family, which include looking after the home or caring for the family; and the conduct of the parties, but only where it would be very unjust to ignore such conduct. A recent landmark case in the House of Lords (*White v White* [2001] 1AC 596 (HL)) made it clear that the implicit objective of section 25 is to achieve a fair outcome and that there should be no discrimination between husbands and wives and their respective roles (i.e. if one spouse stays at home while the other goes out to work, this fact is immaterial). A starting point should be that assets are equally divided, unless there is a good reason for not doing so. Additional cases: *Lambert v Lambert* [2002] EWCA Civ 1685, [2003] 2 WLR 63; *Miller v Miller*; *McFarlane v McFarlane* [2006] UKHL 24, [2006] 2 AC 618; *Charman v Charman* [2007] EWCA Civ 503, 1 FLR 1246. *See also* MAINTENANCE PENDING SUIT; PROPERTY ADJUSTMENT ORDER.

financial relief Any or all of the following: *maintenance pending suit orders, *financial provision orders, *property adjustment orders, and court orders for maintenance during the marriage and for the maintenance of children (*see* CHILD SUPPORT MAINTENANCE). The court has powers to set aside transactions made by a husband or wife with the intention of preventing a spouse from making a claim for financial relief, or to prevent such a transaction from taking place (*see* AVOIDANCE OF DISPOSITION ORDER). Financial relief provisions for children, other than in matrimonial proceedings, are consolidated in the Children Act 1989; for example, it is possible for unmarried parents and those in whose favour a residence order is made to obtain financial relief. In addition, children over the age of 18 have an independent right to seek financial relief from their parents.

Financial Reporting Standards (FRSs) Standards issued by the Accounting Standards Board since 1991, defining the principles on which a company's assets and liabilities should be valued and its profits and losses computed. In many cases FRSs amend or supersede the **Statements of Standard Accounting Practice (SSAPs)** previously issued by the Board. Most of the more recent FRSs have the aim of harmonizing UK practice with the standards issued by the International Accounting Standards Board; from 1 January 2005 these are binding on listed EU companes in their published accounts. *See also* ACCOUNTING PRACTICE.

((⊕)) SEE WEB LINKS
- Summaries of all FRSs in issue from the Financial Reporting Council website
- Website of the International Accounting Standards Board: includes summaries of standards in issue

Financial Services Authority (FSA) A body corporate set up under the Financial Services and Markets Act 2000 to regulate the provision of financial services and markets. The Act contains a general prohibition against any person carrying out any regulated activity unless that person is authorized or exempt. Regulated activities include investment advice, stock broking, deposit taking, and more general consumer transactions involving the provision of mortgages, insurance, and basic banking services. It is an offence, unless exempt, to carry on a regulated activity without authorization. Those in contravention may be unable to enforce transactions and investors who suffer loss may be entitled to compensation. Under the Act, the FSA has powers of investigation in respect of financial crime (e.g. insider dealing), handling the proceeds of crime, and market abuse. Among other powers, the FSA can conduct investigations into breaches of the general prohibition and into the nature of the business or the ownership or control of an authorized person.

financial year 1. For *corporation tax, the year from 1 April to 31 March. The financial year 2015 runs from 1 April 2015 to 31 March 2016. Corporation tax is levied for each financial year separately. If a company makes up its accounts for a period that spans two financial years, the profits arising in the company's period of account must be split between the two financial years in order to ascertain the quantum of corporation tax that is payable. Since 1854, statute has required public accounts to be made up for the same 12-month period ending on 31 March. *Compare* TAX YEAR. **2.** In accounting, any 12-month period for which financial statements are published.

fine *n*. 1. A sum of money that an offender is ordered to pay on conviction. Most *summary offences are punishable by a fine with a fixed maximum, in accordance with a standard scale of five levels. These are currently (2014) as follows: level 1 – £200; level 2 – £500; level 3 – £1,000; level 4 – £2,500; level 5 – £5,000. Under the Criminal Justice Act 2003, before fixing a fine, a court must enquire into the financial circumstances of the offender and the amount of the fine fixed by the court should, in addition, reflect the seriousness of the offence. Sometimes provision is made for imprisonment in cases of failure to pay the fine. A fine may also be imposed instead of, or in addition to, any other punishment for someone convicted on indictment (except in cases of murder). This fine is **at large**, i.e. the amount is at the discretion of the judge. **2.** A lump-sum payment by a tenant to a landlord for the grant or renewal of a lease. *See also* PREMIUM.

firearm *n*. For the purposes of the Firearms Act 1968, any potentially lethal weapon with a barrel that can fire a shot, bullet, or other missile or any weapon classified as a *prohibited weapon (even if it is not lethal). The Act created various offences in relation to firearms. The main offences include: buying or possessing a firearm without a licence; buying or hiring a firearm under the age of 17 or selling a firearm to someone under 17 (similar offences exist under the Crossbows Act 1987 in relation to crossbows); possessing a firearm under the age of 14; supplying firearms to someone who is drunk or insane; carrying a firearm and suitable ammunition in a public place without a reasonable excuse; trespassing with a firearm; possessing a firearm with the intention of endangering life; using a firearm with the intention of resisting or preventing a lawful arrest; having a firearm with the intention of committing an indictable offence; possessing a firearm or ammunition after having previously been convicted of a crime; and having a firearm in one's possession at the time of committing or being arrested for such offences as rape, burglary, robbery, and certain other offences. The Firearms Act 1982 extends the provisions of the 1968 Act to imitation firearms that can be easily converted to firearms and a 1988 Act strengthened controls over some of the more dangerous types of firearms, shotguns, and ammunition.

The Firearms (Amendment) Act 1997, which was enacted in the wake of the 1996 Dunblane massacre, banned all privately owned handguns (i.e. guns that can be held and fired with one hand). Exceptions in favour of private secure gun clubs and some smaller calibre pistols were removed from the Act as passed.

Under the Theft Act 1968 someone who has with him a firearm or imitation firearm while committing *burglary is guilty of aggravated burglary. For the purposes of this Act, a firearm may include an airgun, air pistol, or anything that looks like a firearm. *See also* OFFENSIVE WEAPON; REPEAT OFFENDER.

fire damage An occupier of land or buildings is not liable for a fire that begins there accidentally (Fires Prevention (Metropolis) Act 1774). Liability is imposed if the fire is caused by negligence, nuisance, or a non-natural user of the land or if the fire, having started accidentally, is negligently allowed to spread.

first offender A person with no previous conviction by a criminal court. *See also* SENTENCE.

First-tier Tribunal A body created in 2008 under the Tribunals, Courts and Enforcement Act 2007 to take over the functions of 20 previously existing *tribunals. It currently consists of seven chambers: the General Regulatory Chamber; the Social Entitlement Chamber; the Health, Education and Social Care Chamber; the Tax Chamber; the War Pensions and Armed Forces Compensation Chamber; the Immigration and Asylum Chamber; and the Property Chamber. In most cases appeals against the decisions of the First-tier Tribunal can be made to the *Upper Tribunal, which exercises *judicial review over its decisions.

fiscal year *See* TAX YEAR.

fishery *n. See* PISCARY.

fishery limits The area of sea over which a state claims exclusive fishing rights, except as agreed in treaties with other states. British fishery limits extend to 200 nautical miles from the baselines used for measuring the *territorial waters. Fishery limits may be limited or restricted by bilateral or multilateral fishing treaties or agreements, such as the EU's *Common Fisheries Policy. The UK Merchant Shipping Act 1988 preventing "quota hopping" (*see* QUOTA) in British waters by non-UK EU vessels, such as Spanish and Dutch vessels, was held unlawful by the European Court of Justice in 1996. *See also* EXCLUSIVE ECONOMIC ZONE.

fit for habitation A statutory implied covenant applied to certain tenancies at a very low rent (Landlord and Tenant Act 1985 s 8). Premises are regarded as not reasonably fit for habitation if they are defective in one or more of the following: repair, stability, freedom from damp, natural lighting, ventilation, water supply, drainage and sanitary conveniences, facilities for cooking and for storage and preparation of food, and disposal of waste water. A landlord normally has no obligation to see that premises are fit for habitation when the statutory provisions do not apply. There is an implied term that tenancies of furnished dwelling houses are fit for habitation at the commencement of the tenancy. The environmental health officer employed by the local authority can order the landlord to carry out repairs. *See* HOUSING HEALTH AND SAFETY RATING SYSTEM.

fitness for purpose A standard that must be met by one who sells goods in the course of a business. When the buyer makes known to the seller any particular purpose for which the goods are being bought, there is an implied condition that the goods are reasonably fit for that purpose, except when the circumstances show that the buyer does not rely (or that it is unreasonable for him to rely) on the skill or judgment of the seller.

fixed charge *See* CHARGE.

fixed-date summons Formerly, a summons in the county courts used to initiate actions in which a claim was made for any relief other than the payment of money. Such a claim is now made by means of a *claim form.

fixed penalty notice A notice given to a person who has committed a traffic offence entitling that person to discharge any liability to conviction by payment of a prescribed amount of money in accordance with the Road Traffic Offenders Act 1988, as amended by the Road Traffic Safety Act 2006.

Fixed penalty notices are not, however, confined to road traffic offences and can be issued in respect of a range of offences under the Criminal Justice and Police Act 2001; these offences include throwing fireworks in a thoroughfare, trespassing on a railway, disorderly behaviour while drunk in a public place, and depositing and leaving litter.

fixed-sum credit Any facility (other than *running-account credit) under a *personal-credit agreement by which the debtor is entitled to receive credit, either in one amount or by instalments.

fixed term A tenancy or lease for a fixed period. The date of commencement and the length of a lease must be agreed before there can be a legally binding lease. It may take effect from the date of the grant, an earlier date, or a date up to 21 years ahead (*see* FUTURE LEASE). At the end of the fixed term, the lease or tenancy comes to an end automatically: there is no need for a notice to quit. However, if the tenancy is an *assured tenancy, it will continue at the end of the term as a *statutory periodic tenancy unless it is brought to an end by *surrender of tenancy or a court order. If the tenant remains in possession after the end of the term, a *tenancy at sufferance or a *tenancy at will may arise; if the landlord accepts periodic payments of rent from the tenant after the end of the term, a *periodic tenancy may arise. *See also* HALF A YEAR; LONG TENANCY.

fixed trust A form of *express trust in which the beneficiaries have completely defined and predetermined interests. *Compare* DISCRETIONARY TRUST.

fixture *n.* A chattel that has been annexed to land or a building so as to become a part of it, in accordance with the maxim *quicquid plantatur solo, solo cedit* (whatever is annexed to the soil is given to the soil). Annexation normally involves actual affixation, but a thing resting on its own weight can be regarded as annexed if it can be shown that it was intended to become part of the land or to benefit it (*Holland v Hodgson* (1872) LR 7 CP 328). A chalet used as a dwelling that merely rests on the land but cannot be removed except by destruction is a fixture (*Elitestone Ltd v Morris* [1997] 1 WLR 687 (HL)). However, if an object brought onto land as a chattel deteriorates so as to be irremovable except by destruction, it does not therefore become a fixture (*Mew v Tristmire* [2011] EWCA Civ 912). Fixtures become the property of the freeholder, subject to certain rights of removal (as, for example, in the case of *trade fixtures and certain agricultural fixtures). A vendor of land may retain the right to fixtures as against the purchaser by express provision in the contract.

flag of convenience (FOC) The national flag of a state flown by a ship that is registered in that state but is owned by a national of another state. A state whose law allows this practice can grant, in return for financial considerations, nationality and the right to fly its national flag to virtually any ship. For the ship owners, flags of convenience provide a means of avoiding higher taxes or more stringent safety and environmental regulations in the country of ownership. *See also* FLAG STATE JURISDICTION.

flagrante delicto [Latin] In the commission of an offence. Formerly, certain types of *arrest could only be made when a person was in the act of committing an offence (*see* ARRESTABLE OFFENCE). The phrase is most commonly applied to the situation in which a person finds his or her spouse in the act of committing adultery. Someone who kills his or her spouse in this situation may have a defence of *provocation.

flag state jurisdiction The rule whereby, exceptions applying, a ship on the *high seas is subject only to the jurisdiction of the flag state, i.e. that state permitting it the right to sail under its flag (*see* FLAG OF CONVENIENCE). Case: *Case of the SS Lotus* (1927) PCIJ Rep Series A No 10.

flexible tenancy A form of tenancy introduced by the Localism Act 2011 as an alternative to the grant of a *secure tenancy: a flexible tenancy is granted for a fixed term without security of tenure. It may be granted when an *introductory tenancy or a *demoted tenancy expires.

flexible working *Employees who are parents of children aged under 17 or of disabled children aged under 18 have the legal right to apply to request a change in their working hours and conditions, including the option of working from home. Employers have a duty to consider these requests seriously, but there is no automatic right to work flexibly. The employee, who must have worked for the employer for at least 26 weeks at the date the application is made, must apply in writing and may make only one application a year. The employer must meet the employee to discuss the application within 28 days of the request; within 14 days of the meeting the employer must either agree to the request or explain why it was refused. There is an appeal procedure. If the employer accepts the application, terms and conditions are changed permanently unless the parties agree otherwise. The current government has committed itself to extending the right to request flexible working to all employees, with a view to bringing this into force in 2014.

flexicurity *n.* A labour market model that combines flexibility for employers with job security for workers. It is argued that in order to succeed in increasingly global and competitive markets employers need to be able to adapt quickly to meet prevailing economic and market conditions. As a result, employers want to be able to hire and fire and to introduce new working practices without facing legal sanctions. The growth in the use of temporary and *agency workers and the practice of outsourcing reflects this need. From the worker's point of view, however, flexibility for the employer may mean lack of employment protection. Within the European Union, there has been a move to promote flexible working arrangements while guaranteeing some level of protection for workers. The European Commission has defined flexicurity as a strategy that aims simultaneously to enhance the flexibility of labour markets, work organizations, and labour relations on the one hand, while maintaining employment and income security on the other.

floating charge *See* CHARGE.

flotation *n.* A process by which a public company can, by an issue of securities (shares or debentures), raise capital from the public. It may involve a **prospectus issue**, in which the company itself issues a *prospectus inviting the public to acquire securities; an **offer for sale**, in which the company sells the securities on offer to an **issuing house**, which then issues a prospectus inviting the public to purchase the securities from it; or a **placing**, whereby an issuing house arranges for the securities to be taken up by its own or another's clients in the expectation that they will ultimately become available to the public on the open market. *See also* RIGHTS ISSUE; TENDER OFFER; UNDERWRITER.

FNOs *See* FOREIGN NATIONAL OFFENDERS.

FOB contract (Free On Board contract) A type of contract for the international sale of goods in which the seller's duty is fulfilled by placing the goods on board a ship. Thereafter all costs and the risk of accidental loss or damage passes to the buyer. Insurance during the sea transit is likewise the responsibility of the buyer. If the goods are to travel by air or rail the terms **FOB Airport** or **Free on Rail** (**FOR**) are sometimes used. FOB is a defined *Incoterm in *Incoterms 2010*.

FOC *See* FLAG OF CONVENIENCE.

following trust property *See* TRACING TRUST PROPERTY.

football hooliganism The Sporting Events (Control of Alcohol etc.) Act 1985 contains finable offences of possessing alcohol, being drunk, or causing or permitting the carriage of alcohol on trains and vehicles capable of carrying nine or more passengers; the vehicle must be carrying two or more passengers to or from a "designated sporting event" (mainly Football League club and international fixtures), and normal scheduled coach or train services are excluded. A constable who reasonably suspects that a relevant offence is being or has been committed may stop the vehicle or train and search it or the suspected offender. It is also an offence to be drunk or to possess alcohol or (unless lawful authority is proved) fireworks and similar objects (but not matches or lighters) in the viewing area within two hours before, during, or one hour after the event, or while trying to enter. Under the Public Order Act 1986, persons convicted of the above alcohol-related offences, or offences committed at the football ground, can be excluded by the courts from football matches. Admission to a designated football match is controlled under the Football Spectators Act 1989 and is subject to the control of disorderly behaviour there under the Football (Offences) Act 1991. Under the Football Spectators Act 1989, as amended by the Football (Disorder) Act 2000 and the Football (Disorder) (Amendment) Act 2002, a **banning order** may be made to prohibit an offender from attending a football match in England and Wales. Such an order may also require that the offender surrender his passport to prevent him travelling to a football match abroad (*Gough v Chief Constable of Derbyshire* [2002] QB 459). *See also* OFFENCES AGAINST PUBLIC ORDER.

footpath *n.* Under the Highways Act 1980, any *highway (other than a *footway) over which the public have a right of way on foot only. *Compare* BRIDLEWAY; CARRIAGEWAY; DRIFTWAY.

footway *n.* Under the Highways Act 1980, any way over which the public have a right of way on foot only and which is part of a highway that also comprises a way for the passage of vehicles. *Compare* FOOTPATH.

forbearance *n.* A deliberate failure to exercise a legal right (e.g. to sue for a debt). A forbearance to sue at a debtor's request may be *consideration for some fresh promise by the debtor. A promise not to enforce a claim that is bad in law may still be consideration if the claim is believed to be valid. A requested forbearance, even if it is not binding, may have more limited effects either at common law or in equity (e.g. in certain circumstances it may not be revoked without reasonable notice).

force *n.* In public international law, any action by a state in breach of the norms of international law as stated in the UN Charter and in other international conventions. This may include the use of military, financial, or political methods.

forced heirship A principle in many foreign jurisdictions (e.g. France) under which a person's estate on death must devolve and be divided between specified relatives in specified proportions and such devolution cannot be overridden by a will. *Compare* FREEDOM OF TESTATION.

forced marriage A marriage in which one party does not consent to the marriage and there is some element of duress. A clear distinction is drawn by the courts between a forced marriage, which is void under the Matrimonial Causes Act 1973 s 12(c) and can be annulled by the court, and an arranged marriage, which is lawful. In the latter case families of both spouses play a role in arranging the marriage but the choice whether to accept remains with the individuals (*NS v MI* [2006] EWHC 1646 (Fam), [2007] 1 FLR 444; *P v R (Forced Marriage: Annulment: Procedure)* [2003] 1 FLR 661). Until recently the only civil remedy for a victim would be to apply for a *non-molestation order or an *occupation order under the Family Law Act 1996 or an injunction under the Protection from Harassment Act 1997. Victims of forced marriages may now be protected by a *forced marriage protection order made under pt 4A of the Family Law Act 1996.

(⊕) SEE WEB LINKS

• Website of the Forced Marriage Unit

forced marriage protection order An order providing legal protection for an actual or potential victim of a *forced marriage. The court has wide powers to include a range of provisions, such as those prohibiting a potential victim from being taken outside the UK for the purposes of marrying overseas or preventing someone (typically a member of the family) from molesting or contacting a woman who has left the family and sought refuge elsewhere. An application for such an order can be made by the victim or a third party, such as a relative or teacher.

force majeure [French] Irresistible compulsion or coercion. The phrase is used particularly in commercial contracts to describe events possibly affecting the contract and that are completely outside the parties' control. Such events are normally listed in full to ensure their enforceability; they may include *acts of God, fires, failure of suppliers or subcontractors to supply the supplier under the agreement, and strikes and other labour disputes that interfere with the supplier's performance of an agreement. An express clause would normally excuse both delay and a total failure to perform the agreement.

forcible entry A common-law offence (as amended by various statutes) that applied under certain circumstances when force was used to gain entry to premises. The common-law offence has been replaced by a statutory offence of using or threatening violence against people or property in order to secure entry into premises (Criminal Law Act 1977). The offence only applies if there is someone present on the premises who is opposed to the entry and the offender knows of this. The fact that the offender is the legal owner or occupier of the premises is not in itself a defence. However, there is a special defence if the offender can prove that he was at the relevant time a displaced *residential occupier or protected intending occupier who requires the property for his residence and has a qualifying freehold or leasehold interest, tenancy, or licence and was seeking to gain entry or to pass through premises that form an access to his own place of residential occupation. These provisions do not apply to landlords seeking to regain possession and it is a summary offence to make false statements when claiming to be a protected occupier. It is not an offence, however, for a person unlawfully evicted from his own home to use force to re-enter, subject to the common-law rule that the force must not be excessive. The police may use force to enter with lawful authority. *See also* ADVERSE OCCUPATION.

foreclose down *See* REDEEM UP, FORECLOSE DOWN.

foreclosure *n.* A remedy available to a mortgagee when the mortgagor has failed to pay off a *mortgage by the contractual date for redemption. The mortgagee is entitled to bring an action in the High Court, seeking an order fixing a date to pay off the debt; if the mortgagor does not pay by that date he will be foreclosed, i.e. he will lose the mortgaged property. If, after this order (a foreclosure order nisi) is made, the mortgagor does not pay on the date and at the place (usually a room in the Royal Courts of Justice) named, the foreclosure is made absolute and the property thereafter belongs to the mortgagee. However, the court has discretion to allow the mortgagor to reopen the foreclosure and thereby regain his property. The remedy is unpopular: the mortgagee's *power of sale may be more useful; moreover, if the mortgaged property is worth less than the loan, the mortgagee cannot sue for the balance. *See also* REPOSSESSION.

foreign agreement An agreement or contract the proper law of which is the law of some country other than England and Wales, Northern Ireland, or Scotland. *See* FOREIGN LAW; PROPER LAW OF A CONTRACT.

foreign bill Any bill of exchange other than an *inland bill. The distinction is relevant to the steps taken when the bill has been dishonoured (*see* DISHONOUR).

foreign company A company incorporated outside the UK but having a place of business within the UK. Foreign companies are subject to provisions of the Companies Act 2006 relating to registration, accounts, name, etc. *See* OVERSEA COMPANY.

foreign enlistment The offence under the Foreign Enlistment Act 1870 of enlisting oneself or others (except with the licence of the Crown) for armed service with a foreign state that is at war with a state with which the UK is at peace. A foreign state for this purpose includes part of a province or persons exercising or assuming powers of government. It is also an offence under the Act (again, except with licence) to build or equip any ship for such service or to fit out any naval or military expedition for use against a state with which the UK is at peace.

foreign judgments At common law the judgment of a foreign court may be enforced in England provided that specified requirements are met. In addition, foreign judgments may be registered for enforcement by the English courts under a number of statutory powers, notably those contained in the Administration of Justice Act 1970, the Foreign Judgments (Reciprocal Enforcement) Act 1933, the Civil Jurisdiction and Judgments

Act 1982 (as amended), and the *Judgments Regulation. Part 74 of the *Civil Procedure Rules sets out the relevant procedural rules.

foreign law For the purposes of *private international law, any legal system other than that of England. A foreign legal system may be the system of a foreign state (one recognized by public *international law) or of a law district. Thus the law of Scotland, Northern Ireland, the Channel Islands, and Isle of Man and the law of each of the American or Australian states or Canadian provinces is a separate foreign law. When an element of foreign law arises in an English court, it is usually treated as a question of fact, which must be proved (usually by expert evidence) in each case. The English courts retain an overriding power to refuse to enforce (or even to recognize) provisions of foreign law that are against English public policy, foreign penal or revenue laws, or laws creating discriminatory disabilities or status. *See also* COMMUNITY LAW.

foreign national offenders (FNOs) Under the UK Borders Act 2007 foreign national offenders who have been sentenced to a period of imprisonment of 12 months or longer are subject to automatic *deportation from the UK at the end of their sentence. In such cases the Home Secretary is legally obliged to make a deportation order unless the FNO falls within one of a small number of exceptions. The most important of these are: (i) where deportation would breach the subject's rights under the *European Convention on Human Rights or the UK's obligations under the Convention Relating to the Status of Refugees; (ii) where the subject was under the age of 18 at the time of conviction; (iii) where the subject is being held under the Mental Health Act 1983; and (iv) where the subject is a national of the European Economic Area (EEA) or a dependant of an EEA national. A request for extradition from another government will also take precedence over a deportation order.

Foreign national offenders who are sentenced to less than 12 months' imprisonment may also be deported on the recommendation of the court, as may non-EEA nationals who receive several custodial sentences that in total exceed 12 months within one 5-year period.

foresight *n.* Awareness at the time of doing an act that a certain consequence may result. In the case of some crimes (e.g. *wounding with intent) an *intention by the accused to bring about a certain consequence must be proved before he can be found guilty; foresight is not enough (*see also* ULTERIOR INTENT). However, conviction for many crimes (including *wounding) requires only that the accused foresaw a specified consequence as likely or possible. In all cases where foresight suffices for liability, the court may not assume that the defendant had foresight merely because the particular consequence that occurred was the natural and likely consequence of his acts. *See also* RECKLESSNESS.

forfeiture *n.* Loss of property or a right as a consequence of an offence or of the breach of an undertaking. There are four main situations in which the courts may order forfeiture of property.

(1) Property that is illegally possessed is subject to forfeiture (Proceeds of Crime Act 2002).

(2) Any property relating to an offence under the Misuse of Drugs Act 1971 or the Drug Trafficking Offences Act 1986 (*see* CONTROLLED DRUGS) may be forfeited and either destroyed or dealt with as the court sees fit (this includes the proceeds of the sale of drugs).

(3) Property may be forfeited if it is legally possessed but used (or intended to be used) to commit a crime (e.g. a getaway car) when the owner has previously been convicted

of an offence. Property confiscated under this heading is held by the police for six months and then disposed of.

(4) Most *leases provide for the landlord to terminate the lease when the tenant is in breach of his covenants.

The landlord must follow a particular procedure before effecting forfeiture. From 24 January 1996 a freeholder cannot forfeit a lease for nonpayment of a service charge unless the lessee accepts the charge or the *leasehold valuation tribunal agrees. In the case of forfeiture for nonpayment of rent, the landlord must make a formal demand for the rent unless the lease exempts him from the need to do this. When other covenants have been breached, the landlord must serve a statutory notice on the tenant specifying the breach, requiring him to put it right where this is possible, and requiring compensation in money if appropriate. If the tenant fails to comply with the notice the landlord may proceed with forfeiture. This may be done through court proceedings for possession or, more rarely, by *re-entry. A landlord loses his right of forfeiture if he treats the lease as continuing when he is entitled to forfeit it (by, for example, accepting rent from the tenant). This is known as **waiver of forfeiture**. Some leases contain a waiver clause by which the landlord is deemed not to have waived his right to forfeit even if he accepts rent from the tenant. *See also* CONFISCATION ORDER; RACIAL HATRED; RELIEF FROM FORFEITURE.

forgery *n.* The offence of making a "false instrument" in order that it may be accepted as genuine, thereby causing harm to others. Under the Forgery and Counterfeiting Act 1981, an "instrument" may be a document, a stamp issued by the Post Office or HM Revenue, or any device (e.g. magnetic tape) in which information is recorded or stored. An instrument is considered to be "false" if, for example, it purports to have been made or altered (1) by or on the authority of someone who did not in fact do so; (2) on a date or at a place when it was not; or (3) by someone who is nonexistent. In addition to forgery itself, it is a criminal offence under the Act to copy or use a false instrument, knowing or believing it to be false. It is also an offence merely to have in one's possession or control any one of certain specified false instruments with the intention of passing them off as genuine. It is also an offence to make or possess any material that is meant to be used to produce any of the specified false instruments. These specified instruments include money or postal orders, stamps, share certificates, passports, cheques, cheque cards and credit cards, and copies of entries in a register of births, marriages, or deaths. All the above offences are punishable on indictment by up to ten years' imprisonment and upon summary trial to a *fine at level 5 on the standard scale and/or six months' imprisonment.

The Act also deals with the offences of **counterfeiting currency** (notes or coin), with or without the intention of passing it off as genuine; possessing counterfeit currency; passing it off; making or possessing anything which can be used for counterfeiting; and importing or exporting counterfeit currency. It is also an offence to reproduce any British currency note (e.g. to photocopy a £5 note), even in artwork, and, under certain circumstances, to make an imitation British coin. Some of these offences are subject to the same penalties as forgery.

formal validity of a will In *private international law, a rule determining which country's laws govern the formalities for the *execution of a will where, for example, the testator had a foreign domicile or owned foreign assets. Under English law the position is governed by the Wills Act 1963 s 1: English rules of execution apply if, for example, the will is executed in England or the testator is domiciled in England. *See also* MATERIAL AND ESSENTIAL VALIDITY OF A WILL.

forum *n*. [from Latin: public place] The place or country in which a case is being heard. If a case involving a foreign element is brought in the English courts, the forum is England. *See* LEX FORI.

forum non conveniens [Latin: not in agreement with the judicial forum] A doctrine that permits a court to decline to accept jurisdiction over a case, so that the case may be tried in an alternative forum (i.e. a foreign court). Such decisions are almost entirely at the court's discretion, except that the party seeking a *forum non conveniens* decision must submit to the effective jurisdiction of the alternative court. The stay will be granted by the court if it is satisfied that a foreign court having competent jurisdiction is available and that the case may be tried more suitably for the interests of all the parties and the ends of justice in that court. The factors that courts generally consider in making this decision include the location of witnesses, exhibits, and documents, the language of the witnesses and documents, the citizenship of the claimants, and the law applicable to the dispute.

In general, the burden of proof rests on the defendant to persuade the court to exercise its discretion to grant a stay, but if the court is satisfied that another court is available, the burden will then shift to the claimant to show that there are special circumstances requiring that the trial should nevertheless take place in the first court (*Spiliada Maritime Corporation v Cansulex Ltd (The Spiliada)* [1987] AC (HL) 460, 476 (Lord Goff)).

forum prorogatum [Latin] Prorogated jurisdiction, which occurs when a power is conferred – by the consent of the parties and following the initiation of proceedings – upon the International Court of Justice, which otherwise would not have adjudicated. Such consent can be indicated in an implied or informal way or by a succession of acts (*Anglo-Iranian Oil Case* [1952] ICJ Rep 93).

forum rei [Latin: forum of the thing] The court of the country in which the subject of a dispute is situated.

forum shopping The practice of choosing a country in which to bring a legal case through the courts on the basis of which country's laws are the most favourable. In some instances there is a choice of jurisdiction.

foster child A child who is cared for by someone other than its natural or adopted parents or a person having *parental responsibility (see* FOSTER PARENT). Local authorities are obliged by law to supervise the welfare of foster children within their area and to inspect and control the use of premises as foster homes. Foster children do not include children who are looked after by relatives or guardians or boarded out by a local authority or voluntary organization.

foster parent A person looking after a *foster child. Foster parenthood does not of itself confer *parental responsibility and, unless legal steps are taken to acquire it, foster parents are in a similar position to any other *social parent. Unlike other *de facto* carers, however, all foster parents are subject to legal controls. There is a distinction between *private foster parents and *local authority foster parents.

four unities *See* JOINT TENANCY.

franchise *n*. **1.** (in constitutional law) A special right conferred by the Crown on a subject. Also known as a **liberty**, it is exemplified by the right to hold a market or fair or to run a ferry. **2.** (in constitutional law) The right to vote at an *election. To qualify to vote at a parliamentary election, a person must be a *Commonwealth citizen or a citizen of the Republic of Ireland, must be aged 18 or over, must be shown on the register of electors governing the election (*see* ELECTOR) as resident on the qualifying date in the parliamentary constituency or local government area concerned, and must not be subject to any legal incapacity to vote. Those incapacitated are persons serving sentences of imprisonment, persons convicted during the preceding five years of certain offences relating to elections or to the bribery of public officials, and persons who are incapable of understanding the nature of their acts. Citizens of other EU states may vote in local, European Parliament, and devolved body elections. **3.** (in commercial law) A licence given to a manufacturer, distributor, trader, etc., to enable them to manufacture or sell a named product or service in a particular area for a stated period. The holder of the licence (**franchisee**) usually pays the grantor of the licence (**franchisor**) a royalty on sales, often with a lump sum as an advance against royalties. The franchisor may also supply the franchisee with a brand identity as well as finance and technical expertise. Franchises are common in the fast-food business, petrol stations, travel agents, etc. A franchise contract in the EU must comply with regulation 330/2010 (the vertical *block exemption), which sets out which provisions are permitted and which are banned under EU *competition law; the accompanying Vertical Guidelines contain specific advice on franchise contract terms. *See* VERTICAL AGREEMENTS.

fraud *n.* Dishonestly making a false (untrue or misleading) representation with a view to gain or with intent to cause loss. The Fraud Act 2006 came into force on 15 January 2007 and created a general offence of fraud that replaced the *deception offences created under the Theft Acts of 1968 and 1978. The offence is punishable on indictment by a maximum of ten years' imprisonment or by a fine, or both; on summary conviction it is punishable by a term not exceeding six months' imprisonment or a fine not exceeding the statutory maximum, or both. If the fraud results in injury to the deceived party, he may claim damages for the tort of *deceit. A contract obtained by fraud is voidable on the grounds of fraudulent *misrepresentation. *See also* CONSTRUCTIVE FRAUD. In relation to crime, *see* CHEAT; CONSPIRACY; CYBERCRIME; DEFRAUDING; DISHONESTY; FALSE PRETENCE; FORGERY.

fraud on a power An exercise of a *power of appointment that, although made to an object within the class chosen by the donor, was made in circumstances that render it void. Examples are when the appointor intended to obtain a benefit for himself or another or when there was a deliberate intention to defeat the intentions of the donor of the power.

fraud on the minority An improper exercise of voting power by the majority of members of a company in which votes are not cast for the benefit of the company as a whole. This is now covered by sections 260–64 of the Companies Act 2006. *See also* DERIVATIVE CLAIM.

fraudulent conveyance A transfer of land made without valuable *consideration and with the intent of defrauding a subsequent purchaser. An example of fraudulent conveyance is when A, who has contracted to sell to B, conveys the land to his associate C in order to escape the contract with B. Under the Law of Property Act 1925, B is entitled to have the conveyance to C set aside by the court.

fraudulent misrepresentation *See* MISREPRESENTATION.

fraudulent trading Carrying on business with the intention of defrauding creditors or for any other fraudulent purpose, e.g. accepting advance payment for goods with no intention of either supplying them or returning the money. Such conduct is a criminal offence (Companies Act 2006 s 993) and the court may order those responsible to contribute to the company's assets on a *winding-up (Insolvency Act 1986 s 213-14).

Cases: *Re Patrick & Lyon Ltd* [1933] Ch 786; *Re Maidstone Building Provisions Ltd* [1971] 1 WLR 1085; *Re Augustus Barnett & Son Ltd* [1986] BCLC 170; *Re Cooper Chemicals Ltd* [1978] Ch 262. *See also* WRONGFUL TRADING.

freeboard *n.* Under the Merchant Shipping (Safety and Load Line Conventions) Act 1932, the vertical distance measured amidships from the upper edge of the deck line to the upper edge of the load line mark.

freedom from encumbrance The freedom of property from the binding rights of parties other than the owner. In contracts for the sale of goods, unless the seller makes it clear that he is contracting to transfer only such title as he or a third person may have, there is an implied *warranty that the goods are free from any charge or encumbrance not disclosed or known to the buyer before the contract was made.

freedom of association Article 11 of the *European Convention on Human Rights and the *Human Rights Act 1998 protect **freedom of peaceful assembly** and association with others, including the right to engage in peaceful protests and demonstrations and to form and join trade unions and similar bodies (*Wilson v UK* [2002] 1 IRLR 568 (ECHR)). It is a *qualified right. The state has a duty to protect protesters from those who wish to prevent their assembly or attack them (*Plattform Ärzte fur das Leben v Austria* (1988) 13 EHRR 204).

freedom of expression A right set out in Article 10 of the *European Convention on Human Rights and the *Human Rights Act1998. In the key case *Handyside v UK* (1976) 1 EHRR 737, the European Court of Human Rights declared that: "Freedom of expression constitutes one of the essential foundations of a democratic society, one of the basic conditions for its progress and for the development of every man . . . it is applicable not only to 'information' or 'ideas' that are favourably received or regarded as inoffensive or as a matter of indifference, but also to those that offend, shock or disturb . . . such are the demands of that pluralism, tolerance and broadmindedness without which there is no 'democratic society'." Convention jurisprudence gives different weight to different kinds of expression. The most important expression – political speech – therefore is likely to be protected to a much greater extent than the least important – commercial speech. Freedom of expression is a *qualified right.

freedom of testation A person's right to provide in his will for the distribution of his estate in whatever manner he wishes. The principle is restricted by the powers of the court to set aside a will made by a person of unsound mind (*see* TESTAMENTARY CAPACITY) and to award *reasonable financial provision from an estate to certain relatives and dependants of the deceased under the Inheritance (Provision for Family and Dependants) Act 1975. This is a fundamental principle of English law but does not apply in many other jurisdictions, where *forced heirship rules may apply.

freedom of thought, conscience, and religion A right set out in Article 9 of the *European Convention on Human Rights and the *Human Rights Act1998. Freedom of thought is an *absolute right, but the right to manifest one's beliefs or religion is a *qualified right. The right to proselytize is protected under the Convention (*Kokkinakis v Greece* (App no 14307/88) [1993] ECHR 20). In *Eweida and Others v the United Kingdom* (App no 48420/10) ECHR 15 January 2013 the European Court of Human Rights considered whether UK law adequately protected the applicant's right to manifest her religion (by wearing a Christian cross on a chain around her neck) and decided that suspension from her employment with British Airways was disproportionate; the fact that an employee has the option of resigning from employment does not necessarily defeat a claim from a victim of religious discrimination at work.

free elections Article 3 of the First Protocol to the European Convention on Human Rights and the *Human Rights Act1998 compel the state to hold free *elections at reasonable intervals by secret ballot, under conditions that will ensure the free expression of the opinion of the people in the choice of the legislature. This duty does not apply to local elections (local authorities are not the legislature) but does apply to elections to the European Parliament (*Liberal Party v UK* (1982) (App no 8765/79) 4 EHRR 106; *Matthews v UK* (1999) 28 EHRR 361). There is no duty to use any particular system of voting (proportional representation or first past the post). The Article includes a right to vote which, although not an *absolute right, should not be removed from any person or group of people without justification. The blanket ban preventing convicted prisoners in the UK from voting was ruled a disproportionate interference with this right (*Hirst v UK* (No 2) (App no 74025/01) (2006) 42 EHRR 41); however, MPs subsequently voted to retain the ban despite this ruling.

free from average *See* AVERAGE.

freehold *n.* The most complete form of ownership of land: a legal estate held in *fee simple absolute in possession.

freeing for adoption Formerly, the procedure in which parents gave their consent to the adoption of a child or this consent was dispensed with on statutory grounds. Parents gave their consent in general terms, rather than to an adoption by particular prospective adopters. It was abolished by the Children and Adoption Act 2002 and replaced by a new placement regime (*see* PLACEMENT ORDER).

free movement The movement of goods, persons, services, and capital within an area without being impeded by legal restrictions. This is a basic principle of the *European Community, whose treaty insists on the free movement of goods (involving the elimination of customs duties and quantitative restrictions between member states and the setting up of a *Common External Tariff) as well as the free movement of services, capital, and persons (including workers and those wishing to establish themselves in professions or to set up companies). *See also* EXHAUSTION OF RIGHTS.

Free On Board *See* FOB CONTRACT.

freezing injunction An injunction enabling the court to freeze the assets of a defendant (whether resident within the jurisdiction of the English court or not); it may be obtained under Part 25 of the *Civil Procedure Rules. The injunction prevents the defendant from removing his assets from the jurisdiction of the court, and from disposing of, dealing with, or diminishing the value of his assets. The injunction is draconian and consequently requires clear justification. Any person seeking a freezing injunction must himself disclose all material information to the court. Before the introduction of the Civil Procedure Rules in 1999, freezing injunctions were known as **Mareva injunctions**, from the case *Mareva Compania Naviera Se. v International Bulkcarriers SA* [1980] 1 All ER 213.

freight *n.* **1.** The profit derived by a shipowner or hirer from the use of the ship by himself or by letting it to others, or for carrying goods for others. **2.** The amount payable under a contract (of affreightment) for the carriage of goods by sea.

frolic of his own An action by an employee that is performed outside the scope of his employment, with the consequence that the employer is freed from any *vicarious liability for the act in question. The term was first used in *Joel v Morison* (1834) 6 C & P 501, 503; 172 All ER 1338.

FRSs *See* FINANCIAL REPORTING STANDARDS.

frustration of contract The unforeseen termination of a contract as a result of an event that either renders its performance impossible or illegal or prevents its main purpose from being achieved. Frustration would, for example, occur if the goods specified in a sale of goods contract were destroyed (impossibility of performance: Sale of Goods Act 1979 s 7); if the outbreak of a war caused one party to become an enemy alien (illegality); or if X were to hire a room from Y with the object (known to Y) of viewing a procession and the procession was cancelled (failure of main purpose: *Krell v Henry* [1903] 2 KB 740 (CA)). Unless specific provision for the frustrating event is made, a frustrated contract is automatically discharged and the position of the parties is, in most cases, governed by the Law Reform (Frustrated Contracts) Act 1943. Money paid before the event can be recovered and money due but not paid ceases to be payable. However, a party who has obtained any valuable benefit under the contract must pay a reasonable sum for it. The Act does not apply to certain contracts for the sale of goods, contracts for the carriage of goods by sea, or contracts of insurance.

FSA *See* FINANCIAL SERVICES AUTHORITY.

fugitive offender A person present in the UK who is accused of committing an offence in a Commonwealth country or an overseas territory of the UK and is liable to be surrendered for trial under the Fugitive Offenders Act 1967. The requirements for surrender are similar to those for *extradition to a foreign state, except that no treaty is involved.

full age *See* MAJORITY.

full powers A document produced by the competent authorities of a state designating a person (or body of persons) to represent the state for negotiating, adopting, or authenticating the text of a *treaty, for expressing the consent of the state to be bound by a treaty, or for accomplishing any other act with respect to a treaty. *See also* SIGNATURE OF TREATY.

full representation *See* LEGAL AID.

fully mutual housing association A housing association whose rules restrict membership to people who are tenants or prospective tenants of the association and prevent the granting or assigning of tenancies to those who are not members. Fully mutual housing associations are exempt from the *assured tenancy provisions.

functus officio [Latin: having performed his office] Describing a person who has discharged his duty and whose office or authority is at an end. Once a judgment has been given, the judge is *functus officio*: he has no power to make changes in his decision, which can only be questioned by others presiding in the further courts of appeal.

fundamental breach *See* BREACH OF CONTRACT; INNOMINATE TERMS.

funeral expenses Reasonable funeral expenses are a first charge on the assets of the deceased, payable out of the estate before any other debt or duty. This includes the cost of a tomb or gravestone (*Stanton v Ewart F. Youlden Ltd* [1960] 1 WLR 543; HMRC Statement of Practice SP7/87). Such expenses are deductible in calculating inheritance tax (Inheritance Tax Act 1984 s 172).

furnished holiday accommodation Domestic accommodation anywhere in the EU that is let on a commercial basis and available for letting for at least 210 days each year and actually let for at least 105 days. (Income Tax (Trading and Other Income) Act 2005 s 323.) Each letting during a seven-month period of the year must also be for less than 31 days. When this arithmetical definition is satisfied, the income arising is treated as if it were trading income. A restricted form of loss relief is available, pension contributions can be made on the basis of the letting income, and the income qualifies as earned income (Finance Act 2011, sch 14). Furnished holiday accommodation attracts capital gains tax relief in the form of *rollover relief, *holdover relief, and *entrepreneurs' relief.

furnished tenancy *See* ASSURED TENANCY; PROTECTED TENANCY.

futile *adj.* Describing a medical intervention that has little or no prospect of achieving its intended purpose. In medical law, claims of futility can be used to justify withholding or withdrawing medical treatment at the end of life. However, it is very important to be clear about a particular treatment's intended purpose before claiming that it is futile. Intensive care, for example, cannot be said to be futile simply on the grounds that the patient is unlikely to regain full health, since restoration of full health was never the intended purpose.

future goods Goods to be manufactured or acquired by a seller after a contract of sale has been made. Future goods must be distinguished as the subject of a contract of sale from existing goods, which are owned or possessed by a seller.

future interest Any right to property that does not take effect immediately. An example is B's interest in property held in trust for A for life and then for B. Under the Law of Property Act 1925 future interests in land (with the exception of *future leases) can exist as equitable interests only and not as legal estates.

future lease (reversionary lease) A lease that does not start immediately (in possession) but at some future time. Such leases are capable of being legal estates in land, unlike other future interests. A lease expressed to take effect more than 21 years from the date of the grant is void under the Law of Property Act 1925. A lease that starts more than three months from the date of the grant is required to be registered.

gabella emigrationis [Latin: emigration tax] In public international law, the principle that an alien on leaving a state can take his property away with him on the same conditions as a national; a tax for leaving the country, or a tax upon the property he takes away with him, cannot be levied.

game *n.* Wild animals or birds hunted for sport or food. The Game Acts define these as including hares, pheasants, partridges, grouse, heath or moor game, black game, and bustards. The right to game belongs basically to the occupier, although in leases it is frequently reserved to the landlord rather than the tenant. *See also* POACHING.

gaming (gambling) *n.* Playing a game in order to win money or anything else of value, when winning depends on luck. There are various restrictions upon gaming, depending on whether it takes place in controlled (i.e. licensed or registered) or uncontrolled premises. If the premises are uncontrolled, it is illegal to play a game that involves playing against a bank or a game in which each player does not have an equal chance or the chance of winning is weighted in favour of someone other than the players (e.g. a promoter or organizer), unless the game takes place in a private house in the course of ordinary family life. Thus one cannot play roulette with a zero in uncontrolled premises, but one may play such games as bridge, whist, poker, or cribbage. It is also illegal (subject to one or two exceptions) to game when a charge is made for the gaming or a levy is charged on the winnings. Gaming in any street or any place to which the public has access is illegal, except for dominoes, cribbage, or any game specially authorized in a pub (provided the participants are over 18). If the premises are controlled (either by the grant of a licence or by registration as a gaming club), the restrictions applying to uncontrolled premises apply unless they have been permitted by regulation. Thus casino-type games may be played on controlled premises for commercial profit if permission has been obtained, but only by members of licensed or registered clubs and their guests. There are also restrictions relating to playing on Sundays, and no one under 18 may be present when gaming takes place. It is illegal to use, sell, or maintain gaming machines without a certificate or licence.

gaming contract A contract involving the playing of a game of chance by any number of people for money or money's worth. A **wagering contract** is one involving two parties only, each of whom stands to win or lose something of value according to the result of some future event (e.g. a horse race) or to which of them is correct about some past or present fact; neither party can have any interest in the contract except his stake. In general, gaming and wagering contracts are by statute null and void and no action can be brought to recover any money paid or won under them.

gaming duty A tax levied on the profits of a gaming company in addition to corporation tax. The tax (currently at rates ranging from 15% to 50%: see Finance Act 2012 s 193) is imposed by the Betting and Gaming Duties Act 1981 on the profits of companies registered under the Gambling Act 2005. Schedule 1 of the Finance Act 2007 extends the charge to "remote gaming winnings", which are defined as gaming on the Internet, by telephone, by television, by radio, or equivalent media.

garden leave clause A clause in an employment contract that provides for a long period of notice by the employer, during which the employee will be remunerated in full but will not be required to attend at the workplace. Such clauses are used by employers wishing to safeguard trade secrets or, more importantly, prevent a highly skilled employee from leaving to undertake work for a rival firm. An employee wishing to leave could be required to serve "garden leave" in order to lawfully terminate his existing contract. Throughout the period of garden leave an employee will be subject to all the normal contractual restraints. Employers see the use of such clauses as an expensive but generally reliable alternative to traditional *restraint of trade clauses. These clauses may be enforced by way of injunction without encountering some of the difficulties that arise with respect to restraint of trade clauses, which are notoriously difficult to draft and enforce. It is possible, however, that the court will refuse to enforce a garden leave clause (*William Hill Organization v Tucker* [1998] IRLR 313).

garnishee order The former term for a *Third Party Debt Order.

GATT *See* GENERAL AGREEMENT ON TARIFFS AND TRADE.

Gazette *n*. A publication in which the Crown lists certain statutory notices. It appeared first as the *Oxford Gazette* in 1665, when the court resided at Oxford, and was transferred to London the following year; as the *London Gazette* it has been printed on Tuesdays and Fridays ever since. It contains official announcements of, for example, awards of military decorations, appointments of judges, and the dissolution of partnerships. Similar journals are published in Edinburgh and Belfast (the latter being transferred from Dublin following the establishment of the Irish Free State in 1921). For a businessman or a lawyer the principal use of these publications is to detect those firms that have become insolvent.

gazump *vb*. To raise the price of, or accept a higher offer for, land or buildings on which a sale price has been agreed but no legally binding contract has yet been made (*see* EXCHANGE OF CONTRACTS). The intending purchaser has no legal right either to compel the vendor to sell to him at the agreed price or to recover his wasted expenditure (such as surveyor's and solicitor's charges) unless an agreement, such as a *lock-out agreement, has been signed. The converse practice, in which the buyer reduces an agreed offer immediately before exchange of contracts, is known as **gazundering**.

GBH *See* GRIEVOUS BODILY HARM.

gender reassignment The process by which a **transsexual person** changes his or her sexual characteristics. It is not necessary to do this under medical supervision, nor to have surgery. A transsexual is a person who firmly believes that he or she belongs to the sex opposite to the sex (or gender) to which he or she was assigned at birth, a condition known as **gender dysphoria**. It is important to distinguish a transsexual person from a transvestite, who merely wishes to dress in clothes of the opposite sex. Under the Gender Recognition Act 2004, a transsexual person may apply to the *Gender Recognition Panel for the issue of a Gender Recognition Certificate. Before issuing the certificate the Panel must be satisfied that the applicant has, or has had, gender dysphoria, has lived in his or her acquired gender for the past two years, and intends to continue to live in that gender until death. The certificate entitles the applicant to be legally recognized in his or her acquired gender, to a new birth certificate, and to marry in that gender. Transsexual persons who have not acquired a Gender

Recognition Certificate will not be entitled to have their birth certificates amended and will still only be able to marry in the sex registered at birth. Important cases in this area include *Corbett v Corbett* [1971] P 83 (HL), *Goodwin v UK* (App no 28957/95) (2002) 35 EHRR 18.

The *Equality Act 2010 prohibits discrimination against a person who is proposing to undergo, is undergoing, or has undergone a process, or part of a process, for the purpose of reassigning their sex. In particular, it is discrimination against transsexual people to treat them less favourably for being absent from work because they propose to undergo, are undergoing, or have undergone gender reassignment than they would be treated if they were absent because they were ill or injured.

Case: *KB v National Health Service Pensions Agency* [2004] IRLR 240 (ECJ).

Gender Recognition Panel A panel established by the Gender Recognition Act 2004 to determine applications from transsexual persons who wish to be recognized in their newly acquired gender. A successful applicant will be issued with a **Gender Recognition Certificate**. *See* GENDER REASSIGNMENT.

general act *See* TREATY.

general agent *See* AGENT.

General Agreement on Tariffs and Trade (GATT) An international treaty signed in 1947 to provide for some measure of world free trade with the aim of reducing high tariffs on goods. Its objectives in extending free trade have been achieved in a series of eight negotiations (rounds); the last of these, the Uruguay Round (1986–94), led to the establishment of the *World Trade Organization and further agreement to ensure more free trade around the world.

general and special damages A classification of *damages awarded for a tort or a breach of contract, the meaning of which varies according to the context. **1.** General damages are given for losses that the law will presume are the natural and probable consequence of a wrong. Thus it is assumed that a libel is likely to injure the reputation of the person libelled, and damages can be recovered without proof that the claimant's reputation has in fact suffered. Special damages are given for losses that are not presumed but have been specifically proved. **2.** General damages may also mean damages given for a loss that is incapable of precise estimation, such as *pain and suffering or loss of reputation. In this context special damages are damages given for losses that can be quantified, such as out-of-pocket expenses or earnings lost during the period between the injury and the hearing of the action.

General Anti-Abuse Rule (GAAR) Every tax jurisdiction seeks to ensure that transactions are not taken out of the charge to tax by arrangements that seek merely to avoid a tax charge. In the UK the approach has been to legislate a large number of specific *anti-avoidance provisions for particular circumstances, notably to seek to restrict the availability of a tax relief to those whom the legislature considers to be properly regarded as within the intention of the relieving provisions. Many other jurisdictions have sought to defeat tax arrangements by the enactment of a general anti-avoidance rule (GAAR). The Finance Act 2013 introduces for the first time into UK fiscal legislation a GAAR known as the General Anti-Abuse Rule.

The UK GAAR legislation, which is remarkable for its brevity, imposes or increases a liability to tax by making an adjustment where tax arrangements are "abusive". In contrast to existing anti-avoidance provisions, the key elements in this treatment are defined in relation to the intention of the person subject to tax (or who would be subject to tax if it were not for the steps entered into). Thus, "tax arrangements" are those

arrangements for which "it would be reasonable to conclude that the obtaining of a
*tax advantage was the main purpose, or one of the main purposes". Similarly, "abusive"
arrangements are those that "cannot reasonably be regarded as a reasonable course of
action in relation to the relevant tax provisions". The GAAR has been criticized by many
commentators as creating an additional level of uncertainty in an area of the law where
it is reasonable to strive for certainty. According to the statute, indications that tax
evasions are abusive include: (a) taxable income, profits, or gains being significantly
less than "the amount for economic purposes"; (b) tax deductions or losses being
"significantly greater than the amount for economic purposes"; and (c) "a claim for
repayment or crediting of tax (including foreign tax) that has not been, and is unlikely
to be, paid". This list is declared not to be exhaustive.

General Assembly (of the UN) *See* UNITED NATIONS.

general average *See* AVERAGE.

General Council of the Bar of England and Wales *See* BAR COUNCIL.

General Court The first court of appeal from decisions of the European Commission.
As the **Court of First Instance** it was established under powers conferred by the
*Single European Act 1986 and began to operate in October 1989. Appeals from the
court are to the *European Court of Justice. The court was renamed the General
Court under the *Lisbon Treaty, which extended its jurisdiction.

general defences Common-law defences to any common-law or statutory crimes.
A defendant should be acquitted when the magistrates or jury have a reasonable doubt as
to whether he was entitled to a general defence. By contrast, **special defences** are
confined to individual offences, are usually of statutory origin, and usually place an
evidential burden on the defendant to show that he acted reasonably. *See also* DURESS;
EXCUSE; JUSTIFICATION; MISTAKE; NECESSITY; NON-INSANE AUTOMATISM; SELF-DEFENCE.

general equitable charge A class of *land charge, registrable under the Land
Charges Act (*see* REGISTRATION OF ENCUMBRANCES), that affects a *legal estate in land but
neither arises under a trust nor is secured by deposit of the title deeds.

general improvement area A predominantly residential area in which a housing
authority considers that it should improve or help to improve living conditions by
improving dwellings or amenities (or both). *See also* HOUSING ACTION AREA.

general issue A plea in which every allegation in the opposite party's pleading is
denied. In civil proceedings it is no longer permitted. Instead, under Part 16 of the
*Civil Procedure Rules, each allegation must be specifically admitted or denied. In
criminal cases the defendant may plead the general issue by pleading *not guilty.

general legacy *See* LEGACY.

general lien *See* LIEN.

generally accepted accounting practice (GAAP) *See* ACCOUNTING PRACTICE.

general meeting Under the Companies Act 2006, a meeting of company members
that is not an *annual general meeting. Such a meeting was formerly known as an
extraordinary general meeting. The Companies Act requires adequate notice to be
given of a general meeting, in hard copy form, in electronic form, or by means of a
website (s 308–09). A private company is now exempted from holding general meetings.
However, section 303 of the Act enables 10% of members of a private company to

requisition a general meeting (5% where more than 12 months has elapsed since the last general meeting). Under the 2006 Act many decisions that could formerly only be made at a general meeting of a private company can be made by *written resolution.

general participation clause A clause in the *Hague Conventions of 1899 and 1907. The clause, concerning the conduct of hostilities, stipulates that the Conventions shall be binding upon the belligerents only so long as all belligerents are parties to the Convention. The effect of this clause was to significantly weaken the effectiveness of the Hague Convention rules.

general power *See* POWER OF APPOINTMENT.

general power of investment A power, introduced by the Trustee Act 2000, that allows a trustee to make any kind of investment that he could make if he were absolutely entitled to the assets of the trust fund. Previously, trustees were only permitted to make certain *authorized investments. This much wider general power of investment may be expressly excluded in the trust instrument. There are still some restrictions on investments in land. In exercising the general power of investment, the trustees are required by the Act to consider criteria relating to the suitability of the proposed investment to the trust and the need for diversification of investment within the unique circumstances of the trust. Trustees are also required by the Act to review the investments from time to time with the same standard criteria in mind. Before investing, the trustee must obtain and consider proper advice, unless he reasonably considers it unnecessary or inappropriate to do so.

general principles of law Article 38 of the Statute of the *International Court of Justice requires the Court to apply as sources, in the first instance, (1) *treaties and (2) *customary international law. However, this same article also authorizes the court to apply "the general principles of law recognized by civilized nations". Thus, should neither treaty or custom prove adequate to resolve a contentious question, resort may be had to "general principles" as a subsidiary source. The general principles are commonly recognized as the norms existing in the municipal law of the majority of nations. When such a norm (i.e. the rule against judicial bias) has achieved the requisite degree of usage, it may thus be recognized as a subsidiary source of the substantive content of international law.

general safety requirement A standard of safety that consumer goods must meet in order to comply with the Consumer Protection Act 1987 and the General Product Safety Regulations 1994. The goods are required to be reasonably safe having regard to all the circumstances, e.g. the way the goods are marketed, including any instructions or warnings about their use; their compliance with published safety standards for goods of that kind; and whether reasonable steps could be taken to make them safer. Suppliers of consumer goods who fail to meet the safety requirement commit an offence.

general verdict **1.** (in a civil case) A *verdict that is entirely in favour of one or other party. **2.** (in a criminal case) A verdict either of *guilty or *not guilty. *Compare* SPECIAL VERDICT.

general warrant A warrant for arrest that does not name or describe the person to be arrested, or a search warrant that does not specify the premises to be searched or the property sought. Such warrants are usually illegal, although they may sometimes be expressly authorized by statute (*see* POWER OF SEARCH). Someone arrested under an illegal general warrant can claim damages for *false imprisonment. Sometimes, however,

Parliament grants a general power of arrest while searching premises with a search warrant, e.g. under the Betting, Gaming and Lotteries Act 1963.

general words Words in a *conveyance describing rights and benefits that are incidental to the land (such as easements and profits *à prendre*) and that are conveyed with it. Under the Law of Property Act 1925 such words are no longer necessary, since a conveyance of land is deemed to include all such ancillary rights unless a contrary intention is expressed in the document.

genetic fingerprinting *See* DNA FINGERPRINTING.

Geneva Conventions A series of international conventions on the laws of war, the first of which was formulated in Geneva in 1864. The 1864 and 1906 Conventions protect sick and wounded soldiers; the Geneva Protocol of 1925 prohibits the use of gas and bacteriological warfare; the three Conventions of 1929 and the four Conventions of 1949 protect sick and wounded soldiers, sailors, and prisoners of war, and the 1949 Conventions protect, in addition, certain groups of civilians. The First Protocol of 1977 supplements the 1949 Conventions, extending protection to wider groups of civilians, regulating the law of bombing, and enlarging the category of wars subject to the 1949 Conventions (to include, for example, civil wars). The 1949 Conventions are accepted by many states and are generally considered to embody customary international law that relates to war. *See also* HAGUE CONVENTIONS; MARTENS CLAUSE.

genitor *n.* The biological father of a child as distinct from the legal father.

genocide *n.* Conduct aimed at the destruction of a national, ethnic, racial, or religious group. Genocide, as defined in the United Nations Convention on the Prevention and Punishment of the Crime of Genocide 1948, includes not only killing members of the group, but also causing them serious physical or psychological harm, imposing conditions of life that are intended to destroy them physically or measures intended to prevent childbirth, or forcibly transferring children of the group to another group, if these acts are carried out with the intention of destroying the group as a whole or in part. Destruction of a cultural or political group does not amount to genocide. The Genocide Convention 1948 declares that genocide is an international crime; the parties to the Convention undertake to punish not only acts of genocide committed within their jurisdiction but also complicity in genocide and conspiracy, incitement, and attempts to commit genocide. The Convention has been enacted into English law by the Genocide Act 1969. It is generally considered that the Convention embodies principles of customary international law that bind all nations, including those that are not parties to the Convention. *See also* WAR CRIMES; HUMANITARIAN INTERVENTION.

genuine commercial reasons A number of *anti-avoidance provisions in tax law include a let-out whereby a transaction is not caught under the provisions if it can be shown that it was carried out for "genuine commercial reasons". Such a let-out is found, for example, in the legislation on transactions in securities, which imposes an income tax charge in place of a charge to capital gains tax: the Income Tax Act 2007 s 685 removes the income tax charge if the taxpayer shows that the transaction is carried out for genuine commercial reasons. The 2007 Act is a reenactment of the Taxes Act 1988, which referred to **bona fide commercial reasons**. In the view of the tax-law rewrite committee, there is no difference in the meaning of the two phrases and case law under the former provision continues to be directly applicable. In *Laird Group plc v IRC* [1999] STC 86 it was held that a bona fide commercial reason can include a non-financial reason. Thus, a view that it is important for the future prosperity of a company to maintain family control of that company can be a bona fide commercial reason. A bona fide commercial reason can be unconnected with the company itself. In *Clarke v IRC* [1978] STC 614, a farmer sold shares in a company he controlled in order to raise money to buy another farm. It was held that he made the sale for a bona fide commercial reason and the income tax assessment raised on the sale was cancelled.

ghet *n.* A Jewish religious divorce, executed by the husband delivering a bill of divorce (which must be handwritten according to specific detailed rules) to his wife in the presence of two witnesses. In theory a ghet does not require a court procedure, but in practice it is usually executed through a court because of the many complexities of the relevant religious law. *See also* EXTRAJUDICIAL DIVORCE.

gift *n.* A gratuitous transfer or grant of property. A legally valid gift must normally be effected by deed, by physical delivery in the case of chattels, or by **donatio mortis causa*; the donor must intend ownership to pass as a gift. However, an **imperfect gift** (i.e. one for which the legal formalities have not been observed) may be treated as valid in equity in certain circumstances (*see* ESTOPPEL). A gift by will takes effect only on the death of the testator.

A gift is a disposal for *capital gains tax purposes and tax is potentially payable, unless *holdover relief can be claimed. A gift is likewise a *transfer of value for *inheritance tax purposes. If the gift is made by an individual to an individual or to a trust with an *interest in possession, the gift is a *potentially exempt transfer that will only attract a charge to inheritance tax if the donor dies within seven years of the gift. If the gift is to a *discretionary trust, it is an immediately chargeable transfer.

gift aid A system enabling money donated to a charity by an individual or a company to be treated as if it were a net sum from which tax at basic rate had been deducted. Thus, the charity can reclaim the deemed basic rate credit. If the taxpayer is subject to tax at higher rate, relief at that higher rate can be obtained by the taxpayer bringing the charitable donation into his self-assessment for the tax year in which the donation is made. The taxpayer must make a **gift aid declaration** to the charity. This declaration can, unusually in tax matters, be made retrospectively and specify that all donations made on or after 6 April 2000 shall be treated by the charity as having been made under gift aid. There are equivalent tax-effective arrangements whereby relief is obtained on the gift of land, stocks and shares, or plant and machinery. Tax relief is not available where the gift is a "tainted donation" (essentially one from which the donor or a connected person derives some advantage: Finance Act 2011 sch 3).

gift over A provision in a will or other settlement enabling an interest in property to come into existence on the termination or failure of a prior interest. An example of such a provision would be a gift "to my wife during her lifetime and on her death to my brother". The provision for the brother is a gift over.

gift with reservation Gift by an individual of property where either (1) possession and enjoyment of the property is not bona fide assumed by the donee or (2) the property is not enjoyed to the entire exclusion, or virtually the entire exclusion, of the donor and of any benefit to him by contract or otherwise (Finance Act 1986 s 102 and sch 20).

Where there is a gift with reservation, the gift is charged to *inheritance tax in the normal way. For the purpose of computing inheritance tax at death, however, the property gifted is treated as if it remained in the estate of the donor. There is, thus, potentially a double charge to inheritance tax; in such cases a statutory instrument operates to charge the higher of the two liabilities.

Gillick-competence In medical law, the status of a child under 16 who has sufficient maturity and understanding to *consent to a particular medical treatment. Once a child is deemed by a medical professional to be Gillick-competent, he can be treated without the consent or knowledge of his parents. The refusal to have treatment by a Gillick-competent child can, however, be overridden by the courts, by his parents, or by someone with *parental responsibility. The term refers to the decision in the case *Gillick v West Norfolk and Wisbech Area Health Authority* [1985] 3 All ER 402 (HL).

gipsy (gypsy) *n.* A person of a nomadic way of life with no fixed abode. Formerly, local authorities had a duty to provide sites for gipsies resorting to their areas. (The strict definition of gipsy as a member of the Romany race did not apply for this purpose, but the term did not include travelling showmen or New Age travellers.) Under the Criminal Justice and Public Order Act 1994 this duty is abolished, although local authorities may provide sites if they wish. *See also* TRESPASS; UNAUTHORIZED CAMPING.

glebe *n.* Land possessed as part of the property of an ecclesiastical benefice.

GLO *See* GROUP LITIGATION.

glue sniffing *See* INTOXICATION.

going equipped A person is guilty of "going equipped" if, when not at his place of abode, he has with him any article for use in the course of or in connection with any burglary or theft (Theft Act 1968 s 25). A "place of abode" is not defined in the Act but has a wide meaning (*R v Bundy* [1977] 1 WLR 914 (CA)).

going public The process of forming a *public company or of reregistering a *private company as a public company.

golden handshake A payment, usually very large, made to a director or other senior executive who is forced to retire before the expiry of an employment contract (e.g. because of a takeover or merger) as compensation for loss of office. It is made when a contract does not allow payment in lieu of notice. The first £30,000 is often tax-free.

golden hello A lump-sum payment to entice an employee of senior level to join a new employer. Whether or not the payment is tax-free depends on the nature of the payment.

golden rule *See* INTERPRETATION; INTERPRETATION OF WILLS.

golden share *See* SHARE.

good behaviour A term used in an order by a magistrate (Justice of the Peace Act 1361; Magistrates' Courts Act 1980) or by a Crown Court (Justices of the Peace Act 1968 s 1) upon sentencing. The person named in the order should "be of good behaviour" towards another person (e.g. the victim). The court may order that the person named enter into a *recognizance, and if he does not comply with the order he may be imprisoned for up to six months. The procedure may be used against anyone who has been brought before the court if there is a fear that he may cause a breach of the peace or if he is the subject of a complaint by someone (which need not be based on the commission of a criminal offence). *See* BIND OVER; KEEP THE PEACE.

good consideration *See* CONSIDERATION.

good faith   Honesty. An act carried out in good faith is one carried out honestly. Good faith is implied by law into certain contracts, such as those relating to commercial agency. *See also* UBERRIMAE FIDEI.

good leasehold title   A form of title to registered leasehold land (*see* LAND REGISTRATION) that is equivalent to absolute leasehold title (*see* ABSOLUTE TITLE) except that the landlord's right to grant the lease is not guaranteed. Good leasehold title usually occurs when the lease appears valid on the face of it but the documents proving the landlord's title, or any superior lessor's title, have not been registered at the Land Registry.

good offices   A technique of peaceful settlement of an international dispute, in which a third party, acting with the consent of the disputing states, serves as a friendly intermediary in an effort to persuade them to negotiate between themselves without necessarily offering the disputing states substantive suggestions towards achieving a settlement. A good example occurred during the 1979–80 Iranian hostage crisis, when Iran and the USA resolved the crisis by means of the good offices of the Algerian government. Iran released the US and Canadian hostages to Algeria. *See also* CONCILIATION; MEDIATION.

goods   *pl. n.* Personal chattels or items of property. Land is excluded, and the statutory definition in the Sale of Goods Act 1979 also excludes *choses in action and money. It includes *emblements and things attached to or forming part of land that are agreed to be severed before sale or under a contract of sale. *Compare* SERVICES.

goodwill   *n.* The advantage arising from the reputation and trade connections of a business, in particular the likelihood that existing customers will continue to patronize it. Goodwill is a substantial item to be taken into account on the sale of a business. It may need to be protected by prohibiting the vendor from setting up in the same business for a stated period in competition with the business he has sold.

government circulars   Documents circulated by government departments on behalf of ministers, setting out policies, principles, and practices for the exercise of ministerial powers delegated to public officials. In some instances circulars provide mere administrative guidelines and have no legal effect. However, where circulars give effect to statutory requirements (e.g. circulars providing guidance to local planning authorities under the Town and Country Planning Act 1990) they will have legal effect. In such cases circulars are subject to *judicial review. On matters of general policy where controversial issues are involved, government by circular is not a satisfactory substitute for legislation, nor can such circulars require the performance of unlawful acts (*Gillick v West Norfolk and Wisbech Area Health Authority* [1986] 1 AC 112 (HL)).

government department   An organ of central government responsible for a particular sphere of public administration (e.g. the Treasury). It is staffed by permanent civil servants and is normally headed by a minister who is politically responsible for its activities and is assisted by one or more junior ministers, usually responsible for particular aspects of departmental policy.

government-in-exile   *n.* A government established outside its territorial jurisdiction. Following the German defeat of Poland in 1939, the Polish government transferred its operations to London and thereby became a government-in-exile.

Grand Committee   **1.** Any of the three committees of the House of Commons involved with matters relating to Scotland, Wales, and Northern Ireland. The **Scottish**

Grand Committee consists of the 72 members representing Scottish constituencies. A Bill certified by the Speaker as relating exclusively to Scotland may by standing orders of the House be referred to the Committee for its second reading, and the Committee also debates other purely Scottish matters. The **Welsh Grand Committee**, which consists of the 40 members representing Welsh constituencies and up to 5 others, is purely deliberative. It considers matters relating exclusively to Wales but is not empowered to undertake second readings. The **Northern Ireland Grand Committee** consists of all 18 sitting Northern Irish members and up to 25 others. It debates matters relating exclusively to Northern Ireland. **2.** In the House of Lords, a committee convened to discuss any bill not committed to a *Committee of the whole House. Any member of the House may sit on the committee. The only difference from a Committee of the whole House is that no votes are taken; any changes to the bill must be agreed unanimously.

g

grant *n.* **1.** The creation or transfer of the ownership of property (e.g. an estate or interest in land) by written instrument; for example, the grant of a lease. *See also* LIE IN GRANT. **2.** A *grant of representation. **3.** The allocation of money, powers, etc., by Parliament or the Crown for a specific purpose.

grant for the use and benefit Where a minor or mentally incapable person is appointed executor of a will, a grant of *letters of administration for the use and benefit of the minor or incapacitated person is required to be made to another person. It is only required where the minor or incapacitated person is the only appointed executor or where other executors are not able or willing to act. A *cessate grant is then issued to the minor when he reaches 18. If a person entitled to a grant so wishes, letters of administration for his use and benefit may also be granted to his lawfully constituted attorney (Non-Contentious Probate Rules 1987 r 31–35).

grant of representation Either a grant of *probate or *letters of administration issued by the court to *personal representatives to administer the estate of a deceased person.

grants in aid Central government grants towards local authority expenditure, comprising specific grants for particular services (e.g. the police) and revenue support grants to augment income generally.

gravamen *n.* The substantial grievance or complaint that forms the grounds of an action.

grave hardship (in divorce proceedings) If a divorce petition is based on a five-year under the Matrimonial Causes Act 1973 s 5(1) separation, the respondent may oppose the grant of the *decree nisi on the ground that the dissolution of the marriage will result in grave financial or other hardship and that it would be wrong in all the circumstances to dissolve the marriage. Such applications rarely succeed. *See also* DIVORCE.

Gray's Inn One of the four *Inns of Court, situated in Holborn, London. The earliest claims for its existence are *c.*1370.

Greater London A local government area consisting of the 32 **London boroughs** (12 inner, and 20 outer), the *City of London, and the Inner and Middle Temples. A Greater London Council was established by the Local Government Act 1972 but abolished by the Local Government Act 1985 with effect from 1 April 1986. London borough councils, which are unitary (single-tier) authorities, are elected every fourth year, counting from 1982 (*see also* LOCAL AUTHORITY). In 1998 Londoners voted in favour of government proposals to elect a *Mayor of London and a *London Assembly to operate from 2000; the Great London Authority Act 1999 enacted these proposals (*see also* GREATER LONDON AUTHORITY). The City of London is distinct in both constitution and functions. The Temples have limited independent functions (e.g. public health), but are administered in many respects by the City's Common Council.

Greater London Authority A body created by the Greater London Authority Act 1999 and consisting of the *Mayor of London and the *London Assembly. Its principal purposes are to promote economic development and wealth creation, social development, and the improvement of the environment in Greater London. The *London Development Agency was created to further the first of these aims.

green form *See* LEGAL AID.

green paper *See* COMMAND PAPERS.

grievous bodily harm (GBH) Really serious physical injury (*R v Smith* [1961] AC 290). In *R v Burstow* [1998] 1 Cr App R 177 it was conceded that severe depression could amount to serious bodily harm.

   Under the Offences Against the Person Act 1861 there are several offences involving grievous bodily harm. It is an offence under section 20, punishable by up to five years' imprisonment, to *inflict* grievous bodily harm upon anyone with the intention to cause any amount of harm (however slight) or while reckless to the risk of causing any amount of harm. It is an offence under section 18, punishable by a maximum sentence of life imprisonment, to *cause* grievous bodily harm to anyone with the intention of causing serious injury or of resisting or preventing lawful arrest. It had been thought that there was a distinction between the use of the verbs "inflict" and "cause" but it would now seem that they cover the same activities. If a person intends to cause grievous bodily harm but his victim actually dies, he is guilty of murder, even though he did not intend to kill. The courts have said that judges should not attempt to define grievous bodily harm for the jury, but should leave it to them, in every case, to decide whether the harm caused was really serious. *See also* WOUNDING WITH INTENT.

gross *See* IN GROSS.

gross indecency Formerly, a sexual act considered to be more than ordinary *indecency but not involving actual intercourse. Under the Sexual Offences Act 2003 certain consensual acts formerly categorized as acts of gross indecency were decriminalized, whereas other acts were recategorized under the new offences of *sexual assault and *sexual activity with a child.

gross negligence A high degree of *negligence, manifested in behaviour substantially worse than that to be expected of the average reasonable man. The distinction between negligence and gross negligence can be important in criminal law, notably in cases of **gross negligence manslaughter**. Here, in the words of Lord Hewart CJ in *R v Bateman* (1925) 19 Cr App R8, "in order to establish criminal liability the facts must be such that, in the opinion of the jury, the negligence of the accused went beyond a mere matter of compensation between subjects and showed such disregard for the life and safety of others as to amount to a crime against the State and conduct deserving punishment." Bateman was a doctor who negligently supervised the labour of a woman giving birth with the result that she died. A defendant may therefore be guilty of *manslaughter by gross negligence if: (1) the defendant owed the victim a duty of care; (2) the defendant breached that duty; (3) the breach of duty caused the death of the victim; and (4) the jury decides that the breach is serious enough to be characterized as gross negligence and thus a crime (*R v Adomako* [1995] 1 AC 171 (HL)).

ground rent A rent reserved by a long lease of land. For example when a house or flat is sold on a lease for 99 years, the lessor may reserve a small annual rent payable throughout the term as well as the capital price payable on the grant of the lease. In essence, a ground rent ignores the value of the buildings on the land. *Building leases are sometimes granted in return for a ground rent rather than a capital sum.

group *n.* For tax purposes, two or more companies constitute a group where one company holds more than 50% of the shares in the other company. Ownership must be beneficial. The test is usually applied to the voting share capital only. Where there is a group of companies, the availability of the lower rates of corporation tax is restricted. Where the links are made by share ownership of 75% and over, assets can be passed amongst the companies without a charge to *corporation tax. The transfer of land between companies in a 75% group is exempt from *stamp duty land tax.

group accounts *Accounts required by law to be prepared by a registered company that has a *subsidiary company. Group accounts deal with the financial position of the company and its subsidiaries collectively.

group litigation In civil proceedings, a procedure in which the court makes a **Group Litigation Order** (**GLO**) where a large number of claims give rise to common or related issues of fact or law. Such claims might include personal injury claims arising from a public transport disaster, industrial disease, or the side effects of a medicine. Rules relating to *case management by the court under a Group Litigation Order are set out at Part 19 of the *Civil Procedure Rules. *Compare* REPRESENTATIVE CLAIM.

group relief In contrast to the approach in some other jurisdictions, in the UK the charge to *CORPORATION tax is levied separately on each separate company. There is no aggregating of profits within a group of companies. However, where one member company of a group makes a loss, a claim can be made for that loss to be relieved against the profits of another member of the group. In order to obtain such group relief, at least 75% of the shares of the company surrendering the loss must be held (directly or indirectly) by the company claiming relief. There is also provision for group relief where a loss-making company is owned by a consortium of companies.

Guantanamo Bay A naval base situated at the SE end of Cuba: it has been leased by the USA since the Cuban American Treaty of 1903. Since 2002 the military prison at the base has been used as a detention centre for some 780 alleged terrorists and military combatants, mainly captured in Afghanistan and Iraq. It currently holds about 170 inmates, mostly without charge. In June 2008 the US Supreme Court in *Boumediene v Bush* 553 US (2008) held against the US government with regard to its treatment of certain detainees at the base. The Court held that the Military Commissions Act of 2006 violated the constitutional right of non-US nationals held at Guantanamo Bay by depriving them of a meaningful *habeas corpus review by federal civilian judges. Plans to close the facility were announced in 2009.

guarantee *n.* **1.** A secondary agreement in which a person (the **guarantor**) is liable for the debt or default of another (the principal debtor), who is the party primarily liable for the debt. A guarantee requires an independent *consideration and must be evidenced in writing. A guarantor who has paid out on his guarantee has a right to be indemnified by the principal debtor. *Compare* INDEMNITY. **2.** *See* WARRANTY.

guarantee company *See* LIMITED COMPANY.

guarantee payment Under the Employment Rights Act 1996, the sum that an employer must pay to an employee for whom he is unable to provide work during the whole of any working day or shift. However, an employee is not entitled to a guarantee payment if he is laid off because of industrial action affecting his own or an associated employer, if he unreasonably refuses other suitable work, or if he fails to comply with the employer's reasonable requirements for ensuring that he is available for work if and when needed. Employees only become entitled to a guarantee payment after a month's *continuous employment in the business. The payment is limited to the employee's basic wage for the relevant shift, subject to a maximum prescribed by regulations that are reviewed annually (£24.20 a day in 2013). An employee is not entitled to more than five guarantee payments in any period of three months. The statutory payment is offset by any amount payable to the employee under his employment contract while he is laid off. An employee may complain to an employment tribunal if his employer fails to pay him any sum due as a guarantee payment, and the tribunal can order the employer to pay the sum due.

guard dog A dog kept specifically for the purpose of protecting people and/or property. Under the Guard Dogs Act 1975 it is a summary offence punishable by fine to use a guard dog, or to allow its use, unless either it is secured and cannot roam the premises freely or a handler is controlling it. The Act does not, however, affect civil liability for injuries or damage caused by the dog, which depends on the law of tort (*see* ANIMALS). In some cases the owner may be criminally liable for injury caused by a guard dog; for example, if it kills someone, the owner may be guilty of manslaughter by gross negligence or of constructive *manslaughter. *See also* DANGEROUS ANIMALS.

guardian *n.* One who is formally appointed to look after a child's interests on the death of the child's parents. Under the Children Act s 5 appointment can be made either by the courts during *family proceedings, if it is considered necessary for the child's welfare, or privately by any parent with parental responsibility. A private appointment does not have to be by deed or will but merely made in writing, dated, and signed by the person making it. A guardian automatically has *parental responsibility for the child.

guardian *ad litem* A former term for a *children's guardian. *See* AD LITEM; CHILDREN'S GUARDIAN; LITIGATION FRIEND.

guardianship order An order, made under the Mental Health Act 2007, placing a person over the age of 16 who is suffering a *mental disorder under the guardianship of a local social services authority or (rarely) an approved person. Such an order can only be made if it is judged necessary for the welfare of the individual concerned or the protection of others.

guillotine *n.* A House of Commons procedure for speeding up the passing of legislation: a means whereby government can control the parliamentary timetable and limit debate. The number of days allowed for a Bill's Committee and Report stages is limited by an allocation-of-time order moved by the government; the total time available is then allotted between particular portions of the Bill. When the time limit for any portion is reached, debate on it ceases and all outstanding votes are taken forthwith. *Compare* CLOSURE.

guilty *adj.* **1.** An admission in court by an accused person that he has committed the offence with which he is charged. If there is more than one charge he may plead guilty to some and *not guilty to others. **2.** A *verdict finding that the accused has committed the offence with which he was charged or some other offence of which he can be convicted on the basis of the evidence in the case. *See also* CONVICTION.

guilty knowledge The knowledge of facts or circumstances required for a person to have *mens rea* for a particular crime. Knowledge is usually actual knowledge, but when a person deliberately ignores facts that are obvious, he is sometimes considered to have "constructive" knowledge.

guilty mind *See* MENS REA.

gunboat diplomacy The settling of disputes with weaker states by the threat of *use of force. The phrase derives from the Victorian empire, in which gunboats and other naval vessels were often utilized to coerce local rulers to accept the terms and trade of British merchants. The history of the British navy in the 19th century provides many examples, including the threatened bombardment of Athens at the time of the Don Pacifico affair (1850). More recent examples involve the use of carrier-borne forces in Tanzania and the Persian Gulf in the 1960s.

gypsy *n. See* GIPSY.

habeas corpus A prerogative writ used to challenge the validity of a person's detention, either in official custody (e.g. when held pending deportation or extradition) or in private hands. Deriving from the royal prerogative and therefore originally obtained by petitioning the sovereign, it is now issued by the Divisional Court of the Queen's Bench Division, or, during vacation, by any High Court judge. If on an application for the writ the Court or judge is satisfied that the detention is prima facie unlawful, the custodian is ordered to appear and justify it, failing which release is ordered.

habendum *n.* [Latin: that which is held] A clause of a *conveyance that determines the quantity of interest conveyed. The habendum clause indicates what kind of estate the grantee takes (e.g. *freehold, *tenant in tail, *tenant for life, etc).

habitual residence The place or country in which a person has his home. Habitual residence is necessary in order to establish *domicile.

hacking *n.* Gaining unauthorized access to a computer system. This is currently a summary offence under the Computer Misuse Act 1990; when the Police and Justice Act 2006 (s 35 (3)) comes into force the offence will become triable either way. Under the 1990 Act it is also an offence, triable summarily or on indictment, to engage in hacking with the intention of committing another offence (e.g. theft, diverting funds), or to destroy, corrupt, or modify computer-stored information or programs while hacking. This offence can be committed either through using one computer to gain access to another computer or simply by gaining access to one computer only. *Copyright protection applies. *See also* DATA PROTECTION.

Hague Convention on the Civil Aspects of International Child Abduction
An international treaty signed by more than 50 countries that enables disputes involving the wrongful removal of children to be resolved according to principles set out in the Convention. Generally, any dispute should be resolved in the country where the child is habitually resident and, so long as the application is brought within 12 months of the removal, the court must order the return of the child unless one of the defences set out in the Convention applies. The most important of these are (i) that the child, if returned, would be exposed to physical or psychological harm or would be placed in an intolerable situation; and (ii) that a child who has attained a sufficient age and degree of maturity objects to being returned. *See* CHILD ABDUCTION.

Hague Conventions The Hague Conventions for the Pacific Settlement of International Disputes: a series of international conventions on the laws of war (3 in 1899 and 13 in 1907). The 1899 Conventions established a *Permanent Court of Arbitration, which was active before the Permanent Court of International Justice and the *International Court of Justice functioned. The Hague Conventions are still in force but their provisions are often inapplicable to modern warfare. *See also* GENERAL PARTICIPATION CLAUSE; GENEVA CONVENTIONS; MARTENS CLAUSE.

Hague Rules *See* BILL OF LADING; INTERNATIONAL CARRIAGE.

half a year (in a lease) A *fixed term that begins on a quarter day and ends on the next but one quarter day.

half blood *See* CONSANGUINITY.

half-secret trust (semi-secret trust) A trust whose existence is disclosed on the face of the will or other document creating it but the beneficiaries of which are undisclosed, though known to the secret trustee(s). For example, A may leave property in his will to B "to be held on trust on terms that have already been communicated to him." It is not necessary for the word "trust" to be used. The leading case on half-secret trusts is *Blackwell v Blackwell* [1929] AC 318. *See also* SECRET TRUST.

Hamburg Rules *See* BILL OF LADING; INTERNATIONAL CARRIAGE.

handguns *See* FIREARM.

handling stolen goods Dishonestly receiving goods that one knows or believes to be stolen or undertaking, arranging, or assisting someone to retain, remove, or dispose of stolen goods (*R v Woods* [1960] 1 QB 447). Under the Theft Act 1968, this is an offence subject to a maximum sentence of 14 years' imprisonment. "Stolen goods" include not only goods that have been the subject of *theft but also anything that has been obtained by *blackmail or *deception. The theft or other crime may have occurred at any time and anywhere in the world, provided the handling occurs in England or Wales. There is also a provision to extend the concept of stolen goods to the proceeds of their sale. Thus if A steals goods, sells them for £3,000, and gives part of the money to B, B is guilty of handling if he knows the money represents the proceeds of the sale of stolen goods. If A then buys a car with the rest of the £3,000 and C agrees to dispose of the car for A, knowing or believing that it was bought with the proceeds of sale of stolen goods, C will also be guilty of handling, since he has "undertaken to dispose of stolen goods". The crime is therefore very widely defined; it also covers, for instance, forging or providing new documents and number plates for stolen cars and contacting and negotiating with dealers in stolen property (fences). *See also* DISHONESTY.

Hansard *n.* The name by which the Official Report of Parliamentary Debates is customarily referred to (after the Hansard family, who – as printers to the House of Commons – were concerned with compiling reports in the 19th century). Reporting was taken over by the government in 1908, and separate reports for the House of Commons and the House of Lords are published by The *Stationery Office in daily and weekly parts. The reports, which are available online, contain a verbatim record of debates and all other proceedings (e.g. question time). Members of Parliament have the right to correct anything attributed to them, but may not make any other alterations. In certain circumstances Hansard may be used to discover the will of Parliament, as an aid to judicial statutory interpretation when legislation is unclear. *Compare* JOURNALS.

(⊕) SEE WEB LINKS

• Online version of Hansard: provides verbatim records of proceedings in both Houses of Parliament

harassment *n.* **1.** Under amendments made in 1994 to the Public Order Act 1986, an offence is committed when harassment, alarm, or distress is caused to the victim. Under the Protection from Harassment Act 1997, harassment constitutes a criminal offence and victims of harassment may obtain restraining orders and damages where appropriate. *See* HARASSMENT OF DEBTORS; HARASSMENT OF OCCUPIER; NUISANCE NEIGHBOURS; STALKING; THREATENING BEHAVIOUR. **2.** A form of prohibited *discrimination on grounds of sex, race, age, gender reassignment, sexual orientation, religion or belief, or disability that occurs where someone is subjected to unwanted conduct that has the purpose or effect of violating their dignity or creating an intimidating, hostile, degrading, humiliating, or offensive environment. Case: *Richmond Pharmacology Ltd v Dhaliwal* [2009] UK EAT/045/08, [2009] IRLR 336. Sexual harassment occurs where the unwanted conduct is of a sexual nature.

harassment of debtors Behaviour designed to force a debtor or one believed to be a debtor to pay his debt. This is a criminal offence, punishable by fine, if the debt is based on a contract and the nature or frequency of the acts subject the debtor (or members of his household) to alarm, distress, or humiliation. Harassment also includes false statements that the debtor will face criminal proceedings or that the creditor is officially authorized to enforce payment and using a document that the creditor falsely represents as being official. The offence may overlap with the crime of *blackmail, but it will also cover cases in which the creditor believes he is entitled to act as he does (which might not amount to blackmail).

harassment of occupier The offence of a landlord (or his agent) using or threatening violence or any other kind of pressure to obtain possession of his property from a tenant (the residential occupier) without a court order. The offence is found in the Protection from Eviction Act 1977 and includes interfering with the tenant's peace or comfort (or that of the tenant's household), withdrawing or not providing services normally required by the tenant (e.g. cutting off gas or electricity, even when the bills have not been paid), and preventing the tenant from exercising any of his rights or taking any legal or other action in respect of his tenancy. The Act does not apply, however, to a displaced residential owner, as opposed to a landlord (*see also* FORCIBLE ENTRY). The Criminal Justice and Police Act 2001 (s 42A) states that it is an offence to harass a person in his home. The Protection from Harassment Act 1997 prohibits harassment; the offence is punishable with a jail sentence of up to five years. *See also* NUISANCE NEIGHBOURS.

harbouring *n.* Hiding a criminal or suspected criminal. This will normally constitute the offence of *impeding apprehension or prosecution. *See also* ESCAPE.

hard law *See* SOFT LAW.

harmonization of laws The process by which member states of the EU make changes in their national laws, in accordance with *Community legislation, to produce uniformity, particularly relating to commercial matters of common interest. The Council of the European Union has, for example, issued directives on the harmonization of company law and of units of measurement. *Compare* APPROXIMATION OF LAWS.

hay bote *See* ESTOVERS.

hazardous waste Any waste substance that is considered harmful to human health or the environment because it possesses one or more of 15 properties listed in the EU's Revised Waste Framework Directive (Council Directive 98/2008). A list of such substances can be found in the European Waste Catalogue. There are stringent regulations governing the production, pretreatment, movement, and disposal of all such wastes and imposing a regime of monitoring and inspection. The European legislation has been implemented in the UK by the Landfill Regulations 2002, the Hazardous Waste Regulations 2005 (as amended 2009), the List of Wastes Regulations 2005 (as amended 2009), and the Waste Regulations 2011. *See also* WASTE DISPOSAL.

headings *pl. n.* Words prefixed to sections of a statute. They are treated in the same way as *preambles and may be used to assist in resolving an ambiguity.

Health and Safety Executive (HSE) A body responsible for furthering the general purposes of the Health and Safety at Work Act 1974, for example by giving advice and promoting research and training, and for enforcing the Act through such inspectorates as the Factories and Nuclear Installations Inspectorates. The HSE merged with its associated body, the Health and Safety Commission, on 1 April 2008. Following the merger, the former HSE board became the senior management team. *See also* SAFETY AT WORK.

((()) SEE WEB LINKS
- Website of the HSE: provides information and guidelines on a wide range of health and safety topics, including those applicable to particular industries

Health and Wellbeing Boards New bodies established as part of the major restructuring of the *National Health Service in April 2013. Every 'upper-tier' local authority is now required to establish a Health and Wellbeing Board to act as a forum for local commissioners in the NHS, as well as those in social care, public health, and other related services. The boards are intended to: increase democratic input into strategic decisions about health and social care services; strengthen working relationships between those involved in providing these services; and encourage integrated commissioning.

Healthcare Commission An independent body set up to assess the performance of NHS healthcare and public health services; to award annual performance ratings for each *NHS Trust; and to regulate the independent healthcare sector. Under the Health and Social Care Act 2008 its functions were taken over by the *Care Quality Commission for England.

health records Records kept by the *National Health Service about patients. Access to the health records of living patients is governed by the Data Protection Act 1998, which gives everyone the right to apply for access to their health records, irrespective of when they were compiled. A health record is defined as a record consisting of information about the physical or mental health or condition of an identifiable individual made by or on behalf of a health professional in connection with the care of that individual. Access to the health records of a deceased person continues to be governed by the Access to Health Records Act 1990.

Health Service Commissioners (Health Service Ombudsmen) Commissioners who undertake independent investigations into complaints about the *National Health Service and (since 1996) also investigate complaints about general practitioners, dentists, pharmacists, and opticians. Complaints must be made directly to a Commissioner within one year of the date on which the matter first came to the complainant's notice. Certain matters (e.g. alleged professional negligence) are excluded from investigation. In England the office is held by the *Parliamentary Ombudsman. In Wales, from April 2006, the Public Services Ombudsman for Wales investigates complaints against the Health Service and other public bodies (Public Service Ombudsman (Wales) Act 2005). The Scottish Public Services Ombudsman has been exercising similar functions in Scotland since October 2002.

hearing *n.* Any appearance of a case before a court, including *trial. Under Article 6 of the *European Convention on Human Rights parties have the right to a public hearing. Court hearings may, however, be held in private in certain exceptional circumstances (*see* IN CAMERA). The *Civil Procedure Rules allow for telephone hearings in certain circumstances.

Hearing Officer An officer of the *European Court of Justice whose role was established in 1982 after criticism of the administrative nature of the decision-making process of the Commission in *competition law cases. His terms of reference were published in the Commission's XXth Report on Competition Policy. He organizes and chairs hearings, decides the date, duration, and place of hearings, seeks to ensure protection of the interests of defendants, and supervises the preparation of minutes of hearings. He will, in addition, prepare his own report of a hearing and make recommendations as to the future conduct of the matter.

hearsay evidence Oral or written statements made by someone other than during his *testimony in court but which the court is asked to accept as evidence for the truth of what is stated. In general, hearsay evidence has been inadmissible (the **rule against hearsay**) but this principle has always been subject to numerous exceptions. In civil proceedings, the Civil Evidence Act 1995 abolished the rule against hearsay and provides that what would formerly have been called "hearsay evidence" may be used when a notice of the intention to rely on that evidence is given. It is for the court to decide at trial what weight to put on any particular evidence, whether it is hearsay or not. The admissibility of hearsay evidence in criminal proceedings is now governed by the Criminal Justice Act 2003, which provides that a statement not made in oral evidence in the proceedings may be admissible as evidence of any matter stated if the court is satisfied that it is in the interests of justice for it to be admissible. The Criminal Justice Act 2003 specifically provides for the admissibility of the hearsay evidence of unavailable witnesses and preserves the common law rules relating to the admissibility of *res gestae* and confessions in criminal proceedings. The Act also provides for the admissibility of previous inconsistent statements and other *previous statements, including complaints made by a victim as soon as could reasonably be expected after the offence was committed. In *Al-Khawaja and Tahery v United Kingdom* (2012) 54 EHRR 23 the European Court of Human Rights held that convictions based solely or decisively on hearsay evidence do not necessarily breach Article 6 of the European Convention on Human Rights, which protects the right to a *fair trial.

hedgerow *n.* A row of shrubs or small trees bordering a field or lane. Hedging of ancient origin is protected under the Hedgerow Regulations 1997. Farmers are required to notify local authorities of their intention to uproot a hedgerow, allowing time for a protection order to be issued; the notification period is currently 42 days. Failure to comply with the regulations is punishable by an unlimited fine.

hedonic damages *Compensation in which calculation of the amount paid is based upon an estimation of the future earnings of the injured party. *See* MULTIPLIER; OGDEN TABLES.

heir *n.* Before 1926, the person entitled under common law and statutory rules to inherit the freehold land of one who died intestate. The Administration of Estates Act 1925 abolished these rules of descent and the concept of heirship, except that *entailed interests and in certain very rare cases the property of mental patients devolve according to the old rules. In addition, the Law of Property Act 1925 provides that a conveyance of property in favour of the heir of a deceased person conveys it to the person who would be the heir under the old rules. Where these exceptions apply, an **heir apparent** is the person (e.g. an eldest son) who will inherit provided that he outlives his ancestor; an **heir**

presumptive is an heir (e.g. a daughter) whose right to inherit may be lost by the birth of an heir with greater priority (e.g. a son). *See also* HEIRS OF THE BODY.

heir apparent *See* HEIR.

heirloom *n.* A *chattel that, by custom or close association with land, passed on the owner's death with his house to his heir and did not form part of his residuary estate. Heirlooms now pass to the deceased's personal representatives unless special provision is made for them to pass to the heir direct. When heirlooms are held, together with land, under a settlement, the *tenant for life is entitled under the Settled Land Act 1925 to sell the heirlooms. The price is payable to the trustees as *capital money.

heir presumptive *See* HEIR.

heirs of the body Lineal descendants who were entitled to inherit freehold land under the rules applying on intestacy before the Administration of Estates Act 1925. A conveyance of land "to A and the heirs of his body" created an *entailed interest that devolved to descendants only, according to the old rules. Thus (1) males are first in priority and the principle of primogeniture applies, e.g. an older son is preferred to a younger; (2) in the absence of male heirs, females in equal degree share the land equally; and (3) lineal descendants of an heir represent him, thus the son of an older son who dies will inherit to the exclusion of a younger son.

Helms-Burton Act The Cuban Liberty and Democratic Solidarity (Libertad) Act 1996: an Act of the US Congress under which nationals of third states dealing with US property expropriated by the Cuban revolutionary state, using such property, or benefiting by it may be sued for damages before American courts and even face being barred from entry into the United States. The Act was approved by President Clinton in response to the shooting down by the Cuban Air Force of two light aeroplanes flown by a Cuban-American Organization based in Florida in February 1996. Despite the broad powers in Helms–Burton, no suit was filed in a US court during the Clinton era because the president had suspended that portion of the legislation (Title III) before it took effect and renewed his suspension every six months, as the law allows, until the end of his term. President Clinton's decision to suspend Title III came after the European Union and Canada announced their opposition to the Act. They argued the provisions violate international trade treaties by punishing foreign companies for business conducted outside US borders. The EU brought its case to the World Trade Organization, but dropped its legal challenge in 1998. The USA and EU are still working toward an agreement on the issue. In July 2001 President Bush enacted a six-month waiver of provisions of the 1996 Act that would allow lawsuits against foreign companies who deal with Cuban businesses once claimed by US nationals.

help at court *See* LEGAL AID.

hereditament *n.* **1.** Historically, any real property capable of being passed to an *heir. **Corporeal hereditaments** are tangible items of property, such as land and buildings. **Incorporeal hereditaments** are intangible rights in land, such as easements and profits *à prendre*. **2.** A unit of land that has been separately assessed for rating purposes.

heritage property Property that has been certified by HM Treasury as of national, scientific, historical, or artistic interest. *Inheritance tax is not payable on such property until the property is sold by the donee. Heritage property can include pictures, prints, manuscripts, works of art, or scientific collections. Certification can also be given for land of outstanding scenic or historic interest or land that is essential for the protection of the character or amenities of a building of outstanding historic or archaeological interest.

Her Majesty's Stationery Office (HMSO) Formerly, the government's official publisher. Following privatization in 1996 most of its functions were taken over by The *Stationery Office but certain core functions of HMSO have been retained. These include administration of Crown and Parliamentary copyright, overseeing the functions of the Queen's Printer in relation to Acts of Parliament, statutory instruments, and some other material of an official or legislative nature, and provision of official publications to members of the European Parliament. HMSO now operates within the new *Office of Public Sector Information.

HHSRS *See* HOUSING HEALTH AND SAFETY RATING SYSTEM.

high contracting parties The representatives of states who have signed or ratified a *treaty. From the point of view of international law it is immaterial where the treaty-making power resides (e.g. in a head of state, a senate, or a representative body): this is a question determinable by the constitutional law of the particular contracting state concerned. Other nations are entitled only to demand from those with whom they contract a *de facto* capacity to bind the society that they represent. The House of Lords has held that the determination of who the high contracting parties are is to be based upon the terms of the individual treaty in question. Thus the signatories, as well as the parties, can be considered to be high contracting parties.

High Court Enforcement Officer An officer responsible for the *enforcement of judgments of the High Court by executing writs of *fieri facias*, *writs of possession, and *writs of delivery. *See also* SHERIFF.

High Court of Justice A court created by the Judicature Acts 1873–75. It is one of the Senior Courts of England and Wales. Under Part 7 of the *Civil Procedure Rules, which sets out the rules for starting proceedings, the High Court is restricted to (1) personal injury claims of £50,000 or more, (2) other claims exceeding £15,000, (3) specialist High Court claims that are required to be placed on a specialist list (e.g. the Commercial List), and (4) claims that are required by statute to be commenced in the High Court. The High Court has *appellate jurisdiction in civil and criminal matters. It is divided into the three Divisions: the *Queen's Bench Division, *Chancery Division, and *Family Division.

high hedges Where the owner or occupier of a domestic property believes that his reasonable enjoyment of that property is being adversely affected by a high hedge situated on land owned or occupied by another person, he may complain to the local authority under the Anti-social Behaviour Act 2003 (s 65). A high hedge is one rising to a height of more than two metres. The local authority may issue a remedial notice, which may require the reduction of the hedge to two metres in height. Neighbours are expected to try to resolve matters amicably before approaching the local authority, and frivolous or vexatious claims may be rejected.

high seas Under Article 13(1)(a) of the 1958 Geneva Convention on the High Seas, all parts of the sea that are not included in the *territorial waters or the *internal waters of a state. Article 87 of the UN Convention on the Law of the Sea 1982 guaranteed the principle of freedom of the high seas for both coastal and land-locked states. The high seas as defined by Article 86 of the UN Convention exclude the *exclusive economic zone. However, the freedoms of all states to fly over, navigate, lay submarine cables, etc., in the exclusive economic zone, as stated in the earlier Geneva Convention on the High Seas 1958, have been preserved in Article 58 (1) of the UN Convention.

The English courts have jurisdiction to try offences committed by anyone anywhere on the high seas in a British ship. They also have jurisdiction to try offences committed anywhere in the world on board a British-controlled aircraft while it is in flight. *See also* DEEP SEABED AREA; LAW OF THE SEA; RES COMMUNIS.

highway *n.* A road or other way over which the public may pass and repass as of right. Highways include *footpaths, *bridleways, *driftways, *carriageways, and cul-de-sacs. Navigable rivers are also highways. A highway is created either under statutory powers or by dedication (express or implied) by a landowner and acceptance (by use) by the public. Once a highway has been created, it does not cease to be a highway by reason of disuse. Obstructing a highway is a public nuisance (*see also* OBSTRUCTION), and misuse of the public right to pass and repass over a highway is a trespass against the owner of the subsoil of the highway.

hijacking *n.* Seizing or exercising control of an aircraft in flight by the use or threat of force (the term derives from the call "Hi Jack," used when illegal alcohol was seized from bootleggers during Prohibition in the United States). Hijacking is prohibited in international law by the Tokyo Convention 1963, which defines the conditions under which jurisdiction may be assumed over hijackers, but does not oblige states to exercise such jurisdiction and does not create an obligation to extradite hijackers. There is also a Hague Convention of 1970 and a Montreal Convention of 1971 creating the offences of unlawfully seizing or exercising control of an aircraft by force or threats and of sabotaging aircraft; these conventions provide for compulsory jurisdiction as well as extradition. In English law, hijacking and similar offences are governed by the Hijacking Act 1971, the Protection of Aircraft Act 1973, and the Aviation Security Act 1982.

hire 1. *vb.* To enter into a contract for the temporary use of another's goods, or the temporary provision of his services or labour, in return for payment. In the case of goods, the person hiring them is a bailee (*see* BAILMENT). 2. *n.* **a.** The act of hiring. **b.** The payment made under a contract of hire.

hire purchase A method of buying goods in which the purchaser takes possession of them as soon as he has paid an initial instalment of the price (a **deposit**) and obtains ownership of the goods when he has paid all the agreed number of subsequent instalments and exercises his option to purchase the goods. A **hire-purchase agreement** differs from a *credit sale agreement and a sale-by-instalments contract because in these transactions ownership passes when the contract is signed. It also differs from a contract of *hire, because in this case ownership never passes. Hire-purchase agreements were formerly controlled by government regulations that stipulated the minimum deposit and the length of the repayment period. These controls were removed in July 1982. Hire-purchase agreements were also formerly controlled by the Hire Purchase Act 1965, but most are now regulated by the Consumer Credit Act 1974. In this Act a hire-purchase agreement is regarded as one in which goods are bailed in return for periodical payments by the bailee; ownership passes to the bailee if he complies with the terms of the agreement and exercises his option to purchase.

A hire-purchase agreement often involves a finance company as a third party. The seller of the goods sells them outright to the finance company, which enters into a hire-purchase agreement with the hirer. In this situation there is generally no direct contractual relationship between the seller and the buyer.

historic buildings *See* BUILDING PRESERVATION NOTICE; CONSERVATION AREA; HERITAGE PROPERTY; LISTED BUILDING.

HMOs *See* HOUSES IN MULTIPLE OCCUPATION.

HM Procurator General *See* TREASURY SOLICITOR.

HM Revenue and Customs *See* REVENUE AND CUSTOMS, HM.

HMSO *See* HER MAJESTY'S STATIONERY OFFICE.

holder *n.* The person in possession of a *bill of exchange or promissory note. He may be the payee, the endorsee, or the bearer. A holder may sue on the bill in his own name. When value (which includes a past debt or liability) has at any time been given for a bill, the holder is a **holder for value**, as regards the acceptor and all who were parties to the bill before value was given. A **holder in due course** is one who has taken a bill of exchange in good faith and for value, before it was overdue, and without notice of previous dishonour or of any defect in the title of the person who negotiated or transferred the bill. He holds the bill free from any defect of title of prior parties and may enforce payment against all parties liable on the bill.

holding company *See* SUBSIDIARY COMPANY.

holding out Conduct by one person that leads another to believe that he has an authority that does not in fact exist. By the doctrine of *estoppel, the first person may be prevented from denying that the authority exists. For example, a person who wrongly represents himself as being a partner in a firm will be as liable as if he were in fact a partner to anyone who gives credit to the firm on the faith of the representation.

holding over The action of a tenant continuing in occupation of premises after his lease has expired. If this is without the landlord's consent, the landlord may claim damages from the tenant (*see* MESNE PROFITS). If, however, a landlord accepts rent from a tenant who is holding over, a new tenancy may be created.

holdover relief A relief against *capital gains tax that may be claimed where certain assets are disposed of in the form of a *gift. The effect of the relief is that the gain chargeable to tax is "held over", so that the gain imputed to the donor is reduced to £nil. The amount by which the gain for the donor is reduced also reduces the acquisition cost imputed to the donee. This means that any gain arising from the donee's subsequent disposal of the asset will be correspondingly increased. There are currently two types of holdover relief: (1) where the capital gains tax disposal is also a chargeable transfer for inheritance tax purposes; (2) where the disposal is of a business, of shares in an unquoted trading company, or of agricultural land.

holiday pay Under the Working Time Regulations 1998, all workers are entitled to a period of paid holiday each year (*Byrne Bros Ltd v Baird* [2002] IRLR 96 (EAT)). In 2013 holiday entitlement was 5.6 weeks (28 days for those working a five-day week). There is pro-rata entitlement for part-timers. Employers are allowed to include bank holidays in holiday entitlement. An employee who is unable to take his holidays because of sickness can carry forward that period to the next year: *Revenue and Customs v Stringer* [2009] UKHL 31, [2009] 4 All ER 1205. *See* WORKING HOURS.

holograph *n.* A document written completely by the hand of its author; for example, a will in the testator's own handwriting.

home information pack (HIP) Formerly, a pack of relevant documents compiled by the vendor of land as required by the Home Information Pack Regulations 2006. The pack contained a sale statement, summarizing the terms of the sale; evidence of title; standard searches such as local authority searches and a drainage and water search; and an energy performance certificate, produced by a trained energy assessor. The requirement for a vendor to have such a pack was phased in from 1 August 2007, but suspended on 21 May 2010. Only an energy performance certificate is now required.

homeless person Under the Housing Act 1996, a person who has no living accommodation that he is entitled to occupy, or is unlawfully excluded from his own living accommodation, or whose accommodation is mobile and cannot be placed in a location where he is permitted to reside in it. Certain homeless people (e.g. the elderly or infirm or those with dependent children) have a statutory right to permanent local-authority accommodation or, if they became homeless intentionally, to temporary accommodation.

home-loss payment Additional compensation paid under the Land Compensation Act 1973 to a person on the compulsory acquisition of his property if he has occupied it as his principal residence throughout the preceding five years.

home rights The rights of a spouse or civil partner who is not a co-owner of the *matrimonial home to live in the home. A spouse or civil partner who is in occupation of the home has a right not to be evicted from it, and one who is not in occupation has a right to enter and occupy the home. *See also* OCCUPATION ORDER.

Homes and Communities Agency A body established under the Housing and Regeneration Act 2008 with a remit to deliver more new and affordable homes across all tenures and to drive and invest in regeneration. The Agency aims to provide decent places as well as decent homes, for example by grant funding social housing and investing in infrastructure. *See also* TENANT SERVICES AUTHORITY.

(⊕) SEE WEB LINKS
• Website of the Homes and Communities Agency

Home Secretary The minister in charge of the Home Office, who is responsible throughout England and Wales for law and order generally (including matters concerning the police and the prison and security services) and for a variety of other domestic matters, such as nationality, immigration, race relations, extradition, and deportation. He also advises the sovereign on the exercise of the *prerogative of mercy.

(⊕) SEE WEB LINKS
• Home Office website

homicide *n.* The killing of one human being by another. In English law there is no crime called homicide: what the law does is single out certain homicides that are considered to be unlawful or unjustifiable or inexcusable and make a crime of these. Crimes of unlawful homicide include *murder, *manslaughter, and *infanticide. Homicide can only be committed if the victim is an independent human being (*AG's Reference (No 3 of 1994)* [1997] 3 All ER 936) and the act itself causes the death (*see* CAUSATION). A British citizen may be tried for unlawful homicide committed anywhere in the world. **Lawful homicide** (sometimes termed **justifiable homicide**) occurs when somebody uses *reasonable force in preventing a crime or arresting an offender, in *self-defence or defence of others, or (possibly) in defence of his property, and causes death as a result. *See also* EXCUSABLE HOMICIDE.

homosexual conduct Sexual behaviour between persons of the same sex. Homosexual conduct is now (since 2003) regulated under the criminal law on grounds identical to that of heterosexual conduct.

honest opinion A statutory defence in *defamation. The defendant must show that the statement complained of was a statement of opinion (not of fact), that it indicates the basis of the opinion, and that this opinion could have been held by an honest person. The defence is defeated if the claimant can show that the defendant did not actually hold the opinion. Under the Defamation Act 2013 the defence of honest opinion replaced that of *fair comment.

honorarium *n.* A payment or reward made to a person for services rendered by him voluntarily.

honour clause An express statement in a *contract that an agreement is intended to be binding in honour only. The courts will usually allow it to take effect and so will not enforce the agreement. Case: *Rose and Frank v Crompton* [1925] AC 445 (HL).

horizontal agreements Agreements between companies at the same level of the supply chain; for example, agreements between two or more manufacturers or wholesalers, rather than between a manufacturer and a distributor (*compare* VERTICAL AGREEMENTS). Horizontal agreements that restrict competition may infringe the competition provisions of *Article 101 of the Treaty on the Functioning of the European Union and the Chapter I prohibition in the Competition Act 1998. Most *cartels are horizontal agreements. In 2011 the EU issued Horizontal Guidelines on how such agreements are to be treated under competition law.

hornbook *n.* A mostly US term for a one-volume work summarizing the elementary principles of law in a particular area (e.g. contract law, land law); a legal handbook.

hospital order An order of the Crown Court or a magistrates' court authorizing the detention in a specified hospital (for an initial period of six months, renewable by the hospital managers) of a convicted person suffering from *mental disorder. Unless a *restriction order has also been made, discharge while an order is in force may be authorized by the managers or the doctor in charge or directed by the *Mental Health Tribunal.

hostage *n.* A person who is held as a security. Under the Taking of Hostages Act 1982, it is an offence, punishable in the English courts by a maximum sentence of life imprisonment, to take anyone as a hostage against his will anywhere in the world and to threaten to kill, injure, or continue to hold him hostage in order to force a state, international governmental organization, or person to do or not to do something. This is an extraditable offence, but prosecutions may only be brought with the consent of the Attorney General. *See also* HIJACKING; KIDNAPPING.

hostile witness An *adverse witness who wilfully refuses to testify truthfully on behalf of the party who called him. A hostile witness may, with the permission of the court, be cross-examined by that party and have put to him a *previous statement that is inconsistent with his present testimony. Under the Criminal Justice Act 2003 where the witness admits making a previous inconsistent statement, or his previous inconsistent statement is proved against him, the statement is inadmissible as evidence of any matter stated of which oral evidence by him would be admissible.

hotchpot *n.* The bringing into account, on distribution of an intestate's estate, of certain benefits separately conferred on the beneficiaries. In the case of a total intestacy prior to 1 January 1996 the Administration of Estates Act 1925 (s 47(1)(iii)) expressly brings the *rule against double portions into operation. It provides that property given by the intestate during his lifetime to any of his children must be brought into account, unless a contrary intention is expressed or appears from the circumstances. Thus if A gives £10,000 to his son B, and dies intestate leaving an estate worth £50,000 to which his children B and C are entitled equally, B will in fact receive £20,000 and C £30,000. The rule applies only to lifetime gifts made by way of *advancement (i.e. as permanent provision and not for maintenance or temporary purposes). In the case of a partial intestacy prior to 1 January 1996, benefits conferred by the will on a surviving spouse and on the deceased's issue (i.e. his children, grandchildren, and remoter direct descendants) are also brought into account. The hotchpot rule has been abolished where the deceased died on or after 1 January 1996 by the Law Reform (Succession Act) 1996.

hot pursuit, right of The right of a coastal state to pursue a foreign ship within its *territorial waters (or possibly its contiguous zone) and there capture it if the state has good reason to believe that this vessel has violated its laws. The hot pursuit may – but only if it is uninterrupted – continue onto the *high seas, but it must terminate the moment the pursued ship enters the territorial waters of another state, as such pursuit would involve an offence to the other state (unless during conflict); in these circumstances *extradition should be employed instead. The doctrine applies equally to aircraft that intrude into local airspace.

house bote *See* ESTOVERS.

housebreaking *n.* Forcing one's way into someone else's house. If this is carried out with the intention of committing certain specified crimes in the house, or if, after breaking into a house, certain crimes then take place, the housebreaking amounts to *burglary.

House of Commons The representative chamber of *Parliament (also known as the **Lower House**), composed of 650 **Members of Parliament (MPs)** elected for 533 single-member constituencies in England, 59 in Scotland, 40 in Wales, and 18 in Northern Ireland (*see* ELECTION; FRANCHISE). The total number of MPs may within certain limits be varied as a result of constituency changes proposed by the *boundary commissions.

Various categories of people are disqualified from membership. They include those under 21, civil servants, the police and the regular armed forces, aliens, those declared bankrupt, convicted prisoners and people guilty of corrupt or illegal practices, the holders of most judicial offices (but not lay magistrates), and the holders of a large number of public offices listed in the House of Commons Disqualification Act 1975. Public offices that disqualify include stewardship of the *Chiltern Hundreds and the Manor of Northstead. The number of members who may hold ministerial office is limited to 95. The House of Lords Act 1999 removed an earlier disqualification on hereditary peers from voting and from being elected members of the House of Commons. The Removal of Clergy Disqualification Act 2001 permits clergy of all denominations to be MPs.

The House is presided over by the **Speaker**, who is elected from among themselves by the members at the beginning of each Parliament. The Speaker is responsible for the orderly conduct of proceedings, which must be supervised with complete impartiality, and is the person through whom the members may collectively communicate with the sovereign. The **Leader of the House** is a government minister responsible for arranging the business of the House in consultation with the Opposition.

House of Commons Commission A body established in 1978 to supervise the staffing of the House. It consists of the Speaker, the Leader of the House, and four other members, one of whom is appointed by the Leader of the Opposition.

House of Lords The second chamber of *Parliament (also known as the **Upper House**), which scrutinizes legislation and formerly exercised judicial functions. The House of Lords Act 1999 substantially changed the constitution of the House by excluding hereditary peers from a place in the House as of right, although for a transitional period 92 were allowed to remain on merit. Of these, 75 were elected by their own political party or by cross-bench (usually non-party-political) groups. A further 15 hereditary peers were elected to act as Deputy Speakers or Committee chairmen. Two hereditary royal appointments were also retained: the Earl Marshal and the Lord Great Chamberlain. The other members of the Lords are (as at September 2012) life peers (about 700) or bishops (26), comprising the Archbishops of Canterbury and York, the Bishops of London, Durham, and Winchester, and 21 other Anglican bishops selected according to seniority of appointment. The House is now presided over by the Lord Speaker (a role formerly exercised by the *Lord Chancellor) and its business is arranged, in consultation with the Opposition, by a government minister appointed **Leader of the House**. Long-term reform of the Lords continues to be debated; it is envisaged that the reformed chamber will have about 450 members but there is no agreement as to whether these should be elected, appointed, or some combination of the two.

Until 2009 the Lords was the final court of appeal in the UK in both civil and criminal cases, although it referred some cases to the *European Court of Justice for a ruling. In its judicial capacity the Lords formally adopted opinions delivered by an **Appellate Committee** (of which there were two), drawn from the *Lords of Appeal in Ordinary and others who had held high judicial office. Under the Constitutional Reform Act 2005 the law lords were removed from the legislature to a new *Supreme Court of the United Kingdom, which began sitting at the end of 2009. Under the same Act the judicial functions of the Lord Chancellor were transferred to the *Lord Chief Justice.

House of Lords Appointments Commission A body that recommends people for appointment as non-party-political peers and vets all nominations for membership of the House of Lords. Set up by the Government following the House of Lords Act 1999, which modernizes the Lords, the Commission is an independent nondepartmental public body staffed by civil servants.

houses in multiple occupation (HMOs) Buildings that contain two or more households who share certain facilities, such as a house split into bedsitting rooms with shared bathroom. Certain HMOs are subject to the Housing Authority licensing scheme introduced by the Housing Act 2004. HMOs that are required to be licensed but do not meet licensing standards may be made the subject of an interim management order or a final management order, whereby the Housing Authority steps into the shoes of the landlord.

housing action area An area declared to be such by a housing authority on the grounds that living conditions in it are unsatisfactory and should be dealt with comprehensively over a five-year period. This is done by special measures to improve the standards and management of accommodation and the well-being of the inhabitants. A housing action area may incorporate a *general improvement area.

housing action trust (HAT) A statutory trust set up for a particular area with the objects to secure: the repair and improvement of housing in the area; its proper and effective management; greater diversity of kinds of tenure of the housing; and the improvement of social and living conditions in the area generally. In their areas, housing action trusts can be given power to exercise most of the functions of a housing authority and the planning control and public-health functions of local authorities. Local authority housing can be transferred to a housing action trust by government order if a majority of the tenants agree. A housing action trust must achieve its objects as quickly as possible and is then dissolved and its property disposed of. Housing action trusts were introduced by the Housing Act 1988. Six HATs were established under the Act, all of which have since been wound up.

housing association A non-profit-making organization whose main purpose is to provide housing. A *fully mutual housing association is excepted from the *assured tenancy provisions. The *Housing Corporation can make grants to housing associations registered by them.

housing association tenancy A tenancy in which the landlord is a housing association, a housing trust, or the Housing Corporation. The Housing Act 1996 gave certain housing association tenants a right to buy their homes, and they may be able to obtain a grant towards the purchase price.

housing benefit A benefit payable by local authorities to those with no or very low incomes who pay rent for their housing. There are two types: *rent rebates, paid to the local authority's own needy tenants, and rent allowances, paid to tenants other than their own (e.g. Housing Association tenants). Under the Welfare Reform Act 2012, housing benefit is due to be replaced by *universal credit.

Housing Corporation A government body set up to maintain a register of *housing associations, to promote and assist the development of registered housing associations and unregistered *self-build societies, and to provide dwellings for letting or sale. From 1 December 2008 its functions were taken over by the *Homes and Communities Agency and the *Tenant Services Authority.

housing health and safety rating system (HHSRS) A system introduced by the Housing Act 2004 for dealing with housing that may be unfit for habitation. The local authority is obliged to consider the effect of the housing conditions on the health and safety of occupiers and to decide if they pose a hazard. If they do, the authority must decide what action is required. They may serve a hazard awareness notice, an improvement notice, or, in extreme cases, a demolition notice.

housing subsidy An annual contribution from central government funds, payable under the Housing Act 1985, towards the provision of housing by local authorities and new town corporations.

housing trust A trust set up to provide housing, or whose funds are devoted to charitable purposes and which in fact uses most of its funds for the provision of housing. If it is a *fully mutual housing association, it is exempted from the *assured tenancy provisions. See also HOUSING ACTION TRUST.

hue and cry [French: *huer* to shout; *crier* to cry aloud] Historically, the common-law practice of raising a body of people to pursue those suspected of committing a felony or otherwise endangering their fellow subjects. According to the Sheriffs Act 1887 (reenacting a statute of the time of Edward I): "Every person in a county must be ready and apparelled at the command of the sheriff, and at the cry of the country to arrest the felon", and in default, "shall on conviction by liable to fine and imprisonment, and to an action at the suit of the party injured". This proved a rough-and-ready, if surprisingly successful, method of catching criminals and was widely used prior to the development of the modern police force.

human assisted reproduction Techniques to bring about the conception and birth of a child other than by sexual intercourse between the parties. It includes artificial insemination by the husband (AIH) or by a donor (DI), in vitro fertilization (IVF), and egg and embryo donation. Such methods mean it is no longer possible to base legal parentage solely on genetic links. Under the terms of the Human Fertilization and Embryology Act 2008 s 33, the legal mother is always the woman who has given birth to the child, irrespective of whether she is genetically related to the child. This is so unless a *parental order or an adoption order is made in respect of the child. Where the mother is married, the legal father of the child will be her husband, unless he did not consent to the treatment (s 35). Where the mother has a civil partner, then the civil partner will be the other "parent" (the 2008 Act does not use the term "mother" in such a case: see s 42). Where a couple are neither married nor in a civil partnership, the partner of the mother will usually be the father or parent (in the latter case) so long as certain conditions are met (s 36–37, 43–44). In essence these are that both parties agree to the partner being the parent of the child. The sperm donor whose sperm is used for licensed treatment is never the father of the child (s 41). *See also* SURROGACY.

It is an offence to use female germ cells from an embryo or fetus, or to make use of embryos created from such germ cells, for the purpose of providing a fertility service. Such practice is already banned by the *Human Fertilization and Embryology Authority. The offence is triable only on *indictment and is punishable with up to 10 years' imprisonment.

Human Fertilization and Embryology Authority A body, established under the Human Fertilization and Embryology Act 1990, that monitors, controls, and reviews research involving the use of embryos and issues licences for such research and for treatment in *human assisted reproduction. It must also maintain a register of persons whose gametes are kept or used for such purposes and of children born as a result. Children over the age of 18 can apply to the Authority for information concerning their ethnic and genetic background.

humanitarian intervention The interference of one state in the affairs of another by means of armed force with the intention of making that state adopt a more humanitarian policy, usually the protection of human rights of minority groups. Despite debate, such intervention is not recognized as legal under the UN Charter. However, states continue to rely on humanitarian grounds as justification for military action; examples of humanitarian intervention include Vietnam's invasion of Cambodia (1978), the declaration by the USA, the UK, Russia, and France of an air exclusion zone in southern Iraq in an effort to protect the Shia Marsh Arabs (1992), and military actions to protect the Muslim population of Kosovo (1999). The decision of the *International Criminal Tribunal for the former Yugoslavia in Tadic ("Prijedor") IT-94-1 (November 1999) acted to confirm the fact that a distinction between "international" conflicts and purely "domestic" conflicts has now disappeared. The rules of humanitarian law that are applicable to conflicts between states have also become customary rules applicable to disputes within states.

human rights Rights and freedom to which every human being is entitled. Protection against breaches of these rights committed by a state (including the state of which the victim is a national) may in some cases be enforced in international law. It is sometimes suggested that human rights (or some of them) are so fundamental that they form part of *natural law, but most of them are best regarded as forming part of treaty law.

The United Nations Universal Declaration of Human Rights (1948) spells out most of the main rights that must be protected but it is not binding in international law. There are two international covenants, however, that bind the parties who have ratified them: the 1966 International Covenant on Civil and Political Rights and International Covenant on Economic, Social and Cultural Rights. The United Nations has set up a

Commission on Human Rights, which has power to discuss gross violations of human rights but not to investigate individual complaints. The Human Rights Committee, set up in 1977, has power to hear complaints from individuals, under certain circumstances, about alleged breaches of the 1966 Covenant on Civil and Political Rights. There are also various regional conventions on human rights, some of which have established machinery for hearing individual complaints. The best known of these is the *European Convention on Human Rights (enacted in English law as the *Human Rights Act1998) and the Inter-American Convention on Human Rights (covering South America).

Human Rights Act Legislation, enacted in 1998, that brought most of the rights contained in the *European Convention on Human Rights into domestic law for the whole of the UK on 2 October 2000. In the past the use of the Convention was limited to cases where the law was ambiguous and public authorities had no duty to exercise administrative discretion in a manner that complied with the Convention.

The Act creates a statutory general requirement that all legislation (past or future) be read and given effect in a way that is compatible with the Convention. Section 3 provides that all legislation, primary and secondary, whenever enacted, must be read and given effect in a way that is compatible with Convention rights *wherever possible*.

The Act requires public authorities – including courts – to act compatibly with the Convention unless they are prevented from doing so by statute. This means that the courts have their own primary statutory duty to give effect to the Convention unless a statute positively prevents this. Section 7 gives the *victim of any act of a public authority that is incompatible with the Convention the power to challenge the authority in court using the Convention, to found a cause of action or as a defence. The Act introduces a new ground of illegality into proceedings brought by way of judicial review, namely, a failure to comply with the Convention rights protected by the Act, subject to a "statutory obligation" defence. Secondly, it creates a new cause of action against public bodies that fail to act compatibly with the Convention. Thirdly, Convention rights are available as a ground of defence or appeal in cases brought by public bodies against private bodies (in both criminal and civil cases). Section 7(5) imposes a limitation period of one year for those bringing proceedings.

However, only persons classified as "victims" by the Act are able to enforce the duty to act compatibly with the Convention in proceedings against the authority, and only victims will have standing to bring proceedings by way of judicial review.

The Convention rights that have been incorporated into the Act are: Articles 2 to 12, 14, 16, 17, 18; Articles 1 to 3 of the First Protocol; Articles 1 and 2 of the Sixth Protocol; and the Thirteenth Protocol (individual rights are subjects of entries in this dictionary). *See* ABSOLUTE RIGHT; QUALIFIED RIGHT.

The Act requires any court or tribunal determining a question that has arisen in connection with a Convention right to take into account the jurisprudence of the Strasbourg organs (the European Court and Commission of Human Rights and the Committee of Ministers). This jurisprudence must be considered "so far as, in the opinion of the court or tribunal, it is relevant to the proceedings in which that question has arisen", whenever the judgment, decision, or opinion to be taken into account was handed down.

Section 19 provides that when legislation is introduced into Parliament for a second reading, the introducing minister must make a statement, either (1) to the effect that, in his view, the legislation is compatible with the Convention, or (2) that although the legislation is not compatible with the Convention, the government still wishes to proceed. If it is not possible to read legislation so as to give effect to the Convention, then the Act does not affect the validity, continuing operation, or enforcement of the legislation. In such circumstances, however, section 4 empowers the high courts to make a *declaration of incompatibility. Section 10 and Schedule 2 provide a "fast-track" procedure by which the government can act to amend legislation in order to remove incompatibility with the Convention when a declaration of incompatibility has been made.

The Act gives a court a wide power to grant such relief, remedies, or orders as it considers just and appropriate, provided they are within its existing powers. Damages may be awarded in civil proceedings, but only if necessary to afford *just satisfaction; in determining whether or not to award damages and the amount to award, the court must take account of the principles applied by the European Court of Human Rights.

Sections 12 and 13 provide specific assurances as to the respect that will be afforded to *freedom of expression and *freedom of thought, conscience, and religion: these are `comfort clauses' for sections of the press and certain religious organizations.

The Act does not make Convention rights directly enforceable against a private litigant, nor against a quasi-public body with some public functions if it is acting in a private capacity. But in cases against a private litigant, the Act still has an effect on the outcome, because the court will be obliged to interpret legislation in conformity with the Convention wherever possible; must exercise any judicial discretion compatibly with the Convention; and must ensure that its application of common law or equitable rules is compatible with the Convention.

The Act is not without its critics and some journalists and parliamentarians regularly call for its repeal. In 2011 the government set up a Bill of Rights Commission to review the Act and to consider the creation of an alternative "British Bill of Rights". However, the Commission failed to achieve a consensus before it disbanded in 2012. *See* BILL OF RIGHTS.

(((()))) SEE WEB LINKS

• Information from the website of the Equality and Human Rights Commission

Human Tissue Authority The UK government agency that regulates the removal, use, and storage of human organs and tissue from both the living and the deceased for certain purposes defined by the Human Tissue Act 2004. These purposes include clinical research, clinical audit, and medical education. Anyone handling such material for those purposes should have a licence issued by the Authority.

hybrid Bill *See* BILL.

hybrid power *See* POWER OF APPOINTMENT.

hypothecation *n.* **1.** A mortgage granted by a ship's master to secure the repayment with interest, on the safe arrival of the ship at her destination, of money borrowed during a voyage as a matter of necessity (e.g. to pay for urgent repairs). The hypothecation of a ship itself, with or without cargo, is called **bottomry**; that of its cargo alone is *respondentia*. It is effected by a bond, and the bondholder is entitled to a maritime *lien. **2.** An authority given to a banker, usually as a **letter of hypothecation**, to enable the bank to sell goods or property that have been pledged to it as security for a loan. It applies only when the goods remain in the possession of the pledgor.

ICC *See* INTERNATIONAL CRIMINAL COURT.

identity *n.* (in the law of evidence) *See* EVIDENCE OF IDENTITY.

ignorance of the law *See* MISTAKE.

ignorantia juris non excusat [Latin] Ignorance of the law is no excuse, i.e.
no defence against criminal or other proceedings arising from its breach. The Statutory
Instruments Act 1946 modifies the rule slightly (*see* STATUTORY INSTRUMENT). *See also*
MISTAKE.

ignoring traffic signals Failing to comply with traffic signs, traffic lights, or road
markings (Road Traffic Act 1988). A number of different offences are included in this
category, all concerned with breaches of the rules relating to traffic signals as laid down in
the Highway Code. All these offences are subject to a fine, *endorsement (carrying 3
penalty points under the *totting-up system), and *disqualification at the discretion of
the court. Sometimes charges may also be brought under the head of *careless and
inconsiderate driving or *dangerous driving, depending on the circumstances. It is
also an offence not to comply with road directions given by a uniformed police
officer acting in the course of his duties or engaged in a traffic census or survey.

   Prosecutions for ignoring traffic signals or police directions are subject to a
*notice of intended prosecution.

IHT *See* INHERITANCE TAX.

ILC *See* INTERNATIONAL LAW COMMISSION.

illegal contract A contract that is prohibited by statute (e.g. one between traders
providing for minimum resale prices) or is illegal at common law on the grounds of
*public policy. An illegal contract is totally void, but neither party (unless innocent of the
illegality) can recover back any money paid or property transferred under it (*see* EX TURPI
CAUSA NON ORITUR ACTIO). Related transactions may also be affected. A related
transaction between the same parties (e.g. if X gives Y a promissory note for money due
from him under an illegal contract) is equally tainted with the illegality and is therefore
void. The same is true of a related transaction with a third party (e.g. if Z lends X the
money to pay Y) if the original illegality is known to him. In certain circumstances, illegal
contracts may be saved by *severance.

illegal practices *See* CORRUPT AND ILLEGAL PRACTICES.

illegal trust A trust that contravenes statute, morality, or public policy. Such a trust is
void and of no effect.

illegitimacy *n.* The status of a child born to unmarried parents. Although evidence
of illegitimacy is readily available from the entry in the birth register relating to the

child's parents, it is usual for a short form of birth certificate to be issued, which makes no mention of the parents. Entry in the register of the name of a man who is not married to the mother (which may only be done with the consent of the mother) is evidence of his paternity.

The effect of the Family Law Reform Act 1987 is that, for nearly all purposes, children are to be treated alike, whether or not their parents are married to one another. The parents of illegitimate children have much the same rights, duties, and responsibilities in relation to them as they have for their legitimate children. The father of an illegitimate child is under a duty to maintain the child in the same way as his duty to maintain legitimate children (*see* CHILD SUPPORT MAINTENANCE), but does not automatically have *parental responsibility for that child. Illegitimate children are able to inherit property under wills (unless the contrary intention is apparent) and on intestacy in the same way as if they were legitimate. However, the Family Law Reform Act 1987 did not remove all distinctions between legitimate and illegitimate children, notably in relation to entitlement to British citizenship and succession to the throne of England and to titles of honour.

It is now becoming more usual to use the term "child of unmarried parents" for children born out of wedlock, rather than "illegitimate child". *See also* UNMARRIED FATHER.

illusory appointment The giving of property under a *power of appointment that confers little or no benefit to one or more objects of the power. Before 19th-century legislation such appointments were void; they are now valid under the Law of Property Act 1925.

illusory trust An arrangement that gives the outward impression of being a trust, but is not in fact so, because the apparent trustee has no power to deal with the property of the trust, the authority and power remaining with the settlor. *See also* SHAM TRUST.

IMCA *See* INDEPENDENT MENTAL CAPACITY ADVOCATE.

immediate post-death interest trust As defined by the Inheritance Tax Act 1984 s 49(A), a *trust established under a will such that the beneficiary is entitled to receive the income of the trust immediately on the date of death of the testator. The assets of such a trust are treated as forming part of the estate of the beneficiary for *inheritance tax purposes. A trust arising on an intestacy where a surviving spouse of the intestate has a *life interest in the estate also qualifies as an immediate post-death interest trust.

immigration *n.* The act of entering a country other than one's native country with the intention of living there permanently. Immigration into the UK is subject to control under the Immigration Acts 1971 and 1988, as amended by the Immigration and Nationality Act 1999, the Nationality, Immigration and Asylum Act 2002, and the Immigration, Asylum and Nationality Act 2006. This control extends to all potential entrants except those to whom the legislation gives the *right of abode in the UK (principally those holding *British citizenship) and nationals of other member states of the EU. With minor exceptions, a person subject to immigration control may not enter or remain in the UK except with leave, which may be granted either indefinitely or for a limited period; if leave is granted for a limited period, an immigrant is subject to further conditions (e.g. conditions restricting employment). The 1971 Act itself gave indefinite leave to stay to those not entitled to the right of abode but who were lawfully settled in the UK when it came into force. Whether or not leave is needed, whether it should be granted, and whether a time limit and any other conditions should be imposed are decided initially by immigration officers acting in accordance with immigration rules made by the Secretary of State. Appeals against the decisions of immigration officers are made to immigration adjudicators and thence to the *Immigration and Asylum Tribunal (*see also* ASYLUM). In the case of foreign nationals served with *deportation orders because they are held to be a threat to national security, appeal is to the Special Immigration Appeals Commission (SIAC).

Under the Immigration (*see also* ASYLUM) (Carriers' Liability) Act 1987, the owners of ships and aircraft are liable to pay a £2,000 fine in respect of any person who arrives in the UK on their ship or aircraft and who seeks leave to enter the UK without proper documents (e.g. passport or visa). This provision has since been extended to road hauliers. Under the Immigration, Asylum and Nationality Act 2006 any employer who employs someone who has not been given leave to stay or work in the UK is liable to a civil penalty of up to £5,000 for each employee in breach. Employers must ask employees for evidence of their legal status, such as National Insurance documents, an EU passport, or a valid work permit; this request must be made in a way that does not breach racial discrimination legislation.

Immigration and Asylum Tribunal A tribunal that hears appeals against decisions made by the Home Office in matters of *asylum, *immigration, and nationality. It is now a section within the Immigration and Asylum Chamber of the *First-tier Tribunal.

immoral contract A contract based on sexual immorality, such as a contract of prostitution. Such contracts are *illegal contracts on the grounds that they contravene *public policy.

immovables *pl. n.* Tangible things that cannot be physically moved, particularly land and buildings.

immunity *n.* Freedom or exemption from legal proceedings. Examples include the immunity of the sovereign personally from all legal proceedings (*see* ROYAL PREROGATIVE); the immunity of members of the House of Commons and the House of Lords from proceedings in respect of words spoken in debate (*see* PARLIAMENTARY PRIVILEGE); *judicial immunity; and the immunity from the jurisdiction of national courts enjoyed by members of diplomatic missions and by foreign sovereigns (*see* DIPLOMATIC IMMUNITY; SOVEREIGN IMMUNITY).

impeachable waste *Waste that results in liability on the part of the person who commits it. Thus when a tenant commits impeachable waste his landlord may sue him for damages and/or obtain an injunction to prevent him committing any further waste.

impeding apprehension or prosecution Giving assistance to a person one knows to be guilty of an *indictable offence with the intention of preventing or delaying his arrest or prosecution (e.g. providing a hiding place or destroying evidence). There are also special offences of (1) agreeing not to disclose information that might help to convict or prosecute a criminal (*see* COMPOUNDING AN OFFENCE), (2) refusing to aid a police officer when asked to help stop a breach of the peace, (3) *obstructing a police officer, and (4) *wasting police time by giving them misleading information. *See also* ESCAPE.

imperfect gift *See* GIFT.

imperfect trust *See* EXECUTORY TRUST.

impersonation *n.* Pretending to be another person. It is an offence (rape) to impersonate a woman's husband in order to persuade her to have sexual intercourse (*R v Elbekkay* [1995] Crim LR 163), to impersonate the holder of a Crown office in order to gain access to prohibited places, and to impersonate a police officer, a variety of public officials, a voter, or a juror. Obtaining property, services, or certain financial advantages through impersonation may amount to a crime of *deception.

implementation *n.* The process of bringing any piece of legislation into force. EU directives, which are not directly applicable (*see* COMMUNITY LEGISLATION), are implemented at national level by member states by Act of Parliament or regulation. In the UK this may be done by statute or by statutory instrument or regulation.

implied condition A term or obligation implied by law in a contract, any breach of which will entitle the innocent party not only to damages but to treat the contract as discharged (*see* CONDITION). In a contract of sale of goods there are implied conditions that the seller has the right to sell the goods, that the goods will correspond with the contract description, and, in the case of sales in the course of business, that the goods are of *satisfactory quality and fit for the buyer's declared purpose.

implied contract A contract not created by express words but inferred by the courts either from the conduct of the parties or from some special relationship existing between them.

implied easement An *easement that is implied into a transfer of land. There are four main types of implied easement. Firstly, an *easement of necessity, without which the land would be unusable. Secondly, an easement implied by the common intention of the parties as evidenced by the terms of the transfer or the nature of the property; for example, in *Wong v Beaumont Properties* [1965] 1 QB 173, an easement of ventilation was implied into a lease of a basement restaurant. Thirdly, under the rule in *Wheeldon v Burrows* (1879) 12 Ch D 31, the grant of an easement is implied on a subdivision of land where the right claimed: (i) was used for the benefit of the part transferred before the subdivision; (ii) is continuous and apparent; and (iii) is necessary for the reasonable enjoyment of the part transferred. For example, if a path runs over the retained land to the part transferred, and has been used to benefit the part transferred, a right of way will be implied in the transfer of that part to the new owners unless the contrary is expressed in the transfer. Lastly, section 62 of the Law of Property Act 1925 transfers all existing easements with the land and in certain circumstances will turn *quasi-easements and licences into easements, particularly where the two pieces of land were in separate occupation (for example, one part was leased to a tenant) before the transfer (*Long v Gowlett* [1923] 2 Ch 177).

implied malice *Mens rea* that the law considers sufficient for a crime, although there is no intention to commit that crime. The term is usually now used only in relation to murder, referring to the intention to cause *grievous bodily harm (*R v Woollin* [1999] AC 82 (HL)). *See also* MALICE AFORETHOUGHT.

implied term A provision of a contract not agreed to by the parties in words but either regarded by the courts as necessary to give effect to their presumed intentions or introduced into the contract by statute (as in the case of contracts for the sale of goods; *see* CAVEAT EMPTOR). An implied term may constitute either a *condition of the contract or a warranty; if it is introduced by statute it often cannot be expressly excluded. *Compare* EXPRESS TERM.

implied trust A trust that arises either from the presumed but unexpressed intention of the settlor or by operation of law. Equity imposes an obligation to create such trusts by inference from the facts, including the conduct or relationship of the parties. An implied trust may be subdivided into or overlap with *resulting trusts and *constructive trusts.

impossibility *n.* A *general defence that arises when compliance with the criminal law is physically impossible. This is most likely to arise in the context of crimes of omission. Thus one cannot be found guilty of failing to report a road traffic accident of which one was unaware. However, under the Criminal Attempts Act 1981 one may be convicted of attempting what is physically or legally impossible:

- Physical impossibility owing to ineptitude or to the physical facts of the matter is not a defence (e.g. a thief opens a handbag to remove the contents and the handbag is empty).
- Legal impossibility is not a defence. In *R v Shivpuri* [1987] AC 1 the defendant tried, as he thought, to smuggle drugs into the country: he was found guilty, although the "drugs" turned out not to be a prohibited substance but rather vegetables.

See also ATTEMPT.

impossibility of performance The impossibility of carrying out a contract, which occurs, for example, when it relates to subject matter that does not exist. The event making fulfilment impossible may arise either before or after the contract is made. In the former case (e.g. if X agrees to sell Y a horse that, unknown to either, is already dead) the contract is void for *mistake. In the latter case (e.g. if the horse dies between contract and performance) the contract will be discharged under the doctrine of *frustration of contract.

impotence *n.* The inability of either partner to have normal sexual intercourse (*see also* CONSUMMATION OF A MARRIAGE). In the case of a married couple this is sometimes called **canonical disability** (i.e. a disability recognized by canon law, including that of the Roman Catholic Church, as a ground for annulment of the marriage). If the impotence is permanent and incurable, the marriage is voidable and either party may apply for a nullity decree. Impotence must be distinguished from *wilful refusal to consummate.

imprisonment *n. See* CUSTODY; SENTENCE; FALSE IMPRISONMENT; LIFE IMPRISONMENT.

improvement *n.* (of rented premises) An addition or alteration that improves the premises from the tenant's point of view; it does not necessarily have to increase the value of the premises. In the case of a lease that contains an obligation by the tenant to obtain the landlord's consent before making improvements, the landlord cannot withhold his consent unreasonably. He can, however, claim from the tenant any expense or loss he suffers as a result and he can require the tenant, at the end of the tenancy, to put the premises back into the condition they were in before the improvement was carried out. Some tenants are entitled to compensation for improvements at the end of their tenancy (*see* FARM BUSINESS TENANCY). When rented dwellings lack certain basic amenities, such as a bath, the local authority can require the landlord to provide these amenities and carry out other repairs and improvements after service of an *improvement notice. In the case of business tenancies and agricultural holdings, the tenant can claim compensation for improvements.

improvement notice **1.** A notice requiring any person responsible for a breach of the Health and Safety at Work Act 1974 (or associated legislation) to take steps to remedy the breach or prevent its repetition. *Compare* PROHIBITION NOTICE. **2.** A notice under the Food Safety Act 1990 to the proprietor of a food business specifying measures to be taken to comply with regulations governing the preparation and handling of food.

imputability *n.* The principle that internationally illegal acts or omissions contributing to the damage to foreign property, and caused in some way by organs of the state apparatus, are attributable to the state and therefore incur that state's responsibility. Thus, there must have been state participation in the act before there can be *state responsibility for it. International law treats as irrelevant the question whether, under municipal law, the officials of the state acted beyond their authority, provided they used state organs in performance of the act. Hence, the state has been held liable for the acts of soldiers who joined rioters instead of suppressing them (*Thomas H Youmans (US) v United Mexican States* (1924) 4 RIAA 10).

imputation *n.* In criminal proceedings, an allegation of misconduct or bad *character made by a defendant against another person. Under the Criminal Justice Act 2003, where the defendant adduces evidence attacking another person's character, or where evidence is given of an imputation about another person made by the defendant on being questioned or charged, the defendant may, with *leave of the court, be cross-examined about his own *previous convictions and bad character.

imputation of unchastity A statement imputing unchastity or adultery to a woman or girl was formerly actionable whether or not it has caused actual financial or material loss. The Defamation Act 2013, which now requires serious harm to the reputation of the claimant in all cases, also repealed the provision excepting such a slander from the need to prove special damage. *See* DEFAMATION.

imputation of unfitness or incompetence A statement calculated to disparage someone in his office, profession, calling, trade, or business was formerly actionable whether or not it caused actual financial or material loss. The Defamation Act 2013 now requires serious harm to the reputation of the claimant in all cases, which in the case of a body trading for profit equates to serious financial loss. *See* DEFAMATION.

imputed notice An *agent's knowledge of facts that the law presumes the person employing him (the *principal) to have, irrespective of his actual knowledge of those facts. A purchaser of land has imputed notice of all matters relating to the purchase of which his agent (e.g. a solicitor) has (or ought reasonably to have) knowledge. *See also* ACTUAL NOTICE; CONSTRUCTIVE NOTICE; NOTICE.

inadmissible reason (in employment law) Dismissal for an inadmissible reason is automatically *unfair dismissal, and the employee may apply to an *employment tribunal regardless of his length of continuous employment. Inadmissible or automatically unfair reasons include dismissal based on membership or participation in the activities of an *independent trade union or a refusal to become or remain a member of a union. They also cover situations in which the employee has made a protected disclosure (*see* WHISTLE-BLOWING) or has been dismissed for asserting certain statutory rights, including the right to the national minimum wage or any rights under the Equality Act 2010. It is automatically unfair to dismiss a woman because she is pregnant or for any reason connected with pregnancy. *See also* COMPENSATION.

inalienability *n. See* RULE AGAINST INALIENABILITY.

in bonis [Latin] In the goods of. Cases concerning disposition of property in a will of the deceased can be referred to as *in bonis* or ***in b***.

in camera [Latin: in the chamber] In private. A court hearing must usually be public but the public may be barred from the court or the hearing may continue in the judge's private room in certain circumstances; for example, when it is necessary in the interests of national security or to protect the identity of a witness unwilling to give evidence in public. Part 39 of the *Civil Procedure Rules and Part 16 of the *Criminal Procedure Rules deal with *in camera* hearings.

incapacity (incompetence) *n*. A lack of full legal competence in any respect; for example, the incapacity of mentally disordered persons to conclude valid contracts (*see* CAPACITY TO CONTRACT). A person suffering from incapacity is frequently referred to as a **person under disability**.

incapacity benefit A state benefit that replaced invalidity benefit and sickness benefit in April 1995. From late 2008 incapacity benefit was replaced for all new claims by **Employment and Support Allowance (ESA)**; ESA will in turn be replaced by *universal credit during the period 2013–18.

incest *n*. Sexual intercourse between family members. *Familial sexual offences are now regulated under the Sexual Offences Act 2003.

Inchmaree clause A clause frequently inserted in marine insurance policies to provide cover for a variety of risks that are not covered as *perils of the seas. It provides protection against such events as accidents in loading or discharging cargo or taking on fuel, bursting of boilers, breakage of shafts, and explosions on board ship or elsewhere. It also provides cover for negligence of the ship's master, officers, or crew. The original such clause arose from a legal action brought in 1887 by the owners of a ship named *The Inchmaree* (*Thames and Mersey Marine Insurance Co v Hamilton Fraser and Co* [1887] 12 AC 484 (HL)).

inchoate *adj*. Incomplete. Certain acts, although not constituting a complete offence, are nonetheless prohibited by the criminal law because they constitute steps towards the complete offence. These inchoate offences include *incitement (*Race Relations Board v Applin* [1973] QB 815), *attempt (*Jones* [1990] 1 WLR 1057), and *conspiracy (*R v Anderson* [1986] AC 27).

incitement *n*. Persuading or attempting to persuade someone else to commit a crime. If the other person does not carry out the crime, the person who attempted to persuade him to do so may nonetheless be guilty of the crime of incitement. Incitement may be by means of suggestion, persuasion, threats, or pressure, by words or by implication; for example, advertising an article for sale to be used to commit an offence may constitute incitement to commit that offence. Case: *Race Relations Board v Applin* [1973] QB 815.

incitement to racial hatred *See* RACIAL HATRED.

income support An income-related benefit payable under the Social Security Acts to persons over 16 whose income and savings do not exceed a prescribed amount, and who are not working 16 or more hours a week, and (if applicable) whose spouses, civil partners, or *cohabitants are not working 24 hours or more a week, and who are incapable of or unavailable for work (for example, because they are disabled or a lone parent). Since October 1996 unemployed people who are available for work have received a *jobseeker's allowance rather than income support. Income support is currently being replaced by *universal credit.

income tax A direct tax on a person's wages or salary and on most other sources of income, including unearned income and the profits from an unincorporated business. The amount of tax is based on a person's entire income for the year, less certain *personal allowances, on a progressive scale. The effect is that those with higher incomes pay higher rates of tax.

There are currently three bands of income-tax rates: basic rate, higher rate, and additional rate. The rate applied to income within a band depends on the type of income:

- Dividends within the basic rate are charged at 10%; other income at 20%.
- Dividends subject to higher rate are charged at 32½%; all other income at 40%.
- Dividends subject to additional rate are charged at 37½%; all other income at 45%.

A company not resident within the UK is subject to income tax, and not to corporation tax. Corporate bodies acting as trustees are also subject to income tax.

Several systems of deducting tax at source apply. These include *Pay As You Earn, the *Construction Industry Scheme, and deduction of tax on bank interest. Tax not deducted at source is assessed by the taxpayer under the *self-assessment system. The tax thus self-assessed is collected in a balancing payment on 31 January following the tax year, although many taxpayers are required to make payments on account on 31 January and the following 31 July. The structure of the charge to income tax has been completely changed since 2003 with the enactment of the Income Tax (Earnings and Pensions) Act 2003, the Income Tax (Trading and Other Income) Act 2005, and the Income Tax Act 2007. These three Acts have resulted in the abolition of the former *schedular system for income tax.

incompetence *n. See* INCAPACITY.

incompetent patient (incapacitated patient; patient lacking capacity) Under the Mental Capacity Act 2005, a patient who is unable to take a decision for himself in relation to medical treatment because of an impairment of, or a disturbance in the functioning of, the mind or brain. This would include a person with certain forms of mental illness or with significant learning difficulties as well as a person who is suffering from temporary concussion or loss of consciousness. Unless there is in existence a valid and applicable *advance decision or a *lasting power of attorney, the decision how and whether to treat an incompetent patient will be made by the relevant medical professional in accordance with what he considers to be in that patient's *best interest. In certain cases, for example where a patient is in a persistent vegetative state or in the event of a dispute, the decision will be made by the courts, who also have the power to appoint a *deputy. *Compare* COMPETENT PATIENT.

inconsiderate driving *See* CARELESS AND INCONSIDERATE DRIVING.

incorporation *n.* **1.** The formation of an association that has **corporate personality**, i.e. a legal personality distinct from those of its members. Such a body can own property and incur debts. Company members have no liability to company creditors for such debts (though they may be under some liability to their company). An incorporated company has its own rights and liabilities and legal proceedings in respect of them should be brought by and against it in its own name (*but see* DERIVATIVE CLAIM). It can be convicted of crimes; when *mens rea* is a requirement of the offence, the *mens rea* of the officers responsible may be attributed to the company (*Tesco Supermarkets Ltd v Nattrass* [1972] AC 153 (HL); *Meridian Global Funds Management Asia Ltd v Securities Commission* [1995] 2 AC 500 (PC)). A company is usually incorporated by *registration under the Companies Act 2006 but there are other methods (e.g. by royal charter, public general Act, or private Act of Parliament). *See also* CERTIFICATE OF INCORPORATION; LIFTING THE VEIL. **2.** *See* DOCTRINE OF INCORPORATION.

incorporation by reference **1.** Reference in a will to another document without which the will cannot be understood (the document then forms part of the will). For example, a will leaving a specified sum "to each of the persons listed in my notebook" incorporates the notebook. The document must be clearly identified in the will, in existence at the date of the will, and clearly referred to as being in existence at that date. **2.** Reference to named contract terms, for example on the back of a railway ticket, saying where the terms can be seen for those who want to read them. This will often be sufficient to incorporate the terms by reference into the contract, although the other party may not have taken the opportunity to read the terms. However, there are risks in incorporation; for example, it is harder to enforce an exclusion of liability clause (*see* EXEMPTION CLAUSE) if the terms are merely incorporated by reference.

incorporeal hereditament *See* HEREDITAMENT.

Incoterm *n.* An international trade term. Incoterms, the best known of which are *CIF and *FOB, are used as an international shorthand in commercial agreements. A glossary of these terms, the latest edition of which is **Incoterms 2010**, is published by the International Chamber of Commerce. It sets out definitions of the various Incoterms, which deal with such matters as which party to a contract is responsible for transport of the goods, who insures them in transit, and who arranges payment of customs duties.

(⊕) SEE WEB LINKS

• Incoterms information from the website of the International Chamber of Commerce

incriminate *vb.* To indicate involvement in the commission of a criminal offence. A witness in court need not answer a question if, in the judge's opinion, the answer might expose him to the danger of criminal prosecution. A witness does not have this protection when his answer might lead only to civil action against him.

incumbrance *n. See* ENCUMBRANCE.

indecency *n.* Conduct that the average person would find shocking or revolting. There are common-law offences of outraging public decency and conspiring to outrage public decency (*Shaw v DPP* [1962] AC 220 (HL); *Knuller Ltd v DPP* [1973] AC 435 (HL)). Examples might include *indecent exposure or staging an indecent exhibition. Indecency is a question of fact that is left in each case to the jury to decide.

indecent assault Formerly, an *assault or *battery in circumstances of indecency, such as touching or attempting to touch the genitals of another person without their consent. The Sexual Offences Act 2003 replaced the offence of indecent assault with that of *sexual assault.

indecent exposure *see* EXPOSURE.

indefeasible *adj.* Incapable of being made *void.

indemnity *n.* An agreement by one person (X) to pay to another (Y) sums that are owed, or may become owed, to him by a third person (Z). It is not conditional on the third person defaulting on the payment, i.e. Y can sue X without first demanding payment from Z. If it is conditional on the third person's default (i.e. if Z remains the principal debtor and must be sued for the money first) it is not an indemnity but a *guarantee. Unlike a guarantee, an indemnity need not be evidenced in writing. In many commercial contracts a party will indemnify another, often for liability from third-party claims such as breach of intellectual property rights. There is no duty to mitigate loss when indemnifying and the class of loss is wider, the amount of money recoverable is larger, and the ease of recovery is greater than where there is simply a damages claim for breach of a warranty in a commercial agreement.

An **indemnity insurance** policy is taken out for the benefit of a mortgagee (lender) when a high proportion (often 80%) of the purchase price for a domestic property is borrowed. Such indemnity policies have been held by the courts not normally to be for the benefit of the mortgagor (borrower), although the mortgagor pays the premiums on the policy; only the mortgagee can make a claim. *See also* INSURANCE.

indemnity basis A basis of *assessment of costs under which the receiving party recovers all costs incurred except any that have been unreasonably incurred or are of an unreasonable amount (Civil Procedure Rules Part 44). The receiving party is given the benefit of any doubt on questions of reasonableness.

indemnity principle One of the three principles of *land registration: that the title to registered land is guaranteed by the state, and that compensation will be paid for any loss caused by an error in the register. *See also* CURTAIN PRINCIPLE; MIRROR PRINCIPLE.

indenture *n.* (mainly historical) A deed, generally one creating or transferring an estate in land (e.g. a conveyance or a lease).

independent contractor A person or firm engaged to do a particular job of work, as opposed to a person under a *contract of employment. An independent contractor is his own master, bound to do the job he has contracted to do but having a discretion as to how to do it (*Ready Mixed Concrete (South East) Ltd v Minister of Pensions and National Insurance* [1968] 2 QB 497). A taxi-driver, for example, is the independent contractor of the passenger who hires him. A person who uses an independent contractor is not generally vicariously liable for torts committed by the contractor, but may be in exceptional cases; situations in which *vicarious liability may be incurred include those in which the contractor is employed in particularly hazardous activities, or to perform statutory duties, or to work on or over (but not merely near) the highway, or is specifically authorized to commit a negligent act.

Independent Housing Ombudsman A body set up under the Housing Act 1996 to ensure protection for housing association tenants and to deal with complaints against registered social landlords (not including local authorities).

(⊕) SEE WEB LINKS
• Website of the Housing Ombudsman Service

Independent Mental Capacity Advocate (IMCA) Under the Mental Capacity Act 2005, NHS bodies and local authorities are required in certain situations to instruct an Independent Mental Capacity Advocate to represent people who lack capacity (e.g. those with learning disabilities or mental health problems, including older people with dementia) and who have no family or friends to represent them. The role of the IMCA is to ensure that those persons' rights are respected and to ensure that they are represented when certain serious decisions are being made.

Independent Police Complaints Commission A body corporate established as part of the reforms contained in the Police Reform Act 2002. The Commission replaced the Police Complaints Authority and took over responsibility from that body for the independent investigation of complaints made against the police.

(⊕) SEE WEB LINKS
• Website of the Independent Police Complaints Commission

independent trade union A trade union holding a certificate of independence issued by the *Certification Officer. A certificate will only be issued if the union is not under the domination or control of any employer, group of employers, or employers' association and is not liable to any interference tending towards such control. A union that is refused a certificate of independence may appeal to the *Employment Appeal Tribunal. Trade unions that do not hold a certificate of independence cannot conclude a collective agreement restricting employees' rights to strike and have no statutory right to certain information that employers must disclose to recognized independent trade unions (*see* DISCLOSURE OF INFORMATION). Only officials of independent trade unions have a statutory right to time off work to pursue union activities and duties. Rules regarding the dismissal of an employee for an *inadmissible reason in relation to trade-union membership and activities and rules that prohibit employers from taking other action to deter employees from participating in a union only apply if the union holds a certificate of independence.

indexation allowance When a capital gain is made on the disposal of an asset by a company, the amount of the gain (and therefore the company's liability to tax) is adjusted for inflation by adding indexation allowance to the base cost of the asset. Indexation allowance is calculated by comparing the retail prices index for the month of disposal with the retail prices index for the month of acquisition.

Indexation allowance is not applied when computing the gain made by an individual. Instead, an individual pays *capital gains tax at a rate of 18% (basic rate) or 28% (higher rate), these rates being lower than the rates of 20%, 40%, and 45% applied to income.

index maps Maps kept in the *Land Registry showing the position and extent of every registered estate in land. The index maps can be searched to find out if a particular piece of land has an estate registered in respect of it.

indication of sentence In cases before the Crown Court, the defendant can request that the judge gives an indication of the sentence that is likely to be passed should the defendant plead guilty rather than continue with a trial. The hearing will usually take place in open court and should normally be sought at the *plea and case management hearing. The judge has complete discretion over whether or not to give an indication and is not obliged to give reasons should he decide not to do so. Any indication given is binding on the judge. If the defendant decides not to plead guilty the indication ceases to have effect. Guidance on the procedure is provided in *R v Goodyear* [2005] EWCA Crim 888, [2005] 3 All ER 117.

indictable offence An offence that may be tried on *indictment. Most serious common-law offences are indictable (e.g. murder, rape) and many are created by statute. When a statute creates an offence without specifying how it is to be tried, it is automatically an indictable offence. The most serious indictable offences (**indictable-only offences**) may only be tried in the Crown Court. However, some less serious indictable offences (*offences triable either way) may be tried either in the magistrates' court or in the Crown Court.

indictment *n.* A formal document accusing one or more persons of committing a specified *indictable offence or offences. It is read out to the accused at the trial. An indictment is in a particular form. It is headed with the name of the case and the place of trial. There is then a statement of offence, stating what crime has allegedly been committed, followed by particulars of the offence, with such details as the date and place of the offence, property stolen, etc. If the accused is charged with more than one offence, each allegation and charge appears in a separate paragraph called a **count**. Counts may, however, be **framed in the alternative**, i.e. two or more counts may charge different offences arising out of the same allegation of fact but the defendant may be convicted of only one of them. *See also* BILL OF INDICTMENT; TRIAL ON INDICTMENT.

indigenous peoples Those peoples and nations that have a historical continuity with pre-invasion and pre-colonial societies that developed on their territories and consider themselves distinct from other sectors of the societies now prevailing in those territories (or parts of them). Forming a non-dominant sector of the prevailing society, they exhibit a determination to preserve, develop, and transmit to future generations their ancestral territories, and their ethnic identity, as the basis of their continued existence as peoples, in accordance with their own cultural patterns, social institutions, and legal systems. Examples of indigenous peoples include the Sami (Lapps) in Scandinavia and the Cymry (Welsh) in the United Kingdom.

indirect discrimination A form of prohibited *discrimination based on any of the nine "protected characteristics" covered by the *Equality Act 2010. It occurs where a neutral provision, criterion, or practice is applied to everyone, but the result is to put one group at a particular disadvantage. If it cannot be shown that the application of the provision, criterion, or practice is a proportionate means of achieving a legitimate aim, there will be unlawful indirect discrimination (*Homer v Chief Constable of West Yorkshire Police* [2012] UKSC 15, [2012] 3 All ER 1287; *R (E) v Governing Body of JFS* [2009] UKSC 15, [2010] IRLR 136).

indirect evidence *See* CIRCUMSTANTIAL EVIDENCE.

Individual Savings Account (ISA) A type of savings account on which no tax is payable. There are two types of ISA; (a) a stocks and shares ISA and (b) a cash ISA. A stocks and shares ISA can include some cash; but a cash ISA must be only cash. A taxpayer can invest under the ISA scheme up to £15,000 in total in each tax year. No tax is payable on any of the income from ISA savings and investments, including dividends, interest, and bonuses, and no capital gains tax is payable on gains arising on ISA investments. Money can be withdrawn at any time without losing tax relief.

indivisible contract *See* PERFORMANCE OF CONTRACT.

indorsement *n. See* ENDORSEMENT.

in dubio mitius [Latin: more leniently in case of doubt] A term of art used in the construction of treaties and other legal documents. It indicates that when construing a treaty, the meaning to be preferred in any case of ambiguity is that which is less onerous to the party assuming an obligation, which is less likely to interfere with the territorial and personal supremacy of a party, or which involves fewer general restrictions upon the parties.

inducement *n.* **1.** The promise of some advantage held out by a person in authority in relation to a prosecution to a person suspected of having committed a criminal offence. At common law a confession made after an inducement was inadmissible. It may now render the confession unreliable, and therefore inadmissible, under section 76 of the Police and Criminal Evidence Act 1984. **2.** *See* MISREPRESENTATION.

inducing breach of contract The tort of intentionally persuading or inducing someone to break a contract made by him with a third party. Specific intention to cause breach is required; negligent interference with the claimant's contractual rights will not suffice (*Mainstream Properties Ltd v Young; OBG Ltd v Allan* [2007] UKHL 21, [2007] 2 WLR 920). It is actionable by the party who suffers loss from the breach. Thus a theatre manager may sue the person who induces a singer to break her contract to perform at his theatre (*Lumley v Gye* (1853) 2 E&B 216). The Trade Union & Labour Relations (Consolidation) Act 1992 provides a number of defences and in some instances a defence of *justification is available. Interference with contractual relations, which falls short of actual breach, is no longer actionable under this tort. *See* CAUSING LOSS BY UNLAWFUL MEANS.

industrial building A building in use for the purposes of a trade carried on in a mill, factory, or other similar premises. A special category of *capital allowance, known as industrial buildings allowance, can be claimed for the cost of a qualifying structure (Capital Allowances Act 2001 s 271). A building is a factory only if something is made there (*Vibroplant Ltd v Holland* [1982] 1 All ER 792 (CA)). Other cases that define an industrial building are: *Dale v Johnson Bros* [1951] 32 TC 487; *Saxone Lilley and Skinner (Holdings) Ltd v IRC* [1967] 1 All ER 756 (HL); *Bestway (Holdings) Ltd v Luff* [1998] STC 357 (Ch); *Sarsfield v Dixons Group plc* [1998] STC 938.

industrial democracy Participation in company management by employees. This may take the form of including directors elected by employees on the board of directors. *See also* EMPLOYEES' SHARE SCHEME.

industrial dispute *See* TRADE DISPUTE.

industrial injuries disablement benefit A pension or lump sum payable by the state to a person disabled by injury or a prescribed industrial disease sustained or contracted in the course of his employment. The amount of the benefit depends on the degree of disablement, as medically assessed. To be entitled to benefit, the disablement must be assessed as being at least 14% of total disability (1% in the case of some respiratory diseases and 20% for occupational deafness). The benefit is payable if the claimant is still suffering disability 15 weeks or more after the date of the accident or onset of the disease. The assessment can be reviewed if the claimant's condition changes.

industrial tribunal *See* EMPLOYMENT TRIBUNAL.

inevitable accident An accident that could not have been prevented by the exercise of ordinary care and skill.

in extenso [Latin: at full length] Referring to the citing or transcription of a document from beginning to end with nothing left out.

infant (minor) *n.* Since 1969, a *child under the age of 18. Certain rights (such as rights of parental responsibility, the right to make a child a ward of court, and the right to withhold consent to marriage) only apply to infants. Other rights (such as the right to marry with consent) are governed by different age limits, often 16. Infants have a limited *capacity to contract.

infanticide *n.* The killing of a child under 12 months old by its mother. If the mother can show that the balance of her mind was disturbed because of the effects of the childbirth or lactation, she will be found guilty of infanticide, rather than murder, and punished as though she was guilty of *manslaughter (Infanticide Act 1938 s 1). Most cases of infanticide are dealt with by probation or discharge. *See also* DIMINISHED RESPONSIBILITY.

inferior court Any of the courts that are subordinate to *superior courts, having a jurisdiction limited to a particular geographical area, size of claim, or type of case. Their decisions are normally subject to appeal to a superior court, and the exercise of their jurisdiction may be subject to control by a superior court. In England and Wales, *county courts and *magistrates' courts are inferior courts.

informal patient A patient who is admitted to a hospital or place of care for treatment of a mental disorder but who is not being detained under section 131 of the Mental Health Act. The great majority of such patients have consented to their admission and treatment and are therefore known as **voluntary patients**. They are not subject to any restrictions on leaving the place of care and may refuse any proposed treatment. A **non-voluntary informal patient** is one who lacks the capacity to *consent to admission but who is nevertheless judged to require treatment in his best interest. Such patients previously fell into the so-called *Bournewood gap but are now protected by the provisions of the amended Mental Capacity Act 2005 (*see* DEPRIVATION OF LIBERTY SAFEGUARDS).

information *n.* The written statement by which a prosecutor informs a magistrate of the offence for which a summons or warrant is required. A person who lays an information before a magistrate is an **informant** (*see* LAYING AN INFORMATION). An information must contain a statement that describes the offence in ordinary language, identify any legislation that creates it, and include such particulars of the conduct constituting the commission of the offence as to make clear what the prosecutor alleges against the defendant (Criminal Procedure Rules). The Criminal Justice Act 2003 also provides for a written charge and requisition for the accused to appear before the magistrates.

Information and Consultation Directive European legislation (Council Directive 2002/14) that provides a framework for minimum standards of information and consultation at national level where 50 or more persons are employed in an undertaking. In the UK, the directive was implemented by the Information and Consultation of Employees Regulations 2004. The Regulations apply only to undertakings employing at least 50 employees. The Regulations, which are enforced by the *Central Arbitration Committee, call for the provision of an information and consultation procedure, either at the initiative of the employer or request of the employees. Agreements concluded prior to the coming into force of the Regulations (April 2005) are not not covered by special rules.

informed consent The principle that determines the amount of information to be disclosed by clinicians or researchers to patients undergoing surgery or invasive tests or to subjects involved in a clinical trial in order to render their *consent lawful. In the USA, the doctrine is based upon the "prudent patient" criterion, i.e. the nature, depth, and amount of information is judged by the physician as that required by a prudent patient. In the UK the doctrine is based upon the "prudent physician" criterion, i.e. the nature, depth, and amount of information is judged by the physician as that which is necessary for the patient. Failure to disclose such information will render any treatment unlawful.

informer *n.* A person who gives information to the police about crimes committed by others. An informer who is himself involved in the crimes may sometimes receive a lighter sentence in return for cooperation with the police that leads to the conviction of other offenders. However, the police may not employ their own informers to participate in crimes and then arrest the criminals, and a police informer who pretends to join a plot to commit a crime may himself be guilty of *conspiracy. It is nevertheless generally thought that if a police informer pretends to help in committing a crime with the intention of frustrating it, he will not be considered an *accessory if he fails to prevent the crime taking place.

in gross Existing in its own right and not as ancillary to land or any other thing. For example a profit *à prendre* can exist in gross, conferring rights on persons whether or not they own land capable of benefiting. An easement cannot exist in gross since there must be a dominant tenement.

inherent vice An inherent defect in certain goods that makes them liable to damage. Some fibres, for example, are liable to rot during shipment. If a carrier or insurer of such goods has not been warned of the inherent vice, he will not be liable for damage resulting directly from the defect.

inheritance *n.* **1.** The devolution of property on the death of its owner, either according to the provisions of his will or under the rules relating to intestacy contained in the Administration of Estates Act 1925 as amended. **2.** Property that a beneficiary receives from the estate of a deceased person.

inheritance tax (IHT) A tax on transfers of capital made on or after 18 March 1986. Unlike capital transfer tax (CTT), which preceded it, IHT is designed to operate primarily as a tax on transfers that occur on death. However, in order to prevent too obvious avoidance, the tax also charges retrospectively certain lifetime gifts. Some classes of gifts, such as gifts between husbands and wives and gifts to charities, are totally exempt from IHT. Other classes of gift are liable to IHT if the transferor dies within seven years of making the gift; these are known as *potentially exempt transfers. IHT is payable on a *transfer of value, this being any disposition by which the value of a person's estate is reduced.

(⊕) SEE WEB LINKS

- Inheritance tax area of the HM Revenue and Customs website

inhibition *n.* (in land law) An entry in the proprietorship register relating to registered land (*see* LAND REGISTRATION) that prohibits the registration of any dealing with the land, such as a transfer or mortgage, for a specified time. Such entries were possible under the Land Registration Act 1925, but since the coming into force of the Land Registration Act 2002 (on 13 October 2003), no new inhibitions can be entered. Instead, a *restriction will be entered in similar circumstances.

inhuman treatment or punishment Treatment that causes intense physical and mental suffering (*Ireland v UK* (1978) Series A no 26 2 EHRR 25). The prohibition on inhuman treatment or punishment as set out in Article 3 of the European Convention on Human Rights is part of UK law as a consequence of the *Human Rights Act 1998. This right is an *absolute right. Public authorities have a limited but positive duty to protect this right from interference by third parties.

injunction *n.* A remedy in the form of a court *order addressed to a particular person that either prohibits him from doing or continuing to do a certain act (a **prohibitory injunction**) or orders him to carry out a certain act (a **mandatory injunction**). The remedy is discretionary and will be granted only if the court considers it just and convenient to do so; it will not be granted if damages would be a sufficient remedy.

Injunctions are often needed urgently. A temporary injunction (an **interim injunction**) may therefore be granted at a special hearing pending the outcome of the main hearing of the case. If it is granted, the claimant must undertake to compensate the defendant for any damage he has suffered by the grant of the injunction if the defendant is successful in the main action. If judgment is given for the claimant in the main action, a **perpetual injunction** may be granted. A person who fails to abide by the terms of an injunction may be guilty of *contempt of court. *See also* FREEZING INJUNCTION; QUIA TIMET.

injuria absque damno (injuria sine damno) [Latin: wrong without damage] A controversy in which, although no actual damage was done, a legal wrong still occurred. Thus, in *Entick v Carrington* (1765) 19 How St Tr 1029, 1066 (Lord Camden CJ); 95 ER 807, although no actual damage was caused by the trespass, it still amounted to a legal wrong to be punished by the law through the award of damages to the defendant.

injurious falsehood *See* MALICIOUS FALSEHOOD.

injury *n.* **1.** Infringement of a right. **2.** Actual harm caused to people or property.

injury to aliens A type of *state responsibility that is occasioned following injury to aliens by agents of the host state, the injury being incurred solely because of the nationality of the alien. A state is in consequence accountable for the acts of its agents in treating the aliens differently from the nationals of the host state. The *International Law Commission has published draft articles establishing rules in this area.

inland bill A *bill of exchange that is (or on the face of it purports to be) both drawn and payable within the British Islands or drawn within the British Islands upon some person resident there. All other bills are foreign bills. Unless the contrary appears on the face of a bill, the holder may treat it as an inland bill. The distinction is relevant to the steps taken when a bill has been dishonoured (*see* DISHONOUR).

in limine [Latin] Preliminary: used, for example, to describe an objection.

in loco parentis [Latin] In place of a parent: used loosely to describe anyone looking after children on behalf of the parents, e.g. foster parents or relatives. In law, however, only a guardian or a person in whose favour a residence order is made stands *in loco parentis*; their rights and duties are determined by statutory provisions.

Inner Temple An *Inn of Court situated in the Temple between the Strand and the Embankment, London. The earliest recorded claim for its existence is 1440. Its Hall and Library were destroyed by bombing in World War II but have since been rebuilt.

innocent dissemination *See* DEFAMATION.

innocent misrepresentation *See* MISREPRESENTATION.

innocent passage *See* TERRITORIAL WATERS.

innominate terms (intermediate terms) Terms of a contract that cannot be classified as *conditions or *warranties. The parties to a contract may label the terms of the contract as either conditions or warranties and those labels will usually be respected by the courts provided that the result is reasonable. Similarly, certain terms have traditionally been treated as conditions or warranties even though they have not been labelled as such (for example, time clauses in mercantile contracts are to be treated as conditions: *The Mihalis Angelos* [1971] 1 QB 354). Innominate terms are those that will not fit the above categories. The remedy for breach of an innominate term will depend on whether or not the breach is a **fundamental breach**, i.e. such that the injured party has been deprived of substantially the whole of the benefit of the contract. If the injured party has been so deprived, he will be entitled to treat the contract as repudiated and claim damages. If not, he will be entitled to damages only (*Hong Kong Fir Shipping Co Ltd v Kawasaki Kisen Kaisha Ltd* [1962] 2 QB 26 (CA)). *See also* BREACH OF CONTRACT.

Inns of Chancery Formerly, Inns similar but subordinate to the *Inns of Court, to which they were attached (for example, Staple Inn and Barnard's Inn were attached to Gray's Inn). Originally they were societies in which students prepared for admission to the Inns of Court; later they became societies of attorneys. They were dissolved in the late 19th century.

Inns of Court Ancient legal societies situated in central London; every *barrister must belong to one of them. These voluntary unincorporated associations have the exclusive right of call to the Bar. The early history of the Inns is disputed, but they probably began as hostels in which those who practised in the common law courts lived. These hostels gradually evolved a corporate life in which *Benchers, barristers, and students lived together as a self-regulating body. From an early date they had an important role in legal education. In modern times four Inns survive: *Gray's Inn, *Inner Temple, *Lincoln's Inn, and *Middle Temple.

innuendo *n.* In an action for *defamation, a statement in which the words may be defamatory as a result of a hidden meaning. The hidden meaning must be capable of being understood from the words themselves by people to whom the statement is published. A **true innuendo** is one in which the meaning is hidden in the absence of special facts and circumstances: in this situation the claimant must set out in his *particulars of claim the facts or circumstances that make the words defamatory (*Tolley v J S Fry & Sons Ltd* [1931] AC 333 (HL)). A **false innuendo** is one that an ordinary person, guided by his general knowledge and experience, would infer from the natural and ordinary meaning of the words (*Lewis v Daily Telegraph Ltd* [1964] AC 234 (HL)): in this situation the claimant does not have to support his claim with additional evidence.

in pari delicto, porior est conditio possidentis [Latin: in equal fault the condition of the possessor is more favourable] A maxim meaning that where both parties to a dispute are equally in the wrong, the defendant holds the stronger ground. The law will take notice of an illegal transaction to defeat a suit, but not to maintain one. Thus, in *Taylor v Chester* (1889) LR 4 QB 309 the plaintiff failed to recover money deposited with the defendant as a security for a debt contracted for wine and suppers supplied to the plaintiff by the defendant in a brothel kept by her.

in pari material [Latin: on a like matter] *See* INTERPRETATION.

in personam [Latin: against the person] Describing a court action or a claim made against a specific person or a right affecting a particular person or group of people (*compare* IN REM). The *maxim of equity "equity acts *in personam*" refers to the fact that the Court of Chancery issued its decrees against the defendant himself, who was liable to imprisonment if he did not enforce them.

input tax The *value-added tax liability incurred by a taxable person in respect of goods and services used (or to be used) for the purpose of a business carried on (or to be carried on) by him (Value Added Tax Act 1984 s 24(1)). The VAT that has to be paid by a trader is his *output tax made *less* his input tax.

inquest *n.* An inquiry into a death the cause of which is unknown. An inquest is conducted by a *coroner and often requires the decision of a jury of 7–11 jurors. It must be held in the case of a sudden death whose cause is unknown or suspicious, a death occurring in prison, or when the coroner reasonably suspects that the death was caused by violent or unnatural means. Inquests are not, however, criminal proceedings; witnesses are usually cross-examined only by the coroner and the strict laws of evidence do not apply. If unlawful *homicide is suspected, and criminal proceedings are likely, the coroner will usually adjourn the inquest (and must do so if requested to by a chief police officer). If the inquest jury find that a particular person caused the death in circumstances amounting to an unlawful homicide, that person may stand trial. It is an offence to dispose of a body with the intention of preventing an inquest being held.

inquiry *n.* (in international law) An attempt to discover the facts surrounding an international incident that is the subject of a dispute between two or more parties by means of an impartial investigative body. Such an investigation is intended to promote a successful resolution of the dispute. In treaty law each of the *Bryan Treaties and a number of other treaties between South and Central American states provided for the establishment of permanent commissions of inquiry. In 1967 the UN General Assembly adopted a resolution supporting the institution of such impartial fact-finding and requested the Secretary-General to establish a register of experts whose services could be used by states in specific disputes. Perhaps the most famous example of an inquiry was that following the Dogger Bank incident of 1904, which involved the accidental sinking of British fishing boats by the Russian Baltic fleet. *See also* CONCILIATION; GOOD OFFICES; MEDIATION.

inquiry panels Formal independent panels set up under the Inquiries Act 2005 to look into matters of public concern (e.g. a national disaster or alleged corruption in government). The 2005 Act, which applies throughout the UK, repeals the Tribunals of Inquiry (Evidence) Act 1921, under which **tribunals of inquiry** were previously established. The Act also makes provision for ministers to set the terms of reference, to appoint a chairman to conduct the inquiry, and to appoint additional panel members and assessors where appropriate.

inquisition *n.* A document containing the verdict of a coroner's *inquest. It consists of the **caption** (details of the coroner, jury, and the inquest hearing), the **verdict** (identification of the body and probable cause of death), and the **attestation** (signatures of the coroner and jurors). An **open verdict** may be recorded when there is insufficient evidence of the cause of death.

inquisitorial procedure A system of criminal justice, in force in some European countries but not in England, in which the truth is revealed by an inquiry into the facts conducted by the judge. In this system it is the judge who takes the initiative in conducting the case, rather than the prosecution or defence; his role is to lead the investigations, examine the evidence, and interrogate the witnesses. *Compare* ACCUSATORIAL PROCEDURE.

in re [Latin: in the matter of] A phrase used in the headings of law reports, together with the name of the person or thing that the case is about (for example, cases in which wills are being interpreted). It is often abbreviated to *re.*

in rem [Latin: against the thing] **1.** Describing a right that should be respected by other people generally, such as ownership of property, as distinct from a right *in personam.* **2.** Describing a court action that is directed against an item of property, rather than against a person or group of people. Actions *in rem* are a feature of the *Admiralty Court.

in rixa [Latin] In anger. In *slander actions, the defence that the words used were only spoken in the heat of the moment and were devoid of prior design.

insanity (insane automatism) *n.* (in criminal law) A defect of reason, arising from mental disease, that is severe enough to prevent a defendant from knowing what he did or that what he did was wrong. A person accused of a crime is presumed sane and therefore responsible for his acts, but he can rebut this presumption and escape a conviction if he can prove (*see* BURDEN OF PROOF) that at the time of committing the crime he was insane. For purposes of this defence, insanity is defined by the **M'Naghten Rules**. These were formulated by judges after the trial of Daniel M'Naghten (1843), who killed the Prime Minister's secretary by mistake for the Prime Minister, under the delusion that the government was persecuting him, and was acquitted on the grounds of insanity (*R v M'Naghten* (1843) 10 Cl & F 200; 8 ER 718). According to the rules, the defendant must show that he was suffering from a defect of reason arising out of "a disease of the mind" at the time of committing the act. This would usually include most psychoses, paranoia, and schizophrenic diseases, but psychopaths and those suffering from neuroses or subnormality would not normally fall within the terms of the rules. The defendant must also show that, as a result of the defect of reason, he either did not know the "nature and quality" of his acts, i.e. he did not know what he was doing (*R v Clarke* [1972] 1 All ER 219), or he did not know that his acts were wrong, even if he knew their nature and quality (*R v Windle* [1952] 2 QB 826). If the defendant is suffering from an insane delusion, he is treated as though the delusion was true and will have a defence if there would normally be one on those facts (for example, if he kills someone under the insane delusion that he is acting in self-defence, since self-defence is a defence). Medical evidence may be brought, but the jury are entitled to form their opinion on the facts.

If found to be insane the defendant is given a **special verdict** of "not guilty by reason of insanity" and may be admitted to hospital, may be subject to a supervision order, or may receive an absolute discharge. Magistrates' courts are not empowered to return a special verdict. They will either grant a complete acquittal, if the defendant's evidence of mental abnormality amounts to a denial that he had any necessary *mens rea* for the crime, or they may make a *hospital order, if the crime with which he is charged is one for which they could usually imprison him.

If someone in custody for trial is suffering from mental illness or severe subnormality, he may be detained in hospital and not brought to trial until he is fit. A person who is insane at the time of his trial, in the sense that he does not understand the charge and cannot properly instruct his lawyers, may be found *unfit to plead. *See also* GENERAL DEFENCES; IRRESISTIBLE IMPULSE; NON-INSANE AUTOMATISM.

insider dealing Taking advantage of specific unpublished price-sensitive information to deal in *securities to make a profit or avoid a loss. Under the Criminal Justice Act 1993, dealings by insiders and those who have acquired information from insiders may be a criminal offence. Improperly disclosing such information or encouraging others to deal is also prohibited.

insolvency practitioner A person appointed to officiate in the *winding-up or administration of a company or in bankruptcy proceedings. The Insolvency Act 1986 requires the appointment of a qualified practitioner to act as a *liquidator, an *administrative receiver, an administrator, the supervisor of a *voluntary arrangement, or a *trustee in bankruptcy. Under the Act, a person is only authorized to act in such a capacity if he has met certain statutory requirements, including membership of an approved professional body (such as the Institute of Chartered Accountants of England and Wales or the Insolvency Practitioners Association).

in specie [Latin] In a specific form. If a will creates a trust, the property of which was a house to be enjoyed by the beneficiary *in specie*, the beneficiary must enjoy the house in its bequeathed form and not the proceeds of its sale.

inspection by judge *See* VIEW.

inspection of documents *See* DISCLOSURE AND INSPECTION OF DOCUMENTS.

inspection of property (in civil proceedings) A procedure allowing the High Court or the county courts to order the inspection, preservation, custody, and detention of any property (including land) that is (or may become) the subject matter of proceedings or in respect of which any questions may arise in proceedings (Civil Procedure Rules Part 25). Such an order may be made before the issue of proceedings, in respect of any property that may become the subject matter of subsequent proceedings or which is relevant to issues that will arise in such proceedings. Once proceedings have started, an order may be made in respect of property in the possession of a party, provided that the application is in respect of a physical thing (not details of a manufacturing process, for example), and an order may be made if the property is in the possession of a non-party. In each instance, the order is sought by issuing an application notice supported by evidence.

instant committal A committal without consideration of the evidence, introduced under section 1 of the Criminal Justice Act 1967. *Committal proceedings were abolished in all cases in 2013.

institutional constructive trust *See* CONSTRUCTIVE TRUST.

instrument *n.* A formal legal document, such as a will, deed, or conveyance, which is evidence of (for example) rights and duties. The *European Convention on Human Rights is a **living instrument** in that it must be interpreted in the light of present-day conditions rather than by trying to ascertain the meaning of those who drafted it over fifty years ago. *See also* STATUTORY INSTRUMENT.

insufficient evidence The situation in which the evidence in a trial does not entitle the fact finders to make a certain finding. For example, if there is insufficient evidence for a conviction in a criminal trial, the judge should direct the jury to return a verdict of not guilty.

insulting behaviour *See* THREATENING BEHAVIOUR.

insurable interest An interest (financial or otherwise) in the subject matter of a contract of *insurance, which provides the person insured with the right to enforce the contract. An insurable interest (e.g. ownership of goods insured) distinguishes a contract of insurance from a wager or bet. An interest is required by statute for various types of insurance contract (e.g. life insurance).

insurance *n.* A contract in which one party (the **insurer**) agrees for payment of a consideration (the **premium**) to make monetary provision for the other (the **insured**) upon the occurrence of some event or against some risk. For such contracts to be enforceable, there must be some element of uncertainty about the events insured against and the insured must have an *insurable interest in the subject matter of the contract. (The term **assurance** has the same meaning as insurance but is generally used in relation to events that will definitely happen at some time or another (especially death), whereas insurance refers to events that may or may not happen.) There are two types of insurance: **indemnity insurance**, which provides an indemnity against loss and in which the measure of the loss is the measure of payment (e.g. a fire policy); and **contingency insurance**, which involves payment on a contingent event and in which the sum paid is not measured by the loss but stated in the policy (e.g. a life policy). A contract of insurance is one requiring the utmost good faith (*see* UBERRIMAE FIDEI) and is voidable if a party fails in preliminary negotiations to disclose a fact material to the risk (*see*

NONDISCLOSURE; VOIDABLE CONTRACT). Innocent or fraudulent *misrepresentation may also render the contract voidable, or the contract may be terminated for breach of an essential term (*see* WARRANTY). Particular types of insurance include *life assurance, fire insurance, motor-vehicle insurance (*see* THIRD-PARTY INSURANCE), *marine insurance, liability insurance, and guarantee insurance. There is considerable statutory regulation of insurance business.

Insurers are either **insurance companies** or *Lloyd's underwriters. Insurance companies are regulated by statute, aimed, among other things, at ensuring the insurance companies have sufficient funds to meet all claims made on them. **Insurance brokers** negotiate insurance contracts with insurance companies or Lloyd's underwriters on a commission basis and usually handle claims on their clients' behalf. In the event of a claim the insured receives either the amount agreed in the policy or an appropriate sum that is calculated by an independent **insurance assessor**.

insurance broker *See* INSURANCE.

insurance company *See* INSURANCE.

insurance policy A formal document issued by an insurer setting out the terms of a contract of *insurance. Insurance contracts are not required by law to be in writing. Before the issue of a policy an insurer may issue a **cover note**, which is itself a temporary contract of insurance.

insurance premium tax (IPT) A tax added to insurance premiums payable on or after 1 October 1994. The statutory provision for charging IPT is the Finance Act 1994 (s 48–74; schs 6A, 7, 7A).

insurgency *n.* A state of revolt against constituted authority by rebels who are not recognized as *belligerent communities. Hence, recognition by nation X of a state of insurgency in nation Y means that while the former nation acknowledges a state of rebellion or revolt in nation Y, it is not yet prepared to extend recognition of a state of belligerency to that nation. Such a decision is based upon the relative proportion and success of the rebellion or revolt within state Y.

intangible property *Property that has no physical existence: *choses in action and incorporeal *hereditaments.

intellectual property Intangible property that includes *patents, *trade marks, *copyright, and registered and unregistered *design rights.

Intellectual Property Enterprise Court A *county court established under the Copyright, Design and Patents Act 1988 to exercise a special jurisdiction in cases relating to patents and designs. The court, which was originally known as the **Patents County Court**, provides a cheaper and quicker forum for patent and design cases than the *Patents Court of the High Court. Patents agents have *rights of audience there.

intention *n.* The state of mind of one who aims to bring about a particular consequence. Intention is one of the main forms of *mens rea, and for some crimes the only form (for example, murder). A person is assumed to intend those consequences of his acts that are inevitable but cannot be presumed to intend a consequence merely because it is probable or natural. In the latter case, the jury must decide, on all the available evidence, whether or not in fact the accused did intend the consequences. The jury is entitled to find that the accused intended the consequences of his action if the consequence was a virtual certainty and the defendant recognized it as such (*R v Woollin* [1999] 1 AC 82 (HL)). This is sometimes known as **oblique intention** or **indirect**

intention. Intention is often contrasted with *recklessness and should not be confused with *motive. For some purposes, offences are divided into crimes of *basic intent or *specific intent. *See also* ULTERIOR INTENT.

Intention to injure is also a constituent element of some torts, particularly those dealing with business relations (e.g. *conspiracy, *intimidation, *inducing breach of contract).

intention of testator The meaning that a testator intends his will to have. In interpreting a will, the court seeks to give effect to the intention of the testator as expressed in the will, even if capricious or eccentric. There are rules of construction to enable the testator's intention to be ascertained where it is not clear from the face of the will (*see* ARMCHAIR PRINCIPLE; INTERPRETATION OF WILLS).

intention to create legal relations One of the key constituents of a *contract. An agreement is only enforceable if, *inter alia*, there is an intention that it should be legally binding. As a general rule, the law presumes that familial and social agreements are not intended to be binding (*Balfour v Balfour* [1919] 2 KB 571). The reverse presumption, i.e. that there is an intention to be bound, applies in agreements of a commercial nature (*Edwards v Skyway Ltd* [1964] 1 All ER 4). Both of the above presumptions can be rebutted by bringing forth evidence to the contrary (*Merritt v Merritt* [1970] 1 WLR 1211).

inter alia [Latin] Among other things. The phrase is used to make it clear that a list is not exhaustive.

interest *n.* **1.** In land law, a right in or over land. Such a right may be either legal or equitable. The two most important interests in land are the two legal estates, the *fee simple absolute in possession (freehold) and the *term of years absolute (leasehold). There are also a number of other interests in land that may be legal rather than equitable, the most important of which are legal *mortgages and legal *easements. Other interests in land are equitable, such as the interests of beneficiaries under a *trust of land or a *settlement; in such cases the legal estate is held by trustees. *See also* EQUITABLE INTERESTS. **2.** In general language, a charge made for borrowing a sum of money. For taxation purposes, there is no statutory definition of interest. In *Bennett v Ogston* [1930] 15 TC 374, 379, Mr Justice Rowlatt defined it as "payment by time for the use of money"; *Halsbury's Laws of England* defines it as "the return or compensation for the use or retention by one person of a sum of money belonging to, or owed to, another". An excessive payment cannot be interest (*Cairns v MacDiarmid* [1982] STC 226). The fact that time is used to measure a payment does not suffice to make the payment interest when there is no principal debt (*Re Euro Hotel (Belgravia) Ltd* [1975] 3 All ER 1075 (Ch)).

interested party In criminal proceedings, a person or organization who is not the prosecutor or defendant, but who has some other legal interest in the case.

interest in expectancy Any future interest in property.

interest in possession Despite its crucial importance for *inheritance tax, statute does not define an interest in possession; Viscount Dilhorne described it as "a present right of present enjoyment" (*Pearson v IRC* [1980] STC 318 (HL) 326b). When an individual has an interest in possession over trust property, and that interest in possession was created before 22 March 2006, any charge to inheritance tax is computed by bringing into that person's estate the full capital value of the property over which he has an interest in possession (Inheritance Tax Act 1984 s 49). A lease for life is treated as an interest in possession (s 43(3)). Trusts are often categorized as falling into one of three categories: *bare trust, *discretionary trust, and **interest in possession trust**. Although this threefold division lacks precision and fails to recognize the importance of all the individual terms of a trust, the categorization of certain settlements as "interest in possession trusts" can be a useful starting point. Broadly, such a trust is one in which the beneficiaries are entitled to the income generated by the trust assets for a fixed period or until death. Interest in possession trusts created on or after 22 March 2006 are subjected to the same inheritance tax treatment as discretionary trusts.

interfering with contractual relations *See* CAUSING LOSS BY UNLAWFUL MEANS; INDUCING BREACH OF CONTRACT.

interfering with trade or business The tort of deliberately interfering with the trade or business of another person by unlawful means, thereby causing damage to that person. Liability in this tort is wider than in the tort of *inducing breach of contract, since it is not necessary to show that an existing contract has been interfered with or broken. The operation of the tort in *trade disputes is limited by statute. This tort is now encompassed in that of *causing loss by unlawful means.

interfering with vehicles Under the Criminal Attempts Act 1981, it is an offence, punishable with up to three months' imprisonment and/or a fine, for a person to interfere with a vehicle or anything it carries with the intention that he or someone else will steal the vehicle or any of its contents or take the vehicle without the owner's consent. The offence was introduced when the *sus law was abolished. A constable may arrest anyone he reasonably suspects of this offence. It is also a *summary offence, under the Road Traffic Act 1988, to get onto a vehicle on a road or local authority car park or to tamper with its brakes or other part of its mechanism without lawful authority or reasonable cause. *See also* CONVEYANCE.

interfering with witnesses Attempting to prevent a witness from giving evidence or to influence the evidence he gives. Making improper threats against witnesses may amount to the common-law offence of *perverting the course of justice (*R v Kellett* [1976] QB 372); persuading a witness to tell a lie constitutes – in addition to this – the offence of subornation of *perjury. It is also perverting the course of justice to put pressure upon a witness to give evidence or to pay him money to testify in a particular way. Sometimes interfering with witnesses may also amount to *contempt of court. There is also a separate common-law offence of **tampering with witnesses** when one uses threats to persuade them not to give evidence. *See also* INTIMIDATION.

interim *See* INTERLOCUTORY.

interim appeal (**interlocutory appeal**) An appeal against an order made during the pretrial stage of civil litigation. Generally, appeals from district judges and masters are to the High Court or a county court circuit judge; appeals from a decision of a county court circuit judge are to a High Court judge or to the Court of Appeal; and appeals from a High Court judge are to the Court of Appeal (Civil Division). *See* APPELLATE JURISDICTION.

interim injunction (**interlocutory injunction**) *See* INJUNCTION.

interim judgment (**interlocutory judgment**) A decision by the court in civil proceedings that only deals with part of the matter in dispute. *Compare* FINAL JUDGMENT.

interim measures (in competition law) Temporary sanctions that the European Commission and the UK Office of Fair Trading have powers (by decision and under the Competition Act 1998, respectively) to impose on businesses that are in breach of the competition rules, pending a final decision. This ensures that permanent damage is not done to the party who has complained of a breach of the rules. The interim measures may consist of requiring the offending company to resume supplies of goods to the complainant or to remedy the conduct of which complaint has been made in some other way. *See also* INTERIM RELIEF.

interim payment An order under Part 25 of the *Civil Procedure Rules for payment of a sum of money on account by a defendant of any damages, debt, or other sum of money (excluding costs) that the court may hold him liable to pay to the claimant. When such damages are claimed, it is necessary to show that the defendant has admitted liability; that the claimant has already obtained judgment for damages to be assessed; or that if the action proceeded to trial the claimant would obtain judgment for substantial damages. *See also* PROVISIONAL DAMAGES.

interim proceedings (interlocutory proceedings) The preliminary stages in civil proceedings, such as service of statements of case and disclosure of documents, which occur between the issue of the claim form and the trial. Their principal functions are to define the issues that will have to be decided at the trial.

interim relief (interlocutory relief) A temporary remedy, such as an interim *injunction or *interim payment, granted to a claimant by a court pending the trial.

interim rent Rent that a landlord can request a court to fix for a *business tenancy when he has given the tenant notice to quit or when the tenant has applied for a new tenancy.

interlineation *n.* Writing between the lines of a document. The effect is the same as that of an *alteration.

interlocutory *adj.* During the course of proceedings. Before the introduction of the *Civil Procedure Rules in 1999, the term was applied to certain processes in civil proceedings occurring between initiation of the action and the final judgment (such as interlocutory injunctions). Under the Civil Procedure Rules, it has been replaced by the term **interim**.

intermediary *n.* In criminal proceedings, a person who asks a witness (particularly a child) questions posed by the cross-examining legal representative.

intermediate terms *See* INNOMINATE TERMS.

internal waters All rivers, canals, lakes (excluding international ones), and landlocked seas, the waters of ports, bays, and roadsteads, and the waters on the landward side of the *baseline of the territorial sea. Within its internal waters, a coastal state exercises civil and criminal jurisdiction over foreign merchant ships and also administrative functions, such as enforcing customs and fishing regulations. *Compare* TERRITORIAL WATERS.

International Bank for Reconstruction and Development (IBRD; World Bank) A specialized agency of the United Nations. It developed from the international monetary and financial conference held at Bretton Woods, New Hampshire, in 1944 and was established by 44 nations in 1945. Its central purpose is to spur economic growth in developing states through the provision of loans and technical assistance to their respective governments. The IBRD currently (2009) has 185 members.

international carriage The carriage of persons or goods between two or more nations, which is regulated by various international conventions. The international carriage of goods by sea is governed by the Hague Rules (1924), the Hague–Visby Rules (1968), and the Hamburg Rules (1978, not yet generally adopted); that of goods by road by the Geneva Convention (1956); and that of goods by rail by a convention of 1980. (*See also* CARRIAGE OF GOODS BY AIR). There are also conventions regulating the international carriage of passengers by sea, rail, and road. The UK is a party to various of these conventions and has legislated to give them legal effect; for example, the Carriage of Goods by Sea Act 1971 covers the Hague–Visby Rules. *See* BILL OF LADING.

International Court of Justice A court at The Hague, consisting of 15 judges elected for 9-year terms of office, that has power to determine disputes relating to international law. It was set up by the United Nations in succession to the Permanent Court of International Justice, and all members of the UN are automatically parties to the Statute of the Court. No state may be brought before the Court in contentious proceedings unless it has accepted its jurisdiction, either by agreement in a particular case or by recognition of the authority of the Court in general, in respect of any dispute with another state accepting the general jurisdiction of the Court (the **principle of reciprocity**; *see also* OPTIONAL CLAUSE). The Court may also give advisory opinions (*see* ADVISORY JURISDICTION), which do not bind the parties but are of great *persuasive authority. The Court's first case was that of the Corfu Channel litigation (*Great Britain v Albania* [1949] ICJ Rep 1, 244). The Court decided that the UK had a right to navigate through the Corfu Channel, thus holding Albania responsible for the damage to a Royal Navy vessel. At the point of writing, Albania has still to pay the compensation awarded by the Court.

International Criminal Court (ICC) A permanent court to try individuals for the most serious offences of global concern. In July 1998, 160 nations signed the Statute of Rome in order to establish this court. Crimes within the jurisdiction of the Court are *genocide, *war crimes, and crimes against humanity, such as widespread or systematic extermination of civilians, enslavement, torture, rape, forced pregnancy, persecution on political, racial, ethnic, or religious grounds, and enforced disappearances. Prior to the establishment of the Court offences had been tried by ad hoc tribunals such as the *International Criminal Tribunal for Rwanda. The Court set up by the statute of Rome is both permanent and has a jurisdiction extending to a large number of states. However, the Rome Statute provides that, except when the UN Security Council determines to the contrary, the ICC will be limited to the prosecution of crimes that take place on the territory of states that have ratified the Statute of Rome. The USA, despite having signed the Statute, has stated that it has no intention of ratifying the treaty. The Statute of the Court entered into force on 1 July 2002.

The ICC will be "complementary" to municipal tribunals, which will retain jurisdiction unless they are unable or unwilling genuinely to investigate and prosecute a crime. An incident may be referred to the ICC by the Security Council. Alternatively, a state party can refer a situation to the prosecutor, or the prosecutor can initiate an investigation on his or her own motion. If the prosecutor has determined that there is a reasonable basis to commence an investigation, he or she must inform all state parties and those states that would normally exercise jurisdiction over the alleged crime. Within one month, a state may inform the ICC that it is investigating, or has investigated, the alleged war crimes. The prosecutor must defer to the state's investigation unless the ICC determines that the state is unwilling or unable genuinely to carry out the investigation or prosecution.

By means of the International Criminal Court Act 2001 British tribunals are empowered to try war crimes recognized by the Statute of Rome. The Act enables UK investigative bodies to investigate and prosecute any ICC crimes committed in this country, or committed overseas by a UK national, a UK resident, or a person subject to UK services jurisdiction. It also permits the UK to reach an agreement with the ICC so that persons convicted can serve prison sentences in this country. In July 2005 three British soldiers who had served in Iraq were charged under the Act with "inhuman treatment of persons." They were to be tried by courts martial in the UK. *See also* INTERNATIONAL CRIMINAL TRIBUNAL FOR THE FORMER YUGOSLAVIA.

International Criminal Tribunal for Rwanda (ICTR) A tribunal created in 1994 pursuant to Resolution 955 of the UN Security Council. Given the well-publicized atrocities that took place during the civil strife in Rwanda in 1994, the Security Council exercised its powers under *Chapter VII of the UN Charter with the aim of contributing to the process of national reconciliation and the maintenance of peace in the region. The ICRT was established for the prosecution of persons responsible for genocide and other serious violations of international humanitarian law committed in Rwanda between 1 January 1994 and 31 December 1994. It may also deal with the prosecution of Rwandan citizens responsible for genocide and other such violations of international law committed in the territory of neighbouring states during the same time period. *See* INTERNATIONAL CRIMINAL COURT.

International Criminal Tribunal for the former Yugoslavia (ICTFY) A tribunal created in 1993 pursuant to two resolutions of the UN Security Council (UNSC Res 808 & 827 (1993)). The Security Council, having found that the widespread violations of international humanitarian law occurring within the territory of the former Yugoslavia, including the practice of "ethnic cleansing", constituted a threat to international peace and security, exercised its powers under *Chapter VII of the Charter. The tribunal's statute gives power to hear cases that extend to grave breaches under the Geneva Convention (Article 2), war crimes (Article 3), genocide (Article 4), and crimes against humanity (Article 5) that occurred on the territory of the former Yugoslavia from 1991 onward. The Statute also strips traditional absolute immunity from public officials for their official actions in Article 7(2). *See* INTERNATIONAL CRIMINAL COURT.

international law (*jus gentium*, law of nations) The system of law regulating the interrelationship of sovereign states and their rights and duties with regard to one another. In addition, certain international organizations (such as the *United Nations), companies, and sometimes individuals (e.g. in the sphere of *human rights) may have rights or duties under international law. International law deals with such matters as the formation and recognition of states, acquisition of territory, war, the law of the sea and of space, treaties, treatment of aliens, human rights, international crimes, and international judicial settlement of disputes. The usual sources of international law are (1) *conventions and *treaties; (2) international *custom, in so far as this is evidence of a general practice of behaviour accepted as legally binding (*see* OPINIO JURIS; CUSTOMARY INTERNATIONAL LAW); (3) the *general principles of law recognized by civilized nations.

International law is also known as **public international law** to distinguish it from *private international law, which does not deal with relationships between states.

International Law Commission (ILC) A body established in 1947 by General Assembly Resolution 174 (II) and acting under Article 13 of the United Nations Charter. The ILC consists of 25 members of recognized competence in international law who are elected for five-year periods by the General Assembly from a list of candidates nominated by the member states of the UN. The mission of the ILC is to promote the progressive development of international law by preparing draft conventions on subjects that have not yet been regulated by international law and by codifying the law. It produces annual reports of current problems.

international legal personality Legal personality is principally an acknowledgement that an entity is capable of exercising certain rights and being subject to certain duties on its own account under a particular system of law. In municipal systems, the individual human being is the archetypal "person" of the law, but certain entities, such as limited companies or public corporations, are granted a personality distinct from the individuals who create them (*see* JURISTIC PERSON). Further, they can enter into legal transactions in their own name and on their own account. Under international law, the state is the typical *legal person, and other entities may be considered as the "subjects" of international law in so far as they can enter into legal relations in the international sphere.

international minimum standard (in international law) A minimum standard of treatment that must always be observed with regard to the treatment of foreign nationals. This standard consists of at least the right to life, liberty, and free access to the courts and to the protection of property (especially fair compensation for the nationalization of property). An example of the standard being applied can be found in the *Neer Claim* (1926) 4 RIAA 60. The international minimum standard has proved to be contentious with developing countries, some of whom have argued that it merely advances Western economic imperialism. *See also* ESPOUSAL OF CLAIM; EXPROPRIATION; STATE RESPONSIBILITY. *Compare* NATIONAL TREATMENT STANDARD.

International Seabed Authority *See* DEEP SEABED AREA.

international supply contract A contract for the sale of goods made by parties whose places of business (or habitual residences) are in the territories of different states. The limitations imposed by the Unfair Contract Terms Act 1977 on the extent to which a person may exclude or restrict his liability (e.g. by an *exemption clause) do not apply to such a contract if (1) when it is made, the goods are in carriage (or due to be carried) from one state to another; (2) the offer and its acceptance take place in different states; or (3) the goods are to be delivered in a state other than that in which the offer and acceptance take place. However, other statutes may apply to such contracts, and in many countries the Vienna Convention on the International Sales of Goods and world trade rules under the *General Agreement on Tariffs and Trade (GATT) and the *World Trade Organization (WTO) will apply.

inter partes [Latin: between the parties] *See* WITH NOTICE.

interpleader *n*. A procedure used to decide how conflicting claims against the same person should be dealt with. It applies when there are two or more claims against the applicant (whether or not court proceedings have been issued) that conflict with each other; for example, when two or more people claim the same goods that are being held by the applicant. The court decides how the matter should be dealt with; it may, for example, direct that there should be a court action between the rival claimants.

Interpleader can be of two types. A **stakeholder's interpleader** arises in relation to a person liable on a debt or holding goods or money in respect of which there are rival claims. A **sheriff's interpleader** (in the High Court) or **interpleader under execution** (in the county court) arises in relation to execution of judgment by a *High Court Enforcement Officer or *bailiff who has to deal with rival claims in respect of goods taken under a writ or warrant of execution, when a third party (e.g. a television rental company) claims that the goods seized belong to that third party. The relevant procedural rules are to be found in Schedules 1 and 2 to the *Civil Procedure Rules.

interpretation (construction) *n.* The process of determining the true meaning of a written document. It is a judicial process, effected in accordance with a number of rules and presumptions. So far as is relevant, the rules and presumptions applicable to Acts of Parliament apply equally to private documents, such as deeds and wills.

The principal rules of **statutory interpretation** are as follows:

(1) An Act must be construed as a whole, so that internal inconsistencies are avoided.

(2) Words that are reasonably capable of only one meaning must be given that meaning whatever the result. This is called the **literal rule**.

(3) Ordinary words must be given their ordinary meanings and technical words their technical meanings, unless absurdity would result. This is the **golden rule**.

(4) When an Act aims at curing a defect in the law any ambiguity is to be resolved in such a way as to favour that aim (the **mischief rule**).

(5) The rule *ejusdem generis* (of the same kind): when a list of specific items belonging to the same class is followed by general words (as in "cats, dogs, and other animals"), the general words are to be treated as confined to other items of the same class (in this example, to other *domestic animals*).

(6) The rule *expressio unius est exclusio alterius* (the inclusion of the one is the exclusion of the other): when a list of specific items is not followed by general words it is to be taken as exhaustive. For example, "weekends and public holidays" excludes ordinary weekdays.

(7) The rule in *pari material* (on the like matter): when a prior Act is found to be "on the like matter" it can be used as an aid in construing the statute in question (*R v Loxdale* (1758) 1 Burr 445, 447 (Lord Mansfield); 97 ER 394).

(8) The rule *noscitur a sociis* (known by its associates): when a word or phrase is of uncertain meaning, it should be construed in the light of the surrounding words (*Bourne v Norwich Crematorium Ltd* [1967] 2 All ER 576 (Ch) 578).

Ambiguities may occasionally be resolved by referring to external sources; for example, the intention of Parliament in regard to a proposed Act, as revealed by ministers during its passage through Parliament, may be discovered by reference to *Hansard (Pepper v Hart* [1993] AC 593 (HL)). However, the House of Lords has ruled against the existence of an alleged **social policy rule**, which would enable an ambiguous Act to be interpreted so as to best give effect to the social policy underlying it.Apart from these specific rules, there are some general presumptions relating to the interpretation of statutes. They are presumed:

- not to bind the Crown (including the sovereign personally);
- not to operate retrospectively so far as substantive (but not procedural) law is concerned;
- not to interfere with vested rights (particularly without compensation);
- not to oust the jurisdiction of the courts; and
- not to derogate from constitutional rights or international law.

Nevertheless, clear words or necessary implication may override any of these presumptions.

A *consolidating statute is presumed not be intended to alter the law, but this does not apply to *codifying statutes, which may be concerned with clarifying law that was previously unclear.

Penal and taxing statutes are subject to **strict construction**, i.e. if after applying the normal rules of interpretation it is still doubtful whether or not a penalty or tax attaches to a particular person or transaction, the ambiguity must be resolved in favour of the subject. *See also* INTERPRETATION ACT; INTERPRETATION CLAUSE; PRO BONO PUBLICO.

Interpretation Act An Act of 1978 (originally 1889) that defines a number of common words and expressions and provides that the same definitions are to apply in all other Acts except those specifically indicating otherwise. For example, "person" includes (in addition to an individual) any body of persons corporate or unincorporate.

interpretation clause A clause in a written document that defines words and phrases used in the document itself. In an Act of Parliament it is called an **interpretation section**. *See also* INTERPRETATION ACT.

interpretation of wills The process of determining the true meaning of wills to give effect, as far as possible, to the testator's intention expressed in the will (*see* INTENTION OF TESTATOR). Generally the words used are given their ordinary grammatical meaning. If the words used are ambiguous, either in themselves or in the light of surrounding circumstances, extrinsic evidence may be admitted to assist in ascertaining the testator's intention. The process of construing a will by reference to the circumstances surrounding the testator when he made his will is commonly known as the *armchair principle. Such evidence may not be used to contradict a clear expression in the will. The **golden rule** is to adopt a construction that will avoid an *intestacy, on the basis that if the testator went to the trouble of making a will, he presumably did not intend to die intestate. There are also many detailed rules relating to the meaning of particular phrases and to imprecise gifts for charitable purposes.

interpretive theory of law A theory advanced by US legal philosopher Ronald Dworkin (1931–2013) that rejects *legal positivism on the principal ground that a separation between law and morals is impossible. Law, Dworkin argues, consists not merely of rules, as legal positivists generally claim, but also of what he calls "non-rule standards". When a court has to decide a hard case (i.e., one to which no statute or precedent applies), it will draw on these moral or political standards in order to reach a decision. According to Dworkin, adjudication is and should be interpretive: judges must decide hard cases through an interpretation of the political structure of their community as a whole, from the most profound constitutional rules to the details of, for example, the law of tort or contract. A successful interpretation is one that justifies the practices of the judge's society: it must "fit" with those practices in the sense that it coheres with existing legal materials defining the practices. Moreover, since an interpretation provides a moral justification for those practices, it must present them in the best possible moral light. In other words, the principles to which a judge must appeal will include his own conception of what is the best interpretation of the network of political institutions and decisions of his community. He must ask whether his judgment could form part of a consistent theory justifying this complete network. There is always one "right answer" to every legal problem; it is up to the judge to find it. This answer is "right" in the sense that it coheres best with the institutional and constitutional history of the law. Legal argument and analysis is therefore interpretive in nature.

interregnum *n.* **1.** The period between the death of a sovereign and the accession of his or her successor. **2.** Temporary rule exercised during such a period. In the UK a sovereign's death does not result in an interregnum (*see* DEMISE OF THE CROWN).

interrogation *n.* The questioning of suspects by the police. Suspects are not obliged to answer such questions (*see* RIGHT OF SILENCE), and the right of the police to question suspects is governed by the Police and Criminal Evidence Act 1984 and the *codes of practice made under it. The codes deal with such matters as the rights of the suspect to communicate with third parties, rights to legal advice and to medical treatment, and advice to the police on the administering of a *caution, the provision of interpreters, and the keeping of records concerning all these matters. There are special provisions relating to the interrogation of juveniles, the mentally ill, and the mentally handicapped. The provisions of the 1984 Act and the codes of practice have been amended and updated in the light of the requirements of the *Human Rights Act1998. *See also* CONFESSION.

interrogatory *n.* Formerly, a formal written question submitted by one party to civil litigation to another party and required to be answered on oath. Since 1999, this procedure has been replaced by a **request for further information** under Part 18 of the *Civil Procedure Rules.

in terrorem [Latin] Intimidating. The doctrine of *in terrorem* applies to conditions attached to gifts of personal property in wills or elsewhere. Such conditions are *in terrorem* if it is apparent that the donor does not really intend the recipient to lose the gift, but is merely making an idle threat; for example, when a donor makes a gift subject to a condition against marriage without another person's consent but does not make provision for the disposal of the gift if the recipient does not comply with the condition. Such conditions are void.

interstate trade Trade between states. EU competition rules (*see* COMPETITION LAW) apply only when an anticompetitive agreement or *abuse of a dominant position will affect trade between member states. Whether or not interstate trade is affected is therefore crucial to any competition analysis. Agreements relating to imports or exports are most likely to affect interstate trade, but so might an agreement between two businesses situated in one member state, depending on the terms or effect of the agreement.

intertemporal law The law that international courts apply when a long time has elapsed since the conclusion of a treaty, to take into account changes that have taken place in international law since the treaty was formulated and changes in the meaning of the expressions in the treaty. The existence of a right (e.g. to a territorial claim) should be based not only on the law in effect at the time the right was created, but also on the international law as applied to the continued existence of that right. The legitimacy of a title to territory must be renewed by the claimant state. The classic application of intertemporal law to a dispute can be found in the *Island of Palmas Arbitration* (*Netherlands v US*) (1928) 2 RIAA 829.

intervention *n.* Action taken to intervene in markets, for example to support prices, in the EU or within similar trading groups throughout the world. In the EU it occurs in relation to the *Common Agricultural Policy. The European Commission buys surplus produce at an agreed **intervention price**; the produce may be stored until prices alter. This practice formerly led to butter or meat "mountains", but goods held in intervention in this way have now largely been dissipated.

inter vivos [Latin] Between living people. If a trust is created *inter vivos* it is created during lifetime, as distinct from upon death. *See* SECRET TRUST.

intestacy *n.* The state in which a person dies without having made a will disposing of all his property. A **total intestacy** occurs when the deceased leaves no will at all, a will that only appoints executors but does not dispose of any property, or a will that is invalid (e.g. because the testator lacked *testamentary capacity). A **partial intestacy** arises when a will deals with only part of the testator's estate. The Administration of Estates Act 1925 s 46 as amended and orders made under it govern the manner in which an intestate estate is to be administered, the persons entitled to inherit, and the amounts and proportions of the estate they receive. The rules relating to intestacy reflect the importance accorded to familial relationships: the surviving spouse is given the larger share of the estate (*see* STATUTORY LEGACY).

intestate *n.* A person who dies without leaving a valid will; the deceased may be ruled partially intestate if the will fails to deal with the whole of his estate.

intimidation *n.* **1.** The act of frightening someone into doing something. Intimidation is not in itself a crime, but it may constitute part of a crime. For example, it is a crime to have sexual intercourse with a woman if her agreement was obtained by intimidation. It is a crime to intimidate a juror or witness in relation to proceedings with which he is connected (*see* CONTEMPT OF COURT). If one intimidates someone into handing over money or property, this may amount to theft, and in some cases to blackmail. There are also special statutory offences of threatening to destroy or damage someone else's property and threatening to kill someone. A person who commits a crime when intimidated by others may sometimes have a defence of *duress. See also* THREAT.

Under the Criminal Justice and Public Order Act 1994 it is also an offence to intimidate a person whom the offender believes to be a potential or actual witness or juror. The offender must, however, have an intention to obstruct an investigation or the course of justice although this will be presumed where it is proved that he did an act that intimidates with that intention. Similar offences exist with regard to reprisals against potential witnesses or jurors. **2.** An economic tort in which A, with the intention of harming B, either directly threatens B with some unlawful act or threatens C with an unlawful act in order to make him cause damage to B's interests. Thus if A threatens to do an unlawful act to B's employer (C) unless he dismisses B, and C succumbs to the threat, B has an action for intimidation against A for causing the loss of his job. It is irrelevant that C was entitled to dismiss B and did not act unlawfully: the essence of the tort is A's unlawful threat. The operation of the tort in *trade disputes is limited by statute. *See also* CAUSING LOSS BY UNLAWFUL MEANS.

intoxicating liquor For the purposes of the Licensing Act 1964, spirits, wine, beer, porter, cider (including perry), and any other fermented, distilled, or spirituous liquor. *See also* LICENSING OF PREMISES.

intoxication *n.* The taking, either voluntarily or involuntarily, of alcohol, drugs, or other substances, such as to alter the mood, perception, or judgment of the accused. Intoxication can arise either (1) voluntarily, where a defendant knowingly takes alcohol or drugs; or (2) involuntarily, where he is unaware he is taking an intoxicant or is taking drugs on medical advice. Although intoxication itself is not an offence (*but see* DRUNKENNESS), it is an element in a number of offences. These include *drunken driving, being found drunk in a public place, being drunk and disorderly in a public place, and being drunk in a public place while possessing a loaded firearm. It is also an offence to supply or offer to supply to a person under 18 a substance (e.g. a glue or solvent) whose fumes are likely to be inhaled by that person for the purpose of causing intoxication.

Voluntary intoxication is normally not a defence even if it prevents the defendant from having the necessary *mens rea* (*R v Lipman* [1970] 1 QB 152; *R v Dowds* [2012] EWCA Crim 281 (CA), [2012] 1 Cr App R 455). However, such intoxication is a relevant factor and will be a defence if: (1) it brings about a disease of the mind (e.g. *delirium tremens*) so that the defendant falls within the M'Naghten Rules (*see* INSANITY); or (2) the crime charged is one of *specific intent and intoxication prevents the defendant from having the necessary specific intent. There is no defence of voluntary intoxication to a crime of *basic intent where recklessness can satisfy the *mens rea*.

Involuntary intoxication may be a defence because a person so intoxicated cannot be said to be responsible for his condition and an intent induced in this way does not constitute having the necessary *mens rea* for a crime. However, in *R v Kingston* [1995] 2 AC 355 (HL) the House of Lords held that involuntary intoxication is not a defence to a criminal charge where there *is* evidence of *mens rea*.

Intoxication is not a defence if a person deliberately drinks or takes drugs in order to give himself "**Dutch courage**" to commit a crime (*Attorney-General for Northern Ireland v Gallagher* [1963] AC 349).

intra vires [Latin: within the powers] Describing an act carried out by a body (such as a public authority or a company) that is within the limits of the powers conferred on it by statute or some other constituting document (such as the memorandum and articles of association of a company). *Compare* ULTRA VIRES.

introductory tenancy A tenancy granted by a local authority or housing action trust that is intended as a probationary tenancy for 12 months. This will not be a *secure tenancy until the end of the 12 months. The local authority may also extend the introductory tenancy by a further six months if there are continuing doubts as to the conduct of the tenancy. If the landlord wishes to seek possession during the introductory tenancy, he must serve notice on the tenant, who has 14 days to seek a review. After the review has been completed, the landlord must notify the tenant of the decision and give reasons if the decision to evict stands. *Compare* STARTER TENANCY.

invalid care allowance *See* CARER'S ALLOWANCE.

inventory *n.* A detailed list of assets or property. A lease of furnished premises or a contract for the sale of chattels will usually contain an inventory from which the particular items can be identified. Under the Administration of Estates Act 1925 s 25 (as substituted by the Administration of Estates Act 1971 s 9), personal representatives must produce on oath an inventory of the deceased's estate when called upon by the court (this duty is effectively discharged by lodging an HM Revenue and Customs account).

investigation of a company An inquiry into the running of a company made by inspectors appointed by the Department for Business, Innovation and Skills acting under the Companies Act 2006. It may be ordered by the Secretary of State, on his own initiative or upon application by the shareholders or the company itself, or by the court. Such an inquiry may be held to supply company members with information or to investigate fraud, *unfair prejudice, nominee shareholders, or *insider dealing. The inspectors' report is usually published. Investigations can also be carried out by the Financial Services Authority in accordance with the Financial Services and Markets Act 2000, such as in cases of *insider dealing.

investment company Any company, either private or public, where the *business of the company is holding an investment in one or more other companies. The profits of an investment company are subjected to *corporation tax at the full rate. The lower rate of tax applied to trading companies are not available. Investment companies must give notice in prescribed form to the Companies Registry. Under the Companies Act 1985 they are subject to special provisions in relation to dividends.

invitation to treat *See* OFFER.

invitee *n.* A person permitted to enter land or premises for a purpose in which the occupier of the land has a material interest. An example of an invitee is a customer in a shop. *See* OCCUPIER'S LIABILITY.

in vitro fertilization (IVF) *See* HUMAN ASSISTED REPRODUCTION.

involuntary conduct Conduct that cannot be controlled because one is suffering from a physical or mental condition or is acting under *duress. Involuntary conduct will sometimes give rise to a defence of *insanity or *non-insane automatism, although it may not be a defence if one is aware of one's condition or induced it oneself. Sometimes conduct may be regarded as involuntary if one is in control of one's faculties; for example, when the brakes of a car suddenly fail; this will also afford a defence to a driving offence charge (*Hill v Baxter* [1958] 1 QB 277).

involuntary manslaughter *See* MANSLAUGHTER.

ipsi dixit [Latin: he, himself, said [it]] Describing an instance in which a judge states a legal principle without referring to any precedent or authority for that principle. In such circumstances jurists might comment that the judge made the statement *ipsi dixit* (i.e. he, himself, offered the proposition).

ipso jure [Latin: by the law itself] A phase used to describe legal consequences that arise by the mere operation of law. For example, an existing will is usually revoked *ipso jure* if the testator marries after executing it.

irrationality *n.* One of the common-law grounds of *judicial review of administrative action. It is presumed that public authorities are never empowered to exercise their powers irrationally; therefore irrational action by a public authority is considered to be *ultra vires*. Although it denotes behaviour that falls short of what is to be expected of a rational public authority, the precise parameters of the term are unclear and it has been used to describe a range of behaviour. It is often used interchangeably with the term *Wednesbury* unreasonableness but has become the more common term since the case of *Council of Civil Service Unions v Minister for the Civil Service* [1985] AC 374 (HL), in which the terms irrationality, illegality, and *procedural impropriety were used to define the common law grounds or heads of judicial review.

irrebuttable presumption *See* PRESUMPTION.

irresistible impulse An uncontrollable urge to do something. Irresistible impulse is not usually a defence in law and it will not afford a defence of *insanity, unless it arises out of a disease of the mind as defined by the M'Naghten Rules. When, however, an impulse is irresistible in that the body reacts in an instinctive way to it, there may be a defence of *involuntary conduct. An irresistible impulse may also constitute *diminished responsibility. *See also* PROVOCATION.

irretrievable breakdown (of a marriage) *See* MARITAL BREAKDOWN; DIVORCE.

irrevocable *adj.* Incapable of being revoked. For example, *powers of appointment may be made irrevocable. On the other hand, a testator of sound mind can revoke his will at any time.

ISA *See* INDIVIDUAL SAVINGS ACCOUNT.

Islamic finance *See* ALTERNATIVE FINANCE ARRANGEMENTS; ISTISNA'A.

isonomy *n.* The principle of equality before the law of all the subjects or citizens of the state. It was first stated by ancient Greek writers and is considered to lie at the root of the Western legal tradition.

issue *n.* **1.** The matter in dispute in a court action. **2.** The children or other lineal descendants of a person. **3.** The total of bank notes in circulation within a country.

issued capital *See* AUTHORIZED CAPITAL.

issue estoppel *Estoppel arising in relation to an issue that has previously been litigated and determined between the same parties or their predecessors in title. The issue must be an essential element of the claim or defence in both sets of proceedings. This type of estoppel does not arise in criminal cases and its scope in civil cases is uncertain.

istisna'a In Islamic finance, a practice in which one party agrees to produce specific goods and services made according to certain agreed specifications and price for delivery on a certain date. The production of the goods includes any process of manufacturing, construction, assembling, or packaging. The work may be done by others. *Istisna'a* may also be used in preshipment financing of the acquisition of capital goods and to finance intangible goods such as gas and electricity. *See also* ALTERNATIVE FINANCE ARRANGEMENTS.

itemized pay statement The written statement that, under the Employment Rights Act 1996, an employer must provide for every employee who works eight or more hours a week, on or before each occasion wages or salaries are paid. The statement must contain the following information:

(1) the employee's gross pay for the period;
(2) the amounts and reason for any deductions;
(3) the net amount paid; and
(4) the method of calculating the net pay when different parts are calculated differently (e.g. if the pay is partly a basic wage and partly a commission or bonus payment).

The statement need not contain details of fixed deductions if it contains an aggregate amount of these deductions and the employer has given the employee, either before or at the time of payment, a standing written statement of fixed deductions that contains the following particulars of each deduction:

(1) the amount;
(2) the intervals at which the deduction is made;
(3) the purpose for which it is made.

The standing statement of fixed deductions must be reissued within 12 months of its first being issued and not more than every 12 months after that and it must incorporate any amendments. An employee can apply to an *employment tribunal if his employer fails to provide the statutory statement or reason for deductions. The tribunal can order the employer to provide statements and also to refund any unexplained deductions in respect of a period up to 13 weeks before the application.

IVF In vitro fertilization. *See* HUMAN ASSISTED REPRODUCTION.

J

jactitation of marriage A false assertion that one is married to someone to whom one is not in fact married. Proceedings for jactitation were abolished by the Family Law Act 1986 but an injunction may be sought to restrain such claims being made and may be useful in preventing a presumption of marriage from arising.

Jobseeker's Agreement An agreement that must be signed by a claimant for the *jobseeker's allowance and his JobCentre adviser. The agreement sets out any restrictions on the claimant's availability for work and outlines the type of work being sought and the plans the claimant has made for seeking work.

jobseeker's allowance (JSA) A taxable benefit that replaced both unemployment benefit and *income support for jobseekers from October 1996. Those with National Insurance contributions can claim contribution-based JSA, which is paid for up to six months. Those without NI contributions can claim income-based JSA, which is payable for as long as the claimant satisfies the rules. JSA is only paid to those who are available for work, are actively seeking work, and who have signed a *Jobseeker's Agreement. Income-based JSA is currently being replaced by *universal credit.

joinder of causes of action The combination in the same proceedings of several causes of action. Under Part 7 of the *Civil Procedure Rules the claimant may use a single *claim form to start all claims that can be conveniently disposed of in the same proceedings.

joinder of charges The joining of more than one charge of a criminal offence together in the same *indictment. This may be done when the charges are based on the same facts or are part of a series of offences of the same or similar character.

joinder of defendants Mentioning two or more defendants in one count of an *indictment and trying them together. It is possible to join two or more defendants even if one of them is the principal offender and the other an accessory; if they are separately indicted, however, they cannot subsequently be tried together. Sometimes (e.g. in cases of conspiracy) it is usual to join two or more defendants; one may be convicted even if all his co-conspirators named in the count are acquitted and even though conspiracy by definition requires more than one participant. Two or more defendants may also be joined in one indictment if they are charged with different offences, if the interests of justice require this; for example, if two witnesses commit perjury in relation to the same facts in the same proceedings. Defendants who have been jointly indicted will normally only be tried by separate trials if a joint trial might prejudice one or more of them; for example, when evidence against one accused is not admissible against the other or when the prosecution wish to call one of the defendants to give evidence against another.

joinder of documents The connecting together of two or more documents so that, jointly, they fulfil statutory requirements when one of the documents alone would be insufficient.

joinder of parties In civil proceedings, the combination as claimants or defendants of two or more persons in a single action. Under Part 19 of the *Civil Procedure Rules any number of claimants or defendants may be joined as parties to a claim. The court may order a person to be added as a new party

- if it is desirable to add the new party so that the court can resolve all the matters in dispute in the proceedings;
- if there is an issue involving the new party and an existing party that is connected to the matters in dispute in the proceedings, and it is desirable to add the new party so that the court can resolve that issue.

joint and several Together and in separation. If two or more people enter into an obligation that is said to be joint and several, their liability for its breach can be enforced against them all by a joint action or against any of them by individual action. *See also* JOINT TORTFEASORS.

Joint Committee on Statutory Instruments (Joint Scrutiny Committee) A committee of both Houses of Parliament whose function is to examine most delegated legislation (particularly *statutory instruments of a general character) and to draw Parliament's attention to it on a number of specified grounds; for example, if it imposes a tax, has retrospective effect, has been unduly delayed in publication, or is badly drafted. The Committee consists of seven members appointed by each House.

joint liability In civil proceedings, the liability that exists where parties share a single liability and each party can be held liable for the whole of it (Glossary to the Civil Procedure Rules).

Joint Scrutiny Committee *See* JOINT COMMITTEE ON STATUTORY INSTRUMENTS.

joint tenancy Ownership of land by two or more persons who have identical interests in the whole of the land (*compare* TENANCY IN COMMON). A joint tenancy can arise only when four conditions (the **four unities**) are satisfied.

(1) Each joint tenant must be entitled to possession at the same time.
(2) The estate or interest each has in the land must be identical; each joint tenant is entitled to the whole property and has no exclusive entitlement to any separate part of it (*see* UNDIVIDED SHARES).
(3) Each must have the same *title to the land, i.e. their ownership must be traced from the same instrument, such as a conveyance "to A and B as joint tenants".
(4) Each joint tenant's interest must *vest at and subsist for the same time.

Under a joint tenancy the **right of survivorship** applies: thus ownership of the entire interest in the property passes automatically on the death of one joint tenant to the survivor(s). The last survivor becomes the sole and absolute owner.

Under the Law of Property Act 1925 a distinction is made between a legal and an equitable joint tenancy. When two or more persons hold the *legal estate, they invariably hold it as joint tenants, and the right of survivorship applies. When the conveyance to them contains no words indicating that they are entitled to the property in *undivided shares (words of *severance), there is a presumption that they hold as joint tenants in equity and the right of survivorship again applies (*Stack v Dowden* [2007] 2 AC 432). However, when they take distinct and separate shares, or when the equitable joint tenancy has been terminated (as by notice of severance, *partition, etc.), or when the presumption against joint tenancy can be rebutted (*Jones v Kernott* [2011] UKSC 53, [2002] 1 AC 776), the equitable interest is held by them as tenants in common. However the equitable (or beneficial) interests are structured, the legal estate is always held by joint tenants as trustees upon a statutory *trust of land (Trust of Land and Appointment of Trustees Act 1996; TOLATA), and the trustees are accountable to those who hold the equitable interests – in the proportions to which they are entitled if they are tenants in common – for the property. The owners in equity have many rights under the trust of land, such as the right to be consulted and the right to occupy the property. Any joint tenant may apply to the court under section 14 of TOLATA for an order relating to the exercise by the trustees of any of their functions, including sale of the property. The court may make such order as it thinks fit.

joint tortfeasors Two or more people whose wrongful actions in furthering a common design cause a single injury. For example, if two men searching for a gas leak both applied a naked light to a gas pipe and caused an explosion, they are joint tortfeasors. But if a single injury is caused by several people acting without a common design they are not joint, but **concurrent tortfeasors**. An example of concurrent tortfeasors would be two motorists in separate cars, both driving negligently and causing a collision in which a pedestrian is injured (*Fitzgerald v Lane* [1989] 1 AC 328 (HL)). In both cases, the injured claimant is entitled to sue any or all of the tortfeasors for his whole loss; if he obtains a judgment against one tortfeasor that is not satisfied, he may proceed against the others. A tortfeasor liable for damage may recover contribution from other tortfeasors (whether joint or concurrent) liable for the same damage. *See* CIVIL LIABILITY CONTRIBUTION.

joint venture A commercial undertaking entered into by two or more parties, often by setting up a separate joint-venture company in which all partners have shares, to enable resources and skills to be shared. Joint ventures are defined in a European Commission *notice of 31 December 1994 as "undertakings which are jointly controlled by two or more other undertakings." In practice joint ventures encompass a broad range of operations, from merger-like operations to cooperation for particular functions, such as research and development, production, or distribution. A Commission notice of 23 December 1992 sets out how cooperative joint ventures are treated under the EU competition rules.

joint will A will comprising a single document executed by two or more persons as the will of all of them. It is treated as the separate will of each testator, and probate will be granted separately on the death of each. A joint testator may revoke the will only insofar as it applies to himself. A joint will is a convenient instrument for the exercise of a power conferred on persons jointly to appoint by will (*see* POWER OF APPOINTMENT) but has no other practical benefit and is extremely rare in practice. *Compare* MUTUAL WILLS.

Journals *pl. n.* The authentic record of proceedings in Parliament, as opposed to the verbatim record of debates (*see* HANSARD). There are two series published annually: *Journals of the House of Lords* (beginning in 1509) and *Journals of the House of Commons* (beginning in 1547).

((⊕)) SEE WEB LINKS
- Online version of the Commons Journal (to 1830)
- Online version of the Lords Journal (to 1832)

joyriding *n. See* AGGRAVATED VEHICLE-TAKING.

JP *See* JUSTICE OF THE PEACE.

judge *n.* A state official with power to adjudicate on disputes and other matters brought before the courts for decision. In English law all judges are appointed by the

Monarch, on the advice of the Lord Chancellor; however, since 2006 judges of all ranks have in practice been selected by the Judicial Appointments Commission on a basis of open competition. All judges are experienced legal practitioners. The independence of the higher judiciary is ensured by the principle that they hold office during good behaviour and not at the pleasure of the Crown (*see* AD VITAM AUT CULPAM). They can only be removed from office by a resolution of both Houses of Parliament assented to by the Queen (a power that has never been exercised in England and Wales). Their salaries are a charge on the *Consolidated Fund and are not voted annually. Circuit and district judges may be removed by the Lord Chancellor (with the agreement of the Lord Chief Justice) for incapacity or misbehaviour. All judicial appointments are pensionable and there is a compulsory retirement age of 70 years, but this can be extended to 75 if considered to be in the public interest. *See also* JUDICIAL IMMUNITY. *Compare* MAGISTRATE.

judge advocate A barrister or solicitor appointed to preside in *Court Martial proceedings and who is responsible for advising the court on questions of law. He is appointed by the Judge Advocate General's Department. At the conclusion of the evidence the judge advocate sums up the case to the members of the court. He has no vote on the finding but does vote on sentence.

Judge Advocate-General's Department A department that advises the Secretary of State for Defence and the Defence Council on matters relating to the administration of service law and reviews proceedings of army and air-force courts martial.

judge in his own cause *See* NATURAL JUSTICE.

Judges' Rules Formerly, rules of practice drawn up by the High Court governing the questioning and charging of suspects by the police. They were replaced by the *codes of practice issued under the provisions of the Police and Criminal Evidence Act 1984. *See also* INTERROGATION.

judgment *n.* **1.** A decision made by a court in respect of the matter before it. Judgments may be **interim** (**interlocutory**), deciding a particular issue prior to the trial of the case; or **final**, finally disposing of the case. They may be *in personam*, imposing a personal liability on a party (e.g. to pay damages); or *in rem*, determining some issue of right, status, or property binding people generally. **2.** The process of reasoning by which the court's decision was arrived at. In English law it is the normal practice for judgment to be given in open court or, in some appellate tribunals, to be handed down in printed form. If the judgment contains rulings on important questions of law, it may be reported in the *law reports. *See also* ENFORCEMENT OF JUDGMENT; FOREIGN JUDGMENTS.

judgment creditor A person who has obtained or is entitled to enforce a judgment or order against a debtor (Civil Procedure Rules Part 70). *See also* ENFORCEMENT OF JUDGMENT.

judgment debtor A person against whom a judgment or order has been given or made regarding the payment of a debt (Civil Procedure Rules Part 70). *See also* ENFORCEMENT OF JUDGMENT.

judgment in default *See* DEFAULT.

Judgments Regulation The EU Regulation (Council Regulation (EC) 44/2001) on jurisdiction and the recognition and enforcement of judgments in civil and commercial matters.

judgment summons A *summons, issued on the application of a person entitled to enforce a judgment, that requires a *judgment debtor to appear in court. If it can be shown beyond reasonable doubt that the debtor had the means to pay the debt but has failed to do so, the judge may make an order committing him to prison, suspended for as long as specified instalments are paid. Since the virtual abolition of imprisonment for debt, this procedure has been available only in respect of certain *maintenance orders and judgments for payment of certain taxes and state contributions. Relevant procedural rules are set out in Schedule 2 to the *Civil Procedure Rules.

Judicature Acts Statutes passed in 1873 and 1875 (36 and 37 Vict c 66; 38 and 39 Vict c 77) regulating the organization and powers of the courts and the proceedings therein. The Acts were revolutionary in two senses: firstly, because they represent the first wholesale restructuring and rationalization of the English courts that had taken place since English law began; secondly, because they allowed all the common-law courts to apply the rules and remedies of equity and all the courts of equity to apply the rules and remedies of the common law.

judicial cognizance *See* JUDICIAL NOTICE.

judicial comity The principle that, out of deference and respect, the courts in one state or jurisdiction will give effect to the laws and judicial decisions of another. This rule also applies between different courts in the High Court of Judicature. Thus, a judge for example, of the Queen's Bench Division is not bound to follow a judgment of his brother judge in the Chancery Division. They are on the same level in the judicial hierarchy. However, unless he believes the other judge to have been wrongheaded in the judgment that he earlier made, judicial comity compels him to respect and follow that decision. Case: *AG v Jonathan Cape* [1976] QB 753, 769 F-G (Lord Widgery CJ).

Judicial Committee of the Privy Council A tribunal, created by the Judicial Committee Act 1833, to hear appeals from courts in dependent territories and those Commonwealth countries that have retained appeals to the Privy Council since attaining independence; it also hears appeals under certain statutes. Its members currently comprise Justices of the Supreme Court, Lords of Appeal in Ordinary, and other members of the *Privy Council who have been Lords of Appeal in Ordinary or who have held high judicial office. Certain judges of Commonwealth countries who are Privy Counsellors are also members. The Committee's decisions are not technically judgments but merely advice to the Crown: they do not become final until incorporated into an *Order in Council. For this reason also, until 1966 dissenting opinions were not disclosed. The Committee's decisions are not binding as precedents upon English courts but are merely of *persuasive authority.

judicial deference A concept sometimes deployed by the domestic courts when reviewing the compliance of legislation passed by Parliament with the European Convention on Human Rights. According to the decision of Lord Woolf in *R v Lambert* [2001] UKHL 37, [2002] 2 AC 545: "...legislation is passed by a democratically elected Parliament and therefore the courts under the Convention are entitled to and should, as a matter of constitutional principle, pay a degree of deference to the view of Parliament as to what is in the interest of the public generally when upholding the rights of the individual under the Convention." (Compare, however, Lord Bingham in *A v Secretary of State for the Home Department* [2004] UKHL 56,2 AC 68.) The idea of judicial deference follows from the fact that the *margin of appreciation is not applicable in the domestic courts.

judicial dictum *See* OBITER DICTUM.

judicial discretion The power of the court to take some step, grant a remedy, or admit evidence or not as it thinks fit. Many rules of procedure and evidence are in discretionary form or provide for some element of discretion. In criminal cases, under section 78 of the Police and Criminal Evidence Act 1984, the court may exclude prosecution evidence if its admission would have such an adverse effect on the fairness of the proceedings that the court ought not to admit it. The *Court of Appeal is normally reluctant to review the exercise of discretion by trial judges.

judicial immunity The exemption of a *judge or *magistrate from personal actions for damages arising from the exercise of his judicial office. The immunity is absolute in respect of all words or actions of the judge while acting within his *jurisdiction and extends to acts done without jurisdiction provided that they were done in good faith.

judicial notice (judicial cognizance) The means by which the court may take as proven certain facts without hearing evidence. **Notorious facts** (i.e. matters of common knowledge) may be judicially noticed without inquiry. Some other facts (e.g. matters that can easily be checked in a standard work of reference and are reasonably indisputable) may be judicially noticed after inquiry.

judicial precedent *See* PRECEDENT.

judicial review **1.** The principal means by which the High Court exercises supervision over public authorities in accordance with the doctrine of *ultra vires*. The power of the High Court to exercise judicial review is often referred to as its supervisory jurisdiction. The mechanism for seeking judicial review is by making a claim under the procedure provided for in Rule 54 of the *Civil Procedure Rules. Claims are made to the Administrative Court. The common law grounds on which judicial review may be granted were defined in the case *Council of Civil Service Unions v Minister for the Civil Service* [1985] AC 374 (HL) as illegality, *irrationality, and *procedural impropriety. In terms of the *Human Rights Act1998, judicial review may also be used to challenge action by public authorities that is incompatible with the *European Convention on Human Rights (*R (on the application of GC) v The Commissioner of the Police of the Metropolis* [2011] UKSC 21, [2011], 1 WLR 1230). If the claim for a judicial review is successful, the court may grant a *quashing order, *mandatory order, *prohibiting order, *declaration, or *injunction; it may also award damages in certain circumstances. Under the Tribunals, Courts and Enforcement Act 2007 the newly created *Upper Tribunal has the power of judicial review over decisions of the *First-tier Tribunal. **2.** In European Union law, the *European Court of Justice has a judicial review function provided for under Article 230 of the EC Treaty. In terms of this provision, community acts (i.e. legally binding acts of the community institutions) are challengeable by means of judicial review on the grounds of lack of competence, infringement of an essential procedural requirement, or infringement of the Treaty or any rule of law relating to its application or misuse of powers. Action can be brought by an institution of the EU, a member state, or (in certain limited circumstances) an individual.

judicial separation order An order by the courts that a husband and wife do not have to cohabit. The order does not terminate the marriage but it does free the parties of marital obligations. Judicial (*or* legal) separation is appropriate when there are religious objections to divorce or when the parties have not finally decided upon divorce. The grounds for separation are the same as those for *divorce. The courts have the same powers in relation to financial orders and children as they do when granting a divorce.

judicial trustee A trustee appointed by the court under the Judicial Trustee Act 1906, either as sole trustee or as co-trustee. He is an officer of the court, is subject to the court's control, and is entitled to such remuneration as the court allows. In practice, the *Public Trustee has replaced a trustee appointed under the Act.

jump bail To forfeit *bail by failing to appear at the court or tribunal to answer a charge.

junior barrister Any barrister who is not a *Queen's Counsel. The word "junior" does not necessarily imply youth or lack of seniority: many members of the Bar remain juniors throughout their careers.

jure gestionis [Latin] Describing commercial transactions by bodies that are owned by the state but are not regarded as organs of the state. In international law the state accepts responsibility for such transactions and does not claim immunity. *Compare* JURE IMPERII.

jure imperii [Latin] Describing transactions by state bodies or representatives, such as diplomats. In international law the state maintains immunity from such transactions. *Compare* JURE GESTIONIS.

juridical *adj.* Relating to judicial proceedings or the law. Juridical days were days on which legal business could be transacted.

jurimetrics *pl. n.* The use of scientific techniques, especially the computer analysis of statistical data, to measure the effectiveness of a legal system.

jurisdiction *n.* **1.** The power of a court to hear and decide a case or make a certain order. (For the limits of jurisdiction of individual courts, see entries for those courts.) **2.** The territorial limits within which the jurisdiction of a court may be exercised. In the case of English courts this comprises England, Wales, Berwick-upon-Tweed, and those parts of the sea claimed as *territorial waters. Everywhere else is said to be **outside the jurisdiction**. **3.** The territorial scope of the legislative competence of Parliament. *See* SOVEREIGNTY OF PARLIAMENT.

In international law, jurisdiction can be exercised on a number of grounds, based on the following principles:

(1) the **territorial principle**, i.e. that the state within whose boundaries the crime has taken place has jurisdiction, irrespective of the nationality of the transgressor (*British Nylon Spinners Ltd v ICI* [1952] Ch 19 (CA) 26);

(2) the **nationality principle**, i.e. that a state has the power of jurisdiction over one of its nationals for an offence he has committed in another state (*Joyce v DPP* [1946] AC 347 (HL));

(3) the **protective principle**, i.e. that a potentially injured state can exercise jurisdiction in all cases when its national security is threatened (*US v Archer* 51 F Supp 708 (1943));

(4) the **passive personality principle**, i.e. that a state has jurisdiction if the illegal act has been committed against a national of that state (*Achille Lauro* incident of 1985);

(5) the **universality principle**, i.e. that when the accused has committed a crime in breach of a rule of **jus cogens* (such as a crime against humanity), any party having custody of the alleged lawbreaker is permitted to bring criminal proceedings against him (*Filartiga v Peña-Irala* 630 F 2d 876, 890 (2d Cir 1980)).

juris et de jure [Latin] Of law and from law: an irrebuttable **presumption is so described.

jurisprudence *n.* The theoretical analysis of legal issues at the highest level of abstraction. Jurisprudence may be distinguished from both legal theory and the philosophy of law by its concern with those questions (e.g. about the nature of a particular right or duty, or a particular line of judicial reasoning) that arise within or are implied by substantive legal disciplines. **Legal theory** is often used to denote theoretical enquiries about law "as such" that extend beyond the boundaries of law as understood by professional lawyers (e.g. the **economic analysis of law or **Marxist legal theory). **Legal philosophy** or the **philosophy of law**, as its name implies, normally proceeds from the standpoint of the discipline of philosophy; that is, it attempts to unravel the sort of problems that might concern moral or political philosophers, such as the concepts of freedom or authority.

juristic person (artificial person) An entity, such as a **corporation, that is recognized as having legal personality, i.e. it is capable of enjoying and being subject to legal rights and duties. It is contrasted with a human being, who is referred to as a **natural person**. *See also* INTERNATIONAL LEGAL PERSONALITY.

juror *n.* A member of a **jury. Jurors are chosen from the electoral register; they must be aged between 18 and 70 and must have been resident in the UK for any period of at least five years since the age of 13. Each juror must swear or affirm that he will faithfully try the case and give a true verdict according to the evidence. Certain classes of person, including past and present holders of any judicial office and serving police officers, were formerly ineligible for jury service but this is no longer the case. Anyone who has ever been imprisoned for five years or more, or who has received any sentence of imprisonment or suspended imprisonment within the preceding 10 years, or who is on bail, is disqualified from jury service. *See also* CHALLENGE TO JURY.

jury *n.* A group of **jurors (usually 12) selected at random to decide the facts of a case and give a **verdict. Most juries are selected to try indictable offences in the Crown Court, but juries are also used in some civil cases (including claims in respect of false imprisonment, malicious prosecution, and defamation) and in coroner's inquests. In criminal proceedings the judge will direct the jury on points of law and summarize the evidence (*see* DIRECTION TO JURY), but he must leave the jury to decide all questions of fact themselves. He must also make it clear to them that they are the only **triers of fact and must acquit the defendant unless they feel sure that he is guilty beyond reasonable doubt. The verdict of a jury should, if possible, be unanimous, but when a jury cannot reach a unanimous verdict, a **majority verdict may be acceptable. *See also* CHALLENGE TO JURY.

jus *n.* [Latin] A law or right.

jus accrescendi [Latin] *See* RIGHT OF SURVIVORSHIP.

jus accrescendi inter mercatores pro beneficio commercii locum non habet [Latin: for the advancement of commerce there is no place for the right of survivorship between merchants] A maxim stating the principle that equity will treat as tenants in common (*see* TENANCY IN COMMON) those in partnership whose interest in partnership property is at common law a *joint tenancy. Thus on the death of a partner his interest in the partnership property is part of his estate rather than belonging to the surviving partners.

jus civile [Latin: civil law] **1.** *Municipal law. **2.** The whole body of Roman law.

jus cogens [Latin: coercive law] A rule or principle in international law that is so fundamental that it binds all states and does not allow any exceptions. Such rules (sometimes called **peremptory norms**) will only amount to *jus cogens* rules if they are recognized as such by the international community as a whole. A treaty that conflicts with an existing *jus cogens* rule is void, and if a new *jus cogens* rule emerges, any existing treaty that conflicts with it automatically becomes void. States cannot create regional customary international law that contradicts *jus cogens* rules. Most authorities agree that the laws prohibiting slavery, genocide, piracy, and acts of aggression or illegal use of force are *jus cogens* laws. Some suggest that certain human rights provisions (e.g. those prohibiting racial discrimination) also come under the category of *jus cogens*.

jus gentium [Latin: the law of peoples] *See* INTERNATIONAL LAW.

jus in re aliena [Latin] A right in the property of another (*see* ENCUMBRANCE). It is contrasted with **jus in re propria** – a right in one's own property.

jus naturale [Latin: natural law] The fundamental element of all law. *See* NATURAL LAW.

jus quaesitum tertio [Latin: rights on account of third parties] The general rule that a contract cannot confer rights on a third party: only a party to a contract can sue on it. This rule is now subject to statutory exceptions, principally those created by the Contracts (Rights of Third Parties) Act 1999. In addition, rights may be conferred on third parties by means of a trust.

jus sanguinis [Latin: law relating to blood] The principle that the nationality of children is the same as that of their parents, irrespective of their place of birth. This contrasts with *jus soli*, whereby nationality is dependent on place of birth. In states in which the *jus sanguinis* principle applies (i.e. France and Germany), a conflict of jurisdiction may arise when a child is born of parents who are citizens of another state. For example, a child born in the United States of French parents is an American citizen *jure soli*, but a French citizen *jure sanguinis*. His effective citizenship will depend upon the jurisdiction within which he happens to be in; in the United States he is a US citizen; in France, a Frenchman; in any other country he is both.

Conflicts resulting from the simultaneous presence of these contrasting claims of allegiance are generally settled between states by deferring *jus sanguinis* to *jus soli* when the state asserting its primary claim of allegiance has *de facto* jurisdiction of the individual in question. Most jurisdictions (including the United Kingdom and the United States) now adopt within their nationality law a combination of *jus soli* and *jus sanguinis*.

jus soli [Latin: law relating to the soil (of one's country)] The rule by which birth in a state is sufficient to confer nationality, irrespective of the nationality of one's parents (*compare* JUS SANGUINIS). The United Kingdom and the United States originally adhered to a strict version of this principle. Thus the children of an *alien, born on the territory of the host state, would from their birth adopt the nationality of that state. Most jurisdictions (including the United Kingdom and the United States) now adopt a combination of *jus soli* and *jus sanguinis*.

just and equitable winding-up A *compulsory winding-up on grounds of fairness under the Insolvency Act 1986 (s 122 (1) (g)). This may occur, for example, when the purpose of the company cannot be achieved, when the management is deadlocked or has been guilty of serious irregularities, or, in small companies run on the basis of mutual trust between members, when the majority have exercised their legal rights in breach of a common understanding between the members when the company was formed. No order will be made if another form of *minority protection would be more appropriate (Insolvency Act s 125 (2)); this might, for example, be relief for *unfair prejudice under the Companies Act 2006 (s 994–96). *See also* UNFAIR PREJUDICE.

jus tertii [Latin: right of a third party] A defence raised by a party who is sued in respect of property alleging that some third party has a better claim to the property than the claimant. The Torts (Interference with Goods) Act 1977 provides that this is a good defence to an action in *conversion, but a special procedure is laid down for the joinder of the third party in the action.

justice *n.* A moral ideal that the law seeks to uphold in the protection of rights and punishment of wrongs. Justice is not synonymous with law – it is possible for a law to be called unjust. However, English law closely identifies with justice and the word is frequently used in the legal system; for example, in justice of the peace, Royal Courts of Justice, and administration of justice.

justice of the peace (JP) A person holding a commission from the Crown to exercise certain judicial functions for a particular **commission area**. JPs are appointed on behalf of and in the name of the Queen by the Lord Chancellor and may be removed from office in the same way. On reaching the age of 70 they are placed on a supplemental list and cease to be able to exercise any judicial functions. Their principal function is to sit as *magistrates in the *magistrates' courts but they may also sit in the *Crown Court when it is considering committals for sentence and appeals from magistrates' courts, sign warrants of arrest and search warrants, and take statutory declarations. All High Court judges are *ex officio* justices of the peace for the whole of England and Wales.

justices' clerk *See* CLERK TO THE JUSTICES.

justifiable homicide *See* HOMICIDE.

justification *n.* **1.** Formerly a defence to an action for *defamation that the defamatory statement made was true. Under the Defamation Act 2013 it was replaced by a new defence, *truth. **2.** The defence that interference with the contractual or business relations of another was justified. The scope of the defence is uncertain, but the fact that the wages of chorus girls were so low that they were compelled to resort to prostitution has been held to justify a theatrical performers' protection society inducing theatre owners to break their contracts with the girls' employer (*Brimelow v Casson* [1924] 1 Ch 302). *See* INDUCING BREACH OF CONTRACT. **3.** In criminal law, a category of defence reflecting the determination that the defendant's conduct was not, all things considered, criminally wrongful. *Self-defence and *necessity are often commonly assumed to be central examples of justification. It is often said that justification defences focus on the action, whereas *excuse defences focus on the actor: actions are justified, actors are excused. *See also* DURESS.

justifying bail Demonstrating to a court granting bail that one is capable of meeting the surety specified in the bail (for example, disclosing one's financial resources). A person standing surety for bail must be able to provide the bail out of his own resources. It is a criminal offence (**bail-bonding**) for a defendant who is granted bail to agree to indemnify his surety against any loss arising out of standing surety.

just satisfaction The basis for damages awarded by the European Court of Human Rights (and thus in respect of claims under the *Human Rights Act1998). In many cases where the Court finds a violation it has declined to award any damages on the basis that this finding is in itself sufficient just satisfaction. Subject to this discretion, damages can be obtained for pecuniary loss, nonpecuniary loss, and costs and expenses. Damages awarded by the European Court of Human Rights are generally smaller than those awarded in domestic courts and rarely exceed £1,000.

juvenile court *See* YOUTH COURT.

juvenile offender A person between the ages of 10 and 17 who has committed a crime (*see* DOLI CAPAX); an offender between the ages of 14 and 17 is known as a **young offender**. A juvenile offender cannot be tried on indictment except when charged with: (i) homicide; (ii) a firearms offence carrying a mandatory minimum sentence; (iii) a violent or sexual offence for which an adult could be sentenced to at least 10 years' imprisonment; (iv) certain other offences listed in the Powers of Criminal Courts (Sentencing) Act 2000 s 91, including causing death by dangerous driving; or (v) an offence for which he is jointly charged with someone aged 18 or over when it is considered necessary that they be tried together. In all other cases, juvenile offenders must be tried summarily by a magistrates' court or a *youth court.

A juvenile offender cannot be sentenced to imprisonment; instead he may be sentenced to a *detention and training order of up to two years, half of which is normally served in a young offenders' institute and half in the community. If found guilty of murder or some other grave crime he must be detained in a place and on such conditions as the Home Secretary may determine. The Crime (Sentences) Act 1997 provides that the Parole Board, rather than the Home Secretary, has responsibility for the release of juveniles convicted of murder. A juvenile offender may not be made subject to a *community order but a *youth rehabilitation order may be imposed. He may be fined or bound over (*see* BIND OVER); he may also be discharged (absolutely or conditionally). The procedures for dealing with juvenile offenders are now governed by the Youth Justice and Criminal Evidence Act 1999, the Powers of Criminal Courts (Sentencing) Act 2000, the Criminal Justice Act 2003, and the Criminal Justice and Immigration Act 2008. *See also* CHILD SAFETY ORDER; PARENTING ORDER.

WRITING AND CITATION GUIDE

This section offers a guide to the elements of effective legal writing, and a guide to the accurate citation of legal authorities.

The guides have been written with students in mind, but the advice applies to legal writing in general. Note that particular law schools, solicitors' firms, barristers' chambers, courts, government agencies, and legal publishers all have their own ways of doing things. The basic principles offered in the following guides are meant to be useful to students, academic lawyers, and practicing lawyers in a variety of fields. But the *most* basic principle is that your work must persuade your audience, and for that purpose you may need to tailor your work to the expectations of your reader.

Writing Guide

Much legal writing is awful. So good legal writing stands out. Lawyers who write well do not learn how by being told, but by learning the law. Reading a lot of good and bad legal writing teaches them to get a clear idea of what they want to say, and to pay attention to what the reader (client, judge, teacher, examiner ...) needs to be told. This guide does not try to tell you how to write. It only points out some simple techniques, and some obstacles that you need to clear away in order to make a strong argument.

1. The Task: Answer the question

Make an argument   Provide an answer to the question supported with reasons why the reader should agree. A good argument will explain potential objections, put them at their strongest, and explain why you still arrive at the conclusion you are defending.

Stick to the question set   Do not ramble on about the topic in general. A good answer to a question will leave out material that may be important for other purposes, but is not important for defending your answer to the question. If the question is unclear, explain what you take it to mean. If there is something you do not understand, do not avoid the problem. State the problem.

Be critical   You need to start questioning what the authorities say as early as possible in your work – before you start writing. If you disagree with a scholar, explain why, and if you agree, explain why. Judges are authors with a difference: their reasons for judgment in a case may make the law. But you must still take a critical approach to a judge's reasons for decision. Has the judge misstated what the law was (and perhaps changed the law without saying so)? Are there reasons why a court that has the power to do so ought to overrule the judgment in a future case?

Problem assignments always require you to identify issues (questions on which the resolution of a dispute might turn). But they come in many forms. Keep in mind the following points:

- You still have to make an argument. You cannot stop when you have decided what the issues are and how they should be decided. The reader should know your resolution of the problem, and your reasons for it. Put the potential objections to your view at their strongest, and explain why they do not succeed.

- You may find that the outcome of a dispute can be easily decided on a particular ground. You should still discuss every issue raised, even if you can resolve the dispute without deciding an issue (like a good trial judge, who gives reasons for a resolution of each issue, in case the Court of Appeal overrules on the ground that seemed to dispose of the dispute).

- Your reader will follow you most easily if you list the issues that you will address, and then tackle them one at a time, with a heading to identify your discussion of each issue. Keep it simple.

2. Strategy: Organize, and provide signposts

Organization   The best form of organization will depend on your purposes, but you always need an organization – a shape to your work that helps you to persuade the reader. Here is the easiest approach:

1. Tell the reader your answer to the question in the first sentence.
2. Briefly point out the tasks that need to be accomplished to defend that answer.
3. Create corresponding sections that accomplish each task that your answer sets for you, such as:
   - explaining the meaning of the question
   - giving the reasons for your answer
   - presenting apparent objections
   - responding to those objections
4. Briefly point out why your answer survives the strongest objections, and explain the implications and consequences of your answer.

Sometimes, a less straightforward alternative will prove more effective – such as starting with the facts of a hypothetical case that will quickly show the reader just what you think and why. But you should ordinarily keep your style simple and direct.

The naming of parts   Whatever organization you use, your work will have parts. You can provide headings as a graphic device to highlight sections; it can be useful or distracting depending on the length and complexity of your project. Think about the way in which judges sometimes give headings for the sections of their reasons, and learn from the instances that are helpful to you as a reader. Keep in mind that no law textbook is published without a table of contents and chapter and section headings. But you do not need that apparatus unless it would be helpful to your reader.

Paragraph structure   If you do not use headings, you still need signposts – that is, a way of telling the reader what you are doing at each stage in your work. That can generally be done most effectively using paragraph structure: at the beginning of each paragraph, a strong 'topic sentence' stating the agenda for that paragraph will give the reader confidence in what you are doing. The rest of the paragraph will increase the reader's confidence, if you say something definite and conclusive on the topic introduced at the beginning of the paragraph.

WRITER'S MAXIMS

Write for the layperson, not the expert.   Then the expert will be impressed by your clarity and by the understanding you show.

Avoid the word *clearly*.   If you want to use it, you are probably saying something that you cannot explain.

Proofread your work.   Your work will benefit if you step back and become your own reader. Ask whether the writer has given you what you need to follow the argument, and has made it easy to understand.

Use all the advice you can get from good readers.   You can learn from a piece of work that comes back with a lot of red ink on it. Criticism hurts, but you can make good use of it.

Respect your reader.   You insult a reader's intelligence by waffling, but NOT by making your work easy to follow.

3. Tactics

Using cases   For most legal tasks, you need to read the cases, and use them. But a list of case summaries (even a list of good summaries of all relevant cases) will not accomplish any task.

- Whenever you mention a case you should make it clear how it affects your argument.
- Resist the temptation to throw in everything important or interesting about a case.
- Do not say anything at all about a case other than what the reader needs in order to understand your argument. Stick to the facts and statements of law that you need.
- Judges in their reasons often have a variety of purposes, and they sometimes recite extraneous information. As a result, one crucial lawyer's skill is to learn how to read a case without getting distracted by pointless material. The corresponding writing skill is to describe a case without distracting the reader.

Policy arguments   Be critical: do not stop at citing authority for a proposition of law, but explain whether it makes sense. Do not just say that a rule is good or bad, and never stop with a statement like "this rule is required because certainty is needed to enable businessmen to plan their affairs".

Show:

- that the rule provides more certainty than the alternative (for example, that the rule does not increase uncertainty by leading to unpredictable judicial attempts to evade its effect);
- that the particular form of certainty afforded by the rule is actually valuable in the context in which the rule operates;
- that its value justifies whatever damage the rule may inflict on other interests.

Originality   Never use anyone else's words without using quotation marks and citing the source. When you read, you will make notes that include extracts of the writer's wording, and when you write your finished product you will use your notes. At that point, you must make sure that you do not end up passing off extracts of someone else's prose as your own.

- These points apply equally to the task of stating the facts of a case. It is only by describing the facts for yourself that you will develop the crucial legal skill of examining a situation and deciding what matters.

4. Prose Style I: Eliminate the negative

Having something clear to say is a matter of hard work and good thinking. Clear prose style is largely a matter of eliminating junk. Here are some important forms of rubbish to eliminate from your writing.

Legalese This has two characteristics that lawyers use by habit: redundancy, and clumsiness that sounds like formality.

- Redundancy results partly from fine legal distinctions that make it necessary to use words that look the same to the uninitiated, partly from lawyers' irrational fear of leaving something out, and partly from our heritage of using English, Latin, and Medieval French. You already know many examples:

null and void	cease and desist
force and effect	aid and abet
last will and testament	give, devise, and bequeath

Some of these pairs or triplets have (or once had) distinct meanings in legal use. They lead lawyers into a sloppy reflex of doubling or tripling words:

> in any way, shape, or form
> for all intents and purposes
> part and parcel

Connected with redundancy is a general habit of clumsy wordiness:

said agreement	hereby
aforementioned	such agreement
heretofore	whomsoever

- Compound prepositions and adverbs (and phrases) are a common case of legalistic wordiness:

  > within (for "in")
  > at that point in time (for "then")
  > for the purpose of (for "to")
  > pursuant to (for "under")
  > previous to, prior to (for "before")
  > with regard to (for "about")

Cut out words that add nothing to what you're saying. Never use the word "such" when you mean "so" (e.g. write "the defendant conceded liability, so that damages were the only issue" not "the defendant conceded liability, such that damages were the only issue"). Never use phrases like "said contract".

Vague connectives Your work will be obscure if you suggest that two ideas, doctrines etc. are related, but do not say how.

- Do not say "X involves Y", "X has to do with Y", or "X is related to Y", if you can say how X and Y are related.
- Do not say, "The rule of law is closely connected with the separation of powers", if you can say what the connection is (and if you cannot say what it is, then you have some more work to do).
- Do not use adjectives that set out tendencies, or possible relations ("is constitutive of", "is indicative of"), if you can use verbs that express a relation ("constitutes", "indicates").

Throat clearing Your first words are crucial in any effort at communication. Use them to hook the reader.

- Do not begin by saying, "In order to answer this question, it is necessary to . . .". Leave it out.
- You can also leave out the following:

  > The topic of [. . .] has been very controversial. This essay discusses . . .
  > The problem presents a situation in which . . .
  > The background to the dispute arose as follows.

- Do not say, "*Raffles v Wichelhaus* was a case in which . . . ". Say, "In *Raffles v Wichelhaus*, . . . ".

Passive verbs and nominalization   You will weaken your sentence if you use passive verbs instead of active verbs, or if you turn verbs into nouns. So you should generally say "the defendant did not perform," not "the contract was not performed" or "there was no performance".

- Your sentence will be more informative if you are able to specify the agent, and your sentence will be stronger and more direct if you use an active verb.
- Use nominalization and passive verbs only when they are useful, e.g. for leaving out information that you cannot give, or for reasons of structure in complex sentences.

Queuing prepositions   "In a succession of cases of disputes over contracts for the provision of services . . . " would be better put as, "In successive cases on service contracts . . . ".

5. Prose Style II: Accentuate the positive

Sentence length   If you eliminate the various forms of bad writing listed above, you will end up with shorter sentences. You may want to go further, as Lord Denning sometimes did, and deliberately chop complicated sentences into bite-sized pieces. But the goal is readable prose, not short sentences. Variety in sentence length can be stylistically attractive. But sentence length will take care of itself completely, if you concentrate on a good argument, put as clearly as you can.

Put technical terms to use   Do not try to use jargon to impress people. But as long as the reader knows what you are doing, you can use terms with a special meaning as extremely useful communication techniques.

- It is often best to explain what you mean by a technical term that has a more-or-less standard meaning (e.g. "estoppel", "expectation interest"), either to help the reader to understand you, or to reassure the reader that you understand what you are saying.
- Inventing your own technical terms can be a very useful technique. Explain yourself very clearly, and do it only where it will help the reader.

Using quotations   Do it sparingly and accurately. It is very useful if you find something important in (e.g.) the way a court has expressed itself. But do it only where it is especially valuable: do not make the reader work at understanding what someone else has said, unless they can see the pay-off for the effort.

- You should virtually never use a quotation without commenting on it; you need to show the reader how it serves your purposes.

Timothy Endicott, Fellow in Law, Balliol College, Oxford

THE BASICS:

1. Answer the question. Do not just discuss the general topic.
2. Be specific. Instead of saying, "it has been argued ... ", say who argued it.
3. Give a definite answer to a question, even if the reader may disagree with you. Never leave the reader to work out an answer.
4. Do not just say that an argument is unpersuasive. Show the reader why it is unpersuasive.
5. Use cases. Do not just mention them. Give the court's reasons, and assess them. Tell the reader those aspects of the facts that the reader needs to know in order to understand your argument.
6. Do not use long, obscure words. Make your argument easy to follow.
7. Do not just state the law, but explain the principles behind it, and the difference that those principles make in particular cases.

Guide to Citing Primary Legal Sources

The Oxford Standard for Citation of Legal Authorities ('OSCOLA') is a guide to the citation of sources of law, and also to the citation of books, articles, and other secondary sources. You can find OSCOLA at:

www.law.ox.ac.uk/oscola

The following guide to citing cases and legislation in the United Kingdom is drawn from OSCOLA, which provides further detail and additional examples.

CASES

1. General principles

A case citation identifies the case name (in italics), the neutral citation and the law report, as in the following example:

Radmacher v Granatino [2010] UKSC 42, [2011] 1 AC 534

The two parties, separated with a lower case *v*, are clearly indicated in italics. The next part of the citation is the 'neutral citation' which gives the year of judgment in square brackets, the court, and the judgment number: *Radmacher v Granatino* was the 42nd judgment in the UK Supreme Court (UKSC) in 2010. The third part of the citation is the 'best' report: the year of publication, generally in square brackets, the volume number, the report abbreviation, and the first page of the report. A report of the judgment above can be found in volume 1 of the 2011 series of *Law Reports* called the *Appeal Cases* (AC), beginning on page 534.

There are two main variations to this basic form of case citation. One is that neutral citations were first introduced in 2001. The neutral citation form for each court can be found at www.bailii.org/bailii/citation. Citations of judgments that don't have neutral citations give the 'best' report followed by the court in abbreviated form in parentheses:

Williams v Roffey [1991] 1 QB 1 (CA)

The other main variation is that some law report series have consecutive volume numbers. For these, rather than providing the year of publication in square brackets, the year of the judgment is provided in parentheses at the beginning of the citation. The following citation of a 2009 European Court of Human Rights judgment is from volume 51 of the *European Human Rights Reports* (EHRR), beginning on page 10:

> *Omojudi v UK* (2009) 51 EHRR 10

The OSCOLA style uses very little punctuation. For example, there are no full stops in abbreviations or when using a person or company's initials. Use punctuation only where its omission would cause information to run together, as would happen between the first page of a law report and a pinpoint.

Sample citations   The following are examples of correctly cited cases (post-1865):

> *Donoghue v Stevenson* [1932] AC 562 (HL Sc)
> *R v Radio Authority, ex p Bull* [1998] QB 294 (CA)
> *British Steel plc v Customs and Excise Commissioners* [1997] 2 All ER 366 (CA)
> *Capital & Counties plc v Hampshire CC* [1997] QB 1004 (CA)
> *Rowe v Vale of White Horse DC* [2003] EWHC 388 (Admin), [2003] 1 Lloyd's Rep 418 (CA)
> *R v G* [2003] UKHL 50, [2004] 1 AC 1034
> *R (Smith) v Oxfordshire Assistant Deputy Coroner* [2010] UKSC 29, [2011] 1 AC 1

Some reports series cite to a case number rather than to a page number. This example is from the *Reports of Patent Cases*:

> *Levi Strauss v Tesco* [2002] EWHC 1625 (Ch), [2003] RPC 18

Which is the best report?   The most authoritative reference is to the official *Law Reports* series (*Appeal Cases, Chancery, Family, Queen's Bench* etc). If a case is not reported in the *Law Reports*, cite the *Weekly Law Reports* or the *All England Law Reports*.

Like the official *Law Reports*, the *Weekly Law Reports* are published by the Incorporated Council of Law Reporting (www.lawreports.co.uk), but they do not include argument of counsel. Volume 1 of the WLRs contains cases that the Council does not plan to include in the *Law Reports*, while Volumes 2 (January to June) and 3 (July to December) cover the cases that will be republished in the *Law Reports*. Cite 2 WLR or 3 WLR *only* if the case has not yet come out in the *Law Reports*; there may be changes in the *Law Reports* version.

Case names   Where there are multiple parties, name only the first claimant and first defendant. Where the parties are individuals, omit given names and initials. Abbreviate common words and phrases: use AG for Attorney General, BC for Borough Council, Co for Company, DPP for Director of Public Prosecutions and so on.

Cite a case name in full in the first mention in the text or footnote; it may be shortened thereafter. Thus, "in *Glebe Motors plc v Dixon-Greene*" can be shortened to "in the *Glebe Motors* case" (or "in *Glebe Motors*"). In shipping cases, you can use the name of the ship instead of the full case name (for example, *The Eurymedon*). In criminal cases it is conventional to abbreviate "in *R v Caldwell*" to "in *Caldwell*". In civil cases that kind of abbreviation is also acceptable, subject to the warning that the name chosen must be that which stands first in the full name of the case.

Pinpoint   When citing a case as authority for a proposition, add a pinpoint if possible, to indicate exactly where the passage on which you are relying is to be found. Where the citation ends with the identification of a court by its acronym in brackets, the pinpoint follows that attribution without any comma. Where there is no such attribution, or where there is more than one pinpoint, insert a comma to prevent the numbers running together. Where the pinpoint reference is to the first page of the report, repeat the page number:

> *Beattie v E & F Beattie Ltd* [1938] Ch 708 (CA) 708
> *El Ajou v Dollar Land Holdings* [1993] 3 All ER 717 (Ch) 738, 739–40
> *Associated Newspapers Ltd v Wilson* [1995] 2 AC 454 (HL) 479 (Lord Browne-Wilkinson)

If the case has numbered paragraphs, use the paragraph number in square brackets as a pinpoint, rather than the page number:

> *Thompson Holidays Ltd v Norwegian Cruise Line Ltd* [2002] EWCA Civ 1828, [2003] RPC 32 [23]
>
> *Austin v Southwark LBC* [2010] UKSC 28, [2011] 1 AC 355 [45]–[47] (Baroness Hale)

Attributions to judges   If it is useful for your purposes to name the deciding judge, use the judge's surname followed by the conventional abbreviation identifying their judicial office. Do not use honorifics such as "the Honourable". A High Court judge (a Justice of the High Court) is called "Mr [or Mrs] Justice Smith" (abbreviated "Smith J"). A Court of Appeal judge (a Lord Justice of Appeal or Lady Justice of Appeal) is called "Lord Justice Smith" or "Lady Justice Smith" (abbreviated "Smith LJ"), unless the judge is a peer, in which case he is called, for example, "Lord Smith".

A House of Lords or Supreme Court judge (or "Law Lord") is called "Lord Smith" or "Lady Smith". The President of the Supreme Court is abbreviated as Lord Smith P. Abbreviated forms are not used for Law Lords. If a Law Lord's territorial qualification is stated in the report of a decision (eg Lord Scott of Foscote), you can omit the qualification (or use it the first time you mention the judge, and omit it subsequently).

Cases before 1865   For pre-1865 cases, cite both the nominate reports *and* the *English Reports*, divided by a comma unless there is a pinpoint, in which case by a semi-colon:

> *Boulton v Jones* (1857) 2 H&N 564, 157 ER 232
>
> *Henly v Mayor of Lyme* (1828) 5 Bing 91, 107; 130 ER 995, 1001

If you need to identify the court, spell it out in the text: "The Court of Common Pleas took the view that … ".

2. Scottish cases

The general principles for case citation apply, but the year of the report is not put in brackets. Cite the Session Cases if possible, which includes cases from the Court of Session (SC) and the High Court of Justiciary (JC) as well as from the House of Lords/ Supreme Court. The superior Scottish courts began issuing neutral citations in 2005.

> *Dodds v HM Advocate* 2003 JC 8
>
> *Black v McGregor* [2006] CSIH 45, 2007 SC 69

3. European Union cases

For cases in the Court of Justice of the European Union (CJEU), if possible, cite the official reports, the *European Court Reports* (ECR). If an ECR reference is not available, the second best report is usually the *Common Market Law Reports* (CMLR). You may also cite the *Law Reports*, the WLR, or the All ER in preference to the CMLR. For an unreported case, cite the relevant notice in the *Official Journal* (OJ). If not yet reported in the OJ, then cite the case number, case name, court, and date of judgment.

Since 1989, cases have been numbered and prefixed according to whether they are registered at the CJEU or the General Court (GC). CJEU cases are prefixed C- and GC cases are prefixed T-. Cite the case number before the party names. Do not add a C- to pre -1989 cases. CJEU cases are reported in ECR I- and GC cases are reported in ECR II-. The volume number attaches to the page number as shown in the third example:

> Case 151/73 *Ireland v Council* [1974] 1 CMLR 429
>
> Case 240/83 *Procureur de la République v ADBHU* [1985] ECR 531
>
> Case C-353/06 *Stefan Grunkin* [2008] ECR I-7639

4. European Court of Human Rights cases

Cite the official reports or the *European Human Rights Reports*, providing one in preference to the other throughout. Until 1 November 1998, the official reports were known as Series A and numbered consecutively. The official reports were then renamed as *Reports of Judgments and Decisions* and they are cited as ECHR. The EHRR series is consecutively numbered, but from 2001 case numbers replaced page numbers.

References to unreported judgments should identify the application number, the court and the date of the judgment in place of publication details (current information can be obtained from the ECtHR website and the HUDOC database at www.echr.coe.int).

When pinpointing, use 'para' or 'paras' after a comma.

> *Johnston v Ireland* (1986) Series A no 122
> *Osman v UK* ECHR 1998–VIII 3124
> *Balogh v Hungary* App no 47940/99 (ECtHR, 20 July 2004)
> *A v UK* (2009) 49 EHRR 29, para 120

5. Cases from other jurisdictions

Cite cases from other jurisdictions as they are cited in their own jurisdiction, with one difference: if the name of the series cited does not itself indicate the jurisdiction and the court of decision, and the jurisdiction and court are not obvious from the context of your work, you should indicate these in parentheses at the end of the reference:

> *Roe v Wade* 410 US 113, 163–64 (1973)
> *Waltons Stores (Interstate) Ltd v Maher* (1988) 164 CLR 387 (High Court of Australia)

Resources for citations from other jurisdictions can be found in the Appendix to OSCOLA online.

LEGISLATION

1. Domestic primary legislation

Name of the statute Cite an Act by its short title and date, in roman, without a comma before the date:

> Act of Supremacy 1558
> Literary and Scientific Institutions Act 1854
> Children Act 1995
> Anti-terrorism, Crime and Security Act 2001

For older statutes, it may be helpful to give the appropriate regnal year and chapter number, as in the following citation for the Crown Debts Act 1801. The information in parentheses indicates that the Act was given Royal Assent in the 14th year of the reign of George III. As it was the 90th Act given the Royal Assent in that parliament, it is called "chapter 90", and abbreviated as follows:

> Crown Debts Act 1801 (14 Geo 3 c 90)

Where several jurisdictions are being discussed, it may be necessary to add the jurisdiction of the legislation in parentheses at the end of the citation:

> Water Resources Act 1991 (UK)

Parts of statutes Use the full form at the beginning of a sentence and full or abbreviated forms in the text: the abbreviations are s, ss, para, pt, and sch. Note, however, that paragraph (k) of subsection (4) of section 14 of the Lunacy Act 1934, for example, is expressed as follows:

> Lunacy Act 1934 s 14(4)(k)

In general, it is more convenient to refer to "s 14(4)" rather than "subsection (4)" and to "s 14(4)(k)" than to "paragraph (k)"; if the latter are used, they can be abbreviated to "ss (4)" or "para (k)". Use abbreviations in the footnotes.

2. EU legislation

General principles   Cite EU legislation (Regulations, Directives, and Decisions) and other instruments (Recommendations, Opinions, etc.) by providing the legislation type, number and title, then publication details from the *Official Journal* (OJ) of the European Communities:

> Council Regulation (EC) 1984/2003 of 8 April 2003 introducing a system for the statistical monitoring of trade in bluefin tuna, swordfish and big eye tuna within the Community [2003] OJ L295/1

The OJ citation is given in the order: [year] OJ series number/page. The capital letter 'L' indicating the series stands for Legislation (the C series contains EU information and notices, and the S series contains invitations to tender).

Abbreviations and pinpoints   Give EC Directives, Regulations, and Notices their full name on their first occurrence in a chapter. An abbreviation for the long official title may subsequently be used, or the citation may simply give the document type and number. Full or abbreviated forms may be used for Article (art), Regulation (reg), and Directive (dir). Pinpoints indicating paragraphs or Articles follow the OJ citation, and a comma:

> Council Regulation (EC) 139/2004 on the control of concentrations between undertakings (the EC Merger Regulation) [2004] OJ L24/1, art 5 [in subsequent footnotes use: EC Merger Regulation 139/2004, art 5]

Treaty on European Union (Consolidated Version 2012) [2012] OJ C 326/13, art 3.

3. Legislation from other jurisdictions

Cite legislation from other jurisdictions as it is cited in its own jurisdiction.

Resources for citations from other jurisdictions can be found in the Appendix to OSCOLA.

Kaldor-Hicks efficiency A concept that is often cited in the *economic analysis of law. A Kaldor–Hicks efficiency is said to occur when an alteration in the allocation of resources produces more benefits than costs overall. A *Pareto efficiency arises when at least one person is made better off and no one is made worse off. In practice, however, it is extremely difficult to make any change without making at least one person worse off. Under the Kaldor–Hicks efficiency test, an outcome is efficient if those who are made better off could *in theory* compensate those who are made worse off and so produce a Pareto efficient outcome. Although all Kaldor–Hicks efficient situations are Pareto optimal, in that no further Pareto improvements can be made, the reverse is not true. Conversely, although every Pareto improvement is a Kaldor–Hicks improvement, most Kaldor–Hicks improvements are not Pareto improvements. *See also* COASE THEOREM.

keeping *n.* (of property) *See* THEFT.

keep the peace To behave in such a way as not to cause or threaten a breach of the peace, i.e. a disturbance of public order. Magistrates' courts have very wide powers to *bind over people to keep the peace or to make them enter into *recognizances (either personally or through a surety) to pay a sum of money into court if they fail to keep the peace. The order may be made against a defendant on a criminal charge or merely upon complaint by a member of the public (if there is some evidence that a *breach of the peace may occur). A person may be bound over for any sum of money or any period of time; if he refuses to be bound over or to enter into the recognizance, he may be sentenced immediately to imprisonment (even if he has committed no criminal offence). *See also* GOOD BEHAVIOUR.

kerb crawling The offence by a man of *soliciting a woman for prostitution in a street or public place either from a motor vehicle or having just alighted from one, when the soliciting is persistent or likely to cause annoyance to the woman or nuisance to other people in the vicinity. Case: *DPP v Bull* [1995] QB 88.

kidnapping *n.* Carrying a person away, without his consent, by means of force, threats, or fraud. Kidnapping is a common-law offence that overlaps to some extent with the offences of *child abduction and *false imprisonment. Kidnapping is punishable with a maximum sentence of life imprisonment. A man may be guilty of kidnapping his wife and a parent may be guilty of kidnapping his child (*R v D* [1984] AC 778 (HL)). *See also* HOSTAGE.

kleptomania *n.* A mental disorder leading to the *irresistible impulse to steal.

knock-for-knock An agreement between motor insurance companies that each will pay the claims of its own clients following an accident, irrespective of blame. The agreement seeks to save time and expense. However, one of the parties involved in an accident in such circumstances may still seek to sue the other and, if successful, may claim from the other's insurers.

knock-out agreement An agreement by dealers not to bid against each other at an auction. Such an agreement is illegal (*see* AUCTION RING).

knowhow *n.* Technical information often exploited in conjunction with a *patent. EU Regulation 772/2004 (due to be updated in 2014) governs the terms that may or may not be included in a knowhow licence agreement. *See* TECHNOLOGY TRANSFER.

knowing receipt If a stranger receives trust property knowing it to be in *breach of trust, he will be liable to account to the beneficiaries for that property or for the proceeds of it. *See* ACCESSORY LIABILITY IN BREACH OF TRUST; LIABILITY FOR RECEIPT. *See also* TRACING TRUST PROPERTY.

Kyoto protocol *See* UNITED NATIONS FRAMEWORK CONVENTION ON CLIMATE CHANGE.

k

laches *n.* [from Norman French *lasches*, slackness, negligence] Neglect and unreasonable delay in enforcing an equitable right. If a claimant with full knowledge of the facts takes an unnecessarily long time to bring an action (e.g. to set aside a contract obtained by fraud) the court will not assist him; hence the maxim "the law will not help those who sleep on their rights" and "equity aids the vigilant". The defence of laches is only allowed if there is no statutory limitation period. If there is such a period, the claimant can bring an action at any time up to the expiry of the time stated. *See* ACQUIESCENCE; WAIVER.

lacuna *n.* Literally, a gap: the situation in which there appears to be no law or legal norm applicable in a particular instance. This situation arises most often in *international law.

Lady Day *See* QUARTER DAYS.

land *n.* Those parts of the surface of the earth that are capable in law of being owned and are within the court's jurisdiction. Generally, ownership of land includes the *airspace above it and the subsoil below (**cuius est solum eius est usque ad coelum et ad inferos*: whoever owns land, it is theirs up to the heavens and down to hell). For the purposes of land law, the Law of Property Act 1925 defines land as including mines and minerals (whether or not owned separately from the surface), buildings, and most interests in land. Chattels fixed to the land so that they become part of it are also treated in law as land, under the maxim *quicquid plantatur solo, solo cedit* (*see* FIXTURE).

land certificate A document formerly issued by the Land Registry to the proprietor of registered land as proof of his ownership of it. *See* LAND REGISTRATION. Since 13 October 2003 no new land certificates have been issued as the register is kept entirely in electronic form. However, the land owner will receive a **Title Information Document** containing a printed copy of the entry on the register.

land charge An interest in *unregistered land that imposes an obligation on the landowner in favour of some other person (the **chargee**). If validly created and registered where appropriate under the Land Charges Act 1972 at the *Land Charges Department (*see* REGISTRATION OF ENCUMBRANCES), land charges will normally bind purchasers of the land. Important examples of land charges created by act of the parties include mortgages not protected by deposit of title deeds, binding contracts for sale (including options and rights of pre-emption), *restrictive covenants that affect freehold land, and equitable *easements. Some land charges arise under statute: for example, a spouse's right to occupy the matrimonial home under part IV of the Family Law Act 1996 (a Class F land charge) and the Revenue charge for unpaid inheritance tax (a Class D land charge). **Local land charges**, which arise in favour of local authorities from the exercise of their statutory powers, are registered by the local authority itself and apply to *registered land as well as to unregistered land.

Land Charges Department A department of the Land Registry, maintained under the Land Charges Act 1972 to keep registers of certain interests affecting the rights of persons owning *unregistered land (called **estate owners**). For the interests capable of being registered, *see* REGISTRATION OF ENCUMBRANCES. Registration of land charges against the name of the estate owner constitutes notice to everyone of their existence and generally renders them binding upon purchasers of any interest or estate in the land affected. A person contemplating taking such an interest may apply to the Department for an *official search certificate, which will reveal all interests registered against the estate owner's name.

landfill tax A tax charge on the commercial disposal of waste by way of landfill. It is charged on disposals made on or after 1 October 1996. The statutory provisions that impose the tax are in the Finance Act 1996 s 39–71; sch 5. *See also* WASTE DISPOSAL.

landlord *n.* A person who grants a lease or tenancy. He need not be the outright owner of the tenanted premises (he may, for example, be a lessee himself or even a licensee). A landlord may be an individual, a local authority, a trustee, a personal representative, or a corporation (such as a company). A landlord may provide services to the tenant, such as heating, lighting, and porterage. There are statutory controls on the amount that a landlord can charge for such services and procedures for consultation with the tenants. When there is a change of ownership the new landlord must inform the tenant within two months or when rent is next due, whichever is the later. The kind of security of tenure a tenant has is affected by who his landlord is. *See* ASSURED TENANCY; PROTECTED TENANCY; SECURE TENANCY; RESTRICTED CONTRACT.

land registration The system of registering, at branch offices of the Land Registry, certain legal estates or interests in land. Under the Land Registration Act 1925 compulsory registration was to be introduced in a specified area by Order in Council: registration has now been extended to the whole of England and Wales, and over 90% of all titles to land in England and Wales are now registered. The Land Registration Act 1925 has been superseded by the Land Registration Act 2002 with effect from 13 October 2003. There is no obligation on existing owners to register, but most transactions in land, including sale, gift, legal mortgage, etc., now trigger registration by the new or existing owner. If he fails to do so he does not acquire the legal estate and therefore runs the risk that the vendor or landlord may sell to someone else who can acquire a better title by registration. Existing owners or tenants under a lease having at least seven years to run may register their titles if they wish.

Upon registration of a title the Land Registry allocates a title number. The owner of a registered estate is known as a **registered proprietor**. The entry on the register will consist of three parts, namely:

- The **property register**. This describes the land and any additional rights incidental to it, such as rights of way over adjoining land. The **filed plan** shows the location of the land, usually with a general indication of the position of the boundaries. Registration of precise boundaries is possible under a special procedure involving notice to adjoining owners and hearing their objections.
- The **proprietorship register**. This names the registered proprietor(s) of the land and notes any restriction on their powers to dispose of it (for example, *restrictions, *inhibitions, *cautions, etc.). The register also states the nature of the title, which may be *absolute, *qualified, *possessory, or *good leasehold.

- The **charges register**. This details interests adverse to the proprietor, such as mortgages, restrictive covenants, or easements to which the land is subject.

When a prospective purchaser or mortgagee requires to know the exact state of the register, the Land Registry will issue *official copies or a certificate of *official search on application. A registered proprietor's title is guaranteed by the state subject to *overriding interests, which are not registrable in the charges register. The extent of the guarantee depends on the nature of the title. The register can be altered or rectified by the court in certain circumstances to correct a mistake; compensation is generally paid by the government to a party who suffers loss as a result.

Land Registry A statutory body established under the Land Registration Act 1925 and continued under the Land Registration Act 2002 to maintain registers of certain legal estates in land. Online services are offered to the general public whereby the title information document and/or the filed plan for all titles registered in England and Wales may be downloaded for a small fee (currently £4.00).

 SEE WEB LINKS

- Land Registry online

Lands Chamber A chamber of the *Upper Tribunal that hears disputes concerning compensation for the compulsory acquisition of land and similar questions involving land valuation. It also determines disputes as to the value of land or buildings for inheritance-tax purposes and hears appeals from the Property Chamber of the *First-tier Tribunal. The Lands Chamber took over from the former **Lands Tribunal** in 2008.

lapse *n.* The cancellation of a bequest when the beneficiary dies before the testator. Thus, in general, if A's will leaves property to B but B predeceases A, the gift of property does not take effect. The property becomes part of A's residuary estate and is distributed to his residuary beneficiaries. This rule is subject to the following exceptions:

(1) When property is bequeathed to two or more persons as joint tenants, those who survive the testator take the property.

(2) The Wills Act 1837 s 33 (as substituted by the Administration of Justice Act 1982 s 19) provides that when property is bequeathed or devised to a child or remoter descendant of the testator who predeceases him but leaves issue of his own who are alive at the testator's death, those issue take the property (subject to a contrary intention being expressed in the will). A similar rule applies when property is left in tail (*entailed interest).

(3) Some gifts to charities that cease to exist before the testator's death may be applied *cy-près.

(4) Most importantly, the testator may stipulate what is to happen to the gift if the beneficiary predeceases him. *See* ACCRUER; SUBSTITUTIONAL LEGACY.

lapse of offer The termination of an *offer as a result of the passage of time, death, or the nonfulfilment of a condition. An offer made subject to a specified time limit lapses after that time has passed; all other offers lapse after a reasonable time. Death of the offeree causes an offer to lapse, but death of the offeror does not always do so. The offer remains available for acceptance if the death is unknown to the offeree and the resulting contract could be performed by the offeror's personal representatives. An offer lapses if one or more conditions are not fulfilled. An offer to buy goods, for example, is made on the assumption that they will remain in the same condition until acceptance; it lapses if that ceases to be the case. *See also* REJECTION OF OFFER; REVOCATION OF OFFER.

larceny *n.* Formerly (before 1969), *theft. Larceny was more limited than theft and required an **asportation** (carrying away of the property).

lasting power of attorney A *power of attorney given legal authority by the UK Mental Capacity Act 2005. Under the Act, anyone who has mental capacity may choose another person to make decisions (including decisions regarding health care) on their behalf if they subsequently lose capacity. The donee of such a power must decide what is in the patient's *best interests but can refuse life-sustaining treatment only if express written provision for such a decision was made by the patient in advance (*see* ADVANCE DECISION). *See also* PROXY DECISION.

latent ambiguity *See* AMBIGUITY.

latent defect *See* DEFECT.

law *n.* **1.** The enforceable body of rules that govern any society. *See also* COMMON LAW; NATURAL LAW. **2.** One of the rules making up the body of law, such as an *Act of Parliament.

Law Commission A body established by the Law Commissions Act 1965 to take and keep the law under review with a view to systematically developing and reforming it. In particular, it considers the codification of the law, the elimination of anomalies, the repeal of obsolete and unnecessary enactments, a reduction in the number of separate enactments, and simplification and modernization generally. The Commission consists of a chairman and four other members, appointed by the Lord Chancellor from among the holders of judicial office, barristers, solicitors, and academic lawyers. There is a separate Commission for Scotland.

(⊕) SEE WEB LINKS
• Website of the Law Commission

Law Lords *See* LORDS OF APPEAL IN ORDINARY.

law merchant The international practice of merchants relating to commercial and maritime matters. In early times it influenced Admiralty law and the law administered in local courts. Parts of the law merchant were absorbed into the common law of England (e.g. that relating to negotiable instruments and the transfer of bills of lading).

law officers of the Crown The *Attorney General, *Solicitor General, *Lord Advocate, Solicitor General for Scotland, and Attorney General for Northern Ireland.

law of nations *See* INTERNATIONAL LAW.

law of the sea The rules of international law governing rights over the seas. The seas are divided into several different areas. (1) The *internal waters of a state (e.g. rivers, lakes, ports, and harbours). A state may usually apply its laws to any merchant ship within its internal waters. It may also apply navigation or health regulations to foreign warships in such waters and exclude foreign warships from its ports. (2) The *territorial waters. (3) The *high seas, beyond the territorial waters, which are open to all nations for such purposes as navigation, fishing, laying of submarine cables, and over-flying. Ships on the high seas are usually subject only to international law (for example, in relation to acts of piracy) and the law of the flagstate (usually dependent on registration in that state). There is also a limited right of *hot pursuit. (4) The *continental shelf, which – although geographically part of the high seas – is subject to specific rules.

The law of the sea is contained in customary international law and in the four Geneva Conventions of 1958. Since 1982, when the United Nations Convention on the Law of the Sea came into force, there is a comprehensive code governing the whole of this law, which includes some completely new rules. To date (2009) 156 countries, including the European Community (1998), have established their consent to be bound by this Convention; the UK acceded to the treaty on 25 July 1997. In addition, many nations have subscribed to the related 1994 Agreement Regarding the United Nations Convention on the Law of the Sea. Even though some states chose not to ratify the 1982 Convention, many of the Convention's principles have now passed into the corpus of *customary international law.

Law Reform Committee A body established by the Lord Chancellor in 1952 to consider particular areas of the law that might need reform. It took an active role in the 1960s and 1970s but is now dormant.

law reports Reports of cases decided by the courts, comprising a statement of the facts of every case and the reasons the court gave for judgment. The earliest reports were contained in the *Year Books*, which were published annually between 1283 and 1535. Their authors were anonymous and may have been student lawyers. The *Year Books* were superseded by the so-called nominate reports, i.e. reports written privately by lawyers (e.g. Chief Justice Coke) who appended their names to them. In 1865 the Incorporated Council of Law Reporting, a semiofficial body that publishes the official Law Reports series and *The Weekly Law Reports* (formerly *Weekly Notes*), was established. The *Weekly Law Reports* are reports of important cases selected by the Council, written by lawyers, and approved by the judges involved. There are in addition still a number of commercially published reports, e.g. the *All England Law Reports*, but the Court of Appeal and the House of Lords will cite the reports of the Incorporated Council in preference to other reports where there is a choice. For guidance on the citing of law reports, see the WRITING AND CITATION GUIDE at the centre of this volume.

law sittings *See* SITTINGS.

Law Society The professional body for solicitors in England and Wales, incorporated by royal charter in 1831. The Society exists to further the professional interests of solicitors by providing advice, training, and other services and also represents the profession to government. Until 2007 the Law Society discharged important statutory functions in relation to the admission to practice, the conduct, and the discipline of solicitors; this regulatory role has now been transferred to the *Solicitors Regulation Authority, an independent board of the Society.

(⊕) SEE WEB LINKS
• Website of the Law Society of England and Wales: includes guidance on finding and using a solicitor and advice on common legal problems

lay days (lying days) The number of days specified in a charterparty to enable the charterer to load or discharge cargo. They begin to run as soon as the ship is an **arrived ship**, i.e. has reached the berth or mooring specified in the charterparty. If only a port is specified, the ship must have reached a position within that port at which it is at the immediate and effective disposition of the charterer (the **Reid test**). The charterparty may provide for the payment of dispatch money when the charterer saves days in loading or discharging the cargo. Unless the charterparty provides otherwise (e.g. by restricting them to good-weather working days), lay days are **running days**, i.e. they run consecutively, without any break. *See also* DEMURRAGE.

laying an information Giving a magistrate a concise statement (an **information**), verbally or in writing, of an alleged offence and the suspected offender, so that he can take steps to obtain the appearance of the suspect in court. Information can be laid by any member of the public, although it is usually done by the police. If an arrest warrant is required, the information must be in writing and on oath. Objections cannot normally be made to information laid, on the grounds of formal defects or discrepancies between it and the prosecution's subsequent evidence. But if the defect is fundamental to the charge the information will be dismissed, and if the defendant was misled by a discrepancy, he may be granted an adjournment of the trial.

leader *n.* A *Queen's Counsel or any barrister who is the senior of two counsel appearing for the same party.

Leader of HM Opposition The leader in the House of Commons of the party in opposition to the government that has the greatest numerical strength in the House. By statute a salary is payable to him (in addition to his salary as an MP); any doubt as to his identity is resolved by the Speaker.

Leader of the House *See* HOUSE OF COMMONS; HOUSE OF LORDS.

lead evidence To call or adduce evidence.

leading case A case, the legal reasoning in which establishes an important principle of law. *See* PRECEDENT.

leading question A question asked of a witness in a manner that suggests the answer sought by the questioner (e.g. "You threw the brick through the window, didn't you?") or that assumes the existence of disputed facts to which the witness is to testify. Leading questions may not be asked during *examination-in-chief (except relating to formal matters, such as the witness's name and address, or matters that are not disputed between the parties) but may normally be asked in *cross-examination.

leapfrog procedure 1. (**Supreme Court**) The procedure for appealing direct to the Supreme Court from the High Court or a Divisional Court, bypassing the Court of Appeal. The procedure is only allowed in exceptional cases. All parties must consent and the case must raise a point of law of public importance, which either relates wholly or partly to the interpretation of a statute or of a statutory instrument or is one in respect of which the trial judge is bound by a previous decision of the Court of Appeal or the Supreme Court. The trial judge must certify that he is satisfied as to the importance of the case and the Supreme Court must give permission to appeal in this way. 2. (**Court of Appeal**) The procedure under Part 52 of the *Civil Procedure Rules by which an appeal from a decision of a district judge or master may be transferred to the Court of Appeal. Under the Civil Procedure Rules, which substantially revised *appellate jurisdiction in the civil courts, such an appeal would normally be to a circuit judge or a High Court judge. However, if the appeal is considered to raise an important point of principle or practice, or if there is some other compelling reason, it may be transferred to the Court of Appeal.

lease *n.* A contract under which an owner of property (the *landlord or **lessor**) grants another person (the *tenant or **lessee**) exclusive possession of the property for an agreed period, usually (but not necessarily) in return for rent and sometimes for a capital sum known as a *premium (*Street v Mountford* [1985] AC 809 (HL)). Unless it satisfies the conditions for a *parol lease, a legal lease must be made by a formal document (a *deed), which is itself called a lease. If this is not done, however, there may still be an *agreement for a lease or an *equitable lease. The lessee must have exclusive possession, i.e. the right to control the property and to exclude everyone else from it (subject to any rights of entry or re-entry reserved to the landlord). If possession is not exclusive, there is no lease but there may be a *licence. A lease must be for a definite period that is certain at the date of commencement of the lease (*Lace v Chandler* [1944] KB 368). *See also* LEGAL LEASE.

The deed that creates the lease sets out the terms, which include the parties, the property, the length of the lease, the rent, and other obligations (**covenants**), particularly concerning repairs, insurance, and parting with possession. Certain covenants are implied in all leases (though the lease may vary or exclude them). In the case of the lessor these are:

(1) not to derogate from his grant (i.e. he must not do anything that would make the property unfit for the purpose for which it was let);

(2) *quiet enjoyment.

In the case of the tenant, the implied covenants are:

(1) to pay the rent;

(2) to pay all ordinary rates and taxes;

(3) not to commit *waste; and

(4) to use the property in a tenant-like manner, i.e. to do the sort of small maintenance jobs that any reasonable tenant would be expected to do (he is not, however, responsible for *fair wear and tear or other disrepair that is not his fault).

The different kinds of lease are: tenancy for a *fixed term, *periodic tenancy, *tenancy at sufferance, *tenancy at will, and *tenancy by estoppel. The terms and conditions of leases vary considerably according to the kind of lease and the wishes of the parties. There are many statutory controls that affect leases, particularly in relation to *security of tenure and rent. *See also* ASSIGNMENT; COVENANT TO REPAIR.

leasehold *adj.* Held under a *lease, i.e. for a period of fixed minimum duration. *See* TERM OF YEARS ABSOLUTE.

leasehold ownership Ownership of property under a *lease. The period of ownership depends on the terms of the lease: it may vary from a very short time, such as a week, to a very long period, such as 999 years. The tenant's ownership is also restricted by the terms of the lease. Under the Leasehold Reform Act 1967, holders of long leases (over 21 years) for houses may have a statutory right to purchase the freehold or extend the existing lease by 50 years (*see* ENFRANCHISEMENT OF TENANCY). The Leasehold Reform Act 1993 granted a similar right to leaseholders of flats.

leasehold valuation tribunal A body that handles disputes over service charges and over the purchase of leasehold property by tenants holding long leases; it also appoints managers of leasehold properties when the landlords' managers are not acceptable. Leasehold valuation tribunals started operating in 1997.

leave of the court Permission given by the court.

leave to appeal Permission granted to *appeal against the decision of a court.

legacy *n.* A gift of personal property effected by will (*compare* DEVISE).

• A **general legacy** is a gift of property not identifiable with a specific asset or fund; for example, a simple legacy of "£1000 to A" or "all my shares to B".

• A **specific legacy** is a particular identifiable object, for example a named painting. It is liable to *ademption but is otherwise payable by the deceased's personal representatives in priority to general legacies.

- A **demonstrative legacy** is payable from a specified fund; for example, "£500 from the £1000 kept under my bed". Such a legacy is not adeemed if the testator disposes of the fund during his lifetime and is payable in priority to general legacies.
- A **pecuniary legacy** is a gift of a cash sum and carries interest from one year after the testator's death.
- A **residuary legacy** is one that disposes of the whole of the testator's personal property after payment of debts and specific, demonstrative, and general legacies.
- A *statutory legacy is a legacy provided for in the Administration of Estates Act 1925 on an *intestacy.

legal aid A scheme, first introduced under the Legal Aid Act 1988, whereby the payment of legal costs can be made out of public funds for those unable to meet the costs themselves, provided that the person and the case qualify under the various tests laid down. Under the original scheme civil legal aid had two main components: (i) legal advice and help preliminary to litigation (sometimes known as the **green form** scheme); and (ii) full legal aid, which provided payment for legal advice and assistance at all stages of litigation, including appeals. There was also an intermediate level of help known as **assistance by way of representation (ABWOR)**, under which legal representation was provided for a particular hearing only. In criminal cases, the court determined whether or not legal aid was granted and made a legal aid order if it considered such aid desirable in the interest of justice.

The original legal aid scheme was replaced in April 2000 by the **Community Legal Service**, a scheme administered by the **Legal Services Commission**. Under this arrangement, the green form scheme was replaced by the **legal help** scheme, ABWOR by the **help at court** service, and full legal aid by **full representation**. Three further levels of service were **investigative help**, which provided funding for an investigation of whether or not to proceed with a case; **support funding**, which provided some funds to support high-cost claims but not the majority of the costs; and **specific directions**, by which the Lord Chancellor could authorize support for particular claims, as in test cases or class actions.

The principal aim of these reforms was to cut the costs of legal aid while ensuring that public funds were directed to those most in need. This was to be achieved by excluding various categories of applicant and also by laying down strict criteria for eligibility to each level of service. Central to these criteria was the cost-benefit rule, under which funding could be refused if the benefit to be gained was considered not to justify the level of costs.

Still more radical reforms were introduced under the Legal Aid, Sentencing and Punishment of Offenders Act 2012 and came into force as from 1 April 2013. Further limitations were placed on eligibility, with applicants now being means-tested on their capital as well as their income. At the same time many civil legal services were placed entirely beyond the scope of legal aid provision; in private family law, for example, aid is now effectively limited to those cases in which there are child protection issues or a history of domestic violence. In criminal cases, exceptional funding may be available where a failure to provide aid could constitute a breach of the applicant's right to a fair trial under the European Convention. The Community Legal Service was replaced by the **Legal Aid Agency**, an executive agency of the Ministry of Justice.

(⊕) SEE WEB LINKS

- A guide to claiming legal aid from the GOV.UK website
- Information for legal practitioners from the Ministry of Justice

legal assignment *See* ASSIGNMENT.

legal burden of proof *See* BURDEN OF PROOF.

legal easement *See* EASEMENT.

legal estate Ownership of land or an interest in land either in *fee simple absolute in possession or for a *term of years absolute. Under the Law of Property Act 1925 these are the only forms of ownership that can exist as legal estates in land. All other forms, e.g. life interests and entailed interests, are equitable only.

legal fiction *See* FICTION.

legal fraud *See* CONSTRUCTIVE FRAUD.

legal help *See* LEGAL AID.

legal lease A contract or grant that creates an estate in land for a *term of years absolute. A legal lease must normally be created by deed; however, there are no formal requirements for the creation of a legal lease for a term that takes effect in possession and does not exceed three years at a full market rent without a premium. Under the Law of Property Act 1925, the *assignment of a legal lease of whatever duration must be effected by deed, otherwise it may take effect only as a contract to assign the term. A legal lease for more than seven years must be registered at the Land Registry (*see* LAND REGISTRATION). *Compare* EQUITABLE LEASE.

legal memory The period over which the law's recollection extends. Its commencement was arbitrarily fixed at 1189 by the Statute of Westminster I 1275. Time before legal memory is referred to as **time immemorial**. *Compare* LIVING MEMORY.

legal mortgage *See* MORTGAGE.

Legal Ombudsman A free service that investigates complaints against lawyers in England and Wales. Operational since 2010, it was established under the Legal Services Act 2007 as a replacement for the Legal Complaints Service and Legal Services Ombudsman. Unlike its predecessor bodies, it is a lay organization and a lawyer can not occupy the role of Chief Ombudsman. Its remit is restricted to issues relating to quality of service, as opposed to the quality of legal advice given.

(⊕) SEE WEB LINKS
• Website of the Legal Ombudsman

legal person A natural person (i.e. a human being) or a *juristic person. *See also* INTERNATIONAL LEGAL PERSONALITY.

legal positivism An approach to law that rejects *natural law and contends that the law as laid down (*positum*) should be kept separate – for the purpose of study and analysis – from the law as it ought morally to be. In other words, a clear distinction must be drawn between "ought" (that which is morally desirable) and "is" (that which actually exists). The theory is associated especially with the thought of Jeremy Bentham (1748-1832), John Austin (1790-1859), H. L. A. Hart (1907-1992), and Hans Kelsen (1881-1973), who differ from one another in important respects but generally adhere to the above **separability thesis**. In addition, legal positivists normally adopt the so-called **social fact thesis** (that legal validity is a function of pedigree or related social facts) and the **conventionality thesis** (that social facts giving rise to legal validity are authoritative by virtue of social convention). *See* ANALYTICAL JURISPRUDENCE; PURE THEORY OF LAW; UTILITARIANISM. *See also* INTERPRETIVE THEORY OF LAW.

legal realism A largely instrumental and empirical approach to law developed in the first half of the 20th century in the USA (**American legal realism**) and Scandinavia (**Scandinavian legal realism**). It rejects the view that law is a determinate body of doctrine or that precedents and statutes determine the outcome of legal disputes. Although the * critical legal studies (CLS) movement is often described as its heir, the two movements have little in common apart from their critical approach; in important respects, CLS extends well beyond the scepticism of its alleged progenitor.

legal rights **1.** Rights recognized by the common law courts, as distinct from *equitable rights or interests recognized by the Court of Chancery. In their developed form, legal rights affect everyone whether or not they know (or ought to know) of their existence (hence the expression "legal rights bind the world"). **2.** Generally, all rights recognized by the law (both common law and equity) as having legal existence and effect, as distinguished from moral rights.

legal separation *See* JUDICIAL SEPARATION ORDER.

Legal Services Commission *See* LEGAL AID.

legal theory *See* JURISPRUDENCE.

legal year The period made up, in any year, of the four court *sittings.

legatee *n.* The person to whom a *legacy is given.

legislation *n.* **1.** The whole or any part of a country's written law. In the UK the term is normally confined to *Acts of Parliament, but in its broadest sense it also includes law made under powers conferred by Act of Parliament (*see* DELEGATED LEGISLATION), law made by virtue of the *royal prerogative, and Measures (*see* CHURCH OF ENGLAND). **2.** The process of making written law.

legislature *n.* The body having primary power to make written law. In the UK it consists of Parliament, i.e. the Crown, the House of Commons, and the House of Lords.

legitimacy *n.* The legal status of a child born to parents who were married at the time of his conception or birth (or both). (*See also* LEGITIMATION). There is a **presumption of legitimacy** in all cases when the mother is married, so that children of the marriage are presumed to be the offspring of the mother's husband. This may be rebutted, however, either by showing that the husband was impotent or absent on the date on which the child must have been conceived or, more commonly, by scientific tests. This was traditionally done by *blood tests, which can show that a man is not the father; however, the development of DNA testing now enables paternity to be determined with virtual certainty. Children born of a voidable marriage annulled since 1949 are legitimate; those born of such a marriage annulled between 1937 and 1949 are legitimate only if the grounds of nullity were that the other spouse was of unsound mind or epileptic or suffering from a sexually transmitted disease. Since 1959, children born of a void marriage are treated as legitimate if at the time of their conception or insemination at least one of their parents reasonably thought the marriage was valid and the father was domiciled in England at the time of the child's birth. The Family Law Reform Act 1987 provides that a child conceived, by a party to a marriage, through artificial insemination by a donor, is to be treated as a legitimate child of that marriage. The same Act removed most of the remaining legal distinctions between legitimate and illegitimate children.

Under certain conditions (specified in the Family Law Act 1986) a person may seek a court declaration of his legitimacy (*see* DECLARATION OF PARENTAGE). *See also* ILLEGITIMACY.

legitimate aim A prerequisite for interference with a *qualified right as set out in the European Convention on Human Rights: a signatory state will be able to interfere with a qualified right only if that interference is designed to pursue a legitimate aim and the interference is a proportionate one (*see* PROPORTIONALITY). Legitimate aims include national security, public order, the prevention of crime, etc.

legitimate expectation A principle applied in administrative law. The principle as initially recognized by the courts was confined to legitimate expectation of procedural protection (*Schmidt v Secretary of State for Home Affairs* [1969] 2 Ch 149 (CA)). A **procedural legitimate expectation** arises where a public authority has induced in someone affected by a decision a reasonable expectation that he will be granted a hearing or that some other procedure will be followed before a decision depriving him of some benefit or advantage is taken. A failure to act in accordance with the expectation and provide procedural protection is challengeable on *judicial review (*Council of Civil Service Unions v Minister for the Civil Service* [1985] AC 374 (HL)). More recently the courts have extended protection to substantive legitimate expectations. A **substantive legitimate expectation** is an expectation induced by a public authority that an individual will be granted or retain some substantive benefit. A failure on the part of the public authority to act in accordance with the expectation is considered to be a breach of the rule of law that requires predictability and certainty and is therefore *ultra vires (*R v North and East Devon Health Authority, ex p Coughlan* [2001] QB 213 (CA)). The expectation must be based on either an express undertaking or arise from past conduct on the part of the public authority in order for it to be recognized as legitimate or reasonable (*AG for Hong Kong v Ng Yuen Shiu* [1983] 2 AC 629 (PC); *R (on the application of Patel) v General Medical Council* [2013] EWCA Civ 327, [2013] WLR (D) 128)). *See* NATURAL JUSTICE.

legitimation *n.* The process of replacing the status of illegitimacy by that of legitimacy. A living child may be legitimated if his parents marry one another, provided that the father is domiciled in England or Wales at the date of the marriage. Evidence that the husband recognized the child as his own may be sufficient to establish his paternity for purposes of legitimation. Legitimation takes effect from the date of the marriage and the child is treated thereafter as if he had been born legitimate. Under the Family Law Act 1986, a person may seek a court declaration that he is a legitimated person.

lessee *n.* The person to whom a *lease is granted. *See also* TENANT.

lessor *n.* The person by whom a *lease is granted. *See also* LANDLORD.

letter of attorney *See* POWER OF ATTORNEY.

letter of credence (*lettre de créance*) A formal document by which the head of an accredited state presents its newly appointed diplomatic agent to the head of state of the host country.

letter of credit A document whereby a bank, at the request of a customer, undertakes to pay money to a third party (the **beneficiary**) on presentation of documents specified in the letter (e.g. bills of lading and policies of insurance). The obligation of the bank to pay is independent of the underlying contract of sale and so is not affected by any defects in the goods supplied under the contract of sale. A contract of sale of goods may require the buyer to open an **irrevocable letter of credit** in favour of the seller. This cannot be revoked by the issuing bank or the purchaser of the goods before its expiry date, without the consent of the beneficiary. A **confirmed letter of credit** is one in which the negotiating bank guarantees payment to the beneficiary should it not be honoured by the issuing bank.

letter of intent (memorandum of understanding) A document that sets out the main terms of an agreement between two or more parties and their intention to enter into a binding *contract once certain details have been finalized. A letter of intent is not itself a formal contract but certain of its provisions (e.g. concerning payment for any work completed) may nevertheless be enforceable. Letters of intent are widely used in the UK construction industry, where their usual purpose is to encourage a contractor to begin work on a time-sensitive project before legal formalities have been completed. Recent case law suggests that the courts are increasingly willing to find that a letter of intent constitutes a binding contract, provided that all necessary elements of a contract are present (*Harvey Shop Fitters v ADI Ltd* [2003] EWCA Civ 1757, [2003] 2 All ER 982; *RTS Flexible Systems v Molkerei Alois Müller GmbH & Co Kg* [2008] EWHC 1087 (TCC), [2008] All ER(D) 206). *See also* ACCEPTANCE; QUANTUM MERUIT; QUASI-CONTRACT.

letter of request (rogatory letter, letter rogatory) 1. A letter issued to a foreign court asking a judicial authority to take the evidence of some person within that court's jurisdiction (Civil Procedure Rules Part 34). The resulting *deposition may be read at a subsequent court hearing. Since 2004 there has been a special procedure for taking depositions from persons in member states of the European Union. **2.** A document by which *personal representatives may transfer a deceased's shares to beneficiaries of the estate. In practice there is no advantage over use of a stock transfer form (*see* SHARE TRANSFER) and letters of request are rarely used.

letters of administration Authority granted by the court to a specified person to act as an *administrator of a deceased person's estate when the deceased dies intestate (Non-Contentious Probate Rules 1987 r 22). In certain circumstances, letters of administration may be granted for limited purposes to persons not entitled to deal with the whole estate (*see* AD COLLIGENDA BONA; DURANTE ABSENTIA). *See also* AD LITEM; CUM TESTAMENTO ANNEXO; DE BONIS NON ADMINISTRATIS; PENDENTE LITE.

lex causae [Latin: the law of the case] In *private international law, the system of law (usually foreign) applicable to the case in dispute, as opposed to the *lex fori*.

lex domicilii [Latin] The law of *domicile. In *private international law, the law of the country of domicile determines such matters as capacity to make a will in respect of personal property, the validity of such a will, succession to personal property, consent to marriage, and the proper law of a marriage contract or settlement (*see* PROPER LAW OF A CONTRACT).

lex fori [Latin] The law of the *forum. In *private international law, the law of the forum governs matters of procedure, the mode of trial, most matters relating to evidence, the nature of the remedy available, and most matters of *limitation of actions based on time bars. From the entry into force of Part III of the Private International Law (Miscellaneous Provisions) Act 1995, the provisions of this Act determine the choice of forums in actions in tort.

lex loci actus [Latin] The law of the place where a legal act takes place. In *private international law, this law governs such questions as whether or not property in a bill of exchange or promissory note passes to the transferee and the formal validity of an assignment of an intangible movable (e.g. a share in a trust fund). *See also* LEX LOCI CELEBRATIONIS; LEX LOCI CONTRACTUS.

lex loci celebrationis [Latin] The law of the place of celebration of a marriage. In *private international law, this law governs such questions as the formalities required for a marriage (subject to four special exceptions), whether or not such a marriage is monogamous or polygamous, and possibly what law governs impotence or wilful refusal to consummate a marriage.

lex loci contractus [Latin] The law of the place where a contract was made. In *private international law, this law governs such matters as the formal requirements of a contract and the capacity to incur liability as a party to a bill of exchange. Most other matters relating to contracts are governed by the *proper law of a contract. Case: *Bodley Head Ltd v Flegon* [1972] 1 WLR 680.

lex loci delicti commissi [Latin] The law of the place in which a delict (tort) is committed. In *private international law as applied in most countries in Europe, this law governs liability for torts. In some cases, however, it may be difficult to establish where the tort was committed (for example, when goods negligently manufactured in one country are distributed in another) or the place may be a matter of mere chance (for example, when an aeroplane crashes and lands). For these reasons, England does not accept the theory that liability in tort is governed by the *lex loci delicti*. Case: *Monro v American Cyanamid Corporation* [1944] KB 432.

lex loci situs [Latin] The law of the place where an object is situated. In *private international law, this law usually governs such matters as succession to, title to, and the right to possession of immovables and the essential validity of trusts of immovables (for example, what estates can be created and whether or not gifts to charities are valid).

lex loci solutionis [Latin] The law of the place where a contract is to be performed or a debt is to be paid. In *private international law as applied in England, the *lex loci solutionis* governs the due date for payment of a *bill of exchange but does not usually govern matters relating to the law of contract.

lex mercatoria [Latin: mercantile law] The general body of European usages in commercial matters. Lord Mansfield, by means of the Special Jury, absorbed many of the rules of this system into the common law in the 18th century.

lex non scripta [Latin: the unwritten law] The *common law, as opposed to statute. This may seem a strange term for law that clearly is written to the extent that it is to be found printed in the law reports. However, the term refers to a time before written reports existed, when rules and principles were conveyed by example and retained by memory alone.

lex talionis [Latin] The law of retaliation. This is familiarly found in the biblical expression "an eye for an eye, a tooth for a tooth."

liability *n.* **1.** An amount owed. **2.** A legal duty or obligation. *See* BUSINESS LIABILITY; OCCUPIER'S LIABILITY; PARENTS' LIABILITY; PRODUCT LIABILITY; STRICT LIABILITY; VICARIOUS LIABILITY.

liability for receipt Liability for the receipt of trust property in *breach of trust. The extent to which the recipient will be liable will depend upon the state of his knowledge at the time of receipt. It is a prerequisite to liability that the state of the recipient's knowledge must make it unconscionable for him to retain the benefit of the receipt (*BCCI (Overseas) Limited v Akindele* [2001] Ch 437). If the recipient has disposed of the property received and cannot therefore be holding it on constructive trust, he will be personally liable to the trust. *See also* ACCESSORY LIABILITY IN BREACH OF TRUST; KNOWING RECEIPT.

libel *n.* A defamatory statement made in permanent form, such as writing, pictures, or film (*see* DEFAMATION). Radio and television broadcasts, public performance of plays, and statements posted on the Internet have been treated as being made in permanent form for the purposes of the law of defamation (*Godrey v Demon Internet Ltd* [2001] QB 201). Libel is actionable in tort without proof that its publication has caused special damage (actual financial or material loss) to the person defamed, although the Defamation Act 2013 has introduced a requirement for evidence of serious harm to the claimant's reputation. Libel used also to exist as a crime (**criminal libel**), but the offence was abolished by the Coroners and Justice Act 2009.

liberty and freedom from arbitrary detention A right set out in Article 5 of the *European Convention on Human Rights and now part of UK law as a consequence of the *Human Rights Act 1998. All *detentions must be prescribed by law and detentions must only be for one of the specified purposes set out in Article 5. Those detained must promptly be given reasons for their detention and then at regular intervals have access to a court to test the lawfulness of their continued detention. Arrest is only lawful when based on reasonable suspicion, which is an objective test (*Fox v UK* (1991) 13 EHRR 157). Those remanded in custody pending a criminal trial must be released on bail unless their detention is justified and they shall be entitled to trial within a reasonable time. There is an enforceable right to compensation for unlawful detention.

licence *n.* **1.** Formal authority to do something that would otherwise be unlawful. Examples include a *driving licence, a licence for selling intoxicating liquor (*see* LICENSING OF PREMISES), and a licence by the owner of a patent to manufacture the patented goods. **2.** (in land law) Permission to enter or occupy a person's land for an agreed purpose. A licence does not usually confer a right to exclusive possession of the land, nor any estate or interest in it: it is a personal arrangement between the licensor and the licensee. A **bare licence** (i.e. gratuitous permission to enter or occupy the licensor's land) can be revoked at any time and cannot be assigned by the licensee to a third party (*see* BARE LICENSEE). A **contractual licence** cannot be revoked during the period the parties intended it to last. Neither type is by itself binding on third parties acquiring the land from the licensor. However, if the licence is **coupled with a grant** of property or of an interest in land, the licence may be irrevocable and binding on the licensor's successors in title. For example, if A grants to B the right to catch and remove fish from water on his land, a licence to enter A's land to take up this *profit à prendre* is necessarily implied and will be irrevocable for the duration of the profit. The profit, as a legal interest over A's land, will bind A's successors in title, as will the licence that is irretrievably bound up with it. A bare or contractual licence may become irrevocable by the licensor or binding on a third party acquiring the land from the licensor if the circumstances give rise to a proprietary *estoppel or a *constructive trust. **3.** *See* PAROLE.

licensed conveyancer A person, other than a solicitor, who is qualified to practise *conveyancing. Entry to this profession, which was created in 1985 in response to recommendations by the Farrand Committee, is by examination; the level of competence required, ethics, and professional conduct are regulated by the Council for Licensed Conveyancers.

licensee *n.* **1.** A person who has been granted a licence, most commonly used of one who has been granted a licence by a local authority to sell intoxicating liquor (*see* LICENSING OF PREMISES) or one who has been granted a licence to use intellectual property, such as *patents. **2.** A person with permission to do what would otherwise be unlawful. In relation to land, a licensee is one who enters land with the express or implied permission of the occupier. *See* LICENCE; OCCUPIER'S LIABILITY.

licensing of premises Various activities require the granting of a licence for the premises in which the activity will take place. These include the sale of *intoxicating liquor (for consumption on or off the premises), live music, gaming, bookmaking, the slaughter of animals, and the sale of certain kinds of sexual material. *See also* BREWSTER SESSIONS.

lie in grant To be capable of being transferred by deed. Land and interests in it lie in grant; property that can be transferred by physical delivery **lies in livery**.

lie in livery *See* LIE IN GRANT.

lien *n.* [via Old French from Latin *ligamen*, a binding] The right of one person to retain possession of goods owned by another until the possessor's claims against the owner have been satisfied. The lien may be **general**, when the goods are held as security for all outstanding debts of the owner, or **particular**, when only the claims of the possessor in respect of the goods held must be satisfied. Thus an unpaid seller may in some contracts be entitled to retain the goods until he receives the price (*see also* UNPAID VENDOR'S LIEN), a carrier may have a lien over goods he is transporting, and a repairer over goods he is repairing. Whether a lien arises or not depends on the terms of the contract and usual trade practice. A lien may be waived and can be lost, for example when an owner in possession sells goods to a buyer ignorant of a third party's lien. This type of lien is a **possessory lien**, but sometimes actual possession of the goods is not necessary. In an **equitable lien**, for example, the claim exists independently of possession. If a purchaser of the property involved is given notice of the lien it binds him; otherwise he will not be bound. Similarly a **maritime lien**, which binds a ship or cargo in connection with some maritime liability, does not depend on possession and can be enforced by arrest and sale (unless security is given). The lien accordingly travels with the ship or cargo when possession changes, and is good against a bona fide *purchaser for value without notice. Examples of maritime liens are the lien of a salvor, that of seamen for their wages and of masters for their wages and outgoings, that of a bottomry or respondentia bondholder (*see* HYPOTHECATION), and that over a ship at fault in a collision in which property has been damaged. A maritime lien is enforceable by proceedings *in rem. *See also* SOLICITOR'S LIEN.

life assurance *Insurance providing for the payment of a sum on the occurrence of an event that is in some way dependent upon a human life. In **endowment assurance** the insurer is liable to pay a fixed sum either at the end of a fixed period or at death if the insured should die in the meantime. **Whole-life assurance** provides for the payment of a fixed sum on the death of the insured. **Term** (or **temporary**) **assurance** provides for a fixed sum to be paid in the event of the death of the insured within a specified period.

life estate *See* LIFE INTEREST.

life imprisonment Punishment of a criminal by imprisonment for the rest of his life. The only crime that carries a mandatory sentence of life imprisonment is murder, but there are many crimes (e.g. arson, manslaughter, wounding with intent, and rape) that carry a maximum penalty of life imprisonment, which is imposed in serious cases. An offender aged 21 or over who is convicted of murder must be sentenced to imprisonment for life under section 1(1) of the Murder (Abolition of the Death Penalty) Act 1965. For an offender aged under 21 the current sentence is custody for life (Power of Criminal Courts (Sentencing) Act 2000 s 93).

In practice the imprisonment may often not be for life (*see* PAROLE). When imposing life imprisonment for murder, the judge may make a recommendation that the defendant should serve a **minimum term** (number of years). Under the Criminal Justice Act 2003 sch 21, paras 4 to 11, there is a detailed scheme of general principles that act as guidelines in the determination of the minimum term to be served as part of the mandatory life sentence for murder. Following the decision in *R (Anderson) v Secretary of State for the Home Department* [2003] 1 AC 837, it was ruled that the Home Secretary's power to set a minimum term to be served for life imprisonment for murder was incompatible with article 6(1) of the European Convention on Human Rights, which gives the offender the right to have his sentence imposed by an independent tribunal.

life interest (life estate) An interest in property subsisting only during the lifetime of the person to whom it was granted (e.g. "to A for life") or of some other person (e.g. "to A during the life of B"). The latter type is called an *estate (or interest) *pur autre vie*. Under the Law of Property Act 1925 a life interest in land cannot exist as a legal estate, only as an *equitable interest. Until 1997 the creation of a life interest in land created a settlement, governed by the Settled Land Act 1925. Since that date it creates a *trust of land, governed by the Trusts of Land and Appointment of Trustees Act 1996. *See* SETTLED LAND.

life peerage A nonhereditary peerage of the rank of baron or baroness created by the Crown by letters patent under the Life Peerages Act 1958. The purpose of the Act was to strengthen the composition of the *House of Lords, and there is no limit to the number of peerages that may be created. The peerage of a Lord of Appeal in Ordinary is also for life but is not customarily included among life peerages.

life policy A policy providing a formal embodiment of a contract of *life assurance. The benefit of a life policy can be assigned to a third party.

life tenant *See* TENANT FOR LIFE.

lifting the veil The act of disregarding the veil of *incorporation that separates the personality of a corporation from the personalities of its members and directors. This exceptional course is occasionally sanctioned by statute, for example in relation to *wrongful trading or *fraudulent trading, when it may result in members or directors of a limited company incurring liability. It is also employed by the courts, for example if incorporation has been used to perpetrate fraud or gives rise to unreal distinctions between a company and its subsidiary companies (*Gilford Motor Co Ltd v Horne* [1933] Ch 935; *Jones v Lipman* [1962] 1 WLR 832; *Trustor AB v Smallbone* (No 2) [2001] WLR 1177 (Ch)), but never so as to defeat limited liability (*Ord v Belhaven Pubs Ltd* [1998] 2 BCLC 447; *Adams v Cape Industries plc* [1990] Ch 433; *Petrodel Resources Ltd v Prest* [2013] UKSC 34, [2013] All ER (D) 90); *Woolfson v Strathclyde Regional Council* [1978] UKHL 5, [1978] AC 159; *VTB Capital plc v Nutritek International Corporation* [2012] EWCA Civ 808, [2012] WLR (D) 181). Very occasionally the courts openly disregard corporate personality but more often they evade its inconvenient consequences by deciding that the acts were performed by the corporation acting as agent or trustee for the company members, to whom therefore they should be attributed (*Smith, Stone & Knight Ltd v Birmingham Corporation* [1939] 4 All ER 116).

limitation *n.* Statutory rules limiting the time within which civil actions can be brought. Claims in simple contract and tort must normally be brought within six years of the accrual of the *cause of action (in the case of contracts, within six years of the date of the breach of contract). Special rules apply to actions in respect of land; to *strict liability actions for defective products (*see* PRODUCT LIABILITY); to claims for defamation; and to applications for *judicial review. If the claim is for damages for personal injury or death caused by negligence, nuisance, or breach of duty the limit is normally three years from the accrual of the cause of action or (if later) from the date when the claimant knew of the relevant circumstances; however, the court has a discretion to extend the limitation period. Most **limitation periods** are set out in the Limitation Act 1980 (as amended). Expiry of a limitation period normally provides a defendant with a complete procedural defence to a claim. However, time does not run against persons under a disability (children and persons of unsound mind) until the disability ceases.

limited administration (special administration) The administration of a deceased person's estate for restricted purposes specified by the court in the *letters of administration. Examples of such grants include grants *ad colligenda bona* and *durante absentia* and *grants for the use and benefit during the minority of a child appointed as executor by the will.

limited company A type of company incorporated by registration under the Companies Act 2006 whose members have a limited liability in respect of the company's debts. Most companies are in this category. In a company limited by *shares, members must pay the nominal value (*see* AUTHORIZED CAPITAL) of their shares either upon *allotment or subsequently (*see* CALL). In a company limited by guarantee (a **guarantee company**) members must pay an agreed nominal amount (the guarantee) to their company in the event of a winding-up. The guarantee fund is intended to be for the benefit of company creditors and members' liability to contribute to it cannot be reduced or extinguished by the company. Because payment of the guarantee is postponed guarantee companies often lack a working capital and are therefore more appropriate for charitable or social purposes than for trading.

The name of a limited company must end with the words "Limited" (or "Ltd.") in the case of a private company and "public limited company" (or "plc") in the case of a public company (or their Welsh equivalents; *see* WELSH COMPANY) as a warning to creditors of the limit upon members' liability. *See also* CHANGE OF NAME. *Compare* UNLIMITED COMPANY.

limited executor A person appointed by a will to deal only with specified property, not the whole of the deceased's estate, such as a *literary executor.

limited interest *See* ABSOLUTE INTEREST.

limited liability partnership A legally recognized entity defined under the Limited Liability Partnership Act 2000, which is capable of entering into contracts in its own right and is correspondingly liable for debts under those contracts. Any two or more persons associated for carrying on a lawful business with a view to profit may set up such a partnership under the Act. This type of business organization is intended to combine the flexibility of a traditional *partnership with the corporate notion of limited liability. Under the provisions of the Act there is power to apply sections from both the Partnership Act 1890 and the Companies Act 2006, as appropriate, when dealing with the internal relations of the partners and limited liability, respectively. Persons intending to set up a limited liability partnership must register it with the Registrar of

Companies (*see* REGISTRATION OF A COMPANY). There are also several disclosure requirements that are similar in nature to those required by companies.

limited owner A *tenant for life or a *statutory owner of land comprised in a settlement.

limited owner's charge An equitable charge on land securing repayment to a *limited owner of inheritance tax paid by him to HM Revenue and Customs on the acquisition of his interest. The tax is normally payable out of the trust property but if the limited owner pays it personally (e.g. to avoid having to sell land when the trust money is insufficient to cover the tax) the charge arises to secure his reimbursement. The charge is registrable (*see* REGISTRATION OF ENCUMBRANCES).

limited partnership *See* PARTNERSHIP.

Lincoln's Inn An *Inn of Court situated between Carey Street and Holborn, London. The records of the Inn, the *Black Books*, survive in a continuous series from 1422 to the present. Historically, barristers practising in the *Chancery Division of the High Court belonged to Lincoln's Inn.

linked transaction (under the Consumer Credit Act 1974) A transaction (except one for the provision of security) that is linked to, but not part of, a *regulated agreement (the **principal agreement**) and is entered into by a debtor or hirer with any other person. A linked transaction may comply with a term of the principal agreement (e.g. if the principal agreement requires that the goods be insured with X) or it may be financed by the principal agreement if the latter is a *debtor-creditor-supplier agreement. Alternatively it may be suggested by a creditor or owner to the debtor or hirer. The latter then enters into the linked transaction either to induce the creditor or owner to enter into the principal agreement, or for some other purpose related to the principal agreement, or – when the principal agreement is a *restricted-use credit agreement – for a purpose related to a transaction financed by the principal agreement.

liquidated damages *See* DAMAGES.

liquidated demand A demand for a fixed sum, e.g. a debt of £50. Such a demand is distinguished from a claim for unliquidated *damages, which is the subject of a discretionary assessment by the court.

liquidation *n. See* WINDING-UP.

liquidation committee A committee set up by creditors of a company being wound up in order to consent to the *liquidator exercising certain of his powers. When the company is unable to pay its debts, the committee is usually composed of creditors only; otherwise it consists of both creditors and *contributories. *See also* COMPULSORY WINDING-UP; VOLUNTARY WINDING-UP.

liquidator *n.* A person who conducts the *winding-up of a company. Unless he is the *official receiver, he must be a qualified *insolvency practitioner. *See* LIQUIDATION COMMITTEE; PROVISIONAL LIQUIDATOR.

lis alibi pendens [Latin] A suit pending elsewhere. The fact that there is already litigation pending between the same parties in respect of the same subject matter in another jurisdiction may give the defendant a ground on which he can obtain a *stay of proceedings.

Lisbon Treaty (Reform Treaty) An EU treaty signed by the heads of government of the member states in Lisbon on 13 December 2007. When the *Constitutional Treaty of the European Union failed to be ratified, there was a period of "reflection" that issued in the proposal of the Reform Treaty signed in Lisbon. In terms of its content, the Treaty has many similarities to its predecessor but is seen as following in the EU tradition of amending previous treaties rather than being a stand-alone treaty such as the Constitutional Treaty. The Lisbon Treaty amends the *Maastricht Treaty (now named the Treaty on European Union) and updates the Treaty of Rome (now named the *Treaty on the Functioning of the European Union). More substantive changes include the introduction of majority voting on some EU issues. The new Treaty was intended to come into force before the 2009 elections for the European Parliament but was rejected in a referendum in Ireland in June 2008; following its acceptance in a second referendum the Treaty came into force on 1 December 2009.

lis mota [Latin] A court action that has been set in motion.

lis pendens [Latin] A *pending land action.

listed building A building of special architectural or historic interest specified on a list compiled or approved by the Secretary of State. Listed buildings are graded according to their importance. It may be demolished or altered in character only with listed-building consent granted by the local planning authority (*see* TOWN AND COUNTRY PLANNING) or the Secretary of State. *See also* BUILDING PRESERVATION NOTICE; CONSERVATION AREA.

listed company A company that has satisfied the **listing requirements** of the *Stock Exchange and whose shares may therefore be quoted on its Official List and traded on the main market. Listed companies are subject to continuing obligations of disclosure to the UK Listing Authority.

lists *pl. n.* Calendars of cases awaiting trial. A court may maintain several lists comprising different types of case. Thus in the High Court there is the Queen's Bench nonjury list, the jury list, the *short cause list, etc. A case enters the list after it has been allocated for trial.

literal rule *See* INTERPRETATION.

literary executor An *executor appointed solely to deal with the testator's authorship of published and unpublished works and the copyrights and other rights attaching to them. A literary executor is therefore an example of a *limited executor.

litigant *n.* A person who is a party to a court action (this may include a company or corporation). A litigant may present his case personally to the court (a **litigant in person**). If he does so, he may be assisted by a person who can take notes and advise but cannot assist in the actual presentation of the case (a *McKenzie friend). Alternatively, a litigant may be represented by a *barrister or, where appropriate, a *solicitor. A successful litigant can usually claim his legal *costs from his opponent. If the litigant did not have legal representation he may claim costs for the work he has done himself that would otherwise have been carried out by a lawyer (Civil Procedure Rules Part 48).

litigation *n.* **1.** The taking of legal action by a *litigant. **2.** The field of law that is concerned with all contentious matters.

litigation friend (in civil proceedings) A person responsible under Part 21 of the *Civil Procedure Rules for the conduct and cost of legal proceedings instituted on behalf of, or against, a child or a mentally disordered person. Before the introduction of the Civil Procedure Rules in 1999 such a person was called a **next friend** or a **guardian** *ad litem*. *See also* CHILDREN'S GUARDIAN; OFFICIAL SOLICITOR.

live link In court proceedings, audio and/or video equipment set up in order to enable evidence to be given from outside the court room in which a case is being heard (*see* VIDEO EVIDENCE). A live link may be used so that vulnerable witnesses can give evidence or where witnesses are out of the jursisdiction. Live links are also commonly used for procedural hearings in the magistrates' court and Crown Court when the accused is on *remand, so as to avoid having to arrange for the accused to be transported to court.

lives in being *See* RULE AGAINST PERPETUITIES.

livestock *See* ANIMALS.

living apart The condition required to establish *desertion or separation as evidence that a marriage has irretrievably broken down (*see* DIVORCE). A couple may be living apart for divorce purposes even when living under the same roof, if they are living in separate households. In order to satisfy this test, all form of common life between the parties must have ceased.

living instrument *See* INSTRUMENT.

living memory The period over which the recollection of living people extends. *Compare* LEGAL MEMORY.

living on immoral earnings Formerly, the offence of using money obtained from *prostitution for one's livelihood or upkeep. Under the Sexual Offences Act 2003 (s 52–53) it has been replaced by a number of other offences that involve causing, inciting, or controlling prostitution for gain; the new offences focus on the exploitation of prostitutes, rather than the concept of "immorality".

living together *See* COHABITANTS.

living will *See* ADVANCE DECISION.

Lloyd's A society of *underwriters that was incorporated by Act of Parliament in 1871. Originally Lloyd's only provided marine insurance but they now also provide other kinds. The *insurance is undertaken by syndicates of private underwriters (**names**), each of which is managed by a professional underwriter; since 1992 limited companies have been allowed to become names. Each name underwrites a percentage of the business written by the syndicate and has to deposit a substantial sum with the corporation before being admitted as an underwriter. The public deals with the underwriters only through Lloyd's brokers.

 SEE WEB LINKS
• Lloyd's website

loan capital Money raised by a company issuing *debentures.

loan creditor A creditor of a company, such as a person who holds redeemable *loan capital issued by the company. For the purposes of tax law, loan creditors (other than banks) are participators in *close companies.

loan relationship The Finance Act 1996 abolished the specific tax charge on interest received by a company and the relief for interest paid. Instead, a company is now subject to *corporation tax on the aggregate of its loan relationships. A company is stated to have a loan relationship wherever that company stands in the position of creditor or debtor in respect of any money debt arising from a transaction for the lending of money (Corporation Taxes Act 2009 s 302). Thus, discounts, exchange gains and losses, and increases or decreases in the value of government stock are all aggregated with interest received and paid in computing the sum on which corporation tax is charged.

local Act *See* ACT OF PARLIAMENT.

local authorities and children Local authorities have statutory responsibilities for children in their area. The Children Act 1989 requires local authorities to provide services for *children in need so that wherever possible they may be brought up by their own families, thus avoiding the need for instituting care proceedings. The Act specifies certain services that local authorities must provide. These include: appropriate day care provision for under fives and after school and holiday activities for children of school age; advice, guidance, and counselling; home help; transport or assistance with travel expenses in order to use any of the services provided and assistance with holidays; and family centres for all children in their area. Local authorities are also under a duty to provide accommodation for children whose parents are unable to do so (*see* VOLUNTARY ACCOMMODATION). An important objective of the Children Act is to promote the provision of these services as positive help for children in need. Emphasis is placed on the need for local authorities and families to work in partnership and often on the basis of written agreements. Local authorities also have a duty to investigate when they suspect that children in their area are being ill treated or neglected. If their suspicions are confirmed they must apply for a *care order, an *emergency protection order, or a *supervision order, as appropriate (*see also* SECTION 47 ENQUIRY). In relation to adoption, local authorities are obliged to maintain an *adoption service and to report to the court in respect of non-agency adoption applications. *See also* LOOKED-AFTER CHILD.

local authority A body of **councillors** elected by the inhabitants of a *local government area (*see* FRANCHISE) to exercise local government functions. In England (except *Greater London) areas are governed either by *county councils and *district councils (in a two-tier system) or by *unitary authorities; this mixed system was introduced between 1996 and 1998 with further changes in 2009. There are in addition *parish councils for parishes with 200 or more electors. In Wales the local authorities are the county council, the county borough council, and the *community council. The Welsh county and county borough councils are unitary authorities.

All councillors are elected for four years. A candidate for election to any local authority must be over 21 and a British citizen, a citizen of another Commonwealth country, or a citizen of another member state of the EU, must have sufficient local connection (e.g. residence, local employment, or voting rights), and must not be disqualified (e.g. by reason of holding paid office or employment under the authority).

local authority foster parents Persons with whom the local authority places children in its care, whether on a short-term or a long-term basis, as an alternative to institutional care. *Foster parenthood does not of itself confer *parental responsibility and the child can be removed at any time by the local authority or by the parents (in the case of a *child being looked after by a local authority). Foster parents may, however, acquire parental responsibility if the child has lived with them for one year by applying for a *residence order; if granted this will give security to the foster parents while also preserving the links with the natural family. As an alternative, an application may be made for adoption, during which time the child cannot be removed without permission from the court.

local government A form of government in which responsibility for the regulation of certain matters within particular localities (*local government areas) is delegated by statute to locally elected councillors (*see* LOCAL AUTHORITY).

local government area An area constituting a unit for local government purposes. The local government areas in England (except *Greater London) are the *county, the *unitary authority, the *district, and the *parish. In certain parts of England unitary authorities were introduced to replace nonmetropolitan county and district councils between 1996 and 1998 and again in 2009. In Wales the areas are the county, the county borough, and the *community; counties and county boroughs, which are administered by unitary authorities, replaced the two-tier system of counties and districts in April 1996.

Local Government Ombudsmen *See* COMMISSION FOR LOCAL ADMINISTRATION IN ENGLAND.

local land charge *See* LAND CHARGE; REGISTRATION OF ENCUMBRANCES.

local land charges register *See* REGISTRATION OF ENCUMBRANCES.

local laws Laws applying in only one locality, such as the area of a local authority (*see* BYELAW). In 1996 the Law Commission published a four-volume Chronological Table of Local Legislation to help those wanting to find out whether a local Act has been passed that affects them or their property. The table lists all 26,500 or so local Acts passed since 1797 and states whether or not they are in force and how they have been amended.

local lottery *See* LOTTERY.

Local Safeguarding Children Boards (LSCBs) Boards established by the Children Act 2004 that replace the former Area Child Protection Committees. LSCBs are responsible for local arrangements for protecting children and young people. They provide inter-agency guidelines for child protection and a focal point for organizations that work with children to come together to decide how they will safeguard and promote the welfare of children.

lock-out agreement A contract between a potential purchaser and the vendor of a property in which the vendor agrees that for a fixed period, such as two weeks, he will take the house off the market and not accept any other offers. Meanwhile the purchaser moves towards a quick *exchange of contracts, with the aim of securing the sale within that period. If the vendor breaches the agreement by accepting another offer, he can be sued for *breach of contract. Many vendors will not accept such agreements and some lawyers have argued they are unenforceable.

locus in quo [Latin: the place in which] The place where an event took place. Fact finders may visit the *locus in quo* in order to understand the evidence and the judge and jury may inspect it as part of court proceedings (*see* VIEW).

locus sigilli [Latin: place of the seal] *See* DEED.

locus standi [Latin: a place to stand] The right to bring an action or challenge some decision. Questions of *locus standi* most often arise in proceedings for *judicial review. Section 31(3) Supreme Court Act 1981 provides that the court will not grant leave for judicial review unless the claimant has "sufficient interest" in the matter to which the application relates. However, "sufficient interest" is not defined and this has led to the courts being called upon to determine the issue, as in the notable case *R v IRC ex p The National Federation of Self Employed and Small Businesses Ltd* [1982] AC 617 (HL). Decisions since the IRC case have confirmed that a liberal approach to standing should be taken. The Human Rights Act 1998 s 7 requires that a claimant must be a "victim" of an unlawful act of a public body, a narrower test of standing.

lodger *n.* A person who is given occupation of part of a house in return for rent, where the premises remain under the control of the owner. A lodger normally has a mere *licence rather than a tenancy.

loitering *n. See* SUS LAW.

London *See* CITY OF LONDON; GREATER LONDON.

London Assembly A component of the *Greater London Authority, created by the Greater London Authority Act 1999, consisting of 25 members, of whom 14 are *Constituency Members and 11 are *London Members. The principal functions of the Assembly are to review and investigate actions and decisions of the *Mayor of London and to submit proposals to the Mayor. It may amend the Mayor's budget and it provides members to serve on the Metropolitan Police Authority, the London Fire and Emergency Planning Authority, and the London Development Agency.

London borough *See* GREATER LONDON.

London Development Agency A body created by the Greater London Authority Act 1999 to further the economic development of London, by promoting business efficiency and investment.

London Members Members of the *London Assembly who jointly represent the "Londonwide" constituency. The 11 London Members are elected every four years by voters in London, at the same time as *Constituency Members and the *Mayor of London are elected.

long tenancy For statutory purposes, a *fixed-term tenancy for a period exceeding 21 years. Where the rent is less than two-thirds of the property's rateable value, the tenancy is excluded from being an *assured tenancy. However, it will qualify for special protection if it would have been a *protected tenancy had the rent not been a low one. This allows the tenant to continue the tenancy beyond the fixed term. In such cases, if the landlord wishes to terminate the tenancy at the end of the fixed term, he must serve a statutory notice at least 6 months, but not more than 12 months, before the end of the tenancy. In this notice he can either propose a *statutory tenancy (the terms of which must be agreed with the tenant or settled by a court) or he can claim the right to resume possession of the premises. In the latter case he must have statutory grounds for possession, which correspond to those required for possession of a protected tenancy. If the tenant contests this notice, the landlord must apply for a court order for possession. If this is refused, the tenant will be entitled to a statutory tenancy. Long tenancies made after the coming into force of the Housing Act 1988 are not protected in this way because no new protected tenancies can be made after that date. *See also* ENFRANCHISEMENT OF TENANCY.

long title *See* ACT OF PARLIAMENT.

Long Vacation *See* VACATIONS.

looked-after child A child who is either the subject of a *care order or who is being provided with accommodation by the local authority on a voluntary basis (*see* *VOLUNTARY ACCOMMODATION). The local authority has a duty to safeguard and promote the welfare of such children. It must seek, where possible, to promote contact between the child and its parents, relatives, and others closely connected with the child. Accommodation should be near where the child lives, and siblings should be accommodated together. A written plan should be drawn up before a child is placed; all the people involved in the plan, including the child (so far as is consistent with his age and understanding), should be consulted. Crucially, local authorities also continue to have duties in respect of certain children who have ceased to be looked after by them. In respect of a child of 16 or 17, the local authority must arrange for the child to have a personal advisor and prepare what is called a "pathway plan", which must be kept under regular review. In relation to former looked-after children who are 18 and over, the local authority is under a duty to take reasonable steps to keep in touch with such an individual, to continue with the appointment of his personal adviser, and to keep the pathway plan under review. There is also a duty to give assistance in relation to the child's educational or training needs and in some cases to contribute to living expenses incurred in connection with the pathway plan.

Lord Advocate The chief law officer of the Crown in Scotland, corresponding to the *Attorney General in England. He has ultimate responsibility for criminal prosecutions in Scotland, being assisted by a Solicitor General, advocates depute, and *procurators fiscal. He is normally a supporter of the ruling party and resigns his office upon a change of government, but he is not always a Member of Parliament.

Lord Chancellor Historically, the head of the judiciary, a government minister (in charge of the Lord Chancellor's Department), and Speaker of the House of Lords. He thus combined judicial, executive, and legislative functions. He was entitled to preside over the House when it sat as a final court of appeal; he appointed magistrates and higher judicial officials; and he oversaw such matters as the administration of the courts, the Community Legal Service, law reform, data protection, and human rights. Under the Constitutional Reform Act 2005 the Lord Chancellor was stripped of his judicial functions, which were transferred to the *Lord Chief Justice, and his role as Speaker of the House of Lords. His other functions have been undertaken since 2007 by the *Ministry of Justice, with the Secretary of State taking the historic title of Lord Chancellor.

Lord Chief Justice The head of the judiciary in England and Wales; historically, he ranked second to the Lord Chancellor in the judicial hierarchy but this was altered by the Constitutional Reform Act 2005. It was formerly the practice to appoint the Attorney General when a vacancy in the office occurred but this practice has now been abandoned and recent appointments have been either *Lords Justices of Appeal or *Lords of Appeal in Ordinary. The Lord Chief Justice is *ex officio* a member of the Court of Appeal and is President of its Criminal Division. Under the Constitutional Reform Act 2005 the judicial functions of the Lord Chancellor were transferred to the Lord Chief Justice.

Lord Justice of Appeal An ordinary judge of the *Court of Appeal. The Lord (and Lady) Justices are normally appointed from those holding the post of a High Court judge or those possessing a ten-year High Court qualification under the Courts and Legal Services Act 1990. They become members of the Privy Council on appointment.

Lords, House of *See* HOUSE OF LORDS.

Lords of Appeal in Ordinary (Law Lords) Formerly, up to 12 persons, holders of high judicial office or practising barristers of at least 15 years' standing, who were appointed to life peerages under the Appellate Jurisdiction Act 1876 to carry out the judicial functions of the *House of Lords. Under the Constitutional Reform Act 2005 these functions were transferred to a new Supreme Court and the Law Lords were removed from the legislature.

loss leader A product or service offered for sale by an organization at a loss in order to attract customers. The Competition Act 1998 prohibits *predatory pricing by dominant companies, as does Article 102 of the Treaty on the Functioning of the European Union. Nondominant companies, however, are largely free to set their own resale pricing policy as long as they do not specify the resale prices their customers will sell the products at. *See also* RESALE PRICE MAINTENANCE.

loss of a chance *See* CAUSATION.

loss of amenity Loss or reduction of a claimant's mental or physical capacity to do the things he used to do, suffered as a result of personal injuries, including psychiatric injury. In actions for personal injuries the claimant may recover damages for loss of the amenities of life, in addition to his financial losses and an award for *pain and suffering. Thus loss of the ability to play games or a musical instrument, if these were the claimant's hobbies, will be taken into account in fixing damages. The assessment is based on an objective view of the value of the loss of these amenities to the claimant, and thus may be awarded to a claimant who is expected never to regain consciousness.

loss of control Loss of self-control is not recognized as a *general defence to a criminal charge in English law, though what otherwise would have been murder may be reduced to manslaughter if loss of control is shown (Coroners and Justice Act 2009 (s 54, 55)).

In order to establish a defence of loss of control several different elements need to be addressed. Firstly, it must be established that the killing resulted from a loss of self-control on behalf of the defendant; in a change from the previous law, which was based on the concept of **provocation**, it does not need to be shown that the loss of control was sudden (*R v Ahluwalia* [1992] 4 All ER 889). Secondly, there is the issue of the defendant's characteristics: in a subtle change to the law, the question asked now is whether a person of the defendant's sex and age with a normal degree of tolerance and self-restraint might have acted the same or similarly in the circumstances (the reference is to *all* of the defendant's circumstances provided they do *not* bear on his capacity for tolerance or self-restraint). Thirdly, the loss of self-control needs to have been through a "qualifying trigger". A loss of self-control has a qualifying trigger if it was either i) attributable to the defendant's fear of serious violence from the victim; or ii) attributable to a thing or things done or said (or both) which a) constituted circumstances of an extremely grave character and b) caused the defendant to have a justifiable sense of being seriously wronged.

lost modern grant *See* PRESCRIPTION.

lottery *n.* A game of chance in which the participants buy numbered tickets and the prizes are distributed by drawing lots. Under the Lotteries and Amusements Act 1976, lotteries are usually illegal (*see also* GAMING) unless they are:

(1) on behalf of registered charities or sports;
(2) restricted to members of a private club;

(3) **local lotteries**, promoted in accordance with schemes approved by local authorities and registered with the Gaming Board;

(4) small lotteries that take place as part of an entertainment (e.g. in a bazaar or at a dance).

The **National Lottery** was established by statute (the National Lottery Act 1993).

LSCBs *See* LOCAL SAFEGUARDING CHILDREN BOARDS.

lump-sum award The form in which damages are normally given by a court. The award covers both past losses (up to the time of judgment) and losses likely to be suffered in the future. Historically, the general rule has been that only one award of damages may be made, unless the wrong is a continuing one (such as continuing trespass or nuisance). However, the court now has the power to make orders for damages taking the form of periodical payments when awarding damages for personal injury. In actions for personal injuries in which the claimant may develop some serious disease or suffer some serious deterioration in his condition, *provisional damages may also be given; this enables the claimant to come back for further damages at a future date if the disease or deterioration occurs. Rules relating to the award of provisional damages and periodicial payments under the Damages Act 1996 are set out in Part 41 of the *Civil Procedure Rules. In addition, *interim payments under Part 25 of the Civil Procedure Rules can be ordered pending the final estimation of damages. *See also* STRUCTURED SETTLEMENT.

Maastricht Treaty The Treaty on European Union, which was signed at Maastricht (in the Netherlands) in February 1992 and came into force on 1 November 1993. The Treaty amended the founding treaties of the three *European Communities by establishing a *European Union based on these Communities. It required the defining and eventual implementation of a common foreign and security policy (CFSP), cooperation in justice and home affairs, and – under certain conditions – the introduction of a single currency (*see* EUROPEAN MONETARY UNION). It also introduced the principle of *subsidiarity and increased the powers of the *European Parliament. It has since been amended by the *Amsterdam Treaty and by the *Lisbon Treaty, which renamed it the **Treaty on European Union**.

machinery and plant Generally, the machines, parts of machines, and all other apparatus used for carrying on a business, but excluding stock in trade. An *Annual Investment Allowance on the first £25,000 of expenditure in a financial year and *capital allowances (generally 20%) for the excess over £25,000 are available for the purchase costs of machinery or plant used in a trade, profession, or vocation.

Neither machinery nor plant is defined in the Capital Allowances Act. However, in *Yarmouth v France* [1887] 19 QB 647 Lord Justice Lindley ruled "in its ordinary sense [plant] includes whatever apparatus is used by a business man for carrying on his business – not his stock-in-trade, which he buys or makes for sale; but all goods and chattels, fixed or movable, live or dead, which he keeps for permanent employment in his business". In that case the court ruled that a working horse is plant. Machinery and plant has also been held to include a barrister's law books (*Munby v Furlong* [1977] 2 All ER 953 (CA)), railway locomotives and carriages (*Caledonian Rly Co v Banks* [1880] 1 TC 487), knives and lasts used in the manufacture of shoes (*Hinton v Maden and Ireland Ltd* [1959] 1 WLR 875 (HL)), a swimming pool (*Cooke v Beach Station Caravans Ltd* [1974] 1 WLR 322 (HL)), decorative screens (*Leeds Permanent Building Society v Procter* [1982] 3 All ER 925), and a metal seagull sculpture and other items designed to create "ambience" (*IRC v Scottish and Newcastle Breweries Ltd* [1982] 1 WLR 1450).

McKenzie friend Someone who assists an unrepresented party in court, chiefly by taking notes, organizing papers and giving advice. He has no rights of audience, but may speak if invited to by the judge. A "McKenzie" can help to calm a litigant and is often his only witness to proceedings. The term comes from the case of *McKenzie v McKenzie* [1970] 3 All ER 1034, 1039 h-j, in which Lord Justice Sachs stated that "It is . . . in the public interest that litigants should be seen to have all available aid in conducting cases in court surroundings, which must of their nature to them seem both difficult and strange."

magistrate *n.* A *justice of the peace sitting in a *magistrates' court. Most magistrates are lay persons and have no formal legal qualifications: they receive no payment for their services but give their time voluntarily. There are also, however, *district judges (magistrates' court) (formerly called stipendiary magistrates) in London and other major cities.

magistrates' clerk *See* CLERK TO THE JUSTICES.

magistrates' court A court consisting of between two and seven *magistrates or a single *district judge (magistrates' court) exercising the jurisdiction conferred by the Magistrates' Courts Act 1980 and other statutes. The principal function of magistrates' courts is to provide the forum in which all criminal prosecutions are initiated. In the case of an *indictable offence or an *offence triable either way for which the defendant elects *trial on indictment, the court sits as *examining justices to consider whether or not there is sufficient evidence to justify committing the defendant to the *Crown Court. For a *summary offence or an offence triable either way in which the defendant elects *summary trial, the court sits as a **court of summary jurisdiction**, i.e. as a criminal court of trial without a jury in which justices, assisted by the *clerk to the justices, decide all questions of law and fact.

Magistrates' courts also have a limited jurisdiction in civil matters relating to debt and matrimonial proceedings. Each magistrates' court sits for a **petty-sessions area** and its jurisdiction is generally confined to that area, although it may in some cases extend beyond. A magistrates' court may sit on any day of the year, including (if the court thinks fit) Christmas Day, Good Friday, or any Sunday, but in practice it is unusual for magistrates' courts to sit on public holidays or at weekends.

Magna Carta The Great Charter of Runnymede, acceded to by King John in 1215 after armed rebellion by his barons. It guaranteed the freedom of the church, restricted taxes and fines, and promised justice to all. Confirmed frequently by subsequent feudal kings, it has since been largely repealed as having only symbolic significance.

main purpose rule *See* REPUGNANCY.

main residence For the purposes of *capital gains tax there is an exemption for gains on the disposal of owner-occupied homes. If an individual has more than one residence, he may nominate as his "main residence" the one that he wishes to qualify for exemption.

maintenance *n.* The provision of food, clothing, and other basic necessities of life. A husband or wife is obliged to maintain his or her spouse (*see* FAILURE TO MAINTAIN). Parents are bound at common law to maintain their minor children, and since the Family Law Reform Act 1987 and the Child Support Act 1991 both parents, whether married or not, have a legal responsibility to support their children financially if they can afford to do so (*see* CHILD SUPPORT MAINTENANCE). Neglect or refusal to provide this maintenance is a criminal offence.

Before 1881 it was common for settlements to include a power for the trustees to maintain and educate minors. Since then, a statutory power has existed enabling trustees to pay money for the maintenance, education, or benefit of a minor; this power is subject to any contrary provision in the settlement.

The obligation after a divorce of one spouse to support another or of a parent to support a child of the family is often referred to as maintenance; this is more correctly known as financial provision or *financial relief.

maintenance agreement An agreement between spouses concerning their financial obligations to one another. Maintenance agreements are governed by the provisions of the Matrimonial Causes Act 1973. Any clause that attempts to deny the right of either spouse to apply to a court for financial relief will be void, and the county courts and High Court (and, to a more limited extent, the magistrates' courts) have wide powers to vary the terms of maintenance agreements (*see also* MARRIAGE SETTLEMENT). When one party has died the other spouse may apply to the court, under the special provisions for *dependants, to have the terms of the agreement altered, but only if it was in writing.

maintenance and champerty The promotion or support of litigation by a third party who has no legitimate interest in the proceedings (**maintenance**); or and the support of litigation by a third party in return for a share of the proceeds (**champerty**, an aggravated form of maintenance). The old crimes and torts of maintenance and champerty were abolished by statute in 1967 but a champertous agreement may still be treated as contrary to public policy and so unlawful. An agreement by a lawyer to receive payment in the form of a share of the client's damages (if successful) has traditionally been regarded as champertous in England. A modified form of "no win, no fee" agreement was legalized by the Courts and Legal Services Act 1990, although it is authorized only for certain categories of cases (*see* CONDITIONAL FEE AGREEMENT).

maintenance order A court order providing for payment of sums for the maintenance of a spouse or a child of the family. Strictly speaking the term now applies only to *maintenance agreements incorporated into a court order; orders in the magistrates' courts or High Court on the ground of *failure to maintain and orders in the divorce courts for maintenance are now called *financial provision orders. Power to order payment by direct debit or standing order was introduced by the Maintenance Enforcement Act 1991.

Spouses may try to evade their financial obligations to each other or their children by emigrating. In such cases the Domestic Proceedings and Magistrates' Courts Act 1978 and the Maintenance Orders (Reciprocal Enforcement) Act 1972 grant powers to obtain maintenance from emigrant spouses in certain designated ("convention") countries. For these purposes maintenance orders include any order providing for periodical payments to a person whom the payer is liable to maintain, including children of unmarried parents. The Child Support Act 1991 has greatly curtailed the power of the court to make, vary, or revise maintenance orders; application solely for *child support maintenance must now usually be made to the Child Support Agency rather than the court.

maintenance pending suit A court order for temporary periodical payments during the hearing of a petition for divorce, nullity, or judicial separation.

majority (full age) *n.* The age of 18 years. The state of being below that age is a state of **minority** (*see* INFANT). The age of majority was originally 21 years, but was reduced to 18 by the Family Law Reform Act 1969. This majority applies for the purposes of any relevant legal rule and for the interpretation of any relevant statute, whenever it was made. It does not apply, however, to deeds, wills, and other private documents made before 1969, in which reference is made to majority or minority.

majority rule The principle by which the majority of company members has the power to control the company through voting at a company meeting (*Foss v Harbottle* (1843) 2 Harc 461). There are various ways to safeguard the minority (*see* MINORITY PROTECTION). The rule does not apply where the proposed action requires more than a simple majority vote to be authorized; for example, subject to any entrenched provision in the articles, amending the *articles of association requires approval by 75% of shareholders who attend a *general meeting and who are entitled to vote (*see* ORDINARY RESOLUTION; SPECIAL RESOLUTION). *See also* DERIVATIVE CLAIM; FRAUD ON THE MINORITY.

majority verdict A verdict of a *jury that is reached by a majority. Majority verdicts can be taken in both criminal and civil cases. In criminal cases the verdict need not be unanimous if there are no fewer than 11 jurors and 10 of them agree on the verdict or if there are 10 jurors and 9 of them agree on the verdict. The jury in a criminal case must be given at least two hours in which to try to reach a unanimous verdict; if after this time they reach a majority verdict, and this verdict is guilty, the foreman of the jury must state in open court the number of jurors who respectively agreed to and dissented from the verdict. The procedure for taking majority verdicts is now set out in the *Consolidated Criminal Practice Direction.

making off without payment Leaving without paying for goods or services received and with the intention of avoiding payment, when payment on the spot is expected. This is now an offence punishable by up to two years' imprisonment on indictment or six months' and/or a fine not exceeding the statutory maximum on summary conviction. To obtain a conviction it must be proved that the person who made off knew that payment on the spot was expected (Theft Act 1978 s 3). The offence will usually cover such behaviour as walking out of a restaurant after having had a meal, without paying (even if there was originally no intention not to pay for the meal, and therefore no theft, and no *deception when the meal was ordered; *R v McDavitt* [1981] Crim LR 843); taking a taxi and disappearing without paying; and collecting any items from a shop that has repaired or cleaned them, without paying. *See also* SHOPLIFTING.

mala fide [Latin: bad faith] Describing an act performed fraudulently or dishonestly.

male issue Direct descendants through the male line, e.g. sons and sons of sons (but not sons of daughters).

malfeasance *n.* An unlawful act. *Compare* MISFEASANCE; NONFEASANCE.

malice *n.* **1.** (in criminal law) A state of mind (*see* MENS REA) usually taken to be equivalent to *intention or *recklessness: it does not require any hostile attitude. Malice is said to be **transferred** when someone intends to commit a crime against one person but in fact commits the same crime against someone else (for example, if he intends to shoot X but misses, and instead kills Y: *R v Latimer* [1886] 17 QB 359). Malice is **universal** (or **general**) when the accused has no particular victim in mind (for example, if he shoots into a crowd intending to kill anyone). In both cases this constitutes *mens rea*. **2.** (in tort) A constituent element of certain torts. In the English law of tort, the general rule is that a malicious motive cannot make conduct unlawful if it would otherwise be lawful (*Bradford Corpn v Pickles* [1895] AC 587 (HL)). For example, a right to take water from under one's own land can lawfully be exercised solely in order to cause damage to a neighbour. However, in some cases malice can be relevant. An action for *malicious prosecution requires proof that the prosecution was instigated maliciously, i.e. without reasonable and probable cause. In *defamation, a malicious motive invalidates the defence of *qualified privilege. Malice is also relevant to liability for *conspiracy to injure someone. In *nuisance malice renders an otherwise lawful act unlawful.

malice aforethought The *mens rea* (state of mind) required for a person to be guilty of murder. It is unnecessary for there to be any element of hostility (*see* MALICE) or for the intention to kill to be "forethought" (i.e. premeditated). The term covers:

(1) intention to kill (**direct express malice aforethought**);
(2) intention to cause *grievous bodily harm (**direct implied malice aforethought**);
(3) realizing while doing a particular act that death would be a virtually certain result (**indirect express malice**: *R v Woollin* [1999] AC 82);

(4) realizing that grievous bodily harm would be a virtually certain result from the act, e.g. shooting at someone without wanting to kill him, but realizing that he is virtually certain to suffer a serious injury (**indirect implied malice**).

The prosecution must prove one of these four types of malice aforethought to secure a conviction of murder.

malicious falsehood (injurious falsehood) A false statement, made maliciously, that causes damage to another. The oldest forms of this tort are *slander of title and *slander of goods, but other false and malicious statements (e.g. that a businessman has ceased to trade) can also give rise to an action in tort. Usually actual damage must be proved. Malicious falsehood can overlap with *defamation, but mainly protects property and business interests. More recently this tort has been extended to protect individual economic interests. Cases: *Joyce v Sengupta* [1993] WLR 337 (CA); *Kaye v Robertson* [1991] FSR 62 (CA).

malicious prosecution The malicious institution of legal proceedings against a person. Malicious prosecution is only actionable in tort if the proceedings were initiated both maliciously and without reasonable and probable cause and they were unsuccessful. No one who has been convicted of a criminal charge can sue for malicious prosecution. Making unjustified threats of infringement of trade mark or other *intellectual property rights is also a statutory offence; the person accused of this can apply to the court for a *declaration that they do not infringe these rights.

malicious wounding *See* WOUNDING.

managed service company A company whose business consists wholly or mainly of providing the services of an individual, who receives payments from the company in the form of dividends and payments for expenses rather than salary. From 2007 PAYE is payable on (broadly) all payments made by a managed service company to an individual whose services are provided by that company (Finance Act 2007 sch 3).

management order A court order to appoint a manager for which certain tenants of flats have the right to apply if the court is satisfied that mismanagement has taken place. A Local Housing Authority may also make interim or final management orders in respect of *houses in multiple occupation. *See also* RIGHT TO MANAGE.

managing director A *director to whom management powers have been delegated, either absolutely or subject to supervision, by the other directors of the company under the terms of the articles of association. Managing directors are agents of the company and have wide authority to act on its behalf.

managing trustee *See* CUSTODIAN TRUSTEE.

mandate *n.* **1.** (in private law) An authority given by one person (the **mandator**) to another to take some course of action. A mandate is commonly revocable until acted upon and is terminated by the death of the mandator. A cheque is a mandate from the customer to his bank to pay the sum in question and to debit his account. **2.** (in international law) The system by which dependent territories (such as the former German colonies in Africa) were placed under the supervision (but not the sovereignty) of mandatory powers by the League of Nations after World War I. After World War II, all remaining mandated territories became *trust territories under the United Nations with the exception of South-West Africa (now Namibia) and a strategic trust area consisting of a number of Pacific Islands north of the equator, which were administered by the USA. The mandate over Namibia was terminated by the General Assembly of the UN in 1966, which placed the territory under the direct responsibility of the United Nations; it became an independent state in 1990. The Pacific Islands territories are also now independent states.

mandatory injunction *See* INJUNCTION.

mandatory order A *prerogative order, available on application for *judicial review from the High Court, requiring an inferior court, tribunal, or other public body to perform a specified public duty relating to its responsibilities. Formerly called **mandamus** (from Latin: we command), it was renamed in 1999 under Part 54 of the Civil Procedure Rules.

Manor of Northstead *See* CHILTERN HUNDREDS, STEWARDSHIP OF THE.

manslaughter *n.* Unlawful *homicide that does not amount to the crime of murder. There are two main categories: **voluntary manslaughter** and **involuntary manslaughter**. Voluntary manslaughter arises when a defendant is charged with murder but successfully pleads a partial defence of *provocation (Homicide Act 1957 s 3), *diminished responsibility (s 2), or *suicide pact (s 4). Involuntary manslaughter consists of unlawful killing of another person with a *mens rea* not amounting to *intention. Although the distinctions between forms of involuntary manslaughter remain unclear in law, it is generally understood to consist of **subjective recklessness manslaughter** (*R v Pike* [1961] Crim LR 547), **constructive manslaughter** (also called **unlawful act manslaughter**: *R v Arobieke* [1988] Crim LR 314), **gross negligence manslaughter** (*R v Adomako* [1995] 1 AC 171), and **corporate manslaughter** (Corporate Manslaughter and Corporate Homicide Act 2007). The maximum penalty for manslaughter is life imprisonment. *See also* GROSS NEGLIGENCE.

Mareva injunction *See* FREEZING INJUNCTION.

margin of appreciation A concept created by the European Court of Human Rights to allow a certain amount of flexibility for each signatory state to regulate its own activities and its application of the *European Convention on Human Rights without being subject to negative review by the Court. This flexibility is not available to national courts when considering Convention issues arising within their own countries. However, in some cases the domestic courts, when reviewing decisions of public authorities under the Convention, may defer on democratic grounds to those elected bodies (*see* JUDICIAL DEFERENCE).

marine insurance A form of *insurance in which the insurer undertakes to indemnify the insured against loss of the ship (**hull insurance**), the cargo, any sums paid in freight (**freight insurance**), or any liability to a third party occurring during a sea voyage. A marine insurance contract may be extended to losses on inland waters or to risks on land that may be incidental to a sea voyage. The risks listed in marine insurance policies include *perils of the seas, fire, war perils, pirates, seizures, restraints, jettisons, and *barratry, and the cover may be for a particular voyage, or for a specified time, or both (*see* TIME POLICY). In marine insurance a distinction is made between an *actual total loss and a *constructive total loss; partial loss is subject to *average. The law relating to marine insurance is codified by the Marine Insurance Act 1906 as amended by the Consumer Insurance (Disclosure and Representations) Act 2012. Under this Act marine insurance contracts that are by way of being wagering or *gaming contracts are void; these include contracts in which the insured has no insurable interest as defined in the Act.

mariner's will *See* PRIVILEGED WILL.

marital breakdown The deterioration of a marriage to such an extent that the court will grant a *divorce. The breakdown must be **irretrievable**. Under the Matrimonial Causes Act 1973 this can be evidenced only by *adultery, *desertion, *living apart, or *unreasonable behaviour.

marital privileges Privileges protecting information given by one spouse to the other from disclosure in court. In general, the privilege has now been abolished in both civil and criminal proceedings.

maritime lien *See* LIEN.

market *n.* A facility for the sale and purchase of goods. The concept of an **available market** is important in deciding the amount of damages for breach of contracts of sale of goods: it assumes that goods of the contract description can be sold at a market price fixed by supply and demand. The disappointed buyer or seller will usually, upon breach, make a substitute purchase or sale on the market and his damages will be the difference between the contract price and the market price. *See also* MARKET OVERT.

market maker *See* STOCK EXCHANGE.

market overt An open, public, and legally constituted market or fair. When goods were sold in market overt according to the usage of the market, the buyer acquired a good title to the goods, provided he bought them in good faith and without notice of any defect in the seller's title. This was one of the exceptions to the general principle of *nemo dat quod non habet*, but it was abolished from 3 January 1995 by the Sale of Goods (Amendment) Act 1994.

market testing Testing a particular service to see which supplier – in-house or external – offers the best combination of value for money and quality of service for the user. Launched in 1991, it affects all public services, including the health-care, magistrates', and prison services. Under the Local Government Act 1999, certain authorities are designated as *best value authorities, including the police and fire authorities. Under the Act, these authorities must have regard to economy, efficiency, and effectiveness when exercising their functions.

market value *Inheritance tax is charged on the market value of property at death and *capital gains tax is charged on the market value of an asset at the time of disposal. In both cases, statute gives only a cryptic definition of the term "market value" and its meaning has been established by a line of cases. In 1994 Lord Justice Hoffmann gave a good summary of the process of determining market value in *IRC v Gray* [1994] STC 360 (CA) 371–72: "The property must be assumed to have been capable of sale in the open market – the hypothesis must be applied to the property as it actually existed even if in real life a vendor would have been likely to have made some changes or improvements before putting it on the market. The hypothetical vendor is an anonymous but reasonable vendor who goes about the sale as a prudent man of business. The hypothetical buyer is slightly less anonymous. He is assumed to have behaved reasonably. The concept of the open market involves assuming that the whole world is free to bid and then form a view about what in those circumstances would in real life have been the best price reasonably attainable".

marriage *n.* **1.** The relationship between husband and wife. **2.** A ceremony, civil or religious, that creates the legal status of husband and wife and the legal obligations arising from that status (*see* MARRIAGE CEREMONY). All marriages must be registered by an authorized marriage registrar. The minimum age for marriage is 16 with parental consent (18 without), and capacity to marry in general is governed by the law of *domicile of both parties before the marriage. Relationships within which marriage is prohibited are specified in the Marriage Act 1949, as amended by the Marriage (Prohibited Degrees of Relationship) Act 1986 (*see* PROHIBITED DEGREES OF RELATIONSHIP). Parties to a marriage must be respectively male and female (*see* CIVIL PARTNERSHIP; GENDER REASSIGNMENT), must not be already married to someone else (*see* BIGAMY; POLYGAMY), and must enter into the marriage freely. *See also* MARRIAGE BY CERTIFICATE.

marriage articles The clauses setting out the terms of a *marriage settlement.

marriage brokage contract A contract in which one person undertakes, for financial gain, to arrange a marriage for another. Such contracts are void because they contravene *public policy.

marriage by certificate Marriage authorized by a certificate issued by the Superintendent Registrar of Births, Deaths, and Marriages. All marriages other than those solemnized in the Church of England must be authorized by a certificate (or certificate and licence – *see* MARRIAGE BY CERTIFICATE AND LICENCE); marriages solemnized in the Church of England may be authorized either by a certificate or by a religious procedure (e.g. *banns, common licence, or special licence – *see* MARRIAGE BY RELIGIOUS LICENCE). Notice must be given of the intended marriage to the Superintendent Registrar of the district(s) in which the parties have lived for seven days previously, together with a declaration that there are no lawful obstacles to the marriage and that all necessary consents have been obtained. This notice is made public for 21 days, to give members of the public the opportunity to point out the existence of a lawful obstacle, after which the Registrar must issue a certificate. The marriage must take place within three months from the day the notice was entered in the notice book.

marriage by certificate and licence Marriage authorized by a certificate and licence issued by the Superintendent Registrar. The main difference between this procedure and that of *marriage by certificate alone is its speed – the marriage may take place any time after 24 hours have elapsed from the day of giving notice. This procedure may also be used when only one party has been resident in the district (although the minimum period of residence is 15 days), and the notice of intended marriage need not be publicly displayed. The procedure costs more than marriage by certificate.

marriage by Registrar-General's licence Marriage authorized by a licence issued by the Registrar-General of Births, Deaths, and Marriages. Marriage outside a register office or registered building may now take place in certain other licensed venues, such as stately homes.

marriage by religious licence A marriage in the Church of England based on the grant of an ecclesiastical licence, rather than on publication of *banns. A **common licence** may be granted if one of the parties swears an affidavit that he believes there is no lawful impediment, that at least one of the parties has been resident in the parish for at least 15 days previously (or usually worships at the church), and that (in the case of a minor) the consent of each parent with *parental responsibility (or a person in whose favour a residence order is made) has been obtained. If no caveat is issued against the grant of a licence, the ecclesiastical judge will grant a licence and the marriage may take place immediately. The Archbishop of Canterbury may also grant a **special licence** authorizing a marriage at any time of the day or night in any church, chapel, or other convenient place (even if unconsecrated).

marriage ceremony The ceremony creating the status of marriage. There are four main types of marriage ceremony (excluding marriage in military chapels). In a civil marriage, the ceremony takes place in a register office or other registered venue, with open doors, in the presence of the Superintendent Registrar (who conducts the ceremony), a registrar (who supervises registration formalities), and at least two witnesses. Under the Marriage Act 1983, housebound and detained persons may get married where they reside.

In a Church of England marriage, the ceremony usually takes place in church and is celebrated by a clergyman in the presence of at least two witnesses according to the rite of the Book of Common Prayer (or any alternative authorized form of service). A clergyman may refuse to solemnize the marriage of anyone whose former marriage has been dissolved if the former spouse is still living, or whose marriage would have been void for *affinity of the parties before the passing of the Marriage (Prohibited Degrees of Relationship) Act 1986. The marriage ceremony in Quaker and Jewish marriages is governed by the rules of those religions and need not be celebrated in a registered building, or by an authorized person, or in public. All other religious marriage ceremonies must be celebrated in a registered building designated as a place of meeting for religious worship, with open doors, and in the presence of at least two witnesses and a registrar or previously notified authorized person.

marriage settlement A *settlement made between the parties to a marriage. A settlement made before the marriage ceremony is called an **antenuptial** or **prenuptial settlement**; that made after the marriage is a **postnuptial settlement**. The purpose of a marriage settlement is to provide an income for one spouse or the children, while securing the capital for the other spouse. The courts have power when giving decrees of divorce, nullity, or judicial separation either to order property owned by one spouse to be settled for the benefit of the other spouse and children or to vary the terms of any existing ante- or postnuptial settlement. This power is often used to retain the use of the matrimonial home until the children are independent, as well as to retain the parents' financial investment.

marshalling of assets A process in which the claims of different creditors are directed towards different funds of the same debtor in an attempt to reach a fair result. When there are two creditors and two funds, and one has a claim exclusively on one fund but the other can claim against either fund, the rule of marshalling requires the latter to claim against the fund from which the former is excluded. The aim is, so far as possible, to allocate the assets so as to satisfy all the creditors.

marshalling of assets in probate A form of *marshalling of assets that is applied where a deceased's person assets are to be used to pay off debts of the estate. The Administration of Estates Act 1925 (sch 1 pt II) gives the order of priority in which such assets are to be used to pay off any debts. Section 35 of the same Act also provides that property which is mortgaged is to be used primarily to pay off the mortgage liability. Such rules are not, however, binding on a creditor of the estate, who can enforce his debt against any assets in the estate. If an asset is taken out of order for payment of a debt, then the *personal representatives must adjust matters between beneficiaries by compensating the beneficiary whose asset was used for such payment.

marshalling of securities An application of *marshalling of assets. If A mortgages two properties to B and then mortgages one of the properties in addition to C (who may or may not know of B's mortgage) then B, as first mortgagee, may obtain his money from whichever mortgaged property he chooses. However, if he chooses to obtain his money from the property mortgaged to C, C may if necessary obtain his money from the other property. This right cannot be exercised when a purchaser has obtained the property without knowing of the facts giving rise to the right to marshal.

Martens clause A clause that was included in the Hague Conventions of 1899 and 1907 by the Russian delegate, Friedrich von Martens (1845–1909), and has since then been included in many other treaties. It states that anything not proscribed by the regulations of the treaty will be subject to the international law and will therefore not necessarily be permissible; it also allows the regulations of the treaty to keep pace with the consequences of modern developments in warfare.

martial law Government by the military authorities when the normal machinery of government has broken down as a result of invasion, civil war, or large-scale insurrection. The constitution of the UK does not provide for a declaration (with specified consequences) of martial law: it is no more than a situation capable of arising. While the military authorities are restoring order, their conduct could not be called into question by the ordinary courts of law. After the restoration of order, the legality of their actions would be theoretically capable of examination, but the standards that would be applied by the courts are unknown. Martial law should not be confused with military law; any courts held by the military authorities to try civilians during a state of martial law would not enjoy the status of the Court Martial. *See* SERVICE LAW.

Marxist criminology *See* POSITIVIST SCHOOL OF CRIMINOLOGY.

Marxist legal theory Any approach to legal theory based on the social and economic thought of Karl Marx (1818–1883) and Friederich Engels (1820–1895). This involves a materialist view of social life in which law and the state are accorded a subordinate position as part of the superstructure, as opposed to the fundamental economic infrastructure, of society. *See also* SOCIOLOGY OF LAW.

master *n.* **1.** One of the *Masters of the High Court or the Masters of the Bench (*see* BENCHERS). **2.** The person having command or charge of a vessel. **3.** Formerly, an *employer. *See also* EMPLOYER AND EMPLOYEE.

Master of the Rolls The judge who is president of the Civil Division of the *Court of Appeal. The office is an ancient one and was originally held by the keeper of the public records. Later the holder was a judge of the Court of Chancery and assistant to the Lord Chancellor, with his own court, the **Rolls Court**. Since 1881 he has been a judge of the Court of Appeal only, but retains important duties in relation to public records. He also admits solicitors to practice.

Masters of the Bench *See* BENCHERS.

Masters of the High Court Inferior judicial officers of the *Queen's Bench and *Chancery Divisions of the High Court. Their principal function is to supervise *interim proceedings in litigation and (especially in the Chancery Division) to take accounts. By convention, Chancery Masters used to be solicitors and Queen's Bench Masters used to be barristers. In the provinces a comparable jurisdiction is exercised by *district judges of the High Court. *See also* DISTRICT REGISTRY.

matching broker *See* STOCK EXCHANGE.

material and essential validity of a will In *private international law, a rule determining which country's laws govern the validity of gifts under a will where, for example, the testator had a foreign domicile or owned foreign assets. Under English law a gift is valid in relation to moveable property if it complies with the law of the domicile of the testator, and in relation to immoveable property if it complies with the law of the country in which the property is situate (*lex loci situs*). *See also* FORMAL VALIDITY OF A WILL.

material facts *See* STATEMENT OF CASE.

maternity rights The rights a woman has against her employer when she is absent from work wholly or partly because of her pregnancy or confinement. The current law is contained in the Employment Rights Act 1996 as amended and supplemented by the Maternity and Parental Leave Regulations 1999, as amended. The provisions with respect to maternity pay are governed by the Social Security Contributions and Benefits Act 1992 and its supporting regulations. It is possible for an employer to agree contractually to more generous maternity leave provisions than the statutory minimum. The statutory rights are:

(1) Ante-natal care: all pregnant employees are entitled to reasonable time off work, with pay, for antenatal care, but an employer is entitled to ask for evidence of appointments. An employee who is unreasonably refused time off may complain to an *employment tribunal.

(2) Protection from dismissal: an employee is entitled not to be dismissed because of pregnancy or any reason connected with it. She is treated as having been unfairly dismissed if the principal reason for the dismissal is that she is pregnant, or that she has given birth, or that she has taken maternity leave.

(3) Pay: a pregnant employee who meets certain qualifying conditions based on her length of service and average earnings is entitled to receive **statutory maternity pay** from her employer for up to 39 weeks. To qualify for statutory maternity pay a pregnant employee must have been working for the same employer continuously for at least 26 weeks ending in the 15th week before the week the baby is due, must have been paying National Insurance on earnings of an average of £111 a week (2014), and must give notice of the date she intends to start her maternity leave. If she can satisfy these conditions, she will receive 90% of salary for six weeks followed by a fixed statutory rate for the remaining 33 weeks (set at £138.18 in 2014). Unless the baby is early, payment cannot begin until 11 weeks before the baby is due. Employers can recover 92% of such payments by setting the amount against their National Insurance payments. They can require the employee to provide them with evidence of the baby's birth. An employee who does not qualify for statutory maternity pay but who earns at least £30 per week on average may be entitled to claim the state maternity allowance from the Benefits Agency.

(4) Leave: an employee who continues to be employed by her employer until the beginning of the 11th week before the expected week of confinement is entitled to **maternity leave**. All pregnant employees are entitled to at least 52 weeks' maternity leave, made up of 26 weeks' **ordinary maternity leave** and 26 weeks' **additional maternity leave**. An employee must inform her employer, at least 15 weeks before her expected week of childbirth, that she intends to be absent because of maternity leave. This notice must also state the expected week of confinement, for which she may be required by her employer to produce evidence. The maternity leave period begins either on the date that the employee has previously notified to her employer or on the first day on which she is absent from work wholly or partly because of pregnancy or childbirth, if this is within four weeks of the expected date of confinement.

(5) Return to work: an employee entitled to maternity leave is also entitled to return to work with her employer. An employee who returns after ordinary maternity leave is entitled to return to the same job on the same terms and conditions of

employment as if she had not been absent, unless her job has become redundant, in which case she is entitled to be offered a suitable alternative vacancy. An employee who returns to work after additional maternity leave is entitled to return to the same job on the same terms and conditions of employment as if she had not been absent, unless that is not reasonably practicable; in the latter case, she must be offered a similar job on terms and conditions no less favourable than her original job. If a woman wishes to return to work before the end of her 52 weeks' leave she may do so providing she informs her employer 8 weeks in advance of her proposed return. She need not give notice if she is returning at the end of the 52 weeks. If the employer refuses to allow her to return, the employee is treated as having been dismissed. The dismissal will be treated as unfair unless the employer shows that her job is redundant and that she was offered a suitable alternative, which she refused, or that it was not reasonably practicable to allow her to return and that she was offered suitable alternative employment, which she unreasonably refused.

(6) Compulsory maternity leave: this is the period when the employee is not allowed to work. This is 2 weeks from the date of the birth, or 4 weeks if employed in a factory, or longer if there are special rules.

(7) Contractual terms: throughout the maternity leave period the employee is entitled to continue to benefit from all contractual terms of her employment with the exception of remuneration (money payment). These entitlements may include such things as pension contributions from her employer, company car and personal petrol allowance, and private health insurance.

(8) Health and safety: employers are required to protect the health and safety at work of new and expectant mothers. A new mother is one who has given birth within the last 6 months or who is breastfeeding. If, despite taking all reasonably practicable measures, there is still a risk that could jeopardise the health or safety of a new or expectant mother or her baby, employers must remove any employee who is a new or expectant mother from the risk. The employer must first consider modifying the employee's working conditions and/or hours of work. If this is not practical or if it would not avoid the risk, the employer must offer suitable alternative work if any is available. If that is not possible the employee must be suspended from work for as long as necessary to protect her safety or health or that of her child. An employee on maternity suspension is entitled to be paid at her full normal rate for as long as the suspension continues.

(9) Keeping in touch: during maternity leave employees may do up to 10 days' work. These "keeping in touch days" are paid, but the employee must agree to do the work and the employer may not demand it. In addition, employers must give the employee information that she would have received if she had been at work, including promotion opportunities.

See also PATERNITY LEAVE.

matrimonial causes *See* MATRIMONIAL PROCEEDINGS.

matrimonial home The home in which a husband and wife have lived together. When only one of the spouses owns the matrimonial home the Family Law Act 1996 gives the nonowner certain *home rights, which may be enforced by court order (*see* OCCUPATION ORDER). These rights include a right to live in the matrimonial home while still married. They will bind third parties (such as banks and building societies) if they are registered as a Class F land charge (in the case of previously unregistered land) or if they are protected by a notice (in the case of registered land) – *see* REGISTRATION OF ENCUMBRANCES. The same rights have now been extended to same-sex couples who have registered a *civil partnership. In Scotland similar rights have been granted (for a limited period only) to unmarried cohabitants, under the Matrimonial Homes (Financial Provision) (Scotland) Act 1981. When the legal estate is registered under the Land Registration Act and the wife is in actual occupation, she may also be protected against eviction by a third party if she has an interest in the land, even though she has not registered a notice or caution. Such an interest may be acquired by virtue of her contributions to the mortgage payments or, sometimes, to household expenses, as well as by making improvements in the matrimonial home.

Upon divorce, nullity, or separation the court has wide powers to make orders transferring the matrimonial home from one party to the other or altering their rights in it, in particular to provide for dependent children. County courts and magistrates' courts have powers to grant an occupation order that may exclude a spouse from the matrimonial home (*see* DOMESTIC VIOLENCE) as well as making an order for sale of the matrimonial home in order to redistribute resources.

matrimonial home rights *See* HOME RIGHTS.

matrimonial offence Misbehaviour, such as adultery, desertion, or cruelty, by a party to a marriage. Formerly (before 1969), proof of matrimonial offences provided grounds for divorce and was important in applications in magistrates' courts for financial relief during the marriage.

matrimonial order Formerly, an order made by magistrates under the 1960 Matrimonial Proceedings and Magistrates' Courts Act for periodical payments, custody of children, or noncohabitation clauses. However, both the grounds on which magistrates may exercise jurisdiction and the type of orders they may make are now governed by the 1978 Domestic Proceedings and Magistrates' Courts Act.

matrimonial proceedings (matrimonial causes) Proceedings for *divorce, *judicial separation, or *nullity of marriage. All matrimonial proceedings must be heard in a divorce county court or the Divorce Registry in London. The proceedings may be transferred from the county court to the High Court, and vice versa, at the court's discretion. *See also* FAMILY PROCEEDINGS.

maturity *n.* The time at which a *bill of exchange becomes due for payment. When a bill is payable at a fixed period after date, after sight, or after the happening of a specified event, the date of payment is determined by excluding the day from which the time is to begin to run and including the day of payment. When a bill is payable at a fixed period after sight, the time begins to run from the date of *acceptance if the bill is accepted and from the date of noting or *protest if the bill is noted or protested for nonacceptance.

maxims of equity Short pithy statements used to denote the general principles that are supposed to run through *equity. Although often inaccurate and subject to exceptions, they are commonly used to justify particular decisions and express some of the basic principles that have guided the development of equity. The main maxims are as follows:

- equity acts *in personam;
- equity acts on the conscience;
- equity aids the vigilant;
- equity will not suffer a wrong without a remedy (i.e. equity will not allow a person whom it considers as having a good claim to be denied the right to sue);
- equity follows the law (i.e. equity follows the rules of common law unless there is a good reason to the contrary);

- equity looks at the intent not at the form (i.e. equity looks to the reality of what was intended rather than the way in which it is expressed);
- where the equities are equal, the earlier in time prevails (i.e. where rights are equal in worth or value, the earlier right created takes precedence over the later);
- he who seeks equity must do equity;
- he who comes to equity must come with *clean hands (*see* EQUITABLE REMEDIES*);
- *equality is equity;
- equity looks on that as done which ought to be done (*see* CONVERSION);
- equity imputes an intent to fulfil an obligation (*see* SATISFACTION);
- equity will not assist a volunteer (*see* VOLUNTARY SETTLEMENT).

Mayor of London The head of the *Greater London Authority, elected every four years by the voters in London; the office was created under the Greater London Authority Act 1999. The responsibilities of the Mayor include the promotion of cultural, economic, and social development and improvement of the London environment by use of strategies to reduce air pollution and waste.

Mayor's and City of London Court A court formed in 1922 by the amalgamation of the Mayor's Court and the City of London Court. It had an unlimited civil jurisdiction over matters arising within the City. The Court was abolished by the Courts Act 1971, but the name is retained by the *county court for the City of London, which has normal county court jurisdiction.

Measure *n. See* CHURCH OF ENGLAND.

measure of damages The principle that determines the amount of *damages awarded for a tort or a breach of contract.

mediation *n.* **1.** A form of *alternative dispute resolution in which an independent third party (**mediator**) assists the parties involved in a dispute or negotiation to achieve a mutually acceptable resolution of the points of conflict. The mediator, who may be a lawyer or a specially trained nonlawyer, has no decision-making powers and cannot force the parties to accept a settlement. In family law, for example, mediators assist spouses to resolve disputes that have arisen as a consequence of the breakdown of their marriage by reaching agreement or reducing conflict over future arrangements for children or their finances. Mediation, which is designed to avoid the need to take cases to court, is likely to be extended to many other areas of the law since the publication of Lord Woolf's *Access to Justice* (Final Report) 1996 and the introduction of the *Civil Procedure Rules, in which it is actively encouraged. **2.** (in international law) A method for the peaceful settlement of an international dispute in which a third party, acting with the agreement of the disputing states, actively participates in the negotiating process by offering substantive suggestions concerning terms of settlement and, in general, by trying to reconcile the opposing claims and appeasing any feeling of resentment between the parties involved. *See also* CONCILIATION; GOOD OFFICES.

Mediation, Information and Assessment Meeting (MIAM) From April 2011, a session run by a family mediator in which separating parents attempt to resolve any disputes about the arrangements to be made for their children; in most circumstances, parents will be required to attend a MIAM before making application to the court. A MIAM is not considered appropriate where there are issues relating to child protection or domestic violence.

Medicines and Healthcare products Regulatory Agency (MHRA) A UK government agency that regulates the use of drugs and medical devices. The Agency issues licences for the clinical trial of new products and for their subsequent manufacture and marketing. It also applies the regulations governing the collection, storage, and use of human blood and blood products.

melior est conditio possidentis [Latin: the condition of the party in possession is the better one] A maxim stating that the onus of making out a claim to title in law falls upon the shoulders of the party who makes the claim against the existing possessor.

Member of Parliament (MP) *See* HOUSE OF COMMONS.

Members' interests Interests of Members of Parliament that might affect their conduct as MPs; for example, employments, company directorships, shareholdings, substantial property holdings, and financial sponsorships. By a 1975 resolution of the House, these must be registered for public information. After various allegations of Members not disclosing financial rewards received from outside parties in return for asking questions in the House ("cash for questions"), the rules on disclosure were tightened in 1996, when the Code of Conduct for Members of Parliament with a Guide to the Rules Relating to the Conduct of Members were published.

memorandum in writing Under former provisions of the Law of Property Act 1925, written evidence of a contract for the sale or other disposition of land or of any interest in it. The Act provided that such a contract could not be enforced unless it, or some memorandum or note evidencing the parties' agreement (identifying the parties, the property, the price, and other essentials), was in writing and signed by the party to be held liable on the contract. In practice, a contract would usually be in writing, but a signed memorandum showing that the parties had been bound from the time of an earlier oral agreement was equally acceptable as evidence to support any claim to enforce the contract.

However, the Law of Property (Miscellaneous Provisions) Act 1989 now insists that such a contract can only be made in writing that sets out in one document (or incorporates by reference to other existing documents) all the terms the parties have expressly agreed; the contract must be signed by both parties. A mere memorandum or note evidencing the terms of the agreement will no longer suffice unless it is incorporated in the contract by reference.

memorandum of association A document that must be submitted to the Registrar of Companies by the person(s) wishing to set up a new company. Formerly, under the Companies Act 1985, certain compulsory clauses had to be inserted into the memorandum dealing with the company's identity (**names clause**); its registered address (**registered office clause**); the amount of its *authorized capital (**capital clause**); and the purpose(s) for which the company was formed (**objects clause**). Under the Companies Act 2006, which came into force in late 2010, the memorandum is a much shorter document stating simply that the members wish to form a company.

memorandum of understanding *See* LETTER OF INTENT.

menace *n. See* THREAT.

mensa et thoro [Latin: from board and bed] *See* A MENSA ET THORO.

mens rea [Latin: a guilty mind] The state of mind that the prosecution must prove a defendant to have had at the time of committing a crime in order to secure a conviction. *Mens rea* varies from crime to crime; it is either defined in the statute creating the crime or established by *precedent. Common examples of *mens rea* are *intention to bring about a particular consequence, *recklessness as to whether such consequences may come about (*R v Cunningham* [1957] 2 QB 396), and (for a few crimes) *negligence. Some crimes require knowledge of certain circumstances as part of the *mens rea* (for example, the crime of receiving stolen goods requires the knowledge that they were stolen). Some crimes require no *mens rea*; these are known as crimes of *strict liability. Whenever *mens rea* is required, the prosecution must prove that it existed at the same time as the *actus reus* of the crime (coincidence of *actus reus* and *mens rea*: *R v Le Brun* [1992] QB 61). A defendant cannot plead ignorance of the law, nor is a good *motive a defence. He may, however, bring evidence to show that he had no *mens rea* for the crime he is charged with; alternatively, he may admit that he had *mens rea*, but raise a general defence (e.g. duress) or a particular defence allowed in relation to the crime.

mental disability Under the *Equality Act 2010 it is unlawful to discriminate against people with disabilities in a range of circumstances, including in education and employment. According to the definition in s 6 of the Act, a person with a mental health condition that has a "substantial and long-term" negative effect on his ability to perform normal daily activities is a *disabled person. This would potentially cover many different types of condition, including dementia, depression, bipolar disorder, obsessive compulsive disorder, schizophrenia, and a tendency to self-harm. *See also* MENTAL DISORDER.

mental disorder For the purposes of the Mental Health Act 1983 as amended by the Mental Health Act 2007, any disorder or disability of the mind (s 1(2)). This is a wide term and would include persons suffering from organic brain disorders such as dementia, schizophrenia, and other delusional disorders, personality disorders, autistic spectrum disorders, and in some cases learning disabilities. A person suffering from a mental disorder can be detained and treated in a hospital without his consent. **Detention for assessment** (under s 2) normally takes place on an application to the managers of the relevant hospital by an *approved mental health professional or a *nearest relative. This must be supported in either case by the recommendation of two doctors (or one in the case of an emergency) on the grounds that it is necessary in the interests of the patient's own health and safety or to protect others. The application authorizes detention for up to 28 days (72 hours in the case of an emergency), after which time further detention would be unlawful unless authorized under an application for **detention for treatment** (s 3). The procedure and grounds for detention are similar to those under section 2, one important difference being that if the nearest relative objects to the application a court order must be made to displace the nearest relative and appoint another person (usually a social worker) who will agree to the detention. The application authorizes detention for six months, renewable for a further six months initially and thereafter for periods of one year on a report to the hospital managers by the doctor in charge. Discharge of a patient may be effected by the hospital managers or the doctor in charge and in certain cases by the nearest relative. A patient has a right to appeal to the *Mental Health Tribunal (MHT). In addition, the hospital managers are under a duty to automatically refer any detained patient to the MHT after the first six months of detention. The provision of medical treatment for the mental disorder is regulated by Part 1(v) of the Act. Certain treatments, such as psychosurgery and surgical implantation of hormones to remove sexual drive, cannot be given without the patient's consent and a second opinion. Electroconvulsive therapy cannot be given to a *competent patient who refuses to consent to it and may only be given to an *incompetent patient where it does not conflict with an *advance decision or a decision of a donee of a *lasting power of attorney. Any other treatment may be given for up to three months, beyond which authorization is required from a *Second Opinion

Appointed Doctor (SOAD) if the patient either refuses or is incapable of consenting. *See also* DEPRIVATION OF LIBERTY SAFEGUARDS.

mental disorder impeding choice Under the Sexual Offences Act 2003 it is an offence for a person (A) to engage in sexual activity with a person (B) who has a mental disorder impeding B's choice of whether to engage in sexual activity. B has a mental disorder impeding choice if B lacks the capacity to choose whether to agree to the activity (whether because B lacks sufficient understanding of the nature, or reasonably foreseeable consequences, of what is being done, or for any other reason) or if B is unable to communicate such choice to A. Four separate criminal offences exist under the Sexual Offences Act 2003 designed to protect persons who suffer from a mental disorder impeding choice: sexual activity with a person with a mental disorder impeding choice (s 30); causing or inciting a person with a mental disorder impeding choice to engage in sexual activity (s 31); engaging in sexual activity in the presence of a person with a mental disorder impeding choice (s 32); and causing a person with a mental disorder impeding choice to watch a sexual act (s 33).

Mental Health Act Commission A regulatory body established in 1983 to monitor the operation of the Mental Health Act 1983. Commissioners were responsible for regularly visiting patients detained under the Act, reviewing psychiatric care, investigating certain complaints, and advising ministers. Under the Health and Social Care Act 2008 its functions were taken over by the *Care Quality Commission for England.

mental health treatment requirement A requirement that may be imposed by a sentencing court as part of a *community order or a *suspended sentence order under the Criminal Justice Act 2003 or as part of a *youth rehabilitation order under the Criminal Justice and Immigration Act 2008. An offender who is not insane but who is held to be suffering from a treatable mental health problem may be required to undergo appropriate treatment. Such a requirement can only be imposed with the consent of the offender.

Mental Health Tribunal A body that now forms part of the Health, Education and Social Care Chamber of the *First-tier Tribunal. Its role is to hear applications and references for people detained under the Mental Health Act 1983 (as amended by the Mental Health Act 2007) or living in the community following the making of a conditional discharge, or a community treatment or {guardianship order}. It includes legally and medically qualified members appointed by the Lord Chancellor. There is a separate Mental Health Tribunal for Wales.

MEP Member of the European Parliament. *See* EUROPEAN PARLIAMENT.

mercantile agent A commercial *agent who has authority either to sell goods, to consign goods for the purpose of sale, to buy goods, or to raise money on the security of goods on behalf of his principal.

mercenary *n.* A person recruited to fight in an armed conflict for private gain who is neither a national of a party to the conflict nor a member of its armed forces. Mercenaries are not entitled to combatant status and, if captured, are therefore not entitled to prisoner-of-war status for the purposes of protection under the *Geneva Conventions. British officers undertaking such service (e.g. in Oman) were commonly known as **contract officers**. *See also* FOREIGN ENLISTMENT.

merchantable quality An *implied condition now replaced by *satisfactory quality.

merchant shipping registration *See* SHIP.

mercy *n. See* PREROGATIVE OF MERCY.

mere equity A right affecting property that is less significant than an *equitable right or a *legal right; it does not affect anyone except the parties to the transaction in which it is contained. An example is the right to rectify a document.

merger *n.* **1.** An amalgamation between companies of similar size in which either the members of the merging companies exchange their shares for shares in a new company or the members of some of the merging companies exchange their shares for shares in another merging company. It is usually effected by a *takeover bid. Under current EU mergers law, mergers with a **Community dimension**, i.e. a combined Community-wide turnover of at least 250M euros and a combined worldwide turnover of over 500M euros, must be notified to the EU Mergers Secretariat. However, if each of the merging companies derives two-thirds of its EU business from one and the same member state, the merger does not have to be notified. *Compare* TAKEOVER. **2.** The extinguishing of a lesser interest in land when it comes into the same ownership as a greater one. For example, if a freehold owner acquires the unexpired leasehold estate, the latter may merge into the freehold. Whether or not merger occurs depends on the circumstances of the transaction (thus a leasehold that is subject to a subsisting mortgage will not normally merge with the freehold) and the intention of the parties.

mesne profits Money that a landlord can claim by way of damages from a tenant who continues to occupy property after his tenancy ends, the amount being equivalent to the current market rent of the property. This may be more than the rent that the tenant was paying before the tenancy ended. If the landlord continues to accept the original rent from the tenant at the end of the tenancy, a new tenancy may be created (*see* PERIODIC TENANCY; TENANCY AT WILL).

messuage *n.* A house and its associated garden, outbuildings, and orchard.

MHRA *See* MEDICINES AND HEALTHCARE PRODUCTS REGULATORY AGENCY.

MIAM *See* MEDIATION, INFORMATION AND ASSESSMENT MEETING.

Michaelmas Day *See* QUARTER DAYS.

micro-state *n.* A state with an area of less than 500 square miles and a population under 100,000. Examples of micro-states include Andorra, Antigua and Barbuda, Grenada, and Monaco, all of which have been admitted to membership of the United Nations. Although the UN membership of such small states was contentious, ultimately the principle of universality of membership of states, whatever their size, prevailed over the issue of whether or not they were capable of fulfilling their obligations as members. *See also* RECOGNITION.

Middle Temple One of the four *Inns of Court, situated in the Temple between the Strand and the Embankment, London. The earliest recorded claim for its existence is 1404.

Midsummer Day *See* QUARTER DAYS.

military court The *Court Martial or the *Court of Chivalry.

military law *See* SERVICE LAW. *Compare* MARTIAL LAW.

Military Staff Committee A committee established under Article 47 of the United Nations Charter. Articles 43–47 of the Charter (within *Chapter VII) envisage, through the Military Staff Committee, advance military cooperation for UN collective military security. This body is to advise the Security Council on all questions relating to armed forces placed at the disposal of the latter. It consists of the chiefs of staff of the permanent members of the Security Council, although other members of the United Nations may be invited to sit with it when the efficient discharge of the Committee's responsibilities so requires.

Due to deadlock, principally among the permanent members of the Security Council, the Committee declared that it could make no further progress on the matter of military cooperation for UN collective security measures. Although the Committee still formally exists it has had no real function to perform since its establishment in October 1945. *See also* COLLECTIVE SECURITY; ENFORCEMENT ACTION.

military testament *See* PRIVILEGED WILL.

minerals *pl. n. See* MINING LEASE.

minimum term *See* LIFE IMPRISONMENT.

minimum wage The lowest rate of remuneration that an employer may legally pay. The minimum adult hourly rate (from October 2013) is £6.31. The youth rate for 18–20-year-olds is £5.03 per hour, and for 16–17 year olds £72. Special rules apply to apprentices. Non-compliance by employers may be remedied by civil or criminal sanctions.

mining lease A lease granting a tenant the right to extract minerals from the land for a specified period in return for a rent (which may vary in accordance with the amount or value of minerals extracted).

minister *n.* A person (by *constitutional convention a member of either House of Parliament) appointed to government office by the Crown on the advice of the Prime Minister. He may be a senior minister in charge of a department (normally styled Secretary of State but sometimes Minister), a senior minister without specific departmental responsibilities (e.g. the Lord Privy Seal or a Minister without Portfolio), or a junior minister assisting in departmental business (a Minister of State or a Parliamentary Secretary or Under-Secretary). In the Treasury the ministerial ranks are *Chancellor of the Exchequer, Chief Secretary, Financial Secretary, and Ministers of State.

ministerial responsibility The responsibility to Parliament of the Cabinet collectively and of individual ministers for their own decisions and the conduct of their departments. A minister must defend his decisions without sheltering behind his civil servants; if he cannot, political pressure may force his resignation. Case: *Carltona Ltd v Works Commissioners* [1943] 2 All ER 560 (CA).

Ministry of Justice (MoJ) A UK government department that came into being in May 2007. It is responsible for the courts, judiciary, funding of cases, prisons, sentencing, and the probation service, as well as matters relating to EU law and international justice, human rights and civil liberties, and freedom of information and data protection issues, responsibilities that had previously been shared between the Home Office and the Department for Constitutional Affairs. Many of the functions historically exercised by the *Lord Chancellor are now exercised by the Secretary of State for Justice.

(((⊕))) SEE WEB LINKS

• Website of the Ministry of Justice: includes wide-ranging information on the courts system for both professional and lay users

minor *n. See* INFANT.

minor interests Interests in *registered land that cannot be created or transferred by registered disposition, are not *overriding interests, and could be overridden by a registered proprietor unless protected by registration. Such interests include the equitable interests of beneficiaries under a settlement and all charges that would be registrable at the Land Charges Department if the land had been unregistered (*see* REGISTRATION OF ENCUMBRANCES). Minor interests were protected by registration of a notice, caution, inhibition, or restriction as appropriate until the coming into force of the Land Registration Act 2002. Now only notices or restrictions may be entered. The 2002 Act does not use the term "minor interest" but many commentators still use it.

minority *n.* The state of being an *infant (or minor). *Compare* MAJORITY.

minority clauses Clauses in treaties between states that make special provision for *ethnic minorities. For example, in the Greco-Bulgarian convention of 1919 there was a minority clause that allowed for free migration of minorities between the signatory powers.

minority protection Remedies evolved to safeguard a minority of company members from the abuse of *majority rule. They include *just and equitable winding-up, applying for relief on the basis of *unfair prejudice, bringing a *derivative claim, a *representative claim, or a personal claim, and seeking an *investigation of the company.

minutes *pl. n.* Records of company business transacted at general meetings, board meetings, and meetings of managers. Registered companies are required to keep such records. Minutes of general meetings can be inspected by company members at the registered office or at a place prescribed by regulation (Companies Act 2006 s 358).

mirror principle One of the three principles of *land registration: that the register should provide a true reflection of the interests in the registered land. *Overriding interests are a breach of this principle, as they are binding on purchasers of the land although they do not appear on the register. *See also* CURTAIN PRINCIPLE; INDEMNITY PRINCIPLE.

miscarriage *n.* **1.** A failure of justice or a failure in the administration of justice. **2.** A spontaneous *abortion, i.e. one that is not induced.

mischief rule *See* INTERPRETATION.

misconduct *n.* Incorrect or erroneous conduct. *See* WILFUL MISCONDUCT.

misdemeanour *n.* Formerly (i.e. before 1967), any of the less serious offences, as opposed to *felony.

misdescription *n.* A misleading or inaccurate physical or legal description of property in a contract for its sale. When a vendor cannot convey property corresponding to its description in the contract for sale, a breach of contract results, which at the very least gives the purchaser a right to damages.

If the misdescription is substantial (i.e. it is reasonable to suppose that it constitutes the basis for the purchaser entering into the contract in the first place), the vendor will be unable to enforce the contract against the purchaser. When there is an innocent misdescription, which is not substantial, the contract may be enforced by the vendor, but subject to a suitable reduction in the contractually agreed price, even if the purchaser would prefer to rescind the contract (*see* RESCISSION). Alternatively, the purchaser might prefer to compel the vendor to convey what title he can (despite the misdescription) and receive compensation in addition. If the misdescription operates in the purchaser's favour, the vendor has no right to claim any compensation from him.

Under the Property Misdescription Act 1991, *estate agents and property developers are prohibited from making false or misleading statements about property in the course of their business. Misdescription in this case relates to what purports to be fact and not to mere expressions of opinion. *Compare* MISREPRESENTATION.

misdirection *n.* An incorrect direction by a judge to a *jury on a matter of law. In such cases the Court of Appeal may quash the conviction.

misfeasance *n.* **1.** The negligent or otherwise improper performance of a lawful act. **2.** (in company law) An act by an officer of a company in the nature of a breach of trust or breach of duty, particularly relating to the company's assets. *Compare* MALFEASANCE; NONFEASANCE.

misfeasance in public office The only tort available solely against public authorities or persons holding public office. It consists of an abuse of power by a public authority or person holding public office that is affected by malice or bad faith and that deprives the plaintiff of some benefit or causes him some loss.

misfeasance summons An application, under section 212 of the Insolvency Act 1986, to the court by a creditor, contributory, liquidator, or the official receiver during the course of winding up a company. The court is asked to examine the conduct of company officers and others who are suspected of a breach of a *fiduciary or other duty towards the company and it can order them to make restitution to the company.

misjoinder of parties An incorrect *joinder of parties in an action. In modern practice this does not cause the action to abate but it can be rectified by *amendment.

misleading advertising Advertising that deceives or is likely to deceive those to whom it is addressed or whom it reaches and, because of its deceptive nature, is likely to affect consumers' behaviour or injures or is likely to injure a competitor. The Consumer Protection from Unfair Trading Regulations 2008 and Business Protection from Misleading Marketing Regulations 2008 provide protection against misleading marketing.

(⊕) SEE WEB LINKS
• Advertising Standards Authority website

mispleading *n.* The omission of an essential allegation in a claim form or other statement of case. In modern practice, it can usually be rectified by *amendment.

misprision *n.* Failure to report an offence. The former crime of misprision of felony has now been replaced by the crime of *compounding an offence. However, the common-law offence of misprision of treason still exists; this occurs if a person knows or reasonably suspects that someone has committed treason but does not inform the proper authorities within a reasonable time. The punishment for this offence is forfeiture by the offender of all his property during his lifetime.

misrepresentation *n.* An untrue statement of fact, made by one party to the other in the course of negotiating a contract, that induces the other party to enter into the contract. The person making the misrepresentation is called the **representor**, and the person to whom it is made is the **representee**. A false statement of law, opinion, or intention does not constitute a misrepresentation – unless, in the case of opinion, the representator did not have reasonable grounds for holdings that opinion (*Smith v Land and House Property Co* (1884) 28 ChD 7) or, in the case of statement of intention, it can be shown that there never was such an intention (*Edgington v Fitzmaurice* (1885) 24 ChD 459). Nor does a statement of fact known by the representee to be untrue. Moreover, unless the representee relies on the statement so that it becomes an **inducement** (though not necessarily the only inducement) to enter into the contract, it is not a misrepresentation. The remedies for misrepresentation vary according to the degree of culpability of the representor. If he is guilty of **fraudulent misrepresentation** (i.e. if he did not honestly believe in the truth of his statement, which is not the same as saying that he knew it to be false) the representee may, subject to certain limitations, set the contract aside by *rescission and may also sue for damages. If he is guilty of **negligent misrepresentation** (i.e. if he believed in his statement but had no reasonable grounds for doing so) the representee was formerly entitled only to rescission but may now (under the Misrepresentation Act 1967 or by an action in tort for negligence) also obtain *damages. If the representor has committed merely an **innocent misrepresentation** (one he reasonably believed to be true) the representee is restricted to rescission, subject to the discretion of the court under the 1967 Act to award him damages in lieu. A representee entitled to rescind a contract for misrepresentation may decide instead to *affirm it. *See also* MISDESCRIPTION; NONDISCLOSURE.

missing trader intra-community fraud (carousel fraud) A fraud in which a person (commonly working in conjunction with others overseas) claims repayment of VAT on the export of goods to a fictitious purchaser in another EU country. Commonly the fraud involves a long chain of companies in different member states of the EU. An alternative to carousel fraud is **acquisition fraud**, in which a claim for input tax is made on the acquisition of fictitious goods or services. These two practices have been described by HM Revenue and Customs as "a systematic criminal attack on the VAT system". Specific statutory provisions to counter missing trader intra-community fraud are given in the Finance Act 2003 (s 17–18) and Finance Act 2006 (s 19).

mission *See* DIPLOMATIC MISSION.

mistake *n.* A misunderstanding or erroneous belief about a matter of fact (**mistake of fact**) or a matter of law (**mistake of law**). In civil cases, mistake is particularly important in the law of contract. Mistakes of law have no effect on the validity of agreements, and neither do many mistakes of fact. When a mistake of fact does do so, it may render the agreement void under common-law rules (in which case it is referred to as an **operative mistake**) or it may make it voidable, i.e. liable, subject to certain limitations, to be set aside by *rescission under more lenient rules of equity.

When both parties to an agreement are under a misunderstanding, the mistake may be classified as either a **common mistake** (i.e. a single mistake shared by both) or a **mutual mistake** (i.e. each misunderstanding the other). In the case of common mistake, there is full *consensus ad idem* and the mistake renders the contract void only if it robs it of all substance. The principal (and almost the only) example is when the subject matter of the contract has, unknown to both parties, ceased to exist (*res extincta*; see *Couturier v Hastie* (1856) 5 HLC 673, 10 ER 1065). A common mistake about some particular attribute of the subject matter (e.g. that it is an original, not a copy) is not an operative mistake (*Bell v Lever Bros Ltd* [1932] AC 161 (HL)). In the case of mutual mistake there is no real consensus, but the contract is nevertheless valid if only one interpretation of what was agreed can be deduced from the parties' words and conduct (*Malins v Freeman* (1837) 2 Keen 25, 132 ER 839). Otherwise, the mistake is operative and the contract void (*Raffles v Wichelhaus* (1864) 2 H&C 906, 159 ER 373). When only one party to a contract is under a misunderstanding, his mistake may be called a **unilateral mistake** and it makes the contract void if it relates to the fundamental nature of the offer and the other party knew or ought to have known of it (*Hartog v Colin and Shields* [1939] 3 All ER 566 (HL)). Otherwise, the contract is valid so far as the law of mistake is concerned, though the circumstances may be such as to make it voidable for *misrepresentation.

A deed or other signed document (whether or not constituting a contract) that does not correctly record what both parties intended may be rectified by the courts. When one signatory to a document was fundamentally mistaken as to the character or effect of the transaction it embodies, he may (unless he was careless) plead his mistake as a defence to any action based on the document (*see* NON EST FACTUM: *Lewis v Clay* (1897) 67 LJQB 224).

In criminal cases, a mistake or accident may mean that a person lacked *mens rea*. It has become clear in recent years that a person has a defence if he would have had a common-law defence, such as *consent, *provocation, or one of the *general defences, had the facts been as he mistakenly supposed them to be. If someone commits a crime in ignorance that the law forbids it, he is usually guilty (*ignorantia juris non excusat*: ignorance of the law is no excuse).

Under the Sexual Offences Act 2003, a defendant's mistaken belief in his victim's consent will only relieve the defendant of criminal liability where the mistake is reasonable.

If a defendant makes a mistake as to the civil law that prevents him having the *mens rea* required to be guilty of the crime, he will normally be acquitted of the crime, even if his mistake is unreasonable (for example, if he damages someone else's property in the belief that it is his own, and this belief is caused by a mistake as to the law of property). *See also* GENERAL DEFENCES; INTOXICATION.

mistakes in judgment *See* SLIP RULE.

mistrial *n.* A trial that is vitiated by some fundamental defect.

mitigation *n.* **1.** Reduction in the severity of some penalty. Before *sentence is passed on someone convicted of a crime, the defence may make a plea in mitigation, putting forward reasons for making the sentence less severe than it might otherwise be. A plea in mitigation may deal with matters that mitigate the seriousness of the offence and may also deal with personal or family circumstances of the offender. In raising mitigating factors, *hearsay evidence and documentary evidence of *character are accepted.
2. Reduction in the loss or injury resulting from a tort or a breach of contract. The injured party is under a duty to take all reasonable steps to mitigate his loss when claiming *damages.

mixed action A form of court action combining a claim relating to real property with a claim for damages.

mixed fund A fund of money derived from the sale of both real and personal property.

mixed property *Property that has some of the attributes of both real and personal property. *Emblements are an example.

M'Naghten Rules *See* INSANITY.

mock auction An auction during which (1) any lot is sold to someone at a price lower than his highest bid for it; (2) part of the price is repaid or credited to the bidder; (3) the right to bid is restricted to those who have bought or agreed to buy one or more articles; or (4) articles are given away or offered as gifts. Under the Mock

Auction Act 1961 it is an offence to promote or conduct a mock auction of plate, plated articles, linen, china, glass, books, pictures, prints, furniture, jewellery, articles of household or personal use, ornaments, or any musical or scientific instrument.

mode of trial proceedings A hearing in a magistrates' court that decides whether an *offence triable either way should be heard in the magistrates' court or sent to the Crown Court. *See also* PLEA BEFORE VENUE.

modus operandi [Latin: manner of working] The individual, possibly unique, way in which a person carries out an undertaking. The phrase is often used in criminal investigations. If a criminal has been caught and tried once and his *modus operandi* noted, he will immediately become a suspect again if the police detect a crime with the same "manner of working".

MoJ *See* MINISTRY OF JUSTICE.

molestation *n.* Behaviour that has the effect or intention of annoying or pestering one's spouse (or cohabitant) or children. Such an act need not involve violence or physical assault; harassment (for example by threatening letters or telephone calls) may constitute molestation. Under the Family Law Act 1996, spouses (and in some cases unmarried cohabitants) can apply for a court injunction to prevent molestation (*see* NON-MOLESTATION ORDER). In addition magistrates' courts have similar powers under the 1978 Domestic Proceedings and Magistrates' Courts Act, but only if there is violence and only in relation to married couples. There are procedures for protecting children in an emergency (*see* EMERGENCY PROTECTION ORDER). *See also* BATTERED CHILD; DOMESTIC VIOLENCE; STALKING.

money Bill A Bill that, in the opinion of the Speaker of the House of Commons, contains only provisions dealing with taxation, the Consolidated Fund, public money, the raising or replacement of loans by the state, and matters incidental to these subjects. Such a Bill becomes an Act without the House of Lords' consent (*see* ACT OF PARLIAMENT).

money had and received A former ground for court action that occurred when the defendant was in possession of money that should have belonged to the claimant (for example, when money had been paid to an agent who then failed to pass it on to his principal).

money laundering Legitimizing money from organized or other crime by paying it through normal business channels. EU measures exist to control, on an EU-wide basis, the laundering of money, especially that resulting from organized crime. The Money Laundering Regulations 2007 (SI 2007 No 2157) came into force in December 2007, in compliance with the EU's Third Money Laundering Directive of 2005. Part 7 of the Proceeds of Crime Act 2002 (s 327–29) also creates a series of money-laundering offences.

moneylender *n.* A person whose business it is to lend money. The Moneylenders Acts 1900–27 contained provisions for the control of moneylenders, including the form of their contracts. Under the Acts, the term "moneylender" did not include pawnbrokers, friendly or building societies, corporate bodies with special powers to lend money, those carrying on a banking or insurance business, or businesses whose primary object is not the lending of money. The more extensive provisions of the Consumer Credit Act 1974 have replaced the provisions of the Moneylenders Acts.

monism *n.* The theory that national and international law form part of one legal structure, in which international law is supreme. It is opposed to **dualism**, which holds that they are separate systems operating in different fields.

monopoly *n.* A situation in which a substantial proportion of a particular type of business is transacted by a single enterprise or trader. The Enterprise Act 2002 and Fair Trading Act 1973 contains provisions assigning functions in respect of monopolies to the *Office of Fair Trading and the Competition Commission. It defines a monopoly situation, in relation to the supply of goods and services and the export of goods, as one in which a single enterprise, connected group of companies, or trade association has one-quarter of the relevant business. When the Competition Commission finds that a monopoly situation exists and operates against the public interest, the Minister has powers to remedy or prevent the adverse effects. Sometimes monopolies involving more than one company (complex monopolies) are investigated. The Office of Fair Trading may also investigate joint *abuses of a dominant position that breach Chapter II of the Competition Act 1998 and thus has a choice as to which provisions are used to investigate monopolies.

month *n.* A calendar month or a lunar month (28 days). The common law adopted the lunar month, but the Interpretation Act 1978 provides that the word is to be presumed to mean calendar month in Acts of Parliament, and the Law of Property Act 1925 provides similarly for deeds and other written documents.

moot *n.* A mock trial, often held in university law schools and at the Inns of Court, for students as practice for future advocacy. A hypothetical case is presented to students for preparation and then argued before the judge(s) at the moot. This practice originates in the formal moots held in the medieval Inns of Court, which were considered an essential part of legal education.

moral law The body of laws to which individuals feel themselves subject, often through their religious beliefs. *See also* CANON LAW; NATURAL LAW.

moratorium *n.* The lawful suspension of legal remedies against debtors during times of general financial distress. It can also refer to the duration of the suspension.

mortgage *n.* An interest in property created as a form of security for a loan or payment of a debt and terminated on payment of the loan or debt. The borrower, who offers the security, is the **mortgagor**; the lender, who provides the money, is the **mortgagee**. Virtually any property may be mortgaged (though land is the most common); exceptions include the salaries of public officials. The name is derived from Old French (literally: dead pledge), since at common law failure to repay on the due date of redemption (which in most mortgages is set very early) formerly resulted in the mortgagor losing all his rights over the property. By the rules of equity the mortgagor is now allowed to redeem his property at any time on payment of the loan together with interest and costs (*see* EQUITY OF REDEMPTION). The mortgagee has a right to take possession of the mortgaged property as soon as the mortgage is made, irrespective of whether the mortgagor has defaulted. However, this right (1) must only be used for the purpose of protecting or enforcing the security, (2) may be excluded by agreement, or (3) is subject to a power in the court to adjourn proceedings for possession, to suspend the execution of an order for possession, or to postpone the date for delivery of possession, where the mortgaged property is a dwelling house (Administration of Justice Act 1970 as amended). This right is normally used as a preliminary to an exercise of the mortgagee's power of sale. If there is continued nonpayment of the loan, the mortgagee may sell the mortgaged property under a *power of sale, appoint a *receiver, or obtain a decree of *foreclosure.

Under the Law of Property Act 1925 the only valid **legal mortgages** are (1) a lease subject to *cesser on redemption and (2) a deed expressed to be a charge by way of legal mortgage (*see* CHARGE). Where land is registered, only the charge by way of legal mortgage is permitted and any such charge must be registered as a registered disposition or the mortgage will not take effect at common law. All other mortgages are equitable interests only (*see* EQUITABLE MORTGAGE). All mortgages of registered land are noted in the charges register on application by the mortgagee (*see* LAND REGISTRATION). When mortgaged land is unregistered, a first legal mortgagee keeps the title deeds. A subsequent legal mortgagee and any equitable mortgagee who does not have the title deeds should protect his interests by registration (*see* PUISNE MORTGAGE; REGISTRATION OF ENCUMBRANCES). *See also* PRIORITY OF MORTGAGES.

mortgage action A court action brought by a mortgagee for possession of the mortgaged property or payment of all money due to him, when the mortgagor has failed to pay the amounts due under the mortgage.

mortgagee *n. See* MORTGAGE.

mortgagor *n. See* MORTGAGE.

most favoured nation treatment (MFN treatment) The situation in which a state promises, usually by treaty, to trade with a particular partner on the most favourable tariff terms available for like goods. There might, for example, be a policy in place of taxing the MFN nation's imports at a preferential rate.

motion *n.* Formerly, an application made orally and in open court to a judge for an order. This term has been rendered obsolete by the *Civil Procedure Rules; motions are now referred to as **applications**.

motive *n.* The purpose behind a course of action. Motive is not normally relevant in deciding guilt or innocence (for example, killing to save someone from suffering is still murder or manslaughter), although it may be of some relevance in the crime of *libel. Nor is a bad motive relevant in deciding legal guilt. However, a good motive may be invoked as a reason for mitigating a punishment upon conviction, and a bad motive may provide circumstantial evidence that the defendant committed the crime he is charged with.

motoring offences *See* OFFENCES RELATING TO ROAD TRAFFIC.

motor insurance *See* THIRD-PARTY INSURANCE.

Motor Insurers' Bureau A body set up by the insurance industry, by agreement with the Department of Transport. It provides cover if someone has been injured or killed in a motor accident and in respect of a liability required by the Road Traffic Act to be covered by a contract of insurance when either (1) a judgment against the party liable is unsatisfied, for example because the party is (in breach of the Road Traffic Act) uninsured, or (2) the wrongdoer cannot be identified.

motor vehicle For the purposes of the Road Traffic Acts, any mechanically propelled vehicle intended or adapted for use on the roads. This includes **motor cars** (vehicles of not more than 3050 kilograms in unladen weight, designed to carry loads or up to seven passengers) and **motor cycles** (vehicles of not more than 410 kilograms in unladen weight and having less than four wheels). A car from which the engine has been removed may still be considered to be mechanically propelled if the removal is temporary, but if so many parts have been removed that it cannot be restored to use at a reasonable expense, it ceases to be mechanically propelled. A dumper used for carrying materials at a building site is not intended for use on roads, even if it is in fact used on a road near the building site; and a go-kart is not intended nor adapted for use on the roads (even though it is capable of being used on the roads). *See also* CONVEYANCE.

motorway driving Contravention of the regulations relating to driving on a motorway, as outlined in the Highway Code, is an offence punishable by *endorsement (carrying 3 points under the *totting-up system) and discretionary *disqualification.

MOT test An annual test originally ordered by the Ministry of Transport (now Department for Transport) to be carried out on all motor vehicles over a certain age to ensure that they comply with certain legal requirements relating to vehicle maintenance. The test covers brakes, steering, lights and indicators (including warning lights), windscreen wipers and washers, the exhaust and fuel system, horn, tyres (and to some extent, the wheels), bodywork and suspension (insofar as they affect the brakes and steering), seat belts, and speedometer. It is an offence to put on the road a motor vehicle that has been registered for over three years (five years in Northern Ireland) without a valid test certificate. A certificate is issued for 12 months and must be renewed annually; a vehicle that is subject to a test cannot be licensed without a test certificate (*see* ROAD TAX). It is not an endorsable offence not to have an MOT certificate, but this may invalidate the motorist's insurance and result in a charge of *driving without insurance. An MOT certificate does not indicate that the vehicle is roadworthy in all respects and is not a defence to charges brought under the *vehicle construction and maintenance regulations.

movables *pl. n.* Tangible items of property other than land and goods fixed to the land (i.e. immovables).

MP (Member of Parliament) *See* HOUSE OF COMMONS.

mulct *n.* To impose a fine or other penalty: the term is now rarely used.

multiple admissibility The principle of the law of evidence that if evidence is admissible for one purpose it may not be rejected solely because it is inadmissible for some other purpose. However, the *trier of fact may have to be directed not to consider the evidence when deciding those issues in respect of which it is inadmissible.

multiple agreement (under the Consumer Credit Act 1974) An agreement the terms of which are such that (1) part of it falls within one category of agreement mentioned in the Act and another part within a different category of agreement, which may or may not be mentioned in the Act; or (2) a part or the whole of it is placed within two or more categories of agreement mentioned in the Act. When part of an agreement falls within a category mentioned in the Act, that part is treated for the purposes of the Act as a separate agreement. When an agreement falls within two or more categories, it is treated as an agreement in each of the categories in question.

multiplier *n.* A number used to calculate *damages for future loss or expenses. The multiplier is used to estimate the sum necessary to produce an annuity equivalent to the annual loss or expense for the expected lifetime of the person awarded damages. Multipliers are now found in the *Ogden tables and HM Government establishes a standard notional rate upon which to base the calculation.

multi-track *n.* The track to which a civil case is allocated (*see* ALLOCATION) when the claim is more complex and/or for a higher amount (exceeding £25,000) than those catered for in the *fast track. With the exception of personal injury claims not exceeding £50,000, the jurisdiction for which is retained by the county court, these actions will be based in the High Court. Unlike the *small claims track and the fast track, the multi-track uses tools of *case management rather than standard procedure to process. Those tools include the use of *case management conferences and *pretrial reviews.

municipal law The national, or internal, law of a state, as opposed to international law. *See also* DOCTRINE OF INCORPORATION; PRIVATE LAW; PUBLIC LAW.

muniments *pl. n.* An obsolete term for documents that prove a person's title to land.

murder *n.* Unlawful *homicide that does not fall into the categories of *manslaughter or *infanticide. The *mens rea* for murder is traditionally known as *malice aforethought and the punishment (since 1965) is *life imprisonment. Murder is subject to the special defences of *diminished responsibility, *suicide pact, and *provocation, which serve to reduce the defendant's conviction from murder to voluntary *manslaughter.

mute *adj. See* STANDING MUTE.

mutiny *n.* An offence under the Armed Forces Act 2006 committed by any member of HM forces who combines with one or more other members (whether or not civilians are also involved) to overthrow or resist lawful authority in those forces or any forces cooperating with them. If a civilian is involved, his conduct will be a matter for the ordinary criminal law.

mutual mistake *See* MISTAKE.

mutual society A *building society or an insurance society that is owned by its members, membership being conferred by the making of a deposit with the society or the acceptance of a *mortgage loan from it. During the 1990s and 2000s many mutual building societies converted to public companies by *demutualization.

mutual trading The situation in which the income of a company arises solely from contributions by its members, the members being the owners of the company. The same provisions apply where the entity is an association and not a company. Historically, many insurance companies were created as *mutual societies engaged in mutual trading, as were the *building societies. The "profits" of mutual trading are not subject to UK corporation tax as they are not, strictly speaking, profit but are more correctly regarded as a surplus of contributions. Cases: *English and Scottish Joint Co-operative Wholesale Society Ltd v Assam Agricultural IT Comr* [1948] AC 405, 419 (Lord Normand); *IRC v Eccentric Club Ltd* [1924] 1 KB 390 (HL); *National Association of Local Government Office v Watkins* (1934) 18 TC 499, 506 (Finlay J).

mutual wills Two wills are mutual wills if there is an agreement between the two testators (typically husband and wife) that the wills shall not be revoked. Such an agreement is binding following the death of the first testator. If, following the first death, the will of the second testator is revoked by a new will, then although that new will is admissible to probate any beneficiary prejudiced by the revocation of the previous will has a claim against the second testator's estate. An alternative to mutual wills is for two testators to leave their estate in trust for the survivor of them for life with a *gift over, so that control is retained over the deceased testator's estate.

naked agreement *See* CONSIDERATION.

naked trust *See* BARE TRUST.

name *n. See* BUSINESS NAME; CHANGE OF NAME; COMPANY NAME; SURNAME.

name and arms clause A clause in a settlement providing that the beneficiary forfeits his entitlement unless he uses a specified surname and, if appropriate, coat of arms at all times. The clause is valid only if it is sufficiently precise.

National Assembly for Wales *See* WELSH ASSEMBLY.

National Crime Agency (NCA) A government agency that replaced the former *Serious Organized Crime Agency from October 2013: it also took over certain responsibilities of the UK Border Agency. There are four separate commands: Organized Crime, Economic Crime, Border Policing, and the Child Exploitation and Online Protection Centre. The National Cyber Crime Unit is also a subdivision of the NCA. The purpose of the Agency is to coordinate the response to serious and organized crime across Great Britain: it has no jurisdiction in Northern Ireland.

National Health Service (NHS) A service established for England and Wales in 1948 as a result of the National Health Service Act 1946 and reorganized in 1974, 1982, 1990, 1999 (under the Health Act 1999), 2002 (under the NHS Reform and Health Care Professions Act 2002), and 2013 (under the Health and Social Care Act 2012). It is concerned with the provision of hospital, specialist, general practitioner (medical, dental, ophthalmic, and pharmaceutical), nursing, ambulance, and related services, under the ultimate responsibility of the Secretary of State for Health. In England the Health Service is administered by the National Health Service Executive headed by a Chief Executive.

Following reorganization in 2002, Since 2002 the regional provision of NHS services was managed by *Strategic Health Authorities, whereas local health-care services (e.g. general practitioners, hospitals, ambulances, pharmacies) were managed by *Primary Care Trusts, which commission these services from *NHS Trusts and other provider organizations.

The NHS is currently (2014) undergoing major structural changes, most of which were implemented in April 2013 but some of which are still ongoing. Primary Care Trusts and Strategic Health Authorities have been abolished and new organizations, such as *Clinical Commissioning Groups, will take their place. At the same time, NHS services are being opened up to competition from other providers: these will be regulated by a new regulator, Monitor. There is now an expectation that the vast majority of hospitals and other NHS Trusts will become foundation trusts (*see* NHS FOUNDATION TRUST). Local authorities will assume responsibility for budgets for public health (*see* HEALTH AND WELLBEING BOARDS). The Department of Health will be responsible for strategic leadership of the health system but will no longer be the headquarters of the NHS, nor will it directly manage any NHS organizations. *See also* NHS ENGLAND; PUBLIC HEALTH ENGLAND.

National Insurance A scheme of state-administered social security benefits (including retirement pensions). These were inaugurated by the National Insurance Act 1946 and are now given effect by the Social Security Acts 1975–98. A separate industrial injuries insurance scheme was established by the National Insurance (Industrial Injuries) Act 1946, but the Social Security Acts now govern the payment of *industrial injuries disablement benefit. Entitlement to benefits is determined by decision makers; appeals from their decisions may be made to the *First-tier Tribunal (Social Entitlement Chamber). The scheme is partly funded by **National Insurance Contributions**, which are payable by those with earned income (employed or self-employed) and by employers.

(⊕) SEE WEB LINKS
• Guide to National Insurance Contributions from the HM Revenue and Customs website

nationality *n.* The state of being a citizen or subject of a particular country. *See* BRITISH CITIZENSHIP; BRITISH OVERSEAS TERRITORIES CITIZENSHIP; BRITISH OVERSEAS CITIZENSHIP; BRITISH SUBJECT; BRITISH NATIONAL (OVERSEAS).

nationalized industries Industries that have by statute been taken into public ownership as *corporations. Nationalized industries in the UK have been progressively returned to the private sector through *privatization, mainly by being floated on the Stock Exchange as *public companies.

national treatment standard The doctrine that a state is only bound to treat aliens and their property in the same way as it would treat its own citizens. Opposed to the *international minimum standard, it is seen by its proponents (originally Latin American countries) as counteracting the attempts of economically and politically powerful Western states to use international law to impose their will on less well-developed states. Its effect, however, has been to expose foreign nationals to objectionable standards in states that regularly maltreat their own nationals.

natural child 1. An illegitimate child (*see* ILLEGITIMACY). Until 1969 a gift by will to one's "children" was presumed to exclude natural (illegitimate) children, but there is now a presumption that it does include them. **2.** A child of one's body, as opposed to an adopted child.

naturalization *n.* The legal process by which a person acquires a new nationality. In the UK, *British citizenship or *British Overseas Territories citizenship can be acquired by means of a certificate of naturalization. This is granted by the Secretary of State to an applicant who has satisfied statutory requirements as to residence and other matters and taken an *oath of allegiance. The Nationality, Immigration and Asylum Act 2002 introduced a requirement that applicants should show a knowledge of British life and culture. Under the Borders, Citizenship and Immigration Act 2009 the process of naturalization can be hastened where the applicant has undertaken voluntary community work or other civic activities.

natural justice Rules of fair play, originally developed by the courts of equity to control the decisions of inferior courts and then gradually extended (particularly in the 20th century) to apply equally to the decisions of administrative and domestic tribunals and of any authority exercising an *administrative power that affects a person's status, rights, or liabilities. Any decision reached in contravention of natural justice is void as *ultra vires*. There are two principal rules. The first is the **rule against bias**, i.e. against departure from the standard of even-handed justice required of those who occupy judicial office – **nemo judex in causa sua** (or **in propria causa**): no man may be a judge in his own cause. This means that any decision, however fair it may seem, is invalid if made by a person with any financial or other interest in the outcome or any known bias that might have affected his impartiality (*R v Bow Street Metropolitan Stipendiary Magistrate, ex p Pinochet Ugarte (No 2)* [2000] 1 AC 119 (HL); *Porter v Magill* [2001] UKHL 673, [2002] 2 AC 357; *Davidson v Scottish Ministers* [2004] UKHL 34, [2005] SC 7). The second rule is known as **audi alteram partem**: hear the other side. It states that a decision cannot stand unless the person directly affected by it was given a fair opportunity both to state his case and to know and answer the other side's case (*R v Chief Constable of North Wales Police, ex p Evans* [1982] 1 WLR 1155 (HL); *R v Army Board of the Defence Council, ex p Anderson* [1992] QB 169; *R v Secretary of State for the Home Department, ex p Doody* [1994] 1 AC 531 (HL)). The rules of natural justice provide a minimum standard of procedural fairness and the exact requirements will vary depending on the context.

natural law The permanent underlying basis of all law. The philosophers of ancient Greece, where the idea of natural law originated, considered that there was a kind of perfect justice given to man by nature and that man's laws should conform to this as closely as possible. Theories of natural law have been an important part of jurisprudence throughout legal history. Natural law is distinguished from **positive law**, which is the body of law imposed by the state. Natural law is both anterior and superior to positive law.

natural person A human being. *Compare* JURISTIC PERSON.

natural rights 1. (in *natural law) a. Rights conferred on all individuals by the natural law. b. The fundamental rights found in civilized nations to which all men are entitled without interference by the state. This concept of natural law was particularly popular in the 18th century. It has had great influence in the legal history of the USA, as seen, for example, in the Virginian Declaration of Rights: "All men are by nature equally free and independent and have certain inherent natural rights of which when they enter a society they cannot by any compact deprive or divest their posterity". *See also* HUMAN RIGHTS. 2. (in land law) Rights automatically belonging to a landowner, violation of which constitutes an actionable *nuisance. The most obvious and important of these is the landowner's right to enjoy his land in its natural state and not to have support for it eroded by the activities of his neighbours (for example through excavation or quarrying operations). This right relates to the land rather than to buildings on it, although damages for infringing the natural right of support may reflect the damage done to buildings on the land affected by the neighbours' activities. A natural right to water may exist if it flows naturally through the landowner's property via a defined channel. *Compare* EASEMENT.

naval court A court formerly convened under the Merchant Shipping Act 1894 either by the captain of one of HM ships on foreign station or by a consular officer. Its purpose was to inquire into the abandonment or loss of any British ship, any complaint by an officer or seaman of such a ship, or any other matter requiring investigation in the interests of the owners of the ship or its cargo. It reported to the Department of Trade and Industry and had limited disciplinary powers. A naval court consisted of three to five members, each of whom was either a naval officer, the master of a British merchant ship, a consular officer, or a British merchant.

Inquiries into the fitness or conduct of an officer are now governed by the Merchant Shipping Act 1995, at the instigation of the Secretary of State. Inquiries are held in public and are conducted by a lawyer or judge, assisted by one or more assessors appointed by the Lord Chancellor. The inquiry may cancel or suspend any certificate of competence issued to the officer concerned, or censure him, if satisfied that he did not act to the standards required of him.

naval law *See* SERVICE LAW.

navigation *n.* **1.** The science of directing the course of a vessel or aircraft. Loss occasioned by **improper navigation** may arise even though a vessel is moored. **2.** A right to navigate inland waters.

NCA *See* NATIONAL CRIME AGENCY.

nearest relative A person, usually a family member, who is given certain powers under the Mental Health Act 1983 in respect of a person with a *mental disorder; these include the power to make an application for compulsory admission to hospital. The legal definition is found in section 26, the nearest relative being the person nearest to the top of the list there given, the first four being: (i) husband or wife or civil partner; (ii) son or daughter; (iii) father or mother; (iv) brother or sister. A patient may apply to court to nominate their own nearest relative if the person identified as such by this list is not suitable.

nec clam, nec vi, nec precario [Latin: neither secretly, nor by force, nor with permission] The presumption in law that long enjoyment of land allows for the presumption that the rights to that same land have a legal and legitimate origin.

necessaries *pl. n.* Goods or services suitable to the condition in life and actual requirements of a minor or a person subject to incapacity, e.g. essential clothing. Although such a person's legal *capacity to contract is limited, he must pay a reasonable price for necessaries sold and delivered to him.

necessary in a democratic society An expression set out in a number of the articles of the *European Convention on Human Rights: it makes that particular right a *qualified right and provides a signatory state with a defence of *proportionality. *See also* PRESSING SOCIAL NEED.

necessity *n.* A *general defence to a criminal offence, usually understood as a *justification rather than an *excuse, on the grounds that pressure of circumstances compelled the defendant to commit an illegal act. Necessity involves a situation in which the defendant commits an offence as a result of being faced with the choice of two evils; unlike *duress, the alternative evil is not a threat from another person but some other circumstance, as when the need to reach a fire leads the driver of a fire-engine to go through a red traffic light. The extent to which English law accepts a defence of necessity to a criminal charge (as opposed to one of duress or *self-defence) is unclear. Although this was not in a criminal case, the House of Lords recently ruled that a surgeon may have a defence of necessity if he operates in order to save life (*Re A (Children) (conjoined twins; surgical separation*) [2001] Fam 147). Necessity is not, however, a defence to charges of theft or murder (e.g. when shipwreck victims kill and eat one of their number: *R v Dudley and Stephens* (1884) 14 QBD 273) and it is not usually a defence to driving offences. The definitions of some statutory offences incorporate such expressions as "unlawfully" or "without lawful authority or excuse" and so should admit necessity defences. Other statutory provisions (1) authorize police and fire officers, if necessary, to break into premises when a fire has broken out and do everything necessary to extinguish it; and (2) provide qualified exemption from compliance with traffic lights for fire engines, ambulances, and police vehicles.

Necessity is in some circumstances a defence to an action in tort, but it is generally limited to action taken to protect life or property in an emergency not caused by the defendant's negligence. The steps taken in the emergency must be reasonable.
An exception is in the case of a permanently incapacitated individual, where necessity covers all activities that are in the person's best interests.

negative clearance A former procedure by which the European Commission determined that an agreement notified to it under the competition rules of the Treaty of Rome was exempt from the rules (*see* COMPETITION LAW). The procedure for notifying agreements was abolished on 1 May 2004, when businesses themselves were given the right to assess whether the conditions for exemption in the then Article 81(3) (now 101(3)) were met.

negative resolution *See* DELEGATED LEGISLATION.

neglect *n.* It is a criminal offence for a parent or guardian to neglect their child in a way that is likely to cause unnecessary suffering or injury to health, when the parent is aware of (or reckless as to) the likely consequences of the neglect. Neglect may also be evidence of *negligence and may give rise to a charge of manslaughter if the neglected person dies (*R v Gibbins and Proctor* (1918) 13 Cr App R 134).

negligence *n.* **1.** Carelessness amounting to the culpable breach of a duty: failure to do or recognize something that a reasonable person (i.e. an average responsible citizen) would do or recognize, or doing something that a reasonable person would not do. In cases of professional negligence, involving someone with a special skill, that person is expected to show the skill of a reasonably competent member of his profession (*Bolam v Friern Hospital Management Committee* [1957] 2 All ER 118 (HL)). Negligence may be an element in a few crimes, e.g. *careless and inconsiderate driving, and various regulatory offences, which are usually punished by fine. The main examples of serious crimes that may be committed by negligence are sexual offences under the Sexual Offences Act 2003 and *manslaughter (in one of its forms). *See also* GROSS NEGLIGENCE. **2.** A tort consisting of the breach of a *duty of care resulting in damage to the claimant. Negligence in the sense of carelessness does not give rise to civil liability unless the defendant's failure to conform to the standards of the reasonable man was a breach of a duty of care owed to the claimant, which has caused damage to him. Negligence can be used to bring a civil action when there is no contract under which proceedings can be brought. Normally it is easier to sue for *breach of contract, but this is only possible when a contract exists. Generally, fewer heads of damage can be claimed in negligence than in breach of contract, but the rules limiting the time within which actions can be brought (*see* LIMITATION) may be more advantageous for actions in tort for negligence than for actions in contract. *See also* BOLAM TEST; CONTRIBUTORY NEGLIGENCE; RES IPSA LOQUITUR.

negligent misstatement (negligent misrepresentation, careless statement)
A false statement of fact made honestly but carelessly. A statement of opinion may be treated as a statement of fact if it carries the implication that the person making it has reasonable grounds for his opinion. A negligent misstatement is only actionable in tort if there has been breach of a duty to take care in making the statement that has caused damage to the claimant. There is no general *duty of care in making statements, particularly in relation to statements on financial matters. Responsibility for negligent misstatements is imposed only if they were made in circumstances that made it reasonable to rely on them (*Hedley Byrne v Heller & Partners Ltd* [1964] AC 465 (HL); *Caparo Industries plc v Dickman* [1990] 2 AC 605 (HL)). If a negligent misstatement

induces the person to whom it was made to enter into a contract with the maker of the statement, the statement may be actionable as a term of the contract if the parties intended it to be a term or it may give rise to damages or *rescission under the Misrepresentation Act 1967 (*see also* MISREPRESENTATION).

negotiable instrument A document that constitutes an obligation to pay a sum of money and is transferable by delivery so that the holder for the time can sue upon it in his own name. The transferee can enforce the obligation even if the transferor's title is defective, provided that he accepted the document in good faith and for value and had no notice of the defect. The most important classes of negotiable instruments are *bills of exchange (including cheques) and *promissory notes.

negotiation *n.* (in international law) A diplomatic procedure by which representatives of states, either by direct personal contact or through correspondence, engage in discussing matters of mutual concern and attempt to resolve disputes that have arisen in relations between themselves.

negotiation of a bill The transfer of a *bill of exchange from one person to another so that the transferee becomes the holder. A bill payable to bearer is negotiated by *delivery; a bill payable to order is negotiated by the *endorsement of the holder completed by delivery. The issue of a bill to the payee is not a negotiation.

neighbour principle A principle developed by Lord Atkin in the famous case of *Donoghue v Stevenson* [1932] AC 562 (HL Sc) (Snail in the Bottle case) to establish when a *duty of care might arise. The principle is that one must take reasonable care to avoid acts or omissions that could reasonably be foreseen as likely to injure one's neighbour. A neighbour was identified as someone who was so closely and directly affected by the act that one ought to have them in contemplation as being so affected when directing one's mind to the acts or omissions in question.

nemo dat quod non habet [Latin: no one can give what he has not got] The basic rule that a person who does not own property (e.g. a thief) cannot confer it on another except with the true owner's authority (i.e. as his agent). Exceptions to this rule include sales under statutory powers and cases in which the doctrine of *estoppel prevents the true owner from denying the authority of the seller to sell.

nemo debet bis vexari [Latin: no man ought to be twice vexed] No person should be twice sued upon the same set of facts if there has been a final decision of a competent court. The maxim reflects the principles underlying the doctrine of *estoppel *per rem judicatam* and *issue estoppel.

nemo est heres viventis [Latin: no one is the heir of a living person] A maxim stating that a person's *heir can be ascertained only at the time of his death, since until then his heir apparent may die or be disinherited. Thus an heir apparent has no legal or equitable interest in property he expects to inherit until it actually devolves upon him.

nemo judex in causa sua (nemo judex in propria causa) [Latin: no man may be a judge in his own cause] *See* NATURAL JUSTICE.

nemo tenetur seipsum accusare [Latin: no one is bound to incriminate himself] A maxim reflecting the policy underlying the *privilege against self-incrimination.

neonaticide *n.* The act of killing a baby within the first 24 hours of its life. *See also* INFANTICIDE.

nervous shock *See* PSYCHIATRIC INJURY.

neutrality *n.* The legal status of a state that adopts a position of impartiality toward two other states who are at war with each other. The impartial state accords recognition of the state of belligerency between the two warring parties and this, in turn, creates rights and duties that fall upon all concerned.

neutralization *n.* The guarantee of the independence and political and territorial integrity of (usually) a small power by a collective agreement of great powers, subject to the condition that it will not take up arms against another state, except in self-defence, or enter into any treaty that may compromise its neutrality.

New International Economic Order A special session of the United Nations General Assembly was held in 1974 at which a Declaration (UNGA Res 3201 (S-VI)) and a programme of action (UNGA Res 3202 (S-VI)) on the establishment of a New International Economic Order were adopted. Both documents are concerned principally with economic matters, but their influence is wider and in a number of areas affects the legal position of states as members of the international community. The Declaration states that the new international economic order is to be based on "equity, sovereign equality, interdependence, common interest and cooperation among all states". Its objective is to alter the traditional requirement of effective compensation for nationalization of foreign-owned property. The municipal law of the nationalizing state would thus govern, rather than the customary practice establishing a right of compensation for the taking of alien property.

Newton hearing Where a defendant pleads guilty but disputes certain factual elements of the prosecution case, the judge can give both parties the opportunity to call evidence about the disputed matter. This will usually occur only where there is a substantial divergence between the two parties on a question of fact that might give rise to a difference in the sentence to be imposed. The judge will hear the evidence in the absence of a jury and reach his own judgment. This is known as a Newton hearing from the case *R v Newton* [1982] 77 Cr App R 13. The judge must be satisfied beyond reasonable doubt that the defence version of the facts is wrong.

new trial (retrial) A second trial of a case ordered by an appellate court. In civil proceedings the Court of Appeal has the power to order a new trial or hearing under Part 52 of the *Civil Procedure Rules. In criminal proceedings, the Court of Appeal may order a retrial where there has been a fundamental irregularity in procedure so serious as to render the original trial a mistrial (*see* VENIRE DE NOVO). Under the Criminal Justice Act 2003, the Court of Appeal also has the power to quash a conviction and order the retrial of a person acquitted of a serious offence where there is new and compelling evidence against the acquitted person and it is in the interests of justice for a retrial to be ordered. *See also* REHEARING.

next friend *See* LITIGATION FRIEND.

next of kin A person's closest blood relations. Parents and children (including those of unmarried parents) are treated as being closer than grandparents, grandchildren, or siblings.

NGO *See* NONGOVERNMENTAL ORGANIZATION.

NHS *See* NATIONAL HEALTH SERVICE.

NHS England An independent body within the *National Health Service whose role is to oversee the operation of, and to allocate resources to, the new *Clinical

Commissioning Groups; to commission primary care and specialist services; and to provide national leadership for improving outcomes and driving up the quality of care. It was established as the **NHS Commissioning Board** in October 2012. *See also* PUBLIC HEALTH ENGLAND.

NHS Foundation Trust A type of self-governing hospital, often referred to as a **foundation hospital**, created under the Health and Social Care (Community Health and Standards) Act 2003. Although such hospitals remain part of the *National Health Service, they are not subject to central government control but have freedom to decide locally how to meet their obligations and are accountable to local people. As part of the current (2013–14) reorganization of the Health Service there is now an expectation that the great majority of *NHS Trusts will become Foundation Trusts.

NHS Litigation Authority A Special Health Authority responsible for handling negligence claims made against NHS bodies in England. The Authority also promotes improvement in the standards of patient care and provides an information service for the NHS on human rights case law (*see* HUMAN RIGHTS ACT). It is part of the NHS.

(⊕) SEE WEB LINKS
- Website of the NHS Litigation Authority: includes advice on negligence claims for both patients and clinicians

NHS Trust A self-governing body within the *National Health Service that provides local health and social care services, including hospitals (**Acute Trusts**), mental health services (**Mental Health Trusts**), and patient transport (**Ambulance Trusts**). NHS Trusts are now accountable to *Clinical Commissioning Groups for the delivery of the local services that they have been commissioned to provide. *See also* NHS FOUNDATION TRUST.

Nice Treaty *See* TREATY OF NICE.

nisi *adj.* [Latin] Not final or absolute. *See also* DECREE NISI.

no case to answer In civil proceedings, the defendant may make a submission of no case to answer at the close of the claimant's case on the basis that the claimant has no real prospect of success. If the submission succeeds, judgment will be given for the defendant. In criminal proceedings, the defence may likewise make a submission of no case to answer at the close of the prosecution case. In a *trial on indictment the judge will stop the case and direct the jury to acquit the defendant if (1) there is no evidence that the offence was committed by the defendant or (2) the prosecution evidence, taken at its highest, is such that a jury properly directed could not properly convict upon it.

no-fault compensation A scheme based on the principle that injured persons should receive compensation for their injuries without having to prove fault against any individual. The term is American in origin, and in the USA and Canada it usually refers to insurance-based compensation schemes for injuries occurring in highway accidents. New Zealand introduced a comprehensive no-fault compensation scheme for personal injuries caused by accident in 1974, which replaced actions in tort for personal injuries, but the scope of the original scheme has since been reduced. In the UK, Industrial Injuries Disablement Benefit (IIDB) is a form of no-fault compensation.

noise *n. See* NUISANCE; NUISANCE NEIGHBOURS.

nolle prosequi [Latin: to be unwilling to prosecute] A procedure by which the *Attorney General may terminate criminal proceedings. The Attorney General's decision to enter a *nolle prosequi* is not subject to control by the courts. The procedure is most commonly employed when the accused cannot be produced in court to plead or stand trial owing to some physical or mental incapacity that is expected to be permanent. A *nolle prosequi* does not bar a further prosecution.

nominal capital *See* AUTHORIZED CAPITAL.

nominal damages A token sum of *damages awarded when a legal right has been infringed but no substantial loss has been caused.

nominated court A court nominated to take evidence pursuant to a request by a foreign court.

nomination *n.* **1.** The naming of a person for a vacant post or office or as a candidate in a parliamentary or local-government election. **2.** The naming by a member of a friendly society of a person to take his interest in the society on his death, without the need for a formal will. The member must be 16 or over and the nomination must be made in writing; it may be revoked at any time by the member himself and is, in any event, revoked on his marriage.

nominee *n.* A party who holds legal title to property for the benefit of other(s) but who has no real duties to perform, except very limited ones upon the direction of the beneficiaries. *See also* BARE TRUST.

nominee shareholder A company member who holds the shares registered in his name for the benefit of another. The identity of the person with the true interest may be subject to disclosure and to investigation under the Companies Act.

nomology *n.* The scientific study of laws and law-making.

nonage *n.* The period during which someone is under the age of majority (18 years). *See* INFANT.

non-charitable purpose trust *See* PURPOSE TRUST.

noncommercial agreement A *consumer-credit agreement or a *consumer-hire agreement that is made by a creditor or owner but not in the course of a business carried on by him. Such an agreement is outside certain of the provisions of the Consumer Credit Act 1974.

noncontentious business Any business of a solicitor that is not *contentious business, i.e. it is business of a nonlitigious character.

non-contentious probate business (common form probate) As defined by the Supreme Court Act 1981 s 25, probate business where there is no contention as to the right to obtain probate or administration of an estate. Such business is governed by the Non-Contentious Probate Rules 1987, as issued under the Supreme Court Act 1981.

nondisclosure *n.* **1.** (concealment) (in contract law) The failure by one party, during negotiations for a contract, to disclose to the other a fact known to him that would influence the other in deciding whether or not to enter into the contract. A full duty of disclosure exists only in the case of contracts *uberrimae fidei*, which are usually contracts of insurance. If the person to be insured tells an untruth, the contract will (like any other) be voidable for *misrepresentation; if this person also suppresses a material fact, it will be voidable for nondisclosure. In the case of other contracts, there is no general duty to volunteer information and mere silence cannot constitute misrepresentation (*Bell v Lever Bros Ltd* [1932] AC 161 (HL)). There is, however, a very limited duty of disclosure. A person who does volunteer information must not tell only a partial truth and must correct any statement that subsequently becomes to his knowledge untrue; breach of this duty will render the contract voidable for misrepresentation (*Spice Girls Ltd v Aprilia World Service BV* [2000] EWCA Civ 15, [2001] EMLR 174). **2.** (in civil proceedings) Failure of a party to disclose a document that should have been disclosed in his list of documents (*see* DISCLOSURE AND INSPECTION OF DOCUMENTS). Under Part 31 of the *Civil Procedure Rules the other party may seek an order for **specific disclosure** of the document.

non est factum [Latin, from *non est factum suum*: it is not my deed] A plea that an agreement mentioned in the *statement of case was not the act of the defendant. It may be applicable where the person signing a document had no real understanding of the character or effect of that document. *See* MISTAKE.

nonfeasance *n.* Failure to perform an act required by law. Until 1961, a highway authority guilty of nonfeasance by failing to carry out repair and maintenance was not liable for injuries caused because of this. It was, however, liable for *misfeasance. The defence of nonfeasance was then abolished by statute, but an authority can plead instead the statutory defence that it took all reasonable care to secure that the highway was not dangerous.

nongovernmental organization (NGO) A private international organization that acts as a mechanism for cooperation among private national groups in both municipal and international affairs, particularly in economic, social, cultural, humanitarian, and technical fields. Under Article 71 of the United Nations Charter, the Economic and Social Council is empowered to make suitable arrangements for consultation with NGOs on matters within its competence.

non-insane automatism Unconscious *involuntary conduct caused by some external factor where there is no claim of *insanity. A person is not criminally liable for acts carried out in a state of non-insane automatism, since his conduct is altogether involuntary (*Hill v Baxter* [1958] 1 QB 277). Examples of such acts are those carried out while in a state of concussion or hypnotic trance, a spasm or reflex action, and acts carried out by a diabetic who suffers a hypoglycaemic episode. Non-insane automatism is not a defence, however, if it is self-induced (for example, by taking drink or drugs).

nonjoinder *n.* A plea in *abatement alleging that the claimant had failed to join all necessary parties in the action. In modern practice this does not cause the action to abate but it can be rectified by *amendment. Rules dealing with the addition and substitution of parties are set out in Part 19 of the *Civil Procedure Rules.

non licet [Latin] Not permitted.

non liquet [Latin: it does not appear clear] An instance in which statute and previous case law seem to produce no clear legal answer to a new legal problem. In theory, a *non liquet* can never occur in English law: if not statute law, then certainly English common law, will provide an answer to any new legal problem that might emerge. Therefore, English judges are bound to give a decision in every case competently submitted to them. In practice *non liquets* do exist in English law, as they do in every other legal system.

non-molestation order A wide-ranging order under the Family Law Act 1996 s 42 that prohibits the respondent from "molesting" the applicant. *Molestation is not limited to acts of physical violence but includes conduct that harasses or threatens the applicant. An order can be made against anyone with whom the applicant is "associated"; this includes a spouse or civil partner, a cohabitant, a relative, or any person with whom the applicant has been in an intimate relationship. The order can also be made to protect a **relevant child**; this will usually be the biological child of the applicant or respondent but also includes any child who is living (or expected to live) with the applicant or respondent. In deciding whether to make the order, the court will look in particular at the need to secure the health, safety, and wellbeing of the applicant or of any relevant child. Breach of such an order is a criminal offence. *See also* DOMESTIC VIOLENCE.

nonprovable debt A debt that cannot be claimed in the course of bankruptcy proceedings. Examples are *statute-barred debts and debts that cannot be fixed or estimated. *Compare* PROVABLE DEBT.

non-refoulement *n.* [French: no forcing back] In public international law, the principle that a nation state is prohibited from expelling a legitimate refugee to his or her country of origin. It is governed by Article 33 of the Convention on the Status of Refugees. *See* ASYLUM.

non-resident parent A parent who is not living with his or her child and who may be liable to pay *child support maintenance. Non-resident parents were formerly known as **absent parents**.

nontariff barriers Special impositions (such as licences) or other restrictions that pose barriers to free trade in a particular commodity or service.

non-user *n.* The failure to exercise a right over land, which may be extinguished if the non-user continues for a sufficient period. *See* LIMITATION.

Northern Ireland Assembly A body established under the Northern Ireland Act 1998. It consists of 108 elected members and has limited primary legislative powers in such areas as agriculture, the environment, economic development, health, education, social security, and (from 2008) policing. Its powers are discharged by an Executive Committee of 12 ministers, which is appointed on a power-sharing basis. The Assembly was suspended in October 2002 but restored in May 2007. *See* DEVOLUTION.

noscitur a sociis [Latin: known by its associates] *See* INTERPRETATION.

notary (notary public) *n.* A legal practitioner, usually a solicitor, who attests or certifies deeds and other documents and notes or *protests dishonoured bills of exchange. **Ecclesiastical notaries** are usually diocesan registrars and the legal secretaries of bishops; **general notaries** may practise anywhere in England and Wales; and **district notaries** practise in a limited area. Diplomatic and consular officials may exercise notarial functions outside the UK.

not guilty **1.** A denial of the charges by an accused person in court. If there is more than one charge, the accused may plead guilty to some and not guilty to others. **2.** A *verdict finding that an accused person has not committed the offence with which he was charged. *See also* ACQUITTAL; INSANITY.

notice *n.* **1.** Knowledge of a fact. A person is said to have *actual notice of anything that he actually knows; *constructive notice of anything that he ought reasonably to know (for example, any fact that he would have discovered if he had made any inquiry that a reasonable person would have made); and *imputed notice of anything of which any agent of his has actual or constructive notice. **2.** (in employment law) Formal notification, given by either of the parties to a contract of employment, that the contract is to be terminated after a specified period. The period of notice to which each party is entitled is governed by the contract, subject to statutory minimum periods if the employee has been continuously employed in the business (*see* CONTINUOUS EMPLOYMENT) for more than four weeks. An employee who has been so employed for up to two years is entitled to a week's notice; one employed for a longer period is entitled to one week's notice for each year's continuous employment up to 12 years. Thus an employee who has been employed for 20 years must be given a statutory minimum of 12 weeks' notice, although his employment contract may entitle him to a longer period, which takes priority. An employee with four weeks' continuous employment must give at least one week's notice of his resignation. An employee whose conduct justifies immediate dismissal is treated as waiving his right to notice, as is an employer whose conduct amounts to *constructive dismissal. A fixed-term contract cannot be terminated by notice unless the contract expressly provides for this. **3.** (in land law) An entry against a registered title that may be lodged by a person with a right or interest in the land comprised in the title. The rights and interests that may be protected by a notice are listed in the Land Registration Act 2002, and a notice must always specify the right or interest it seeks to protect. A notice may be "agreed", which requires the consent of the registered proprietor, or "unilateral", in which case it is essentially hostile in nature. The registered proprietor may apply for cancellation of a unilateral notice. The notice protects the priority of the noted interest in the land; that is, a purchaser will be bound by that interest. **4.** (in *Community legislation) A nonbinding document. Notices are often issued by the European Commission to explain further details of a competition regulation, for example in relation to exclusive distribution and purchasing agreements, cooperation agreements, subcontracting agreements, agency agreements, and the distinction between cooperative and concentrative *joint ventures. Notices are not binding on the Commission, whereas regulations are; however, in practice it would be very rare for the Commission to depart from policies set out in a notice.

notice of abandonment *See* ABANDONMENT; CONSTRUCTIVE TOTAL LOSS.

notice of discontinuance In civil proceedings, a notice served by a claimant under Part 38 of the *Civil Procedure Rules voluntarily giving up all or part of a claim. In general, a claimant may discontinue all or part of a claim at any time by filing a notice of discontinuance with the court and serving copies on the other parties. Where there is more than one defendant, the claimant may discontinue all or part of a claim against all or any of the defendants. The permission of the court may be required if the claimant wishes to discontinue a claim where an interim injunction has been granted; where the claimant has received an interim payment; or where there is more than one claimant.

notice of dishonour A notice that must be given by the holder of a *bill of exchange to the drawer and to each endorser when the bill has been dishonoured; any drawer or endorser to whom notice is not given is discharged. The notice must identify the bill and state that it has been dishonoured by nonacceptance or nonpayment. The notice must be given within a reasonable time of the *dishonour (to which strict rules apply). Certain excuses are recognized for failure to give notice or delay.

notice of intended prosecution A written notice issued to someone charged with any of certain specified driving offences stating that he or she will be prosecuted. These offences are: *speeding, *dangerous driving, *careless and inconsiderate driving, *ignoring traffic signals, and leaving a car in a dangerous position (*see* OBSTRUCTION). If the offender was not warned when he committed the offence that he might be prosecuted for it, he cannot normally be subsequently prosecuted unless he is served with either a summons or a notice of intended prosecution within 14 days of committing the offence (*Gibson v Dalton* [1980] RTR 410). If he is prosecuted nonetheless, he may appeal against his conviction. If the notice was posted by registered or recorded mail so that it would normally have arrived within the 14 days, the motorist cannot plead that he did not receive it within that time. It is not necessary to serve a notice of intended prosecution when: (1) an accident happened at the time of the alleged offence owing to the presence on the road of the car involved in the alleged offence; (2) it was not possible to find out the name and address of the accused (or registered owner) in time; or (3) the motorist is charged with *causing death by dangerous driving, *causing death by careless or inconsiderate driving, or *drunken driving.

notice of transfer A procedure used in cases of serious and complex fraud, and in certain cases involving child witnesses, whereby the prosecution can, without seeking judicial approval, have the case sent direct to the Crown Court without the need to have the accused committed for trial (Glossary to the Criminal Procedure Rules).

notice to quit The formal notification from a landlord to a tenant (or vice versa) terminating the tenancy on a specified date. The notice must be clear and unambiguous and it must terminate the tenancy in relation to the whole of the rented property: a notice to quit part of the property can be valid only if specifically allowed by the tenancy. When the tenant lives in the rented property, the notice to quit must be in a statutory form that tells the tenant his legal rights. Otherwise no particular form is required for a notice to quit.

The period of notice varies according to the kind of tenancy and any agreement between the parties. In the case of periodic tenancies for which no period has been agreed the following periods apply: a yearly or longer tenancy – six months; a monthly tenancy – one month; a quarterly tenancy – one quarter; a weekly tenancy – one week. The notice must be given so that it expires at the end of one of the periods of the tenancy, for example in a yearly tenancy beginning on 1 January, the notice must expire on 31 December. If tenants have statutory protection this can affect the length of the notice to quit. Thus residential tenants must be given at least four weeks' notice, tenants of *agricultural holdings must be given a year's notice, and tenants of *business tenancies are entitled to at least six months' notice. In these cases a tenant may be entitled to continue in occupation of the rented property even after the notice to quit has expired. If the landlord treats the tenancy as continuing after the notice to quit has expired, a new tenancy may be created.

notice to treat A notice required to be given, under the Compulsory Purchase Act 1965, by an acquiring authority to all persons interested in or having power to sell and convey or release land proposed to be compulsorily acquired (*see* COMPULSORY PURCHASE). The notice must give particulars of the land concerned, demand particulars of the recipient's estate and interest in the land and of his claim in respect of it, and state that the acquiring authority is willing to negotiate for the purchase of the land and regarding compensation payable for damage.

noting a bill *See* PROTEST.

not negotiable Words marked on a crossed cheque indicating that a transferee for value of the cheque gets no better title to it than his transferor had. Since the Cheques Act 1992 most banks have printed cheques that are not negotiable. A bill of exchange so marked is not transferable.

not proven A *verdict used in Scottish courts when the prosecution case has not reached a sufficient standard of proof to establish the accused person's guilt, but there is some doubt about his innocence. The effect is the same as a verdict of not guilty.

nova causa interveniens *See* NOVUS ACTUS INTERVENIENS.

novation *n.* The substitution of a new contract for one already existing. The new contract may be between the same parties or it may involve the introduction of a new party, as in the case of the substitution of debtors. If A owes B £1,000 and B owes C £1,000, novation would occur if all three agreed that the existing debts were to be extinguished and that A is to pay C a new debt of £1,000. Novation should be distinguished from *assignment of a commercial agreement, in which no new agreement is needed and the benefit of a contract is transferred to the assignee.

novus actus interveniens (***nova causa interveniens***) [Latin: a new intervening act (or cause)] An act or event that breaks the causal connection between a civil wrong or crime committed by the defendant and subsequent happenings and therefore relieves the defendant from responsibility for these happenings. In tort the chain of *causation may be broken by the claimant (*McKew v Holland* [1969] 3 All ER 1621 (HL)), natural events (*Carslogie Steamship Co Ltd v Royal Norwegian Government* [1952] AC 292 (HL)), or a third party (*Knightley v Johns* [1982] 1 WLR 349 (CA)).

no win, no fee *See* CONDITIONAL FEE AGREEMENT; DAMAGES-BASED AGREEMENT; MAINTENANCE AND CHAMPERTY; SUCCESS FEE.

nudity *See* EXPOSURE.

nudum pactum [Latin: naked agreement] *See* CONSIDERATION.

nuisance *n.* An activity or state of affairs that interferes with the use or enjoyment of land or rights over land (**private nuisance**) or with the health, safety, or comfort of the public at large (**public nuisance**). Private nuisance is a tort, protecting occupiers of land from damage to the land, buildings, or vegetation or from unreasonable interference with their comfort or convenience by excessive noise, dust, fumes, smells, etc. An action is only available to persons who have property rights (e.g. owners, lessees) or exclusive occupation. Thus, for example, lodgers and members of a property owner's family cannot sue in private nuisance (*Hunter v Canary Wharf Ltd* [1997] AC 655 (HL)).

Physical damage is actionable when the damage is of a type that is reasonably foreseeable and provided it does not arise solely because the claimant has put his land to a hypersensitive use. Interference with comfort is actionable when it is considered unreasonable as judged by a number of factors, the most important of which is the nature of the locality. The main remedies are damages and an injunction. Alternatively there is a limited right to abate (i.e. remove) the nuisance. Where a statutory framework and remedy exist, there is no common-law action in nuisance and such a regulatory scheme is compliant with the Human Rights Act 1998 (*Marcic v Thames Water Utilities Ltd* [2003] UKHL 66, [2004] 2 AC 42).

Public nuisance is a crime. At common law it includes such activities as *obstruction of the highway, carrying on an offensive trade, and selling food unfit for human consumption. The Attorney General or a local authority may bring a civil action for an injunction on behalf of the public but a private citizen may obtain damages in tort only if he can prove some special damage over and above that suffered by the public at large (*Benjamin v Storr* (1874) LR 9 CP 400).

Statutory nuisances are created by provisions dealing with noise, public health, and the prevention of pollution and permit a local authority to control neighbourhood nuisances by the issue of an *abatement notice. The Protection from Harassment Act

1997 and also the Criminal Justice and Police Act 2001 (s 42A) enable individuals to be protected from harassment by their neighbours (*see* NUISANCE NEIGHBOURS).

nuisance neighbours People who disturb the lives of those living nearby by interfering with their *quiet enjoyment of their homes. The Protection from Harassment Act 1997 and the Criminal Justice and Police Act 2001 (s 42A) provide enhanced protection for those suffering *nuisance (including noise) from their neighbours. Restraining orders can be obtained, which require the offender to do what the court orders (e.g. not to communicate, go near, or harass their neighbours); in some circumstances *eviction may be ordered. Offenders threatening violence can be jailed for up to five years and/or be subjected to an unlimited fine; even if the harassment does not give rise to fear for safety, the offender faces up to six months in jail and/or a fine not exceeding the statutory maximum.

nulla poena sine lege [Latin: no punishment without a law] The principle that a person can only be punished for a crime if the *punishment is prescribed by law. The punishment may be specified by a statute as a term of imprisonment or fine or it may be based on common-law principles. With the exception of treason and murder, for which the punishment is fixed, all statutory punishments are expressed in terms of the maximum possible punishment; judges have discretion to impose a lesser punishment according to the circumstances. At common law punishment is said to be **at large**, i.e. the amount of the fine or length of the prison sentence is entirely at the judge's discretion. In many cases, however, there are now statutes specifying the maximum punishment for common-law offences. Magistrates' courts are subject to shorter maxima than Crown courts.

nullity of marriage The invalidity of a marriage due to some defect existing at the time the marriage was celebrated (or, sometimes, arising afterwards). A marriage may be null in the sense that it is **void**, i.e. it was never in the eyes of the law a valid marriage (and the "spouses" are legally merely cohabitants). It may alternatively be **voidable**, i.e. valid until made void by a court decree of *annulment, which (since 1971) does not end the marriage retrospectively (so that, for example, the children of a marriage that is annulled will not be regarded as illegitimate). The main grounds for nullity are: close relationship, lack of age, lack of consent, and nonconsummation (*see* CONSUMMATION OF A MARRIAGE). When granting a decree of nullity the court has wide discretionary powers to make orders for *financial provision or *property adjustment. *See also* LEGITIMACY.

nullum crimen sine lege [Latin: no crime without a law] The principle that conduct does not constitute crime unless it has previously been declared to be so by the law; it is sometimes known as the **principle of legality**. Some serious offences are well-defined common-law offences (although the details relating to their definition may often be unclear until ruled upon by the judges); many regulatory offences (e.g. those involving road traffic and the manufacture of products) are constantly being created by statute. The principle is violated by the power occasionally attributed to judges to create new offences in order to punish morally harmful conduct.

nunc pro tunc [Latin: now instead of then] A phrase used of a judgment entered in such a way as to have legal effect from an earlier date. Under Part 40 of the *Civil Procedure Rules a judgment or order generally takes effect from the day when it is given or made, or such later date as the court may specify.

nuncupative will An oral statement directing how property is to be distributed after death. Except in the case of *privileged wills and *donatio mortis causa*, such statements have no effect in English law.

oath *n.* A pronouncement swearing the truth of a statement or promise, usually by an appeal to God to witness its truth. An oath is required by law for various purposes, in particular for *affidavits and giving evidence in court. The usual **witness's oath** is: "I swear by Almighty God that the evidence which I shall give shall be the truth, the whole truth and nothing but the truth". Those who object to swearing an oath, on the grounds that to do so is contrary to their religious beliefs or that they have no religious beliefs, may instead *affirm.

oath of allegiance An oath to be faithful and bear true allegiance to the Crown. It is taken by members of both Houses at the opening of every new Parliament, by certain officers of the Crown on their appointment, and by those who become British citizens, British Overseas Territories citizens, British Overseas citizens or British subjects by registration, or British citizens or British Overseas Territories citizens by naturalization.

obiter dictum [Latin: a remark in passing] Something said by a judge while giving judgment that was not essential to the decision in the case. It does not form part of the *ratio decidendi* of the case and therefore creates no binding precedent, but may be cited as *persuasive authority in later cases.

objection to indictment A procedure in which the accused in a *trial on indictment attempts to prove some objection to the indictment on legal grounds (e.g. that it contravenes, or fails to comply with, an enactment). The objection is raised by application to quash the indictment.

objects *pl. n.* The purposes for which a company has been formed. Unless stated in the *articles of association, a company has unrestricted objects (Companies Act 2006 s 31). *See* MEMORANDUM OF ASSOCIATION.

objects of a power Persons in whose favour a *power of appointment may be exercised, i.e. potential appointees.

obligation *n.* **1.** A legal duty. **2.** A *bond by deed.

obliteration *n.* The deletion of words in a will. An obliteration is valid only if the words deleted are indecipherable or if the *alteration is properly signed and witnessed.

obscene publication Under the Obscene Publications Acts 1959 and 1964, any published article containing material that "tends to deprave or corrupt".

It is an offence to publish an obscene article or to have an obscene article for publication for gain. For the purposes of the Acts, obscenity is not limited to pornographic or sexually corrupting material: a book advocating drug taking or violence, for instance, may be obscene. Whether or not particular material is obscene (i.e. whether it tends to "deprave or corrupt") is a question of fact in each case, to be decided by the jury, and expert evidence is not usually permitted. Material that merely tends to shock or disgust is not obscene. The intention or motive of the author in writing or depicting the material is irrelevant.

"Publishing" an obscene article includes distributing, circulating, giving, hiring, or lending the article, offering it for sale or hire, or transmitting it through the telephone system (i.e. over the Internet). Offering for sale or hire does not include displaying the material in a shop, which is merely an invitation to treat and not an *offer. An "article" may be material that is to be looked at, rather than read, and can also include a negative of a film or any article used to reproduce material to be read or looked at.

Publishing an obscene article is an offence of *strict liability. However, there is a defence of **lack of knowledge** if the defendant can show he had not examined the article and had no reason to suspect that publishing it would constitute an offence. Under the Obscene Publications Act 1959 there is also a special defence of **public good**, which applies when the defendant shows that publication of the article was justified as being in the interests of science, literature, art, or learning. This defence permits the calling of expert opinion as to the literary or artistic merits of a work, as in the famous test case *R v Penguin Books Ltd* (1960) 161 Crim LR 176 (*Lady Chatterley* case). The offence of possessing an obscene article in the expectation that it will be published for financial gain is also subject to the defences of lack of knowledge and public good.

If a magistrate suspects that obscene articles are kept in any premises for the purpose of publication for gain, he may issue a warrant authorizing the police to search for and seize the articles. If they prove to be obscene, the magistrate may order them to be forfeited.

The Acts do not apply to material published by means of television or broadcasting, but they do apply to cinema screening and theatre performances, subject to the rule that prosecutions in such cases require the consent of the Director of Public Prosecutions or the Attorney General, respectively. These offences, too, are subject to the public good defence. The Criminal Justice Act 1994 for the first time set out legislative guidelines for the censorship of films and videos and gave the Home Office powers to overrule the decisions of the British Board of Film Censors in some circumstances.

There are also various special offences relating to obscenity, for example:

- publishing obscene advertisements;
- sending unasked for material describing sexual techniques;
- sending through the post any "indecent or obscene article" (this offence is limited to sexual obscenity).

It is also an offence to take, make, distribute, or possess indecent photographs or pseudo-photographs of a child; a "pseudo-photograph" is an image, created by computer graphics or any other means, that resembles a photograph and can include electronically stored data that can be converted into such images.

The maximum penalty for these offences is five years' imprisonment, a fine, or both on indictment (Obscene Publications Act 1959 s 2(i), as amended by the Criminal Justice and Immigration Act 2008, s 71); or six months' imprisonment, a fine not exceeding the statutory minimum, or both summarily. The Criminal Justice and Immigration Act s 63 also created a new *strict liability offence of possessing an "extreme pornographic image", this being defined as an image that realistically depicts sexual acts with an animal, with a corpse, or that would be likely to cause serious injury or death.

obscene telephone calls   It is a *summary offence to make an obscene, offensive, or annoying telephone call. The maximum punishment is six months' imprisonment and/or a *fine on level 5 (Communications Act 2003 s 127; Protection from Harassment Act 1997).

obstructing a police officer The offence of hindering a police officer who is in the course of doing his duty (Police Act 1996 s 89). "Obstruction" includes any intentional interference, e.g. by physical force, threats, telling lies or giving misleading information, refusing to cooperate in removing an obstruction, or warning a person who has committed a crime so that he can escape detection (e.g. warning a speeding driver that there is a police trap ahead). It is not, however, an offence merely not to answer, or to advise someone not to answer, police questions that he does not have to answer. A police officer is acting in the course of his duty if he is preventing or detecting crime (in particular, breaches of the peace) or obeying the orders of his superiors. However, he is not acting in the course of his duty when he is merely assisting the public in some way unconnected with crime. When the obstruction amounts to an *assault, the offence is punishable by imprisonment and/or a fine. One may be guilty of this offence even if the police officer was in plain clothes.

obstruction *n.* The offence of causing or allowing a motor vehicle, trailer, or other object to stand on a road in such a way that it is likely to impede other road users (Road Traffic Act 1988 s 22) or to use a vehicle on the road in a similar way (e.g. by driving unreasonably slowly: Road Traffic Act 1988 s 3). It is unnecessary to show that any other vehicle or person has in fact been obstructed. This offence is punishable by a fine. It is also an offence to leave a motor vehicle on a road in such a position or in such circumstances that it is likely to cause danger to other road users. This offence requires a *notice of intended prosecution and is punishable by a fine, *endorsement (which carries 3 penalty points under the *totting-up system), and discretionary *disqualification.

obstruction of recovery of premises *See* RECOVERY OF PREMISES.

occupation *n.* **1.** (in land law) The physical possession and control of land. Under the Land Registration Act 2002 the proprietary rights of a person in actual occupation may be an *overriding interest binding a purchaser of registered land, unless inquiry is made of that person and the rights are not disclosed or the occupation is not obvious on a reasonably careful inspection of the land (*Williams and Glyn's Bank Ltd v Boland* [1981] AC 487 (HL)). Under the Family Law Act 1996, spouses have rights of occupation in the *matrimonial home by virtue of marriage, which may be capable of protection as *land charges. **2.** (in international law) The act of taking control of territory belonging either to no one (**peaceful occupation**) or to a foreign state in the course of a war (**belligerent occupation**). Peaceful occupation is one of the methods of legally acquiring territory, provided the occupier can show a standard of control superior to that of any other claimant. Denmark acquired Greenland in this way, and the UK acquired Rockall. A belligerent occupant cannot acquire or annex the occupied territory during the course of the war. Certain provisions for the protection of enemy civilians in the Hague and Geneva Conventions are applied to those parts of the enemy territory that have been effectively occupied. A belligerent occupier must retain in force the ordinary penal laws and tribunals of the occupied power, but may alter them or impose new laws to ensure the security and orderly government of the occupying forces and administration. The government in exile is also regarded as continuing to represent the occupied state in international law without any special *recognition being necessary. *See also* CESSION; SUCCESSION.

occupation order Any of various orders under the Family Law Act 1996 relating to occupation of the *matrimonial home in cases of *domestic violence or where a marriage or relationship has broken down. The orders can enforce the rights of co-owning spouses or civil partners, or spouses or civil partners with *home rights, to occupy the home and provide for the exclusion of the respondent from the home or from any part of it. The orders can also extend similar rights to nonowning ex-spouses, whether or not they are actually in occupation, and also – under certain circumstances – to cohabitants or ex-cohabitants.

occupier *n.* A person in possession of land or buildings as owner, tenant, or trespasser. If he is a trespasser he may obtain a right to lawful occupation if the owner accepts money from him as rent, in which case a tenancy may be created, or through *adverse possession for a sufficient period.

occupier's liability The liability of an occupier of land or premises to persons on the land for the condition of the premises and things done there. The occupier for this purpose is the person or persons exercising control over the premises (*Wheat v Lacon* [1966] AC 522 (HL)). The common-law rules on occupier's liability have been replaced by statutes. The English statutes distinguish between visitors and other persons on land. The Occupiers' Liability Act 1957 imposes on an occupier the *common duty of care to all his visitors (i.e. those who enter by his invitation or with his permission) to see that they will be reasonably safe in using the premises for the purpose for which they were invited or permitted to be there. The duty of care may vary according to the type of visitor, e.g. children. Under the Occupiers' Liability Act 1984, an occupier only owes a duty to persons other than visitors (i.e. trespassers and persons who enter lawfully but without the occupier's permission) if the occupier is aware or has reasonable grounds to know of a danger on the premises and that a person may be in the vicinity of the danger and the risk is one against which he may reasonably be expected to offer some protection. The duty, if any, is confined to taking such care as is reasonable in all the circumstances to see that the danger due to the state of the premises does not cause death or personal injury to the person concerned. The duty may be discharged by taking such steps as are reasonable to give warning of the danger or to discourage persons from incurring the risk. There is no duty under either Act to warn of obvious risks (*Tomlinson v Congleton Borough Council* [2003] UKHL 47, [2004] 1 AC 46).

In Scotland, the Occupiers' Liability (Scotland) Act 1960 requires an occupier to show to *all* persons entering the premises such care as is reasonable in all the circumstances of the case.

occupying tenant A person in possession of premises in accordance with his rights under a lease or tenancy agreement, or as a *statutory tenant, assured agricultural occupier, or a *protected occupier, or under his rights as a tenant with a *restricted contract.

offence *n.* A *crime. The modern tendency is to refer to crimes as offences. Offences are either *indictable or *summary; the distinction between *arrestable and nonarrestable offences was abolished by the Serious Organized Crime and Police Act 2005.

offences against international law and order Crimes that affect the proper functioning of international society. Some authorities regard so-called international crimes as crimes of individuals that all or most states are bound by treaty to punish in accordance with national laws passed for that purpose. Examples of this type of crime are *piracy, *hijacking, and *war crimes. The International Law Commission has formulated Draft Articles on State Responsibility, which attempt to define international crimes for which individual states are liable. It gives as examples: (1) a serious breach of an international obligation essential to safeguard international peace (e.g. aggression) or peoples' rights to self-determination (e.g. colonial domination by force); (2) a widespread and serious breach of obligations essential to safeguard individuals (e.g. slavery, *genocide, or apartheid) or the environment (e.g. massive pollution).

offences against property Crimes that affect another person's rights of ownership (or in some cases possession or control). The main offences against property are *theft, offences of *fraud, *deception and *making off without payment, *criminal damage, *arson, *forgery, and *forcible entry. Some offences against property, such as *burglary, *robbery, and *blackmail, may also contain elements of *offences against the person.

offences against public order Crimes that affect the smooth running of orderly society. The main offences against public order are *riot, *violent disorder, *affray, *threatening behaviour, stirring up *racial hatred, public *nuisance, and *obstruction of highways. *See also* RAVE; TRESPASS.

offences against the person Crimes that involve the use or threat of physical force against another person. The main offences against the person are unlawful *homicide, *infanticide, illegal *abortion, *causing death by dangerous driving, *causing death by careless or inconsiderate driving, and *causing death by careless driving when under the influence of drink or drugs (fatal offences against the person); and *torture, *rape, *wounding, causing or inflicting *grievous bodily harm, *assault, aggravated assault, *battery, *kidnapping, and sexual offences (nonfatal offences against the person). *See also* POISON.

offences against the state Crimes that affect the security of the state as a whole. The main offences against the state are *treason and *misprision of treason, *sedition (and incitement to *mutiny), offences involving *official secrets, and acts of terrorism. *See also* TERRORISM.

offences relating to road traffic Crimes that are associated with driving vehicles on public roads and related acts. The main offences in this category are *careless and inconsiderate driving, *causing death by careless or inconsiderate driving, *causing death by careless driving when under the influence of drink or drugs, *dangerous driving, *causing death by dangerous driving, *drunken driving, *driving while disqualified, *driving without insurance, *driving without a licence, *speeding, *ignoring traffic signals, *parking offences, and *obstruction. Some road traffic offences require *notice of intended prosecution. Road traffic offences carry various penalties or combinations of penalties, such as fines, *endorsement of driving licence, *disqualification from driving, and in some circumstances imprisonment. The court may also make a *driving-test order. Many road traffic offences (especially the minor ones) are offences of *strict liability. *See also* DRIVING LICENCE; MOT TEST; ROAD TRAFFIC ACCIDENTS; ROAD TAX; SEAT BELT; VEHICLE CONSTRUCTION AND MAINTENANCE.

offence triable either way A crime that may be tried either as an *indictable offence or a *summary offence. Such crimes include offences of deception or fraud, theft, bigamy, and sexual activity with a child under the age of 16.

When an offence is triable either way, the magistrates' court must decide, on hearing the initial facts of the case, if it should be tried on indictment rather than summarily (for example, because it appears to be a serious case). Even if they decide that they can deal with the matter adequately themselves, they must give the defendant the choice of opting for trial upon indictment before a jury. There are three exceptional cases, however:

(1) If the prosecution is being conducted by or on behalf of the Attorney General, Solicitor General, or Director of Public Prosecutions, and they apply for trial on indictment, the case must be tried on indictment.

(2) If the case concerns criminal damage or any offences connected with criminal damage (except arson), and the damage appears to be less than £5,000, the case must be tried summarily.

(3) If the defendant is under 18, he must be tried summarily unless he is charged with (a) homicide; (b) an offence for which he is charged jointly with someone over 17, and it is thought necessary that they should be tried together; (c) a violent or sexual offence for which an adult could be sentenced to 10 years' imprisonment or more; (d) a firearms offence carrying a mandatory minimum sentence; or (e) certain other specified offences that can be punished by long periods of detention.

offence triable only on indictment An offence that can be tried only in the Crown Court. *See* INDICTABLE OFFENCE. *Compare* OFFENCE TRIABLE EITHER WAY; OFFENCE TRIABLE ONLY SUMMARILY.

offence triable only summarily An offence that can be tried only in a magistrates' court. *See* SUMMARY OFFENCE. *Compare* OFFENCE TRIABLE EITHER WAY; OFFENCE TRIABLE ONLY ON INDICTMENT.

offender *n.* One who has committed a *crime. *See also* DANGEROUS OFFENDER; FIRST OFFENDER; FUGITIVE OFFENDER; JUVENILE OFFENDER; REPEAT OFFENDER.

offensive weapon Any object that is made, adapted, or intended to be used to cause physical injury to a person. Examples of objects made to cause injury are revolvers, coshes, and daggers; objects adapted to cause injury include bottles deliberately broken to attack someone with and sawn-off shotguns. In theory any object may be intended to be used to cause injury, but articles commonly intended for such use include sheath knives (or any household knife), pieces of wood, and stones.

It is an offence under the Prevention of Crime Act 1953 to have an offensive weapon in one's possession in a public place. This offence is punishable summarily by up to six months' imprisonment and/or a *fine at level 5 on the standard scale or on indictment with up to four years' imprisonment and/or a fine, and the court may order the weapon to be forfeited. There are special exceptions for those, such as soldiers or police officers, who carry offensive weapons in the course of duty (*Houghton v Chief Constable of Greater Manchester* (1986) 84 Cr App R 319) and in cases of "reasonable excuse", but the defendant must prove that he comes within these categories. Self-defence is not usually a reasonable excuse unless there is an imminent and particular threat.

It is also an offence (finable only), under the Criminal Justice Act 1988, to possess in a public place a bladed or sharply pointed article (other than a folding penknife with a blade of three inches or less). Here, it is a defence to prove that the article was for use at work, for religious reasons (e.g. a Sikh's dagger), or part of a national costume, or that there was authority or good reason for its possession. The 1988 Act also gives the Home Secretary power to prohibit the manufacture, sale, hire, and importation of certain offensive weapons. *See also* FIREARM; WEAPON OF OFFENCE; PROHIBITED WEAPON.

offer *n.* An indication of willingness to do or refrain from doing something that is capable of being converted by *acceptance into a legally binding *contract. It is made by an **offeror** to an **offeree** and is capable of acceptance only by an offeree who knows of its existence (*Taylor v Allon* [1966] 1 QB 304). Thus, a person giving information cannot claim a reward if he did not know that a reward was being offered. An offer must be distinguished from an **invitation to treat**, which is an invitation to others to make offers, as by displaying goods in a shop window (*Gibson v Manchester City Council* [1979] 1 WLR 294 (CA); *Fisher v Bell* [1961] 1 QB 394). It must also be distinguished from a **declaration of intention**, which is a mere statement of intent to invite offers in the future, as by advertising an auction. *See also* COUNTEROFFER; LAPSE OF OFFER; REJECTION OF OFFER; REVOCATION OF OFFER.

offer of amends A procedure introduced by the Defamation Act 1996, whereby a defendant in an action for *defamation may make a written offer to publish an apology or correction and pay damages. The defendant may not rely on any other defence. Acceptance of such an offer will terminate any defamation proceedings and parties settle between themselves.

Office for the Supervision of Solicitors (OSS) Formerly, the body that dealt with complaints about solicitors; it was replaced by the *Solicitors Regulation Authority in 2007.

Office of Fair Trading (OFT) A public body, first established in 1973, that reviews the carrying on of commercial activities in the UK relating to the supply of goods or services to consumers in the UK and identifies *monopolies and other *anticompetitive practices. From 1 April 2003, as a result of the Enterprise Act 2002, the OFT was established on a statutory basis as a corporate body and a new board took on the powers of the former Director General of Fair Trading. Under the terms of the Enterprise and Regulatory Reform Act 2013, the OFT was replaced by a new body, the *Competition and Markets Authority, in April 2014.

Office of Public Sector Information (OPSI) A government body established in 2005 to provide a wide range of services relating to the finding, reuse, and trading of public sector information. In particular, it maintains the government's Information Asset Register. The Office has a lead role in implementing the Freedom of Information Act 2000 and the EU's Public Sector Information Directive, which came into force in 2005. Together with *Her Majesty's Stationery Office (HMSO), it now operates from within the National Archives.

 SEE WEB LINKS
• OPSI website

official copy An exact copy of an official document, supplied and marked as such by the office that holds or issues the original. Official copies are generally admissible in evidence to the same extent as the original. Thus official copies of entries recorded at the Land Registry are used in *conveyancing as evidence of title to registered land, and an official copy grant of probate may be used to prove an executor's right to receive or deal with the deceased's assets.

Official Custodian for Charities A corporation sole created by the Charities Act 1960 for the purpose of acting as a custodian trustee of property held for charitable purposes. It is now governed by the Charities Act 1993 and is currently a member of the Charity Commission staff.

Official Journal The official organ of the European Union, usually published every day and in each of the official languages of the EU. It is currently divided into two parts. One part (designated L) contains *Community legislation and bears references in the style "OJ [1997] L 23". The other (designated C) contains proposals of the European Commission, reports of proceedings in the European Parliament, notices concerning matters in the European Court, and other matters of general information; it carries references in the style "OJ [1997] C 23". There is a daily supplement containing publication of notices of public works and supply contracts and invitations to tender (*see* PUBLIC PROCUREMENT). The *Official Journal* can be bought from The Stationery Office and is published daily on the Internet.

official receiver The person appointed by the Department for Business, Innovation and Skills who acts in *bankruptcy matters as interim receiver and manager of the estate of the debtor, presides at the first meeting of creditors, and takes part in the debtor's public examination. In the *compulsory winding-up of a company, he often becomes *provisional liquidator when a winding-up order is made.

official referee Until 1972, a judicial officer of the *Supreme Court to whom certain matters could be referred, usually cases involving prolonged examination of accounts or large numbers of small items (such as building claims). The office was abolished by the Courts Act 1971 but the functions previously discharged by official referees can now be discharged by *circuit judges nominated to take **official referees' business**. The official referee's court is now known as the **Technology and Construction Court** and official referees as **judges of the Technology and Construction Court**.

official search A search, in response to an applicant's *requisition, into the registers of local land charges, the *Land Charges Department, or the *Land Registry (as appropriate) in order to disclose any registered matter relevant to the requisition. A certificate is issued by the registrar giving details of encumbrances that the search has revealed. In the case of the land charges register, a purchaser is not bound by any encumbrance that a proper search fails to reveal, the official search certificate being conclusive according to its tenor. If an entry is made in the land charges register after the date of the certificate and before completion of the purchase (other than in pursuance of a *priority notice entered on the register on or before the date of the certificate), it will not affect the purchaser if the purchase is completed within 15 working days after the issue of the certificate.

In the case of registered land, a purchaser seeking to become the registered proprietor is only bound by what is on the register and by *overriding interests. When a purchaser has applied for an official search of the register, his subsequent application to register the document effecting the purchase of the property concerned takes precedence over any entry made by a third party in the register during the priority period (30 days from the time the application for the search was delivered). Should an official search fail to reveal a registered interest, the newly registered owner is bound by that interest, but may be entitled to a statutory indemnity. A local land charge search certificate is valid only at the time it is issued and a purchaser is bound by any local charge registered subsequently. Since December 1990 the Land Registry has been open to public inspection: it is therefore possible to discover, on payment of a fee, whether any specific property has been or is about to be registered. The Land Registry also operates an online search facility. The registers of local land charges and the Land Charges Department are also open to public inspection.

official secrets For the purpose of the Official Secrets Acts 1911–89, information that is categorized as a secret code or password or that is intended to be (or might be) useful to an enemy. Under the Acts it is an offence for a Crown servant (or any other person subject to the provisions of the Acts) to disclose any information relating to UK security or intelligence matters without lawful authority.

It may be an offence for any person to do any of the following:

- to make a sketch, plan, model, or note that might be useful to an enemy of the United Kingdom;

- to obtain, record, or communicate to anyone else a secret official code or password or any information or document that is intended to be useful to an enemy;
- to enter, approach, inspect, or pass over (e.g. in an aircraft) any prohibited place. Such places include naval, military, or air-force establishments, national munitions factories or depots, and any places belonging to or used by the Crown that an enemy would want to know about.

For all three offences the prosecution must prove that the act was done for a purpose that prejudices the safety or interests of the state. Even if no particular prejudicial act can be proved, someone may be convicted if it appears from the circumstances of the case, his conduct, or his known and proven character that his purpose was prejudicial to the interests of the state. There is also a presumption (which may be disproved by the defendant) that any act done within the scope of the three offences without lawful authority is prejudicial to the state's interests. All three offences are punishable by up to 14 years' imprisonment. (*R v Prime* (1983) S Cr App Rep (s) 127).

It was also an offence under the Official Secrets Act 1911, section 2, for the holder of a Crown office who had any document or information as a result of his position to pass it on to an unauthorized person, keep it, or use it in any other way that prejudiced the state's interests. The information concerned did not have to be secret or confidential and the defendant did not have to be aware that harm might result from his act. The offence was punishable by up to two years' imprisonment, and anyone who received the information knowing or suspecting that it was given in breach of the Acts was liable to the same punishment.

Owing to widespread disquiet at the "catch all" nature of these provisions, the Official Secrets Act 1989 replaced section 2 of the 1911 Act with provisions protecting more limited classes of information from disclosure. Under the 1989 Act a member or former member of the security and intelligence services, or any other person notified that he is subject to this provision, commits an offence, punishable with up to two years' imprisonment and/or a fine, if without lawful authority he discloses or purports to disclose any information, document, or other article relating to security or intelligence. Similarly, Crown servants and "government contractors" are prohibited from making disclosures that damage security services' operations, endanger UK interests abroad, or result in the commission of an offence and from negligently failing to prevent such disclosures. Other offences relate to the disclosure by an ordinary citizen of protected information communicated in confidence by a Crown servant.

It is also an offence to attempt to commit, or incite, or aid and abet any of the above offences and to do any act of preparation for any of these offences. All such acts are subject to the same penalties as the offence they relate to. Thus, for example, buying paper in the knowledge that someone else plans to use it to sketch a military installation could be a preparatory act carrying a sentence of up to 14 years' imprisonment. *See also* SABOTAGE; SPYING; TREACHERY; TREASON.

Official Solicitor An officer of the Senior Courts who, when directed by the court, acts as *litigation friend (next friend) or childrens' guardian for those under a disability who have no one else to act for them; he may also be called upon to intervene and protect the interests of children. He can be appointed *judicial trustee in proceedings relating to disputed trusts.

OFT *See* OFFICE OF FAIR TRADING.

Ogden tables A work of reference that gives the most detailed guidance yet on how the courts should assess *damages for personal injury and accidental death. The aim of the tables is to provide a realistic estimate of discounted future earnings, allowing for the chances that the claimant might die before retirement age and might also have spent time not working owing to sickness, unemployment, etc. *See* MULTIPLIER.

Old Bailey *See* CENTRAL CRIMINAL COURT.

oligopoly *n.* Control of a market by a small number of suppliers, which may or may not lead to the operation of a *cartel. *Compare* MONOPOLY.

Ombudsman *n. See* COMMISSION FOR LOCAL ADMINISTRATION IN ENGLAND; INDEPENDENT HOUSING OMBUDSMAN; LEGAL OMBUDSMAN; PARLIAMENTARY OMBUDSMAN.

omission *n.* A failure to act. It is not usually a crime to fail to act; for example, it is not usually a crime to stand by and watch a child who has fallen into a river drown. Sometimes, however, there is a duty on a person to act, either because of the terms of a contractual duty, or because he is a parent or guardian of a minor, or because he has voluntarily assumed a duty (e.g. looking after a disabled relative), or through a statutory imposition of such a duty. In such cases, omission may constitute a crime. Usually this will be a crime of *negligence (e.g. manslaughter, if the victim dies because of the defendant's omission); if it is a deliberate omission with a particular intention (e.g. the intention of starving someone to death) it will amount to murder. *See also* NEGLECT.

Similarly, there is no general liability in the law of tort for failing to act, but there are some situations where the law imposes a duty to take action to prevent harm to others. Thus occupiers of premises are under a duty to see that their visitors are reasonably safe (*see* OCCUPIER'S LIABILITY).

omnia praesumuntur rite et solemniter esse acta [Latin: all things are presumed to have been done correctly and solemnly] *See* PRESUMPTION.

on all fours with Where the principles involved in two cases are deemed to be directly analogous, the later case is said to be "on all fours with" the earlier one. The notion of *precedent then allows for the application of *stare decisis* - the maxim that, in the interests of consistency, like case should be decided in like manner. It is important to note that when jurists refer to a "like" case they do not mean that the facts are (necessarily) alike. What matters to the common lawyer is that the principle by which the earlier case was decided (the *ratio decidendi*) is applicable to the later case. Any similarity as to factual detail is incidental.

onomastic *adj.* Describing a signature that is written in a different handwriting from that of the document to which it is attached.

onus of proof *See* BURDEN OF PROOF.

onus probandi *See* BURDEN OF PROOF.

open contract A contract for the sale of land in which the only express terms are the identity of the parties, the property, and the price. An open contract is valid if it is in writing or, for contracts made before the Law of Property (Miscellaneous Provisions) Act 1989 came into force, it is evidenced by writing (*see* MEMORANDUM IN WRITING) or *part performance. Other necessary terms are implied, including:

(1) a condition that the vendor must convey an unencumbered freehold title, although the purchaser is bound by any defect of which he knew and which cannot be removed;

(2) the vendor must within a reasonable time produce at his own expense an abstract of title beginning with a *root of title at least 15 years old or, in the case of registered land, the documents specified by the Land Registration Act 2002;

(3) a condition that the vendor will convey as *beneficial owner;

(4) the purchaser must deliver any *requisitions on or objections to the title within a reasonable time after receiving the abstract;

(5) the conveyance must be prepared by the purchaser at his own expense;

(6) the vendor must give vacant possession on completion;

(7) the transaction must be completed within a reasonable time: if it is not, the vendor is entitled to interest on the unpaid price and the purchaser to the income of the property from the time when completion should have occurred.

In the case of contracts made by correspondence, statutory conditions set out in regulations made under the Law of Property Act 1925 apply (*see* STATUTORY FORM OF CONDITIONS OF SALE). A vendor cannot insist on preparing the conveyance himself (a contractual term to this effect is void), but apart from this the implied and statutory conditions may be dispensed with, varied, or supplemented by agreement between the parties. In practice, the forms of contract generally used specify the parties' rights and obligations much more precisely.

open court A courtroom that is open to the public. A *hearing must usually be held in open court but in some circumstances may be held *in camera.*

open for signature When states have negotiated a treaty they settle its form and content by drawing up a text setting out its provisions. In expressing their agreement with this body of text, states are said to "adopt" the text. However, this is distinct from their agreement to be bound by its provisions, which occurs when representatives with full powers have signed the text. In the interval between adoption and signature the treaty is said to be "open for signature".

opening speech 1. A speech made by the prosecution counsel at the beginning of a criminal trial, briefly outlining the case against the accused and summarizing the evidence that the prosecution intends to call to prove its case. 2. The speech made by counsel for the claimant at the beginning of a civil trial.

open procedure *See* PUBLIC PROCUREMENT.

open space An area in a *conservation area so designated by the Secretary of State for the Environment and consequently requiring "special attention" for planning purposes.

open the floodgates A metaphor used by jurists to reflect the fear of opening up one area of law to a flood of litigation. Such an opening can easily be created either by statute or by case law and judges often express their fear of "opening the floodgates," – that is, to claims in law "undeterminant in amount, time and class" (*Ultramarine Corp. v Touche* 174 NE 441 (NY 1931) per Cardozo J at 444).

operative mistake *See* MISTAKE.

operative part *See* DEED.

operative words The part of a conveyance that effects the essence of the transaction; for example, the words "the Vendor hereby conveys Blackacre to the Purchaser in fee simple", or, as most commonly used now on the Land Registry form TR1, "the transferor transfers the property to the transferee". No specific form of words is necessary provided that the intention is clear.

opinio juris [Latin, from *opinio juris sive necessitatis* (whether the opinion of law is compulsory)] An essential element of *custom, one of the four sources of *international law as outlined in the Statute of the *International Court of Justice. *Opinio juris* requires that custom should be regarded as state practice amounting to a legal obligation, which distinguishes it from mere usage.

opinion *n.* **1.** A judgment in the Supreme Court (as formerly in the House of Lords. **2.** (counsel's opinion) A barrister's advice on a particular question. **3.** Advice on a case given by an *Advocate-General before a final judgment of the *Court of Justice of the European Union.

opinion evidence Evidence of the opinions or beliefs of a witness, as opposed to evidence of facts about which he can give admissible evidence. At common law, under the **opinion rule**, opinion evidence is in general inadmissible; however, this rule is subject to many exceptions, so that a witness of fact may give *evidence of identity, as well as evidence of matters of impression and narrative. Expert witnesses may give their opinions on any matter falling within their expertise that falls outside the experience and knowledge of the court. *See also* HEARSAY EVIDENCE.

OPSI *See* OFFICE OF PUBLIC SECTOR INFORMATION.

option *n.* A right to do or not to do something, usually within a specified time. An enforceable option may be acquired by contract (i.e. for consideration) or by deed to accept or reject an *offer within a specified period. An option to acquire land or an interest in it on specified terms will only bind third parties if it is registered (*see* REGISTRATION OF ENCUMBRANCES). If an option to buy does not specify the price it will only be valid if it specifies a means for determining the price, e.g. by a valuation to be made by a specified third party who is or will be under a duty to act. Thus an option to buy at a price to be agreed is void for uncertainty.

On financial markets, options to sell or to buy a fixed quantity of a commodity, currency, security, etc., at a particular price are purchased for a certain sum of money, which is forfeited if they are not taken up. An option to sell is known as a **put option**, that to buy is a **call option**, and an option to either sell or buy is a **double option**. Under the Companies Act 1985, directors, shadow directors, and the spouses or children of either are prohibited from buying or selling options in the shares of their own company. *See* SHARE OPTION.

optional clause An arrangement under which nations may give voluntary consent to the jurisdiction of the *International Court of Justice prior to a dispute taking place with another member state. Such consent can be given by the state depositing a declaration that it accepts the *compulsory jurisdiction of the court under Article 36(2) of the Statute of the United Nations until such time as notice may be given to withdraw that declaration. The original hope was that in the spirit of good international relations all, or the majority, of states would grant their consent. This hope applied particularly to the permanent members of the Security Council, whose principal function is to maintain international law and order. At present only 65 states have deposited a declaration under Article 36(2); the only permanent member of the Security Council to have done so is the UK, and its consent is subject to a reservation. France withdrew its consent following the *Nuclear Test Case* [1974] ICJ Rep 253 concerning French nuclear testing in the Pacific. The USA withdrew its declaration under the optional clause so as to attempt to deprive the Court of jurisdiction in the *Nicaragua Case* [1984] ICJ Rep 392, in which it was the defendant.

option to purchase A right to purchase land from the owner at some time in the future on agreed terms. The option remains in force for an agreed time. Such an option should be registered as an *estate contract if it affects unregistered land, or as a notice on the charges register of registered land. If it is correctly registered it may be enforced against any owner of the land, not just the person who granted it.

oral agreement A contract made by word of mouth, as opposed to one made in writing. *See also* IMPLIED CONTRACT.

oral evidence Generally, spoken evidence given by a witness in court, usually on *oath. Under the Criminal Justice Act 2003 oral evidence includes evidence that, by reason of any disability, disorder, or other impairment, a person called as a witness gives in writing or by signs or by way of any device. *See also* VIDEO EVIDENCE.

orality *n.* The principle that evidence must normally be given orally and subject to *cross-examination.

order *n.* **1.** A decision of the court other than a *judgment (which is the final decision of the court in relation to a claim). Rules relating to judgments and orders are to be found in Part 40 of the *Civil Procedure Rules. **2.** The document bearing the seal of the court recording its decision in a case. **3.** A subdivision of the *Rules of the Supreme Court and the County Court Rules, some of which are retained in Schedules 1 and 2 to the *Civil Procedure Rules.

order of committal An order sending someone to prison for *contempt of court (Glossary to the Criminal Procedure Rules).

order of discharge A court order resulting in the *discharge of a bankrupt.

orders for accounts and inquiries Interim orders that may be made at any stage of civil proceedings directing accounts to be taken or specified inquiries to be made by the court (Civil Procedure Rules Part 25). Accounts and inquiries are usually taken or made by a master or district judge.

Orders in Council Government orders of a legislative character made by the Crown and members of the Privy Council either under statutory powers conferred on Her Majesty in Council (*see* DELEGATED LEGISLATION; STATUTORY INSTRUMENT) or in exercise of the *royal prerogative. *Compare* ORDERS OF COUNCIL.

Orders of Council Orders of a legislative nature made by the Privy Council under statutory powers conferred on the Council alone. They relate mainly to the regulation of certain professions and professional bodies. *See* DELEGATED LEGISLATION. *Compare* ORDERS IN COUNCIL.

ordinance *n.* One of the forms taken by legislation under the *royal prerogative, normally legislation relating to UK dependencies.

ordinarily resident In the UK *capital gains tax rules, an individual "ordinarily resident" in the UK is subject to the tax even if not actually resident in the UK. Such a status might be held by an individual imprisoned in a foreign jail or a backpacker during the gap year between school and university. However, even a short period of not being resident in the UK is, for most individuals, likely to involve a period of not being ordinarily resident. In *Reed v Clark* [1985] STC 323 the court held that the musician Dave Clark had ceased to be ordinarily resident in the UK when he went to San Francisco for 13 months to avoid paying UK tax on the sale of his music. In *Shah v Barnet*

London Borough Council [1983] 2 AC 309 (HL) Lord Scarman said: "Ordinarily resident refers to a man's abode in a particular place or country which he has adopted voluntarily and for settled purposes as part of the regular order of his life for the time being, whether of short or of long duration".

"Ordinarily resident" is also the test applied to determine whether an individual qualifies for a local authority award or loan to finance the cost of university education. Decided cases appear to follow the same rationale as is used to determine the liability to capital gains tax.

Although "ordinarily resident" is also the test adopted for eligibility for child tax credits and for various social security benefits, the approach taken by the courts in these areas appears to be different. For these purposes, ordinarily resident appears to be equated with *habitual residence.

It is possible to be ordinarily resident in more than one country at the same time (*R v Secretary of State for the Home Department* ex Chugtai [1995] Imm AR 559). In contrast, it is not possible to be habitually resident in more than one country at the same time (*Re V (Abduction: Habitual Residence)* [1995] 2 FLR 992). An individual who unexpectedly returned to the UK after 15 months overseas was held to have abandoned his ordinary residence on his departure, even though he was not absent for an entire tax year (*Turberville v HMRC* [2010] UKFTT 69 (TC)).

ordinary legislative procedure Under the *Lisbon Treaty, the main procedure by which the *European Parliament and the *Council of the European Union work together to consider and enact legislation. It extends the existing *codecision procedure to a much wider area of legislation, including the EU budget, and has the effect of giving greater authority to the European Parliament.

ordinary resolution A decision reached by a simple majority (i.e. of more than 50%) of company members voting in person or by proxy. It is appropriate where no other type of resolution is expressly required by the Companies Act 2006 or the *articles of association. *Compare* SPECIAL RESOLUTION.

ordinary share *See* SHARE.

original evidence **1.** Evidence of a statement made by a person other than the testifying witness, which is offered to prove that the statement was actually made rather than to prove its truth. Thus, if in an action for slander a witness testifies that he heard the defendant defame the claimant, his testimony is original evidence. The use of the term distinguishes such evidence from *hearsay evidence. **2.** *See* DIRECT EVIDENCE.

originating summons A form of originating *process in the High Court now rendered obsolete by the Civil Procedure Rules. Under the Rules, it has been replaced by the *Part 8 claim form.

origin system A system for protecting products in which each is identified by means of an **appellation of origin**, which is similar to a trade mark but may only be used for a product from a particular region. The regulations, which cover many products, were agreed in March 1996. The scheme stops manufacturers, etc., from other regions from using local names, such as Stilton cheese, Newcastle Brown Ale, and Jersey Royal potatoes.

ouster *n.* The act of wrongfully dispossessing someone of any kind of *hereditament, such as freehold property.

ouster of jurisdiction The exclusion of judicial proceedings in respect of any dispute. There is a presumption that statutes and other documents (e.g. contracts) do not oust the jurisdiction of the courts. *See* INTERPRETATION.

outer Bar (utter Bar) Junior barristers, collectively, who sit outside the bar of the court, as opposed to *Queen's Counsel, who sit within it.

output tax The *value-added tax that is charged by a taxable person on making a supply of goods or services. *Compare* INPUT TAX.

outraging public decency *See* CONSPIRACY.

outsider jurisprudence *See* CRITICAL RACE THEORY.

outstanding term *See* SATISFIED TERM.

outworker *n. See* TELEWORKING.

overcrowding *n.* For statutory purposes a dwelling is overcrowded when two or more people of opposite sexes over the age of ten, and not married to one another or cohabiting, are obliged, because of lack of space, to sleep in the same room. There is also a test for overcrowding based on the number of people living in the dwelling compared with the number of rooms and the floor area of those rooms. Local authorities have a duty to prevent overcrowding and can take action against an owner-occupier, a landlord, or a tenant. *See* HOUSING HEALTH AND SAFETY RATING SYSTEM.

overreaching *n.* The process by which interests in land are converted on sale of the land into corresponding interests in the *capital money arising from the sale.

Where land is held on a *trust of land, the Law of Property Act 1925 provides that a purchaser of the land shall take free of the beneficiaries' interests, provided that the purchase money is paid to at least two trustees or a trust corporation (*City of London Building Society v Flegg* [1988] AC 54 (HL)). A mortgagee exercising his *power of sale is able to overreach the mortgagor's estate and *equity of redemption and convey the land free from the equitable right: the mortgagor's rights are transferred to the purchase money, the mortgagee being trustee of any such funds remaining after paying off the mortgage debt. A sale by the tenant for life of settled land also overreaches the interests of the beneficiaries.

Overreaching in general affects only equitable rights.

overriding interests Certain rights and interests in registered land, listed in Schedules 1 and 3 of the Land Registration Act 2002, that are not protected by registration but, unless overreached, will bind the registered proprietor and any third party acquiring the land or any interest in it. The list includes legal *easements and *profits *à prendre*, rights of persons in actual occupation (*Williams and Glyn's Bank Ltd v Boland* [1981] AC 487 (HL)), and leases granted for terms of up to seven years.

overriding objective The paramount duty of the court to deal with cases justly. In civil proceedings this includes ensuring the parties are on an equal footing, dealing with the case proportionately, ensuring it is dealt with expeditiously and without undue expense, and allocating an appropriate share of the court's resources (*Civil Procedure Rules Part 1). In criminal proceedings it includes acquitting the innocent and convicting the guilty, dealing with the prosecution and defence fairly, and recognizing the rights of a defendant, particularly those under Article 6 of the *European Convention on Human Rights (*Criminal Procedure Rules Part 1). Parties must prepare and conduct cases in accordance with the overriding objective and may be subject to an adverse order for costs if they fail to do so.

overrule *vb.* To set aside the decision of a court in an earlier case. Because of the doctrine of *precedent, a court can generally only overrule decisions of courts lower than itself. The setting aside of the judgment of a lower court on appeal is called a **reversal**.

oversea company A *foreign company with an established place of business in the UK. Such companies are obliged to comply with certain formalities, such as filing their constitution or charter at *Companies House and giving details of their directors and of who is authorized to accept service of legal proceedings and notices in the UK.

overseas divorce A divorce, annulment, or legal separation obtained overseas. There are different rules for the recognition of overseas divorces in the UK, according to whether or not they are obtained through judicial proceedings. An overseas divorce obtained through proceedings is recognized if: it is effective under the law of the country in which it was obtained; and either party to the marriage was habitually resident in, domiciled in, or a national of the country where it was obtained. An overseas divorce obtained otherwise than through proceedings is recognized if: it is effective under the law of the country where it was obtained; both parties were domiciled in that country, or one party was domiciled in that country and the other party was domiciled in another country that recognizes the divorce as valid; and neither party was habitually resident in the UK in the year preceding the divorce. *See also* EXTRAJUDICIAL DIVORCE.

owner-occupier *n.* A person who has legal ownership of a dwelling in which he lives or in which he lived before letting it on an *assured or *regulated tenancy. For statutory purposes, the term includes a tenant under a *long tenancy.

ownership *n.* The exclusive right to use, possess, and dispose of property, subject only to the rights of persons having a superior interest and to any restrictions on the owner's rights imposed by agreement with or by act of third parties or by operation of law. Ownership may be **corporeal**, i.e. of a material thing, which may itself be a *movable or an *immovable; or it may be **incorporeal**, i.e. of something intangible, such as of a copyright or patent. Ownership involves enjoyment of a number of rights over the property. The owner can alienate (i.e. sell or give away) some of these rights while still retaining others; for example, an owner of land may grant a right of way or a patent owner may grant a licence to manufacture the patented goods. Ownership may be held by different persons for different interests, for example when a freehold owner grants a lease or when land is held on a trust of land for persons with interests in succession to one another. More than one person can own the same property at the same time. They may be either joint owners with a single title to the property (*see* JOINT TENANCY); or owners in common, each having a distinct title in the property that he can dispose of independently (*see* TENANCY IN COMMON).

A person may be both the legal and beneficial owner, or the legal ownership of property may be separate from the beneficial (equitable) ownership (i.e. the right to enjoy the property), as when a trustee owns the legal estate in land for the benefit of another.

A legally valid transaction may confer specific rights to use, possess, or deal with property without conferring ownership of it; for example, a contract may appoint a person as the owner's agent for the sale of specified land.

See also ESTATE.

PACE Acronym for the Police and Criminal Evidence Act 1984. *See* CODE OF PRACTICE.

pact *n*. *See* TREATY.

pacta sunt servanda [Latin] Agreements are to be kept; treaties should be observed. *Pacta sunt servanda* is the bedrock of the customary international law of *treaties and, according to some authorities, the very foundation of international law. Without such an acceptance, treaties would become worthless.

pacta tertiis nec nocent nec prosunt [Latin] Treaties do not create either obligations or rights for third states without their consent.

paedophile *n*. A person who is sexually attracted to children (of either sex). Sexual activity with any child under the age of 16 is illegal. A range of specific new offences in this area was created by the Sexual Offences Act 2003. *See* CHILD ABUSE.

paid-up capital The amount actually paid to a company for shares allotted or issued to a shareholder. If a shareholder makes a full payment of the purchase price of the share, the amount received is referred to as **fully paid-up capital**. If the company permits the shareholder to make only partial payment of the total purchase price, such shares are referred to as **partly paid-up shares**, with the remaining balance recorded in the company's accounts as an amount that the company may *call upon in the future (**uncalled capital**). *See* AUTHORIZED CAPITAL.

pain and suffering The psychological consequences of personal injuries, in terms of pain, shock, consciousness that one's life expectancy has been shortened, embarrassment caused by disfigurement, etc. Damages are assessed on the extent to which the claimant actually experiences these feelings.

palatine courts Originally, courts of the counties palatine of Durham, Lancaster, and Chester. In modern times, only the Chancery courts of Durham and Lancaster survived, but their jurisdiction was transferred to the High Court by the Courts Act 1971. *See also* VICE CHANCELLOR.

Panel on Takeovers and Mergers *See* CITY CODE ON TAKEOVERS AND MERGERS.

paperless trading *See* ELECTRONIC DATA INTERCHANGE.

paper owner *See* ADVERSE POSSESSION.

parallel import A product bought in one state and imported into another by the purchaser, often to take advantage of price differences between states; such products are also known as **grey market** goods. Parallel importation usually takes place outside supplier-authorized official distribution networks. Within the EU measures taken to prevent parallel imports in the Single Market will infringe *Article 101 of the Treaty on the Functioning of the European Union (*see* EXPORT BANS). While it is permitted to restrict an exclusive distributor from soliciting sales outside his exclusive area, absolute territorial protection may not be given, either by contract terms or by conduct or oral arrangements.

paramount *adj.* (in land law) Superior; having or denoting a better right or title.

paramount clause *See* BILL OF LADING.

parcels *pl. n.* **1.** Plots of land. **2.** *See* DEED.

pardon *n.* The withdrawal of a sentence or punishment by the sovereign, on advice of the Home Secretary, under the *prerogative of mercy. Once a pardon is granted, the accused cannot be tried and if he has already been convicted, he cannot be punished. The responsibility is upon him, however, to plead the pardon as a bar to prosecution or punishment; if he does not do so as soon as possible, he may be held to have waived it. A person may also be granted a **reprieve**, i.e. the temporary suspension of a punishment (for example, if he becomes insane after sentence is passed).

parent *n.* The mother or father of a child. The term also includes adoptive parents but does not usually include *step-parents. At common law parents have **parental rights** over their children while they are minors, which include the right to physical control of the child, to control their education and determine their religion, to consent to medical treatment, to administer their property, to represent them in legal proceedings, and to discipline them reasonably. They also have **parental duties**, notably to maintain and educate their children, which can be legally enforced. Where parents are married both exercise parental rights jointly. If they are unmarried and the father does not have *parental responsibility for the child, then the mother has exclusive parental rights. The father will, however, still have a legal duty to maintain the child: *see* CHILD SUPPORT MAINTENANCE. Parental rights decline as the child grows older; in any dispute over their enforcement the welfare of the child is the paramount consideration (*see* WELFARE PRINCIPLE). *See also* PARENTS' LIABILITY; SECTION 8 ORDERS.

parental leave Time off work given to parents. The statutory provisions are contained in the Maternity and Parental Leave Regulations 1999 as amended, which set down key elements regarding such time off, although employers and employees are free to agree an improved contractual scheme.

In order to exercise the right to parental leave the employee must have been employed for a minimum of one year, must give employers a minimum of 21 days' notice, must have or expect to have responsibility for the child, and must take any leave for the purpose of caring for the child. Up to 18 weeks' parental leave is available in respect of any individual child; it must be taken before the child is five years old. *Adoption leave (for employees who adopt a child) is available on the same basis, with the proviso that the leave must be taken within five years of the placement of the child (or before the child's 18th birthday, whichever is earlier). In the case of a disabled child (i.e. one for whom an award of disability living allowance has been made), up to 18 weeks leave may be taken any time up to the child's 18th birthday.

In the absence of any contractual agreement on the operation of parental leave, the statutory provisions lay down default provisions. These state that leave must be taken in blocks of a week or more and that the maximum annual leave allowance is four weeks in respect of any individual child.

Employers may postpone the leave but only if their business would be unduly disrupted. Fathers and prospective adoptive parents who want to guarantee that they can be present at the birth or placement of their child may book time off work without postponement. No notice is required to be given by employees returning to work, and on return employees are entitled to work in their same job provided the leave was for 4 weeks or less. Employees may complain to an *employment tribunal if the employer prevents or attempts to prevent them from taking parental leave. An employee who takes parental leave is protected from dismissal for taking it.

Currently parental leave is unpaid. *See also* DEPENDANTS' LEAVE; MATERNITY RIGHTS; PATERNITY LEAVE. Changes are planned for parental leave so that after 18 weeks of maternity leave the remaining period would be classed as parental leave, and would be available to either parent.

parental order A court order made under section 54 of the Human Fertilization and Embryology Act 2008 which provides for a child born as a result of a *surrogacy agreement to be treated in law as the child of the applicants (the commissioning couple) rather than that of the surrogate mother (the mother who gave birth to the child). Once made, the order severs all legal ties with the surrogate mother; in this way it is similar to an *adoption. Certain conditions must be satisfied before the order can be made. The child must have his or her home with the applicants, and the application must be made within 6 months of birth. The applicants must be married, in a civil partnership, or in an "enduring relationship", and one of the applicants must be genetically related to the child. Crucially, the surrogate mother must fully and freely and with full understanding of what is involved have agreed unconditionally to the making of the order. Additionally, if the child has another parent (for example, the surrogate mother's husband (*see* *human assisted reproduction) then that parent also has to consent.

parental responsibility All the rights, duties, powers, and responsibilities that by law a parent of a child has in relation to the child and his or her property. The concept was introduced by the Children Act 1989, replacing *custody. Parental responsibility is automatically conferred on both parents if married. Where parents are not married, the father will automatically have parental responsibility for a child born on or after 1 December 2003 so long as he is registered as the child's father (Children Act 1989 s 4(1)(a)). Otherwise an unmarried father can acquire parental responsibility either by agreement with the mother or by applying to court for a *parental responsibility order. Both parents retain parental responsibility on divorce. Under the Children Act 1989 s 4A a step-parent who is married to, or is the civil partner of a parent, can obtain parental responsibility either by agreement or by a court order. Other persons may also acquire parental responsibility by virtue of being granted other orders. For example, anyone in whose favour a *residence order is made acquires parental responsibility for the duration of that order, and a *care order or an *emergency protection order confer parental responsibility on the relevant local authority. In all these cases, parental responsibility is shared with the parents. *See also* SPECIAL GUARDIANSHIP ORDER; STEP-PARENT.

parental responsibility agreement A formal agreement usually between the mother and unmarried father of a child conferring *parental responsibility on the father. An agreement can also be made to confer parental responsibility on a step-parent (the spouse or civil partner of the child's parent). In this case the agreement of both parents with parental responsibility is required. The agreement must be made on a set form, be signed and witnessed, and be registered in the Principal Registry of the Family Division in London. Once made, the agreement cannot be revoked by either party. Only a court may bring a parental responsibility agreement to an end – on the application of either party with parental responsibility or by the child himself if he has been given permission by the court to apply.

parental responsibility order An order made by a court conferring *parental responsibility on an *unmarried father. In determining whether or not to make such an order, the court must treat the child's welfare as its paramount consideration. Courts will usually grant a parental responsibility order to a father who is able to demonstrate some degree of commitment and attachment to his child. It is rare for a court not to make an order and these will be cases where the father has behaved irresponsibly or would be likely to abuse parental responsibility if it were granted. A parental responsibility order may be revoked by a court.

parent company *See* SUBSIDIARY COMPANY.

Parenting Agreement As proposed by the Family Justice Review (2012), a written agreement in which parents set out the arrangements to be made for their children in the event of divorce or separation, including where the child would live, contact with the other parent, financial issues, etc. Such an agreement would have weight as evidence in any subsequent dispute.

parenting order An order, introduced by the Crime and Disorder Act 1998, that requires the parent or guardian of a child under the age of 16 to comply, for a period not exceeding 12 months, with such requirements as the court considers necessary for preventing offences being committed by this child. Parents whose children have been made the subject of a *child safety order may be required to attend courses that will assist them with their parenting skills. The rationale behind the introduction of such orders was that inadequate parental supervision is thought to be strongly associated with youth offending.

parents' liability Parents are not liable for their children's torts, but they may be liable for their own negligence in failing to supervise or train young children, where the absence of supervision or training has led a child to cause damage to others. There is no fixed age determining a child's liability for its own torts. A child may, however, be too young to form the intention necessary for a particular tort. In cases in which the negligence or contributory negligence of a child is in question, the test applied is whether the child's conduct measured up to the standard of care to be expected from an average child of that age.

Parents are not legally responsible for their children's crimes, although they may be required by a court to pay their *fines.

parent with care *See* CHILD SUPPORT MAINTENANCE.

Pareto efficiency A concept often invoked in the *economic analysis of law; it was first described by the Italian economist Vilfredo Pareto (1848–1923). An alteration in the allocation of resources is Pareto efficient when it leaves at least one person better off than he was prior to the change and nobody worse off. A state of **Pareto optimality** occurs when no further improvements can be made without one party becoming a loser. *Compare* KALDOR-HICKS EFFICIENCY; COASE THEOREM.

par in parem non habet imperium [Latin: equals do not have authority over one another] In public international law, the principle that one sovereign power cannot exercise jurisdiction over another sovereign power. It is the basis of the *act of state doctrine and *sovereign immunity.

pari passu [Latin: with equal step] Proportionally, without preference. The principle that where there are competing claimants, (e.g. in bankruptcy proceedings) assets should be distributed on a *pro rata* basis, in accordance with the size of the claim.

parish *n.* A *local government area in England (outside Greater London) consisting of a division of a *district (though not all districts are so divided). All parishes have meetings and many have an elected parish council, which is a *local authority with a number of minor local governmental functions (e.g. the provision of allotments, bus shelters, and recreation grounds). A parish council may by resolution call its area a town, itself a town council, and its chairman the town mayor. The Local Government and Rating Act 1997 gives extra powers to parish councils in relation to rights of transport and crime prevention.

Paris Treaty The treaty, signed in Paris on 18 April 1951, that formed the *European Coal and Steel Community. Many of its provisions were similar to those of the later *Treaty of Rome, establishing the EEC, for example in the fields of *competition law and *state aid. The Treaty expired in 2002.

parking offences Offences relating to parking a motor vehicle. These include parking a vehicle within the limits of a pedestrian crossing or wherever signs or kerb markings indicate that parking is prohibited or restricted and failing to comply with the regulations associated with the use of parking meters. If the accused can show that road markings or signs indicating parking restrictions were absent or deficient, he may be acquitted. Parking offences are punishable by fine only; they are not subject to endorsement. *See also* OBSTRUCTION.

parlementaire *n.* [from French *parlementer*, to discuss terms; parley] An agent employed by a commander of a belligerent force in the field whose function is to go in person within the enemy lines for the purpose of communicating or negotiating openly and directly with the enemy commander.

Parliament *n.* The legislature of the UK, consisting of the sovereign, the House of Lords, and the House of Commons. Under the Parliament Act 1911, the maximum duration of any particular Parliament is five years, after which its functions expire. In practice, a Parliament's life always ends by its earlier **dissolution** by the sovereign under the *royal prerogative; this proclamation also summons its successor. The date of dissolution was usually chosen by the Prime Minister but the Fixed-term Parliaments Act 2011 fixed the date of the next general election as 7 May 2015. The life of a Parliament is divided into sessions, normally of one year each, which are ended when Parliament is prorogued (also under the prerogative) by a royal commission. Each House divides a session into sittings, normally of a day's duration, which end when a motion for adjournment is passed. The functions of Parliament are the enactment of legislation (*see* ACT OF PARLIAMENT), the sanctioning of taxation and public expenditure, and the scrutiny and criticism of government policy and administration. *See also* SOVEREIGNTY OF PARLIAMENT.

Parliamentary Commissioner for Administration *See* PARLIAMENTARY OMBUDSMAN.

parliamentary committees *See* COMMITTEE OF THE WHOLE HOUSE; GRAND COMMITTEE; JOINT COMMITTEE ON STATUTORY INSTRUMENTS; STANDING COMMITTEE; SELECT COMMITTEE.

parliamentary counsel Civil servants (barristers or solicitors) who draft government Bills, government amendments to Bills, and any procedural motions required in connection with the passing of Bills. In 1996 proposals to contract out this activity to private practice lawyers were considered.

Parliamentary Ombudsman (Parliamentary Commissioner for Administration) An independent official appointed under the Parliamentary Commissioner Act 1967 (as amended by the Parliamentary and Health Service Commissioners Act 1987) to investigate complaints by individuals or corporate bodies of injustice arising from maladministration by a government department or by certain nondepartmental public bodies, such as the Arts Councils and the *Housing Corporation. Appointment of the Ombudsman is by the Crown on the Prime Minister's advice. The Ombudsman may investigate complaints only if they are submitted to him in writing through a Member of Parliament; investigation is entirely at his discretion. If he upholds a complaint and it is not remedied, he reports this to Parliament. Complaints of maladministration by devolved bodies in Wales and Scotland are investigated by the Welsh Administration Ombudsman and the Scottish Parliamentary Commissioner for Administration, respectively. *See also* HEALTH SERVICE COMMISSIONERS.

(⊕) SEE WEB LINKS
• Website of the Parliamentary and Health Service Ombudsman

parliamentary papers Papers published on the authority of either House of Parliament. They include Bills, the Official Reports of Parliamentary Debates (*see* HANSARD), and reports of parliamentary committees.

parliamentary privilege Special rights and immunities enjoyed by the Houses of Parliament and their members to enable them to carry out their functions effectively and without external interference. They are conferred mainly by the common law but partly by statute; they can be extended by statute but not by the resolution of either House.

The Commons have five main privileges:

(1) The right of collective access to the sovereign through the Speaker.
(2) The right of individual members to be free from civil (but not criminal) arrest. Since the abolition of imprisonment for debt, this privilege has been of only minor significance, but it would still shield a member against (for example) imprisonment for disobeying a court order in civil proceedings.
(3) The individual right to freedom of speech. This substantial privilege means that a member cannot be made liable either civilly (e.g. for defamation) or criminally (e.g. for breach of the Official Secrets Acts) for anything said by him in the course of debates or other parliamentary proceedings. Under the Parliamentary Papers Act 1840 members are also not liable for statements repeated in reports published on the authority of the House.
(4) The collective right to exclusive control of its own proceedings, so that it can (for example) exclude the public, prohibit reporting, and expel any member whom it may consider unfit to sit.
(5) The collective right to punish for any **breach of privilege** or other **contempt**. Examples of breaches of privilege are initiating defamation proceedings in respect of privileged words and the reporting of secret proceedings. Other contempts include any conduct prejudicial to the proper functioning or dignity of the House, e.g. by refusing to give evidence to a committee, bribing members, or insulting the House. Members may be punished for contempt by expulsion, suspension, or imprisonment; others by reprimand or imprisonment. Imprisonment is terminated by prorogation. Whether or not particular conduct amounts to a contempt, and if so what punishment (if any) is appropriate, is considered by the Committee of Privileges, whose report the House is free to accept or reject after debate.

The privileges of the Lords are similar, except that members have an individual right of access to the sovereign and the House can fine for contempt and imprison for a fixed term, which is not affected by prorogation.

parol contract *See* SIMPLE CONTRACT.

parole (release on licence) *n.* The conditional *release of a prisoner from prison. Under the Criminal Justice Act 2003, anyone sentenced to imprisonment for more than 12 months must be released on licence after serving one-half of the sentence, providing the offender is not a *dangerous offender. The conditions of the offender's parole will be determined by the Secretary of State, with advice from the probation service. Parole remains in force until the end of the offender's sentence. If a prisoner on parole commits an offence during the period of his original sentence, he may have to serve any part of the original sentence still outstanding. In such cases limitations are imposed on his right to be considered again for parole.

parol evidence 1. In court proceedings, evidence given orally, as opposed to *documentary evidence. **2.** *See* EXTRINSIC EVIDENCE; PAROL EVIDENCE RULE.

parol evidence rule The common law principle that *extrinsic evidence cannot generally be given to contradict, alter, or vary the terms of a written document, unless there are allegations of mistake, illegality, or fraud. Under the parol evidence rule, a written contract cannot normally be contradicted by any evidence of prior oral or written statements by the parties (e.g. statements made during the negotiations).

parol lease A lease that is made either orally or in writing, but not by deed, and fulfils certain conditions. These are that it takes effect in possession immediately it is made; it is for a period less than three years; and it is at the full market rent. *Periodic tenancies usually fulfil these conditions. Parol leases are the exception to the general rule that leases are not legally enforceable unless they are made by deed (Law of Property Act 1925 s 54(2)).

Part 8 claim form A form of originating *process used in cases in which the issues are likely to be ones of law or the interpretation of documents. It should not be used when disputed questions of fact are involved, for which proceedings begun by normal *claim form are more appropriate. A Part 8 claim form must state that Part 8 of the Civil Procedure Rules applies and must set out the question the claimant wants the court to decide or the remedy that he seeks. Any evidence relied upon must be filed and served with the claim form. Part 8 claims are allocated as *multi-track proceedings.

Part 20 claim A claim other than a claim by the claimant against the defendant. It includes (1) a *counterclaim by the defendant against the claimant; (2) a counterclaim by the defendant against a third party (i.e. a person who is not a party to the current proceedings), normally with the claimant; and (3) a claim by the defendant for an *indemnity or a *contribution from either a third party or from a party to the current proceedings. If the defendant to a claim alleges that a third party is liable to indemnify him or contribute to any judgment, or is someone that they seek to counterclaim against in addition to the claimant, he must bring that party into the proceedings by issuing a Part 20 claim form. Once done, the third party becomes known as the **Part 20 defendant.**

A defendant can issue a Part 20 claim form without requiring permission of the court if it is issued before or at the time of the filing of his defence. Directions in such a case will be dealt with as part of the normal system of *case management appropriate to the track to which the case has been allocated. If the time in which the defence must be filed has expired, permission is required from the court. This is normally sought by the use of an application notice filed at court and supported by evidence of reasons why the third party be introduced into the proceedings. If granted, the court will issue directions at that time. In any event, the court will consider further directions as to the future conduct of the proceedings when the time for filing the defence to the Part 20 claim by the third party or co-defendant has expired.

Part 36 offers and payments Under the *Civil Procedure Rules, offers and payments made by parties in the pretrial period in an attempt to encourage a settlement out of court. A **Part 36 payment** (formerly called **payment into court**) is made into the court; it can only be made once legal proceedings have started and only in respect of money claims. A **Part 36 offer** (formerly called a **Calderbank letter** or **offer**) can be made in the period before the start of proceedings or – in respect of nonmonetary claims – after proceedings have started. Both procedures place pressure on the other party to the litigation to settle.

In the case of a Part 36 payment, the other party is notified of the payment and that it may accept or reject the payment as a settlement. In the event of a rejection and the litigation proceeding to trial, the amount awarded is compared with the amount paid in. If the amount awarded is less than the sum previously paid into court, costs since the time of payment in will be awarded against the successful claimant. Part 36 offers have a similar purpose and effect in that the court will consider the contents of the offer when it considers the issue of costs, after finding liability and settling the amount of damages.

partial loss (in marine insurance) Any loss of the subject matter of an insurance policy other than an *actual total loss or a *constructive total loss. In the case of a partial loss there is a lesser measure of indemnity than in the case of a total loss. *See also* AVERAGE.

partibility *n.* (of chattels) *See* PARTITION OF CHATTELS.

participator *n.* Any person having a share or interest in the capital or income of a company. This includes:
- any person who possesses, or is entitled to acquire, share capital or voting rights;
- any loan creditor;
- any person who possesses a right to receive a premium on redemption;
- any person who is entitled to secure that income or assets will be applied directly or indirectly for his benefit.

particular average *See* AVERAGE.

particular lien *See* LIEN.

particulars *pl. n.* Details of an allegation of fact made by either side in civil proceedings. Under Part 16 of the *Civil Procedure Rules details of a claim (the **particulars of claim**) may be set out in the *claim form or served separately on the defendant. *See also* STATEMENT OF CASE.

parties *pl. n.* **1.** Persons who are involved in some transaction, e.g. the parties to a deed or a contract. **2.** Persons who are involved in litigation, either civil or criminal. A party is defined in the Glossary to the *Criminal Procedure Rules as a person or organization directly involved in a criminal case, either as prosecutor or defendant. *See also* JOINDER OF PARTIES.

partition *n.* **1.** The division of a territory into two or more units, each under a different government. **2.** The division of supreme power over a territory between different governments (e.g. federal and state). **3.** The formal separation, effected by deed, of land held in common ownership into parts, so that each co-owner takes his part solely, beneficially, and free from any rights of the others. Partition of land cannot be enforced without the consent of all the co-owners. **4.** The transfer to different companies of parts of a trade or undertaking (or two or more trades or undertakings) of a company. This is usually by means of a distribution agreement or a demerger under the Income and Corporation Taxes Act 1988. *Compare* PARTITION OF CHATTELS.

partition of chattels The division between co-owners of chattels held in undivided shares, so that each takes his part of the goods solely and absolutely. If chattels are **partible** (i.e. capable of being divided), the court may order partition under the Law of Property Act 1925 on the application of a co-owner.

partnership *n.* An association of two or more people formed for the purpose of carrying on a business with a view to profit. Partnerships are governed by the Partnership Act 1890. Unlike an incorporated *company, a partnership does not have a legal personality of its own and therefore partners are liable for the debts of the firm. On leaving the firm they remain liable for debts already incurred; they cease to be liable for future debts if proper notice of retirement has been published. A **limited partnership** is governed by the Limited Partnership Act 1907. It consists of **general partners**, who are fully liable for partnership debts, and **limited partners**, who are liable to the extent of their investment. Limited partners lose their limits of liability if they take part in management. A **partnership at will** is one for which no fixed duration has been agreed. Any partner may end the partnership at any time provided that he gives notice of his intention to do so to all the other partners, subject to any restriction in the partnership deed. *See also* LIMITED LIABILITY PARTNERSHIP.

part performance A doctrine of equity that a contract required to be evidenced in writing will still be enforceable even if it is not so evidenced provided that one of the parties does certain acts by which the contract is partly performed. For an act to bring the doctrine into play (i.e. a sufficient act of part performance) that act must be performed by the person alleging the contract to exist and must relate unequivocally to the contract; an example would be taking possession of property alleged to have been sold (under a contract entered into before 21 September 1989) to the person who takes possession. It is unclear whether mere payment of money is a sufficient act of part performance.

This doctrine applied primarily to contracts for the sale of land. However, such contracts entered into on or after 21 September 1989 are required, under the Law of Property (Miscellaneous Provisions) Act 1989, to be in writing (not merely evidenced in writing) if they are to be valid. Acts of part performance will not, as such, validate an unwritten land contract, although they may, in particular circumstances, give rise to a proprietary *estoppel or a *constructive trust.

part-time worker Under the Part-time Workers (Prevention of Less favourable Treatment) Regulations 2000, any worker whose hours are less than those of a full-time worker in that employment. Part-time workers are entitled to no less favourable treatment than full-timers; however, this applies only where (a) there is a full-time worker on a similar contract and (b) the only reason for the less favourable treatment is that the worker is a part-timer. Employers have a defence if they can objectively justify the less favourable treatment on some other ground. Case: *Matthews v Kent and Medway Towns Fire Authority* [2004] IRLR 697 (CA).

party wall A wall or fence in premises that is shared with another owner or tenant in adjacent premises. The Party Wall Act 1996, which came into force on 1 July 1997, imposes obligations on owners carrying out works on party walls or fences. They must notify the adjoining owner or tenant in advance if they intend to repair a party wall or fence or build on a boundary; any damage that occurs as a result of the work must be repaired.

passing off Conducting one's business in such a way as to mislead the public into thinking that one's goods or services are those of another business. The commonest form of passing off is marketing goods with a design, packaging, or trade name that is very similar to that of someone else's goods. It is not necessary to prove an intention to deceive: innocent passing off is actionable.

passport *n.* A document, issued under the *royal prerogative by the Home Office through its executive agency the Passport Agency, that provides prima facie evidence of the holder's nationality. It is not required by law for leaving the UK, but it is required for entry into most other countries. Within the European Union, EU nationals are sent through quicker channels of entry although they are still subject to occasional passport checks, despite the Schengen Agreement reached by most EU states to abolish internal border checks, which came into force on 26 March 1995, and the creation of the *Single Market in the EU, which came into force on 1 January 1993. Concerns such as drug smuggling have made member states of the EU reluctant to abandon internal controls. The issue of a passport is purely discretionary and the government may withdraw or revoke a passport at will. Under the Immigration Act 1988, a person seeking entry into the UK on the basis of his *right of abode there must either produce an appropriate passport or a certificate showing such an entitlement, issued by or on behalf of the UK government. The British Visitor's Passport has been abolished and only a full British passport is adequate for foreign travel. Children need their own passports. However, children included on a parental passport before 5 October 1998 may continue to travel abroad on that passport either until reaching the age of 16 or until the passport is submitted for an amendment. The English courts have power to order the surrender of a foreign passport to protect the interest of children who might otherwise be removed unlawfully from the UK by a foreign parent. Similar powers to order surrender of a UK passport are contained in the Family Law Act 1986.

(((●))) SEE WEB LINKS

• Website of HM Passport Office

past consideration *See* CONSIDERATION.

pasture *n.* A *profit *à prendre* or *common conferring rights of grazing over another's land or on common land, which may be limited to particular types of animal, to fixed numbers of animals, or (in the case of a common) to as many animals as the land will support.

patent *n.* The grant of an exclusive right to exploit an invention. In the UK patents are granted by the Crown through the **Intellectual Property Office** (**IPO**: formerly the Patent Office), which is an executive agency of the Department for Business, Innovation and Skills. An applicant for a patent (usually the inventor or his employer) must show that the invention is new, is not obvious, and is capable of industrial application. An expert known as a **patent agent** often prepares the application, which must describe the invention in considerable detail. The IPO publishes these details if it grants a patent. A patent remains valid for 20 years from the date of application (the **priority date**) provided that the person to whom it has been granted (the **patentee**) continues to pay the appropriate fees. During this time, the patentee may assign his patent or grant licences to use it. Such transactions are registered in a public register at the Patent Office. If anyone infringes his monopoly, the patentee may sue for an *injunction and *damages or an *account of profits. However, a patent from the IPO gives exclusive rights in the UK only: the inventor must obtain a patent from the European Patent Office in Munich and patents in other foreign countries if he wishes to protect the invention elsewhere. For patents internationally the Patent Co-operation Treaty procedure can be used. A *COMMUNITY PATENT covering all EU states except Spain and Italy is likely to become available in 2014. *See also* UTILITY MODEL.

(()) SEE WEB LINKS
- Advice on applying for a patent from the Intellectual Property Office website
- Website of the Chartered Institute of Patent Agents: includes an introduction to patents and other forms of intellectual property

patent ambiguity *See* AMBIGUITY.

patent defect *See* DEFECT.

patentee *n*. A person who has been granted a *patent.

Patents County Court *See* INTELLECTUAL PROPERTY ENTERPRISE COURT.

Patents Court Collectively, the *Patents County Court and the **Patents Court of the High Court**. The latter forms part of the *Chancery Division of the High Court, having jurisdiction over matters arising under the Patents Acts 1949–77, the Registered Designs Acts 1949–61, and the Defence Contracts Act 1958, as well as the inherent jurisdiction of the High Court. Two *puisne judges of the Chancery Division with special experience of patent law are assigned to hear cases, but they will be assisted by special scientific advisers.

paternity leave After the birth of a child an *employee who has or expects to have responsibility for bringing up the child, and who is the father of the child or the mother's husband or partner, may take either one week or two consecutive weeks' paternity leave (not odd days). The employee must have worked for the employer for 26 weeks ending with the 15th week before the baby is due. The leave may start from the date of the birth (whether this is earlier or later than expected) or from another date but it must be completed within 56 days of the birth (or, if the child is born early, within the period from the actual date of birth up to 56 days after the first day of the expected week of birth). During paternity leave, most employees are entitled to **statutory paternity pay (SPP)**. SPP is paid by employers for either one or two consecutive weeks as the employee has chosen. The rate is the same as the standard rate of Statutory Maternity Pay (*see* MATERNITY RIGHTS). Employees must inform their employers of their intention to take paternity leave by the end of the 15th week before the baby is expected, unless this is not reasonably practicable. They must tell their employer when the baby is due, how much leave they want, and when they want it to start. Employees are entitled to return to the same job after paternity leave and are protected from suffering unfair treatment or dismissal for taking, or seeking to take, such leave. Fathers may also claim additional paternity leave by taking some of the leave to which the mother would have been entitled. If the mother is not entitled to maternity rights, additional paternity rights do not apply. If the mother has taken at least 20 weeks maternity leave and has returned to work, the father may claim up to 26 weeks paternity leave. During the leave the father is entitled to be paid at the same rate as statutory maternity pay but the payment period cannot extend beyond the 39 weeks of the mother's entitlement to statutory maternity pay. Changes are planned for *parental leave that will supersede some of the rules on paternity leave. *See also* ADOPTION LEAVE; DEPENDANTS' LEAVE; PARENTAL LEAVE.

patient lacking capacity *See* INCOMPETENT PATIENT.

patient with capacity *See* COMPETENT PATIENT.

pawn (pledge) *n.* An item of goods transferred by the owner (the **pawnor**) to another (the **pawnee**) as security for a debt. (The word is also used for the transfer itself.) A pawn involves a *bailment and the pawnor remains owner of the goods; the pawnee is liable for failure to take reasonable care of them. If the pawnor fails to repay the loan at the agreed time, the pawnee has the right at common law to sell the pawn; he must account to the pawnor for any surplus after discharging his debt. **Pawnbrokers** are dealers licensed to lend money at a specified rate of interest on the security of a pawn. Pawnbroking is regulated by provisions of the Consumer Credit Act 1974 (replacing the Pawnbrokers Acts 1872 and 1960) with regard to such matters as pawn receipts, rates of interest, redemption period and procedure, consequences of failure to redeem, and realization of the pawn. Under the Act, a pawn can be redeemed at any time within six months, or longer if agreed by both parties. At the end of the redemption period ownership of the pawn passes to the pawnbroker if the redemption period is six months and the value of the debt is £25 or less. If it is more than £25 the pawnbroker may sell the pawn after giving the pawnor notice, but the pawnor may still redeem the pawn at any time until it is sold. The pawnbroker must account to the pawnor for any surplus from the proceeds of sale after discharging his debt but he may claim any balance of the debt if the proceeds are insufficient.

Pay As You Earn (PAYE) A system for collecting *income tax in which the employer deducts tax direct from the employee's pay. HM Revenue and Customs gives every employee a code number, which the employer uses, together with tax tables (now ususally in the form of computer software), to work out how much tax to deduct. The employer is then responsible for paying the tax to the Revenue by the 19th day of the following month.

((⊕)) SEE WEB LINKS
• An introduction to PAYE for employers from the HM Revenue and Customs website

payment by post The payment of a debt by the posting of notes, a cheque, or some other negotiable instrument. If the letter is lost in the post, the debt is not discharged unless the creditor has expressly or by implication requested payment by post and the debtor has sent a properly addressed letter.

payment in due course Payment made at or after the *maturity of a *bill of exchange to the holder of the bill by a payer in good faith and without notice that the holder's title to the bill is defective. A bill is discharged by payment in due course by or on behalf of the drawee or acceptor. When a bill is paid by the drawer or endorser it is not discharged and the party paying may have rights on it.

payment into court In civil proceedings, the payment by a defendant, into an account maintained by the court, of a sum in satisfaction of any or all of the claims made against him. Under the *Civil Procedure Rules, this is now referred to as **Part 36 payment**. *See* PART 36 OFFERS AND PAYMENTS.

payroll deduction scheme An arrangement under which an employee instructs his employer to pay a sum out of his salary to a specified charity. Tax relief is granted on the charitable donation, so that the employee is subjected to income tax on only the amount he receives after the donation (Finance Act 2000 s 38).

pay statement *See* ITEMIZED PAY STATEMENT.

PCC *See* POLICE AND CRIME COMMISSIONER.

PCPs *See* POLICE AND CRIME PANELS.

PCT *See* PRIMARY CARE TRUST.

peaceful assembly *See* FREEDOM OF ASSOCIATION.

peaceful enjoyment of possessions A right set out in Article 1 of the First Protocol to the European Convention on Human Rights and now part of UK law as a consequence of the *Human Rights Act1998. This right is a *qualified right; as such, the public interest can be used to justify an interference with it providing that this is prescribed by law, designed for a legitimate purpose, and proportionate. Therefore the state may deprive individuals of their possessions and control of the use of property providing that this is prescribed by law, in the public interest, and proportionate.

peculate *vb.* To rob or embezzle, especially from public funds.

pecuniary legacy *See* LEGACY.

peer-reviewed statements A statutory defence in *defamation. It applies to statements published in a scientific or academic journal that have been reviewed both by the editor of the journal and by an independent assessor. The defence, which extends the scope of *qualified privilege, was introduced by the Defamation Act 2013.

penal notice *See* CONTEMPT OF COURT.

penal statute A statute that creates a criminal offence or provides for any penalty (e.g. a forfeiture) enforceable in civil proceedings. It is subject to strict construction (*see* INTERPRETATION).

penalty *n.* **1.** A *punishment for a crime. A penalty must be clearly stated before it can be enforced. When statute creates an offence and specifies a penalty without saying how the offence is to be tried, there may be an implication that it is to be imposed by a magistrates' court. **Retrospective penalties** are penalties imposed by the criminal law for behaviour that was not an offence at the time it occurred. This is contrary to the principle of the common law and to Article 7 of the European Convention on Human Rights and therefore the Human Rights Act 1998. **2.** A sum specified in a contract as payable on its breach but not constituting a genuine estimate of the likely loss. Case: *Dunlop Pneumatic Tyre Co Ltd v New Garage and Motor Co Ltd* [1915] AC 79 (HL). *See* DAMAGES. **3.** A sum that may be levied on a taxpayer who fails to make a correct tax return as required by statute. Where a taxpayer fails to make a return, a fixed penalty is leviable. Where a taxpayer fraudulently or negligently delivers an incorrect return, the penalty is calculated as a percentage of the tax lost by the taxpayer's fraud or negligence. HM Revenue and Customs has the power to mitigate a penalty. Tax penalties have been held to be punishments for crime. Under Article 6 of the European Convention on Human Rights, therefore, the imposition of a tax penalty is subject to the citizen's right to a fair trial (*King v Walden* [2001] STC 822 (Ch)). *See also* SURCHARGE.

penalty points *See* TOTTING UP.

pendente lite [Latin] Until trial. When a will or the right to administer an estate is being disputed in a *probate action, the High Court may if necessary appoint an administrator *pendente lite* to deal with the estate until the proceedings have been resolved. Once the proceedings have been resolved, the grant *pendente lite* is terminated and the person entitled as a result of the probate action may take out a *grant of representation. An administrator *pendente lite* cannot distribute any of the estate without leave of the Court (Supreme Court Act 1981 s 117).

pending land action Proceedings in court that relate to land or to some interest in it. The claimant should register the pending action as a land charge for unregistered land, or by the entry of a notice or restriction for registered land as soon as the proceedings begin. If he fails to do this a purchaser acquiring the land without knowing of the action will not be bound by the outcome.

penology **1.** The study of penal policy and the methods and processes used to punish crime. Its subjects include the nature, purpose, and effectiveness of *punishment. *See also* CRIMINOLOGY. **2.** More specifically, the study of prison management.

pension *n.* Income paid to a person who has reached the state *retirement age (retirement pension) or who has retired from employment and benefits from a company pension or an annuity purchased under a personal pension scheme (*see also* STAKEHOLDER PENSION). Contributions to a company pension scheme are made net of tax. Pensions paid are taxable in the hands of the recipient, although a proportion of the fund accumulated in a personal pension scheme can be taken as a tax-free lump sum on retirement. *See also* STATE SECOND PENSION.

(⊕) SEE WEB LINKS
- Information about state pension provision from the Directgov website
- Website of the Pensions Regulator: includes codes of practice and guidance for employers, trustees, and their advisers

pension earmarking A provision for financial relief on granting a divorce or judicial separation that, when the pension of one spouse (the main earner) becomes payable, part of its benefits will be paid to the other spouse. Thus on the death of the main earner, all payments will cease. *See also* PENSION SHARING ORDER.

pension sharing order An order that may be made by the court on granting a divorce, whereby the spouse with little or no pension either becomes a member of the main earner's pension scheme in her or his own right or, alternatively, receives a transfer of a designated percentage of this scheme into her or his own pension arrangement. Unlike *pension earmarking, pension sharing does not apply to *judicial separation.

peppercorn rent An insignificant rent reserved for the purpose of showing that a lease or tenancy is granted for valuable *consideration.

per autre vie *See* ESTATE PUR (OR PER) AUTRE VIE.

per capita [Latin: by heads] For each person. Distribution of an estate or fund *per capita* is an equal distribution in the specified shares among all those entitled to it. *Compare* PER STIRPES.

percipient witness *See* DIRECT EVIDENCE.

per curiam (*per cur.*) [Latin] By the court. A proposition *per curiam* is one made by the judge (or, if there is more than one judge, assented to by all).

peremptory challenge *See* CHALLENGE TO JURY.

peremptory norm *See* JUS COGENS.

peremptory pleas *See* PLEAS IN BAR.

perfect and imperfect rights Legally recognized rights. Perfect rights are enforceable through court action but imperfect rights are not.

perfect trust *See* EXECUTED TRUST.

performance bond *See* BOND.

performance of contract The carrying out of obligations under a contract. Performance by both parties discharges the contract completely; performance by one party discharges him alone. The rules relating to performance distinguish between a **divisible contract** and an **indivisible** (or **entire**) **contract**. In a divisible contract the obligations of the parties are independent of each other, so that one party can demand performance by the other without rendering performance himself. Thus a landlord, though liable to be sued by his tenant for not carrying out a repairing covenant, is not prevented by his own default from enforcing the tenant's covenant to pay rent. Most contracts, however, are indivisible, i.e. the obligations of the parties are interdependent. Neither party can demand performance unless he himself either has performed or is ready and willing to do so. At common law, complete and precise performance was originally required, so that a party who rendered anything short of this (for example, a builder who carried out the contract work, but defectively in some respects) could recover nothing for his efforts. This extreme position was subsequently modified by the doctrine of **substantial performance**. A party who has substantially performed his obligations can now recover the contract price, reduced by damages awarded to the other party in respect of the defects (*Hoenig v Isaacs* [1952] 2 All ER 176 (CA)).

A **tender of performance** is the equivalent of performance, so that a seller who tenders the correct goods is discharged from the contract (and entitled to damages for breach) if the buyer rejects them. **Vicarious performance** (e.g. by a subcontractor) is good performance, except when personal performance is demanded by the contract. *See also* PART PERFORMANCE; SPECIFIC PERFORMANCE.

performers' rights The rights of performers, such as musicians, in the live performance of their works, to prevent others recording their performances. The rights are also infringed if anyone broadcasts a qualifying performance under the Copyright, Designs and Patents Act 1988 without consent or imports a recording of such a performance knowing that it was an illicit recording. The right is owned by the performer, although in commercial practice many performers enter into exclusive recording contracts in relation to their works, which give recording rights to a record company; in this case the company obtains *copyright in the sound recording and the performer loses his rights for the duration of the contract. The Copyright Term Directive 93/98 harmonized EU law in this area. Performers' rights must be protected under national law; the right must exist for 50 years from the end of the calendar year in which the performance takes place. Directive 2011/77, which is due to be implemented in the UK in November 2013, will extend this period to 70 years after death.

perils of the seas One of the heads of risk included in a marine insurance policy. It covers the insured against loss caused by fortuitous accidents or casualties of the seas, e.g. such events as unusual violence of wind or waves, striking submerged rocks, and collisions with other ships. The ordinary action of wind and waves in causing wear and tear is not, however, regarded as a peril of the seas.

per incuriam [Latin] Through lack of care. A decision of a court is made *per incuriam* if it fails to apply a relevant statutory provision or ignores a binding precedent.

periodic tenancy A tenancy in which rent is payable at fixed intervals, usually weekly, monthly, quarterly, or yearly. The tenancy continues automatically from one period to another until terminated by *notice to quit. Periodic tenancies can be created by express agreement. Alternatively they can be created by implication when rent is accepted by the owner of the land from the person who occupies it. This may arise, for example, when a tenant under a *fixed-term tenancy remains in possession at the end of his tenancy and the landlord continues to accept rent from him. The length of notice required to terminate the tenancy is usually the same as one of the periods of the tenancy (*Prudential Assurance Co Ltd v London Residuary Body* [1992] 2 AC 386).

perished goods Under the Sale of Goods Act 1979, goods under a contract of sale that have been either totally destroyed or so damaged that they no longer fit the contract description. The Act provides that a contract is void if it relates to specific goods that, unknown to the seller, have perished before it is made. If the goods perish after the contract is made, this event will make the contract void unless the risk has by then passed to the buyer (*see* TRANSFER OF RISK). These two propositions give statutory recognition to common-law rules relating to *mistake and *frustration of contract, respectively.

perjury *n.* The offence of giving false evidence or evidence that one does not believe to be true (even if it is in fact the truth). It is punishable by up to seven years' imprisonment and/or a fine. The offence may be committed by any witness who has taken the oath or affirmed, by the defendant at any stage of the trial, and by an interpreter. Perjury is only committed, however, in judicial proceedings, which include any proceedings before a court, tribunal, or someone with the power to hear evidence on oath (e.g. Commissioners of Income Tax hearing appeals against tax assessments). The evidence given must be relevant to the proceedings and must be given with knowledge that it is false or recklessly.

The Perjury Act 1911 also creates various offences related to perjury. These include making a **false statement** on oath in nonjudicial proceedings and making a false statement or declaration relating to marriage (e.g. to obtain a licence to marry or make an entry in a register of marriage) or to the registration of a birth or death. These offences are punishable by up to seven years' imprisonment on indictment. The offences of making a false statement in a statutory declaration or in any account, balance sheet, or document required to be made by Act of Parliament are punishable by up to two years' imprisonment. *See also* SUBORNATION.

Permanent Court of Arbitration A standing panel of jurists established in 1900 under the 1899 *Hague Convention for the pacific settlement of disputes. Despite the name, it is neither permanent nor is it a court. Rather, it is a mechanism for promoting the creation of arbitration tribunals as required. Although resort to the Court is infrequent, it is by no means redundant: its facilities have been used, for example, by the Iran–United States Claims Tribunal, established in 1981.

permanent establishment Most tax treaties operate so that business profits are taxed in the country of the taxpayer's *residence, unless the taxpayer has a "permanent establishment" in the other territory. In the model double tax agreement drawn up by the Organization for Economic Cooperation and Development, a permanent establishment is defined as a "fixed place of business through which the business of an enterprise is wholly or partly carried on". The model agreement goes on to state specifically that the term "permanent establishment" includes a place of management, branch, office, factory, workshop, mine, oil or gas well, quarry, or any other place of extraction of natural resources. *See* DOUBLE TAXATION RELIEF.

permissive waste A kind of *waste that occurs when a tenant fails to maintain the property he leases and allows it to deteriorate.

per my et per tout [Norman French: by the half(?) and by all (the meaning of *my* is uncertain)] Denoting the unity of possession that is an essential characteristic of joint ownership of land. *See also* JOINT TENANCY.

perpetual injunction *See* INJUNCTION.

perpetual trusts *See* RULE AGAINST PERPETUAL TRUSTS.

perpetuation of testimony A procedure formerly used for the recording of evidence in civil cases in which there was a danger that it might be lost (e.g. because of the death of a witness) before it could be used in a future action. It was rarely ordered and is now no longer used.

perpetuity *n. See* RULE AGAINST PERPETUITIES.

persistent offender Formerly, a person whose previous criminal record made him liable to be given an extended sentence of imprisonment. *Compare* REPEAT OFFENDER.

persistent vegetative state (PVS) The condition of living without consciousness or the ability to initiate voluntary action, as a result of brain damage. People in the vegetative state may sometimes give the appearance of being awake and conscious, with open eyes. They may make random movements of the limbs or head and may pick or rub with the fingers, but there is no response to any form of communication and no reason to suppose that there is any awareness of the environment. The law currently allows medical treatment to be withdrawn from patients in PVS but permission must first be granted by the courts.

personal Act *See* ACT OF PARLIAMENT.

personal allowances Certain fixed sums that are deductible from total income in calculating the taxable income of an individual before income tax is imposed (Income Tax Act 2007 s 35–37). Personal allowances are not available to trustees or *personal representatives. These categories of persons are subject to income tax on total income, without deductions. The UK now has only the following categories of personal allowance:

- the principal allowance available to all individuals resident in the UK, and to certain non-resident individuals;
- age allowance;
- married couple's allowance for those born before 6 April 1935;
- blind person's allowance.

The value of the personal allowances increases each year by the increase in the retail prices index, but it is open to Parliament to specify a different amount.

personal chattel *See* CHATTEL.

personal contract *See* DERECOGNITION.

personal-credit agreement An agreement made between an individual (the debtor) and any other person (the creditor) by which the creditor provides the debtor with credit of any amount. Personal-credit agreements (a concept under the Consumer Credit Act 1974) exclude loans, etc., to companies. *See also* CONSUMER-CREDIT AGREEMENT.

personal property (personalty) All *property that does not comprise land or incorporeal *hereditaments.

personal protection order An order formerly made under the Domestic Proceedings and Magistrates' Courts Act 1978 for the protection against violence of a spouse or a child of the family. Such protection is now provided by a *non-molestation order under the Family Law Act 1996.

personal representative A person entitled to deal with a deceased person's estate in accordance with his will or under the rules relating to intestacy. Personal representatives include *executors and *administrators of all descriptions.

personal service The *service of a document on a party in accordance with Part 6 of the *Civil Procedure Rules. A document is served personally on an individual by leaving it with that individual; on a company by leaving it with a person holding a senior position in the company (a director, the treasurer, secretary, chief executive, manager, or other officer); and on a partnership by leaving it with a partner or person who has control or management of the partnership business at its principal place of business.

personalty *n. See* PERSONAL PROPERTY.

personal union An arrangement in which two or more states share a single head of state. A personal union does not create a single international person; rather, each state retains its separate legal personality. For example, in 1603 James VI of Scotland became monarch of England (styled as James I) but continued to be monarch of Scotland (styled as James VI).

persona non grata [Latin: an unacceptable or unwelcome person] A *diplomatic agent who is unacceptable to the receiving state. The sending state should recall such an agent; if this fails to occur, the host state may ignore the presence of the agent or expel him from its territory.

per stirpes [Latin: by the roots] According to descent. When property in an estate or fund is distributed *per stirpes*, beneficiaries a generation removed from the primary class of beneficiaries receive between them the share attributable to their ancestor. For example, a will may leave property to A and B in equal shares with provision that if either predeceases the testator, the deceased beneficiary's children take his share in equal shares *per stirpes*. If, on the testator's death, both A and B have already died, A leaving two children and B three, A's children will each receive a quarter of the property, and B's children one-sixth each. *Compare* PER CAPITA.

persuading to murder The statutory offence, which is punishable by a maximum sentence of life imprisonment, of persuading or encouraging any person to murder anyone else (*R v Kayani* [1997] 2 Cr App R (S) 313). A foreigner temporarily in England who persuades someone to commit a murder abroad may be guilty of the offence of inciting terrorism overseas (Terrorism Act 2000).

persuasive authority A decision or other pronouncement of law that, under the doctrine of *precedent, a court may but need not apply when deciding the case before it. Persuasive authorities include decisions of courts of equal or lesser standing, decisions of courts outside the English legal system (particularly, courts of Commonwealth countries having systems based on the common law), *obiter dicta*, and the opinions of eminent textbook writers.

persuasive burden of proof See BURDEN OF PROOF.

perverse verdict A *verdict of a jury that is either entirely against the weight of the evidence or contrary to the judge's direction on a question of law.

perverting the course of justice Carrying out an act that tends or is intended to obstruct or defeat the administration of public justice. Common examples are inventing false evidence to mislead a court (in either civil or criminal proceedings) or an arbitration tribunal, making false statements to the police, stealing or destroying evidence, threatening witnesses, and attempting to influence jurors. The maximum penalty is life imprisonment and/or a fine. The common-law offence of perverting the course of justice overlaps with certain forms of *contempt of court and with the separate offence of tampering with witnesses. It is not an offence, however, to offer money to someone to persuade him not to proceed with an action in the civil courts; nor is it an offence to offer to pay reasonable compensation to the victim of a crime, if he will agree not to take criminal proceedings (Criminal Law Act 1967 s 5(1)). However, once he has made a statement to the police in connection with possible proceedings, it is an offence to attempt to induce him to withdraw or alter his statement.

petition *n*. A written application for a legal remedy or relief that is only available if statute or rules of procedure permit it. Examples are a petition for *divorce, an *election petition, a *bankruptcy petition, or a petition for winding up a company (see COMPULSORY WINDING-UP).

petition of right See CROWN PROCEEDINGS.

petroleum revenue tax A tax levied on the profits from sales of oil and gas extracted in the UK or on the continental shelf. The rate of tax (from 1 July 1993) is 50%, and the tax is abolished for new oilfields that get development consent on or after 16 March 1993.

petty patent See UTILITY MODEL.

petty sessions A court of summary jurisdiction now known as a *magistrates' court. The term was formerly used to denote a meeting of two or more *justices of the peace other than a general or *quarter sessions.

PHE See PUBLIC HEALTH ENGLAND.

philanthropic purposes Purposes that are narrower than *benevolent purposes but wider than charitable purposes. See CHARITABLE TRUST.

philosophy of law See JURISPRUDENCE.

physician-assisted suicide Any direct or indirect act of a doctor that is intended to enable a patient to end his own life, typically by providing the patient with medication or a prescription for medication in sufficient quantities to cause death. This is a crime under section 2 of the Suicide Act. *See* ASSISTED SUICIDE.

picketing *n.* Attendance by employees and their trade union representatives peacefully at or near a place of work for the purpose of persuading others to work or not to work, or to exchange information, in contemplation or furtherance of a *trade dispute. There is no specific legal right to picket, nor any prohibition on picketing, but there is a concept of lawful picketing in the Trade Union and Labour Relations (Consolidation) Act 1992. Pickets have no immunity from prosecution for committing criminal offences and they have no right to compel others to stop or to listen to the pickets' views. However, employees and their trade union representatives picketing their own place of work in contemplation or furtherance of a trade dispute are immune from civil legal action for inducing others to break commercial or employment contracts with the employer involved in the dispute.

Pickets lose their immunity if the action is taken without being first authorized by a ballot of the members of the union involved, or if the reason for the action is that the employer is employing a person who is not a trade union member.

"Flying pickets", who are neither employees nor trade union representatives of employees at the workplace picketed, have no immunity. The courts will grant injunctions to stop or prevent unlawful picketing. A *code of practice on picketing is published by the Department for Business, Innovation and Skills.

It is arguable that the incorporation of the European Convention on Human Rights into English law via the *Human Rights Act 1998 may have an impact on the law affecting picketing. Article 10, the right of *freedom of expression, and Article 11, the right to freedom of peaceful assembly (*see* FREEDOM OF ASSOCIATION), could be used to challenge some of the existing restrictions laid down in English law. As picketing is a form of public demonstration (in an industrial context) the imposition of restrictions could raise the civil-liberties aspects of such restrictions sufficiently to amount to breaches of either or both of these Articles.

Cases: *Middlebrook Mushrooms Ltd v TGWU* [1993] ICR 612; *Steel v United Kingdom* (1998) EHRR 603.

piracy *n.* **1.** (piracy *jure gentium*) Any illegal act of violence, detention, or robbery committed on a private ship for personal gain or revenge, against another ship, people, or property on the high seas. Piracy may also be committed on or against an aircraft. Piracy also includes operating a pirate ship or aircraft and inciting or assisting any other act of piracy. However, acts committed for political purposes are not piracy; nor are any acts committed by a warship or government ship or aircraft. Piracy is an international crime and all nations may exercise jurisdiction over pirates, regardless of the nationality of the ship or aircraft or the pirates. A ship or aircraft involved in piracy is also subject to seizure by any state. British courts have traditionally exercised such jurisdiction, and the power to do so is confirmed in the Tokyo Convention Act 1967.

English municipal law has created certain offences of piracy that are not covered by international law, but they are not subject to the jurisdiction of the English courts unless committed on board a British ship or within British territorial waters. Examples of such offences are revolt by the crew of a ship against their master and hijacking of the ship by the crew. These offences, if tried as piracy, are subject to life imprisonment (the death penalty for piracy accompanied by acts endangering life, or by an assault with intent to murder, has been abolished; *see* CAPITAL PUNISHMENT). In English law the offence is contained in the Piracy Acts of 1837 and 1850. **2.** (in marine insurance) One of the risks covered by a marine insurance policy, which extends beyond the criminal offence to include a revolt by the crew or passengers and plundering generally. **3.** Infringement of *copyright, *trade marks, or other *intellectual property rights. The owner's usual remedy is to obtain an *injunction to end the infringement, although piracy is often also a criminal offence. In 2012 Ofcom proposed a draft Code on Internet piracy.

piscary (fishery) *n.* A *profit *à prendre* or *common conferring the right to take fish from water on another's land.

placement order A court order introduced by the Children and Adoption Act 2002 s 21 that authorizes a local authority to place a child who is under a *care order for *adoption with prospective adopters. The placement order will give *parental responsibility to the local authority and to the prospective adopters with whom the child is placed. Normally the consent of a parent or guardian is required before an order can be made; however, consent can be dispensed with if the court considers that it is in the best interests of the child to do so. The placement order will last until an adoption order is made, or until it is revoked.

place of safety order *See* EMERGENCY PROTECTION ORDER.

plaint *n.* Formerly, a statement in writing of a cause of action, used to initiate actions in the county courts. It has been replaced by the *claim form under Part 7 of the *Civil Procedure Rules.

plaintiff *n. See* CLAIMANT.

planning permission *See* TOWN AND COUNTRY PLANNING.

plant *n. See* MACHINERY AND PLANT.

plc (public limited company) *See* LIMITED COMPANY; PUBLIC COMPANY.

plea *n.* In criminal proceedings, a formal statement made in court by an accused person as a response to the charge made against him. *See also* GUILTY; NOT GUILTY; PLEA BARGAINING; PLEAS IN BAR.

plea and case management hearing A pretrial hearing held in all cases sent or transferred to the Crown Court. At the hearing the defendant will enter a *plea and the court will exercise its *case management powers. A plea and case management hearing questionnaire must be completed by the prosecution and defence prior to the hearing. Rules dealing with the management of cases in the Crown Court are set out in Part 3 of the *Criminal Procedure Rules and in the *Consolidated Criminal Practice Direction. *See* PRELIMINARY HEARING. *See also* CASE MANAGEMENT CONFERENCE.

plea bargaining In criminal proceedings, an agreement between the prosecution and the defence by which the accused agrees to plead guilty to a lesser charge in return for an offer by the prosecution (for example, to offer no evidence on a more serious charge against the accused). Although a *plea must always be made voluntarily and free from any improper pressure, a defendant in the Crown Court is entitled to seek an indication from the judge of the maximum sentence that would be imposed if he were to plead guilty.

plea before venue An initial hearing in the magistrates' court at which the defendant indicates his intended plea. If the plea is guilty, the case will proceed to *summary trial in the magistrates' court. If not guilty, it will go forward to *mode of trial proceedings.

plead *vb.* To make a *plea.

pleading *n.* In colloquial usage, the *claim form, *defence, or other *statement of case used in civil proceedings. Although the term no longer has any formal meaning under the *Civil Procedure Rules, it continues to be used informally by lawyers and lay people.

pleading guilty by post In criminal proceedings, a procedure that allows a person to plead guilty to certain minor *summary offences by letter without appearing at the court (Criminal Justice Act 2003 s 12, 308).

pleading in the alternative In civil proceedings, the practice of including in a *statement of case two or more inconsistent allegations and inviting the court to grant relief in respect of whichever allegation it finds to be well-founded. Under the *Civil Procedure Rules a party may be entitled to set out alternative claims or separate defences in a statement of case, but this is subject to the requirement in Part 22 of the Rules that statements of case must be verified by a *statement of truth.

pleas in bar (peremptory pleas) Pleas in *trials on indictment setting out some special ground for not proceeding with the indictment. Pleas in bar include the pleas of *autrefois acquit, *autrefois convict, and the plea of pardon.

plebiscite *n.* A public referendum or vote by the population of a territory to determine its choice of a sovereign or a *cession of territory to another state. Under the Treaty of Versailles 1919 doubtful boundaries were determined by plebiscites, as in the cases of boundaries between Poland and Germany in Upper Silesia and in certain sections of the boundary with East Prussia (arts 88, 94–97).

pledge *n. See* PAWN.

plene administravit [Latin: he has fully administered] The defence of a personal representative who has completed administration of a deceased's estate to a creditor's action to recover a debt of which he had no knowledge. Unless the creditor can prove that the personal representative still holds assets of the estate, he will obtain a judgment enforceable only against any such assets coming into the personal representative's hands in the future.

plight and condition If it appears from the state of a will that another document may have been attached (e.g. there are pin holes or marks from a paperclip) or there is evidence to suggest an attempt to revoke the will (e.g. there are signs of burning or tearing) then an *affidavit of plight and condition may be required before a *grant or representation is issued. Such an affidavit would be signed by a person with knowledge of the condition of the will when it was made or found, or by another person able to provide evidence as to the reason for the state and condition of the will.

plough bote *See* ESTOVERS.

poaching *n.* Taking game without permission from private land or from land on which the killing of game is restricted. Wild animals cannot usually be stolen; there are, however, various statutory offences to cover poaching that do not amount to theft. For example, the Deer Act 1991 creates offences relating to taking, killing, or injuring deer or trespassing on land with the intention of committing any of these acts. Conviction may involve *forfeiture of the game taken or of the equipment and vehicles used in poaching. There are also special offences relating to taking or destroying fish in private waters or in waters with a private right of fishery. There is special legislation dealing with the poaching of endangered species.

PoCA list Abbreviation for Protection of Children Act list; a list that identifies people unsuitable for employment in child-care roles. The list was previously held by the Independent Safeguarding Authority but is now held by the Disclosure and Barring Service of the Home Office. The Protection of Children Act 1999 requires that all members of certain professions (such as teachers) be checked against the list prior to employment. A person included on the list may appeal to the Upper Tribunal.

poison *n.* A substance that, if ingested, is capable of endangering life or injuring health. It is an offence (punishable by up to five years' imprisonment) to cause someone to consume a poison or any other noxious substance (which can include drugs or alcohol administered in such quantities as to be harmful) with the intention of injuring or annoying them, even if no injury results (Offences Against the Person Act 1861 s 24). It is also an offence (punishable by up to ten years' imprisonment) to cause someone to consume such substances so that their life is endangered or they suffer grievous bodily harm as a result, even if this was not intended (Offences Against the Person Act 1861 s 23). Administering poison with the intention of killing someone or causing them serious harm may amount to an attempt to murder or to cause *grievous bodily harm. In both cases the attempt will be punishable with a maximum sentence of life imprisonment.

A person who uses or who threatens to use a noxious substance or other noxious thing in order to cause harm or intimidate in regard to an act of terrorism will fall under the Anti-terrorism, Crime and Security Act 2001 (s 113).

The sale of poisons is controlled by various statutes, principally the Medicines Act 1968 and Poisons Act 1972.

Police and Crime Commissioner (PCC) Under the Police Reform and Social Responsibility Act 2011, which applies to England and Wales, an elected official whose role is to set policing priorities in each local police area. The PCC replaces the existing police authorities everywhere except in London, where these responsibilities are transferred to the office of the directly elected mayor. The first PCCs were elected in November 2012; elections will be held again in May 2016 and thereafter every four years.

The PCCs must swear an oath of impartiality to emphasize that they are there to serve the whole community. Their job is to ensure that the policing needs of the community are met as effectively as possible by bringing the public closer to the police, and building confidence in the system. The PCC has the power to appoint and dismiss chief constables. He or she is also responsible for setting the policing budget, including the precept (council charge for the police). PCCs must engage with the public and consult with victims of crime when setting policing priorities. They are responsible for setting and updating a Police and Crime Plan and are accountable to the newly established *Police and Crime Panels.

The legislation protects the operational independence of the police. Chief constables retain control and direction of their forces' officers and staff.

Police and Crime Panels (PCPs) Local bodies established in 2011 to examine the actions and decisions of each *Police and Crime Commissioner and to make sure that relevant information is available to the public, thereby promoting accountability. The main focus is on strategic matters, such as whether the PCC has achieved the aims in his Police and Crime Plan and consulted appropriately with the public and victims of crime. The PCPs are empowered to make (and publish) reports and to issue recommendations on such matters as the appointment of a chief constable or the level of the precept (council charge for the police); in the latter case, they may veto the proposed charge if they vote to do so by a two-thirds majority. A Panel may hold public meetings to question the PCC or to discuss his annual report. It will also handle any non-criminal complaints against the PCC or his deputy (criminal complaints being the province of the *Independent Police Complaints Commission). Panels include at least one elected representative from each local authority within the police area.

police court A *magistrates' court.

police force A body of police officers maintained for a police area by a *Police and Crime Commissioner. Currently, there are 43 **police areas** in England and Wales, many of which are based on county boundaries but some of which, such as Thames Valley Police, cover more than one county.

police officer A person who, whatever his rank within a police force, holds the ancient office of **constable**, i.e. one who has undertaken to serve the Crown as an officer of the peace. His office is, in law, independent. He is not technically a Crown servant, since the Crown neither appoints him nor pays him, nor is he a local authority employee. *See* POLICE FORCE.

police protection of children In cases of real urgency, the police have powers to pick up and hold children for their protection under the Children Act 1989 s 46. Where a police officer has reasonable cause to believe that a child would otherwise be likely to suffer significant harm, he may remove that child to suitable accommodation; that child is then said to be have been taken into police protection. Alternatively, the police may take steps to ensure that parents do not remove a child from a hospital, or other place. These powers are similar to those conferred by an *emergency protection order but the police have the authority to act without a court order. However, the powers conferred do not include any rights of search and entry, so if the police need to enter premises to search for a child, they will have to seek an emergency protection order. Typically, these powers are used to pick up and hold abandoned children and runaways. Children can be held for up to 72 hours.

political asylum *See* ASYLUM.

political offence An offence committed for a political purpose or inspired by a political motive, for which the alleged offender cannot be extradited (*see* EXTRADITION) or surrendered as a *fugitive offender. The act could be a combination of a politically motivated but criminally implemented act, or it may be more narrowly political, or it may be criminal activity that resulted from an attempt to escape a political system or discriminatory persecution. In all cases, however, the offence results from a dispute between the fugitive and the state that applies for extradition on some issue connected with the political control or government of the country.

pollution *n.* Any action rendering the environment impure. Statutes relating wholly or partly to **air pollution** include the Clean Air Act 1993, the Health and Safety at Work Act 1974, the Control of Pollution Act 1974, the Environmental Protection Act 1990, and the Environment Act 1995, which control the emission of smoke into the atmosphere, the emission of noxious or offensive substances, and the composition of petrol and other fuels. Directive 2008/50/EC combined most of the existing legislation into a single directive. The UK failed to achieve compliance with the limits placed on nitrogen dioxide by the deadline 1 January 2010 and the Supreme Court granted a declaration that there had been a breach of article 13 of the Air Quality Directive *(R (on the application of ClientEarth) (Appellant) v Secretary of State for the Environment, Food and Rural Affairs (Respondent)* [2013] UKSC 25). **Water pollution** generally is governed by the Control of Pollution Act 1974 and the Environmental Protection Act 1990, under which it is an offence (among other things) to allow polluting matter to enter rivers or other inland waters or to impede their flow so as to aggravate pollution due to other causes. Management of water supplies is governed primarily by the Water Act 2003, which implemented the EU's *Water Framework Directive, and the Water Resources Act 1991. Control of pollution by oil is covered by the Prevention of Oil Pollution Act 1971. Pollution by the deposit of waste on land is governed primarily by the Control of Pollution Act 1974, which permits household, commercial, and industrial waste to be deposited only on licensed sites (*see* WASTE DISPOSAL). Local authorities are required by the Act to collect and dispose of household waste free of charge; for the purposes of refuse disposal by their residents, they are also, by the Refuse Disposal (Amenity) Act 1978, obliged to provide free refuse dumps. Additional powers in relation to waste disposal are contained in the Clean Neighborhoods and Environment Act 2005. EU legislation in this area includes the Landfill Directive 1999, the Waste Incineration Directive 2000, and the Waste Framework Directive 2008. The European Integrated Pollution Prevention and Control (IPPC) Directive 1996, implemented in the UK through the Pollution Prevention and Control Regulations 2000, regulates pollution from noise and vibrations as well as emissions to air, land, and water. The Environmental Liability Directive 2004 imposes obligations on operators of activities that cause or threaten to cause environmental damage. Environmental damage is defined in the regulations and generally includes only more serious damage to water, land, and certain species and habitats. *See also* HAZARDOUS WASTE.

polygamy *n.* The practice of having more than one spouse. English law considers a marriage **actually polygamous** if there is in fact more than one spouse, and **potentially polygamous** if there is only one spouse but the marriage was contracted under a system of law that permits polygamy. No polygamous marriage may be validly contracted in England. If it is celebrated abroad, however, it will be recognized if at the time it was celebrated neither spouse was domiciled in England; if either spouse was at that time domiciled in England the marriage will be void. For the purposes of the Social Security Contributions and Benefits Act 1992 a polygamous marriage is to be treated as valid at any time while it is monogamous in fact.

Ponsonby Rule In the UK, the rule that treaties that require *ratification should be laid before Parliament 21 days before signature and ratification. This practice has on occasion been abandoned (December 1924–1929), ignored (1961), or waived (at various times).

port *n.* A place or town with access to the sea to which ships may conveniently come and at which they may load and unload. In charterparties and marine insurance policies, the word is construed in this commercial sense, as understood in the shipping business. For pilotage or revenue purposes, a port may extend over a larger geographical area than the commercial port.

port alert *See* ALL-PORTS WARNING SYSTEM.

portion *n.* Funds or other property given or left to a child by his parent or someone standing *in loco parentis* and intended to make permanent provision for him or to establish him in life (e.g. a sum provided to set the child up in business). Sums provided for the child's maintenance or education or to supplement his income do not qualify. A portion may be brought into *hotchpot and may be presumed to adeem a legacy (*see* ADEMPTION; SATISFACTION) unless there is evidence that the testator intended the portion to be disregarded on his death.

port tranquillity doctrine The principle that a nation may exercise jurisdiction over a foreign vessel in one of its ports when activity on board that vessel disturbs the tranquillity of the port. In bilateral treaties, this provides a common exception to the usual rule that cedes primary jurisdiction over vessels to the state of the vessel's nationality. The position of warships, however, is different. Since Chief Justice Marshall in *The Schooner Exchange v M'Faddon* (1812) 7 Cranch 116 declared that a public armed ship constitutes a part of the military force of the nation, it has been accepted that warships are immune from the jurisdiction of any foreign sovereign. This does not mean that a visiting warship may flout port regulations; if it does so, it may be required to leave port. Nor does it mean that events occurring on board the ship take place outside the jurisdiction of the port state. It merely means that the ship cannot be arrested or taxed and that the local authorities have no competence with respect to crimes committed on board unless the captain surrenders the offender to them. In any respects, the immunity may be waived (*Chung Chi Cheung v The King* [1939] AC 160 (PC)) and in no sense is a ship to be regarded as a territorial enclave.

positive discrimination Actively favouring one category of people over others because they are considered to be disadvantaged and thereby discriminating against those others. Positive discrimination is illegal in the UK (although it is not unlawful to treat disabled people more favourably than non-disabled people). "Positive action" is, however, permitted. This introduces measures designed to alleviate disadvantage experienced by people who share a "protected characteristic" (*see* EQUALITY ACT 2010), to reduce under-representation, and to meet particular needs. An example might be training if targeted to particular groups. Any such measures must be a proportionate way of achieving the relevant aim. In relation to recruitment and promotion at work, the Equality Act 2010 allows (but does not require) an employer to select recruits or candidates from under-represented groups, where they are equally well qualified as the other candidates. This is in line with European Law (*Badeck C-158/97* [001] 2 CMLR 79).

Special rules apply to the selection of Parliamentary candidates (Equality Act 2010).

positive law *See* NATURAL LAW. *See also* LEGAL POSITIVISM.

positivist school of criminology One of the two major schools of *criminology. In contrast to the *classical school, which assumes that criminal acts are the product of free choice and rational calculation, the positivist sees the root causes of crime in factors outside the control of the offender. These are to be identified using empirical methods, in particular the analysis of statistics.

The earliest form of positivism, which arose in the late 19th century, involved an attempt to correlate criminal behaviour with certain physiological traits. This led to the identification of a genetic "criminal type"—an idea that is now wholly discredited. Later, psychological positivists used detailed studies to link personality traits with particular crimes and to identify those formative experiences (e.g. parental neglect) that might produce a general predisposition to law-breaking. Alternatively, sociological positivists have sought the causes of crime in factors external to the offender, such as poverty, alienation, high population density, and exposure to deviant subcultures (e.g. gangs or drug-takers). One particularly influential approach was that taken by the **Chicago School** of the mid 20th century, which used ecological methods to study the breakdown of social order in inner-city neighbourhoods. Other social positivist approaches include **Marxist criminology**, which sees crime as an inevitable product of class conflict and the capitalist system, and **critical criminology**, which focuses on the role of power elites in defining what and who is regarded as criminal (*see* MARXIST LEGAL THEORY). More recently, there has been a general retreat from social theory and a more pragmatic emphasis on crime prevention. *See also* SOCIOLOGY OF LAW.

possession *n.* Actual control of property combined with the intention to use it, rightly or wrongly, as one's own. In the case of land, possession may be actual, when the owner has entered onto the land, or possession in law, when he has the right to enter but has not yet done so. Possession includes receipt of rent and profits, or the right to receive them. *See also* QUIET POSSESSION.

possessory lien *See* LIEN.

possessory title Ownership of land that can only be proved by evidence of the requisite period of *adverse possession or possession coupled with a defective documentary title. A proprietor of registered land having only possessory title is not protected against any adverse estate, interest, or right subsisting or capable of arising up to the time when the title was first registered.

possibility *n.* (in land law) An interest in land that depends on the occurrence of an uncertain future event. A **bare possibility**, such as a *spes successionis*, i.e. a person's expectation of inheriting land under the will of a testator who is still alive (i.e. depending on the testator dying without having revoked the will), confers no legal or equitable interest. A **possibility coupled with an interest** (e.g. B's rights under a conveyance "to A for life, and if C is living at A's death then to B") can be transferred by will or by deed. *See also* POSSIBILITY OF REVERTER.

possibility of reverter The interest of a person who has conveyed land to another until the occurrence of some specified event (which may never happen). The *determinable interest thus created will end automatically should this future event occur, and the legal estate will revert to the grantor. Thus, when A conveys land to B until he marries, A has a possibility of reverter when B marries (although if B dies unmarried, the possibility of reverter is lost). *See* SETTLED LAND.

post-adoption contact Contact between a child and its birth family after an *adoption order has been made. Contact after adoption is a contentious issue, the traditional view under English law being that it was contrary to the very nature of adoption. However, this position was relaxed when the House of Lords decided in *Re C (Adoption Order: Conditions)* [1998] 2 FLR 259 (HL) that the court had power to attach a condition to an adoption order that preserved contact between a child and his siblings. Since the coming into force of the Children Act 1989 the courts have had the power to make a *contact order in addition to an adoption order. Under the Children and Adoption Act 2002 the court is now under a duty when making an adoption order to consider whether arrangements should be made to allow the child to maintain links with his birth family.

postliminy *n.* [Latin: *postliminium*: return behind one's threshold] The right by which persons or things seized by the enemy during war are restored to their former status on return to their original jurisdiction.

postmodernist legal thought Postmodernism is best understood as a broad, multidisciplinary assault on the values of the Enlightenment, especially its ideal of objective human knowledge achieved through the exercise of reason in pursuit of universal truths. Postmodernist accounts of law are sceptical of formalism, essentialism, Utopianism, and even democracy. Nevertheless, postmodernist legal thought has an important political object. It attacks, amongst other contemporary phenomena, the overarching presence of the state, the increasing globalization of markets, and the universalizing of values. It has also promoted a new pragmatism that advances a set of economic, ecological, and political goals with special attention to the predicament of women, minorities, the dispossessed, and the poor. *See also* FEMINIST LEGAL THEORY.

post-mortem *n.* [Latin: after death] *See* AUTOPSY.

postnuptial settlement *See* MARRIAGE SETTLEMENT.

potentially exempt transfer (PET) A transfer made by an individual to another individual. A PET does not attract a liability to *inheritance tax at the time of the gift. A potentially exempt transfer is exempt from any charge after the passage of seven years without the transferor dying; if the transferor dies in that period, it becomes a chargeable transfer (Inheritance Taxes Act 1984 s 3A(4)).

power *n.* A legal discretion (as opposed to a *duty) to carry out or refrain from carrying out any act. When powers affect the rights of others (e.g. the powers of *trustees and *administrative powers), their exercise can be challenged in the courts. An act that goes beyond the scope of a power as specified in the instrument creating it (e.g. a trust deed or statute) is invalid; so, too, is any act carried out in abuse of a power (e.g. when it is exercised after taking irrelevant considerations into account, for improper motives, or capriciously). *See also* ULTRA VIRES.

power in the nature of a trust *See* TRUST POWER.

power of appointment A right given to someone to dispose of property that is not his, within bounds established by the owner of the property (it is sometimes called a **mere** or **bare power**; *compare* TRUST POWER). The owner of the property (the **donor** of the power) gives a power to another (the **donee** of the power, or **appointor**) to appoint (give) the property to a person (the **appointee**) chosen by the appointor. The power may be **general** (under which an appointment may be made to anyone, including the donee or the appointor himself), **special** (an appointment may be made only within a class chosen by the donor), or **hybrid** (an appointment may be made to virtually anyone except a small class). The appointees have very limited rights – much more limited than those of beneficiaries under a trust. An appointment is void if it is made to someone not within the class chosen or if it is a *fraud on a power.

power of arrest (in cases of domestic violence) A power attached to, for example, an *occupation order that enables a police constable to arrest without warrant a person whom he has reasonable cause for suspecting of being in breach of the order to which it is attached.

power of attorney (letter of attorney) A formal instrument by which one person empowers another to act on his behalf, either generally or in specific circumstances. A power to execute a *deed must itself be given by a deed.

power of sale **1.** The right of a mortgagee to sell mortgaged property if the mortgagor has not repaid his loan by the contractual date of redemption. This power arises when the contractual date (stated in the mortgage document and usually very early in the period of the mortgage) has passed, but may only be exercised if interest due under the mortgage is two months in arrears, if there has been a breach of certain terms in the mortgage by the mortgagor, or if notice has been served on the mortgagor to repay the loan and the loan (or part of it) has not been repaid within three months of the notice. If the mortgagee sells the property under the power of sale, he owes a duty to the mortgagor to act with reasonable care (*Cuckmere Brick Co Ltd v Mutual Finance Ltd* [1971] Ch 949) and hold on trust any money surplus to that needed to pay his expenses and mortgage debt for the mortgagor's benefit. **2.** The right of a *tenant for life under the Settled Land Act 1925 to sell the settled land for the best price in money that can be obtained. Such a sale *overreaches the interests of the subsequent beneficiaries.

power of search The legal right to search people or property. Private people have no powers of search, but various statutes, notably the Police and Criminal Evidence Act 1984, confer such powers on police or other officials, often on the authority of a **search warrant** issued by a magistrate or a High Court judge. The 1984 Act empowers the police to stop and search any person or vehicle found in a *public place for stolen or prohibited articles and to detain a person or vehicle for such a search. (An article is "prohibited" if it is either an *offensive weapon or made or adapted for use in connection with *burglary, *theft, taking a *conveyance, or obtaining property by *deception or *fraud.) Before such a search the police officer must state his station and object. If out of uniform, he must produce evidence of his status. He must always give his grounds for the search if asked and must record details of it. A magistrate may issue a search warrant to an officer if he is satisfied that there are reasonable grounds for believing that a serious *indictable offence has been committed and material evidence is to be found on the premises. Under the Theft Act 1968, for example, police may obtain a warrant to search for stolen goods when there are reasonable grounds for believing that they are in someone's possession or on his premises. Under certain circumstances the police are given powers of search without requiring either a warrant or any superior authorization; for example, under section 23 of the Misuse of Drugs Act 1971 (*see* CONTROLLED DRUGS) and sections 44–45 of the Terrorism Act 2000 (*R (Gillan) v Metropolitan Police Commissioner* [2006] UKHL 12, [2006] 2 AC 307: *see* TERRORISM). The police also have a general power, when arresting someone for an indictable offence, to enter and search any place in which the suspect is believed to be. Statutes sometimes give powers of search to public officials, e.g. customs officers or Revenue officers.

Police powers of stop and search were extended under the Criminal Justice and Public Order Act 1994. Where a senior police officer reasonably believes that an incident involving serious violence may take place in his area he may issue an authorization (valid for 24 hours, extendable for up to 24 hours) for persons and vehicles (which can include caravans, ships, aircraft, and hovercraft and their passengers) to be stopped and searched if he thinks it expedient to do so to prevent violence. A constable in uniform may stop and search any person for the purpose of seeing whether that person is carrying an offensive weapon or an instrument that has a blade or a sharp point. Failure to stop is a *summary offence punishable by one month's imprisonment and/or a *fine on level 3. Failure to cooperate might amount to *obstructing a police officer in the execution of his duty. Similar powers are available to senior police officers to authorize searches for periods of 28 days to prevent acts of terrorism. Both failure to stop and wilful obstruction of a constable are *summary offences for the purpose of this power and are punishable by six months' imprisonment and/or a *fine on level 5.

power reserved by executor If an *executor does not wish to act as an executor following the death of the testator, but wishes to reserve the right to come in to prove the will as an executor at a later date, then (provided there are other executors willing to take out a grant) the non-proving executor can allow the other executors to proceed, with power expressly reserved to him. That executor can apply later to become an executor by way of *double probate. *Compare* RENOUNCING PROBATE.

power to manage The power to direct the affairs of a company, particularly as this is distributed between the *general meeting and the board of directors. The distribution of power is usually made clear in the company's constitution; for example, the model *ARTICLES OF ASSOCIATION contained in schedule 1-3 of the Companies (Model Articles) Regulations 2008 provide that (subject to a limited number of exceptions) there is a wide power of management vested with the board of directors. At common law, however, the general meeting can exercise a residual power to act where the board of directors is unable to do so (*Barron v Potter* [1914] 1 Ch 595).

power to sue The authority by which a *legal person can institute legal proceedings. In the case of a company, where there is a wrong done to the company, the company is the proper person to act against the wrongdoer (*Foss v Harbottle* (1843) 67 ER 189). However, the organ of the company that is empowered to exercise that function will depend on the company's constitution. Under the model *articles of association contained in schedules 1-3 of the Companies (Model Articles) Regulations 2008, the power is vested with the board of directors, which may, as a matter of management, decide not to sue. However, under the same model articles, the *general meeting can intervene by passing a *special resolution. Alternatively, the general meeting can use a residual power to commence proceedings where the board is unable to act (*Alexander Ward & Co Ltd v Samyang Navigation Co Ltd* [1975] 1 WLR 673 (HL)) or can act as the decision-making body where the directors are themselves the wrongdoers.

practice *n.* **1.** The mode of proceeding to enforce a legal right. It is virtually synonymous with *procedure, but is sometimes used to denote informal rules of procedure as distinct from those derived from rules of court. **2.** A book on practice and procedure, such as the *Civil Procedure Rules.

Practice Directions **1.** Published statements, usually issued by the head of the court or division to which they relate, indicating the procedure to be followed in particular matters or the court's intended policy in certain cases. Unlike *rules of court, they have no statutory authority. They are normally published in the law reports. Masters' Practice Directions, issued by the Queen's Bench Masters, concern the administration of the *Queen's Bench Division. **2.** Instructions found in the *Civil Procedure Rules of 1999 that supplement those rules and act as aids to their interpretation. *See also* PRE-ACTION PROTOCOLS.

practice form A form to be used for a particular purpose in court proceedings, the form and purpose being specified by a *Practice Direction.

practice master *See* CENTRAL OFFICE.

practising certificate An annual certificate issued by the *Solicitors Regulation Authority to a solicitor entitling him to practise. The fee chargeable includes the premium of an insurance policy indemnifying the solicitor against the consequences of professional negligence. Barristers obtain an annual practising certificate from the *Bar Council after they have successfully completed a twelve-month pupillage and have attended further education courses required by the Bar Council.

praecipe *n.* [Latin: command] **1.** A court document on which a party writes the particulars of a document that he wishes to have prepared or issued. Under Schedule 1 to the *Civil Procedure Rules, before a *writ of execution is issued in the High Court, a *praecipe* for its issue signed by the solicitor of the person entitled to execution must be filed at court. In county court procedure, this document is now known as a **request**. **2.** Formerly, a writ requiring the sheriff to command the defendant either to do a certain thing or to show cause why he had not done it.

pray a tales *See* TALES DE CIRCUMSTANTIBUS.

prayer *n.* A formal request contained in a *petition to a court for the relief sought by the petitioner. The term is now almost always associated with actions for *divorce, where the prayer is the section of the petition that sets out the orders the court is asked to make. This is a throw-back to the time (prior to 1857) when divorce was a matter entirely confined to ecclesiastical courts.

pre-action protocols Protocols introduced in 1999 to speed up the early parts of the litigation process. Pre-action protocols encourage greater contact between the parties at the earliest possible opportunity in order to encourage better and earlier exchange of information with a view to fair and early settlement of claims. There are now nine protocols:

- construction and engineering disputes;
- defamation;
- personal injury;
- clinical disputes;
- professional negligence;
- judicial review;
- disease and illness claims;
- housing disrepair;
- possession claims based on rent arrears.

Pre-action protocols can be enforced by the court and are seen as an aspect of the courts' new responsibility of *case management under the *Civil Procedure Rules.

preamble *n.* The part of a statute that sets out its purposes and effects. It follows immediately after the long title and date of royal assent. Preambles are now virtually confined to statutes originating in private Bills.

precarious possession Possession of property at the will of another person.

precatory trust *See* PRECATORY WORDS.

precatory words Words that accompany a gift of property in a document, hoping, desiring, trusting, or requesting that the donee will dispose of the property in a particular way. It is often difficult to decide whether there is sufficient certainty of intention to create a trust (**precatory trust**) or whether the property is an absolute gift to the recipient. The courts have tended to construe gifts so as not to create a trust, unless there is no doubt that a trust was intended (*Lambe v Eames* (1871) 6 Ch App 597; *Re Adams & Kensington Vestry* (1884) 27 ChD 394). However, some more recent cases have indicated a reversal of this trend, especially where the settlor has not taken legal advice (*Comiskey v Bowring-Hanbury* [1905] AC 84; *Paul v Constance* [1977] 1 WLR 1338 (CA); *Rowe v Prance* [1999] 2 FLR 787 (Ch)).

precedent *n.* A judgment or decision of a court, normally recorded in a *law report, used as an authority for reaching the same decision in subsequent cases. In English law, judgments and decisions can represent **authoritative precedent** (which is generally binding and must be followed) or **persuasive precedent** (which need not be followed). It is that part of the judgment that represents the legal reasoning (or *ratio decidendi*) of a case that is binding, but only if the legal reasoning is from a superior court and, in general, from the same court in an earlier case. Accordingly, *ratio decidendi* of the *House of Lords are binding upon the *Court of Appeal and all lower courts and are normally followed by the House of Lords itself. The *ratio decidendi* of the Court of Appeal are binding on all lower courts and, subject to some exceptions, on the Court of Appeal itself. *Ratio decidendi* of the High Court are binding on inferior courts, but not on itself. The *ratio decidendi* of inferior courts do not create any binding precedent.

precept *n.* A lawful demand or direction, particularly a demand from a rating authority to another authority to levy rates for the benefit of the former. For example, a district council's rates include an amount that it collects as a result of a precept from its county council.

predatory pricing The practice, undertaken largely by dominant businesses, of pricing goods or services at such a low level that competitors are forced to leave the market. While small companies are entitled to price as they wish, provided this is not in collusion with other companies, dominant businesses must comply with *Article 102 of the Treaty on the Functioning of the European Union and the Competition Act 1998; predatory pricing may be an *abuse of a dominant position contrary to these provisions. Companies can be fined for engaging in predatory pricing.

predecessor *n.* (in land law) A person through whom an owner's title to land is traced. Examples are a previous owner who sold, bequeathed, or settled the land and a mortgagee who exercised his power of sale.

pre-employment health questionnaires The *Equality Act 2010 provides that it is generally unlawful for an employer to ask questions about disability or health before making a conditional or unconditional job offer. The rule, which applies to all enquiries by or on behalf of an employer (e.g. by a recruitment agency), is intended to prevent disability or health issues being used to reject applicants at an early stage in the recruitment process. It would be unlawful, therefore, to ask applicants to list on an application form how many days' sick leave they have taken in the last year. The rule covers questions to third parties, such as an ex-employer, as well as to applicants. It is, however, permissible to make a job offer that is conditional on the applicant passing a medical examination or answering health-related questions. In addition, there are certain specific exceptions to the general rule. First, the employer is allowed to ask whether the applicant is able to take part in an assessment to test his ability to do the job and whether any *reasonable adjustments will be needed for that, or in the interview process. Second, the employer may ask whether an applicant will be able to carry out an intrinsic part of the job. If a job requires manual handling, for example, it may be asked whether the person is able to lift and carry. However, the employer is under a duty to make reasonable adjustments and this must be considered in dealing with the answer given by the applicant. Third, it is lawful to collect information for the purposes of monitoring the composition of the workforce, but this information must not be used in the recruitment process (and should be kept separate from that). Fourth, it is lawful to ask whether an applicant has a particular disability where having that disability is an occupational requirement of the job (e.g. where the employer is seeking to employ a support worker with experience of a particular disability). Fifth, it is permissible to seek information where the employer wishes to take positive action to benefit disabled people, for example, by way of guaranteed interviews.

If an employer makes an enquiry outside the exceptions, this is unlawful. Enforcement is by the *Equality and Human Rights Commission (EHRC), not the individual. However, if the employer asks a prohibited question and the applicant is rejected, the applicant may make a claim to the employment tribunal alleging disability discrimination (*see* DISABLED PERSON).

pre-emption *n.* The right of first refusal to purchase land in the event that the grantor of the right should decide to sell. For example, if A makes a covenant that for five years he will not sell his land other than to B at £5000, A cannot be forced to sell (*compare* OPTION TO PURCHASE) but B's right of pre-emption prevents him from selling other than on the stated terms for five years. A right of pre-emption is valid only if it is sufficiently precise. A right of pre-emption created in registered land after 13 October 2003 is registrable as a restriction on the proprietorship register of the affected land.

pre-emptive right **1.** The right of some shareholders under the Companies Act 1985 to be offered a proportion of certain classes of newly issued securities before they are offered to anyone else and upon terms at least as favourable. (*See also* RIGHTS ISSUE.) **2.** The right conferred by the articles of association upon shareholders in some private companies to be offered, on specified terms, first refusal of the shares of any shareholder wishing to transfer his holding.

preference *n.* **1.** The favouring by an insolvent debtor of a particular creditor (for example by paying one creditor in full when there is no prospect of paying the others). If the debtor subsequently becomes bankrupt (in the case of an individual) or goes into insolvent liquidation (in the case of a company), and was motivated by a desire to improve the position of the creditor, the court can order that the position be restored to what it would have been had that creditor not been given preference. The court can also make orders when the debtor has given property away or sold it at an undervalue. In respect of companies, the relevant provisions are sections 238–39 of the Insolvency Act 1986. **2.** A floating *charge created within one year before the commencement of *winding-up in favour of an existing creditor. It is invalid if the company was insolvent at the time it was created unless the creditor provided some fresh benefit to the company at that time, e.g. by way of loan or goods supplied. If the charge was created in favour of a person connected with the company, the period is two years and it is not necessary to show that the company was insolvent at the time of its creation.

preference share *See* SHARE.

preferential debts The debts of a company on winding-up or of an individual on bankruptcy that have priority over unsecured debts and those secured only by floating *charge. They are defined in the Insolvency Act 1986 and include debts to the trustees of occupational pension schemes and to employees in respect of outstanding remuneration. Debts owed to the Crown (i.e. to HM Revenue and Customs) ceased to be preferential debts from 2003.

preferment *n.* In criminal proceedings, the act of bringing a *bill of indictment before an appropriate court. To **prefer** is defined in the Glossary to the *Criminal Procedure Rules as to bring or lay a charge or indictment.

pregnancy *n.* (in employment law) *See* MATERNITY RIGHTS.

pregnancy *per alium* [Latin: by another] Pregnancy of a woman at the time of her marriage by someone other than her husband. If the husband was unaware of the true facts of the pregnancy, the marriage is voidable.

prehearing review *See* EMPLOYMENT TRIBUNAL.

pre-incorporation contract A contract purportedly entered into by a person on behalf of a company at a time when the company has not been formed. Under section 51 of the Companies Act 2006, subject to any agreement to the contrary, the person purporting to act for the company, or as an agent of the company, is personally liable on the contract (*Phonogram Ltd v Lane* [1982] QB 939). Such a person can also enforce a pre-incorporation contract (*Braymist Ltd v Wise Finance Co Ltd* [2002] EWCA Civ 127, [2002] 3 WLR 322).

prejudice *n.* Preconceived judgment. *See* UNFAIR PREJUDICE; WITHOUT PREJUDICE.

preliminary hearing In cases sent to the Crown Court, a pretrial hearing in which the judge gives preliminary *case management directions in relation to the service of prosecution evidence and the *defence statement. A preliminary hearing is not required in all cases but may be ordered where case management issues call for such a hearing, the case is likely to last for more than four weeks, it is desirable to set an early trial date, or the defendant is a child or young person. Relevant provisions are set out in the *Consolidated Criminal Practice Direction. *See* PLEA AND CASE MANAGEMENT HEARING.

preliminary inquiries A set of inquiries presented by an intending purchaser of land or property to the intending vendor at an early stage in the transaction. Sometimes known as **precontract inquiries**, they relate to the state and condition of the property rather than to the title. Printed standard forms of inquiries are available. A vendor who gives false or misleading replies can be liable for misrepresentation, but a vendor's replies may be (and often are) noncommittal and evasive. Nowadays, vendors are often required to complete a Seller's Property Information Form as an alternative (*see* CONVEYANCING).

preliminary issue (preliminary point of law) In civil proceedings, an issue ordered to be tried before the main trial of the case. An order for the trial of a preliminary issue may be made by the court if the preliminary issue (which may be a question of law) will be decisive or potentially decisive in the case. Under Part 3 of the *Civil Procedure Rules the court has the power to dismiss or give judgment on a claim after a decision on a preliminary issue.

premises *pl. n.* **1.** Land or buildings; a parcel of land. **2.** *See* DEED.

premium *n.* **1.** The sum payable (usually annually) by the insured to the insurer under a contract of *insurance. Since October 1994 household and motor insurance premiums have been subject to a duty known as **insurance premium tax** (5% in 2006). **2.** A lump sum that is sometimes paid by a tenant at the time of the grant, assignment, or renewal of his lease or tenancy. It was illegal to demand a premium in respect of a *protected tenancy but this does not apply to *assured tenancies. When a premium is paid on the issue of a lease for less than 50 years, a proportion of the premium paid is treated as income subject to income tax. The part of the premium not subject to income tax is then subject to capital gains tax as a part disposal. A premium is defined as "including any like sum whether payable to the immediate or superior landlord or to a person connected with such landlord". Cases: *Elmdene Estates Ltd v White* [1960] AC 528 (HL); *Clarke v United Real (Moorgate) Ltd* [1988] STC 273; *R v Birmingham (West) Rent Tribunal* [1951] 2 KB. **3.** *See* CAPITAL.

prenuptial agreement (antenuptial agreement) An agreement entered into before marriage, usually to limit the claims one spouse can make on divorce from the other. These agreements are not binding in the UK, but may be taken into account by the court in determining how to distribute assets and income on divorce or judicial separation. Traditionally prenuptial agreements carried very little weight with the courts because they were deemed to be against public policy; however, recent cases, in particular the Supreme Court decision in *Granatino* v *Radmacher* [2010] UKSC 42, WLR (D) 260 have indicated a change of attitude. The courts will now give effect to a properly drawn up agreement that is freely entered into and where each party has received legal advice and has a full appreciation of its implications – unless in the circumstances prevailing it would be unfair to do so. An agreement that failed to meet the needs of either party or that failed to compensate them for their losses would be considered unfair, as would an agreement that prejudiced the reasonable requirements of any *child of the family. Additional cases: (*M v M (Prenuptial Agreement)* [2002] 1 FLR 654; *K v K (Ancillary Relief: Prenuptial Agreement)* [2003] 1 FLR 120; *Crossley v Crossley* [2007] EWCA Civ 1491, [2008] 1 FLR 1467).

pre-owned asset regime An income tax charge imposed on an individual who receives a benefit from an asset that he previously owned and which he passed to a new owner without (broadly) making a commercial sale. The income tax charge applies from 6 April 2005 and is only imposed where the asset is no longer treated for inheritance tax purposes as part of the estate of the person receiving the benefit. The income tax charge under the pre-owned asset regime is applied to three classes of asset: (1) land, (2) chattels, and (3) intangible property.

preparatory hearing A hearing before a judge of the Crown Court, before the jury are sworn, in a case of serious or complex fraud for the purpose of identifying issues likely to arise in the case and assisting in their comprehension and management. *See also* SERIOUS FRAUD OFFICE.

prepense *adj.* Preconceived or contrived beforehand. *See* MALICE AFORETHOUGHT.

prerogative of mercy The power of the Crown, on the Home Secretary's advice, to pardon a criminal offence absolutely (and thereby relieving the defendant of all the consequences of conviction), to commute a sentence to a milder form, or to remit a sentence in part.

prerogative orders Orders issued by the High Court in exercising its supervisory jurisdiction over inferior courts, tribunals, and public authorities. They include *mandatory orders, *prohibiting orders, and *quashing orders. Relevant rules are set out in Part 54 of the *Civil Procedure Rules. *See also* HABEAS CORPUS; JUDICIAL REVIEW.

prescribed by law A prerequisite for interference with any right in the European Convention of Human Rights: any such interference will be unlawful if it is not prescribed by law (or "in accordance with the law"). To be "prescribed by law" there must be a legal regime governing the interference in question. Moreover, that law must be both adequately accessible (in that citizens must be able to understand whether or not the law applies in a given case) and formulated with sufficient precision to enable citizens to regulate their conduct (*Sunday Times v UK* (1979) 2 EHRR 245).

prescribed limit The maximum amount of alcohol a person is legally allowed to have in his blood if he is driving or in charge of a motor vehicle on a road or public place (*R v Bolton Justices, ex p Khan* [1999] Crim LR 912: *see* DRUNKEN DRIVING). The level is currently fixed at 35 micrograms of alcohol in 100 millilitres of breath, 107 milligrams of alcohol in 100 millilitres of urine, or 80 milligrams of alcohol in 100 millilitres of blood.

prescription *n.* **1.** (in land law) The acquisition for the benefit of one's own land (the dominant tenement) of an *easement or *profit *à prendre* over another's land (the servient tenement) by uninterrupted use over a long period. A person claiming a right by prescription must show that his use did not have the servient owner's permission and was not kept secret or exercised by force. Under the Prescription Act 1832 most easements may be acquired by prescription over 20 years, the period being extended when the servient owner is under a disability (e.g. a child or person of unsound mind), although 40 years' use establishes an absolute and indefeasible right. The periods are

30 and 60 years in the case of profits. An absolute easement of light is acquired after 20 years' use. Rights can also be acquired at common law under the doctrine of **lost modern grant**, under which the court deems a grant to have been made if there has been 20 years' use of the right. Common law prescription requires proof of continuous use since time immemorial, i.e. since 1189, and is therefore practically obsolete. **2.** (in international law) The acquisition of title to territory through an uncontested exercise of sovereignty over an extended period of time. Prescription presupposes a prior sovereign authority whose control and administration over the territory in question has lapsed through (1) failure to occupy, (2) failure to administer, (3) abandonment or neglect, (4) a wrongful original claim, or (5) failure to contest a new claim. In the *Island of Palmas Arbitration* (1928) 2 RIAA 829 the tribunal accepted the principle that "the actual continuous and peaceful display of state functions is in case of dispute the sound and natural criterion of territorial sovereignty", and found that the evidence demonstrated that the Netherlands had been exercising undisputed sovereignty over the island for more than 200 years.

pre-sentence report A report, normally prepared by a probation officer or youth offending team worker, made with a view to assisting a criminal court to determine the most suitable method of dealing with an offender. It is based on interviews with the offender. The report considers the offence itself, the culpability of the offender, and the offender's circumstances, as well as the risk of the offender re-offending and of harm to the public. It also gives the probation officer's opinion on the suitability of particular kinds of sentence, such as a *community sentence. Under the Criminal Justice Act 2003 a court will normally order a pre-sentence report before imposing a sentence of imprisonment or making a *community order with requirements.

presentment *n.* The act of presenting a *bill of exchange to the person upon whom it is drawn for his *acceptance or for payment. When a bill is payable after sight, presentment for acceptance is necessary in order to fix its *maturity. Bills must normally be presented for payment; otherwise the drawer and endorsers are discharged. There are rules as to the time and place of presentment.

presents *pl. n. See* DEED.

preserved county A *county that remains in existence for certain legal purposes, such as licensing legislation, although it has been abolished as a *local government area after local government reorganization.

presiding judge A *puisne judge appointed by the Lord Chancellor to supervise the work of a particular circuit (*see* CIRCUIT SYSTEM). Each circuit has two presiding judges with the exception of the South-Eastern circuit, which has the Lord Chief Justice and two puisne judges. There is a Senior Presiding Judge for England and Wales.

pressing social need A concept used by the European Court of Human Rights as the basis for assessing whether or not an interference with a *qualified right is *necessary in a democratic society (*Sunday Times v UK* (1979) 2 EHRR 245).

presumption *n.* A supposition that the law allows or requires to be made. Some presumptions relate to people, e.g. the presumption of innocence and of sanity (see entries below). Others concern events, e.g. the presumption of legality (***omnia praesumuntur rite et solemniter esse acta***: all things are presumed to have been done correctly and solemnly). Most relate to the *interpretation of written documents, particularly statutes. Almost every presumption is a **rebuttable presumption**, i.e. it holds good only in the absence of contrary evidence. Thus, the presumption of innocence is destroyed by positive proof of guilt. An **irrebuttable presumption** is one that the law does not allow to be contradicted by evidence, as, for example, the presumption that a child below the age of 10 is incapable of committing a crime (*see* DOLI CAPAX). *See also* EQUITABLE PRESUMPTIONS.

presumption of advancement *See* ADVANCEMENT.

presumption of death A common-law presumption that someone has died. The presumption will be made if a spouse has been missing for at least seven years (with nothing to indicate that he or she is still alive) or by proof of other reasonable grounds (e.g. that the spouse was on a ship that sank). *See also* DECREE OF PRESUMPTION OF DEATH AND DISSOLUTION OF MARRIAGE.

presumption of due execution If on the face of it a will appears to be duly executed, a court will not inquire further into the circumstances of its execution, but will presume that all formalities were properly observed, unless there is positive and reliable evidence to the contrary. *See* EXECUTION OF WILL.

presumption of innocence The legal presumption that every person charged with a criminal offence is innocent until proved guilty. Although this is termed a "presumption" it is in fact a fundamental principle underlying the criminal law, which has been reinforced by the Human Rights Act 1998 (*see* FAIR TRIAL). *See* BURDEN OF PROOF.

presumption of legality *See* PRESUMPTION.

presumption of legitimacy *See* LEGITIMACY.

presumption of negligence *See* RES IPSA LOQUITUR.

presumption of sanity The legal presumption that every person charged with a criminal offence was sane (and therefore responsible in law) at the time he is alleged to have committed the crime. *See* INSANITY.

presumption of survivorship *See* COMMORIENTES.

presumptive evidence *See* PRIMA FACIE EVIDENCE.

pretrial review A *case management hearing in civil proceedings. It may be held at any time after a case has been allocated to the *multi-track. Relevant rules are set out in Part 29 of the *Civil Procedure Rules. *See* CASE MANAGEMENT CONFERENCE.

previous convictions (in the law of evidence) In civil proceedings, evidence that a party or witness has been convicted of a criminal offence on a previous occasion is normally inadmissible, unless it is relevant to any issue in the proceedings. In criminal proceedings, the admissibility of evidence of the previous convictions of the defendant or a witness is governed by the Criminal Justice Act 2003. *See* ANTECEDENTS; CHARACTER.

previous statement (in the law of evidence) The evidence of a statement made on a previous occasion by a witness giving evidence in proceedings. The Criminal Justice Act 2003 provides that a statement not made in oral evidence in the proceedings may be admissible as evidence of any matter states if the court is satisfied that it is in the interests of justice for it to be admissible. *See* HEARSAY EVIDENCE.

price *n.* In a contract of sale, the money *consideration given in exchange for the transfer of ownership. In a contract of *sale of goods the price may be fixed by the contract, it may be left to be fixed in a manner agreed by the contract, or it may be determined by the course of dealing between the parties. If the price is not determined in any of the above ways, the buyer must pay a reasonable price. Under the Consumer Protection from Unfair Trading Regulations 2008 (formerly the Consumer Protection Act 1987), it is a criminal offence to give a misleading indication of the price of goods, services, accommodation, or facilities; for example, when the consumer might reasonably expect the price indicated to cover matters for which an additional charge is in fact made.

prima facie [from Latin *prima facies*, first appearance] At first appearance; on the face of things.

prima facie case A case that has been supported by sufficient evidence for it to be taken as proved should there be no adequate evidence to the contrary. A prima facie case is defined in the Glossary to the *Criminal Procedure Rules as a prosecution case that is strong enough to require the defendant to answer it.

prima facie evidence **1. (presumptive evidence)** Evidence that is sufficient to discharge any evidential *burden of proof borne by a party and that may be sufficient to discharge the persuasive burden of proof if no evidence in rebuttal is tendered. **2.** Evidence of a fact that is of sufficient weight to justify a reasonable inference of its existence but does not amount to conclusive evidence of that fact.

Primary Care Trust (PCT) Formerly, a self-governing body within the NHS that had responsibility for ensuring that the organizations providing health and social care services in a local community were working effectively; these included hospitals, dentists, opticians, mental health services, patient transport, pharmacies, and opticians. From 2013 PCTs were replaced by *Clinical Commissioning Groups under the Health and Social Care Act 2012.

primary evidence Evidence, such as the original of a document, that by its nature does not suggest the existence of better evidence *See* BEST-EVIDENCE RULE; SECONDARY EVIDENCE.

primary facts Facts found by the trial court to be established on the basis of the testimony of witnesses and the production of real or documentary evidence. Appellate courts are generally unwilling to change the trial court's findings concerning primary facts, but may reverse its decisions concerning the inferences to be drawn from them.

Prime Minister The head of the UK government, who is appointed by the Crown to select and preside over the *Cabinet and bears ultimate responsibility for the policy and machinery of government. The Prime Minister also advises the Crown on such matters as the creation of peerages and the making of senior appointments (e.g. the Ombudsman). Like the Cabinet, the office derives from *constitutional convention, which requires that the person appointed is the leader of the party with the greatest number of Members of Parliament.

principal *n*. **1.** (in criminal law) The person who actually carries out a crime. (Formerly, the actual perpetrator was known as the **principal in the first degree** and a person who aided and abetted was called **principal in the second degree**, but the former is now known as the principal and the latter as the secondary party.) The law on principals and *accessories is codified in the Accessories and Abettors Act 1861 s 8 (as amended by the Criminal Law Act 1977) for indictable offences and the Magistrates' Courts Act 1980 s 44 for summary offences. A person can be a principal even if he does not carry out the act himself; for example, if he acts through an innocent agent, such as a child, or if he is legally responsible for the acts of another (e.g. because of *vicarious liability). Note also that even if for some reason the secondary party is incapable of committing the offence as a principal he can still be convicted of the offence: in *Ram v Ram* [1893] 17 Cox CC 609 a woman was found guilty of aiding and abetting in a rape (even though a woman cannot commit rape as a principal). **2.** (in the law of agency) The person on whose behalf an *agent acts. **3.** (in finance) The sum of money lent or invested, as distinguished from the interest.

Principal Registry *See* PROBATE REGISTRY.

principle of legality *See* NULLUM CRIMEN SINE LEGE.

priority *n. See* PRIORITY OF ASSIGNMENT; PRIORITY OF MORTGAGES; PRIORITY OF TIME.

priority notice In the case of unregistered land, a notice lodged at the Land Charges Department of the intended registration of a charge. The priority notice is lodged at least 15 days before the intended charge is to take effect, and the subsequent registration of the charge will be effective from the time the charge was created, provided the application for registration is presented within 30 days after the priority notice. Thus when A is about to convey land to B, who is to give a restrictive covenant in A's favour, A may lodge a priority notice before completing the transaction and register the covenant afterwards. This will ensure that the covenant will bind any purchaser or mortgagee from B whose interest may arise before A can register the covenant as a charge.

priority of assignment The order in which two or more *assignments of a chose in action takes effect. This order is determined according to the date of receipt of the notice of assignment by the legal owner of the property assigned.

priority of mortgages The order in which two or more mortgages of the same property take effect. If there are several mortgages of the same property, and its value is less than the amount due on the mortgages, the respective claims of the mortgagees must be determined. Before 1926, priority often depended on the date order in which the mortgages were created. Since 1925 the order of priority in the case of *registered land is according to the date order in which the respective mortgages are registered. A first mortgagee of *unregistered land usually retains the title deeds and has priority over others except prior mortgages that are registered as a land charge in the Land Charges Registry. Otherwise the order is governed by the order of registration. Priority of equitable interests is determined by the date at which notice is received by the trustees. *See also* CONSOLIDATION OF MORTGAGES; TACKING.

priority of time When there are two or more competing equitable interests, the equitable maxim *qui prior est tempore potior est jure* (he who is earlier in time is stronger in law) applies. This means that the first in time prevails over the others. For example, where a property is subject to two mortgages, the one granted first has priority (*see* PRIORITY OF MORTGAGES). However, the priority can be affected by the existence of a purchaser for value without notice, fraud, estoppel, gross negligence, registration, and overreaching.

privacy *n.* The right to be free from unwarranted intrusion and to keep certain matters from public view, as recognized in Article 8 of the European Convention on Human Rights and the *Human Rights Act 1998. The right includes privacy of communications (telephone calls, correspondence, etc.); privacy of the home and office; environmental protection (including freedom from excessive noise: *Hatton v UK* [2003] 37 EHRR 611);

the protection of physical integrity; protection from unjustified prosecution and conviction for those engaged in consensual nonviolent sexual activities; and protection from being photographed and described in circumstances where the individual has a reasonable expectation of privacy (*Campbell v MGN Ltd* [2004] UKHL 22, [2004] 2 AC 457), including by way of CCTV cameras (*Peck v UK* (App no 44647/98) (2003) 36 EHRR 41). Other cases have involved the search of a person by the police in a public place (*Gillian and Quinton v UK* (App no 4158/05) (2010) 50 EHRR 45), the notion of personal autonomy or self-determination (*Pretty v UK* (App no 2346/02) (1998) 26 EHRR 241), and retention of DNA profiles on a police database (*S and Marper v UK* (App no 30562/04) (2008) 48 EHRR 1169). This right is a *qualified right. Public authorities have a limited but positive duty to protect privacy from interference by third parties. Note, however, that there is no common law tort of invasion of privacy under English Law (*Wainwright v Home Office* [2003] UKHL 53, [2004] 2 AC 406). *See also* BREACH OF CONFIDENCE.

private Act *See* ACT OF PARLIAMENT.

private Bill *See* BILL.

private carrier *See* CARRIER.

private company A residuary type of *registered company defined by section 4(1) of the Companies Act 2006 as any company that is not a *public company. This form of company is prohibited from offering its shares to the public at large (Companies Act s 755). Although not a strict requirement under the Act, it is common to find such companies placing restrictions on the *transfer of shares and confining them to other (often family) members. As with a public company, a private company can consist of only one *company member. Many of the restrictions that apply to public companies (such as those relating to the issuing of shares, the holding of meetings, and *financial assistance) are relaxed under the Companies Act 2006 in respect of private companies.

private defence Action taken in reasonable defence of one's person or property. It can be pleaded as a defence to an action in tort. The right of private defence includes the defence of one's family and, probably, of any other person from unlawful force.

private foster parent A person who cares for and accommodates in his home for more than 28 days a child under 16, in respect of whom that person is neither a parent, relative, or guardian. Such a child is defined as a privately fostered child under the Children Act 1989 and as such is governed by Part 1X of the Children Act 1989. *Foster parents, unlike other carers, are subject to local authority control. The status of foster parenthood does not of itself confer *parental responsibility and hence the child may be removed from the foster parent's care at any time by its parents. A foster parent may acquire parental responsibility in several ways: an application can be made for a *residence order in respect of the child, or the foster parent may apply for adoption or seek appointment as a special guardian (*see* SPECIAL GUARDIANSHIP ORDER). *Compare* LOCAL AUTHORITY FOSTER PARENTS.

private international law (conflict of laws) The part of the national law of a country that establishes rules for dealing with cases involving a foreign element (i.e. contact with some system of foreign law). For example, if a contract is made in England but is to be fulfilled abroad, it will be necessary to decide which law governs the validity of the contract. This is known as the question of **choice of law**. Generally, under the Rome Convention (1980; in force from 1 April 1991), the parties' choice of law in a written contract is respected; rules are set down in the Convention stating which laws apply if the parties to the contract have not made a choice. Sometimes the courts must also decide whether or not they have jurisdiction to hear the case and whether or not to recognize a *foreign judgment (such as a divorce obtained abroad).

Private international law must not be confused with public *international law.

private law The part of the law that deals with such aspects of relationships between individuals that are of no direct concern to the state. It includes the law of property and of trusts, family law, the law of contract, mercantile law, and the law of tort. *Compare* PUBLIC LAW.

private life *See* PRIVACY.

private member's Bill *See* BILL.

private nuisance *See* NUISANCE.

privatization *n.* A programme of denationalization – removing the provision of public utility services from the public sector into the private sector under the auspices of public companies with public shareholders. The shareholders may or may not include the government, but increasingly do not. *See also* NATIONALIZED INDUSTRIES.

privilege *n.* **1.** A special right or immunity in connection with legal proceedings conferred upon a person by virtue of his rank or office. For example, Members of Parliament enjoy certain privileges in relation to arrest, which, however, do not extend to arrest in connection with indictable offences (*see* PARLIAMENTARY PRIVILEGE). *See also* ABSOLUTE PRIVILEGE; QUALIFIED PRIVILEGE. **2.** (in the law of evidence) The right of a witness when testifying to refuse to answer certain types of question, or of a party when disclosing documents to withhold disclosure or inspection of certain types of document on the ground of some special interest recognized by law.

Privileges are divided into two groups: **public interest privilege** and **private privilege**. The Crown has always been able to claim public interest privilege in relation to secrets of the state and other matters whose confidentiality is essential to the functioning of the public service (*see* CROWN PRIVILEGE; PUBLIC INTEREST IMMUNITY). A similar privilege may be claimed by private parties when some overriding public interest is involved. Under Part 31 of the *Civil Procedure Rules a party may make a *without notice application for an order permitting him to withhold disclosure of a document on the ground that disclosure would damage the public interest. *See* DISCLOSURE AND INSPECTION OF DOCUMENTS.

Private privileges include the **privilege against self-incrimination**, (according to which a witness may refuse to answer a question the answer to which might tend to expose him to criminal proceedings) and **legal professional privilege**. Legal professional privilege includes **legal advice privilege** (which protects confidential communications between lawyers and clients made with a view to obtaining or providing legal advice) and **litigation privilege** (which protects documents prepared by lawyers, and communications between lawyers and third parties, made with a view to existing or contemplated litigation). A privilege also attaches to *without prejudice communications made as part of an attempt to settle a claim. *See also* MARITAL PRIVILEGES.

privileged communication 1. A confidential official communication that may be withheld from production in court proceedings because disclosure of its contents would be against the public interest. **2.** A communication between parties in a confidential relationship, such as solicitor and client, evidence of which may not be given without the consent of the party to whom the privilege belongs. **3.** (in the tort of *defamation) A communication protected by *absolute privilege or by *qualified privilege.

privileged will A will that is valid even though it does not comply with the formal requirements of the Wills Act 1837 (e.g. in being written but not witnessed or in being oral) or is made by a minor. The right to make a privileged will is conferred by the 1837 Act (as extended by the Wills (Soldiers and Sailors) Act 1918) on any soldier in actual military service (a **soldier's will** or **military testament**) and any mariner or seaman at sea (a **mariner's will**). It also applies to airmen on actual military service and, on normal principles of statutory interpretation, to females as well as to males (for example, a female secretary aboard an ocean liner has been held to be a mariner at sea). **Actual military service** has been very widely interpreted. It is not confined to service as a combatant during time of war, but extends to service in any other capacity (e.g. as an auxiliary or a trainee) and to service when war is merely imminent. Service with an occupying force after a war is also included, as is service in support of the civil power against terrorists. **At sea** has received a similarly wide interpretation. A member of the naval forces is treated as being at sea if he is in an equivalent position to a soldier or airman on actual military service (e.g. if he is on shore leave during wartime).

privilege of witness *See* PRIVILEGE.

privity *n.* The relationship that exists between people as a result of their participation in some transaction or event; for example, *privity of contract and *privity of estate.

privity of contract The relationship that exists between the parties to a contract. The common law doctrine of privity of contract established that only the parties to the contract, i.e. those that provided *consideration, could sue or be sued under the contract. Third parties could not derive rights from, nor have obligations imposed on them by, someone else's contract. This position has now been modified by the Contracts (Rights of Third Parties) Act 1999. By the provisions of the Act, a person or class of persons can enforce a term of a contract to which he is not a party provided that the term purports to confer a benefit on him or the contract expressly provides for such enforcement. The Act does not, however, interfere with the principle that a person cannot incur obligations under a contract to which he has not provided consideration.

privity of estate The relationship of landlord and tenant under the same lease; as long as the relationship continues, the landlord and tenant may enforce obligations, such as covenants, under the lease against each other. For example, if L grants a lease to T, but T then assigns his lease to A, L and A have privity of estate. Similarly, if L then sells his reversion to R, R and A now have privity of estate. There is no privity of estate between different leasehold estates. If instead of assigning his lease to A, T instead sublets the property to S, S and L do not have privity of estate.

Privy Council A body, headed by the President of the Council, that formerly advised the Crown on government policy but has been superseded in that role by the *Cabinet. Its functions are now mainly formal (e.g. a few members are summoned to make *Orders in Council), but it has limited statutory powers of legislation (*see* ORDERS OF COUNCIL) and it also advises the sovereign, through committees, on certain judicial matters (*see* JUDICIAL COMMITTEE OF THE PRIVY COUNCIL) and other matters of a nonpolitical nature (e.g. the grant of university charters). There are about 350 Privy Counsellors, who include members of the royal family, all Cabinet ministers, the Speaker and other holders of high nonpolitical office, and persons honoured for public services. A Privy Counsellor is addressed as "Right Honourable".

prize court A municipal court that, in accordance with *international law, deals with questions relating to **prize**, i.e. ships, aircraft, or goods captured during wartime at sea or in port by the naval or air forces of a belligerent power. Prize law entitles the belligerent state to expropriate not only enemy vessels and goods but also neutral property suspected of carrying *contraband or running a *blockade. The Supreme Court of Judicature (Consolidation) Act 1925 constituted the High Court a prize court; jurisdiction in prize was vested in the Probate, Divorce and Admiralty Division until its transfer in 1970 to the Admiralty Court (part of the Queen's Bench Division). Prize appeals go to the Judicial Committee of the Privy Council.

probate *n.* A document issued by the Family Division of the High Court, on the application of *executors appointed by a will, to the effect that the will is valid and that the executors are authorized to administer the deceased's estate. When there is no apparent doubt about the will's validity, probate is granted in **common form** on the executors filing an *executor's oath. Probate granted in common form can be revoked by the court at any time on the application of an interested party who proves that the will is invalid. When the will is disputed, probate in **solemn form** is granted, but only if the court decides that the will is valid after hearing the evidence on the disputed issues in a *probate action. All parties who knew of the probate action and of their interest in the estate are bound by the court's order, whether or not they were parties to the action.

probate action Proceedings in court to determine, for example, whether or not a disputed will is valid or to seek revocation of a previous grant of probate. Contentious probate business is dealt with by the Chancery Division of the High Court. A will may be challenged on the grounds that it was not properly executed (*see* EXECUTION OF WILL), that the testator lacked *testamentary capacity, that it has been revoked, that it is fraudulent, or that there was *undue influence.

Probate, Divorce and Admiralty Division A division of the *High Court of Justice created by the Judicature Acts 1873–75 to take over the jurisdiction formerly exercised by the Court of Probate, the Court for Divorce and Matrimonial Causes, and the High Court of Admiralty. The Division was renamed the *Family Division by the Administration of Justice Act 1970: the Admiralty jurisdiction was transferred to the *Queen's Bench Division and the contentious probate jurisdiction to the *Chancery Division.

probate registry Any registry of the High Court *Family Division to which an application for a *grant of representation (i.e. a grant of *probate or of *letters of administration) can be made. In addition to the Principal Registry in High Holborn, London, there are various district probate registries and probate subregistries.

probation hostel Premises for the accommodation of persons who may be required to reside there by *community rehabilitation orders.

probation officer An officer whose duties include supervising persons bound by (for example) *community rehabilitation orders, *supervision orders, or *community punishment orders. A probation officer advises, assists, and befriends these and others (e.g. persons who have been released from prison or are on bail) and inquires into the circumstances of offenders in order to assist the court to determine how best to deal with them.

probation order *See* SUPERVISION ORDER.

pro bono publico [Latin: for the public good] **1.** Describing legal work that is carried out unpaid for the good of the general community. *Pro bono* work is increasingly performed by law students, who are provided with indemnity insurance for the purpose. On the high streets it has been carried out for many years by the Citizens Advice Bureaux. **2.** The principle that when the courts are engaged in the act of *interpretation of statutes, they should always do so for the public good (*Remon v City of London Real Property Co Ltd* [1921] 1 KB 49).

procedural impropriety A failure on the part of a public authority to act in accordance with the requirements of procedural fairness and in compliance with the common-law rules of *natural justice. In *Council of Civil Service Unions v Minister for the Civil Service* [1985] AC 374 (HL) the terms procedural impropriety, illegality, and *irrationality were used to denote the common-law grounds or heads of *judicial review of administrative action. Case: *Bank Mellat v HM Treasury* [2013] UKSC 38.

procedure *n.* (in court proceedings) The formal manner in which legal proceedings are conducted. *See also* ADJECTIVE LAW; PRACTICE; RULES OF COURT.

process *n.* **1.** A document issued by a court to require the attendance of the parties or the performance of some initial step in the proceedings by a defendant. When it is used to initiate proceedings it may be known as the **originating process**. Under the *Civil Procedure Rules (Part 7) proceedings are normally initiated by the issue of a *claim form. **2.** *See* ABUSE OF PROCESS.

procès-verbal [French] An informal record or memorandum of international understandings arrived at in negotiations. It is frequently a preliminary step in concluding a *treaty.

procurator fiscal In Scotland, an officer of the sheriff court (roughly equivalent to the English county court). Appointed by the *Lord Advocate, he must be a qualified advocate or solicitor. His duties include initiating preliminary investigations into criminal cases in his district, taking written statements (precognitions) from witnesses, conducting the prosecution, and conducting inquiries into sudden or suspicious deaths.

Procurator General *See* TREASURY SOLICITOR.

procure *vb.* **1.** To produce by endeavour (*AG's Reference (No 1 1975)* [1975] QB 773). Procurement is one form of *accessory liability in criminal law (*see also* AID AND ABET; COUNSEL). In order to be liable as an accessory for having procured an offence, it is necessary that the accessory's conduct be causally related to the principal's offence. Case: *DPP v K and B* [1997] 1 Cr App R 36. **2.** Formerly, to induce someone to become a prostitute or to engage in sexual activity in various prohibited circumstances. The former offences of procurement have been replaced by new offences created under the Sexual Offences Act 2003.

procuring breach of contract *See* INDUCING BREACH OF CONTRACT.

procuring disclosure of personal data An offence committed by someone who obtains personal information about an individual that is stored on a computer when he knows or believes that he is not a person to whom the data user is registered to disclose this data. Other offences are committed when the data procured in this way is offered for sale or sold. *See also* DATA PROTECTION.

production of documents *See* DISCLOSURE and INSPECTION OF DOCUMENTS.

product liability The liability of manufacturers and other persons for defective products. Under the Consumer Protection Act 1987, passed to conform with the requirements of European law, the producer of a defective product that causes death or personal injury or damage to property is strictly liable for the damage. A claim may only be made for damage to property, other than to itself, if the property was for private use or consumption and the value of the damage caused exceeds £275. A product is defined to include any goods or electricity, including component parts, raw materials, and agricultural products. A product is defective if its safety is not such as persons generally are entitled to expect. The persons liable for a defective product are:

- the producer (i.e. the manufacturer, including producers of component parts and raw materials);
- a person who holds himself out to be producer by putting his name or trade mark on the product;
- a person who imports the product into the European Union;
- a supplier who fails, when reasonably requested to do so by the person injured, to identify the producer or importer of the product.

There are several defences to liability under the Act, for example *contributory negligence; that the defect is attributable to compliance with a requirement imposed by law; that the defendant did not supply the product or did not supply it in the course of business; that the defect did not exist at the relevant time; and that the state of scientific and technical knowledge at the relevant time was not such that a producer of such products could be expected to have discovered the defect. Actions must be started within three years from the date when the claimant first had a cause of action or (if later) first knew or should have known the material facts, but not later than ten years from when the product was put into circulation. Liability under the Act may not be excluded by any contract or notice.

Compensation for defective products can also be obtained under the general principles of contract and tort. The purchaser of a defective product may sue the seller for *breach of contract in failing to supply a product that conforms to the contract (including its *implied conditions). An action in tort can be brought by anyone whose person or property is damaged by a defective product against the person whose *negligence caused the damage; this person may be the manufacturer or someone else, such as a distributor or a repairer.

Regulations establishing a new product-safety regime, based on the requirements of the EU's General Product Safety Directive, entered into force in the UK in October 2005. They apply to new and second-hand consumer products and place general duty on all suppliers of consumer goods to supply products that are safe for normal or reasonably foreseeable use.

profession *n.* Until 2005, profits from a profession were taxed under Schedule D Case II of the income tax legislation, whereas profits from a *trade were taxed under Schedule D Case I. Although there is no longer a separation of cases, profits of professions are taxed differently from those arising from a trade in a number of ways. Perhaps the most important distinction is that the value of goods gifted by a trader must be brought into the calculation of taxable profits (*Sharkey v Wernher* (1955) 36 TC 275), but there is no tax charge on the value of a professional service gifted (*Mason v Innes* (1967) 44 TC 326). An isolated transaction can be a trade, whereas it can never be a profession (*Wain v Cameron* [1995] STC 555 (CH)). Income from a *vocation is taxed in the same way as income from a profession.

Statute does not define "profession". In *IRC v Maxse* [1919] 12 TC 41 (CA) 61, Lord Justice Scrutton said: "A profession involves the idea of an occupation requiring either purely intellectual skill, or if any manual skill as in painting or sculpture or surgery, skill controlled by the intellectual skill of the operator . . . " In that case, it was held that a journalist "whose contributions have any literary form" carries on a profession; but a newspaper reporter carries on a trade.

The traditional approach of the courts is to say that a company cannot carry on a profession as the profits of a profession must be dependent mainly upon the personal qualification of the person by whom it is practised, and that can only be an individual (*William Esplen, Son and Swainston v IRC* [1919] 2 KB 731, 734). However, the Law Society now accepts registration of solicitors practising as a limited company, and other professional bodies act likewise. It may be that this change would now lead a court to accept that a company can carry on a profession (in *Newstead v Frost* [1980] 1 WLR 135 (HL) the court refused to decide the point).

profit-and-loss account A document presenting in summary form a true and fair view of the company's profit or loss as at the end of its financial year. It must show the items listed in one of the four formats set out in the Companies Act 2006. Its function is to show as profit or loss the difference between revenue generated and the expenditure incurred in the period covered by the account. *See also* ACCOUNTS.

profit à prendre The right to take soil, minerals, or produce (such as wood, turf, or fish) from another's land (the servient tenement) or to graze animals on it. It may exist as a legal or equitable interest. The right may be enjoyed exclusively by one person (a **several profit**) or by one person in common with others (a **common**). A profit may exist **in gross** (i.e. existing independently of any ownership of land by the person entitled) and may be exercisable without any limit on the amount of produce taken. It may be sold, bequeathed, or otherwise dealt with. Profits existing for the benefit of the owner's land (the dominant tenement) are generally exercisable only to the extent to which the dominant tenement can benefit. They may be *appurtenant, when the nature of the right depends on the terms of the grant; or *pur cause de vicinage* (Norman French: because of vicinity), in respect of cattle grazing the dominant tenement and straying onto the unfenced adjacent servient tenement. Profits may be created by express or implied grant or by statute; profits appurtenant may also arise by *prescription (or presumed grant). They may be extinguished (1) by an express release; (2) by the owner occupying the servient tenement; or (3) by implied release (e.g. through abandonment, which may be presumed through long *non-user, through changes to the dominant tenement that make enjoyment of the right unnecessary or impossible, or through an irreversible alteration of the servient tenement).

profits *pl. n.* Income tax on an individual's trading income or property income is charged on "profits": corporation tax is charged on the "total profits" of a company. However, in contrast to the approach taken in a number of Continental countries, the UK Taxes Acts do not provide a formulation of the measure of profit. The earliest judicial formulation as to what constitutes "profit", as a measure on which a tax liability is to be charged, was given in 1888 by Lord Herschell: "The profit of a trade or business is the surplus by which the receipts from the trade or business exceed the expenditure" (*Russell v Aberdeen Town and County Bank* [1888] 13 AC 418 (HL) 424). In recent years courts have tended to take the profits for tax purposes as those shown in the accounts of the enterprise as drawn up in accordance with generally accepted *accounting practice (*Herbert Smith v Honour* [1999] STC 173 (Ch); *Jenners Princes Street Edinburgh Ltd v IRC* [1998] STC (SCD) 196; *Tapemaze v Melluish* [2000] STC 189).

programme requirement A requirement that may be imposed by a sentencing court as part of a *community order or a *suspended sentence order under the Criminal

Justice Act 2003 or as part of a *youth rehabilitation programme under the Criminal Justice and Immigration Act 2008. The offender is required to take part in an accredited programme that is designed to change the attitudes and behaviours that led to his offending.

prohibited activity requirement A requirement that may be imposed by a sentencing court as part of a *community order or a *suspended sentence order under the Criminal Justice Act 2003 or as part of a *youth rehabilitation programme under the Criminal Justice and Immigration Act 2008. The offender is required to refrain from a specified activity or activities for a specified period.

prohibited degrees of relationships Family relationships within which marriage is prohibited (and, if celebrated, is void) although sexual intercourse within such a relationship may not amount to *incest. A man, for example, may not marry his grandmother, aunt, or niece; a woman may not marry her grandfather, uncle, or nephew. Since 1986, there are fewer relationships of *affinity within which marriage is prohibited. For example, a man may now marry his mother-in-law provided his former wife and his former wife's father are both dead.

prohibited steps order A court order prohibiting a person from taking certain specified steps in relation to a named child (e.g. taking him or her abroad) without the consent of the court. A prohibited steps order can be made against anyone, regardless of whether he or she has *parental responsibility for the child in question. *See* SECTION 8 ORDERS.

prohibited weapon A weapon suitable only for use by the armed forces and having no normal function in civilian life (Firearms Act 1968 s 5). Prohibited weapons include automatic firearms, weapons designed or adapted to discharge a poisonous liquid or gas, and ammunition containing poisonous substances (*R v Weaver* [2007] EWCA Crim 3485). It is an offence (punishable with up to two years' imprisonment) to produce, sell, buy, or possess any prohibited weapon without the permission of the Defence Council. *See also* FIREARM; OFFENSIVE WEAPON.

prohibiting order A *prerogative order, obtained by an application for *judicial review, in which the High Court orders an inferior court, tribunal, or public authority not to carry out an *ultra vires act (for example, hearing a case that is outside its jurisdiction). It is available in cases in which, had the act been carried out, the remedy would have been a *quashing order and it is governed by broadly similar rules. Formerly called a **prohibition order**, it was renamed in 1999 under Part 54 of the Civil Procedure Rules.

prohibition notice A notice under the Health and Safety at Work Act 1974 specifying activities that, in the opinion of an inspector, involve a risk of serious personal injury and prohibiting them until specified safeguards have been adopted. *Compare* IMPROVEMENT NOTICE.

prohibitory injunction *See* INJUNCTION.

prolixity *n.* Excessive length or repetitiveness in statements of case, affidavits, or other documents.

promise *n.* An undertaking given by one person (the **promisor**) to another (the **promisee**) to do or refrain from doing something. It is legally binding only if contained in a *contract or made by *deed.

promissory estoppel *See* ESTOPPEL.

promissory note An unconditional promise in writing, made by one person to another and signed by the maker, engaging to pay a specified sum of money to (or to the order of) a specified person or to the bearer, either on demand or at a fixed or determinable future time. Promissory notes are *negotiable instruments and many of the provisions in the Bills of Exchange Act 1882 apply with necessary modifications to promissory notes. Promissory notes are not presented for acceptance and the party primarily liable is the maker of a note. A bank note is a promissory note issued by a bank; the sum of money mentioned on the note is payable to the bearer on demand.

promoter *n.* **1.** A person engaged in the formation or *flotation of a company (*Twycross v Grant* (1877) 2 CPD 469 (CA)). A promoter stands in a *fiduciary relationship to the company; his functions may include drafting a *prospectus or listing particulars, negotiating preliminary agreements, instructing solicitors, and obtaining directors. Solicitors, bankers, and other professionals involved in the company, but acting merely in their professional role, are not regarded as promoters. **2.** One who introduces a private *Bill.

proof *n.* **1.** In the law of evidence, the means by which the existence or nonexistence of a fact is established to the satisfaction of the court, including testimony, documentary evidence, real evidence, and *judicial notice. Since most facts with which a court is concerned are not capable of being tested empirically, proof in the legal sense is quite different from proof in the context of mathematics or science. The uncorroborated evidence of one credible witness is sufficient proof for most purposes in the law. *See* STANDARD OF PROOF. **2.** (*informal*) The written statement of a prospective witness obtained by a solicitor. A witness is said not to have **come up to proof** if he fails to testify in accordance with his proof.

proof beyond reasonable doubt The *standard of proof required in criminal proceedings. It is often paraphrased by the judge instructing the jury that they must be "satisfied so that they are sure" of the guilt of the accused. *See also* BURDEN OF PROOF.

proof of age The age of a person may be proved by *direct evidence, such as the testimony of someone present at the person's birth, and in some cases by inferences from his appearance. It is usually proved by producing a birth certificate, under the exception to the hearsay rule relating to statements in *public documents, and evidence that the person in question is the person referred to in the birth certificate.

proof of birth Birth is usually proved by the production of a birth certificate, which is admissible under the exception to the hearsay rule relating to statements in *public documents, together with evidence identifying the person in question with the person referred to in the birth certificate.

proof of handwriting Handwriting may be proved by the testimony of the person whose handwriting it is or by that of someone who saw him execute the document in question. It may also be proved by the opinion of someone familiar with the handwriting of the alleged writer or by comparison with a proved example of the writer's handwriting. Expert *opinion evidence may also be admissible.

proof of marriage Legally valid evidence that a *marriage was celebrated. This will usually be shown by possession of a marriage certificate and proof of identity, but may also be shown by other forms of evidence.

proper law of a contract The system of law that is applied in *private international law to a contract with foreign elements. Which system governs the contract will depend on the intention of the parties to the contract, to be determined in each case by considering the terms of the contract, and all the surrounding facts. If the parties have expressly agreed which law should govern the contract, that law will normally be applied by virtue of the Rome Convention (1980; in force from 1 April 1991). If, as is usual, they have not expressly agreed, the courts try to infer their intention from all the circumstances; if it cannot be inferred, they will apply the system of law with which the contract has "its closest and most real connection". In the UK the Rome Convention is implemented by the Contracts Applicable Law Act 1990.

property *n.* Anything that can be owned. A distinction is made between **real property** (land including incorporeal *hereditaments) and **personal property** (all other kinds of property) and between **tangible property** (that which has a physical existence, e.g. chattels and land) and **intangible property** (*choses in action, including *intellectual property, and incorporeal hereditaments). For purposes of the law of *theft, property includes all real, personal, and intangible property, although land can only be stolen under certain specified conditions. For purposes of the law of *criminal damage, property does not include intangible property.

property adjustment order An order made by the court under the Matrimonial Causes Act 1972 s 24 in proceedings for divorce, separation, or nullity that affects rights of ownership of property belonging to either spouse. Such orders include the transfer of property from one spouse to another, settling property for the benefit of the other spouse or children, varying marriage settlements, or extinguishing rights under such settlements. The courts have exceptionally wide discretion in making property adjustment orders, and each case will depend on its own facts. The general aim of the discretion, and factors to be considered, are identical with those listed in relation to *financial provision orders; two other factors to be considered are the need to provide adequate housing for both spouses, and especially for minor children, and the need to allow each spouse a share in the capital value of the family assets, especially the *matrimonial home. The courts have power to order the sale of the matrimonial home or to make the home subject to a deferred trust for sale, e.g. until the children grow up. As in the case of financial provision orders, the court must achieve a *clean break wherever possible. Property adjustment orders are often awarded in addition to financial provision orders and may only be made on or after the granting of the decree of divorce, separation, or nullity.

property in goods A right of *ownership in chattels.

property register *See* LAND REGISTRATION.

proponent *n.* The party who bears the evidential, and in some cases the persuasive, *burden of proof in relation to an issue in litigation.

proportionality *n.* **1.** A principle of European Union law requiring that action taken by the EU does not go beyond what is necessary to achieve the objectives of the EC Treaty. Originally developed by the *European Court of Justice as a general principle of EC law, it is now incorporated into Article 5 of the Treaty on the Functioning of the European Union (TFEU), together with *subsidiarity. It is a requirement for validity of EU legislation and breach of the principle of proportionality can thus be used as a ground for *judicial review of acts of the EU institutions under Article 263 of the TFEU. In order to be proportionate, action must be appropriate, necessary, and not impose an excessive burden on those affected by it (Case C-84/94 *UK v Council* [1996] ECR I-5755). UK courts have been applying the proportionality doctrine since 1973 in EU cases and suggestions have been made that it should become a full head of judicial review. However, in *R v Secretary of State for the Home Department ex p Brind*

[1991] UKHL 4, [1991] 1 AC 696, the House of Lords emphatically rejected the doctrine's incorporation while conceding that future reform may occur. Since the passage of the Human Rights Act 1988, judges have discussed whether the *Wednesbury* unreasonableness test for judicial review is adequate protection for *Convention rights and whether in deciding whether a decision is unreasonable, the court might also consider whether it was proportionate (*R v Secretary of State for the Home Department ex p Daly* [2001] UKHL 2623, [2001] 2 AC 532). **2.** A central provision of the *European Convention on Human Rights. It applies particularly to the *qualified rights and where the expression "necessary in a democratic society" is contained within the article. Whether or not such a right has been violated will depend on whether the interference with the right is proportionate to the legitimate aim pursued by that interference. Thus even if a policy that interferes with a Convention right might be aimed at securing a legitimate purpose (e.g. the prevention of crime), this will not in itself justify the violation if the means adopted to secure the purpose are excessive in the circumstances. The principle is applied in the UK courts in cases under the Human Rights Act.

propositus *n.* [Latin] **1.** The person immediately concerned with an issue. **2.** An ancestor through whom descent is traced. **3.** A testator when making his will.

propounder *n.* A person in a *probate action who claims that a disputed will is valid.

proprietary estoppel *See* ESTOPPEL.

proprietor *n.* One who owns land. In the case of registered land, the registered proprietor is the person entitled to the *legal estate and is recorded as such in the proprietorship register (*see* LAND REGISTRATION). The owners of equitable interests are protected by registration of their *minor interests in the appropriate manner.

proprietorship register *See* LAND REGISTRATION.

prorogation *n. See* PARLIAMENT.

proscribed organization An organization or association declared to be forbidden by the Home Secretary under the *Terrorism Act 2000, because it appears to be concerned with terrorist activities.

prosecution *n.* The pursuit of legal proceedings, particularly criminal proceedings. The term is also used for the party instituting the proceedings. Criminal prosecutions are normally in the name of the Crown and the duty of conducting them now falls principally upon the *Crown Prosecution Service. The consent of the *Attorney General may be required before prosecution for some offences, as in cases involving national security. A private individual may bring a prosecution (most often for assault), as might a corporation (as for theft from a shop).

prosecutor *n.* **1.** The person who institutes criminal proceedings on behalf of the Crown. *See* PROSECUTION. **2.** The representative of the above in court, conducting the litigation.

prospectus *n.* A document inviting the public to invest in shares or debt securities of a public company (*see* FLOTATION). The prospectus of a *listed company, or the listing particulars in respect of debt securities of a listed company, must contain the information required by the Financial Services Authority. The prospectus of an unlisted company must comply with the Financial Services and Markets Act 2000.

prostitution *n.* The exchange of money for sex. By definition, prostitution involves at least two parties: the prostitute, who accepts money in exchange for engaging in sexual activity (or in virtue of whose sexual activity money is paid to a third-party profiteer), and the prostitute user, who pays money in order to engage in sexual activity with the prostitute. Prostitution commonly involves one or more third-party profiteers, including pimps (who offer prostitutes for the purpose of exploiting their prostitution for gain or profit), brothel managers, or traffickers (Sexual Offences Act 2003 s 57–60). Prostitution per se is not illegal, but there exist several offences relating to prostitution, including *soliciting, *kerb crawling, keeping or managing a *brothel, causing or inciting prostitution for gain, controlling prostitution for gain, trafficking into the UK for sexual exploitation, trafficking within the UK for sexual exploitation, trafficking out of the UK for sexual exploitation, paying for the sexual services of a child, causing or inciting child prostitution or pornography, controlling a child prostitute or a child involved in pornography, and arranging or facilitating child prostitution or pornography. Case: *R v Massey* [2007] EWCA, [2008] 1 WLR 937.

protected characteristics *See* EQUALITY ACT 2010.

protected child A child whom someone wishes to adopt and over whom a local authority must exercise supervision. Under the 1976 Adoption Act, such supervision is only required when the child was not placed for adoption by an adoption agency; in agency cases, the agency itself will be responsible for supervision.

protected goods (under the Consumer Credit Act 1974) Goods that are the subject matter of a regulated *hire purchase or *conditional sale agreement of which the debtor is in breach, but under which he has already paid to the creditor one-third or more of the total price of the goods, which remain in the ownership of the creditor. The creditor may not recover possession of the goods except on an order of the court, which may allow the debtor further time to pay. The restriction does not apply if the debtor has terminated the agreement.

protected occupancy The right of an agricultural worker to occupy a *tied cottage with statutory protection similar to that of a *protected tenancy. Protected occupancies were replaced by *assured agricultural occupancies by the Housing Act 1988, but protected occupancies already in existence continue to have the same protection as before. *See also* FARM BUSINESS TENANCY.

protected person A head of state (or a member of a corporate head of state), head of government, or minister for foreign affairs, or any member of his family accompanying him; or a representative or official of a state or of an intergovernmental international organization who is entitled under international law to special protection from personal injury or any member of his family who is also a member of his household. The Internationally Protected Persons Act 1978 incorporates into English law the provisions of the 1974 New York Convention on Crimes against Internationally Protected Persons. The Act gives jurisdiction to English courts to try those charged with committing certain serious acts against protected persons (e.g. rape, assault, causing actual bodily harm, wounding or inflicting grievous bodily harm, kidnapping, and certain attacks on premises), even if the alleged acts were committed outside the UK. It also creates offences of threatening to commit any of the above acts anywhere in the world, and extends jurisdiction to various types of attempts and assistance. It is no defence to any of these offences that the defendant did not know that the victim was a protected person.

protected shorthold tenancy *See* ASSURED SHORTHOLD TENANCY.

protected site A site for which planning permission has been granted for one or more mobile homes to be set up.

protected state A state that, although nominally sovereign, is under the protection of another state. Usually the protected state allows the protector full control over its external affairs but retains control over its internal affairs. Examples are the Kingdom of Bhutan under the protection of India and the State of Brunei under British protection. A protected state is sometimes called a **protectorate**.

protected tenancy A contractual residential tenancy in which the tenant has the right to a *fair rent and *security of tenure. Protected tenancies have been replaced by *assured tenancies under the Housing Act 1988, but protected tenancies already in existence continue to have the same protection as before. To qualify as a protected tenancy, the premises must be let as a separate dwelling that is within certain rateable value limits and must have been created before the Housing Act 1988 came into force (15 January 1989). There are some exceptions, including lettings to students, holiday lettings, local authority housing, and lettings in which the rent includes payment for board or attendance. If a landlord wishes to terminate a protected tenancy he must first terminate the contractual tenancy in the usual way (*see* NOTICE TO QUIT). A *statutory tenancy then comes into existence and the landlord can obtain possession only by a court order. To do this he must have suitable grounds, such as nonpayment of rent, provision of suitable alternative accommodation for the tenant, or if the landlord needs the property for himself or one of his family to live in.

There were formerly two kinds of protected tenancy: controlled and regulated. All controlled tenancies have now been converted into *regulated tenancies. (*See* CONVERTED TENANCY.) **Furnished tenancies** have the same protection as unfurnished tenancies, but they are more likely to fall within one of the exceptions to protection. *See also* ASSURED SHORTHOLD TENANCY; SECURE TENANCY; RESTRICTED CONTRACT.

protection and indemnity association (or club) An association of shipowners formed to meet, out of funds contributed by its members, liabilities that arise from maritime activities and are not covered by insurance.

protectionism *n.* The practice of protecting states or EU interests by imposing trade barriers and customs duties to prevent imports from abroad. Protectionism is the opposite of free trade. As a party to the *General Agreement on Tariffs and Trade and the *World Trade Organization, the EU seeks to ensure free trade not only between the members of the EU and the *European Economic Area but also with other countries, although not to the same extent as within the EU.

protective award An award made by an employment tribunal ordering an employer to continue to pay wages for a "protected period" to employees who have been made redundant in breach of the consultation requirements laid down in the Trade Union and Labour Relations (Consolidation) Act 1992 (*see* COLLECTIVE REDUNDANCY; DISCLOSURE OF INFORMATION). In the absence of special circumstances rendering it not reasonably practicable to comply with these requirements, an employment tribunal is empowered to make a protective award of up to 90 days. The Act provides that the protected period should be just and equitable in all the circumstances having regard to the seriousness of the employer's default. Each employee covered by the award is entitled to one week's pay for each week of the protected period. If the employer fails to make any or all of the payments due for this period, the individual employee may complain, within three months, to an employment tribunal, which may order payment (*Susie Radin Ltd v GMB* [2004] EWCA Civ 180, [2004] ICR 893).

protective trust (alimentary trust) A trust for a period no longer than the beneficiary's life, the period ending if certain events (commonly including the bankruptcy of the beneficiary) take place. At the occurrence of such an event, the income of the property is applied at the absolute discretion of the trustees for a class that includes the beneficiary or his family, the beneficiary no longer having any right to receive the income himself. The protective trust is governed by section 33 of the Trustee Act 1925.

protector *n.* A person appointed by a trust instrument, in addition to any trustees, upon whom rights or powers may be conferred. Such rights or powers are usually concerned with regulating the activities of the trustees in relation to the way in which they carry out the trusts. Although a protector does not have any trust property vested in him, he will usually be concerned to ensure that the trusts are carried out in accordance with the settlor's wishes. Protectors are rarely used in English trusts but are commonly used in trusts domiciled in offshore jurisdictions, such as the Isle of Man and Jersey. In some places, such as the Bahamas and the British Virgin Islands, the role of protector has statutory recognition.

protest *n.* **1.** An express indication that an act is not to carry an implication that might otherwise attach to it. For example, when a payment is made **under protest**, the payer does not agree that he is liable for the payment. **2.** A procedure by which a *notary provides formal evidence of the *dishonour of a bill of exchange. When a *foreign bill has been dishonoured by nonacceptance or nonpayment it is handed to the notary, who usually presents it again. If it is still dishonoured, the notary attaches a slip showing the answer received and other particulars – a process called **noting**. The protest, in the form of a formal document, may then be drawn up at a later time.

protocol *n.* **1.** The original draft of a document. **2.** An international agreement of a less formal nature than a *treaty. It is often used to amend treaties. It may also be an instrument subsidiary or ancillary to a *convention, in which case it may deal with points of interpretation and reservations. **3.** A code of procedure. **4.** Minutes of a meeting setting out matters of agreement.

provable debt A debt in respect of which a creditor can claim a share of a bankrupt's assets. A provable debt must either be incurred by the bankrupt before a bankruptcy order is made against him or arise after the order is made as a result of an obligation that existed beforehand. *Compare* NONPROVABLE DEBT.

proving a will Obtaining *probate of a will or *letters of administration *cum testamento annexo*. A *CODICIL to a will also needs to be proved with the will.

provisional damages Damages given in personal injury cases when the injuries sustained may cause in the future some serious disease or other serious deterioration in the claimant's physical or mental condition. Under the Supreme Court Act 1981 s 32A the court has the power to make an immediate award of damages on the basis of the claimant's present condition and to order that he can come back within a specified time for a further award if the disease or condition develops.

provisional liquidator A person appointed by the court to conduct the *compulsory winding-up of a company pending the appointment of a *liquidator. Either the *official receiver or a qualified *insolvency practitioner may be appointed.

provisional orders Orders made by government ministers but requiring confirmation by Act of Parliament (a Provisional Order Confirmation Act) before becoming law. They do not, therefore, constitute *delegated legislation. Provisional orders were formerly used extensively, primarily to confer powers on local authorities, but have been largely superseded by *special procedure orders.

proviso *n.* A clause in a statute, deed, or other legal document introducing a qualification or condition to some other provision, frequently the one immediately preceding the proviso itself.

In criminal appellate procedure, **applying the proviso** occurs when the Court of Appeal uses the power conferred by the proviso to section 2 of the Criminal Appeal Act 1968. This empowers the court to dismiss an appeal if it considers that no miscarriage of justice has occurred, even though it believes that the point raised in the appeal might be decided in favour of the appellant.

provocation *n.* *See* LOSS OF CONTROL.

proxy *n.* A person (not necessarily a company member) appointed by a company member to attend and vote instead of him at a company meeting (Companies Act 2006 s 324). Directors often offer themselves as proxies by sending out proxy forms with the notice of the meeting. When this is done at company expense, forms must be sent to all company members alike. In the case of a *listed company, the form must enable members to direct the proxy whether to vote for or against the resolution; in other cases, it may specify that the proxy is to use his discretion. The *articles of association may confer more extensive rights on members or proxies than are conferred by the Companies Act (s 331).

proxy decision A decision made with or on behalf of a person who lacks full legal capacity to *consent to or refuse medical treatment (*see* INCOMPETENT PATIENT). In the case of children under the age of 16 years who are not *Gillick-competent, their parents will usually be asked to take a proxy decision about their care. For adults, a person previously nominated by the patient while competent (a donee of a patient's *lasting power of attorney) may make this decision. The decision itself may be based on either a judgment of the patient's *best interests or a judgment as to what he or she would wish in the circumstances (a *substituted judgment). *See also* ADVANCE DECISION.

psychiatric injury A recognized psychiatric illness (such as post-traumatic stress disorder) that is caused by sudden shock, as distinct from normal grief, sorrow, or anxiety. There is no general *duty of care for psychiatric injury. A distinction is made between **primary victims** and **secondary victims** (*Page v Smith* [1995] AC 155 (HL)). A primary victim is someone within the range of foreseeable physical injury, typically a participant in the accident; damages are recoverable for psychiatric injury as for physical injury, even if no physical injury has occurred. Secondary victims are those outside the range of foreseeable physical injury, such as witnesses or relatives of the accident victims. For these victims the duty of care is strictly limited and control factors of proximity apply (*Alcock v Chief Constable of South Yorkshire Police* [1994] 1 AC 310 (HL)). Psychiatric injury was formerly known as **nervous shock**.

psychopathic disorder Formerly, under the Mental Health Act 1983, a form of *mental disorder resulting in abnormally aggressive or seriously irresponsible conduct. The Mental Health Act 2007 amended the 1983 Act to create a single category of mental disorder or disability.

Public Accounts Committee A nondepartmental select committee of the House of Commons, established in 1861 to examine government expenditure and report on any irregularity or other matter to which it considers that attention should be drawn. It has 15 members and a chairman who is customarily a member of the Opposition.

public Act *See* ACT OF PARLIAMENT.

publication *n.* **1.** (in the law of *defamation) The communication of defamatory words to a person or persons other than the one defamed. In the English law of tort, publication to at least one other person must be proved. Communication between husband and wife does not amount to publication, but communication by the defendant to the spouse of the claimant is sufficient. Dictation of a defamatory statement to a secretary or typist is publication, but return of the document by the secretary to its author is not. Publication to persons other than the one defamed is not required in Scottish law or in criminal libel. **2.** (in copyright law) The issuing of reproductions of a work or edition to the public. Protection under the Copyright, Designs and Patents Act 1988 may depend on whether the work has been published. **3.** *See* OBSCENE PUBLICATION.

publication on a matter of public interest A statutory defence in *defamation that applies to statements of both fact and opinion. The statement must be on a matter of public interest and the defendant must reasonably believe it is in the public interest to publish it. The defence was introduced by the Defamation Act 2013 as a replacement for the so-called Reynolds defence of "responsible journalism" (*see* QUALIFIED PRIVILEGE).

public authorities (in human rights law) Under the *Human Rights Act1998 (s 6) "public authorities" have duties to refrain from breaching the rights in the Act and victims are provided with remedies (s 7). Government departments, local authorities, and courts and tribunals are all public authorities. A private body carrying out public functions is not a "public authority" (*YL v Birmingham City Council* [2007] UKHL 27, [2008] 1 AC 95) unless it is a care home (Health and Social Care Act 2008 s 145); however, a social landlord such as a housing association will be subject to the Human Rights Act (*R (Weaver) v London and Quadrant* [2009] EWCA Civ 587, [2010] 1 WLR 363).

public Bill *See* BILL.

public body Any body, corporate or otherwise, that performs its duties and exercises its powers for the public benefit, as opposed to private gain. Under the Local Government Act 1972, public bodies include local authorities, trustees, commissioners, and those who have duties to provide cemeteries and markets and act for the improvement of any place, or who have powers to issue or levy *precepts. The Public Bodies Act 2011 empowered ministers to abolish or reform those public bodies listed in its schedules, with the aim of increasing accountability and controlling costs.

public company A type of registered company that can offer its shares to the public (Companies Act 2006 s 4; *compare* PRIVATE COMPANY). Its certificate of incorporation must state that it is a public company (s 761), that its name ends with the words "public limited company" or plc (s 58), and that its *authorized capital is at least the authorized minimum (£50,000 or prescribed euro equivalent: s 763). It cannot do business until it has allotted shares with a nominal value corresponding with the authorized minimum (s 761). It cannot allot shares except upon payment of one-quarter of their nominal value plus any *share premium (s 586). £12,500 is therefore its minimum capital. It thus may not have much wealth or substance, although many assume the contrary. Under the Companies Act 2006 an undertaking to do work or perform services is not an acceptable *consideration for shares in a public company (s 585), and other non-cash considerations are subject to independent valuation. *See also* FLOTATION; STOCK EXCHANGE.

public corporation A corporation established to perform a public function, frequently commercial but not necessarily so (it may be social, advisory, or of any other character). Thus bodies established to manage nationalized industries are public corporations, as are such bodies as English Nature. A public corporation is normally a **statutory corporation**, i.e. established by Act of Parliament; exceptions include the British Broadcasting Corporation, which was established by royal charter. The *privatization programme that has been in operation in the UK since the 1980s has reduced the number of public corporations as their functions have been taken over by public companies and the government has divested itself, either wholly or substantially, of the statutory and financial commitment to the provision of public utilities (such as telecommunications, water, electricity, and gas). As these corporations have been privatized, *regulatory agencies have been established as watchdog bodies.

public document A document concerned with a public matter, made under a public duty to inquire into all the circumstances recorded and meant for public inspection. Statements in public documents, such as public registers, are generally admissible as an exception to the rule against *hearsay evidence.

public duties Certain public officers, including magistrates, councillors, school and college governors, and members of health authorities, are entitled under the Employment Rights Act 1996 to time off work to fulfil their official duties. An employee entitled to time off work for public duties does not have a statutory right to be paid for his periods of absence. No specific right to time off for jury service is given, but failure to attend jury service is contempt of court, therefore an implied right to time off probably exists.

public examination In *bankruptcy proceedings, an investigation into the affairs, dealings, and property of a debtor. It takes place in open court and the debtor is compelled to attend and answer questions on oath.

public general Act *See* ACT OF PARLIAMENT.

public good A special defence to some charges under section 4 of the Obscene Publications Act 1959 (*R v Penguin Books* [1961] Crim LR 176). *See* OBSCENE PUBLICATION.

Public Health England (PHE) A new organization created as part of the restructuring of the *National Health Service in 2013. The role of Public Health England is to coordinate a national public health service, to build an evidence base to support local public health services, to provide leadership to the public health delivery system, and to support the development of the public health work force. An executive agency of the Department of Health, PHE works with local and national government, industry, and the NHS. *See also* NHS ENGLAND.

public house Under the Local Government Act 1966, any premises licensed for the sale of intoxicating liquor for consumption on the premises, this (apart from any ancillary or incidental trade or business) being the only trade carried on there.

public interest immunity A doctrine that authorizes the nondisclosure of information or documents relevant to litigation on the basis that disclosure of such evidence is against the public interest. According to the doctrine of *Crown privilege, only the Crown could apply to the court to suppress evidence on this basis, it being accepted that a ministerial affidavit or certificate to the effect that the production of certain evidence would be contrary to the public interest was conclusive. Crown privilege has now been replaced by public interest immunity, which enables any party or witness in any proceedings to apply for nondisclosure (*R v Lewes Justices, ex p Home Secretary* [1973]

AC 388). Where a claim of public interest immunity is made, it is for the court to weigh the interests of justice against the reasons for the claim of immunity. In the majority of cases this requires the court to inspect the documents. If, in the view of the court, the public interest would not be prejudiced by disclosure, production of the documents will be ordered (*Conway v Rimmer* [1968] AC 910 (HL); *Burmah Oil v Bank of England* [1980] AC 1090 (HL); *Air Canada v Secretary of State for Trade (No 2)* [1983] 2 AC 394 (HL); *R v Chief Constable of West Midlands Police, ex p Wiley* [1995] AC 274 (HL)).

publicist *n.* An international legal scholar whose works, in accordance with Article 38(1)(d) of the Statute of the *International Court of Justice, are a subsidiary source for determining the rules of public international law. The Court has so far found no occasion to rely on this particular source.

public law The part of the law that deals with the constitution and functions of the organs of central and local government, the relationship between individuals and the state, and relationships between individuals that are of direct concern to the state. It includes constitutional law, administrative law, tax law, and criminal law. *Compare* PRIVATE LAW.

public limited company (plc) *See* LIMITED COMPANY; PUBLIC COMPANY.

public mischief Conduct damaging the interests of the community; for example, making bogus telephone calls to the police. Until 1975 this was regarded as a crime but it is now no longer so regarded, nor is conspiracy to effect a public mischief. There is, however, a special statutory offence of *wasting police time (Criminal Law Act 1967 s 5) and it is also an offence if a person knowingly gives or causes to be given a false alarm of fire to a person acting on behalf of a fire rescue authority (Fire and Rescue Services Act 2004 s 49). *See also* BOMB HOAX; SENDING DISTRESSING LETTERS.

public morals The basic moral structure of society. Judges have occasionally said that they retain a general overriding discretion to punish as crimes behaviour that is destructive of public morals but it is not at all clear to what extent they should do so. The abolition of the crimes of homosexual conduct and suicide was based on the assumption that matters of morals that do not directly harm other people should not be the subject of criminal legislation. Cases: *Shaw v DPP* [1962] AC 220 (HL); *Knuller (Publishing, Printing and Promotions) Ltd v DPP* [1973] AC 435 (HL). *See also* CORRUPTION OF PUBLIC MORALS.

public nuisance *See* NUISANCE.

public office Employment in the *Civil Service or in any other capacity in which remuneration is provided by Parliament or the Consolidated Fund. Holders of public office include government ministers, councillors and local government officers, judges, and magistrates.

public or general rights *See* DECLARATION CONCERNING PUBLIC OR GENERAL RIGHTS.

public place A place to which the public has access. The main offences relating to public places are: (1) being found drunk or being drunk and disorderly in a public place; (2) carrying a *firearm, *offensive weapon, or bladed article in a public place; (3) *soliciting in a public place; and (4) displaying support for a *proscribed organization in a public place. *See also* OFFENCES AGAINST PUBLIC ORDER.

public policy The interests of the community. If a contract is (on common-law principles) contrary to public policy, this will normally make it an *illegal contract. In a few cases, however, such a contract is void but not illegal, and is treated slightly more leniently (for example, by *severance). Contracts that are illegal because they contravene public policy include any contract to commit a crime or a tort or to defraud the revenue, any contract that prejudices national safety or the administration of justice, and any *immoral contract. Contracts that are merely void include contracts in *restraint of trade and in *restraint of marriage and *marriage brokage contracts.

public procurement Obtaining goods or services for the use of the public sector. Procurement in this sector is often formalized, and contracts for public works, supplies, or services, which can be large, are advertised for formal tender. In the 1970s the EU, finding that most public contracts in the EU were placed with local suppliers, issued directives requiring that large public supply and works contracts must be advertised throughout the EU and be open to all who meet the requirements set out in them. These directives have been amended and revised and now extend to cover services and utility contracts. Three alternative procedures for submitting tenders are set out in the directives; of these, the **open procedure** is generally regarded as the fairest and is the one that must most often be used. The basic principle for all three procedures is that if the value of a contract for public works, supplies, or services (or of a contract for utilities whether in the public sector or not) is over a certain minimum financial level, the contract must be advertised in the EU's *Official Journal* and suppliers from all EU states are entitled to put in tenders. The company winning the contract must be chosen fairly in accordance with formulae set down in the relevant directive. When the procedure is not followed, there is a right to claim damages under separate remedies directives.

public prosecutor *See* DIRECTOR OF PUBLIC PROSECUTIONS.

public trust A trust for the benefit of the public, which may or may not be a *charitable trust.

Public Trustee A public officer, appointed by the Lord Chancellor under the Public Trustee Act 1906, who is a *corporation sole under that name and who may act as an executor, the administrator of an estate of a deceased person, a *custodian trustee, a *judicial trustee, or an ordinary trustee. The Public Trustee cannot accept certain trusts, e.g. those exclusively for charitable or religious purposes, those governed by foreign law, or those involving the management of a business. He has a duty to administer small estates unless there is some good reason for his refusal.

puff *n.* An exaggerated claim about a product made in an advertisement or other promotional material. Claims of this kind that are not likely to be taken literally by consumers are considered part of the normal rhetoric of advertising: as such, they are not prohibited by the Fair Trading Act 1973.

puisne *adj.* [from Old French *puisné*, later born] Inferior; of lesser rank.

puisne judge Any ordinary judge of the High Court. Puisne judges are referred to as (for example) "Mr Justice Smith", even though they are knighted upon appointment. They must be barristers of at least seven years' standing or circuit judges of two years' standing.

puisne mortgage A legal mortgage of unregistered land in which the mortgagee does not keep the title deeds of the land as security. Usually a first mortgagee retains the deeds; thus subsequent mortgages will be puisne and should be protected by registration (*see* REGISTRATION OF ENCUMBRANCES).

punctationes *pl. n.* [Latin: points] In public international law, negotiations on the items that are to be contained within a future treaty. Any agreement reached on these points is not binding, unless it is included in a preliminary treaty.

punishment *n.* A penalty imposed on a defendant duly convicted of a crime by an authorized court. The punishment is declared in the *sentence of the court. The two basic principles governing punishment are *nullum crimen sine lege* (no crime without a law) and *nulla poena sine lege* (no punishment without a law).

There are various different theories about the nature and purposes of punishment, and these can have quite different implications for sentencing and for penal policy in general. The provisions of the English legal system reflect four main approaches to the issue of punishment, based on ideas of retribution, deterrence, incapacitation, and rehabilitation.

The theory of **retribution** holds that a criminal merits his just punishment because he has done something morally or socially evil. In some forms, the theory implies that the punishment should be proportionate to the harm done, rather than to the moral guilt of the criminal. Ultimately, the retributive view holds that punishment is a requirement of *natural law that does not require further justification in terms of outcomes or results (e.g. its effects on the offender or on society at large). However, most modern defences of retribution would emphasize its role in reinforcing the moral values of society and expressing the public's outrage at certain crimes.

The main challenge to the idea of retribution for its own sake comes from the utilitarian view that all punishment is evil, in so far as it adversely affects human happiness, and can therefore only be justified in so far as it prevents greater unhappiness or harm (*see* UTILITARIANISM). This is the basis of the theory of **deterrence**, in which the punishment is aimed at deterring the criminal from repeating his offences (specific deterrence) or deterring others from committing similar acts (general deterrence). *See also* CLASSICAL SCHOOL OF CRIMINOLOGY.

Utilitarian theory can also be used to justify the **incapacitation** of offenders in the public interest. Most obviously, custodial sentences may be required to protect the public from further harm, particularly when the crimes involve violence. This principle has influenced modern approaches to the sentencing of *dangerous offenders and *repeat offenders and lies behind the practice of electronic tagging.

Utilitarian thinking also holds that, where possible, sentences should be designed to assist in the **rehabilitation** or **reform** of the criminal. Sentences may therefore involve an element of training or education and may sometimes include a requirement for medical or psychological treatment (e.g. in cases of drug addiction or certain behavioural problems). The idea of rehabilitation is generally accepted in relation to young offenders, and is also reflected in the system of *parole, under which the length of a period of detention may be made dependent on the offender's good or bad behaviour (*see also* SPENT CONVICTION).

Legislators and judges have to bear in mind all these concepts in laying down and applying *sentences. For example, the extent to which crimes should be punished without proof of *intention or *recklessness (e.g. crimes of *negligence and *strict liability) depends on which theory of punishment one adopts. Parliament has created a large number of so-called **regulatory offences** (e.g. road traffic offences and offences relating to production of food), which usually do not involve moral guilt and are often punished despite the absence of *mens rea*. It is also a matter of considerable controversy whether or not the criminal law should punish morally objectionable conduct that does not obviously harm anyone (e.g. *corruption of public morals).

The European Convention on Human Rights (signed 1950) forbids the use of "inhuman or degrading" punishment; this prohibition is now part of UK law as a consequence of the *Human Rights Act 1998 (*see* DEGRADING TREATMENT OR

PUNISHMENT; INHUMAN TREATMENT OR PUNISHMENT). Similarly, the prohibition on the use of **arbitrary punishment**, as set out in Article 7 of the Convention, is now incorporated into the Human Rights Act. This provision makes unlawful the use of criminal penalties that are not prescribed by law.

punitive damages *See* EXEMPLARY DAMAGES.

pur autre vie *See* ESTATE PUR (OR PER) AUTRE VIE.

pur cause de vicinage *See* PROFIT À PRENDRE; COMMON.

purchaser *n.* **1.** (in land law) Any person who acquires land otherwise than by mere operation of law. Thus a purchaser may be a mortgagee or one to whom land is given or bequeathed as well as one who buys land for money or other consideration. A tenant in tail (whose interest devolves upon him automatically on his ancestor's death) is not a purchaser, nor is one who acquires title by *adverse possession. **2.** A *buyer.

purchaser for value without notice One who acquires land either in return for money or other consideration having monetary value and who does not know and has no reason to know of an encumbrance that adversely affects the land. Such a purchaser is not bound by certain equitable encumbrances, such as restrictive covenants created before 1926 or the rights of beneficiaries under a trust in unregistered land. However, in order to take free of encumbrances, such a purchaser must act in good faith (*bona fide*), and, in any event, most equitable encumbrances are capable of registration (*see* REGISTRATION OF ENCUMBRANCES) and a purchaser is deemed to know of any interest that is registered. Some encumbrances in registered land may be *overriding interests and will bind a purchaser whether he knows of them or not. Legal encumbrances (such as legal easements) always bind a purchaser of the land whether or not he knows of their existence.

pure economic loss *See* ECONOMIC LOSS.

pure theory of law A form of *legal positivism propounded by the Austrian theorist Hans Kelsen (1881–1973) that seeks to expunge all "impurities" from its "scientific" account of law. Such impurities include psychology, sociology, ethics, and political theory. If we are to arrive at a scientific (as opposed to a subjective, value-laden) theory of law, Kelsen claims, we need to restrict our analysis to the "norms" of positive law, i.e. those norms that provide that if conduct X is performed, then sanction Y should be applied by an official to the offender. The theory therefore rules out all that cannot be objectively known, such as the social purpose of law, or its political functions. Law has only one function: the monopolization of force. Every society has a basic norm (*Grundnorm*) that must be accepted by the officials of that society for there to be an effective and valid legal order.

purpose trust (non-charitable purpose trust, trust of imperfect obligation) A trust that is not for the benefit of a human beneficiary and is not a *charitable trust. Such trusts are normally invalid as they offend the *beneficiary principle. Exceptions include trusts for the care of specific animals (*Re Dean* (1889) 41 Ch D 552), trusts for the provision and upkeep of tombs and monuments (*Mussett v Bingle* [1876] WN 170; *Re Hooper* [1932] 1 Ch 38), and trusts for the saying of masses (*Re Hetherington* [1990] Ch 1). The categories of purpose trust that have been recognized by the courts will not be extended (*Re Endacott* [1960] 2 Ch 232). Valid purpose trusts are subject to the *rule against perpetual trusts.

putative father A man alleged to be the father of an illegitimate child. If the court accepts the mother's allegations, the man is declared the putative father and may be ordered to make periodical payments for the maintenance of the child by the Child Support Agency (*see* CHILD SUPPORT MAINTENANCE) or to pay a lump sum by the court. The putative father's name may also be entered on the child's birth certificate. *See also* ILLEGITIMACY.

p

QC *See* QUEEN'S COUNSEL.

qua *prep.* [Latin: who] In the character or capacity of; in virtue of being. For example, it might be stated that "The beneficiary, *qua* beneficiary, is entitled to benefit from the trust".

qualified acceptance An *acceptance of a bill of exchange that varies the effect of the bill as drawn; for example, either by making payment by the acceptor dependent on fulfilling a condition or by accepting to pay part only of the amount for which the bill is drawn (a **partial acceptance**). A qualified acceptance is distinguished from a **general acceptance**, which assents without qualification to the order of the drawer. The holder of a bill may refuse to take a qualified acceptance; if he does not obtain an unqualified acceptance he may treat the bill as dishonoured by nonacceptance. If a qualified acceptance is taken (subject to an exception as to partial acceptances) and the drawer or an endorser has not authorized the holder to take a qualified acceptance or does not subsequently assent to it, such drawer or endorser is discharged from his liability on the bill.

qualified privilege The defence that a statement cannot be made the subject of an action for *defamation because it was made on a privileged occasion and was not made maliciously, for an improper motive. Qualified privilege covers statements made fairly in situations in which there is a legal or moral obligation to give the information and the person to whom it is given has a corresponding duty or interest to receive it (*Watt v Longsdon* [1930] 1 KB 130) and when someone is acting in defence of his own property or reputation. Qualified privilege also covers fair and accurate reports of public meetings and various other public proceedings. The privilege attaching to professional communications between solicitor and client is probably qualified, rather than absolute (*see* ABSOLUTE PRIVILEGE). Prior to the Defamation Act 2013, newspaper articles on matters of public interest, where the investigation and reporting of the issues was responsible and fair, could raise a defence of qualified privilege, if they meet a test of "responsible journalism" (*Reynolds v Times Newspapers Ltd* [2001] 2 AC 127 (HL); *Jameel v Wall Street Journal Europe Sprl* [2006] UKHL 44, [2007] 1 AC 359). Book publishers and authors may also rely on this species of qualified privilege of responsible journalism (*Michael Charman v Orion Publishing Group Ltd* [2007] EWCA Civ 972). This variant of qualified privilege was developed through further case law under the general heading of the **Reynolds defence**. Under the 2013 Act the Reynolds defence was replaced by a defence of *publication on a matter of public interest. *See also* PEER-REVIEWED STATEMENTS. **Reportage**, or neutral reporting without adoption or embellishment of the allegations or assertions being reported, will also be subject to qualified privilege (*Roberts v Gable* [2007] EWCA Civ 721, [2008] 2 WLR 129).

    The Defamation Act 1996 lists various types of statement that are subject to qualified privilege. Schedule I part I lists types of statement that have "qualified privilege without explanation or contradiction": it would not be possible to sue for such statements, unless made with malice. Schedule I part II lists types of statement that are "privileged subject to explanation or contradiction": these statements may lose their protection if the person defamed is not given adequate opportunity to explain or contradict them.

qualified right A right set out in the European Convention on Human Rights that will only be violated if the interference with it is not proportionate (*see* PROPORTIONALITY). An interference with a qualified right that is not proportionate to the *legitimate aim being pursued will not be lawful. *Compare* ABSOLUTE RIGHT.

qualified title Ownership of a legal estate in registered land subject to some exception or qualification specified in the register. If, for example, X applies to register his title to land and there is some possibility that part of it may already have been sold to another person, X's title may be registered subject to the rights of anyone having a better title to that part. The state's guarantee of good title does not protect the proprietor in respect of the specified qualification. *Compare* ABSOLUTE TITLE.

qualifying child For the purposes of the Child Support Act 1991 (*see* CHILD SUPPORT MAINTENANCE), a child who is under the age of 16, or under the age of 19 and receiving full-time education, and who has not been married. This definition applies only to "natural" children (i.e. children of both parties) or adopted children; it does not include stepchildren. *See also* CHILD OF THE FAMILY.

qualifying floating charge holder A creditor with a floating *charge over the whole or substantially the whole of a company's assets. In accordance with the Insolvency Act 1986, as amended by the Enterprise Act 2002, the holder of such a charge has the power to appoint an administrator without obtaining a court order (*see* ADMINISTRATION ORDER). *See also* ADMINISTRATIVE RECEIVER.

quamdiu se bene gesserit [Latin: as long as he shall behave himself well] A clause found in grants of certain offices (as that of judge or recorder) to secure the office holders in their posts so long as they shall not be guilty of abusing them. The opposite clause is ***durante bene placito*** [Latin: during the pleasure of the grantor]. Under the Act of Settlement 1701 (12 and 13 Will 3 c 2) judges hold their positions *quamdiu se bene gesserint*. They can only be removed upon the address of both Houses of Parliament (Article 3 clause 7).

quango *n.* quasi-autonomous non-governmental organization: a body appointed wholly or partly by the government (but not constituting a department of government) to perform some public function, normally administrative or advisory and frequently involving the distribution of public moneys. Examples are the Competition Commission and the Student Loans Company.

quantum *n.* (of damages) The amount of money awarded by way of damages.

quantum meruit (Latin: as much as he deserved) A legal principle that enables the provider of goods or services to recover fees for the provision of those goods or services. However, it will not necessarily enable those working "subject to contract" or at their own risk to recover fees. It can be used where the contract is silent about the amount to be paid and has also been applied in relation to some *letters of intent. Where there is no contract, it can enable a supplier to obtain "restitution" for work done but only where certain stringent conditions are made and the buyer benefits from the work. *See* QUASI-CONTRACT.

quantum valebat [Latin: as much as it was worth] An action to claim the value of goods that were sold without any price having been fixed, when there was an implied promise to pay as much as they were worth.

quarantine *n.* A period of isolation of people or animals that have been in contact with a communicable disease. The period was originally 40 days (hence the name, which is derived from the Italian *quarantina*), but is now approximately the incubation period of the suspected disease. Quarantine is imposed, for example, by public health regulations relating to ships and aircraft or by orders made under the Animal Health Act 1981.

quarter days 25 March (**Lady Day**), 24 June (**Midsummer Day**), 29 September (**Michaelmas Day**), and 25 December (**Christmas Day**). Rents are sometimes made payable on these days.

quarter sessions Originally, a *court of record with quarterly meetings of the *justices of the peace for a county. City and borough quarter sessions were presided over by the recorder sitting alone. In modern times quarter sessions became a court for the trial of offences triable on indictment, other than those that had to be tried at *assizes. Quarter sessions were abolished by the Courts Act 1971 and their jurisdiction is now exercised by the *Crown Court.

quash *vb.* To invalidate a conviction made in an inferior court or to set aside a decision subject to judicial review. *See also* QUASHING ORDER.

quashing order A *prerogative order, obtained by an application for *judicial review, in which the High Court orders decisions of inferior courts, tribunals, and administrative authorities to be brought before it and quashes them if they are *ultra vires or show an *error of law on the face of the record. As it is discretionary, a quashing order may be refused if alternative remedies exist. Originally called ***certiorari***, it was renamed in 1999 under Part 54 of the Civil Procedure Rules.

quasi-contract *n.* A field of law covering cases in which one person has been unduly enriched at the expense of another and is under an obligation *quasi ex contractu* (as if from a contract) to make restitution to him. In many cases of quasi-contract, the defendant has received the benefit from the claimant himself. The claimant may have paid money to him under a mistake of fact, or under a void contract, or may have supplied services under the mistaken belief that he was contractually bound to do so. In that case, he is entitled to be paid a reasonable sum and is said to sue on a *quantum meruit (as much as he deserved). Alternatively, the claimant may have been required to pay to a third party money for which the defendant was primarily liable. The defendant's receipt of the benefit need not necessarily, however, have been from the claimant. It is enough that it was at the latter's expense, and he may therefore be liable in quasi-contract for money paid to him by a third party on account of the claimant.

quasi-easement *n.* A right in the nature of an *easement enjoyed over a plot of land for the benefit of another plot owned by the same person: it would be an easement if the two plots of land were owned and occupied by different persons. If the second plot (the quasi-dominant tenement) is sold, the purchaser will acquire a full easement under the Law of Property Act 1925 s 62 provided the two parcels were occupied by different persons immediately before the sale. For example A, the owner of Blackacre and Whiteacre, lets Whiteacre to B, who uses a track across Blackacre. If A then sells the freehold estate in Whiteacre to B, B acquires an easement of way over the track (*International Tea Stores Co v Hobbs* [1903] 2 Ch 165). If the plots are not separately occupied an easement may still arise in favour of the purchaser of the quasi-dominant tenement if the easement claimed is permanent in nature, identifiable from inspection of the land, and used by the grantor (vendor) at the time of the conveyance for the benefit of the quasi-dominant tenement (*Wheeldon v Burrows* (1879) 12 Ch D 31).

quasi-judicial *adj.* Describing a function that resembles the judicial function in that it involves deciding a dispute and ascertaining the facts and any relevant law, but differs in that it depends ultimately on the exercise of an executive discretion rather than the application of law.

queen *n.* **1.** The sovereign if female (*see* CROWN). **2.** The wife of the sovereign (**queen consort**). **3.** The widow of a sovereign (**queen dowager**).

Queen *n.* By the Royal Titles Act 1953, "Elizabeth II by the Grace of God of the United Kingdom of Great Britain and Northern Ireland and of Her other Realms and Territories Queen, Head of the Commonwealth, Defender of the Faith". The Act empowers Her Majesty to adopt by proclamation such other style and titles as she may think fit. *See also* CROWN.

Queen's Bench Division The division of the *High Court of Justice whose principal business is the trial of civil actions based upon contract or tort. It also has important appellate functions in relation to appeals from *magistrates' courts and certain tribunals and exercises supervisory jurisdiction over all inferior courts. The *Admiralty Court and *Commercial Court are part of the Queen's Bench Division.

Queen's Bench Masters *See* MASTERS OF THE HIGH COURT.

Queen's Counsel (QC) A senior *barrister of at least ten years' practice who has received a patent as "one of Her Majesty's counsel learned in the law". QCs are now appointed by an independent selection panel of the highest calibre supported by a secretariat. Applicants are assessed against a competence framework. In court they sit within the bar and wear silk gowns (hence they are also known informally as **silks**). If the monarch is a king these barristers are known as **King's Counsel** (**KC**).

Queen's evidence Evidence given on behalf of the prosecution by an accused person who has pleaded guilty and is thus no longer on trial in the proceedings and who then acts as a witness against his accomplices. Such evidence is generally considered less reliable than other evidence because the witness is likely to minimize his own role and exaggerate that of his accomplices.

Queen's Proctor A solicitor who, under the direction of the Attorney General, gives legal advice to the courts on difficult or disputed legal problems involving divorce and who intervenes, generally to prevent a divorce from being made absolute, in cases in which not all the material facts were before the court earlier. The office of Queen's Proctor is held by the *Treasury Solicitor.

Queen's Regulations *See* SERVICE LAW.

Queen's Speech (Speech from the Throne) A speech prepared by the government and read by the Queen to Parliament (assembled in the House of Lords) at the beginning of a parliamentary session. It outlines the government's principal legislative and policy proposals for the session.

questioning of suspects *See* INTERROGATION; RIGHT OF SILENCE.

Quia Emptores [Latin: whereas purchasers (the first words of the preamble)] A statute of 1290 (still in force today) that forbids the creation of any new tenures (i.e. **subinfeudation**) other than by the Crown. Owners of land wishing to transfer the property may only do so by selling it, not by creating a new lord–tenant relationship. This is the basis of the modern system of conveying estates. The leasehold (or landlord and tenant) relationship fell outside the feudal system of tenures (only one of which effectively now remains, namely the freehold tenure of **socage**) and so can still be freely created as outside the scope of the statute. *See* FEUDAL SYSTEM.

quia timet [Latin: because he fears] An *injunction granted for the purpose of quieting a present apprehension of a probable future injury to property. In order to succeed in a *quia timet* action, the claimant must prove imminent danger of a substantial kind or that the apprehended injury, if it does come, will be irreparable (*Colls v Home and Colonial Stores* [1904] AC 179 (HL)).

quicquid plantatur solo, solo cedit [Latin: whatever is annexed to the soil is given to the soil] *See* FIXTURE.

quiet enjoyment One of the obligations of a landlord, which is implied in every *lease unless specifically excluded. It entitles the tenant to possess and use the land he leases without unlawful interference from the landlord or anyone claiming rights through the landlord.

quiet possession Freedom from disturbance in the enjoyment of property. In contracts for the sale of goods, unless the seller makes it clear that he is contracting to transfer only the title that he or a third person has, there is an implied *warranty that the buyer will enjoy quiet possession of the goods. This warranty is broken not only if the seller and those claiming through him interfere with the buyer's quiet possession but also if the interference is by a third party claiming by virtue of a better title to the goods. The corresponding covenant upon the sale of land extends only to interferences by the seller and those claiming through him.

qui facet per alium facit per se [Latin: he who acts through another, acts through himself] The traditional basis of *vicarious liability. It means, for example, that an employer is liable for the consequences of any act done by employees in the ordinary course of their duties and responsibilities. *See* FROLIC OF HIS OWN.

Quistclose trust A trust that arises when property has been transferred for a specified purpose but that purpose then fails. The name is derived from *Barclays Bank Ltd v Quistclose Investments Ltd* [1970] AC 567 (HL). Such a trust has the effect of "ringfencing" the property concerned (usually money) and protecting it from the claims of third parties (usually creditors). The exact nature and classification of the Quistclose trust has remained elusive. Theories range from it being a form of *resulting trust (the view taken in *Twinsectra v Yardley* [2002] 2 AC 164 (HL) (Lord Millett)), an entity consisting of a primary and a secondary trust (*Barclays Bank v Quistclose Investments* (Lord Wilberforce)), or a contractual arrangement that limits the use that the recipient may make of the money, such that a resulting trust arises in favour of the donor or lender when the purpose for which the money was advanced fails. Notwithstanding the dicta of Lord Millett in *Twinsectra*, there continues to be vigorous academic debate on the true classification of the Quistclose trust.

***qui tam* action** [Latin: who as well]. A method, now virtually extinct, by which the civil law can be enforced by private action. The incentive for such a private action is that the claimant is entitled to a share of the fine. It was often used in the past for effective enforcement of the law against Sunday trading.

quit rent *See* RENTCHARGE.

quittance *n.* A document that acknowledges payment of a debt.

quorum *n.* **1.** The minimum number of people who must be present at a meeting in order for business to be transacted. The required number is usually laid down in the *articles of association, constitution, or rules of the company or other body concerned. *See also* GENERAL MEETING. **2.** Formerly, an indication in a Commission of the Peace of the particular justices (called **justices of the quorum**) required, at least one of whom had to be present in order for business to be done.

quota *n.* A limited quantity or number of goods or other items that are permitted by a state or body to be imported, exported, or manufactured. For example, in the fishing industry the EU sets national quotas for fishing catches (*see* COMMON FISHERIES POLICY). In the practice of "quota hopping", British vessels are bought by nationals of other EU states (especially Spain and the Netherlands) in order to qualify as UK-based and therefore acquire the catch quotas allocated to the UK in respect of those vessels. Attempts by the UK to prevent this practice have been held as unlawful by the European Court of Justice (*see* FISHERY LIMITS).

quotation *n.* A listing of a share price on the London *Stock Exchange. A price may be obtained by accessing the **Stock Exchange Electronic Trading System** (**SETS**).

q

R Abbreviation for *Rex* or *Regina* [Latin: King or Queen]. Criminal prosecutions on indictment are brought in the name of the Crown, since a crime is viewed as a wrong against the public at large, or the state, represented by the monarch. Hence the formula *R v Defendant* (the Crown against the defendant).

Race Directive An EU directive (Council Directive 2000/43) that prohibits *discrimination on grounds of racial or ethnic origin. It covers employment, training, membership of workers', employers', or professional organizations, social protection (including social security and healthcare), social advantages, education, and access to the supply of goods and services (including housing). *See* RACE DISCRIMINATION.

race discrimination *Discrimination on the grounds of colour, race, nationality, or ethnic or national origins (*Mandla v Dowell Lee* [1983] 2 AC 548 (HL); *R (E) v Governing Body of JFS* [2009] UKSC 15, [2010] IRLR 136). The *Equality Act 2010 prohibits direct discrimination, *indirect discrimination, *harassment, and *victimization.

The functions of the Commission for Racial Equality were taken over in 2007 by the *Equality and Human Rights Commission. Individual complaints in the field of employment are dealt with by *employment tribunals; other complaints are dealt with in specified county courts. *See also* RACIAL HATRED.

racial harassment *See* HARASSMENT; RACIST ABUSE; THREATENING BEHAVIOUR.

racial hatred Hatred against a group of people because of their colour, race, nationality, or ethnic or national origins. The Public Order Act 1986 (s 18) contains six offences of **stirring up racial hatred**, which all require proof of words, behaviour, or material that are threatening, abusive, or insulting; for there to be an offence, the person must intend to stir up racial hatred or, having regard to all the circumstances, realize that racial hatred is likely to be stirred up. All offences are punishable with up to two years' imprisonment and/or a fine and require the Attorney General's consent before proceedings can be instituted.

The offences are as follows.

(1) Using *threatening behaviour or words or displaying threatening written material. This offence may be committed in a public or private place, but it is a defence for the accused person to prove (*see* BURDEN OF PROOF) that he was inside a dwelling and had no reason to believe that his behaviour or display would be seen or heard by someone outside that or another dwelling. Even if the intention to stir up racial hatred is not proved, the accused can still be guilty of the offence if he is proved to have either intended his behaviour or material to be threatening or been aware that it might be so. The offence does not extend to behaviour or written material that is used solely for inclusion in a radio or television programme. A constable may *arrest without warrant anyone he reasonably suspects is committing this offence.

(2) Publishing or distributing to the public threatening written material. It is a defence for the accused to prove that he was unaware of the material's contents and did not suspect that it was threatening.

(3) Presenting or directing the public performance of a play that involves the use of threatening words or behaviour. The actual performers do not commit or *aid and abet the offence, and recordings or broadcasts of plays can only involve the offence if outsiders attend. It is a defence for the accused to prove that he was unaware and had no reason to suspect that (a) the performance would involve use of the threatening words, or (b) the offending words were threatening, or (c) racial hatred would be likely to be stirred up during the performance.

(4) Distributing, showing, or playing a recording of visual images or sound to the public. It is a defence for the accused to prove that he was unaware of the recording's content and did not, and had no reason to, suspect that it was threatening.

(5) Providing, producing, or directing a radio or television programme involving threatening images or sounds. The offence is limited to broadcasts by satellite, community radio services, cable, pirate stations, and the like; it does not extend to BBC or IBA programmes. It is a defence if the accused can prove either of the following: (a) that he was unaware and had no reason to suspect that the offending material was threatening; or (b) that he was unaware and had no reason to suspect that (i) the programme would involve the offending material and that it was not reasonably practicable for him to remove the material or (ii) the programme would be broadcast or that racial hatred would be likely to be stirred up by it. Defence b(ii) is unavailable to those providing the broadcasting service. A broadcaster who uses the offending words can also commit the offence; defences (a) and b(ii) are available to him.

(6) Possessing threatening written material or a sound or visual recording with a view to its being distributed or broadcast, or (written material only) published, or (a recording only) shown or played. The offence does not extend to the BBC or IBA, and defence (a) above is available. The police are given entry and search powers in connection with the last offence.

Courts can order forfeiture of offending material after convictions.

Although hatred against a religion is not directly covered by the legislation, the Crime and Disorder Act 1998 introduced a series of racially aggravated offences and these provisions were extended by the Anti-terrorism, Crime and Security Act 2001 so as to include religiously aggravated offences (*Taylor v DPP* (2006) 170 JP 485). The Protection from Harassment Act 1997 provides remedies for those harassed on racial grounds and the Crime and Disorder Act 1998 (s 32) creates a racially or religiously aggravated form of this offence (*see* RACIST ABUSE); offenders may receive jail sentences of up to two years, a fine, or both.

racist abuse *Harassment of someone as a consequence of the harasser's biased views of that person's racial origins. The Protection from Harassment Act 1997 provides that offenders who make others fear for their safety can be jailed. Section 32 of the Crime and Disorder Act 1998 creates a racially or religiously aggravated form of this offence and offenders may receive for indictable offences jail sentences of up to two years, a fine, or both.

rack rent **1.** The yearly amount of rent that a tenant could reasonably expect to pay on the open market; a rent representing the gross annual value of the holding. *Compare* GROUND RENT. **2.** In non-legal usage, any extortionate rent.

***Ramsay* principle** In *W T Ramsay Ltd v IRC* [1981] AC 300 (HL) the House of Lords considered a claim that certain self-cancelling transactions could be used to create a non-taxable gain and a tax relievable loss. The Lords applied what became known as the *Ramsay* doctrine, stating that the court was entitled to look at the whole transaction and so to conclude that the taxpayer had not suffered a loss. The *Ramsay* principle is considered by some commentators to be a judicial limitation on the *Westminster doctrine established 45 years earlier. It is interesting to note that the decision of the House of Lords in *IRC v Duke of Westminster* was by a majority: the most senior Law Lord on the panel decided against the Duke by proposing an argument that was effectively that adopted 45 years later in *Ramsay v IRC*.

The *Ramsay* doctrine was developed in *IRC v Burma Oil Ltd* [1982] STC 30 (HL) and *Furniss v Dawson* [1984] STC 153 (HL), then effectively limited in *MacNiven v Westmoreland Investments* [2001] STC 237 (HL); on one view, it was finally put to rest in *Barclays Mercantile v Mawson* [2005] STC 1 (HL). In *Astall v Revenue and Customs Commissioners* [2010] STC 137 (CA) tax was imposed by ignoring two elements of a composite transaction as being of no commercial validity.

rape *n.* Under the Sexual Offences Act 2003, a criminal offence in which a person (A) intentionally penetrates the vagina, anus, or mouth of another person (B) with his penis, where B does not *consent to the penetration and where A does not reasonably believe that B consents. Whether A's belief in B's consent is reasonable is to be determined having regard to all the circumstances, including any steps A has taken to ascertain whether B consents. The *mens rea element for rape in the 2003 Act sets a standard of negligence whereby the defendant's honest but unreasonable belief in his victim's consent will not negate liability. Formerly, the defendant's honest belief in the victim's consent would negate liability, irrespective of whether that belief was reasonable (*DPP v Morgan* [1976] AC 182 (HL)). The offence of rape, as defined under the 2003 Act, covers some activities criminalized as *indecent assault under the former law (e.g. non-consensual penile–oral penetration) and some activities categorized as buggery under the former law (e.g. non-consensual penile–anal penetration). The maximum penalty for rape or attempted rape is life imprisonment, but this is rarely imposed. Owing to the requirement that rape be committed through penetration with a penis, it is clear that it can only be committed as a principal by a man; a woman can only be convicted of rape as an accessory (*Ram v Ram* [1893] 17 Cox CC 609). A husband can be convicted for raping his wife (*R v R* [1992] 1 AC 599) and a boy under the age of 14 may be convicted of rape (Sexual Offences Act 1993 s 1: formerly, boys of this age were deemed incapable of rape even if intercourse had taken place). A man or boy can be the victim of a rape. *Compare* ASSAULT BY PENETRATION; SEXUAL ASSAULT.

rape of a child under 13 It is a specific criminal offence under the Sexual Offences Act 2003 to engage in sexual intercourse with a child under the age of 13. *Consent is irrelevant to determining whether the offence has been committed. A person commits the offence if he intentionally penetrates the vagina, anus, or mouth of another person with his penis, and the other person is under 13. The maximum penalty is life imprisonment. Owing to the requirement that rape of a child under 13 can only be committed through penetration with a penis, it is clear that the offence can only be committed as a principal by a man; a woman can only be convicted of the offence as an accessory. The victim cannot be convicted as an accessory, even if the offence takes place with the victim's voluntary assistance, since the offence is designed to protect the victim (*R v Tyrrell* (1894) 1 QB 710 (CCR)). *Compare* ASSAULT OF A CHILD UNDER 13 BY PENETRATION; SEXUAL ACTIVITY WITH A CHILD.

rape offence Any one of the offences of rape, attempted rape, aiding, abetting, counselling, or procuring rape or attempted rape, incitement or conspiracy to rape, and burglary with intent to rape. In cases where the defendant to a rape offence pleads not guilty, the Sexual Offences (Amendment) Act 1976 limits the right to ask questions about the alleged victim's sexual experiences. It also prohibits (subject to special leave of the court) the reporting of details about the case that might enable members of the public to identify the victim. If such details are published, the publishers may be fined.

rapporteur *n.* An official of the European Parliament or of some other EU body whose job is to help discussions progress in connection with a particular matter and to prepare a report on it. In the European Court of Justice the judge in charge of drafting a judgment is known as the judge-rapporteur.

rates *pl. n.* Local taxes charged on property by local authorities to pay for the services they provide. The community charge ("poll tax") replaced domestic rates (i.e. those payable by private householders) in April 1990 in England and Wales (in 1989 in Scotland), but was itself replaced by the *council tax in April 1993. Owners of business and other nondomestic property remain liable to pay nondomestic rates based on a **Uniform Business Rate** (UBR), fixed by central government, and a local valuation of the property.

ratification *n.* **1.** Confirmation of an act. If, for example, X contracts with Y as agent for Z, but has in fact no authority to do so, Z may nevertheless adopt the contract by subsequent ratification. An unenforceable contract made with a minor can become enforceable if the minor ratifies the contract when he comes of age. **2.** (in international law) The approval of a *treaty, usually by the head of state (or by the head of state and legislature). This takes place when documents of ratification are either exchanged or deposited with a named depositary. Normally a treaty states expressly whether it will bind a party as soon as it is signed by that party's representative or whether it requires ratification. The Vienna Convention on Treaties (1969) provides that when a treaty does not specify whether or not ratification is required, reference will be made to the party's intention. Performance of a treaty may amount to implicit ratification. In the UK the expression "Parliament has ratified a treaty" is misleading, for it is the Crown that signs and ratifies a treaty on behalf of the UK. Parliament, if invited by HM Government, may give its approval for the Crown to do so, but it is the Crown, upon the advice of the responsible minister, that ratifies the treaty. Legislation is nearly always necessary to give effect to the treaty in domestic law, but that is not ratification. **3.** (in company law) A resolution of a general meeting sanctioning some irregularity in the running of a company. Some irregularities cannot be sanctioned, such as acts that are *ultra vires* or a *fraud on the minority.

ratio decidendi [Latin: the reason for deciding] The principle or principles of law on which the court reaches its decision. The *ratio* of the case has to be deduced from its facts, the reasons the court gave for reaching its decision, and the decision itself. It is said to be the statement of law applied to the material facts. Only the *ratio* of a case is binding on inferior courts, by reason of the doctrine of *precedent.

rational choice theory *See* CLASSICAL SCHOOL OF CRIMINOLOGY.

rave *n.* An assembly, unlicensed by the local authority, of 20 or more people, partly or entirely in the open air, at which amplified music is played during the night and is likely to cause serious distress to local inhabitants. Under the Criminal Justice and Public Order Act 1994 a police officer of at least the rank of superintendent may issue directions to participants to leave if it is reasonably believed that two or more people are preparing for a rave or ten or more people are waiting for one to start or are already participating in an event that will attract 20 or more participants. A *summary offence is committed by anyone (excluding the occupier, a member of his family, and an employee or agent) who fails to leave as soon as reasonably practicable or who re-enters within seven days; it is punishable by up to three months' imprisonment and/or a fine on level 4. A uniformed police officer may arrest without warrant anyone refusing to leave. He may also stop and turn back within five miles of a rave anyone whom he believes to be travelling to the rave. Failure to comply is a summary offence punishable by a fine on level 3.

There are supplementary powers of entry for the purpose of clearing the land and seizing and removing vehicles and sound equipment. Any sound equipment under the control of a person convicted under these provisions may be made the subject of a *forfeiture order.

reading down Interpreting statutory provisions that appear to create a *reverse burden of proof so that an evidential burden alone is placed on the defendant (*see* BURDEN OF PROOF). This may be necessary under section 3 of the Human Rights Act 1998, which requires that "so far as is possible", legislation must be read and given effect in a way that is compatible with the *European Convention on Human Rights.

real *adj*. **1.** Relating to land. *See also* REAL ESTATE; REAL PROPERTY. **2.** Relating to a thing, rather than to a person. *See also* REAL EVIDENCE.

real estate Under the Administration of Estates Act 1925, all interests in land held by the deceased at death excluding interests in money charged on land.

real-estate investment trust (REIT) A company that is resident in the UK, owns at least three properties that are let to third parties, and distributes at least 90% of its profits to its shareholders (Finance Act 2006 s 103–45). A real-estate investment trust is exempt from UK corporation tax. The distributions made by an REIT are not treated as dividends, but are taxed in the hands of shareholders as if they were rent received directly by those shareholders.

real evidence Evidence in the form of material objects (e.g. weapons). When an object is admitted in evidence, it is usually marked as an *exhibit. Documents are not usually classified as real evidence, but may be treated as such if the physical characteristics of the document (rather than its content) are of significance. Some authorities include evidence of identification and the demeanour of witnesses within the classification of real evidence. Photographs, video, and sound recordings may be treated as real evidence or as documentary evidence (*Taylor v Chief Constable of Cheshire* [1986] 1 WLR 1479).

real property (realty) Freehold land including incorporeal *hereditaments. *See* PROPERTY.

real security **1.** A mortgage. **2.** A *rentcharge secured on freehold land.

realty *n. See* REAL PROPERTY.

real union A treaty arrangement in which two or more states unite in order to make them one *international legal personality. A real union does not create a single state; each state can revive its own international personality should the real union be dissolved. An example of a real union was that between Sweden and Norway between 1814 and 1905.

reasonable adjustments Under the *Equality Act 2010 the employer or potential employer of a *disabled person is under a duty to make "reasonable adjustments". The duty has three requirements that apply where a disabled person would otherwise be placed at a substantial disadvantage compared with people who are not disabled. The first involves making adjustments to any provision, criterion, or practice imposed by the employer that creates such a disadvantage (e.g. where rules on sickness absence have a disproportionate impact on a disabled employee: *O'Hanlon v Commissioners for HM Revenue and Customs* [2007] EWCA Civ 283, [2006] IRLR 404). The second involves making changes to physical barriers in the workplace (e.g. providing a wheelchair ramp). The third involves providing an auxiliary aid or auxiliary service (e.g. special computer software). A failure to comply with any of these requirements is discrimination against a disabled person. The duty applies to employees and job applicants, but only where the employer is aware of the disability or could reasonably be expected to be aware of it.

The duty is subject to a test of reasonableness. This is judged objectively rather than from the point of view of the employer and will take account of such factors as: how effective the change will be in avoiding the disadvantage; its practicality and cost (judged against the employer's resources); and the availability of financial support. Cases: *Fareham College Corporation v Walters* [2009] IRLR 991; *Archibald v Fife Council (Scotland)* [2004] UKHL 32, [2004] ICR 954.

reasonable doubt *See* PROOF BEYOND REASONABLE DOUBT.

reasonable financial provision Under the Inheritance (Provision for Family and Dependants) Act 1975, the financial provision that the *dependants of a deceased person can reasonably expect to receive from his estate. If the deceased's will does not make such provision, or he dies intestate and the intestacy laws do not make such provision, the dependants may apply to the court for provision. A spouse or *civil partner is entitled to reasonable financial provision even if he or she already has enough resources for maintenance; in all other cases, reasonable financial provision is limited to the amount required for maintenance.

reasonable force At common law a person may use reasonable force in *self-defence (*R v Rose* (1884)15 Cox CC 540) and, in extreme circumstances, may be justified in killing an attacker (*R v Clegg* [1995] 1 AC 482 (HL)). Reasonable force may be used in defending one's property (*Revill v Newbery* [1996] 1 All ER 291), and if someone intrudes on one's property at night, one might be justified in treating this as a threat not merely to property, but to personal safety. An occupier of premises (even if he is not the owner) and possibly even a licensee (such as a lodger) may use reasonable force against a trespasser. The Criminal Law Act 1967 permits the use of reasonable force in order to prevent crime, to lawfully arrest a criminal or suspected criminal (or to help in arresting him), or to capture someone who has escaped from lawful detention. The Act extends to both police and private citizens. It is not altogether certain whether the statutory right includes the right to kill.

It is a statutory offence to set spring guns or mantraps, except in a private house between sunset and sunrise. One may use a dog in self-defence if this use is reasonable (*see* GUARD DOG).

If a person mistakenly thinks that he is entitled to use reasonable force when he is not he may use such force as is reasonable in the circumstances as he believed them to be (*R v Shaw* [2001] 1 WLR 1519). It seems, however, that this does not apply if he made a mistake of law, rather than fact, or if the defendant's mistake was based on intoxication (*R v O'Grady* [1987] QB 995). The defence of self-defence in so-called "householder cases" where a householder is surprised by an intruder was clarified and strengthened by the Criminal Justice and Immigration Act 2008 s 76, as amended by the Crime and Courts Act 2013 s 43. A defence of self-defence is available where a householder uses disproportionate force, mistakenly believing this level of force to be reasonable in the circumstances, but not where he uses "grossly disproportionate force". *See also* FORCIBLE ENTRY.

reasonable person An ordinary citizen, famously referred to by Lord Devlin as the "man on the Clapham omnibus". The standard of care in actions for *negligence is based on what a reasonable person might be expected to do considering the circumstances and the foreseeable consequences. The standard is not entirely uniform: a lower standard is expected of a child, but a higher standard is expected of someone, such as a doctor, who purports to possess a special skill.

rebus sic stantibus [Latin: matters so standing; in the existing state of matters] A phrase used when a state or international organization seeks to avoid or renegotiate its treaty obligations because a change of circumstances has rendered the objective of the treaty difficult or impossible. The Vienna Convention on the Law of Treaties 1969 distinguishes between supervening impossibility of performance and fundamental change of circumstances (Articles 61 and 62).

rebuttable presumption *See* PRESUMPTION.

rebutter *n.* Formerly, a pleading served by a defendant in reply to the claimant's *surrejoinder. Such a pleading was very rare in modern practice and no longer exists under the *Civil Procedure Rules.

recall of witness The further examination of a witness after his evidence has been completed. The judge may permit the recall of a witness even after the close of a party's case to allow *evidence in rebuttal.

recaption *n.* The retaking of goods that have been wrongfully taken or are being wrongfully withheld. It is a form of *self-help.

receiver *n.* **1.** A person appointed by the court under Part 69 of the *Civil Procedure Rules to preserve and protect property during the course of litigation. *See also* EQUITABLE EXECUTION. **2.** A person appointed under the terms of a *debenture or by the court to realize assets charged and apply the proceeds for the benefit of those entitled. Notice of appointment must be given to the Registrar of Companies and must appear upon business documents. The receiver may have power to manage the company. *See also* ADMINISTRATIVE RECEIVER; OFFICIAL RECEIVER. **3.** In criminal proceedings, a person appointed with certain powers in respect of the property and affairs of a person who has obtained such property in the course of criminal conduct and who has been convicted of an offence.

receivership order An order of the court that a person's assets be put into the hands of a *receiver.

receiving *n.* Acquiring exclusive control of stolen property or joint possession of it with the thief or another receiver. Thus if someone merely examines stolen goods in the presence of the thief, he is not guilty of receiving. Before 1968 this was an offence in itself, but it is now one form of the wider offence of *handling stolen goods (Theft Act 1968 s 22).

receiving order   Formerly, a court order made during the course of *bankruptcy proceedings that placed the debtor's property under the control of the *official receiver or of a *trustee in bankruptcy.

recidivism   *n.* An offender's relapse into crime after serving a sentence, especially when this proves habitual. *See* REPEAT OFFENDER

reciprocity   *n.* A provision of the Statute of the * International Court of Justice (ICJ) under which a state may limit its consent to the Court's *compulsory jurisdiction. This form of consent to suit imposes the prior condition that in any future litigation that state may invoke a claimant state's narrower terms of general consent to ICJ jurisdiction. Reciprocity thus enables the consenting state to avoid suit on the same basis that would be available to the claimant state, if the latter were a defendant in similar ICJ litigation. *See* OPTIONAL CLAUSE.

recitals   *pl. n. See* DEED.

recklessness   *n.* A form of *mens rea* that amounts to less than *intention but more than *negligence. Many common-law offences can be committed either intentionally or recklessly, and it is now common for statutes to create offences of recklessness. Recklessness has normally been held to have a subjective meaning of being aware of the risk of a particular consequence arising from one's actions but deciding nonetheless to continue with one's actions and take the risk where it is unreasonable to do so (*R v G* [2004] 1 AC 1034 (HL), overruling *MPC v Caldwell* [1982] AC 341 (HL)).

recognition   *n.* (in international law) **1.** The process by which one state declares that another political entity fulfils the conditions of statehood (*see* STATE) and that it is willing to deal with it as a member of the international community. Recognition usually takes place when a new state comes into being. Some authorities believe that recognition is constitutive, i.e. it is one of the conditions that create a state in international law (*see* CONSTITUTIVE THEORY). Most, however, regard it as being merely declaratory, i.e. an acceptance of a fact that already exists (*see* DECLARATORY THEORY).

    With the collapse of the Soviet Union and Yugoslavia in the 1990s it became imperative for states of the European Union to adopt a common policy with regard to recognition of the newly emerging sovereign states of E and SE Europe. In December 1991 the EC published its Declaration on Yugoslavia and on the Guidelines on the Recognition of New States. This made it a precondition of recognition that the new state should respect human rights and oppose the proliferation of nuclear weapons. In August 2008, following the Russian intervention in Georgia, Russians recognized the breakaway states of South Ossetia and Abkhazia. Only Venezuela and Belarus followed suit. **2.** Acceptance of a government as the legal representative of the state. This may be *de facto* or *de jure*. The distinction is a fluid one, often involving a political element, since international law allows states discretion as to whether or not to accord recognition and of which kind. The according of recognition of either kind is usually an acknowledgment that the government recognized has effective control, but the decision to give merely *de facto* recognition may reflect a wish not to show approval of the nature of the government concerned (and at the same time to be able to continue to give *de jure* recognition to the ousted government). The significance of the distinction (which is of little legal consequence) therefore depends on the intention of the recognizing government. Recognition may be express or implied (for example, by entering into diplomatic relations with a new government). *See also* ESTRADA DOCTRINE; TOBAR DOCTRINE.

    For purposes of English municipal law, the question of whether or not a state is recognized is sometimes relevant. Thus: (1) only a recognized state is entitled to *sovereign immunity from jurisdiction; (2) an unrecognized state cannot sue in English courts; and (3) when a foreign law is to be applied under the principles of *private international law, this can only be the law of a recognized state or subsidiary body set up by it. A Foreign and Commonwealth Office certificate stating that an entity is or is not recognized by the British government is usually taken as conclusive evidence in the courts. Since 1980 Britain has abandoned the practice of recognizing governments – only states are now the subject of express recognition (*Sierra Leone Telecommunications Co Ltd v Barclays Bank Plc* [1998] 2 All ER 821 (HL)).

recognition issue A trade dispute as to whether a particular trade union should be recognized by an employer as having the right to negotiate terms and conditions of employment on behalf of its members among the employer's workforce.

recognition procedure (in employment law) A statutory procedure introduced by the Employment Relations Act 1999 by which a trade union can secure the legal right to enter into *collective bargaining with an employer. As well as the benefit the trade union and its members secure from the fact of bargaining, a recognized trade union becomes entitled to all rights bestowed by employment legislation on recognized trade unions. The procedure enables unions to seek statutory recognition for collective bargaining if they fail to secure a voluntary agreement with the employer concerned.

The statutory procedure is given in Schedule A1 (as amended) of the Trade Union and Labour Relations (Consolidation) Act 1992. Statutory recognition can be requested by one or more independent trade unions, in the first instance from the employer. Such an approach (often with the assistance of *ACAS) may result in a voluntary agreement being made between the parties. Following a failure to arrive at a voluntary agreement a trade union may then refer the request to the *Central Arbitration Committee (**CAC**). If satisfied that the trade union has at least 10% membership among the group of workers it is seeking to represent, the CAC will then proceed to establish the viability of the union's request.

The CAC must satisfy itself that the proposed bargaining union is an appropriate unit and take into account such factors as the need for effective management, the relative views of the parties to the dispute, the existing national and local arrangements for bargaining, and the need to avoid fragmentation of existing bargaining units. Crucially the CAC must determine that the necessary support exists at the workplace for collective bargaining. In determining this issue a ballot may be held. However, if the CAC is satisfied that a majority of the workers in the unit are currently members of the applicant union, it may decide that a ballot is not needed. If a ballot is held (and it must be held if less than 50% of the workers are union members), the result must show that a majority of those voting support the union and that those voting in favour constitute at least 40% of the workers in the bargaining unit. The CAC then issues a declaration that the union is entitled to recognition on the basis either that a majority of the workers are union members or that a majority support collective bargaining. When this declaration has been made, the parties are given 30 days to negotiate a method of conducting collective bargaining. Failure to arrive at an agreement will result in a further reference to the CAC. If after a further period of arbitration no voluntary agreement can be reached by the parties, the CAC is empowered to specify a method for collective bargaining. This method then takes effect as a legally binding agreement between the parties.

The statutory procedure also contains provisions for the derecognition of a trade union.

recognizance *n.* An undertaking by an offender (or by sureties on his behalf) to forfeit a sum of money under certain conditions. Recognizances may be entered into to answer to judgment, i.e. to appear before the court for pronouncement of judgment on a specified date. This procedure may be appropriate if the accused wishes to appeal against conviction. Alternatively, recognizances may be used in addition to or in place of any other sentence or judgment, the offender being obligated to keep the peace and be of good behaviour. Magistrates have wide powers of binding over upon recognizances under the Statute of Westminster 1361 (which enacted into statute the laws of justices of the peace), the Bail Act 1976, and the Magistrates' Courts Act 1980; they may punish failure to comply with the order with imprisonment. *See* BIND OVER; KEEP THE PEACE.

reconciliation *n*. The coming together of estranged spouses. It is the general policy of the law to encourage reconciliation, and there are special organizations to help with this. Solicitors in divorce cases must certify whether or not they have discussed the possibility of reconciliation with their clients, and proceedings may be adjourned if the court feels there is a chance of reconciliation. When divorce cases are heard under the *special procedure the court will have no opportunity to judge whether there is a chance of reconciliation. If spouses have lived together for more than six months after separation in cases of divorce applications based on adultery, unreasonable behaviour, desertion, or separation, there is a presumption of law that they have become reconciled and a divorce is refused.

reconstruction of a company The transfer of the property of a registered company in a *voluntary winding-up to another company in exchange for shares in that company to be distributed among members of the company in liquidation. The liquidator effects the reconstruction with the authority of a *special resolution (members' voluntary winding-up) or the consent of the court or *liquidation committee (creditors' voluntary winding-up). A member who does not agree to the arrangement can require the liquidator to buy his shares. *See also* SCHEME OF ARRANGEMENT.

reconversion *n*. The imaginary process by which a fictional *conversion is considered not to have taken place: the property is reconverted in law to the state that, in fact, it has always held.

record *n*. The documents constituting an authentic account of the proceedings before a court, including the *claim form or other originating process, the statements of case, and the *judgment or order, but usually not the evidence tendered. The record of an inferior court is the only part of the proceedings that can be considered by the High Court when deciding whether to grant a *quashing order.

recorder *n*. **1.** A barrister or solicitor appointed as a part-time judge. Recorders agree to make themselves available regularly and for at least four weeks a year. Recorders may sit in both the Crown Court and county court. **2.** Formerly, a member of the Bar appointed to preside at City or borough *quarter sessions.

recovery *n*. Regaining possession of land from an unlawful occupier by proceedings in the High Court or a county court. *See* RECOVERY OF PREMISES.

recovery of costs *See* BILL OF COSTS.

recovery of premises The right to regain possession of property from which one has been unlawfully dispossessed (*see* FORCIBLE ENTRY) or the right of a court officer to enforce a judgment for this (Criminal Law Act 1977 s 7). It is a summary offence, punishable by up to six months' imprisonment and/or a *fine at level 5 on the standard scale, to resist or intentionally obstruct a court officer in the process of enforcing such a judgment, whether or not one knows that he is a court officer. There is, however, a specific defence if one can show that one believed that he was not a court officer. This offence covers most action taken by squatters to resist eviction, such as physical assaults, boarding up doors, or merely refusing to leave.

recreational charity A charity that provides facilities for leisure-time occupation in the interests of social welfare. After doubts expressed in the courts, Parliament confirmed in the Recreational Charities Act 1958 that these trusts were valid, as long as the facilities were provided with the aim of improving the conditions of life for those for whom they were primarily intended and were available to the public or a section of it. The 1958 Act was repealed in its entirety by the Charities Act 2011 and provision in relation to recreational charities is made thereunder.

rectification *n.* The correction of a document if it does not correctly express the common intention of the parties to it. Conveyances, leases, contracts, and certain registers of companies may be rectified on application to the court; the court exercises the jurisdiction to rectify with very great caution and only on the most cogent evidence. Parties to a document may, by agreement, rectify it without the court's consent, provided that the rights of third parties are not affected.

rectification of will Under the Administration of Justice Act 1982 s 20, a court has power to rectify a will that fails to carry out the intentions of the testator. However, this only arises when the court is satisfied that the failure was caused by clerical error or through a misunderstanding of the testator's instructions. An application for rectification should as a general rule be made within six months from the date on which a *grant of representation was first taken out.

recuse *vb.* To remove somebody, especially from a jury, because of potential prejudice.

redaction *n.* A document that has been edited so that certain items of confidential or sensitive information do not appear. For example, a court may rule that the names of third parties mentioned in a transcript should be deleted. Similarly, *data protection laws may require that some names and details are removed from information before it is made available to the public.

red bag *See* BLUE BAG.

reddendum *n.* The clause in a *lease that specifies the amount of the rent and when it should be paid.

redeemable share *See* SHARE.

redeem up, foreclose down A maxim applied in the context of *priority of mortgages. When there are successive mortgages of the same property, a mortgagee who is second or below in the order of priority may buy out (redeem) an earlier mortgagee. Any mortgagee may be redeemed by a mortgagee with a lower priority. If the matter is complicated and a court action is necessary, any person who might suffer in such an action must be made a party to it, i.e. the mortgagor and any mortgagees of lower priority to the mortgage being redeemed. Any person seeking to redeem by action must not only redeem any mortgages standing between him and the prior mortgage; he must also foreclose all subsequent mortgagees and the mortgagor. The principle does not apply to redemptions out of court.

redemption *n.* *See* EQUITABLE RIGHT TO REDEEM; EQUITY OF REDEMPTION.

redress *n.* *See* REMEDY.

reduction of capital A reduction of a company's share *capital in accordance with the Companies Act 2006. Section 641(1)(a) of the Act states that a private company can reduce its share capital provided that: (i) it passes a *special resolution to do so; (ii) the resolution is supported by a solvency statement; and (iii) the reduction is not restricted or prohibited by the company's articles. Alternatively, a private or public company can, subject to any restriction or prohibition in the articles, reduce its share capital on the passing of a special resolution confirmed by the court (s 641(1)(b) and 645–51). A reduction of capital can also occur where there is a permitted redemption or repurchase of a private company's own shares out of capital under sections 709–23 of the Companies Act.

redundancy *n.* **1.** (in employment law) The situation in which an employee fills a job that no longer needs to be done. Under the Employment Rights Act 1996, dismissal for redundancy occurs when the reason is wholly or mainly that the employer has ceased or intends to cease carrying on the business in which the employee was employed, that he is transferring the business in which the employee works to another location, or that he needs fewer employees to carry out the work in the place in which the employee is employed. An employee dismissed in such circumstances is entitled to a statutory *redundancy payment if he has been continuously employed in the business (*see* CONTINUOUS EMPLOYMENT) for two years prior to the *effective date of termination of his employment. He may be disqualified from receiving payment if the employer has offered him suitable alternative employment, starting within four weeks after his old employment ends, and the employee unreasonably refuses it. He may however try out alternative employment for up to four weeks without forfeiting his redundancy payment, if he decides not to accept this employment and his refusal is reasonable.

An employee who is laid off (i.e. not provided with work) or kept on short-time working, otherwise than as a result of industrial action, for four or more weeks continuously, or for six or more weeks (not more than three consecutively) in any 13-week period, may claim a redundancy payment in certain circumstances. He must give his employer at least the minimum required period of *notice terminating his employment, stating his intention to claim a redundancy payment. This notice must be given within four weeks after the end of the relevant period of lay-off or short-time working. However, the employer is not liable to give him a redundancy payment if he honours a written undertaking, given within seven days after receiving the employee's notice, to restore full-time working within four weeks after the employee's notice, for at least 13 weeks without interruption.

An employee who is dismissed for redundancy must be given reasonable time off during the notice period to seek other employment. If he is offered a new job starting before his notice expires, the employee may bring forward the termination of his old employment. However, the employer can challenge his right to a redundancy payment if he justifiably requires the employee to work for the full notice period. An employee forfeits his redundancy payment if, during the notice period, his employer justifiably dismisses him for misconduct other than strike action.

Disputes concerning redundancy and redundancy payments are determined by application to an *employment tribunal. The tribunal can also make a *protective award to employees on the application of an *independent trade union when the employer has failed to give sufficient notice of his intention to declare collective redundancies (*see* DISCLOSURE OF INFORMATION). *See also* COLLECTIVE REDUNDANCY. **2.** (in statements of case) The inclusion of unnecessary or irrelevant material. The court may order redundant material in a statement of case to be struck out.

redundancy payment The sum that an employee dismissed because of *redundancy is entitled to receive from his employer under the Employment Rights Act 1996. The sum is the total of:

(1) one and a half weeks' pay for each year of the employee's *continuous employment in which he was aged 41 or more;

(2) one week's pay for each year's service between the ages of 22 and 41; and

(3) half a week's pay for each year below the age of 22.

The sliding scale based on age has been retained despite laws on *age discrimination, as the government believes that it is justifiable.

Continuous employment exceeding 20 years is ignored, and a maximum amount of weekly pay to be used in the calculation is prescribed by regulations and reviewed annually. In 2013 the limit was £450. Redundancy costs are met entirely by the employer. An employer may be obliged under a collective agreement or individual employees' contracts of employment to pay sums in excess of the statutory requirement.

re-engagement order An order made by an *employment tribunal directing an employer who has been found to have unfairly dismissed an employee (*see* UNFAIR DISMISSAL) to provide him with comparable or other suitable employment in a post different from that from which he was dismissed (*compare* REINSTATEMENT ORDER). A re-engagement order might be made, for example, when the employee's former job no longer exists following a reorganization, but he could be similarly employed in a different post. The order is accompanied by the tribunal's directions specifying the nature and remuneration for the new employment, benefits that must be restored to the employee, and the date by which he is to be re-engaged. An employer cannot be forced to comply with the order; if he fails to do so the tribunal will award *compensation on the usual principles together with an additional award.

re-entry *n.* Repossession by a landlord of land held under a lease when he effects *forfeiture. There are restrictions on re-entering residential premises without a court order. The normal method of enforcing a right of re-entry is therefore by issuing court proceedings for possession. *See also* EVICTION.

re-examination *n.* The questioning of a witness by the party who originally called him to testify, following the *cross-examination of the witness by the opposite party. *Leading questions may not be asked in re-examination. Re-examination must be confined to matters arising out of the cross-examination; new matter may only be introduced with the permission of the judge.

referee *n.* **1.** A person to whom a dispute is referred for an opinion. *See also* OFFICIAL REFEREE; REFERENCE. **2.** A person who provides a character reference for another.

reference *n.* **1.** The referral by a court of a case (or an issue arising in a case) to another court or an arbitrator (**referee**) for a decision or opinion. In the High Court any action or any question or issue of fact arising from it may be referred to an *official referee for trial. In the county courts, a case may be referred to the district judge for an opinion and report. Under the Treaty of Rome, a court may refer to the *European Court of Justice a question of Community law for a preliminary ruling and must do so if it is a court from which there is no appeal within the national system. **2.** (in succession) *See* INCORPORATION BY REFERENCE.

referential settlement A settlement incorporating by reference terms of an earlier settlement, either with or without variations. If the two settlements are inconsistent, a referential settlement may give rise to difficult questions relating to the precise meaning of the documents, when taken together.

referral order An order of the court requiring an offender aged 10–17 years to attend a youth offender panel and to agree a contract with the panel; this will typically involve reparation to the victim or the community as a whole and participation in a programme designed to address the offending behaviour. Where a young person is charged with a criminal offence for the first time and pleads guilty, the court will in almost every case impose a referral order. The order may last from 3 to 12 months.

reform *n. See* PUNISHMENT.

Reform Treaty *See* LISBON TREATY.

refresher *n.* A fee payable to a barrister for each additional day in court after the first day; it is usually much lower than the *brief fee.

refreshing memory A procedure in which a witness may, while testifying, remind himself of matters about which he is testifying by referring to a document made on an earlier occasion. Under the Criminal Justice Act 2003 a witness in criminal proceedings may at any stage while testifying refresh his memory from a document or transcript of a sound recording made or verified by the witness on an earlier occasion.

refugee *n. See* ASYLUM; STATELESSNESS.

refuse disposal *See* WASTE DISPOSAL. *See also* POLLUTION.

regent *n.* A person exercising all the royal functions while the sovereign is under 18 or totally incapacitated. Under the Regency Acts 1937 and 1953, the regent is the person next in line to the throne who is of age and is a Commonwealth citizen domiciled in the UK. *Compare* COUNSELLORS OF STATE.

register *n.* The formal records kept by a magistrates' court.

registered company A company incorporated by registration under the Companies Act 2006 (*see* REGISTRATION OF A COMPANY). There are several types of registered company (*see* LIMITED COMPANY; PRIVATE COMPANY; PUBLIC COMPANY; UNLIMITED COMPANY). *Compare* STATUTORY COMPANY.

registered design A design registered at the Designs Registry, which is part of the Intellectual Property Office (*see* PATENT). Registration gives monopoly rights over the outward appearance of an article, including its shape, configuration, pattern, or ornament, but not over the underlying idea. Works of sculpture, wall plaques, medals, and printed matter primarily of a literary or artistic character cannot be registered. It is also possible to register a Community Design Right, which is a registered design providing protection throughout the EU. *See* DESIGN RIGHT.

registered land Land to which the title in question is registered (*see* LAND REGISTRATION). Land subject to compulsory registration on dealing may be both registered and unregistered; for example, the freehold owner's title may not be registered if he acquired the land before compulsory registration was introduced in the area, but if he grants a lease for more than seven years the tenant's leasehold title must be registered. Strictly, it is the legal estate or title that is registered, not the land itself. Since over 90% of all titles to land in England and Wales are now registered, this is now the "normal" way for ownership of land to be recorded, replacing title deeds.

registered office The official address of a registered company. It must be notified to the Registrar of Companies before *registration of the company and it must appear on company letter-heads and order forms. Documents may be served to a company's registered office (or other place as prescribed by regulation) and various registers and records may be inspected there.

Register of Companies The official list of companies registered at Companies House (*see* REGISTRATION OF A COMPANY).

register of members A record of the names, addresses, and shareholdings of members of a registered company, which is kept at the registered office or wherever it is compiled. The register must be kept open for public inspection (members free) for at least two hours daily; it may not be closed for longer than 30 days in any year.

registrable disposition A disposition of a registered estate (i.e. an estate in *registered land) or registered *charge that is required to be completed by registration under the Land Registration Act 2002 s 27. Such dispositions include transfers of the estate (e.g. a sale), the grant of a lease out of the estate for more than seven years, and the grant of a legal charge over the estate. If the registrable disposition is not registered as required, it fails to take effect at law—that is, the interest granted takes effect as an *equitable interest only. Once a registrable disposition is registered, it is a **registered disposition**.

registrar *n.* **1.** An official responsible for compiling and keeping a register, e.g. the Registrar of Companies. The judges of the Chancery Division of the High Court include six judges known as the Bankruptcy Registrars. **2.** In the *Court of Appeal, the officer (Registrar of Civil Appeals) responsible for superintending the prehearing stages of appeals in the Civil Division of the court. **3.** (district registrar) *See* DISTRICT JUDGE.

registration as citizen or subject A method by which certain persons can, either by right or at the Secretary of State's discretion, acquire *British citizenship, *British Overseas Territories citizenship, or *British Overseas citizenship or become *British Nationals (Overseas). Some people can also become *British subjects by registration. An *oath of allegiance must be taken by most adult applicants. *Compare* NATURALIZATION.

registration of a company *Incorporation of a company by complying with the registration requirements of the Companies Act 2006. To register a company, section 9 of the Act requires the delivery to the Registrar of Companies of a *memorandum of association (s 8), an application for registration (s 9–12), a statement of compliance (s 13) and *articles of association (s 18).

registration of birth The recording of a birth by a Registrar General of Births and Deaths under the Births and Deaths Registration Act 1953. Where parents are married, both parents are under a statutory obligation to register the birth within 42 days of its occurrence. Where the child is born to an unmarried mother, only the mother is under this obligation. Registration of the *unmarried father's name will normally require the co-operation and joint attendance by both parents. Independent registration of the father is only allowed on the production of proof of parentage, or a court order such as a *parental responsibility order. The Welfare Reform Act 2009 contains provisions, not yet in force, that will require unmarried parents to jointly register the births of their children. The mother will be required to name the father unless it would be impossible, impracticable, or unreasonable to do so.

A **birth certificate** may be obtained from the Registrar, the Superintendent Registrar, or the General Register Office; a short form of the certificate, relating to the child's name, sex, and date of birth but not parentage, may also be obtained (*see* ILLEGITIMACY). Children may consult the birth register to discover who their registered parents are and adopted children over the age of 18 have a right to see their original birth certificate. *See also* HUMAN FERTILIZATION AND EMBRYOLOGY AUTHORITY.

registration of commons *See* COMMON LAND.

registration of death The recording of a death by the Registrar of Births and Deaths under the Births and Deaths Registration Act 1953. This must take place within five days of the death or, if written notice of the death is given to the Registrar within that period, within 14 days. It may be effected by any relative of the deceased present at the death or during the last illness, by any other relative, by any person present at the death, or by the occupier or any inmate of the premises on which the death occurred. The informant must supply details of the date and place of death, the name, sex, address, and occupation of the deceased, and the cause of death. A **death certificate** may be obtained from the Registrar, the Superintendent Registrar, or the General Register Office.

registration of encumbrances Registration of *land charges and other interests affecting the rights of landowners. If registered, these charges are binding on third parties who acquire the land affected or any interest in it. If not registered, however, they will not bind most third parties and thus lose their effectiveness as interests or rights of occupation in the land itself. A person contemplating buying or taking an interest (e.g. a mortgage) in land should therefore search the relevant registers to ensure that there are no charges registered that would influence him against proceeding. The registers are therefore always searched in any *conveyancing transaction by the purchaser or his solicitor. There are four relevant registers:

(1) **Local land charges**, arising in favour of a local authority from the exercise of its statutory powers, are recorded in a **local land charges register** maintained by the authority concerned in relation both to registered and unregistered titles. Examples include rights to the repayment of improvement grants, compulsory purchase and smoke control orders, and planning decisions affecting the development or use of premises. Local land charges do not appear in any national register.

(2) When the title to land is registered (*see* LAND REGISTRATION), encumbrances other than local land charges can be protected by registration of the appropriate entry in the charges register of the title at the Land Registry. This may be as a *minor interest, protected by a *notice or by a *restriction. Some encumbrances also rank as *overriding interests and so do not require registration.

(3) In the case of *unregistered land, registers are maintained by the *Land Charges Department of the following types of interest recorded against the names of persons owning land:

(a) Land charges, comprising **Class A**: certain statutory charges registered on the application of the chargee; **Class B**: similar charges registered automatically; **Class C**: (i) *puisne mortgages, (ii) *limited owners' charges, (iii) *general equitable charges, and (iv) *estate contracts; **Class D**: (i) HM Revenue charges for *inheritance tax, (ii) *restrictive covenants created after 1925 and affecting freehold land, and (iii) equitable *easements created after 1925; **Class E**: annuities created before 1926 and registered after 1925; and **Class F**: spouses' and civil partners' rights of occupation under the Family Law Act 1996.

(b) *Pending land actions relating to land or any interest in it, and petitions for bankruptcy.

(c) Writs or orders of the court imposing a charge on, or appointing a receiver or sequestrator of, land, and all bankruptcy orders.

(d) *Deeds of arrangement affecting land. Land charges remain registered until discharged by the chargee or the court. Registration of pending land actions, writs and orders, and deeds of arrangement must be renewed every five years.

(4) A floating charge on the assets (including land) of a limited company and any other charge on a company's land that was created before 1970 for securing money need only be registered at the Companies Registry, under the Companies Act 1985. A fixed charge on a company's land created after 1969 should be registered both at the Companies Registry and the Land Charges Department (or charges register of the registered title as appropriate).

Although a chargee is protected by registration against all persons acquiring any interest in the land affected, the Law of Property Act 1969 provides that a purchaser is bound only by registered charges of which he knew or ought to have known when the contract was made. Thus if the purchaser discovers an undisclosed registered charge before completing the contract, he may rescind or pursue other contractual remedies against his vendor as the circumstances allow. If he completes the transaction, however, he will be bound by the charge.

registration of marriage The official recording of details relating to a marriage after it has been solemnized. (It is not to be confused with registration of notice of an intended marriage.) The details usually registered include the names, ages, occupations, and addresses of the parties, names and occupations of their fathers, and place of solemnization of the marriage. Certified copies of the details may be issued on request.

registration of merchant ships *See* SHIP.

registration of title *See* LAND REGISTRATION.

registration of treaties Under Article 102 of the United Nations Charter, every treaty and every international agreement entered into by any member of the United Nations must be registered as soon as possible with the Secretariat and published by it. The sanction for failing to do so is that any treaty that has not been registered cannot be invoked before an organ of the United Nations (such as the *International Court of Justice). Hence, in practical terms, a non-registered treaty is unenforceable. Registration attempts to ensure that international agreements are public documents as opposed to secret treaties (such as some landmark treaties that preceded the World Wars of the 20th century).

regulated agreement Any *consumer-credit agreement or *consumer-hire agreement under the Consumer Credit Act 1974, other than one specifically exempted by the Act. Exempted agreements include debtor-creditor-supplier agreements secured by a land mortgage, in which the creditor is a local authority or building society who finances the purchase of that land or the provision of dwellings on the land, and *debtor-creditor agreement secured by a land mortgage. The Act also enables the Secretary of State to exempt other consumer-credit agreements in which the number of payments to be made by the debtor does not exceed a specified number or the agreement has a connection with a country outside the UK.

regulated mortgage contract A legal *mortgage subject to regulation by the Financial Conduct Authority. These are first legal mortgages on land in the UK granted in respect of loans to individuals or trustees. At least 40% of the land must be used as a dwelling by the borrower, or the beneficiaries of a trust, or a relation of the borrower.

regulated tenancy A *protected tenancy or a *statutory tenancy. It is a protected tenancy until the contractual element is terminated, when it becomes a statutory tenancy. Regulated tenancies have been replaced by *assured tenancies by the Housing Act 1988.

regulations of the EU *See* COMMUNITY LEGISLATION.

regulatory agency Any of the nonministerial government departments with statutory duties of control over privatized industries. Each of the statutes that provided for the *privatization of services formerly provided by public corporations also made provision for the establishment of a regulatory agency for the service in question; these agencies include the Office of Communications (Ofcom), the Office of Gas and Electricity Markets (Ofgem), the Office of Water Services (Ofwat), the Office for Standards in Education (Ofsted), and the Office of the National Lottery (Oflot).

rehabilitation *n.* Treatment aimed at improving an offender's character or behaviour (including education, counselling, employment, training, etc.) that is undertaken with the goal of reintegrating the offender into society. *See* PUNISHMENT. *See also* SPENT CONVICTION.

rehearing *n.* A second hearing of a case already adjudicated upon. In criminal proceedings, an *appeal to the Crown Court against conviction before a magistrates' court consists of a rehearing before a judge sitting with two lay magistrates in which the evidence is heard again and fresh evidence may be introduced. An appeal to the Court of Appeal is usually limited to a reading of the original trial evidence. In civil proceedings, Part 52 of the *Civil Procedure Rules provides that every appeal will be limited to a review of the decision of the lower court unless the court considers that in the circumstances of an individual appeal it would be in the interests of justice to hold a rehearing. *See also* NEW TRIAL.

Reid test *See* LAY DAYS.

reinstatement order An order made by an *employment tribunal directing an employer who has been found to have unfairly dismissed an employee (*see* UNFAIR DISMISSAL) to restore him to his former job (*compare* RE-ENGAGEMENT ORDER). The employee is to be treated as if he had not been dismissed and is therefore entitled to recover any benefits (such as arrears of pay) that he has lost during his period of unemployment. However, pay in lieu of notice, *ex gratia* payments by the employer, state unemployment or supplementary benefits, and other sums he has received because of his dismissal or any subsequent unemployment will be taken into account. An employer cannot be forced to comply with an order for reinstatement; if he fails to do so, *compensation will be awarded to the employee on the usual principles together with an additional award.

reinsurance *n.* The procedure in which an insurer insures himself with another insurer against some or all of his liability for a risk that he has himself underwritten in an earlier *insurance contract. Reinsurance is undertaken when the potential loss attached to the risk is too great for the insurer to bear alone. A valid contract of insurance gives the insurer an *insurable interest to support a reinsurance.

REIT *See* REAL-ESTATE INVESTMENT TRUST.

rejection of offer The refusal of an *offer by the offeree. Once an offer has been rejected, it cannot subsequently be accepted by the offeree. A counter-offer ranks as a rejection, but a mere inquiry as to the possibility of varying some term does not. *See also* LAPSE OF OFFER; REVOCATION OF OFFER.

rejoinder *n.* Formerly, a pleading served by a defendant in answer to the claimant's *reply. Such a pleading could only be served with the court's permission.

relation back The treating of an act or event as having legal effect from a date earlier than that on which it actually takes place. Thus a grant of *probate relates back to the date of the testator's death.

relator *n.* A person at whose request an action is brought by the *Attorney General to enforce some public right. The Attorney General must consent to the issue of proceedings and has discretion in deciding whether to bring an action on behalf of the relator.

release *n.* **1.** The renunciation of a right of legal action against another. The fact that a release has been granted should be specifically pleaded as a defence if the person who granted it subsequently initiates court proceedings. **2.** Any document by which one person discharges another from any claim with respect to a particular matter. **3.** The freeing of a person formerly detained, either upon *discharge when sentencing him, at the end of a prison sentence, or on *parole or licence. Conditions for the release of prisoners on licence are set out in the Criminal Justice Act 2003.

release on licence *See* PAROLE.

relevance (in the law of evidence) The relationship between two facts that renders one more or less probable from the existence of the other, either taken by itself or in connection with other facts. The fundamental rule of the law of evidence is that all evidence that is relevant is admissible, and all evidence that is irrelevant is inadmissible. However, even relevant evidence must be excluded if it falls within one of the *exclusionary rules.

relevant child *See* NON-MOLESTATION ORDER.

relevant evidence *See* RELEVANCE.

relevant facts *See* RELEVANCE.

relevant property trust From April 2008, any trust that is not an *interest-in-possession trust, an age *18–25 trust, or a trust established for a bereaved minor or a disabled person is a relevant property trust for *inheritance tax purposes. A relevant property trust is taxed (i) on creation, (ii) whenever there is a distribution to a beneficiary, and (iii) on each tenth anniversary of the settlement. *See also* ACCUMULATION AND MAINTENANCE SETTLEMENT; DISCRETIONARY TRUST.

relevant transfer A situation that may arise when a business or part of a business (the transferor) changes ownership and staff transfer to the new owner (the transferee). If the change of ownership falls within the scope of the amended Transfer of Undertakings Protection of Employment (**TUPE**) Regulations 2006, then there is an automatic transfer of an employee's contract of employment. The Regulations resulted from EC Directive 77/187, known as the Acquired Rights Directive, the main objective of which was to safeguard employees' rights in the event of a change of employer. This is now Directive 2001/23. Employees are protected via TUPE where there is a relevant transfer but this is not always a straightforward issue. Because the Acquired Rights Directive is very wide in its scope, both the Court of Justice of the European Union and national courts have taken a wide view of what situations amount to a relevant transfer. The simplest situation is where one company acquires another and staff transfer. More complex situations that may qualify as relevant transfers include contracting out services, the transfer of contracts and franchises, and the transfer of leases. The 2006 Regulations explicitly state that a relevant transfer will include a "service provision change" provided certain conditions are met. This gives greater protection to workers where services have been subject to outsourcing. In 2013 the current government launched a consultation to gauge support for a repeal of this provision.

There are a number of important issues where a relevant transfer occurs. First there is an automatic transfer of the transferor's rights and obligations arising from the employment relationship they have with their staff. Because of this the employee's terms and conditions (with exceptions in the area of pension rights) must be maintained by the new employer (the transferee). There are some circumstances in which changes to the terms and conditions may be agreed by employer and employee, in particular where the transferor employer is subject to insolvency proceedings.

Secondly, a relevant transfer cannot be the basis for dismissal unless an employee can be shown to have been dismissed for economic, technical, or organizational reasons. Where an employee, being aware of a proposed transfer, informs either the transferor or the transferee that he objects to the transfer, his transfer does not take effect and his contract of employment is terminated, but he has no claim for unfair dismissal. If a dismissal occurs as a direct result of the transfer this is automatically unfair. If an employer seeks to argue a dismissal was for an economic, technical, or organizational reason, it is not *automatically* unfair but it can still be found unfair depending on the employer's procedure.

Finally, TUPE provides for a consultative process to ensure the exchange of information between the transferee, the transferor, and the staff who may be affected. The transferor has a duty to inform and consult with a recognized independent trade union when any of its members may be affected by the transfer. The employer must inform union representatives in writing, long enough before the relevant transfer to enable consultations to take place, of the fact that a transfer is to take place; when this is to occur and the reasons for it; the legal, economic, and social implications of the transfer for the affected employees; and the measures the employer is to take (if any) in relation to those employees. If there are no employee representatives, information must be given to all employees. The transferee has a duty to provide the transferor with sufficient information to enable him to give these facts. During consultations the employer has a duty to consider any representations made by trade union or staff representatives and reply to them; if he rejects them he is obliged to give his reasons for doing so. If any employer fails to inform or consult, a complaint may be presented to an employment tribunal within three months of the completion of the relevant transfer. The employer can argue that his failure to perform a particular duty was due to special circumstances but that he took all reasonably practicable steps to inform and consult. Although this is a potential defence, tribunals interpret it very narrowly. Insolvency does not amount to special circumstances. If the complaint is upheld, the tribunal can order the employer to pay appropriate compensation not exceeding 13 weeks' pay for the employee(s) in question.

relief *n.* **1.** *See* REMEDY. **2.** A tax concession; for example, a personal allowance (*see* INCOME TAX) or roll-over relief (*see* CAPITAL GAINS TAX). **3.** Payment by a feudal tenant following succession to him of land after the death of the former tenant.

relief from forfeiture A discretionary power of the courts to restore a lease to a tenant or *subtenant when the landlord claims or has exercised his right of *forfeiture.

remainder *n.* An interest in land that comes into effect in possession only when a prior interest ends. For example if A settles land on B for life then on C in fee simple, C's interest is in remainder until B dies. All interests in remainder are necessarily equitable (*see* FEE SIMPLE ABSOLUTE IN POSSESSION). A settlement may create several successive remainders; for example, a settlement on A for life, remainder to B for life, remainder to C in tail, remainder to D in fee simple. B, C, and D are called **remaindermen**. There can be no remainder after a fee simple. *See also* REVERSION.

remainderman *n. See* REMAINDER.

remand *vb.* To commit an accused person to custody or release him on *bail during an adjournment. After arrest a suspect is normally kept at the police station until he is brought before the magistrates. If the offence with which he is charged is triable summarily or is an indictable offence that is being tried summarily (*see* OFFENCE TRIABLE EITHER WAY), the court may adjourn the case and remand the accused. If the offence is being tried on indictment, the court may likewise adjourn the case and remand the accused before inquiring into the offence as examining justices. Remand in custody has traditionally been made for no more than eight clear days, excluding the day on which the accused was remanded and the day on which he is to appear again before the court (the "eight-day rule"). If the accused had to be remanded for more than eight days, he was normally released on bail unless there was some special reason why bail should be refused. However, the court could remand a suspect for a further period (or any number of further periods) of eight days after the end of the original remand order. If the period of time spent on remand became excessive, the accused could apply for bail. However, following claims that eight-day remand hearings served no useful purpose and wasted prison service resources, the Home Secretary was empowered in 1988 to provide remand periods not exceeding 28 days for accused persons aged 17 or over, in particular areas or classes of case. The abolition of the eight-day rule was extended, by the Criminal Procedure and Investigations Act 1996, to those under 17 for offences alleged to have been committed on or after 1 February 1997. A remand order may also be made upon adjournment of a trial at any stage, at the request of either the prosecution or the defence, or after conviction, if the court wishes to obtain a report before sentencing. Bail must normally be granted, however, when remanding for reports.

Upon remand the suspect is sent to the local prison. *Juvenile offenders may be remanded instead to local authority accommodation. Under the Criminal Justice and Public Order Act 1994, the court may remand a juvenile offender to secure accommodation in a *community home or a registered children's home, provided the charge or conviction is for a violent or sexual attack, the offence is one for which an adult could be imprisoned for at least 14 years, or there is a recent history of absconding and the charge or conviction relates to an imprisonable offence committed while remanded to the local authority. As a result of major amendments to the Children and Young Persons Act 1969, the minimum age for being remanded to secure accommodation has been reduced to 12.

remedial constructive trust *See* CONSTRUCTIVE TRUST.

remedy (redress, relief) *n.* Any of the methods available at law for the enforcement, protection, or recovery of rights or for obtaining redress for their infringement. A **civil remedy** may be granted by a court to a party to a civil action. It may include the common law remedy of *damages and/or the *equitable remedies of *quantum meruit* (*see* QUASI-CONTRACT), *injunction, decree of *specific performance, or *declaration.

remission *n.* Cancellation of part of a prison sentence. Formerly, a prisoner could earn remission of one-third of his sentence by good behaviour in prison and was released upon remission without any conditions. However, a prisoner serving an *extended sentence, or a prisoner serving more than 18 months' imprisonment, who was under the age of 21 when sentenced, could only be released on licence (*see* PAROLE). Remission of a sentence for good conduct was abolished by the Criminal Justice Act 1991 and the Criminal Justice Act 2003, which specifies the conditions now required for the early release of prisoners.

remittance basis An individual *resident, but not domiciled, in the UK is subject to UK income tax and capital gains tax on a remittance basis during the first six years in which he is so resident. For later years, the remittance basis is applied if the individual so elects and he pays a fee of £30,000 for the tax year; the charge is increased to £50,000 for an individual who has been resident in the UK more than 11 years in the previous 14 years (Income Tax Act 2007, s 809A-809Z7). When the remittance basis applies, income arising from a foreign source is only subject to UK income tax if it is remitted to the UK and gains arising on the disposal of a foreign asset are only subject to UK capital gains tax insofar as they are remitted. In general, a remittance for this purpose is a transfer of money; the import of goods purchased abroad is not a remittance until the goods are sold (*Scottish Provident Institution v Farmer* [1912] 6 TC 34). In *Grimm v Newman* [2002] STC 1388 (CA) a non-domiciled husband gave his English-domiciled wife a gift of cash and the wife remitted the cash to the UK. The Court of Appeal held that this was not a remittance by the husband and did not give rise to any income tax liability as the gift was perfected overseas. This is a modern re-enunciation of the rule laid down by the High Court in *Sharon v Carter* [1936] 20 TC 229 (Ch). In *Slattery v Moore Stephens* [2003] EWHC 1869 (Ch) [2003] STC 1379, the High Court awarded damages against an accountancy firm for failing to advise a client of the tax saving available to him from the application of the remittance basis. Case law on what is a remittance is now subject to the statutory provisions of the Income Tax Act 2007 s 809L (enacted by the Finance Act 2008 sch 7).

remoteness of damage The extent to which a defendant is liable for the consequences of his wrongful act or omission. In contract, the defendant compensates for damage only if it was within his **reasonable contemplation**. He is presumed to have contemplated (and is therefore liable for) damage likely to result from the breach according to the usual course of events. Unusual damage resulting from special circumstances is regarded as within his contemplation only if a reasonable man, knowing what he knew or ought to have known, would have thought it liable to result.

In tort there is no single test to determine whether or not damage is too remote. In actions for *negligence and other forms of liability based on fault, the defendant is responsible only for damage of the type he should have foreseen, but if damage of that type is foreseeable, it is no defence that the extent of the resulting damage is greater than could have been expected. In torts of *strict liability, the defendant may be liable even for unforeseeable damage. Thus the keeper of an animal belonging to a dangerous species is liable for any damage it causes, whether foreseeable or not.

renewal of lease The grant of a fresh *lease on similar terms to those of a pre-existing lease between the same parties. A lease sometimes contains a clause that gives the lessee an option to renew the lease when it expires. If the renewal is to be on the same terms, including the option to renew, the lease is known as a **perpetually renewable lease**; by statute, however, it is instead deemed to be a lease for 2000 years.

renouncing probate An executor's refusal, after the testator's death and in signed writing filed at a probate registry, to accept the office of executor. In such circumstances, if there are no other executors appointed, the person who would be entitled on intestacy to apply for *letters of administration may apply for a grant of letters of administration *cum testamento annexo*. An executor cannot renounce if he has already started to deal with the estate – he will become an *executor *de son tort. *Compare* POWER RESERVED BY EXECUTOR.

rent *n.* Payment by a tenant to his landlord under the terms of a *lease or *tenancy agreement. The obligation to pay rent is implied in all leases. If the tenant fails to pay his rent, the landlord can take action for *forfeiture of the lease, bring a court action against the tenant to claim the rent due, or, if the premises are commercial, exercise distress (a new procedure for taking control of goods will also be available when the Tribunals, Courts and Enforcement Act 2007 sch 12 comes into force). The manner and time of payment is as specified in the lease or tenancy agreement. If there is no express provision, rent should be paid to the landlord or his agent at the end of each *rental period or, in the case of a *fixed term, at the end of each year. The tenant can only deduct from the rent amounts that the lease or tenancy agreement allows. If the parties wish, the rent need not be paid in money: it may be in the form of service to the landlord or payment in kind. However, the amount of rent must be certain or capable of being ascertained at the date for payment (*Greater London Council v Connolly* [1970] 2 QB 100). *See also* FAIR RENT.

rental period A period in a lease or tenancy for which the tenant must make a payment of rent. In the absence of agreement, this is yearly in the case of a *fixed term. For other periods, *see* PERIODIC TENANCY.

rent assessment committee A committee that decides any dispute concerning the amount of a *fair rent determined by a rent officer for a tenancy of a dwelling-house under the Rent Act 1977 (where it still applies). This is subject to the Rent Acts (Maximum Fair Rent) Order 1999, which imposed a limit on fair rents by reference to a formula based on a variation in the Retail Price Index. A rent assessment committee may also, on application by a tenant, determine whether a proposed increase in rent for an *assured tenancy (under the Housing Act 1988) is what the landlord could obtain on the open market and, if not, it may fix what this should be. *See also* RENT TRIBUNAL.

rent book A book or other document used to record rent paid and other tenancy details. A landlord must give his tenant a rent book when there is a weekly tenancy of residential property unless a substantial proportion of the rent is payment for board.

rentcharge *n.* A periodic payment of money charged on land, but excluding rent payable under a lease or tenancy and sums payable as interest. Depending on the manner in which the rentcharge arose, it may be called a **chief rent** or **fee farm rent**, but the effect is similar. A rentcharge owned on terms equivalent to a fee simple absolute in possession or term of years absolute can be a legal interest in land, but one subsisting on other terms (e.g. for life) is an equitable interest, registrable as a *general equitable charge. If the rent falls into arrears, the owner of the rentcharge may (on 40 days' arrears) enter the land and take its income until the debt is paid or lease the land to trustees who have powers to raise the money. On 21 days' arrears, he may enter the land and seize the debtor's goods as security for the rent (*see* DISTRESS). In general, a deed creating a rentcharge also reserves to its owner the right to forfeit the debtor's interest in the land if the rent is not paid. The Law of Property (Amendment) Act 1926 provides that freehold land subject to a rentcharge owner's right of forfeiture (a right of re-entry) can still qualify as a fee simple absolute in possession.

A rentcharge may also be secured on another rentcharge, rather than directly on land. For example, A grants a rentcharge (R1) over his land of £50 a year to B, who grants a rentcharge (R2) secured on R1 of £25 a year to C. If B is more than 21 days in arrears,

C may appoint a receiver to collect the £50 from A and to pay C his £25 plus the expenses of the recovery, and account to B for any surplus.

The Rentcharges Act 1977 prohibits the creation of new rentcharges after 21 August 1977, except for (1) certain charges, usually in favour of the landowner's family, the effect of which is to make the land subject to a *trust of land; and (2) **estate rentcharges**. The latter are usually reserved by a developer selling plots on an estate subject to covenants given by the purchasers to protect the character of the estate; they entitle the owner of the rentcharge to enforce the purchasers' covenants even after all the plots have been sold off.

rent officer An official appointed by central government who determines *fair rents and keeps a register of all fair rents in his local area. There is an appeal from the Rent Officer to the *rent assessment committee. Under the Housing Act 1988, rent officers are given additional functions relating to housing benefit and rent allowance subsidy.

rent rebate A rent subsidy paid by local authorities to their own needy tenants, as part of *housing benefit. The conditions vary from one local authority to another.

rent registration 1. The registration by a rent officer of a *fair rent determined by himself or a rent assessment committee under the Rent Act 1977. This procedure is now abolished except for rents already so fixed. 2. The registration by a local authority of a *restricted contract rent determined by a rent tribunal or rent assessment committee. Since the passing of the Housing Act 1988, rents of new tenancies are not registered.

rent service 1. Any rent payable where a landlord and tenant relationship exists. 2. Originally, a rent payable to a feudal lord.

rent tribunal A tribunal to whom the determination of the rent properly payable under a *restricted contract may be referred. Rent tribunals also have power to grant limited security of tenure, but only if the contract was made before the commencement of the Housing Act 1980. Until that Act they were distinctly constituted bodies, but their functions are now carried out by *rent assessment committees sitting as rent tribunals. No new restricted contracts can be made since the passing of the Housing Act 1988.

renunciation *n*. In public international law, the relinquishment by a state of its title to territory without formal *cession in a treaty. This has often been demanded by the victor in a conflict as a form of war reparation.

renvoi *n*. [French: sending back] The doctrine whereby the courts of one country in certain circumstances apply the law of another country in resolving a legal dispute. A problem arises in private international law when one country's rule as to conflict of law refers a case to the law of a foreign country, and the law of that country refers the case either back to the law of the first country (**remission**) or to the law of a third country (**transmission**). For example, under English conflict rules, if a person dies intestate, the succession to his personal property is governed by the law of the country in which he is domiciled. Under Italian conflict rules, however, succession to personal property in such cases is governed by the law of the intestater's nationality. Thus if an English national dies intestate while domiciled in Italy, a *renvoi* problem will arise – English law will refer the matter to the law of his domicile (i.e. Italian law) and Italian law would refer the matter to the law of his nationality (i.e. English law).

repairs *pl. n.* (in landlord and tenant law) *See* COVENANT TO REPAIR.

reparation order An order of the court made against a child or young person who has been convicted of an offence, requiring him to make specific reparations to the victim or to the community at large (Glossary to the Criminal Procedure Rules). It usually requires the offender to undertake specific activities relevant to the offence: for example, a person convicted of criminal damage may be required to spend time restoring damaged property.

reparations *pl. n.* (in international law) **1.** Compensation for injuries or international torts (breaches of international obligations). Whenever possible, international courts or arbitration tribunals will rule that reparations be made by means of restitution in kind; if this is not possible, compensation is by payment of a sum equivalent to the value of restitution in kind. The aim of reparations is to eradicate the consequences of the illegal act. It is not clear, however, whether there is an obligation to make reparations for all breaches of international law. **2.** Payments made by a defeated state to the conquering state to compensate for damage suffered by the victor.

repatriation *n.* A person's voluntary return from a foreign country to that of which he is a national. *Compare* DEPORTATION.

repeal *n.* The total or partial revocation of a statute by one passed subsequently. A statute is normally repealed by express words, but if provisions of a later statute are inconsistent with those of an earlier one this will imply that Parliament intended a repeal. Repeal does not affect any transaction that has been completed under the repealed statute.

repeat offender An offender who commits the same offence on more than one occasion. Under the Criminal Justice Act 2003, in sentencing an offender the court must treat each previous conviction as an aggravating factor, having regard to (a) the nature of the prior offence and its relevance to the current offence and (b) the time that has elapsed since the prior conviction.

replevin *n.* A procedure to recover goods that have been taken out of the claimant's possession (usually by way of distress for unpaid rent), the effect of which is to restore them to the claimant provisionally, pending the outcome of an action to determine the rights of the parties.

reply *n.* A statement of case served by the claimant in a civil action in answer to the *defence (Civil Procedure Rules Part 15). It is often contained in the same document as a defence to a *counterclaim.

reportage *See* QUALIFIED PRIVILEGE.

repossession *n.* (of mortgaged property) The right of a mortgagee to obtain vacant possession of the property occupied by a mortgagor, in accordance with the terms of the mortgage. All mortgagees have a right to possession of the property from the time the mortgage is granted unless they have contracted out of the right (*Four Maids Ltd v Dudley Marshall (Properties) Ltd* [1957] Ch 317). It is, however, unusual for a mortgagee to exercise such a right unless the mortgagor has defaulted in some way. If property is occupied the mortgagee will usually obtain a court order for possession. *See also* MORTGAGE; POWER OF SALE.

representation *n.* **1.** The state of being represented, e.g. by an elected representative in the House of Commons (*see also* PARLIAMENT), by a defending counsel in court, or by an agent acting on behalf of his principal. **2.** (in succession) Taking the place of another. The court grants to executors or administrators the right to represent the deceased, i.e. to collect, sell, and transfer the deceased's assets (in accordance with the will or intestacy rules) as if they were the owners. Under the Wills Act 1837 a *devise or *legacy in favour of a child or remoter descendant of the testator who predeceases him leaving descendants of his own does not lapse but is inherited by those surviving descendants, who therefore represent their deceased ancestor (*see* PER STIRPES). **3.** (in contract law) A statement. A person who has been induced to enter into a contract on the basis of a statement that is untrue or misrepresents a material fact may sue for damages or for rescission of the contract (*see* MISREPRESENTATION). Under the Consumer Credit Act 1974 a representation includes a *condition, *warranty, or any other statement or undertaking, either oral or in writing. Many contracts exclude all prior representations from terms of the contract, although in consumer contracts such an exclusion may be void if unfair.

representation order In criminal proceedings, an order authorizing payment of legal aid for a defendant (Glossary to the Criminal Procedure Rules).

representative claim A claim brought under Part 19 of the *Civil Procedure Rules by or against one or more persons as representative(s) of a larger group. All the persons represented must have the same interest in the proceedings, and therefore a representative claim cannot generally be brought if each member of the group has a separate claim for damages. Under the Civil Procedure Rules judgment in a representative claim is binding upon all the persons represented in the claim. *Compare* DERIVATIVE CLAIM; GROUP LITIGATION.

reprisals *pl. n.* Retaliatory measures taken by one state against another to settle a dispute occasioned by the other's illegal or unjustified conduct. Reprisals include boycotts, *embargoes, and limited military action. A military reprisal, if otherwise than for the purpose of lawful self-defence under Article 51 of the United Nations Charter, is now illegal under international law. Examples of reprisals include the expulsion of Hungarians from Yugoslavia in 1935, in retaliation for alleged Hungarian responsibility for the murder of King Alexander of Yugoslavia, and the bombardment of the Spanish port of Almeria by German warships in 1937, as a reprisal for an alleged bombing of the battleship *Deutschland* by Spanish Republican forces. Perhaps the most famous recent example was the US bombing of Libya in April 1986, by way of reprisal for alleged Libyan involvement in an explosion at a discotheque in Berlin, which killed 50 US service personnel.

republication of will The re-execution with proper formalities of an existing will, or of a *codicil to it that contains some reference to the will, which has the effect of confirming that will. When republished, the will takes effect as if made at the date of republication. A republication may have the effect of validating an unattested alteration made to the will before its re-execution or the execution of the confirmatory codicil. *Compare* REVIVAL OF WILL.

repudiation *n.* **1.** (in contract law) **a.** An anticipatory *breach of contract. **b.** A minor's disclaimer of a contract that is voidable because of his minority (*see* CAPACITY TO CONTRACT; RESCISSION). **2.** (in international law) A state's disclaimer of its obligations under a treaty. There is no question that such repudiation is a violation of international law unless it can be justified on one of the accepted grounds for securing release from the obligation to comply with the treaty. The grounds upon which a treaty can be held to be invalid are laid down in Articles 46–53 of the Vienna Convention on the Law of Treaties.

repugnancy *n*. Contradiction or inconsistency in the terms of a document. Generally the court construes documents to give effect to the parties' primary intention (the **main purpose rule**). If this cannot be established and the document's provisions are directly contradictory, the court treats the later provision as effective in the case of a will and the earlier one in the case of a deed. Thus a transfer of property to A and B "as beneficial joint tenants in equal shares" confers a *joint tenancy unless it was effected by will, when it will be treated as conferring a *tenancy in common in equal shares.

reputation *n*. The estimation in which a person is generally held. *See* CHARACTER; DEFAMATION.

reputed ownership Goods that at the beginning of the bankruptcy of a trader are in his possession with the consent of the true owner and in circumstances suggesting that the bankrupt is the owner are said to be in the bankrupt's reputed ownership. Such goods are treated as the bankrupt's own goods and are therefore available for distribution to his creditors.

request for further information (in civil proceedings) A written request made by a party under Part 18 of the *Civil Procedure Rules seeking clarification or information in relation to a matter in dispute in the proceedings. A request should be concise and strictly confined to matters that are reasonably necessary and proportionate to enable that party to prepare his own case or to understand the case he has to meet. A court has the power under Part 18 of the *Civil Procedure Rules to order a party to clarify any matter in dispute in the proceedings or to give additional information in relation to any such matter.

requisition *n*. **1.** (in land law) An application to the Land Registry, the Land Charges Department, or a local authority for a certificate of *official search to reveal whether or not land is affected by encumbrances. **2.** (in conveyancing) A request by an intending purchaser or mortgagee arising from the *abstract of title supplied by the owner. For example if an abstracted deed shows that the land is affected by encumbrances contained in an earlier deed that has not been abstracted, the purchaser will raise a requisition demanding proper evidence of the encumbrances. **3.** (under *emergency powers) The compulsory acquisition of property for use by the armed forces or civil authorities. The power to make regulations for the requisitioning of property (with or without compensation) is currently contained in the Civil Contingencies Act 2004.

reregistration *n*. The procedure enabling a registered company to change its status, e.g. from limited to unlimited or from public to private (or, in either case, vice versa).

resale *n*. *See* RIGHT OF RESALE.

resale price maintenance The fixing by a supplier of the price at which his goods may be sold by others. This may be attempted by contractual arrangements or by non-legal means, such as blacklisting by trade associations. Resale price maintenance is now prohibited by the Competition Act 1998 and Article 101 of the Treaty on the Functioning of the European Union. Provisions in contracts of sale between suppliers and dealers fixing minimum prices are void, and it is illegal to withhold supplies on the grounds of adverse pricing. Fines of 10% of turnover can be imposed for breach of these provisions. Formerly, resale price maintenance was permitted for books and certain non-prescription drugs, but even these exceptions have now been declared illegal. In 2003 ten businesses, including the Football Association and Manchester

United FC, were fined a total of £18.6M by the *Office of Fair Trading for fixing the price of Umbro replica football kit in breach of the Competition Act 1998.

rescission *n.* The setting aside of a *voidable contract, which is thereby treated as if it had never existed. Rescission is an irrevocable step and can be effected by any clear indication of intention to be no longer bound by the contract; this intention must be either communicated to the other party or publicly evidenced in some way. Rescission can also be effected by a formal action (a remedy developed by the courts of equity). There are limits on the right of rescission. It cannot be exercised unless *restitutio in integrum* is possible, i.e. unless it is possible to restore both parties to their original positions (*Erlanger v New Sombrero Phosphate Co* (1878) 3 App Cas 1218 (HL)), and it cannot be exercised if this would involve upsetting rights acquired by third parties (*Phillips v Brooks Ltd* [1919] 2 KB 243). Thus, a buyer of goods cannot rescind if he cannot return the goods, and a seller of goods cannot rescind if they have been resold to a third party.

The setting aside of a proprietary contract by a minor is normally called **repudiation** rather than rescission, but there is no distinction in substance. The treating of a contract as discharged by breach (*see* BREACH OF CONTRACT) is frequently, but misleadingly, called rescission. It does not operate retrospectively and is permissible whether or not *restitutio* is possible.

res communis [Latin: common thing] An area of territory that is not subject to legal title of any state. Examples would be the *high seas (see Article 2 of the Geneva Convention on the High Seas and Article 89 of the 1982 Convention on the Law of the Sea) and outer space (see UN General Assembly Resolutions 1962 (XVII), 1721 (XVI), and 1884 (XVIII)). *See* COMMON HERITAGE OF MANKIND PRINCIPLE.

rescue *n.* **1.** Action to save people or property from danger. There is no general duty to rescue people or property from danger, though a master of a ship is bound by statute to render assistance to people in danger at sea. Voluntary attempts to rescue people in danger are encouraged by the law. Someone injured in such a rescue attempt may recover damages from the person whose negligence created the danger (*Baker v Hopkins* [1959] 3 All ER 225). The rescuer is not regarded as having assumed the risk of being injured provided the rescue was reasonably necessary and the rescuer did not act with reckless disregard for his own safety. Courts are similarly reluctant to find that his injuries were due to *contributory negligence. Attempts to rescue property may not be treated so sympathetically. **2.** The forcible removal of a person in the custody of the law, which is a criminal offence. **3.** The recovery of property that has been taken by way of *distress. If the distress was unlawful, the owner is entitled to recover it.

resealed probate A grant of *probate issued in one country and approved (and sealed again) by the court of another, giving the executor authority to deal with the testator's property in that second country.

reservation *n.* **1.** (in international law) A unilateral statement made by a state, when signing, ratifying, accepting, approving, or acceding to a treaty, in order to exclude or modify the legal effect of certain provisions of the treaty in their application to that state. This device is used by signatory states to exempt particular policies from challenge. The UK has made one reservation in relation to the *right to education in Article 2 of the First Protocol to the European Convention on Human Rights. The *Human Rights Act 1998 also excludes public authorities from duties under Article 2 where this reservation applies. **2.** (in land law) The creation of an easement or other right in a conveyance of land that is for the benefit of land retained by the vendor or transferor.

For example, if A is selling Blackacre but requires a right of way over it for access to land he is retaining, the conveyance of Blackacre to the purchaser will reserve the right of way for the benefit of A's retained land. Such a reservation may be implied in circumstances of necessity. *See* EASEMENT OF NECESSITY.

reservation of title *See* RETENTION OF TITLE.

reserve capital *See* AUTHORIZED CAPITAL.

reserve forces The non-regular armed forces of the Crown, comprising the Royal Fleet Reserve, Royal Naval Reserve, Royal Marines Reserve, Army Reserve, Territorial Army, Royal Air Force Reserve, and Royal Auxiliary Air Force. They are governed by the Reserve Forces Act 1996, which creates safeguards for reservists and their employers when the former are called out or recalled into operational service. These include: a formal right to seek exemption from, or deferral of, call out or recall; financial assistance to reservists whose military salary is less than their civilian pay; payments to cover the additional costs incurred by employers when their staff are called out or recalled; and the establishment of independent Appeal Tribunals to hear appeals from reservists or employers who are dissatisfied with the Ministry of Defence's decision on their application under any of the safeguards. The civilian employment of all reservists who are called out or recalled is protected under the Reserve Forces (Safeguard of Employment) Act 1985 and the reservist also has the protection of the Reserve and Auxiliary Forces (Protection of Civil Interest) Act 1951.

res extincta [Latin] Matter that has ceased to exist. *See* MISTAKE.

res gestae [Latin: things done] The events with which the court is concerned or others contemporaneous with them. In the law of evidence, *res gestae* denotes both a rule of *relevance according to which events forming part of the *res gestae* are admissible and an exception to the hearsay rule under which statements forming part of the *res gestae* are admissible. The Criminal Justice Act 2003 specifically preserves the common law rules relating to the admissibility of *res gestae* in this second sense by providing that in criminal proceedings a statement is admissible as evidence of any matter stated if:

(1) the statement was made by a person so emotionally overpowered by an event that the possibility of concoction or distortion can be disregarded;

(2) the statement accompanied an act that can be properly evaluated as evidence only if considered in conjunction with the statement;

(3) the statement relates to a physical sensation or a mental state (such as intention or emotion). *See* HEARSAY EVIDENCE.

residence *n.* **1.** The country (or territory) in which a person has his home or a company is held to be based. The term has been defined in various ways for different purposes. For tax purposes, the principles are derived from case law rather than Acts of Parliament (*see* RESIDENT). For some purposes it is possible to be a resident of more than one country at the same time. *See also* DOMICILE; HABITUAL RESIDENCE; PERMANENT ESTABLISHMENT. **2.** The dwelling in which an individual resides. *See* MAIN RESIDENCE.

residence order An order made by a court that settles the question of who is to provide accommodation and day-to-day care for a child. It is usually made in cases where the parents have divorced or separated. The parent who will not have the child living with him (the "non-resident parent") loses the right physically to look after the child but continues to have *parental responsibility. Although the Children Act 1989 indicates that there is no need for the resident parent to consult the non-resident parent before taking decisions in relation to the child, case law seems to draw a distinction between serious matters (such as a change of school or a decision to circumcise a child), which do require consultation, and trivial or minor day-to-day matters, which do not (*Re G (Parental Responsibility: Education)* [1994] 2 FLR 964; *Re J (Specific issue orders: Muslim upbringing and Circumcision)* [2000] 1 FLR 571 (CA)). Generally, a residence order is made in favour of one parent and a *contact order in respect of the other. However, in some cases the court will grant a joint residence order requiring that the child's time be split between the two homes. Residence orders are usually made in favour of one or other parent of a child, but may be made in respect of nonparents. In such a case the residence order confers parental responsibility on the holder.

residence requirement A requirement that may be imposed by a sentencing court as part of a *community order or a *suspended sentence order under the Criminal Justice Act 2003 or as part of a *YOUTH REHABILITATION order under the Criminal Justice and Immigration Act 2008. It requires that the offender resides at a specified place for a specified period.

resident *adj.* (in revenue law) A person who is resident in the UK is subject to UK income tax (or UK corporation tax for companies) on income arising anywhere in the world. A person who is not resident in the UK is subject to UK income tax (or UK corporation tax) only on income arising from a source within the UK. A person resident in the UK is subject to UK capital gains tax (or corporation tax on capital gains, in the case of a company) on gains arising from the disposal of assets anywhere in the world. A person not resident in the UK is not subject to UK capital gains tax, unless the gain is made on the disposal of the assets of a UK resident's *permanent establishment.

Statute does not give a test to determine whether a person is resident, other than to declare that an individual who spends 183 or more days in the UK in a tax year is resident for that year (Income Tax Act 2007 s 831) and to treat every company incorporated within the UK as resident in the UK (Finance Act 1998 s 66(1)). When one of these tests is not applicable, the test derives from a series of decided cases. HM Revenue and Customs also treats any individual as resident if, taking four successive years, he is present in the UK for more than 90 days on average per year. Such a simple arithmetical calculation has not, however, always been followed in decided cases (*IRC v Brown* [1926] 11 TC 292 (HL)). The determination of residence of partners, trustees, and personal representatives follows a mixture of case law, practice, and statutory provision that parallels the approach adopted for individuals. *See also* ORDINARILY RESIDENT.

residential occupier A person who is living in a property as a result of his contractual rights, his statutory rights, his rights under a rule of law, or because other people are restricted by law from removing him. It is an offence to force a residential occupier to leave the property without complying with the proper procedure (Protection from Eviction Act 1977). *See* ADVERSE OCCUPATION; EVICTION; FORCIBLE ENTRY; HARASSMENT OF OCCUPIER.

Residential Property Tribunal (RPT) A statutory body that must be consulted about the exercise of certain powers by Housing Authorities. It will also arbitrate on disputes over the exercise of those powers. The body was introduced by the Housing Act 2004 *See* FAIR RENT.

(⊕) SEE WEB LINKS
• Introduction to the Residential Property Tribunals from the Ministry of Justice website

residuary devise *See* DEVISE.

residuary estate (residue) The property comprising a deceased person's estate after payment of his debts, funeral expenses, costs of administration of the estate, and all specific (and demonstrative) bequests and devises. If a will does not dispose of the whole of a testator's property, the residue passes to those entitled under the rules applying on *intestacy.

residuary legacy *See* LEGACY.

residue *n. See* RESIDUARY ESTATE.

resile *vb.* To withdraw from something, such as an agreement, position, or statement.

res inter alios acta alteri nocere non debet [Latin: a transaction between strangers ought not to injure another party] A maxim stating that the sworn evidence of a witness in one cause cannot be made available in another cause between other parties (*Dimond v Lovell* [2000] 2 WLR 1121).

res ipsa loquitur [Latin: the thing speaks for itself] A principle often applied in the tort of *negligence. If an accident has occurred of a kind that usually only happens if someone has been negligent, and the state of affairs that produced the accident was under the control of the defendant, it may be presumed in the absence of evidence that the accident was caused by the defendant's negligence (*Scott v London and St Katherine Docks Co* (1865) 3 Hurl. & C. 596).

resisting arrest Taking any action to prevent one's arrest. A person may use *reasonable force to resist an illegal arrest (*Christie v Leachinsky* [1947] AC 573 (HL)). If he resists a legal arrest, however, he lays himself open to a charge of assaulting or *obstructing a police officer in the course of his duty. The fact that the police officer was in plain clothes is no defence to such a charge. The House of Lords has ruled that it is the right and duty of every citizen to take reasonable steps to prevent a breach of the peace by detaining the offender (Criminal Law Act 1967 s 3). The offender therefore has no right to resist such an arrest on the grounds of *self-defence; if he uses force to do so, he may be guilty of an assault.

res judicata [Latin: a matter that has been decided] The principle that when a matter has been finally adjudicated upon by a court of competent jurisdiction it may not be reopened or challenged by the original parties or their successors in interest. It is also known as **action estoppel**. It does not preclude an appeal or a challenge to the jurisdiction of the court. Its justification is the need for finality in litigation. *See also* ESTOPPEL.

resolution *n.* **1.** A decision reached by a majority of the members at a company meeting. *See* ELECTIVE RESOLUTION; ORDINARY RESOLUTION; SPECIAL RESOLUTION; WRITTEN RESOLUTION. **2.** The decision of a meeting of any other assembly, such as the *United Nations General Assembly. Such a resolution, strictly speaking, has no binding effect on either the Security Council or the United Nations as a whole. Academics have treated such resolutions as containing a kind of *soft law.

respondent *n.* The defending party to an application, appeal, or petition to the courts. *Compare* DEFENDANT.

respondentia *n. See* HYPOTHECATION.

responsible clinician Under the Mental Health Act 1983, the clinician charged with overall responsibility for a patient who is subject to detention or a *Community Treatment Order. *Compare* APPROVED CLINICIAN.

restitutio in integrum [Latin] Restoration to the original position. *See* DAMAGES; RESCISSION.

restitution *n.* The return of property to the owner or person entitled to possession. If one person has unjustifiably received either property or money from another, he has an obligation to restore it to the rightful owner in order that he should not be unjustly enriched or retain an unjustified advantage. This obligation exists when, for example, goods or money have been transferred under compulsion (duress), under mistake, or under a transaction that fails because of illegality, lack of formality, or for any other reason or when the person who has taken the property has acquired a benefit through his actions without justification.

In certain circumstances the courts may make a **restitution order** in respect of property. Under the Powers of Criminal Courts (Sentencing) Act 2000, if someone is convicted of any offence relating to stolen goods the court may order that the stolen goods or their proceeds should be restored to the person entitled to recover them. The court will only exercise this power, however, in clear cases that do not involve disputed questions of fact or law. Under the Police (Property) Act 1897, magistrates' courts are empowered to make a restitution order in favour of a person who is apparently the owner of property that has been obtained by the police in connection with any crime, even when no charge can be brought or the goods are seized under a search warrant. If the owner cannot be found, the court may make any order it thinks fit (usually an order for sale by auction). The police have no power to retain property lawfully seized merely because they think the court will probably make a restitution order.

restorative justice An approach to justice that focuses on the idea of repairing the harm done by a crime as opposed to simply seeking retribution. In practice this will usually mean that an offender is required to make specific *restitution to the victim as well as reparation to the community as a whole. The restorative process requires that the offender should be confronted with the consequences of his actions and, where appropriate, this may involve a mediated encounter with the victim of the crime. The offender may also be required to participate in a programme of activities or interventions designed to prevent him from reoffending. The restorative justice approach has been increasingly influential in youth sentencing (*see* REPARATION ORDER; REFERRAL ORDER).

restraint of marriage A condition in a contract or other disposition intended to prevent someone from marrying. Such conditions are usually (unless they are very limited) void, as they are considered to be against *public policy.

restraint of trade A contractual term that limits a person's right to exercise his trade or carry on his business. An example is a term in an employment contract or partnership agreement prohibiting a party from engaging in a similar business for a specified period after the relationship ends. Such a term is void unless the party relying on it shows that it does not offend *public policy; it must also be reasonable as between the parties. Many such terms are reasonable and therefore valid (*Wincanton Ltd v Cranny* [2000] IRLR 716 (CA)). *See also* GARDEN LEAVE CLAUSE.

restraint on alienation Provisions in a grant or conveyance of land that purport to prevent the owner from disposing of it. Restraints of an absolute nature are generally void. Partial restraints on alienation may be upheld by the courts.

restraint order An order of the court prohibiting a person from dealing with any realizable property held by him (Glossary to the Criminal Procedure Rules).

restraints of princes (in marine insurance) Political or executive acts causing loss or damage, as distinct from such acts as riots or ordinary judicial processes. Such acts, more common in time of war, need not be done by officials of governments, but may be done by individuals exhorted or compelled to them by the states of which they are nationals.

restricted contract For the purposes of the Rent Act 1977, a contract granting someone the right to occupy a dwelling for a rent that includes payment for the use of furniture or for services. A contract creating a *regulated tenancy is not, however, a restricted contract. No new restricted contracts can be made since the Housing Act 1988 came into force. However, the occupant may qualify for *security of tenure as an *assured tenant.

restricted-use credit agreement (under the Consumer Credit Act 1974) A regulated *consumer-credit agreement that either (1) finances a transaction (which may or may not form part of the agreement) between the debtor and the creditor, e.g. a purchase of goods; (2) finances a transaction between the debtor and a person (the supplier) other than the creditor; or (3) refinances any existing indebtedness of the debtor's, to either the creditor or another person.

restriction *n.* (in land law) A limitation of the right of a registered proprietor to deal with the land or charge in a registered title. For instance, a beneficiary may enter a restriction against his trustees if the trust provides that the land may not be sold without the beneficiary's consent. A restriction may also be entered by, or with the concurrence of, the registered proprietor, and there are cases in which the Chief Land Registrar is obliged to enter a restriction (for example, when persons are registered as joint proprietors, and the survivor will not have power to give a valid receipt for *capital money arising on a disposition of the land).

restriction order An order placing special restrictions (for a specified period or without limit of time) on the discharge from hospital of a person detained there by a *hospital order. It may be made by the Crown Court (but not a magistrates' court) when this appears necessary for the public protection, and its principal effects are that discharge may be authorized only by the Home Secretary and may be subject to conditions (e.g. subsequent supervision by a mental welfare officer).

restrictive covenant An obligation created by *deed that curtails the rights of an owner of land; for example, a covenant not to use the land for the purposes of any business. A covenant imposing a positive obligation on the landowner (the covenantor), for example to repair fences, is not a restrictive covenant. Third parties who acquire freehold land affected by a restrictive covenant will be bound by it if it is registered (*see* REGISTRATION OF ENCUMBRANCES) or, in the case of covenants created before 1926, if they are aware or ought to be aware of it (*see* CONSTRUCTIVE NOTICE) (*Tulk v Moxhay* (1842) 2 Ph 774). The covenant may also be enforceable by successors of the original beneficiary (the covenantee) if it was annexed to (i.e. expressly taken for the benefit of) the covenantee's land or if the benefit of it was expressly assigned. Section 78(1) of the Law of Property Act 1925 has been interpreted as providing a form of statutory annexation (*Federated Homes v Mill Lodge Properties* [1980] 1 WLR 594 (CA)). Thus, unless there is an express stipulation to the contrary, all covenants shall be deemed binding on successors to the original covenantee. The benefit of a covenant will not be annexed, however, if the covenantee's land is not actually capable of benefiting from the covenant; for example, if it is too far away to be affected, or if the benefited land is not identified with sufficient certainty. Restrictive covenants contained in leases are not registrable but are nevertheless generally enforceable between third parties (*see* COVENANT RUNNING WITH THE LAND). *See also* BUILDING SCHEME.

restrictive endorsement An *endorsement that prohibits the further negotiation (transfer) of a *bill of exchange (for example, "Pay X only") or states that it is a mere authority to deal with the bill as thereby directed and not a transfer of ownership of the bill (for example, "Pay X or order for collection"). A restrictive endorsement gives the endorsee the right to receive payment of the bill and to sue any party to it that his endorser could have sued, but gives him no power to transfer his rights as endorsee unless it expressly authorizes him to do so.

Restrictive Practices Court A superior *court of record created by the Restrictive Trade Practices Act 1956. Its jurisdiction was to determine matters arising under the legislation controlling *restrictive trade practices and *resale price maintenance, principally whether or not restrictive agreements registered with the Director General of Fair Trading were contrary to the public interest. It was abolished under the Competition Act 1998 and its functions taken over by the *Office of Fair Trading.

restrictive trade practices Arrangements in industry designed to maintain high prices or earnings or to exclude outsiders from a trade or profession. Examples include *resale price maintenance contracts, agreements between manufacturers to restrict output so that demand remains unsatisfied and a high price is maintained, similar agreements concerning the provision of services, and rules restricting entry to a trade or profession. Under the Competition Act 1998, as supplemented by the Enterprise Act 2002, certain types of restrictive agreement are presumed to be against the public interest (and therefore void). The *Office of Fair Trading (OFT) has powers to investigate anti-competitive agreements and may declare whether or not an agreement breaches the competition rules. The European Commission has similar powers under Article 101 of the Treaty on the Functioning of the European Union.

resulting trust An *implied trust that arises by operation of law. Such a trust has arguably been abolished in the context of land by section 60(3) of the Law of Property Act 1925. A distinction has often been made between **automatic resulting trusts** and **presumed intention resulting trusts**, although many leading commentators have now abandoned this terminology. There are a number of situations that will give rise to a resulting trust:

- where a trust fails to dispose of the entire *beneficial interest, the trust property that is undisposed of will "result" back to the settlor (*Re Vandervell's Trusts* [1971] AC 912 (CA));
- where there is a voluntary conveyance of property to a third party, there will be a rebuttable presumption of a resulting trust (*Hodgson v Marks* [1971] Ch 892);
- where the purchase money for property is paid by A and B and legal title to the property is held in B's name alone, there will be a presumption that B holds the property on trust for himself and A in beneficial shares equal to the proportion of their contribution.

In addition to the well-established circumstances in which a resulting trust will arise, there has been considerable support for the proposition that *Quistclose trusts are a form of resulting trust, although this analysis is by no means universally accepted. The courts have sometimes unhelpfully used the terminology of *constructive trusts and resulting trusts interchangeably (*Gissing v Gissing* [1971] AC 886 (HL)), particularly in the context of the family home.

retention of title (**reservation of title**) A stipulation on a contract of sale that the right of ownership of the goods shall not pass to the buyer until the buyer has paid the seller in full or has discharged all liabilities owing to the seller. It is also known as a **Romalpa clause**, from the case *Aluminium Industrie Vaassen BV* v *Romalpa Aluminium Ltd* [1976] 1 WLR 676. Where such clauses seek to claim rights over goods made using the original products or otherwise amount to a registrable *charge they will be void for want of registration at Companies House. They require careful drafting to ensure validity.

retirement age (in the state pension scheme) The age at which an individual can start to receive a state retirement *pension. For many years, the state retirement age in the UK was 65 for men and 60 for women. However, since 2010 the government has gradually harmonized retirement ages for both men and women in order to comply with EU law on *equal pay; the state retirement age will be 65 for both sexes in 2018, 67 in 2028, and 70 in the 2060s.

retirement of jury The withdrawal of the *jury from the court at the end of the trial so that they may decide on their verdict in private.

retirement of trustees A right of trustees to be released from their trusteeship. Originally trustees were not allowed to retire, but retirement is now possible subject to certain safeguards. Under the Trusts of Land and Appointment of Trustees Act 1996, when there is no person nominated to appoint new trustees in the trust instrument and the beneficiaries are of full age, sound mind, and absolutely entitled, the beneficiaries may give a written direction to the trustees to retire from the trust.

retorsion (**retortion**) *n.* A lawful means of retaliation by one state against another. It is usually provoked by an equally lawful, but discourteous, act of the other state, such as trade discrimination measures that single out foreign nationals or by hostile propaganda produced via government-controlled sources of information. Thus, if the productions of a particular state are discouraged or kept out of a country by differential import duties, or its subjects are put at a disadvantage as compared with other foreigners, the state affected may retaliate by like laws and tariffs. *See also* REPRISALS; SANCTION; SELF-HELP.

retour sans protêt [French: return without protest] A direction on a *bill of exchange to the effect that the bill should be returned without *protest if it is dishonoured.

retrial *n. See* NEW TRIAL.

retribution *n. See* PUNISHMENT.

retrospective legislation (**retroactive legislation**) Legislation that operates on matters taking place before its enactment, e.g. by penalizing conduct that was lawful when it occurred. There is a presumption that statutes are not intended to have retroactive effect unless they merely change legal procedure (*see* INTERPRETATION).

retrospective penalties *See* PENALTY.

return *n.* **1.** A formal document, such as an *annual return or the document giving particulars of shares allotted and to whom (**return of the allotment**), which must be delivered to the Companies Registry within one month of *allotment. **2.** The official result of the votes cast in an election.

returning officer An election official who is responsible for conducting an election in one or more constituencies and returning the results. Under the Representation of the People Act 1983, the sheriff of a county or chairman of a district council in England or

Wales is designated as returning officer for parliamentary elections in a constituency in his county or district.

Revenue and Customs, HM The UK government department responsible for the care, management, and collection of direct and indirect taxes, National Insurance contributions, and customs and excise duties within the UK. Its other responsibilities include the payment of *tax credits and child benefit. It is governed by a small board known as the Commissioners of Revenue and Customs, but the day-to-day administration is carried out by civil servants. HM Revenue and Customs was formed from a merger of the Board of Inland Revenue and the Board of Customs and Excise in April 2005. A Revenue and Customs Prosecution Office, responsible for the prosecution of all revenue and customs cases, was established at the same time.

( ) SEE WEB LINKS
• Website of HMRC: provides details of all UK tax rates, codes, and allowances

reversal of judgment The alteration of a *judgment on appeal.

reverse burden of proof The situation in which the legal *burden of proof is (exceptionally) placed on the defendant in a criminal case. *See* READING DOWN.

reversion (reverter) *n.* The interest in land of a person (called the **reversioner**) who has granted some lesser interest than his own to another but has not disposed of the whole of his own interest. For example, if A grants land to B for life, A has an interest in reversion, since the land reverts to him on B's death. Similarly, a person who lets or sublets land to another retains an interest in reversion. The reversionary interest of a lessor can subsist as a legal estate, but the reversion after any other interest than a lease is necessarily an equitable interest.

reversionary lease *See* FUTURE LEASE.

reverter *n. See* REVERSION.

reverter of sites Reversion of land donated for charitable purposes to the donor or his successors in title when the land ceases to be used for the specified purposes. Many of these donations occurred under 19th-century statutes to enable voluntary schools, libraries, museums, and churches and chapels to be established. Since that time, many of these charitable purposes have ceased, and it has often proved difficult to trace the beneficial owners entitled to the reverter. Under the Reverter of Sites Act 1987, when a charitable purpose comes to an end, the trustees holding the land are given a right to manage it and keep it in repair. If the beneficial owner remains unidentifiable, the land can be sold and the proceeds used for charitable purposes. Case: *Fraser v Canterbury Diocesan Board of Finance* [2005] UKHL 65, [2006] 1 All ER 315.

revival of will The re-execution with proper formalities of a will that has been revoked other than by destruction, or the execution of a *codicil to it, showing the testator's intention that the will should be effective notwithstanding the earlier revocation. Under the Wills Act 1837 these are the only ways in which a will that has been revoked can be revived. A revived will operates as if executed at the time of its revival. *Compare* REPUBLICATION OF WILL.

revocation of offer The withdrawal of an *offer by the offeror so that it can no longer be accepted. Revocation takes effect as soon as it is known to the offeree (from whatever source); offers can be revoked at any time before acceptance unless they are coupled with an *option (*Routledge v Grant* (1828) 4 Bing 653, 130 ER 920). *See also* LAPSE OF OFFER; REJECTION OF OFFER.

revocation of probate The cancellation by the court of a grant of probate that was obtained by fraud or mistake. The revocation does not affect those who have purchased assets of the estate from the executors before the revocation.

revocation of will The cancellation of a will. The testator may revoke his will by destroying it with that intention, by making a new will inconsistent with the original, or by making a new will expressly revoking the original (Wills Act 1837 s 20). A will is automatically revoked by the testator's valid marriage or civil partnership, unless it appears from the will that at the time it was made the testator was expecting to marry a particular person or enter into a civil partnership with a particular person and that he intended his will not to be revoked by the marriage or civil partnership (Wills Act 1837 s 18, 18B; Civil Partnership Act 2004 s 71). A particular disposition in a will may similarly take effect in spite of the marriage. The dissolution of a marriage or civil partnership does not revoke a will but sections 18A and 18B of the Wills Act 1837 (as amended by the Administration of Justice Act 1982 s 18 and the Civil Partnership Act 2004 s 71) provide that in the event of divorce or annulment any devise or bequest to a former spouse lapses in the absence of contrary intention in the will and any appointment of the former spouse as an executor does not take effect.

Reynolds defence *See* PUBLICATION ON A MATTER OF PUBLIC INTEREST; QUALIFIED PRIVILEGE.

right *n.* **1.** Title to or an interest in any property. **2.** Any other interest or privilege recognized and protected by law. **3.** Freedom to exercise any power conferred by law. *See also* HUMAN RIGHTS; NATURAL RIGHTS.

right of abode The right to enter the UK and live and work in the UK with no restrictions under UK *immigration control. The Immigration Act 1971 gave the right of abode to all citizens of the UK and Colonies who either owed their status to their own (or a parent's or grandparent's) birth, *registration, or *naturalization in the UK or were or became at any time settled in the UK and had at that time been ordinarily resident there for at least five years. Commonwealth citizens had the right of abode if one of their parents was a citizen of the UK and Colonies by reason of birth in the UK. As from 1 January 1983 the Act was amended by the British Nationality Act 1981 to confine the right of abode to British citizens as defined by that Act (*see* BRITISH CITIZENSHIP) and to *Commonwealth citizens enjoying it before the Act came into force. Since 2002 nearly all holders of *British Overseas Territories citizenship have also had the right of abode. Nationals of other EU states are exempt from most restrictions under UK immigration control but do not have the right of abode. The Immigration, Asylum and Nationality Act 2006 contains several provisions empowering the Home Secretary to deprive a person of right of abode if it is considered that such deprivation is "conducive to the public good".

right of action **1.** The right to take a particular case to court (*see* CLAIM). **2.** A chose in action (*see* CHOSE).

right of audience The right of an *advocate to be heard in legal proceedings. Barristers have full rights of audience in all courts. Traditionally, solicitors only appeared in the county courts and magistrates' courts but they may now obtain higher rights of audience in the Crown Court, the High Court, the Court of Appeal, and the House of

Lords. Many administrative tribunals have no rules concerning rights of audience and a party may be represented by any person he chooses.

* Guide to higher rights of audience for solicitors from the SRA website

right of common *See* COMMON.

right of establishment The right under the Treaty of Rome of a national of a member state of the European Community to engage in and manage businesses in any other member state.

right of light An *easement giving the owner of a dominant tenement the right to the access across the servient tenement of a sufficient quantity of light for the ordinary purposes to which the dominant tenement may be put. No easement can be acquired for a greater amount of light than is necessary for such purposes. *See* ANCIENT LIGHTS.

right of re-entry *See* RE-ENTRY.

right of resale The right that the seller in a contract of sale has to resell if the buyer does not pay the price as agreed. When the goods are perishable or the *unpaid seller gives notice to the buyer of his intention to resell, and the buyer does not pay the price within a reasonable time, if the seller is in possession of the goods he may resell them and recover from the first buyer damages for any loss.

right of silence The right of someone charged with an offence or being tried on a criminal charge not to make any statement or give any evidence. Often cited as a prime example of the fairness of the English criminal system, being intended to protect the innocent, it was also criticized as unduly hampering the conviction of the guilty and has therefore been modified. If a suspect fails to mention something at the time of his arrest or charge that is later relied on in his defence, this may result in a court at a subsequent trial drawing such inferences as appear proper (*see* CAUTION). Sometimes, however, statute obliges him to answer, as in certain fraud investigations by the *Serious Fraud Office (although this has been held contrary to the European Convention on Human Rights: *Murray v UK* (1996) 22 EHRR 29).

Failure of an accused aged 14 or over to give evidence in his own defence or refusal to answer questions without good cause will also allow such inferences to be drawn. Inferences may also be drawn from a suspect's failure to account for any object, mark, or substance found on his person, in his clothing or footwear, or otherwise in his possession at the time of arrest. The police officer must reasonably believe that such items are attributable to an offence and inform the suspect accordingly. Inferences may also be drawn from a suspect's failure to account for his presence at a particular place.

right of support 1. An *easement conferring on the owner of the dominant tenement the right to have buildings on his land supported by those on the servient tenement. For example, houses forming a semidetached pair are likely to have mutual rights of support. **2.** For the right to preserve support for land in its natural state, *see* NATURAL RIGHTS.

right of survivorship (*jus accrescendi*) The right of a joint owner of property to acquire absolute ownership of the entire property on the death of the other owner(s). *See* JOINT TENANCY.

right of water 1. An *easement conferring on the owner of a *dominant tenement rights in connection with water, such as the rights to take water or to discharge water onto another's land, or a right to enter another's land to open sluice gates in order to prevent flooding of the dominant tenement. **2.** A *natural right to use water flowing through a channel on one's land.

right of way The right to pass over another's land. It may exist as a public right exercisable by anyone; as an *easement for the benefit of a particular piece of land; or as a *licence, purely personal to the person to whom it is granted.

rights issue A method of raising share *capital for a company from existing members rather than from the public at large. Members are given a right to acquire further shares, usually in proportion to their existing holding and at a price below the market value of existing shares. This right may be sold (**renounced**) to a third party. *See also* PRE-EMPTIVE RIGHT.

right to air The right to a flow of air over land or buildings from neighbouring premises. It may be enjoyed on any terms agreed by personal arrangement between neighbouring landowners, but can only exist as an *easement if the right can be sufficiently defined. Thus an easement for the flow of air through a specific ventilation passage may exist, but a right to a general flow of air over the chimneys of a house does not qualify as an easement so is not an interest in the land itself.

right to begin The right of a party at trial to present his case to the court first (to **open the case**) by making the opening speech and presenting his evidence. The right to begin generally belongs to the party who carries the persuasive *burden of proof. In criminal cases the prosecution will have the right to begin. In civil cases the claimant generally begins, but the defendant may do so where he has the burden of proving the issues to be decided at trial.

right to buy *See* SECURE TENANCY.

right to education A right set out in Article 2 of the First Protocol to the European Convention on Human Rights and now part of UK law as a consequence of the *Human Rights Act 1998. It is not limited to primary and secondary education (*Leyla Sahin v Turkey* (App no 44774/98) (2007) 44 EHRR 5) and does not create a duty to fund or subsidize private education. The right involves a duty to respect the religious and philosophical convictions of the parents regardless of whether or not the child is in the state sector; this includes the right not to have corporal punishment imposed upon one's children (*Campbell and Cosans v UK* (1982) (App no 7511/76 4 EHRR 293) but see also *R (Williamson) v Secretary of State for Education and Employment* [2005] UKHL 15, [2005] 2 AC 246). The courts have decided that the display of crucifixes in Italian state schools did not violate this provision (Lautsi v Italy [2011] ECHR 30814/06) but nor did the prohibition on wearing the hijab in state universities in Turkey (*Leyla Sahin v Turkey* as above). As a specific type of disadvantaged and vulnerable minority, the Roma in the Czech Republic have been afforded special protection (*DH v Czech Republic* (2007) (App no 57325/00) 47 EHRR 3).

right to life A right set out in Article 2 of the European Convention on Human Rights and now part of UK law as a consequence of the *Human Rights Act 1998. The right to life does not make the use of the death sentence unlawful (*but see* CAPITAL PUNISHMENT). Article 2 makes unlawful the use of lethal force where the use of force was greater than that which was absolutely necessary (this is a higher test than imposed by section 3 of the Criminal Law Act 1967). The right to life also imposes a duty on public authorities to take reasonable measures to protect life from threats from third parties (*Osman v UK* (2000) 29 EHRR 245 but also see *Van Colle v Chief Constable of Hertfordshire* [2008] UKHL 50, [2009] 1 AC 225). Article 2 also imposes a duty to ensure that any investigation of a death that might have been caused by a public body or that takes place where the state has a higher duty of care (e.g. a death in custody), is independent and effective (*Jordan v UK* (2003) 37 EHRR 2).

right to manage (RTM) A group right for leaseholders of flats to manage the building they live in without proving that their manager is at fault or paying any premium. The right must be exercised through a special company (an **RTM company**) set up by leaseholders for that purpose. A number of conditions must be met for this right to be exercisable, notably that two-thirds of the flats must be occupied by qualifying tenants. A qualifying tenant is any leaseholder whose lease was originally granted for a period exceeding 21 years. Where an RTM company has acquired RTM, it will be responsible for the management functions under all of the leases held by qualifying tenants in the building, such as services, repairs, maintenance, insurance, and management of the whole or part of the premises.

right to marry A right set out in Article 12 of the European Convention on Human Rights and now part of UK law as a consequence of the *Human Rights Act. The right is not a particularly strong one; it only exists subject to the national laws governing the exercise of this right. However, the courts have imposed some restrictions on those laws in that barring transsexuals from marrying was ruled a violation (*Goodwin v UK* (2002) (App no 28957/95) 35 EHRR 447; *Bellinger v Bellinger* [2003] UKHL 21).

right to roam The right provided by the Countryside and Rights of Way Act 2000. If land is designated as *access land, the public has the right of access to it for the purposes of open-air recreation. There are statutory powers to extend the rights of access to foreshore and other coastal land. The right of access is limited to access on foot, and there are strong restrictions on activities that may be pursued. For example, there is no right to play organized games, hang-glide, para-glide, hunt, shoot or fish, or swim in nontidal waters.

riot *n.* An offence committed when 12 or more persons, present together, intentionally use or threaten unlawful violence (*see* VIOLENT DISORDER) for a common purpose. The collective conduct must be such as would have caused a reasonable person to fear for his safety, though no-one else need be present. A person is only guilty of riot if he intended to use violence or was aware that his conduct might be violent. The offence of riot is found in the Public Order Act 1986, though it can be committed in private as well as in public places. It replaces the common-law offence of riot and is punishable with up to ten years' imprisonment and/or a fine. Under the Riot (Damages) Act 1886, when property has been destroyed, damaged, or stolen in the course of a tumultuous riot, the owner is entitled to compensation out of public funds. *See also* AFFRAY.

road *n.* For purposes of offences relating to road traffic, any *highway or other route to which the general public has access. A road must be a route leading from one place to another, and this is always a question of fact. It may include a hotel forecourt, a road privately owned but to which the public has access, or a bridge over which a road passes, but a car park is usually not regarded as a road (*Oxford v Austin* [1981] RTR 416). Some traffic offences are defined to cover roads and "other public places".

road rage Aggressive behaviour while driving motor vehicles on roads. Although there is no specific road rage offence, such behaviour may involve breach of other laws. If the aggressor causes injury he may face a conviction for *dangerous driving or for some other similar offence.

road tax A tax (formally called **vehicle excise duty**) that must be paid in respect of any mechanically propelled vehicle used, parked, or kept on a public road. It is an offence to fail to pay it. Electrically propelled vehicles and invalid vehicles do not have to be taxed, and no tax is required when a motorist is driving to and from a prearranged *MOT test. It is also an offence to fail to display a tax disc showing that the vehicle has been taxed, unless one has applied for a new disc before the old one expired and it is within 14 days from the date of expiry. The tax disc must be displayed on the nearside lower corner of the windscreen. Failure to pay road tax or display the tax disc is punishable by fine, but is not subject to endorsement.

road traffic accidents If an accident has been caused by the presence of a motor vehicle on a road and results in injury to anyone or damage to anyone else's vehicle or to property on the road or neighbouring land (e.g. someone's garden wall), it is an offence for the driver of the vehicle not to stop, unless he can show that he did not know that the accident happened. It is also an offence to refuse to give one's name and address to anyone who reasonably requires it (e.g. a police officer or another driver or pedestrian involved in the accident), unless one reports the accident to the police as soon as possible (not later than 24 hours after it occurred). If a person has been injured in a road accident, it is an offence not to produce one's certificate of insurance (*see* THIRD-PARTY INSURANCE) for a police officer or anyone else with reasonable grounds for asking for it, unless one reports the accident to the police not later than 24 hours after it occurred (*DPP v Drury* [1989] RTR 165) and, at the same time or within five days, produces the certificate of insurance at any police station one specifies. *See also* ACCIDENT RECORD BOOK.

Failure to stop after an accident or give particulars is an endorsable offence (carrying 5–10 penalty points under the *totting-up system) and is subject to a *fine at level 5 on the standard scale and to discretionary *disqualification.

robbery *n.* The offence of using force against any person, or putting them in fear of being subjected to force, in order to commit a theft, either before the theft or during the course of it. It is also robbery to threaten to use physical force in these circumstances, even if the person threatened is not frightened by the threats. The degree of force required is a question of fact in each case to be decided by the jury; nudging someone so that he loses his balance may constitute sufficient force (*R v Dawson* (1976) 68 Cr App R 170 (CA)). The force must, however, be directed against the person, rather than his property. Robbery and assaults with intent to rob are punishable by a maximum sentence of life imprisonment (Theft Act 1968 s 8).

rogatory letter *See* LETTER OF REQUEST.

rollover relief A relief that enables a charge to *capital gains tax or *corporation tax to be deferred when the proceeds from the disposal of an asset are reinvested in a new asset (Taxation of Chargeable Gains Act 1992 s 152–59). Any gain arising from the disposal of the new asset will be correspondingly increased (unless the gain is once more "rolled over"). The relief is only available for the following types of asset: a building for the purposes of trade; any land used only for the purposes of trade; fixed *machinery and plant; ships, aircraft, and hovercraft; goodwill; satellites, space stations, and space vehicles; milk quotas and potato quotas; ewe and suckler cow premium quotas; fish quotas; rights of a member of a Lloyd's Syndicate; oil licences.

Romalpa clause *See* RETENTION OF TITLE.

Rome Treaty *See* TREATY OF ROME.

root of title The document from which an owner of unregistered land traces his ownership. A good root must be at least 15 years old, deal with the whole legal and beneficial ownership of the land, describe it sufficiently to identify it, and cast no doubt on the title. A vendor must supply and the purchaser must accept such a root unless their contract provides otherwise.

rout *n.* An old public-order offence approximating to *riot.

royal assent The agreement of the Crown, given under the *royal prerogative and signified either by the sovereign in person or by royal commissioners, that converts a Bill into an *Act of Parliament or gives a Measure (*see* CHURCH OF ENGLAND) the force of an Act. It is the duty of the Clerk of the Parliaments to endorse the date on which it was given immediately after the long title.

royal prerogative The special rights, powers, and immunities to which the Crown alone is entitled under the common law. Most prerogative acts are now performed by the government on behalf of the Crown. Some, however, are performed by the sovereign in person on the advice of the government (e.g. the dissolution of Parliament) or as required by constitutional convention (e.g. the appointment of a Prime Minister). A few prerogative acts (e.g. the granting of certain honours, such as the Order of the Garter) are performed in accordance with the sovereign's personal wishes.

The Crown has limited powers of legislating under the prerogative, principally as respects the civil service and UK dependent territories. It does so by Order in Council, ordinance, letters patent, or royal warrant. The dissolution and prorogation of Parliament and the granting of the royal assent to Bills take place under the prerogative. Originally the fountain of justice from which the first courts of law sprang, the Crown still exercises (through the Home Secretary) the *prerogative of mercy and retains the right (through the Attorney General) to stop a prosecution by entering a *nolle prosequi*. In foreign affairs, the sovereign declares war, makes peace and international treaties, and issues passports under the prerogative. Many appointments (e.g. the higher judiciary, archbishops, and diocesan bishops) are made under the prerogative, and a variety of honours, including new hereditary peerages, are conferred by the Crown as the fountain of honour. The sovereign is head of the armed forces, and, although much of the law governing these is now statutory, their disposition generally remains a matter for the prerogative. There is a prerogative power, subject to the payment of compensation, to expropriate or requisition private property in times of war or apprehended war. Miscellaneous prerogative rights include the rights to *treasure trove and to *bona vacantia*. An important immunity of the sovereign is the prerogative of perfection. The common-law maxim that "the King can do no wrong" resulted in the complete immunity of the sovereign personally from all civil and criminal proceedings for anything that he or she might do. This personal immunity remains, but actions may now be brought against the Crown under the Crown Proceedings Act 1947 (*see* CROWN PROCEEDINGS).

If a statute confers on the Crown powers that duplicate prerogative powers, the latter are suspended during the existence of the statute unless it either abolishes them or preserves them as alternative powers.

royal proclamation A document by which the sovereign exercises certain prerogative powers (e.g. the summoning and dissolution of Parliament) and certain legislative powers conferred on her by statute (e.g. the declaration of a state of emergency; *see* EMERGENCY POWERS).

royal title *See* QUEEN.

royalty *n.* A sum payable for the right to use someone else's property for the purpose of gain. Royalties are paid on *wasting assets, which have a limited lifespan. For example, the royalty paid by a licensee to mine someone's land is a fixed sum per tonne of the mineral he extracts, and an author's royalty is similarly determined by the total number of his books the publisher sells. Royalties are paid generally for the licensing of *intellectual property.

RPT *See* RESIDENTIAL PROPERTY TRIBUNAL.

RSC *See* RULES OF THE SUPREME COURT.

RTM *See* RIGHT TO MANAGE.

rubric *n.* [From Latin: red earth] The title of a statute, such titles formerly being published in letters of red. The rubric serves to show the intent of the legislature and thus forms a means by which the Act can be interpreted. The term is also, more rarely, used to refer to the headnote to a case.

rule against bias *See* NATURAL JUSTICE.

rule against double portions A rule designed to ensure, as far as possible, equality between children entitled under a settlement and under a will, both made by the same person. Thus if a father promises to pay substantial sums of money to certain of his children to advance them and at his death the money has not been paid, but the children (together with others) are entitled to legacies under his will, the payment of the legacies and the moneys due under the settlement will be considered together. Thus if an advancement of £10,000 and a legacy of £5000 are due to one son and a legacy of £10,000 is due to another son, the first son will not receive his legacy, to ensure equality between the children. *See* HOTCHPOT.

rule against inalienability A rule that prevents property from being rendered incapable of transfer within the perpetuity period, i.e. a life presently existing plus a period of 21 years. A gift that prevents transfer within this period is void. The rule is similar to the *rule against perpetual trusts.

rule against perpetual trusts The rule that prohibits noncharitable trusts from lasting beyond the perpetuity period, i.e. a lifetime presently existing plus a period of 21 years. Provisions concerning the relevant perpetuity period are to be found in the Perpetuities and Accumulations Act 2009, which applies only to instruments taking effect after its commencement on 6 April 2010. Earlier instruments will continue to be governed by the Perpetuities and Accumulations Act 1964. A trust that may last beyond that period is void. *Compare* RULE AGAINST INALIENABILITY; RULE AGAINST PERPETUITIES.

rule against perpetuities (rule against remoteness of future vesting) A rule developed by the *common law to enable a court to declare void any future or postponed interest in property that might possibly vest (i.e. become enjoyable as of right) outside the **perpetuity period**. This comprises (1) the lifetimes of persons mentioned (or mentioned by implication) in the disposition who are alive at that time and whose existence governs the timing of the vesting of the future interest (the relevant **lives in being**), plus (2) 21 years, plus (3) (in the case of a posthumous beneficiary) any actual period of gestation. The period runs from the date of execution of the deed or, if the disposition is contained in a will, from the death of the testator. The purpose of the rule is to prevent land being tied up for an indefinite period, which would hinder its ultimate disposal.

The common law rules relating to perpetuities have been supplemented (though not replaced) by the Perpetuities and Accumulations Act 1964. When a disposition would otherwise be void under the common law rules, the Act allows a period in which one can **wait and see** whether the interest will in fact vest within the perpetuity period; only if it becomes clear that it cannot do so will the disposition be void. For these purposes, the perpetuity period is varied in that the Act provides a new list of lives in being (the **statutory lives in being**). The Act also provides for a fixed perpetuity period unrelated to lives.

rule against remoteness of future vesting *See* RULE AGAINST PERPETUITIES.

rule in *Howe v Dartmouth* The principle that *trustees must act impartially between successive beneficiaries and not favour the interests of one beneficiary (e.g. a life tenant) over another (e.g. a remainderman), unless the trust instrument expressly provides that this rule is not to apply or makes it impossible for the trust assets to be applied evenly as between beneficiaries. The rule originates from the case of *Howe v Earl of Dartmouth* (1802) 7 Ves 137, which established that assets of a trust created by will should be converted, despite the absence of an express direction to do so, as long as the trust property is comprised of residuary personal estate, the property is of a wasting or reversionary character, and there is expressed an intention that the legatees should enjoy the same thing in succession.

rule in *Keech v Sandford* The rule that a trustee is prevented from retaining the benefit of a lease that is renewed in his own name, the lease having previously been held on trust. If a trustee does renew for his own benefit a lease that was previously the subject matter of the trust, even in circumstances where there is no desire for or prospect of the lease being renewed for the benefit of the trust, the trustee will be irrebuttably presumed to be a *constructive trustee for those who were beneficially interested in the original lease. This rule is derived from the case of *Keech v Sandford* (1726) Sel Cas Ch 61 in which a lease was renewed in the name of the trustee, for the trustee's own benefit, despite the fact that the lessor had refused to renew the lease in favour of the trust. It has been held that the rule applies to all persons acting in a fiduciary capacity and is not confined to trustees (*Re Biss* [1903] 2 Ch 40).

rule in *Re Hastings Bass* The principle that in some circumstances the court can set aside a disposition by trustees if it is clear that the trustees would (or perhaps might) not have acted as they did had they: (i) taken into account considerations that they ought to have taken into account; or (ii) declined to take into account considerations that they ought not to have taken into account. The principle emanated from the case of *Re Hastings Bass* [1975] Ch 25 and was initially concerned only with the need to protect beneficiaries against aberrant trustees. However, the way in which the rule was applied in some subsequent cases attracted much criticism. In *Pitt v Holt* and *Futter v Futter* [2013] UKSC 26, the Supreme Court greatly narrowed the scope and effect of the principle. It is now clear that if trustees, having discharged their duty by taking appropriate professional advice (on, for example, the tax consequences of a transaction), make the wrong decision on wrong advice then their decision stands and the transaction will not be voided. This potentially exposes trustees to liability even though they have acted in accordance with skilled professional advice.

rule in *Re Pettit* The tax rule that applies when an agreement states that the payer is to pay Q £100 "free of tax". The payer is then required to make a payment to Q of £100; this is equivalent to £128.20 gross and the recipient's income is therefore taken to include not £100 but £128.20 (*Re Pettit, Le Fevre v Pettit* [1922] 2 Ch 765). Illogically, the rule does not apply to court orders (*Jefferson v Jefferson* [1956] 1 All ER 31).

rule in *Re Rose* The rule under which a *gift is held to be effective where the donor has made every reasonable effort to divest himself of the property and to vest it in the donee, but the transfer has been left incomplete by the failure of a third party to perform certain legal formalities. The rule originated from the case *Re Rose* [1952] Ch 499. *See* VOLUNTARY SETTLEMENT.

rule in *Rylands v Fletcher* The principle that a person "who for his own purposes brings on his lands and collects and keeps there anything likely to do mischief if it escapes, must keep it in at his peril, and if he does not do so, is *prima facie* answerable for all the damage which is the natural consequence of its escape". It was first stated in the case *Rylands v Fletcher* (1868) 3 HL 330, in which the defendant had a reservoir built on his land that caused flooding of the claimant's mine. The rule creates a tort of strict liability for extraordinary and unusual things, accumulated on the land, that give rise to an exceptionally high risk of danger or mischief if they escape. There must be an escape on to another's land and only those with an interest in land may sue, as this tort is considered to be a species of *nuisance (*Transco plc v Stockport Metropolitan BC* [2003] UKHL 61, [2004] 2 AC 1). The rule only protects rights to and enjoyment of land and liability is limited to damage of a type that is reasonably foreseeable (*Cambridge Water Co Ltd v Eastern Counties Leather plc* [1994] 2 AC 264 (HL)).

rule in *Saunders v Vautier* A rule under which the beneficiaries of a trust, if of full age (18), sound mind, between them wholly entitled to the trust property, and in agreement, may direct the trustees to end the trust and transfer the trust property to themselves as beneficiaries absolutely. It is named after the case *Saunders v Vautier* (1841) 49 ER 282.

rule in *Strong v Bird* A rule that operates to perfect an otherwise imperfect *gift where the intended donee acquires the gift property by indirect means. The rule originated in the case of *Strong v Bird* (1874) LR 18 Eq 315, which was concerned not with a gift but with the extinguishment of a debt in circumstances where the deceased creditor had appointed his debtor as executor under his will. The court concluded that the right to sue for the repayment of the debt was voluntarily abandoned when the creditor appointed the debtor as his executor. The principle was subsequently extended to apply to gifts that had been promised but which, at the time of the testator's death, remained within the property of the testator's estate. In circumstances where the intended donee was appointed executor and came by the intended gift as a consequence of his executorship, the rule would also apply (*Re Stewart* [1908] 2 Ch 251). This extension of the doctrine has been accepted in the Court of Appeal (*Re Freeland* [1952] Ch 110). The rule is limited to circumstances in which there is a present intention to make a gift at the time of the donor's death and does not apply in the context of an intention to make a gift at some time in the future.

rule in *Wilkinson v Downton* The principle that where a defendant has wilfully committed an act or made a statement calculated to cause physical harm, and which does cause physical harm (including psychiatric injury), it is actionable. The tort requires actual intention to injure or a reckless disregard as to the consequences. This tort can be differentiated from *trespass to the person as the cause of harm is indirect (*Wainwright v Home Office* [2003] UKHL 53, [2004] 2 AC 406; *C v D* [2006] EWHC 166 (QB)).

rule of law 1. The supremacy of law. 2. A feature attributed to the UK constitution by Professor Dicey (*Law of the Constitution*, 1885). It embodied three concepts: the absolute predominance of regular law, so that the government has no arbitrary authority over the citizen; the equal subjection of all (including officials) to the ordinary law administered by the ordinary courts; and the fact that the citizen's personal freedoms are formulated and protected by the ordinary law rather than by abstract constitutional declarations.

rules of court Rules regulating the practice and procedure of a court, usually made by a rule committee acting under a statutory power. *See also* CIVIL PROCEDURE RULES; CROWN COURT RULES.

Rules of Oleron Ancient maritime laws promulgated in France in about 1160 and subsequently published in English. They include Article VI, "Rules of Maintenance and Cure" under which a ship owner is responsible for the medical care of a seaman injured in performance of duties on the ship.

Rules of the Supreme Court (RSC) Formerly, rules governing the practice and procedure of the *Supreme Court of Judicature. The rules were made under a statutory power by the Supreme Court Rule Committee, a body appointed by the *Lord Chancellor and comprising himself, the *Master of the Rolls, the heads of the Divisions of the High Court, and four practitioners. The Rules were revoked in 1999 by the *Civil Procedure Rules, which have re-enacted some of the rules of the RSC.

running-account credit (under the Consumer Credit Act 1974) A facility under a *personal-credit agreement that enables a debtor to receive periodically from the creditor or a third party cash, goods or services to an amount or value that does not exceed the *credit limit (if any), taking into account payments made by or to the credit of the debtor. Examples are bank overdrafts and credit cards.

running days *See* LAY DAYS.

running with the land *See* COVENANT RUNNING WITH THE LAND.

Rylands v Fletcher *See* RULE IN RYLANDS V FLETCHER.

Sabbath *n. See* SUNDAY TRADING.

sabotage *n.* Damage to or destruction of property, especially the property of an employer during a strike or of the state for political reasons. Sabotage as such is not an offence, although it may be treated as *criminal damage (*Chandler v DPP* [1964] AC 763 (HL)). The courts have, however, interpreted the phrase "prohibited place" in the Official Secrets Act 1911 to bring sabotage against the state within the scope of that Act, even though it is clear that Parliament's intention was only to prohibit spying.

safe haven A zone of territory within a sovereign state demarcated by the United Nations (or other international organization) as a refuge to which a persecuted *ethnic minority can choose to retire. While within such a zone the ethnic minority is afforded military protection by the body that established the zone. The international community set up safe havens in Iraq and the former Yugoslavia in response to acts of systematic persecution carried out by the government of the sovereign state concerned against part of its own population. *See also* HUMANITARIAN INTERVENTION.

safety at work Every employer has a common-law duty to take reasonable care for his employees' health, safety, and welfare at work: he may be sued in the courts for damages if an employee is injured through the employer's negligence or failure to observe the safety regulations. The employer cannot contract out of this liability and, under the Employers' Liability (Compulsory Insurance) Act 1969, must insure against his liability for employees' injuries and diseases sustained or contracted at work. The Health and Safety at Work Act 1974 further requires employers to ensure, as far as is reasonably practicable, that their working methods, equipment, premises, and environment are safe and to give such training, information, and supervision as will ensure their employees' health and safety (*see* HEALTH AND SAFETY EXECUTIVE). Anyone employing more than five persons must maintain a written statement of his general policy concerning his employees' health and safety (dealing, for example, with safety rules and protective clothing) and must keep them informed of it. He must also give relevant information to the *safety representatives of his employees' trade unions and establish a *safety committee where appropriate.

There are special rules governing the protection of the health and safety of pregnant women and new mothers (*see* MATERNITY RIGHTS).

Employees also have a duty to take reasonable care for their own health and safety, for example by complying with safety regulations and using protective equipment supplied to them. Employers and employees who fail to comply with the requirements of the Health and Safety at Work Act 1974 face prosecution in the criminal courts. An employee dismissed for health and safety reasons is under certain circumstances regarded as having been unfairly dismissed. It is also regarded as automatically unfair to select an employee for redundancy on certain grounds connected with health and safety.

safety committee A committee that, under the Health and Safety at Work Act 1974, an employer must establish within three months after a written request from at least two employees' *safety representatives. The employer must consult with the safety representatives as to the composition of the committee and must also display a notice in his premises informing his employees of its composition and the workplaces it covers. The *code of practice published by the Health and Safety Commission suggests that safety committees' responsibilities should include monitoring accidents and disease occurring in the workplace and developing improved safety rules and systems of work and training of employees with regard to safety.

safety representatives Employees appointed by trade unions to represent the interests of their colleagues regarding their health, safety, and welfare at work. Regulations made under the Health and Safety at Work Act 1974 give a trade union recognized as having negotiating rights on behalf of a group or class of employees the right to appoint at least one of those employees as a safety representative. The representatives' statutory powers include the investigation of accidents and industrial diseases occurring at the workplace and inspection of the premises to determine their causes. The employer must allow them time off work with pay to train for and perform their duties and to attend meetings of *safety committees. In workplaces where there is no recognized trade union the employer must consult directly with the employees or with an elected representative of employee safety. Dismissal of a safety representative for reasons connected with that role is automatically unfair, being an *inadmissible reason. There is no maximum limit on compensation in such cases. *See also* DISCLOSURE OF INFORMATION.

sale *n.* A contract involving the *sale of goods or a similar contract involving the transfer of land.

sale by description A contract of sale of goods containing words identifying its subject matter, e.g. 1000 tonnes of Western White Wheat. Even when the subject matter of the contract is physically ascertained at the time of contracting, e.g. a particular motor car, the contract may contain words of description or identification. The goods delivered must match their description in the contract; otherwise the seller is in breach of an *implied condition of the contract and the buyer, if he acts promptly, may reject the goods.

sale by sample A contract of sale of goods made on the basis that the bulk of goods to be delivered to the buyer will match a sample submitted by the seller. If the bulk does not match the sample the seller is in breach of an *implied condition of the contract and the buyer may reject the goods. The seller must give the buyer a reasonable opportunity of comparing the bulk with the sample and the goods must be free from any defect making them unmerchantable that would not be apparent on reasonable examination of the sample.

sale of goods A contract by which a seller transfers or agrees to transfer the ownership of goods to a buyer in exchange for a money price. If ownership is to pass at a future time the contract is called an **agreement to sell**. The contract, which need not be in writing, may contain *express terms. Terms may also be implied by law (*see also* IMPLIED CONDITION); for example, that the seller has a right to sell, that the goods correspond with the description under which they are sold, and that the goods are of *satisfactory quality and are reasonably fit for the buyer's purpose. Unless the parties agree otherwise the seller must hand over the goods in exchange for the price and the buyer must pay the price in exchange for the goods. Much of the law governing the sale of goods is codified in the Sale of Goods Act 1979, as amended by the Sale and Supply of Goods to Consumers Regulations 2002.

( ) SEE WEB LINKS

• Quick Facts on the Sale of Goods Act from the Department of Business

sale on approval *See* SALE OR RETURN.

sale or return (sale on approval) The delivery of goods to a person on terms that allow him to keep the goods for a time before he decides whether or not to buy them. Unless otherwise agreed, such a person becomes the owner if he signifies his approval of the goods or carries out any other act adopting the transaction. He will also become the owner if he retains the goods beyond the time fixed for their return, or, if no time has been fixed, beyond a reasonable time.

salus rei publicae suprema lex [Latin: The safety (or welfare) of the state is the supreme law] A maxim of Roman law reflecting the implied assent of every member of society that his own individual welfare shall, in cases of necessity, yield to that of the general community. It implies that the property, liberty, and life of the individual may, under certain extreme circumstances, be placed in jeopardy or even sacrificed for the public good.

salvage *n.* The service rendered by a person who saves or helps to save maritime property. Salvage may be the subject of an express agreement. In the absence of any agreement, a salvor is entitled by law to an award (also known as salvage), which is assessed by the court and payable out of the salvaged property, if he shows that the property was in real danger and that he acted with some skill and in a purely voluntary capacity. The award can also take account of the saving of life, but this alone gives no claim to an award as there is no property saved out of which payment can be ordered. The rules apply equally to aircraft. However, no award of salvage may be made unless the ship or aircraft is on or over the sea or tidal waters. Property saved in a nontidal river cannot be subject to a salvage claim.

salvage of trust property A power that existed before 1926 for the court to authorize a payment for preserving (or salvaging) trust property (e.g. repairing buildings) even though the document creating the trust did not permit such payment. A wider power was given by statute in 1925, under which the court can authorize any transaction that is expedient.

salvo *n.* [Latin: without] A saving clause: a derogation from the main purpose or intent of a document in writing (e.g. a will or statute).

sanction *n.* **1.** A *punishment for a crime. *See* NULLA POENA SINE LEGE. **2.** A measure taken against a state to compel it to obey international law or to punish it for a breach of international law. It is often said that international law is deficient because it lacks the power to impose sanctions or even to compel states to accept the jurisdiction of courts (*see* INTERNATIONAL COURT OF JUSTICE). There are, however, certain sanctions that can be applied. A state may, in certain cases, use force in self-defence, or as a sanction against an act of aggression, or as a reprisal (for example, by expropriating property belonging to citizens of a country that had previously carried out unlawful acts of expropriation). It may also act by way of *retorsion. There are also certain powers of sanction available under the United Nations system, such as economic (and, at least in theory, military) sanctions, although the powers of the Security Council to impose sanctions are subject to veto. *See also* ANGARY.

Sanderson order *See* Bullock order.

sanity *n. See* presumption of sanity.

***sans recours* (without recourse to me)** A stipulation that the drawer or an endorser of a *bill of exchange may add to his signature, thus repudiating his liability to the holder. If the bill is dishonoured, the holder has no recourse to the drawer or endorser who has made such a stipulation.

SARs (Substantial Acquisition Rules) Rules, administered by the Panel on Takeovers and Mergers, governing the acquisition of substantial shareholdings in public companies. *See* City Code on Takeovers and Mergers; concert party; dawn raid.

satisfaction *n.* **1.** The fulfilment of a claim. *See also* accord and satisfaction. **2.** The principle that a gift in a will may cancel, or be cancelled by, some other obligation of or provision made by the deceased. For example, a legacy to a creditor of the deceased that is equal to or in excess of the debt will be presumed to be made in satisfaction of the debt, so that only the legacy is payable. Likewise, if a testator makes a will containing a gift by way of *portion and subsequently makes a lifetime portion gift to the same person, then the lifetime gift may be presumed to be made in satisfaction of, and so as to cancel, the gift in the will. *See also* ademption.

satisfactory quality An *implied condition that goods sold in the course of business will meet the standard that a reasonable person would regard as satisfactory. In assessing this, account is taken of any description of the goods, the price (if relevant), and all other circumstances. The quality of goods includes their state and condition, taking account of their fitness for purpose, appearance and finish, freedom from minor defects, safety, and durability. Most commercial agreements exclude the implied conditions and replace them with express *warranties, although unreasonable exclusions in standard-form contracts, even between two businesses, may be void under the law relating to *unfair contract terms. Satisfactory quality replaced the term **merchantable quality** by the Sale and Supply of Goods Act 1994.

satisfied term The expired period of an interest in land for a term of years created for a specific purpose that has been fulfilled. For example, when land under a *strict settlement is assigned to trustees for a term of years on trust to raise capital sums for members of the settlor's family, the term is satisfied when the sums have been raised. Under the Law of Property Act 1925, the estate or interest in the land ceases when the purpose is fulfilled. A term of years that has not expired although the purpose for which it was created has been fulfilled is called an **outstanding term**.

***Saunders v Vautier* *See* rule in Saunders v Vautier.

saviour siblings *See* embryo selection.

scandalous statement A statement that is irrelevant and abusive. Under the Bar Code of Conduct a barrister when conducting proceedings in court must not make statements or ask questions that are merely scandalous or intended or calculated only to vilify, insult, or annoy either a witness or some other person.

schedular system A system formerly used to classify various sources of income for *income tax purposes and still applicable for corporation tax. The Finance Act 1803 established a set of five *schedules for the taxation of income. Tax was only imposed if the income fell within one of the specified schedules, each of which contained its own rules for the assessment of that income. The principles of this system were described by

Lord Radcliffe in his ruling in *Mitchell and Edon v Ross* [1961] 40 TC 11 (CA) 61: "Before you can assess a profit to tax you must be sure that you have properly identified its source or other description according to the correct Schedule: but, once you have done that, it is obligatory that it should be charged, if at all, under that Schedule and strictly in accordance with the rules that are there laid down for assessments under it. It is a necessary consequence of this conception that the sources of profit in the different Schedules are mutually exclusive".

This basic scheme continued until 2002, there then being tax charges imposed under Schedule A, Schedule D, Schedule E, and Schedule F (Schedule D was subdivided into six separate cases and Schedule E into three cases). The Income Tax (Earnings and Pensions) Act 2003 abolished Schedule E and replaced it with three categories of income: "employee income", "pension income", and "social security income". The Income Tax (Trading and Other Income) Act 2005 likewise abolished Schedules A, D, and F for income tax, replacing them with four categories: "trading income", "property income", "savings and investment income", and "miscellaneous income". Nevertheless, the two Acts of 2003 and 2005 specify an income tax charge applying to categories of income that look remarkably like subdivisions of the old schedules. In the Revenue view, the principle of exclusivity of income tax schedules continues to apply to the new categories of income. Schedules A, D, and F have been retained for corporation tax purposes.

schedule *n.* An appendix to an Act of Parliament or other legislation that deals with points of detail supplementary to the main part.

scheme *n.* A document, normally approved by the court, that contains provisions for the management or distribution of property or for resolving a dispute concerning allegedly conflicting rights. For example, the court or the *Charity Commission may approve a scheme for the management of a charitable trust.

scheme of arrangement **1.** An agreement between a debtor and his creditors to arrange the debtor's affairs to satisfy the creditors. The debtor usually agrees to such an arrangement in order to avoid *bankruptcy. If the arrangement is agreed when no bankruptcy order has been made, it is governed primarily by the ordinary law of contract. However, if it is for the benefit of the debtor's creditors generally, or if the debtor is insolvent and it is for the benefit of at least three of his creditors, it is a *deed of arrangement and subject to statutory control unless it is a voluntary arrangement. An arrangement agreed after a bankruptcy order has been made is governed by the statutory provisions relating to bankruptcy (*see* VOLUNTARY ARRANGEMENT). **2.** An agreement between a company and its creditors or members when the company is in financial difficulties or to effect a *takeover. It must be approved by a majority in number (holding 75% in value) of those creditors or members at separate meetings and sanctioned by the court. All creditors or members involved in the scheme are bound by it, although the court can make special provision for those who dissent (Companies Act 1985). Agreements with company creditors can often be more conveniently concluded by *voluntary arrangement under the Insolvency Act 1986.

Schengen Agreement The agreement between most member states of the European Union (but not the UK) to abolish internal border controls. It came into force on 26 March 1995. *See also* PASSPORT.

school attendance procedures Procedures invoked by a local education authority (LEA) under the Education Act 1996 to secure a child's registration and attendance at school. An LEA must serve a **school attendance order** where it is not satisfied that a child is being educated according to section 7 of the Act. If this is not complied with, a parent commits a criminal offence punishable by a fine and, where the parent knows that his child is failing to attend school regularly, by imprisonment for up to three months. LEAs may prefer the civil option of an *education supervision order.

Scottish Parliament A body established by the Scotland Act 1998 (and operative from July 1999), having 129 elected members (**Members of the Scottish Parliament; MSPs**) and possessing limited primary legislative powers over such matters as health, school education, and forestry, as defined within the Act. It may alter the basic rate of income tax in Scotland by up to three pence in the pound. The **Scottish Executive** (the devolved government of Scotland) is formed by the party or parties with the majority of seats in the Parliament. *See* DEVOLUTION.

Scott Schedule A document commonly used for giving *particulars when a claim is in respect of a large number of individual items (e.g. a landlord's claim for dilapidations). The Scott Schedule is divided into columns providing for

(1) the consecutive numbering of the items;
(2) the full description of each item;
(3) the contention of each party against each item as to liability or amount; and
(4) a column for the use of the court. It is named after a former official referee.

SCT *See* SUPERVISED COMMUNITY TREATMENT.

scuttling *n.* Sinking a ship (particularly with a view to making a fraudulent insurance claim) by making or opening holes in its hull to allow the entry of water.

SDT *See* SOLICITORS REGULATION AUTHORITY.

seal *n.* Wax impressed with a design and attached to any document as a sign of its authenticity; alternatively, an adhesive wafer or anything else intended to serve the purpose of a seal may be used. The Glossary to the Civil Procedure Rules defines a seal as a formal mark that the court puts on a document to indicate that the document has been issued by the court. Under the terms of the Law of Property (Miscellaneous Provisions) Act 1989, *deeds no longer require a seal in order to be validly executed.

search **1.** *vb.* To examine the registers maintained by the Land Registry, the Land Charges Department, or the registers of local land charges during an *official search. **2.** *n. See* POWER OF SEARCH.

search before Crown Court The searching of a person before the Crown Court when that person has been ordered by the court to pay a fine or to pay money for some other reason (e.g. where the court has made a compensation order or where a person has forfeited a *recognizance). Any money found on the person may be applied towards payment of the fine or other sum payable by him, with any balance being returned to him.

search of ship The right that a belligerent power has during wartime, under public international law, to search any ship of a neutral power on the high seas in order to discover whether it is carrying *contraband.

search order A form of interim mandatory *injunction made by the High Court under the jurisdiction conferred upon it by section 7 of the Civil Procedure Act 1997. Such an order requires a defendant to permit a claimant or his representatives to enter the defendant's premises to inspect, copy, or remove material evidence that it is feared the defendant might otherwise destroy or remove in order to frustrate the claimant's action. Because of its nature, a search order is granted without notice to the defendant.

It will be granted in limited circumstances, and only where it is deemed absolutely necessary. A search order may *prima facie contravene the defendant's right to privacy under Article 8(1) of the European Convention on Human Rights. However, the qualification under Article 8(2) would permit the use of such orders where necessary. The *privilege against self-incrimination does not apply. Until 1999 a search order was known as an **Anton Piller Order**, from the case *Anton Piller KG v Manufacturing Processes* [1976] All ER 779 (CA).

search warrant *See* POWER OF SEARCH.

seat belt A belt fitted in a motor vehicle, designed to restrict the forward movement of a driver or front-seat passenger in the event of an accident. All passenger vehicles with seating for fewer than 13 passengers and most four-wheeled goods vehicles registered after 1 January 1965 must comply with statutory regulations governing seat belts, although the details of these regulations vary according to the date when the vehicle was first registered. It is compulsory for all drivers and front-seat passengers in cars registered after 1964, light vans registered after 1966, and three-wheeler vehicles registered after 1969 to wear seat belts at all times when the vehicle is moving, and for back-seat passengers to wear seat belts when these are fitted, subject to certain exceptions. These exceptions are:

(1) drivers carrying out any manoeuvre that includes reversing (passengers must still wear their seat belts during such manoeuvres);
(2) drivers making local delivery or collection rounds in specially adapted vehicles (e.g. milkmen in milk vans);
(3) anyone whose seat belt has become faulty during the drive or who has already arranged to have a faulty belt repaired;
(4) anyone whose belt has locked on a steep hill;
(5) anyone supervising a learner who is reversing;
(6) certain categories of people with a special exemption certificate on medical grounds.

Any front-seat passenger over the age of 14 is responsible for wearing his own seat belt, but the driver of the car is responsible for ensuring that front-seat passengers under the age of 14 wear a seat belt. Children under the age of one must wear an approved child restraint. Over the age of one they can wear an adult seat belt, preferably with an approved booster cushion to raise them to a suitable height. Alternatively they can sit in the back seat fitted with an approved restraint. When more passengers are carried than there are seat belts available, the passengers who do not have seat belts do not break the law by not being restrained. Thus in a four-seater car with a fifth passenger sitting in the middle of the back seat, the middle back passenger does not break the law by being unrestrained.

Failure to wear a seat belt carries a *fine at level 2 on the standard scale and may also be regarded as *contributory negligence in a claim for injuries sustained in a road traffic accident, leading to a reduction in damages.

sea waybill A receipt for goods that contains or evidences the contract for the carriage of goods by sea and also identifies the person to whom delivery of the goods is to be made by the carrier in accordance with that contract. A sea waybill is not a *bill of lading: it is commonly used in container transport and, unlike a bill of lading, does not have to be produced at the port of discharge in order to obtain delivery.

seaworthy *adj.* **1.** Having at the start of a voyage the degree of fitness (as respects the ship, her crew, and her equipment) for that particular voyage that a careful owner might be expected to require of his ship. **2.** The suitability of a particular ship to carry a particular cargo. Obligations relating to seaworthiness are implied by law in charterparties and imposed by the Hague Rules in bills of lading. A marine insurance policy incorporates by statute a warranty that the insured ship is seaworthy.

secession *n.* The action of breaking away or formally withdrawing from an alliance, a federation, a political or religious organization, etc. An example of secession is the attempted withdrawal of the Confederate States from the United States in the War of Secession (1861–65).

secondary evidence Evidence that by its nature suggests the existence of better evidence (e.g. a copy of a document). *See* PRIMARY EVIDENCE.

secondary party An *accessory to a crime. *See also* PRINCIPAL.

secondary use *See* SHIFTING USE.

Second Opinion Appointed Doctor (SOAD) An independent consultant psychiatrist appointed by the *Mental Health Act Commission to make certain decisions regarding the treatment of a person with *mental disorder.

Secretary of State *See* MINISTER.

secret profits Profits made by an *agent during the course of his agency without the knowledge or authorization of his principal. The principal may require the agent to account for secret profits.

secret trust A trust whose existence is not made public, thereby giving the impression that the trust property is in fact an outright gift to its recipient, the secret trustee. For example, A makes a gift in his will to B on the secret understanding between them that B will hold the property on trust for C. Secret trusts, while normally associated with a will, have been created upon *intestacy where the settlor has made an arrangement with an intestate successor (*Sellack v Harris* (1708) 2 Eq Ca Ab 46). Doctrinal difficulties regarding the recognition of secret trusts have arisen because of their apparent failure to comply with the requirements of the Wills Act 1837 (s 9). This requires all testamentary dispositions to be in writing, signed by the testator. However, the modern theory of secret trusts suggests that secret trusts are created *inter vivos*, hence the Wills Act does not apply. Further difficulties arise in connection with the proper classification of secret trusts. It has not yet been conclusively determined whether secret trusts are *express trusts or *constructive trusts. This has a bearing on what formalities should apply to the creation of such trusts, particularly the application of section 53(1)(b) of the Law of Property Act 1925 where the trust property is land. The leading case on fully secret trusts is *Ottoway v Norman* [1972] Ch 698.

section *vb.* To issue an order for the compulsory admission of a patient with a *mental disorder to a psychiatric hospital for assessment and treatment under the appropriate section of the Mental Health Act 1983.

section 8 orders Court orders under the Children Act 1989 that settle practical details concerning the child's care and upbringing in any family proceedings in which the child's welfare is a matter for consideration (such as matrimonial, wardship, or adoption proceedings). Section 8 orders, which replace the old access, custody, and care and control orders, include *residence orders, *contact orders, *prohibited steps orders, and *specific issues orders.

Section 8 orders are only necessary when there is a dispute between the parents or others in relation to a child and are usually only made in respect of children up to the age of 16. In determining whether or not to make such an order, the court must treat the child's welfare as paramount.

section 12 doctor A registered medical practitioner who is approved to give one of the medical recommendations required for the compulsory admission of a patient to hospital under the Mental Health Act 1983. To be approved under section 12 a doctor must have special experience in the treatment of diagnosis of mental disorder.

section 37 investigation An investigation of a child's circumstances ordered by the court to be carried out by a local authority when the court has cause for serious concern about the child's upbringing. The order may be made in any *family proceedings, for example when an application for a residence or contact order is being made by a parent (*see* SECTION 8 ORDERS). The local authority carrying out the investigation must consider whether it should apply for a *care order or a *supervision order or assistance for the child or its family or take any other action with respect to the child.

section 47 enquiry An enquiry carried out by a local authority in order to enable it to decide whether or not it should take any action to safeguard and promote the welfare of a particular child. The local authority is under a duty to carry out such an investigation if it has reasonable cause to suspect that a child is suffering or likely to suffer significant harm, or is the subject of an *emergency protection order, or is in *police protection. As a result of its enquiries a local authority might decide that no action is required; alternatively, it may decide that the family in question is in need of support and provide the appropriate services, or it may apply for an emergency protection order, a *care order, a *supervision order, or a *child assessment order. If, in the course of its enquiries, a local authority is denied access to a child, it should immediately apply to court for an emergency protection order.

sector theory A proposed basis for national claims to sovereignty over both the Arctic and Antarctica. The sector theory delineates a meridian line from the pole to the farthest extremity of the contiguous state's land mass. All territory within that sector is thereupon purported to be under the sovereignty of the claimant state. It should be noted that this theory is not universally recognized as the sole basis for claiming territory in these regions.

secure accommodation Accommodation provided for a child looked after by a local authority (*see* LOOKED-AFTER CHILD) in which his or her liberty is restricted. Such accommodation can only be used where the criteria in the Children Act 1898 s 25 are met. The child in question must either (i) have a history of absconding from other accommodation and be likely to suffer significant harm if he absconds again, or (ii) be likely to injure himself or others if he does not have his liberty restricted. A local authority can keep a looked-after child in secure accommodation for up to 72 hours without a court order, but beyond this court sanction is required. Secure accommodation should only be used as a last resort.

secured creditor A person who holds some security, such as a mortgage, for money he has lent. If the debtor becomes bankrupt the creditor has a choice. He may surrender his security and claim the amount of the debt from the bankrupt's assets; he may realize or evaluate the security and claim any balance of the debt in excess of the value of the security; or he may rely on the security and not make any claim in the bankruptcy proceedings. *Compare* UNSECURED CREDITOR.

secure tenancy A residential tenancy in which the tenant has statutory protection if he occupies the rented property as his home. It applies only if there is a certain kind of landlord, such as a local authority, the *Housing Corporation, or a *housing action trust. Certain tenants are excluded from protection; these include students, the occupants of almshouses, licensed premises, and accommodation for the homeless, and those renting accommodation on long leases or who have a *service tenancy.

If a secure tenancy is for a fixed term, the tenancy continues at the end of the term as a *periodic tenancy. A landlord can only terminate a secure tenancy by serving a notice on the tenant in a special statutory form and can only obtain possession with the tenant's consent or, if this is refused, by a court order. An order is granted only if the landlord has statutory grounds similar to those required in the case of an *assured tenancy. When the holder of a secure tenancy dies, his spouse or a member of his family who has lived with him for the past 12 months can succeed him as tenant. Under certain conditions, secure tenants have a right to buy their rented property, at a discount on the market value of the property, and with their landlord supplying a mortgage. The Housing Act 2004 gives landlords the right to suspend completion of a right-to-buy sale where some types of court action relating to antisocial behaviour are pending. The Housing Act 1988 contains provisions for the transfer of public-sector housing to the private sector and to housing action trusts. *See also* INTRODUCTORY TENANCY.

securities *pl. n.* Loosely, *stocks, *shares, *debentures, *bonds, or any other rights to receive dividends or interest. Strictly, the term should only be used for rights backed by some sort of security, as in the case of debentures.

security In criminal proceedings, a sum of money deposited to ensure that the defendant attends court (Glossary to the Criminal Procedure Rules).

Security Council (of the UN) *See* UNITED NATIONS.

security for costs A sum payable by a claimant to a civil action as a condition of being permitted to continue with the action. The court has discretion as to whether or not to order security for costs and may exercise it only in four circumstances:

(1) when the claimant is ordinarily resident out of the area of the jurisdiction;
(2) when the claimant is suing on behalf of someone who will be unable to pay the defendant's costs if ordered to do so;
(3) when the claimant's address is dishonestly not stated or incorrectly stated on the originating process;
(4) when the claimant has changed his address during the course of the proceedings in order to evade the consequences of the litigation. A defendant may not be ordered to give security for costs. When security is ordered the claimant is usually ordered to pay a sum into court.

security of tenure Statutory protection given to tenants that restricts landlords' rights to obtain possession and may give the tenant a right to demand a new tenancy at the end of a *fixed term. The conditions for obtaining possession vary according to the kind of tenancy, but a court order is usually required. *See* AGRICULTURAL HOLDING; ASSURED AGRICULTURAL OCCUPANCY; ASSURED SHORTHOLD TENANCY; ASSURED TENANCY; BUSINESS TENANCY; LONG TENANCY; PROTECTED OCCUPANCY; PROTECTED TENANCY; SECURE TENANCY; STATUTORY TENANCY.

sedition *n.* The speaking or writing of words that are likely to incite ordinary people to public disorder or insurrection. Sedition is a common-law offence (known as **seditious libel** if the words are written) if it is committed with the intention of

(1) arousing hatred, contempt, or disaffection against the sovereign or her successors (but not the monarchy as such), the government of the UK, or either House of Parliament or the administration of justice;

(2) encouraging any change of the law by unlawful means; or

(3) raising discontent among Her Majesty's subjects or promoting ill-will and hostility between different classes of subjects. There must be an intention to achieve these consequences by violence and disorder. An agreement to carry out an act to further any of these intentions is a criminal *conspiracy.

seduction *n.* **1.** Enticement to have sexual intercourse. Until 1971 parents could sue a seducer for loss of earnings or services resulting from the seduction of their child, but this has now been abolished. It is an offence for a parent to cause or encourage the seduction of a child under the age of 16, the *age of consent. **2.** The offence under the Incitement to Disaffection Act 1934 of maliciously and advisedly endeavouring to persuade any member of HM forces to abandon his duty or allegiance to the Crown.

seisin *n.* Possession of a freehold estate in land. Historically, availability of certain remedies for a landowner depended on being able to show seisin. In old conveyances, owners are sometimes said to be **seised** of land. In modern times it is unnecessary to distinguish between seisin and possession, the latter being the basis of most remedies available to a landowner. *See also* UNITY OF SEISIN.

select committee A committee appointed by either House of Parliament or both Houses jointly to investigate and report on a matter of interest to them in the performance of their functions. Examples are the committees of the Commons that examine government expenditure or the activities of government departments and the nationalized industries, and the *Joint Committee on Statutory Instruments.

self-assessment *n.* A system enabling taxpayers to assess their own *income tax and *capital gains tax liabilities for the year. Under self-assessment, the requirement to calculate taxable income and any capital gains using all the complexity of the Taxes Acts lies solely with the taxpayer. If a *market value for an asset is required, the taxpayer must supply it. If information is not available until after the due date for the submission of a tax return (normally 31 January the following fiscal year), the taxpayer must supply an estimate. The liability calculated by the taxpayer himself under the self-assessment process is a debt that can be collected, if necessary, by County Court or High Court action, even though the Revenue has taken no action to create the debt. A company, similarly, produces its own self-assessment to *corporation tax.

(((()))) SEE WEB LINKS

- Guide to self-assessment from the HM Revenue and Customs website
- Guide to corporation tax self-assessment from the HM Revenue and Customs website

self-build society A *housing association whose object is to provide, for sale to or occupation by its members, dwellings built or improved principally by their own labour.

self-defence *n.* **1.** A defence at common law to charges of *offences against the person (including homicide) when *reasonable force is used to defend oneself, or one's family, or anyone else against attack or threatened attack (*R v Rose* (1884)15 Cox CC 540). The scope of the defence often overlaps with the statutory right to use reasonable force to prevent a crime (Criminal Law Act 1967 s 3), but also extends to cases in which the statutory right is inapplicable (for example, when the attacker is for some reason not guilty of a crime). There is no rule of law that a person must retreat before acting in self-defence (*R v McInnes* (1971) 1 WLR 1600). In cases where a householder is confronted by an intruder on his property, the defence of self-defence has been clarified and strengthened by the Criminal Justice and Immigration Act s 76, as amended by the Crime and Courts Act 2013 s 43. If a householder acting in self-defence uses more force than was strictly necessary in the circumstances and kills or causes serious injury to the intruder, he may still have a defence of self-defence if he can show that the level of force used was not grossly disproportionate in the circumstances as he genuinely believed them to be, even if this belief was, in fact, mistaken. In deciding whether the force used was justified or reasonably thought to be justified, the jury must bear in mind the difficulty of quickly assessing the correct amount of force to be used in an alarming situation. Case: *R v Martin* [2002] 2 WLR 1 (CA). *See also* GENERAL DEFENCES. **2.** One of the very few bases for a legal use of force under international law. Under *Chapter VII (Article 51) of the United Nations Charter, the inherent right of self-defence is preserved. Reference to "inherent right" has promoted the belief that the pre-Charter right of self-defence in customary international law is specifically preserved by the Charter. However, the pre-existing right is arguably wider in scope than that allowed for by the terms of Article 51 and may arguably also allow for *anticipatory self-defence. The UK relied on the argument of self-defence in the Falklands Conflict of 1982. *See also* SELF-HELP; USE OF FORCE.

self-determination *n.* (in international law) The right of a people living within a non-self-governing territory to choose for themselves the political and legal status of that territory. They may choose independence and the formation of a separate state, integration into another state, or association with an independent state, with autonomy in internal affairs. The systems of *mandates and trusteeship marked a step towards recognizing a legal right of self-determination, but it is not yet completely recognized as a legal norm. It is probably illegal for another state to intervene against a liberation movement and it may be legal to give assistance to such a movement. *See also* ERGA OMNES OBLIGATIONS.

self-employed *adj.* In business on one's own account, i.e. not engaged as an employee under a *contract of employment. Statutory employment provisions do not apply to the self-employed. A self-employed person may nevertheless be the employer of others.

self-executing treaty A treaty that is intended to bind states internally, as opposed to one that is intended to bind them externally. The vast majority of treaties are non-self-executing: that is, following their signature (and later ratification) the signing state is bound viz-a-viz other signatory states but, until it transforms the terms of the treaty into municipal law, it does not bind its own subjects (*The Parlement Belge* (1879) 4 PD 129). Self-executing treaties, on the other hand, require no such transformation by statute. In English law this rare type of treaty would include those that cede territory.

self-help *n.* **1.** Action taken by a person to whom a wrong has been done to protect his rights without recourse to the courts. Self-help is permitted in certain torts, such as *trespass and *nuisance. A trespasser may be evicted provided only reasonable force is used. A nuisance may be abated (*see* ABATEMENT). *See also* RECAPTION. **2.** Independent and self-directed action taken by an injured state against the transgressing state in order to gain redress. Until the middle of the 20th century the right of self-help was claimed by states as one of the essential attributes of *sovereignty. In the absence of an international executive agency, an injured state undertook on its own account the defence of the claim it was making. Forcible measures falling short of war might prove sufficient; failing these, war might be resorted to as the ultimate means of self-help. Since self-help was regarded at international law as a legal remedy, the results secured by it were recognized by the international community as a final settlement of the case. Since the establishment of the United Nations, self-help with regard to *use of force can only be legal in so far as it forms part of a legitimate claim to *self-defence. The remaining forms of self-help are countermeasures, such as *retorsion and *reprisals.

seller *n.* The party to a contract of *sale of goods who transfers or agrees to transfer ownership of the goods to the buyer. The term may also be used in the context of the transfer of the ownership of land, but a seller of land is more usually called a **vendor**.

Seller's Property Information Form *See* CONVEYANCING.

semble *n.* [Latin: it seems] Used to suggest that a particular point may be doubtful. A good example of this can be found in the case of *Hedley Byrne v Heller & Partners* [1963] 2 All ER 575 (HL) 576 E-F. Here Lords Reid, Morris, and Hodson establish a proposition concerning a bank's provision of the creditworthiness of a client to another party. In such instances, they state, there is no legal duty on the bank beyond that of giving an honest answer. This is the belief of their lordships. They could, of course, be wrong in law. This is a matter to be tested in future cases concerning the same point.

semiconductor topography Etching on a computer chip otherwise known as a **mask work** or **right**: an *intellectual property right protecting the layout of a semiconductor chip or integrated circuit. Such rights are protected in the EU under directive 87/54.

semi-secret trust *See* HALF-SECRET TRUST.

sending distressing letters The finable offence, under the Malicious Communications Act 1988, of sending to someone a letter or some other article that conveys an indecent or grossly offensive message, a threat, or information that is false and known or believed by the sender to be false. Sending an indecent or grossly offensive article is similarly punishable. The sender must have aimed to cause distress or anxiety. If the material contains a threat, there is a defence similar to that available on a *blackmail charge. *See also* HARASSMENT.

sending for trial The procedure by which *offences triable either way and *indictable offences are transferred to the Crown Court without the need for a committal hearing in the magistrates' court. The relevant law and rules of procedure are set out in Part 9 of the *Criminal Procedure Rules.

Senior Courts The higher courts of England and Wales, excluding the *Supreme Court of the United Kingdom: namely, the *Crown Court, the *High Court of Justice, and the *Court of Appeal. Until 2009 these courts were known collectively as the *Supreme Court of Judicature.

sentence *n.* Any order made by a court when dealing with an offender in respect of his offence, including imprisonment (which may take the form of a *concurrent sentence or *suspended sentence), a fine, a *community order, or an absolute or conditional *discharge. Criminal sentencing is now governed by the Criminal Justice Act 2003, which requires courts to take into account the following purposes of sentencing: punishing offenders, reduction of crime (including its reduction by deterrence), the reform and rehabilitation of offenders, the protection of the public, and the making of reparations by offenders to persons affected by their offences (*see* PUNISHMENT). This provision, however, does not apply where the penalty for an offence is fixed in law (such as the life sentence required upon conviction for murder). Under the 2003 Act, the **Sentencing Guidelines Council** is empowered to promulgate sentencing guidelines for various offences, which sentencing judges must take into account in relevant cases. Sentences may be increased if the offence was racially or religiously aggravated, or was based on hostility towards the victim on the basis of his actual or presumed sexual orientation or disability.

Before the sentence is imposed, the prosecution must present the judge with the accused's *antecedents and the defence may then make a plea in *mitigation of the sentence. The sentencing court will normally obtain a *pre-sentence report prior to imposing a custodial sentence or a community order with requirements upon a defendant. Sentence must be pronounced in open court by the presiding judge and is almost always pronounced in the presence of the accused. The sentence may be altered (or rescinded) within 28 days by the trial court, and there is a power to postpone sentence for up to six months (*see* DEFERRED SENTENCE). Magistrates' courts may not impose sentences of imprisonment exceeding six months upon any defendant, and they may not impose any sentence of imprisonment upon first time offenders or defendants who are not legally represented in court. Where the magistrates' court considers that its powers of sentencing are insufficient for the case, it may commit an offender to the Crown Court for sentencing. There is usually a right of appeal against sentence to the *Court of Appeal. The *Attorney General may refer cases to the Court of Appeal (with its permission) when Crown Court sentences appear unduly lenient. *See also* DANGEROUS OFFENDER; JUVENILE OFFENDER; REPEAT OFFENDER.

separability thesis *See* LEGAL POSITIVISM.

separate trials *See* JOINDER OF DEFENDANTS.

separatim *adv.* [Latin: separately] Apart from anything already pleaded. The term may be used, for example, to introduce a secondary line of defence that is unrelated to the main defence.

separation *n. See* JUDICIAL SEPARATION ORDER; LIVING APART.

separation agreement An agreement between husband and wife releasing each other from the duty to cohabit. Such an agreement will only be valid (subject to the ordinary rules of the law of contract) if the marriage has already broken down; it will be void (contrary to public policy) if they enter into it to provide for the contingency that the marriage may break down at some future date. Separation agreements often contain further clauses (such as nonmolestation clauses, maintenance clauses, *dum casta* clauses) or an agreement not to bring other matrimonial proceedings based on past conduct ("*Rose v Rose* clauses"). Under the Family Law Act 1996 such orders will not be granted unless the interests of the children are settled first. A spouse may also relinquish his rights or powers in relation to his children, but the court has an overriding discretion not to enforce such provisions if they are not for the children's benefit. A separation agreement in writing may be a *maintenance agreement and governed by the Matrimonial Causes Act 1973.

separation of powers The doctrine that the liberty of the individual is secure only if the three primary functions of the state (legislative, executive, and judicial) are exercised by distinct and independent organs. It was propounded by Montesquieu (*De l'Esprit des Lois*, 1748), who regarded it as a feature of the UK constitution. In fact, however, while the judiciary is largely independent, the legislature and the executive depend on one another and their members overlap. The doctrine had a great influence over the form adopted for the constitution of the USA and many other countries.

separation order *See* JUDICIAL SEPARATION ORDER.

sequestration *n.* A court order in the form of a writ to (usually four) commissioners (**sequestrators**), ordering them to seize control of a person's property. The order may be made against someone who is in *contempt of court because he has not complied with a court order (such as an injunction). The property is detained until he complies with the order. Relevant procedural rules are set out in the schedules to the *Civil Procedure Rules.

seriatim *adv.* [Latin: severally and in order] A term used by way of a blank denial to any allegation that has been made by a claimant, as if to blot out any possibility of admitting any liability to the various claims made.

Serious Fraud Office (SFO) A body established in 1987 to be responsible for investigating and prosecuting serious or complex frauds. The *Attorney General appoints and superintends its director. The director is empowered to investigate any suspected offence that appears to involve serious fraud and may employ any suitable person to help in the investigation. Serious and complex fraud cases go straight to the Crown Court, which can hold *preparatory hearings to clarify issues for the jury and settle points of law.

(🌐) SEE WEB LINKS
• SFO website

Serious Organized Crime Agency (SOCA) A former body corporate established under the Serious Organized Crime Agency and Police Act 2005 to replace the National Crime Squad, the National Criminal Intelligence Service, and the investigative and enforcement arm of the Customs and Excise. Its role was to prevent, detect, and prosecute serious organized crime in the UK. SOCA was replaced by a new *National Crime Agency (NCA) in 2013.

SERPS *See* STATE SECOND PENSION.

servant *n.* An *employee.

service *n.* **1.** The steps required by rules of court to bring documents used in court proceedings to a person's attention. Under Part 6 of the *Civil Procedure Rules service of a document may be made by leaving the document with the person concerned (*see* PERSONAL SERVICE); by first class post; by leaving the document at the *address for service given by that person; through a document exchange (DX); or by fax or other means of electronic communication. The Civil Procedure Rules also provide for service by an alternative method (formerly known as **substituted service**) where there is good reason, as where the defendant is evading service. **2.** (contract of service) *See* CONTRACT OF EMPLOYMENT. **3.** *See* SERVICES.

Service Civilian Court A court, provided for by the Armed Forces Act 2006, for the trial outside the British Isles of lesser offences committed by certain civilians, e.g. the families of servicemen. The court consists of a single *judge advocate and may sit in any place other than the British Isles. *See* SERVICE LAW.

Service Complaints Commissioner An official, appointed by the Secretary of State for Defence under the Armed Forces Act 2006, to act as an independent person to whom complaints may be made by any person who believes that a member of the armed forces has a complaint arising from the service. The commissioner may refer the complaint to a relevant officer in the armed forces and can monitor progress thereafter. The Commissioner reports to the Secretary of State and Parliament annually.

service inquiry A panel convened by naval, army, or air force authorities under the Armed Forces Act 2006 to investigate and report upon the facts of any happening (e.g. the death or serious injury of service personnel or the loss or destruction of service property) and to make recommendations to prevent a recurrence.

service law The specialized code of criminal law that regulates the conduct of members of the armed forces.

Service law is the collective name for what was historically known as **naval law, military law,** and **air force law** (military law was the branch relating to the army, but the expression was frequently used to describe all three branches). Its primary source is the Armed Forces Act 2006, which effectively consolidated and aligned the Army Act 1955, the Air Force Act 1955, and the Naval Discipline Act 1957 to create a single body of service law applicable to all the armed forces. Supplementary sources are the **Queen's Regulations** for each service, which are made by *royal prerogative (or *Orders in Council in the case of the Royal Navy).

The Act requires annual renewal. Every fifth year a new Armed Forces Act will enable it to continue in force for one year and will provide that for each of the following four years it may be continued in force by an Order in Council that has been approved by resolution of each House of Parliament. The next such Act is therefore due in 2016. The purpose of this procedure (which also applied to the three earlier single service Acts) is to ensure that Parliament has an annual opportunity of debating matters relating to the armed forces.

Service law is a specialized code of criminal law. Its essential concern is the maintenance of discipline and it embodies a variety of offences (including *desertion, malingering, and insubordination) that have no counterpart in the ordinary criminal law. Since 1 April 1997 it has been an offence against service law to fail to provide a urine sample for the purpose of a service compulsory drug test; in addition, the service authorities have been empowered to take fingerprints or DNA samples from those convicted of service offences, for criminal records purposes. Many provisions of criminal law have direct application to the armed forces, while others require specific secondary legislation to take account of service requirements.

Commanding officers have powers of dealing with minor offences summarily and, with effect from 2 October 2000, a member of the armed forces may appeal against the commanding officer's finding and/or award to a **Summary Appeal Court**. The Summary Appeal Court, consisting of a *judge advocate and two officers or warrant officers may uphold, quash, or vary the commanding officer's finding or award. However, the tribunal primarily responsible for the trial and punishment of offences is the *Court Martial, which consists of a *judge advocate and up to seven serving officers (including warrant officers). A defendant may appeal against conviction and/or sentence to the Court Martial Appeal Court, which is headed by the Lord Chief Justice.

Service law applies to members of the armed forces wherever they may be. In the UK, a member of the armed forces is subject both to service law and to the ordinary criminal law. When he or she is not in the UK, the ordinary criminal law does not in general apply to a member of the forces; the Act therefore provides that it is an offence under service law for any member to do anything that constitutes an offence under the ordinary criminal law. The effect of this general provision is to create, in the case of a member of the armed forces who is in the UK, a duality of offences. If, for example, a soldier in the UK steals, he or she commits an offence against both the ordinary criminal law and service law. The soldier cannot, however, be punished under both.

Although service law applies primarily to members of the armed forces, certain classes of civilians are also subject to it (who are referred to as being subject to service discipline). These include civilians employed outside the UK within the limits of the command of any officer commanding a body of the regular forces and the families of members of the armed forces residing with them outside the UK. This has led to the establishment of the Service Civilian Court.

service out of the jurisdiction *Service of a *claim form, petition, or application notice outside England and Wales. The rules concerning service out of the jurisdiction, obtaining permission of the court to serve out of the jurisdiction, and the procedure for serving out of the jurisdiction are set out in Part 6 of the *Civil Procedure Rules. Under the Civil Jurisdiction and Judgments Act 1982 and the *Judgments Regulation, service out of the jurisdiction on a defendant domiciled in a Regulation State does not need permission of the court. In other cases permission of the court may be granted if the grounds specified in the Civil Procedure Rules are satisfied. In general, some particular connection must be shown between the defendant or the subject matter of the proceedings and the jurisdiction of the English courts.

Service Prosecuting Authority *See* Director of Service Prosecutions.

services *pl. n.* For *value-added tax purposes, there are two categories of taxable supply: a supply of *goods and a supply of services. Anything done for a *consideration that is not a supply of goods is a supply of services. For examples, see Case 230/87 *Naturally Yours Cosmetics Ltd v Customs and Excise Comrs* [1988] STC 879 (ECJ) (procuring a gathering at which goods are sold); *GUS Merchandise Corpn Ltd v Customs and Excises Comrs* [1981] STC 569 (CA) (agreeing to act as agent); *Customs and Excise Comrs v High Street Vouchers Ltd* [1990] STC 575 (redeeming vouchers at a discount); *Ridgeons Bulk Ltd v Customs and Excise Comrs* [1994] STC 427 (QB) (covenanting to refurbish premises); *Mirror Group Newspapers Ltd v Customs and Excise* [2000] STC 156 (issuing shares).

service tenancy A tenancy in which the landlord is also the tenant's employer and the premises were let as a condition of that employment. Although such a tenancy may be an *assured tenancy, the landlord can apply to the county court for possession when he ceases to employ the tenant. The court has a discretion whether or not to grant possession in this case.

servient tenement Land that is subject to an encumbrance, such as an easement, profit *à prendre*, or restrictive covenant, created for the benefit of other land, called the **dominant tenement**.

servitude *n.* A restriction upon the exercise of a state's sovereignty over its territory. For example, in 1856 Russia agreed by treaty not to fortify its own islands in the mouth of the Gulf of Bothnia.

set-off *n.* **1.** A monetary cross-claim that is also a defence to the claim made in the action by the claimant. **2.** The deduction of monies owed against sums due to be paid. Many commercial contracts contain express terms prohibiting set-offs.

setting aside An order of a court cancelling or making void some other order or *judgment or some step taken by a party in the action. In certain circumstances judgment in *default may be set aside or varied under Part 13 of the *Civil Procedure Rules.

setting down for trial Formerly, the final stage of the interlocutory (interim) proceedings in an action begun by writ in the High Court. This is now dealt with through the procedure for *allocation for trial.

settled *adj.* *Ordinarily resident in the UK and not subject under immigration law to any restriction on length of stay there. *See* BRITISH CITIZENSHIP; IMMIGRATION.

settled land Land that is the subject of a *settlement under the Settled Land Act 1925, i.e. land in which two or more beneficial interests exist in succession to one another or land that is subject to certain other fetters on the owner's powers. No such settlements can be created after 1996; most of the arrangements described below can now exist as *trusts of land with the exception of *entailed interests, which can no longer be created. Existing settlements continue until coming naturally to an end. The categories were as follows:

(1) Land held in trust for any persons by way of succession; for example, in trust for A for life then B for life then C in fee simple.
(2) Entailed interests.
(3) Land owned subject to a *gift over on a specified event.
(4) Land owned for a *determinable interest.
(5) Land conveyed to a person under 18 years (a minor cannot own or convey a legal estate in land).
(6) Land in which a future interest may come into possession on a specified event. For example, when land is left to A and B provided they respectively attain the age of 18, the elder is absolutely entitled to a half share on reaching 18 but may become entitled to the whole of the land absolutely if the younger dies during minority.
(7) Land charged voluntarily (i.e. without *consideration) or in consideration of marriage or by way of family arrangement with payment of any rentcharge or capital sum; for example, when the owner charges his land with payment of income to his wife during her life or widowhood.

A settlement made during the life of the settlor was effected by a **trust instrument** and a **vesting deed**. The trust instrument declared the beneficial interests in the land and appointed two or more individuals, or a trust corporation (e.g. a bank), as **trustees of the settlement** (*see* SETTLED LAND ACT TRUSTEES). The vesting deed transferred the legal estate in the settled land to the immediate beneficiary; it also had to identify the trustees of the settlement. A will that effected a settlement constituted the trust instrument; the legal estate devolved upon the testator's personal representatives on trust to vest it, by deed or *assent, in the immediate beneficiary. When the legal estate could not be transferred to the immediate beneficiary (e.g. because he was under 18), it had to be vested in a *statutory owner.

The purpose of the 1925 Act was to balance the protection of beneficiaries with future interests against the principle that the person immediately entitled in possession should not be prevented by the existence of future interests from prudently managing and dealing with the land. Thus the Act conferred on the immediate beneficiary powers to sell the land at the best price reasonably obtainable, to exchange it for other land, and to grant certain leases (up to 50 years, or 100 years for mining, or 999 years for building or forestry). These transactions *overreached the interests of the subsequent beneficiaries, who acquired corresponding interests in the capital money or income arising from them. The immediate beneficiary could also mortgage the land to raise money to pay off other encumbrances, to give equality of value on an exchange, and to pay for certain improvements. He could insist that the cost of certain improvements (such as rebuilding the principal mansion house and installation of drainage and electricity) be paid out of capital. His statutory powers could be extended by the terms of the settlement but could not be excluded or restricted. The Act imposed on the immediate beneficiary, in exercising these powers, the duties of a trustee for all parties having a beneficial interest in the land. The beneficiary thus had a dual role. When the immediate beneficiary sold or otherwise disposed of settled land, the vesting deed formed the basis of his title. The purchaser was not concerned with the interests of beneficiaries whose rights are overreached (*see* CURTAIN PROVISIONS) but had to pay the price to the trustees of the settlement or, at the direction of the immediate beneficiary (the tenant for life or the person exercising the powers of the tenant for life), into court.

Settled Land Act trustees (trustees of the settlement) Two or more individuals or a trust corporation (such as a bank) who are trustees of *settled land. Their primary function is to receive *capital money arising on a sale or other disposition of the land by the immediate beneficiary and to hold it in trust for those entitled under the settlement. Their consent is also necessary before the immediate beneficiary can validly exercise certain of his statutory powers; for example, to vary rights (such as easements) over other land that benefit the settled land.

The trustees were generally appointed by the trust instrument but must be named in the vesting deed. If no trustees were appointed, the Settled Land Act 1925 provides that they will be either

(1) trustees having a power of sale of other land comprised in the settlement and held on similar trusts;
(2) trustees having a future power of sale of the settled land;
(3) persons appointed by the beneficiaries if they are of full age and entitled to dispose of the whole settled estate; or
(4) the settlor's personal representatives, when the settlement is effected by will.
Trustees can also be appointed by the court.

settled property Property that is the subject matter of a *settlement.

settlement *n.* A disposition of land or other property, made by deed, will, or very rarely by statute (as in the Duke of Marlborough Annuity Act 1706), under which trusts are created by the *settlor designating the beneficiaries and the terms on which they are to take the property. Settlements are of many different kinds; for example, *marriage settlements, *strict settlements, *voluntary settlements, and, particularly, settlements under the Settled Land Act 1925 (*see* SETTLED LAND). All new settlements of land now take effect (since 1997) as *trusts of land.

settlement agreement A legally binding agreement under which parties can agree to end an employment relationship on specified terms, usually including a payment by the employer to the employee. The validity of such agreements is governed by the Employment Rights Act 1996. They must be in writing and the employee must have received independent advice from an appropriate person (e.g. a lawyer, trade union official, or advice worker). The effect of the agreement is that the employee waives his right to make a claim to the *employment tribunal on the matters covered in the agreement. Prior to the Enterprise and Regulatory Reform Act 2013, settlement discussions could be conducted confidentially where the *without prejudice rule applied. However, this rule did not apply if there was no existing dispute between the employer and employee; in such cases discussions in the course of negotiation could be used as evidence in a later tribunal claim. To encourage the settlement of disputes outside the tribunals, the 2013 Act amends the Employment Rights Act 1996 so that employers and employees can discuss settlement before a dispute arises, knowing that it will remain confidential. Confidentiality does not apply where the employee alleges dismissal for an automatically unfair *inadmissible reason. In addition, where either party behaved "improperly" in making or negotiating the offer, the tribunal may consider this as evidence in an unfair dismissal claim. An employer who improperly pressures an employee into entering a settlement agreement should be aware that this can amount to *constructive dismissal. Guidance is provided in a statutory ACAS Code of Practice. Settlement agreements were sometimes formerly called **compromise agreements**.

Settlement Code A set of statutory provisions (now enacted in the Income Tax Trading and Other Income Act 2005 s 619–48) under which income arising from property that has been gifted is taxed as if it were income of the donor and not of the donee. Broadly, the provisions apply whenever there is a *gift and the circumstances are such that it is possible for either income or capital to pass back to the donor at a later date. They thus apply to an outright gift, as well as to a gift into trust. The Settlement Code is designed for three purposes. The first is to attempt to ensure that a trust cannot be used as a piggy bank, in which income can be taxed at a lower rate than that which applies to the settlor, but is then passed back to the settlor. The second is to restrict income-splitting opportunities within the family between parents and minor children. The third is to restrict the possibility of income being assigned to a person subject to a lower rate of tax, while the capital asset is not gifted. In *Jones v Garnett* [2007] UK HL 35, four of the five judges in the House of Lords declared that the issue of shares to the wife of a company selling the services as a computer consultant of her husband was a settlement. However, the House of Lords unanimously decided that the exemption in the settlement code applied, so that the dividends paid to the wife were correctly treated as her income and were not taxable as income of the husband.

settlement of action The voluntary conclusion of civil litigation by agreement of the parties. Settlement may be made at any time and may be recorded in a consent order. Settlement may be followed by the claimant filing a *notice of discontinuance under Part 38 of the *Civil Procedure Rules. *See also* TOMLIN ORDER.

settlor *n.* A person who creates a *settlement. In a broad sense the term includes testators; in a more restricted sense it signifies one who settles property during his life.

several *adj.* Separate (in contrast to "joint"), as in *joint and several or *several tenancy.

several tenancy Ownership of land by one person absolutely, not jointly or in common with another. *Compare* JOINT TENANCY; TENANCY IN COMMON.

severance *n.* **1.** The conversion of an equitable *joint tenancy in land into a *tenancy in common. Severance may be effected, for example, by mutual agreement of the joint tenants, by the bankruptcy of one of them, by sale of the land or of one joint tenant's interest, or by written notice to the other joint tenants. It is not possible to sever a legal joint tenancy, since a tenancy in common cannot exist as a legal estate. Any words in a conveyance of land to two or more people that show an intention that they take separate shares will be construed as **words of severance** creating an equitable tenancy in common, rather than a joint tenancy. **2.** The separation of the good parts of a contract from the bad, which are rejected. The doctrine of severance applies to any contract which contains clauses that are void by statute or common law, or even, in some cases, illegal, provided there are no *public policy grounds against severing (*see* VOID CONTRACT). The courts will, if possible, save the contract from total invalidity by severing the offending part and the rest of the contract will stand under what is known as the "blue pencil" test. When little remains after severance, the whole contract terminates. Many commercial contracts contain a clause stating that void provisions may be severed. **3.** An order amending an *indictment so that the accused is tried separately on any count or counts of the indictment.

severance pay Money to which an employee is entitled at common law upon the termination of his contract of employment; for example, pay in lieu of notice, when he is dismissed with inadequate notice or none. An employee dismissed before the expiry of a fixed-term contract that has no provision for notice can claim damages in the courts to compensate him for the loss of pay he would have earned during the rest of the term, unless he was dismissed for a breach of contract entitling the employer to dismiss him. *See also* REDUNDANCY PAYMENT; UNFAIR DISMISSAL; WRONGFUL DISMISSAL.

sex change *See* GENDER REASSIGNMENT.

sex discrimination Discrimination on the ground of sex under the *Equality Act 2010 The Act makes it unlawful to discriminate because of sex not only in relation to terms of employment (for example, pay) but also in relation to recruitment, promotion, and dismissal. It is unlawful to treat a woman less favourably than a man (or vice versa) "because of sex" (direct discrimination). The Act also covers *indirect discrimination. An example of the latter might occur where an employer insists on full-time working, which is more difficult for women to satisfy because of child-care responsibilities. It is unlawful to victimize someone who has complained of illegal discrimination (*see* VICTIMIZATION). It is also unlawful to harass or sexually harass someone (*see* HARASSMENT).

The Act provides that it will not be unlawful sex discrimination if being male or female is an occupational requirement, this being a proportionate means of achieving a legitimate aim. The Equality Act is within the remit of the *Equality and Human Rights Commission and is enforced by *employment tribunals.

See also EQUAL TREATMENT DIRECTIVE.

sex offenders *See* SEXUAL OFFENCE.

sex selection *See* EMBRYO SELECTION.

sex trafficking *See* TRAFFICKING FOR SEXUAL EXPLOITATION.

sexual activity with a child It is a specific criminal offence under the Sexual Offences Act 2003 to engage in sexual activity with a child under the age of 16. *Consent is irrelevant to determining whether the offence has been committed. A person (A) over the age of 18 commits the offence if he intentionally touches another person (B), where the touching is sexual, B is under the age of 16, and A does not reasonably believe that B is over 16. If B is under the age of 13 the defendant is liable to a charge of *sexual assault of a child under 13 and the question of his mistaken belief in B's age becomes irrelevant. The maximum penalty varies according to the touching involved, ranging from 6 months' imprisonment and a fine to 14 years' imprisonment. The victim cannot be convicted as an accessory to this offence, even if the offence takes place with the victim's voluntary assistance, since the offence is designed to protect the victim (*R v Tyrrell* (1894) 1 QB 710 (CCR)). *Compare* ASSAULT OF A CHILD UNDER 13 BY PENETRATION; RAPE OF A CHILD UNDER 13.

sexual assault A criminal offence under the Sexual Offences Act 2003 in which a person (A) intentionally touches another person (B), where the touching is sexual, where B does not *consent to the touching, and where A does not reasonably believe that B consents. Whether A's belief in B's consent is reasonable is to be determined having regard to all the circumstances, including any steps A has taken to ascertain whether B consents. The *mens rea* element for sexual assault in the 2003 Act sets a standard of negligence whereby the defendant's honest but unreasonable belief in his victim's consent will not negate liability. Formerly, the defendant's honest belief in the victim's consent would negate liability, irrespective of whether that belief was reasonable (*DPP v Morgan* [1976] AC 182 (HL)). The offence of sexual assault covers many of the activities that were previously criminalized as indecent assault. The maximum penalty is 10 years' imprisonment. *Compare* RAPE; ASSAULT BY PENETRATION.

sexual assault of a child under 13   It is a specific criminal offence under the Sexual Offences Act 2003 to engage in sexual touching of a child under the age of 13. *Consent is irrelevant to determining whether the offence has been committed. A person commits the offence if he intentionally touches another person, where the touching is sexual, and where the other person is under 13. The maximum penalty is 14 years' imprisonment. *Compare* ASSAULT OF A CHILD UNDER 13 BY PENETRATION; RAPE OF A CHILD UNDER 13; SEXUAL ACTIVITY WITH A CHILD.

sexual intercourse   The penetration of the vagina by the penis (*Kaitamaki v R* [1984] 2 All ER 435 (PC)). For the purposes of sexual offences involving intercourse, penetration need only be slight and rupture of the hymen or ejaculation is not required (*R v Hughes* (1841) 9 C&P 752). *See also* UNLAWFUL SEXUAL INTERCOURSE.

sexual intercourse with an animal   Under the Sexual Offences Act 2003 (s 69) a person commits an offence if he or she:

(i) intentionally penetrates the anus or vagina of a living animal with his penis; or
(ii) intentionally allows his or her anus or vagina to be penetrated by the penis of a living animal.

sexually transmitted disease   Any infectious disease transmitted through sexual contact (such as HIV infection, syphilis, or gonorrhoea). If a spouse at the time of marriage was, unknown to his (or her) partner, suffering from a sexually transmitted disease this constitutes a ground for annulment of the marriage under the Matrimonial Causes Act 1973 s 12(e).

sexual offence   Any crime that involves sexual intercourse or any other sexual act. The main crimes in this category are *rape, *assault by penetration, and *sexual assault. There are also a range of offences governing sexual activities with children. Sex offenders are obliged to register with the police and tell police every time they move. Failure to register a change of address within 14 days is punishable on summary conviction with up to six months' imprisonment and a fine not exceeding the statutory maximum and on indictment with imprisonment for up to five years.

Sexual Offences Prevention Order   A civil preventative order introduced by sections 104 to 113 of the Sexual Offences Act 2003; it can be made only where the court thinks it necessary for the purpose of protecting the public or any particular members of the public from "serious sexual harm" from an offender but can be drafted in any way the court sees fit to achieve this purpose. The order can be made by the magistrates' court or Crown Court at the point of sentence or by complaint to a magistrates' court in respect of someone previously convicted of a sexual offence where that person's behaviour suggests the possibility of reoffending. The penalty for breaching an order is up to five years' imprisonment. The order can be for a fixed period but of not less than five years. Comprehensive guidance was provided in *R v Smith* [2011] EWCA Crim 1772, [2012] 1 WLR 1316 where the Court of Appeal warned against the excessive use of such orders and advised that there must be a real rather than remote risk of harm arising from the commission of further offences.

sexual penetration of a corpse   Under the Sexual Offences Act 2003 (s 70) a person commits an offence if he intentionally penetrates any part of the body of a dead person with part of his own body or anything else and this penetration is sexual in nature.

sex with an adult relative Under the Sexual Offences Act 2003 (s 64) a person aged 16 or over commits an offence if he has penetrative sex with another person over the age of 18 and who is his parent (includes adoptive parent), grandparent, child, grandchild, brother, sister, half-brother, half-sister, uncle, aunt, nephew, or niece.

SFO *See* SERIOUS FRAUD OFFICE.

shadow director A person who is not a director of a company but who gives instructions (rather than professional advice) upon which the directors are accustomed to act (Companies Act 2006 s 251). Certain statutory provisions (for example, those relating to transactions requiring approval of members) apply to both shadow directors and directors proper.

sham marriage A marriage entered into for some ulterior motive, without the intention of cohabiting with the other party. Such marriages will usually nonetheless be deemed valid, unless one of the parties (e.g. a person trying to escape extradition) deceives the other party as to his identity or the marriage is entered into to escape a threat to life, limb, or liberty (e.g. to enable a person imprisoned under harsh conditions to leave his or her country) or to escape imprisonment.

sham plea *See* FALSE PLEA.

sham transaction A transaction in which the parties intend to create one set of rights and obligations but perform acts or enter into documents that they intend should give third parties, often HM Revenue and Customs or the court, the appearance of creating different rights and obligations. Cases: *Snook v London and West Riding Investments Ltd* [1967] 2 QB 786 (CA); *Hitch's Executors v Stone* [2001] STC 214 (CA).

sham trust A trust that is created for the purpose of safeguarding property from one's creditors in the event of bankruptcy or insolvency. In such a case the requisite intention to create a trust is not present if it is clear that its existence is meant only as an "insurance" and it will be considered a sham (*Midland Bank v Wyatt* [1995] 1 FLR 696). *See also* ILLUSORY TRUST.

share *n.* A unit that measures the holder's interest in and liability to a company. Because an incorporated *company is in law a separate entity from the company membership, it is possible to divide and sell that entity in specified units (*see* CAPITAL). In the case of a company limited by shares (*see* LIMITED COMPANY) the liability of shareholders is confined to the purchase price of the shares. Once purchased, these units of the company become intangible property in their own right and can be bought and sold as an activity distinct from the trading activities of the company in question. While the company is a going concern, shares carry rights in relation to voting and sharing profits (*see* DIVIDEND). When a *limited company is wound up the shareholders have rights to share in the assets after debts have been paid. If there are no such assets shareholders lose the amount of their investment but are not liable for the company's debts (*see* FRAUDULENT TRADING; WRONGFUL TRADING).

    Preference shares usually carry a right to a fixed percentage dividend, e.g. 10% of the nominal value (*see* AUTHORIZED CAPITAL), before ordinary shareholders receive anything and holders also have the right to the return of the nominal value of their shares before ordinary shareholders (but after creditors). Holders of **participating preference shares** have further rights to share surplus profits or assets with the ordinary shareholders. Preference shares are generally **cumulative**, i.e. if no dividend is declared in one year, holders are entitled to arrears when eventually one is paid. Usually preference shareholders can vote only when their *class rights are being varied.

S

Ordinary shares constitute the risk capital (also called equity capital), as they carry no prior rights in relation to dividends or return of nominal value. However, the rights they do carry are unlimited in extent: if the company is successful, the ordinary shareholders are not restricted to a fixed dividend (unlike the preference shareholders) and the high yield upon their shares will cause these to increase in value. Similarly, if there are surplus assets on a winding-up, the ordinary shareholders will take what is left after the preference shareholders have been satisfied. Because ordinary shareholders carry the risk of the enterprise, they generally have full voting rights in a *general meeting (though some companies issue nonvoting ordinary shares to raise additional capital without diluting the control of the company).

Redeemable shares are issued subject to the proviso that they will or may be bought back (at the option of the shareholder or the company) by the company. They cannot be bought back unless fully paid-up and then only out of profits (*see* CAPITAL REDEMPTION RESERVE) or the proceeds of a fresh issue of shares made for the purpose.

A **golden share** enables the holder, usually the government, to outvote all other shareholders on certain types of company resolution.

share capital *See* CAPITAL. *See also* AUTHORIZED CAPITAL.

share certificate A document issued by a company evidencing that a named person is a company member and stating the number of shares registered in his name and the extent to which they are paid up. A company can be precluded by *estoppel from denying its accuracy. Ownership of shares can be registered electronically using the Bank of England's CREST system. *Compare* SHARE WARRANT.

share option **1.** *See* OPTION. **2.** A benefit sometimes offered to employees in which they are given the option to buy shares in the company for which they work at a favourable fixed price or at a stated discount to the market price. The difference between the value of the share acquired (or its sale proceeds) and the amount paid to exercise the option is subject to income tax and (usually) National Insurance contributions. The arrangement under which certain Revenue-approved share option schemes enabled the employee to pay capital gains tax rather than income tax on any gains was ended by the Finance Act 2006.

share premium The amount by which the price at which a share was issued exceeds its nominal value (*see* AUTHORIZED CAPITAL). Share premiums must be credited by the company to a **share premium account**, which is subject to the rules relating to *reduction of capital and can only be used for certain purposes, e.g. issuing bonus shares (*see* BONUS ISSUE).

share transfer (**stock transfer**) A document transferring registered shares to a new owner. Formerly, a share transfer in proper form had to be delivered to the company before it could place the transferee's name on the register of members (Stock Transfer Act 1963). The whole process can now be carried out instantaneously using the Bank of England's electronic share settlement scheme. *See* TRANSFER OF SHARES. *See also* STAMP DUTY RESERVE TAX.

share warrant A document issued by a company certifying that the bearer is entitled to the shares specified in it. The name of the bearer will not appear on the register of members until he surrenders the warrant to the company in return for *transfer of the shares, but he may be regarded as a company member under the provisions of the articles of association. The company is contractually bound to recognize the bearer as shareholder. *Compare* SHARE CERTIFICATE.

SHAs *See* STRATEGIC HEALTH AUTHORITIES.

sheriff *n.* The principal officer of the Crown in a county. The former responsibilities of the sheriff for the *enforcement of judgments of the High Court by writs of *fieri facias*, possession, and delivery have now been vested in *High Court Enforcement Officers.

sheriff's interpleader *See* INTERPLEADER.

shifting use (secondary use) Formerly, a *use that operated to terminate a preceding use. For example, if property was given to X to the use of A, but then to the use of B when C paid £100 to D, B had a shifting use, which arose when C made the specified payment.

ship *n.* For the purposes of the Merchant Shipping Act 1995 (which consolidated the Merchant Shipping Acts 1894 to 1994 and other enactments relating to merchant shipping), the word "ship" includes every description of vessel used in navigation (s 313). A central register of British ships is kept. For the purposes of ownership, a British ship is notionally divided into 64 shares. Each share may be in different ownership, but no share may be in the ownership of an alien or a foreign company. Co-owners will commonly appoint a **ship's husband** or managing owner to manage the ship. The definition of "British ship" in the then Merchant Shipping Act 1988, in relation to fishing rights, has been challenged under EU law (*see* FISHERY LIMITS; QUOTA).

shipwreck *n. See* WRECK.

shock *n. See* PSYCHIATRIC INJURY.

shoplifting *n.* Dishonestly removing goods from a shop without paying for them. Shoplifters could be charged with *making off without payment under the Theft Act 1978, but it is more usual to charge them with *theft under the Theft Act 1968. It is not legally necessary to remove the goods from the shop precincts in order to be guilty of shoplifting, but in practice it is advisable to wait until the accused has left the shop before stopping him, as it is then easier to prove the intention to steal (*see also* ARREST). A cashier in the shop who deliberately rings up a lower price than the true price may be guilty of aiding and abetting theft.

short cause list A list of cases for hearing for which the trial is expected to last less than four hours.

short notice A lesser period of notice for the calling of a company meeting. In the case of an *annual general meeting of a public company, it may be agreed by all members entitled to attend and vote at it (Companies Act 2006 s 337); for other meetings of a public company 95% of the shareholders must agree. In the case of a private company the requisite majority is 90% or such higher majority not exceeding 95% as specified in the *articles of association (Companies Act 2006 s 307 (5) (6)). There are strict requirements for the details to be given for short notice and service of the notice.

short title *See* ACT OF PARLIAMENT.

sickness benefit *See* INCAPACITY BENEFIT.

sic utere tuo ut alienum non laedas [Latin] Use your own property in such a way that you do not injure other people's: a maxim often used in cases of nuisance. It is misleading, since only an unreasonable interference with a neighbour's property is actionable as a nuisance.

signature of treaty The formal and official affixing of names to the text of a *treaty by the representatives of the negotiating states, either as a means of expressing the definitive consent of the state to be bound by the terms of the treaty or as an expression of provisional consent subject to *ratification, acceptance, or approval.

signature of will *See* EXECUTION OF WILL.

silence *n. See* RIGHT OF SILENCE.

silk *n. See* QUEEN'S COUNSEL.

similar-fact evidence Evidence that a party, especially the accused, has on previous occasions misconducted himself in a way similar to the misconduct being alleged against him in the proceedings before the court. The admissibility of similar-fact evidence in criminal proceedings is now governed by the Criminal Justice Act 2003. *See* ANTECEDENTS; CHARACTER.

simple contract (parol contract) Any *contract other than one made by *deed.

simple trust *See* BARE TRUST.

simpliciter *adj.* [Latin: simple] Indicating that a word or phrase in a document is used absolutely, unconditionally, and free from any shades of meaning given to it by surrounding words or phrases. For example, if the word "yard" is found in a document, it means that the word is used in its most natural sense. Thus it is not a "stockyard", which is a particular type of yard.

sine die [Latin] Without a date. To adjourn a case *sine die* is to adjourn it without setting a date for a future hearing.

single administrative document (SAD) A single document declaring an import into an EU state. This is an improvement on the system it replaced, in which many documents were required before a product could be imported into the EU.

Single European Act The legislation passed in 1986 in the European Community (in force from 1 July 1987) that committed all member states to an integrated method of trading with no frontiers between countries by 31 December 1992. It was the first Act to amend the principles of the then *Treaty of Rome. The main creation of the Single European Act is the *Single Market for trading in goods and services within the EU.

Single Market The concept of a single integrated market that underlies trading in the European Union, as codified in the *Single European Act 1986. The Single Market came into force on 1 January 1993. The measures covered by the legislation included: the easing of entry requirements for those from other EU member states; the acceptance throughout the market of professional qualifications; the acceptance of national standards for product harmonization; open tendering for public supply contracts; the free movement of capital between states; a reduction of state aid for certain industries; and the harmonization of some duties.

single-member company *See* PRIVATE COMPANY.

single-union agreement A collective agreement within a company or establishment that recognizes only one *independent trade union for the purposes of *collective bargaining. The selection of the union to be recognized for this purpose is frequently now based on the so-called *beauty contest. This agreement does not restrict the rights of individual employees to belong to a union of their choice or not to belong to a union. However, their only access to collective bargaining is through the single union.

sittings *pl. n.* The four periods of the legal year during which the full range of judicial business is transacted in the Senior Courts. The sittings are Michaelmas, Hilary, Easter, and Trinity. Sittings were substituted for *terms by the Judicature Act 1873. The dates of the sittings of the Court of Appeal and the High Court are set out in a Practice Direction to Part 39 of the *Civil Procedure Rules. *See also* VACATIONS.

situs *n.* The place in which an *asset is held to be located. The location determines the proper law to be applied in identifying the rights and liabilities associated with the asset. For *capital gains tax, the disposal of a foreign situs asset does not give a charge to UK capital gains tax if three conditions are satisfied:

(1) the person making the disposal is not domiciled within the UK:

(2) this person has been in the UK for less than seven years, or has opted (and paid the fee for) *remittance basis; and

(3) the proceeds of the disposal are not remitted to the UK. For *inheritance tax, an asset with a foreign situs is an excepted asset. Hence if it is held beneficially by an individual who is not domiciled within the UK at the time of the transfer, no tax is chargeable upon it.

skeleton argument In court proceedings, a document prepared by a party or his legal representative that sets out the basis of the party's argument, including any arguments based on law. The court may require such documents to be served on the court and on the other party prior to a trial.

slander *n.* A defamatory statement made by such means as spoken words or gestures, i.e. not in permanent form. Subject to narrow exceptions, slander is only actionable on proof that its publication has caused special damage (actual financial or material loss), not merely loss of reputation. Traditionally, the exceptions were when the slander implied:

(a) the commission of a criminal offence punishable by imprisonment;

(b) infection with a contagious disease;

(c) unchastity in a woman: or

(d) was calculated to disparage a person in his office, business, trade, or profession.

The Defamation Act 2013 has abolished exceptions (b) and (c) and now requires serious harm to the claimant's reputation in all cases, which for a body trading for profit equates to serious financial loss.

See DEFAMATION.

slander of goods (disparagement of goods) A false statement, made maliciously, that disparages the quality of goods manufactured and sold by the claimant. It is a form of the tort of *malicious falsehood. In order to be actionable, the statement must allege some specific defect in the claimant's goods. A mere assertion by a rival trader that his goods are better is not sufficient, even if the claim was false and malicious.

slander of title A false statement, made maliciously, that impugns a vendor's title to sell property. It is a form of the tort of *malicious falsehood.

slavery *n.* The prohibition on slavery or forced labour as set out in Article 4 of the European Convention on Human Rights is now part of UK law as a consequence of the *Human Rights Act 1998. There are exceptions to this prohibition for prisoners, military service, normal civic obligations, and in emergencies. The prohibition does not extend to the imposition of having to do *pro bono* work as part of training as a lawyer (*Van der Mussele v Belgium* (1983) 6 EHRR 163).

slip rule The rule permitting the correction of any accidental slip or omission in judgments or orders. Such errors can be corrected at any time by the court on application without an appeal (Civil Procedure Rules Part 40). The Crown Court has the power to alter a sentence or other order within 56 days of the date it was made (Powers of Criminal Courts (Sentencing) Act 2000 s 155).

small agreement 1. (under the Consumer Credit Act 1974) A regulated *consumer-credit agreement for credit not exceeding £50, other than a hire-purchase or conditional-sale agreement, or a regulated *consumer-hire agreement that does not require the hirer to make payments exceeding £50. In both cases the agreement is either unsecured or secured by a guarantee or indemnity only. Some small agreements are outside certain provisions of the Act. **2.** (under the Competition Act 1998) An agreement in which the parties are exempt from the imposition of penalties (fines) for anticompetitive practices. Section 39 of the Act provides the exemption, and the Competition Act 1998 (Small Agreements and Conduct of Minor Significance) Regulations 2000 defines an anticompetitive agreement as "small" when both parties to it have a total turnover of under £20M. However, no exemption applies for a price-fixing agreement. Moreover, small agreements are not exempt from other provisions of the 1998 Act, and thus restrictive clauses in them may still be void.

small claims track The track to which a civil case is allocated when the claim is for an amount of no more than £10,000. The limit is £1000 for claims for general damages in personal injury cases; it is also £1000 in certain landlord and tenant actions. The hearing is relatively informal and in public, and there are generally no experts, no formal rules of evidence, and often no adverse cost award to a losing party.

With the approval of the court parties may consent to use the small claims track even if their claim value exceeds £10,000.

SMEs Small and medium enterprises: in EU law, these are businesses having fewer than 250 employees, a balance-sheet total of no more than €43 million, and an annual turnover of no more than €50 million. SMEs are encouraged by the European Commission through various aid programmes. Different definitions of small and medium-sized companies appear in the UK Companies Act and corporation tax legislation.

smuggling *n.* The offence of importing or exporting specified goods that are subject to customs or excise duties without having paid the requisite duties (Customs and Excise Management Act 1979 s 170). Smuggled goods are liable to confiscation and the smuggler is liable to pay treble their value or a sum laid down by the law (whichever is the greater); offenders may alternatively, or additionally, receive a term of imprisonment (*R v Czyzewski* [2004] 1 Cr App R (S) 289). A penalty of up to £5,000,000 can be imposed on a manufacturer of cigarettes or hand-rolling tobacco if the manufacturer supplies cigarettes etc. to persons who "are likely to smuggle them into the United Kingdom" (Tobacco Products Duty Act 1979 s 7A–D, inserted by Finance Act 2006 s 2).

SOAD *See* SECOND OPINION APPOINTED DOCTOR.

SOCA *See* SERIOUS ORGANIZED CRIME AGENCY.

Social Chapter The *Maastricht Treaty on European Union 1992 included a Social Chapter that laid down EU policies on workers' rights and other social issues. The objectives of the Social Chapter are to promote employment, improve living and working conditions, establish dialogue between management and workers by means of works councils, implement proper social protection, and develop human resources with a view to lasting high employment. The social provisions include unpaid *parental leave for new parents and the principle of *equal pay for male and female workers for equal work. It was not until 1997 that the British government finally agreed to the incorporation of these social aims and objectives into the main body of the founding Community Treaty with the signing of the *Amsterdam Treaty. This has led to a number of changes to UK law, including the implementation of unpaid parental leave and *European Works Councils and new rights for *part-time workers.

social fact thesis *See* LEGAL POSITIVISM.

social fund A fund currently administered by the Department of Work and Pensions. It was established in 1988, under the Social Security Act 1986, and replaced single payments of supplementary benefit for one-off needs. Until April 2013 there were two distinct parts of the social fund. The **regulated social fund** covered one-off payments for specific circumstances, such as winter fuel payments and Sure Start maternity grants. **The discretionary social fund** covered one-off payments for emergencies, such as community care grants, budgeting loans, and crisis loans. From April 2013 the discretionary social fund was abolished. Budgeting loans and crisis loans for benefit disallowance or sanction will become part of *universal credit. All other crisis loan expenditure and community care grants will become the responsibility of local authorities.

social inquiry report *See* PRE-SENTENCE REPORT.

social parents (*de facto* **carers)** Any persons, such as *step-parents or *foster parents, who are not biological or adoptive parents but who take care of children and are otherwise interested in their upbringing. Such persons do not have *parental responsibility simply by virtue of looking after a child, although they may acquire it by a court order. In the absence of such an order, the social parent has limited powers, and can only do what is possible in all the circumstances to safeguard and promote the child's welfare.

social policy rule *See* INTERPRETATION.

Societas Europaea (European Company) An entity created by the merger of two or more companies resident in different states of the European Union. The status of a Societas Europaea is given in EU Council Regulation 2157/2001. The treatment of the profits of a Societas Europaea for UK tax purposes is given in the Finance (No 2) Act 2005 (s 51–65).

socio-legal studies A field of enquiry that is mainly preoccupied with empirical studies of the institutions of the law (e.g. the courts, the jury, the police, and the legal profession), rather than with providing a theoretical account of the "law in action". *Compare* SOCIOLOGY OF LAW.

sociology of law The application of a sociological approach to questions of the origin, nature, and operation of the law and legal system. Sociologists of law generally regard law as merely one, albeit an important and ubiquitous, feature of society, rejecting the idea (most closely associated with *legal positivism) that there can be a value-free explanation of law. The sociologist of law, therefore, is concerned to analyse and interpret the part played by law and legal administration in effecting certain observable forms of conduct or behaviour. He will attempt to present certain "types" of society in which the role or function of law may be examined. His purpose will generally be an explanation of society based on an examination of law as a form of social control. **Sociological jurisprudence** is an older discipline, associated especially with the theorists Emile Durkheim (1858–1917), Max Weber (1864–1920), and Karl Marx (1818–1883), that seeks to provide a scientific account of the nature of law in society from a variety of standpoints. *See* MARXIST LEGAL THEORY.

socius criminis [Latin: associate in crime] An *accomplice, especially one who has agreed to give evidence for the prosecution. *See* QUEEN'S EVIDENCE.

sodomy *n.* *See* BUGGERY.

soft law (in international law) Guidelines of behaviour, such as those provided by treaties not yet in force, resolutions of the United Nations, or international conferences, that are not binding in themselves but are more than mere statements of political aspiration (they fall into a legal/political limbo between these two states). Soft law contrasts with **hard law**, i.e. those legal obligations, found either in *treaties or customary international law (*see* CUSTOM), that are binding in and of themselves.

software *n.* Computer programs, which are protected by *copyright under the Copyright, Designs and Patents Act 1988. EU Directive 2009/24 (replacing 91/250) on the legal protection of computer programs provides that all member states must protect computer programs by copyright law. The directive also provides a right to make back-up copies of software and a very limited *decompilation right. A right to repair is also included, unless a software licence prohibits this. The UK implemented the directive by the Copyright (Computer Programs) Regulations 1992, which amend the 1988 Act.

(((●))) **SEE WEB LINKS**
- Website of the Federation Against Software Theft
- Website of the Business Software Alliance

solatium *adj.* [Latin: to console] Describing additional *damages allowed in certain lawsuits as a solace for wounded feelings.

soldier's will *See* PRIVILEGED WILL.

solemn form *See* PROBATE.

sole solicitor A solicitor who is the sole principal of a practice, rather than one who practises in partnership with others.

soliciting *n.* **1.** The offence by a prostitute of attempting to obtain prospective clients in a street or public place (Street Offences Act 1959 s 1). It is punishable by a *fine at level 2 on the standard scale on a first conviction and at level 3 on a subsequent conviction. Any act committed by the prostitute (even smiling provocatively) may constitute soliciting (*DPP v Bull* [1995] QB 88), but an advertisement inviting men to visit her is not soliciting. "Street" is widely defined to include roads, lanes, bridges, courtyards, alleyways, passages, etc., open to the public, as well as doorways and entrances of houses on the street, and ground adjoining and open to the street. If a prostitute in a private house attracts the attention of men in the street (for example by tapping on the window and inviting them in, or even merely by sitting at the window illuminated by a red light), this may be considered soliciting "in a street". **2.** The offence by a man of persistently accosting a woman in a public place for the purpose of prostitution (*see also* KERB CRAWLING) or persistently accosting anybody in a public place for immoral purposes.

"Persistently" requires either a number of single invitations to different people or more than one invitation to the same person (Sexual Offences Act 2003 s 1–2, 4).

solicitor *n.* A legal practitioner admitted to practise under the provisions of the Solicitors Act 1974. Solicitors may take a three-year law degree at university, then a one-year legal practice course (LPC), followed by two years as an employee under a training contract (previously called **articles of clerkship**), after which they are admitted as solicitors. Those taking a non-law degree will need to spend at least one further year at a university undertaking a graduate diploma in law (GDL) before undertaking the legal practice course. Practising solicitors must possess a *practising certificate. Solicitors form much the larger part of the English legal profession (*compare* BARRISTER), often undertaking the general aspects of giving legal advice and conducting legal proceedings. They have *rights of audience in the lower courts but may not act as advocates in the Senior Courts (except in chambers) or the Supreme Court unless they have acquired a relevant *advocacy qualification under the terms of the Courts and Legal Services Act 1990. A solicitor may be sued for professional negligence and owes the duties of a *fiduciary to his client; these include the duty to preserve the confidentiality of the client's affairs.

solicitor and own client basis of costs A basis of *assessment of costs on which is calculated the sum that a privately represented client must pay his own solicitor. On this basis, all costs are allowed provided that they are of a reasonable amount and have not been unreasonably incurred.

Solicitor General A law officer of the Crown immediately subordinate to the *Attorney General. The Solicitor General is usually a Member of Parliament of the ruling party. He acts as deputy to the Attorney General and may exercise any power vested by statute in the latter (unless the statute otherwise provides) if the office of Attorney General is vacant or the Attorney General is unable to act through illness or has authorized him to act.

Solicitors Disciplinary Tribunal (SDT) A tribunal established under the Solicitors Act 1974 for hearing applications and complaints against solicitors. It has the power to strike the name of a solicitor off the roll and to restore the name of a solicitor previously struck off, suspend a solicitor from practice, and order the payment of a penalty. The members of the tribunal are practising solicitors of not less than ten years' standing and some lay members. They are appointed by the *Master of the Rolls. Appeals from decisions of the tribunal can be brought to the High Court of the Master of the Rolls. *See also* SOLICITORS REGULATION AUTHORITY.

(⊕) SEE WEB LINKS
• Website of the Solicitors Disciplinary Tribunal

solicitor's lien The right of a solicitor to retain papers or property of his client as security for the payment of his costs. There are two types of lien: a retaining lien, i.e. a right to retain property already in his possession until he has been paid costs due to him; and a lien on property recovered or preserved, i.e. a right to ask the court to direct that personal property recovered under a judgment obtained by his exertions stand as security for his costs of the recovery. By statute the second type of lien has been extended to confer upon the court the power to make a *charging order over real and personal property recovered or preserved in proceedings by the solicitor.

Solicitors Regulation Authority (SRA) The regulatory arm of the *Law Society: an independent body established in 2007 to regulate the professional practice, conduct, and discipline of solicitors. The SRA admits solicitors to the profession and issues annual *practising certificates, without which a solicitor may not practice. It also publishes the **SRA Code of Conduct** and may take action against solicitors who are found to have breached it; serious cases are referred to the *Solicitors Disciplinary Tribunal.

(((∰))) SEE WEB LINKS

- Full text of the SRA Code of Conduct 2011 from the website of the Solicitors Regulation Authority

***solus* tie** A form of *restraint of trade sometimes incorporated into a mortgage, often for the acquisition of certain types of commercial premises, most often petrol stations and public houses (*Esso Petroleum Co Ltd v Harper's Garage (Stourport) Ltd* [1968] AC 269 (HL)). A *solus* tie seeks to limit the mortgagor's choice of commercial supplier by incorporating a provision into the mortgage deed that determines the source from which the mortgagor may obtain his supplies during a predetermined period. *Solus* ties and other restraint of trade clauses can be found in contracts other than mortgage contracts: the principles that underpin the law's dislike of such clauses, which are held to impose an unreasonable restraint on the borrower, are of general application and do not originate from the law of mortgages.

sources of international law The sources of public international law are to be found in Article 38(1) of the Statute of the *International Court of Justice. They are *treaties, *customary international law, *general principles of law, and, as subsidiary sources, judicial decisions and the teachings of the most highly qualified *publicists of the various nations.

sovereign *n. See* CROWN.

sovereign immunity The exemption of the sovereign or other head of a foreign state and foreign governmental departments from the jurisdiction of the English courts. The principles governing this exemption are now contained in the State Immunity Act 1978 and are consistent with the European Convention on State Immunity. The immunity granted is no longer absolute; it is subject to numerous exceptions outlined in the Act (*see* ABSOLUTE THEORY OF SOVEREIGN IMMUNITY). Subject to modifications, the Diplomatic Privileges Act 1964 extends to foreign sovereigns the same privileges and immunities as are granted to heads of diplomatic missions. It is now clear under English law that such immunity does not apply to former heads of state who are alleged to have committed crimes against humanity.

sovereignty *n.* Supreme authority in a state. In any state sovereignty is vested in the institution, person, or body having the ultimate authority to impose law on everyone else in the state and the power to alter any pre-existing law. How and by whom the authority is exercised varies according to the political nature of the state. In many countries the executive, legislative, and judicial powers of sovereignty are exercised by different bodies. One of these bodies may in fact retain sovereignty by having ultimate control over the others. But in some countries, such as the USA, the powers are carefully balanced by a constitution. In the UK sovereignty is vested in Parliament (*see* SOVEREIGNTY OF PARLIAMENT).

In international law, it is an essential aspect of sovereignty that all states should have supreme control over their internal affairs, subject to the recognized limitations imposed by international law. These limitations include, in particular, the international law of *human rights and the rules forbidding the use of force. However, no state or international organization may intervene in matters that fall within the domestic jurisdiction of another state. The concept of state sovereignty was outlined, among other things, in a declaration on Principles of International Law (Resolution 2625), proclaimed by the General Assembly of the United Nations in 1970.

sovereignty of Parliament The constitutional principle that the legislative competence of Parliament is unlimited. No court in the UK can question its power to enact any law that it pleases. In practice, however, Parliament does not assume unlimited authority; it can legislate only for territories that are recognized by international law to be within its competence, i.e. the UK, the Channel Islands and the Isle of Man, and UK Overseas Territories. The *Welsh Assembly, *Scottish Parliament, and *Northern Ireland Assembly have devolved power in certain areas.

Speaker *n. See* HOUSE OF COMMONS; HOUSE OF LORDS.

special administration *See* LIMITED ADMINISTRATION.

special agent *See* AGENT.

special business Business that can only be transacted at a general meeting if its general nature has been specified in the notice convening the meeting. *See* ANNUAL GENERAL MEETING.

special damages *See* GENERAL AND SPECIAL DAMAGES.

special defences *See* GENERAL DEFENCES.

special endorsement *See* ENDORSEMENT.

special guardianship order An order, introduced by the Children and Adoption Act 2002, primarily to provide permanence and stability for looked-after children (*see* CHILD BEING LOOKED AFTER BY A LOCAL AUTHORITY) as a less permanent alternative to adoption. The special guardianship order confers many of the rights of a parent, including *parental responsibility, on the **special guardian**, which means in effect that he will be able to make almost any decision about the child's upbringing. The following persons can apply for an order:

- anyone who for at least one year immediately prior to the application has been the child's *local authority foster parent;
- the holder of a *residence order in respect of the child;
- any guardian of the child.

Unlike adoption, a special guardianship order does not terminate the parental status of birth parents and is therefore likely to be appropriate where there are good reasons why the child should retain formal links with his birth family. The advantage of a special guardianship order over a residence order is that the local authority is under a statutory duty to provide a package of services, including financial support, to a special guardian.

Special Health Authorities Authorities established in 1977 to provide a health service to the whole of England, not just a local community: an example is the National Blood Authority. They are independent but can be subject to ministerial direction like other NHS bodies.

special hospital A hospital controlled and managed by the Home Secretary for persons suffering from *mental disorder who require detention under special security conditions, because of their dangerous, violent, or criminal propensities. The term is no longer in formal use: the Health Act 1999 (amending the Mental Health Act 1983) instead refers to "hospitals providing high-security psychiatric services". There are currently three such hospitals: Ashworth, Broadmoor, and Rampton.

speciality *n.* The principle that the state requesting the *extradition of a fugitive from another state must, in order for the request to succeed, specify the crime for which the accused is to be extradited. Further, the requesting state must only try the individual for the crime specified in the extradition request. *See also* DOUBLE CRIMINALITY.

special measures In court proceedings, measures that can be put in place under the Youth Justice and Criminal Evidence Act 1999 to provide protection and/or anonymity to a witness, such as a screen separating a witness from the accused. Rules dealing with applications for special measures directions are set out in Part 29 of the *Criminal Procedure Rules.

special notice The 28 days' notice that is required to be given to a registered company of an intention to propose certain resolutions at a *general meeting of the company (Companies Act 2006 s 312). These resolutions are:
(1) removing or failing to reappoint an auditor (Companies Act s 511, 515); and
(2) removing a director before his term of office expires or appointing a new director to replace him at the same meeting (Companies Act 2006 s 168 (2)).

special parliamentary procedure *See* SPECIAL PROCEDURE ORDERS.

special plea A *plea in bar of arraignment, e.g. *autrefois acquit* or *autrefois convict*.

special power *See* POWER OF APPOINTMENT.

special procedure (in divorce proceedings) A speedy, simple, and cheap procedure for uncontested divorce cases introduced in the mid-1970s. A district judge scrutinizes the divorce application and, if satisfied that the ground is made out, issues a certificate to that effect. The divorce is then formally granted in open court; neither party need appear. The introduction of the special procedure revolutionized divorce law and is now used in the majority of cases.

special procedure material (in court proceedings) Material acquired or created in the course of a trade, business, profession, occupation, or office that is held subject to an express or implied undertaking to hold it in confidence, or subject to a statutory restriction on disclosure or obligation of secrecy. Under the Police and Criminal Evidence Act 1984, a *warrant enabling access to special procedure material for the purposes of a criminal investigation can only be obtained from a *circuit judge. *See* EXCLUDED MATERIAL.

special procedure orders A form of *delegated legislation consisting of orders made by government ministers under powers that are expressed in the enabling statute to be exercisable by order subject to **special parliamentary procedure**. The Statutory Orders (Special Procedure) Act 1945 applies to such legislation. This requires that the order be laid before Parliament together with a certificate by the minister responsible specifying that all the requirements of the enabling Act have been fulfilled. Petitions for its annulment or amendment may be presented. Special procedure orders, which have largely replaced provisional orders, are used primarily to confer powers on local authorities. The *compulsory purchase of land must also in certain cases (e.g. land owned by local authorities or the National Trust) be effected by a special procedure order.

special resolution A decision reached by a majority of not less than 75% of company members voting in person or by proxy at a general meeting (Companies Act s 283).

special trust *See* ACTIVE TRUST.

specialty *n. See* DEED.

special verdict **1.** A verdict of not guilty by reason of *insanity. **2.** A verdict on particular questions of fact, without a general conclusion (in criminal cases) as to guilt or (in civil cases) in favour of the claimant or the defendant. The judge asks the jury their opinion on the facts, but decides the general question himself. Such verdicts in criminal cases are very rare. *Compare* GENERAL VERDICT.

specification *n.* **1.** (in *patent law) A document that must be lodged with an application for a patent for an invention. It must contain a description of the invention, a claim defining the matter for which the applicant seeks protection, and any drawing referred to in the description or claim. **2.** A general document in which a commercial buyer or seller describes goods to be bought or sold. It is sometimes incorporated into the contract by reference.

specific delivery *See* WRIT OF DELIVERY.

specific devise *See* DEVISE.

specific goods Goods specifically identified at the time a contract of sale is made, e.g. a named car with a specified registration number. If the subject matter is not so identified, the contract is for the sale of *unascertained goods. In a contract for the sale of specific goods the seller is bound to deliver the identified goods and no others.

specific intent Any offence for which only *intention will suffice as the *mens rea* element may be considered an offence of specific intent. *Compare* BASIC INTENT. *See also* INTOXICATION.

specific issue order A court order to a person having parental responsibility for a child that deals with any specific issues concerning the child's upbringing, such as education or medical treatment. *See* SECTION 8 ORDERS.

specific legacy *See* LEGACY.

specific performance A court order to a person to fulfil his obligations under a contract. For example, when contracts have been exchanged for the sale of a house, the court may order a reluctant seller to complete the sale. The remedy is a discretionary one and is not available in certain cases; for example, for the enforcement of a contract of employment or when the payment of damages would be a sufficient remedy.

specimen of blood A specimen of blood for analysis, used as an alternative to a *specimen of breath in cases involving *drunken driving. A police officer may require a specimen of blood if he reasonably believes that he cannot demand a breath specimen for medical reasons, if an approved and reliable device for taking a breath specimen is unavailable or cannot be used, or if the defendant is suspected of being unfit to drive and a doctor believes that his condition is due to a drug. A police officer may also ask for a blood specimen if the suspect is in hospital (subject to the consent of the doctor treating him). A suspect may be asked to give a blood specimen under these conditions even if he has already given a breath specimen.

  A blood specimen may only be taken with the defendant's consent and by a medical practitioner, otherwise it cannot be used as evidence in any proceedings (*DPP v Jackson* [1999] 1 AC 406). It must be analysed by a qualified analyst, who must sign a certificate stating how much alcohol he found. The suspect may ask to be given half the specimen for his own analysis, which may be used to contradict the prosecution's evidence; if he has asked for but was not given half of the sample, the other half may not be used in evidence against him. A *specimen of urine may sometimes be taken as an alternative to a blood specimen.

In all other respects the law relating to blood specimens is the same as that relating to breath specimens.

specimen of breath A specimen of breath for analysis taken from a person suspected of *drunken driving. It is this specimen that usually forms the evidence for a prosecution and conviction for offences of drunken driving and should not be confused with the preliminary *breath test. The specimen may be required whenever the police are investigating any of these offences, but only if the suspect is at the police station. Usually he will have been brought to the station under arrest as a result of a positive breath test or refusal to undergo such a test. It is an offence not to provide a specimen without a reasonable excuse, and the police officer should warn a suspect of this when asking for the specimen. This offence is punishable by fine or imprisonment, endorsement (which carries 10 penalty points under the *totting-up system), and discretionary disqualification (in cases of being in charge of a vehicle) or compulsory disqualification (in cases of driving or attempting to drive).

The suspect must give two breath specimens, which should be measured by means of an approved electronic device (not the *breathalyser used for the preliminary breath test) that automatically prints out the level of alcohol in the breath. A print-out of the lower of the two readings is used as evidence in a subsequent trial, together with a signed certificate by a police officer that it refers to the defendant's specimen given at the stated time (Road Traffic Act 1988 s 8). The defendant must be given a copy of these documents at least seven days before his trial, and he may serve notice not later than three days before the trial that he requires the police officer who signed it to attend the hearing. At his trial, a defendant may bring evidence to show that he drank more alcohol between the time of the alleged offence and giving the specimen and that this accounted for his exceeding the prescribed limit. It is an offence, however, to deliberately drink more alcohol in order to make it difficult to prove his guilt.

Once a suspect has given a specimen he is free to leave the police station, but the police may detain him if they reasonably suspect that he is likely to continue driving with an excess alcohol level or while unfit to drive. Under certain circumstances the suspect can provide either a *specimen of blood or a *specimen of urine instead of a breath specimen. If the breath specimen records a reading of more than 35 but less than 50 micrograms of alcohol per 100 ml of breath (and prosecution is intended), the suspect is entitled to ask that it should be replaced by a blood or urine specimen.

specimen of urine A specimen of urine for analysis, used as an alternative to a *specimen of breath in cases involving *drunken driving. A specimen of urine may be required when there are objections to taking a breath specimen and when a medical practitioner thinks that a *specimen of blood should not be taken for medical reasons. A urine specimen must be provided within one hour after it has been asked for (*DPP v Baldwin* [2000] RTR 314); two specimens are asked for, and it is the second specimen that is used as evidence in a subsequent trial. In all other respects the law relating to urine specimens is the same as the law relating to blood and breath specimens.

speeding *n.* Driving a motor vehicle at a speed in excess of that permitted. Unless road signs specifically indicate otherwise, the speed limit on roads in built-up areas is 30 mph. On other roads, the limit for cars and vans weighing up to 2 tonnes when fully laden is 60 mph on single carriageways and 70 mph on dual carriageways and motorways (unless towing a trailer or caravan, when the limit is 50 mph and 60 mph respectively).

Buses, coaches, and lorries weighing more than 7.5 tonnes laden can drive at speeds of up to 50 mph on single carriageways, 60 mph on dual carriageways, and 70 mph on motorways. The limit for goods vehicles weighing more than 7.5 tonnes is 40 mph on single carriageways, 50 mph on dual carriageways, and 60 mph on motorways.

The penalty for speeding is a fine, *endorsement (carrying 3–6 penalty points under the *totting-up system), and discretionary *disqualification. When section 17 of the Road Safety Act 2006 is brought into force, the range of penalty points will increase. A person cannot be convicted of a speeding offence on the evidence of one witness alone, but the evidence of two police officers unsupported by a speed-measuring device may be enough to secure a conviction. Speeding may itself be evidence of *careless and inconsiderate driving or *dangerous driving, but it is an offence in its own right even if it caused no danger. Speeding offences are subject to the requirement of a *notice of intended prosecution.

spent conviction A conviction that, after a specified number of years known as the **rehabilitation period**, may in all subsequent civil proceedings be treated as if it had never existed (Rehabilitation of Offenders Act 1974). The length of the rehabilitation period depends on the gravity of the offence, and some convictions are not subject to rehabilitation (e.g. when the sentence was life imprisonment). Dismissal from a job on the grounds of an undisclosed spent conviction may amount to *unfair dismissal. Similarly, to deny that one has been convicted if the conviction is spent does not amount to *perjury or *deception. Malicious publication of statements about a person's spent convictions can make the publisher liable for defamation, even if the statements are true. The provisions relating to spent convictions do not apply in criminal proceedings, but counsel and the court should, as far as possible, avoid referring to a spent conviction and references to it in open court may only be made with express leave of the judge in the interests of justice. A spent conviction in a record should be marked as such. *See also* CRIMINAL RECORDS BUREAU.

spes successionis [Latin: hope of succeeding] *See* POSSIBILITY.

split trial A trial in the *High Court (or, exceptionally, in the county courts) in which the issues of liability and amount of damages are tried separately.

spoliation *n.* The material alteration or destruction of a document in writing, so as to render it invalid as evidence.

sponsion *n.* An agreement or promise made by a public official, most usually a senior officer in time of war, either without authority or in excess of the authority under which it was purported to be made. Such an agreement requires ratification by the government or state concerned.

sponte sua [Latin: of one's own accord] Referring to an order made by the court on its own initiative, rather than at the request of one of the parties. Common examples are when the court dismisses an action or transfers it to another jurisdiction.

spouse *n.* A person's lawfully married husband or wife. From 5 December 2005 the word includes, for taxation purposes, a civil partner who has been through the registration process for a same-sex *civil partnership. Many provisions in the tax code apply specifically to transactions between spouses. For *capital gains tax, the special treatment given to transfers of assets between spouses ends for the tax year in which the spouses cease to live together (Taxation and Capital Gains Act 1992 s 58). For *inheritance tax, the special treatment of transfers between spouses continues until the final divorce decree (Inheritance Tax Act 1984 s 18).

springing use Formerly, a *use that arose on the occurrence of a future event. If property was given to X to the use of A when A married, A had a springing use that arose on his marriage.

spying (espionage) *n.* Obtaining or passing on to an enemy information that might prejudice the safety or interests of the state or be useful to an enemy. *See* OFFICIAL SECRETS.

squatter *n.* A person unlawfully occupying land. *See* ADVERSE OCCUPATION; ADVERSE POSSESSION; TRESPASS.

squatter's title *See* ADVERSE POSSESSION.

SRA *See* SOLICITORS REGULATION AUTHORITY.

stakeholder pension Employers with five or more employees have to make a stakeholder pension available to their staff. The term includes both occupational pensions and personal pension plans. The elements of a stakeholder pension scheme are:

- Anyone who is not a member of an occupational pension scheme can pay up to £3,600 a year into a stakeholder pension, even if he has no earnings.
- Contributions over £3,600 can be made based on earnings. From 6 April 2006 a contribution can be made of up to 100% of earnings.
- All contributions are paid net of basic rate tax. The pension provider then obtains a sum equivalent to basic rate tax from HM Revenue and Customs.
- There are provisions for carrying back a contribution to an earlier tax year.
- Detailed regulations limit the charges that can be levied by the pensions provider to (generally) 1% of the premium paid.

(⊕) SEE WEB LINKS

- Guide to stakeholder pensions from the GOV.UK website

stakeholder's interpleader *See* INTERPLEADER.

stalking Persistent threatening behaviour by one person against another. The Protection from Harassment Act 1997 creates two offences relating to stalking. If the harasser's behaviour makes the victim fear for his or her safety, the maximum penalty is two years' imprisonment and/or an unlimited fine. When the behaviour does not lead to a fear of violence but does cause distress, the maximum penalty is six months in prison and/or a fine not exceeding the statutory maximum. The behaviour must have taken place on more than one occasion and the prosecution must show that a reasonable person would realize that the behaviour would have the effect of causing the victim to fear violence or feel harassed (*Kelly v DPP* (2002) 166 JP 621). Both offences are immediately arrestable without a warrant, and the police have power to search the harasser's property. The courts may make a restraining order immediately after convicting a person of either of the two offences. In Scotland the common law has always provided protection against stalking through the offence of breach of the peace. *See also* MOLESTATION.

stamp duty A tax collected by stamping the legal documents giving effect to certain transactions. The tax has been imposed continuously since the enactment of the Stamp Duty Act 1694. Stamp duty is a tax on a document and not on a transaction or a person. Currently, the primary charging statute is the Stamp Act 1891. Since 1 December 2003 stamp duty proper has been charged solely on traditional stampable documents relating to shares and securities (including bearer instruments). A transfer of shares or securities that is made without a stampable document (i.e. electronically) is charged to *stamp duty reserve tax. A transfer of land is now charged to *stamp duty land tax.

The rate of duty is ½% of the consideration given, the charge always being rounded up to the nearest multiple of £5. The tax is remarkably efficient to collect, the collection costs being lower than for any other UK tax.

stamp duty land tax (SDLT) A tax charged on the consideration given for the sale of land in the UK (Finance Act 2003 s 42–124 and schs 3–19). Unlike *stamp duty, which it replaces for land transactions, stamp duty land tax is a tax on transactions, not a levy on documents. There are different rates of SDLT for residential land and for non-residential land. For residential land, SDLT is charged at a rate of 1% where the price paid is between £125,001 and £250,000; 3% where the price is between £250,001 and £500,000; 4% where the price is between £500,001 and £1,000,000; 5% where the price is between £1,000,001 and £2,000,000, and 7% where the price paid is over £2,000,000. For transfers of non-residential land, the rate is 1% on a price between £150,001 and £250,000; 3% on a price between £250,001 and £500,000; and 4% on a price above £500,000. There is a special rate of 15% for properties sold for over £500,000 to corporate bodies. Interest is charged on late payment and penalties are imposed that parallel those for income tax and corporation tax.

stamp duty reserve tax (SDRT) A tax levied on the transaction when a shareholding is transferred without a document, or when the document is kept outside the UK. The majority of transactions on UK exchanges are now electronic and "paperless". Like *stamp duty, stamp duty reserve tax is charged on the consideration given, not on the market value of the shareholding. The charge to stamp duty reserve tax is given by the Finance Act 1986 s 86–99 (as amended) and statutory instruments issued under that Act.

standard basis (of assessment of costs) *See* COSTS.

Standard Conditions of Sale A published set of conditions of sale that are designed to be used as standard conditions in domestic and commercial transfers of land. These replace the two former sets of standard conditions, the Law Society's Conditions of Sale and the National Conditions of Sale. In practice these conditions are used in the vast majority of contracts for the sale of land.

standard-form contract A commercial contract (e.g. a routine contract of carriage or insurance) that is concluded on terms issued by the offeror in standard form and allows for no effective negotiation. In French law such a contract is known as a *contrat d'adhésion*.

standard investment criteria *See* GENERAL POWER OF INVESTMENT.

standard of proof The degree of proof required for any fact in issue in litigation, which is established by assessing the evidence relevant to it. In criminal proceedings the standard of proof is *proof beyond reasonable doubt. In civil proceedings the standard of proof is proof on the balance of probabilities. *See also* BURDEN OF PROOF.

standing committee A committee of the House of Commons appointed to take the committee stage of public Bills allotted to it by the government. There are about 8 such committees (the number varies according to need), each consisting of between 16 and 50 members who are nominated by a Committee of Selection to reflect the political composition of the House as a whole. *Compare* COMMITTEE OF THE WHOLE HOUSE.

standing mute The refusal of the defendant in a *trial on indictment to plead to the indictment. A jury must be empanelled to say whether the defendant is **mute**

of malice (i.e. is wilfully refusing to plead) or is **mute by visitation of God** (i.e. is suffering from some physical or mental impairment that is preventing him from pleading). If the verdict of the jury is mute of malice the court may order a plea of *not guilty to be entered. If the verdict of the jury is mute by visitation of God, the jury may then go on to consider whether the defendant is *unfit to plead. In criminal proceedings a deaf mute is a competent witness and may plead to an indictment, take an oath, and be examined and cross-examined through an interpreter using sign language.

stare decisis [Latin: to stand by things decided] A maxim expressing the underlying basis of the doctrine of *precedent, i.e. that it is necessary to abide by former precedents when the same points arise again in litigation.

starter tenancy A type of probationary tenancy introduced by registered social landlords (i.e. housing associations) across some or all of their housing stock. These tenancies do not have security of tenure but are treated as *assured shorthold tenancies. *Compare* INTRODUCTORY TENANCY.

state *n.* A sovereign and independent entity capable of entering into relations with other states (*compare* PROTECTED STATE) and enjoying *international legal personality. To qualify as a state, the entity must have:

(1) a permanent population (although, as in the case of the Vatican or Nauru, this may be very small);

(2) a defined territory over which it exercises authority (although its borders, as in the case of Israel, need not be defined or undisputed);

(3) an effective government. There are currently over 180 states. When a new state comes into existence, it is automatically bound by the principles of international law. For some purposes, entities that do not normally qualify as fully fledged states may nonetheless be treated as such. Liechtenstein, for example, was refused admission as a state to the League of Nations (and did not become a member of the United Nations until 1990), but is a party to the Statute of the International Court of Justice, which is only open to states. *See also* BOUNDARY; JURISDICTION.

state aid Government assistance, often to local businesses, which is usually of a financial nature and discriminates against businesses trying to compete with them. Articles 87–89 of the *Treaty of Rome and provisions in the *Paris Treaty regulate the granting of such aid. Article 87 prohibits state aid, but the EU may approve certain types of state aid that are beneficial. About 30 cases a year are challenged by the European Commission under these provisions.

State Earnings Related Pension *See* STATE SECOND PENSION.

statelessness *n.* The absence of a recognized form of nationality, whereby an individual has refugee status. This means that he or she lacks both a legal place of *domicile and is not afforded the protection afforded by a legal connection with any particular state. *See* ASYLUM.

statement of affairs **1.** A document that must be prepared by a debtor after a *bankruptcy order has been made against him except when the bankruptcy order was made on his own petition or when the court excuses him. It gives details of his assets, debts and liabilities, the names and addresses of his creditors, and what securities they hold. The debtor must send the statement to the official receiver, and the creditors are entitled to inspect it. A debtor who wrongly fails to submit a statement of affairs is guilty of *contempt of court. **2.** *See* VOLUNTARY WINDING-UP.

statement of arrangement for children A statement of proposed arrangements for the children of divorcing parents, which must be filed before a divorce is granted. The statement must be scrutinized by the court, which may make certain orders in respect of the children.

statement of case A formal written statement in a civil action served by each party on the other, containing the allegations of fact that the party proposes to prove at trial (but not the evidence by which they are to be proved) and stating the remedy (if any) that the party claims in the action. Before the introduction of the *Civil Procedure Rules in 1999, statements of case were called **pleadings**. Statements of case include *claim forms, *particulars of claim, *defences, *counterclaims, and replies to defences. All statements of case must include a *statement of truth. Statements of case must contain only **material facts**, i.e. those facts essential to the party's claim or defence, and not the subordinate facts that are the means of proving them. It is customary to include the inferences of law that the party claims are to be drawn from the facts stated, although this is not essential. Allegations of law as such (legal arguments) are not permitted. Since the purpose of statements of case is to define clearly the issues in the action and to give the parties notice of the other side's case, sufficient details must be given of each allegation. Rules of procedure dealing with statements of case are set out in Part 16 of the Civil Procedure Rules.

statement of claim Formerly, a pleading served by the claimant in an action begun by writ of summons in the High Court. Under the *Civil Procedure Rules, statements of claim are now known as *particulars of claim.

Statement of Objections A document issued by the European Commission setting out the case against a business that has infringed the rules of competition law under *Articles 101 and 102 of the Treaty on the Functioning of the European Union. The statement will set a reasonable time limit for a reply, which can be extended (about 2–3 months is the usual period initially given). In the UK the Competition Act 1998 also empowers the *Office of Fair Trading to initiate proceedings for breach of UK competition law by way of issuing a Statement of Objections.

statement of reasons for dismissal A written notice of the reasons for an employee's dismissal or for the nonrenewal of a fixed-term contract. Under the terms of the Employment Rights Act 1996, a dismissed employee having two years' *continuous employment may demand such a statement from his employer and may complain to an employment tribunal if the statement is refused or not provided within 14 days. If an employee is dismissed during her pregnancy or after the birth of her child in circumstances in which her maternity leave period ends by reason of the dismissal, the employee is entitled to such a statement without making any request and irrespective of the period of continuous employment (*see* MATERNITY RIGHTS).

statement of terms of employment A statement in writing that an employer must give to certain employees under the terms of the Employment Rights Act 1996. Not later than two months after the beginning of employment, the employer must give the employee a statement setting out the following information:

- the names of employer and employee;
- the date employment began;
- the date when the employee's continuous employment began;
- the scale or rate of remuneration or method of calculating remuneration;
- the intervals at which remuneration is paid;
- the hours of work;

- the holiday entitlement (which must be sufficiently specific to allow the employee's holiday entitlement to be precisely calculated);
- the procedure to be adopted in the event of incapacity for work as a result of sickness or injury (including sick pay provisions, if any);
- pensions and pension schemes;
- the length of notice the employee is obliged to give and entitled to receive to terminate the contract;
- the title of the job the employee is employed to do or, as an alternative to the job title, a brief description of the work;
- if the employment is not intended to be permanent, the period for which it is expected to continue or, if it is for a fixed term, the date it is intended to end;
- either the place of work or, if the employee is required to work at various places, an indication that this is the case;
- any collective bargaining agreements that directly affect the terms and conditions of employment.

Where there are no particulars to be given (for example, if there is no pension scheme), this must be indicated.

If the employee is required to work outside the UK for more than one month there is a requirement for additional information to be given relating to the length of the period of this employment, the currency in which remuneration is to be paid in that period, details of additional remuneration or benefits connected with working outside the UK, and the repatriation arrangements.

The statement must also include a note giving certain details of the employer's disciplinary and grievance procedures and stating whether or not a pensions contracting-out certificate is in force. The note of disciplinary and grievance procedures must cover any disciplinary rules and dismissal procedures that apply to the employee.

Some of these particulars may be provided by way of reference to documents other than the written statement, provided the employee has reasonable opportunities to read these documents in the course of his employment.

If any amendment is made to any of these terms after the statement has been (or should have been) issued, the employer must give the employee a written statement setting out the details of the change not later than one month after the change has been made.

Failure to comply with any of these requirements gives the employee the right to complain to an *employment tribunal at any time during the currency of the employment, or within three months of the employment coming to an end.

The written statement, although providing evidence of the terms of employment, is not itself the *contract of employment.

statement of truth A statement that the party putting forward a document, or the maker of a witness statement, believes that the facts stated in the document are true. Under Part 22 of the *Civil Procedure Rules statements of case and witness statements must be verified by a statement of truth. Under Part 35 an expert's report must be verified by a statement of truth. The court may strike out a statement of case that is not verified by a statement of truth, and may direct that a witness statement not verified by a statement of truth shall not be admissible as evidence. Proceedings for contempt of court may be brought against a person who makes, or causes to be made, a false statement in a document verified by a statement of truth without an honest belief in its truth.

Statements of Standard Accounting Practice (SSAP) *See* FINANCIAL REPORTING STANDARDS.

state of emergency *See* EMERGENCY POWERS.

state responsibility The obligation of a state to make reparation arising from a failure to comply with a legal obligation under international law. *See also* ESPOUSAL OF CLAIM.

State Second Pension (SSP; S2P) A scheme run by the UK government to provide a pension for employees in addition to the basic state retirement *pension. It was introduced in April 2002 to replace the existing **State Earnings Related Pension (SERPS)**. Contributions are made through National Insurance payments. Those wishing to contract out of SSP may currently subscribe to an occupational pension scheme or a personal pension scheme; from 2012, however, it is only possible to contract out through a defined-benefit scheme operated by an employer.

Stationery Office, The (TSO) The privatized body that, on 1 October 1996, took over the functions of *Her Majesty's Stationery Office (HMSO) in selling government and related legislative material. All Acts of Parliament and government regulations can be purchased from TSO, which also maintains the United Kingdom Official Publications database (UKOP). HMSO remains in public ownership and is now part of the *Office of Public Sector Information (OPSI).

((⊕)) SEE WEB LINKS
• TSO's online bookstore (parliamentary and legal)

status *n.* A person's legal standing or capacity. The term derives from Roman law, in which it referred to a person's freedom, citizenship, and family rights. Status is an index to legal rights and duties, powers, and disabilities.

statute *n. See* ACT OF PARLIAMENT.

statute-barred debt A debt that has not been recovered within the period allowed by the legislation relating to *limitation of actions. Such a debt can no longer be recovered by action. The limitation period for debts due on promises made by deed is 12 years from the date the debt became due. For other debts the limitation period is six years from the date the debt became due. However, in certain contracts of loan that do not provide for repayment of the debt by a fixed date and in which repayment is not conditional on a demand by the creditor, the six-year period will not start to run until the creditor makes a demand in writing for repayment of the debt. The Limitation Act 1980 sets out these periods.

statute book The entire body of existing statutes.

statute law The body of law contained in Acts of Parliament. *Compare* CASE LAW.

statutorily protected tenancy A tenancy that has *security of tenure and, in some cases, statutory control of rent.

statutory adoption pay *See* ADOPTION LEAVE.

statutory advertisement An advertisement asking any creditors to come forward placed by a *personal representative under the Trustee Act 1927 s 27. This enables the personal representative to escape liability for unknown debts.

statutory assignment *See* ASSIGNMENT.

statutory authority A defence to an action in *nuisance or under the *rule in *Rylands v Fletcher*, where the damage complained of is an inevitable result of some act authorized by statute (*Allen v Gulf Oil Refining* [1981] AC 101 (HL)).

statutory company A *company incorporated by the promotion of a private Act of Parliament. *Compare* REGISTERED COMPANY.

statutory corporation *See* PUBLIC CORPORATION.

statutory declaration A *declaration made before a Commissioner for Oaths in a prescribed form.

statutory demand A standard form used for the enforcement of debts. It typically sets out a demand by a creditor to a debtor to honour payment of an amount owing. The amount may be due immediately or at a future date (if the creditor has reasonable grounds for believing that it will not be paid at this date). The demand will also specify a period of three weeks for repayment or other satisfactory solution. Failure to comply with the demand by the debtor will be evidence of an inability by the debtor to pay creditors and can be used to support a *compulsory winding-up petition under section 124 of the Insolvency Act 1986.

Statutory Form of Conditions of Sale Standard terms of contract for the sale and purchase of land, published by the Lord Chancellor under the Law of Property Act 1925. They cover, for example, the vendor's obligations in proving his title to the land, the completion of the transaction, and the payment of interest by the purchaser if he fails to complete on the due date. The Statutory Form applies automatically to contracts made by correspondence subject to any express agreement between the parties, and any valid contract for the sale and purchase of land may be expressed to incorporate the Statutory Form.

statutory instrument Any *delegated legislation (not including subdelegated legislation) to which the Statutory Instruments Act 1946 applies. This includes both

(1) delegation made under powers conferred by an Act passed after 1947, either on the Crown or on a government minister, and expressed by that Act to be exercisable by Order in Council in the former case or by statutory instrument in the latter; and

(2) delegation made under powers conferred by pre-1947 legislation.

The 1946 Act requires statutory instruments to be numbered, printed, and published by the Queen's printer. They are numbered consecutively for each calendar year in the order in which the printer receives them; for example, the first statutory instrument to be received in 1993 would be cited as "S.I. 1993 No. 1". Moreover, as a modification of the rule *ignorantia juris non excusat* (ignorance of the law is no excuse), the Act makes nonpublication a defence to proceedings for contravening a statutory instrument unless other adequate steps had been taken to bring it to the public notice. The Act is also concerned with certain aspects of parliamentary control. It standardizes negative resolution procedure for statutory instruments by providing that, if the enabling statute simply makes them subject to annulment by resolution of either House of Parliament, they are to be laid before Parliament for 40 days and liable to annulment during that period. It further provides that any statutory instrument required to be laid (either because of that rule or because the enabling statute expressly says so) must be laid before becoming operative unless there is good reason to the contrary (in which case, an explanation must be given to the Lord Chancellor and the Speaker). *See also* JOINT COMMITTEE ON STATUTORY INSTRUMENTS.

statutory interpretation *See* INTERPRETATION.

statutory legacy Under the Administration of Estates Act 1925 s 47, the legacy to which a surviving spouse is entitled on an *intestacy. Where the intestate leaves a surviving spouse and children, the spouse receives a legacy of £250,000 before the division of residue. Where there are no children the spouse receives a legacy of £450,000.

statutory lives in being *See* RULE AGAINST PERPETUITIES.

statutory maternity pay *See* MATERNITY RIGHTS.

statutory owner A person having the powers of an immediate beneficiary of *settled land, where the beneficiary himself is under 18 or there is no immediate beneficiary (for example, in a discretionary settlement in which no beneficiary has been appointed). The statutory owner is either the person of full age on whom the powers are conferred by the settlement; the trustees of the settlement (*see* SETTLED LAND ACT TRUSTEES); or, in a settlement made by will on a beneficiary under 18, the testator's personal representatives until a vesting instrument has been effected.

statutory paternity pay *See* PATERNITY LEAVE.

statutory periodic tenancy A *periodic tenancy that comes into operation on the expiration of an *assured tenancy for a *fixed term unless that tenancy is terminated by a court order or *surrender of the tenancy. The statutory periodic tenancy is on the same terms as the fixed term tenancy before it expired, except for the condition for terminating the tenancy at the end of the term. However, the landlord or tenant can apply to a *rent assessment committee to vary the terms of the tenancy. *See also* ASSURED SHORTHOLD TENANCY.

statutory rules and orders *See* STATUTORY INSTRUMENT.

statutory sick pay (SSP) Weekly payments by employers to employees unable to work because of sickness; it is payable, after the first three days of sickness, for a period of up to 28 weeks, after which employees can claim Employment and Support Allowance (ESA). Formerly employers were entitled to a partial or full reimbursement for SSP by the government but reimbursement is now available only where an employer pays out, in any income-tax month, SSP exceeding 13% of his liability to pay National Insurance contributions in that month. In such circumstances that excess can be recouped.

statutory tenancy A tenancy that comes into existence when the contractual element of a *protected tenancy is terminated and the former protected tenant continues to live in the property (a company cannot be a statutory tenant). A statutory tenancy continues only for as long as the tenant lives in the property (therefore it will end if the tenant attempts to sublet). When the tenant dies, however, the statutory tenancy can be transmitted to his spouse if she was living in the dwelling immediately before the tenant's death. If there is no spouse, the tenancy can be transferred to another member of the tenant's family who was living with him for the previous two years. This is known as a **statutory tenancy by succession**. The terms of a statutory tenancy are, in general, the same as those of the original contractual tenancy. If there is no provision for notice in the original tenancy, the tenant must give three months notice to terminate his tenancy. A landlord can terminate a statutory tenancy only by obtaining a court order for possession. Statutory tenancies are being phased out as no new protected tenancies can be created after the Housing Act 1988. *See* ASSURED TENANCY.

statutory trust **1.** Until 1997, a trust created by statute when land was held by trustees on trust pending its sale (*see* TRUST FOR SALE). Any income from the land prior to its sale and the proceeds of sale itself was held in trust by the trustees. Since 1997, statutory trusts have been replaced by *trusts of land governed by the Trusts of Land and Appointment of Trustees Act 1996. **2.** A trust that arises on an *intestacy where the *issue of the deceased are entitled to the whole or part of the estate. The terms of such trusts are set out in the Administration of Estates Act 1925 s 27, which provides for a child's share to be held in trust until the age of 18 on a *per stirpes basis.

statutory will A will made through the *Court of Protection on behalf of a person who lacks *testamentary capacity.

stay of execution An order suspending the *execution of the judgment or order of a court.

stay of proceedings An order imposing a halt on civil proceedings (apart from taking any steps allowed by the Civil Procedure Rules or the terms of the stay). A stay is usually ordered because of some misconduct by the claimant. Proceedings may be continued if a stay is lifted.

step-parent *n.* A person who is married to the father or mother of a child but is not the natural parent of the child. A step-parent has no automatic legal status in relation to his or her step-children, but will usually qualify to apply, as of right, for a *section 8 order in respect of the child by virtue of being married to the child's natural parent. Until recently step-parents could only acquire *parental responsibility either by applying to court for a *residence order (which automatically confers parental responsibility) or by applying to adopt the child together with the child's natural parent. The Children Act 1989, as amended by the Adoption and Children Act 2002, has given the court a new power to confer parental responsibility on the step-parent, so long as both natural parents agree. There is a policy of discouraging step-parent adoption since the effect will be to irrevocably sever the child's legal ties with its other natural parent.

Stimson Doctrine In public international law, the doctrine that an aggressor cannot acquire territory by conquest alone. The doctrine was enunciated in 1931, when Japanese troops took over Manchuria, until then part of China, and set up the puppet state of Manchukuo. Almost all states considered that Japan was guilty of aggression and the US Secretary of State, Henry L. Stimson, announced that his government would not recognize any territorial changes brought about by force alone. The same principle informed the non-recognition resolution (662/1990) of the UN Security Council following the annexation of Kuwait by Iraq in 1990.

stipendiary magistrate *See* DISTRICT JUDGE (MAGISTRATES' COURT).

stirring up racial hatred *See* RACIAL HATRED.

stock *n.* **1.** A fixed-interest loan raised by the government or a local authority. **2.** Shares in a registered company that have been converted into a single holding with a nominal value equal to that of the total of the shares. For example, a holder of 100 shares of £1 each will have £100 stock after conversion. **3.** *See* LOAN CAPITAL.

Stock Exchange London Stock Exchange plc, formerly the International Stock Exchange of the UK and the Republic of Ireland Ltd, is the UK body responsible for marketing company securities. Admission to the Official List, and hence to the main market, is available only to shares of large public companies that have published *accounts for the three years preceding the application and that have satisfied the listing requirements of the UK Listing Authority (an arm of the *Financial Conduct Authority). These rules ensure that sufficient information is supplied, both on admission and subsequently, to enable investors to assess the merits of the shares. Admission to the **Alternative Investment Market** (**AIM**) is available to smaller companies who meet the statutory requirements. Deals in listed shares will usually be arranged through a member of the Stock Exchange acting as a market intermediary and taking a commission. Intermediaries who will themselves buy or sell the securities as principals are called **market makers**. Face-to-face dealing on the floor of the exchange has now been virtually abolished by the Stock Exchange Electronic Trading System (SETS).

SEE WEB LINKS
• Website of the London Stock Exchange: includes information for companies, traders, and private investors

stock transfer *See* SHARE TRANSFER.

stop notice **1.** A court procedure available to protect those who have an interest in shares but have not been registered as company members. The notice prevents the company from registering a transfer of the shares or paying a dividend upon them without informing the server of the notice. **2.** A notice served by a local planning authority when they consider that any activity specified in an *enforcement notice should be prevented before the time for compliance given by that notice. It takes effect on a date specified therein, which is 3 to 28 days after service, and a site notice may be posted, drawing attention to its provisions.

stoppage *in transitu* A remedy available to an *unpaid seller of goods when the buyer has become insolvent and the goods are still in course of transit. If the seller gives notice of stoppage to the carrier or other bailee of the goods, he is entitled to have them redelivered to him and may then retain possession of them until the price is paid or tendered. If the right is not exercised, the goods will fall into the insolvent buyer's estate and go towards satisfying his creditors generally.

stowaway *n.* A person who secretes himself upon a ship and goes to sea. This is a criminal offence under the Merchant Shipping Act 1894.

Strategic Health Authorities (**SHAs**) Authorities established in 2002 to manage the *National Health Service locally and provide a key link between the Department of Health and the NHS. They hold all local NHS organizations (apart from *NHS Foundation Trusts) to account for performance and are responsible for developing plans for improving health services in their local area. The number of SHAs was reduced from 28 to 10 in 2006 and they were abolished in 2013.

street offence Any offence relating to the use of public streets. Examples are *obstruction, failing to obey police regulations about movement of traffic or pedestrians, *kerb crawling, and *soliciting.

strict construction *See* INTERPRETATION.

strict liability **1.** (in criminal law) Liability for a crime that is imposed without the necessity of proving **mens rea* with respect to one or more of the elements of the crime. There are few crimes of strict liability at common law but such crimes are often created by statute, particularly to control or regulate daily activities; examples include offences relating to the production and marketing of food and *offences relating to road traffic. The usual penalty for crimes of strict liability is a fine. Most crimes of strict liability do, however, require *mens rea* in respect of at least some of the elements of the crime. In some cases statute provides for strict liability, but then allows a defence if the accused can prove (*see* BURDEN OF PROOF) that he had no reason to know of or suspect certain facts, so that, in effect, the crime becomes one of *negligence. *Insanity or *non-insane automatism is a defence to all crimes, including crimes of strict liability. **2.** (in tort) Liability for a wrong that is imposed without the claimant having to prove that the defendant was at fault. Strict liability is exceptional in the law of tort, but is imposed for torts involving dangerous animals (*see* ANIMALS) and dangerous things (the *rule in *Rylands v Fletcher*), *conversion, *defamation, *product liability, and some cases of *breach of statutory duty. It is no defence in these torts that the defendant took reasonable care to prevent damage, but various other defences are admitted.

strict settlement A trust conferring beneficial interests in land that render it *settled land, governed by the Settled Land Act 1925. Generally the purpose of a strict settlement is to create successive interests that will keep the land in the settlor's family. The usual form of marriage settlement gave a life interest to the husband with remainder (after provisions for the wife during widowhood and for younger children of the marriage) to the first and other sons in *tail, a further remainder to any daughters as tenants in common in tail, and a final remainder to the husband in fee simple. The beneficiaries under a strict settlement have equitable interests in the land. Since 1997, such settlements exist as a *trust of land.

strike *n.* A cessation of work or refusal to work by employees acting together in connection with a *trade dispute to secure better terms and conditions of employment for themselves and/or other workers. A trade union cannot call its members out on strike unless it has held a secret ballot and the majority agree to the action. Under the Trade Union and Labour Relations (Consolidation) Act 1992, as amended, trade union ballots for industrial action must be fully postal and, if a ballot involves 50 or more members, it must be subject to independent scrutiny. Seven days' notice of the union's intention to ballot its members on industrial action must be given to the employer and the union must provide the employer with details of the ballot result and give him at least seven days' written notice of those members it intends to call out on strike. A strike ballot remains effective for four weeks. This period may be extended to eight weeks if the union and employer agree. The Trade Union and Labour Relations (Consolidation) Act 1992 provides for a "Citizen's Right" for any individual to sue the union if he is deprived (or likely to be deprived) of any goods or services because of unlawfully organized industrial action.

strike out In civil proceedings, an order of the court ordering written material to be deleted so that it may no longer be relied upon. Under Part 3 of the *Civil Procedure Rules the court has the power to strike out a party's *statement of case if it appears to the court that (1) the statement of case discloses no reasonable grounds for bringing or defending the claim; (2) the statement of case is an abuse of the court's process or is otherwise likely to obstruct the just disposal of the proceedings; or (3) there has been failure to comply with a rule, Practice Direction, or court order.

striking off **1.** The removal of a solicitor's name from the roll of solicitors, either at his request or for misconduct. **2.** A similar procedure in other professions (e.g. the erasure of a doctor's name from the register of general medical practitioners). **3.** The removal of a limited company from the companies register, often because it has failed to file accounts.

structured settlement A form of *settlement of action used in cases of serious personal injuries in which it is agreed, or the court orders, that the injured person will receive, in addition to a *lump-sum award for losses already suffered, further payments on a periodic basis to cover future needs. The periodic payments are funded by an annuity purchased by the defendant and can be index-linked to provide for inflation. The courts now have the power to vary periodical payment orders as set out in the Damages (Variation of Periodical Payments) Order 2005.

structure plan A written statement formulating a local planning authority's policy on development and land use, including environmental improvement and traffic management policy.

subdelegated legislation Legislation made under powers conferred by *delegated legislation or by subdelegated legislation itself (in which case it is technically sub-subdelegated legislation). Subdelegated legislation is quite common (as when the parent Act authorizes a minister to make regulations and these in turn authorize others to make orders), but sub-subdelegated legislation is rare (though examples have existed in wartime); the chain has not in practice been further extended. Subdelegated legislation is not subject to any form of parliamentary control but it is subject to judicial control by means of the doctrine of *ultra vires*.

subject to contract *See* ACCEPTANCE.

sub judice rule **1.** A rule limiting comment and disclosure relating to judicial proceedings, in order not to prejudice the issue or influence the jury. *See* CONTEMPT OF COURT. **2.** A parliamentary practice in which the Speaker prevents any reference in questions or debates to matters pending decision in court proceedings (civil or criminal). In the case of civil proceedings, he has power to waive the rule if a matter of national interest is involved.

sublease (subtenancy, underlease) *n.* A *lease granted by a person who is himself a lessee of the same property. The sublease must be shorter than the main lease. Thus a lessee with a lease for 10 years can grant a sublease for a period up to 10 years less one day. The formalities for creating and terminating a sublease are the same as those for a lease. There is often a covenant in a lease prohibiting subletting. If a lessee sublets in breach of the covenant the sublease will be valid, but the landlord may have a right of *forfeiture of the lease. In some cases the lease specifies that the lessee may only sublet with the landlord's consent. In this case, the landlord may not withhold his consent unreasonably and he cannot charge a fee for giving his consent unless there is express provision for this in the lease. If the main lease is forfeited, any sublease automatically comes to an end, subject to that subtenant's right to apply for *relief from forfeiture. However, the surrender of a lease does not affect any sublease.

subletting *n.* The granting of a *sublease.

submortgage *n.* A mortgage of a mortgage. A **submortgagor** is a person who holds a mortgage over another's land and charges that mortgage as security for a debt he owes to a third party (the **submortgagee**). If the submortgagor defaults, the submortgagee may sell the mortgage (but not the land) and recover the debt from the proceeds.

sub nomine (sub nom) [Latin: under the name] A phrase used in law reports when the name of the case has changed through the process of appeal. For example, before the House of Lords we have the case of *R v Shaw* [1961] 1 All ER 330, in which Frederick Shaw was found guilty on three counts by the Central Criminal Court. Leave to appeal was granted by the Court of Criminal Appeal in respect of counts 1 and 2. Owing to the public policy issues involved in these counts, the case for the Crown was brought by the *Director of Public Prosecutions. The case was then entitled *Shaw v DPP* [1961] 2 All ER

446. Thus, the House of Lords report will state in its details of the appeal process: "*Shaw v DPP* reported *sub nom R v Shaw* [1961] 1 All ER 330".

subordinate legislation *See* DELEGATED LEGISLATION.

subornation *n.* Procuring another to commit an offence. Normally subornation is included in the offence of aiding, abetting, or procuring (*see* ACCESSORY), but there is a special statutory offence of **subornation of perjury**.

subpoena *n. See* WITNESS SUMMONS.

subrogation *n.* The substitution of one person for another so that the person substituted succeeds to the rights of the other. Thus an insurer who indemnifies his insured against the loss of goods may be subrogated to the insured person's rights against a third party whose negligence caused the loss.

sub rosa [Latin: under the rose] In secret or in confidence. The rose was a Roman symbol of secrecy.

subscribing witness A person who signs a written document as an attesting witness to the signature of another.

subsidiarity *n.* A principle of the European Union, introduced by Article 3A of the *Maastricht Treaty, ensuring that in areas which do not fall within the exclusive competence of the EU, it shall not take action unless the objectives of the proposed action cannot be adequately achieved by individual member states. Thus it provides for legislation at national level when EU measures are not required.

subsidiary company A company controlled by another company, its **holding** (or **parent**) **company**. For general purposes, such control is established when the holding company has a majority of the voting rights attached to its shares (either by virtue of its ownership of those shares or because of an agreement with other shareholders) or the right to appoint or remove a majority of its board of directors. If company A controls company B, which itself controls company C, then company C is the subsidiary of both company B and company A. For the purposes of *group accounts, a wider definition applies: the subsidiary need not be incorporated (*see* COMPANY) and control can also be established in other ways, e.g. when the holding company has the right, under the subsidiary's *articles or *memorandum of association, to exercise a dominant influence over it.

Substantial Acquisition Rules *See* SARS.

substantial damages *See* DAMAGES.

substantial donor A person who makes a series of gifts to a charity that total £25,000 or more in any 12-month period or £100,000 or more during a six-year period. The charity is penalized by the denial of tax relief (or, sometimes, the imposition of a tax charge) if a property is sold to, or purchased from, or is let to, or is let from that substantial donor. This tax treatment also applies to the provision of services, exchanges of property, the provision of financial assistance and investment by the charity in the business of a substantial donor (Taxes Act 1988 s 506A and Income Tax Act 2007 s 543–57, inserted by Finance Act 2006 s 54).

substantial performance *See* PERFORMANCE OF CONTRACT.

substantive law The part of the law that deals with rights, duties, and all other matters that are not matters purely of practice and procedure. *Compare* ADJECTIVE LAW.

substituted judgment A decision made by someone on behalf of an *incompetent patient that is judged to reflect what the patient would have wanted had he had the mental capacity to decide for himself. This test for decision making, used in the USA, is to be contrasted with the *best interest test used in English law. *See* PROXY DECISION.

substituted service *See* SERVICE.

substitutional legacy (substitutional gift) A legacy that (1) passes to descendants of a beneficiary who is named in a will if this beneficiary has predeceased the testator or (2) passes to other persons by express provisions in the will (e.g. a legacy of £10,000 to A but if he predeceases then to B). The Wills Act 1837 s 33 provides for automatic substitution where property is gifted by will to a child or remoter issue of the testator (subject to contrary intention being expressed in the will). If there is no substitutional legacy and s 33 does not apply, the legacy *lapses. *See also* ACCRUER; REPRESENTATION.

subtenancy *n. See* SUBLEASE.

subtenant *n.* A tenant who holds a *sublease.

sub-trust (derivative trust) *n.* A trust created out of a trust such that A holds property on trust for B and B then declares himself to be trustee of his beneficial interest for C. If, in making such a *declaration of trust, B has no duties to perform as trustee (because A continues to perform all such duties), then B will simply drop out of the picture leaving the original trustee, A, holding in trust for C (*Grainge v Wilberforce* (1889) 5 TLR 436). This is not a genuine example of a sub-trust. If B, however, by declaring the trust in favour of C, has some duty to perform in his capacity as trustee, then a genuine sub-trust will have been created and B will not drop out of the picture.

success fee (contingency fee) In civil proceedings, an additional fee that may be payable to a legal representative where there is a *conditional fee agreement and the case proves successful. The success fee must be expressed as a percentage of the other costs payable under the agreement.

succession *n.* **1.** The law and procedures under which beneficiaries become entitled to property under a testator's will or on intestacy. **2.** (in international law) The transfer of sovereignty over a territorial entity from one subject of international law (i.e. one state) to another. As a result of succession, an existing state becomes totally extinguished (as when Tanganyika and Zanzibar ceased to exist in 1964 on the formation of Tanzania) or a state transfers part of its territory to another state.

successive interests Where interests under a trust succeed each other on the occurrence of specified events. For example to A for his lifetime, then to B until he reaches the age of 25, then to C absolutely.

sue *vb.* To make a claim for a remedy in the civil courts by issuing court proceedings.

sufferance *n. See* TENANCY AT SUFFERANCE.

suicide *n.* The act of killing oneself intentionally. Since 1961 suicide itself is not a crime, but there is a special statutory crime (punishable by up to 14 years' imprisonment) of aiding, abetting, counselling, or procuring a suicide. In practice very few prosecutions are brought for this offence. Doing nothing to stop someone else from committing suicide is not abetting it, but euthanasia (mercy killing) in the form of giving assistance to the sufferer (rather than actually killing him) may amount to aiding (*R v Wallis* (1983) 5 Cr App R (S) 342). When two people agree that one of them shall kill the other and then commit suicide (a **suicide pact**), the one who does the killing is guilty, if he survives, not of murder but of manslaughter.

sui generis [Latin: of its own kind] Forming a class of its own; unique.

sui juris [Latin: of his own right] Describing the status of a person who is of full age and capacity. *Compare* ALIENI JURIS.

suit *n.* A court claim. The term is commonly used for any court proceedings although originally it denoted a suit in equity as opposed to an action at law.

summary assessment *See* ASSESSMENT OF COSTS.

summary conviction A *conviction in a magistrates' court. The magistrates are the judges of both fact and law and must either convict the accused or dismiss the case. The usual form of words for a conviction is "We find the case proved", and a conviction may be returned on a simple majority verdict. Under the Magistrates' Courts Act 1980, the magistrates may remand the accused for a medical examination if they are satisfied that he has committed the act he is charged with, but are in doubt as to his mental condition and whether or not to make a hospital order. Such a finding has the force of a conviction for purposes of the accused's right to be granted bail.

summary financial statement A statement providing financial information about a company that is derived from its annual *accounts. *Listed companies may opt to supply this abbreviated form of the accounts to their members in place of the full accounts, but only if the members do not object (Companies Act 2006 s 426–32).

summary judgment A procedure under Part 24 of the *Civil Procedure Rules by which the court may decide a particular claim or issue without a trial. The court may give summary judgment against a claimant or defendant on the whole of a claim or on a particular issue if it considers that the claimant has no real prospect of succeeding on the claim or issue, or that the defendant has no real prospect of succeeding on the claim or issue, or that the defendant has no real prospect of successfully defending the claim or issue, and there is no other compelling reason why the claim or issue should be disposed of at a trial. Part 53 of the Civil Procedure Rules sets out rules relating to the summary disposal of defamation claims in accordance with the Defamation Act 1996.

summary offence An offence that can be tried summarily, i.e. before magistrates. Most minor offences (e.g. common assault and battery) are triable only summarily; some more serious offences are *offences triable either way (i.e. they can be tried either summarily or on indictment in the Crown Court). Prosecutions for summary offences must be started within six months of the commission of the offence, unless statute expressly provides to the contrary. *Compare* INDICTABLE OFFENCE.

summary trial Trial by magistrates without a jury. All summary offences are tried in this way, as well as some *offences triable either way. The main procedural principles followed in *trial on indictment also apply to summary trial, but there are some differences of which the most important are as follows.

(1) The accused does not usually have to be present at the hearing.

(2) Objections cannot usually be made either to information laid before the magistrates or to a summons or warrant served on the defendant on the grounds of "defects of substance or form" (unless they are fundamental defects).

(3) In the case of summary offences, the accused may send in a written plea of guilty, together with a statement of mitigation, and the case may then be tried without the prosecution or defence appearing.

summing up A judge's speech at the end of a trial by *jury, in which he explains to the jury what its functions are, directs the members of the jury on any relevant points of law, and summarizes the evidence that has been given in the trial.

summons *n.* A court order to an individual to appear in court at a specified place and time. The term is now used only in certain categories of criminal cases for appearance at a magistrates' court. Before the introduction of the *Civil Procedure Rules in 1999, it was used in civil cases for hearings in the county court and applications to a judge sitting in chambers about procedural matters prior to the court hearing. Such orders are now made by **application notice**. *See also* WITNESS SUMMONS.

Summons Production Centre *See* CLAIM PRODUCTION CENTRE.

Sunday trading The opening of shops for trading on a Sunday, which is governed by the Sunday Trading Act 1994 as consolidated in the Employment Rights Act 1996. Small shops may open at will on a Sunday. Large shops with a floor area over 280 square metres may open on Sundays, provided that they open for no more than six hours between 10.00 a.m. and 6.00 p.m. Shops may not open on Easter Sunday and, under the Christmas Day (Trading) Act 2004, large shops may not open on Christmas Day. Fines can be levied for breach of the requirements. The Act also controls noisy unloading on a Sunday.

Shop workers (other than those specifically employed to work only on Sundays) have the right not to be dismissed or selected for redundancy for refusing to work on Sundays. They are also protected from suffering any other detriment (for example, loss of overtime or denial of promotion) for refusing to work on Sundays. Shop workers who have been employed by the same employer since August 1994 are automatically protected and may simply tell the employer that they do not wish to work on Sundays. All other shop workers can opt out of Sunday working by giving their employer three months' notice, in writing, that they do not wish to work on Sundays. Any worker may opt in to Sunday working if they wish. A complaint about infringement of these rights is to an *employment tribunal. Workers other than shop workers are governed by the terms of their contracts of employment, which may require Sunday working.

superior court Any of the higher courts of the legal system, whose jurisdiction is not limited, for example, by geography or by value of the subject matter of the claim and whose decisions have weight as *precedents. In English law, the superior courts are the *Supreme Court, the *Court of Appeal, the *High Court, and the *Crown Court, together with the *Judicial Committee of the Privy Council. Decisions of superior courts are not subject to judicial review by the High Court. *Compare* INFERIOR COURT. *See also* SENIOR COURTS.

superior orders A plea that certain conduct does not constitute a crime because it was committed in obedience to the orders of a superior (usually a superior officer in the armed forces). It could arise, for example, on the unjustified shooting of a rioter when the military are restoring order. UK law does not recognize the plea as a defence in itself. If an order is manifestly unlawful (for example, an order to commit genocide or crimes against humanity), a soldier's duty is to disobey it. If, however, an unlawful order is not manifestly so, the plea could be raised as establishing that the soldier did not have the necessary *mens rea.*

Supervised Community Treatment (SCT) Arrangements under which patients can be discharged from detention in hospital under the Mental Health Act 1983 but are subject to conditions set out in a *community treatment order.

supervision order An order of the court placing a child under the supervision of a local authority or a probation officer whose duty it is to advise and assist the child (Powers of Criminal Courts (Sentencing) Act 2000 s 63). The court can make a supervision order only if certain *threshold criteria are satisfied. A supervisor may have wide powers, for example to ensure that the child lives as directed or attends specified activities; in addition, the supervisor may apply for an **education supervision order** if the child is of compulsory school age and not receiving adequate education. A supervision order does not confer *parental responsibility and initially lasts only for one year with a possible extension for up to a maximum of three years. *Compare* CARE ORDER.

supervision requirement A requirement that may be imposed by a sentencing court as part of a *community order or a *suspended sentence order under the Criminal Justice Act 2003 or as part of a *youth rehabilitation order under the Criminal Justice and Immigration Act 2008. It places an offender under the supervision of a probation officer or other responsible officer. A community order with a supervision requirement replaces the former **community rehabilitation order** (often referred to as a **probation order**).

support services Services that a local authority is under a duty to provide for *children in need and their families under Part 111 of the Children Act. One of the primary purposes of such services is to prevent, wherever possible, the circumstances under which it becomes necessary for compulsory action to be taken (e.g. for the local authority to apply to court for a *care order or an *emergency protection order).

suppression of documents The dishonest destruction, hiding, or defacing of any valuable security (i.e. almost any document creating, extinguishing, or transferring a right in money or property), will or similar document, or any original document (but not a copy) belonging to or filed in any court or governmental department (Theft Act 1968 s 20(1)). If done with the purpose of gaining as a result, or causing loss to someone else, it is an offence punishable by up to seven years' imprisonment on indictment; or six months, a fine not exceeding the statutory maximum, or both, summarily. *See also* FORGERY.

supra protest *See* ACCEPTANCE SUPRA PROTEST.

supremacy *n.* The prevalence of one law or document over another that conflicts with it. Within the European Union, EU law prevails over national law (*R v Secretary of State for Transport ex p Factortame Ltd (No 1)* [1990] 2 AC 85 (HL)). There are many instances of national law being overturned by the *European Court of Justice when a member state has ignored provisions of the Treaty of Rome. However, in certain areas, for example competition law, national laws may be permitted when they are stricter than provisions in EU law.

Supreme Court of Judicature A court created by the Judicature Acts 1873–75 to take over the jurisdiction of all the higher courts, other than the House of Lords, existing at that time. It did not sit as a single court but comprised the *High Court of Justice, the *Court of Appeal, and the *Crown Court. On the establishment of the Supreme Court of the United Kingdom in 2009 these courts were renamed the *Senior Courts of England and Wales. *See also* RULES OF THE SUPREME COURT.

Supreme Court of the United Kingdom A court established under the Constitutional Reform Act 2005 to replace the *Lords of Appeal in Ordinary sitting in the

*House of Lords as the highest appeal court in the UK. In October 2009 the judges lost their right to speak and vote in the Lords and began to sit in the nearby Supreme Court. The maximum number of judges appointed to hear cases in the Supreme Court is 12 (including a president and deputy president).

surcharge *n.* A charge levied on the taxpayer if income tax, capital gains tax, or National Insurance contributions are unpaid 28 days after the due date. The basic surcharge of 5% is raised to 10% if the liability remains unpaid six months after the due date. *See also* PENALTY.

surety *n.* **1.** Security in the form of money to be forfeited upon nonappearance in court, offered either by the defendant himself or by other people of suitable financial resources, character, and relationship to the defendant. **2.** Any person who offers security for another. *See* BAIL; RECOGNIZANCE.

surname *n.* A family name. Upon marriage a wife is entitled to take her husband's surname (and title or rank) and to continue using it after his death or divorce (unless she uses it for fraudulent purposes), although she is not obliged to do so. A legitimate child, by custom, takes the name of his father and an illegitimate child that of his mother (although the father's name may be entered on the birth registration if both parents agree or an affiliation order names the man as the putative father). Upon adoption a child automatically takes the name of his adoptive parents. *See also* CHANGE OF NAME.

surprise *n.* An unexpected event that causes a party to be put at some disadvantage in litigation. Many of the rules of pretrial procedure in the *Civil Procedure Rules are designed to prevent surprise. For example, under Part 16 of the Rules matters that might otherwise take the other parties by surprise must be set out in a party's *statements of case. Similarly, under Part 32 of the Rules the court will order a party to serve on the other parties any witness statement of the oral evidence which that party intends to rely on in relation to any issues of fact to be decided at trial.

surrebutter *n.* Formerly, a pleading served by a claimant in reply to the defendant's *rebutter. Such a pleading was very rare in modern practice and is not mentioned in the *Civil Procedure Rules.

surrejoinder *n.* Formerly, a pleading served by a claimant in answer to the defendant's *rejoinder. Such a pleading was very rare in modern practice and is not mentioned in the *Civil Procedure Rules.

surrender of tenancy The termination of a *lease, which occurs when a tenant gives up his interest to his landlord. Surrender can be express or implied. Express surrender is usually in the form of a deed. When the lease is for less than three years, no deed is needed provided that the tenant signs a written agreement to surrender. Implied surrender occurs when the actions of both parties show that they consider the lease to be at an end; for example, when the tenant gives up possession and the landlord reoccupies the property.

surrender to custody To give oneself into the custody of the court or police at an appointed time and place. It is the primary condition of all releases on *bail to surrender to custody; in order to achieve this, the court may attach conditions to the bail, such as the provision of a *surety or restrictions on movement. Failure to surrender to custody is an offence (Bail Act 1976 s 6: *see* ABSCONDING). The police may arrest without warrant anyone whom they reasonably believe is not going to surrender to custody or anyone whom they have been informed by a surety (who wishes to be relieved of his undertaking) is not going to surrender.

surrogacy *n.* An arrangement in which a woman ("the carrying mother") agrees to bear a child and to hand over that child, on birth, to another person or persons ("the commissioning parents"). The carrying mother may have been artificially inseminated with the sperm of the commissioning father or donated gametes from the commissioning parents may be used to create an embryo that is then carried to term by her. In the latter case, the carrying mother will be genetically unrelated to the child. Nevertheless, in both cases the carrying mother is deemed in law under the Human Fertilization and Embryology Act 1990 to be the mother of the child. The surrogacy arrangement is not enforceable at law and hence if the surrogate mother wishes to keep her child, the commissioning parents cannot force her to hand the child over. Where the child is handed over on birth the commissioning parents must take steps to become the legal parents. This they may do by applying to court for either an adoption order or, more commonly, a *parental order under the Human Fertilization and Embryology Act 1990. The Surrogacy Arrangements Act 1985 prohibits commercial agencies from engaging women to act as surrogate mothers. Breach of the prohibition is punishable with a fine of up to £2000 or three months' imprisonment. Surrogate mothers and commissioning parents are exempt from liability. Advertising surrogacy services is punishable with a similar maximum fine.

surveillance *n.* Keeping watch on a suspect. The Police Act 1997 and the Regulation of Investigatory Powers Act 2000 provide a formal system for authorization of intrusive surveillance operations by chief police officers. A team of independent commissioners oversees the arrangements and investigates complaints. Police and customs officials are also required to seek prior approval from a commissioner for authorizations in particularly sensitive cases – such as those involving legal *privilege, for example – except in cases of emergency. *See also* ELECTRONIC SURVEILLANCE.

survival of cause of action on death At common law all causes of action in personal actions (i.e. contract and tort) died with the person in whom they were vested (*actio personalis moritur cum persona*). By statute, however, all such causes of actions, except for defamation and claims for certain types of loss, survive against or for the benefit of the deceased. *See also* FATAL ACCIDENTS.

survivorship *n. See* COMMORIENTES; RIGHT OF SURVIVORSHIP.

survivorship clause A provision in a will such that a gift to a person is conditional upon that person surviving the deceased by a specified time period. For example, a legacy in a will of "£10,000 to my son James if he survives me by 30 days". Such a clause avoids the *commorientes rule. For inheritance tax reasons survivorship clauses should not exceed six months (Inheritance Tax Act 1984 s 92).

sus law The law that formerly empowered the police to arrest any reputed thief or suspected person found loitering with intent to commit an arrestable offence. This law caused much public concern and was abolished by the Criminal Attempts Act 1981. *See* INTERFERING WITH VEHICLES.

suspended sentence A sentence of imprisonment that does not take effect immediately. Under the Criminal Justice Act 2003, a court that passes a suspended sentence may order the offender to comply with one or more of a number of specified requirements, including an *unpaid work requirement, an *activity requirement, a *programme requirement, a *prohibited activity requirement, a *curfew requirement, an *exclusion requirement, a *residence requirement, a *mental health treatment requirement, a *drug treatment requirement, an *alcohol treatment requirement, a *supervision requirement, and (in the case of an offender aged under 25) an *attendance centre requirement. If during the specified period the offender fails to comply with a requirement imposed by the court, or commits a further offence, the court may order that the original sentence is to take effect. *See also* COMMUNITY ORDER.

symbolic delivery *See* DELIVERY.

synallagmatic contract *See* BILATERAL CONTRACT.

synod *n.* A deliberative assembly of the clergy. *See* CHURCH OF ENGLAND.

Table A Model *articles of association that apply to companies limited by shares unless other articles excluding or modifying them are delivered to the Companies Registry when the company is registered. The company is subject to the Table A in force at the time it was registered. **Tables B**, **C**, **D**, **E**, and **F** specify forms of *memorandum of association and *articles of association to be adopted by particular types of company.

tacking *n.* The situation in which a mortgagee makes a second advance to the mortgagor and attaches his second advance to the first one, so that it has priority over the claims of any intervening mortgagee. Since 1926 this can occur only with consent of the subsequent mortgagee, or where the first mortgagee has no notice of the subsequent mortgagee, or under an obligation imposed by the mortgage. Charges on registered land are excluded from these rules, but similar rules are provided by section 49 of the Land Registration Act 2002.

tail *n.* An *entailed interest.

tail general An *entailed interest under which the class of descendants who can succeed to the land is not limited to the issue of a specified spouse of the first tenant in tail. *Compare* TAIL SPECIAL.

tail male An *entailed interest under which only male descendants of the original tenant in tail can succeed to the land. If the male line dies out, the land goes to the person next entitled in *remainder or in *reversion. The interest may be general or special: *see* TAIL GENERAL; TAIL SPECIAL.

tail special An *entailed interest under which only the descendants of the first tenant in tail and a specified spouse can succeed to the land; for example, when land is settled on "John and the heirs of his body begotten on Mary". *Compare* TAIL GENERAL.

tainted acquittal In criminal proceedings, an acquittal affected by interference with a witness or a juror (Glossary to the Criminal Procedure Rules).

takeover *n.* The acquisition of control by one company over another, usually smaller, company (the **target company**). This is usually achieved (1) by buying shares in the target company with the agreement of all its members (if they are few) or of only its *controllers; (2) by purchases on the *Stock Exchange; or (3) by means of a *takeover bid. *Compare* MERGER. *See also* CITY CODE ON TAKEOVERS AND MERGERS; CONCERT PARTY; DAWN RAID.

takeover bid A technique for effecting a *takeover or a *merger. The bidder makes an offer to the members of the target company to acquire their shares (either for cash or in exchange for shares in the bidding company) in the hope of receiving sufficient acceptances to obtain voting control of the target company. Unless there is a *scheme of arrangement – and providing that the court does not order otherwise – if members holding not less than 90% in value of the shares involved in the bid accept the offer, the bidding company can compulsorily acquire the shares of the remaining members (Companies Act 2006 s 979).

taking at sea A risk commonly covered in policies of marine insurance, which includes seizure or capture of a vessel by enemies or pirates.

taking without consent *See* CONVEYANCE.

talaq *n.* An Islamic divorce, usually effected by a triple declaration ("I divorce you") by the husband to the wife in front of witnesses. In some Moslem countries this may be done informally; in other countries it must be pronounced before an authorized officer of the court. It may also be effected by a written **talaqnama**. *See also* EXTRAJUDICIAL DIVORCE.

tales de circumstantibus [Latin: such of the bystanders] If a sufficient number of jurors do not appear upon trial, either party may **pray a tales**, that is, require a supply of such persons from the environs of the court in order to make up the deficiency (Juries Act 1974 s 6, 11).

tangible property *Property that has a physical existence, e.g. chattels and land but not *choses in action nor incorporeal *hereditaments (which are **intangible property**).

tax *n.* A compulsory contribution to the state's funds. It is levied either directly on the taxpayer by means of *income tax, *capital gains tax, *inheritance tax, and *corporation tax; or indirectly through tax on purchases of goods and services (*see* VALUE-ADDED TAX) and through various kinds of duty, e.g. *road tax, *stamp duty, and duties on betting and gaming.

The characteristics necessary for a charge to be correctly termed a tax were considered by the Court of Appeal and by the House of Lords in *Aston Cantlow Parochial Church Council v Wallbank* [2001] EWCA Civ 713; [2003] UKHL 37, [2004] 1 AC 546. In that case, the Court of Appeal ruled that a charge made by the Church Council for the cost of church repairs is a tax and is rendered invalid by the European Convention on Human Rights, which forbids capricious taxation. However, the House of Lords declared that the charge imposed by the Church Council is not a tax, as a Parochial Church Council is not a public body.

taxable person *See* VALUE-ADDED TAX.

taxable supply *See* VALUE-ADDED TAX.

tax advantage In many specifically directed *anti-avoidance provisions, as in the *General Anti-Abuse Rule enacted in 2013, the ability of the Revenue to impose an additional tax charge requires a "tax advantage" to be identified. A tax advantage is defined in statute as either: (a) a relief or increased relief from, or a repayment or increased repayment, of tax; or (b) the avoidance or reduction of an assessment to tax, whether effected by receipts accruing in such a way that the recipient does not pay or bear tax on them or by a deduction in computing profits or gains. This definition has been given a wide meaning by the courts (*Cleary v IRC* [1967] 2 All ER 48; *Emery v IRC* [1981] STC 150; *Bird v IRC* [1988] STC 312). The House of Lords has held that the quantum of the tax advantage is to be calculated by contrasting the non-taxable receipt with a similar receipt that had accrued in a taxable manner.

taxation of costs *See* ASSESSMENT OF COSTS.

tax avoidance The lawful arrangement or planning of one's affairs so as to reduce liability to tax. If a person marries in order to reduce his tax burden he is practising tax avoidance: if he tells the Revenue that he is married when he is not, he is guilty of *tax evasion. As Denis Healey once said: "The difference between tax avoidance and tax evasion is the thickness of a prison wall".

In other respects, however, the concept of tax avoidance is not so easily identified. According to Lord Nolan: "The hallmark of tax avoidance is that the taxpayer reduces his liability to tax without incurring the economic consequences that Parliament intended to be suffered by any taxpayer qualifying for such reduction in his tax liability" (*IRC v Willoughby* [1997] 1 WLR 1071 (HL)). By contrast, Lord Hoffmann has suggested that the closer one tries to look at the concept of tax avoidance the more one finds that it is not a concept at all: "Tax avoidance schemes either work or they do not . . . It is not that the statute has a penumbral spirit which strikes down devices or stratagems designed to avoid its terms or exploit its loopholes" (*Norglen Ltd v Reeds Rains Prudential Ltd* [1999] 2 AC 1, 13–14 (HL)).

The phrase "tax avoidance" has crept into statute. The Finance Act 2004 Part VII is entitled "Disclosure of Tax Avoidance Schemes". However, in the 14 sections in that part of the Act the phrase "tax avoidance scheme" is never used; instead, reference is consistently made to "notifiable arrangements". Statutory use of the term "tax advantage" is, by contrast, frequent. *See also* ANTI-AVOIDANCE PROVISIONS; GENERAL ANTI-AVOIDANCE RULE; RAMSAY PRINCIPLE.

tax credit A social security payment that is administered by HM Revenue and Customs rather than by the Department for Work and Pensions. **Child tax credit** is a means-tested social security benefit for all those, whether in or out of work, who have responsibility for children. **Working tax credit** is available to low-paid workers and is usually payable by employers through the pay packet; it may also be available to those who have a disability that puts them at a disadvantage in getting a job.

Tax credits represent the first attempts to integrate the tax and benefit system. The measure of income for tax-credit purposes is based on income tax rules and credits are given based on the income tax year. Unlike income tax, however, the income measured is the joint income of a couple with responsibility for a child for whom the claim is made. For this purpose, the income of an unmarried couple is aggregated in the same way as the income of a married couple. Under the Welfare Reform Act 2012, tax credits are due to be replaced by *universal credit.

tax evasion Any illegal action taken to avoid the lawful assessment of taxes; for example, by concealing or failing to declare income. *Compare* TAX AVOIDANCE.

taxing master *See* COSTS OFFICER.

taxing statute An Act of Parliament that imposes tax. Where there is any dispute about the application of a taxing statute, the onus of proof lies with the person who is seeking to apply it. Thus, where there is a dispute as to the levying of a tax, it is the Revenue authority that has the onus of proving the charge applied to the transaction. Where a relief is claimed, the taxpayer has the onus of proving that the statutory provision provides the relief in the circumstances in which it is being claimed.

tax point The date on which a taxable supply becomes liable for *value-added tax. The rate of tax chargeable on the supply is the rate in force at the tax point, and the supply must be accounted for in the tax period in which the tax point occurs. If the supply is a straightforward sale of goods, the tax point is normally the date on which the customer takes possession of the goods. For the supply of services, the tax point is normally the date on which the service is completed. In the case of hirings, rentals, continuous or metered supplies (e.g. electricity), and supplies that are subject to progress payments, the tax point is either the date on which an invoice is issued or the date on which payment is received, whichever is earlier. If the supplier issues a tax invoice, this must show the tax point.

tax year (fiscal year) The year of assessment for *income tax and *capital gains tax purposes, running from 6 April to 5 April in the following year. This is by contrast with the *financial year, which runs from 1 April to 31 March. Prior to 1752, the tax year began on Lady Day, which is 25 March, being one of the four days in the year on which rent was traditionally paid. In 1752, Great Britain moved to the Gregorian calendar and eleven days were "lost" in the move. In order to avoid advancing the date of payment of tax, the tax year was extended to 5 April and has remained at that date ever since. Income tax (and capital gains tax) is imposed for a single year. If the Finance Act is not passed by Parliament, there is no taxation for that year. Each Finance Act, thus, imposes a charge to tax for a specified tax year.

Technology and Construction Court *See* OFFICIAL REFEREE.

technology transfer The licensing of *intellectual property. EU regulation 772/2004 provides *block exemption from *Article 101 (EU competition law) for certain categories of patent, software copyright, and *knowhow licence (and also for trade mark, design, copyright, and other intellectual property licences that are ancillary to such a licence). The regulation, which is due to be updated in 2014, sets out those restrictions that are void and anti-competitive and must be avoided in such licences, known as the "hard core list". It was issued in 2004 with accompanying intellectual property guidelines.

telephone tapping Secretly listening to telephone conversations by interfering with the line. It is illegal except when authorized by the Home Secretary under the Regulation of Investigatory Powers Act 2000. In England telecommunications interception evidence is normally inadmissible at trial. In 2009 the government dropped plans to allow such evidence to be used in court. Foreign interception evidence may be admissible at trial, as may evidence of intercepted telephone calls made from a prison. *See also* ELECTRONIC SURVEILLANCE.

teleworking *n.* A form of employment in which employees use information technology to enable them to work mainly from home. The advantages to the employer are the elimination of transport problems, reduction in office overheads, and increased flexibility. Teleworkers are distinguished from **outworkers** or **home workers** in that the former are engaged in white-collar work, as opposed to the manual tasks often performed by poorly paid outworkers.

temporary employee An *employee who is employed for a specified period or for a specific task. Under the Fixed-term Employees (Prevention of Less Favourable Treatment) Regulations 2002, they are entitled to be treated no less favourably than permanent employees if they are doing the same or similar work. It is open to the employer to justify less favourable treatment if he can show a good reason. Note that the Regulations, unlike those applying to *part-time workers, extend only to employees and not to *workers.

tenancy *n.* Broadly, the interest of one who holds land by any right or title. The term is often used in a more restricted sense, as a synonym for *lease.
    The broader use of the term falls into two categories: *joint tenancy and *tenancy in common. *See also* TENANT FOR LIFE.

tenancy at sufferance A tenancy that arises when a tenant is *holding over and the landlord has not indicated whether or not he agrees to the tenant's continued occupation. If the landlord gives his express agreement, the tenancy becomes a *tenancy at will: if the landlord accepts periodic payments by way of rent, the tenancy becomes a *periodic tenancy.

tenancy at will A tenancy that can be terminated by the landlord or the tenant at any time. A tenancy at will usually arises by implication, when the owner of land allows a person to occupy it although he has no *fixed term, *periodic tenancy, or *licence (for example, when a landlord agrees to the tenant *holding over). More rarely, a tenancy at will may be created by express agreement, as, for example, when a landlord permits the tenant to occupy premises before the formal grant of a lease or the transfer of the freehold. If the landlord starts to accept rent on a periodic basis, an ordinary *periodic tenancy is created. A tenant who holds over after a fixed-term *assured tenancy expires may have a *statutory periodic tenancy. A tenancy at will of business premises does not have the statutory protection given to a *business tenancy. In the case of residential premises, however, the usual statutory protection from *eviction will apply. A tenancy at will can be terminated by the landlord demanding possession or if either he or the tenant dies or parts with his interest in the land.

tenancy by estoppel A lease that exists despite the fact that the person who granted it had no legal right to do so (because, for instance, the landlord holds no estate in the land). Such a tenancy is binding on the landlord and tenant but not on anyone else (although see *Bruton v London & Quadrant Housing Trust* [2000] 1 AC 406 (HL)). If the landlord subsequently acquires an estate, the estoppel is "fed" and the lease becomes a full legal lease (*EH Lewis & Son Ltd v Morelli* [1948] 2 All ER 1021; *Macley v Nutting* [1949] 2 KB 55).

Tenancy Deposit Scheme Any deposit paid by the tenant of an *assured shorthold tenancy commencing after 6 April 2007 must be protected by the landlord depositing the amount or insuring it with one of four recognized Tenancy Deposit Schemes. Failure to do so can result in the landlord being fined. In the event of any disagreement as to the amount of deposit to be returned, the dispute may be resolved by the Scheme (Housing Act 2004).

tenancy for years A tenancy for a *fixed term.

tenancy from year to year A yearly *periodic tenancy.

tenancy in common Equitable ownership of land by two or more persons in equal or unequal *undivided shares. Each co-owner may sell or dispose of his share by will, and a share does not pass automatically by the right of survivorship on the death of a co-owner but forms part of his estate (*compare* JOINT TENANCY). Under the Law of Property Act 1925 the legal estate is held by the co-owners as joint tenants on trust for themselves as equitable tenants in common, and a *trust of land is implied.

tenant *n.* A legal person who is granted a *lease or a *tenancy. A tenant need not be an individual; for example, a company can be a tenant.

tenantable repair The maintenance of a property in a condition fit for letting to a tenant. The phrase is sometimes used in a *covenant to repair. The use of the word "tenantable" has no significant effect on the parties' usual obligations under the covenant.

tenant for life (life tenant) A person owning land for an equitable interest that subsists for the whole of his life but terminates on his death (*see also* LIFE INTEREST). The statutory powers of a tenant for life are laid down by the Settled Land Act 1925 (*see* SETTLED LAND). *See also* TRUST OF LAND.

tenant in tail A person entitled in possession or on the death of his ancestor to an *entailed interest.

tenant *pur autre vie* See ESTATE PUR (OR PER) AUTRE VIE.

Tenant Services Authority A body established under the Housing and Regeneration Act 2008 to administer the regulatory framework established by that Act. This gives local authority tenants more say in how their homes are managed, changes the way housing services are provided (including creating a level playing field for members of the armed forces applying for local authority housing), and reforms the Right to Buy Scheme. In 2011 its functions were transferred to the *Homes and Communities Agency (HCA) and to a new Housing Ombudsman Service.

tenant's fixtures Fixtures attached to rented property by a tenant that the tenant is entitled to remove at the end of the tenancy. These are: *trade fixtures, ornamental and domestic fixtures (such as blinds and mirrors) whose removal does no serious damage, and (subject to certain statutory rules) agricultural fixtures. Tenants are not entitled to remove any other fixtures.

tender *n.* **1.** An offer to supply (or to purchase) goods or services. Normally a tender must be accepted to create a contract, except when the invitation to tender states unequivocally that the lowest (or highest) tender will be accepted. If the tender is to supply goods as required by the other party, it may be a standing offer and creates contracts as and when particular orders are placed. Whether or not the tenderer can withdraw from supplying future orders depends upon the terms of the tender, in particular whether the tenderer binds himself (for consideration) to execute all orders. **2.** An offer of performance, acceptance of which requires the concurrence of the other party, e.g. the tender of the price of goods by a buyer to a seller.

tender before claim A defence to a civil claim that, before the claimant started proceedings, the defendant unconditionally offered to the claimant the amount due or, if no specified amount is claimed, an amount sufficient to satisfy the claim.

tender offer An offer of a company's securities to the public (*see* FLOTATION) at a uniform price (above a specified minimum) that is determined by the bids received and ensures that all the securities are taken up.

tenure *n.* Under the *feudal system, the relationship between lord and tenant, which determined the conditions under which the land was held. Today the term is used to indicate the nature of a legal estate in land, i.e. freehold or leasehold. The only tenurial relationship of practical significance in modern law is that of landlord and tenant (or leasehold). *See also* SECURITY OF TENURE.

term *n.* **1.** Originally, any of four periods of the year during which judicial business had to be transacted. For this purpose terms were abolished by the Judicature Acts 1873–75, and the legal year is now divided into *sittings and *vacations. In the *Inns of Court the year is still divided into terms that have the same names as the court sittings but are shorter. A student **keeps term** as part of the qualification for call to the Bar by dining in his Inn on a specified number of occasions during the term. **2.** Any provision forming part of a contract. A term may be either a *condition, a warranty, or an *innominate term, depending on its importance, and either an *express term or an *implied term, depending on its form. **3.** The duration of a leasehold interest in land. *See* TERM OF YEARS.

term for years *See* TERM OF YEARS.

term of years (term for years) An interest in land that subsists for or by reference to some specified period of time. It includes interests subsisting for less than a year (e.g. a lease for six months) and periodic tenancies (e.g. a weekly, monthly, or yearly tenancy determinable by notice to quit). It can also include time-share agreements, e.g. of one specified week in each of a number of years. The commencement date and maximum duration of the term must be identifiable before the lease takes effect. *See also* TERM OF YEARS ABSOLUTE.

term of years absolute A leasehold estate in land: a *term of years that may or may not be brought to an end by notice, forfeiture, or any other event except the death of any person. Thus a lease "to X for 25 years if Y shall so long live" is not a valid term of years absolute. Under the Law of Property Act 1925 a term of years absolute can exist as a *legal estate provided it is created in the required manner, i.e. by deed in the case of a term of three years or more. Note that some legal leases may not create a term of years (*Bruton v London and Quadrant Housing Trust* [2000] 1 AC 406 (HL)). *See* CONTRACTUAL TENANCY.

terra nullius *See* DISCOVERY.

territoriality *n.* (in international law) The principle that states should not exercise their jurisdiction outside the area of their territory. They are entitled, however, to exercise jurisdiction within their territory over acts committed by their citizens outside their territory, and all states have jurisdiction over *offences against international law and order. The territory of a state for purposes of jurisdiction includes its ships and aeroplanes. A state may exercise jurisdiction over crimes that are either originated within its territory but completed outside or originated outside its territory and completed inside.

territorial limits The geographical limits within which an Act of Parliament operates, which include, in the UK, the territorial sea up to the 12-mile limit. The limits are restricted by international law (*see* SOVEREIGNTY OF PARLIAMENT).

territorial waters The band of sea between the limit of the *internal waters of a state (*see* BASELINE) and the *high seas, over which the state has certain specified rights. These rights are governed by a 1958 Geneva Convention, which is taken to represent the position under customary international law. New rules were proposed in a 1982 United Nations Convention on the Law of the Sea (*see* LAW OF THE SEA). A coastal state exercises sovereignty over its territorial waters, which includes, in particular, the following:

(1) An exclusive right to fish and to exploit the resources of the seabed and subsoil of the seabed and exclusive use of the airspace above the territorial sea.

(2) The exclusive right to use the territorial waters to transport people and goods from one part of the state to another.

(3) The right to enact laws concerning navigation, immigration, customs dues, and health, which bind all foreign ships.

(4) The right to ask a warship that ignores navigation regulations to leave the territorial waters.

(5) Certain powers of arrest over merchant ships and people on board and jurisdiction to try crimes committed on board such ships within the territorial waters.

(6) The right to exclude fighting in the territorial waters during a war in which the coastal state is neutral. All foreign ships, however, have a right of **innocent passage** through the territorial sea, i.e. the right to pass through, provided they do not prejudice the peace, security, or good order of the coastal state (submarines must navigate on the surface). *See also* HOT PURSUIT, RIGHT OF.

The extent of the territorial sea is usually measured from the low-tide mark on the shore, but in estuaries and small bays it is measured from a **closing line** between two points on the shore, which delimits the state's internal waters. The width of the territorial sea is a matter of dispute in international law. Traditionally it has been fixed at 3 nautical miles (*see* CANNON-SHOT RULE), but many states have claimed 12 miles or more, and this will probably become the normal width. The Territorial Sea Act 1987 fixes the territorial waters of the UK at 12 nautical miles. Beyond the territorial sea, states have a **contiguous zone**, not exceeding 24 nautical miles, in which they may exercise jurisdiction over certain infringements of their customs, fiscal, immigration, or sanitary regulations. In recent years many states (including the UK) have also claimed **exclusive fishery zones** extending 200 miles beyond the low-tide mark. The UK is subject to the EU's *Common Fisheries Policy in relation to fishing. *See also* EXCLUSIVE ECONOMIC ZONE.

terrorism *n.* The use or threat of violence for political, religious, or ideological ends. The Terrorism Act 2000 abolished all the previous statutory provisions relating to terrorism, apart from a number of specific provisions that continue to exist under the Northern Ireland (Emergency Provisions) Act 1996, the Terrorism (Temporary Provisions) Act 1989, and the Criminal Justice (Terrorism and Conspiracy) Act 1998. The Terrorism Act 2000 defines terrorism in section 1 as:

- the use or threat of action that involves serious violence against a person or serious damage to property, endangers a person's life, creates a serious risk to the health or safety of the public or a section of the public, or is designed to interfere with or disrupt an electronic system; or
- the use or threat of violence designed to influence the government or intimidate the public or a section of the public

where the use or threat of such action or violence is made for the purpose of advancing a political, religious, or ideological cause. The Act also provides that the action referred to may include action taken or threatened outside the UK.

The 2000 Act contains provisions that allow for certain organizations to be declared as **proscribed organizations**. It then becomes an offence to be a member of such an organization. The Act also contains detailed provisions as to property defined as being "terrorist property" and the forfeiture of such property. There are detailed provisions relating to the investigation of terrorist activities that grant the police and security services special and extra powers. These include special powers to stop and search, detain, and interrogate those suspected of involvement in terrorist activities.

Like previous legislation relating to terrorism, the 2000 Act was intended primarily to deal with the situation in Northern Ireland. However, since the terrorist attacks on the United States on 11 September 2001 the focus has shifted to the threat of international terrorism. Accordingly, the Antiterrorism, Crime and Security Act 2001 included measures designed to cut off the funding of international terror groups, to ensure the security of the UK's aviation and nuclear power industries, and to restrict access to dangerous substances that could be used in terrorist attacks. More controversially, Part 4 of the Act gave the Secretary of State powers to detain certain classes of foreign nationals for an indefinite period without charge or trial on the basis that they were suspected of involvement in terrorism. This provision required a *derogation from the European Convention of Human Rights and was declared unlawful by the House of

Lords in December 2004 (*A v Secretary of State for the Home Department* (2004) UKHL 56, [2005] 2 AC 68). The Prevention of Terrorism Act 2005 repealed these so-called Part 4 powers and replaced them with a system of **Control Orders**, under which the Secretary of State could impose an order placing various restrictions on the movements or activities of named individuals (whether they were UK nationals or not). Although a control order was automatically subject to judicial review, there was no obligation to disclose the evidence on which it was based either to the person made subject to the order or to his legal counsel of choice. In June 2006 the High Court quashed six of the control orders then in force, as being contrary to the Human Rights Act. Although this decision was reversed by the House of Lords, the Law Lords upheld a similar appeal in June 2009. From January 2012 control orders were replaced by **Terrorism Prevention and Investigation Measures** (**TPIMs**), a change that removed some of the more extreme restrictions that could be imposed under the previous regime (e.g. a total ban on mobile phone use) but retained the use of secret evidence. TPIMs expire automatically after two years but can be renewed if the Secretary of State believes that new evidence has emerged.

The Terrorism Act 2006 was passed in the wake of the London bombings of 7 July 2005. It gives police the power to hold terrorist suspects for up to 28 days without charge and creates a range of new offences including the encouragement or "glorification" of terrorism, training for terrorism, and the dissemination of terrorist literature. The Counter-Terrorism Act 2008 created a further offence of publishing certain classes of information "likely to be useful" to terrorists.

testament *n.* A *will. Strictly speaking, a testament is a will dealing only with the testator's personal property, not his land. This is not a distinction of current practical importance, in that a modern will deals with both personal and real property.

testamentary capacity The ability to make a legally valid will. Persons under 18 years (apart from members of the armed forces on active service – *see* PRIVILEGED WILL) and mental patients do not have testamentary capacity. The testator must, at the time he makes his will, understand the nature of the document, the property of which he is disposing, the persons who have a natural claim to provision from his estate, and the manner in which he provides for his estate to be distributed. *See also* UNDUE INFLUENCE.

testamentary expenses Costs incurred by a deceased's personal representatives in administering his estate.

testamentary freedom *See* FREEDOM OF TESTATION; FORCED HEIRSHIP.

testamentary guardian A person appointed by will to be the *guardian of a child under 18 (Children Act 1989 s 5).

testamentary intention The principle that a person's will must reflect his true wishes. Thus a will executed as a result of coercion, fraud, or undue influence will be set aside by the court.

testamentary trust A trust contained in a will.

testate *adj.* Having left, at one's death, a legally valid will.

testator *n.* A person who makes a will.

testatum *n. See* DEED.

test case In civil proceedings, a case brought to test a principle of law that, once established, can be applied in other cases. When there are a number of claimants with similar claims, a test case may be brought by one of them, after which the remainder of the claims may be settled out of court on the same basis. *Compare* REPRESENTATIVE CLAIM.

testimonium *n. See* DEED.

testimony (testimonial evidence) *n.* The evidence of a witness in court, usually on oath, offered as evidence of the truth of what is stated.

textbooks *pl. n.* Textbooks may be cited in court to assist in the interpretation of the law. They have no authority as a source of law but merely provide an expert opinion as to the current state of the law. There was formerly a convention that only the works of dead authors could be cited, but modern practice also allows citation of living authors. The **Books of Authority**, i.e. the works of Glanvil, Bracton, Littleton, Coke, and Blackstone, are treated as having the same authority as cases of the same period.

TFEU *See* TREATY ON THE FUNCTIONING OF THE EUROPEAN UNION.

thalweg, rule of the [from German: literally, valley line] The rule for determining the *boundary line between two states that are separated by a navigable river containing a newly formed island. According to this rule, the boundary line moves with the centre of the navigable channel, i.e. it is delineated as being the centre of the course with the strongest current, so that the newly formed island must lie on one side of it or the other. In the case of *Iowa v Illinois* 147 US 7 (1893) the expression "middle of the Mississippi River" was interpreted as the "middle of the main channel" or "thread of the stream". On non-navigable rivers, however, the middle line of the river will mark the boundary between the two states between which it flows. Thus, a newly formed island might well fall partly on one side of the boundary line and partly on the other. *See also* ACCRETION; AVULSION.

theft *n.* The dishonest appropriation of property belonging to another with the intention of permanently depriving the other of it (*see* DISHONESTY). "Appropriation" is defined in the Theft Act 1968 as the assumption of the rights of the owner of the property and includes any act showing that one is treating the property as one's own, which need not necessarily involve taking it away. For example, switching price tags from one item to another in a shop to enable one to buy goods at a lower price could amount to an appropriation (*R v Morris* [1984] AC 320 (HL)), as could purporting to sell someone else's property (*R v Pitham and Hehl* (1976) 65 Cr App R 45). If a person acquires property without stealing it, but later decides to keep the property unlawfully, he may be regarded as having appropriated it (*AG's Reference (No 1 of 1983)* [1985] QB 182). For example, if A lends his golf clubs to B for a week and B subsequently decides to keep the clubs or sell them, this indicates that B has assumed the rights of the owner unlawfully. "Property" includes all tangible and intangible objects and choses in action (e.g. bank balances) but there are special rules in the Theft Act 1968 governing land and wild plants and animals (*see* POACHING). Property belongs to anyone who either owns it or has physical possession or control of it. The Act expressly states that a person is not dishonest if he believes (even if unreasonably) that he is legally entitled to appropriate the property or that the owner would consent or could not be discovered by taking reasonable steps. The punishment for theft is up to ten years' imprisonment.

Under the Theft Act 1978, obtaining goods or services without paying for them is now covered by the offence of *making off without payment (*see also* SHOPLIFTING). Cases in which property is obtained by deception are usually dealt with as *deception or *fraud offences. Theft involving the use of force may amount to *robbery. *See also* BURGLARY; CONVEYANCE.

therapeutic privilege The right of a doctor to withhold information from a patient when it is feared that disclosure could cause immediate and serious harm to the patient (e.g. because he or she is suffering from severe depression). In exceptional cases, the need to withhold information may be considered to override the requirement to obtain *informed consent before proceeding with treatment. In such a case therapeutic privilege could be used as a legal defence against the charge of *battery or *negligence.

thin capitalization An arrangement in which a company is incorporated (typically in another jurisdiction) with a small share capital and financed by a large loan from its parent company. The arrangement is often designed to give tax relief on the interest payment on the loan, whereas no relief would be available on dividends paid on shares. In the UK a special tax regime is applied in certain instances of thin capitalization, so that excessive interest paid on the loan is treated as if it were a non-tax-deductible dividend (Taxation (International and Other Provisions) Act 2010 s 152).

thing *n.* *See* CHOSE.

Third Party Debt Order Under Part 72 of the *Civil Procedure Rules, the procedure by which a judgment creditor may obtain a court order against a third party who owes money to, or holds money on behalf of, the judgment debtor. The order requires the third party to pay the money (or part of it) to the judgment creditor. *See* GARNISHEE PROCEEDINGS.

third-party insurance Insurance against risks to people other than those that are parties to the policy. It is illegal to use, or allow anyone else to use, a motor vehicle on a road unless there is a valid insurance policy covering death, physical injury, or damage caused by the use of the vehicle in Great Britain. It also covers any liability resulting from the use of a vehicle (or a trailer) that is compulsorily insurable in EU countries. The policy is only considered valid when a certificate of insurance has been issued.

There is a duty upon anyone driving a motor vehicle to give his name and address and that of the car owner and to produce the certificate of insurance whenever asked to do so by a police officer. He may, however, produce it within five days at any police station he specifies at the time he was asked to produce it. There is also a duty to give details of one's insurance to any person making a claim against it or to any chief police officer who is checking whether the legal requirements of insurance are complied with. Breach of any of these duties is punishable by fine. *See also* DRIVING WITHOUT INSURANCE.

third-party proceedings Proceedings brought by a defendant to a civil action against a person not already a party to the action. Such proceedings are now made under Part 20 of the *Civil Procedure Rules and known as *Part 20 claims.

threat *n.* The expression of an intention to harm someone with the object of forcing them to do something. A threat (or **menace**), or the action of threatening someone (*see* INTIMIDATION), is an ingredient of many crimes. *See* BLACKMAIL; BOMB HOAX; CRIMINAL DAMAGE; DURESS; FORCIBLE ENTRY; INTIMIDATION; RACIAL HATRED; RAPE; SENDING DISTRESSING LETTERS; THREATENING BEHAVIOUR; VIOLENT DISORDER.

threatening behaviour It is an offence, punishable with up to six months' imprisonment and/or a fine, to use towards another person threatening, abusive, or insulting words or behaviour. It is a similar offence to distribute or display anything that is threatening, abusive, or insulting. In both cases it must be proved either that the accused person had the specific intent (*see* INTOXICATION) to cause the other person to believe that immediate unlawful violence would be used against him or, simply, that the threatened person was likely to believe that violence would be used against him. A constable may *arrest without warrant anyone he reasonably suspects is committing either of these offences.

It is also an offence, punishable with a fine, to use threatening or disorderly behaviour, or to display anything that is threatening, abusive, or insulting, within the hearing or sight of anyone likely to be harassed, alarmed, or distressed by it. Here, it is a defence if the accused person proves (*see* BURDEN OF PROOF) either that he had no reason to believe that there was anyone within hearing or sight who was likely to be harassed, alarmed, or distressed, or that he was inside a dwelling (any living accommodation, including a hotel bedroom) and had no reason to believe that the behaviour or display would be heard or seen by someone outside, or that his conduct was reasonable. A constable may *arrest without warrant anyone he reasonably suspects of committing this offence if, after warning him to stop, the person repeats the offence.

All these offences were introduced by the Public Order Act 1986 to replace similar offences; they may be committed in private as well as public places unless the behaviour or display took place inside a dwelling. A further offence of intentionally causing harassment (primarily aimed at racial harassment) was introduced by the Criminal Justice and Public Order Act 1994; it is punishable by a fine and/or six months' imprisonment. *See also* RACIAL HATRED; RACIST ABUSE; STALKING; VIOLENT DISORDER.

three certainties *See* TRUST.

three-tier system A system for allocating cases between *Crown Court centres. First-tier centres deal with both criminal and High Court civil cases and are served by High Court *puisne judges, *circuit judges, and *recorders. Second-tier centres deal only with criminal cases, but are served by the same kinds of judge as first-tier centres. Third-tier centres deal only with criminal cases and are served by circuit judges and recorders only.

threshold criteria The minimum preconditions that must be met before the court is able to make a care or supervision order. These are set out in the Children Act 1989 and are that the child is suffering or likely to suffer significant harm either caused by the care or lack of care given to it by its parents or because the child is beyond parental control. *See also* CARE ORDER; SUPERVISION ORDER.

tidal waters Under the Merchant Shipping Act 1995, any part of the sea and of a river within the ebb and flow of the tide at ordinary spring tides, excluding harbours.

tied cottage A dwelling provided for the tenant of a *service tenancy, usually in relation to agricultural workers' accommodation. *See also* AGRICULTURAL DWELLING-HOUSE ADVISORY COMMITTEE; ASSURED AGRICULTURAL OCCUPANCY.

time charter *See* CHARTERPARTY.

time immemorial *See* LEGAL MEMORY.

time policy A marine insurance policy that covers a ship against risks arising in the course of any voyage during a specified period. It differs from a **voyage policy**, covering risks arising in a specified voyage of any duration. A policy may, however, be **mixed**, i.e. restricted in cover as to both time and voyage. *See also* DEVIATION.

time provisions in contracts Provisions in contracts that relate to the time within which acts are to be performed. The question often arises whether or not a time provision constitutes a *condition of the contract. If it does, it is said that time is **of the essence**.

In general, time is of the essence only if the contract says so or if an intention that it should be so is to be inferred from the nature of the transaction or the circumstances surrounding it (for example "ready to load" clauses in shipping contracts: *Bunge Corporation v Tradax Export SA* [1981] 1 WLR 711 (HL)). Most suppliers' contracts, however, include an express term that time is not of the essence.

timeshare lease *See* DISCONTINUOUS LEASE.

title *n.* **1.** A person's right of *ownership of property. Someone with a **good title** has adequate evidence to establish his right. *See* ABSOLUTE TITLE; QUALIFIED TITLE; TITLE DEEDS. **2.** The heading of an *Act of Parliament, which may be a **long title** or a **short title**. **3.** The name of a particular court action, which is derived from the heading of the originating *process that initiated it.

title deeds Documents that prove a person's ownership of land and the terms on which he owns it. In the case of unregistered land they consist of all *conveyances, *mortgages, and other documents tracing ownership of the land back to a good *root of title at least 15 years old. There are no title deeds to registered land, but the purchaser can search the register of title and obtain an *official copy.

Tobar doctrine The doctrine that *recognition of a government should only be granted if that administration came to power by legitimate democratic means. Named after its creator, the Ecuadorian Minister of Foreign Relations, it was first adopted by five Central American states in 1907 and embodied in a treaty. After later US approval, the doctrine became known as the **Wilsonian policy**. Although it had the laudable aim of trying to maintain stability in a notoriously unstable part of the world, the doctrine has been applied inconsistently; since the end of World War II, the USA and many other states have favoured the more pragmatic *Estrada doctrine.

TOLATA (TLATA) Acronym for the Trusts of Land and Appointment of Trustees Act 1996. *See* TRUST OF LAND.

Tomlin order In civil proceedings, a form of order used to give effect to a compromise of litigation in the High Court. It is based on a *Practice Direction issued by Mr Justice Tomlin in 1927. The order is made by consent of the parties and states that on terms agreed between them (which are scheduled to the order) all further proceedings are to be stayed except for the purpose of putting the agreed terms into effect. Relevant rules of procedure are found in Part 40 of the *Civil Procedure Rules.

tonnage tax A means of calculating the charge to *corporation tax for a shipowning company. When a company elects to pay tonnage tax, it is subject to corporation tax by reference to the tonnage of its shipping, irrespective of the profit or loss made (Finance Act 2000 sch 22).

tools of trade A workman's tools, which he is entitled to keep if he is made bankrupt. They include all tools, books, vehicles, and other items of equipment necessary for the bankrupt's personal use in his employment, business, or vocation.

tort *n.* [Old French: harm, wrong; from Latin *tortus*, twisted or crooked] A wrongful act or omission for which *damages can be obtained in a civil court by the person wronged, other than a wrong that is only a *breach of contract. The law of tort is mainly concerned with providing compensation for personal injury and property damage caused by *negligence. It also protects other interests, however, such as reputation (*see* DEFAMATION), personal freedom (*see* ASSAULT; FALSE IMPRISONMENT), title to property (*see* CONVERSION; TRESPASS), enjoyment of property (*see* NUISANCE), and commercial interests (*see*

INTIMIDATION; *conspiracy; *passing off). It must usually be shown that the wrong was done intentionally or negligently, but there are some torts of *strict liability. Most torts are actionable only if they have caused damage, but torts whose main function is to protect rights rather than to compensate for damage (such as trespass) are actionable without proof of damage. The person principally liable is the one who committed the tort (the **tortfeasor**) but under the rules of *vicarious liability one may be liable for a tort committed by another person. The main remedy for a tort is an action for damages, but in some cases an *injunction can be obtained to prevent repetition of the injury. Other remedies are *self-help and orders for specific restitution of property.

Some torts are also breaches of contract. Negligent driving by a taxi-driver that causes injury to his passenger is both the tort of negligence and breach of the contract to carry the passenger safely to his destination. The passenger may sue either in tort or for breach of contract, or both. Many torts are also crimes. Assault is both a crime and a tort. *Dangerous driving is a crime and may give rise to an action in tort if it causes injury to another person. The crime is prosecuted by agents of the state in the name of the Crown. It is left to the injured person to seek compensation from the wrongdoer by means of an action in tort.

tortfeasor *n.* One who commits a *tort. *See also* JOINT TORTFEASORS.

tortious *adj.* Having the nature of a *tort; wrongful.

torture *n.* Under section 134 of the Criminal Justice Act 1988, the offence committed by a public official (or someone with the official's acquiescence) of intentionally inflicting severe physical or mental suffering on any person anywhere in the world. It carries a maximum sentence of life imprisonment. Under this Act, the accused had a defence if he proved that his conduct was legally authorized, justified, or excusable. However, the prohibition on torture as set out in Article 3 of the European Convention on Human Rights is now part of UK law as a consequence of the *Human Rights Act. This right is an *absolute right, and torture can never be justified as being in the public interest, no matter how great that public interest might be. Public authorities have a limited but positive duty to protect this right from interference by third parties. In December 2005 the House of Lords unanimously overturned a ruling by the Court of Appeal to the effect that evidence obtained under torture in other jurisdictions could lawfully be admitted in British courts (*A and others v Secretary of State for the Home Department* (No 2) [2005] UKHL 71, [2006] 2 AC 221). *See also* DEPORTATION.

total loss (in marine insurance) *See* ACTUAL TOTAL LOSS; CONSTRUCTIVE TOTAL LOSS. *Compare* PARTIAL LOSS.

totting up The system under which offences endorsed on a driving licence are added up to empower the courts to order *disqualification from driving. Until 1 November 1982, certain road offences (listed in a Schedule to the Road Traffic Act 1972) were totted up if, within three years before committing the latest offence, the accused had been convicted and had his licence endorsed on two occasions. Since that date the system has been altered. All traffic offences that are subject to compulsory or discretionary disqualification are now assigned a number of **penalty points** (reflecting the gravity of the offence). When a person is convicted of any of these offences, and his licence is endorsed but he is not disqualified, the endorsement states the number of points for that offence. If he is disqualified for the offence, the penalty points that would normally apply to that offence are not endorsed. When the penalty points endorsed within the past three years – together with the points acquired on the latest offence – amount to 12 or more, the court must order disqualification for a minimum of six months, but the points applying to the latest offence are not endorsed. If the accused has already been disqualified within the three years before the latest endorsable conviction, the minimum disqualification is for one year; if he has been disqualified more than once, the minimum is two years. Mitigating circumstances are still permitted (to prevent disqualification or shorten the period), but only upon proof of exceptional hardship. When several offences are committed together, the licence is only endorsed with the points relating to the gravest offence. If a person is disqualified under this system, all previous points are eliminated, and he gets back a clean licence after disqualification. If a driver is convicted of an endorsable offence and accumulates 6 or more penalty points within two years of passing a driving test, his licence is revoked and he must retake the test. Under the Road Traffic Offenders Act 1988 (sch 2, as amended) penalty points for the most important offences are set out as follows:

- 3–11 points – any offence involving obligatory disqualification for which disqualification was not ordered because of special reasons or mitigating circumstances;
- 10 points – being in charge when unfit or with excess alcohol in the body (*see* DRUNKEN DRIVING); failing to provide a *specimen of breath;
- 5–10 points – failing to stop after a *road traffic accident; failing to report an accident;
- 3–9 points – *careless and inconsiderate driving;
- 6–8 points – *driving without insurance;
- 7 points – *driving while disqualified;
- 3–6 points – *driving without a licence; driving under age
- 4 points – failing to provide a specimen for a preliminary (roadside) *breath test;
- 3 points – *speeding (if a fixed penalty, otherwise 3–6 points); leaving a car in a dangerous position (*see* OBSTRUCTION).

All endorsements on the licence before 1 November 1982 count as 3 points. When the relevant provisions of the Road Safety Act 2006 come into force the range of penalty points will increase.

touting *n.* Seeking business by approaching potential customers. Under section 166 of the Criminal Justice and Public Order Act 1994 it is a summary offence (punishable by a fine) for unauthorized persons to offer or display for sale, in a public place, a ticket for a designated football match or other sporting event for which more than 6000 tickets are issued. Similarly, it is a summary offence (punishable by a fine) for taxi operators to solicit persons to hire vehicles to carry them as passengers unless they are licensed operators within an authorized scheme that permits such soliciting.

town and country planning A system of controlling the use of land administered by **local planning authorities** under the Town and Country Planning Act 1990, which is subject to supervisory powers of the Secretary of State. These authorities include both county and district councils (or unitary authorities) and also, in Greater London, the London borough councils and the Court of Common Council of the City. The background to control is the **development plan**. Councils formulate and keep under review structure plans of general policy for their areas, and the other authorities maintain local plans of detailed policy for theirs. The structure plan and local plan for an area constitute its development plan. The machinery of control is **planning permission**, without which no *development of land may take place. The Secretary of State has granted permission for certain classes of development ("permitted development") by a general development order applicable throughout England and Wales; permission may be granted for particular cases by special development orders. In all other cases permission is a matter for local planning authorities (normally at district or borough level), with a right of appeal to the Secretary of State against its refusal or against conditions attached to it. The implementation of control is by local planning authorities, primarily by serving an *enforcement notice.

town clerk The office held by the head of the permanent staff (normally a qualified solicitor) of some local authorities. Under the Local Government Act 1972, the office ceased to be obligatory and most authorities now appoint a chief executive instead.

TPIMs Abbreviation for Terrorism Prevention and Investigation Measures; *see* TERRORISM.

tracing *n.* The process that enables the original owner of property to identify his property or its substitute in the hands of a third party. Both the common law and equity have developed their own rules of tracing, the common-law rules being more limited. At common law, where the property being traced is money, the rules do not allow tracing to continue once the money has become part of a mixed fund (i.e. money mixed in a bank account with other money). Tracing in equity does permit the tracing of money through a mixed fund. However, tracing in equity is first dependant upon there being a fiduciary relationship (*Westdeutsche Landesbank Girozentrale v Islington London Borough Council* [1996] AC 669 (HL)). It is not, however, necessary for there to be a pre-existent fiduciary relationship: it may be that circumstances will have given rise to such a relationship. This requirement has been criticized on the basis that the courts are too willing to find a fiduciary relationship where one would not otherwise have been found to exist, particularly in a commercial context (*Chase Manhattan Bank NA v Israeli-British Bank (London) Ltd* [1981] Ch 105), in order to facilitate the operation of tracing in equity. The different rules for tracing at common law and in equity have also been severely criticized (*Foskett v McKeown* [2001] 1 AC 102 (Lord Millett)). Tracing should be distinguished from "following", which simply involves tracking the same product from one place to another, because tracing enables the identification of new property by which the original property has been substituted (proceeds of sale, for example).

tracing trust property The right of a beneficiary under a *fiduciary relationship to recover trust property or its value if it is wrongfully disposed of by the fiduciary. The right exists against anyone except a person who has purchased the trust property without notice of the fiduciary obligation; a beneficiary may, for example, recover the property from a trustee who has mixed trust property with his own funds, or from a person to whom the property has wrongly been given. *See* LIABILITY FOR RECEIPT.

track (in civil proceedings) *See* ALLOCATION; CASE MANAGEMENT.

trade *n.* The *income tax charge on trading income (previously Schedule D Case I; *see* SCHEDULAR SYSTEM) only applies when there is "a trade" (Income Tax Trading and Other Income Act 2005 s 5). If there is no trade, a transaction is likely to be subject to capital gains tax and not income tax. (This gives a lower tax charge.) When deciding whether there is a trade, courts have in the past adopted the formulation of the Royal Commission on the Taxation of Profits and Income (1955 Cmd 9474, 116), which stated that the existence of a trade might be determined by considering six **badges of trade**, namely:

(1) the subject matter of the transaction;
(2) the length of period of ownership of the property realized in the transaction;
(3) the frequency or number of similar transactions by the same person;
(4) supplementary work on or in connection with the property realized;
(5) the circumstances that were responsible for the realization;
(6) motive.

A more modern approach was followed by the court in *Rosemoore Investments v Inspector of Taxes* [2002] STC (SCD) 325, in which, in order to determine whether there was a trade, the company's activities were examined by reference to nine badges of trade:

(1) repetition: a one-off transaction can be an adventure in the nature of trade but the lack of repetition points towards there being no trade;
(2) whether a transaction is related to the trade of the taxpayer (if so, it is more likely to be a trade);
(3) the nature of the subject matter: this is not conclusive but may be a valuable pointer;
(4) the way in which the transaction was carried through;
(5) the source of finance;
(6) whether work was done on the object purchased for resale;
(7) whether the object purchased for resale was broken down into lots;
(8) whether the purchaser intended to resell at the time of purchase;
(9) whether the object purchased and resold provided employment or an income pending resale.

Illegal acts can constitute a trade. In *IRC v Aken* [1990] 1 WLR 1374 (CA) the Court of Appeal held that prostitution is a taxable trade even though a prostitute cannot enforce her bargains and in the course of carrying on her trade criminal offences had been committed by the taxpayer. A single transaction can be a trade. *Compare* PROFESSION.

trade description Any direct or indirect indication of certain characteristics of goods or of any part of them, such as their quantity, size, fitness for their purpose, time or place of origin, method of manufacture or processing, and price. Under the Trade Descriptions Act 1968, it is a criminal offence to apply a trade description to goods that is false or to supply or offer to supply any goods to which such a description is applied (*see* FALSE TRADE DESCRIPTION).

trade dispute Any dispute between workers and their own employer relating to one or more of the following:

- terms and conditions of employment;
- the engagement or nonengagement, suspension, or dismissal of any employee;
- allocation of duties between employees;
- disciplinary matters;
- trade union membership or nonmembership;
- facilities for trade union officials;
- negotiating machinery and the recognition of trade unions' negotiating rights on behalf of employees.

Under the Trade Union and Labour Relations (Consolidation) Act 1992, a person cannot be sued in *tort for an act that is committed in contemplation or furtherance of a trade dispute on the grounds that it induces or threatens any breach or interference with the performance of a contract. Generally such immunity extends only to the acts of employees against their own employer (*see also* PICKETING). Moreover, there is no immunity in respect of action taken to enforce a *closed-shop agreement.

The 1992 Act gives similar immunity to trade unions for their acts committed in contemplation or furtherance of a trade dispute provided the act concerned is authorized by a majority vote in favour of the action in a secret ballot of the union's members. A trade union member can obtain a court order preventing industrial action being taken if it has not been authorized by a ballot. When the immunity does not apply, a union is only liable in respect of action that has been authorized or endorsed by a responsible person (which includes the principal executive committee, general secretary, president, paid officials, or committees to whom they report). The president, general secretary, or principal executive committee may repudiate such authorization or endorsement provided they act promptly and notify the person giving the authorization or endorsement in writing and without delay.

When a trade union's immunity does not apply and it is ordered to pay damages (other than for causing personal injury or for breach of duty concerning the ownership control or use of property, or for *product liability under the Consumer Protection Act 1987), the amount awarded may not exceed specified limits. These range from £10,000 for a union with under 5000 members to £250,000 for a union with 100,000 or more members, and the limits may be varied by statutory instrument. Payment of damages awarded against a trade union or employers' association may not be enforced against certain protected property, including its political and pension funds and the personal assets of its trustees, members, or paid officials, as distinct from assets they hold for the union's or association's purposes.

trade fixture A fixture attached to rented premises by a tenant for the purpose of his trade or business. A tenant can remove trade fixtures at any time during his tenancy, as well as at the end of it. *See also* TENANT'S FIXTURES.

trade mark A distinctive symbol that identifies particular products of a trader to the general public. The symbol may consist of a device, words, or a combination of these. A trader may register his trade mark at the Register of Trade Marks, which is at the UK Intellectual Property Office (*see* PATENT). He then enjoys the exclusive right to use the trade mark in connection with the goods for which it was registered. Any person or firm that has a trade connection with the goods may register a trade mark. For example, he may be the manufacturer, a dealer, importer, or retailer. Under the Trade Marks Act 1994 (and EU directive 89/104), registration is initially for ten years; it is then renewable. Trade marks can be registered for ever. However, the right to remain on the register may be lost if the trade mark is not used or is misused. The owner of a trade mark may assign it or allow others to use it. If anyone uses a registered trade mark without the owner's permission, or uses a mark that is likely to be confused with a registered trade mark, the owner can sue for an *injunction and *damages or an *account of profits. Unregistered marks are protected by *passing off. Since 1 April 1996 *Community Trade Marks can now be obtained. These are cheaper than trade marks obtained by registration in several individual EU states. Trade marks are an example of *intellectual property.

(((●))) **SEE WEB LINKS**

- Advice on applying for and managing trade marks from the Intellectual Property Office website
- Website of the Institute of Trade Mark Attorneys: includes an introduction to trade marks and other forms of intellectual property

trade mark at common law A *trade mark that is not registered in the Register of Trade Marks but is identified with particular goods through established use. The trade mark's owner may bring an action for *passing off in the case of infringement.

trade secret Some process or product belonging to a business, disclosure of which would harm the business's interests. The courts will generally grant injunctions to prohibit any threatened disclosure of trade secrets by employees, former employees, and others to whom the secrets have been disclosed in confidence. There is a relationship of trust and confidence between employer and employee that may be destroyed if the employee discloses a trade secret, providing a reason for dismissal; such a dismissal may be fair if the procedure adopted complies with the necessary requirements. Cases: *Faccenda Chicken Ltd v Fowler* [1986] 2 Ch 117 (CA); *Herbert Morris Ltd v Saxelby* [1916] 1 AC 688 (HL). *See* RESTRAINT OF TRADE; UNFAIR DISMISSAL.

trade union An organization whose members are wholly or mainly workers and whose principal purposes include the regulation of relations between workers and employers or employers' associations. Unions' affairs are regulated by the Trade Union and Labour Relations (Consolidation) Act 1992. This provides that: secret ballots must be held for election of unions' executive committees and before any industrial action backed by the union (*see* STRIKE); union funds cannot be used to indemnify individuals for fines imposed by a court for a criminal offence or contempt of court; and unions' accounting records must be open to inspection by their members, who can challenge any unlawful use of the funds through the courts. There is a right for trade union members not to be unjustifiably disciplined by their union (for example for failing to take industrial action). A member can apply to an *employment tribunal for a declaration that he has been unjustifiably disciplined. The employment tribunal can award compensation if the claim is upheld. Trade-union members seeking to enforce their union membership rights can obtain advice and financial and legal assistance from the *Certification Officer.

(((⊕))) SEE WEB LINKS
• Website of the TUC: includes a comprehensive guide to employment rights

trade union official An officer of a trade union (or of a branch or section of it) or a person elected or appointed in accordance with the union's rules to represent a group of its members. An employee who is a trade union official is entitled to time off work, paid at his normal rate, for certain purposes. These must be official union duties concerning industrial relations between his employer and any associated employer and their employees or training approved by the Trades Union Congress and relevant to his union duties.

trading stamps Stamps bought from a trading-stamp company by a retailer and given to his customers when they purchase goods. The customer obtains stamps in proportion to the goods purchased, and when he has collected enough stamps he can exchange them for goods from the trading-stamp company. The issue of trading stamps was first regulated by the Trading Stamp Act 1964, now replaced by Regulatory Reform (Trading Stamps) Order 2005. Each stamp must be clearly marked with a monetary value and the name of the issuing company. The retailer aims to cover the cost of the stamps by profits from the increased custom he hopes they will attract. Schemes such as supermarket clubcard points are now much more common than those involving stamps.

trafficking for sexual exploitation Under the Sexual Offences Act 2003 (s 57) a person commits an offence if he intentionally arranges or facilitates the arrival in, or the entry into, the United Kingdom of another person for the purpose of sexual exploitation of that person. Trafficking within the UK for sexual exploitation is covered by s 58 of the Act and trafficking out of the UK by s 59.

traffic offences *See* OFFENCES RELATING TO ROAD TRAFFIC.

transfer *n.* (in land law) A deed by which ownership of registered land is conveyed. *See also* CONVEYANCING.

transfer direction A direction that a person serving a sentence of imprisonment who is suffering from a mental disorder be transferred to a hospital and be detained there for treatment (Glossary to the Criminal Procedure Rules).

transfer of proceedings In civil proceedings, the process by which a case is transferred to the most appropriate court. Rules governing the transfer of proceedings are contained in Parts 26 and 30 of the *Civil Procedure Rules.

transfer of risk The passing from the seller of property to the buyer of the incidence of the loss if the property is damaged or destroyed. The Sale of Goods Act 1979 provides that, unless it is otherwise agreed, goods remain at the seller's risk until ownership passes to the buyer. After that they are at the buyer's risk, whether or not delivery has been made.

transfer of shares A transaction resulting in a change of share ownership. It traditionally involved (1) a contract to sell the shares; (2) their transfer by delivery of a *share warrant or execution of a *share transfer; and (3) entry of the transferee's name on the register of members of the company. The process can now be carried out electronically using the CREST system. Shares in private companies and partly paid shares may be subject to restrictions on transfer. *See also* STAMP DUTY; STAMP DUTY RESERVE TAX; TRANSMISSION OF SHARES.

transfer of undertakings *See* RELEVANT TRANSFER.

transfer of value *Inheritance tax is charged when there is a "transfer of value" that is not exempted by any statutory provision. A transfer of value is any disposition made by the transferor as a result of which the value of his estate immediately after the disposition is less than it would be but for the disposition (Inheritance Tax Act 1984 s 3(2)). Statute declares the reduction in the estate not to be a transfer of value if it can be shown that the transfer was not intended to confer any gratuitous benefit and occurred as part of a commercial transaction. A disposition for maintenance of the family (which is very restrictively defined) is also declared by statute not to be a transfer of value.

transfer pricing The scheme of pricing goods or services that pass from one division of a company to another, or from one company to another company in the same *group. Transfer pricing has been used to move profits from one jurisdiction to another to minimize tax on profits. However, the Taxation (International and Other Provisions) Act 2010 pt 4 has the effect that tax is charged on profits computed by reference to prices that would be paid by an unconnected third party, irrespective of the price actually charged. These provisions apply to large companies and certain medium-sized companies.

transferred malice *See* MALICE.

transform *vb.* To convert a rule contained within a treaty, or that is a by-product of a treaty, into domestic law by means of primary or secondary UK legislation. Without such a transformation, the rule cannot be applied as law by a British court. Hence, before the transformation of the UK's treaty obligations under the *European Convention for the Protection of Human Rights by the Human Rights Act 1998, British courts could not directly apply the provisions of the Convention. With regard to obligations under EU law, the term **transpose** is used in preference to transform. The so-called "doctrine of transformation" is opposed to the *doctrine of incorporation.

transmission of shares A *transfer of shares that occurs automatically, by operation of law, upon bankruptcy (from the bankrupt to his trustee in bankruptcy) or upon death (to the personal representatives of the deceased). The transferees do not become company members until the company enters their names upon the register of members; in the meantime they are unable to attend or vote at company meetings. *See also* TRANSFER OF SHARES.

transnational corporation An enterprise consisting of commercial entities in more than one state that are linked by ownership or otherwise. Transnational corporations operate in such a way that they exercise a uniform, cohesive, and common policy in order to further their economic interests. This policy can allow them to wield significant influence over the activities of those states in which they carry out their commercial activities, i.e. by exerting pressure over the direction of domestic policy of the host states.

transparency *n.* An essential condition for those operating in a market, which ensures that the rules to which they are subject are made obvious. Generally, it ensures that the reasons behind measures and the applicable regulations are clear to all, so that all are treated fairly.

transpose *vb. See* TRANSFORM.

transsexual person *See* GENDER REASSIGNMENT.

travaux préparatoires [French] Preparatory works that form a background to the enactment of legislation; for example, recommendations of Royal Commissions and consultative documents published by the government. They may not be used by the courts as an aid to interpreting the legislation. *See* INTERPRETATION.

traverse 1. *vb.* In civil proceedings, to deny an allegation of fact made in a *statement of case. **2.** *n.* (in civil proceedings) The denial itself. Under Part 16 of the *Civil Procedure Rules a defence must state which allegations in the *particulars of claim are denied. In addition, where the defendant denies an allegation he must state his reasons for doing so; if he intends to put forward a different version of events to that put forward by the claimant, he must state his own version. A defendant who fails to deal with an allegation may be taken to admit that allegation.

treachery *n.* Conduct that assists an enemy. This was defined under the Treachery Act 1940 as an offence relating to World War II, which was punishable by death. There is now, however, no specific crime of treachery: acts of this sort are usually dealt with under the *Official Secrets Acts or, in some cases, as *treason.

treason *n.* Conduct comprising a breach of allegiance owed to the sovereign or the state. Under the Treason Act 1351, high treason included violating the king's wife, eldest unmarried daughter, or wife of the king's eldest son; openly attempting to prevent the heir to the throne from succeeding; and killing the chancellor or any judge while performing their duties. Treason was redefined by the Treason Act 1795 and the principal forms now include: (1) compassing the death or serious injury of the sovereign or his (or her) spouse or eldest son; (2) levying war against the sovereign in his (or her) realm, which includes any insurrection against the authority of the sovereign or of the government that goes beyond *riot or *violent disorder; (3) giving aid or comfort to the sovereign's enemies in wartime. The penalty for treason (fixed by law) was formerly death but is now life imprisonment.

treasure trove Formerly, items of gold and silver found in a concealed place, having been hidden by an owner who was untraceable. Under medieval law they belonged to the Crown, but only if it could be proved at a coroner's inquest that the owner had intended to retrieve the items and had not merely abandoned them. If the items were lost or abandoned, the finder acquired a right to possess them. The Treasure Act 1996 (in force from September 1997) altered the law in this field; the Act and the Code of Practice made under it apply only to England, Wales, and Northern Ireland. The definition of treasure now includes any object at least 300 years old and containing more than 5% precious metal (excluding single coins). The Crown is now entitled to receive *all* treasure and will pay a reward to the finder. The Act creates a new offence of failing to report the discovery of treasure, with a maximum penalty of a £5000 fine or three months' imprisonment (or both). The Code of Practice sets out guidelines on such matters as which objects should be reported; how finders can seek advice from museums and archaeologists in the event of a large find; government policy on the payment of *ex gratia* rewards, including rewards to landowners and rewards for finds resulting from trespass; and policy and procedures for reaching valuations, including the commissioning of reports from independent experts and provisions for finders to submit their own valuations.

Treasury Counsel   Advocates appointed by the Attorney General to undertake work for a number of government departments. They are appointed after open competition through advertisements in the national press. The Attorney General maintains four panels of junior counsel to undertake civil and EU work for the government. There are three London panels (A panel for senior juniors, B panel for middle juniors, and C panel for junior juniors) and a regional panel. The size of the panels is determined by need. Sitting above these panels are **First Treasury Counsel** who are the main advocates for the government in civil litigation affecting the Crown. First Treasury Counsel must do exclusively government work for the duration of their appointment.

Treasury Solicitor (HM Procurator General and Treasury Solicitor)   A solicitor who advises the Treasury on legal matters, instructs parliamentary counsel on Bills, instructs counsel to appear on behalf of the Crown in civil cases involving Treasury issues, and acts as *Queen's Proctor. Between 1883 and 1908 the office was combined with that of *Director of Public Prosecutions. The Treasury Solicitor's Department is the largest division of the Government Legal Service; the Treasury Solicitor is the head of this service.

treaty   *n.* An international agreement in writing between two states (a **bilateral treaty**) or a number of states (a **multilateral treaty**). Such agreements can also be known as *conventions, **pacts**, *protocols, *final acts, **arrangements**, and **general acts**. Treaties are binding in international law and constitute the equivalent of the municipal-law contract, conveyance, or legislation. Some treaties create law only for those states that are parties to them, some codify pre-existing customary international law, and some propound rules that eventually develop into customary international law, binding upon all states (e.g. the Genocide Convention). Federal states, colonial states, and public international organizations are sometimes also able to enter into treaty obligations. The Vienna Convention on the Law of Treaties (1969) defines in detail the rules relating to inter-state treaties and is itself generally considered to declare or develop customary international law in this area. Treaties are normally concluded by the process of *ratification. *See also* HIGH CONTRACTING PARTIES; RESERVATION; SIGNATURE OF TREATY.

In the UK the power to make or enter into treaties belongs to the monarch, acting on the advice of government ministers, but a treaty does not become part of municipal law until brought into force by an Act of Parliament.

Treaty of Nice   A treaty that was signed by the member states of the European Union on 26 February 2001 and that came into force on 1 February 2003. The Treaty's main purpose was to prepare the EU institutions for the enlargement to 25 member states in May 2004. It also extended the policy areas covered by the *codecision procedure, giving more power to the European Parliament. *See also* CONSTITUTIONAL TREATY OF THE EUROPEAN UNION.

Treaty of Paris   *See* PARIS TREATY.

Treaty of Rome (Treaty Establishing the European Community)   The treaty founding the European Economic Community (subsequently known as the *European

Community) and the European Atomic Energy Community (*see also* EUROPEAN UNION). The treaty was signed in Rome on 25 March 1957 by its founder members, i.e. Belgium, West Germany, France, Italy, Luxembourg, and the Netherlands. It was subsequently amended by the *Single European Act, the *Maastricht Treaty, and the *Amsterdam Treaty and has now been replaced (under the *Lisbon Treaty) by the *Treaty on the Functioning of the European Union.

Treaty on European Union (TEU) The updated and amended version of the *Maastricht Treaty that now forms part of the *Lisbon Treaty of 2009.

Treaty on the Functioning of the European Union (TFEU) The updated and amended version of the *Treaty of Rome that forms part of the *Lisbon Treaty of 2009 and is now the basis for European law. Most provisions were moved over from the Rome Treaty with a few amendments and differences in numbering.

tree preservation order An order made by a local planning authority (*see* TOWN AND COUNTRY PLANNING) prohibiting, in the interests of amenity, the felling of a tree (or trees) without its consent. *See also* CONSERVATION AREA.

trespass *n.* A wrongful direct interference with another person or with his possession of land or goods. In the middle ages, any wrongful act was called a trespass, but only some trespasses, such as trespass by force and arms (*vi et armis*), were dealt with in the King's Courts. The distinguishing feature of trespass in modern law is that it is a direct and immediate interference with person or property, such as striking a person, entering his land, or taking away his goods without his consent. Indirect or consequential injury, such as leaving an unlit hole into which someone falls, is not trespass. Trespass is actionable *per se*, i.e. the act of trespass is itself a *tort and it is not necessary to prove that it has caused actual damage.

There are three kinds of trespass: to the person, to goods, and to land. **Trespass to the person** may be intentional or negligent, but since negligent physical injuries are remedied by an action for *negligence, the action for trespass to the person is only brought for direct and intentional acts, in the form of actions for *assault, *battery, and *false imprisonment. **Trespass to goods** includes touching, moving, or carrying them away. It may be intentional or negligent, but *inevitable accident is a defence. **Trespass to land** usually takes the form of entering it without permission. It is no defence to show that the trespass was innocent (e.g. that the trespasser honestly believed that the land belonged to him). Trespass to land or goods is a wrong to possession rather than to ownership. Thus a tenant of rented property has the right to sue for trespass to that property. Trespass to land is a tort but not normally a crime: the notice "Trespassers will be prosecuted" is therefore usually misleading.

However, trespass may sometimes constitute a crime. Thus squatters may be guilty of a crime (*see* ADVERSE OCCUPATION); it is a crime to trespass on diplomatic or consular premises or premises similarly protected by immunity; and it is a crime to enter and remain on any premises as a trespasser with a *weapon of offence for which one has no authority or reasonable excuse, or to be on any premises, land, or water as a trespasser with a *firearm for which one has no reasonable excuse. Under the Sexual Offences Act 2003 it is an offence to trespass with intent to commit a sexual offence. The Criminal Justice and Public Order Act 1994 created the offences of aggravated trespass and collective trespass. The summary offence of **aggravated trespass** occurs when a trespasser in the open air seeks to intimidate, obstruct, or disrupt a lawful activity, such as hunting; an offender can be arrested and failure to leave the land on the direction of a senior police officer is also an offence. **Collective trespass** occurs when two or more people are trespassing with the purpose of residing on land belonging to another person.

The police have powers to direct collective trespassers to leave if they have caused damage, used threatening or abusive words towards the occupier, or brought six or more vehicles (which may be caravans) onto the land (*see also* UNAUTHORIZED CAMPING). Failure to leave or re-entry within three months is a summary offence for which a uniformed police officer has a power of arrest. Both collective and aggravated trespass are punishable by a fine and/or three months' imprisonment. *See also* AIRSPACE; BURGLARY; TRESPASSORY ASSEMBLY.

trespass *ab initio* [Latin: trespass from the beginning] A form of trespass that occurs when a person enters land with authority given by law, e.g. to arrest a criminal or search for stolen goods, and subsequently commits an act that is an abuse of that authority. The authority is cancelled retrospectively and the entry is deemed to have been a trespass from the beginning (Six Carpenters Case (1610) 8 Co Rep 146a).

trespass by relation A form of trespass based on the legal fiction that a person's actual possession of land dates from the moment he became entitled to possession. It arose from the rule that only the possessor of land can sue for trespass to it. When someone entitled to immediate possession of land enters into possession of it at some later date, his possession is deemed to relate back to the moment he became entitled to it to enable him to sue for acts of trespass committed in the intervening period.

trespassory assembly An assembly of more than 20 people in the open air on land to which the public has no right, or a limited right, of access, when the occupier has not consented to the event and it is likely to result in serious disruption to the life of the community or significant damage to land, monuments, or buildings of historical, architectural, archaeological, or scientific importance. A chief office of police may apply to prohibit such an assembly if he reasonably believes it is going to be held. Knowingly organizing or inciting a trespassory assembly are *summary offences punishable by a *fine on level 4 and/or three months' imprisonment; knowingly taking part attracts a fine on level 3. A uniformed police officer has powers of arrest for these offences as well as a power to stop people proceeding to such an assembly.

trial *n.* The hearing of a civil or criminal case before a court of competent jurisdiction. Trials must, with rare exceptions (*see* IN CAMERA), be held in public. At the trial all outstanding issues of law and fact arising in the case will be determined. *See also* SUMMARY TRIAL; TRIAL ON INDICTMENT.

trial at bar *Trial on indictment before three or more judges of the *Queen's Bench Division and a jury: formerly used for the trial of criminal cases of exceptional public importance. The last such trial was that of Sir Roger Casement for treason in 1916 and the procedure was abolished by the Courts Act 1971.

trial on indictment The trial of a person charged with an *indictable offence by jury in the *Crown Court. The *indictment is read out to the accused at the start of the trial. *Compare* SUMMARY TRIAL.

tribunal *n. See* ADMINISTRATIVE TRIBUNAL; DOMESTIC TRIBUNAL; EMPLOYMENT TRIBUNAL.

tribunal of inquiry *See* INQUIRY PANELS.

Tribunals Service *See* COURTS AND TRIBUNALS SERVICE, HM.

trier of fact A member of a court who has the duty to decide questions of fact. In criminal trials on indictment, and in civil trials with a jury, the jury is the trier of fact. However, in summary trials the magistrates (or district judge) decide all issues of law and of fact. Similarly, in civil trials by judge alone the judge decides all issues of law and of fact.

TRIPS The Agreement on Trade Related Aspects of Intellectual Property Rights 1994: the international agreement on *intellectual property rights that arose from the Uruguay Round of the *General Agreement on Tariffs and Trade (*see* WORLD TRADE ORGANIZATION). It is designed to reduce distortions and impediments to international trade while taking account of the need to promote effective protection of intellectual property rights. It also aims to ensure that measures to enforce these rights do not themselves become barriers to legitimate trade. TRIPS sets out how participating nations will protect intellectual property rights: for copyright they should comply with some provisions of the *Berne Convention; computer programs and databases will also be protected by copyright. Trade marks and patents should be protected in accordance with the Paris Convention for the Protection of Intellectual Property (1971), with additional protection for designs and the layout of integrated circuits. Less-developed countries were given until 2013 for compliance (January 2016 for pharmaceutical patents), with a subsequent extension to 2021.

trover *n.* The original form of the modern action in tort for *conversion of goods. Trover was based on a fictitious allegation that the claimant had lost the goods and the defendant found them and converted them to his own use. The old form of action has disappeared, but its name is still sometimes used as a synonym for conversion.

trust *n.* **1.** An arrangement in which a *settlor transfers property to one or more *trustees, who will hold it for the benefit of one or more persons (the **beneficiaries** or *cestuis que trust*, who may include the trustee(s) or the settlor) who are entitled to enforce the trust, if necessary by action in court. The trust, recognized originally in Chancery, is based on confidence and developed from the *use; it has been described as the most important contribution of *equity to English jurisprudence. The beneficiary has rights against the trustee and may also have rights over the property in the hands of others (*see* TRACING). When a sole beneficiary is 18 or over, of sound mind, and entitled to all the trust property, he may require the trustees to transfer that property to him; this applies equally when all the beneficiaries are 18 or over, of sound mind, acting together, and likewise entitled. For a trust to exist, the **three certainties** must be present (*Knight v Knight* (1840) 3 Beav 148 (HL)): these are certainty of intention (i.e. to create a trust), certainty of subject matter (the property in the trust), and certainty of objects (those who will or may benefit under the trust).

   Declarations of trust can be made orally except where land is concerned, in which case compliance with section 53 (1)(b) of the Law of Property Act 1925 is necessary. *Express trusts are, however, usually found in professionally drafted documents. Trusts are sometimes used to protect an individual's (or company's) ownership of property, when it is feared that the possessor of the property may become insolvent. However, where the sole purpose of a trust is to put property beyond the reach of creditors, the trust may fail for lack of genuine intention to create a trust (*Midland Bank v Wyatt* [1995] 1 FLR 697). *See* ACTIVE TRUST; CHARITABLE TRUST; DISCRETIONARY TRUST; EXECUTED TRUST; EXPRESS TRUST; IMPLIED TRUST; PROTECTIVE TRUST; SECRET TRUST; STATUTORY TRUST. **2.** (in the *National Health Service) *See* NHS TRUST; PRIMARY CARE TRUST.

trust corporation The *Public Trustee, or a corporation either appointed by the court to act as trustee or entitled under rules created under the Public Trustee Act 1906 to be a custodian trustee, or certain other persons (e.g. the Treasury Solicitor). A trust corporation may exercise all the powers that would otherwise require two trustees (e.g. selling land). The clearing banks and others have subsidiary companies that are trust corporations.

trust deed A deed setting out the terms of a trust.

trustee *n.* A person having a nominal title to property that he holds for the benefit of one or more others, the beneficiaries (*see* TRUST). Trustees may be individuals or corporate bodies (*see* TRUST CORPORATION) and can include such specialists as *judicial trustees, *custodian trustees, and the *Public Trustee. A trustee must show a high standard of care towards his beneficiaries, and must not allow his interests to conflict with those of his beneficiaries. He is not entitled to profit from the trust, although a professional trustee is authorized to receive remuneration for his services under part V of the Trustee Act 2000 in the absence of any other express entitlement. It is not unusual for remuneration of trustees to be authorized by the *trust instrument itself. Other legislation permits the payment of fees to *Public Trustees, *judicial trustees, and *custodian trustees. Trustees may refuse their office, retire, or resign, but they remain liable for acts carried out during their trusteeship. The power to appoint replacement trustees is usually given either to the beneficiaries or to the remaining trustees; in default the court will appoint replacement trustees. Trustees have a wide range of powers and duties, including a duty to act equally between the beneficiaries and a power to advance money to them (*see* ADVANCEMENT). In the exercise of their duties they are answerable to the court.

trustee *de son tort* [from Latin: of his own wrongdoing] A person unconnected with a trust who takes it upon himself to act as a trustee. He is thereafter liable as if he had been appointed a trustee.

trustee in bankruptcy A person in whom the property of a bankrupt is vested for the benefit of the bankrupt's creditors. The trustee in bankruptcy (either a licensed *insolvency practitioner or the *official receiver) must collect the bankrupt's assets, sell them, and distribute the proceeds among those with valid claims against the bankrupt. Some claims take preference over others (*see* PREFERENTIAL DEBTS).

trustee investments *See* AUTHORIZED INVESTMENTS.

trusteeship *n. See* TRUST TERRITORY.

trustees of the settlement *See* SETTLED LAND ACT TRUSTEES.

trust for sale A trust in which the trustees have an obligation to sell the property and hold the proceeds of sale in trust for the beneficiaries. Such a trust used to be imposed by statute in situations in which land is owned by two or more persons jointly or as tenants in common. Since 1997, all such trusts, including those already in existence in 1997, have become *trusts of land. Under the Administration of Estates Act 1925, an intestate's estate is held by his administrators on trust for sale. If his property includes land, this will now be a trust of land. Trusts for sale may be expressly created, but if the property of the trust includes land, it will be a trust of land, and a power to postpone sale will be implied.

trust instrument A deed under which property is vested in trustees upon trust to apply it for the benefit of the beneficiaries specified in the deed. In the case of *settled land, the trust instrument appoints the trustees of the settlement, sets out the interests to which the beneficiaries are entitled and any powers conferred in extension of those contained in the Settled Land Act 1925, and bears any *ad valorem* stamp duty payable in respect of the settlement. A will admitted to probate may also act as a trust instrument.

trust of imperfect obligation *See* PURPOSE TRUST.

trust of land Any trust of property that consists of or includes land. These trusts were introduced by the Trusts of Land and Appointment of Trustees Act 1996 (TOLATA). Since

1997, where land is owned by more than one person or by a number of persons in succession, a trust of land will be imposed. In this respect the trust of land replaces both statutory *trusts for sale and Settled Land Act settlements (*see* SETTLED LAND). Land in co-ownership must be held by trustees of land, of which there must be not more than four individuals, or a trust corporation. Often, the trustees and the beneficiaries are the same people; for example, a husband and wife who own their home jointly will usually be both trustees and beneficiaries of the trust of land. The point of imposing such a trust is to allow *overreaching to take place on a sale or other disposition of the property. The trustees of land have all the powers of a beneficial (outright) owner, but have duties to consult the beneficiaries and manage the land for their benefit. The beneficiaries have the right to occupy the land if it is suitable for that purpose. *See also* JOINT TENANCY; TENANCY IN COMMON.

trust power (power in the nature of a trust) A *power of appointment held by trustees. The trustees are bound to consider whether or not to exercise the power, which donees of a mere power are not obliged to do, and to that extent objects of a trust power have rights similar to, but perhaps weaker than, those of beneficiaries under a trust.

trust property Property subject to a *trust, normally held by trustees (it may include trust documents, which affect the trust). If trust property is wrongfully disposed of, it may be recovered by the beneficiaries (*see* TRACING TRUST PROPERTY).

trust territory Any of the territories formerly under a League of Nations *mandate, which after 1945 were placed under the **trusteeship** of the United Nations until ready for independence. All trust territories are now independent states.

truth *n.* A statutory defence in *defamation; the defendant must show that the facts in the statement complained of are substantially true. It was introduced by the Defamation Act 2013 as a replacement for the defence of *justification.

TSO *See* STATIONERY OFFICE, THE.

TUPE Transfer of Undertakings (Protection of Employment) Regulations 2006. *See* RELEVANT TRANSFER.

turbary *n.* A *profit *à prendre* or *common conferring the right to take peat or turf from another's land, for use as fuel.

turning Queen's evidence *See* QUEEN'S EVIDENCE.

turpis causa [Latin] A disreputable cause. *See* EX TURPI CAUSA NON ORITUR ACTIO; ILLEGAL CONTRACT.

twin-track planning *See* CONCURRENT PLANNING.

two-counsel rule A rule of etiquette of the Bar that required junior counsel to be instructed to assist Queen's Counsel when the latter appeared in court or in chambers. This rule has now been abolished, but two counsel are often instructed when the weight of the case justifies it.

uberrimae fidei [Latin: of the utmost good faith] Describing a class of contracts in which one party has a preliminary duty to disclose material facts relevant to the subject matter to the other party. *Nondisclosure makes the contract voidable (*see* VOIDABLE CONTRACT). Examples of this class are *insurance contracts, in which knowledge of many material facts is confined to the party seeking insurance.

ubi jus ibi remedium [Latin: where there is a right there is a remedy] The principle that where one's right is invaded or destroyed, the law gives a remedy to protect it or damages for its loss. Further, where one's right is denied the law affords the remedy of an action for its enforcement. This right to a remedy therefore includes more than is usually meant in English law by the term "remedy", as it includes a right of action. Wherever, therefore, a right exists there is also a remedy. *Ashby v White* (1703) 14 St Tr 695, 92 ER 126 (or rather the classic judgment of Lord Chief Justice Holt in that case) is usually cited to exemplify the maxim. This principle, which has at all times been considered so valuable, gave occasion to the first invention of that form of action called an **action on the case**. Such actions played a major part in the development of the law of *tort.

UBR Abbreviation for Uniform Business Rate. *See* RATES.

ulterior intent An element of the **mens rea* for certain crimes that requires an intention to bring about a consequence beyond the criminal act (*see* ACTUS REUS) itself. Crimes of ulterior consent include burglary with intent (*see* BURGLARY) and *wounding with intent. In the former, the ulterior intent is the intention to commit one of three crimes (theft, causing grievous bodily harm, or causing criminal damage) having entered the building as a trespasser (the *actus reus*). Case: *R v Jones and Smith* [1976] 1 WLR 672. *Compare* BASIC INTENT; SPECIFIC INTENT.

ultra vires [Latin: beyond the powers] Describing an act by a public authority, company, or other body that goes beyond the limits of the powers conferred on it. *Ultra vires* acts are invalid (*compare* INTRA VIRES). The *ultra vires* doctrine applies to all powers, whether created by statute or by a private document or agreement (such as a trust deed or contract of agency). In the field of public (especially administrative) law it governs the validity of all *delegated and *subdelegated legislation. This is *ultra vires* not only if it contains provisions not authorized by the enabling power but also if it does not comply with any procedural requirements regulating the exercise of the power. Subdelegated legislation that is within the terms of the delegated legislation authorizing it may still be invalid if the power to make that legislation did not include the power to subdelegate (*see* DELEGATUS NON POTEST DELEGARE). The individual can normally establish the invalidity of delegated or subdelegated legislation by raising the point as a defence in proceedings against him for contravening it. The doctrine also governs the validity of decisions made by inferior courts or administrative or domestic tribunals and the validity of the exercise of any *administrative power. The decision of a court or tribunal is *ultra vires* if it exceeds jurisdiction, contravenes procedural requirements, or disregards the rules of natural justice (the power conferring jurisdiction being construed as requiring the observance of these). The exercise of an administrative power is *ultra vires* not only if unauthorized in substance, but equally if (for example) it is procedurally irregular, improperly motivated, or in breach of the rules of natural justice. The remedies available for this second aspect of the doctrine are *quashing orders, *prohibiting orders, *declaration, and *injunction (the first two of these are public remedies, not available against decisions of domestic tribunals whose jurisdiction is based solely on contract).

An act of a registered company may be *ultra vires* if it is beyond the *objects (if any) in its *articles of association. By virtue of section 39 of the Companies Act 2006, to the extent provided for by that section, such acts are valid, as the section states that an act cannot be questioned on the ground of lack of capacity by reason of anything contained in the company's constitution. However, by virtue of section 41 of the Act, where the *ultra vires* act is with a third party, who is a director or connected to a director of the company, the act is voidable. These provisions are subject to section 42 of the Companies Act 2006 in relation to companies that are charities.

umpire *n. See* ARBITRATION.

UN *See* UNITED NATIONS.

unascertained goods Goods that are not specifically identified at the time a contract of sale is made. For example, in a contract for the sale of 1000 tonnes of soya bean meal, the seller may deliver any 1000 tonnes that answer the contract description. When the correct quantity has been set aside for delivery to the buyer, the goods are described as **ascertained**. Ownership does not pass to the buyer until the goods have been ascertained. *Compare* SPECIFIC GOODS.

unauthorized camping The summary offence of camping in vehicles on land without the consent of the occupier, or on land forming part of a highway, or on any other unoccupied land and failing to comply with a direction to leave by the local authority (Criminal Justice and Public Order Act 1994 s 77). It is also an offence to re-enter the land within three months. The local authority may direct the removal of vehicles or any other property; it may also apply to a magistrates' court for an order authorizing removal. A vehicle does not have to be fit for use on the roads and includes any body or chassis, with or without wheels, and any caravan. Both the offences are punishable by a *fine on level 3. Defences of illness, mechanical breakdown, or immediate emergency may be available. Local authorities may establish caravan sites for *gipsies but are no longer under a duty to do so. *See also* TRESPASS.

unchastity *n. See* IMPUTATION OF UNCHASTITY.

UNCID Uniform Rules of Conduct for Interchange of Trade Data by Teletransmission: a set of rules for *electronic data interchange that were drawn up by the International Chamber of Commerce in 1988. These rules can be incorporated into contracts if the parties wish to do so.

uncollected goods *See* DISPOSAL OF UNCOLLECTED GOODS.

unconditional surrender *See* CAPITULATION.

unconscionable bargain *See* CATCHING BARGAIN.

undefended cause 1. In civil proceedings, the situation in which the defendant fails to file an *acknowledgment of service; fails to file a *defence; or fails to appear, or to be represented, at the hearing of the case. If a defendant fails to file an acknowledgment of service or a defence, the claimant may obtain judgment in *default under Part 12 of the *Civil Procedure Rules. However, under Part 13 of the Rules the court has power to set aside or vary a judgment entered in default if the defendant has a real prospect of successfully defending the claim, or if it appears to the court that there is some other good reason why the judgment should be set aside or varied or the defendant should be allowed to defend the claim (*see* SETTING ASIDE). **2.** An application for divorce, nullity, or separation not contested by the respondent. This may be because: (1) the respondent declares he does not intend to contest the divorce; (2) he gives notice of his intention to defend but fails to file an answer within the time allowed; (3) he files no answer at all; or (4) the answer filed has been struck out.

underlease *n. See* SUBLEASE.

undertaking *n.* **1.** A promise, especially in legal proceedings, that creates an obligation. A solicitor who breaks such a promise will be in breach of disciplinary rules. **2.** A business, such as a company, partnership, or sole trader. *Article 101 of the Treaty on the Functioning of the European Union (formerly Treaty of Rome) applies to agreements between undertakings. EU case law has established that some state bodies of a trading nature, as well as charities and trade associations, may under certain circumstances be classed as undertakings.

underwriter *n.* **1.** A member of an insurance company or a *Lloyd's syndicate who decides whether or not to accept a particular risk for a specified premium. In general, the public only deal with underwriters through a broker. **2.** An individual, finance company, or issuing house who undertakes for a commission to acquire a specified number of shares in a company if those shares are not taken up by the public during a *flotation.

In both cases the underwriter may relieve himself of part of his liability by effecting similar arrangements with **subunderwriters**.

undischarged bankrupt A person who has been made bankrupt and who has not yet received an order of discharge from the court. Such a person is disqualified from holding certain offices, which include justice of the peace, councillor, and Member of Parliament. He must not obtain credit for more than £500 without informing the creditor that he is an undischarged bankrupt, and he must not carry on a business without disclosing the name under which he was made bankrupt to those who deal with him. *See* BANKRUPTCY.

undisclosed principal *See* AGENT.

undivided shares The equitable interests in land owned by tenants in common. Each co-owner has a specified (but not necessarily equal) share in the property, which he may dispose of separately from the others. Such shares are held under a *trust of land. *See also* TENANCY IN COMMON.

undue influence Influence that prevents someone from exercising an independent judgment with respect to any transaction. A contract or gift procured by the exercise of undue influence is liable to be set aside by the courts. A will may likewise be held to be invalid if it is shown that the testator made it under conditions of undue influence (*see* TESTAMENTARY INTENTION). The exercise of undue influence must normally be proved affirmatively - it must be shown that there is a dealing or transaction in which an unfair advantage has been taken of another person. In the case of certain transactions, however, some relationships (for example, between parent and child, husband and wife, doctor and patient, solicitor and client) may be presumed to involve undue influence in the absence of evidence to the contrary. For example, banks should advise spouses to seek independent legal advice before mortgaging the family home at the behest of the other spouse for business loans (*Royal Bank of Scotland v Etridge (No 2)* [2001] UKHL 44, [2001] 3 WLR 1021).

unduly lenient sentence Where it appears that the Crown Court has been unduly lenient in sentencing an offender, the Attorney General may, with the leave of the Court of Appeal, refer the case to that court for review. Only certain types of case can be reviewed, including murder, rape, robbery, and sex crimes relating to children (Criminal Justice Act 1988 s 33). The procedure on referral is set out in Rule 20 of the *Criminal Procedure Rules.

unemployment benefit *See* JOBSEEKER'S ALLOWANCE.

unenforceable contract A contract that, although valid, cannot be enforced by action because it is neither **evidenced in writing** nor (when this is a permissible alternative) supported by a sufficient act of *part performance. Two classes of contracts are involved – guarantees, and contracts for the sale of land entered into before 21 September 1989. By the Statute of Frauds 1677 (in the case of guarantees) and the Law of Property Act 1925 (for land contracts), no contract of either class is enforceable unless its existence and its terms are evidenced by some written note or memorandum signed by the defendant or his agent. By the equitable doctrine of part performance, a land contract entered into before 21 September 1989 (but not a guarantee) can be enforced if, alternatively, the claimant has carried out some act that can be taken as evidencing the existence of the contract. Note that land contracts entered into on or after 21 September 1989 will not even be valid unless they are in writing; the requirement of writing is no longer merely an evidential one.

unenforceable trust A trust that is valid but cannot be directly enforced by a beneficiary. An example would be a trust of land in respect of which there is no compliance with section 53(1)(b) of the Law of Property Act 1925. *See* PURPOSE TRUST.

unfair consumer practices *See* CONSUMER PROTECTION.

unfair contract terms Contractual terms relating to the exclusion or restriction of a person's liability that, under the Unfair Contract Terms Act 1977 and Unfair Terms in Consumer Contracts Regulations 1999, are either ineffective or effective only so far as is reasonable. *See* EXCLUSION AND RESTRICTION OF NEGLIGENCE LIABILITY; EXEMPTION CLAUSE; INTERNATIONAL SUPPLY CONTRACT.

unfair dismissal The dismissal of an employee that an employment tribunal finds is unfair. Under the Employment Rights Act 1996 employees have the right not to be unfairly dismissed, provided they have served the required period of *continuous employment. However, employees dismissed for an *inadmissible reason have this right whatever their age or length of service. An employee who considers he has been unfairly dismissed can apply within three months after the *effective date of termination of his employment contract to an employment tribunal for *reinstatement, *re-engagement, or *compensation. The tribunal will make an award unless the employer can show that the principal reason for the dismissal was the employee's incapability, lack of qualifications, or conduct; redundancy; the fact that it would be illegal to continue employing him; or some other substantial reason. In addition to establishing a reason for the dismissal, the employer must also have acted reasonably in dismissing the employee.

There are some exceptions to the statutory protection, notably in the case of some employees who work outside Great Britain *Lawson v Serco Ltd* [2006] UKHL 3, [2006] ICR 250.

unfair prejudice Unfair conduct on the part of those entrusted to run and control a company in respect of (usually minority) *company members. Any member affected may apply to the court under the Companies Act 2006 s 994, and the court is empowered under the Act to make such order as it thinks fit (s 996). Commonly, the unfair conduct consists of actions having the effect of seriously diminishing the value of the complainant's shareholding. The usual remedy sought, or given, is for the purchase of the petitioner's shares at a fair price. *See also* MINORITY PROTECTION.

unfavourable witness An *adverse witness who is not hostile towards the party who called him to testify. An unfavourable witness may not be cross-examined by that party. *See* HOSTILE WITNESS.

UNFCCC *See* UNITED NATIONS FRAMEWORK CONVENTION ON CLIMATE CHANGE.

unfitness or incompetence *See* IMPUTATION OF UNFITNESS OR INCOMPETENCE.

unfit to plead In criminal proceedings, describing an accused person who is under a disability (such as mental incapacity) that would constitute a bar to his being tried. The test of unfitness to plead is whether the accused will be able to comprehend the course of proceedings so as to make a proper defence. The relevant procedure is governed by the Criminal Procedure (Insanity) Act 1964.

Unified Patent Court *See* EUROPEAN PATENT COURT.

Uniform Business Rate (UBR) *See* RATES.

unilateral contract A contract in which one party (the promisor) undertakes to do or refrain from doing something if the other party (the promisee) does or refrains from doing something, but the promisee does not undertake to do or refrain from doing that thing (*Carlill v Carbolic Smoke Ball Co* [1893] 1 QB 256). An example of a unilateral contract is one in which the promisor offers a reward for the giving of information. *Compare* BILATERAL CONTRACT.

unilateral discharge *See* ACCORD AND SATISFACTION.

unilateral mistake *See* MISTAKE.

unincorporated body An association that has no legal personality distinct from those of its members (*compare* CORPORATION). Examples of unincorporated bodies are *partnerships and *clubs.

union membership agreement *See* CLOSED-SHOP AGREEMENT.

unitary authority An all-purpose *local authority created under the Local Government Act 1992 and subsequent legislation to replace the two-tier system of local government by *county and *district councils. Unitary authorities were established in Wales (and Scotland) in April 1996 and in certain nonmetropolitan counties in England between 1996 and 1998 (with further changes in 2009); single-tier authorities also administer the former metropolitan county areas (since 1986) and the Isle of Wight (since 1995).

United Nations (UN) An international organization, based in New York and Geneva, set up by the United Nations Charter in 1945 to replace the League of Nations. The main aims of the UN are:

- to maintain international peace and security and to bring about settlement of international disputes by peaceful means;
- to develop friendly relations among nations;
- to achieve international cooperation in solving international problems of an economic or cultural nature and in promoting respect for human rights.

The Charter sets out certain fundamental principles, which include the undertaking to refrain from using or threatening force against the territory or political independence of any state.

The Charter established six principal organs, of which the most important are the General Assembly, the Security Council, the Economic and Social Council, and the *International Court of Justice. The **General Assembly** is the debating forum of the UN, consisting of all the member states; it can pass resolutions, but these are not legally binding upon member states. The **Security Council** has five permanent members (China, France, Russia, the UK, and the USA), and ten temporary members elected for two-year periods. Its resolutions are binding on member states, but each permanent member has the right to veto a resolution. It is empowered, under certain conditions, to make recommendations and take measures to maintain the peace, including the establishment of peacekeeping military forces in sensitive areas.

The **Secretariat** serves as the permanent liaison between the main organs of the United Nations and between these organs and such specialized agencies as the United Nations High Commissioner for Refugees (UNHCR) and the United Nations Children's Fund (UNICEF). It prepares every session of the General Assembly and the Economic and Social Council and is headed by the UN Secretary General, the chief administrative officer of the UN.

The United Nations has lost credibility as an international legal organization because it has often been divided upon issues on the basis of political (rather than legal) factors or has passed resolutions of a political nature. Nevertheless it remains important as the only world organization (almost all independent states are members of the UN) and as a forum for discussion and development of international law.

⊕ SEE WEB LINKS
- Website of the United Nations Office (Geneva)

United Nations Framework Convention on Climate Change (UNFCCC) An International treaty under which 192 countries have committed themselves to cooperate on measures aiming to reduce the threat of global warming. The text was adopted in 1992 and came into force in March 2004. At a subsequent conference held in Kyoto, Japan, in 1993 a protocol to the convention was adopted under which 38 industrialized countries agreed to reduce their emissions of the six main greenhouse gasses by an average of 5.2% from 1990 levels by 2012. The EU target is 8% and that of the UK 12.5%. The **Kyoto protocol**, which finally came into force in 2005 after its ratification by Russia, constitutes the first legally binding treaty on climate change. However, the refusal of the United States to sign the protocol means that it is unlikely to be followed by any similar agreement setting specific, binding targets.

Uniting for Peace Resolution A resolution passed by the General Assembly (GA) of the *United Nations in 1950 in which the GA assumed the authority to determine what constituted a threat to the peace, a breach of the peace, or an act of aggression. In the event of any of these occurring, the GA resolved to invite member states to take collective action, including the use of armed force. It is highly doubtful that this attempt by the General Assembly to usurp the role of the Security Council has any legal authority to allow it to act in this way. It has been seen more as a declaration of the frustration of the nonaligned countries at the superpower stalemate that previously existed in the Security Council.

unit trust A *trust enabling small investors to buy interests in a diversity of companies and other investments. These investments are held by trustees (responsible for holding the investments and collecting and distributing income), who enter into a trust deed with the managers of the fund (who select, buy, and sell the investments). The managers sell units to investors, who thus acquire an interest in the fund proportionate to their investment. There is a service charge that provides the remuneration of the managers. Unit trusts are subject to regulation and supervision by the Department for Business, Innovation and Skills.

unity of personality Formerly, the common-law doctrine that husband and wife were one person in the eyes of the law. This doctrine has now been almost entirely abolished. However, the court still has jurisdiction to stay proceedings in tort brought by one spouse against another if there will be no substantial benefit from it; a husband and wife may not be convicted of criminal conspiracy together with each other (unless a third person is involved); and there are certain limitations on criminal proceedings in relation to theft of property belonging to one's spouse.

unity of seisin The ownership of two plots of land by the same person. Easements and other rights over a *servient tenement for the benefit of a *dominant tenement are extinguished if both tenements come into the same ownership.

universal credit A new social security payment for people who are looking for work or on a low income, which is being introduced from 2013 with the aim of simplifying the benefits system and cutting costs. A single payment will eventually replace a range of working-age benefits, including income-based *jobseeker's allowance, *income support, working *tax credit, child tax credit, and *housing benefit.

unjust enrichment *See* QUASI-CONTRACT.

unlawful act notice A notice served by the *Equality and Human Rights Commission on an individual or organization where it is discovered after investigation that there has been a breach of the equality legislation. The notice may require the offender to prepare an action plan or may recommend action to be taken. There is a right of appeal against the notice.

unlawful assembly *See* VIOLENT DISORDER.

unlawful interference with trade *See* INTERFERING WITH TRADE OR BUSINESS. *See also* CAUSING LOSS BY UNLAWFUL MEANS.

unlawful possession of drugs *See* CONTROLLED DRUGS.

unlawful sexual intercourse Sexual intercourse that occurs in any of the *sexual offences involving intercourse, including intercourse with a person under the age of 16 or a mentally defective person.

unlawful trust *See* VOID TRUST.

unlawful wounding *Wounding or *wounding with intent that is not justified by, for example, self-defence or by statutory powers given to the police to arrest criminals.

unless order An order of the court instructing a party to comply with directions specified in the order and also stating the consequences of noncompliance with the order within a specified time. Any sanction for noncompliance attaching to such an order must be proportionate to the request being ordered.

unlimited company A type of *registered company whose members have an unlimited liability (Companies Act 2006 s 3(4)). Thus on winding-up, the company can make demands upon its members until it has sufficient funds to meet the creditors' claims. The risk that members of unlimited companies assume is balanced by certain advantages: an unlimited company (unless it is a parent or subsidiary of a limited company) does not have to deliver its *accounts to the Registrar of Companies and it has more freedom to deal with its capital than a limited company. Unlimited companies may be formed with an *authorized capital, thus enabling them to issue shares and raise working capital, but members' liability is not limited to the nominal value of these shares.

unliquidated damages *See* DAMAGES.

unmarried father A father of a child who is not married to the mother of his child. In law, there is no automatic presumption of paternity in respect of the unmarried father; however, the effect of registration of the name of a man as the father of a child creates a rebuttable presumption of paternity. In other cases a *declaration of parentage may be sought. A father who is registered as such will automatically have *parental responsibility for any child born after 1 December 2003. In all other cases, the father can only acquire parental responsibility by entering into a *parental responsibility agreement with the mother or by obtaining a *parental responsibility order from the courts. Such orders are readily granted where the father establishes a positive attachment and commitment to a child (*Re H* (*Minors*) (*Local Authority: Parental Rights*) (no 3 [1991] Fam 151 (CA); *Re C & V* (*Contact and Parental Responsibility*) [1998] 1 FLR 392 (CA); *Re S* (*Parental Responsibility*) [1994] 2 FLR 68). Examples of circumstances in which parental responsibility orders have been refused include where the father was serving a long-term prison sentence and where a father displayed sadistic behaviour in relation to the child (*Re H* (*Parental Responsibility*) [1998] 1 FLR 855 (CA)). On the whole, the legal status of an unmarried father without parental responsibility is limited; he has no right to look after the child physically, no right to participate in decisions regarding his upbringing, and no right to veto adoption proceedings. It is to be noted that all these limitations will be overcome by obtaining parental responsibility. An unmarried father without parental responsibility does, however, have an obligation to maintain his child financially (*see* CHILD SUPPORT MAINTENANCE); is in the same position as all other parents for the purposes of succession; has a right to reasonable contact if his child is in care; and has a right to be consulted by a local authority about decisions taken in relation to the child. *See also* REGISTRATION OF BIRTH.

unopposed proceedings Proceedings in which any person entitled to oppose fails to take any step (or any further step) in the proceedings, having been given an opportunity to do so.

unpaid seller A seller of goods who has not been paid in full for them or who has received a cheque or other *negotiable instrument that has not been honoured. Although ownership of the goods may have passed to the buyer, an unpaid seller has certain rights against the goods themselves. Under the Sale of Goods Act 1979, these rights are: (1) a possessory *lien (particular, not general); (2) a right of *stoppage *in transitu*; and (3) a *right of resale.

unpaid vendor's lien An equitable right arising in favour of a vendor of land against the purchaser (and those taking title through him as *volunteers) if the vendor has given *possession of the land to the purchaser before receiving the whole of the purchase price. This form of *lien gives the vendor no right to possession of the land but entitles him to seek a court order for the sale of the property to ensure that he is paid the money owing by the purchaser.

unpaid work requirement A requirement that may be imposed by a sentencing court as part of a *community order or a *suspended sentence order under the Criminal Justice Act 2003 or as part of a *youth rehabilitation order under the Criminal Justice and Immigration Act 2008. The offender is required to carry out between 40 and 300 hours of unpaid work, usually for a charity or community project. The unpaid work requirement is effectively a replacement for the former **community punishment order** (often referred to as **community service**).

unreasonable behaviour Behaviour of a respondent that may be evidence that a marriage has broken down irretrievably, entitling the petitioner to a *divorce. Such conduct need not be unreasonable in itself – the real test is whether it is reasonable to expect the petitioner to continue living with the respondent, taking into account the behaviour of both parties and their particular personalities and characteristics (*Livingstone-Stallard v Livingstone-Stallard* [1974] Fam 47). The behaviour may be "positive" (for example, persistent drunkenness, violence, or obsessive conduct) or "negative" (for example, neglect or indifference); a petition may succeed even if the respondent is not responsible for the behaviour, due (for example) to an illness (*Thurlow v Thurlow* [1976] Fam 32).

unreasonableness (of administrative action) *See* WEDNESBURY UNREASONABLENESS. *See also* IRRATIONALITY.

unregistered company A *company that is incorporated otherwise than by registration under the Companies Acts. Unregistered companies, which include *statutory companies and *foreign companies, are subject to some provisions of the Companies Act 2006. *Compare* REGISTERED COMPANY.

unregistered land Land to which the title in question is not registered at the Land Registry. The vast majority of land has become registered as the system of land registration now demands the compulsory registration of all land on transfer. *Compare* REGISTERED LAND. *See also* REGISTRATION OF ENCUMBRANCES.

unsecured creditor A person who has lent money without obtaining any security. *Compare* SECURED CREDITOR.

unsolicited goods Goods sent to someone (other than a trader) who has not asked for them to be sent. It is not in itself an offence to send unsolicited goods (except for matter describing human sexual techniques or advertisements for such matter), but it is a criminal offence to demand payment for them. A person who receives unsolicited goods is an involuntary bailee of them (*see* BAILMENT) and may not destroy or damage them. If he disposes of them, he might be guilty of theft. Statute, however, permits him to treat them as his own property after six months (or 30 days if he has asked the sender to take them back).

unsworn evidence Evidence given by a child under the age of 14 in a criminal case, which must be given unsworn in accordance with the provisions of the Youth Justice and Criminal Evidence Act 1999. In order to give evidence in criminal proceedings a child must be capable of giving intelligible *testimony. The test for unsworn evidence is whether the witness can understand questions put to him and whether he can give answers which can be understood to those questions.

unsworn statement Formerly, a statement made from the dock by an accused person while not on oath. The evidentiary effect of such a statement was much disputed and the right to make one was abolished by the Criminal Justice Act 1982.

uplift *n.* The amount by which a solicitor is allowed to increase a claim for *costs above the basic charge for the work involved. *See also* CONDITIONAL FEE AGREEMENT.

Upper Tribunal A superior *court of record created in 2008 under the Tribunals, Courts and Enforcement Act 2007 as a common means of handling appeals against decisions of lower tribunals. It is the first tribunal to have the power of *judicial review. The Tribunal presently consists of four chambers: the Administrative Appeals Chamber; the Tax and Chancery Chamber; the *Lands Chamber; and the Immigration and Asylum Chamber. Appeals against decisions of the Upper Tribunal can be made to the Court of Appeal in certain circumstances. In *R (Cart) v Upper Tribunal* [2011] UKSC 28, [2012] 1 AC 663 the Supreme Court held that judicial review would occur only where the Tribunal had committed an *error of law on the face of the record or a *procedural impropriety resulting in a denial of natural justice.

urine specimen *See* SPECIMEN OF URINE.

usage *n.* A long-established and well-known practice in a particular market or trade. It may affect the interpretation of, and the nature of *implied terms in, a contract made in that market or trade.

use *n.* [possibly from Latin: *opus*, benefit] Formerly, a right, recognized only in Chancery, of a beneficiary (the *cestui que use*) against the legal owner of land. The medieval common law recognized only legal rights, which were often restricted in nature, but the Chancery protected those to whose use or benefit land was given, although they were not the legal owners. If A held property to the use of B, A was the legal owner (**feoffee to uses**) and B was the beneficiary (*cestui que use*). Uses gave flexibility and helped the evasion of feudal incidents (the medieval equivalent of tax liability). In 1535 the Statute of Uses executed the use, i.e. converted the rights of a *cestui que use* to legal rights, but the statute proved ineffective (*see* USE UPON A USE); it was repealed and uses were abolished in 1925.

use and occupation Possession and/or use of land ⟨by a⟩ person in unlawful occupation of it. A person claiming to recover possession of the land by proceedings in court can also claim a money sum to compensate him for the defendant's unlawful use and occupation.

use classes *See* DEVELOPMENT.

use of force The use of offensive military action, whether amounting to war or not, is prohibited under Article 2(4) of the United Nations Charter. The only exceptions to this strict rule are as follows: (1) when the use of force is by way of an *enforcement action (Article 39 within *Chapter VII of the UN Charter); (2) when force is used for the purposes of *self-defence under Chapter VII (Article 51); and (3) controversially, when a state uses force for the purposes of self-defence under *customary international law (arguably preserved by Article 51). Resort to force upon any other basis is illegal under international law. The leaders of states (and their confederates and agents) who are responsible for initiating such illegal conflicts can be individually tried for *war crimes.

user *n.* The use or enjoyment of property.

use upon a use Formerly, a right recognized by the Chancery after the Statute of Uses 1535 (*see* USE). In a situation in which A held property to the use of (i.e. for the benefit of) B, who held to the use of C, the Statute made B the legal owner but did not affect the second use to C (the use upon a use), who remained entitled to the benefit. The second use eventually developed into the *trust.

usual covenants The covenants that a good conveyancing practitioner would insert in a *lease. When an *agreement for a lease does not specify the terms of the lease, there is a term implied in the agreement that the lease will contain the usual covenants. The following are generally accepted as usual: by the landlord, a covenant for *quiet enjoyment; by the tenant, to pay rent, to pay tenants' rates and taxes, to keep the premises in repair, and to allow the landlord to enter to inspect the state of repair. There is also a condition for *re-entry for nonpayment of rent. Whether or not any other covenant is usual is a matter of evidence.

usufruct *n.* The right of reaping the fruits (*fructus*) of things belonging to others, without destroying or wasting the subject over which such rights extend. An example would be the right of the wife of a deceased person to live in an estate house until her own death.

utilitarianism The approach to morality that regards pleasure or the satisfaction of desire as the exclusive element in human good, and treats the morality of acts and rules as wholly dependent on the consequences for human welfare. Its premise is the proposition that the fundamental objective of morality and justice is that happiness should be maximized. Thus the leading Utilitarian Jeremy Bentham (1748–1832) devised a "felicific calculus" by which we might test the "happiness factor" of any action. A distinction is drawn between two forms of utilitarianism: **act utilitarianism** and **rule utilitarianism**. The former adopts the position that the rightness or wrongness of an action is to be judged by the consequences, good or bad, of the action itself. The latter argues that the rightness or wrongness of an action is to be judged by the goodness or badness of the consequences of a rule that everyone should perform the action in like circumstances. Since the early 19th century utilitarian thought has had a major influence on thinking about punishment and other aspects of penal policy. *See* PUNISHMENT. *See also* CLASSICAL SCHOOL OF CRIMINOLOGY; ECONOMIC ANALYSIS OF LAW; LEGAL POSITIVISM.

utility model (petty patent) A type of short-term *patent that is available in many EU and other jurisdictions but not the UK. A utility model is usually much easier to obtain than a full patent and gives the holder an exclusive right to exploit an invention for a limited period of time (generally 7 to 10 years).

uti possidetis [Latin: as you possess] A principle usually applied in international law to the delineation of borders. When a colony gains independence, the colonial boundaries are accepted as the boundaries of the newly independent state. This practice, first adopted for the sake of expediency by the Spanish American colonies when they declared independence, has since been employed elsewhere in the world following the withdrawal of empire.

The principle of *uti possidetis* is also applied to the status of movable public property of belligerent states. Unless a peace treaty provides to the contrary, each party will retain such property as was in its possession on the day the hostilities ceased.

utter Bar *See* OUTER BAR.

vacantia bona [Latin: empty goods] *See* BONA VACANTIA.

vacant possession The exclusive use of land, to which a purchaser is entitled on completion of the transaction unless he has contracted to buy subject to another's right of occupation.

vacations *pl. n.* The periods between the end of any of the *sittings of the Senior Courts and the beginning of the next sitting, i.e. the Long Vacation, Christmas Vacation, Easter Vacation, and Whitsun Vacation. Provisions relating to the hearing of High Court cases in vacation are set out in a Practice Direction to Part 39 of the *Civil Procedure Rules. The vacation judge is the High Court judge listed to deal with such matters.

vaccine damage payment A tax-free lump-sum payment made, under the Vaccine Damage Payments Act 1979, in compensation for severe disablement caused by a vaccine administered under the British government's vaccination programme.

vagrant *n.* A person classified under the Vagrancy Act 1824 as an "idle and disorderly person", a "rogue and vagabond", or an "incorrigible rogue". The first of these groups includes pedlars who trade without a licence, prostitutes who behave indecently in a public place, and those who beg in a public place. Rogues and vagabonds include those with a second conviction for being idle and disorderly, those who collect charity under false pretences, and tramps who do not make use of available places of shelter. Incorrigible rogues include those with a second conviction for being rogues and vagabonds. Vagrants are usually liable to imprisonment for between one month and one year, depending on which class they fall under, although beggars and tramps sleeping rough are liable only to fines. The Act also provides for various powers to search them or their property.

valuable consideration *See* CONSIDERATION.

value *n.* Valuable *consideration.

value-added tax (VAT) A tax payable on a wide range of supplies of goods and services by way of business. As well as straightforward sales, **taxable supplies** include hirings, rentals, the granting of rights, and the distribution of promotional gifts. VAT is also payable on imports. The amount of tax payable is a percentage of the value of the supply (at present 15%, temporarily reduced from 17.5%, except for domestic fuel, which is charged at 5%) and the liability for the tax arises at the time of the supply (*see* TAX POINT). Any person, firm, or organization that makes regular taxable supplies above a certain annual value must register with HM Revenue and Customs, who administer the tax. A registered person (known as a **taxable person**) must collect from his customers the tax due on the supplies that he makes. This is known as his **output tax**. He pays the tax to HM Revenue and Customs on a periodic basis (usually quarterly), but in doing so he may reclaim any VAT that he has himself paid in the course of his business (his **input**

tax). The entire tax is therefore borne by the ultimate consumer. VAT came into force on 1 April 1973, replacing purchase tax and selective employment tax. *See also* EXEMPT SUPPLY; ZERO-RATED SUPPLY.

(⊕) SEE WEB LINKS
• VAT area of the HM Revenue and Customs website

valued policy An insurance policy that specifies the value of the property insured as agreed between the parties. A policy is not valued merely because it specifies an amount as the sum insured, for that is no more than an estimate of value by the person insured. The essence of a valued policy is that it is based on an agreed valuation, which is conclusive; the insured will recover its full amount even if this exceeds the actual value of the property at the time of loss.

value received Words that may appear on a *bill of exchange indicating either that value has been received by the drawer from the payee or by the acceptor from the drawer. Such words are not necessary; every party whose signature appears on a bill is presumed, unless the contrary is proved, to have become a party for value.

vandalism *n.* Defacing or damaging property. There is no offence of vandalism as such, but it will usually constitute an offence of *criminal damage.

variance *n.* In civil proceedings, a discrepancy between a statement in the *statements of case and the evidence adduced in support of it at trial. In modern practice, it can be rectified by *amendment.

variation of trust A trustee is normally obliged to carry out a trust according to its precise terms; if he fails to do so, he is liable to be sued by his beneficiaries. There are, however, circumstances (both under the court's own jurisdiction and by statute) in which a trust may be varied, and a wide discretion is given to the court, under the Variation of Trusts Act 1958, to vary a trust, provided (usually) that the variation is for the benefit of those on whose behalf the court is acting.

variation to an estate *See* DEED OF VARIATION.

VAT *See* VALUE-ADDED TAX.

VC *See* VICE CHANCELLOR.

VCT *See* VENTURE CAPITAL TRUST.

VDU *See* VISUAL DISPLAY UNIT.

vehicle *n. See* MOTOR VEHICLE.

vehicle construction and maintenance There are detailed rules governing the manufacture and subsequent maintenance of motor vehicles, failure to comply with which may constitute a criminal offence. The main rules deal with such matters as the brakes and steering system, mirrors, windscreen wipers and washers, petrol tanks, door hinges and latches, silencers, pollution prevention, indicators, speedometers, lights, and tyres. There are also regulations governing the use of a motor vehicle. Breach of the regulations relating to brakes, steering system, or tyres or breach of any of the regulations relating to construction, maintenance, or use in a manner that causes or is likely to cause danger is an offence punishable by *endorsement (and carrying 3 penalty points under the *totting-up system) and discretionary disqualification. Other breaches are subject to fines but not to endorsement. There are also special offences relating to the sale or attempted sale of vehicles whose use on the roads would be a breach of the regulations, to the fitting of parts to a vehicle in such a way that its subsequent use would be in breach of the regulations, and to selling or supplying parts whose fitting would cause the vehicle's subsequent use to be in breach of the regulations. These offences do not apply, however, if the defendant proves that the vehicle was sold for export or that he reasonably believed that it would not be used in Britain in an unlawful condition. *See also* MOT TEST.

vehicle insurance *See* THIRD-PARTY INSURANCE; DRIVING WITHOUT INSURANCE.

vehicle interference *See* INTERFERING WITH VEHICLES.

vendor *n.* A seller, particularly one who sells land.

venire de novo [Latin: to come anew] An order made by the Court of Appeal (Criminal Division) ordering a *new trial where there has been a fundamental irregularity in procedure so serious as to render the original trial a mistrial. Originally, it was a writ (***venire facias de novo juratores***) addressed to the sheriff, ordering him to cause new jurors to try the case afresh.

venture capital trust (VCT) An *investment company listed on the London Stock Exchange that specializes in investing in companies of the same kind as those that can qualify under the *Enterprise Investment Scheme. This enables individuals to spread the risk over a number of qualifying companies. The investor buys shares in the VCT, and fund managers invest the money raised in trading companies; the profits are paid out as dividends. The investor is entitled to relief from income tax and capital gains tax.

verdict *n.* **1.** A *jury's finding on the matters referred to it in a criminal or civil trial. The jury is asked to give its decision to the court separately for each of the questions it was asked to consider. A jury must try to reach a unanimous verdict but in both criminal and civil proceedings a *majority verdict may be accepted in certain circumstances. If in criminal proceedings the jury cannot agree a verdict at all they are discharged and the accused may be retried by a different jury. In criminal proceedings a jury may decide that the accused is not guilty of the offence charged but guilty of some lesser offence (*see* ALTERNATIVE VERDICT). *See also* GENERAL VERDICT; PERVERSE VERDICT; SPECIAL VERDICT. **2.** The finding of a coroner's inquest. *See* INQUISITION.

vergens ad inopiam [Latin] On the brink of insolvency. The concept is important in the Scots law relating to bankruptcy proceedings.

vertical agreements Agreements between businesses at different levels of the supply chain; for example, agreements between suppliers and distributors or between wholesalers and retailers (*compare* HORIZONTAL AGREEMENTS). EU regulation 330/2010 exempts certain vertical agreements from the competition rules. Vertical Guidelines accompany the regulation to explain its scope. The EU exemption applies provided that clauses from a list of banned clauses are not included in the agreement concerned and a 30% market share threshold is not exceeded. Many vertical agreements benefit from *block exemption protection.

vest *vb.* **1.** To confer legal ownership of land on someone. **2.** To confer legal rights on someone.

vested in interest Indicating a present right to a future interest in property. For example, if property is left by will "to A for life, remainder to A's first son", A being childless at the testator's death, A's first son's right to the property is vested in interest as soon as he is born and his interest is a **vested remainder**. *Compare* VESTED IN POSSESSION.

vested in possession Indicating an immediate right to the enjoyment of an interest in property. *Compare* VESTED IN INTEREST.

vested remainder *See* VESTED IN INTEREST.

vested rights Rights that have accrued to a person, as opposed to rights that he may or may not acquire. There is a presumption that Acts of Parliament are not intended to interfere with vested rights, particularly without payment of compensation. *See* INTERPRETATION.

vesting assent A document that transfers ownership of *settled land from personal representatives of a deceased tenant for life or statutory owner to the beneficiary entitled to it under the settlement. The assent must be signed by the personal representatives but need not be executed as a deed and it should contain the same information required to be included in a vesting deed by the Settled Land Act 1925.

vesting declaration A statement in a deed appointing new trustees that the trust property is to vest in them, i.e. be in their possession.

vesting deed *See* SETTLED LAND.

vesting order An order of the High Court creating or transferring a legal estate in land. Such an order may be made, for example, when an equitable mortgagee exercises his power of sale: the court may make an order vesting the land in the purchaser.

veto *n.* **1.** (in international law) The power given to any permanent member of the Security Council of the *United Nations to refuse to agree to any nonprocedural proposal (there is no such power in relation to procedural matters) and thereby defeat it. An abstention is not equivalent to a veto. The President of the Security Council has power to determine which questions are nonprocedural. The General Assembly of the UN passed a *Uniting for Peace Resolution in 1950, providing for the Assembly to take over some of the functions of the Security Council when the Council's work has been paralysed by use of the veto. This resolution, however, was only a political gesture and failed to overcome the veto power. **2.** (in EU law) **a.** The power of a member state in the *Council of the European Union to block legislation when a unanimous decision in favour of a measure is required. Although much EU legislation only requires a qualified majority decision of the Council, unanimity votes are required in such areas as taxation, budgets, foreign policy, and the admission of new member states. **b.** The power of the *European Parliament to reject legislation proposed by the Commission by means of the *codecision procedure.

vexatious proceedings Proceedings brought with no reasonable prospect of success and for the purpose of annoying the other party. A **vexatious litigant** is a person who has habitually and persistently and without any reasonable ground instituted vexatious civil proceedings, made vexatious applications in any civil proceedings, or instituted vexatious prosecutions. Under the Supreme Court Act 1981 the court has power, on an application by the Attorney General, to make a "civil proceedings order", a "criminal proceedings order", or an "all proceedings order" in respect of a vexatious litigant. A civil proceedings order or an all proceedings order prevents a vexatious litigant from instituting, continuing, or making an application in any civil proceedings covered by the order without permission of the court. Relevant provisions are set out in the Practice Direction to Part 3 of the *Civil Procedure Rules.

viable *adj.* (in medical law) Capable of being born alive and living a separate existence. The legal age of viability of a fetus is 24 weeks, but some fetuses now survive birth at an even earlier age. *See* ABORTION; CHILD DESTRUCTION.

vicarious liability (vicarious responsibility) Legal liability imposed on one person for torts or crimes committed by another (usually an employee but sometimes an *independent contractor or agent), although the person made vicariously liable is not personally at fault. An employer is vicariously liable for torts committed by his employees when he has authorized or ratified them or when the tort was committed in the course of the employees' work. Thus negligent driving by someone employed as a driver is a tort committed in the course of his employment, but if the driver were to assault a passing pedestrian for motives of private revenge, the assault would not be connected with his job and his employer would not be liable. The test is whether the tort is so closely connected with the employment that it would be fair and just to hold the employer vicariously liable (*Lister v Hesley Hall* [2002] 1 AC 215 (HL)). Employers have been found vicariously liable for bullying in the workplace (*Majrowski v Guy's and St Thomas's NHS Trust* [2006] UKHL 34, [2006] IRLR 695) and for the stabbing of a guest by a bouncer outside a nightclub (*Mattis v Pollock (t/a Flamingo's Nightclub)* [2003] EWCA Civ 887, [2003] ICR 335). The purpose of the doctrine of vicarious liability is to ensure that an employer pays the costs of damage caused by his business operations. His vicarious liability, however, is in addition to the liability of the employee, who remains personally liable for his own torts. The person injured by the tort may sue either or both of them, but will generally prefer to sue the employer.

Vicarious criminal liability may effectively be imposed by statute on an employer for certain offences committed by an employee in relation to his employment. Thus it has been held that an employer is guilty of selling unfit food under the Food Act 1984 when his employee does the physical act of selling (the employee is also guilty, though in practice is rarely prosecuted). Likewise, an employer may be guilty of supplying goods under a false trade description when it is his employee who actually delivers them. For an offence that normally requires *mens rea*, an employer will only be vicariously liable if the offence relates to licensing laws. For example, if a licensee has delegated the entire management of his licensed premises to another person, and that person has committed the offence with the necessary *mens rea*, the licensee will be vicariously liable.

Vicarious liability for crimes may be imposed in certain other circumstances. The registered owner of a vehicle, for example, is expressly made liable by statute for fixed-penalty and excess parking charges, even if the fault for the offence was not his. If the offence is a regulatory offence of *strict liability, the courts often also impose vicarious liability if the offence is defined in the statute in a way that makes this possible.

vicarious performance *See* PERFORMANCE OF CONTRACT.

vicarious responsibility *See* VICARIOUS LIABILITY.

Vice Chancellor (VC) 1. Formerly, the judge who was the effective head of the *Chancery Division of the High Court (the *Lord Chancellor was the nominal president but in practice rarely, if ever, sat in the Division). In 2005 this office was renamed Chancellor of the High Court. **2.** Formerly, a judge of the *palatine courts. The title is still held by the judge assigned to exercise Chancery jurisdiction in Lancashire.

victim *n.* (in human rights law) A person who is actually and directly affected by an act or omission that is incompatible with the European Convention on Human Rights, or a person who is at risk of being directly affected. Only victims have a right to take proceedings. *See* HUMAN RIGHTS ACT.

victimization *n.* In the context of the law against *discrimination on grounds of any of the "protected characteristics" covered by the *Equality Act 2010 the situation in which someone is subjected to a detriment because he has brought a complaint under the legislation or has assisted someone else to do so. The victim may complain to an *employment tribunal.

victim personal statement A written statement that may be given by a victim of a crime, or a member of their family, explaining the impact of the crime on their life. The statement may affect whether or not an accused person is granted bail and may be referred to by the judge in sentencing.

video evidence Evidence from witnesses provided on video, either by video recording or through *live link. In civil proceedings, rules relating to the giving of evidence by live video link are set out in Part 32 of the *Civil Procedure Rules; guidance on videoconferencing in civil proceedings is set out in the Practice Direction to Part 32 of the Rules. In criminal proceedings a *special measures direction may permit a witness to give video-recorded evidence or evidence by means of a live television link. The Criminal Justice Act 2003 allows for the increased use of evidence through a live television link: relevant rules are set out in Part 29 of the *Criminal Procedure Rules.

view *n.* (in court proceedings) An inspection by a judge, or by a judge and jury, of any place or object (such as a bus) that cannot be brought to court, and with respect to which any question arises in the course of litigation. A view is part of the evidence in the case, and a judge should not hold a private view of a public place in the absence of the parties. A view should normally be attended by the judge and the parties, as well as by the jury and the accused in criminal proceedings.

vinculo matrimonii [Latin: bond of marriage] *See* A VINCULO MATRIMONII.

vindictive damages *See* EXEMPLARY DAMAGES.

violence for securing entry *See* FORCIBLE ENTRY.

violent disorder An offence committed when three or more persons, present together, use or threaten unlawful violence (*R v Mahroof* (1988) 88 Cr App R 317). The collective conduct must be such as would have caused a reasonable person to fear for his safety, though no-one else need be present. "Violence" includes violent conduct towards property as well as persons and extends to conduct causing or intended to cause injury or damage. It therefore includes throwing a missile at someone though it does not hit him or falls short. The offence is found in the Public Order Act 1986, though it can be committed in private as well as in public places. It replaces the common-law offence of **unlawful assembly** and is punishable with up to five years' imprisonment and/or a fine. Violent disorder differs from *riot in the smaller minimum number of participants, the absence of need to prove community of purpose, and a lesser maximum punishment. As with *affray, a person is only guilty if he intended to use or threaten violence or was aware that his conduct might be violent or threaten violence. For this purpose, an intoxicated person is taken to be aware of what a sober person would have been aware. If the police fear that a violent event may take place they may now exercise stop-and-search powers (*see* POWER OF SEARCH).

It is also an offence, punishable with six months' imprisonment and/or a fine, to do any of the following, without legal authority, in order to compel a person to do (or not to do) something he has a right to do (or not to do): use violence towards or intimidate that person, his wife, or children or injure his property; persistently follow him; hide his property or hinder his use of it; watch or beset him or his place of residence, work, or business; or follow him with two or more others in a disorderly manner in a street or road. This offence is aimed mainly at disorderly *picketing. However, it is lawful to watch or beset a place (other than a residence) for the sole purpose of peacefully obtaining or communicating information or peacefully persuading any person to work or not to work.

violent offender order (VOO) A civil preventative order introduced by section 98(1) of the Criminal Justice and Immigration Act 2008; it can be made in respect of an offender where the court thinks it necessary for the purpose of protecting the public from the risk of "serious violent harm" and can be drafted in any way the court sees fit to achieve this purpose. For example, the order may prohibit the offender from going to a specified place or premises, from attending a specified event, or from having contact with a specified person. A VOO can only be imposed on an offender aged 18 or over who has received a custodial sentence of 12 months or longer in respect of a violent crime, or who has been made the subject of a *hospital order or *supervision order for such a crime. The order is imposed by the magistrates' court on application from the police service. Breach of a VOO may result in up to five years' imprisonment.

visiting forces Commonwealth forces stationed in the UK and any other forces from abroad designated by Order in Council, including their civilian components. The Visiting Forces Act 1952 empowers the service courts of such forces to exercise jurisdiction over their members according to their national law (but not to carry out the death penalty). It exempts their members from trial by UK criminal courts in the case of offences committed on duty, against other members, or against the property of the force or other members. The Income and Corporation Taxes Act 1988 confers certain exemptions from UK taxation on members of visiting forces.

visitor *n.* **1.** A person appointed to visit and inspect an institution and, in particular, to inquire into internal irregularities. Many universities have a visitor (frequently the Crown), and judges are visitors of the Inns of Court. Boards of Visitors, appointed for prisons by the Home Secretary, act as disciplinary tribunals for breaches of the Prison Rules. A Lord Chancellor's Visitor is appointed under the Mental Health Act 1983 to visit patients and inquire into their ability to manage their affairs. **2.** A person who enters land or premises at the invitation or with the permission of the occupier. *See* OCCUPIER'S LIABILITY.

visual display unit (VDU) A computer screen. The EU's visual display screen directive on health and safety and the visual display units (computer screens) directive 90/270 protects employees by setting out requirements for such matters as risk assessments of computers used at work and by providing for free sight tests and footstools for staff and regular breaks from VDU work.

vitiate *vb.* To destroy or impair the legal effect of a document; for example, a contract may be vitiated by fraud.

vocation *n.* Income from a vocation is taxed in the same way as income from a *profession. According to the ruling of Mr Justice Denman in *Partridge v Mallandaine* (1886) 2 TC 179, 180, which held that the profits of an (illegal) bookmaker were taxable, a vocation "is analogous to the word 'calling' it means the way in which a person passes his life, and it is a very large word indeed". A dramatist (*Billam v Griffith* (1941) 23 TC 757), a racing tipster (*Graham v Arnott* (1941) 24 TC 157), and a jockey (*Wing v O'Connell* [1927] IR 84) have all been held to be carrying on a vocation but not a perennial gambler (*Graham v Green* [1925] 2 KB 37), nor a film producer (*Asher v London Film Productions Ltd* [1944] KB 133).

void *adj*. Having no legal effect.

voidable *adj*. Capable of being avoided (set aside).

voidable contract A contract that, though valid when made, is liable to be subsequently set aside (*compare* VOID CONTRACT). Voidable contracts may arise through *misrepresentation, some instances of *mistake, *nondisclosure, and duress (*see* ECONOMIC DURESS; UNDUE INFLUENCE). Certain proprietary contracts entered into by minors are also voidable (*see* CAPACITY TO CONTRACT). The setting aside of a voidable contract is effected by *rescission.

voidable marriage *See* NULLITY OF MARRIAGE.

voidable trust A trust that can be set aside, e.g. a trust created by an *infant. It may be repudiated by the infant on his attaining majority (18) or shortly thereafter; if the trust is not repudiated, it becomes valid and binding. A trust may also be set aside if it is made as a result of fraud, duress, or undue influence.

void contract A contract that has no legal force from the moment of its making (*compare* VOIDABLE CONTRACT). Void contracts occur when there is lack of *capacity to contract and by the operation in some instances of the doctrine of *mistake. An *illegal contract is void. In addition, certain contracts (e.g. *gaming and wagering contracts) are declared void but not illegal by statute, and certain contracts that are at common law contrary to *public policy are merely void but not illegal. Under UK and EU *competition law on restrictive trade practices, clauses infringing those laws are void but usually the rest of the contract continues. Contracts that are void or, in certain cases, illegal may be saved by *severance.

void marriage *See* NULLITY OF MARRIAGE.

void trust (unlawful trust) A trust that it is against the policy of the law to enforce. Such trusts include those that offend the *rule against perpetuities or the *rule against inalienability or that are contrary to public policy. If a trust is void, the property in the trust will normally be held on *resulting trust for the settlor or his estate.

voir dire (*voire dire*) [Norman French: to speak the truth] **1.** In criminal proceedings, the preliminary examination by a judge of a witness to determine his competence or of a juror to determine his qualification for jury service. **2.** An inquiry conducted by the judge in the absence of the jury into the admissibility of an item of evidence (e.g. a *confession).

volenti non fit injuria [Latin: no wrong is done to one who consents] The defence that the claimant consented to the injury or (more usually) to the risk of being injured; in negligence cases it is more often expressed as **voluntary assumption of risk**. Knowledge of the risk of injury is not sufficient; there must also be (even if only by implication) full and free consent to bear the risk (*Simms v Leigh Rugby Football Club Ltd* [1969] 2 All ER 923). A claimant who has accepted the risk of injury has no action if the injury occurs. The scope of the defence is limited by statute in cases involving business liability and public and private transport.

voluntary *adj*. Without valuable *consideration.

voluntary accommodation Accommodation provided under the Children Act s 20 by a local authority for children whose parents are temporarily unable to look after them or for children who have been abandoned. (It is important to distinguish between a child who is being accommodated by a local authority and a child who is the subject of a *care order.) The purpose of a local authority in supplying accommodation is to support *children in need and their families; it is not a means for the local authority to gain control of the child against the parents' wishes. The local authority does not acquire *parental responsibility for a child who is accommodated; parents with parental responsibility must consent to their child being accommodated and may remove the child without notice and without the consent of the local authority. This is in contrast to a child who is the subject of a care order, where the local authority acquires parental responsibility for that child and may act against the parents' wishes.

voluntary arrangement 1. (**individual voluntary arrangement: IVA**) An agreement between a debtor and his creditors concerning the payment of his debts under the provisions of the Insolvency Act 1986. An IVA, which is often used as an alternative to bankruptcy, takes the form of either a *scheme of arrangement or a *composition. It can be made either before *bankruptcy proceedings are initiated or between an *undischarged bankrupt and his creditors. The court makes an order, called an **interim order**, to protect the debtor from bankruptcy and other court proceedings while an agreement is worked out. The debtor presents his proposals to a creditors' meeting to which all his creditors must be invited. If the meeting agrees with the debtor's proposals, the **approved voluntary arrangement** becomes binding on all the debtor's creditors, whether or not they attended the meeting. The approved voluntary arrangement does not have to be registered as a *deed of arrangement. The meeting's decision is reported to the court, which may discharge the interim order if no agreement has been reached. An *insolvency practitioner (the **supervisor**) is appointed to supervise the carrying out of an approved voluntary arrangement. He may petition for a bankruptcy order if the debtor fails to comply with the terms of the arrangement. 2. (**company voluntary arrangement: CVA**) A similar agreement between a company in financial difficulties and its creditors. Under the Insolvency Act 1986 it must be approved by meetings of both the company and the creditors; if it affects the priority of *preferential debts, the consent of the preferential creditors is required. If the arrangement is approved it becomes binding from the date of the creditors' meeting; there is no interim order. It is supervised by a **nominee**, who must be a qualified *insolvency practitioner. An *administration order may be granted to assist the conclusion of a voluntary arrangement.

voluntary assumption of risk *See* VOLENTI NON FIT INJURIA.

voluntary bill procedure A procedure, governed by Part IV of the Consolidated Criminal Practice Direction, that enables the prosecution to apply to a judge of the High Court to obtain consent for preferring a voluntary *bill of indictment against a defendant. This enables a Crown Court trial without preliminary procedures in the magistrates' court.

voluntary confession *See* CONFESSION.

voluntary conveyance *See* VOLUNTARY DISPOSITION.

voluntary disposition A conveyance or other transfer of ownership of land, made otherwise than for valuable *consideration. Under the Law of Property Act 1925, a voluntary disposition made with intent to defraud a purchaser can be set aside at the instigation of the purchaser.

voluntary liquidation *See* VOLUNTARY WINDING-UP.

voluntary manslaughter *See* MANSLAUGHTER.

voluntary patient *See* INFORMAL PATIENT.

voluntary settlement A *settlement made without valuable *consideration. For any voluntary settlement of property to be valid it must be properly constituted (*Milroy v Lord* (1862) 4 De GF 264 (QB)); hence the maxim "equity will not assist a volunteer". In the case of an outright gift the property should have passed from the donor to the donee and there must have been donative intent at the time of the transfer. In the case of a *trust there must either have been a valid declaration that the settlor holds the property on trust for another, or a valid declaration of trust together with the transfer of the trust property to the trustee(s). In short, for a voluntary settlement to be valid the donor must have done everything necessary in order to render the settlement binding upon him. Exceptions to this rule have been established, most notably in *Re Rose* [1952] Ch 499 (CA), in which the Court of Appeal held that it was sufficient for the settlor to have done everything in his own power to render the transfer effectual even though a third party still had a function to perform in order to perfect the transfer (*see* RULE IN RE ROSE). Recent decisions have also relaxed the strictness of the approach in *Milroy v Lord* (*T Choithram International SA v Pagarani* [2001] 1 WLR 1 (PC); *Pennington v Waine* [2002] EWCA (iv 227, [2002] 1 WLR 2075). The maxim "equity will not perfect an imperfect gift" has arguably been infringed as a consequence of this more relaxed approach.

voluntary waste A kind of *waste that occurs when a tenant takes positive action that damages the land he leases.

voluntary winding-up (voluntary liquidation) A *winding-up procedure initiated by a resolution of the company in accordance with section 84 (1) of the Insolvency Act 1986. In a **members' voluntary winding-up**, the directors must make a statutory **declaration of solvency** within the five weeks preceding the resolution (s 89). This declaration states that the directors have investigated the affairs of the company and are of the opinion that the company will be able to pay its debts in full within a specified period, not exceeding 12 months from the date of the resolution. The liquidator is appointed by the company members. A **creditors' voluntary winding-up** arises when no declaration of solvency has been made (s 90) or when the liquidator in a members' voluntary winding-up disagrees with the forecast made by the directors (s 95–96). In these circumstances the company must hold a meeting of its creditors and lay before it a **statement of affairs** disclosing its assets and liabilities. A *liquidator may be nominated by the company and by the creditors; the creditors' nominee is preferred unless the court orders otherwise (s 100). If the company nominee acts as liquidator prior to the creditors' meeting he can only exercise his powers with the consent of the court. The creditors can also appoint a *liquidation committee (s 101).

In both types of voluntary winding-up the powers of the directors are restricted after the resolution for voluntary winding-up has been passed and they cease when a liquidator has been appointed.

volunteer *n.* **1.** A person who, in relation to any transaction, has not given valuable *consideration. **2.** A person who engages in an activity that involves spending time, unpaid, doing something for the benefit of others. Volunteers may offer their services under a formal arrangement with public, private, or voluntary (charitable) organizations, or may volunteer informally within their community. In general terms, because volunteers are unpaid they do not qualify as *employees or *workers for the purpose of employment protection rights. Nor are they protected under the *Equality Act 2010 from discrimination (*X v Mid-Sussex Citizens Advice Bureau* [2012] UKSC 59, [2013] IRLR 146).

VOO *See* VIOLENT OFFENDER ORDER.

voting *n.* **1.** (in a registered company) The process of casting a vote on a motion proposed at a company meeting. Initially the vote is taken upon a show of hands, i.e. each company member present in person has one vote. If the result is disputed, it is usually possible for the chairman or members (present in person or by *proxy) to demand a **poll**, in which votes are cast (in person or by proxy) in accordance with the number and class of *shares held. Particulars of these voting rights are usually stated in the *articles of association. Members may agree among themselves how they will cast their votes in relation to particular types of resolution (**voting agreement**). **2.** (in a parliamentary or local-government election) *See* ELECTION; FRANCHISE.

voyage charter *See* CHARTERPARTY.

voyage policy *See* TIME POLICY.

voyeurism *n.* Under the Sexual Offences Act 2003 (s 67-68) a person commits the offence of voyeurism if, for the purposes of sexual gratification, he observes another person performing a private act and he knows that the other person does not consent to be observed for his sexual gratification (*R v Bassett* [2008] EWCA Crim 1174, [2009] 1 WLR 1032). A person is similarly guilty if he records (or uses equipment with the intention of recording) a person performing a private act for the sexual gratification of a third party and the person so recorded does not consent.

vulnerable adult An adult patient who has capacity to consent to medical treatment (*see* COMPETENT PATIENT; INCOMPETENT PATIENT) but who is nevertheless judged to be in need of protection, usually because of disability, learning difficulties, or old age. The Department of Health issues special guidelines to safeguard such patients from abuse or neglect.

vulnerable beneficiary A beneficiary who falls within one of three categories: (1) a person who by reason of mental disorder is incapable of administering his property or managing his affairs; (2) a person in receipt of either attendance allowance or of disability living allowance at the highest or middle rate; (3) a person under the age of 18, at least one of whose parents has died. The Finance Act 2005 (s 23–45) introduced a new system for taxing income and capital gains arising in a fund held on trust for such a beneficiary. Tax is calculated as if the income and gains had been received by the beneficiary, regardless of whether any payment is made to him by the trustees. In order to qualify for this treatment, no income arising to the trustees can be paid to any person who is not a vulnerable beneficiary as defined by the Act.

v

wagering contract *See* GAMING CONTRACT.

wait and see principle *See* RULE AGAINST PERPETUITIES.

waiver *n.* **1.** The act of abandoning or refraining from asserting a legal right. **2.** The instrument that declares the act of waiving. **3.** Variation of a contract.

waiver of privilege *See* ABSOLUTE PRIVILEGE.

waiver of tort Giving up the right to sue for damages for a tort in favour of some other remedy, e.g. a restitution action for money that the tortfeasor has made from the tort.

war *n.* The legal state of affairs that exists when states use force to vindicate rights or settle disputes between themselves. States can engage in hostilities (e.g. reprisals) without being in a technical state of war, and they can be in a state of war without much fighting taking place. At common law a state of war could not exist until there had been a formal declaration of war or commencement of hostilities by the Crown. The legal condition of war automatically terminates diplomatic relations and certain types of treaties between the participants. Normal intercourse and commerce between British subjects and those of a power with which the Crown is at war are prohibited.

In the Kellogg–Briand Pact (also known as the Pact of Paris) of 1928, the contracting parties renounced war as an instrument of national policy and undertook to settle their disputes by peaceful means. The United Nations Charter declares that all parties to it "shall refrain . . . from the threat or use of force against the territorial integrity or political independence of any state" or in a manner inconsistent with the Charter, and this is commonly accepted as an accurate statement of customary international law. Nonetheless it appears that states still retain a right of *self-defence, at least if they have been the victims of armed attack and until the Security Council can act. The Security Council is also authorized to use force (or to call upon states to do so) under certain circumstances in order to protect the peace, although in practice this power has not been invoked (*see* USE OF FORCE). The right of self-defence includes a collective right to assist other states acting in self-defence.

The Hague Conventions and Geneva Conventions provide rules governing the conduct of wars and stating the rights and duties of both combatants and noncombatants during war. However, they do not deal with all aspects of warfare or all types of war. There have also been various specific conventions governing particular issues, including a 1972 convention on the use or possession of bacteriological and toxic weapons, a 1976 convention on the military use of environmental modification techniques, and a 1981 convention and three protocols on cruel or indiscriminate non-nuclear weapons. Civil wars are not usually illegal from the point of view of international law, but it is uncertain whether or not other states may legally help either the insurgents or the established authorities (*see* BELLIGERENT COMMUNITIES, RECOGNITION OF; INSURGENCY). The 1977 First and Second Protocols to the Geneva Conventions of 1949, respectively, extend some of the laws of war to civil wars and wars of national liberation (*see* SELF-DETERMINATION).

See also AGGRESSION; HUMANITARIAN INTERVENTION; MARTENS CLAUSE; OCCUPATION; OFFENCES AGAINST INTERNATIONAL LAW AND ORDER; WAR CRIMES.

war crimes Any violation of the laws or customs of war amounting to a criminal act. According to the Charter of the Nuremberg International Military Tribunal of 1946, war crimes include murder, ill-treatment, or deportation of civilian populations, murder or ill-treatment of prisoners of war, killing hostages, plundering property, and wanton destruction of population centres or devastation that is not justified by military necessity. The Nuremberg Tribunal also defined a new category of **crimes against humanity**, consisting essentially of murder, extermination, enslavement, deportation, and other inhumane acts committed against any civilian population before or during World War II and persecution on political, racial, or religious grounds (but only if the persecution is connected with war crimes or crimes against peace); these acts are crimes against humanity whether or not they violate the domestic law of the country where the crime was committed. It is now arguable that this definition is of general application and is wider than that of war crimes. In consequence, the prohibition of crimes against humanity denies the right of any state to treat its citizens as it pleases. This has had major implications for the relationship between state *sovereignty and *humanitarian intervention.

The Tribunal also created a third category of **crimes against peace**, i.e. planning, preparing, or waging a war of aggression or a war in violation of international treaties. It is generally considered that these definitions now form part of customary international law.

War crimes tribunals were established at the end of World War II with jurisdiction to try and punish those who allegedly committed war crimes while acting in the interests of the European Axis countries or Japan. More recently, under *Chapter VII of the UN Charter, the UN Security Council has set up *ad hoc* war crimes tribunals in relation to the conflicts in the former Yugoslavia (1993) and Rwanda (1994). *See also* INTERNATIONAL CRIMINAL COURT.

The War Crimes Act 1991 gives jurisdiction to UK courts to try those charged with war crimes committed in German-held territory during World War II, irrespective of the accused's nationality at the time. Prosecutions may be brought with the consent of the Attorney General for *homicide offences.

By means of the International Criminal Court Act 2001, British tribunals are able to try war crimes recognized by the Statute of Rome. The Statute of Rome established the *International Criminal Court.

Indictments against the former Serbian leader Slobodan Milošević for war crimes committed during the breakup of Yugoslavia were issued by the *International Criminal Tribunal for the former Yugoslavia in May 1999; in June 2001 he was arrested in Serbia and removed to stand trial in the Hague. The trial process was aborted by Milošević's sudden death in March 2006. *See also* INTERNATIONAL CRIMINAL TRIBUNAL FOR RWANDA.

ward of court 1. A minor under the care of a *guardian (appointed by the parents or the court), who exercises rights and duties over the child subject to the general control and discretion of the court. **2.** A minor in respect of whom a *wardship order has been made and over whom the court exercises parental rights and duties. A child becomes a ward of court when a wardship order is made and remains a ward until he reaches the age of 18 or the court orders that he should cease to be a ward. Any child who is actually in England or Wales (or ordinarily resident in England or Wales) may be made a ward of court, even though he is neither domiciled there nor a British subject. Marriage of a ward does not necessarily terminate the wardship.

wardship *n.* The jurisdiction of the High Court to make a child a *ward of court and assume responsibility for its welfare. The jurisdiction is almost unlimited, although subject to consideration of the child's welfare and, to some extent, the rights of other persons and the public interest. The court exercises detailed control of the ward: it may appoint the Official Solicitor to act as his children's guardian and may order either parent to make periodical payments for his maintenance. Wardship proceedings are heard in private and the usual rules of evidence may be relaxed (e.g. in respect of hearsay evidence). The court may enforce its orders by injunction; breach of this or tampering with the ward may constitute contempt of court.

Circumstances in which wardship proceedings are useful include:

- where parents refuse to consent to medical treatment and it is necessary to take long-term decisions about the child;
- where third parties, such as the press, are intruding in a child's life;
- where a child is about to be kidnapped and removed from the jurisdiction. Wardship offers immediate and effective protection in such a case since the moment an application is made, the child becomes a ward of court, and hence can be stopped at a port or airport.

The Children Act 1989 has restricted the use of wardship by local authorities and has considerably reduced the need for wardship in private law proceedings, since individual disputes about a child can frequently be settled by a *specific issue order or a *prohibited steps order. Cases: *Re C (A Baby)* [1996] 2 FLR 43 (CA); *Re W (Wardship: Discharge: Publicity)* [1995] 2 FLR 466 (CA); *A v Liverpool CC* [1982] AC 363 (HL).

war injuries It is normal in the UK on the outbreak of war to enact provisions (e.g. the Personal Injuries (Emergency Powers) Act 1939) excluding civil liability for injuries caused by the discharge of missiles, the use of weapons, explosives, etc.

warned list *See* CAUSE LIST.

warning of caveat A notice given to a person who has entered a *caveat warning him to appear and state what his interest is.

warrant *n.* **1.** A document authorizing some action, especially the payment of money. A **warehouse** (or **wharfinger's**) **warrant** is issued when goods are taken into a public warehouse and must be produced when they are removed. This document is negotiable and transferable by endorsement. *See also* ENFORCEMENT OF JUDGMENT; SHARE WARRANT. **2.** A written document issued by a magistrate for the *arrest of a person or the search of his property (*see* POWER OF SEARCH). When a suspect has fled abroad and there is an extradition treaty covering the offence he is suspected of, the magistrate who has jurisdiction over the place in which the offence was allegedly committed may issue an arrest warrant to enable the Director of Public Prosecutions and the Home Secretary to extradite the suspect. *See also* GENERAL WARRANT.

warrant backed for bail *See* BACKED FOR BAIL.

warrant of commitment An order of the court sending someone to prison.

warrant of detention A court order authorizing the *detention of an arrested person.

warrant of distress A court order giving the power to seize goods from a debtor to pay his creditors. *See* DISTRESS.

warrant of execution *See* WRIT OF EXECUTION.

warranty *n.* **1.** (in contract law) A term or promise in a contract, breach of which will entitle the innocent party to damages but not to treat the contract as discharged by breach. *Compare* CONDITION. *See also* INNOMINATE TERMS. **2.** (in insurance law) A promise by the insured, breach of which will entitle the insurer to treat the contract as discharged by breach. The word therefore has the same meaning as *condition in the general law of contract. **3.** Loosely, a manufacturer's written promise as to the extent he will repair, replace, or otherwise compensate for defective goods; a *guarantee.

war risks Under the Marine and Aviation Insurance (War Risks) Act 1952, risks arising from hostilities, rebellion, revolution, and civil war or from civil strife resulting from such events.

waste *n.* **1.** Any alteration of tenanted property that is caused by the tenant's action or neglect. It includes damage, deterioration, and improvement (*see* AMELIORATING WASTE; EQUITABLE WASTE; PERMISSIVE WASTE; VOLUNTARY WASTE). Landlords can take action against tenants who cause waste (*see* IMPEACHABLE WASTE). The extent of a tenant's liability varies according to the kind of tenancy. Most tenants are liable for equitable and voluntary waste. *Fixed-term tenants are also liable for permissive waste, as are yearly *periodic tenants (but only to the extent that they must keep the premises wind- and water-tight). A *tenant for life under a *settlement is prima facie liable for ameliorating waste, rarely liable for permissive waste, and usually liable for voluntary and equitable waste (unless exempted or made "unimpeachable of waste" by the terms of the settlement). **2.** *See* POLLUTION.

wasted costs order A court order against a legal representative that disallows, or orders him to meet the whole or any part of, costs found to have been incurred as a result of improper, unreasonable, or negligent acts or omissions.

waste disposal Under the Control of Pollution Act 1974 household, commercial, and industrial waste may be disposed of only in licensed sites. Local authorities are generally required to collect household waste free of charge, although there is often a charge for garden waste or large items. There is a charge for the collection of waste from business premises. Local authorities are also obliged to provide free refuse dumps for the disposal of household waste. Householders and businesses now have a duty of care in respect of waste removed from their property by builders, gardeners, scrap-metal merchants, etc. If the contractors are not registered with the *Environment Agency as authorized carriers of waste, the householder may be liable for a fine. Waste has traditionally been buried in landfill sites but recent European and UK legislation has placed strict controls on the amount and type of material sent to landfill. The current regulatory framework is provided by the Landfill Directive 1999 and the Landfill Regulations 2002 (effective 2004). The treatment and storage of scrap motor vehicles is governed by the End Of Life Vehicles (ELV) Directive 2001, which came into effect in the UK in 2003. Stringent controls on emissions from the incineration of waste were introduced by the Waste Incineration Directive (WID), which applies to all UK installations from December 2005. There are special regulations dealing with the treatment, carriage, and disposal of *hazardous waste. *See* POLLUTION.

wasting assets Property forming part of a deceased's estate and having a reducing value (e.g. a leasehold interest in land). Unless the will directs otherwise, the personal representatives have a duty to sell such assets.

wasting police time An offence committed by someone who causes wasteful employment of the police by making a false report about an offence or by implying that a person or property is in danger or that he has information relevant to a police inquiry. The consent of the Director of Public Prosecutions is required for prosecutions for this offence, which is punishable by a fine and/or imprisonment (Criminal Law Act 1965 s 5).

water *n. See* RIGHT OF WATER.

Water Framework Directive An EU directive (2000/60 EC) that establishes a legal framework for the protection and sustainable use of lakes, rivers, and other large bodies of water. Its main aims are to improve water quality by the control of *pollution, reduce the dangers of flooding and drought, and prevent the deterioration of wetlands and other aquatic ecosystems. The directive has been implemented in the UK by the Water Act 2003 and the Water Environment and Water Services (Scotland) Act 2003. Further directives aiming to protect groundwater and to reduce the discharge of 33 "priority substances" have since been adopted at European Level.

water pollution *See* POLLUTION; WATER FRAMEWORK DIRECTIVE.

waybill *n. See* SEA WAYBILL.

weapon of offence Any *offensive weapon or any article made, adapted, or intended for incapacitating someone (e.g. a rope to tie someone with or pepper to make him sneeze). There are special offences of aggravated *burglary and of *trespass with a weapon of offence. *See also* FIREARM.

wear and tear *See* FAIR WEAR AND TEAR.

Wednesbury unreasonableness One of the common law grounds of *judicial review of administrative action, as formulated in the case of *Associated Provincial Picture Houses Ltd v Wednesbury Corporation* [1948] 1 KB 223 (CA). The term denotes behaviour on the part of a public authority that is particularly perverse or absurd (*R v Secretary of State for the Environment, ex p Nottinghamshire County Council* [1986] AC 240 (HL)). However, recent cases indicate that the standard of unreasonableness may be applied with varying degrees of stringency. In cases involving matters of government policy or public expenditure, the courts are reluctant to intervene and tend to apply a more stringent standard of unreasonableness, referred to as super-*Wednesbury*. A less stringent standard is applied in cases where human rights are at issue, referred to as sub-*Wednesbury* (*R v Ministry of Defence, ex p Smith* [1996] QB 517 (CA)). The term is often used interchangeably with the term *irrationality.

weekly tenancy A weekly *periodic tenancy.

welfare law Law enacted to give effect to society's responsibility for the well-being of individuals. It relates to such matters as social security (*see* NATIONAL INSURANCE) and income support, employment protection, health and safety at work, and housing. Many of the services available to individuals under welfare law are covered by the Department for Work and Pensions (formerly Social Security). The Welfare Reform Act 2012 marks the biggest overhaul of the benefits system since the 1940s. It will merge several benefits into a new *universal credit and makes significant changes to housing benefit and disability benefits. The Act also creates new responsibilities for local authorities.

welfare principle The principle that, when making a decision in relation to a child's upbringing, the child's welfare must be the court's paramount consideration (Children Act 1989 s 1). This means that the child's **best interests** are at all times the court's sole concern and that other factors (such as the "rights" of the parents) are only relevant to the extent that they assist the court in ascertaining the best solution for the child (*J v C* [1970] AC 668). The Children Act 1989 does not define welfare but it introduced a checklist of factors to which the court must have regard when deciding whether to make certain orders such as *section 8 orders and *care orders. These factors include: the ascertainable wishes and feelings of the child concerned (considered in the light of his age and understanding); the physical, emotional, and educational needs of the child together with his age, sex, and background; any harm that the child has suffered or is likely to suffer; and how capable his parents or any other relevant persons (e.g. a step-parent) are of meeting his needs. Under the Act any delay in determining the question of upbringing is deemed likely to prejudice the welfare of the child. However, a court will only make an order if it considers that this is the only means of ensuring the child's welfare. *See also* ADOPTION.

well *n.* The open space at the centre of a courtroom, between the bench and the tables used by counsel. It is a breach of court etiquette for anyone who is not a court employee to enter this area; generally, if a lawyer wishes to present papers to the judge, he will hand them to a clerk for this purpose. A lawyer may only cross the well to "approach the bench" with express permission from the judge.

Welsh Assembly The National Assembly for Wales, a body established in 1999 under the Government of Wales Act 1998. The Assembly has 60 elected salaried members. Until 2007 the Assembly did not have legislative or taxing powers, exercising instead a diverse range of functions, such as housing, education, economic development, and flood defence; it also took over many of the powers and responsibilities of the Secretary of State for Wales. The Assembly gained limited primary legislative powers under the Government of Wales Act 2006 and, following a referendum in July 2012, gained direct law-making powers, without the need to consult Westminster. *See* DEVOLUTION.

Welsh company A company that is registered as having its *registered office in Wales (Companies Act 2006 s 88). Welsh companies may lodge documents at the Register of Companies in Welsh and may adopt in their name the Welsh equivalents for "limited" (*cyfyngedig*) and "public limited company" (*cwmni cyfyngedig cyhoeddus*, or c.c.c.). An English translation must be provided.

***Westminster* doctrine** The principle that a person is entitled to make any lawful arrangement of his affairs that he sees fit in order to reduce liability to tax. The Duke of Westminster paid his gardener a wage of £3 a week. By agreement with the gardener he stopped paying the wage and, instead, entered into a covenant to pay him an equivalent amount. Under the law that applied to the tax years in question (1929–30 and 1931–32) the gardener's wage would not have given rise to a tax deduction but the covenant reduced the Duke's liability to surtax. When the case came before the House of Lords, Lord Tomlin stated: "Every man is entitled if he can to arrange his affairs so that the tax attaching under the appropriate Acts is less than it otherwise would be. If he succeeds in ordering them so as to secure that result, then, however unappreciative the Commissioners of Inland Revenue or his fellow taxpayers may be of his ingenuity, he cannot be compelled to pay an increased tax" (*IRC v Duke of Westminster* [1936]

AC1 (HL)), *Compare* RAMSAY PRINCIPLE. *See also* GENERAL ANTI-ABUSE RULE; TAX AVOIDANCE.

wharf *n.* Under the Merchant Shipping Act 1894, any premises (including quays and docks) in or upon which goods landed from ships may be lawfully placed.

whistle-blowing *n.* The disclosure by an employee of information regarding his employer's business. In certain circumstances (with respect to disclosures of wrongdoing by the employer and provided the employee reasonably believes that the disclosure is in the public interest) employees are given legal protection from retaliation by the employer. The Public Interest Disclosure Act 1998 inserts provisions into the Employment Rights Act 1996 that protect employees from dismissal, or detriment, with respect to certain types of disclosures. Contractual provisions attempting to oust the operation of the Act (e.g. the use of "gagging clauses" in an employment contract) are rendered void by the Act.

Qualifying disclosures must relate to any of the following:

- criminal offences;
- failure to comply with a legal obligation;
- a miscarriage of justice;
- a danger to the health or safety of any individual;
- damage to the environment;
- deliberate covering up of information tending to show any of the above matters.

Qualifying disclosures may be made to the employer or to a legal adviser, a minister of the Crown, or a prescribed regulator. If an employee is unable to make disclosures to any of these named persons, or fears retaliation in making such disclosures, then wider disclosure may be made (as long as this is not for personal gain). Wider disclosure could be, for example, to the police, the media, a Member of Parliament, or a non-prescribed regulator. Workers and employees who are dismissed or subjected to a detriment as a result of making a qualifying disclosure to an appropriate recipient can, within three months of such action, make a complaint to an employment tribunal. A dismissal on such grounds is automatically unfair and there is no upper limit on the compensation that may be awarded. If, however, an employment tribunal considers that a disclosure has been made in bad faith, it may reduce any compensation awarded to the worker for the detriment or dismissal he has suffered by up to 25%. Case: *Street v Derbyshire Unemployed Workers' Centre* [2004] EWCA Civ 964, [2004] IRLR 687. *See also* INADMISSIBLE REASON.

white paper *See* COMMAND PAPERS.

whole blood *See* CONSANGUINITY.

widow's benefit A benefit formerly payable to widows. In April 2001 it was renamed *bereavement benefit and now applies equally to men and women.

wild animals *See* ANIMALS; DANGEROUS ANIMALS; POACHING.

wilful *adj.* Deliberate; intended: usually used of wrongful actions in which the conduct is intended and executed by a free agent.

wilful default The failure of a person to do what he should do, either intentionally or through recklessness; for example, nonappearance at court.

wilful misconduct Intentionally doing something that is wrong, or wrongfully omitting to do something, or doing something or omitting to do something that shows reckless indifference as to what the consequences may be.

wilful neglect Deliberate or intentional failure to perform a duty.

wilful neglect to maintain *See* FAILURE TO MAINTAIN.

wilful refusal to consummate The unjustified decision not to consummate a marriage, which may be grounds for annulment of the marriage. There will be no wilful refusal if the unwillingness to consummate is temporary, due to shyness, or due to some physical abnormality that cannot be safely corrected by surgical means. *See also* CONSUMMATION OF A MARRIAGE.

Wilkinson v Downton *See* RULE IN WILKINSON V DOWNTON.

will *n.* A document by which a person (called the **testator**) appoints *executors to administer his estate after his death, and directs the manner in which it is to be distributed to the beneficiaries he specifies. To be valid, the will must comply with the formal requirements of the Wills Act 1837 (*see* EXECUTION OF WILL), the testator must have *testamentary capacity when the will is made, and he must make it of his own free wishes without any *undue influence. A will can be amended by the execution of a *codicil or a duly executed alteration. It can be revoked by the testator destroying it with that intention, or making another will. It may be revoked in part through partial destruction (with the necessary intent), *obliteration of words (rendering them indecipherable) or through signed and attested alterations (such as scoring out words). It is automatically revoked if the testator marries or enters into a civil partnership, except where at the time it was made the testator was expecting to marry a particular person or enter into a civil partnership with a particular person and he intended his will to survive the act of marriage or civil partnership. Following death, the validity of the will is confirmed by the court issuing a grant of *probate. *See also* INTERPRETATION OF WILLS; JOINT WILL; MUTUAL WILLS; NUNCUPATIVE WILL; PRIVILEGED WILL; REVOCATION OF WILL.

winding-up (liquidation) A procedure by which a company can be dissolved. It may be instigated by members or creditors of the company (*see* VOLUNTARY WINDING-UP) or by order of the court (*see* COMPULSORY WINDING-UP). In both cases the process involves the appointment of a *liquidator to assume control of the company from its directors. He collects the assets, pays debts, and distributes any surplus to company members in accordance with their rights.

withdrawal of issue from jury A procedure enabling a judge, who is satisfied that there is insufficient evidence to discharge the evidential *burden of proof borne by a party, to discharge the jury and enter judgment for the opponent if the issue is decisive of the litigation. If the issue is not decisive of the litigation as a whole, he may direct the jury to find against that party in respect of that issue.

with notice Describing a court hearing at which both parties attend, one of them having given the other notice of the time and place of hearing. Prior to the Civil Procedure Act 1999 such a hearing was described as *inter partes*.

without notice Describing an application to the court by one party (or side), without the presence of the other. This is usually associated with either (1) actions in which the claimant seeks *judicial review from a judge of the High Court or (2) actions in which one party wishes to apply to the court without the other party being aware of it, as in applications for a *search order or a *freezing injunction. Prior to the Civil Procedure Act 1999 a without notice application was described as *ex parte*.

without prejudice A phrase used to enable parties to negotiate settlement of a claim without implying any admission of liability. Letters and communications used in such negotiation and headed "without prejudice" cannot be adduced as evidence in any court action without the consent of both parties. However, they may be relevant when costs are discussed in court: thus the phrase "without prejudice save as to costs" is often added on settlement correspondence. Whether or not a letter or discussion is "without prejudice" and therefore cannot be disclosed to the court depends on whether it was a genuine attempt to settle a dispute, not on whether the words "without prejudice" were written on a letter or spoken in a meeting. The reason such discussions are kept secret from the court is that the courts are keen to encourage settlement of disputes without recourse to the courts, and if settlement discussions could be disclosed it might deter parties from settling disputes.

without recourse to me *See* SANS RECOURS.

witness *n.* **1.** A person who observes the signing of a legal document in case it is subsequently necessary to verify the authenticity of the signature. He adds his own signature to the document as a witness. Many legal documents are only valid if properly witnessed (*see* DEED; WILL). **2.** In court proceedings, a person who gives *evidence, either by way of a written statement or orally. In court, witnesses are required either to give evidence on *oath or to *affirm that their evidence is true. Most people are qualified to give evidence in any case (*see* COMPETENCE) but there are certain exceptions; for example, when the judge considers the witness mentally unfit to give evidence. In civil cases a child who is too young to understand the nature of an oath is not a competent witness, although in criminal cases a young child may be allowed to give *unsworn evidence. There is no minimum age below which a child cannot give evidence, but the judge has a discretion to determine whether or not a child is too young to be a competent witness. Most competent witnesses can be compelled to give evidence (a witness who refuses to answer is in *contempt of court) but again there are exceptions. For example, a witness cannot be compelled to answer a question that may *incriminate him. *See also* ADVERSE WITNESS; COMPELLABLE WITNESS; HOSTILE WITNESS.

witnessing part *See* DEED.

witness's oath *See* OATH.

witness summons **1.** In civil proceedings, a document issued by the court under Part 34 of the *Civil Procedure Rules requiring a witness to attend court to give evidence or to produce documents to the court. A witness summons was formerly known as a **subpoena**, a summons requiring a person to give evidence being a **subpoena** *ad testificandum* and a summons requiring him to produce documents being a **subpoena** *duces tecum*. **2.** In criminal proceedings, a document served on a witness requiring him to attend court to give evidence. The procedure for applying to the magistrates' court for the issue of a summons to witness under the Magistrates' Courts Act 1980, and to the Crown Court for a witness summons under the Criminal Procedure (Attendance of Witnesses) Act 1965, is set out in Part 28 of the Criminal Procedure Rules.

women employees *See* EQUALITY CLAUSE; EQUAL PAY; EQUAL TREATMENT DIRECTIVE; MATERNITY RIGHTS; SAFETY AT WORK; SEX DISCRIMINATION.

Woolf Reforms *See* CIVIL PROCEDURE RULES.

words of art Words whose legal interpretation has been fixed so that the legal effect of their use is known.

words of limitation Words in a conveyance of land that define the interest transferred; for example, "in fee simple".

words of procreation The words in a settlement of land that created an *entailed interest. Unless the land was expressly settled on the beneficiary "and the heirs of his body" or "in tail", an entailed interest would not result.

words of purchase The words in a conveyance of land that identify the person to whom the property is transferred.

words of severance *See* SEVERANCE.

work done and materials supplied, contract for A contract the substance of which is that skill and labour must be exercised in carrying out the contract, in addition to supplying the materials used in the work. Examples are contracts by an artist to paint a portrait and by a builder to fit double glazing. Such a contract is distinct from a contract of sale of goods, in which the substance of the contract is a product to be sold.

worker *n.* Under UK employment legislation, "worker" is a wider category than that of *employee. In particular, it may encompass those who would describe themselves as self-employed. The Employment Rights Act 1996, section 203(3), defines a worker as "an individual who has entered into or works under ... (a) a *contract of employment, or (b) any other contract ... whereby the individual undertakes to do or perform personally any work or services for another party to the contract whose status is not ... that of a client or customer of any profession or business undertaking carried on by the individual". Some employment legislation extends to both employees and workers (e.g. the national minimum wage) while some covers only employees (e.g. protection against *unfair dismissal). A worker is distinguished from someone in business on his own account because the worker is heavily dependent on the employer for his work. Case: *Byrne Bros Ltd v Baird* [2002] IRLR 96 (EAT).

work-in *n.* Industrial action in which employees occupy their workplace against the will of their employer and continue working. Generally such action constitutes *trespass, and the employer can apply to the court for an order that the employees restore possession of the premises to him.

working day 1. For banking and financial purposes, any day other than Saturday, Sunday, and *bank holidays. *See also* SUNDAY TRADING. **2.** (of a court) Any day other than Sunday or holidays, called a *dies juridicus*. A day on which no legal business can be carried on is called a *dies non*.

working hours The EU Working Time Directive (93/104) 1993 required all member states to limit the working week of employees to 48 hours (except when employees have agreed otherwise). The provisions of this Directive were implemented in the UK in the Working Time Regulations 1998. Key elements of the Regulations require a maximum working week of 48 hours, daily rest breaks, weekly rest periods, and annual paid leave (*see* HOLIDAY PAY). The Regulations also contain protections with respect to night working. They are enforced by the Health and Safety Executive. The Regulations extend to *workers who are not employees.

working tax credit *See* TAX CREDIT.

World Bank *See* INTERNATIONAL BANK FOR RECONSTRUCTION AND DEVELOPMENT.

World Trade Organization (WTO) An international trade organization formed under the *General Agreement on Tariffs and Trade (GATT) to replace GATT and implement measures agreed at the Uruguay Round (1994) by 2002. It began operating on 1 January 1995. The WTO's aims are to continue the work of GATT in agreeing international trading rules and furthering the liberalization of international trade. The WTO extends its jurisdiction into such aspects of trading as intellectual property rights (*see* TRIPS). WTO rules are very important in international trade contracts. The highest authority of the WTO is the Ministerial Conference, held at least every two years. By 2013 the WTO had 157 member states.

• WTO website

wounding *n.* Breaking the continuity of the skin or of a membrane (such as that lining the cheeks or lips). Scratching, bruising, burning, or breaking a bone without tearing the skin do not constitute wounding (*Moriarty v Brookes* (1834) 6 C&P 684; *JJC (a minor) v Eisenhower* [1984] QB 331). **Malicious wounding** is an offence punishable by up to five years' imprisonment. It requires an intention to cause some physical harm (not necessarily a wound) or foresight of the risk of causing physical harm (Offences Against the Person Act 1861 s 20). A person is not guilty of this offence if he intended only to frighten his victim but in fact accidentally wounded him, although he would be guilty of *assault or *battery.

wounding with intent Causing a wound to any person with the intention of *wounding, causing *grievous bodily harm, or resisting the lawful arrest of any person (Offences against the Person Act 1861 s 18). Wounding with intent carries a maximum sentence of life imprisonment.

wreck *n.* **1.** (shipwreck) The destruction of a ship at sea, as by foundering in a storm or being driven onto rocks. **2.** The remains of a wrecked ship. **3.** Goods cast up by the sea from a wrecked ship.

writ *n.* An order issued by a court in the sovereign's name directing some act or forbearance. Originally, a writ was an instrument under seal bearing some command of the sovereign.

writ of delivery In civil proceedings, a *writ of execution to enforce a judgment or order for the delivery of goods. It directs the *High Court Enforcement Officer (formerly the sheriff) to seize the goods and deliver them to the claimant or to recover their assessed value. If the writ does not offer the defendant the option of retaining the goods by paying their assessed value, it is known as a **writ of specific delivery**. In the county court a judgment or order for the delivery of goods is enforced by a bailiff under a warrant of delivery. Relevant procedural rules are set out in Schedules 1 and 2 to the *Civil Procedure Rules.

writ of execution In civil proceedings, a writ used in the *enforcement of a judgment. Writs of execution include a writ of *fieri facias, a *writ of possession, a *writ of delivery, and a writ of *sequestration. In the county court execution is effected by a bailiff under a **warrant of execution**. Relevant procedural rules are set out in Schedules 1 and 2 to the *Civil Procedure Rules.

writ of possession In civil proceedings, a writ directing the *High Court Enforcement Officer (formerly the sheriff) to enter upon land to give vacant possession to the claimant. It is used to enforce a judgment or order for the possession of land. In the county court a judgment or order for the recovery of land is enforced by a bailiff under a **warrant of possession**. Relevant procedural rules are set out in Schedules 1 and 2 to the *Civil Procedure Rules.

writ of summons Formerly, a writ by which a civil action was commenced in the High Court. Civil proceedings in the High Court are now initiated through a *claim form under Part 7 of the *Civil Procedure Rules.

written resolution A resolution passed outside a *general meeting by members of a private company. It can be passed as an *ordinary resolution or as a *special resolution (Companies Act 2006 s 296). A written resolution is not permitted to dismiss a director or auditor of the company (s 288(2)).

wrong *n.* An illegal or immoral act. A distinction must be drawn between moral wrongs and legal wrongs. Some moral wrongs, such as murder or theft, are also crimes punishable by law. But many moral wrongs are not legal wrongs and some legal offences, such as parking offences, are not generally regarded as morally blameworthy. Legal wrongs may be criminal or civil. *Crimes are offences against society as a whole, not merely against the victim of the crime. Civil wrongs, such as *torts, *breaches of contract, and interferences with property rights, are wrongs to the individuals affected.

wrongful dismissal The termination of an employee's contract of employment in a manner that is not in accordance with that contract. Thus when an employee is dismissed without the notice to which he is entitled (in circumstances that do not justify summary dismissal) or when the employer prematurely terminates the employee's fixed-term contract, the employee is entitled to claim damages in the courts or an employment tribunal at common law for wrongful dismissal. The court's jurisdiction concerns only the parties' contractual rights and not their statutory rights under the employment protection legislation (*compare* UNFAIR DISMISSAL). If a breach of statutory rights arises, an employee may also bring a claim for unfair dismissal. However, this must be done before an employment tribunal.

wrongful interference with goods Under the Torts (Interference with Goods) Act 1977, any of various torts to goods. It includes *conversion, *trespass to goods, negligence so far as it results in damage to goods or to an interest in goods, and any other tort that results in damage to goods or an interest in goods.

wrongful trading Carrying on business knowing that the company has no reasonable prospect of avoiding an insolvent *winding-up (Insolvency Act 1986 s 214). Such knowledge may be implied if a reasonably diligent person would have realized the position (*Re Produce Marketing Consortium Ltd* (No 2) [1989] 1 WLR 745; *Re Rod Gunner Organization Ltd* [2004] EWHC 316 (Ch)). Directors responsible may be ordered to contribute to the assets of the company when the winding-up occurs unless they can prove that, after acquiring the relevant knowledge, they endeavoured to minimize loss to the company's creditors, e.g. by initiating a winding-up or administration of the company. *See also* FRAUDULENT TRADING.

WTO *See* WORLD TRADE ORGANIZATION.

year and thereafter from year to year Words sometimes used in a tenancy agreement, the effect of which is that the tenant has a *fixed-term tenancy for the first year, followed by a yearly *periodic tenancy.

Year Books *See* LAW REPORTS.

yearly tenancy A yearly *periodic tenancy.

yielding and paying Words that usually introduce the clause in a *lease that specifies the rent. *See also* REDDENDUM.

York-Antwerp rules *See* AVERAGE.

young offender *See* JUVENILE OFFENDER.

young workers *See* CHILD EMPLOYEE.

youth rehabilitation order A community sentence that may be imposed on an offender aged 18 or under. It imposes one or more specified requirements, which may include an *activity requirement, a *curfew requirement, an *exclusion requirement, a *mental health treatment requirement, an *unpaid work requirement, a *supervision requirement, a *drug treatment requirement, a *residence requirement, a *programme requirement, a *prohibited activity requirement, or an *attendance centre requirement. Under the Criminal Justice and Immigration Act 2008 youth rehabilitation orders replaced the previous system of youth community orders. *See also* COMMUNITY ORDER.

youth court A *magistrates' court exercising jurisdiction over crimes committed by *juvenile offenders and other matters relating to children under 18. It was formerly called a **juvenile court**. The court consists of either three lay *magistrates (at least one of whom should normally be a man and one a woman) or a single *district judge (magistrates' court) (normally accompanied by a lay magistrate of the opposite sex). All these magistrates are selected from the **youth court panel**, whose members are thought to be specially qualified to deal with juveniles and who have received additional training for this purpose. The proceedings of the court are not open to the general public, access being very restricted and determined by the Children and Young Persons Act 1933, section 42 (as amended) and by the Home Office and Lord Chancellor's Department Joint Circular on access to youth courts (1998). The press may not publish the identity of any juvenile concerned in the court's proceedings unless the court or the Home Secretary so orders, although reporting restrictions are lifted on conviction. Court proceedings are generally more informal than in the magistrates' court for adult offenders, and hearings can be heard in locations other than other court buildings, although generally they will be in existing magistrates' courts.

youth custody *See* DETENTION AND TRAINING ORDER.

zealous witness A *witness who displays undue favouritism towards one party in the case.

zebra crossing A road crossing for pedestrians, identified by studs and alternating black and white stripes on the carriageway and lighted yellow globes (normally flashing) at each end. Pedestrians take precedence over vehicles on crossings uncontrolled by police or traffic wardens, and it is an offence for vehicles to wait or overtake within their limits.

zero-rated supply A supply of goods or services that is specified in the Value Added Taxes Act 1994 as being liable to a *value-added tax charge of 0%. A zero-rated supply differs from an *exempt supply in that the VAT attributable to it is allowable for *input tax credit. Schedule 8 of the Act lists 16 groups of zero-rated supplies:

(1) food;
(2) sewerage services and water;
(3) books etc.;
(4) talking books and wireless sets;
(5) buildings and civil engineering works;
(6) protected buildings;
(7) international services;
(8) transport;
(9) caravans and houseboats;
(10) gold;
(11) bank notes;
(12) drugs, medicines, aids to the handicapped, etc.;
(13) imports, exports, etc.;
(14) tax-free shops;
(15) charities, etc.;
(16) clothing and footwear.

The EU Sixth Directive obliges member states to charge VAT on supplies. The European Commission accepts that the UK discharges this liability by charging VAT at 0% on the specified categories of supply.

Abbreviations

The following is a list (by no means comprehensive) of abbreviations commonly found in legal writing. It includes abbreviations for law report series and legal journals as well as those conventionally used in case names and citations of statutes. For detailed advice on citing cases and legislation, see the WRITING AND CITATION GUIDE at the centre of this book.

AC	Law Reports: Appeal Cases	CLR	Commonwealth Law Reports
Admin	Administrative Court of the High Court	Cmd	Command Papers (1919–56)
AG	(1) Attorney General	CMLR	Common Market Law Reports
	(2) Advocate General	Cmnd	Command Papers (1957–)
AJCL	American Journal of Comparative Law	Com Ct	Commercial Court of the High Court
AJIL	American Journal of International Law	CPS	Crown Prosecution Service
All ER	All England Law Reports	Cr App R	Criminal Appeal Reports
Anglo-Am LR	Anglo-American Law Review	Crim LR	Criminal Law Review
		DC	Divisional Court
App no	application number (of European Court of Human Rights cases)	dir	directive
		DPP	Director of Public Prosecutions
art	article	EAT	Employment Appeal Tribunal
BC	Borough Council		
BCC	British Company Law Cases	ECC	European Commercial Cases
BTR	British Tax Review	ECHR	European Court of Human Rights
c	chapter (*pl.* cc)		
C	Command Papers (1870–99)	ECJ	European Court of Justice
CA	Court of Appeal	ECR	European Court Reports
CC	County Council	EG	Estates Gazette
CCR	Crown Cases Reserved	EHRR	European Human Rights Report
Cd	Command Papers (1900–18)		
CEC	(1) European Community Cases	EJIL	European Journal of International Law
	(2) Commission of the European Communities	EMLR	Entertainment and Media Law Reports
CFI	Court of First Instance	Ent LR	Entertainment Law Review
Ch	(1) Chancery Division of the High Court	Eq	Law Reports: Equity
	(2) Law Reports: Chancery Division	ER	English Reports
		ET	Employment Tribunal
CJ	(after the name of a judge) Lord Chief Justice	EWCA Civ	Court of Appeal, Civil Division (England and Wales)
cl	clause	EWCA Crim	Court of Appeal, Criminal Division (England and Wales)
CL	Current Law Monthly Digest		

EWHC	High Court (England and Wales)	Lloyd's Rep	Lloyd's Law Reports
		LR	Law Reports
Exch	Law Reports: Court of Exchequer	MLR	Modern Law Review
		MR	Master of the Rolls
Exor	Executor	NLJ	New Law Journal
ex p	*ex parte* (on the part of)	OJ	Official Journal of the European Union
Exrx	Executrix		
F	(1) Family Division of the High Court	ors	others
		P	Law Reports: Probate
	(2) Federal Reporter	PAD	Planning Appeal Decisions
Fam	Law Reports: Family Division		
		P & CR	Property and Compensation Reports
FCR	Family Court Reporter		
FLR	Family Law Reports	para	paragraph
FSR	Fleet Street Reports	Pat	Patents Court of the High Court
F Supp	Federal Supplement		
HL	House of Lords	PC	Judicial Committee of the Privy Council
HRLJ	Human Rights Law Journal		
ICC	International Criminal Court	PCIJ	Permanent Court of International Justice
ICJ	International Court of Justice	PD	Practice Direction
		pt	part
ICR	Industrial Cases Reports	Pty	proprietary
ILM	International Legal Materials	QB	(1) Queen's Bench Division of the High Court
ILR	International Law Reports		(2) Law Reports: Queen's Bench Division
Imm AR	Immigration Appeals Reports		
		r	rule (*pl.* rr)
IRC	Inland Revenue Commissioners	R	The Queen/King
		reg	regulation
IRLR	Industrial Relations Law Reports	Res	Resolution
		RIAA	Reports of International Arbitration Awards
ITR	Industrial Tribunals Reports		
		s	section
J	(after the name of a judge) Justice	Sc	Scottish
		SC	Scottish Session Cases
JC	Scottish Justiciary Cases	sch	schedule
JPEL	Journal of Planning and Environmental Law	S Ct	Supreme Court Reporter
		SI	statutory instrument
KB	(1) King's Bench Division of the High Court	ss	(1) subsection
			(2) sections
	(2) Law Reports: King's Bench Division	STC	Simon's Tax Cases
		St Tr	State Trials and Proceedings
LBC	London Borough Council		
LC	Lord Chancellor	sub nom	*sub nominee* (under the name)
LCJ	Lord Chief Justice		
L Ed	Lawyers' Edition	supp	supplement
LGR	Local Government Review	TC	(1) Tax Cases
LJ	(after the name of a judge) Lord Justice/Lady Justice		(2) Technology and Construction Court

TLR	Times Law Reports	UNSC	United Nations Security Council
UKHL	House of Lords (United Kingdom)	US	United States Reports (i.e. Supreme Court decisions)
UKSC	Supreme Court of the United Kingdom		
UNGA	United Nations General Assembly	WLR	Weekly Law Reports
		WN	Weekly Notes

Online Legal Resources

Recent years have seen a proliferation of online legal resources, ranging from specialist databases to sites offering advice, information, and legal services to the layperson. The following is a selection of authoritative, quality-controlled sites that provide free information on essential legal topics. These resources are widely used by law students and legal professionals but can be navigated quite easily by those with no previous background in legal research. To access any of these websites, go to the dictionary's web page at http://www.oup.com/uk/reference/resources/law, click on **Web links** in the Resources section, go to **Appendix web links**, and then click through to the relevant site.

Portals

- Lawlinks: a portal maintained by the University of Kent. Annotated links provide access to a wide range of resources, including primary materials (cases and statutes).

- Access to Law: a links directory compiled by librarians at the Inner Temple, London. The site provides links to materials on civil procedure, courts and tribunals, case law, and legislation, as well as to specific subject areas.

- Infolaw: the UK's first source of online legal information. Its lawfinder service, which is widely used by lawyers, provides access to numerous resources, including Acts and cases.

- Intute Law: a gateway service developed by Social Sciences: Intute, a consortium led by staff at the Universities of Bristol and Birmingham. There are links to a wide range of resources, including primary and secondary materials.

- Lawbore: the law portal of City University, London. The resource is designed primarily for law students, with links arranged according to subject area.

- Venables: a directory compiled by Delia Venables. Links provide legal information for individuals, companies, students, and (especially) legal practitioners.

Legislation

- Bailli: the website of the British and Irish Legal Information Institute. This is the most comprehensive free-access database for primary English law materials.

- Legislation Database: the official online database for primary legislation in the UK, as maintained by the National Archives. The website provides full texts for all UK legislation since 1988, including statutory instruments and Acts of the devolved institutions. Primary legislation can be viewed both with and without later amendments. Most earlier (pre-1988) legislation is now also available at this site although sometimes in unamended form only.

- Houses of Parliament website: provides details of all bills currently before Parliament (including full text and current status) and verbatim reports of debates in both Houses.

- Europa: provides direct access to European Union law, including treaties, legislation, and case law.

- Ecolex: a comprehensive resource for environmental legislation worldwide. Ecolex provides details of treaties, national legislation, EU directives and regulations, and court decisions.
- Electronic Information System for International Law (EISIL): a directory of links to treaty collections, UN resolutions, and other primary materials compiled by the American Society of International Law. There are also links to regional and intergovernmental organizations.

Case Law

- Bailli: see under Legislation above.
- House of Lords: full text of all judgments of the House of Lords from November 1996 to July 2009.
- Supreme Court: judgments of the Supreme Court of the UK since it was established in October 2009.
- Law Reports: website of the Incorporated Council of Law Reporting, compilers of the official Law Reports and Weekly Law Reports. It provides summaries of important cases since January 2005, including industrial cases and decisions of the European Court of Justice.
- Swarb: David Swarbrick's site provides a substantial case-law database, extracts from statutes, and advice and information on legal topics.
- Scotcourts: recent significant judgments of the Scottish courts, together with court rules and other information.
- Employment Appeals: decisions of the Employment Appeal Tribunal from 2000 onwards.
- Interights: summaries of important human rights decisions from courts and tribunals around the world.

Advice

- Advice Now: an independent not-for-profit service providing advice on everyday legal matters (consumer rights, employment law, divorce, compensation claims, buying and selling property, etc.).
- Civil Legal Advice: online or telephone advice service from the Legal Aid Agency.
- Your Rights: a layperson's guide to the Human Rights Act 1998 provided by Liberty, the UK human rights and civil liberties organization.
- Chambers and Partners: a database of lawyers and law firms in 175 countries compiled by the publishers of the Chambers guides. Searchable by region and area of expertise, it also features merit rankings based on interviews with clients.

More History titles from OUP

The Oxford Companion to Black British History
David Dabydeen, John Gilmore, and Cecily Jones

The first reference book to explore the full history of black people in the British Isles from Roman times to the present day.

'From Haiti to Kingston, to Harlem, to Tottenham, the story of the African Diaspora is seldom told. This Companion will ensure that the history of Black Britain begins to take its rightful place in mainstream British consciousness.'

David Lammy, MP, former Minister for Culture

A Dictionary of World History

Contains a wealth of information on all aspects of history, from prehistory right up to the present day. Over 4,000 clear, concise entries include biographies of key figures in world history, separate entries for every country in the world, and subject entries on religious and political movements, international organizations, and key battles and places.

The Concise Oxford Dictionary of Archaeology
Timothy Darvill

The most wide-ranging, up-to-date, and authoritative dictionary of its kind.

'Comprehensive, proportionate, and limpid'

Antiquity

More Literature titles from OUP

The Oxford Companion to Charles Dickens
edited by Paul Schlicke

Reissued to celebrate the bicentenary of Charles Dickens's birth, this companion draws together an unparalleled diversity of information on one of Britain's greatest writers; covering his life, his works, his reputation, and his cultural context.

Reviews from previous edition:
'comes about as close to perfection as humanly possible'

Dickens Quarterly

'will prove invaluable to scholars, readers and admirers of Dickens'

Peter Ackroyd, *The Times*

The Oxford Companion to the Brontës
Christine Alexander and Margaret Smith

This Companion brings together a wealth of information about the fascinating lives and writings of the Brontë sisters.

'This book is a must ... a treasure trove of a book'

Irish Times

The Oxford Companion to Classical Literature
edited by M. C. Howatson

A broad-ranging and authoritative guide to the classical world and its literary heritage.

Reviews from previous edition:
'a volume for all seasons ... indispensable'

Times Educational Supplement

'A necessity for any seriously literary household.'

History Today

More Art Reference from Oxford

The Grove Dictionary of Art

The 34 volumes of *The Grove Dictionary of Art* provide unrivalled coverage of the visual arts from Asia, Africa, the Americas, Europe, and the Pacific, from prehistory to the present day.

'succeeds in performing the most difficult of balancing acts, satisfying specialists while ... remaining accessible to the general reader'

The Times

Oxford Art Online
www.oxfordartonline.com

Oxford Art Online is the home of Grove Art Online, the unsurpassed authority on all aspects of art from pre-history to the present day.

A Dictionary of Modern and Contemporary Art
Ian Chilvers and John Glaves-Smith

This dictionary boasts worldwide coverage of modern and contemporary art from 1900 to the present day.

The Oxford Dictionary of American Art and Artists
Ann Lee Morgan

The first single-volume dictionary of American art in thirty years.

'Concise, clear and very informative ... There is really nothing comparable'

Choice

Oxford Companions

'Opening such books is like sitting down with a knowledgeable friend. Not a bore or a know-all, but a genuinely well-informed chum ... So far so splendid.'

Sunday Times [of *The Oxford Companion to Shakespeare*]

For well over 60 years Oxford University Press has been publishing Companions that are of lasting value and interest, each one not only a comprehensive source of reference, but also a stimulating guide, mentor, and friend. There is a wide range of Oxford Companions available at any one time, covering topics such as music, art, and literature, as well as history, warfare, religion, and wine.

Titles include:

The Oxford Companion to English Literature
Edited by Dinah Birch
'No guide could come more classic.'

Malcolm Bradbury, *The Times*

The Oxford Companion to Music
Edited by Alison Latham
'probably the best one-volume music reference book going'

Times Educational Supplement

The Oxford Companion to Theatre and Performance
Edited by Dennis Kennedy
'A work that everyone who is serious about the theatre should have at hand'

British Theatre Guide

The Oxford Companion to Food
Alan Davidson
'the best food reference work ever to appear in the English language'

New Statesman

The Oxford Companion to Wine
Edited by Jancis Robinson
'the greatest wine book ever published'

Washington Post

Oxford Quick Reference

The Concise Oxford Dictionary of English Etymology
T. F. Hoad

A wealth of information about our language and its history, this reference source provides over 17,000 entries on word origins.

'A model of its kind'

Daily Telegraph

New Oxford Rhyming Dictionary

From writing poems to writing birthday cards, and from composing advertising slogans to music lyrics, this dictionary has what every writer (or budding writer) needs. It contains rhymes for over 45,000 words, including proper names, place names, and foreign terms used in English.

'All wordsmiths are bound to enjoy feeling indebted (fetid, minareted, rosetted...)'

Julia Donaldson (author of *The Gruffalo*)

The Oxford Dictionary of Slang
John Ayto

Containing over 10,000 words and phrases, this is the ideal reference for those interested in the more quirky and unofficial words used in the English language.

'hours of happy browsing for language lovers'

Observer

Oxford Quick Reference

The Concise Oxford Companion to English Literature
Dinah Birch and Katy Hooper

Based on the best-selling *Oxford Companion to English Literature*, this is an indispensable guide to all aspects of English literature.

Review of the parent volume:
'the foremost work of reference in its field'

Literary Review

A Dictionary of Shakespeare
Stanley Wells

Compiled by one of the best-known international authorities on the playwright's works, this dictionary offers up-to-date information on all aspects of Shakespeare, both in his own time and in later ages.

The Oxford Dictionary of Literary Terms
Chris Baldick

A best-selling dictionary, covering all aspects of literature, this is an essential reference work for students of literature in any language.

A Dictionary of Critical Theory
Ian Buchanan

The invaluable multidisciplinary guide to theory, covering movements, theories, and events.

'an excellent gateway into critical theory'

Literature and Theology

Oxford Quick Reference

A Dictionary of Marketing
Charles Doyle

Covers traditional marketing techniques and theories alongside the latest concepts in over 2,000 clear and authoritative entries.

'Flick to any page [for] a lecture's worth of well thought through information'

Dan Germain, Head of Creative, innocent ltd

A Dictionary of Media and Communication
Daniel Chandler and Rod Munday

Provides over 2,200 authoritative entries on terms used in media and communication, from concepts and theories to technical terms, across subject areas that include advertising, digital culture, journalism, new media, radio studies, and telecommunications.

'a wonderful volume that is much more than a simple dictionary'
Professor Joshua Meyrowitz, University of New Hampshire

A Dictionary of Film Studies
Annette Kuhn and Guy Westwell

Features terms covering all aspects of film studies in 500 detailed entries, from theory and history to technical terms and practices.

A Dictionary of Journalism
Tony Harcup

Covers terminology relating to the practice, business, and technology of journalism, as well as its concepts and theories, organizations and institutions, publications, and key events.

Oxford Quick Reference

Concise Medical Dictionary

Over 12,000 clear entries covering all the major medical and surgical specialities make this one of our best-selling dictionaries.

'"No home should be without one" certainly applies to this splendid medical dictionary'

Journal of the Institute of Health Education

'An extraordinary bargain' *New Scientist*

A Dictionary of Nursing

Comprehensive coverage of the ever-expanding vocabulary of the nursing professions. Features over 10,000 entries written by medical and nursing specialists.

A Dictionary of Dentistry
Robert Ireland

Over 4,000 succinct and authoritative entries define all the important terms used in dentistry today. This is the ideal reference for all members of the dental team.

A Dictionary of Forensic Science
Suzanne Bell

In over 1,300 entries, this new dictionary covers the key concepts within Forensic Science and is a must-have for students and practitioners of forensic science.

Oxford Quick Reference

The Oxford Dictionary of Dance
Debra Craine and Judith Mackrell

Over 2,600 entries on everything from hip-hop to classical ballet, covering dancers, dance styles, choreographers and composers, techniques, companies, and productions.

'A must-have volume ... impressively thorough'

Margaret Reynolds, *The Times*

The Oxford Guide to Plays
Michael Patterson

Covers 1,000 of the most important, best-known, and most popular plays of world theatre.

'Superb synopses ... Superbly formatted ... Fascinating and accessible style'

THES

The Oxford Dictionary of Music
Michael & Joyce Kennedy & Tim Rutherford-Johnson

The most comprehensive, authoritative, and up-to-date dictionary of music available in paperback.

'clearly the best around ... the dictionary that everyone should have'

Literary Review